Strategic Management
Concepts, Decisions, Cases

Strategic Management
Concepts, Decisions, Cases

Strategic Management
Concepts, Decisions, Cases

Second Edition

Lester A. Digman
University of Nebraska

**BPI
IRWIN**

Homewood, IL 60430
Boston, MA 02116

© RICHARD D. IRWIN, INC., 1986 and 1990

Associate publisher: Martin F. Hanifin
Developmental editor: Kama Brockmann
Project editor: Ethel Shiell
Production manager: Ann Cassady
Cover designer: Sam Concialdi
Compositor: Carlisle Communications, Ltd.
Typeface: 10/12 Times Roman
Printer: R. R. Donnelley & Sons Company

Library of Congress Cataloging-in-Publication Data

Digman, Lester A.
    Strategic management : concepts, decisions, cases / Lester A.
 Digman.—2nd ed.
      p.   cm.
    Includes bibliographical references.
    ISBN 0-256-06673-6
    1. Strategic planning. 2. Strategic planning—Case studies.
 I. Title.
 HD30.28.D54 1990
 658.4'012—dc20   89–36637
                                         CIP

To Ellen, Stephanie, Sarah, and Mark

Editor's Note

There are many reasons why you would benefit from using Les Digman's *Strategic Management: Concepts, Decisions, Cases,* second edition. The book is:

- Well-written.
- Well-organized.
- Meticulously researched.
- Comprehensive and rigorous.
- Very ''real world.''

Also, this edition includes a variety of outstanding and thought-provoking cases. Here's what one reviewer said about the text:

> Digman's approach mirrors my own in certain ways. First, I believe a text should be entertaining. That may be a bit strong to describe Digman's work, but at least it is interesting. He does an excellent job of holding the reader's attention with a liberal dose of short real-world examples to clarify conceptual points. In fact, he does as good a job of this as any text I've read.
>
> Further, the chapters tend to flow well from beginning to end. Too many authors attempt to break chapters up into subchapters with ''special applications,'' ''new directions,'' and/or ''international'' approaches to the material in the chapter. Digman does a very nice job of just incorporating those and other topics right into the central flow of the chapter. That's a much more effective approach.

This text has been carefully developed and edited to serve the needs of strategic management educators and students throughout the English-speaking world. We hope that you find it useful.

Preface

This second edition—as was the first edition—is written for strategic management and business policy students at high-quality business schools, whether at the undergraduate or master's level. The strategy and policy fields have undergone significant changes during the past four years; those changes—both in substance and process—are incorporated in this revised text. Therefore, this text reflects both the academic and practitioner state of the art in these fields.

The viewpoint taken in this text agrees with that of Paul Cook and Joseph Bower of Harvard, that the policy field includes "all the messy, unsolved, and perhaps undefined problems" characterizing the management of an organization. As soon as such problems are sufficiently well understood, they can be incorporated as part of the subject matter in one of the functional disciplines.

STRUCTURE AND FOCUS OF THE TEXT

As in the first edition, the focus in this book is on strategic issues and decisions, with cases selected to illustrate those issues. The text starts with specific, easier-to-comprehend situations and concepts (such as business-level strategies) before moving to less-familiar, more general topics (such as corporate-level strategies). The process of strategic management is explored, along with the latest techniques, frameworks, and tools of strategic analysis, as an aid to making strategic decisions. The point of view in this text is that organizations and their managers are primarily concerned with the need to make the appropriate strategic decision, given the environment, issues, and situation facing the organization. The process, tools, and techniques of strategic management are helpful and necessary in making those decisions, but should not be the primary focus of the book.

The book also recognizes that corporate planning people and other staff and functional managers, *as well as* line and general managers, have a role in the process of dealing with these decisions. Furthermore, the strategic management focus includes strategy implementation and control, as well as strategic planning (since management—strategic or operational—includes implementation and control as well as planning). Emphasis is on "best available practice" in strategic issue management.

Part I of this book presents the latest and most important concepts, processes, and roles comprising this clearly important discipline. Chapter 1 defines the field, traces its development, examines its value, and describes its elements. Chapter 2 investigates the strategic management process and practices including the critical roles and responsibilities of management.

Part II assesses the strategic situation facing the organization, including defining the business (mission, stakeholders, competencies, and resources) in Chapter 3; overall opportunities and threats present in the general environment (Chapter 4); and the competitive environment (industry, market, and competitor analysis) in Chapter 5.

In Part III we specifically address strategic decision making—formulating, evaluating, and selecting strategies. Chapter 6 treats business-level topics, including generic, differentiation, and scope strategies. Chapter 7 examines multibusiness strategies (coordination, diversification, venturing, and restructuring). Chapter 8, in turn, deals with developing and evaluating strategic options, including the use of critical success factors and competitor analysis.

Strategic planning systems and techniques, plus strategy implementation and control, are discussed Part IV with Chapter 9 concentrating on strategic decision support systems and techniques as well as the related area of strategic planning systems. Chapter 10 treats the critical areas of implementing and controlling strategic performance, including the managerial skills required as well as how to design a reward system geared to strategic performance. Levels of control are examined, as are strategic and operational audits.

Part V extends the concept into two areas, first examining the unique features of common organizational types, such as start-up ventures, small businesses, not for profits, the public sector, and the increasingly dominant service organization in Chapter 11. Chapter 12 completes the text portion by discussing trends and directions, including the field's state of the art and likely areas of attention as the field moves into its second generation.

This textbook is in the mainstream of the field in that it fulfills the integrative, capstone needs of the policy course, cast in a strategic management framework. It is state of the art in that it presents the very latest strategic management material cast in a strategic decision framework. The body of knowledge is tied to the essential viewpoints, tasks, and analyses required to *perform* the strategic management function. Thus, the reader will be required (and shown how) to perform strategic planning, implementation, and control, rather than simply being exposed to text material that talks *about* strategic management. Included are data, guides, and checklists on: *(a)* which types of strategies are appropriate; *(b)* what a given strategy requires and consists of; and *(c)* probable outcomes. In short, the text pulls the field together for the masters or undergraduate class and instructor, and moves in the direction toward which the field and the course are evolving. This text presents the field in a natural framework while adding emerging concepts.

THE CASES

A critical factor in the case portion of a text on strategic management and policy is the balance or complement of the cases selected. The cases included in Part VI were selected from a review of hundreds of cases, screened from a list of several thousand strategy- and policy-related cases. Careful consideration was given to the quality of the case, a balance of strategic issues and decisions, a wide representation of industries, varying company sizes, cases of varying length and complexity, geographical balance, how current the case is, and organizations in which students and faculty are likely to have an interest.

The cases are grouped into eight sections representing the primary strategic *issue or decision* facing the organization:

Defining the business: Vision, Values, Mission, Policies

Start-up Strategies: New Ventures

Growth and Share-Building Strategies

Corporate Size and Focus: Diversification and Restructuring

Coping with Environmental Change and Turbulence

Strategy Change, Renewal, and Turnaround

Strategy Refinement and Control

Strategy Implementation and Planning

In addition, the cases reflect most major types of organizations competing in a number of different industries. At least four of the cases have "industry pairs" for comparison purposes. Further, the geographical balance of the cases closely approximates the population of the various regions of the United States in which they are headquartered, and most are national and international in scope and recognition. Canadian, British, and Swedish companies are also represented.

Also included in Part VI is student-oriented material on learning by the case method—what it is, how it works, and how to analyze a case.

INSTRUCTOR'S MANUAL

An essential aid to the faculty member is a high-quality instructor's manual, particularly for a case-oriented course. Unlike many, the instructor's manual for this text was prepared by the book's author, ensuring consistency and high quality. Extensive classroom testing and student research has gone into the teaching note for each case, in many instances including direct input by the case authors themselves. The complete manual includes the following:

- Thorough, logical, and consistent analysis of each case, including a detailed update.
- Detailed course outlines and schedules.

- Extensive test bank, including objective and essay questions and answers.
- Transparency masters.
- Suggestions and hints for covering the material in each part/chapter.
- Detachable pages, for ease of classroom use.

STRATEGY NEWSLETTER

It is important that the instructor keep abreast of significant developments in the field, both theory and practice. Sometimes this is a difficult task, given the preparation and grading demands of a case-oriented course. Likewise, it is important and always of interest to students to know the "latest scoop" concerning the cases they are analyzing. This is particularly true regarding dynamic organizations, industries, and individuals—the situation facing many of the cases in this book. For this reason, adopters will receive a "Strategy Newsletter," at least for each semester, providing synopses of important new developments in the field plus the latest happenings and results experienced by the case organizations. In this way, faculty members will be able to keep themselves and their students as current as is possible on the field and the cases.

NOTE FOR THE INSTRUCTOR

This textbook does *not* utilize a special computer package for case analysis—an approach currently popular with some authors and faculty members—even though such programs are useful in helping students analyze finances, ratios, and alternatives using spreadsheets. Why not? One of the current major trends in strategic management is toward creative, intuitive solutions to strategic problems, and away from step-by-step "mechanical analytical" approaches. Improper reliance on analytical aids can have several side effects:

1. By structuring the situation for the students, they are less likely to learn the most valuable aspects of strategic decision making (creative problem solving.)
2. They can leave students with the misconception that the primary aspect of strategic management and policy decisions is numerical analysis and manipulation.

While quantitative financial analysis *is* important to strategy and policy decisions, and is *necessary,* it is not *sufficient.* In strategy and policy courses, the goal is not to *teach* financial analysis, but to *use* it. To the extent that computer packages *reduce* the students' preoccupation with quantitative manipulations, allowing and assisting them to focus on key strategic issues, they are valuable. To the extent that they overstructure case situations and reduce creative, intuitive thinking, they do the student a disfavor. At present, the benefits of the former do not outweigh the risks of the latter, in my estimation.

In summary, it is my view that data should not be preorganized for students. They should be required to pull important financial and other data from the case (using *their* judgment); this data can be analyzed using independent spreadsheet computer packages on PCs at virtually all quality institutions of higher education.

ACKNOWLEDGMENTS

One can never adequately thank everyone who played a role in the completion of a textbook. With that in mind, let me single out the authors of the cases included in this book, both for their outstanding work and their permission to use the cases. Second, special mention is due for the authors of the many cases that were graciously sent to me for review, but which I was not able to include. I am especially indebted to adopters of the first edition—the people *really* responsible for the existence of this vastly improved second edition. Their faith and confidence will not be forgotten. Special mention must also be made of the researchers and practicing managers who have advanced the state of the art of the field to its present level, and of those who will continue to do so in the future, leading the field into its second generation.

I will be forever grateful to my academic cohorts and professional society colleagues from various institutions who have helped and assisted my academic career progression. Special thanks are due to my friends and colleagues at the University of Nebraska: Fred Luthans, for encouraging my return to academics and for encouraging me to undertake this task; Sang Lee, for his continuing support and encouragement; and Gary Schwendiman for resources and a supportive environment.

My former and present doctoral students are due a debt of gratitude for the challenge and research assistance they provide, as well as for the feedback and impetus to keep current in one's field. Special mention should go to the following persons who contributed significantly in the form of examination questions, comments, and suggestions:

Phil Crossland
University of Missouri—Kansas City

Pat Feltes
Southwest Missouri State University

Karen Fowler
San Diego State University

Neil Gilchrist
Northeast Missouri State University

Phil Hall
University of Nebraska

Jim Hoffman
Florida State University

Paul Mallette
Colorado State University

Rebecca Morris
University of Nebraska at Omaha

Bob Spagnola
University of Denver

Neil Swanson
Southwest Missouri State University

Soen Tjan
Creighton University and Indonesian Institute for Management Development

I am indebted to the many reviewers of the first and second editions for their insightful comments and suggestions. First edition reviewers include:

Richard Bettis
Southern Methodist University

H. Kurt Christensen
Northwestern University

Joel Cook
Texas A&M University

Raymond L. Cook
University of Texas

Arnold C. Cooper
Purdue University

Tim Davis
Cleveland State University

Roger Evered
Naval Post Graduate School

Edward Freeman
University of Minnesota

Harvey Hegarty
Indiana University

R. Duane Ireland
Baylor University

Kenneth E. Marino
University of Kentucky

Hugh M. O'Neill
University of Connecticut

Richard L. Pyle
University of Massachusetts at Boston

William R. Soukup
University of San Diego

John M. Stengrevics
Boston University

Gerardo Ungson
University of Oregon

D. Robley Wood, Jr.
Virginia Commonwealth University

Second edition reviewers include:

B. R. Baliga
Texas Tech University

Geoffrey R. Brooks
University of Oregon

Phillip D. Jones
Xavier University

Marshall Schminke
The University of Iowa

James B. Thurman
George Washington University

Joseph Rosenstein
University of Texas at Arlington

E. K. Valentin
Weber State College

Jean M. Lundin
Northern Michigan University

J. Michael Geringer
University of Western Ontario

Ken Thompson
DePaul University

In addition, I gratefully acknowledge the case authors:

1. The Farm Management System
   Walter S. Good, University of
   Manitoba
   with assistance from John Fallows

2. The National Jazz Hall of Fame
   Cornelius A. deKluyver, University
   of Virginia
   with assistance from Jonathan
   Giuliano, John Milford, Bruce
   Cauthen

3. Apple Computer, Inc. (1986)
   Sexton Adams, North Texas State University
   Adelaide Griffin, Texas Woman's University
   with assistance from Rusty Crews, Cherie Lyon, Russell Neely, John Williams, North Texas State University

4. The Douglasville Athletic Club Venture
   Frank R. Hunsicker, West Georgia College
   Gordon E. Johnson III, West Georgia College

5. Infosoft, Inc.
   L. L. Roos, University of Manitoba
   with assistance from C. Bhakar

6. The NFL versus the USFL
   Michael E. Porter, Harvard University
   with assistance from Laurence M. Baer, Lee C. Field III, Robert J. Haber, Robert Randell, Stephen Rogers

7. Burger King's Battle for the Burgers
   Larry D. Alexander, Virginia Polytechnic Institute and State University
   with assistance from Thomas W. Ripp

8. The Limited, Inc. (1986)
   Sexton Adams, North Texas State University
   Adelaide Griffin, Texas Woman's University
   with assistance from Jeff Friant, Elsie Fletcher, North Texas State University

9. Circuit City Stores, Inc.
   Eleanor G. May, University of Virginia
   with assistance from James Olver

10. American Greetings
    Daniel G. Kopp, Southwest Missouri State University
    Lois M. Shufeldt, Southwest Missouri State University

11. Hallmark Cards, Inc.
    Daniel G. Kopp, Southwest Missouri State University
    Lois M. Shufeldt, Southwest Missouri State University
    with assistance from Kim L. Stoops

12. Mesa Petroleum Co. (C)
    Robert R. Gardner, Southern Methodist University
    M. Edgar Barrett, Southern Methodist University
    with assistance from Mark Rich, Francis C. Stiff

13. Turner Broadcasting System, Inc.
    Neil H. Snyder, University of Virginia
    Melanie D. Sheip, Morgan Guaranty Trust

14. Goodyear Tire and the Goldsmith Challenge
    Bernard E. Deitzer, University of Akron
    Alan G. Krigline, University of Akron
    Thomas C. Peterson, University of Akron

15. Global Marine, Inc.
    James W. Clinton, University of Northern Colorado

16. Gotham Utilities Co.
    Adelaide Griffin, Texas Woman's University
    Sexton Adams, North Texas State University
    with assistance from Holly Feder, Linda McKee, Texas Woman's University

17. Manville Corporation (1988)
    Arthur Sharplin, McNeese State University

18. The New Chrysler Corporation: Fall and Rise
    M. Resa Vaghefi, University of North Florida
    with assistance from Richard E. Miller

19. Deere and Co.
    Peter G. Goulet, University of
    Northern Iowa
    Lynda L. Goulet, University of
    Northern Iowa

20. Strategic Management at the
    Amherst H. Wilder Foundation
    John M. Bryson, University of
    Minnesota
    Paula J. King, University of
    Minnesota
    William D. Roering, University of
    Florida
    Andrew H. Van de Ven, University
    of Minnesota

21. The Kellogg Company and the
    Ready-to-Eat Cereal Industry
    Joseph A. Schenk, University of
    Dayton
    Dan S. Prickett, Mead Data Central,
    Inc.
    Stanley J. Stough, University of
    Dayton

22. The Lincoln Electric Co. (1985)
    Arthur Sharplin, McNeese State
    University

23. Food Lion, Inc.
    Neil H. Snyder, University of
    Virginia
    with assistance from Janet L.
    Caswell

24. The American Food Corporation
    Barry Allen Gold, Pace University

25. The NASA Space Shuttle Disaster
    Robert Marx, University of
    Massachusetts
    Charles Stubbart, University of
    Massachusetts
    with assistance from Virginia Traub,
    Michael Cavanaugh

26. AB Volvo
    Jyoti N. Prasad, Western Illinois
    University
    Hans J. Bocker, Western Illinois
    University
    Fazal J. Seyyed, Western Illinois
    University
    with assistance from Megan E.
    Sutton

Finally I owe a debt to the office staff at the University of Nebraska, particularly Joyce Anderson, Cathy Jensen, and Cheryl Heinzman. Again, my wife Ellen deserves special mention for her assistance and understanding, as do our children, Stephanie, Sarah, and Mark for putting up with—and often without—me while the book was being written and revised.

Lester A. Digman

Major Changes in This Edition

In addition to being *totally* updated, revised, and streamlined, this edition contains **all new cases,** with most of the chapter profiles new, and all are current and pertinent to the chapter material. A few of the text-material changes found in this edition include:

- A description of the strategic management process as more creative, innovative, and intuitive, as is the practice in leading companies.
- An emphasis on shorter, flexible and adaptable, and contingency-based plans.
- An updated simplified model of the strategy process, better reflecting the various elements and their relative roles.
- Examples illustrating how strategies evolve in practice, including intended versus realized strategies.
- A new section dealing with service organizations and strategies.
- New material on distinctive competencies, competitive and comparative advantages and the value-added chain, and sustainable advantages, plus a new model relating these topics to corporate- and business-level strategies.
- A new model of competition, to complement Porter's 5-forces model.
- Significantly expanded material on public sector organizations, including a completely new model of the strategic process in this type of organization.
- The latest material on corporate restructuring, including concentration and focus strategies.
- Critiques and evaluations of topics and practices such as the experience curve, portfolio models, generic strategies, strategic business units, diversification strategies, and others.
- Contingency-based guidelines on topics such as top-down versus bottom-up planning, and types of structure (including M-form and U-form) versus diversification strategy and resulting performance.
- Data describing performance results of various strategies, tying together the mission, goals, strategies, actions, and results via examples.
- New material on topics such as strategic alliances, guerrilla strategies, decisional quicksand, corporate renewal, corporate culture, and others.

- Expanded and updated treatment of stakeholders, technology strategies and productivity, the role of economic cycles, international/global strategies, social/demographic changes, and strategic groups.
- New material or strategic control, focusing on premises, implementation, and strategic surveillance.
- Expanded coverage of the role of vision, plus other important strategic management skills and abilities.
- The latest comprehensive framework of generic strategies, representing the combined wisdom of the top writers in the field.
- Expanded coverage of strategic decision making, particularly in "high-velocity" environmental settings.
- Expanded treatment of international strategies, especially sources of global competitive advantage.
- Use of a current application example—the financial services industry—to illustrate the interactive effects of a dynamic general environment, a changing competitive environment, and resulting strategic responses.
- Revised, recast, and refocused material on critical success factors, scenarios, implementation (including CEO and management selection, development, and succession), and the changing role of the board of directors.
- The latest organizational practices in leading companies such as G.E., Coca-Cola, and ITT.
- A complete reassessment and extensive treatment of the state-of-the-art of the field, emerging trends, and likely practices in the coming second generation.

About the Author

LESTER A. DIGMAN, PH.D.

Les Digman is the Leonard E. Whittaker/American Charter Professor of Management at the University of Nebraska, where he also serves as director of Graduate Studies in Management. A graduate of the University of Iowa, Professor Digman specializes in strategic management, strategic decision making, management of technology, and executive development.

He has written 4 books, made contributions to 10 others, published 25 journal articles (including those in *Harvard Business Review, Organizational Dynamics, Operations Research,* and others), written 30 conference proceedings papers, presented 38 professional papers, and authored 17 reports and monographs. He has consulted with scores of private and governmental organizations in the United States, Sweden, Germany, and Korea.

Dr. Digman is a member of the Strategic Management Society, the Planning Forum, the Academy of Management, the Decision Sciences Institute, the Institute of Management Sciences, the Operations Research Society of America, and others. He has served as program chair and president of the Midwest Decision Sciences Institute, as well as coordinator of the Institute's Doctoral Student Consortium. He is listed in *Who's Who in Finance and Industry.*

Contents

Part I

Strategic Management: Concepts, Processes, and Roles

The Essence of Strategic Management

LEARNING OBJECTIVES

After reading Chapter 1, you should be able to:

Define and understand strategic management and its purpose.

Realize that effective strategic management is a flexible, adaptive, and creative process.

Appreciate the differences and relationships between strategic and operational management.

Understand the elements, components, and analysis required for effective strategic management.

Understand the roles of strategic planning and control in strategic management.

Describe the reasons for increasing strategic management and planning by organizations.

Describe the characteristics common to successful organizations.

Why is it that some organizations perennially seem to be more successful than others, typically leaving the competition in the dust? It may be, as one expert observes, that there are three types of people in this world—those who *make* things happen, those who *watch* things happen, and those who *wonder* what happened. Which are you? Time management expert Alan Lakein and the well-known entrepreneur Ted Turner have similar analogies. Lakein says you can either decide, drift, or drown; Turner says, ''Do something! Lead, follow, or get out of the way!'' A common element among the leaders, doers, movers, and shakers is the ability to make effective strategy and policy decisions. These organizations are also able to turn those decisions into reality—to implement them—and to operate the organization efficiently, as well. How they do it is what this book—and this course—is all about.

<table>
<tr><td>

PROFILE

</td><td>

IBM® Corporation

International Business Machines Corp. is one of the largest and most successful organizations in the world, by almost any measure. International Business Machines possesses the enviable record of going from "also ran" in the early 1950s to number one in its industry five years later. In 1988, IBM had profits of $5.5 billion on sales of $60 billion, making it first in profits and fourth in sales among U.S. industrial companies.[1] In addition, IBM is the leading seller in virtually all of the 130 countries in which it does business. But this industrial giant has not been acting as you might expect from a giant—it has entered new markets, pursued new technologies, and trimmed unnecessary fat.

An example of "Big Blue's" ability to make strategic decisions at the right time was its move into the personal computer market. Apple® had been selling personal computers—largely to individuals—for several years, with sales multiplying from $1 million in 1977 to $582 million in 1982. IBM, however, waited until it was convinced that enough of a market existed to warrant entry, and that the machines were starting to be used in offices rather than as home computers. An IBM task force then developed the personal computer in one year, and within a short time it became the industry standard and sales leader.

IBM's move into personal computers gives a glimpse of the workings of the company and its previous CEO, Chairman John R. (Johnny) Opel, and its current CEO, John Akers. They are products of a corporate culture and system that has produced capable managers not only within the company, but "alumni" in key positions with other firms in computer and related industries. In fact, the IBM culture, beliefs, and principles become a way of life for its people. Some analysts have noted that Big Blue was the model for a number of management techniques widely used by the Japanese. (In fact, IBM first used quality circles in the early 1960s, intensively trains its people, and has never laid off an employee for financial reasons.)

How can a company of this size remain flexible despite the elaborate systems and procedures of planning its size requires? IBM people explain that the result of planning at IBM isn't just a "plan," it is a way of communicating. Planning *is* important at IBM, because it helps generate information and helps people communicate. "But if you think, as many corporate planners do, that you're going to plan the future, you're crazy. The important things are just unplannable."[2]

</td></tr>
</table>

---

[1]"The Business Week Top 1000," *Business Week,* 1989 Special Issue, April 14, 1989, p. 14.

[2]"How the Best Get Better," *Business Week,* September 13, 1987, p. 99.

In fact, even an IBM occasionally encounters obstacles and must make major changes. Changes in the computer industry—including growth of the personal computer (PC) market—make the industry more fast moving and dynamic in the 80s. As a result, IBM's performance was disappointing to some, as faster-moving competitors capitalized on the company's inertia and aloofness. But how does one change a giant—quickly? Akers responded by instituting a major reorganization to decentralize decision making, plus a plan to "reinvent IBM" by changing its corporate culture. The goals of both moves were the same; to force the company and its decision making to be closer and more responsive to its customers.[3]

IS STRATEGIC PLANNING "IN" OR "OUT?"

Writers introducing *Business Week*'s new feature, "Corporate Strategies," in 1978 posed the question, "What is the business concept that has become the major thrust and emphasis in the management of U.S. corporations today?" Their answer was *strategic planning,* and their reason: "the discipline helps corporate officers anticipate and cope with a variety of forces beyond their operating control."[4]

While we saw tremendous growth in strategic planning in the 60s and 70s, the 80s have seen a reaction to this growth. A number of companies reduced their strategic planning staffs, creating the appearance of a decline in the field. It became "in" to say that strategic planning was "out"—"dead"—that this buzz-phrase had come and gone, and now was on the decline. Perhaps as a reaction to its earlier growth, pundits told the story of how strategic planning had even penetrated the Kremlin! In fact, at one recent May Day parade, Mikhail Gorbachev and his staff were reviewing the latest Soviet weapons as they paraded by the reviewing stand. The weapons grew steadily more threatening— beginning with small arms, followed in order by jeeps, howitzers, combat vehicles, tanks, tactical missiles, intermediate-range missiles, ICBMs, and finally multiple-warhead ICBMs. Lastly, to everyone's confusion, came a cadre of 50 or so men in suits, carrying briefcases. Who were these people; the KGB? No, they were the new strategic planners; everyone *knows* how much damage *they* can do!

But is strategic planning in decline? Nothing could be further from the truth—but it has changed, and changed significantly in recent years. We do have fewer strategic planners today in many organizations, just as we have fewer mainframe computer operators. But has computing declined? No, it has been decentralized. Strategic planning has also been decentralized and dispersed

---

[3]R. E. Carlyle, and Jeff Mead, "The Rise of an Information Utility," *Datamation,* January 1, 1989, p. 26.

[4]"Publishers Memo," *Business Week,* January 9, 1978, p. 5.

throughout the organization, with many of its functions being performed by the people who should have been doing them all along—line managers and their immediate staffs.

Today, line managers—the people who run the companies—are themselves becoming more deeply involved in *strategic decisions*. As an example, strategic decision making is the focus of a month-long executive development seminar AT&T conducts for all of its future top managers. Why? The program coordinator explains that strategic decision making is "the most crucial aspect of managing, particularly in higher-level positions where the kinds of decisions a manager is called upon to make usually are complex and multifaceted."[5] The 1984 breakup of the Bell System—obviously a major strategic move—reinforces the need for such training.

These examples reflect the changing role of *strategic management* (of which strategic decision making and planning are a part) and typify what is happening in business. Strategic management is in a refinement phase, similar to what happened with operations management a generation ago, management science in the 1950s and 60s, and human resource management in the 60s and 70s. According to Michael Kami (a pioneer and well-known consultant in strategic planning), as recently as 1952 only two companies did any type of formal strategic planning: General Electric and IBM.[6] The technique began to grow rapidly during the late 1960s, and since then has been installed as a formal management process in most large companies and in many medium-sized and smaller companies.[7] Today, the *practice* of strategic management—its use in organizations—is in some ways ahead of the *teaching* of its concepts in most colleges and universities. Nonetheless, students of management wanting to adequately prepare for the future should learn all they can about the concepts and practice of strategic management.

WHAT IS STRATEGIC MANAGEMENT?

Conceptually, strategic planning is very simple. Stripped of its complexities, a strategy consists of the *means* an organization chooses to move it from point A (where it is now) to point B (where is must be at some time in the future). As shown in Figure 1.1, the organization must first assess where it is at present. In reality, this step is not so simple; "where we are" includes defining the market; the industry; the competitors; our resources, strengths, and weaknesses; technology; economic factors; customer needs and preferences; demographics;

---

[5]"Where Will All the Leaders Come From?" *Bell Telephone Magazine*, 6 (1980), p. 2.

[6]Michael Kami, *Strategic Planning for Changing Times* (Dayton, Ohio: Cassette Recording Co., 1984).

[7]William D. Guth, ed., *Handbook of Business Strategy* (Boston: Warren, Gorham & Lamont, 1985), p. vii.

FIGURE 1.1   The Essence of Strategy

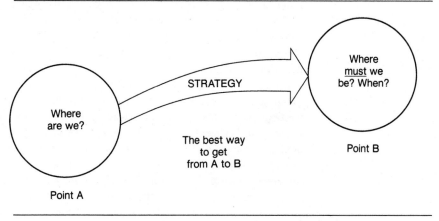

international effects; regulatory influences; and a host of other factors. Determining "where we must be" and "when we must be there" is even more difficult, because it requires us to predict changes in all of the previously mentioned factors. Choosing the "best way to get from A to B" is obviously a judgmental matter, and is only as good as our ability to assess points A and B.

Versus Strategic Planning and Long-Range Planning

In the previous discussion, the terms *strategic management* and *strategic planning* were used as if they were interchangeable. While they are related, in reality there are differences between them. Strategic planning describes the *periodic* activities undertaken by organizations to cope with changes in their *external* environments. Strategic management is a *continuous* process that involves attempts to match or fit the organization with its changing environment in the most advantageous way possible. It clearly includes adapting the organization itself (via internal changes) to fit the external environment.

In this light, strategic management is a broader, more encompassing concept than is strategic planning. Strategic management focuses on strategic decisions—whenever they are required—as well as on the strategic planning required to put them into practice. Thus, strategic management represents the intersection, or marriage, of organization theory, microeconomics (the theory of the firm), and industrial organization. Organization theory joins the roles of individuals and the goals of the organization at the enterprise level. Theory of the firm, in turn, brings goal-oriented enterprises together at the market level. Strategic management deals with both the behavior of the organization within its external market *and* its internal roles, processes, structure, and decisions, to enable the organization to function as best it can within that external environment.[8]

Many people use the terms *strategic management, strategic planning,* and *long-range planning* interchangeably. This is unfortunate. Just as management consists of much more than planning, strategic management encompasses more than strategic planning.

Strategic planning involves formulating and evaluating alternative strategies, selecting a strategy, and developing detailed plans for putting the strategy into practice. In contrast, strategic management, as a minimum, includes strategic planning *and* strategic control, because plans at any level—operating, management, or strategic—are not likely to be accomplished without effective controls. *Strategic control,* then, consists of ensuring that the chosen strategy is being implemented properly and that it is producing the desired results. Plans without effective controls are like a ship without a navigator; the captain may plan to sail from point A to point B, but the navigation process—controlling—is what actually gets him or her there. Controlling is the process of comparing actual conditions with planned conditions, analyzing the differences, and making necessary changes.

Long-range planning, planning for events beyond the current quarter or year, is not synonymous with strategic management (or strategic planning, for that matter). Certain strategic actions and reactions can be relatively short range and may include more than just planning aspects. Furthermore, not all long-range planning is strategic. It is perfectly reasonable to have long-range operating or technical plans that are not strategic. As an example of this distinction, several years ago, Bendix attempted to acquire Martin-Marietta. As a result, Martin-Marietta had to make a number of unplanned strategic decisions within a very short time frame in response to the takeover threat. While Bendix began acquiring Martin's shares, Martin decided to fight by trying to acquire Bendix— a move known as a "Pac-Man" strategy. In fact, both companies ended up holding controlling interest in the other, and deeply in debt. Bendix, however, made a tactical error in that it had to wait 30 days before assuming control of Martin, while Martin (incorporated in a different state) could assume control of Bendix in 10 days. More short-term strategic decisions were required—this time by Bendix—which sought out a "white knight" (a firm willing to take over Bendix on friendly terms) and which it found in Allied Corp. In this complicated situation, one can see a number of strategic decisions and actions being taken on an unplanned basis by all three of the firms involved. However, it should be noted that most strategic decisions—those that change the character or direction of the organization—have long-term ramifications, even if they were not planned in advance, although they usually are.

---

[8]J. C. Spender, "The Business Policy Problem and Industry Recipes," in *Advances in Strategic Management,* vol. 2, ed. R. Lamb (Greenwich, Conn.: JAI Press, 1983), p. 215.

"Now, this one is a tactical rock, and that big one is a strategic rock."

Source: *Datamation* 29, no. 11 (November 1983), p. 178

Simply put, strategic decision making involves determining how to get from point A (where we are now) to point B (where we need to be at some time in the future). Strategic planning involves determining the details of getting from A to B, and strategic management consists of controlling the entire process and its accomplishment.

The key concept in the definitions given above is *strategy,* the organization's preselected means or approach to achieving its goals and objectives while coping with current and future external conditions. A strategy is a pattern in the organization's important decisions and actions, and consists of a few key areas or things by which the firm seeks to distinguish itself.[9] *Tactics,* on the other hand, are specific actions the organization might undertake in carrying out its strategy. These terms will be explained more fully later in the text, but first some background information may be helpful.

A Military Analogy

The terms *strategy* and *tactics* have been borrowed directly from the military. In the military sense, strategy involves the overall approach or means used to

---

[9]Kami, *Strategic Planning for Changing Times.*

combat the enemy, such as defending enclaves or large areas of the countryside, or using complementary deployments of air, sea, and land forces to attack the enemy.

Tactics, on the other hand, relate to specific means of carrying out a strategy: how to define the enclaves or the countryside; how to carry out the land, sea, or air attack; how many planes, ships, or tanks to employ; the conduct of each skirmish or battle.

Much can be learned from the military when applying strategy and tactics to the management of organizations, whether in the business sector, in government, health care, or in other areas. For example, World War II General George Patton reportedly said that it is virtually impossible to win a war using the wrong strategy, even though your tactics may be perfectly carried out. On the other hand, tactical errors may not cause you to lose the war if the correct overall strategy is being employed. In a business sense, attempting to market the wrong mix of products may not succeed, even though the marketing plan for each product is expertly carried out. In turn, the organization with the correct product mix can be successful, even if errors are made in the individual marketing plans.

Characteristics of Strategic Decisions

A strategic decision can be defined as one that significantly affects what an organization does and how it does it. That is, a strategic decision would involve changes in one or more of the following: the organization's basic concept, its role in society; the mix of markets in which the organization competes; the choice of products and services within those markets; or how the firm competes within its markets. As the definition suggests, strategic decisions are complex and wide ranging.

In addition, there are several interrelated factors that contribute complexity and uncertainty to strategic decisions. As examples, firms typically pursue multiple objectives; strategic decisions have long time horizons; there are a number of interested (and often opposing) groups in each firm; strategic decisions by definition involve values, risks, and uncertainties, and involve many intangibles, assumptions, and judgments. In addition, strategic decisions tend to involve high stakes and are difficult to evaluate; and there also tends to be no individual or group possessing an overall expertise in a given decision area.[10] For these reasons, strategic decisions are seldom simple or clear-cut at the time they are made, and often not in retrospect, either.

As defined by Henry Mintzberg of McGill University in Montreal, Quebec, a strategy is a *pattern* in a stream of actions. This pattern is the result of strategic decisions made by the firm. The firm's strategy, however, is not always

---

[10]Gus W. Grammas, "Quantitative Tools for Strategic Decision Making," in *Handbook of Business Strategy,* ed. W. Guth (Boston: Warren, Gorham & Lamont, 1985), p. 15–5.

FIGURE 1.2   Intended versus Realized Strategy

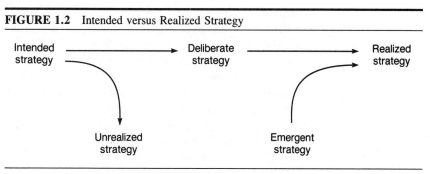

Source: Henry Mintzberg, J. P. Brunet, and J. A. Waters, "Does Planning Impede Strategic Thinking?" in *Advances in Strategic Management,* vol. 4, ed. Robert Lamb and Paul Shrivastava, (Greenwich, Conn.: JAI Press, 1986), p. 4.

completely preplanned. As Figure 1.2 illustrates, the *intended* strategy may not be fully realized. For one reason or another, portions of the intended strategy may not materialize, while other patterns may emerge despite or in the absence of management's intentions.[11]

As an example of this, as well as an illustration of how strategies must be flexible, consider the following case. Valcom, Inc., began as a division of Valmont Corporation, the largest manufacturer of center pivot irrigation systems for agriculture. The Valcom strategy was to sell IBM personal computers and software to farmers through Valmont's dealers. Within three months, sales had exploded, but not for the reasons anticipated. A sales analysis showed that less than 1 percent of sales were to farmers; the customers were bankers, small businesses, and so on, in small towns—areas without a PC outlet. So Valcom changed its strategy, selling computers to everyone in nonurban areas through company-owned and franchised stores. A subsequent sales analysis caused a further strategy refinement—a focus on businesses in smaller communities largely through franchised dealers.[12]

Strategy Making Requires Vision and Creativity.   Unfortunately, some writers have tended to describe strategic management and strategic planning as a "rational," specific step-by-step process. While we do attempt to systematize elements of the process in large organizations, the most effective strategic decision makers tend to be intuitive and creative, employing an adoptive, flexible process. In fact, the majority of strategic decisions are "event driven" rather

---

[11]Henry Mintzberg, J. P. Brunet, and J. A. Waters, "Does Planning Impede Strategic Thinking?" in *Advances in Strategic Management,* vol. 4, ed. Robert Lamb and Paul Shrivastava, (Greenwich, Conn.: JAI Press, 1986), p. 4. Also see Mintzberg's article, "Crafting Strategy," *Harvard Business Review,* 65, no. 4 (July–August 1987), p. 66.

[12]William L. Fairfield, Keynote Address to the Third Nebraska Conference on Productivity and Entrepreneurship, Lincoln, Nebraska, April 11, 1988.

than programmed in advance; therefore, they are "unplanned." Thus, strategy is often less an exercise in applied logic than it is "an exercise in preferences, choices, and matches."[13] The significance of this statement will become clearer as our discussion of strategy progresses.

An important key to effective strategic decision making is the proper integration of analysis and intuition. Formal planning can help in developing strategy, particularly in complex organizations, but it's not the whole story. In fact, formal planning tends to drive out creative strategic thinking.[14] The reason we do formal planning is that we *have* to in order to manage the process in complex organizations, even though it is somewhat detrimental to the making of the most effective strategic decisions—it is a necessary evil. The goal is to make the correct strategic decisions, not the development of detailed plans.

The best strategists tend to have a *vision* of their organization—a clear understanding of what the firm is about and where it is headed. This vision is the "glue" that holds things together through turbulent times and business fluctuations. It guides competitive strategy, and does not require exhaustive analysis.[15] In fact some managers consider this vision to be at the very core of strategic planning—defining it as helping your organization "create, maintain, and implement a long-term or strategic vision."[16]

Control versus Breakthrough.   It is also helpful to look at strategic decisions from the perspectives both of planning and of control. Most of what are considered problem-solving activities are related to the control function; that is, an attempt to bring the organization's performance back "under control." The other side of the control coin involves Juran's "breakthrough" concept.[17] Briefly, this concept holds that management's goal, once things are "under control," is to attempt to achieve a higher level of performance through conscious efforts. This means making certain changes that may reduce control in the short run, but are designed to improve performance (quality, output, effectiveness, efficiency, and cost) when things are brought under control at the new, but higher, level of performance. Again, this approach involves risk and short-term disruption, but it recognizes that "control" is not the manager's

[13]A Van Cauwenbergh and R. Martens, "Simplicity behind Strategy: A Reflection on Strategic Management Theory versus Practice," in *Advances in Strategic Management,* ed. R. Lamb and P. Shrivastava (Greenwich, Conn.: JAI Press, 1983), p. 118.

[14]Henry Mintzberg, J. P. Brunet, and J. A. Waters, "Does Planning Impede Strategic Thinking? Tracking the Strategies of Air Canada from 1937 to 1976," in *Advances in Strategic Management,* vol. 4, ed. Lamb and Shrivastava (Greenwich, Conn.: JAI Press, 1986), p. 3.

[15]Amar Bhide, "Hustle as Strategy," *Harvard Business Review* 64, no. 5 (September/October 1986), p. 65.

[16]Major General Perry M. Smith (USAF), "Creating a Strategic Vision: The Value of Long-Range Planning," *Air University Review,* 37, no. 6 (September/October 1986), p. 16.

[17]J. M. Juran, *Managerial Breakthrough: A New Concept of the Manager's Job* (New York: McGraw-Hill, 1964).

ultimate goal; performance improvement is. This type of planning decision requires that the manager be able to realistically assess and evaluate the risks of the attempted breakthrough strategy. Also, the managerial action required is more positive. The manager engages in "opportunity finding" activities, rather than in the more reactive "problem-solving" approach.

Strategic versus Operating Management

Most of us are more aware of the operational than of the strategic aspects of a business. Operating management deals with the ongoing, day-to-day "operations" of the business. It involves producing, marketing, and selling the goods and services the organization provides. The organization chart, management information system, plant management, supervisory activities, sales meetings, and other functions are all focused on delivery of the firm's goods and services as efficiently as possible. Thus, when you "see" the organization, you see it *operating,* and you see the structure, systems, procedures, and facilities employed to permit it to operate as efficiently as possible.

On the other hand, the strategic function of the organization is more difficult to observe. The strategic function may be performed by some of the same people, but is separate and distinct from the operating function. Strategy is typically not reflected on the organization chart, nor can it be seen by studying operating systems and procedures, departments, plants, and facilities. However, it is linked to operations in that its main purpose is to ensure that the organization is capitalizing on its comparative advantages and distinctive competencies to take advantage of any opportunities the environment may provide, creating a competitive advantage. To accomplish this end, all of the operating elements of the organization must function *effectively,* the organization must "do the right things," as well as *efficiently,* "doing things right." Effectiveness means that the firm is producing the goods and services that the market wants; efficiency merely means that the firm is producing its goods and services at minimum cost. As an illustration of the relative importance of these two management responsibilities, ask yourself the following question: What good is it to be an efficient producer of Edsels? On the other hand, for 17 years, Polaroid held an exclusive patent on the instant camera. How critical is efficiency when you have monopoly on a product? In certain types of markets and stages of the product life cycle, efficiency may be *very* important and may, in fact, constitute a strategy—that of being the lowest-cost producer, as is discussed in Chapter 6.

As shown in Figure 1.3, the strategy is the primary determinant of success or failure in fulfilling the mission and achieving the organization's goals and objectives. The choice of strategy is based on comparative advantages and distinctive competencies of the firm—its strengths—and provides a framework or envelope for the effective and efficient tactics and operations necessary to carry out the strategy.

FIGURE 1.3   Strategy is the Primary Determinant of Success or Failure

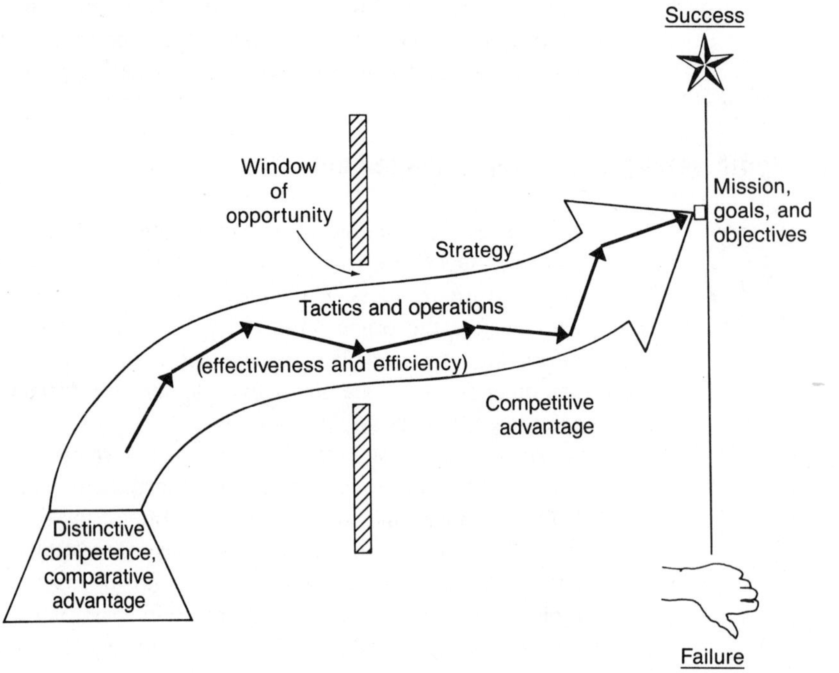

To summarize, remember that there are *two* essential areas of management responsibility: strategic management and operating management. Neither can be neglected and they complement one another. However, our concern here is with the strategic element alone.

The Environmental Interface

In the previous discussion, strategic management was defined as effectively matching or fitting the organization to its environment. Actually, the strategic process is an attempt to achieve a productive fit between the organization's *external* environment (economic, competitive, social, political/legal, technological) and its *internal* situation (structure, systems and procedures, climate, and physical, financial, technical, and human resources). This is shown schematically in Figure 1.4. In doing this, the organization must consider the threats and opportunities present in the external environment, and the strengths and weaknesses present internally.

FIGURE 1.4   The Environmental Fit

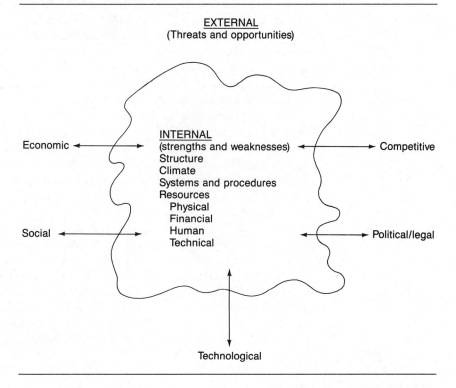

EXTERNAL
(Threats and opportunities)

Economic

INTERNAL
(strengths and weaknesses)
Structure
Climate
Systems and procedures
Resources
  Physical
  Financial
  Human
  Technical

Competitive

Social

Political/legal

Technological

The concept of environmental fit implies that there are certain things the organization may want to accomplish, but may not be able to or may choose not to, because of internal weakness or external risks. The strategic manager must carefully assess the marketplace, the competition, laws and regulations, taxes and interest rates, the business cycle, customer needs and desires, and any other pertinent factors in an attempt to locate opportunities for the organization. At the same time, it must be recognized that opportunities and threats often are opposite sides of the same coin; any change in the environment *at the same time* presents opportunities and threats. No opportunity is risk free; the strategic manager must weigh the risks against the rewards of any potential action. In addition, opportunities not recognized or seized by your firm may be taken by your competitors, turning them into very real threats. Thus, timing is important; opportunities must be recognized and taken advantage of when appropriate, and not too early or too late. Opportunities decay with time; on the other hand, an idea whose time has not yet come is not a viable opportunity.

Through planning, the firm ideally tries to *induce* change, or cause changes to occur that will put the organization in a relatively better position vis-à-vis the competition. Thus, the firm seizes or creates opportunity for itself and creates a threat for the competition, forcing the competition to react, much as Philip Morris did by applying advanced marketing techniques to its Miller Beer subsidiary. The firm does not always have this luxury, however, but nonetheless should strive to *control* change, or through advance planning, have some influence over what happens, even though the firm may not have induced the change. As a minimum, the organization must be able to *react* effectively to changes over which it has no influence or control, although this is a decidedly less desirable situation for the firm to find itself in.

What the organization is able to do in the way of seizing opportunities or responding to threats depends on its internal strengths and weaknesses. It must *realistically* assess its management skills and depth, finances, production facilities, marketing abilities, technological base, structure and systems—in other words, perform a resource audit—to determine what it can or cannot do. Not all things are possible. For example, Braniff chose to expand rapidly after airlines were deregulated. However, the carrier's accompanying increases in fixed and operating costs greatly exceeded the added revenues, and forced the company into bankruptcy. IBM, however, with its superior resources, was able to enter the microcomputer market and successfully move into a leadership position in a very short time.

In general, management should strive to build on, improve, and broaden its strengths and reduce its weaknesses. This usually is the result of effective strategic management and opens the door for a broader range of strategic alternatives in the future. In general, those who succeed seem to be those who select a realistic niche in the market and build from there.

Components of Strategies

Any strategy contains four components:

1. The *scope* or domain of action within which the organization tries to achieve its objectives.
2. The skills and resources that the organization will use to achieve its objectives—its *distinctive competence*.
3. Advantages the organization expects to achieve over its competitors through its skill and resource deployments—its *competitive advantage*.
4. *Synergies* that will result from the way the organization deploys its skills and resources.[18]

Therefore, a ''cardinal feature of each strategy is the selection of a few relationships on which the company seeks to distinguish itself.''[19]

---

[18]C. W. Hofer and Dan Schendel, *Strategy Formulation: Analytical Concepts* (St. Paul, Minn.: West Publishing, 1978), p. 25.

[19]W. H. Newman, ''Commentary,'' in *Strategic Management,* ed. D. Schendel and C. W. Hofer (Boston: Little, Brown, 1979), p. 46.

At the business level, the company can choose to compete either selectively in one or more niches, or across the board. It can choose to compete in the same way that the rest of the industry competes, or it can try to change the rules. If the firm is a market leader, and if its competitive advantage is sustainable, playing the same game as the rest of the industry tends to be the best strategy. If it is not a market leader, the firm can explore ways to gain an advantage—either by focusing on a niche in which it has an advantage, or by exploring ways to change the game to its advantage.[20] For example, Miller Brewing marketed Lite, a low-calorie beer, as a new market segment, and changed the way the industry competed.

HISTORY AND EVOLUTION OF STRATEGIC MANAGEMENT

Though much of the terminology and many of the concepts of strategic management are taken from military history, specific recognition of the strategy concept in management theory and practice is relatively new. As we will see in Chapter 3, the growth in size, complexity, and diversity of our economic and social organizations has created an increased need for formal strategic management. In the late 1800s, most businesses were relatively small, simple, and specialized. The rate of environmental change was also relatively slow, and major discontinuities in the environment were uncommon. For this type of organization and situation—a relatively simple organization in a relatively stable environment—the task of achieving a productive match or fit with that environment (the essence of strategic management) was relatively easy. Most firms followed an *implicit* type of strategy, since strategic decisions were relatively uncomplicated and were required relatively infrequently. Today, many small businesses still operate this way; however, the increased rate and abruptness of environmental change requires increased use of strategic management by small as well as large firms.

Need for Planning Has Increased

Figure 1.5 indicates that as organizations grow in terms of size, product line, diversity, geographical coverage, organizational complexity, and vertical integration (as well as operating in a less stable environment), their need for formal strategic management increases—perhaps exponentially. If change is slow and predictable, it is easy to plan for the future, and the plan is likely to remain valid for extended periods of time. Planning can be a simple and infrequently needed function. On the other hand, in a rapidly changing and discontinuous environ-

---

[20]F. W. Gluck, "The Dilemmas of Resource Allocation," *Journal of Business Strategy* 2, no. 2 (Fall 1981), p. 67.

FIGURE 1.5   Conditions Requiring Formal Strategic Management

Environmental change rate	Slow	⟶	Rapid
Environmental change type	Continuous	Increased ⟶	Discontinuous
Geographical	Local	Need for ⟶	Multinational
Product line	Single	Formal ⟶	Broad
Product types	Related	Strategic ⟶	Diverse
Organization	Functional	Management ⟶	Multidivisional
Size	Small	⟶	Large

---

ment, valid plans are difficult to develop and are likely to have short life spans. Unfortunately, some managers become frustrated by the likelihood that their plans will be outmoded and perhaps invalidated, in certain instances soon after the plans are completed. The managers conclude that planning is an impossible task. But planning is much more important and critical in this situation, even though the process is more difficult and the resulting plans may be imprecise and short lived.

Through the first half of the 20th century, U.S. businesses and their environment grew steadily more complex, requiring progressively more attention to strategic management. But gradual change tends not to be noticed until it is perhaps too late (as in the case of the person who puts on two pounds a year and then discovers that his old army uniform no longer fits). We may have a gnawing feeling that things aren't working as well as they should (or once did), but may not be aware of the change or the need for a new approach because of the very gradual nature of the change.

Discontinuous changes, however, such as World War II, are readily apparent, even if the appropriate response to the change isn't. You know that things are different, and a new approach is required on your part. The years following World War II saw a dramatic increase in diversification and geographical (multinational) expansion by U.S. firms. There was an abrupt move toward the right side of the chart in most of the areas shown in Figure 1.5. In response to this shift, firms began to devote increasing effort to planning and strategy formulation to enable them to compete more effectively in their various markets. In the late 1960s, another rapid (if not discontinuous) change occurred in many of the organizations themselves. The trend toward multibusiness organizations (whether diversified firms or conglomerates) became evident, and in modified form continues today as cash-rich firms such as Philip Morris seek acquisition and buy-out candidates. As will be seen later, the multidivisional company needs to consider strategic alternatives not only at the individual business, product, or market level, but also at the corporate level. That is, in what businesses (products, markets) should the company compete, and how should these businesses be integrated to meet *corporate-level* goals and objectives?

FIGURE 1.6 Increasing Challenges Require Additional Strategies

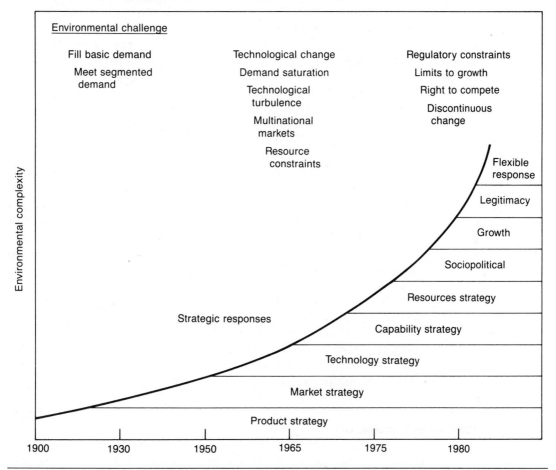

Source: Adapted from H. I. Ansoff, "The Changing Shape of the Strategic Problem," in *Strategic Management: A New View of Business Planning and Policy,* ed. D. Schendel and C. W. Hofer (Boston: Little, Brown, 1979), p. 30.

More Areas Require Strategic Attention

Several researchers in the field of strategic management have developed models describing the evolution of the external environment and the organizations' strategic response. Ansoff, as an example, analyzed the changing environmental challenges facing organizations during this century and the managerial responses, competitive strategies, and entrepreneurial strategies employed to cope with them.[21] Ansoff's major conclusions are summarized in Figure 1.6, which

---

[21]H. Igor Ansoff, "The Changing Shape of the Strategic Problem," in *Strategic Management: A New View of Business Policy and Planning,* ed. D. Schendel and C. W. Hofer (Boston: Little, Brown, 1979), p. 30.

shows that markets, products, and technology progressively have become more diverse and complex. We have gone from trying to satisfy basic unfilled demands for goods and services (a production economy) to a situation where basic needs long since have been met, and ''needs'' must be created through product differentiation, planned obsolescence, and consumer manipulation (a marketing economy). More recently, increased environmental turbulence has necessitated resource conservation and contingency or surprise preparedness strategies. The firm now spreads its risks through diversification and a search for new areas for expansion, such as through products that conserve resources, ecology markets, and Third World markets. Strategies are needed to cope with a much larger number of environmental influences today than was true in the early 1900s, when a strategy of meeting existing unfulfilled demand was sufficient. Today, more strategies are required as progressively more areas become problems.

Additional environmental trends, threats, and opportunities are likely to appear in the future, and specific strategies will be required to cope with them. Real or artificial constraints on growth (rate and size) may require a limited-growth strategy. Challenges to the firm's right to compete in certain markets may require the firm to prove that it should be permitted to do so, necessitating a legitimacy strategy. The increasing rate of environmental change in general, when the rate exceeds the firm's ability to respond, may require an explicitly flexible response or surprise management strategy.

The point is: as more and more environmental constraints—and opportunities— emerge, more and more explicit areas of strategic attention are presented to the firm. This clearly increases the need for, the importance of, and the complexity of a firm's strategic management activities.

Time Compression and Instability

In the past, fluctuations in the variables affecting strategic decisions were relatively small and infrequent. As shown in Figure 1.7, the size of the fluctuations has increased, and they occur more frequently than in the past. This trend is likely to continue into the future, making the environment even more dynamic than it had been.

One obvious example of this phenomenon is interest rates. The prime rate during the 1950s and 60s was typically in the neighborhood of 5 percent, with a range of from 4 to 6 percent. In the mid-1970s, the prime rate averaged over 10 percent, and typically ranged from 7 to 12 percent. So far in the 1980s, it has been as high as 17 percent while averaging about 11 or 12 percent. Another example is the price of gold, which has been as high as $800 per ounce and as low at $285 in the past few years. Similar instances have involved fluctuations in: other interest rates; the value of the dollar; stock prices; the demand for and prices of many products, including gasoline, farm equipment, lumber, airline tickets, and others. Motor-home demand was once as high as 500,000 units per

FIGURE 1.7   Increasing Frequency and Amplitude of Change

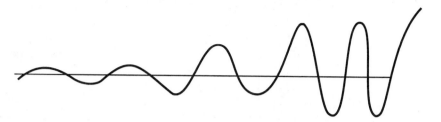

Past	Present	Future
Less frequent fluctuations	More frequent fluctuations	Higher frequency of fluctuations
Small fluctuations	Increased size of fluctuations	Large fluctuations

year. With the energy crisis, demand dropped to 40,000 units, later rose to 400,000, and more recently was in the neighborhood of 200,000 units.[22]

How does a company plan under such circumstances? First of all, as pointed out earlier, planning is at once more important and more difficult in such an environment, and requires a change in strategic response. With greater fluctuations in sales, a firm must lower its break-even point to remain profitable, even if its average level of sales does not change. It will be operating at lower levels of output than before, which will result in lower profits or greater losses during those increasingly more frequent periods of low output. On the other hand, the higher peak demands necessitate more, not less, maximum capacity. These two phenomena may require more flexible, automated plants, outside sources of supply, producing to inventory, or other strategies. The point is that a greater number of strategic decisions must be made more frequently, and with less time for analysis than in the past. This trend is likely to continue or even accelerate in the future, making the organization's strategic management activities and decisions even more essential than they are today.

Increased Rate of Change

In describing "future shock" some years ago, Alvin Toffler pointed out that the last 50,000 years of human existence could be represented by some 800 sequential life spans of 60-plus years each. Of those 800 life spans:

[22]Kami, *Strategic Planning for Changing Times.*

FIGURE 1.8   Increasing Rate and Magnitude of Change

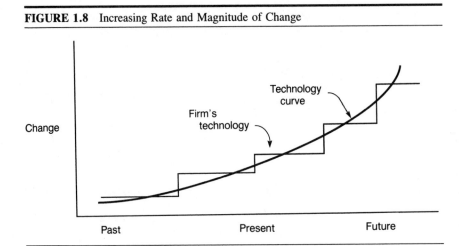

- The first 650 were spent in caves.
- Only the last 70 saw communication from one lifetime to another.
- Only the last 6 saw the widespread printed word.
- Only the last 4 saw time measured with precision.
- Only the last 2 saw the electric motor.
- Only the current lifetime has seen the overwhelming majority of material goods we take for granted today[23]

This rate of change can be illustrated for a manufacturing firm as it adopts new technology, as shown in Figure 1.8. In the past, as a firm adopted a new technology or production method, it could expect to employ that method for an appreciable period of time before it fell behind the latest methods. At present, that period of time has shortened, and the amount of change required at each step has increased. In the future, it is likely that even more dramatic (and risky) changes will be required, with increasing frequency. Again, we can see that more significant strategic decisions must be made more frequently and with greater risk because of the rapidity and magnitude of change.

As General Motors' Michael Naylor points out, business is analogous to a race. But it is a race that never ends; winning today *only* earns you the right to compete again tomorrow!

DOES PLANNING PAY?

We have made a case, conceptually at least, that strategic management is important to the success of a company, and becomes more important as

---

[23]Alvin Toffler, *Future Shock* (New York: Random House, 1970), p. 14.

organizations and their environments become more complex. The bottom line, however, is whether or not the increased effort expended on strategic management can be shown to produce improved performance. Do firms that plan experience better levels of sales, growth, return on investment, or earnings?

This is a difficult question to answer. First of all, organizations may show mixed results depending on the criteria selected to measure performance: sales might be increasing while ROI decreases, growth rate might be diminishing while ROI and earnings improve, and so on. Also the company's performance is subject to a number of nonstrategic—or operating—factors, such as the effectiveness of its sales force, manufacturing efficiencies, accounting policies, and performance of its people. In addition, the economy, competitive actions, interest rates, tax rates, acts of God (such as airplane crashes), product safety concerns (such as with nuclear reactors and Tylenol), and other environmental influences can significantly affect performance.

However, strategic management involves forecasting and developing an effective fit with the environment. Firms practicing strategic management should be in a better position to forecast and cope with (or at least react to) the types of environmental conditions just mentioned. So they should exhibit better performance, at least on the average and in the long run. What do the studies tell us?

Strategic Planning Pays

A number of early studies indicate that strategic planning pays, as shown in Table 1.1. Most of these studies examined the performances (using a number of commonly accepted criteria) of companies in various industries. Companies using formal planning systems or approaches were compared with companies that did not. The Thune and House study, for example, matched 18 medium-to-large companies on the basis of industry, size, and growth rate.[24] One member of each pair used formal planning systems and one did not. Over the seven years of the study, the formal planners significantly outperformed the informal planners in every area measured—sales growth, earnings per share, stock price, return on equity, and ROI. In addition, those adopting formal systems for the first time significantly bettered their previous performance in the areas observed—sales, earnings per share, and stock price. The Herold study extended the drug and chemical portion of the Thune and House study for four more years and found similar results.[25] In fact, formal planners increased their lead over the others.

---

[24]Stanley Thune and R. House, "Where Long-Range Planning Pays Off," *Business Horizons,* August 1970, pp. 81–87.

[25]D. M. Herold, "Long-Range Planning and Organizational Performance: A Cross-Validation Study," *Academy of Management Journal,* March 1972, pp. 91–102.

TABLE 1.1 Studies on Relationship between Planning and Performance

Study	Sample Type (number)	Categorization on Planning	Performance Measures	Findings
Thune and House (1970)	Industrial firms (36)	Strategy, goals, action programs for 3 years	Sales, stock prices, EPS, ROE, ROA, 6–11 years	Formal planners' performance superior
Ansoff, et al. (1970)	U.S. manufacturing firms (62)	Systematic establishment and implementation of plans	Twenty-one financial measures	Planners outperformed nonplanners. Planners performed more consistently
Herold (1972)	Industrial firms (10)	Strategy, goals, action programs for 3 years	Pretax profit, R&D expenditures, 7 years	Formal planners outperformed informal planners
Fulmer and Rue (1974)	U.S. firms in durable, nondurable and service industries (386)	Three-year written document with objectives and strategy	Sales growth, net margin, ROA, 3 years	No across-the-board relationship found
Karger and Malik (1975)	Industrial firms (38)	Five-year written plan for firm, divisions and plants plus detailed 1–2 year plan	Thirteen financial measures, 10 years	Planners outperformed nonplanners on almost all measures
Wood and LaForge (1979)	U.S. banks (41)	Nonplanners, partial planners, comprehensive planners	Net income, ROE, 5 years	Comprehensive planners outperformed nonplanners. No relationship between comprehensive and partial planners
Kudla (1980)	Manufacturing firms plus others (129)	Nonplanners, incomplete planners, and complete planners	Monthly stock returns adjusted for market effects and risk	Planning had a negligible impact on returns and transitory impact on reduction of risk
Leontiades and Tezel (1980)	Fortune 1,000 firms (61)	CEO's and CPO's perception of importance and contribution of planning	ROE, ROA, price earnings ratio, sales and EPS growth, 4–7 years	No relationship
Robinson, Vozikis and Pearce (1981)	Small firms (51)	Not explicitly defined	Sales growth, profitability, sales per employee, employment growth	Planning found to enhance effectiveness

Study	Sample	Planning measure	Performance measure	Findings
Lindsay, et al. (1981)	U.S. firms in durable, nondurable and service industries (144)	Impoverished, programmed, and progressive planners	Sales and earnings growth, net margin, ROA, 5 years	No consistent relationship between planning and performance
Robinson and Pearce (1983)	Small banks (85)	Formal versus nonformal planners	Profit margin, loan growth, ROA, ROE, 3 years	No relationship
Welch (1984)	N.Y. Stock Exchange firms (49)	Strategic versus nonstrategic planners	Average price/earnings multiple, 5 years	Strategic planner's P/E multiple higher
Fredrickson and Mitchell (1984)	Forest products firms (27)	Level of comprehensiveness	Average return on assets, sales growth, 5 years	Negative relationship between comprehensiveness and performance
Fredrickson (1984)	Paint and coating manufacturers (38)	Level of comprehensiveness	Average return on assets, sales growth, 5 years	Positive relationship between comprehensiveness and ROA, no relationship with sales growth
Rhyne (1986)	Fortune 1,000 firms, (89)	Continuum of planning sophistication	Total return to investors, 4 and 10 years. Return on equity	Superior 10-year results from externally focused long-term systems
Pearce, Robbins, and Robinson (1987)	Eastern manufacturing firms (97)	Degree of planning formality	ROA, ROS, sales growth, overall performance	Formal strategic planning positively associated with organizational performance

Source: Adapted from L. C. Rhyne, ''The Relationship of Strategic Planning to Financial Performance,'' *Strategic Management Journal* 7, no. 5 (September–October 1986), pp. 424–25, reprinted by permission of John Wiley & Sons, Ltd., and including the following sources: H. I. Ansoff, J. Avner, R. G. Brandenburg, F. E. Portner, and R. Radosevich. ''Does Planning Pay? The Effect of Planning on Success of Acquisition in American Firms.'' *Long-Range Planning* 3, no. 2 (1970), pp. 2–7; J. W. Fredrickson. ''The Comprehensiveness of Strategic Decision Processes: Extension, Observations, Future Directions.'' *Academy of Management Journal* 27 (1984), pp. 445–66; J. W. Fredrickson and T. R. Mitchell. ''Strategic Decision Processes: Comprehensiveness and Performance in an Industry with an Unstable Environment.'' *Academy of Management Journal* 27 (1984) pp. 399–432; R. M. Fulmer and L. W. Rue. ''The Practice and Profitability of Long-Range Planning.'' *Managerial Planning* 22, no. 6 (1974), pp. 1–7; D. M. Herold, ''Long-Range Planning and Organizational Performance: A Cross-Evaluation Study.'' *Academy of Management* 15 (1972), pp. 91–102; D. W. Karger and Z. A. Malik. ''Long-Range Planning and Organizational Performance.'' *Long-Range Planning* 8, no. 6 (1975). pp. 60–64; R. J. Kudla. ''The Effects of Strategic Planning on Common Stock Returns.'' *Academy of Management Journal* 1 (1980), pp. 5–20; M. Leontiades and A. Tezel. ''Planning Perceptions and Planning Results.'' *Strategic Management Journal* 1 (1980), pp. 65–76; W. M. Lindsay, W. R. Boulton, S. Franklin, and L. W. Rue. ''Strategic Management Effectiveness: A Longitudinal Study.'' Unpublished paper presented to the Academy of Management Annual Meeting, San Diego, 1981; J. A. Pearce II, D. K. Robbins, and R. B. Robinson, Jr. ''The Impact of Grand Stratety and Planning Formality on Financial Performance.'' *Strategic Management Journal* 8, no. 2 (March–April 1987), pp. 125–34; L. C. Rhyne, ''The Relationship of Strategic Planning to Financial Performance.'' *Strategic Management Journal* 7, no. 5 (September–October 1986), pp. 423–36; R. B. Robinson and J. A. Pearce. ''The Impact of Formalized Planning on Financial Performance in Small Organizations.'' *Strategic Management Journal* 4 (1983), pp. 197–208; R. B. Robinson, G. S. Vozikis, and J. A. Pearce. ''Stage of Development as a Contingency on the Strategic Planning Performance Relationship: An Empirical Study within a Small Firm Environment.'' Unpublished paper presented to the Academy of Management Annual Meeting, San Diego, 1981; S. S. Thune, and R. J. House. ''Where Long-Range Planning Pays Off.'' *Business Horizons* 13, no. 4 (1970), pp. 81–87; J. B. Welch, ''Strategic Planning Could Improve Your Share Price.'' *Long-Range Planning* 17, no. 2 (1984), pp. 144–47; D. R. Wood and R. L. LaForge. ''The Impact of Comprehensive Planning on Financial Performance.'' *Academy of Management Journal* 22 (1979), pp. 516–26.

The Ansoff et al.,[26] Karger and Malik,[27] and Wood and LaForge[28] studies produced further indications that formal planners outperform the others in a variety of industries.

Some of the more recent studies began to investigate types and degrees of sophistication of planning systems, not just the oversimplified formal versus informal dichotomy. Several of these studies showed the degree of formality and comprehensiveness of the planning system to be related to improved performance measures.

Strategic Planning Doesn't Always Pay

On the other hand, a few of the early studies cast doubt on the value of formal planning. Rue and Fulmer found that planning paid off in certain industries but not in others, and paid off more for larger firms that for smaller ones.[29] In durable goods industries, manufacturers using formal planning outperformed the others in each case; however, the reverse was true in service industries. Whether the effect of planning varies from manufacturing to service industries, or whether the three-year study produced erroneous results is open to question. However, a Canadian study by Sheehan found that growth rate declined as the degree of planning increased from nonplanners to low, medium, then high.[30] It should be noted that Sheehan used growth rate alone as a performance measure; it may well be that firm size was an overriding factor, because, for example, small firms tend to have higher-percentage growth rates and employ less formal planning systems than do their larger counterparts. Thus, the results of the Sheehan study are somewhat open to question.

Several of the late studies showed no consistent relationship between planning measures and performance, and one study found a *negative* relationship between a plan's level of comprehensiveness and performance, as measured by a five-year return on assets and sales growth. This study—by Fredrickson and Mitchell—studied the comprehensiveness versus performance relationship under varying environments. Specifically, comprehensive approaches did not lead to improved performance under uncertain environmental conditions, but they did in relatively

---

[26]H. I. Ansoff, J. Avner, R. G. Brandenburg, F. E. Portner, and R. Radosevich, *Acquisition Behavior of U.S. Manufacturing Firms, 1946–65* (Nashville, Tenn.: Vanderbilt University Press, 1971).

[27]Delmar W. Karger, and E. A. Malik, "Long-Range Planning and Organizational Performance," *Long-Range Planning,* December 1975, p. 63.

[28]D. R. Wood, Jr., and R. L. LaForge, "The Impact of Comprehensive Planning on Financial Performance," *Academy of Management Journal,* September 1979, pp. 516–26.

[29]L. W. Rue and R. M. Fulmer, "Is Long-Range Planning Profitable?" *Academy of Management Proceedings,* 1973, pp. 66–73.

[30]G. A. Sheehan, "Long-Range Planning and Its Relationship to Firm Size, Firm Growth, and Firm Growth Variability," Ph.D. dissertation, University of Western Ontario, 1975.

certain environments.[31] To add additional fuel to the controversy, however, several just-completed studies have found that high performers in fast-changing environments tend to use more thorough, structured approaches. These contemporary results will be discussed in more detail in Chapters 2 and 8.

What Have We Learned?

We have not proved conclusively that planning pays, but only that most well-conducted research studies suggest that planning pays. Even those studies did not *prove* that planning improved performance, but only that the two are correlated. It could be just as likely that high performers have the resources and time to engage in strategic planning, although the Thune and House, and Herold studies would suggest otherwise. If better-controlled studies can more closely identify the planning-performance link, a stronger case will emerge for the value of planning.

In addition, many studies largely dealt with formal versus informal planners, *not* planners versus nonplanners, as one might mistakenly conclude. "Every business enterprise from the smallest partnership to the largest corporation has a planning process. It may be informal and unstructured, but planning must be done if rational decisions are to be made. The mechanics reflect the nature of the industry, its management style, and systems peculiar to individual companies."[32] So the comparison is *how,* not *whether,* planning is done. Further, as will be discussed in Chapter 9, many formal planning systems serve as a means for *implementing* rather than *formulating* strategy; therefore, strategy formulation still may occur on an informal basis in firms utilizing a formal planning system. If this is the case, the studies of formal versus informal planning have merely shown that more systematized *implementation* of strategies tends to yield better performance—a conclusion worth noting on its own.

Other writers have reported a vague discontent with strategic planning among top managers. The managers question the value added by strategic planning processes that are increasingly more time-consuming and sophisticated. J. Quincy Hunsicker, of the management consulting firm McKinsey & Company, observes that top management is most frustrated by the "disproportion between the time and money expended on the strategic planning effort and the substantive value of the resulting strategies."[33] This should not be surprising since top management is more directly involved in strategy formulation than in strategy implementation, and formal planning aids implementation more than it assists in formulation.

---

[31]Fredrickson and Mitchell, "Strategic Decision Processes."

[32]D. R. Welsh and R. W. Lee, "Adapting Systems to Cope with Multiple Futures," *Management Focus* 26, no. 1 (January/February 1979), p. 6.

[33]J. Quincy Hunsicker, "The Malaise of Strategic Planning," *Management Review,* March 1980.

Finally, most of the studies focused on "bottom-line" measures—profits, growth, and so on—measures which are subject to a variety of powerful influences in addition to planning systems and approaches. In addition, most firms today "plan"; any simple planner versus nonplanner dichotomy has long since vanished, forcing researchers to look for other factors. The evaluation measure should probably *not* be firm performance, but should be the following:

1. The *development* of high-quality *strategies,* regardless of the type of system employed.
2. The *appropriateness* of the planning *system,* given the firm's industry, size, diversification, and the like.

In sum, the deciding factor is the *quality* of the strategies implemented by the firm, not the degree of formalization of the planning process. It is reasonable to conclude that larger, more complex firms are likely to require a more formalized planning process, even if it is directed primarily toward the implementation of strategies. On the other hand, if increasing formalization of any step of the process—formulation or implementation—causes the firm to become less flexible and less responsive to a dynamic environment, the firm will be defeating the very purpose of strategic management; that is, achieving a beneficial fit with the environment. More *formalized* planning is not necessarily more *effective* planning, although formalization tends to ensure that the process will not be ignored.

OTHER CHARACTERISTICS OF SUCCESSFUL ORGANIZATIONS

We have concluded that the development of high-quality strategies, coupled with and aided by the appropriate planning systems and approaches, are important to an organization's success. But strategies alone are not enough. Other researchers (such as the work described in the following paragraphs) have found other contributing factors which are likely to complement effective strategies. Organizations that employ *both* approaches stand an even higher likelihood of success than is probable with either approach by itself.

Tom Peters: Search, Passion, and Chaos

Thomas Peters, formerly of McKinsey & Company and Stanford University, conducted a study of well-managed companies to determine the common factors that contribute to their successes. Peters' study (conducted in conjunction with Robert H. Waterman, Jr.) initially looked in-depth at 10 companies that had been successful over long periods of time and continued to lead their industries: IBM, Texas Instruments, Hewlett-Packard, 3M, Digital Equipment, Procter & Gamble, Johnson & Johnson, McDonald's, Dana, and Emerson Electric. While the companies differ in many ways, Peters found eight common attributes that they adhere to and work hard to maintain:

1. *Bias toward action.* The companies are action oriented; their approach is "do it, fix it, try it." They don't analyze a problem to death before acting (paralysis by analysis), and make progress in small steps rather than through sweeping, grand plans. In this way, if the action turns out to be a mistake, they reverse the action quickly and do something else—they are flexible, incremental, and responsive. They focus quickly on problems, typically appointing a "czar" or a task force (of *line* managers) to solve them.

2. *Simple form and lean staff.* The structure or form of an organization is not an end in itself; it is a *means* to an end. The best organization structure is the simplest structure that works, regardless of how it looks on paper. Many of these companies are divided into small, entrepreneurial units that manage to get things done. Staffs are kept as small as possible to avoid bureaucracies. (Staffs have a way of growing and generating their own workload—for example, reports and analyses—that sap line managers' energies if not kept in check.)

3. *Closeness to the customer.* Successful companies tend to view the customer as an integral part of their businesses, rather than as an outsider. The companies are "customer driven." Their goods and services are designed, above all, to satisfy the customer's needs. Contrast this with the technology-, product-, or strategy-driven companies that produce products because they can be built, then try to convince customers to buy them. A classic example of a product/technology-driven company is Polaroid. Its "instant movie camera" could be built, but customers decided they did not need it. In fact, IBM does not allow managers to hold staff jobs for more than three years, because they tend to lose touch with customers.

4. *Productivity improvement through people.* The companies surveyed believe that productivity can be improved by motivating and stimulating employees, largely through giving them autonomy, feedback, and recognition programs. In fact, much of the feedback and recognition programs—for example, progress charts in the plant, badges, pins, medals, and slogans—may sound simplistic, but they work.

5. *Operational autonomy.* Well-managed companies authorize their managers to act like entrepreneurs, giving them the authority to make a wide range of decisions on their own. These companies do not unduly constrain their managers by making it impossible for them to fail—or succeed. The managers know they are in charge, and the companies rarely force them to go against their best judgment.

6. *Stress on a key business value.* The companies studied by Peters focus on a corporate value that is important to their success, yet simple enough to be clearly understood—and internalized—even by the lowest-level employees. The value may involve customer service or productivity improvement. At Iowa Beef Processors, the focus is on being the lowest-cost producer, a value that gives the company a definite strategic advantage over the competition and "drives" other decisions.

7. *Doing what they know best.* All of the companies surveyed have been able to define their strengths and build on them. They resist the temptation to move into attractive businesses that require skills the company does not have. One executive states, ''Never acquire any business you don't know how to run.'' A cigarette company diversifying into high-technology or land development or motion pictures may be asking for trouble; on the other hand, marketing beer may be a natural extension of their consumer-product strengths.

8. *Simultaneous loose/tight controls.* At first glance this may appear inconsistent; how can controls be both loose *and* tight? Successful companies control a few variables tightly, but allow flexibility and leeway in others. They do not control everything tightly, nor do they give their managers free rein on everything. There are several measures—such as return on sales or output per employee—that top management uses for control and that subordinate managers *must* meet. The subordinate has the flexibility, autonomy, and leeway he or she needs by *not* being closely measured on other variables.[34]

Reevaluating "Excellence."   Peters and Waterman expanded their research and published it in book form in 1982.[35] The book was wildly successful—hitting a management nerve—and sold over 5 million copies. The book was largely an attack on managers who rely too heavily on financial analysis and controls. As time went on, however, the book's message began to lose some of its luster. By 1984, several of the ''excellent'' companies were experiencing serious financial difficulties. Peters' response was to write a sequel, *A Passion for Excellence,* with Nancy Austin.[36] The new book attempted to identify the sources of longer-term excellence, rather than the broadbrush approach of the first book.

Critics pointed out that the entire thrust of the books is on doing things right, without examining whether the companies were doing the right things.[37] Further questions were raised by academic studies which showed that ''nonexcellent'' companies outperform the ''excellent'' ones—at least in terms of shareholder returns.[38] In reality, all this may illustrate is that the ''excellent'' companies had this fact reflected in their stock prices at the beginning of the study, making them vulnerable to any bad news. In any event, Peters has become increasingly pessimistic about the ability of American corporations' ability to compete in foreign markets, reflected in his latest book, *Thriving on Chaos.*[39]

---

[34]Thomas J. Peters, ''Putting Excellence into Management,'' *Business Week,* July 21, 1980, p. 196.

[35]Thomas J. Peters and Robert H. Waterman, Jr., *In Search of Excellence* (New York: Harper & Row, 1982).

[36]T. J. Peters and Nancy Austin, *A Passion for Excellence* (New York: Random House, 1985).

[37]Milton Leontiades, ''Editorial: A Memo to the CEO,'' *Planning Review,* 14, no. 2 (March 1986), p. 4.

[38]W. G. Simpson and Timothy Ireland, ''Managerial Excellence and Shareholder Returns,'' *The Journal of the American Association of Individual Investors,* August 1987.

[39]T. J. Peters, *Thriving on Chaos* (New York, Alfred A. Knopf, 1987).

Enter Renewal

If Peters thinks that American industry cannot compete globally, his original cohort—Robert Waterman—does not share his view. Waterman says that *In Search of Excellence* merely *described* the excellent company, and his book—*The Renewal Factor*—tells managers what is needed to *become* excellent and to stay there. Renewal involves retaining the best of the past, but changing with the times. It involves moving from strength to strength, effectively managing change, adapting their cultures, strategies, systems, products, and structures to survive and prosper—even through severe crises. Eight themes underlie effective renewal:

1. *Informed opportunism.* Information is their main strategic advantage, and flexibility is their main strategic weapon. They assume opportunity will keep knocking, but it will knock softly and in unpredictable ways.
2. *Direction and empowerment.* Managers at renewing companies define the boundaries, and their subordinates figure out the best way to do the job within them. Managers give up some control to regain results.
3. *Friendly facts, congenial control.* Renewing companies love information that provides context and removes decision making from the realm of mere opinions. Their people regard financial controls as the benign checks and balances that allow them to be creative and free.
4. *A different mirror.* Leaders are open and inquisitive. They get ideas from almost anyone in and out of the hierarchy such as customers, competitors, even next-door neighbors.
5. *Teamwork, trust, politics, and power.* Renewers stress the value of teamwork and trust their employees to do the job. While relentless at fighting office politics, they acknowledge politics are inevitable in the workplace.
6. *Stability in motion.* Renewing companies undergo constant change against a base of underlying stability. They understand the need for consistency and norms. But they also realize that the only way to respond to change is to deliberately break the rules.
7. *Attitudes and attention.* Visible management attention, rather than exhortation, gets things done. Action may start with the words, but it has to be backed by symbolic behavior that makes those words come alive.
8. *Causes and commitment.* Commitment results from management's ability to turn grand causes into small actions so that everyone can contribute to the central purpose.[40]

CONCLUSIONS

Formal strategic planning has been with us since the early 1950s, even though organizations have always made strategic decisions. As organizations grow

---

[40]R. H. Waterman, *The Renewal Factor: How the Best Get and Keep the Competitive Edge* (New York: Bantam Books, 1987).

larger and more complex, and as environments become more dynamic and unstable, firms have tended to turn increasingly to formal strategic planning activities. A strategy is defined as a means, approach, or pattern of actions designed to achieve goals and objectives, focusing on a few key or critical areas. A strategy attempts to achieve a productive fit between the organization and its environment, and exists at several different levels of organizational activity.

Strategic decisions are those that tend to change the character or direction of an organization or one of its units, and strategic management is the continuous process of formulating, analyzing, evaluating, selecting, implementing, and controlling strategies by the organization, whether formal or informal. The value of the process depends on the quality of the implemented strategies, rather than on the formality of the process.

The Process and Practice of Strategic Management

LEARNING OBJECTIVES

After completing Chapter 2, you should be able to:

Define the four levels or types of strategic management.

Understand the strategic management process, including its role and key components.

Describe the specific steps in formulating and analyzing strategies.

Describe the relationship between strategies and policies.

Realize that effective strategic management is a continuous, regular, planned process.

Understand the roles and responsibilities of various management levels in the strategic process.

Define the term *general manager,* and appreciate the general manager's perspective.

Understand the roles of line and staff managers, including those in corporate planning, in the strategic process.

Chapter 1 examined the growing importance of strategic management by organizations competing in today's increasingly complex environments. Strategic management, as was shown, involves the match, or fit, the organization achieves with its environment, using its distinctive competencies to achieve competitive advantages and synergies. This chapter explores the process and key components of strategic management from an overall, or integrated, perspective. Specific steps in the process will be elaborated on in later chapters.

In addition, organizations are run by people; strategies and policies are formulated by people; strategic and operational decisions are made by people; and the decisions are implemented and planned by people. Those primarily responsible for strategic decisions are the managers overseeing the organization and its major divisions—the general managers. This chapter examines the essence of managerial roles and responsibilities, with particular emphasis on strategy and policy-related aspects.

To reiterate a point made in Chapter 1, effective planning and strategic management are flexible, adaptive processes. Successful organizations adapt themselves to the business environment; they are successful because they have managers who learn quickly and cause their organizations to respond effectively. However, most organizations "learn" more slowly than individuals do. Therefore, an important aspect of the corporate planning function is to cause the company to speed up its learning processes; that is, recognizing environmental change, digesting the new information, confirming it, and acting on it. Some companies—Shell Oil, for example—consider the prime value of the planning function to be speeding up the organizational learning process, not just "making plans." They do this through changing the way executives see and think about their markets, competitors, and businesses, using what-if scenarios, computer models, and other techniques to be discussed in later chapters. Many times, the ability to learn faster than competitors is the only real sustainable advantage a company has.[1] On the other hand, frequent strategy shifts may cause an organization to lose its focus or direction.[2] Balancing the need to respond quickly while maintaining a sense of direction is no easy task.

PROFILE   ### ConAgra's Simplified Planning System

Many firms follow relatively simple and flexible planning approaches with excellent results. More detail and structure at the expense of flexibility and ease of use is not necessarily an improvement, and may even be a detriment. Flexibility, simplicity, and ease of use *are* important characteristics of planning systems. Planning systems should be no more formal, structured, or detailed than necessary.

One example of a company that stresses simple planning is ConAgra, a highly successful food processor located in Omaha, Nebraska. Mike Harper, CEO, states that "simplicity is the key to planning at ConAgra," and the goal is to become the best-earning food company in the United States, with a number 1

---

[1]Arie P. DeGeus, "Planning as Learning," *Harvard Business Review* 66, no. 2 (March–April 1988), p. 70.

[2]Robert Lamb and Paul Shrivastava, eds., *Advances in Strategic Management*, vol. 5 (Greenwich, Conn.: JAI Press, 1988), p. xi.

objective of "making shareholders rich"—an average return of over 20 percent after taxes. ConAgra has deliberately located its independent divisions away from Omaha to reinforce their independence. Some of ConAgra's credos include:

1. Outside directors should offer advice, but not be too involved in planning.
2. The basic test for acquisitions is whether they fit strategically. Much time and money is spent on research, using outside consultants, before making an acquisition decision.
3. A system of 30-minute, Monday morning conference calls keeps the divisions in touch.
4. Executives are given adequate incentives to meet company goals.

An example of simple, clear thinking is illustrated by how the company decided to become a major force in raising chickens. Two pounds of feed are needed to produce one pound of meat on a chicken. Three pounds of feed, however, are required for a hog, and seven to eight pounds for cattle. Thus, chickens are cheaper, more efficient sources of food. An important strategic factor in this emphasis on chickens was also government attempts to improve citizens' diets.[3]

PROFILE   ***Incremental Decisions at GM***

Strategic decisions—like many other organizational decisions—often are made in an evolutionary, incremental manner. General Motors, for example, uses an iterative process to make tentative decisions on the way it thinks the auto market will go. As GM managers get more data, these tentative decisions are continuously modified. Strategy really *evolves* as a series of incremental steps, not on a definitive planned schedule. In fact, it is often difficult to say precisely who decided something and when. This is as it should be, because strategic management is an ongoing, continuous process, involving executives who are constantly thinking strategically.[4]

LEVELS OF STRATEGIC MANAGEMENT

Organizations, particularly multidivisional, multinational corporations, are complex entities. Management—strategic and operational—of these complex entities is a complicated and difficult task. As the saying goes, for every complex

---

[3]D. C. Beeder, "Fastest-Growing Food Company: Simplicity Helps ConAgra Grow," *Omaha World-Herald,* April 20, 1983, p. 18.

[4]Michael E. Naylor, "Keynote Address," 18th Annual Meeting, Decision Sciences Institute, Honolulu, Hawaii, November 1986.

problem there is a simple solution, and it's almost always wrong. Strategic management is not a simple matter. Every organization must address several levels, types, or areas of strategic management. For example, each organization has to determine its place in society: what its contribution will be, which sector of the economy it will be part of, whether to be profit or not for profit, and so on. Decisions must be made regarding how the firm will compete in its market or markets. Also, the firm must decide how the functional areas of the business need to be managed to support its market strategy most effectively and efficiently. Along with this, strategic guidelines must be developed to ensure that the firm's line, or operating, management manufactures and delivers the products and services in a cost-effective manner. Finally, for firms competing in more than one business area or market, a strategy of integration and interrelationships between the various businesses must be developed. Various authors have described these areas, types, or levels of strategies differently, but the essential issues can be addressed using four levels: an enterprise strategy, a corporate-level strategy, a business-unit strategy, and functional/operational strategies, as described in Table 2.1.

Enterprise Strategy

Every organization, regardless of size or sector of the economy, has a societal-role strategy. This strategy may not be implicitly or formally stated, but it exists nevertheless. Called "enterprise" strategy by Ansoff,[5] this strategy concerns the organization's mission, purpose, and role in society. It addresses questions such as: Why does this organization exist? What is it attempting to provide to society? What sector(s) of the economy is it part of? How does it function in society—as a not-for-profit or profit-making firm, in a regulated or unregulated industry? What form of ownership exists? Who comprises the board of directors?

The firm's enterprise strategy also influences its relationships with its environment, particularly its relationships with those who have an interest in what the organization does and how it conducts its business. Sometimes called "stakeholders" (having a stake in the firm), these include investors, creditors, suppliers, customers, management, employees, and local governments and citizens, to name a few. One reason organizations are regulated to various degrees is that the government has accepted the role of representing the interests of the relatively powerless small stakeholders in the firm.

An enterprise needs a clear, unambiguous concept of its mission and purpose—its role in society—to guide the formation of corporate policies and

---

[5]H. I. Ansoff, "The Changing Shape of the Strategic Problem," paper presented at a special conference on Business Policy and Planning Research: The State of the Art, Pittsburgh, May 1977.

TABLE 2.1 Strategy Levels

Strategy Types	Applies to	Focus
Enterprise	All organizations	Mission, purpose, role in society
Corporate	Multibusiness organizations	Which businesses and their interrelationships
Business unit	All organizations	How to compete most effectively
Functional/operating	All organizations	Fuctional and operational business-unit support

strategies in other areas. Thus, the enterprise strategy acts as a framework or envelope within which other, more specific types of strategies will operate. For example, the 1982 antitrust agreement between AT&T and the Justice Department significantly changed the societal role of that organization—from a regulated provider of local and long-distance telephone service and equipment to an unregulated, high-technology provider of long-distance voice and data communication services, equipment, and anything else it wishes to provide. AT&T's enterprise strategy guided it in the decisions to accept a relatively unregulated growth opportunity while giving up the regulated, lower-profit, local phone businesses.

Corporate Strategy

Corporate strategy addresses the questions: What set of businesses should the firm compete in? and How should they be integrated? While this type of strategy is most applicable to organizations competing in more than one market—the multibusiness firm—in a sense it applies to all firms. That is, the single-business firm is pursuing a corporate-level strategy by choosing to compete in only one business, rather than several.

The primary concerns of corporate strategy are: What should the firm's "portfolio" of businesses be, now and in the future? How do the businesses complement or reinforce one another, and how are corporate-level resources to be allocated to the various business units? Corporate-level strategy deals with questions of diversification, acquisition/divestiture, and the starting of new ventures or divisions, for example. Its basic concern is with the current and future rationale for deciding which businesses comprise the total corporation. Techniques helpful in developing corporate-level strategies will be discussed in Chapter 7.

Business-Unit Strategy

For single-business companies and for each business unit or market comprising the multibusiness corporate portfolio, a strategy must be developed focusing on how to compete in that product or market or industry segment. The focus of business-unit strategy is on what is appropriate for the product's stage in the life cycle, on the competitive environment, on the firm's distinctive competencies to develop or pursue, and on the niches it should seek, as well as on how to integrate the various functional areas of the business (notably, product design, manufacturing, and marketing) to produce a competitive advantage. The focus is also on the relative emphasis placed on each functional area and the level of resources each one is allocated. Numerous strategic factors important to business-unit success are presented in Chapter 6.

Functional and Operations Strategies

The success of the individual business strategy depends not only on how well the firm positions itself and competes in the given market segment, but also on how well it coordinates the various functions and operations required to design, manufacture, market, deliver, and support the product or service. Functional strategy involves what should be done in each of the key functional areas, given the relative emphasis placed on them and the resources allocated to each. For example, if the firm's business-unit strategy is to broaden its offerings in a particular market, how should the products complement one another with regard to cost, quality, features, and other factors? If a strategy of expanding market share is to be followed, will the marketing strategy involve increased advertising? Will quantity discounts, expansion of outlets, or the use of manufacturers representatives be necessary? How will this strategy affect the manufacturing, distribution, and finance functions?

Operations strategies also are needed to manage operating units and line areas—such as manufacturing plants, sales offices, retail outlets, and parts and distribution warehouses—in a cost-effective manner. At both the functional and operating levels, the major emphasis is on maximizing resource productivity by capitalizing on any possible synergies and distinctive competencies that the firm may possess. The goal is to support the business-unit, corporate, and enterprise strategies. At the corporate level, management—and the strategies—tend to be financially oriented; at the business-unit level, strategies are often marketing oriented. At the functional and operations levels, these strategies are implemented, and it is here that the people—for example, the R&D, sales, manufacturing, and plant managers—are found who many times make the difference in whether or not a higher-level strategy will be successful.

WHO IS INVOLVED IN STRATEGIC MANAGEMENT?

To understand strategic management, we must know where strategic decisions are made in organizations, what levels of management are involved, the roles of line and staff, and the skills required.

Managers and Strategic Decisions

In large organizations, several levels of management may be involved in strategic decision making at any given time. The majority of strategic decisions, however, will emanate from both the corporate level and the division or business-unit level. Does this mean that others have little or no role in such decisions?

To answer this question, one must understand how decisions are made in organizations. In reality, very few decisions are made *totally* by one person. A "decision" is the result of a stream or sequence of inputs and actions by a number of people. For example, a salesperson may inform the sales manager that a competitor is working on a "new and improved" line of products (according to information gleaned informally from a customer or other source). The sales manager may recommend to the division managers that a similar product should be developed, and research and engineering will likely be asked for feasibility and schedule estimates. Assuming that the effort is a major one, with effects on the product lines of other divisions (and needing funding from the corporate level), corporate staff input and analysis will be required. Finally, a recommendation will be made to the corporate president, who decides either to go ahead or drop the new line. The president *made* the decision—or did he? This decision was shaped by everyone involved in the process, from the salesperson who gathered the intelligence information, to the functional and staff people at division and corporate levels, who performed the analyses, to those at various levels who made the recommendations and finally to the president, who made the "choice." Thus, many people and levels can be involved in a significant strategic decision made by top management.

Henry Singleton, the well-respected former chief executive officer of the Teledyne Corporation, believes that a CEO's most important function is to foresee trends and act on them to help his company. When facing strategic decisions, Singleton demands maximum flexibility and the right to change his positions when the external environment warrants it. For his efforts and successes, *Forbes* has concluded that "when the history of this era is written, Dr. Henry E. Singleton will probably be one of its towering figures."[6] The point is that top managers are less responsible for *making* strategic and other decisions than they are for *managing* the decision process—making sure that the right decisions are made.

---

[6]Robert J. Flaherty. "The Singular Henry Singleton," *Forbes,* July 9, 1979, p. 45.

FIGURE 2.1   The Team at the Top

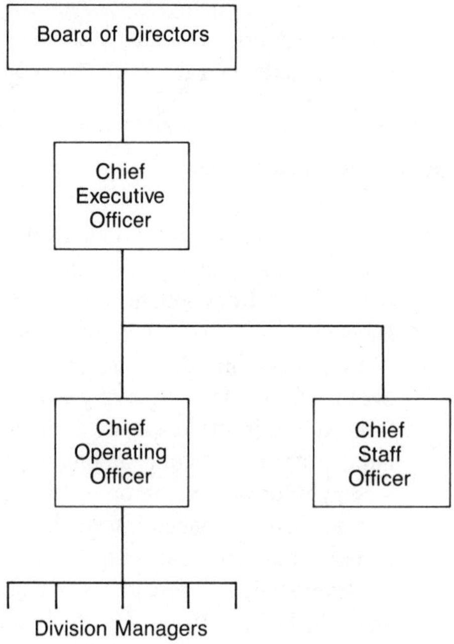

```
              ┌──────────────────┐
              │ Board of Directors│
              └──────────────────┘
                       │
              ┌──────────────────┐
              │      Chief        │
              │    Executive      │
              │     Officer       │
              └──────────────────┘
                       │
          ┌────────────┴────────────┐
  ┌──────────────┐          ┌──────────────┐
  │    Chief      │          │    Chief      │
  │  Operating    │          │    Staff      │
  │   Officer     │          │   Officer     │
  └──────────────┘          └──────────────┘
          │
  ┌───┬───┬───┬───┐
  │   │   │   │   │
    Division Managers
```

The Team at the Top

The people *responsible* for major strategic decisions, of course, are the board of directors, the chief executive officer (CEO), the chief staff officer (CSO), the chief operating officer (COO), and the division managers—the team at the top (see Figure 2.1). The board's role (discussed in more detail in Chapter 12) is rather limited in most strategic decisions. Truly major decisions, however—such as those involving mergers, acquisitions, or divestitures—typically may require board input and approval. Most lesser strategies, particularly at the business unit or division level, do not. The CEO's prime strategic function, perhaps even more than *making* such decisions, is to provide strategic leadership to other executives and managers—shaping the premises offered by other executives, calling for changes, and focusing the attention of the organization on what he or she feels is important.[7]

---

[7]J. L. Bower and Yves Doz, ''Strategy Formulation: A Social and Political Process,'' in *Strategic Management: A New View of Business Policy and Planning*, ed. D. E. Schendel and C. W. Hofer (Boston: Little, Brown, 1979).

A good leader pulls together the right people and sets the agenda; then lets people make their own decisions.[8] Even so, the role of the CEO has changed in the past five years. A recent study of 897 chief executives indicated that more than one fifth say they plan to become more involved in strategic planning in the next five years. As Harvard's Andrall Pearson states, "If top managers don't get involved in the details of the markets they compete in, they're going to get killed by people who do."[9]

The essence of strategy is the purposeful management of change, so that the firm can achieve competitive advantages in each of the businesses in which it competes.[10] In this regard, the job of top management is becoming more one of *changing things* (strategic) than *running things* (operational).[11]

The corporate planning staff under the CSO, coordinates the analytical functions of the organization, managing the planning process. Included in this function are: the analysis of environmental information, assessments of the firm's capabilities, the generation of strategic alternatives, and the review of implementation plans for completeness. The responsibility for strategic *decisions* lies with *line* managers, such as the CEO, COO, and division or business unit managers. Table 2.2 highlights the relative roles and responsibilities of the key decision levels for various organizational strategies.

Line and Staff Involvement

Planning staffs in U.S. and United Kingdom corporations typically *do not* decide on strategies, at least not at the corporate level. In fact, in their study of corporate planning, Taylor and Irving found that *planning is a line job.* "The role of the planner, therefore, is not to *do* the planning, but to design, sell, and direct the planning effort" or process.[12] However, at the divisional or functional levels, the planner's role may be somewhat different. He or she may be more of a "doer" than a manager of the process.

The emphasis on the line aspects of planning is indicated by recent cutbacks. An article in *Business Week* pointed out that the trend recently has been to cut back sharply on the number of staff jobs in organizations—a trend that is likely to be permanent. In fact, in 1982, GE cut its corporate-level strategic planning

---

[8]Alan M. Webber, "Gerald R. Ford: The Statesman as CEO," *Harvard Business Review,* 65, no. 5 (September–October 1987), p. 76.

[9]"A CEO's Life: Money, Security, and Meetings," *The Wall Street Journal,* July 7, 1987, p. 27.

[10]Arnoldo C. Hax and N. S. Majluf, "The Concept of Strategy and the Strategy Formation Process," *Interfaces* 18, no. 3 (May/June 1988), p. 102.

[11]Derek F. Abell, "Keynote Address," 20th Annual Conference, Decision Sciences Institute, November 1988.

[12]Bernard Taylor and P. Irving, "Organized Planning in Major U.S. Companies," *Long-Range Planning,* June 1971.

TABLE 2.2 Strategic Decision-Making Roles and Responsibilities

	Decision Level			
Hierarchy of Strategy	*Board of Directors*	*CEO*	*Corporate Management*	*Division Management*
Enterprise strategy				
Formulation	Primary			
Assessment		Primary		
Implementation		Primary	Contributory	
Monitoring	Primary			
Corporate strategy				
Formulation	Contributory	Primary		
Assessment	Primary			
Implementation			Primary	
Monitoring	Contributory	Primary		
Business strategy				
Formulation			Contributory	Primary
Assessment		Contributory	Primary	
Implementation				Primary
Monitoring			Primary	

Source: R. H. Rock and Marv Eisthen, "Implementing Strategic Change," in *The Strategic Management Handbook,* ed. K. J. Albert (New York: McGraw-Hill, 1983), p. 16–7. Reproduced with permission.

department from 60 to 25 people.[13] A study by Arthur D. Little of 12 major corporations also showed a general cutback in corporate staff, including corporate strategic-planning staffs. Some of the planners have been transferred to division levels, with other positions eliminated completely.[14]

Such cutbacks often are meant to emphasize that strategic planning must be performed *by* line managers, not *for* them. In fact, large centralized planning groups may have interfered at times with planning by line managers. Michael Kami, for example, feels that one to two planners per business unit is sufficient.[15] The view now is that if implementation is to become part of the plan, "the planners must be the same people who will be responsible for carrying out the plan.[16] Given this line emphasis, the role of corporate planning, then, includes the following:

1. Developing a framework for strategic planning and providing the data base.
2. Identifying and evaluating new product and market opportunities.

[13]"A New Era for Management," *Business Week,* April 25, 1983, p. 50.

[14]R. M. Tomasko, "Subbing Division, Line Work for Corporate Staff," *The Wall Street Journal,* March 28, 1983, p. 14.

[15]Michael Kami, *Strategic Planning for Changing Times* (Dayton: Cassette Recording Co., 1984).

[16]S. G. Brandt, *Strategic Planning in Emerging Companies* (Reading, Mass.: Addison-Wesley Publishing, 1982), p. 54.

3. Monitoring, reviewing, and revising the strategic plan.
4. Forecasting economic conditions and trends.
5. Developing contingency plans and alternate scenarios.
6. Predicting the uncertain future.[17]

But Who Is Responsible?

The General Manager.   Earlier, the statement was made that general managers are the people primarily responsible for strategic decisions. Who are these people and how do their jobs differ from those of other types of managers?

A general manager is someone responsible for the totality of an organization, a division of the organization, or a significant operating element (such as a subsidiary). A functional manager, by contrast, is responsible only for certain activities of that organizational element, such as marketing, manufacturing, finance, or engineering. The general manager, in turn, is responsible for *all* activities of his or her (usually multifunctional) organizational unit. Business policy and strategic management, of necessity, take the view of the general manager because they are concerned with the total organization (or a complete division or subsidiary).

Their Unique Responsibilities.   General managers, particularly those at the corporate level of an organization, tend to have responsibilities that differ from those of other managers. They are primarily responsible for managing other managers. No longer can this person function as a "playing coach" or expert practitioner. Many people get by in middle-level management jobs by working harder and longer. At the corporate executive level, however, this approach will not succeed for long (if at all) because the job is just too big. The time demands are very much greater than they are at lower levels, and a different approach is required. The need to delegate is critical—not just assigning work to people, but defining responsibilities and delegating responsibility (not tasks). Inherent in this is recognizing which issues are important, which and how much risk to take, and how much challenge a subordinate is capable of accepting and carrying out. There are qualitative, rather than quantitative, differences between executive and middle-level jobs; it is not a case of more of the same and broader responsibilities.

Key corporate-level general management functions include:

1. *Managing the strategic process.* This level of management is responsible for *creating* the appropriate structure and systems so that the organization's objectives are met effectively and efficiently, and so that resources are allocated properly. At lower levels, these things are largely "givens"; at upper levels, very little is given, especially in the long run. The main focus is what should the objectives be, rather than how they should be met. It is by creating the

---

[17]"Corporate Planning: Piercing Future Fog in the Executive Suite," *Business Week,* April 28, 1975, p. 46.

appropriate structure and systems that corporate management influences strategic and operational decisions, not by making or controlling those decisions directly.

2. *Managing relationships.* While division-level managers must successfully manage a number of relationships, the thrust of this task changes at the corporate level. Here the relationships between and among the corporate level and the division level units is a key concern. The issue again becomes more of what the roles and relationships should be, rather than how to live with them. In addition, the corporate level must develop a productive relationship with the board of directors. Further, the executive's use of corporate staff must be specified, as must the important relationship between corporate staff and division management.

3. *Managing executive development.* In the final analysis, the quality of the organization's managers—corporate and divisional—determines the success of the firm. What kinds of executives are needed? How should and can they be developed or acquired? What is the executive succession plan? How are candidates identified and their performance evaluated? Corporate-level management is responsible for these vital decisions.[18]

Some experts liken the job of the general manager to that of the wagon master, the leaders of the westward movement. Like wagon masters, effective general managers realize that their own success is inseparable from that of their fellow travelers. In this light, the leaders must realize that they have two important jobs—to reach the goal and to maintain morale along the way.[19]

THE STRATEGIC MANAGEMENT PROCESS

In complex organizations, formal processes are necessary to ensure that strategic analyses and decisions are made and carried out in a coordinated, integrated manner. In addition, a certain degree of structure is required so that the firm maintains its sense of purpose, focus, and direction. Ideally, the organization's planning processes will allow the CEO's vision to flow from the top down, and strategic plans incorporating that vision to emanate from the operating divisions.[20] Doing so requires a balance between formal, or synoptic, planning processes and less-structured, or incremental, processes. Recent research has shown that more formal processes result in better strategic decisions when the organization faces a relatively turbulent environment, and incremental approaches work best in stable

[18]H. E. R. Uyterhoeven, R. W. Ackerman, and J. W. Rosenblum, *Strategy and Organization,* rev. ed. (Homewood, Ill.: Richard D. Irwin, 1977).

[19]Jack S. Ninomiya, "Wagon Masters and Lesser Managers," *Harvard Business Review* 66, no. 2 (March–April 1988), p. 84.

[20]Ray Stata, "The Role of the Chief Executive Officer in Articulating the Vision," *Interfaces* 18, no. 3 (May/June 1988), p. 3.

environments.[21] At this point, it is appropriate to investigate an overall model of the process, which can be implemented with the appropriate degree of formality or flexibility to fit the organization and its environment.

In studying the process of strategic management and its components, various authors have developed models representing their view of the process. For example, Kenneth Andrews[22] and his co-workers at Harvard, William F. Glueck,[23] George Steiner,[24] A. A. Thompson and A. J. Strickland,[25] and D. E. Schendel and C. W. Hofer[26] have all made major contributions in furthering the development of a comprehensive model of the strategic management process. The model described below integrates and incorporates the best features and major contributions of each of these landmark models.

An Integrated Model

As discussed in Chapter 1, strategic management includes both strategic planning and strategic control. Strategic planning, in turn, includes formulating and evaluating alternative strategies, choosing a strategy, and developing plans for putting it into practice. To formulate a strategy, the decision maker must take into account values and expectations of the stakeholders, the organization's mission and purpose, goals and objectives, the external environment and the internal capabilities of the firm, as well as major policies. Taken together with those of strategic control, these tasks comprise the strategic management process, and are described in the following paragraphs and illustrated in Figure 2.2. Its key elements are examined in depth in later chapters.

Overview of the Process

Briefly, the process begins with top management's vision and a value analysis. The values and expectations of external stakeholders (e.g., stockholders, customers, suppliers, society, the community, and creditors) and the internal

---

[21]Rebecca J. Morris, "The Effect of Environmental Turbulence on the Design of Effective Strategic Information Systems," Ph.D. dissertation, University of Nebraska, 1988.

[22]Kenneth Andrews, *The Concept of Corporate Strategy,* rev. ed. (Homewood, Ill.: Richard D. Irwin, 1980).

[23]W. F. Glueck, *Business Policy: Strategy Formation and Management Action,* 2nd ed. (New York: McGraw-Hill, 1976); and W. F. Glueck, *Business Policy and Strategic Management,* 3rd ed. (New York: McGraw-Hill, 1980).

[24]G. A. Steiner, *Strategic Planning: What Every Manager Must Know* (New York: Free Press, 1979), p. 17.

[25]A. A. Thompson, Jr., and A. J. Strickland III, *Strategy Formulation and Implementation* (Plano, Tex.: Business Publications, 1980).

[26]D. E. Schendel and C. W. Hofer, *Strategic Management: A New View of Business Policy and Planning* (Boston: Little, Brown, 1979).

FIGURE 2.2   Integrated Model of Strategic Management

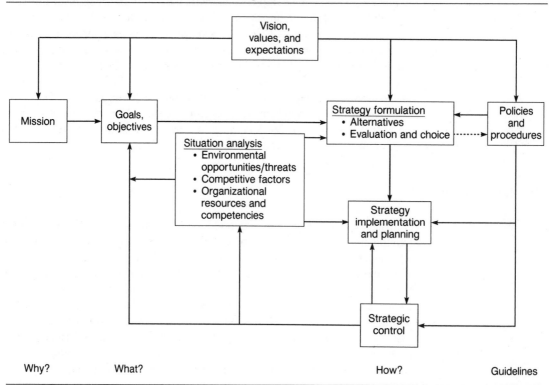

stakeholders (e.g., top management, other management, staff, and other employees) most importantly affect the organization's mission or purpose. They also affect the firm's policies, or the guidelines within which it operates, as well as the goals and objectives the firm sets for itself, and the strategies proposed and selected by the firm.

The firm's mission, goals and objectives, policies, and analyses of the external and internal environments provide the major bases for strategy formulation, including development, evaluation, and choice of strategic alternatives.

While certain authors define policies as dealing with implementation of strategies, it is more correct to consider them as constraints guiding strategy formulation and selection. For example, if a firm has a policy of not diversifying into unrelated businesses, this policy would obviously affect the growth strategy alternatives open to the company; that is, it would cut down the number of strategies available if no such policy existed. On the other hand, strategies can, at times, result in policy changes. Using the same example, if a particularly desirable opportunity arose for the company to diversify into an unrelated business, it is entirely possible that the company would reevaluate the policy prohibiting it from taking this advantage. In general, however, the major direction of influence is from policies to strategies, rather than vice versa.

Just as tactics can be thought of as actions taken within a strategic framework, procedures can be considered to be specific expressions of policies. That is, procedures are guides to the day-to-day activities of the firm, designed to ensure that the firm operates within the broader guidelines of its policies. For example, if a firm has a policy of strongly protecting employee privacy, this will be reflected in procedures governing how the company's personnel records are prepared, disseminated, and stored. Obviously, a firm will have many levels of policies and many levels of procedures, but generally procedures can be thought of as supporting, implementing, or ensuring adherence to certain policies. Unfortunately, however, many employees are not aware of or do not see the connection between certain procedures that impinge on their work and the policies the procedures support. In addition, procedures have a tendency to remain in place long after their reason for being has expired, sometimes even after the policy they were designed to support has been changed. Both situations should be guarded against because, as indicated, policies guide strategy formulation, as well as strategy evaluation and choice. Likewise, procedures guide the strategy evaluation and choice process, and, perhaps to a greater degree, strategy implementation and planning.

Strategic control completes the process shown in Figure 2.2, answering the questions of: (1) whether the strategy implemented is the one that was chosen (or has it been changed in the implementation and detailed planning processes); and (2) whether the results are those that were expected. If the answer to either of these questions is negative, corrective action must be taken. The action can be directed to those areas where changes are required or appropriate, starting with modifications of detailed plans, and progressing through changing or modifying the strategy selected, selecting an entirely new strategy, or perhaps even modifying the goals and objectives of the firm (if it is judged that *no* strategy is likely to result in their accomplishment).

ELEMENTS OF THE STRATEGIC PROCESS

In general, following the framework of Figure 2.2, the organization's mission or purpose, a result of its enterprise strategy, defines *why* the organization exists and why it competes in certain sectors or industries. Within this mission or purpose, the firm addresses *what* it intends to accomplish, both in the long and short run. *Goals* are the broad directions or results the firm wants to accomplish, while *objectives* relate to more specific targets. Goals tend to involve longer-term or continuing results, and may not have a specific time frame for their accomplishment. Objectives, on the other hand, are more specific ends to be met within the framework of the broader goals, and usually relate to a given period. That time frame, however, can be long and/or short run. Thus, goals tend to be unrelated to time, but objectives include a time horizon. For example, a firm may have the goal of becoming a ''leader in the industry.'' To support this, a long-term objective of having the largest share of the market by 1995 may be chosen, with shorter-range objectives of increasing market share by 2 percent in each of the next five years.

Defining why the organization exists and competes as it does and what it attempts to accomplish is not enough. The organization must decide *how* it plans to do this. The ''how'' question is the basis of the firm's strategy—its general approach and its specific plans. Just as there are many ways to skin a cat, there may be several strategies that could achieve the desired goals and objectives. Guidelines in the form of policies help to define which strategic alternatives mesh with the organization's value system and its general philosophies of doing business. Each of these areas will be addressed in greater detail in the following paragraphs.

But first, let's look at a real-world example of how some of the parts of the process fit together. Quaker Oats states that its mission is ''to create shareholder value by consistently achieving our financial objectives of superior returns and growth.''[27] In line with this mission, the company publicly stated its goals and objectives in 1981. The goals, strategies, actions, and results are as follows:

1. Goals and objectives
   a. Maintain return on equity of 20 percent.
   b. Achieve real earnings growth averaging 5 percent.
   c. Increase dividends.
   d. Maintain strong bond and paper ratings.
2. Strategies
   a. Remain a leading marketer of strong consumer brands.
   b. Achieve better than average real growth in grocery and Fisher-Price brands.
   c. Improve profitability of low-return businesses or divest.
3. Actions
   a. Divestitures: 1982—restaurant division; 1983—chemicals division; 1987—specialty retailing.
   b. Acquisitions: 1982—Ardmore Farms (food service); 1983—European Pet Foods; 1984—Stokely-Van Camp; 1987—Golden Grain, Gaines.
   c. New product introductions: 1982—chewy granola bars; 1983—Fisher-Price toys for older kids; 1984–87—various food products.
4. Results
   a. By 1985: 8.5 percent compound growth; growth categories represent 52 percent of grocery sales.
   b. By 1986: ROE exceeds 20 percent; 63 percent of grocery sales from market-leading brands.
   c. By 1987: returns reach all-time high in grocery products.[28]

---

[27]*Annual Report 1987*, Quaker Oats Co., Chicago, inside cover.
[28]Ibid.

An important part of Quaker's success was and is effective strategic management. Again, the following paragraphs and chapters provide the fundamentals necessary to achieve successful results.

The Organization's Mission or Purpose

The starting point in formulating an organization's strategy is its mission or purpose; that is, the definition of the organization's role in society and the economy. The firm's mission defines why it exists and why it competes in certain selected sectors or industries and not in others. The mission flows from the values of stakeholders, the people and groups with an interest in the organization, including the public and their representatives (the government). For any but a newly formed organization, the past plays a major role in the current mission or purpose of the firm; the basic mission reflects previous competitive practices and performance.

A firm's mission is a broad statement, providing a general direction for business activities and a basis for the coherent selection of desired ends (goals and objectives) and means to achieve them (strategies). Institutions in our society may have missions that relate to charitable, religious, social, or economic realms. Within these realms, an organization may have a more specifically focused mission, such as providing transportation products, communication services and equipment, and financial services. For example, Control Data Corp.'s mission statement reads as follows:

"Control Data is in the business of applying micro-electronics and computer technology in two general areas: computer-related hardware; and computing-enhancing services, which include computation, information, education and finance."[29]

Firms without specified mission statements can run into difficulties similar to those experienced by the conglomerates of the late 1960s. Many of these firms began wild and unrelated diversification moves into businesses and industries with profit and growth being the only reasons. If they had a mission, it seemed to be solely "to make money" or "to grow." While profits are essential to business and growth may be a desirable goal, they do not define purpose. History has shown that many firms without statements of mission encountered serious difficulties in later years, because they had no clear concept of what their business was.

In this context, all U.S. federal government agencies must develop a mission statement that guides and limits their activities and defines their role. Unfortunately, many firms in the private sector have not given sufficient attention to this critical area. The mission or purpose of most small firms and new ventures may

---

[29]John A. Pearce II and Fred David, "Corporate Mission Statements: The Bottom Line," *The Academy of Management Executive* 1, no. 2 (May 1987), p. 111.

be readily apparent (even though not formally stated). But when these firms are able to grow and diversify, a mission statement becomes important to guide and focus the direction of that growth and diversification. We will discuss development of the mission statement, as well as goals and objectives, in more depth in Chapter 3.

Goals and Objectives

Once a firm has defined its purpose, the next step is to define what it attempts to accomplish. Goals are broad directions the firm wishes to pursue or results it wishes to accomplish within its mission. Statements of goals might include the following:

1. Becoming a leading producer in the construction equipment industry.
2. Realizing a continuing high level of profits and return on investment.
3. Steady, stable growth in sales, profits, and dividends.
4. Maintenance of a stable, productive work force through all phases of the business cycle.

Many other goals could be cited. The point is that they are broad and general, and can be pursued on a continuing basis—they may never be satisfied completely. Goals provide direction for the firm and its employees.

However, goals are not sufficient. Statements of intentions and directions that are never really (or specifically) achieved make it difficult to assess and evaluate corporate and individual performance. Thus, objectives provide more specific ends to be met within the framework of the broader goals, and they involve specific time frames for accomplishment. An organization's objectives should cover varying time frames, ranging from general, long-range objectives to quite specific short-term objectives. The number of objectives (or targets) is likely to increase as the time frame becomes shorter and shorter.

It is important that goals and objectives be consistent and support one another. Goals must be developed within a defined mission, and objectives must be developed to support specific goals.

Goals and objectives provide the targets for which strategies are developed, and (particularly in the case of objectives) become important in the implementation of those strategies. Goals and objectives exist at the enterprise, corporate, business-unit, and functional and operational levels of a firm; in other words, all areas in which the firm is involved.

Assessing the Strategic Situation

To create a productive match between an organization and its external environment, the firm must understand both the general external environment and its competitive environment, in addition to organizational factors (and by implication, its values and the resulting mission, goals and objectives, and policies). These areas are outlined briefly here and treated in more depth in Part II (Chapters 3, 4, and 5).

The General Environment: Opportunities and Threats.

The external environment consists of factors over which the organization has little direct control. For most firms, this would include a number of economic factors, social factors, political-legal factors, and technological factors. A firm may have *some* influence in one or more of these areas; for example, an invention by one firm may help it change its technological environment. Some firms also may exert greater control than others over certain environmental factors. However, environmental factors are typically beyond direct control of most firms.

Environmental analysis is important because the environment is constantly changing, and the organization may need to change, as well, to maintain its productive fit. To keep up with the external environment, management must watch for changes and trends of strategic significance. The changes and trends are brought into and disseminated within the organization by means of a strategic information system, which probably functions separately from the firm's operating or management information system. Since responding to change requiries a certain amount of lead time, forecasting those changes is an important organizational activity. Numerous quantitative as well as qualitative approaches to environmental forecasting have been developed and are discussed in Chapter 9.

The more rapid and discontinuous the change, the greater the need for environmental analysis and forecasting so that the firm can anticipate and react. In a stable, unchanging environment, there is less need for analysis and forecasting; these tasks are relatively simple and can be performed with great precision and little risk of error. A turbulent environment, however, puts a premium on analysis and forecasting, but makes the tasks very difficult, imprecise, and risky.

Any change creates, simultaneously, both threats and opportunities. But whether a given change is a threat or an opportunity depends on how accurately the firm diagnoses and understands the change and its significance, as well as what the firm decides (and is able) to do about it. Thus, management must be aware of changes, interpret their impacts (the most difficult task), and take appropriate action. Obviously, a firm with limited resources that prevent it from capitalizing on new situations will find changes creating more threats than opportunities.

The major environmental, forces affecting most firms include:

1. The economy, including tax rates, interest rates, price controls, business cycles, inflation, and general overall condition. Some sectors and products (such as housing, autos, and resorts) are more susceptible to economic factors than are others (such as food, medical care, and other necessities).
2. Technology, including product design, production processes, related cost factors, product quality, the general rate of technological change and innovation, and raw materials.

3. Social factors, including consumer preferences, values, demands for product safety, demographics, lifestyle changes, roles of women and minorities, career expectations, and others.
4. Political/legal considerations, including government regulations, restrictions, the political climate (in Washington, the statehouse, and overseas), antitrust legislation, import/export restrictions, environmental and consumer protection laws, product liability, and OSHA regulations.

Changes in any one of these areas can have significant impacts on the firm, its products, its markets, its ability to compete, and its methods of doing business. Analyzing the environment is not an easy task. It is often easier to forecast the changes themselves than to accurately determine their effects, or the timing of those impacts. American Motors foresaw the change to smaller cars as early as the 1950s and produced compact cars well in advance of the competition. The public, however, was not yet ready to buy them in sufficient quantities to support the company.

The Industry Environment: Competitive Factors.   In addition to its general economic environment, competitive factors within the organization's industry or sector of the economy provide a number of more specific opportunities and threats. For example, direct and indirect competition from other firms, the market structure, market size, costs of entry and exit, market changes and niches, and distribution channels all are important determinants of the strategic situation facing the firm.

Industry structure—whether the market is local, regional, national, or global—as well as the number and composition of *strategic groups* (firms following similar strategies) within the industry are important considerations. Also important are factors relating to the product life cycle, such as whether the market is in a rapid growth, shakeout, or maturity stage. Last, factors relating to capital intensity as well as experience curve effects must be considered.

The Organization: Resources and Competencies.   The internal situation must be analyzed, as well. Three dimensions affect the capabilities of an organization and influence its strengths and weaknesses: (1) the values and expectations of stakeholders; (2) the goals and objectives of management; and (3) the organization's resources and competencies. Influencing these factors are the size, type, and stage of development of the organization (e.g., whether it is large or small, concentrated or diversified, young or mature, and the like).

Many stakeholders may actually be external to the firm (such as society, the community, suppliers, creditors, customers, and the government). Others clearly are internal (top and other levels of management, staff, and other employees), while a third external group can be considered quasi insiders (investors). Whether the stakeholders are internal, external, or on the boundary, their collective impact determines the set of values and expectations directing and guiding the firm, which is an element of the internal situation. As was shown in

Figure 2.2, the resulting values and expectations ultimately define the mission, goals and objectives, and policies of the firm.

In the short run, the stakeholders having the most immediate impact on the firm's strategies are management, particularly top management. Strategies are formulated by people (primarily top management) within the existing environment, and management's individual and collective goals and objectives are a potent and direct influence on strategic decisions.

Strategy Formulation

Strategy formulation, described more fully in Chapters 6, 7, and 8, is a decision-making process that builds on the analysis of the strategic situation, as determined by the general, industry, and internal factors. It involves a determination of strategic alternatives, or the means by which the organization is able to meet its goals and objectives, given its available resources and competencies. Strategy formulation essentially is problem solving in unstructured situations, and most important, involves selecting the right problems to solve.

The key to effective strategy formulation lies in finding the major variables the firm can manipulate to improve its match with the environment. This requires an understanding of which strategic directions and alternatives are appropriate for the current and future situation facing the firm. At the business level, for example, this would include strategies for positioning and distinguishing the business, plus strategies for increasing, refining, or reducing its scope. At the corporate level, strategies of business integration, diversification, concentration, and restructuring are included. It includes analyzing factors for each level of strategy—enterprise, corporate, business, and functional—and is both a social/ political and analytical/conceptual process. That is, strategy formulation may employ analytical tools such as financial analysis and management science techniques, but is still the result of the values, goals, and judgments of the group of individuals comprising the firm.

Two categories of strategies may be required, depending on the environment. Our concern so far has been with *initiating actions* (sometimes called action strategies) that define means of dealing with expected environmental circumstances. On the other hand, if the environment is too complex or changes too rapidly to develop meaningful action strategies to cope with it, *response actions* (sometimes called preparedness strategies) may be necessary. These are predetermined contingency plans that can be implemented in the event a certain set of circumstances occurs in the environment. The result is a strategy for coping with unforeseen events, or a preparedness strategy, which consists of contingency plans that can be implemented when and if needed.

In general, strategy evaluation consists of first making sure that no obvious strategic alternative has been overlooked, then systematically narrowing down the list to the ''best'' alternatives based on factors critical to the firm's success. Procedures for doing this are discussed in Chapter 8.

It is not unusual for seemingly obvious alternatives to be overlooked during strategy formulation. One such alternative, always present, is to *not* change strategy at all. If certain proposed strategies are no more likely than the current strategy to accomplish the firm's goals and objectives, they should be rejected.

Evaluating strategic alternatives requires criteria for acceptance or rejection. These may be "go/no go," absolute criteria for acceptance or rejection; for example, that all alternatives must result in a certain level of return on investment and not require that the firm borrow more than a given amount of money. Any alternative not meeting these criteria will be rejected and dropped from further evaluation. Other criteria may not be so clear-cut. In these instances, a "scorecard" for each alternative may be developed and used as a basis for selecting the strategy with the best overall score. In evaluating alternatives, as in quality control testing, candidates should be subjected to the most demanding criteria first, with as many alternatives as possible rejected as early as possible. Examples of how to perform these tasks are given in Chapter 8.

Strategy Implementation and Planning

After a strategy has been evaluated and selected, the critical implementation phase begins. Implementation is vitally important because a brilliant strategy poorly put into action may be no more effective than a well-implemented but otherwise less desirable strategy. In short, a strategy is only as good as its implementation.

While strategy formulation and evaluation are sometimes performed apart from the organization's operating structure, processes, and systems, implementation is largely an administrative task that occurs within these functions. Consequently, individuals who are not involved in formulation and evaluation (operating managers and staff at various levels), and who use existing organizational procedures are largely responsible for implementation. This transfer of responsibility is critical to the success of a strategy.

In the implementation phase, a master plan is required to turn strategy into reality. Chapter 9 shows how a master plan is developed and Chapter 10 outlines the major actions and schedules required to implement the strategy. A master plan becomes the basis for more detailed and shorter-term planning and scheduling at progressively lower operating levels of the firm. It also includes any structural, system, process, or personnel changes required for implementation, as well as resource requirements and budgets. Resource allocation decisions are made at this time, and are reflected in the budgets and schedules of the implementing units of the firm.

Most of what we have come to know as strategic planning, including the use of formal planning systems and techniques, occurs in this implementation phase. It is here, also, that alternative, or contingency, plans are developed, in case actual events do not correspond to the assumptions of the master strategic plan.

Strategic Control

Strategic control involves evaluation of whether or not a strategy is being implemented as intended, and whether or not the desired results are being achieved. If not, corrective action may be required to modify the implementation activities or even the strategy itself. In addition, the internal situation and external environment of the firm likely will change with time, and their impacts must also be periodically reevaluated as part of the strategic control process.

A critical element in strategic control, as well as in strategy formulation, is the strategic information system, which is described in Chapter 9. A strategic information system is vital to determining strategic results (some of which may be determined by the organization's management information system), as well as to be aware of important environmental changes, trends, and "surprises."

Japan Does It Differently

The role of the planning staff is to assist in, not to make, planning and strategy decisions. It is not uncommon in U.S. firms to have a top-management group or decision-making body of three to five people, called the office of the president, the management committee, the senior executive committee, or the planning committee. In contrast, a study by Toyohiro Kono found that, in the 1950s, Japanese businesses adopted the concept of a management committee comprised of 8 to 10 senior executives, with sole responsibility for general management and strategic decisions (and little responsibility for operational decisions).[30] In addition to this body, the average Japanese planning department employs 12 people and acts as a strategic staff, working closely with top management and participating in the initiation and formulation of strategies.

In the United States, on the other hand, the corporate planning staff typically numbers three to five people, and functions more as a coordinator of the strategic planning process, with the planning decisions made by heads of operating divisions and top management.

Kono further found that long-range planning is used widely by large firms in both countries—by 85 percent of the firms in the United States and by 88 percent in Japan. The plan is formal and written in about 75 percent of these firms in both countries. The components of the plans also are very similar. However, preparation of the plan differs greatly. In the United States, planning is largely a bottom-up process. Two thirds of American firms rely on operating units to prepare plans. Most of the remaining third use an interactive process involving operating- and corporate-level managers. Japanese corporations, contrary to what might be expected with the Ringi (bottom-up) system, rely primarily on

---

[30]Toyohiro Kono, "Comparative Study of Strategy, Structure, and Long-Range Planning in Japan and in the USA," *Management Japan* 13, no. 1 (Spring 1980), p. 20.

top-down or interactive processes, and depend heavily on their planning departments. In fact, planning departments prepare the long-range plans in 86 percent of Japanese firms, versus 39 percent in U.S. firms. Division management performs this task in 87 percent of U.S. firms, versus 39 percent in Japan (the slight overlap is caused by shared responsibility). Thus, significant differences exist between the two countries in the area of responsibilities for the preparation, review, and final approval of long-range plans.

ORGANIZATIONAL PLANNING PROCESSES

A strategic planning system (SPS) is a structured way of formulating, implementing, and controlling the firm's strategies. Strategic planning systems are formalized approaches for doing the job of strategic planning. While some may be less structured and less formal than others, they still provide management with a *systematic approach* to planning.

One of the important decisions management must make is how formal this systematic approach should be. Research has shown that tailor-made planning systems tend to be the most effective. However, the design and operation of the planning system must be consistent with the organization's structure and processes in general. In addition, planning systems typically cannot be transplanted from one firm to another, but must be adapted to the needs of each firm.

Strategic, Tactical, and Operational Planning

The difference between strategic and operational planning—that of the future (strategic) versus the short term (operational)—was discussed in Chapter 1. In addition, planning is done at the tactical and scheduling and dispatching levels. Table 2.3 illustrates the relationships between the four major levels of planning.

Strategic planning typically involves issues significantly affected by elements in the organization's external environment. It also includes decisions that can greatly change the character or direction of the organization.[31] It deals with what the firm is to be in the future, reflecting the firm's role in the environment, and includes what businesses the firm should be in, how they should be financed, and how scarce resources should be allocated.

Tactical planning deals with the implementation and support of longer-range (strategic) plans. It includes capital budgeting, facility expansion or shut down, price setting, and product-line and market development decisions. Tactical plan-

---

[31]W. R. King and D. I. Cleland, *Strategic Planning and Policy* (New York: Van Nostrand Reinhold, 1978), p. 9.

TABLE 2.3   Relationships between Planning Levels

Strategic planning

Which business should the firm be in?

How should they be financed?

How should scarce resources be allocated across business sectors?

Tactical planning

What are the optimal patterns of capital investment and divestment for implementing some longer-range plan?

What decisions about facility location, expansion, or shutdown will maximize profitability?

What products should be added to or deleted from the product line?

What is the optimal product pricing pattern?

Operations planning

What is the optimal operating plan (raw material acquisition, product sources, inventory levels, distribution system configuration, route and mode of distribution, and so on) to meet specified system objectives, consistent with some longer-term plan, with existing facilities in the next planning period (e.g., month, quarter, year)?

What is the best operating plan on which to base plans for production and dispatch?

Scheduling and dispatching

What specific operations or sequences of operations should be performed with which existing facilities, to meet specified output requirements in the next operational period (for example, hour, day, week)?

Source: Reprinted by permission of D. S. Hirshfield, "From the Shadows," *Interfaces* 13, no. 2 (April 1983), p. 74. Copyright 1983 The Institute of Management Sciences.

ning is often concerned primarily with future facilities or product planning, and its time horizon is related to the lead time for new, major facilities or products.

Operational planning allocates tasks to specific existing facilities to achieve particular objectives in each planning period.

The most specific form of planning—*scheduling and dispatching*—involves the assignment and sequencing of specific existing resources (people, machines, raw materials, and so forth) to manufacture or deliver given quantities of products, consistent with a longer-interval operating plan (such as a quarterly operations plan).

As can be seen in Table 2.3, strategic planning involves the greatest scope and the least specificity or detail, while the opposite is true for scheduling and dispatching.

People at all levels of the organization have strategic, tactical, and operational views of the environment within which they work. As shown in Figure 2.3, upper-level management's concerns are primarily long range and strategic, but management at this level must also think in terms of tactical and operational

FIGURE 2.3   Strategic, Tactical, and Operational Views at Various Organizational Levels

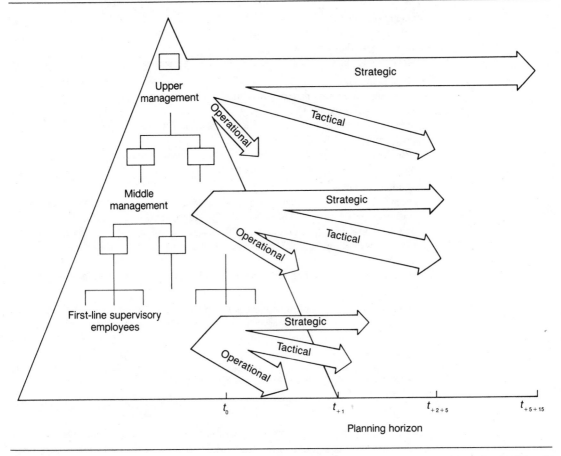

Source: L. K. Swim and D. S. Sink, "Cooperative Labor-Management Strategic Planning in a Unionized Steel Plant." Reprinted from *IE Management News,* Summer 1984, p. 9, with permission from Institute of Industrial Engineers, 25 Technology Park/Atlanta, Norcross, GA 30092.

matters. Middle-level managers' concerns are primarily medium range and tactical, while at lower levels, the emphasis is primarily short range and operational. Therefore, each level of the organization has strategic, tactical, and operational concerns, but the relative proportion devoted to each and their time horizon varies by level.

Statements of Strategy

Differences of opinion exist on how explicitly an organization's strategies should be stated and how widely they should be disseminated. Researchers have found that firms may operate with several versions of a strategy, some widely publicized and some confidential. For example, a firm may employ the following:

1. *Corporate strategy for the annual report.* This is usually a "sterilized" and edited version, intended to convey to shareholders a sense of direction and an assurance that management knows where it wants to take the company.
2. *Corporate strategy for the board of directors, financial analysts, and middle managers.* More explicit than the previous version, this is still a relatively simple, camouflaged statement of strategy.
3. *Corporate strategy for top management.* Since the CEO needs top management's support, they are usually privy to and participate in a full discussion of potential strategic moves and countermoves by the firm.
4. *The CEO's private corporate strategy.* If the CEO is a strategic thinker, he or she may be mulling over a range of strategic moves that are, as yet, disclosed to almost no one.[32]

From this breakout, one can see the CEO's strong influence in creating the vision and shaping the strategies of the company. The CEO also controls the flow of information and the degree of participation in the process.

Top-Down or Bottom-Up?

It was stated earlier that strategic planning in U.S. corporations is primarily a bottom-up process for implementing the CEO's vision of the future. In this way, division managers responsible for an individual business-unit develop the strategies and plans for that unit. This approach has some well-known advantages. However, recent research shows that this approach is not *always* the best, nor should it be used under all conditions. For diversified corporations, interrelationships between businesses become an important factor, requiring more top-down strategy making. Michael Porter's research indicates that "multipoint competition"—where firms are challenged on many industrial fronts—requires top-down strategy and lots of initiative from the top levels of the firm. Stellar performances from individual business-unit managers are no longer enough to assure the success of this type of firm, and senior executives must take a proactive role in strategy development and implementation.[33]

This view is corroborated and expanded by a recent study of 10 leading British companies, which found that there are conditions under which either method—top-down or bottom-up—may be preferable. For example, if corporate development and coordination of individual businesses is the key objective of the firm, headquarters should make the strategy and accept the fact that the motivation of managers and performance of their units may suffer. If unit financial performance

---

[32]Hax and Majluf, "The Concept of Strategy," p. 103.

[33]Donald F. Heany, "Porter's Competitive Advantage Revisited," *Planning Review* 14, no. 1 (January 1986), p. 27.

matters most, headquarters should let unit managers determine strategy, and accept less coordination between the businesses. Also, if a balance of the two is sought, be prepared to accept increased ambiguity.[34]

Group Approaches

An interesting set of alternative ways of making group strategic decisions involves the dialectic inquiry, devil's advocate, and group consensus approaches. The dialectic inquiry approach involves debates between managers backing diametrically opposed sets of recommendations. Devil's advocacy relies on critiques of single sets of recommendations and assumptions (where an individual or group plays the "devil's advocate" role). Consensus approaches involve an interactive sharing of information and evaluation of assumptions, alternatives, and recommendations, with challenge likely to occur only when there is lack of agreement. Recent research results show that both the dialectic inquiry and devil's advocacy methods led to higher-quality recommendations and assumptions than did consensus. Dialectic inquiry was more effective than devil's advocacy in surfacing assumptions. However, consensus groups expressed more satisfaction and harmony within the group, as well as greater acceptance of the group's decisions.[35] Again, a trade-off seems to exist, depending upon which factor or set of factors is more important to the firm.

Skills Required for Strategic Managers

The skills required for effective strategic management can be looked at in two ways. One is to focus on the general skills required to analyze, formulate, and implement strategies, and these are addressed here. The second is to focus on the skills required to function effectively with certain strategies, which—along with a more detailed treatment of specific strategy-related skills—is addressed in Chapter 10.

Conceptual and Synthesis Skills.   Upper levels of management must be adept at conceptualizing. They must possess *vision;* they must be able to see the enterprise as a whole and how the organization fits (and *can* fit) into its overall environment. This skill is critical for strategic managers. Strategic decision makers must visualize things that do not yet exist. They must have a vision of what their organization or division can become and can do. Required is an ability to see the situations in their entirety—a synthesis skill. This includes being able

---

[34]Michael Goold and Andrew Campbell, "Many Best Ways to Make Strategy," *Harvard Business Review*" 65, no. 6 (November–December 1987), pp. 70–76.

[35]D. M. Schweiger, W. R. Sandberg, and J. W. Ragan, "Group Approaches for Improving Strategic Decision Making," *Academy of Management Journal* 29, no. 1 (March 1986), pp. 51–70.

to understand the role of the organization in its environment and how environmental changes can and will affect the company. Synthesis skill is required to assess what the various functions and divisions of the company must do to successfully implement a strategy, and what the effects will be on each division and function. Conceptual and synthesis skills are difficult to teach, unlike specific technical and analytical skills, such as accounting, engineering, and effective writing and speech making.

Technical and Analytical Skills. Nonetheless, strategic decision making requires more than conceptual/synthesis skills. Technical and analysis skills are required, as well, and may be important elements in synthesizing and conceptualizing. Just as an artist must be able to work with paints, brushes, and the like to put what he or she conceptualizes on canvas, the strategic manager must be able to analyze trends, prepare plans and budgets, make presentations, sell his or her ideas, and implement them. In either case, having the vision or the concept is necessary, but not totally sufficient.

In addition, the skills needed vary by level in the corporate hierarchy. At lower levels of administrative responsibility, the major need is for technical skills and for human skills in working with, for, and leading others. At higher levels, managerial effectiveness depends largely on human and conceptual skills. At the top, conceptual skill becomes the most important of all for successful performance.[36] This identification of the skills most needed at various levels of responsibility is important in the selection, training, and promotion of managers. Technical skills may enable a person to be promoted to first-line management; for example, supervisor. Technical *plus* human skills can get you to middle-level management, but conceptual skills are required for effective performance in general management and executive-level positions. The primary responsibility at the executive level in an organization is that of policy formulation. In other words, the direction in which the organization is going to proceed and how it will conduct its activities are the prime executive-level concerns. Middle management, in turn, is primarily responsible for interpreting and implementing these goals and policies, while the supervisory level is responsible for accomplishment—producing the goods or delivering the services.

Combination of Skills. Strategic decision makers also must be able to function in the political environment of organizations, which requires well-developed human skills. They must have a willingness and desire to make decisions by integrating and balancing elements, assessing risks, communicating and enlisting support, and employing a sense of timing. Also required is a combination of analysis and synthesis skills—a diagnostic ability—since strategic and organizational situations do not present themselves as concretely and

---

[36]Robert L. Katz, "Skills of an Effective Administrator," *Harvard Business Review,* July–August 1975, p. 49.

neatly as do technical or financial facts. Making strategic decisions in complex organizations is a delicate art, requiring a balance of vision, entrepreneurship, and politics. The strategic decision maker must be able to sense needs, build awareness, broaden support, create pockets of commitment, crystallize a developing focus, obtain increased commitment, and keep the process moving forward.[37]

CONCLUSIONS

Understanding and following a logical and complete process of strategic management helps to ensure that no important factors will be overlooked in formulating and implementing strategies. This increases the likelihood that the organization will employ the best strategies that it possibly can—those that result in the best possible fit between the firm's external environment, its distinctive competencies and resources, and the values and expectations of its stakeholders. Following a regular schedule for the process further ensures that the firm's strategic management activities will yield maximum benefits.

In addition, strategic management requires the perspective of the general manager. General managers must act both as strategists and as organization builders, and many times must sail through uncharted waters, managing when no precedent exists. Strategic decisions are evaluated by the board of directors, but are the responsibility of *line* general managers, supported by corporate planning staffs that perform analyses and manage the planning processes. Successful, respected companies tend to keep their processes flexible and simple; they do not use long-term plans as straitjackets, but as guides.

---

[37]J. B. Quinn, "Strategic Goals: Process and Politics," *Sloan Management Review* 19, no. 1 (Fall 1977), p. 21.

Part II

Practicing Strategic Management: Assessing the Strategic Situation

Chapter 3

Defining the Business: Mission, Stakeholders, Competencies, and Resources

LEARNING OBJECTIVES

After completing Chapter 3, you should be able to:

Understand the key points in assessing the critical strategic internal factors affecting the firm.

Describe the major types of business organizations and how they differ.

Understand typical growth and evolutionary patterns of organizations.

Realize that organizations have differing needs and opportunities at different stages in their development.

Realize that an organization is made up of and influenced by a number of stakeholder groups with varying values and expectations.

Describe the important features and characteristics of effective mission statements and goals and objectives.

Appreciate the major resources on which an organization relies and how they relate to organizational strengths and weaknesses.

In Part I, we discussed the concepts, processes, and roles required for effective strategic management. While following a logical process is very helpful in analyzing, making, and implementing strategic decisions, keep in mind that the process is a means to an end, not an end in itself. That end is the formulation and successful implementation of the proper strategies for the situation at hand. In Part II, we will deal with the first phase of practicing strategic management: assessing the strategic situation. Here, we are dealing with strategy *content*. This assessment involves a clear concept and definition of the organization, including its stakeholders, its mission, and its competencies and resources (Chapter 3); the firm's general environment in terms of overall opportunities and threats (Chapter 4); and the competitive environment, including the industry, the market, and competitors (Chapter 5).

When we speak of the firm or the organization, we refer to its internal characteristics—the vision of top management, the values and expectations of its stakeholders, its mission, its goals and objectives, and its competencies and resources. Together, these factors define the organization's strengths and weaknesses and determine its ability to pursue given strategic alternatives. As John Rockwell, senior vice president of Booz Allen & Hamilton management consultants says, "More and more companies are understanding that the match of corporate capacity with marketplace needs is what the game is all about."[1]

This chapter first looks at the role of the values and expectations of stakeholders in defining the business, including its mission and its goals and objectives. Next, we discuss the growth and development patterns through which organizations typically progress, because organizations face different strategic concerns at different stages in their life cycle, and the size and diversity of an organization are important determinants of which strategies the firm can and should pursue. Finally, an assessment is made of the firm's distinctive competencies and its resources.

PROFILE

Defining the Mission at Ford

Ford Motor Company is one of the world's largest corporations, with sales of $92 billion and a 25 percent return on equity in 1988. One person responsible for this performance is former CEO Phillip Caldwell, who has strong feelings about the importance of an organization's mission. He believes that the best strategic planning is based on:

> carefully collected and organized facts arranged to serve your interests. I'm not much on hip shooting and the mystical approach.
>
> The first thing I want to know about a plan is, what are you trying to accomplish? What's the mission? Then I recommend that you take a lot of time to describe it carefully. . . . Make defining the mission a continuous process—but make sure you do it as accurately as possible.
>
> Once that's done, I want to know your game plan. I remember when I was involved in the Pacific Theatre in World War II. The Joint Chiefs of Staff ordered Admiral Nimitz

---

[1]"Listening to the Voice of the Marketplace," *Business Week,* February 21, 1983, p. 90.

to "seize and occupy the Marianas Islands." The mission was very clear. But the question then became, how do you go about seizing and occupying the Marianas Islands? Somebody had to develop a game plan. And to do that, they had to use human, physical, and financial resources, as well as working out the timing. . . . then someone had to figure out how to go about deploying all those resources.[2]

PROFILE   **NCR Manages for Its Stakeholders**

Some experts claim that companies not managed to maximize returns to shareholders are vulnerable to attack. NCR Corp., however, attempts to manage with all of its *stakeholders* in mind—employees, customers, suppliers, and communities where NCR has plants—not just shareholders. NCR's CEO, Charles E. Exley Jr., feels that it is his responsibility to balance the shareholders' interest in the long-term prosperity of the company against their understandable interest in yearly dividend increases and steady quarterly earnings increases. He believes that considering the interests of all stakeholders is the best way to do this, which in turn maximizes value over the long run—even for shareholders.[3] His approach seems to work: NCR has one of the higher returns on equity in the EDP industry, has relatively low debt, and has seen its stock and earnings rise significantly during the past several years.

STAKEHOLDER VALUES AND EXPECTATIONS

Two important parts of creating a firm's enterprise strategy include analyses of the firm's stakeholders and their values and expectations. As defined in Chapter 2, stakeholders are individuals and groups with a positive "stake" in how well the organization performs, including investors, directors, managers, employees, unions, customers, suppliers, creditors, the community, the state and region, society in general, and perhaps others, all of whom provide resources to the organization. Many of these people and interest groups have differing expectations of the firm; top management's responsibility is to deal with, and satisfy, as many of them as possible. Obviously, management will not be able to fully meet or even reconcile all expectations. At best, an uneasy equilibrium may exist that temporarily accommodates conflicting demands. Nonetheless, management should remember that the price of resource inputs from stakeholders is a certain degree of satisfaction of their needs, conflicting as they might be. William Dill of New York University observed that environmental turbulence is less of a threat for companies that spent time listening to and assessing what

---

[2]"Some Better Ideas from Ford Motor's CEO," *Planning Review* 12, no. 5 (September 1984), p. 8.
[3]George Melloan, "NCR's Exley Manages for His 'Stakeholders'," *The Wall Street Journal,* June 16, 1987, p. 27.

stakeholders say about the powers they are and are not willing to delegate to corporations and corporate management.[4]

Who Are the Stakeholders?

Again, stakeholders are those individuals or groups who have a stake, or claim, against the firm. As shown in Table 3.1, this group is extensive, although many of the stakes are dissimilar and even conflicting. Satisfying their expectations and incorporating their values is an important management task, part of the firm's social and economic responsibilities. From one perspective, management *must* satisfy stakeholder wants, because—collectively, if not individually—stakeholder groups have a great impact on a firm's performance. Although various stakeholder groups can exert their influence in different ways, an obvious example involves stockholder power. In fact, choosing the firm's CEO may be the ultimate decision the stockholders (through the board of directors) can make, because the CEO's values and beliefs shape the way their companies operate, and their aspirations mold the corporate environment.[5]

Satisfying Stakeholder Wants

Again, some writers have said that the overriding purpose of management is to maximize stockholder wealth. While this is a major management concern, the needs of other stakeholders must be met, as well, and balanced against the interests of stockholders. However, public corporations clearly have obligations to present and potential shareholders, including disclosure of information about their firms, such as the nature and activities of the business, financial and policy matters, tender offers, special problems, and opportunities facing the firm. Disclosure should be frequent and the information should be pertinent to the shareholders' investment decisions.

But stockholders are only one group of stakeholders. Organizations have been described as collections of internal and external stakeholders. Given this view, the task of management—including strategic management—becomes one of satisfying stakeholders' wants and needs and of managing the relationships between, and often conflicting demands of, various stakeholders. In fact, some authors feel that the ultimate objective of strategy should be to address

[4]W. R. Dill, "Commentary," in *Strategic Management: A New View of Business Policy and Planning* (Boston: Little, Brown, 1979), p. 49.

[5]Alan M. Webber, "The CEO Is the Company," *Harvard Business Review* 65, no. 1 (January-February 1987), p. 114.

TABLE 3.1   A Claimant View of Company Responsibility

Claimant	*Nature of the Claim*
Stockholders	Participation in distribution of profits, additional stock offerings, assets on liquidation; vote of stock, inspection of company books, transfer of stock, election of board of directors, and such additional rights as established in the contract with the corporation.
Creditors	Legal proportion of interest payments due and return of principal from the investment. Security of pledged assets; relative priority in event of liquidation. Participate in some management and owner prerogatives if certain conditions exist within the company (such as default of interest payments).
Employees	Economic, social, and psychological satisfaction in the place of employment. Freedom from arbitrary and capricious behavior on the part of company officials. Share in fringe benefits, freedom to join union and participate in collective bargaining, individual freedom in offering up their services through an employment contract. Adequate working conditions.
Customers	Service provided with the product: technical data to use the product; suitable warranties; spare parts to support the product during customer use; R&D leading to product improvements; facilitation of consumer credit.
Suppliers	Continuing source of business: timely consummation of trade credit obligations; professional relationship in contracting for, purchasing, and receiving goods and services.
Governments	Taxes (income, property, and so on), fair competition, and adherence to the letter and intent of public policy dealing with the requirements of fair and free competition. Legal obligation of businessmen (and business organizations); adherence to antitrust laws.
Unions	Recognition as the negotiating agent for employees. Opportunity to perpetuate the union as a participant in the business organization.
Competitors	Norms established by society and the industry for competitive conduct. Business statesmanship on the part of peers.
Local communities	Place of productive and healthful employment in the community. Participation of company officials in community affairs, regular employment, fair play, purchase of reasonable portion of product of the local community, interest in and support of local government; support of cultural and charity projects.
The general public	Participation in and contribution to society as a whole; creative communications between governmental and business units designed for reciprocal understanding; bear fair proportion of the burden of government and society. Fair price for products and advancement of state of the art technology which the product line involves.

Source: From W. R. King and D. I. Cleland, *Strategic Planning and Policy* (New York: Van Nostrand Reinhold, 1978), p. 153. © 1978 by Litton Educational Publishing Inc. Reprinted by permission of Van Nostrand Reinhold Company.

TABLE 3.2   Strategic Assumptions Analysis

Issue: Joint Venture in Manufacturing

Stakeholder	Position
Senior management	Yes
Direct customers	Strong yes
End-product customers	Yes
Plant management	Weak yes
R&D management	No
Investment bankers	Strong yes
Overall assessment	Yes

Source: Adapted from James R. Emshoff and Arthur Finnel, "Defining Corporate Strategy," *Sloan Management Review,* Spring 1979, pp. 41–52.

stakeholders' benefits.[6] How can this be done? Two writers in the field, Richard Mason and Ian Mitroff, have proposed a strategic assumption surfacing and testing technique (SAST) to assist management in this task.[7] The first step in their approach is to identify the full range of relevant stakeholders. This is necessary because whether or not an organization achieves its goals depends inevitably on the assumption it makes about its stakeholders and their behavior.

Further, since assumptions of some stakeholders are more crucial to the success of a strategy than are those of others, the various stakeholders should be rated on a scale of importance. Next, each strategic assumption should be rated on a scale of certainty; that is, how certain are you of the validity of each assumption? The result of these two ratings—importance and certainty—reveals the likely impact of each assumption on the organization and its strategy. Finally, implementation becomes a matter of developing an action plan for each important stakeholder.

A simpler and perhaps more practical approach to assessing stakeholder positions on issues is the Strategic Assumptions Analysis technique, developed at the Wharton School. This approach simply requires management to judge each major stakeholder group's position on the issue, consider the strength and importance of their position, and arrive at an overall assessment and decision, as Table 3.2 illustrates.[8] Whether this approach or the more involved SAST approach is used, each is a systematic means of specifically incorporating stakeholder wants, needs, and desires into the strategic planning process. In fact,

---

[6]Arnoldo C. Hax and N. S. Majluf, "The Concept of Strategy and the Strategy Formation Process," *Interfaces* 18, no. 3 (May-June 1988), p. 102.

[7]R. O. Mason and Ian Mitroff, "A Telelogical Power-Oriented Theory of Strategy," in *Advances in Strategic Management,* vol. 2, ed. R. Lamb (Greenwich, Conn.: JAI Press, 1983), p. 31.

[8]James R. Emshoff and Arthur Finnel, "Defining Corporate Strategy," *Sloan Management Review,* Spring 1979, p. 41.

FIGURE 3.1   Inputs to the Company Mission

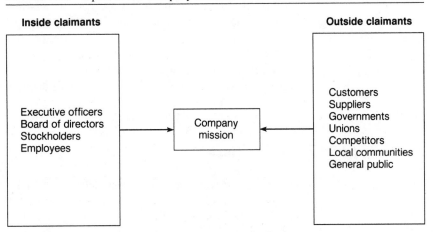

Source: J. A. Pearce II, Richard B. Robinson, Jr., and Kendall Roth, "The Company Mission as a Guide to Strategic Action," in *Strategic Management and Planning Handbook,* ed. W. R. King and D. I. Cleland (New York: Van Nostrand Reinhold, 1987), p. 79.

consideration of the claims of inside and outside stakeholders is an important input to determination of the company's mission, as shown in Figure 3.1

DEFINING THE MISSION

The organization's mission defines *why* the organization exists and guides *what* it should be doing. It specifies what the organization's business is now or will be in the future. It also states the kind of organization the firm is or wants to be.

This mission is the most important element of strategic management, or, for that matter, of the organization itself. Without a mission, there is no clear statement of why the company exists. More and more companies are developing formal mission statements, because such statements can provide management and personnel with a shared sense of opportunity, direction, significance, and achievement. Unfortunately, it is not easy to develop an effective mission statement. Some organizations work a year or two before they come up with an adequate one. But in the process of developing a mission statement, a company will learn more about itself and its latent opportunities.[9]

Some organizations endeavor to conceal their true purpose beneath obscure and all-inclusive terminology. An umbrella statement such as "our purpose is to serve the food needs of the nation" can refer to anything from farming in

---

[9]A. A. Thompson and A. J. Strickland III, *Strategy and Policy: Concepts and Cases,* rev. ed. (Plano, Tex.: Business Publications, 1982), p. 7.

Nebraska, to delivering bread, to running a Kentucky Fried Chicken franchise. It is simply too broad to guide management action. Since mission statements are not carved in stone, there is no real danger of the organization locking itself in by being too specific. A statement is properly dynamic and may, from time to time, be fine tuned. This is particularly true of mission statements for diversified organizations expanding into many businesses. Even without diversification, however, a well-conceived mission statement seldom will stay current for more than a decade or two.

Defining and Redefining the Business

However, unless a firm has a clear definition of purpose, it is impossible to design a mission statement with sharply focused objectives, strategies, and policies. Managerial effectiveness begins with clarity of purpose—with a clear concept of the business.

At least three questions must be answered when defining or redefining a business:

1. Which groups of customers or clients does the firm wish to attract?
2. Which functions does the business wish to perform?
3. What technology will the firm use? (In other words, *how* will the needs of the customers and clients be satisfied?)[10]

The answers to these questions determine how broadly or narrowly focused the firm's mission should be, as well as the degree of differentiation of its products and markets. AT&T, for example, was forced to redefine its business after it agreed to divest its operating telephone companies. According to its new mission statement, "AT&T's business is the electronic movement and management of information—in the United States and around the world."[11] This revised mission statement puts AT&T clearly in the information industry via electronic media. The stated mission would seem to preclude it from handling written information (a basic mission of the postal service), but would not prevent AT&T from entering computer information systems markets. Actually, AT&T's mission is somewhat more limited than its stated mission would seem to imply; it can provide long-distance service but not local phone service.

The mission of the U.S. Postal Service (USPS), in turn, is stated as follows:

The function of the United States Postal Service, an independent establishment of the Federal Government, is to provide **prompt, reliable and economical services** to customers in all urban, suburban, and rural areas through the collection, transmission

---

[10]Derek F. Abell, *Defining the Business: The Starting Point of Strategic Planning* (Englewood Cliffs, N.J.: Prentice-Hall, 1980).

[11]*AT&T 1984 Annual Report,* p. 5.

and delivery of personal, educational, literary and business communications and parcels.[12]

This statement identifies the USPS as part of the public sector, describes the breadth of its customer base, limits the types of items it will handle, and indicates a desired quality of service.

Relationship to Goals, Objectives, Strategies, and Policies

The mission should be a company's driving force, a sort of "invisible hand" that guides it. The mission combines with objectives and goals to define exactly what an organization seeks to achieve through its activities. Strategy is the master plan for achieving the desired results, while policy sets up the framework for implementing the strategy. Over time, circumstances inevitably change and complications arise. These prompt the organization to modify its purpose, as well as its objectives, strategies, and policies. Developing a consistent, compatible relationship among these four items is a continuous task.

Amid changes and complications, purposes, desired results, and the means of achieving them take on different meanings for various levels of an organization. The CEO tries to provide benefits for stakeholders by fulfilling the firm's mission, while his or her management team also tries to fulfill that mission by meeting goals and objectives.

Properties of Effective Mission Statements

To be effective, a mission statement must be: (1) market oriented, (2) feasible, (3) motivating, and (4) specific.

Market Oriented. A clear mission statement defines the business domain in terms of the market to be served. Business domain here refers to product class, technology, customer group, market need, or any combination of these. A well-defined, market-oriented mission statement would state that the business is formed to serve a particular customer group, meet a particular type of need, or both.

Feasible. The mission statement must not define a market too narrowly or too broadly. For example, a product-oriented statement such as "we manufacture slide rules" is too narrow. It leaves no room for expansion when such items as the electronic calculator are developed. On the other hand, a mission statement such as "we manufacture communication equipment" is too broad for a company that makes pencils. The mission statement has to determine the middle

---

[12]Stan Payne, Letter to Omaha Division Employees, USPS Field Division, Omaha, Nebr. November 17, 1988.

path for operations, to allow for growth while not getting the company into unrealistic business ventures beyond its capabilities. For example, a prune company can be described as a dried fruit company, as a fruit company, or ultimately as a food company. (It may be a bit farfetched, however, to label it a laxative company or a pharmaceutical company).[13]

Motivating.   A successful mission statement motivates. It inspires employees to work by making them feel that their efforts are significant and a contribution to the betterment of society. If possible, the mission should be stated as an accomplishment external to the firm. In this way, the employees can feel that they are producing a product or service for the benefit of the target consumer group. Workers are inclined to be more productive if they feel they are helping the consumer rather than just making a larger profit for the company.

Specific.   The mission statement must be specific enough to include major policies, and it must give specific guidelines enabling management to choose from among alternative courses of action. The policies in the mission statement should express the value system of the company and the tone of its dealings with customers, suppliers, distributors, competition, and other market participants. On the other hand, a mission statement should not be overly specific. An effective mission statement should serve the company for many years. It should not have to be updated every few years just because the environment has changed or because a new, unrelated opportunity has come up. However, a company should revise its mission statement if the statement is no longer appropriate or does not define an optimal course for the company.[14]

Are Mission Statements of Value?

In reality, many corporate mission statements are of little value, consisting of pious platitudes and necessities. Of what value is stating "We hope to provide products of the highest quality?" A mission should not describe what a firm *must* do to *survive*; it should describe what the firm *chooses* to do in order to *thrive*.

To be of value, a mission statement should include statements such that progress or performance in achieving the mission can be measured. Second, a mission statement should differentiate the company from other companies, and should define the business the company *wants* to be in—not merely the business it *is* in. In addition, a mission statement should be relevant to a wide range of stakeholders and, most importantly, it should be inspiring and motivating.[15]

---

[13] Philip Kotler, *Principles of Marketing,* (Englewood Cliffs, N.J.: Prentice-Hall, 1980), pp. 74–76.

[14]Ibid.

[15]Russell L. Ackoff, "Mission Statements," *Planning Review* 15, no. 4 (July-August 1987), p. 30.

A recent study of Fortune 500 firms attempted to determine if the mission statements of the high performers differed from those of the low performers. The study found a significant difference; the higher performers prepared publicly available *written* mission statements that included the organization's:

- Company philosophy—including the firm's basic beliefs, values, and broad aspirations.
- Self-concept—the company's view of itself, including its competitive strengths.
- Desired public image.

In other words, significantly more of the high-performing organizations had mission statements that addressed the above three areas. The conclusion is that the high performers have more comprehensive mission statements, and the three areas (corporate philosophy, self-concept, and desired image) are especially important components to include in an organization's mission statement.[16] The implication is that the successful firms are clear on these three issues, which somehow translate into improved performance. Every person in the organization should have a full understanding of the firm's mission.

DETERMINING GOALS AND OBJECTIVES

Another important aspect of strategic management involves goals and objectives which define *what* it is the organization hopes to accomplish, both over the long and short term. They are expected results, or targets, that support the organization's purpose. Goals and objectives are typically applied in certain specific areas, including:

1. Growth—including corporate growth rate, eventual size and growth, as well as relative size of business units.
2. Financial—including profits, cash flow, return on investment, dividends, and ratios.
3. Product/service—including development of new products/services, innovation, and quality.
4. Marketing—including customer base, advertising, sales, market penetration, market expansion, and customer service.
5. Operating—including inventory, cost control, production processes, and plant operations.
6. Personnel—including human-resource planning, management development, turnover, and labor relations.
7. Social responsibility—including regulations, pollution control, and community involvement.

---

[16]John A. Pearce II and Fred David, "Corporate Mission Statements: The Bottom Line," *The Academy of Management Executive* 1, no. 2 (May 1987), p. 112.

A look at the goals and objectives of the postal service shows the inclusion of a number of the seven areas, even though the postal service is a public sector organization. Specifically, the overall goals of the USPS are:

1. Respond to the needs of postal customers by providing a full range of services that are prompt, reliable, and economical.
2. Maintain the integrity of the postal service on the basis of sound fiscal and operational policies.
3. Provide postal employees with career opportunities, working conditions, and compensation comparable to generally accepted practices in the private sector.[17]

In support of these overall goals, the postmaster general has developed a set of general objectives to be achieved by the year 2000:

1. To manage our resources in such a way to obviate the need for future rate increases.
2. To restore public and customer confidence and satisfaction in the postal service and return service levels (as defined by the overnight, second-, and third-day service, Express Mail, and so on) to at least those levels experienced in 1986–87.
3. To provide a workplace climate which recognizes the value of the individual and stimulates participation and individual initiative.[18]

While these goals and objectives are largely in the product/service, operating, and personnel areas, they are appropriate to the postal service's situation and support its mission.

Hierarchy of Objectives

An important responsibility of management at each level of the organization is ensuring that lower-level goals reinforce one another. That is, the goals and objectives of division A must complement those of division B so that the organization is working toward the same ends and not at crosspurposes.

The important point is that all goals and objectives must support the organization's mission and must complement those of other departments of the firm—they must be consistent. Also, goals and objectives of lower-level departments must support those at higher levels of the organization. For this reason, it is helpful to think in terms of a hierarchy of objectives: primary, secondary, and subobjectives.

Primary objectives for the firm are typically finance and profit related, and may include: (*a*) return on capital employed; (*b*) return on shareholders' capital;

---

[17]Payne, Letter.
[18]Ibid.

and (*c*) levels of sales, profits, and rate of growth. These are typically broken down into specific targets for each division and profit center.

Secondary objectives are additional targets the firm and its divisions wish to attain, but are considered to be less important than the primary objectives. Examples would be customer satisfaction goals, equal opportunity targets, product quality levels, and the like.

Subobjectives support the achievement of the firm's primary and secondary goals. For example, one objective of a firm may be to achieve a 15 percent ROI after taxes. Subobjectives that support this goal may include increasing manufacturing efficiency to a certain level, reducing sales and distribution costs, and bringing higher-margin products on-line by a certain date.

In short, goals and objectives are required at every level of the organization and for each level of strategy: enterprise, corporate, business unit, and functional.

Further, goals and objectives must be achievable. They should *not* be so high that achievement is unlikely. Success breeds success: therefore, achievable goals tend to result in more divisions (and people) feeling that they are winners rather than losers—an important climate for the successful firm.

Also, while short-term accomplishments are important, long-term goals and objectives are even more important. Recent popular opinion holds that American managers pay undue attention to short-term financial results (and that business school graduates are trained this way, as well). However, a recent study of top executives at leading U.S. industrial firms indicates that this is not true—the overriding objective is long-term self-sustaining growth. Managers are most concerned with the long-term survival of their companies, and with minimizing their dependence on external sources of funds and on narrow product lines.[19] This is as it should be.

Management's Goals and Objectives

Managers are human, and, like most human beings, tend to put self-interest before anything else. This includes preserving their jobs. Instead of trying to maximize corporate earnings, managers *satisfice,* that is, attempt to meet a satisfactory performance level for themselves and for the corporation, while doing whatever it takes to ensure their job tenure and promotion chances. Much of their behavior, then, is directed toward maximizing not stockholder returns or wealth, but returns to themselves in the form of money, promotions, satisfaction, and security. In this context, you should *not* assume that outside directors truly represent stockholder interests and can effectively "control" management. Even

---

[19]Gordon Donaldson and Jay W. Lorsch, *Decision Making at the Top: The Shaping of Strategic Direction* (New York: Basic Books, 1983), pp. 7–10.

outside directors owe their board seats to inside directors (management), and many will act to preserve their tenure on the board.[20]

In general, managers attempt to meet certain thresholds in areas such as profitability, to ensure survival of the firm and permit the pursuit of other goals, as a means of furthering their careers. Thus, long-term profit satisfaction, rather than maximization, and the satisfaction of other corporate needs, best describe the goals and objectives of both management and the organization.

ORGANIZATIONAL TYPE AND STAGE OF DEVELOPMENT

Defining the business—including development of goals and objectives, as well as assessing the organization's resources and competencies—is affected by the organization's current characteristics. That is, organizations face different strategic and policy concerns at different stages in their life cycle; start-ups, high-growth firms, mature businesses, and shrinking organizations face very different strategic situations. Also, the size and diversity of a firm are important determinants of which strategies the firm can and should pursue from this point on. Therefore, it is important to understand basic organizational growth and development patterns as they impact the strategic situation.

The process and content of strategic planning are affected by the size, maturity, and diversification of an organization. Such things as how to grow, how rapidly to grow, how much and what type of diversification, internal versus acquisition growth and diversification, horizontal or vertical integration, forward versus backward integration, domestic versus international growth, the type of departmentation, all are, in fact, strategic decisions.

These factors apply to all types of organizations, from the traditional medium-to-large business firm to public-sector organizations, other not-for-profit organizations, new ventures, small businesses, international businesses, and even to professional and service organizations such as CPA firms. The focus in this section is on strategy processes and content as applied to organizations in general, concentrating on those aspects applicable to traditional medium-to-large business firms. For certain other kinds of organizations, unique characteristics, features, and needs that may affect strategic decisions and processes are treated in detail in Chapter 11.

Types of Organizations

There are many types and sizes of organizations. Appropriate strategies for organizations not only vary with their relative size (large businesses and agencies *are* different from small businesses and agencies), but also with the *type* of

---

[20]Paul Solman and Thomas Friedman, *Life and Death on the Corporate Battlefield* (New York: Simon & Schuster, 1983).

organization. One major strategic decision involves the type of business an organization wishes to become (or is at present). Here strategic issues facing four generic *types* of business—the single-product business, the dominant-product business, the diversified company, and the multi-industry company, shown in Figure 3.2, will be examined.[21] (The term *business* is used broadly and is not limited to private-sector organizations.)

Single-Product Businesses. The single-product business receives over 95 percent of its revenues from a single line of goods or services. This type of business is almost always departmentalized along functional lines, regardless of its size. Many small businesses are of this type, although some single-product firms, such as Caterpillar, as well as banks and insurance companies, are relatively large. The major corporate-level strategic decision in this type of company deals with how to grow—within the single product line (for example geographically), or by broadening the line and ceasing to be a single-product firm.

Dominant-Product Businesses. This type of business is somewhat diversified, but a single line of goods or services still accounts for 70 to 95 percent of revenues. The dominant-product business is usually managed along functional lines. A separate subsidiary division, or divisions, is often created for the remaining product or services lines—a partial move to a multidivisional structure. Again, financial institutions typify larger dominant-product businesses, but another example is Deere & Company, where farm equipment dominates, yet industrial equipment, lawn equipment, and recreational products also are manufactured.

Dominant-product businesses may be vertically integrated, diversified into products linked in some way to the dominant product, diversified to exploit a particular advantage they possess, or diversified on an unrelated basis. The corporate strategic questions here are how much to diversify, into which areas, and the relationship (if any) to the dominant product.

Diversified Businesses. Diversified organizations typically receive over 30 percent of their revenues from products outside their main business. This type of business is typically large and organized along divisional lines, sometimes called M-form (for multidivision form) structure. The product lines relate to one another in many ways that are the same as in the dominant-business firm. Yet no one business dominates to the degree that it does in the dominant-business firm. Corporate-level strategy relates largely to the ''portfolio'' of businesses comprising the firm, and to their relationships. For example, diversification moves can lead the firm into businesses that are *related* in some way, or *unrelated,* or some combination.

---

[21]Leonard Wrigley, ''Divisional Autonomy and Diversification,'' Ph.D. dissertation, Harvard Business School, Cambridge, Mass., 1970.

FIGURE 3.2   Types of Businesses

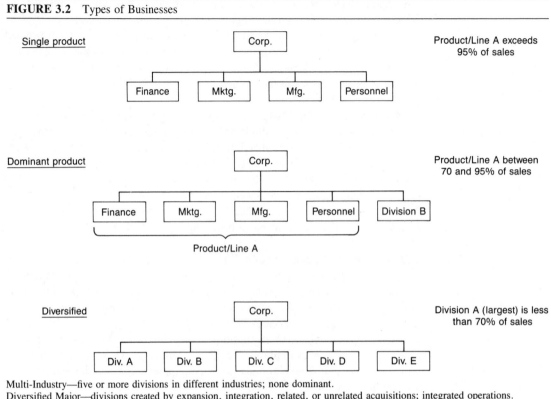

Single product — Product/Line A exceeds 95% of sales

Dominant product — Product/Line A between 70 and 95% of sales

Diversified — Division A (largest) is less than 70% of sales

Multi-Industry—five or more divisions in different industries; none dominant.
Diversified Major—divisions created by expansion, integration, related, or unrelated acquisitions; integrated operations.
Conglomerate—divisions/subsidiaries operate independently.

Multi-Industry Firms.   This type of business is a subtype of the diversified firm. The multi-industry, or multimission, organization is characterized by a relatively large number of businesses, none of which is significantly bigger than the others. While the diversified company might have three divisions accounting for, say, 50, 30, and 20 percent of sales, the true multi-industry firm might have five or more divisions in a number of *different* industries.

Multi-industry firms, then, have diversified into a number of *unrelated* industries, and no one product line comes close to dominating the others. Multi-industry corporate strategies typically deal with managing the portfolio of businesses, as well as the type of diversification methods to be followed. Some multidivision firms manage their divisions on a closely related basis—sharing technology, for example, and transferring employees between divisions. Others manage the divisions separately, acting as a holding company for the divisions, which operate quite independently. A conglomerate tends to treat its subsidiaries not so much as divisions as independent companies owned by the parent corporation; in fact, each subsidiary typically has its own president and CEO. While this arrangement appears similar to the holding company, conglomerates typically treat their subsidiaries as investments that can be bought or sold and are acquired through aggressive financial transactions.

Another way of classifying multi-industry firms is in terms of "diversified majors" versus conglomerates. Diversified majors are formed largely through *internal* expansions, through vertical or horizontal *integration,* through *concentric* acquisitions (acquisitions into industries or companies somehow related to existing divisions), or through *unrelated* acquisitions.

The diversified company (including the multi-industry company) is the most important form of industrial organization in the United States in terms of sales and assets. This type of company comprises about 80 to 85 percent of the Fortune 500 industrials, which account for two thirds of the output, investment, and employment, and three fourths of the profits of U.S. industry.[22]

Patterns of Organizational Evolution

As organizations increase in size, they often change from a single-product firm to a dominant business, a diversified major, or a multi-industry firm. In addition, at any stage in this progression, the firm can expand geographically into foreign markets, becoming progressively more global or multinational. There are, however, typical patterns, or stages of development, that organizations pass through as they grow, develop, and mature.

It is important to understand these stages, because strategies and modes of operation appropriate for one stage may be inappropriate for another. Goals, objectives, strategies, organization structure, and management styles tend to differ from stage to stage.

A number of researchers have proposed models depicting these growth patterns. For example, Downs[23] studied the life cycle of government bureaus. Lippitt and Schmidt[24] proposed a three-stage model of development for companies, as did Scott.[25] While each of these models approaches organizational growth and development somewhat differently, there is a degree of commonality.

---

[22]Norman Berg and R. A. Pitts, "Strategic Management: The Multi-Business Corporation," in *Strategic Management,* ed. D. Schendel and C. W. Hofer (Boston: Little, Brown, 1979), p. 339.

[23]A. Downs, "The Life Cycle of Bureaus," in *Inside Bureaucracy,* ed. A. Downs (San Francisco: Little, Brown, and Rand Corp., 1967), p. 296.

[24] G. L. Lippitt and W. H. Schmidt, "Crises in a Development Organization," *Harvard Business Review* 45, no. 6 (November–December 1967), p. 102.

[25]W. R. Scott, *Stages of Corporate Development—Part 1,* Case No. 9–371-294 (Boston: Intercollegiate Case Clearing House, 1971).

The models usually progress from the start-up stage through various intermediate stages to that of a large mature organization, often a multidivisional (perhaps multinational) corporation. Two models that are particularly helpful in understanding an organization's growth patterns are Greiner's evolution and revolution model and Galbraith and Nathanson's model.

Greiner's Evolution and Revolution Model.

Greiner suggests that organizations progress through five sequential stages as they grow and mature.[26] There is a distinct strategy, structure, and management style appropriate for each phase, but inappropriate for other phases. Further, the approach appropriate for each phase has certain limitations, that prevent the organization from growing beyond a certain size. When this limit is reached, the organization must change in certain ways to progress to the next phase. That is, it must make certain "revolutionary" or dramatic changes, or its growth will be effectively halted.

Greiner's model, shown in Figure 3.3, begins with a small, informal organization growing because of the creative ideas of its founders (Phase I). If the firm grows and prospers, this informal, entrepreneurial approach may begin to cause problems. A need arises for a strong, professional manager to take charge and lead the firm toward unified objectives. If this happens, the firm can grow through Phase II under strong, centralized leadership.

However, this approach also has its limits. As the firm grows and expands, centralized decision making becomes a bottleneck and subordinate managers begin to demand more autonomy. The firm becomes too large and diverse for a few top managers to make all the important decisions. Only by increased delegation of authority and responsibility can the burden on top management be eased, and the firm can grow through the third phase. Again, this approach eventually reaches its limit as diverse, autonomous divisions begin to drift apart. In fact, they may begin to function almost as separate companies, with differing financial, personnel, and operating policies as well as strategies. There is a need to regain control over these diverse subunits, which is usually met by creating corporate staff groups to coordinate and control planning, decision making, and operations of the units.

However, a large organization with too much coordination and control can become bureaucratic, and faces a "red-tape" crisis. Greiner suggests that this can be overcome by collaborative approaches, such as matrix management, team building and group rewards, project teams, and the like, to create increased motivation, purpose, and excitement. The next crisis may be one of information overload and psychological saturation ("burnout"). In short, firms face very different problems and need different solutions as they grow and mature through the five phases. Again, structure, strategies, and management approaches must be appropriate to the phase the firm currently is in.

---

[26]Larry Greiner, "Evolution and Revolution as Organizations Grow," *Harvard Business Review* 50, no. 4 (July–August 1972), p. 37.

FIGURE 3.3   Greiner's Five-Phase Growth Model

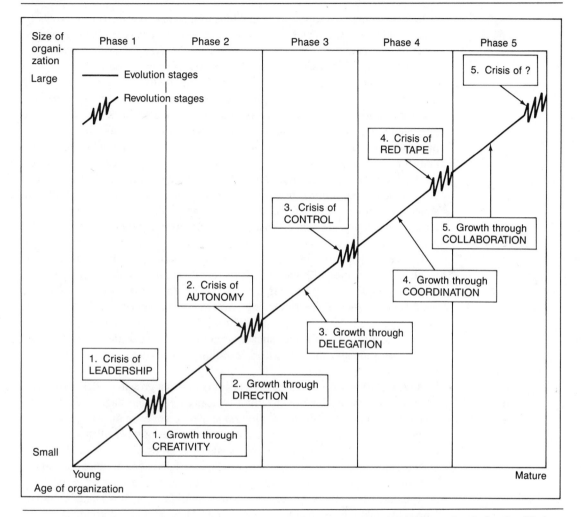

The Galbraith and Nathanson Model.   Galbraith and Nathanson also studied organizational growth patterns in some depth, and offer models that shed additional light on the growth process and the strategies it requires.[27] Their model focuses more on organizational types and characteristics at various stages

---

[27]Jay R. Galbraith and D. A. Nathanson, *Strategy Implementation: The Role of Structure and Process* (St. Paul, Minn.: West Publishing, 1978), p. 118.

of development. Figure 3.4 shows likely growth patterns in the Galbraith and Nathanson model.

In their model, as the simple (analogous to the single-product) firm grows (in sales volume, assets, and employees), it almost always adopts a simple functional structure. At this point, however, the type of *growth* strategy it pursues dictates the type of structure the firm will adopt in the next stage of its evolution. The firm can grow in two ways—internally, or by acquisitions. If growth is internal, related diversification is usually the pattern, and the firm becomes multidivisional. This is also the case if related lines are acquired. If unrelated acquisitions are made, the firm becomes a holding company. The predominant path, however, is to pursue a strategy of vertical integration, which calls for a centralized functional form of organization. After reaching this stage, the typical firm begins related diversification strategies (either through internal growth or by acquisition), taking the company to the point where a multidivisional (M-form) structure is called for. As one might suspect, companies can move between organization types at this point, depending on their strategies and actions.

The next major strategy is almost always international expansion, which results in the firm requiring a global structure (functional, holding company, or, typically, multinational). In Figure 3.4, Galbraith and Nathanson describe a number of characteristics (including corporate-level strategies) that typify the major organizational types in their framework. This figure can be used in two ways; to identify the characteristics appropriate for a particular type of organization, or to identify the *type* of organization by studying its characteristics.

Further Observations.   You should bear in mind that growth models such as the above describe paths that organizations typically follow and stages they typically go through *if they progress to the final stage*. Not all (or even most) organizations progress to the final stages; some stop at various stages or types of structure along the way. Some even regress to previous stages or types. Some fail and cease to exist at some point. Some are acquired and exist as divisions of other companies, and some lose their identity entirely after an acquisition or merger.

A model recently developed by Miller and Friesen at Canada's McGill University takes these factors into account. Their model incorporates a birth phase (in which a new firm is attempting to become a viable entity), a growth phase (after the firm has established its distinctive competencies and enjoys some initial product-market successes), and a maturity phase (which follows growth as sales levels stabilize, the level of innovation falls, and a more bureaucratic structure is established). In addition, they include a decline phase (which results from stagnation as markets dry up and the firm declines with them. Profitability drops because of external factors and a lack of innovation.) Further, they include a revival phase, which is typically a phase of diversification and expansion of product and market scope. In this phase, firms typically adopt divisionalized structures to cope with more complex and heterogeneous markets and emphasize

FIGURE 3.4 Characteristics of Organizational Types

TYPE / CHARACTERISTIC	(S) Simple	(F) Functional	(H) Holding	(M) Multidivisional	(G) Global — (M)
Strategy	Single product	Single product and vertical integration	Growth by acquisition, unrelated diversity	Related diversity of product lines— internal growth, some acquisition	Multiple products in multiple countries
Interunit and Market Relations	[diagram]	[diagram] MKT	[diagram] MKT MKT MKT	[diagram] MKT MKT MKT	[diagram] MKT MKT MKT / MKT MKT MKT
Organization Structure	Simple functional	Central functional	Decentralized profit centers around product divisions Small headquarters	Decentralized product or area division profit centers	Decentralized profit centers around worldwide product or area divisions
Research and Development	Not institutionalized Random search	Increasingly institutionalized around product and process improvements	Institutionalized search for new products and improvements Decentralized to divisions	Institutionalized search for new products and improvements Centralized guidance	Institutionalized search for new products which is centralized and decentralized in centers of expertise
Performance Measurement	By personal contact Subjective	Increasingly impersonal based on cost, productivity, but still subjective	Impersonal based on return on investment and profitability	Impersonal based on return on investment profitability with some subjective contribution to whole	Impersonal with multiple goals like ROI, profit tailored to product and country
Rewards	Unsystematic, paternalistic Based on loyalty	Increasingly related to performance around productivity and volume	Formula-based bonus on ROI or profitability Equity rewards	Bonus based on profit performance but more subjective than holding Cash rewards	Bonus based on multiple planned goals More discretion Cash rewards
Careers	Single function specialist	Functional specialists with some generalist interfunctional moves	Cross function but intradivisional	Cross functional, inter-divisional, and corporate-divisional moves	Interdivisional Intersubsidiary Subsidiary/corporate moves
Leader Style and Control	Personal control of strategic and operating decisions by top management	Top control of strategic decisions Some delegation of operations through plans, procedures	Almost complete delegation of operations and strategy within existing businesses Indirect control through results and selection of management and capital funding	Delegation of operations with indirect control, through results Some decentralization of strategy within existing business	Delegation of operations with indirect control through results according to plan Some delegation of strategy within countries and existing businesses Some political delegation
Strategic Choices	Need of owner versus needs of firm	Degree of integration Market share Breadth of product line	Degree of diversity Types of business Acquisition targets Entry and exit from businesses	Allocation of resources by business Entry and exit from businesses Rate of growth	Allocation of resources across businesses and countries Exit and entry into businesses and countries Degree of ownership and type of country involvement

more sophisticated planning and control systems.[28] While elements of decline and revival are inherent in some of the earlier models (such as Greiner's crises and revolutionary changes), treating them explicitly, as Miller and Friesen have done, adds to understanding of the processes.

Miller and Friesen's revival phase is analogous to corporate *renewal,* which is characteristic of many firms from time to time. In fact, most established (and many young) firms go through significant periods of decline and renewal, some externally caused and some internal. Figure 3.5 illustrates this process.

Also, nothing was said about the *rate* of progression from stage to stage; some firms progress rapidly, some slowly, some in spurts, and so forth. What is important to realize, however, is that patterns of development seem to be somewhat consistent, and that structures, strategies, and other characteristics at one stage or type are not the same as the characteristics at other stages. It is also worth noting that our understanding of *how* organizations of varying types and sizes function is incomplete. Some observers have suggested studying small businesses, implying that there is more knowledge of larger businesses. This may be true if "big business" is defined as anything larger than a "small business." However, most organization studies tend to focus on medium-sized organizations or a department or division of a large organization. In reality, relatively little is known about the way the *very large* businesses function.[29] The point is that there are qualitative as well as quantitative differences among organizations of different sizes and types.

FIGURE 3.5   Organizational Growth and Renewal

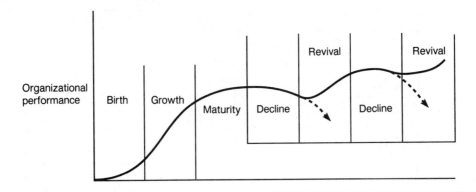

---

[28]Danny Miller and Peter H. Friesen, "A Longitudinal Study of the Corporate Life Cycle," *Management Science* 30, no. 10 (October 1984), p. 1161.

[29]David S. Brown, *Managing the Large Organization,* (Mt. Airy, Md.: Lomond Publications, 1982), jacket.

COMPETENCIES AND RESOURCES

Regardless of the type, developmental stage, and size of the organization, a firm is able to do only what it has the knowledge, skill, ability, and resources to accomplish. In other words, its capabilities are determined by its competencies and its resources. An organization's *distinctive competencies* are those relatively few things that the organization does particularly well, and if properly focused, can enable it to achieve competitive advantages and successfully achieve its goals and objectives.[30] Typical sources of distinctive competence include financial, managerial, functional, and organizational capabilities, as well as the company's reputation and history.[31] In short, if a company has superior abilities in producing or marketing a product or service, or has superior skills or resources in other competitively important areas, it may have a source of competitive advantage which can be an important part of its strategies. Competitive advantage will be discussed more fully in Chapters 5 and 8.

Resources

A final consideration in any assessment of a firm's strengths and weaknesses is *resources*. In general, organizations possess six types of resources that they can employ toward the achievement of objectives:

1. *Financial resources,* such as cash flow, debt capacity, the availability of new equity, and cash and other liquid resources on hand.
2. *Physical resources,* such as plants and equipment, buildings, land, inventories, vehicles, and other facilities.
3. *Human resources,* such as management, supervisors, production employees, staff specialists, salespeople, and engineers.
4. *Technology,* such as patents, licenses, designs, production methods, proprietary information, and technological skills.
5. *Organizational resources,* such as systems, procedures, management techniques, decision-making models, company reputation, and goodwill.[32]
6. *Information,* such as knowledge of markets, the competition, the economy and other environmental influences, customer and supplier data and plans, technological advances, internal operating data, and the like.

---

[30]Mark R. Hurwich and Richard A. Furniss Jr., "Measuring and Rewarding Strategic Performance" in *Handbook of Business Strategy,* ed. W. D. Guth (Boston: Warren, Gorham & Lamont, 1985), p. 24:22.

[31]Kenneth R. Andrews, *The Concept of Corporate Strategy,* rev. ed. (Homewood, Ill.: R. D. Irwin, 1980), p. 69.

[32]Charles W. Hofer and Dan Schendel, *Strategy Formulation: Analytical Concepts* (St. Paul: Minn.: West Publishing, 1978), p. 145.

One reason many small businesses fail and strategies in larger firms do not succeed is that management has attempted to do more than the firm's resources will permit or support. The business that tries to grab a large market share when it does not have sufficient capital, people, or experience is likely to fail. For this reason, strategies must be evaluated in terms of their resource requirements and the ability of the organization to support those requirements—spreading a firm too thin is a recipe for failure. In addition, resources are relative. American Motors had more financial assets than General Mills and Armstrong Cork, and outsold National Cash Register and Campbell Soup, but it did not compete in those industries; it competed in the automotive industry. Chrysler had 10 times the assets of AMC, Ford 20 times, and GM 40 times. In the auto industry, AMC's otherwise substantial assets were marginal, at best. A company's strengths and weaknesses must be evaluated not in absolute terms but in relation to its competitive environment, including other companies pursuing similar strategies.

The Resource Audit

In terms of internal strengths and weaknesses, the resource audit provides the best assessment. A resource audit can determine which external opportunities can be taken advantage of. According to Harvard's Hugo Uyterhoeven, the resource audit encompasses three main dimensions:

1. Operational, focusing on what it takes to succeed in a particular market, industry, or field of endeavor. What are the key requirements for success?
2. Financial, focusing on assets, earnings, cash, and sources and uses of funds. What are the current financial resources of the firm and what can the firm afford to commit to a given strategy from internal as well as external (debt and equity) sources?
3. Management, focusing on human resources, particularly the ability to plan and implement strategies. Does the firm have enough of the necessary skills and abilities, given the requirements of the external environment and the strategy?[33]

The operational dimension consists of what it takes to succeed in a particular business or market. Does the company possess the technological capability to compete? Can it produce and distribute the product in sufficient volume at an acceptable level of quality? Are its costs competitive? Are the products aimed at the proper segments, and does the company possess distinctive competencies in important areas? In other words, will the company be able to effectively compete in this market? Out of this analysis will come an assessment of what the company *can* and *cannot* do.

---

[33]H. Uyterhoeven, R. W. Ackerman, and J. R. Rosenblum, *Strategy and Organization: Text and Cases in General Management*, rev. ed. (Homewood, Ill.: Richard D. Irwin, 1977).

The financial dimension focuses on money—such as cash flow and debt capacity. Ratio analysis, funds flow analysis, computer-based financial models, and other similar measurements are helpful in determining a business's intermediate- and long-term financial resources and requirements. The strategist is primarily interested in the following financial elements:

1. What are the asset requirements per dollar of sales? If the company's strategy calls for an increase in sales, how much will have to be invested in operating assets to support those sales?
2. What does the company earn? What will be its return on sales and on the assets required to support those sales?
3. How much cash is generated? Cash flow in broad terms is defined as cash receipts minus cash disbursements—it equals profits plus depreciation minus dividends. This figure determines how much *internally* generated cash will be available to support future investments.
4. How has the company committed its resources? How much of the internally generated cash is already committed? The *remainder* is the amount available for reinvestment. This figure should be compared to the reinvestment required to support the strategy. If sufficient funds are not available internally, how much can be gotten externally, from loans or additional equity? The company's debt capacity must be analyzed if external funding will be required.

The management dimension centers on the company's human resources. In many ways, a company's management is its most critical resource and perhaps the most constraining. Certainly, management is the most difficult resource to assess. However, the company's management capabilities must be equal to environmental requirements and to the demands of strategies chosen, and management must be able to use the firm's operational and financial resources effectively. As Bob Daugherty, chairman of Valmont Industries (supplier of agricultural products and services, and largest producer of center-pivot irrigation systems) states: "We want to have a management team capable of running a company 10 times as large as we are now."[34] The strategy, in Daugherty's view, ensures that management is not his company's constraining resource. If it is, what good is having all the other resources to permit growth?

CONCLUSIONS

The organization's internal characteristics (including management's vision and the values and expectations of its stakeholders); its mission, goals and objectives; and its competencies and resources combine to determine what the organization is trying to accomplish and how successful it is likely to be. Together, these

---

[34]R. Daugherty, visiting executive speech, University of Nebraska, April 1983.

factors comprise a key aspect of assessing the strategic situation, which must be done before strategy alternatives are formulated. In addition, the general environment must be analyzed in terms of its overall opportunities and threats (Chapter 4), and the competitive environment must be assessed, including the industry, markets, and competitors (Chapter 5). The strategy alternatives open to the company can be selected from a number of generic strategic options, which are discussed in Chapters 6 and 7. Also important is the realization that organizations go through fairly typical patterns or stages of development as they grow from single-product businesses. The growth strategies that they pursue often dictate changes in structure and processes, and needs tend to change as the organization becomes more and more successful in its endeavors.

Analyzing the General Environment: Overall Opportunities and Threats

LEARNING OBJECTIVES

After completing Chapter 4, you should be able to:

Appreciate the importance of the impact of the general environment.

Delineate the major environmental influences affecting the firm.

Realize that general environmental conditions may have a significant bearing on the choice of strategic alternatives.

Understand the major macro- and microeconomic influences on the firm.

Describe basic technology and productivity-related influences.

Describe social, political, legal, and regulatory influences and processes.

PROFILE   *Kustom Electronics*

Kustom Electronics of Kansas City is the nation's leading producer of police radar systems. Until the mid-1970s, Kustom's markets were mature and experiencing little growth, and the company was flirting with losses. However, the OPEC oil embargo changed all that. How? To save oil, Congress mandated a nationwide 55 MPH speed limit in 1974, which gave birth to a new industry—the radar detector—and also gave new life to the CB-radio industry. To combat the ''fuzzbusters,'' ''super snoopers,'' and other radar detectors motorists were using, the police were interested in purchasing new, more advanced radar equipment that the motorists' fuzzbusters could not detect. They also were interested in longer-range, more powerful equipment to thwart the CB warning network the drivers had developed. Kustom, therefore, began producing and selling radar equipment that operated on a higher frequency band than the motorists' detectors were able to intercept.

Electrolert (which manufactures fuzzbusters) and other manufacturers of detectors then added multiband capability to their equipment, generating more sales for themselves in the process. Radar manufacturers, in turn, again modified their products to counter the more sophisticated detectors. In fact, the situation became a continual game of countermeasures.

Thus, a new U.S. industry was created, and new life was given to a stable, mature company—by a seemingly unrelated political event in the Middle East. Each competitive response, in turn, gave a shot in the arm to the opposition by creating the demand for new products.

Subsequent changes in the international political and economic environments—such as competition between OPEC countries, plus creation of an energy conservation ethic—have increased oil production and reduced relative demand. This has led to increased supplies of oil, lower prices, and pressure to raise interstate highway speed limits to 65 MPH—an event in the legal environment likely to *reduce* the demand for Escorts, fuzzbusters, and in turn, police radar units.

PROFILE   Deere & Company

During the 1970s, the revenues of Deere & Company grew faster than those of Xerox and nearly twice as fast as those of IBM and Texas Instruments. Earnings kept pace, increasing almost sixfold during the same period. This record of performance, particularly for a large corporation, would satisfy all but the most ardent growth enthusiasts. But Deere is a farm and construction equipment company, not an electronics, semiconductor, or other high-tech business. What caused this outstanding record?

According to industry observers, Deere is the industry's most efficient producer, has the strongest dealer network, the newest factories, and boasts the lowest inventory-to-sales ratio in the industry. This enviable position was achieved largely as a result of perceptive strategic decisions made since the mid-1950s, when Deere was operating in the shadow of the industry leader, International Harvester.

Deere had conducted extensive research into the future of farming. Management concluded that long-run trends would result in a reduction in the number of and an increase in the size of farms, requiring larger equipment and fewer—but larger—dealers. Deere capitalized on this trend away from labor toward heavy machinery by spending twice as much on R&D as its competitors—4 cents of every sales dollar—to design larger tractors and equipment. At the same time, Deere began to focus on the 20 percent of farmers who earn most of the cash income. These strategies paid off, with Deere passing IH in the mid-1960s.

Thus, innovation, service, and efficiency have been the strategies that contributed to Deere's success. In fact, more than half of their manufacturing facilities are less than 10 years old. Their new tractor plant in Waterloo, Iowa, for example, is one of the most modern in the world, with the latest in manufacturing technology and computer control. Deere is the industry's lowest-cost producer, and can break even operating at 45 percent of capacity at the Waterloo plant.

However, the strong dollar of the mid-80s and agricultural self-sufficiency in more and more foreign markets dramatically reduced U.S. farm exports, causing a crisis in our farm economy. Even though Deere is the dominant U.S. producer and has been increasing its market share, the demand for farm equipment has dropped, causing Deere's sales and profits to fall as well. Thus, the company took advantage of environmental changes and appropriate strategies to achieve its dominant position, but recently has fallen victim to a lengthy decline by its industry, caused by other environmental influences.

THE IMPORTANCE OF ENVIRONMENTAL INFLUENCES

A number of factors have major bearing on the *content* of the strategies of an organization. These factors dictate the types of strategies the firm should pursue. This chapter examines the role of general factors external to the firm (the economy, technology, social factors, and political/legal considerations).

Key to this process is the ability to identify early those social, technological, political, economic, competitive, legal, and other issues that may significantly affect the operation and strategic success of the firm. (An *issue* is a "condition or pressure, either internal or external to an organization, that, if it continues, will have a significant effect on the functioning of the organization or its future interests.")[1]

Strategic issues are those major trends, developments, and progressions of events that materially affect the strategy and operations of the organization. Strategic issues tend to be broad, multifaceted, and closely interrelated; examples include the women's movement and civil rights. Normally, such issues affect both the external environment in which the organization must operate and the internal activities of the organization.[2] Such issues must be considered in the strategic planning process, in the operational execution of those plans, and

---

[1]James K. Brown, *This Business of Issues: Coping with the Company's Environments* (New York: The Conference Board, 1979), p. 1.

[2]J. E. Dutton and Edward Ottensmeyer, "Strategic Issue Management Systems: Forms, Functions, and Contexts," *Academy of Management Review* 12, no. 2 (April 1987), p. 355.

whenever the strategy is confronted by an external trend or event. They can emerge at virtually any time and with little prior notice. Customarily, strategic issues pose basic questions in four general areas:

1. *The external environment:* How to gain better understanding of the socio-political, technological, and economic changes affecting the organization's strategic and operating environment.

2. *Resource capabilities:* How to determine the organization's human resource needs and responsibilities while following the present strategy or change in strategy.

3. *The alignment of business units:* How to organize and position the product and market groups to best support the strategy.

4. *Communication:* How to get the strategy and/or issues fully communicated, understood, and applied throughout the organization.

Strategic issues can include such concerns as energy shortages and embargoes, pollution control, industry deregulation, consumerism, equal rights, employee safety and privacy, unstable foreign economies and governments, and changing consumer tastes, to name just a few. As James Farley, chairman of Booz Allen & Hamilton Inc. management consultants has pointed out, "For all of us, there will be far less room in the 1980s for strategic mistakes, for the cost of mistakes will be very high, indeed."[3]

The Need for Environmental Analysis

Environmental analysis has become a key task in strategic planning in the last two decades. The match, or fit, between the internal strengths and resources of the firm and the opportunities in its environment is the crux of strategic management. Knowledge of the environment becomes critical as the firm seeks these propitious matches with the opportunities in its environment. The firm must also analyze its environment to avoid, to the extent possible, any problems or threats that might arise. Michael Kami, former head of planning for IBM and recently head of his own firm, Corporate Planning, Inc., has stated that successful organizations plan from the outside in—not from the inside out—because the environment shapes the future of the organization. Furthermore, Kami contends a company can influence changes in internal issues or trends, and can, in effect, manage them.[4] External issues and trends, however, remain far less amenable to management control. In fact, the firm's environment can be

---

[3]James B. Farley, "Winners and Losers in the Eighties," *World Business Weekly,* April 28, 1980, p. 5.

[4]Michael J. Kami, *Kami Strategic Assumptions: Fall '82 Update* (Lighthouse Pt., Fla: Corporate Planning, 1982).

looked on as the product of the strategic decisions of others: government, competitors, customers, society, and a host of other outside influences. Events external to the firm have important effects on future results.

During the 70s and 80s, there has been a growing recognition of the need to understand environmental influences and changes in order to devise successful strategies for the firm. Several indications of this recognition include:

- An increased realization that organizations are *open*—not closed—systems. Systems theory tells us that an open system is *dependent* upon input from its environment for survival and growth. Therefore, an organization is dependent upon its environment, and should look upon this interaction as a necessity and an opportunity, not merely as a threat.
- An increased awareness of environmental change and turbulence and their impact upon a firm, the industry, and society in general. Coupled with this realization is the notion that management needs to study and *understand* the environment in order to think strategically.
- Along with the previous points, increased efforts to include environmental analysis in the organization's strategy formulation processes, in order to ensure that important external changes and information are included in the firm's strategic decisions.[5]

Environmental analysis then, is the process of seeking information about relationships and events *outside* the company that will help management chart the company's future actions. Environmental analysis helps identify those parts of the environment the firm can concentrate on and attack competitively—the organization's *domain*.[6] One problem in such analysis is that environmental influences often are complex and sometimes unpredictable. However, the mere fact that the environment is changing does not mean that it is unpredictable. For example, demographic changes due to the baby boom—their effects on retirement plans, population aging, and the like—are predictable. On the other hand, environmental changes that don't follow known patterns—such as oil embargoes, natural disasters, and political changes—are more difficult to anticipate, and are less predictable.

In addition, a quickening *pace* of change requires a firm to focus more directly on the environment, since the firm will experience more changes (even if they are predictable) in a given period of time. As a result, the firm will find itself making more strategic decisions in a given time frame. The more dynamic the environment, the greater the impact on the firm's strategies.

---

[5]Liam Fahey and V. K. Narayanan, *Macroenvironmental Analysis for Strategic Management* (St. Paul, Minn.: West Publishing, 1986), p. 1.

[6]Sol Levine and P. E. White, ''Exchange as a Conceptual Framework for the Study of Interorganizational Relationships,'' *Administrative Science Quarterly* 5 (1961), pp. 583–601.

FIGURE 4.1   Sources of Turbulence

Factor	Turbulence Level				
	Low				*High*
Market scope	Local	Regional	National	International	Global
Success factors	Economic only	+ Technological		+ Sociopolitical	
Type and predictability of change	Familiar	Gradual		Discontinuous	Novel
Speed of change	Slow	Moderate		Rapid	Faster than response

Source: Adapted from H. I. Ansoff, "Strategic Response in a Turbulent Environment," *Handbook of Business Strategy,* ed. W. D. Guth (Boston: Warren, Gorham & Lamont, 1985), p. 4–4.

Increased environmental turbulence is the result of four contributing factors, as shown in Figure 4.1. Briefly, these factors are:

1. *Market scope,* proceeding from local to regional, national, international, and global markets. As market scope expands, the relevant environment is subject to more and more sources of turbulence.
2. *Success factors.* As a greater number of factors become critical to the firm's success, again the firm is subject to turbulence from a greater number of sources.
3. *Type and predictability of change.* Obviously, familiar and gradual changes are less upsetting than are discontinuous and novel changes.
4. *Speed of change.* In the past, changes occurred more slowly than they do today. As the pace quickens, the environment becomes more turbulent, and the pace can ultimately exceed the firm's ability to respond to it.[7]

In addition, since environmental analysis is a critical factor in strategic management, it should not be surprising that a definite relationship has been shown to exist between a firm's efforts to analyze the environment and its subsequent financial performance.[8]

Which Factors Are Important?

Which environmental factors are most important for a firm to analyze? Figure 4.2 shows a model for environmental analysis which suggests that the firm, the

---

[7]H. I. Ansoff, "Strategic Response in a Turbulent Environment," *Handbook of Business Strategy,* ed. W. D. Guth (Boston: Warren, Gorham & Lamont, 1985), p. 4–4.

[8]P. H. Grinyer, and David Norburn, "Strategic Planning in 21 U.K. Companies," *Long-Range Planning,* August 1974, p. 80.

FIGURE 4.2   A Model for Environmental Analysis

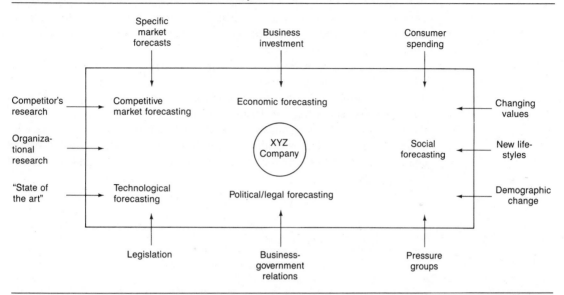

Source: Adapted from Ian Wilson, "Socio-Political Forecasting: A New Dimension to Strategic Planning." *Michigan Business Review,* July 1974, p. 19.

XYZ Company, should direct its environmental analysis toward five major directions: economic, technological, competitive, social, and political/legal forecasting.[9] Michael Kami, on the other hand, gears his environmental analysis toward five major areas as well, but with a somewhat different focus on economic, government, business, social, and international environments.

Other authors distinguish between the *general* environment (economic, technological, social, political, regulatory, and others) and the *industry* or operating environment (the market, industry structure, and suppliers, customers, and others with whom the firm deals directly).

Fahey and Narayanan[10] offer a clear and cogent framework of the relevant environments surrounding an organization—the general environment, the competitive or industry environment, and the task environment. At the broadest level lies the general environment—or macroenvironment—which influences all industries functioning within it. Again, the macroenvironment includes the economic, technological, social, and political/legal segments.

---

[9]Ian H. Wilson, "Socio-Political Forecasting: A New Dimension to Strategic Planning," *Michigan Business Review,* July 1974, pp. 19–20.

[10]Fahey and Narayanan, *Microenvironmental Analysis,* p. 25.

However, not all aspects of the general environment may be relevant to the firm; analyzing all aspects of the macroenvironment would be impossible and unnecessary. The firm should focus on those aspects of the general environment judged *relevant* to the firm's strategic situation, as shown in Figure 4.3.

Within the general environment lies the competitive or industry environment, which includes those businesses of a firm competing in a particular industry. The firm's most specific environment is the task environment, which refers to the customers, suppliers, competitors, agencies, and so on, directly related to the firm. The task environment is specific to the firm and is not necessarily shared by all competitors within an industry. This chapter examines factors comprising the general environment, while the industry environment is treated in Chapter 5.

FIGURE 4.3   Levels of Environment

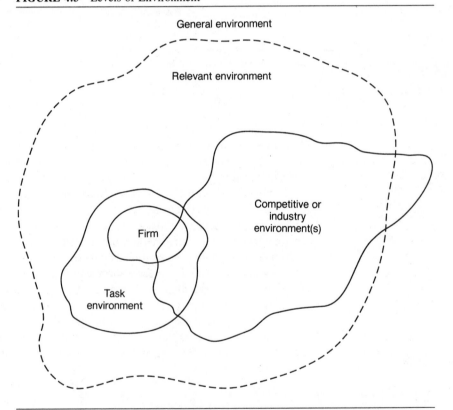

Environmental Analysis Practices

In a recent survey of corporate practices in environmental assessment (EA), almost half of the responding firms had recognized EA as a formal step in the planning process. A relatively small number, 20 percent, actually had a formal EA unit or department within the formal planning section. Factors that contributed to the firms' use of environmental analysis were size, length of time a formal planning process had been installed, the use of longer planning horizons, changing environmental factors that were considered important from one cycle to the next, commitment to an explicit strategic planning activity, and the ability to use analytic forecasting techniques.[11]

Another recent survey found that 73 percent of the firms responding had organized environmental analysis activities. This study concluded that the perceived usefulness of environmental analysis increased as the primary users were at higher organizational levels (those more concerned with the organization's interactions with the environment). Top-level strategic decision makers perceived environmental analysis as useful because of such factors as: ''Increased general awareness by management of environmental changes, better strategic planning and decision making, greater effectiveness in government matters, sound diversification and resource allocation decisions, and better energy planning.''[12]

Also interesting are studies that identify the specific environmental factors organizations choose to analyze. A fairly recent study found a relationship between the type of firm, its strategy, and the critical environmental system identified by that firm. Capital-intensive firms such as public utilities viewed the financial environment as the preeminent environmental influence. Other firms identified the economic or the regulatory system as the most significant factor based on their lines of business and the nature of their industries. Thus, the strategic considerations of the firm will contribute to the structuring of the environmental analysis.[13]

Recent studies have shown an important link between environmental analysis and *critical success factor (CSF)* analysis. These success factors are key areas in which the business must be satisfactory to survive and in which it must excel to competitively flourish; they might include low costs, high quality, innovation, diversification, and flexibility. Identifying critical success factors for a business is a key basis for structuring environmental analysis. The environment is scanned

[11]H. E. Klein and R. E. Linneman, ''Environmental Assessment: An International Study of Corporate Practice,'' *Journal of Business Strategy* 5, no. 1 (1984), pp. 66–75.

[12]J. Diffenbach, ''Corporate Environmental Analysis in Large U.S. Corporations,'' *Long-Range Planning* 16, no. 3 (1983), pp. 107–16.

[13]L. Fahey and W. R. King, ''Environmental Scanning for Corporate Planning,'' *Business Horizons,* August 1977, pp. 61–71.

for opportunities or threats in terms of CSFs, and competitors are analyzed with regard to these factors.[14]

In summary, macroenvironmental analysis is useful because it is a key aspect of strategic management. It should provide an understanding of the current and potential *changes* occurring in the environment. It provides important *intelligence* for strategic decision makers, and therefore should precede attempts at strategy formulation and implementation. Last, the analysis has implications for both the content and the process of strategic management. Concerning content, it should foster *strategic thinking* by managers, increasing their understanding of the context within which the firm operates and sparking ideas for strategic actions. In the process area, the analysis and strategic actions can affect the organization's structure and ways of doing business.

THE ECONOMY

The economy is very important to the success of a firm or an industry. Assume, for example, that an objective of management is to maximize the wealth of its stockholders. Research by Martin Zweig, a well-known stock market analyst, has shown that roughly two thirds of the movement in a stock's price is explained by the movement of the stock market in general, and another fourth is explained by the action of the firm's industry. Therefore, the bulk of management's objective is affected by factors external to the firm and beyond its control. Further, the market is significantly influenced by economic variables, such as interest rates, corporate profits, and gross national product (GNP).

But how does the economy affect the firm's sales and profits? The level of the economy directly influences these factors in several important ways. The stage of the economic cycle has a direct bearing on GNP, disposable income, the level of investment, and sales. It is easier to increase sales in an economic upturn than during a recession. Therefore, strategies that may be successful in prosperous times may well fail in a recession. On the other hand, it takes time to implement a strategy. Waiting until an economic expansion is under way to build a new plant may mean that the firm will have added capacity late in the expansion, perhaps just in time for the next downturn.

In addition, inflation, interest rates, and currency valuations have much to do not only with the total economy and customer behavior, but also with the decisions a firm makes. A strategy promising a rate of return of 15 percent may be very attractive with inflation at 3 percent and interest rates at 7 percent, but totally unacceptable with inflation at 12 percent and interest rates at 16 percent. Inflation forces strategists to adopt a shorter-term perspective, focusing on asset

---

[14]J. R. Leidecker and A. V. Bruno. "Identifying and Using Critical Success Factors," *Long-Range Planning* 17, no. 1 (1984), pp. 23–32.

growth rather than on inflation-dominated profits. As an example, many firms had difficulty adapting to the inflationary period of the 1970s, with high interest rates, little real investment, and inflation-eroded profits. The resulting low equity prices forced firms to forgo the stock and bond markets as sources of capital, or accept them as very expensive sources. The alternative, short-term borrowing, was even more expensive. In the early 1980s, inflation decelerated abruptly, again catching many firms unprepared for a ''disinflationary'' economy. Firms could no longer repay debts with money that would be cheaper in the future, so many began to focus on sharply reducing expenses and the ratio of debt to capital. In periods of disinflation, when the value of assets is declining, companies with real assets, such as natural resources, fare less well than those with consumer products and other items with high ''value added.'' The opposite was true during the inflationary 1970s.

Such factors not only affect the performance of a given business unit, but also directly influence corporate-level strategies, such as which industries to compete in. In a stagnant economy, companies compete more fiercely to maintain sales, inevitably putting pressure on profits. Fiscal policies, such as tax rates and depreciation allowances, also exert significant pressures on profits and dividends.

Economists refer to factors relating to the general state of an economy as *macroeconomic* factors. Such influences on a business would include inflation, fiscal and monetary policies (including taxes, government spending, and interest rates), unemployment, consumption, investment, tariffs, and the like. *Microeconomic* factors, on the other hand, typically deal with firm behavior in various types of markets, including production, pricing, and distribution decisions. *Industrial organization* economists, however, typically concern themselves with industry structure, competition, and competitive behavior of firms.

Becoming increasingly important—critically so since the mid-80s—are international economic influences. Included here are factors such as the relative productivity of the economies of our trading partners and competitors, the effects of currency exchange rates on imports and exports, and trade and tariff policies of the countries. Microeconomic, macroeconomic, and international economic factors are part of the general environment and are discussed in the following paragraphs. Competitive factors are part of the industry environment and are discussed in Chapter 5.

Microeconomic Factors

At the microeconomic or firm level, the economic models available to guide decision makers in most industries are insufficient. While relatively well-developed models exist to guide firms in perfectly competitive and monopolistic markets, models of monopolistically competitive and oligopolistic markets are less well defined. As Table 4.1 shows, perfectly competitive markets account for only 4 percent of total U.S. GNP and 6 percent of private-sector GNP. (Perfectly competitive markets are those in which no single supplier is able to exert any effect on prices or quantities, and products are perfect substitutes for one another. Agricultural products are an example.)

Monopolistic markets—where there is only one supplier (even though substitutes may exist, such as gas for electricity)—also account for a small percentage of output.

Monopolistic competition exists in markets where there are a number of producers, but the products are differentiated in some way and are close substitutes for one another. Many consumer products have these characteristics, including soaps, cigarettes, beer, and soft drinks. Such products account for 28 percent of total GNP and 44 percent of private-sector output.

Oligopolies are characterized by few suppliers, with possibly one dominating the market. Examples would be autos, computers, and perhaps oil companies. Such markets total 24 percent of total GNP and 38 percent of the private sector. Although monopolistic competitions and oligopolies represent 52 percent of total GNP and 82 percent of private-sector production, models of their behavior are inferior to models of perfectly competitive and monopolistic markets, and offer little to corporate decision makers.

As an added point, at first glance it might appear that microeconomic factors would apply only to traditional, private-sector, for-profit firms. On closer analysis, however, it becomes evident that most organizations in our economy and society are subject to similar influences. For example, many government programs—such as medicare, social security, and postal services—have close substitutes or even competitors in other sectors of the economy. The postal service competes with Federal Express, United Parcel Service, Western Union, and even fax machines and the telephone companies. To a degree, even the military departments—army, navy, air force, and marines—compete with one

---

TABLE 4.1   Market GNP Contribution

Market Type	Example	Percent of GNP	Percent Private-sector GNP
Perfect competition	Agricultural products	4%	6%
Monopolistic competition	Soap, beer, cigarettes	28	44
Oligopoly	Autos, computers	24	38
Monopoly	Utilities	7	11
Other	Government, education	37	—

Source: Adapted from ''Domestic Business Report,'' *Commerce America* 1, no. 10 (May 10, 1976). p. 12.

another. Thus, many government and other services are not truly monopolies, but find themselves in oligopolistic or even monopolistically competitive markets—a realization that may have important strategic implications in offering, targeting, and pricing their services.

Often our perception of events in markets or sectors of the economy is flawed. For example, it has become popular to discuss the U.S. farm economy in terms of a 1973–80 boom period followed by a post-1980 collapse, suggesting that agriculture's decline since 1980 represents a new situation, sharply differing from earlier years. A closer analysis, however, shows that farm labor productivity has increased over sevenfold since 1950, greatly lessening the need for farm labor. Also, real net farm income and prices for farm products have declined to 50–60 percent of their 1950 levels, interrupted only by the increase of the early 70s. Therefore, farming fundamentals—primarily relative prices and real income—have been declining for many years. In such an environment, only the most productive and efficient units are likely to survive.[15]

In fact, a recent report found that 25 nations now have a surplus of food, and by the year 2030 the United States will need 40 percent fewer acres to produce food than in 1987! Again, only the most productive land and farms are likely to survive, with major implications not only for individual farms, but for entire states and regions with marginal land, weather, and growing seasons.[16]

Macroeconomic Factors

The type of economy in which a firm competes—laissez-faire, managed capitalistic, or socialistic—has a great influence on strategic decisions. The first decision in this context is whether or not to compete in certain countries or industries. Within the U.S. economy, for example, various degrees of regulation exist. Transportation, utilities, drugs, hospitals, and other industries have been highly regulated, while other industries have not. Deregulation of the airline, financial services, trucking, and natural gas industries has dramatically changed the environment for many companies, creating a new set of opportunities and threats in their industries.

In other capitalistic economies, the environment may be very different from that in the United States. Sweden, for example, taxes the typical blue-collar worker at a marginal rate of 55 percent and an executive at 85 percent. In fact, the rate can go as high as 99 percent. Individuals actually can *lose* money as a result of a salary increase, because of the loss of government allowances for such things as housing, coupled with the high tax rates. One Swedish company

---

[15]M. T. Belongia, ''The Farm Sector in the 1980s: Sudden Collapse or Steady Downturn?'' *The Review,* Federal Reserve Bank of St. Louis, November 1986, pp. 17–25.

[16]Fred Thomas, ''Federal Report Sees Fewer Acres Farmed in Future,'' *Omaha World-Herald,* August 7, 1987, p. 17.

calculated that it would cost the company the equivalent of $255,000 to provide each of its top five executives with a $1,000 after-tax raise.[17]

Japan also has a managed capitalistic economy, but one that is distinctly different from Sweden's. After World War II, Japan adopted economic policies that fostered economic growth. These involved a mix of macro-level monetary and fiscal policies coupled with micro-level industrial policies. Macroeconomic planning includes projecting economic growth and setting goals for the economy. These plans are an important means of achieving national consensus on long-range economic goals and the direction of the economy. Following World War II, the Economic Planning Agency was created to prepare national economic plans that were approved by the Japanese legislature. These plans initially focused on economic recovery.

Japan's economic development since the occupation can be categorized into four stages. The first stage, 1951 to 1954, centered on reconstruction and rebuilding basic industries. In stage two, 1955 to 1964, the focus was on catching up with other industrialized countries through development of heavy and chemical industries, creation of an "open economy," improving the balance of payments, and closing gaps in the development of areas within the country. In stage three, 1965 to 1974, the emphasis was on social development and welfare, including urban development, housing, pollution control, computer technology, and power generation. The current fourth stage continues stage three's targets, with a focus on adjusting to stable growth, conserving resources, improving the quality of life, and further developing technology.[18] Thus, the Japanese seem to have had a logical set of economic goals in place, which guided their economic policies and became the basis for the development of more detailed stategies and plans.

An additional example of macroeconomic influence involves the complicated domestic effects of fiscal and monetary policies on selected industries, such as agricultural production and equipment. Because of the large federal deficits in the early to mid-1980s, the Federal Reserve Board held interest rates relatively high to reduce inflationary pressures. According to some, this attracted foreign investment, which greatly strengthened the dollar, making exports expensive and imports cheap. This encouraged imports and discouraged exports, such as farm products. In turn, farm prices, receipts, and land values declined, causing farm bankruptcies, low sales of farm equipment, and bank failures due to nonperforming loans. Others have held, however, that these events resulted more from increased farm production in South America, China, India, and the Soviet Union, greatly reducing demand for U.S. farm products.

Finally, economic cycles are important to a firm's strategies. The timing of plant expansions, new product introductions, and financial investments should

---

[17]L. A. Digman, Personal Interview with Leif Philippson, MoDo KP AB Personnel Director, March 3, 1981.

[18]U.S. General Accounting Office, *Industrial Policy: Japan's Flexible Approach,* GAO/ID-82-32, June 23, 1982.

consider whether the economy is in the early or late stages of an economic expansion, as well as the likely occurrence and severity of the next recession. Again, government fiscal and monetary policies, as well as the ability of the federal government to take corrective action in the event of a downturn, can be important considerations. For example, Alfred Malabre, economics editor of *The Wall Street Journal,* observed in 1987 that the federal government had been taking actions to prolong the economic expansion of the 80s that left it few options to deal effectively with any ensuing downturn. He stated that ''If we get into a recession, we have no tools at our disposal to correct it,'' and to do so would require deficits of $400–$500 billion per year, or increasing the money supply at 30–40 percent rates. As a result, he forecasted a 30 percent chance of hyperinflation (similar to Germany after World War II), a 30 percent chance of hyperdeflation (akin to the Great Depression), with the most probable outcome being massive government intervention, perhaps even nationalization of financial institutions.[19] Obviously, operating in such ''uncharted waters'' could have major strategic implications for companies.

International Factors

It is apparent that international factors are closely woven into the fabric of the economic environment, and are becoming even more so. In recent years, much of our national debt has been financed by foreign investors, as have our stock market operations. Low wage rates and increasing foreign productivity make it desirable for manufacturing facilities to be located in foreign countries, accelerating our trend to a service economy. In addition, such factors increase the trade deficit, as more and more such products are imported into the United States. To attract these funds back into the United States in the form of investments, interest rates must be kept relatively high, further discouraging domestic investment.

A declining dollar, however, tends to offset wage rate differentials, as does increasing reliance on high technology and automated manufacturing. In fact, in 1986, the United States was the only major nation to cut its labor costs, resulting from increases in manufacturing productivity and a decline in the value of the dollar. In October 1987, factory workers in West Germany, Norway, and Switzerland received *higher* average hourly pay than in the United States, with Sweden and the Netherlands close behind. Japan's $11.20 was 85 percent of U.S. wages, with Brazil, Mexico, Hong Kong, South Korea, Singapore, Taiwan, and Portugal all less than 20 percent of the U.S. figure.[20] When compared with economic output, the U.S. position appears favorable. Workers in

[19]Robert Wrubel, ''Cliffhanger,'' *Financial World,* November 17, 1987, pp. 126–29.

[20]Gene Koretz, ''Economic Trends,'' *Business Week,* November 23, 1987, p. 26.

the United States produced an average of $38,900 of output in 1987, 23 percent more than the higher-paid German workers, and 41 percent more than Japanese workers.[21]

In addition, the changing costs of manufacturing in the United States versus foreign countries have reversed much of what we have only recently learned. In the early 80s, Japanese auto manufacturers, for example, were able to build a car in Japan for $2,400 less than U.S. companies could build one here. By 1987, however, as the dollar depreciated from 240 to 140 yen per dollar, this cost relationship was reversed; that is, it became cheaper to build cars in the United States. For this reason, Japanese manufacturers began importing U.S. components and parts. Japanese trade publications cited numerous cases of this in mid-1987, including companies such as Yamaha, Mitsubishi Electric, NEC, Honda, Toyota, Mitsubishi Motors, and Hitachi Construction Machinery Co.[22] The point is that changing currency values can dramatically change the relative costs of manufacturing in one country versus another, complicating international marketing and production decisions.

Conventional opinion also fears Japanese purchases of U.S. businesses, real estate, and farms. In fact, polls show that Americans regard economic rivals, particularly Japan, as a greater threat to their security than military adversaries. A closer look, however, shows that the Japanese are not the largest investors in the United States; the British are. British investments in the United States totaled $75 billion in early 1988; up 34 percent from a year earlier. The Netherlands with $47 billion ranked second, while Japan was third with $33 billion. While this is up 25 percent from a year earlier, it is still less than 1 percent of our economy.[23]

The major international variable on the economic horizon is Europe, which is planning to become one united market in 1992. Should U.S. firms view this significant happening as an opportunity or a threat? It is likely to be an opportunity for firms already there, as trade barriers within Europe come down, and as a large, unified market of 320 million consumers emerges. For outsiders, however, it is likely to be a threat as a major new competitor emerges, perhaps with barriers to entry and import restrictions.[24] The positions of U.S. companies in 1992 and beyond will be the result of strategic analyses and decisions made now.

In conclusion, like international factors, the macroeconomy and related policies have much to do with how a firm can and should compete. They influence both the freedom to pursue certain strategies and the effect of government monetary and fiscal policies on the firm and its customers. As we discussed earlier, microeconomic factors, such as the economic structure of the market, also play an important role in strategic management.

---

[21]"Losing the Lead," *The Wall Street Journal,* October 24, 1988, p. A1.

[22]"Japan's Manufactured Imports Rise Sharply in First Half of '87," *JETRO Monitor,* October 1, 1987, p. 4.

[23]Monroe W. Karmin, "Economic Outlook," *U.S. News & World Report,* November 7, 1988, p. 65.

[24]"Reshaping Europe: 1992 and Beyond," *Business Week,* December 12, 1988, p. 48.

TECHNOLOGY

The role of technology in corporate and business-unit strategy is extremely important, yet is poorly understood by many writers on strategic management. "High technology" has become a buzz phrase in our society, and is looked on by many to solve a country's growth, development, productivity, and balance-of-payments problems. Yet technology receives short shrift in many discussions of strategic management. Nonetheless, it is the high-tech companies—Texas Instruments, IBM, Hewlett-Packard, Genentech, Merck, Teledyne, Apple Computer, and many others—that have become the focus of attention by strategic analysts, even though the role of technology is underdeveloped and ignored relative to other important strategic areas such as marketing and finance.[25] Technology *creates* many of the products and advances that must be strategically financed and marketed. It helps a firm produce its products more efficiently than does its competition. Technology creates not only new products, but also entire industries. For these reasons, strategic planning is of little value if technology isn't taken into account.

However, many misconceptions abound concerning technology. For example, most people would probably consider computers to be a high-technology industry and automobile manufacturing to be a lower-technology, "smokestack" industry. Lester Thurow of MIT, however, observes that while computers may be high-technology *products,* their *manufacture* is not; it requires lower-level skills and is more labor intensive than many people realize. Autos, on the other hand, now employ sophisticated processes and robotics in their manufacture, and the industry has many high-technology characteristics. In addition, autos themselves have become much more technologically complex in recent years with the addition of sophisticated electronic engine controls and sensors, nonskid braking systems, and electronic instruments and displays.

Management's Role

The strategic implications of technology are not limited to high-tech industries, however. New methods have greatly reduced the size required for steel mills to produce efficiently, automated teller machines and electronic funds transfer are transforming much of banking, radial treads have revolutionized the tire industry, and so on. Management must therefore be able to *understand* the technology of the products and processes it manages. Otherwise, it cannot make strategic and operational decisions about those products and processes. The critical decisions are: (1) which technology to pursue and when to pursue it; (2) how to manage the

---

[25]H. Dudley Dewhirst, "Strategic Management of Research and Development," presented at national meeting of American Institute for Decision Sciences, 1982.

transition from one technology to another; and (3) how to prepare the corporation for technological change. Managers must be able to assess the limits of their firm's technologies, as well as those of alternative approaches, before they can answer questions about which areas to pursue. In this light, technology is too important to be left only to engineers. Development of technologies and innovations is the responsibility of scientists and engineers, just as fighting a war is the responsibility of the generals. But generals should not decide whether or not we will fight, just as engineers should not decide which technologies should be incorporated into products or processes; these are strategic decisions that management must understand and make.

Managers must understand that technological breakthroughs result in more rapid obsolescence of existing products, which can be either an opportunity or a threat. It may be wise for a firm to postpone introducing an innovation because of its effect on existing products. Also, all innovations—technological or otherwise—should be put into their proper perspective; they create a degree of uniqueness. How and when this uniqueness, or distinction, is exploited is the basis for a strategic decision.

The selection of technology is a major element in business strategy. While it is not as strategically important for some firms as for others, for many firms, it is *the* central element of strategy.[26] In a study of rapidly growing firms, *INC.* magazine found that an increase in R&D spending of 1.5 percent (measured in percent of sales) translated into a 10 percent sales gain 18 months later.[27] In a study of the larger firms in the pharmaceutical and chemical industries, Bruce Old found that R&D expenditures over Years 1–10, plus capital expenditures in Years 5–15, correlated 0.85 with increases in profits in Years 1–20.[28] Thus, R&D pays off for large companies as well as for smaller firms.

Managers of firms may choose to achieve growth through technology in one of three ways:

1. Internally, by a strategically managed R&D program.
2. By a mix of internal and external means. Internally, by scanning the technological environment plus establishing a limited R&D program; externally, by providing venture capital for new technology, or licensing or acquiring firms with promising technology.
3. By acquiring or licensing technology only after its acceptance and feasibility have been demonstrated.[29]

Again, the choice is often broader in scope than it might initially appear; the ramifications extend beyond the R&D functional-level strategy.

---

[26]R. A. Burgelman and M. A. Maidique, *Strategic Management of Technology and Innovation* (Homewood, Ill.: Richard D. Irwin, 1988), p. 12.

[27]"The More They Spend on R&D, the Faster They Grow," *INC.*, August 1981, p. 44.

[28]"Bruce S. Old, "From the Boardroom: Corporate Directors Should Rethink Technology," *Harvard Business Review*, January–February 1982, p. 6.

[29]Dewhirst, "Strategic Management."

Service Technology

In addition to products, technology affects the delivery of services as well. In fact, technologies have restructured the service industries extensively in recent years. For example, new technologies have created economies of scale in services by making larger organizations possible and efficient, as in rental cars, brokerage clearinghouses, and medical care. Second, technology permits increased economies of scope, or the offering of new or additional services to customers with little added cost. Examples include Federal Express's Zap Mail, resulting from its advanced electronic communications network (even though the venture was not competitive with proliferating facsimile machines), and the insurance companies' new products, also arising from their electronic networks.

In addition, technology in services permits new levels of complexity to be managed (as in computerized legal research), the breaking down of traditional boundaries between industries (such as banks, insurance companies, and brokerage houses), and an increase in international competitiveness. Services are a critical factor in manufacturing competitiveness, including items such as transportation, communication, financing, insurance, health care, and other costs. Overall, Japanese productivity has consistently lagged behind the United States because of our more productive service sector, even though they excel in certain mass-manufacturing fields.[30]

Process Technology and Productivity

Products and services are directly affected by technology, as are manufacturing and service processes and their relative productivity. Productivity is defined as output (products produced or services delivered) per unit of resource input (labor and capital). Much has been written about the productivity growth in countries such as Japan versus the United States. In reality, the value of output per labor hour in the United States as a percentage of Japan in 1980 was as follows:[31]

Sector	Percent
Private domestic business	167%
Agriculture	771
Electricity, gas, water	129
Transportation and communication	232
Trade	175
Finance and insurance	68
Business services	211
Manufacturing	127

---

[30]J. B. Quinn and C. E. Gagnon, "Will Services Follow Manufacturing into Decline?" *Harvard Business Review* 64, no. 6 (November–December 1986), pp. 95–103.

[31]Ibid.

Thus, while Japanese productivity has been increasing more rapidly than the United States in recent years, the absolute level of U.S. productivity is above that of Japan, even in manufacturing. Granted, manufacturing employment in the United States has declined slightly in recent years; however, the share of manufacturing output has not changed. This increased productivity has caused the manufacturing sector to *appear* to decline, because its share of employment and total spending have declined; but its output has not declined.[32]

On the other hand, there are those who say that the U.S. advantage in productivity may continue to erode, partly because of social factors. For example, we have a large number of young people entering the legal and finance fields—versus science, engineering, and manufacturing—as compared to other countries. As some have observed, this results in a society adept at *administering* wealth, rather than *creating* it.[33] Other social factors—demographic changes— may have impacted productivity, as well. The U.S. economy has had a tremendous increase in labor supply during the past 15 years, due to the baby boom and the increasing numbers of women entering the work force. As Figure 4.4 shows, an increase in labor supply lowers its cost relative to capital, resulting in lower capital expenditures. Productivity, which is often defined as output per labor-hour, appears not to grow as a result.

But the possibility of massive increases in productivity is on the horizon. Carver Mead, a professor of computer science at Cal Tech and a long-time expert

---

FIGURE 4.4   Labor, Capital, and Productivity

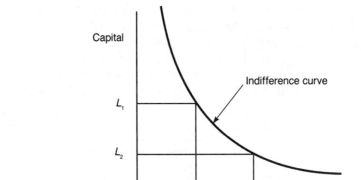

---

[32]J. A. Tatom, "Why Has Manufacturing Employment Declined?," *The Review,* Federal Reserve Bank of St. Louis, December 1986, pp. 15–23.

[33]Allan Murray, "The Outlook: The U.S. Economic Role May Face Long Decline," *The Wall Street Journal,* August 17, 1987, p. 1.

in the field, points out that the entire Industrial Revolution enhanced productivity 100-fold. The microelectronic revolution has already enhanced productivity in information-based technology by a factor of more than a million, with the promise of yet another 10,000-fold increase in the cost-effectiveness of technology in the next decade. The important point, however, is not the increasing productivity of computing; it is that these advances are spilling over into other industries, increasing their productivity as well. For example, people in other industries—computers, telephones, office equipment, autos, toys, transportation, and many more—will be able to *design* their own custom chips, which will be *manufactured* by the semiconductor industry. Major productivity enhancements will come about because of this custom-designed chip software, the greatest source of its added value.[34]

Corporate-Level Responsibilities

To this point, we have been discussing technology strategies independent of the levels of strategic decisions faced by the organization. Technology represents one of several functional-level strategies for the organization. At the business level, the various functional strategies must be integrated and coordinated; that is, the technology, marketing, financial, and other strategies must relate and reinforce one another. So, most of what we have been discussing would apply to the technology of a given business unit or product line—in short, business-unit technical planning.

However, corporate-level strategies must integrate business-unit strategies; corporate-level technical planning is more than the sum of the technical plans of the business units. Technical planning at the corporate level must realize and strive for synergies from related technologies across business units; a corporate technology portfolio should exist and must involve planning. Key technologies that must be supported and pushed forward by the corporate level rather than by business units must be identified at the corporate level. In addition, technological considerations may require that the firm evaluate its business units, possibly adding or divesting certain units. For example, NBI of Boulder, Colorado, was a strong competitor in the word processing industry. Industry experts, however, felt that companies not competing in integrated office systems (including word processing, computers, message systems, and the like) would be at a definite disadvantage in this industry. Since NBI lacked the technology to compete across the board in office automation (versus dedicated word processing), they attempted to acquire a company with the required technology.[35]

---

[34]George Gilder, ''You Ain't Seen Nothing Yet,'' *Forbes,* April 4, 1988, p. 89.

[35]William Celis III and Hank Gilman, ''NBI Sets Offer for Computer Consoles, Inc.,'' *The Wall Street Journal,* January 14, 1985, p. 5.

Common Mistakes

While technological decisions ultimately must be made by general managers, nontechnical people often misunderstand technology and innovation, and make errors in judgment as a result. Some of the major mistakes managers make include:

1. Seeking the optimal or best-possible technology, as opposed to that which is "good enough." Remember that need, desirability, and economic factors, not the maximum level of sophistication, should determine the level of technological sophistication of a product. If a company's product is very much more advanced than that of a competitor, money may be wasted in its design, manufacture, and service, because it may be too advanced for many customers. Remember that the market and economics determine a product's success, state-of-the-art technology does not.
2. Assuming that most innovations will be successful. Many are not, because they are not enough of an improvement to warrant the development cost, or because they have design or quality problems. In addition, they may improve in both of the above areas but still fail in the marketplace.
3. Putting greater emphasis on radical new technology than on extensions of what is currently available. Evolutionary advances are less risky than breakthroughs in many ways, as well as being more cost effective. While new technologies, such as solar power and electric cars, may be exciting, they are often not commercially feasible.
4. Believing that the organization will produce innovations without effective controls, such as procedures, work standards, schedules, and objectives. Scientific and engineering people are more productive when their efforts are targeted toward definite objectives.[36]

Technology is important because it is an organizational resource as well as an environmental influence. Technology takes on varying degrees of centrality in the strategies of different companies, as well as within companies. And it can be a key corporate strategic weapon that drives the other strategic actions of the firm.

SOCIAL FACTORS

Social factors in the environment involve issues and information that are essentially people oriented. They are the broadest and least specific factors the firm must consider. Social factors, while including social issues affecting the firm, are not synonymous with social responsibility. Social responsibility has been described as

---

[36]Lowell Steele, "Managers' Misconceptions about Technology," *Harvard Business Review,* November–December 1983, p. 133.

the "obligation of businessmen to pursue those policies, to make those decisions, or to follow those lines of action which are desirable in terms of the objectives and values of society."[37] While social factors and issues arise from the environment and may affect a firm's social responsibility, the resulting social responsibility actions more properly become part of the firm's societal role, or enterprise, strategy. As part of our discussion of social factors, we will examine demographic factors; income, employment, and influence factors; and values, attitudes, and preferences.

Demographic Influences

Demographic factors can have significant impacts including, for example, the baby boom of the late 1940s and 1950s and the subsequent decline in birthrates which have resulted in a progressively aging work force. As the population bulge moves through the years—like a pig through a python—there are many effects. People fortunate enough to be born during low-birthrate years go to uncrowded schools and colleges, and experience high demand for their services in terms of job opportunities and relatively rapid promotions. For the baby-boom generation, the opposite is true.

Other demographic factors have important impacts as well. When the baby-boom generation entered the work force in the 1970s, many more women also chose to work and pursue new career opportunities. These two factors, as discussed earlier, have caused the work force to grow more rapidly than normal, resulting in relatively high unemployment and cheaper labor. When labor is cheap relative to capital equipment costs, productivity tends to grow less rapidly, with attendant side effects. Also, increased mobility of the work force tends to accentuate growth in certain geographical areas and declines in others.

In addition, because of healthier lifestyles, improved health care, and a declining birthrate, our society's average age is steadily increasing. In fact, by the year 2000, it is anticipated that there will be 100,000 Americans aged 100 years or older. Many will be in good health and able to work well past traditional retirement ages. This phenomenon is occurring worldwide, and has a number of important implications for retirement plans and health-care services.

Two opposing trends are also occurring. The baby-boomers are having babies of their own, creating an "echo" of the original baby boom. This boomlet will have a considerable effect on youth-related products and services. On the other hand, our society is seeing more and more singles; therefore, fewer children will result, and more money will likely be spent on adult luxuries, amusements, and conveniences.

---

[37]Howard R. Bowen, *Social Responsibilities of the Businessman* (New York: Harper & Row, 1953), p. 6.

Income, Employment, and Influence

Some experts have concluded that standards of living have been dropping for up to 10 years, requiring either two wage earners per household, or a reduced living standard. Further, Americans traditionally have expected to move up the social and economic ladder with each generation. Not only is that no longer the case, but the middle class is being squeezed. Between 1973 and 1985, there has been a 9 percent drop in households with incomes between $20,000 and $50,000, with gains at the high and low ends. One reason is a cut in the middle-management ranks of many companies, making it increasingly difficult for lower- and middle-level employees.[38]

An often overlooked social factor is that countries with less population growth than others can expect to have declining global influence. It is difficult to compete militarily (in terms of troops and defense expenditures), as well as economically for small countries or those with below-average population growth.[39]

Values, Attitudes, and Preferences

Another important social factor is people's attitudes, both as employees and as consumers. What people want, demand, and are able to get from their jobs depends on a host of factors, including supply of and demand for their skill. Few would have thought a few years ago that unions would agree to wage reductions in the recessionary early 1980s.

Sometimes, people's values and attitudes change faster than companies can change products and services to accommodate them. For example, during most of the 1970s, people were chastising U.S. auto manufacturers for not producing enough smaller cars. But customers continued to purchase large cars over compacts. And Japanese automakers moved into the market for small, inexpensive automobiles. As Kotler and Fahey point out, sales of ''Japanese cars were going nowhere in the United States until the price of oil shot up. Had fuel costs not escalated, most Americans would still be preferring and driving large cars.''[40] This is borne out by Charles Hofer's observation that in 1978 Chrysler could not produce a sufficient number of full-sized cars to satisfy the demand. Scarcely a year later, that same public was ''calling for Chrysler's head'' and

---

[38]Jonathan Peterson, ''Much-Heralded Service Economy Has Arrived,'' *Lincoln Journal,* September 24, 1987, p. 28.

[39]Alan L. Otten, ''Some Thinkers Expect Population to Drop and Trouble to Result,'' *The Wall Street Journal,* June 18, 1987, p. 1.

[40]Philip Kotler and Liam Fahey, ''The World's Champion Marketers: The Japanese,'' *The Journal of Business Strategy* 3, no. 1, Summer 1982, pp. 3–13.

criticizing the company's management for "not building the small cars the public wanted."[41] Ford had a similar experience. To meet the corporate average fuel economy (CAFE) levels mandated by the federal government, the company had to artificially discourage buyers of their large-engined cars by adding a surcharge.[42]

After the second (Iranian) oil embargo in 1980, a great number of Americans shifted to the type of car the Japanese had been producing for years (in fact, the *only* size car they had been producing for export—the subcompact). Since Detroit had not been producing such cars for as long a time as the Japanese, or in the same quantities, the Japanese were much farther ahead on the experience curve, giving them a cost and quality advantage. Kotler and Fahey also observed that the "Japanese companies were doubly lucky that U.S. auto manufacturers responded slowly rather than swiftly to the increased demand for small cars—and triply lucky that Detroit's first small cars were poorly designed."[43]

In addition, consumers' tastes for fad or gimmick products change rapidly and sometimes almost without notice. Products such as food processors were hot sellers for several years, but fell on hard times in 1982. One customer stated that the product is used for 30 seconds, and it takes 30 minutes to clean. Not only that, "it seems silly to pay $100 for a machine that converts everything you put into it into baby food." High prices, customer fatigue, and boredom play a part in rapidly changing preferences for such items, putting a premium on producing products that are "innovative and exciting."[44]

The United States traditionally has been called the "melting pot," because of its diverse immigrant heritage. During periods of high immigration and for perhaps several generations thereafter, people seem to have a desire to join, to be accepted, and to be like everyone else. This behavior creates mass markets. Increasingly, however, U.S. citizens seem to have been searching for their heritage, their identity, and uniqueness. The resulting mass of subcultures, or pluralism, is the opposite of a melting pot, and breaks the mass market down into smaller segments, with important implications for producers of goods and services.[45]

Another change sweeping the United States involves neotemperance: it is becoming "in" *not* to drink, or to drink very sparingly. Based on the perceptions that drunk driving had increased and that drinking-related auto deaths were increasing, people began demanding tougher laws. Coupled with the physical

---

[41]C. W. Hofer, "New Frontiers in Strategic Management," visiting scholar speech, University of Nebraska, November 12, 1980.

[42]Fred Secrest, "The Automobile Industry," visiting executive speech, University of Nebraska, February 1981.

[43]Kotler and Fahey, "The World's Champion Marketers," p. 4.

[44]Srully Blotnick, "Why Customers Aren't Buying," *Forbes,* August 16, 1982, p. 103.

[45]Michael Kami, *Strategic Planning for Changing Times* (Dayton, Ohio: Cassette Recording Co., 1984).

fitness craze and attempts to stamp out teenage drug abuse, people began to look more closely at their own drinking habits, resulting in a reduction of the use of alcohol. While drinking is much lower than it has been throughout most of U.S. history, the *perception* that it is higher and affecting people's safety and well-being parallels a more basic change in society, Americans "have overcome their post-Prohibition distaste for meddling with other people's personal behavior." In fact, "the evidence is overwhelming that Americans are finding it increasingly acceptable—and sometimes desirable—to try to alter other people's behavior." It seems that concern with community rights outweighs the ideal of absolute personal liberty.[46]

Another major social behavior change—with ramifications for industries as well as workplace policies—concerns smoking. By 1987, the adult smoking rate had dipped to a new low of 26.5 percent, and to many Americans, the habit is not only unhealthy but unfashionable (perhaps the stronger influence of the two). In an attempt to arrest the rate of decline in this industry, R. J. Reynolds announced plans to introduce Premier, a cigarette with "little smoke, no ash, no odor, and no tar."[47] The product may make smoking safer, but not more fashionable. In fact, the cigarette was pulled off the shelves after only five months of test marketing, making it one of the most expensive new product flops in decades.[48]

Lastly, the world seems to be trending toward a more homogeneous society, as communication and travel become more widespread. One analyst observed that there is less difference between teenagers in New York, Tokyo, and Geneva than there is between the teenagers and their parents.

In conclusion, between 1965 and 1980, corporations were hit with a succession of social changes (minority rights, consumerism, environmentalism, women's rights); by the politics of oil, Vietnam, Watergate, and sentiment against institutions and multinational corporations; by changes in consumer tastes and behavior ("natural" foods, health consciousness, conservation, emphasis on value); and by new work-life values (individual rights, assertiveness, participation). But coping with social change is not simply corporate social responsibility; it is related to work force productivity and availability, as well as to costs and profitability. It is also related to corporate credibility, acceptance, and support, resulting in a firm's freedom to act and implement its strategies. It is better to adopt a proactive stance concerning social change than to adopt a reactive one. As Figure 4.5 shows, as social issues intensify, corporate options

---

[46]"The Sobering of America: A Push to Put Drinking in Its Place," *Business Week*, February 25, 1985, p. 112.

[47]John Helyar, "RJR Unveils Cigarette that Produces Little Smoke; Marketing May Be Tricky," *The Wall Street Journal*, September 15, 1987, p. 2.

[48]Peter Waldman, "RJR Nabisco Abandons 'Smokeless' Cigarette," *The Wall Street Journal*, Mar. 1, 1989, p. B1.

FIGURE 4.5 The Corporate Impact of Evolving Societal Expectations

Stage	I Societal expectation	II Political issue	III Legislation/regulation	IV Litigation/penalties
Example	Women demand equal treatment in the labor market	• Equal pay for equal work • Equal pay for work of comparable worth	• Equal Pay Act, 1963 • Civil Rights Act, 1964	• EEOC actions • Civil suits

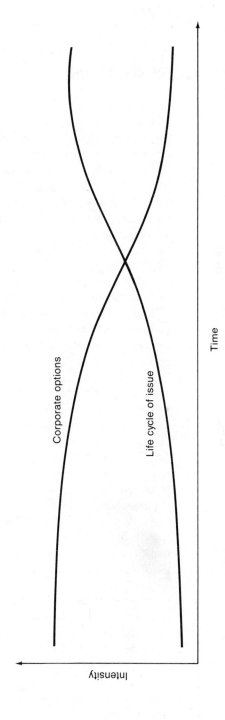

Corporate options

Life cycle of issue

Time

Intensity

Source: Ian Wilson, ''Evaluating the Environment: Social and Political Factors,'' in *Handbook of Business Strategy*, ed. W. D. Guth (Boston: Warren, Gorham & Lamont, 1985), p. 3–3.

decrease. Furthermore, social issues can quickly become political and even legal issues,[49] as will be discussed in the following section.

POLITICAL/LEGAL CONSIDERATIONS

Government is often the major factor in the political and legal environment of a firm or industry. Laws and regulations are usually formulated by government bodies, and can have dramatic effects on a company's strategic alternatives, as our previous discussions of deregulation pointed out. Further, firms must comply with antitrust laws, pollution laws, safety regulations, EEO programs, and a host of other constraints. However, other regulations and guidelines also constrain firms; industries and professions sometimes enforce standards of conduct and practice over and above those imposed by any government body. For this reason, and because regulations and constraints are the *result* of a political/legal process, the strategist needs a framework for analyzing political activity that may have an effect on the company.

Figure 4.6 describes a model of the political processes affecting company strategy. Obviously, political factors influence government and other regulatory policies, which can affect the company's distinctive competence, competitive positions, and even its values. A company can use several options to forge a corporate political strategy. The purpose of the strategy is influencing the political factors and, in turn, the regulatory policies that affect the company. Instead of thinking only of competitors, managers should view their company as one of a number of *players* in a political arena, and should assess the agendas of all the other players. These may include—in addition to competitors—unions, legislative bodies, government agencies and officials, trade and industry groups, consumer groups, other interest groups, and the media. All of the players, while pursuing their own agendas, create *issues* that may affect the company. These issues are not raised and dealt with in the marketplace, but in *forums*, such as the legislature, the media, or others. Managers must be aware that in such environments, strategy is not simply formulated but is in large measure *negotiated* with the other players.

In dealing with or confronting issues, two things must be addressed: (1) the issue's potential for political dramatization by one or more of the players; and (2) the pattern of cooperation and conflict that the issue encourages—in other words, who is likely to line up on which side of the issue. This requires assessment of who the players are with regard to the issue, as well as what motivates them. Who the players are, what their agendas are, what alliances and adversaries are likely to emerge, and how powerful they are must be considered. The manager must know the setting and rules of the forum in which the players will deal with the

---

[49]Ian Wilson, "Evaluating the Environment: Social and Political Factors," in *Handbook of Business Strategy,* ed. W. G. Guth (Boston: Warren, Gorham & Lamont, 1985), p. 3–3.

FIGURE 4.6   Political/Legal Strategy Process

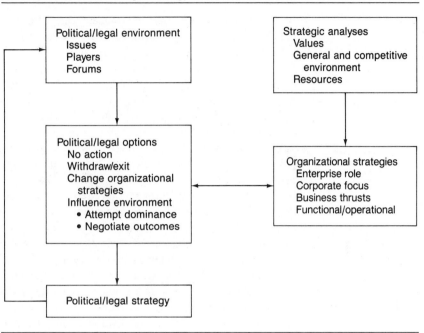

issue. "Facts" may count less than how well a player is able to utilize a particular forum.

How can managers respond to or influence political activity? Four basic options exist: do nothing and suffer the consequences; exit the business or market; modify the firm's strategy to offset or capitalize on the issue; or seek greater influence over the political environment. The latter can be done by attempting to dominate the other players (a high-risk approach) or by attempting to negotiate a relatively desirable outcome with them.

The result of this process is the firm's political strategy, which attempts to achieve a balance or fit between the company and its political environment. Some specific goals for this strategy should include:

1. Attempting to frame an issue in a favorable way.
2. Assembling a coalition of players with similar to overlapping agendas.
3. Seeking to choose the most favorable forum for the company and the coalition.[50]

---

[50]J. L. Badaracco, Jr., *Note on Corporate Strategy and Politics*, Case No. 9-382-151 (Boston: Harvard Business School, 1982).

CONCLUSIONS

In conclusion, the general environment can have a significant impact on an industry, a firm, and its task environment. As an example, the financial services industry has experienced revolutionary changes since the 60s. Several interacting forces—economic, international, regulatory, and technological—have drastically changed the type and degree of competition within the industry (as well as the definition of the industry itself). As a result, the industry no longer faces the "3-6-3 environment" (pay depositors 3 percent interest, lend money at 6 percent, and tee off at 3 P.M.).

What caused the change? In the macroeconomic arena, declining industry growth, double-digit inflation, and volatile interest rates have all introduced major instabilities in the industry, tending to shift the focus of financial investments from long term to short term. In the regulatory area, increased deregulation has caused the lines separating the various segments of the financial services industry (between banks, S&Ls, credit unions, securities firms, and the like) to be increasingly blurred. Technologically, computerized telecommunications and electronic technology have increased the scope, scale, and volume of transactions. In the process, it has integrated geographical markets, reduced labor intensiveness, and facilitated networking (such as fund transfer and automated teller machines—ATMs). Lastly, internationalization has been a factor as well. Increased competition from foreign lenders, the growth of multinational firms and international financial markets, electronic technology, and related factors have contributed to this trend. The end result of these environmental changes has been to make the financial services industry more competitive than ever before.[51]

Assessing the strategic situation is the first phase in determining the content of the proper strategies for a firm. This assessment often begins with an analysis of the general environment of the firm, in terms of economic, technological, social, and political/legal influences. They are important collectively as well as individually, and often override industry or organizational variables and strategies. We discussed a number of significant environmental events, and described several techniques for dealing with each of the environmental factors. In Chapter 9, information systems for dealing with environmental and other strategic information will be discussed, while the next chapter—Chapter 5— discusses the competitive and industry environment.

---

[51]David Rogers, "Environmental Change in the Financial Services Industry," in *Advances in Strategic Management,* ed. Robert Lamb and Paul Shrivastava, vol. 5 (Greenwich, Conn.: JAI Press Inc., 1988), pp. 90–94.

Chapter 5

The Competitive Environment: Industry, Market, and Competitor Analysis

LEARNING OBJECTIVES

After completing Chapter 5, you should be able to:

Describe the primary determinants of the intensity of competition facing a business unit.

Appreciate the differences between local, regional, national, international, multinational, and global businesses, markets, and industries.

Understand the role of strategic groups and market structure.

Realize the importance of stage of the product/market life cycle in strategy formulation.

Describe the concept and use of the experience curve.

The third major aspect in assessing the organization's strategic situation involves analyzing the industry, or competitive, environment. The effects of competition and market structure, including industry and strategic-group memberships, are part of this environment. As was mentioned in Chapter 4, the competitive or industry environment affects those businesses of a company which compete within a particular industry. Therefore, the individual businesses comprising a corporation may face very different competitive environments, depending on the characteristics of the industries in which they compete. In this light, *businesses—*

not companies or firms—face competitive environments. A diversified company may face a number of competitive environments.

In addition, firms and businesses face task environments, directly related to the firm or business and not necessarily to the industry as a whole. Our focus in this chapter is to address those aspects of the industry and task environments *relevant* to the competitive situation facing the business. As such, we may touch upon elements of a business's task and industry environments in analyzing the impact of the industry, markets, and competitors upon the focal business. Industries and markets can range from local to global, and can progress through definite life-cycle stages, as can products. A final industry-related factor discussed in this chapter is the experience curve and its strategic implications.

PROFILE   **USX Corp.**

For years, U.S. Steel (now USX Corp.) dominated an oligopolistic industry with little foreign competition. In fact, the company continued to operate as if this were still the case long after it had become just another competitor in a rapidly changing international market.

J. P. Morgan put the company together in the early 1900s by merging 10 companies to prevent Andrew Carnegie from expanding his steel empire. Put together for defensive purposes, the company maintained a short-term, centralized, autocratic climate for most of its history. In recent years, however, problems have begun to surface. U.S. Steel's domestic market share dropped to less than 16 percent in 1982, down from over 50 percent earlier. Some of this was as a result of foreign competition; the firm was in a global market, and domestic market share became a meaningless statistic. Management reacted to changes and foreign competition defensively, pleading for government protection against imports. They even mounted an advertising campaign against the Environmental Protection Agency.

Here was a mature company in a mature industry undergoing major restructuring to adjust to a more competitive, global industry. Suddenly the firm was threatened by innovative foreign upstarts with no respect for its leadership position. Actually, while U.S. Steel may have been the leader of an oligopolistic *domestic* industry, it was merely another competitor producing a commodity product in a monopolistically competitive *global* industry.[1]

PROFILE   **The Video Rental Industry**

Revenues of the videocassette rental industry skyrocketed to $5.6 billion in 1986 from $76 million in 81, and are expected to reach $10 billion in the early 90s—obviously a high-growth industry. Yet, with video rental outlets cropping

---

[1]"The Toughest Job in Business," *Business Week,* February 25, 1985, p. 50.

up in convenience stores, record shops, electronic outlets, book stores, supermarkets, and discount stores to compete with the neighborhood video specialty shops, the video rental industry is becoming overcrowded. In fact, rental rates in many areas are off sharply and profits are slim to nonexistent for many outlets—a case of "profitless prosperity."

Why is this the case in an obvious high-growth industry? It is an industry with very low and inexpensive barriers to entry; thus, competitors expanded faster than the market. The industry is likely to undergo a "shakeout," whereby marginal outlets will be forced to close. In addition, the industry is further threatened by "rack jobbers"—firms which set up and service displays of 200 or so cassettes in convenience stores and other high-traffic locations, sharing the revenue. On the other end, video "superstores" are emerging, with 7,500 or so tapes, serviced by central distribution centers. In the process, the medium-sized outlet, unable to match neither the selection and prices of the superstores nor the convenience and prices of the rack jobbers, may be forced out.[2]

DETERMINANTS OF COMPETITION

Competition can be defined as vying for customers or resources. Often, however, people concentrate on firms competing for buyers or customers when describing the competitive environment, ignoring the equally important competition for resources that may occur. As Figure 5.1 shows, however, competition can (and does) arise from either source. In Case 1, two businesses compete intensely for customers, but do not compete for resources. In Case 2, however, two businesses do not compete for customers (as in the case of a monopoly), but compete intensely for resources. Which case contains the greater degree of competition? We cannot answer this question, but we should realize that both can describe relatively competitive environments. As Figure 5.2 illustrates, the two cases just discussed would likely represent situations of moderate total competitive pressure on the business. In Case 1 (competing for customers), significant marketing-oriented competition is apt to exist, but little purchasing-oriented competition. In Case 2 (competing for resources), the reverse is true. The most intensely competitive situation would exist where a business competes for *both* customers and resources, and the least competitive would be where minimal competition exists for customers and resources.

Competitive Forces

The terms *competition* and *rivalry* are often considered to be synonymous. Harvard's Michael Porter points out, however, that rivalry is but one of a number of factors, or forces, determining the degree of competition within an industry. Porter's studies of structural factors and strategic groups within industries

---

[2]W. M. Alpert, "What's Wrong with This Picture?" *Barrons,* September 21, 1987, p. 8.

FIGURE 5.1   Firms Compete for Customers and Resources; Two Cases

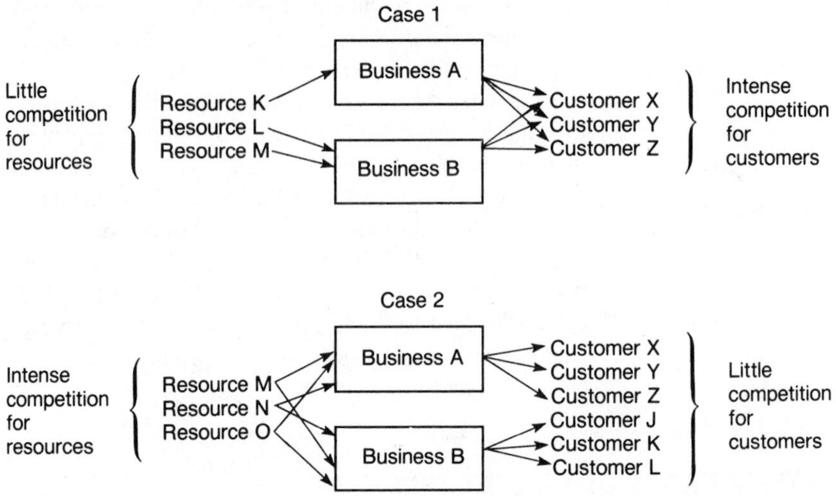

Case 1

Little competition for resources

Resource K
Resource L
Resource M

Business A

Business B

Customer X
Customer Y
Customer Z

Intense competition for customers

Case 2

Intense competition for resources

Resource M
Resource N
Resource O

Business A

Business B

Customer X
Customer Y
Customer Z
Customer J
Customer K
Customer L

Little competition for customers

concluded that the state of competition in an industry depends on the five basic competitive forces shown in Figure 5.3. The combined strength of these forces determines the profit potential in the industry, in terms of return on invested capital.

Threat of New Entrants.   New entrants bring increased competition to an industry. Entry depends on the barriers existing—economies of scale, product differentiations, capital requirements, access to distribution channels, cost advantages for established competitors, and certain government and legal constraints—as well as on the possible reactions of existing competitors.

FIGURE 5.2   Intensity of Competition

Competition for Resources	*Intense*	Intense competitive pressure	Moderate pressure (purchasing) —Case 2
	Minimal	Moderate pressure (marketing) —Case 1	Little competitive pressure
		Intense	*Minimal*

Competition for Customers

FIGURE 5.3   Forces Driving Industry Competition

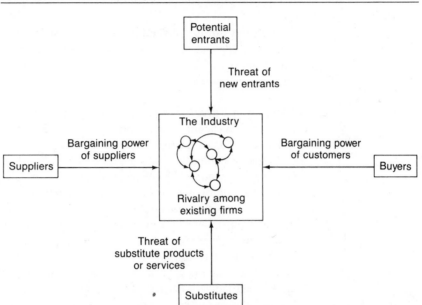

Source: Adapted from and reprinted with permission of The Free Press, a Division of Macmillan, Inc., from *Competitive Strategy* by Michael E. Porter, p. 4. Copyright © 1980 by The Free Press.

Rivalry among Existing Firms.   Rivalry, or attempts to improve the firm's position within the industry, can have noticeable effects on the firm's competitors, because firms in an industry are mutually dependent. The intensity of the rivalry is greatest when the following factors are present:

1. Competitors are numerous and roughly equal in size and power.
2. Industry growth is slow.
3. Fixed or storage costs are high.
4. The product or service is not differentiated from those of competitors.
5. Capacity normally is added in large increments.
6. Competitors have diverse goals, objectives, strategies, origins, and "personalities."
7. Companies rate the need to succeed in the industry as high.
8. High exit barriers exist, based on costs, interrelationships with other divisions, company commitment, or legal restrictions. Obviously, the worst case exists in an industry with high exit but low entry barriers, while the reverse would be the ideal.

Threat of Substitution.   All firms in an industry, even monopolies, compete with industries and companies producing substitute products. Saccharin, fructose, aspartame, and sugar are examples of substitute products, as are heat pumps, furnaces, and air conditioners.

Bargaining Power of Customers.   Buyers attempt to force down prices as well as to demand higher quality, better services, and other concessions. The need to make such concessions to buyers with bargaining power increases rivalry and reduces profits.

Bargaining Power of Suppliers.   Suppliers can increase rivalry and reduce profits by their ability to raise prices, reduce services, and allocate purchases.[3]

The five forces determine the attractiveness of an industry, because their collective strength determines industry profitability. They determine profitability because they influence the elements of return on investment—prices, costs, and required levels of investment. The main point is that each of the forces is a function of industry *structure,* which is relatively stable. However, businesses— through their strategies—can influence the five forces, and industry structure can change over time. In short, industry profitability is a function of industry structure—the five forces—not product, process, or technological characteristics, per se. For example, the forces are favorable in pharmaceuticals and soft drinks, and industry participants can earn high returns. Returns are inherently low in industries where one or more of the forces is unfavorable, such as steel, rubber, and video games. Thus, when the forces are favorable, returns are likely to be attractive; when they are unfavorable, returns are likely to be disappointing, *despite management's efforts.*[4]

Competitive Advantage and the Value Chain

Competitive advantage is the advantage a firm gains over its competitors because it is better able to transform resources, or inputs (labor, capital, raw materials, purchases) into goods and services at maximum profit. To do so, a company must either be able to transform these inputs into goods and services at a lower cost, or perform them in a way that leads to differentiation (greater value) and a premium price.[5] Competitive advantage, however, should not be confused with comparative advantage, which is derived from the relative costs of the inputs between countries, regions, states, cities, and other location factors. Obviously, comparative advantage is a contributing factor to a firm's competitive advantage,[6] as are its distinctive competencies.

---

[3]Michael Porter, *Competitive Strategy* (New York: Free Press, 1980), chaps. 1 and 7.

[4]Michael E. Porter, *Competitive Advantage* (New York: Free Press, 1985), pp. 4–7.

[5]M. E. Porter and V. E. Millar, "How Information Gives You Competitive Advantage," *Harvard Business Review* 63, no. 4 (July–August 1985), p. 150.

[6]Bruce Kogut, "Designing Global Strategies: Comparative and Competitive Value-Added Chains," *Sloan Management Review,* Summer 1985, p. 15.

FIGURE 5.4   The Generic Value Chain

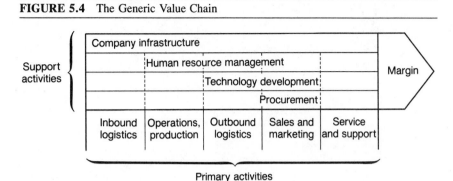

Source: Adapted from and reprinted with permission of The Free Press, a Division of Macmillan, Inc., from *Competitive Advantage* by Michael E. Porter, p. 37. Copyright © 1985 by Michael E. Porter.

Competitive advantage influences the decision of what activities and technologies along the *value-added chain*—the chain of activities a firm performs in creating the value that causes customers to buy the product or service—that the firm should concentrate its investment and managerial resources in. The value chain is the process by which technology is combined with material and labor inputs, and then the resulting product or service is assembled, marketed, and distributed.[7] Ideally, maximum value, in the eyes of the consumer, is added by this process at low cost, resulting in the firm's competitive advantage.

The value chain is the basic tool for systematically examining the activities a business performs and how they interact, and is necessary in order to determine its sources of competitive advantage. That is, one cannot understand competitive advantage by studying a business as a whole; it must be dissected into its "strategically relevant activities" to understand the *sources* of competitive advantage (cost leadership or differentiation, according to Porter).[8]

As Figure 5.4 shows, value-producing activities fall into nine categories: five primary activities and four support activities. Primary activities are those involved in producing the product or service, its marketing and delivery, and its post-sale service and support. Support activities provide the resource inputs and company infrastructure so that the primary activities can occur. Also, the way the activities are linked together often affects the cost or effectiveness; a sort of interaction effect.[9]

Competitive advantage can be created in the value-added chain by actions which lower costs, enhance differentiation of the product or service, and optimize the firm's competitive scope—the breadth of activities performed. In some instances, broadening the competitive scope (broadening product lines, more vertical integration, selling in more markets, and the like) may increase

---

[7]Ibid.

[8]Porter, *Competitive Advantage*, p. 33.

[9]Porter and Millar, "How Information Gives You Competitive Advantage," p. 150.

FIGURE 5.5   The Components of a Competitor Analysis

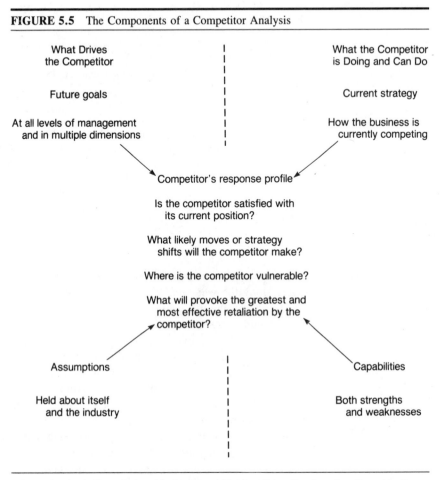

Source: Reprinted with permission of the Free Press, a Division of Macmillan, Inc., from *Competitive Strategy* by M. E. Porter, p. 49. Copyright 1980.

value added (and profits). In other instances, narrowing the competitive scope (targeting and focusing on particular market segments, customers, or regions) may add more value and provide a competitive advantage.[10]

Competitor Analysis

It is important to evaluate competitive advantages of the firm, but it is equally important to evaluate the capabilities of competitors. In large measure, a competitor analysis closely resembles the analysis of a firm's strengths and weaknesses. Figure 5.5 illustrates the major components of a competitor

---

[10]Porter and Millar, "How Information Gives You Competitive Advantage," p. 151.

analysis. This information, presented in a form such as that shown in Table 5.1 permits a comparative evaluation of competitors based on key factors and criteria. This form can be used to evaluate relative strength, as well as to compare the strengths and weaknesses of competitors with those of your firm.

Another method of analysis is to compare the position of the business with that of its competitors with regard to relative quality and price—in other words, relative value. As Figure 5.6 shows, the interaction of customers and suppliers in the marketplace tends to align products along a "price-performance curve," so that strong competing products offer roughly the same perceived value. For example, economy products offer both low price and low quality, and better products command higher prices. Products offering less value than those on the curve are likely to lose out, while those offering greater value are likely to win. Research has shown that products—and businesses—offering greater value have a far better chance of gaining market share and growing than do the rest. Further, changes in relative quality have a more potent effect on market share

TABLE 5.1   Competitor Evaluation Form

| | Competitors | | | |
Item	A	B	C	D
Name				
Estimated sales ($000)				
Estimated share of market				
Price advantage*				
Quality advantage*				
Technology base*				
Sales force base*				
Distribution advantage*				
Cost advantage*				
Overall				
Standing in industry (today)*				
Standing in industry (next year)*				
Seriousness of competition (today)*				
Seriousness of competition (next year)*				
Seriousness of competition (two years ahead)*				
Anything special to which we must react?				
Soon				
Next year				
Longer range threat				

*Evaluate on the following scale: 1 = great, highest, best; 2 = above average; 3 = average; 4 = below average; 5 = worst, no threat, very poor.

Source: Reprinted with permission of The Free Press, a Division of Macmillan, Inc., from *Strategic Planning: What Every Manager Must Know* by G. A. Steiner, p. 139. Copyright 1979.

FIGURE 5.6   Value and the Price-Performance Curve

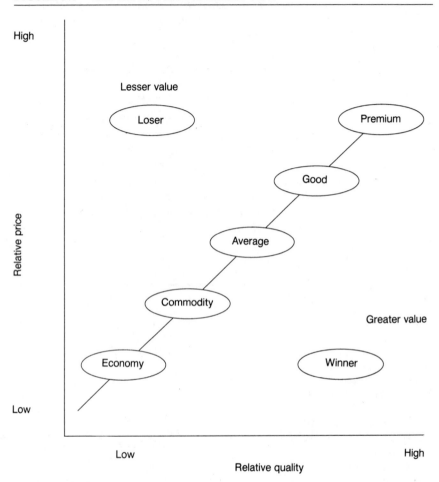

Source: Adapted from Bradley T. Gale and Richard Klavans, *Formulating a Quality Improvement Strategy,* PIMS Letter No. 31 (Cambridge, Mass.: The Strategic Planning Institute, 1984), pp. 3–6.

than price changes do, and quality improvements are harder for competitors to follow than are price changes.[11] In summary, it is important to compare and analyze the position of your business relative to competitors in the industry to determine relative positions with respect to the industry's price-performance curve.

---

[11]Bradley T. Gale and Richard Klavans, *Formulating a Quality Improvement Strategy,* PIMS Letter No. 31. (Cambridge, Mass.: The Strategic Planning Institute, 1984), pp. 3–6.

THE EFFECT OF MARKET AND INDUSTRY STRUCTURE

Another factor in the firm's competitive environment involves the type of market and industry structure it faces. For example, the scope of the market and industry within which the firm competes are very important considerations. Is the firm competing in a broad market, such as General Motors in automobiles, or does it compete in certain segments of that market, as Mercedes Benz does and Checker did? Is the industry or service area local, regional, national, international, or even global? What is the intensity of the rivalry between the competitors? What strategic groups (firms following similar strategies) exist?

These factors, discussed in this section, are related to industrial organization and microeconomics. However, they are sufficiently different from the general economic environment and related closely enough to the firm to warrant a separate and more detailed look. Also, these factors are not fixed—they can change. Remember our previous discussion of banking. For years, banking was a relatively stable, protected industry. Bank charters were difficult to acquire, and change in the industry was slow. The advent of savings and loans provided some competition for deposits, but each financial institution had its own market niche. Then came high interest rates and money market accounts. Financial institutions such as Dreyfus and Fidelity permitted customers to write checks on their accounts, and started to compete with banks. Deregulation blurred the distinction between savings and loans and banks, and both found themselves in a more competitive environment. Many banks were ill prepared for life without the shelter of regulation.

Not only did deregulation permit price competition for deposits, but it also increased the range of services that nonbank institutions could offer. For the first time in banking history, institutions other than banks were able to offer checking deposits and have broader lending powers. And the Depository Institutions Act of 1982 changed the regulations governing deposits, allowing savings and loans to act more like banks, thus creating another competitive force. The financial effect on the industry has been an increase in the cost of funds due to more permissive interest rate ceilings plus increased competition from financial service institutions other than banks. The net effect of this is a squeezing of profits from both ends for banks.

Deregulation may also result in a reduction in the number of banks. Several studies predict that by the early 90s or sooner, the number of banks in the United States, currently 14,000, will have shrunk to 10,000 or fewer. Some extremists are even predicting 7,000. All agree that by the 90s, banking will be a totally different industry.[12]

This trend can already be observed. Intensified competition (including that from other types of financial institutions, insurance companies, brokerage-based

---

[12]Robert O. Metzger and Susan E. Rau, "Strategic Planning for Future Bank Growth," *Bankers Magazine* 165, no. 4 (July-August 1982), p. 58.

firms, and giant retailers) will increase the number of bank consolidations and buyouts. Many banks have found themselves unprepared and financially crippled by the competitive environment and have had to sell out. Larger banks (realizing the loss in market share and/or profitability) and nonbank financial institutions are seeking acquisitions to add to their portfolio to increase market share.

Furthermore, the size of most banks' markets is changing. It used to be that a bank in Sioux Falls, South Dakota, for example, competed only with other banks in the same city. Then came savings and loans. Then competition with national organizations such as General Motors Acceptance Corp. (GMAC) for auto loans. Then money market funds and total investment packages such as those offered by Sears (through Allstate and Dean Witter) and Merrill Lynch (through its cash management account). Finally, de facto interstate banking has been offered by Citibank and First Interstate, and is likely to intensify greatly when and if banking laws are further relaxed.

Defining the Market

Market characteristics can change, markets themselves can change, and measures such as "market share" and "market growth" can depend on how one defines the market. Thus, there is no one way to define a market. But markets tend to be described, if not defined, in terms of several dimensions.

1. *Products*. Products or services comprising a market can be defined narrowly (the market for microwave ovens) or broadly (the market for all ovens, or even all appliances). In general, useful ways of categorizing products in terms of their markets would include groupings relating to similar functions and/or similar technology.
2. *Customers*. Are the products sold to similar or different types of customers?
3. *Geography*. Markets often are defined in terms of geographical regions.
4. *Components versus goods*. Is the product a raw material, component, or subassembly sold to other producers, or is it sold to end users?
5. *Multidimensional factors*. While a market may be defined in terms of each of the four factors above, it may also be defined in terms of combinations of factors.

In general, as Harvard's Robert Buzzell states,

> Market definition is an important and difficult step in the process of strategy formulation. For the management of a business unit (BU), determining the scope of the *served* market is a basic strategic decision. In most cases, there are choices to be made about what kinds of customers to serve, what types of products to offer, the geographic scope of the BU's market, and the level(s) of production/distribution on which to operate. The strategy employed by a BU is largely determined by the definition of its served market. To complicate matters, an appropriate served market definition at one point in time may not be appropriate later on, because of changes in customer needs, technology, or competitors' activities. . . . managers may need to use several different

definitions of "the market" to satisfy different purposes. To summarize this point, . . . Assume that the BU sells . . . [150 units] to only two customer or product segments, with market shares of 50 percent in Segment A and 67 percent in Segment B—or 60 percent for the two segments combined. Beyond these two served segments, there is an "immediately adjacent" market in which the BU makes no sales—but into which it could expand by directing marketing efforts to new types of customers, broadening its product offering, etc. If the size of this unserved portion of the market is 500 units, then the BU's share of its "total market" is (150/750) or 20 percent.

For purposes of evaluating the BU's competitive effectiveness, it seems reasonable to say that *all* of the "market shares" just cited—share in each served segment, combined share in both segments, and share of total market including unserved segments—are relevant measures.

Finally, for purposes of evaluating possible future growth opportunities and potential competitive threats, a still broader view of "the market" will be necessary. Potential competitors may include firms selling in the "immediately adjacent" market; firms operating in related cost sectors; those in other geographic regions, including overseas markets; and producers of functionally related products whose offerings might be modified so as to compete directly with those of the business unit. All of these possibilities are, furthermore, two-way streets—and each represents a potential direction for the BU's future growth as well as a possible source of new competition.[13]

Thus, while General Motors may appear secure in the fact that it controls over 35 percent of the U.S. auto market, it competes against not only Ford and Chrysler, but against a number of Japanese and European automakers. Since GM is a full-line producer, and foreign companies compete in the United States, perhaps it should consider its share of the *world* market. On this score it would not fare so well (even in comparison to Ford, which is a major producer in Europe). In contrast, Mercedes Benz has a very small share of the total market, but it does not compete across the board. If one defines its market as luxury sedans and coupes, its share of this *served* market is much greater.

On the other hand, some markets, such as those for laundries and bakeries, are inherently local. Some are regional, such as cement production (limited by transportation costs). And some are national, international, and even global.

Defining the Industry

Equally important and related to the definition of the market is the definition of the industry. An *industry* is a group of firms offering products or services that are close substitutes for each other.[14] An industry is also a group of producers and sellers of close substitute outputs who supply a common group of buyers. An industry, then, is defined in terms of both product or service and of customers.

---

[13]From Robert D. Buzzell, *Note on Market Definition and Segmentation,* 9–579–083, p. 27. Boston: Harvard Business School, 1978. Reprinted by permission.

[14]Arnoldo C. Hax and N. S. Majluf, *Strategic Management* (Englewood Cliffs, N.J.: Prentice-Hall, 1984), p. 261.

In analyzing industry structure, economists often consider the basic determinants of supply and demand because an "industry" tends to involve common factors that affect both. Supply-related factors include: (1) raw materials, (2) technologies, and (3) the type of work force. Demand-related factors are: (1) price elasticities of products and services, (2) rates of growth, (3) cyclical characteristics of demand, and (4) the method of purchase. These supply and demand factors interacting over time produce an industry structure with several key strategic aspects:

1. The number and size of buyers and sellers.
2. The degree of product differentiation.
3. Requirements and conditions for entry into the industry, for exit from the industry, and for positioning within the industry.
4. Cost structure, particularly the relationship between fixed and variable costs.
5. The degree of vertical integration, both backward and forward.[15]

While industry structure may change over the product life cycle, structural factors are important in determining the appropriate corporate, business, and functional strategies; the purpose of these strategies is to provide a strong position for the firm relative to its competition and market environment.

Global Industries.   A *global* industry is one that *requires* global operations to compete effectively. In contrast, an *international company* is usually thought of as a primarily national firm that operates in one or more foreign markets, but its basic orientation is still toward its home country.[16] A *multinational company* is one that operates in a number of different countries. The true multinational not only sells its products in foreign countries, as might be the case with an international firm, but also has production and other operating facilities in a number of countries.

Refining our definition further, it is necessary to distinguish between global competition, global businesses, and global companies. *Global competition* occurs when companies "cross-subsidize" national competitive battles (use financial resources accumulated in one part of the world to wage a competitive battle in another) in pursuit of global sales and distribution. *Global businesses* (or markets) are those in which the minimum efficient volume is not present in the company's domestic market. *Global companies,* in turn, sell in key foreign markets, employing cross-subsidization, international competition, and world-scale volume. Therefore, a company must distinguish between offshore sources and large-scale plants and the ability to compete in competitors' key markets.[17]

---

[15]Abraham Katz, "Evaluating the Environment: Economic and Technological Factors," in *Handbook of Business Strategy,* ed. W. D. Guth (Boston: Warren, Gorham & Lamont, 1985), pp. 2–6.

[16]Porter, *Competitive Strategy,* p. 276.

[17]G. Hamel and C. K. Prahalad, "Do You Really Have a Global Strategy?" *Harvard Business Review* 63, no. 4 (July–August 1985), pp. 139–48.

TABLE 5.2   Some Global Industries and Competitors

Industry	*Principal Competitors*
Watches	Timex, Seiko, Citizen
Automobiles	General Motors, Ford, Fiat, Toyota, Nissan, Volkswagen
Motorcycles	Honda, Kawasaki, Suzuki
Construction equipment	Caterpillar, Komatsu
Farm equipment	Deere, Massey Ferguson
Oil	Exxon, Shell, Mobil, British Petroleum
Chemicals	Hoechst, BASF, Bayer, Imperial, Dow

In most cases, a firm can choose whether or not to operate on an international or multinational basis without incurring any significant disadvantages. The global industry, however, presents significant strategic disadvantages to any firm that chooses to compete on a limited scale. Some examples of global industries are oil production, television manufacturing, motorcycles, sewing machines, and automobiles. While many of the structural factors and market forces that affect global industries are the same as those in domestic or single-country markets, the concepts apply on a global scale. That is, a true global market is more than the sum of individual country markets—it must be considered as an entity.[18] In a global industry, any firm pursuing a domestic, international, or even a multinational strategy is essentially pursuing the equivalent of a niche strategy. Examples of global industries and competitors are shown in Table 5.2.

Kenichi Ohmae, a well-known Japanese management expert, considers farming a global industry. As a result, he states that large farms run like factories are the only kind that can compete in the new global market for agricultural products. In fact, Japan already buys more agricultural commodities from the United States than from any other country, and Ohmae says both countries should stop subsidizing their producers and free them to efficiently produce their products wherever it is advantageous to do so—in Japan, the United States, or other countries.[19]

How to Compete Globally.   In order to compete globally—as well as locally, regionally, or on a national basis—a firm must achieve competitive advantages. In order to achieve competitive advantage, a firm must satisfy three goals: it must conduct its operations efficiently; it must successfully manage the risks it assumes in carrying out those activities; and it must be able to innovate and adapt to current and future changes in the market. Taking strategic actions that optimize achievement of these three goals is the source of competitive advantage.[20]

---

[18]Richard D. Robinson, *International Business Management,* rev. ed. (Hinsdale, Ill.: Dryden Press, 1978) p. 17.

[19]Kenichi Ohmae, "Myths about Farmers Complicate U.S.-Japan Relations," *Sunday Journal-Star,* May 3, 1987, p. F–3.

[20]Sumantra Ghoshal, "Global Strategy: An Organizing Framework," *Strategic Management Journal* 8, no. 5 (September–October 1987), p. 427.

TABLE 5.3   Achieving Global Competitive Advantage

Strategic Objectives	Sources of Competitive Advantage		
	National Differences	*Scale Economies*	*Scope Economies*
Achieving efficiency in current operations	Benefiting from differences in factor costs—wages and cost of capital	Expanding and exploiting potential scale economies in each activity	Sharing of investments and costs across products, markets and businesses
Managing risks	Managing different kinds of risks arising from market or policy-induced changes in comparative advantages of different countries	Balancing scale with strategic and operational flexibility	Portfolio diversification of risks and creation of options and sidebets
Innovation and adaptation	Learning from societal differences in organizational and managerial processes and systems	Benefiting from experience—cost reduction and innovation	Shared learning across organizational components in different products, markets or businesses

Source: Adapted from Sumantra Ghoshal, ''Global Strategy: An Organizing Framework,'' *Strategic Management Journal* 8, no. 5 (September–October 1987), p. 428.

Multinational firms competing globally, however, must achieve *global* competitive advantages. The multinational has three ways of achieving such competitive advantage. As shown in Table 5.3, it can exploit national differences—differences in input and output markets among the countries in which it operates. It can also seek to benefit from size—scale economies—in its various activities. In addition, it can exploit synergies—economies of scope—that may exist because of its diversity of activities and operations. In short, the key to successful global strategies is to manage the interactions between these different objectives and sources of advantage—to use all three sources of competitive advantage to optimize efficiency, risk, and adaptation simultaneously in a worldwide business.[21]

With regard to economies of scale and scope, the small, entrepreneurial company may be at a disadvantage in world markets. Companies in the United States have not been losing out to small foreign competitors but to huge, protected Japanese firms embedded in stable, concentrated, coordinated alliances. In this light, only the large, integrated corporations are apt to be able to compete effectively.[22]

---

[21]Ibid.

[22]Charles H. Ferguson, ''From the People Who Brought You Voodoo Economics,'' *Harvard Business Review* 66, no. 3, (May–June 1988), p. 55.

Global Advantages. A global industry requires a global strategy to succeed—thinking of the world as one market and one production base instead of as a collection of national markets and production facilities. A number of advantages can accrue to global companies. Michael Porter describes nine, including:

1. *Comparative advantage.* Certain countries, for example, offer sufficiently skilled labor at wage rates significantly lower than those in developed countries. In the mid 80s, Outboard Marine Corp. (OMC) closed its plant in Galesburg, Illinois. Part of the business went to a Mexican subsidiary, because among other factors, labor rates were less than one third of those at the old plant.
2. *Production economies of scale.* It may be that optimal plant size exceeds the product demand in a given country; if so, a larger plant may supply markets in two or more countries.
3. *Global experience.* The Japanese approach of producing for several markets simultaneously gives a competitive cost advantage in comparison to the firm that pursues a foreign market *after* saturation in the domestic market.
4. *Logistical economies.* The fixed costs of oil tankers, for example, dictate a global approach so that the costs can be spread over a higher volume of operations.
5. *Marketing economies.* Pharmaceutical research, for example, is very expensive. Marketing pharmaceutical products in several countries spreads those costs over a larger number of sales.
6. *Purchasing economies.* Buying on a large scale often enables a firm to buy at reduced prices. The oil companies are a prime example.
7. *Product differentiation.* In some industries, an international presence helps products sell in other countries. In fashion and cosmetics, for example, a presence in Paris helps sell the products elsewhere. Likewise, U.S. cigarettes are in demand around the world, as are Cuban cigars and German beers.
8. *Proprietary technology.* It is advantageous to sell any product involving a great deal of unique research in multinational markets. Computers, semiconductors, automobiles, and aircraft are prime examples.
9. *Production or service mobility.* In certain industries, such as heavy construction or oil exploration, the equipment and people are readily transportable to locations where the service is needed.[23]

Global Impediments. Porter also lists a number of impediments to global competition:

1. *Economic impediments.* Factors such as high transportation and storage costs, differing product needs in different countries, differing distribution channels, the need for local sales forces and repair facilities, unduly short lead times,

---

[23]Porter, *Competitive Strategy,* pp. 278–81.

differing market segmentation, and lack of demand in other countries mitigate against global operation.

2. *Managerial impediments*. Rapidly changing technology, differing marketing tasks, and requirements for intensive localized marketing or service complicate management across geographical boundaries, perhaps to such an extent that international approaches become undesirable.

3. *Institutional impediments*. A host of government impediments, such as tariffs, quotas, other laws, tax and labor policies, and other policies may impede international business. In addition, certain firms and their managers may not have the vision to think and to compete in international terms.[24]

In summary, global companies have an advantage in certain (global) industries—they can set up operations in areas of the world where their product can be produced at a cost advantage. However, this comparative advantage can be gained only to the extent that resources—such as capital, technology, management, and products—can be moved from country to country.[25] The former board chairman of Korea's large conglomerate, Daewoo Corporation, stated that global manufacturing is spreading through "transnationalization," or joint ventures between multinational companies in global industries—such as between his company and General Motors.[26]

Strategic Groups.   While it is important to define the market and the industry, a more useful concept than total industry definition is often the identification of "strategic groups" within industries. The most relevant unit of industry analysis may be the strategic group to which the business belongs.

As an example, Figure 5.7 shows the variation in the relationship between return on equity (ROE) and market share for three industries. Only brewing seems to adhere to the across-industry trend of ROE rising with increased market shares. However, a different picture emerges from a closer look at the brewing industry if it is divided into three strategic groups—local, regional, and national firms. As Figure 5.8 shows, ROE declines with increasing share *within* each of the groups, but increases *between* groups. A regional brewer, for example, attempting to pick up market share may find a lower ROE *until* the firm goes national.

As this example illustrates, looking only at the industry can be misleading; you need to look further. Michael Porter points out that "the first step in structural analysis within industries is to characterize the strategies of all significant competitors along these dimensions. This activity then allows for the mapping of the industry into strategic groups. A strategic group is the group of firms in an industry following the same or a similar strategy" and having similar strategic characteristics. "An industry could have only one strategic group if all the firms

[24]Ibid. pp. 281–87.

[25]Patrick F. Dolan, "Strategic Planning for Multinational Corporations," in *Handbook of Business Strategy*, ed. W. D. Guth (Boston: Warren, Gorham & Lamont, 1985), pp. 13–14.

[26]Duk Choong Kim, in a speech, given at the University of Nebraska, January 22, 1985.

FIGURE 5.7 Relationship between Market Share and ROE

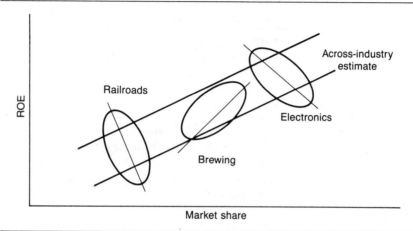

Source: K. J. Hatten, "Quantitative Research Methods, in Strategic Management," in *Strategic Management: A New View of Business Policy and Planning,* ed. D. Schendel and C. W. Hofer (Boston: Little, Brown, 1979), p. 456. Reprinted by permission.

FIGURE 5.8 ROE and Market Share for Brewing Industry

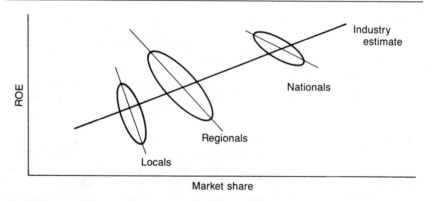

Source: K. J. Hatten, "Quantitative Research Methods in Strategic Management," in *Strategic Management: A New View of Business Policy and Planning,* ed. D. Schendel and C. W. Hofer (Boston: Little, Brown, 1979), p. 455. Reprinted by permission.

followed essentially the same strategy. At the other extreme, each firm could be a different strategic group. Usually, however, there are a small number of strategic groups which account for the essential strategic differences among firms in the industry."[27]

---

[27]Porter, *Competitive Strategy,* p. 129.

TABLE 5.4   Strategic Groups in the U.S. Pharmaceutical Industry

Group Description	Firms
1. Large, R&D-intensive, prescription products, broad range of products, competing in many segments.	Abbott American Home Bristol-Myers Pfizer SmithKline Warner-Lambert
2. Large, advertising intensive, prescription and nonprescription products, fewer prescription segments, and narrower product range than (1).	Lilly Merck Upjohn
3. Medium-sized, "me-too" product strategy, heavy promotion.	Johnson & Johnson Schering-Plough Squibb Sterling Drug
4. Medium-sized, lacking R&D competence, otherwise like (3).	Searle Syntex
5. Small, prescription products, narrow product range, selective market participation, me-too development, heavy professional promotion.	Carter-Wallace Marion Morton-Norwich Richardson-Vicks Robins Rorer
6. Small, very focused product line, narrow scope, negligible R&D.	Lederle

Source: Adapted from K. O. Cool and Dan Schendel, "Strategic Group Formation and Performance: The Case of the U.S. Pharmaceutical Industry, 1963–1982," *Management Science* 33, no. 9 (September 1987), p. 1115.

Strategic groups, then, can be defined as the set of firms competing within an industry which pursue similar strategies and employ similar combinations of scope and resource commitments.[28] They are essentially inhabitants of similar niches in the marketplace. The reason that the strategic group concept is important is that the major issue in industry analysis involves which strategies will best suit organizations with particular resource capabilities—a good strategy for one firm may not suit another.[29] Strategic groups identify firms which have chosen to utilize similar resource capabilities in similar ways. Table 5.4 defines six strategic groups within the U.S. pharmaceutical industry as an example, based upon scope and resource commitments.

---

[28]K. O. Cool and Dan Schendel, "Strategic Group Formation and Performance: The Case of the U.S. Pharmaceutical Industry, 1963–1982," *Management Science* 33, no. 9 (September 1987), p. 1106.

[29]K. J. Hatten and M. L. Hatten, "Strategic Groups, Asymmetrical Mobility Barriers and Contestability," *Strategic Management Journal* 8, no. 4 (July–August 1987), p. 341.

TABLE 5.5   Inventive Strategic Groups in the Pharmaceutical Industry

Core Firms	Related Firms	Unrelated Firms
Abbott Labs	Johnson & Johnson	American Home
Becton-Dickinson	SmithKline	C. R. Bard
Lilly	Sterling Drug	Baxter-Travenol
Pfizer	Warner-Lambert	Bristol-Myers
Schering-Plough		Marion Labs
Squibb		Merck
Upjohn		Robins
		Syntex

Based upon inventive activity, however, a somewhat different set of strategic groups emerges for the pharmaceutical industry. As shown in Table 5.5, the industry can be grouped into "core firms" (firms "typical" of the industry in terms of inventive activity); "related firms" (those significantly different from but still related to the technical core, either positively or negatively); and "unrelated firms" (those which vary markedly from the core firms, either positively or negatively). Thus, strategic group membership can be defined in a variety of ways.[30]

In Porter's view, both the industry and strategic group membership determine a firm's profitability; these underlying factors include:

1. Common industry characteristics.
   a. Industrywide structure elements that determine the strength of competitive forces and that apply equally to all firms. These traits include rate of growth of industry demand, overall potential for product differentiation, structure of supplier industries, and aspects of technology, which provide the overall context of competition for firms in the industry.

2. Characteristics of strategic group.
   a. The height of *mobility barriers* protecting the firm's strategic group.
   b. The *bargaining power* of the firm's strategic group with customers and suppliers.
   c. The vulnerability of the firm's strategic group to *substitute products*.
   d. The exposure of the firm's strategic group to *rivalry from other groups*.

3. The firm's position within its strategic group.
   a. The degree of competition *within* the strategic group.
   b. The *scale* of the firm relative to others in its group.

---

[30]Philip D. Crossland and L. A. Digman, "Using Time-Series Analysis to Identify an Industry's 'Inventive Strategic Groups'," *Proceedings of the 20th Annual Conference*, Decision Sciences Institute, November 1988.

     c. Costs of entry into the group.

     d. The ability of the firm to execute or *implement* its chosen strategy.[31]

Upon observation, it is apparent that many of the factors listed above are related to Porter's five-forces model of industry competition. Therefore, the factors which determine competition apply to strategic groups within industries as well as to industries as a whole. For example, entry barriers depend on the particular strategic group the firm wishes to join, and can vary from group to group within an industry. In addition, there may be barriers to shifting from one strategic group to another. Therefore, an important element of formulating competitive strategy within an industry is choosing the strategic group or niche in which to compete.

Financial Services: A Changing Industry.   At the beginning of this section, we discussed the changing financial services industry in terms of the effects of those changes on banks. In Chapter 4, we pointed out that a number of environmental forces have been at work since the 60s to cause revolutionary changes for the entire industry, not just for banks. As we mentioned, these converging forces were macroeconomic, regulatory, international, and technological in nature. It appears that the forces of change are still at work, as one of the "rescue plans" proposed for the savings and loan industry would abolish many of the remaining distinctions between commercial banks and thrift institutions.[32]

Whatever the outcome of the latest crisis, the forces for change are forcing major changes in the industry, resulting in a new market structure and an industry much more competitive than ever before. As a living example of industry change, let us take a glance at the dynamics of industry change that commercial banks and S&Ls are facing as they attempt to reposition themselves, both to survive and to enhance their performance.

The regional banks, for example, are being challenged by newly merged, larger regional banks, sometimes called *superregionals*. One consequence of these mergers may be a change in the balance of power in commercial banking, because the superregionals possess advantages over both the regionals and the national money center banks. For example, they can still claim their regional identification, autonomy, and attraction by customers, which the nationals do not have. In addition, they have fewer bad loans, more access to midsize corporations, and operate in more protected markets than the nationals. Vis-à-vis the regionals, the superregionals possess new economies of scale and scope, and are no longer easy takeover targets.

Foreign banks are another vigorous new competitor. Not subject to U.S. regulations and anxious to penetrate American markets, foreign banks operate

---

[31]Porter, *Competitive Strategy,* p. 42.

[32]Alan Murray and Paulette Thomas, "The Bush Bailout Plan for Savings and Loans Could Spell Extinction," *The Wall Street Journal,* February 7, 1989, p. A1.

with a big advantage. The Japanese, for example, are radically altering the industry by following the approaches that made them strong competitors in automobiles and electronics.

Last, the "nonbank banks" are becoming big players in consumer lending; in fact, only two of the largest five consumer lenders are banks. The largest is the General Motors Acceptance Corporation (GMAC), with Sears fourth and Ford Motor Credit fifth. Other big players include General Electric, American Express, Merrill Lynch, J. C. Penney, and Prudential Bache. Some of the factors enabling the nonbanks to approach dominance of the consumer lending market include their merchandising skills, their ability to segment markets and package services, and their effectiveness at lobbying in Washington.

In summary, commercial banks are finding themselves competing in a drastically changed market. As Citibank's former CEO Walter Wriston observed, "We had a monopoly and it was lovely; now there's a market and we're losing market share."[33] We will return to the financial services industry in Chapter 8, as we examine some of the strategic options appropriate to their new competitive environment.

THE PRODUCT/MARKET LIFE CYCLE

As students of marketing are aware, products, markets, and entire industries go through definite life cycles of the type shown in Figure 5.9: from the introductory, embryonic, or development stage to a more rapid growth stage—including a resulting shakeout—to a low-growth maturity stage, and finally to an aging or actual decline stage. Another important factor in achieving competitive advantage involves developing strategies appropriate to the life-cycle stage of the product/market/industry, since appropriate strategies vary from stage to stage. Important stages and their recommended strategies are discussed in the following paragraphs.

Introductory and Growth Stages

In the introductory stage, sales growth tends to be slow due to buyer unfamiliarity and inertia. This stage requires heavy start-up investments in research, manufacturing, and marketing. It tends to be unprofitable, and involves a negative cash flow and high risks. At this stage, there tend to be few competitors. The strategic objectives should be to achieve a commanding competitive position, if possible, including elimination of design, product, and marketing defects, development of awareness of the product and its benefits, and sales to early adopters.

---

[33]David Rogers, "Environmental Change in the Financial Services Industry," in *Advances in Strategic Management,* ed. Robert Lamb and Paul Shrivastava, vol. 5 (Greenwich, Conn.: JAI Press, 1988), pp. 94–98.

FIGURE 5.9   Product/Market Life-Cycle Stages

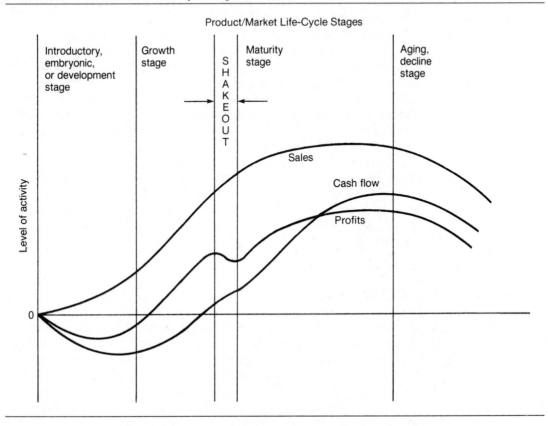

In the growth stage, the product begins to "take off" in sales. This attracts other producers. As sales of products such as cellular phones begin to grow more rapidly, the product starts to become profitable. Strategic objectives should be to establish a strong brand identity and develop a distribution system capable of meeting the rapidly growing demand. The goal of both objectives is to capture and maintain a large share of this demand, so that money invested during the introductory phase will begin (and continue) to pay off. The ideal situation is to have the customer identify the firm's product with the market, as was the case with Apple® computers and ATARI® video games. Cash flow remains negative during most of this phase, however, as investments are made in such areas as additional plant capacity.

Shakeout Stage

As shown in Figures 5.9 and 5.10, a shakeout phase typically occurs toward the latter part of the growth stage. In the early growth stage, margins are such that

FIGURE 5.10   Growth/Maturity Transition

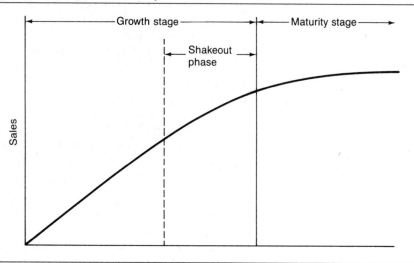

relatively inefficient producers may survive and even prosper. Rivalry focuses on product performance, access to distribution channels, identifying market segments, and highlighting special product features to enable sales to grow with the rapidly expanding market. In the shakeout phase, however, the *rate* of growth begins to decline, although growth is still occurring. Margins begin to fall, and firms with inferior products, poor distribution, high costs, or inappropriate segmentation come under pressure. Weaker competitors begin to be cleared from the market; those with efficient production, selling, and distribution are likely to survive and prosper because of reduced competition caused by the shakeout. The strategic objective during shakeout is to maintain and strengthen market niches or segments, through dealer and customer loyalty. In this stage, cash flow tends to turn positive for successful competitors. Keep in mind, however, that shakeouts can and do occur at *any* stage in the life cycle.

Maturity Stage

In the maturity stage, sales may continue to grow. But this growth is due mainly to replacement purchases of the product, new purchases owing to population growth or other stable factors, and inflation. In the maturity stage, relative stability reigns. Marginal producers have been cleared from the industry, and few (if any) new entrants are attracted because of the reduced growth rate. Profits peak in this phase, as do cash flows. Strategy shifts to a more defensive posture, as the firm attempts to protect itself from competitor erosion of market share and profits. This is done by paying constant attention to product improvement and refinement, as well as to trying new or refined promotional and distribution efforts.

In a mature market, without innovation or distinct changes in the environment, the primary way a firm can pick up major improvements in market share is through the mistakes of its competitors. Attention should be focused on efficiency—becoming the low-cost producer—through operations management approaches such as productivity improvement, cost control, and backward integration. The firm's product differentiation and pricing strategies are designed to *preserve* the firm's competitive position and to put pressure on competitors. This will enable the firm to take advantage of any strategic mistakes competitors make. As the maturity stage progresses, growth in sales to new customers may fall below the growth rate of the new-customer population, leaving largely replacement sales. Eventually, even replacement sales may begin to decline, resulting in an actual decline in total sales. However, profits and cash flow still may be strong, because expenditures and capital investments are minimal.

Decline Stage

Finally, it becomes clear that the product's future is limited. Buyers are shifting to newer products, and definite signs of old age and decline are evident for the industry—thus, the decline stage. Beset by declining sales and excess capacity, producers begin to drop out of the industry; the business can, however, extend its life span through product refinements and pricing strategies. The basic strategy now should be to milk the business of all possible profits and cash flow, using this money for investment in other products in earlier stages of the life cycle. But staying with products in the decline phase can have some advantages. If the firm is well established in the market and is a low-cost producer, it is likely that some competitors can be enticed to leave the market, leaving voids the remaining producers can capture. Phillip Morris, for example, continues to increase its cigarette sales by picking up sales from others who have departed.

Tables 5.6 and 5.7, adapted from Wasson[34] and Fox,[35] outline a number of descriptors and appropriate business strategies for the various stages in the product life cycle. These tables provide guidelines for business and functional-level actions and strategies for each stage, although exceptions can and do occur.

Some Cautions

While the preceding section and tables present the typical life cycle, certain caveats must be kept in mind. One is that the duration of the stages varies widely from industry to industry, as can the rate and height of the growth curves.

---

[34]Chester R. Wasson, *Dynamic Competitive Strategy and Product Life Cycles*, (St. Charles, Ill.: Challenge Books, 1974), pp. 247, 248.

[35]Harold W. Fox, "A Framework for Functional Coordination," *Atlantic Economic Review* 23, no. 6, (1973), pp. 10, 11.

TABLE 5.6 Wasson's Hypotheses about Appropriate Strategies over the Product Life Cycle

Dynamic Competitive Strategy and the Market Life Cycle

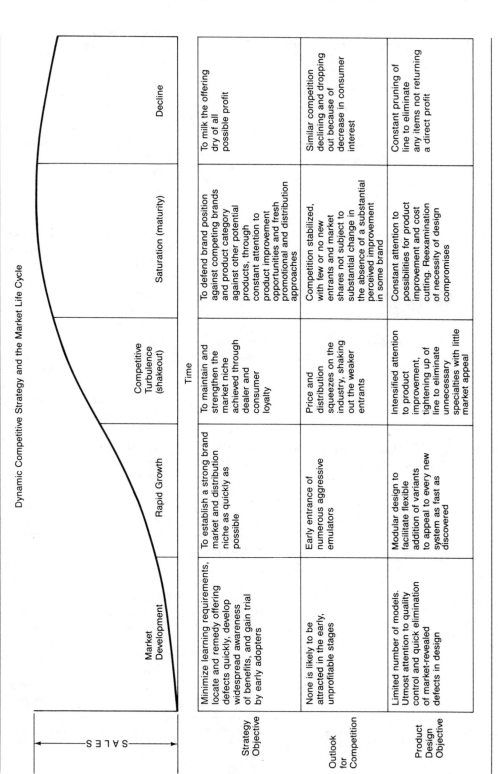

	Market Development	Rapid Growth	Competitive Turbulence (shakeout)	Saturation (maturity)	Decline
Strategy Objective	Minimize learning requirements, locate and remedy offering defects quickly, develop widespread awareness of benefits, and gain trial by early adopters	To establish a strong brand market and distribution niche as quickly as possible	To maintain and strengthen the market niche achieved through dealer and consumer loyalty	To defend brand position against competing brands and product category against other potential products, through constant attention to product improvement opportunities and fresh promotional and distribution approaches	To milk the offering dry of all possible profit
Outlook for Competition	None is likely to be attracted in the early, unprofitable stages	Early entrance of numerous aggressive emulators	Price and distribution squeezes on the industry, shaking out the weaker entrants	Competition stabilized, with few or no new entrants and market shares not subject to substantial change in the absence of a substantial perceived improvement in some brand	Similar competition declining and dropping out because of decrease in consumer interest
Product Design Objective	Limited number of models. Utmost attention to quality control and quick elimination of market-revealed defects in design	Modular design to facilitate flexible addition of variants to appeal to every new system as fast as discovered	Intensified attention to product improvement, tightening up of line to eliminate unnecessary specialties with little market appeal	Constant attention to possibilities for product improvement and cost cutting. Reexamination of necessity of design compromises	Constant pruning of line to eliminate any items not returning a direct profit

Source: Adapted from Chester R. Wasson, *Dynamic Competitive Strategy and Product Life Cycles* (St. Charles, Ill.: Challenge Books, 1974), pp. 247, 248.

TABLE 5.7   Fox's Hypotheses about Appropriate Business Strategies over the Product Life Cycle

Stage	Functional Focus	Department		
		R&D	Production	Marketing
Precom-mercialization	Coordination of R&D and other functions	Reliability tests	Production design Process planning Purchasing department lines up vendors and subcontractors	Test marketing Detailed marketing plan
Introduction	Engineering: debugging in R&D production, and field	Technical corrections (engineering changes)	Subcontracting Centralize pilot plants; test various processes; develop standards	Induce trial: fill pipelines; publicity
Growth	Production	Start successor product	Centralize production Phase out subcontractors Expedite vendors output; long runs	Channel commitment Brand emphasis Reduce price if necessary
Maturity	Marketing and logistics	Develop minor variants Reduce costs through value analysis Originate major adaptations to start new cycle	Many short runs Decentralize Import parts, low-priced models Routinization Cost reduction	Short-term promotions Cooperative advertising Forward integration Routine marketing research; panels, audits
Decline	Finance	Withdraw all R&D from initial version	Revert to subcontracting; simplify production line Careful inventory control: stock spare parts	Withdraw most promotional support Selective distribution Careful phaseout, considering entire channel

Source: Reprinted by permission from *Atlanta Economic Review* (now *BUSINESS* Magazine). ''A Framework for Functional Coordination,'' by Harold W. Fox, November–December 1973, pp. 10, 11.

	Department			
Physical Distribution	*Finance*	*Other*	*Customers*	*Competition*
Plan shipping schedules, mixed carloads Rent warehouse space, trucks	LC plan for cash flows, profits, investments, subsidiaries	Final legal clearances (regulatory hurdles, patents)	Panels and other test respondents	Neglects opportunity or is working on similar idea
Plan a logisitics system	Accounting deficit; high net cash outflow Authorize large production facilities	Help develop production and distribution standards	Innovators and some early adopters	(Monopoly) Disparagement of innovation Legal and extra-legal interference
Expedite deliveries Shift in owned facilities	Very high profits, net cash outflow still rising Sell equities	Short-term analyses based on return per scarce resource	Early adopters and early majority	(Oligopoly) A few imitate, improve, or cut prices
Reduce costs and raise customer service level Control finished goods inventory	Declining profit rate but increasing net cash inflow	Spearhead cost reduction, value analysis, and efficiency drives Price cuts bring price wars; possible price collusion	Early adopters, early and late majority, some laggards; first discontinued by late majority	(Monopoly competition) First shakeout; yet many rivals
Reduce inventory and services	Retrenchment Sell unneeded equipment Export the machinery	Accurate sales forecast very important	Mainly laggards	(Oligopoly) After second shakeout, only a few rivals

Consider, for example, "fad" products such as hula-hoops or pet rocks, in which the whole cycle can be completed in one year or less. ATARI® video games seemed to have a two-year growth and maturity stage but Nintendo's success seems longer lasting. Also, an industry does not always go through each of the stages. Or it may spend very little time in any given stage. CB radios, for example, went through a very long introduction stage, a growth stage of one or two years, little (if any) maturity stage, then into decline. Industry growth sometimes revitalizes, or renews, after a period of decline (this was true in the motorcycle, bicycle, and radio broadcasting industries), as if an entirely new life cycle began at some point. Others appear to skip the introductory phase altogether.[36] Still others either abort during the introductory phase and never make it any further, or go directly into decline.

In general, many businesses expect in the neighborhood of seven years of losses plus an even longer period of negative cash flow in the growth stage for products now in the early embryonic stage. After that, profitable maturity *can* go on for a long time. The life-cycle theory suggests that, over time, every business drifts to the right—toward decline—and that its financial performance changes. A corporate strategy that expects large and rising profits from an embryonic or aging business is not realistic. Expecting high profits in the growth and maturity stages, however, is reasonable.

THE EXPERIENCE CURVE

Pricing strategies offer another source of competitive advantage. One possible source of cost advantage to a business results from experience effects, enabling the firm to price its product more attractively than competitors. For example, the price of a four-function, hand-held calculator produced by Texas Instruments was about $150 in 1971. Five years later, an equivalent model was priced in the $15 range, and by 1990 cost less than $5. In inflation-adjusted terms, the price of calculators dropped 99 percent in 19 years. Why? One of the main reasons is the learning or "experience" curve, as its use in strategic analysis is called.

The learning-curve concept was first observed in 1925 when the commander of Wright-Patterson Air Corps Base noticed that the number of direct labor-hours required to assemble each plane decreased as more and more aircraft were assembled. With further study, it was found that as production doubled, labor-hours tended to decrease by a relatively stable amount. If the decrease was, for example, 15 percent, the result would be an 85 percent learning curve. This means that the time required to assemble the 20th plane is 85 percent of the time required to assemble the 10th plane, the 40th requires 85 percent of the time for the 20th, and so on. Table 5.8 lists times for various units, assuming a value of 100 for the 10th unit.

---

[36]Porter, *Competitive Strategy*, p. 158.

TABLE 5.8   85 Percent Curve Values

Unit	Labor Index
10	100
20	85
40	72
80	61
160	52
320	44
640	38

Figure 5.11 shows the learning curve graphically, and Figure 5.12, shows the same data plotted on double log paper (logarithmic scale for each axis), in which case the relationship becomes a straight line.

The learning curve, with labor costs falling with cumulative volume, has important implications for competitive strategy. Firms with marketing and pricing strategies geared to accumulating experience much faster than do their competitors may be able to achieve significant cost advantages over their competitors. For example, if one firm has produced a total of 320 units, its cost

FIGURE 5.11   The Learning Curve

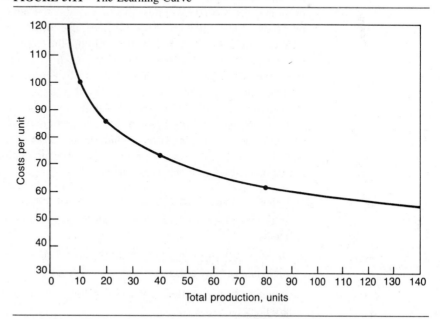

FIGURE 5.12   The Learning Curve on Log-Log Scales

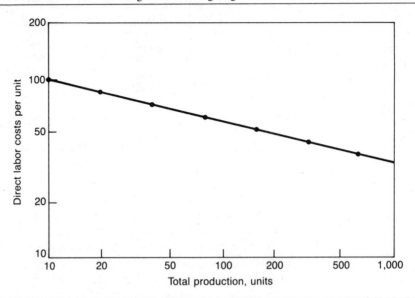

per unit will be at a labor index of 44, which is 15 percent less than the cost for a competitor that has produced only 160 units. The first producer can make more profit than the second (assuming that they charge the same price), or he can price his product lower, pick up additional sales, and lower his labor costs even more.

According to the Boston Consulting Group, the learning-curve concept applies not only to direct labor but to all costs, such as production, marketing, and economies of scale. BCG studies indicate that most cost elements, including nonlabor items, decline in such a way that total cost follows a composite "experience curve." Of course, all costs must be expressed in real terms (constant dollars) to observe the effect. Inflationary effects can be added to determine actual cost. BCG has found that the costs of most value-added items decline in the 20 to 30 percent range each time cumulative experience doubles. Factors contributing to this effect include:

1. Labor efficiency (indirect as well as direct labor).

2. Improved processes and methods, such as innovations and process improvements.

3. Product redesigns that result in faster production, less consumption of material, and lower costs.

4. Product standardization, such as the use of components common to other products.

FIGURE 5.13   Profit Effects of Experience Curve

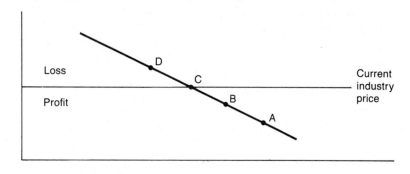

5. Economies of scale; the cost per unit of capacity increases less rapidly than does the level of capacity.
6. Substitution, including less expensive processes and cheaper materials.

Experience Curve Pricing

If a firm prices its product at a fixed percentage over costs, prices should decline at the same rate as the experience curve. However, the producer with the highest cumulative production will be rewarded with the lowest costs, encouraging some producers to price initial items below cost. In this way, the lower price will encourage more customers to purchase the product, resulting in a faster growth in sales, which puts the producer farther out on the experience curve than its competitors. This "dominant producer" greatly influences average costs for the industry. If the dominant producer's costs are declining, for example, at an 80 percent rate, so must the costs of other producers, if they are to survive. The other producers must be able to match the experience effects. Furthermore, the dominant producer will be able to set his prices lower than those of others because of his position on the curve, making production less profitable (or even unprofitable) for competitors. This is shown in Figure 5.13. Competitor A, having greater cumulative production and lower costs, has a higher profit margin. In fact, C is breaking even and D is losing money. Only by catching up in cumulative production can C and D compete, unless they are able to place themselves on a separate experience curve with a greater slope than the competitors' (which may be possible).

As Harvard's G. B. Allan observed, prices and costs often exhibit relationships similar to those shown in Figure 5.14. In Phase 1, prices may be less than average costs if firms base their prices on anticipated costs to gain an early volume and experience lead.

FIGURE 5.14   Common Price versus Cost Relationships

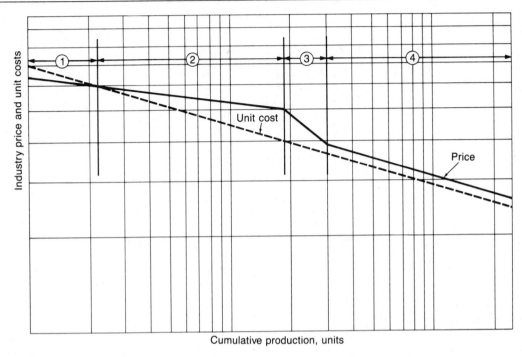

These prices often remain stable for a period of time (Phase 2) if production is less than demand. As supplies increase, however, this temporary situation is likely to change. One or more producers will try to increase their revenues by lowering prices and increasing their sales volume. Or others will be attracted by the high profit margins, producing a degree of overcapacity, usually resulting in price reductions. The typical result is Phase 3, where prices decline faster than costs, causing marginal producers to be shaken out of the market. When profit margins return to "normal" levels, the shakeout ends, and prices follow costs down the experience curve (Phase 4). Such shakeouts occurred in chemicals in the late 1950s and in semiconductors in the early 60s.[37]

The experience curve concept can be employed to determine strategies appropriate to the life-cycle stage and competitive position. In the growth stage (15 percent or greater growth per year, where experience doubles in five years or less), gaining and holding a dominant market position is the most desirable strategy. A firm may accomplish this position through price reductions, improved

[37]G. B. Allan, *Note on the Use of Experience Curves in Competitive Decision Making*, Case No. 9–175–174 (Boston: Harvard Business School, 1976), pp. 9–10.

TABLE 5.9   Experience Position and Stage Strategies

Experience Curve Position	Life-Cycle Stage		
	Growth	*Maturity*	*Decline*
Cumulative output exceeds competitors'.	Reduce prices to discourage new entrants and maintain capacity utilization.	Innovate, improve quality, and increase sales efforts to hold share.	Cut expenses by attempting to improve efficiency.
Cumulative output trails competitors'.	Attempt to increase share or seek a niche that can be dominated.	Innovate to create a new experience curve, or maintain share through low costs and prices. If not able, withdraw.	Withdraw.

service, quality or support, or by concentrating on a market segment or niche in which dominance can be obtained.[38] Table 5.9 provides guidelines for experience-based strategies for several combinations of competitive position and growth rate (indicated by life-cycle stage).

Some Cautions

If experience curve effects hold, eventual market dominance should be determined early in the product life cycle, since trailing firms will find it difficult to overtake the market leader. How then was IBM able to enter the personal computer market late and rapidly catch Apple and Radio Shack? Because IBM was able to transfer its substantial experience in larger computers to the microcomputer market. In addition, product or process innovations can both change the shape of the curve and make it obsolete. For example, a significant product innovation by a previous follower can force an entire industry "back to zero," putting the innovator in the lead with the new product. And not all firms follow the same experience curve. A firm with a more steeply sloping curve (such as an 80 percent versus the 85 percent experience factor we are using) can reach a lower cost position with less total production than can a firm with a flatter experience curve. Finally, Hax and Majluf of MIT report that experience effects

---

[38]Ibid.

vary with different activities in the firm, and the total effect depends on the *relative* influence of these activities. For example, their experience suggests the following typical learning effects:[39]

Activity	Experience Factor (percent)
R&D	95%
Manufacture of parts and components	75
Subassembly	70
Marketing	90
Distribution	85
Retailing	95

Thus, in our microcomputer example, IBM was able to transfer its considerable experience in R&D, manufacturing, assembly, and marketing. It was at a disadvantage in distribution and retailing of small computers. But this was outweighed by IBM's previous experience in the other areas.

Finally, the use of experience curve strategies depends upon how easy it is for firms to protect (or acquire) experience from competitors. When a firm is able to protect its proprietary experience, entry barriers for others are high. As diffusion of learning increases, entry barriers erode rapidly, however, making late entry feasible for competitors. In addition, experience curve pricing is a viable strategy only when there is little or no diffusion of experience. Also, the Strategic Planning Institute has found that changes in product quality have a far more potent—and lasting—effect on market share than do changes in price. Therefore, it may be time to swing the pendulum away from the experience curve drive for market share and toward effective quality control and customer perceived quality improvements.[40] These findings underscore the danger of simple strategy prescriptions based on the experience curve. Only rarely is it in a firm's best interests to attempt experience curve pricing.[41]

CONCLUSIONS

Analyzing the organization's relevant industry and competitive environment is the third major aspect of assessing the firm's strategic situation. An important part of this analysis is to correctly define the market or market segment that the

---

[39]Arnoldo C. Hax and N. S. Majluf, "Competitive Cost Dynamics: The Experience Curve," *Interfaces* 12, no. 5 (October 1982), p. 58.

[40]Gale and Klavans, *Formulating a Quality Improvement Strategy,* p. 9.

[41]M. B. Lieberman, "The Learning Curve, Diffusion, and Competitive Strategy," *Strategic Management Journal* 8, no. 5 (September–October 1987), p. 451.

company is trying to serve. Also important and related is the industry of which the business unit is a part. Markets can range from local to global, and industries can cover a similar range. In fact, there appears to be a trend toward transnationalization and globalization of industries.

While businesses are demographically and structurally part of an industry, they may be strategically related to a subset of firms within an industry—the strategic group. Competition in markets occurs between firms in industries and strategic groups, and depends on five major factors: the threats of new entrants, and of substitutes, the bargaining power of suppliers, and of customers, and the degree of rivalry among existing competitors.

Industries and products can progress through definite life-cycle stages, each suggesting generic strategic thrusts. Another important consideration is that of learning or experience effects, which can provide important strategic advantages when used properly (or prove disastrous if used improperly). Pricing behavior with increasing industry experience has been shown to be related to and affected by the product's life-cycle stage.

Part III

Strategic Decision Making: Formulating and Evaluating Strategic Alternatives

Business-Level Strategies: Generic, Differentiation, and Scope

LEARNING OBJECTIVES

After completing chapter 6, you should be able to:

Describe the general strategic options available to business units.

Understand the importance of positioning the business.

Discuss key strategies for distinguishing the business, including differentiation, scope, and supporting functional strategies.

Describe strategies for increasing the scope of the business, including penetration, market development, product development, and geographical expansion.

Relate strategies appropriate for redefining and reducing the scope of the business; that is, defense and renewal, retrenchment and turnaround, and endgame strategies.

Business-level strategies deal with how a given business unit of the organization should compete, as well as how the various functional strategies supporting the business—marketing, financial, production, research and development, and the like—should be integrated to support the business-level strategy. Concern in this chapter is with the basic business-level options; functional strategies other than innovation are not treated in depth here, since they are adequately covered in other courses in the business school curriculum. While there are numerous individual strategic options a business can pursue, the approach in this chapter is to group them into related or similar types or categories. Basic strategic thrusts for businesses are discussed, including the following:

1. Strategies for positioning the business at the proper point in the stream of product/service development activities.

2. Distinguishing the business; defining distinguishing characteristics in terms of differentiation, scope, and functions that enable the business to achieve competitive advantage.

3. Increasing the scope of the business; strategies for developing and expanding the business through increased penetration, market development, product development, and geographical expansion (including international).

4. Redefining and reducing the scope of the business; strategies for contraction, retrenchment, turnaround and renewal, as well as retreat and product termination.

Strategies for extending the firm into other businesses are treated separately in Chapter 7 as multibusiness strategies.

The approach in this chapter is not to present any single author's conceptualization of basic business strategies, even though a number of credible frameworks exist. Beginning with Miles and Snow's types of organizational adaptation (Defenders, Prospectors, Analyzers, Reactors)[1] at least five schemes deserve mention here. Notable contributions toward development of a conceptual framework of "generic" business strategies have been made in recent years by Derek Abell[2] and Michael Porter.[3] Most recently, however, authors have been judging the widely espoused framework of Michael Porter (cost leadership, differentiation, and focus strategies) to be deficient in important areas, and have proposed improvements. Improved frameworks have been proposed by Chrisman, Hofer, and Boulton,[4] Hofer[5] again, and Henry Mintzberg.[6] The approach

---

[1]R. E. Miles and C. C. Snow, *Organizational Strategy, Structure, and Process* (New York: McGraw-Hill, 1978), p. 29.

[2]Derek F. Abell, *Defining the Business: The Starting Point of Strategic Planning* (Englewood Cliffs, N.J.: Prentice-Hall, 1980).

[3]Michael E. Porter, *Competitive Advantage: Creating and Sustaining Superior Performance* (New York: Free Press, 1985).

[4]J. J. Chrisman, Charles W. Hofer, and W. R. Boulton, "Toward a System for Classifying Business Strategies," *The Academy of Management Review* 13, no. 3 (July 1988), p. 413.

[5]Charles W. Hofer, *Generic Business Strategies: Some Typological Considerations,* paper presented at Midwest Decision Sciences Institute Meeting, April 1988.

[6]Henry Mintzberg, "Generic Strategies: Toward a Comprehensive Framework," in *Advances in Strategic Management,* ed. Robert Lamb and Paul Shrivastava, vol. 5 (Greenwich, Conn.: JAI Press, 1988), pp. 1–68.

in this chapter was to consider the arguments behind each of the frameworks and to rationalize and incorporate the strongest points of each.

PROFILE

Motorola, Inc.

Motorola is a U.S. electronics and semiconductor company involved in a competitive struggle with the Japanese. The company has recently made several acquisitions and management changes designed to give it a strategically interrelated, yet reasonably diversified corporate portfolio. Until the mid-1970s, the company was "simply reacting to the ideas that the operating guys had. Now we're strategizing. We're thinking about where we want the company to go," says Keith Bane, vice president and director of corporate strategy.

Motorola has developed a "library" of formal strategies, one for each of its more than 40 businesses. The firm uses five-year and one-year plans, with monthly operating reports to let headquarters know whether a division is straying from its plan. Each business also develops a "technology road map" to forecast technologies that will be needed for the next two generations of products.

In 1982, Motorola was the top U.S. producer of the 64K RAM computer memory chip, and today is one of the leaders in the latest technology, the 32-bit 68040 chip. The company's current goal is to succeed in the information-processing business, capitalizing on its unique combination of communications, data processing, software, and silicon foundry. Motorola's stated challenge is to manage that uniqueness into a leadership position.[7]

PROFILE

Goodyear Tire & Rubber Co.

In August 1978, Goodyear announced plans to build a $75 million tire technical center in Akron, Ohio, as part of a $374 million program begun in 1972 to increase its market share and profitability in the U.S. tire industry. This was at a time when Goodyear's competitors were diversifying away from the tire business, the result of five consecutive years of slow growth and poor profits.

Goodyear saw the opportunity to grow by picking up market share from competitors who were retrenching and diversifying out of the industry. By investing in new plants and modern technology, Goodyear hoped to lower its costs and increase its profits, reversing the reasons the competitors were leaving. This contrarian, preemptive action probably hastened the departure of some competitors, making the Goodyear strategy somewhat of a self-fulfilling prophecy and increasing its share of (and influence over) the tire market.[8]

---

[7]"Motorola's New Strategy," *Business Week*, March 29, 1982, p. 128.

[8]"Goodyear's Solo Strategy," *Business Week*, August 28, 1978, p. 67.

As the example shows, growth and retrenchment strategies can be followed by competitors in the same market at the same time. The success of a strategy depends not only on what your firm does, but on what the competition does, as well. Had major competitors—such as Uniroyal, Firestone, or Michelin—attempted a strategy similar to Goodyear's, the results could have been unfortunate for all involved.

POSITIONING THE BUSINESS

The initial business-level strategic question involves *position;* where should the business be positioned in the industry chain or stream. That is, where should its "center of gravity" be located in the industry chain from raw materials to primary manufacturer to fabricator to assembler to wholesaler/distributor to retailer? Should its primary focus be "upstream," "midstream," or "downstream" in the chain? Upstream (or primary) industries tend to be capital intensive, process oriented, standardization focused, and efficiency oriented. Further downstream, businesses tend to be more people intensive, concerned with product innovation, interested in segmentation, customization, and differentiation, and in search of marketing pull. Therefore, the decision as to where to position the business can strongly influence—even dictate—the strategies to be employed in distinguishing the business.[9]

DISTINGUISHING THE BUSINESS

Porter's Generic Strategies

Porter defines three business-level generic strategies: cost leadership, differentiation, and focus (or scope).[10] In Porter's framework, *cost leadership* strategies are where the business attempts to achieve and maintain a competitive advantage through lower unit costs of production and distribution. This advantage enables the business to either sell at a lower cost or make a greater profit than the competition. This is the type of strategy that Henry Ford employed to gain dominance in the automobile market during the 20s.

Competitors in commodity businesses (where the products or services are essentially the same and differentiation is on the basis of price) *must* strive to be low-cost producers. An example is Iowa Beef Processors, whose key corporate value—appropriately—is to be *the* lowest-cost producer. In addition, the business must be a low-cost producer in the total relevant market, which may be global. This may mean closing high-cost plants and opening others that are lower

---

[9]Mintzberg, "Generic Strategies," pp. 6–12.
[10]Michael E. Porter, *Competitive Strategy* (New York: Free Press, 1980), p. 35.

cost owing to either automation or location in areas where labor and distribution costs are low (e.g., in the South or in foreign countries).

Product or service differentiation strategies attempt to achieve competitive advantage by providing features that set your product or service apart from the competition. If a low-cost position is not possible, uniqueness—perceived or real value that causes customers to pay more—is essential. General Motors, under the leadership of Alfred P. Sloan, used differentiation strategies to build its market position during the 30s. Differentiation can be based on the product, service, quality, cost control, financing, or whatever. Examples of differentiated products are designer jeans, Izod sportswear, Corona beer, and Cabbage Patch dolls. Braniff tried to differentiate itself by painting its planes bright colors; unfortunately for them, this uniqueness was not enough to overcome an overly ambitious expansion program which forced the company into Chapter 11 bankruptcy.[11]

Today, many successful businesses differentiate themselves from the pack by offering premium quality and superior service. One such business—Sewell Village Cadillac in Dallas—realizes that the service department is critically important in keeping customers satisfied, as well as in repeat business. In fact, they give customers biographical sketches of their mechanics (who averaged $80,000 a year in 1986) as well as their *home* phone numbers.[12]

Honda Motors ranks fourth in auto sales in the United States, but it ranks only third in Japan, behind Toyota and Nissan. In order to improve its position in its home market, Honda is attempting to differentiate its products from those of its two larger competitors. Honda's marketing surveys showed that young, urban Japanese customers—particularly women—wanted something unique. So, Honda is exporting Ohio-made Hondas to Japan, with two differentiating features: left-hand drive (versus Japan's standard right-hand drive); and three medallions reading "Honda of America Manufacturing, Inc. Import Edition." Plus, the cars can now be manufactured more cheaply in the United States than in Japan.[13]

Porter also discusses *focus* strategies, which attempt to gain competitive advantage by narrowing the competitive scope of the business to specific segments. In line with his cost leadership and differentiation strategies, the business would either attempt to employ a cost focus or differentiation focus within the targeted segment of the market.

Porter holds that a business should strive for either a strong cost-leadership position or a strong differentiation position. He holds that a strong position in either is necessary to create a competitive advantage, and is superior to a moderate position in each (being "stuck in the middle"), because doing so offers

---

[11]Michael Kami, *Strategic Planning for Changing Times* (Dayton, Ohio: Cassette Recording Co., 1984).

[12]Steve Jordon, "Author: Endless Service Is the Means to Success," *Omaha World-Herald,* November 18, 1987, p. 58.

[13]Robert T. Grieves, "Made in America," *Forbes,* April 18, 1988, p. 98.

FIGURE 6.1   Generic Business Strategies and ROI

Differentiation Position

		Low	High
Cost Position	*Low*	Pure cost strategy (ROI = 28.6%)	Cost and differentiation strategies (ROI = 30.2%)
	High	No competitive advantage (ROI = 4.9%)	Pure differentiation strategy (ROI = 22.1%)

no clear competitive advantage. Recent studies have evaluated the effectiveness of cost leadership and differentiation strategies, alone and in combination. As Figure 6.1 shows, four possible types of competitive advantage are possible, given high and low levels of cost and differentiation. As the figure also shows, a favorable position in both costs and differentiation tends to yield the highest return on investment, with the pure individual strategies yielding somewhat less favorable results. As might be expected, businesses with neither fared much less well.[14]

Strategies of Differentiation

Mintzberg, in evaluating Porter's framework, suggests that cost leadership is not really a competitive strategy, but is more a comparative advantage that makes a different strategy—*price differentiation*—possible. What attracts customers is the price, not the producer's cost position. Following this line of reasoning, Porter's cost leadership and differentiation strategies become one strategy—differentiation.[15]

Numerous examples of organizations attempting to distinguish themselves in the competitive marketplace exist. Maytag's investment in quality, resulting in products that last longer and need less service (thus, the lonely Maytag repairman) comes to mind. Upon closer examination, seven strategies of differentiation exist.

---

[14]R. E. White, "Generic Business Strategies, Organizational Context and Performance: An Empirical Investigation," *Strategic Management Journal* 7, no. 3 (May–June 1986), pp. 217–31.

[15]Mintzberg, "Generic Strategies," p. 14.

Price Differentiation.   The most basic way to differentiate a product or service is to charge less for it than competitors do. This is often the major source of differentiation in commodity markets, where products are not differentiated in any other way.

Image Differentiation.   Sometimes, differentiation can be created in the mind of the customer, even if no real basis for differentiation exists. Marketing and advertising attempt to create images of products to cause customers to want to buy those products. A few years ago, Smirnoff vodka raised its prices, enhancing its image as a premium product. The mystique behind Coors beer, Corona beer, and Chivas Regal scotch involves image differentiation, as does the branding of oranges as Sunkist and bananas as Chiquita. Cosmetic features and packaging, as well as many other real and perceived differences can contribute to a product's image—both negatively and positively.

Support Differentiation.   This type of differentiation attempts to set the product or service apart by offering something in addition to the basic purchase. That may be selling related (credit, delivery, free assembly), service related (free return policy, extended warranties, free repair), or inclusion of a complementary product or service (free lessons, a users' association, and the like).

Design Differentiation.   Here we refer to "true" differentiation—the product or service is different from competitors by design. The differences can be minor or cosmetic (as designer jeans) or major (e.g., instant cameras).

Quality Differentiation.   Quality variations have to do with features of the product that make it "better"; no different by design, but better. Thus, the product can be essentially the same as competing products, but may possess greater reliability, durability, and/or superior performance.

Undifferentiated Products.   The lack of differentiation is also a strategy, whether by choice or circumstance. Commodity products are by definition undifferentiated, as are "generic" products, medicines, and the like. The "copycat" strategy falls into this category, even though many businesses try to differentiate themselves in other ways, even in commodity markets.

Functional Differentiation.   Lastly, it is worth mentioning that differentiation strategies are often related to functional-level strategies. For example, price, image, support, design, and quality differentiation strategies are all rooted in some functional area. The source of these differences usually emanates from strategies in design, processing, sourcing, delivery, or support areas of the business. Supporting functional strategies are discussed further later in this chapter.[16]

---

[16]Ibid., pp. 17–21.

Strategies of Scope

Strategies of differentiation identify what is distinct about a business's products and services in the marketplace. The orientation is toward the product and adopts the perspective of the customer, since differentiation has to be perceived by the customer to have any effect. Another set of strategies adopt the perspective of the producer, focusing on the served market. These latter strategies—strategies of scope—identify the markets the business is pursuing, as perceived by management. Scope—or focus, in Porter's terminology—pertains to market definition; how the business perceives its markets. Scope is related to market segmentation (in reality, segmentation is one aspect of the scope strategy of a business). As part of scope, segmentation refers to the business's approach to its markets; how it targets its various *types* of products to its markets. Differentiation, on the other hand, refers to distinctive product *characteristics*.[17]

Unsegmented Strategy.   In the unsegmented approach, the business views the market as one large segment; a mass market of basically homogeneous buyers buying the same product. Typical of this approach would be general products, promoted by general advertising, and sold through mass merchandisers. An example is the brewing industry, particularly before the changes introduced by Philip Morris via their Miller division. The trend today is clearly away from unsegmented market strategies.

In recent years, U.S. markets have been undergoing a trend to extremes, or polarization. We see full service versus no service, top-of-the-line versus discount products, global versus local markets, and the like. Targeting one's products at the middle or average may miss both extremes, as Sears found out several years ago. The retailer was squeezed from above and below, with little distinctive competence or clear image.

Segmentation Strategy.   In reality, segmentation is a continuous variable ranging—on the one hand—from very little segmentation (essentially unsegmented markets) to almost complete segmentation (customized products). Whatever the degree of segmentation, a business can choose to be *comprehensive,* attempting to serve all segments, or *selective,* carefully targeting only certain segments. Department stores are an example of the comprehensive approach, offering a complete line of products, grouped by department. Another example is General Motors in automobiles, offering a product in every price range, size, and category. Companies pursuing selective segmentation would include Deere & Co. in tractors, targeting the large equipment market. Mercedes-Benz and BMW would be other examples, concentrating only on certain segments of the market.

---

[17]Ibid., p. 25.

In deciding on a segment or segments of the market to target, it is important that the firm focus on the correct segments. For example, MIT's David Birch points out that most of the growth in our economy is coming from small companies; but not *all* small companies are growing. His research has shown that 83 percent of the growth in new jobs, for example, has come from just 5 percent of companies—the fastest growing 5 percent. Also, 88 percent of these fastest growing companies employed fewer than 100 people when he began his study. What does this mean? Historically, many suppliers have focused their marketing and selling efforts on large companies, because they are easiest to identify and contact. However, growth will come by focusing sales efforts on rapidly growing small companies.[18]

Niche Strategies.   Businesses that focus only on a single segment of the market are pursuing specialization or *niche* strategies. Porter's focus strategy is in one sense a niche strategy. An organization can specialize in a variety of ways—by product type, by type of customer or channel, by geographical area, or by function (such as oil exploration).[19] In general, then, a niche is a relatively small segment of a market, such as luxury automobiles, sports cars, generic products, no-frills airlines, limited geographical areas, and the like. Wal-Mart discount stores and ValCom computer stores pursue market niches, in that they both focus on relatively small communities. George Mason University concentrates on two academic niches—conservative economics and information technology—and one athletic niche—basketball.[20]

A business should try either to be big, or focus on niches in the market. If the latter, the firm should always try to dominate the niche, whatever it is. However, a niche doesn't last forever; if the niche is growing, it will attract big competitors with superior resources, as Apple learned when IBM entered the PC market. It may be advisable for a firm to sell out if its niche or niches are growing too large.[21]

Guerrilla Warfare Strategies.   In one light, niche strategies—pursuing a segment of the market small enough to defend—are the business equivalent of guerrilla warfare. Guerrilla warfare is often the only effective strategy for small, counterinsurgency movements. This approach is also appropriate for small, aggressive businesses that do not have the resources to slug it out head to head with the large competitors. The guerrilla's defensible niche could be geographic, or exceptional service, or some other aspect that a larger company may find difficult—or uneconomical—to attack. According to Columbia's Kathryn Harrigan, Rolls-Royce pursues a guerrilla/niche strategy in dominating the ultraluxury segment of the auto market.

---

[18] David L. Birch, ''The Booming Hidden Market,'' *Inc.,* October 1987, p. 15.

[19]Mintzberg, ''Generic Strategies,'' p. 29.

[20]Kae H. Chung, *Management: Critical Success Factors* (Boston: Allyn and Bacon, 1987), p. 202.

[21]Kami, *Strategic Planning.*

For guerrilla strategies to be successful, several precepts are important:

1. *Choose a defensible guerrilla base.* Choose specialized marketplaces, ignored customers, offer customized, differentiated products, excellent service, and the like—all in areas that larger competitors are not likely to offer.
2. *Keep the base secure.* Focus on a limited span of activities geared to your base.
3. *Divert the enemy from your base.* Distract competitors with diversionary tactics, secondary product lines, and the like.
4. *Surprise the enemy.* Fall back, retreat, then turn and fight when competitors least expect it.
5. *Outwit the enemy.* Analyze market changes and move to capture new segments or niches before competitors realize that changes are taking place.
6. *Control information.* Again, use smokescreens, rumors, and disinformation to distract and confuse competitors.
7. *Build and sustain a strong corporate culture.* Take pains to maintain and reinforce your corporate values, which are different from those of your large competitors.[22]

Customizing Strategies.   Finally, a business can pursue the ultimate in segmentation; products or services oriented to a single customer. In effect, each customer represents a unique market segment. Again, degrees of customization exist in actuality, ranging from pure customization through tailored customization to standardized customization. Examples of pure customization would be the architecturally designed house and any special project.

In tailored customization, a basic design is adapted to meet a customer's needs or specifications, such as a tailored suit or the typical custom-built house. In standardized customization, individualized end products are assembled from standard components. Thus, the product is customized, but from a limited set of choices or options.[23] Examples would include ordering a hamburger at Wendy's to selecting carpeting, fixtures, and wall covering for the typical tract house.

Functional Strategies

As was stated earlier, the bulk of the sources for product or service differentiation are functional in nature. That is, differentiation by price, image, support, design, and quality are each based on one of the functional strategy areas, as shown in Figure 6.2.

---

[22]Kathryn R. Harrigan, "Guerrilla Strategies for Underdog Competitors," *Planning Review* 14, no. 6 (November 1986) pp. 4–12.
[23]Mintzberg, "Generic Strategies," pp. 30–31.

FIGURE 6.2   Functional Strategy Areas

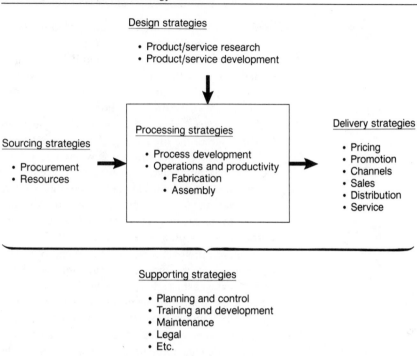

Design strategies

- Product/service research
- Product/service development

Sourcing strategies

- Procurement
- Resources

Processing strategies

- Process development
- Operations and productivity
  - Fabrication
  - Assembly

Delivery strategies

- Pricing
- Promotion
- Channels
- Sales
- Distribution
- Service

Supporting strategies

- Planning and control
- Training and development
- Maintenance
- Legal
- Etc.

Source: Adapted from Henry Mintzberg, ''Generic Strategies: Toward a Comprehensive Framework,'' in *Advances in Strategic Management,* ed. Robert Lamb and Paul Shrivastava, vol. 5 (Greenwich, Conn.: JAI Press, 1988), p. 13.

One of the important aspects of business-level strategy involves determining the proper integration of functional-level strategies (product design, manufacturing, marketing, and finance, in particular) for the business. With the exception of product design and development—or innovation—functional strategies are treated in other courses in the business school curriculum. As Richard Cyert, president of Carnegie-Mellon University has observed, business schools do not do an adequate job of educating MBAs about new technology and its management. They are led to think that ''the key to management is finance and marketing, when in fact it is new technology. Managers don't have the background to make decisions'' in this vital area.[24] The management of technology involves planning and strategies concerning entrepreneurship, research, technology development, invention, and innovation.

---

[24]''U.S. Business Schools Criticized for Failing to Educate MBAs about New Technology,'' *The Chronical of Higher Education,* June 24, 1987, p. 16.

Technology Strategies.   A firm can employ four broad strategies with regard to technology, according to Maidique and Patch:[25]

1. *First to market*. This offensive strategy attempts to get the product to market before the competition does, creating a temporary monopoly. A strong commitment to applied research and development is required. Users of this strategy are Cray Research (in large computers) and Apple (in microcomputers). A major risk with this strategy is that there may not be a market for the product, as was the case with Polaroid's instant movie camera.

2. *Second to market*. The "fast-follower" strategy involves entry in the early growth stage of the life cycle and quick imitations of innovations developed by a competitor. This strategy may involve lower R&D expenditures, but requires flexibility and responsiveness. Zenith (versus RCA) and Japan (versus the United States) have used this strategy, as has IBM in both mainframes and microcomputers. This somewhat more defensive strategy lets the first-to-market pioneers test the market and perhaps develop it to the point warranting entry on a larger scale.

3. *Cost minimization*. This late-to-market approach involves market entry in the later growth stages and attempts to avoid development costs and to exploit cost advantages through economies of scale, joint product lines, and process efficiencies. U.S. manufacturers of small cars have taken this approach, as did Wendy's in fast-food restaurants (versus McDonald's and Burger King).

4. *Market segmentation*. This specialized strategy attempts to serve niches or pockets of demand through special applications of the basic technology. Entry can occur in almost any stage of the life cycle, and is often practiced by smaller, lower-volume producers.

These technology strategies and their primary functional requirements are shown in Table 6.1.

STRATEGIES FOR INCREASING SCOPE

The third business-level strategy area deals with strategies for increasing the scope of the business; ways to develop and extend the core mission of the business. A core business can be elaborated in a number of ways, as shown in Figure 6.3. The organization can choose to expand with existing products in existing markets through *penetration* strategies, or in new markets via *market development* strategies. It can also choose to introduce new products in existing markets via *product development* strategies, or in new markets through *diversification*. Diversification strategies are beyond the scope of a single business unit,

---

[25]M. A. Maidique and Peter Patch, *Corporate Strategy and Technological Policy*, Case No. 9–679–033. (Boston: Harvard Business School, 1978, revised 1980).

TABLE 6.1 Technology Strategy and Functional Policy

Technology Strategy	Policy Requirements						
	R&D	Manufacturing	Marketing	Finance	Organization	Timing
First to market	Requires state of the art R&D	Emphasis on pilot and medium-scale manufacturing	Emphasis on stimulating primary demand	Requires access to risk capital	Emphasis on flexibility over efficiency; encourage risk taking	Early—entry inaugurates the product life cycle
Second to market	Requires flexible, responsive and advanced R&D capability	Requires agility in setting up manufacturing, medium scale	Must differentiate the product; stimulate secondary demand	Requires rapid commitment of medium to large quantities of capital	Combine elements of flexibility and efficiency	Entry early in growth stage
Cost minimization late to market	Requires skill in process development and cost-effective product	Requires efficiency and automation for large-scale production	Must minimize selling and distribution costs	Requires access to capital in large amounts	Emphasis on efficiency and hierarchical control; procedures rigidly enforced	Entry during late growth or early maturity
Market segmentation	Requires ability in applications, custom engineering, and advanced product design	Requires flexibility on short to medium runs	Must identify and reach favorable segments	Requires access to capital in medium or large amounts	Flexibility and control required in serving different customers' requirements	Entry during growth stage or later

Source: Adapted from Modesto Maidique and Peter Patch, *Corporate Strategy and Technological Policy*, Case No. 9–679–033. Boston: Harvard Business School, 1978, p. 24. Reprinted by permission.

FIGURE 6.3   Strategies for Increasing Scope

	Existing Products	*New Products*
Existing Markets	Penetration strategies	Product development strategies
New Markets	Market development strategies	Diversification strategies

Source: Adapted from H. Igor Ansoff, *Corporate Strategy* (New York: McGraw-Hill, 1965) p. 109.

and will be discussed as part of multibusiness strategies in Chapter 7. We do, however, treat an important type of market development strategy—geographical expansion (particularly international expansion)—separately in this chapter because of its unique aspects.

Penetration Strategies

Penetration strategies involve attempts to achieve a greater share of existing product sales in existing markets. This can be done by expansion, in essence taking share from existing competitors, or by taking over or acquiring all or part of a competing business. A firm must be careful not to merely attempt to "buy market share," because the real source of *profitable* growth in market share is sustainable competitive advantage—not just expansion.

Growth is a prime goal for most firms and businesses. Many compensation plans reward managers not only for profits but also for growth and increases in market share. But the product life-cycle curve shows that it is relatively easy to grow during the "growth" stage (although increasing market share may not be as easy), and that growth *and* share increases are much more difficult to achieve in the maturity and decline stages. However, growth can be *managed* by portfolio decisions at the corporate level: start up or acquire growth businesses and divest declining businesses. At the business-unit level, that luxury does not exist. Growth and share building must occur *within* a given business and industry. What opportunities for growth and share building exist in the various life-cycle stages?

Share-building strategies are intended to strengthen the competitive position of the business. But such changes require heavy investment—investments far above those made by the typical firm in the industry. Therefore, access to capital (internally or from outside) is typically required. In addition, certain life-cycle stages are more likely to result in significant changes in share than are others. For example, the shakeout stage typically reduces the number of competitors, as does the decline stage, allowing others to pick up share. Also, different factors are more important in determining competitive strength in different stages. Early stages reward product design, quality, positioning, and availability; shakeout and later stages reward segmentation, service, pricing, and distribution. Thus, in the absence of merger-induced growth in share, the firm needs major advantages over competition to increase share, unless a competitor makes a strategic error.

Growth strategies, in turn, do not necessarily attempt significant gains in share, but try to enable the business to grow at least as fast as the market is growing—especially in the market's growth stage. Such strategies also require adequate resources to match market growth (and provide a defense against potential shakeout), as well as other weapons to continue growth in the latter stages of the market life cycle.

Managed Growth. Growth must be managed—a firm must have a strategy specifying *how rapidly* it plans to grow. Unmanaged growth can destroy a firm just as wildly growing cancer cells can destroy the body. A company must consolidate its gains to support future growth, just as the stock market needs to "back and fill" from time to time, even in a bull market. The question of how fast a business or company should grow depends on whether future profitability (such as return on equity—ROE) is greater or less than the cost of capital required to support the growth. If ROE can be expected to exceed the cost of capital, the more growth the business can achieve, the better. If, on the other hand, ROE is likely to be less than the cost of capital, financing additional growth does not make sense; it costs more than it returns. If a business in this position cannot sufficiently improve its profitability, it should reduce its size (perhaps by divesting low-profit businesses).[26]

Assuming that the business recognizes its long-term versus short-term growth potential, what are some specific approaches that can contribute to growth and share building in its markets? Research by Buzzell and Wiersema has shown that gains in market share are associated with improvements in product quality, new-product introductions, and marketing budget increases, but price reductions *seldom* are used as a means for building share. Further, businesses with "high" market shares tend to lose share over time, while those with "low" share tend to gain.[27]

Grow through Franchising. Innovative companies, as they review their competitive position, may find themselves the worried owners of businesses with low market share. As they consider the strategies suggested to improve the situation, they are faced with the knowledge that to make a substantial change in their position as a follower in a high-growth industry, they must consider the

---

[26]W. E. Fruhan, Jr., "How Fast Should Your Company Grow?" *Harvard Business Review* 62, no. 1 (January–February 1984), p. 84.

[27]R. D. Buzzell and R. D. Wiersema, "Successful Share-Building Strategies," *Harvard Business Review* 59, no. 1 (January–February 1981). p. 135.

dilemma of increasing market share while satisfying resource constraints. For firms requiring widespread outlets and convenient availability of service and production, one viable option is to create a franchise system. Franchising offers a company access to capital investment at little risk, as well as offering cost sharing, economies of scale due to increased size, motivated management, and widespread brand identification. The successful franchisor can then remain strictly in franchising, buy up the franchises as they become available to develop a wholly owned chain of company stores, or practice a combination strategy.[28]

Product Development Strategies

Unlike penetration strategies, product development strategies attempt to increase the scope of the business by bringing out new products within existing markets. One way of doing this is through a *product extension* strategy, which consists of offering new or modified products in the same basic business. Another approach is to engage in *product line proliferation*—virtually complete coverage of a given line of products. Again, this approach is related to market segmentation, intending to end up with comprehensive product segmentation (as with General Motors in automobiles). A variation of this strategy involves product line fortification, or attempts to fill voids in existing product lines, in effect preempting competitors' moves to do so.[29]

Preemptive/Strategies.   A preemptive strategy is one that attempts to disrupt the "normal" course of industry events and in the process change the rules—to create new industry conditions to the disadvantage of the competition. It is defined as "a major move by a focal business, ahead of moves by its adversaries, that allows it to secure an advantageous position from which it will be difficult to dislodge because of the advantages it has captured by being the first mover."[30]

An example of a preemptive move was Goodyear's decision to expand its capacity ahead of industry demand, hoping to gain market share by discouraging competitors from expanding. Another example of a preemptive move was Philip Morris' decision to segment the beer market and apply its advanced marketing skills to this formerly tradition-bound industry with its Miller brand. In the process, it changed the industry, forcing the industry to play by a new set of rules. With airline deregulation, the opportunity existed for new competitors to enter with new ways of operating. Early entrants, such as America West, and Midway, and expansion by others, preempted such moves by existing or potential competitors. Other examples involve introducing products before the

---

[28]Pat Feltes and L. A. Digman, "Franchising as a Share Building Strategy," *Proceedings of Midwest American Institute for Decision Sciences Meeting,* April 1986.

[29]Mintzberg, "Generic Strategies," pp. 37–38.

[30]Ian C. MacMillan, "Preemptive Strategies," in *Handbook of Business Strategy,* ed. W. D. Guth (Boston: Warren, Gorham & Lamont, 1985), p. 9–2.

competition, gaining early acceptance by customers, and perhaps even temporary monopolies. Polaroid, Frigidaire, Xerox, Hoover, and Kleenex were so
successful at this that their brand names became synonymous with the product.

Preemptive Opportunities and Characteristics.   There are several characteristics of preemptive strategies to keep in mind. First, they entail a degree of risk,
as in game theory, since the strategist is making assumptions, which may not be
correct, about the resulting behavior of competitors. Second, preemptive moves
need not affect *all* competitors or their actions, only the major ones—enough to
make a significant difference. Third, the results of preemptive moves are not
permanent, and competitors will eventually respond. A good example of this is
the brewing industry, where Anheuser-Busch changed its tactics in response to
Miller's marketing strategies, and came back a much stronger competitor.[31]

Actually, preemptive strategies are not confined to direct moves against the
competition. Opportunities exist along the entire product chain from raw material
supply sources to distribution and service after the sale, as shown in Table 6.2.
In addition, opportunities for preemption occur at all stages of the life cycle,
from preintroduction to decline.[32]

Preemptive Bankruptcy.   A heretofore unsuspected preemptive strategy sur-
faced in the early 1980s—bankruptcy. The increased competition due to airline
deregulation was causing Continental Airlines severe profit problems. Continental was coming out third best in its battle with United and Frontier at its Denver
hub. Frank Lorenzo, CEO of Texas Air (Continental's parent), decided that the
company had no choice but to become a discount carrier, hoping to develop a
new distinctive competence. However, the company was locked into long-term,
high-cost labor agreements with its unions. Lorenzo took the high-risk action of
declaring chapter 11 bankruptcy, briefly shutting down, and starting up as a
nonunion carrier with much lower pay scales. The move worked and was upheld
in the courts; the airline was soon profitable, with Frontier's survival at stake.

Johns Manville filed for bankruptcy when it faced $2 billion in litigation over
claims of asbestos-related illnesses, but had only $1.7 billion in net assets.
Manville was not trying to duck its liabilities, but to keep afloat.

Given that it has been upheld in the courts, it is possible that the bankruptcy
strategy may be tried by more firms.[33]

Contrarian Preemptive Strategies.   The best time to expand may be when
the market is *temporarily* in decline, as long as the competition is cutting back.
For example, recession may be the best time for businesses to pick up market
share. During recessions, firms, particularly weaker competitors, often cut back.
A recent study showed that the average surviving industrial business picks up
0.63 percent of share in recessions, and loses 0.10 percent during expansionary
times (when new competitors arrive and competition expands, as well).

---

[31]Ibid.

[32]Ibid., p. 9–18.

[33]Marcia Bishop, "Bankruptcy as a Business Strategy: The Manville Experience," *Planning
Review* 13, no. 2 (March 1985), p. 12.

TABLE 6.2 Sources of Preemptive Opportunities

Supply Systems
1. Secure access to raw materials or components.
2. Preempting production equipment.
3. Dominating supply logistics.

Product
1. Introducing new product lines.
2. Developing dominant design.
3. Positioning.
4. Securing accelerated approval from agencies.
5. Securing product development and delivery skills.
6. Expanding scope of the product.

Production Systems
1. Proprietary processes.
2. Aggressive capacity expansion.
3. Vertical integration with key suppliers.
4. Securing scarce and critical production skills.

Customers
1. Segmentation.
2. Building early brand awareness.
3. Training customers in usage skills.
4. Capturing key accounts.

Distribution and Service Systems
1. Occupation of prime locations.
2. Preferential access to key distributors.
3. Dominance of distribution logistics.
4. Access to superior service capabilities.
5. Development of distributor skills.

Source: Ian C. MacMillan, "Preemptive Strategies," in *Handbook of Business Strategy,* ed. W. D. Guth (Boston: Warren, Gorham & Lamont, 1985), p. 9–9. Reprinted with permission. All rights reserved.

Significant share gainers during recessions were those firms that *increased* their advertising by 28 percent or more, which resulted in a 1.5 percent increase in share. Big increases in advertising in normal or fast-growth periods, however, yielded only a 0.2 percent increase in share.[34]

Market Development Strategies

Market development strategies are attempts to promote existing products in new markets, in effect broadening the scope of the business by finding new market

---

[34]"Marketing . . . When to Gain Market Share," *The Wall Street Journal,* July 8, 1982, p. 17.

segments or new channels.[35] An example might be a manufacturer of brand name products agreeing to produce store-brand products. One particularly successful market development strategy is to enter "emerging" markets or industries.

Emerging industries are either newly formed *or* are industries reformed, as a result of technological change, changes in consumer needs, changes in cost structures, or similar factors. As Intel's Robert Noyce stated, get into unpopulated or underpopulated industries and markets if you want to grow.[36] One way (perhaps the most obvious way) to do this is to enter the market earlier than do competing firms, ideally in the embryonic or early growth stage.

Another way is through segmentation or reformulation. Most of the businesses achieving major gains in market share do so by focusing their efforts on selected segments—often segments that were relatively small at first. Philip Morris offers two examples: Merit cigarettes and Lite beer. Merit concentrated on a high-growth segment of a declining industry, and brought with it high growth. Lite beer did the same. In fact, one might conclude that such segments actually are new subindustries with their own life cycles. Creating or discovering such a segment enables the business to avoid often self-defeating attempts to gain share and growth in the perhaps mature or declining broader market. Other examples include Honda motorcycles, compact cars, fast-food restaurants, and other niches or segments that follow the characteristics of emerging markets and may be early in their life cycles.

First-Mover Strategies.   Businesses that enter markets early (pioneers, or "first-movers") tend to outperform later entrants.[37] First-mover advantages tend to arise from three primary sources:

1. *Technological leadership*. If they are able to build a favorable position on the experience curve and/or through patent or R&D success, the firm may be able to gain advantage through sustainable leadership in technology.
2. *Preemption of assets*. If the first-mover firm can preempt rivals in the acquisition of scarce assets (e.g., purchasing input factors at temporarily low prices, acquisition of desirable geographical and market segment locations, and preemptive investment in plant and equipment), it may gain advantage.
3. *Buyer switching costs*. Later entrants must invest extra resources to attract customers from the first-mover firm, and buyers often tend to stick with the first supplier that meets their needs satisfactorily.[38]

---

[35]Mintzberg, "Generic Strategies," p. 35.

[36]"Intel: The Microprocessor Champ Gambles on Another Leap Forward," *Business Week,* April 18, 1980, p. 92.

[37]Mary Lambkin, "Order of Entry and Performance in New Markets," *Strategic Management Journal* 9, special issue (Summer 1988), p. 127.

[38]M. B. Lieberman and D. B. Montgomery, "First Mover Advantages," *Strategic Management Journal* 9, special issue (Summer 1988), p. 41.

Other studies also confirm the above findings, that pioneers tend to have substantially larger market shares, even after a market has matured. Therefore, late entrants should recognize that the odds are against their receiving a large market share, and a niche strategy should be given serious consideration. Pioneers should continue to defend their position against late entrants through product-line extensions.[39]

Geographical Expansion Strategies

Geographical expansion is actually a form of market development which takes an existing product line to new geographical areas. Growth can come through geographic expansion—international or domestic. Philip Morris, Coca-Cola, and Pepsi achieved significant growth by expanding into countries where demand for their products was not as saturated as it was in the domestic market. Overseas, these firms were early in the market life cycle. The geographical growth strategies employed domestically by the makers of J&B and Cutty Sark scotches provide an interesting contrast. Cutty Sark went nationwide early and became the top-selling brand. J&B's parent, Paddington Corp., having fewer resources, meanwhile followed a different method—an "enclave" approach. Just as an army establishes a beachhead and branches out from there, J&B first concentrated on the New York market. In a short time, J&B—through intensive marketing—became the number 1 seller in New York with 40 percent of the market. Next, it concentrated on Chicago, then on the West Coast. In time, J&B, with its intensive, concentrated approach, overtook Cutty Sark, market area by market area. A similar approach was employed successfully by Vlasic Pickles. For firms not hampered by limited capacity or resources, the reverse approach may be best, as the Japanese have shown by entering domestic and foreign markets simultaneously.

International Strategies.   As companies grow, more and more wind up competing in foreign markets. When domestic markets become more mature and/or saturated, expansion into foreign markets offers the firm the opportunity to continue its growth. In addition, some foreign markets may be at an earlier stage of the life cycle for a given product than is the case in advanced industrial areas, such as the United States, Canada, Japan, or Western Europe.

International business is different from domestic business in several important ways. It involves operating effectively within different national sovereignties, under disparate economic systems and conditions, within different value systems, and across great distances. The implications of these differences for

---

[39]W. T. Robinson and Claes Fornell, *Market Pioneering and Sustainable Market Share Advantages,* PIMS Letter No. 39 (Cambridge, Mass.: Strategic Planning Institute, 1986), pp. 3–6.

management are numerous. Different nations have different political, legal, monetary, and social systems. Each legal system, for example, involves a unique set of rights and obligations concerning property, taxation, regulation, contracts, and ownership. These differences often require new forms of organization, new management skills, and different accounting and control systems. The firm that choses to compete internationally is taking a big step; in many ways it may be easier to enter an additional domestic business than to expand internationally.

Forms of International Business.   From an organizational perspective, there are a number of ways of conducting international business. As shown in Figure 6.4, the degree of parent company control increases as one goes from licensing agreements to branch operations to joint ventures to subsidiary operations. In

FIGURE 6.4   Basic Organizational Forms for Multinational Operations

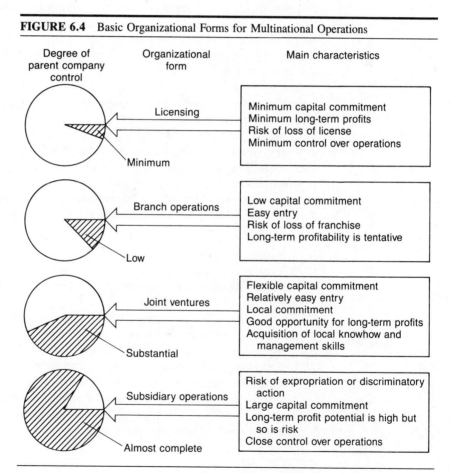

Source: J. G. Hutchinson, *Management Strategy and Tactics* (New York: Holt, Rinehart & Winston, 1971), p. 508.

addition to increasing control, the amount of required capital, risk, and profit potential also increases.

Licensing grants a foreign firm the right to handle specified products in the country. Most companies begin foreign sales, however, by establishing a branch office in the foreign market. With this approach, sales offices and warehouses must be established, but manufacturing is performed elsewhere. Sometimes, a joint venture with a foreign firm (or a consortium with several firms) is used, enabling the companies to share investment, skills, and profits. The advantage of this method is that the distribution and marketing skills of the firm can be helpful in a foreign country, and these skills increase the likelihood of successful operations. Laws in some countries (such as Mexico) effectively *require* joint ventures. The most predominant method, however, is to form a wholly owned subsidiary incorporated under the laws of the host country. For example, Seagram Co. Ltd. of Canada operates a wholly owned subsidiary in the United States—Joseph E. Seagram & Sons. Sandoz, the large Swiss multinational pharmaceutical company, has subsidiaries in a number of countries, including Sandoz, Inc. (prescription drugs) and Dorsey Labs (over-the-counter drugs) in the United States.

Stages of "Internationalization."   Most businesses that operate in foreign countries evolve into international, multinational, or global operations over time. They tend to begin with low stakes in foreign operations, then develop a growing corporate dependence on foreign operations, and finally evolve into global corporate structure (as opposed to domestic plus international divisions). The three typical phases, including typical corporate viewpoints, organizational arrangements, and managerial emphasis for each are shown in Figure 6.5.

As reported by Robinson, "decisions by which a firm commits resources to a foreign market differ from comparable domestic decisions in several important respects:

1. They are more expensive in that more variables are involved. It is more difficult to apply familiar measures; special legal and financial and area skills are required; the amount of time-consuming communication and travel is greater.
2. They are less likely to be stimulated by an internal company market survey and more likely to be the result of external pressure on the firm.
3. They are more likely to be the result of selective analysis of market opportunities, rather than universal and comparative analysis.
4. They are less subject to quantitative analysis because a subjectively derived discount rate is applied to anticipated earnings; the rate may be someone's guess as to political risk (that is, continuity of relevant law: contract, tax, exchange control, labor, property)."[40]

---

[40]Richard Robinson, *International Business Management,* 2nd ed. (Hinsdale, Ill.: Dryden Press, 1978), p. 27.

FIGURE 6.5   Typical Phases in the Internationalization of Organizations

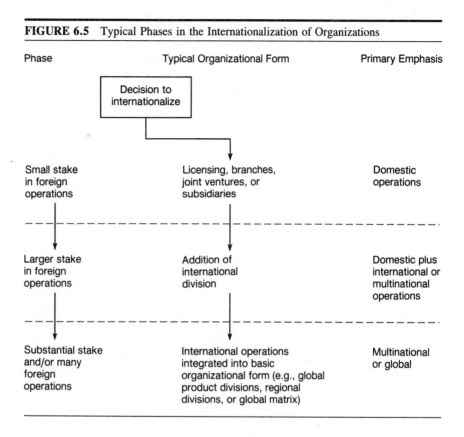

Phase	Typical Organizational Form	Primary Emphasis
	Decision to internationalize	
Small stake in foreign operations	Licensing, branches, joint ventures, or subsidiaries	Domestic operations
Larger stake in foreign operations	Addition of international division	Domestic plus international or multinational operations
Substantial stake and/or many foreign operations	International operations integrated into basic organizational form (e.g., global product divisions, regional divisions, or global matrix)	Multinational or global

Strategies and Alternatives.   The first strategic choice the firm must make is whether or not to compete internationally. If it decides to do so, the next concern is what type of international competition to pursue. Porter lists four alternatives:

1. *Protected niche.* The firm seeks out countries where government restrictions exclude global competitors by requiring local ownership or participation, high tariffs, and so on. The firm works out arrangements to allow it to compete selectively in such protected markets, perhaps through licensing or joint ventures.

2. *National focus.* The firm chooses to out-compete global firms by pursuing an approach focused on the unique needs of individual national markets, taking advantage of differences in national markets.

3. *Global focus.* The firm targets a particular segment of an industry in which to compete on a global basis. An example is Caterpillar in earth-moving equipment.

4. *Broad line global competition.* The firm competes worldwide in the full product line of the industry.[41]

Whatever approach the firm selects, it must realize that a number of substrategies must be developed, many of which will differ from the firm's domestic functional and product/market strategies. Robinson has outlined nine such substrategies, that fall into three areas: basic strategies (including sales, supply, and public affairs), input strategies (including labor, management, ownership, and financial), and structural strategies (legal and control).[42] The problem is to develop an interrelated and consistent set of substrategies. These should support the organization's overall international strategy and fit the environment's threats and opportunities, as well as the firm's strengths and weaknesses.

International Environmental Trends.   According to Porter, several trends are important for international competition:

1. *Reduction in differences among countries.* A narrowing of differences in income, factor and energy costs, marketing practices, and channels of distribution tend to reduce impediments to international competition.
2. *More aggressive industrial policies.* Governments such as those of Japan, West Germany, South Korea, Singapore, Taiwan, and Hong Kong follow very aggressive industrial policies that are likely to change international competition and heighten international rivalry.
3. *Protection of distinctive assets.* An obvious example is the OPEC cartel. Other examples are low-cost labor and other natural resources. As a result, it becomes more difficult for outside firms to "exploit" a country's strategic advantages.
4. *Freer flow of technology.* This makes it easier for other firms and countries to upgrade their products.
5. *Emergence of new, large-scale markets.* The opening up of China and Russia, and the advancement of newly developing countries such as India offer potentially huge future markets.
6. *Competition in newly developing countries.* As countries develop, they also become potential competitors.[43]

Assessing Foreign Risks.   Inherent in the above discussion was the suggestion that doing business in foreign countries is a different ball game. It involves more than just deciding to pursue an international or multinational strategy, or recognizing that an industry requires global strategies. It involves more than selecting the specific type of strategy by which the firm will compete internationally. Attention must be given to the risks unique to international business—risks over and above those that must be analyzed in evaluating domestic

---

[41]Porter, *Competitive Strategy*, p. 294.
[42]Robinson, *International Business Management*, p. 23.
[43]Porter, *Competitive Strategy*, pp. 295–96.

strategies. Two such risks relate to areas critical to the success of international operations: currency fluctuations and foreign risks (political turmoil, financial instability, expropriation or confiscation of assets, or increasing tariffs).

1. *Currency Fluctuations.* A strong dollar sounds attractive. However, this usually means that other currencies are weaker in relative terms. And an increase in the value of the dollar relative to foreign currencies adversely affects a firm's earnings in two ways. First, foreign assets on the firm's balance sheet are worth fewer dollars; this is a one-time charge against earnings and lowers profits. Second, there is an ongoing profit and loss effect as sales and profits generated abroad continue to represent fewer dollars. Furthermore, a stronger dollar makes U.S. exports relatively more expensive to foreigners, and imports to the United States cheaper. Of course, the reverse is true when the dollar weakens. The implications of such changes can be enormous. In 1981, the net effect of currency translations on IBM's balance sheet and income statement was a charge against earnings of nearly 35 cents a share for the first nine months; this works out to about $200 million![44] Anyone with a calculator can figure out what happened to companies with assets in Mexico, where the value of the peso dropped from 22 per dollar to 2,500 per dollar since 1976. For a multinational company, even the amount of cash and inventories located in various countries can have a substantial effect on assets and profits. Thus, currency fluctuations can greatly affect the success or failure of an international strategy.

2. *Other Risks.* In 1960, Texaco lost a $60 million refinery (costing the equivalent of $298 million in 1990 prices) when the Castro government seized all foreign assets in Cuba. For firms with assets in foreign countries, the risk of government instability, political turmoil, and other risks are *major* considerations, and can wipe out years of work and investment almost overnight. For this reason, it is of critical importance to consider such risks when engaging in international strategies. But how does one evaluate or quantify such possibilities? The prudent firm would be wise to employ a surprise matrix and contingency planning approach to cover such events, as described in Chapter 9. In addition, business information firms such as Frost and Sullivan, Business International, and others attempt to assess such risks. As an example of such an analysis, Table 6.3 provides 18-month and five-year forecasts for a number of countries. When a firm is involved in international operations, its profits must reflect these added risks. In addition, international expansion is not always (or even usually) more profitable. A recent research study found that high-technology firms employing domestic, export, or direct foreign investment strategies showed no significant difference in financial performance. Thus, international strategies did not improve their performance, nor did these strategies hurt the firms' performance.[45]

---

[44]J. A. White, "IBM Earnings Dropped 22% in Third Period," *The Wall Street Journal,* October 14, 1981, p. 4.

[45]P. M. Feltes and L. A. Digman, "The Effect of International Trading Strategy on Financial Performance," *Proceedings of Pan Pacific Conference VI,* May 1989.

TABLE 6.3 Risk Forecast for Selected Countries to 1994

Country	Regimes and Probabilities	Turmoil	Transfer	Investment	Export		Real GDP Growth	Inflation	Current Account
Argentina									
8/88	*Peronists 45%	High	C−	C	D+	1984–88	1.4	363.2	−2.76
	*Peronists 40%	Moderate	C−	C−	D	1989	1.0	250.0	−3.20
						1990–94	1.8	200.0	−2.60
Australia									
11/88	Hawke 85%	Low	A	A	A−	1984–88	4.4	7.1	−8.66
	Hawke 45%	Low	A−	A	A−	1989	2.5	5.5	−10.00
						1990–94	2.5	5.0	−7.50
Austria									
5/88	Grand Coalition 70%	Low	A+	A	A+	1984–88	1.7	2.9	−0.03
	Grand Coalition 60%	Low	A+	A+	A+	1989	1.3	2.2	+0.24
						1990–94	1.6	2.4	+0.22
Brazil									
12/88	*Center Left 55%	Moderate	C−	C	C	1984–88	5.7	345.2	−0.50
	*Center Left 55%	Moderate	C	C−	C−	1989	2.0	600.0	+3.00
						1990–94	3.5	200.0	+2.00
Canada									
12/88	PC Majority 85% (55%)	Low	A	A (A−)	A	1984–88	3.9	4.2	−4.44
	PC 40%	Low	B+	B+	B	1989	2.0	6.0	−8.50
						1990–94	2.5	5.0	−6.00
China									
11/88	Reformers 55%	Low	B−	B	C+	1984–88	10.5	8.1	−4.25
	Reformers 50%	Low	B	B−	C+	1989	10.0	13.0	−2.50
						1990–94	8.0	11.5	−2.75
Costa Rica									
11/88	*PLN 50%	Low	B−	A−	B−	1984–88	4.1	13.8	−0.26
	*PLN 50%	Moderate	C+	A	B	1989	3.0	18.0	−0.20
						1990–94	3.0	18.0	−0.15
Denmark									
9/88	KVR Coalition 65%	Low	A	A+	A+	1984–88	2.1	4.5	−2.88
	Non-Socialist 55%	Low	A−	A	A−	1989	1.0	3.5	−2.50
						1990–94	1.5	3.0	−1.75
East Germany									
11/88	Current Politburo 90%	Low	C	C	C	1984–88	4.0	1.8	+0.89
	Current Politburo 65%	Low	A−	B−	B	1989	2.5	2.5	+1.00
						1990–94	3.5	2.5	+1.50
Egypt									
12/88	Mubarak 70%	Moderate	C	B+	C	1984–88	3.1	20.1	−1.94
	Mubarak 55%	Moderate (Low)	C (B−)	C− (C+)	C (C+)	1989	2.0	25.0	−2.50
						1990–94	2.5	25.0	−2.00

Country (date)	Party / coalition	Stability	Grade	Grade	Grade	Period			
El Salvador 9/88						1984–88	1.5	27.1	−0.15
	Arena 55%	Very high	C	C+	C−	1989	1.0	40.0	−0.25
	Right Wing 45%	Very high	D−	D−	D−	1990–94	1.0	25.0	−0.25
France 9/88						1984–88	2.0	4.3	−1.26
	Socialist minority 65%	Low	A+	A+	A+	1989	1.8	2.8	−1.80
	*Rocard 45%	Low	A+	A+	A+	1990–94	2.5	3.8	−1.50
Greece 8/88						1984–88	1.7	18.2	−2.03
	Pasok 40%	Moderate	C	B	B−	1989	3.0	15.0	−1.00
	Pasok 40%	Low	C+	C+	C	1990–94	2.5	12.0	−1.50
Guatemala 6/88						1984–88	1.2	16.8	−0.17
	Christian Democrats 55%	High	B−	B−	C	1989	5.3	12.5	−0.08
	Christian Democrats 40%	Moderate	B−	B	B−	1990–94	4.2	11.13	−0.08
Hong Kong 6/88						1984–88	8.7	5.5	+2.08
	Appointed 90%	Low	A+	A	A+	1989	8.5	8.0	+2.00
	Apponted 85%	Low	A+	A	A+	1990–94	8.3	8.5	+1.55
Hungary 12/88						1984–88	1.3	8.7	−0.52
	Pragmatic Reform 80%	Low	B	A−	B	1989	1.5	15.0	−0.60
	Pragmatic Reform 65%	Low	B+	B+	B	1990–94	1.5	10.0	−0.50
India 10/88						1984–88	4.9	8.3	−4.22
	Gandhi 50%	Moderate	B	B−	B−	1989	1.0	10.0	−3.50
	Gandhi 45%	High	B−	B−	B−	1990–94	2.5	8.0	−3.00
Indonesia 12/88						1984–88	3.9	7.9	−2.23
	Suharto 90%	Low	C+	A−	B	1989	4.0	10.0	0.00
	Suharto 60%	Moderate	B−	B−	C+	1990–94	5.0	8.5	+1.00
Iran 11/88						1984–88	−0.7	28.4	+0.68
	Alliance 80%	Moderate	B−	C+	B−	1989	2.5	35.0	−1.00
	Alliance 65%	Moderate	B	C+	B−	1990–94	3.0	20.0	−0.30
Iraq 10/88						1984–88	1.1	22.8	−3.57
	Saddam Hussein 85%	Moderate	C+	B−	B−	1989	3.5	25.0	−1.50
	Saddam Hussein 55%	Moderate	B	C	C+	1990–94	3.0	25.0	−0.50

TABLE 6.3 (continued)

Country	Regimes and Probabilities	Turmoil	Transfer	Investment	Export		Real GDP Growth	Inflation	Current Account
Ireland 11/88	Fianna Fail Minority 60%	Low	A	A	A+	1984–88	1.9	4.5	−0.25
	Fianna Fail 60%	Low	A−	A	A−	1989	2.0	2.5	+1.00
						1990–94	2.5	2.5	+1.00
Israel 12/88	Likud-led 70%	Moderate	C+	A−	B−	1984–88	3.6	153.6	−0.10
	Likud-led 65%	Moderate	C+	B+	B	1989	3.5	22.0	−0.50
						1990–94	3.1	17.0	0.00
Italy 8/88	DC-Center Left 65%	Low	B+	A+	A	1984–88	3.1	7.1	−1.48
	*Center Left 65%	Low	B+	A	A−	1989	2.3	4.5	−1.25
						1990–94	2.5	5.0	−1.00
Jamaica 11/88	*Manley 55%	Low	B	A−	B+	1984–88	1.3	17.1	−0.20
	*Manley 45%	Low	B−	B	C	1989	3.0	15.0	−0.15
						1990–94	2.5	20.0	−0.30
Japan 7/88	Takeshita 75%	Low	A+	A	A+	1984–88	4.3	1.2	+67.00
	*New LDP Leadership 55%	Low	A+	B+	A	1989	5.4	1.3	+86.02
						1990–94	4.2	2.4	+78.00
Libya 12/88	Qaddafi 65% (50%)	Moderate	B−	C+	C(C+)	1984–88	−0.9	8.9	−0.14
	*Military 45% (50%)	Moderate	B(C)	C+(C−)	C+(C−)	1989	0.0	8.0	−0.50
		(Very high)				1990–94	1.5	7.0	+0.50
Malaysia 12/88	Mahathir 70%	Moderate	A−	B+	B+	1984–88	3.9	1.6	+0.34
	Mahathir 60%	Moderate	A−	B	B−	1989	6.0	2.5	+0.40
						1990–94	4.5	2.5	+0.50
Mexico 10/88	*Nationalist PRI 55%	Moderate	B	B	B−	1984–88	1.0	88.7	+2.14
	*Nationalist PRI 55%	Moderate	B	B	B−	1989	2.5	75.0	+3.50
						1990–94	3.0	50.0	+4.00
Netherlands 12/88	CDA-Liberals 70% (45%)	Low	A(A+)	A(A+)	A+	1984–88	2.4	1.3	+4.38
	*CDA-Labor 50%	Low	A	A(A−)	A(B+)	1989	2.5	1.5	+4.50
						1990–94	2.0	3.0	+2.70

Country / Date	Scenario					Period			
New Zealand 7/88	Lange 85%	Low	A−	A	A	1984–88	2.2	10.0	−1.60
	Lange 45%	Low	B+	B	B−	1989	1.0	5.5	−1.25
						1990–94	1.1	7.0	−1.18
Nicaragua 6/88	Pragmatic FSLN 55%	High	C	C	C	1984–88	−2.2	700.5	−0.71
	Pragmatic FSLN 50%	High	C−	D	D−	1989	−1.5	840.0	−0.63
						1990–94	−2.0	450.0	−0.72
Norway 5/88	Labor Minority 75%	Low	A+	A+	A+	1984–88	3.5	6.9	−1.72
	Labor Minority 40%	Low	A+	A+	A+	1989	1.0	6.8	−6.00
						1990–94	1.3	6.2	−4.75
Pakistan 12/88	*Bhutto 40%	High	C	B	C	1984–88	6.6	5.4	−0.89
	*Bhutto 40%	Very high	D	C−	D	1989	5.0	12.0	−1.00
						1990–94	4.0	10.0	−0.75
Panama 11/88	Noriega-PRD 50%	High	B	B+	B−	1984–88	−1.5	1.1	+0.16
	*Moderate PRD 40%	High	B−	C−	C+	1989	−2.0	3.5	−0.12
						1990–94	2.0	5.0	−0.10
Philippines 9/88	Aquino 65%	Very high	B−	B	C+	1984–88	0.4	17.2	−0.27
	Aquino 40%	Very high	C−	D+	D+	1989	6.0	7.0	−0.65
						1990–94	5.5	6.5	−0.80
Poland 11/88	Jaruzelski 75%	Low	D+	C+	C−	1984–88	4.1	25.3	−0.91
	Jaruzelski 65%	Low	B−	B−	B−	1989	4.5	57.0	−0.37
						1990–94	3.8	41.0	−0.69
Portugal 9/88	PSD 85%	Low	A−	A+	A	1984–88	2.9	15.5	+0.45
	PSD 55%	Low	A	B+	A	1989	3.0	8.0	+0.75
						1990–94	3.5	6.5	+1.00
Puerto Rico 12/88	Hernandez-Centrist 80% (60%)	Low	A+	A+	A+	1984–88	4.3	1.8	−0.07
	Hernandez-Centrist 50% (60%)	Low	A	A+	A	1989	4.5	3.5	−0.03
						1990–94	3.9	3.3	+0.04

TABLE 6.3 *(concluded)*

Country	Regimes and Probabilities	Turmoil	Transfer	Investment	Export		Real GDP Growth	Inflation	Current Account
Saudi Arabia 5/88	Fahd 75%	Low	A−	B+	A−	1984–88	−2.9	−1.1	−12.31
	Fahd 60%	Low	B+	C+	C+	1989	0.0	1.1	−7.60
						1990–94	1.0	2.6	−8.30
Singapore 10/88	*Goh Chok Tong 60%	Low	A	A+	A+	1984–88	5.1	1.0	+0.27
	*Goh Chok Tong 55%	Low	A+	A+	A+	1989	7.0	2.5	+0.70
						1990–94	6.0	4.0	+0.75
South Africa 12/88	Pragmatic NP 55% (60%)	High	B+	C+	B−	1984–88	2.2	15.4	+2.18
	Right Wing 40%	Very high	C	D	D+	1989	2.5	12.0	+3.00
						1990–94	2.0	10.0	+2.00
South Korea 12/88	Roh 65%	Moderate	A−	B+	A−	1984–88	9.2	3.7	+4.44
	Roh 60%	High	C+	C+	C+	1989	8.0	8.0	+10.00
						1990–94	8.0	6.5	+7.00
Spain 8/88	Socialists 80%	Moderate	A−	A	A−	1984–88	3.6	7.8	+1.18
	Socialists 70%	Moderate	B	B+	A−	1989	3.7	4.0	−3.30
						1990–94	3.0	3.0	−3.50
Sweden 10/88	Social Democrats 70%	Low	A+	A	A+	1984–88	2.4	5.9	−0.56
	Social Democrats 50%	Low	A	A	A	1989	2.2	5.6	−1.49
						1990–94	2.0	6.1	−1.00
Syria 5/88	Assad 65%	Moderate	C−	C+	C−	1984–88	2.3	54.5	−0.69
	Assad 50%	Very high	C−	D+	C−	1989	1.0	110.0	−0.34
						1990–94	1.5	65.0	−0.32
Taiwan 8/88	Collective KMT 85%	Low	A	A−	A+	1984–88	9.1	0.3	+12.09
	Collective KMT 70%	Low	A	A+	A+	1989	7.0	1.0	+10.58
						1990–94	7.8	3.0	+11.29
Thailand 12/88	Chatichai-Military 45%	Low	B	B+(A−)	B	1984–88	5.4	2.3	−1.05
	*Chaovalit 40%	Moderate	B(B+)	B−	C+(B−)	1989	6.5	5.0	−1.50
						1990–94	5.0	5.5	−0.50

Country / Regime	Turmoil	Transfer	Investment	Export	Period	GDP Growth	Inflation	Current Account
USSR 11/88								
Gorbachev 80%	Low	C+	C−	B−	1984–88	2.8	3.5	−0.98
Gorbachev 55%	Low	B+	B	B+	1989	3.0	5.0	−1.50
					1990–94	3.0	5.0	−1.50
United Kingdom 10/88								
Thatcher 80%	Low	A+	A	A+	1984–88	3.3	4.5	−1.23
Conservatives 60%	Low	A+	A	A	1989	2.5	4.5	−14.00
					1990–94	2.8	5.0	−7.00
United States 12/88								
*Bush-Centrist 80%	Low	A+	A+	A+	1984–88	3.6	3.4	−133.21
*Centrist 60%	Low	A+	A	A−	1989	2.5	5.0	−130.00
					1990–94	2.0	5.5	−100.00
West Germany 7/88								
CDU-CSU-FDP 75%	Low	A+	A+	A+	1984–88	2.5	1.2	+31.73
*SPD-FDP 50%	Low	A+	A+	A+	1989	3.0	1.5	+41.75
					1990–94	2.8	2.0	+39.62
Yugoslavia 11/88								
Collective 55%	Moderate	C	B+	C+	1984–88	1.6	114.6	+1.08
*Centralization 50%	Moderate	B−	A−	C+	1989	1.5	120.0	+0.60
					1990–94	2.0	50.0	+1.00

Note: Under each "Country" is the date of the 1989 update or report, followed by the 18-month (second line) and five-year (third line) political forecasts: the "Regimes" most likely to hold power and their "Probabilities," risk ratings for "Turmoil" (low to very high), and risk ratings (A+ the least to D− the most) for financial "Transfer," direct "Investment," and "Export" to the country. Parentheses indicate a changed forecast. An asterisk means a noncumbent regime. The list of "Economic Indicators" contain most recently issued economic data and forecasts, including a previous five-year average, a one-year forecast or estimate, and a five-year forecast (average). "Real GDP Growth" and "Inflation" are expressed as percentages, and "Current Account" figures are in billions of U.S. dollars.

Source: Adapted from W. D. Coplin and M. K. O'Leary, "1989 World Political and Economic Risk Forecast," *Planning Review* 17, no. 1 (January/February 1989), pp. 30–33.

In summary, a strategy of international expansion holds an inherent attractiveness and mark of success for many firms. For many whose domestic markets are saturated, it may be a requirement for future growth, and certain industries effectively demand global strategies. But international expansion is not without a number of problems and significant risks. A firm should look hard when deciding whether or not to pursue an international strategy to determine if the benefits truly outweigh the costs.

Combined Factors

Successful share-building strategies often involve a combination of several competitive factors. Typically, better results are achieved by using a balanced, consistent marketing program or a mix of strategic factors. Buzzell and Wiersema have cited L'eggs pantyhose as an example. Hanes used a combined approach when it introduced L'eggs in 1971. Heavy advertising and promotion speeded up customer trial of the product. This facilitated acceptance by retailers. And direct distribution ensured that L'eggs seldom would be out of stock, allowing customers to develop repeat buying routines.[46]

STRATEGIES FOR REDEFINING AND REDUCING SCOPE

A quick glance at the product life-cycle curve yields an obvious conclusion: not all firms and businesses can be in growth markets. Additionally, the maturity and decline stages are often much longer than the growth phase. Therefore, a firm must face the possibility that many of its business units are likely to be in limited growth or even decline at any given time. How should firms handle this situation? What should their strategies be? While "growth" sounds more exciting than maturity, don't forget that profits and cash flow are greater during the maturity phase than in any other stage; even in the aging and decline phase profits and cash flows often equal or exceed those of the growth stage. In fact, recent research has shown that mature businesses that actively invested in highly differentiated positions, low-cost operations, or defensible niches performed significantly better than did those attempting to milk such businesses for diversification funds. In fact, the industry leaders produced *better* results than did the leaders in rapidly growing high-technology fields.[47]

The 30 years following World War II are often referred to as the golden years of economic growth. Not since the Industrial Revolution of the late 1800s had the United States seen such growth in the number and scope of businesses. With the

---

[46]Buzzell and Wiersema, "Successful Share-Building Strategies," p. 143.

[47]W. K. Hall, "Survival Strategies in a Hostile Environment," *Harvard Business Review* 58, no. 5 (September–October 1980), p. 75.

booming economy of the 1950s and 1960s came an emphasis on growth and expansion. The main concerns of businesses were capital investments, expanding market share, and increasing sales. A company whose annual report did not show significant growth from year to year was viewed as stagnant and a poor investment. The prosperity of the time lulled people into a belief that the good times would last forever, and there would never be any need to worry about a business decline.

The rapidly changing, hostile environment of the 1970s burst the public's idealistic bubble, and suddenly survival, not growth, was the key word to industry. The attitude that a business which could not survive was simply poorly managed disappeared quickly. Suddenly, business was faced with high interest rates, increasing raw-material costs, and skyrocketing energy costs. After nearly 30 years of prosperity, many managers were in a situation where they did not know what to do. Little research had been done on the retrenchment and turnaround strategies needed by many businesses in the slower growth environment. In addition, many found themselves with excess capacity, having built for growth that failed to materialize.

Thus, businesses need to be redefined and possibly reduced in scope under certain conditions, usually due to changes in the competitive or general environments. Redefining, or reconceiving, the business may also be required because some firms lose sight of their essence—their vision, their distinctive competencies and competitive advantages. The question then becomes one of how to recapture, rediscover, or recreate this essence. Mintzberg suggests that three approaches are possible:[48]

1. *Redefining the business.* This approach requires the firm to reconceive the business, to use innovative means to redefine markets, functions, or products—the very concept of the business—to gain a new competitive advantage. Redefinition strategies are essentially creative, designed to change the rules, as Timex did with watches, Miller for beer, and cable for television programming.

2. *Recombining businesses.* In certain instances, it may be advantageous to combine various activities, either within or between existing businesses, in order to create a new concept of market scope, or segmentation. 3M was early to define the "coating and bonding" business, and Procter & Gamble the "personal care" industry. The recombination must exist in more than name only; critics question whether there ever was a " transportation" business.

3. *Relocating the core.* As changes in the industry, the business, and its strategic position take place, the firm may need to change the "center of gravity," or position in the stream, of the business. The business can be shifted further upstream or downstream, can change the relative emphasis of functions, or

---

[48]Mintzberg, "Generic Strategies," pp. 54–61.

make relocation changes in conjunction with moves to redefine and recombine the business as described above.

In examining situations warranting scope redefinition and reduction actions, it is helpful to think in terms of defense and renewal strategies, retrenchment and turnaround strategies, and "endgame" strategies. These concepts are discussed in the remaining sections of this chapter.

Defense and Renewal Strategies

The further one progresses in the product/market life cycle, the more important defensive strategies become. There is less margin for error, and improvements in performance are likely to be incremental, rather than dramatic, as they were in the earlier stages. Put another way, businesses in mature markets may find the risk/reward ratio from a bold action less favorable than it was in earlier stages. Market-share improvements tend to be won in the trenches, by hard work and attention to detail day after day and year after year.

A serious strategic or even tactical error can cause hard-earned ground to be quickly lost, and it may take years to recover. For example, Schlitz switched to lower-cost ingredients for its beer in the 1970s, causing a rapid loss of market share. The company quickly corrected its mistake, but was never able to regain its sales even though some industry experts felt that their subsequent product was superior to the competition. In this context, the easiest and cheapest way to increase market share is through the mistakes of competitors. Thus, the patient firm that does not become overanxious and overambitious will likely be the long-term beneficiary, particularly in mature markets.

The maturity phase is also an opportune time for actions that may renew or revive the products and services of the business. Such actions can include product innovations, new technologies, service and distribution innovations, process innovations, management improvements, and the like, and may even serve to put the industry or a segment on a new growth curve. An obvious example of this was the creation of the fast-food segment of the already mature restaurant industry.

Segmentation Tactics.   Numerous experts prescribe differentiation strategies for businesses in mature industries. One way to achieve differentiation is by segmenting the market in some productive way, such as by appealing to singles, Yuppies, or the elderly, for example. Often products or services can be repositioned to appeal to such defined segments. Another approach is using multiple branding to promote similar products to different customers, as the cigarette industry has done. In general, segmentation tends to create identifiable market niches, one or more of which may be pursued by the business.[49]

---

[49]R. G. Wilson, "Competitive Business Strategies," in *Handbook of Business Strategy,* ed. W. D. Guth (Boston: Warren, Gorham & Lamont, 1985), p. 8–4.

Quality Improvements.   Another major competitive strategy for mature industries centers on quality. Improving the quality of the product or service can result in improved sales and market share. This can be done by product improvements or by building in additional features or services (such as delivery, on-time service, quick repair, extended warranties, and the like). Actions taken to enhance the product's image and reliability—such as Ford's "Quality is Job 1" campaign—are obvious examples.

Efficiency Improvements.   Low-cost strategies are important in mature markets, especially if a business does not have a dominant position or a defensible niche. Economies of scale, purchasing, common interchangeable parts, selective consolidations of facilities, automation, and the like can contribute to efficiency and lower costs.[50]

Rest of the World Strategy.   Excess capacity is indeed a problem that lowers efficiency and productivity and raises unit costs. But excess capacity can be a problem even in industries that are not slowing down. In electric power generation, for example, the capacity that must be available to meet peak loads results in excess at other times. Most cyclical industries, such as auto and farm equipment manufacturing, find themselves with excess capacity at some times and shortages of capacity at other times.

The ideal would be to operate at some level of output corresponding to the most economical level of production, which defines the plant's optimal capacity. But how can a firm (or industry) be responsive to market demands without having significant excess capacity from time to time?

The Japanese approach has been to employ a "rest of the world" strategy. They focus on certain markets—say the domestic market and one additional— and use other markets as a buffer. In this way, by using the other market to fill the gap between what is demanded in their primary markets and their capacity, they can operate near optimal capacity. For example, as shown in Figure 6.6, a company attempts to satisfy as much of its domestic market as it can, as well as one export market. If plant capacity exceeds the total of these two markets, additional sales can be made to the rest of the world, but only on an "as available" basis.[51]

Retrenchment and Turnaround Strategies

Chrysler's recent turnaround is familiar to all and has made a folk hero of its architect, CEO Lee Iacocca. Other more recent but less spectacular turnarounds were staged by Ford and Peugeot in automobiles, and Control Data in computers.

---

[50] Ibid., p. 8–7.

[51] Alan Zakon, invited address to Business Policy and Planning Division, Academy of Management National Meeting, August 1987.

FIGURE 6.6   "Rest of the World" Strategy

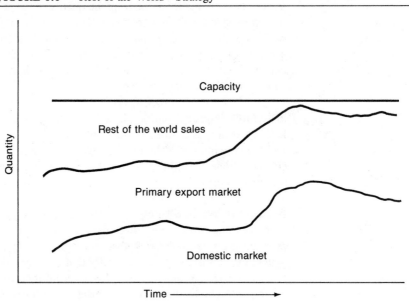

Turnaround strategies are attempts to arrest and reverse the decline of a business. As in the case of Chrysler, reasons for the decline can be external (recessions, declining demand, competitive pressures, and the like), internal (largely mismanagement and poor planning), or both. Successful turnaround strategies typically have short- and long-term aspects, but the short term is clearly the most important in survival situations such as Chrysler's. Why? Because if the short-term actions fail, *there will be no long term*—the survival of the business is at stake. Without this clear realization, turnaround strategies are not likely to succeed. In fact, actions may be required that are clearly detrimental in the long run. Without them, however, the firm may not exist to reap any long-term benefits.

Retrenchment Actions.   The best turnaround is the one that does not have to happen; prevention is a lot better than the cure. On a personal basis, it is obviously better for an individual to exercise and follow a proper diet than to have coronary bypass surgery. The business that watches its general and competitive environments, thinks strategically, and regularly examines and redirects its use of resources is not likely to find itself needing a turnaround. The business has made a regular practice of controlling its resources and retrenching regularly.

   Retrenchment involves defensive actions taken when the market is saturated or in actual decline, when the company is in financial or other trouble, or during recessions. During the 1980–83 recession, for example, Chrysler shrank (retrenched) in size to the extent that its break-even point was half of what it was before survival actions were taken, and also sold its profitable tank business. Chrysler used a retrenchment strategy and selective shrinking as part of its survival and turnaround actions. Braniff, on the other hand, was not so adept at retrenchment actions, and was forced to cease operations in 1982, although it later resumed operations as a much smaller carrier.

Retrenchment actions in some ways are the reverse of strategies for increasing scope. A negative penetration strategy, for example, would amount to *contraction*—cutting back on investment or service to reduce its commitment to a certain market and/or product. The opposite of a product development strategy is *product line rationalization*—actions taken to simplify or even eliminate a particular product line to get rid of unprofitable excesses or overlaps. The inverse of a market development strategy obviously involves *market contraction,* or reducing the number of segments. Again, the goal here is to periodically purge the excesses gained from proliferating market segments.[52] In reality, many organizations analyze and take actions to redefine and reduce business scope at the same time they are increasing scope in other areas.

Warning Signals.   What are some of the danger signals that indicate impending trouble? John Harris of Booz Allen & Hamilton offers 12 danger signals that are remarkably similar for both industries and companies. Companies that are in turnaround situations typically exhibit one or more of the following characteristics:

1. *Decreasing market share.* This is perhaps the most telling signal of a major problem. It may be masked temporarily by sales increases due to market growth or inflation. However, the company's competitive position is eroding, portending future trouble.
2. *Declining constant dollar sales.* Inflation-adjusted declines in sales in comparison to industry criteria (such as sales per square foot of retail space) indicate trouble.
3. *Decreasing profitability.* This can show up as lower dollar profits, lower return on sales or investment, or similar measures.
4. *Increasing reliance on debt.* A substantial rise in debt or the debt-to-equity ratio, or a lowered credit rating can cause significant problems.
5. *Restricted dividend policies,* such as lowered or eliminated dividends. Do not confuse this with actions taken to effect a turnaround, however, once the need is recognized.
6. *Inadequate reinvestment in the business.* Adequate reinvestment in plant, equipment, and maintenance is required for a business to remain competitive. Deferral indicates that the company is mortgaging its future for the short term.

---

[52]Mintzberg, ''Generic Strategies,'' pp. 34–38.

7. *Proliferation of new ventures.* Such actions, if done while ignoring the basic business, may be attempts to cover up problems and a search for a bailout. Diversification should supplement, not replace, the basic business of the firm.
8. *Lack of planning.* Unplanned growth or inattention to environmental changes and strategy is sure to create problems.
9. *CEO resistant to the ideas of others.*
10. *Management succession problems.*
11. *An overly passive board.*
12. *Inbred management.* Management that feels nothing can be learned from outsiders, professional conferences, competitors, and the like is headed for trouble.[53]

Action Is Needed.   While such danger signals may be present, they are valuable only if recognized and acted on. Many firms ignore such signals until it may be too late. Or management prevents action from being taken. At some point, however, the firm must face the music, and *someone* has to intervene and take charge. Once consensus has been achieved that trouble exists, the turnaround can begin. Figure 6.7 portrays actions typically required as part of a turnaround effort.

Extraordinary powers must be granted to those responsible for the turnaround. The "turnaround team" needs to select and focus on *one or two* activities offering the greatest opportunity to affect company performance. Singleness of purpose is crucial—the company cannot tolerate business as usual. The cause of the decline must be isolated, and corrective actions taken. In turnaround situations, achieving a positive cash flow, not profits, becomes all important. Profit-making, but cash-absorbing, assets may have to be sold to generate cash. In any event, cash outflows must be stopped in the short run, with a goal of restoring profitability as the next step. Curtailing investments and dividend payments are obvious ways to conserve cash. Others are price increases and cost and asset reduction programs.

Turnaround Options.   Four major turnaround options exist. Depending on the firm's position in relation to its break-even point, the following actions may be taken:

1. *Cost-cutting strategies.* If the firm has high direct labor costs, high fixed expenses, or is close to the break-even point, cost-cutting may be most appropriate. Such actions usually take effect relatively quickly.
2. *Asset-reduction strategies* may be needed if the firm is far from its break-even point, since there is no way to cut costs sufficiently. Assets or capacity unneeded in the next two years or so should be the first to go.

---

[53]J. M. Harris, "Corporate Turnaround Strategy," in *The Strategic Management Handbook*, ed. K. J. Albert (New York: McGraw-Hill, 1983), chap. 20.

FIGURE 6.7   Schematic Diagram of a Turnaround Strategy

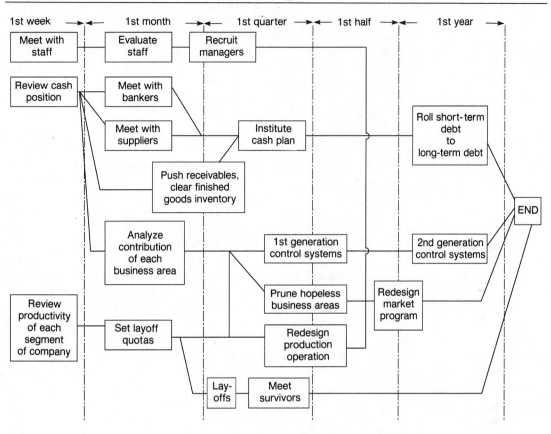

Source: D. D. Wyckoff, *Turnaround Management* (Boston: HBS Case Services, No. 9–686–057, 1986), revised 9/87 by Christopher Hart, p. 10.

3. *Revenue-increasing strategies*. If the firm is close to covering its fixed costs and has low variable costs (such as direct labor costs), revenue increasing approaches such as price increases may be most beneficial. This option is an alternative to asset reduction strategies if the assets are likely to be needed within the next year or two. Keep in mind that revenue-increasing strategies may not pay off as quickly as cost-cutting or asset-reduction approaches.

4. *Combination strategies*. If the firm is covering fixed costs but significantly below its break-even point, a combination of the previous three approaches may be most fruitful.[54]

---

[54]C. W. Hofer and Dan Schendel, *Strategy Formulation: Analytical Concepts* (St. Paul, Minn.: West Publishing, 1978), p. 173.

Whatever action is pursued, the focus must be on short-term cash flow, while minimizing long-term damage. Whether or not a turnaround strategy is required, keeping a low break-even point should be considered essential for any business; therefore, periodic retrenchment may be warranted. Financial leverage can be increased by automation, such as the use of robotics or, in banking, automatic teller machines. Automation provides depreciation, which labor does not. From a human standpoint, it is better to have a thriving business with 30 percent fewer people, than a business with 100 percent fewer people because of bankruptcy.

However, one must keep a core of key, motivated, and talented people. Subcontracting all nonessential activities (such as janitorial, grounds keeping, maintenance, and the like) is one way to keep the organization lean. In addition, modern technology—such as shared data bases—can sometimes eliminate a whole layer of management. Honda Motors has only five levels of management, and the Roman Catholic Church with 24,000 churches and 52 million members has only three; most large corporations have many more.[55]

In summary, firms would prefer never to have to use turnaround strategies. However, because of the dynamic nature of the environment in which firms must compete and mistakes on their part, they are sometimes forced to. The major factor causing a firm to use such strategies is declining demand. However, success is possible even in hostile environments, particularly if the firm can achieve the lowest delivered cost position and the highest product, service, and quality position in the industry. If possible, the firm should attempt to gain or defend a leadership position in the industry.

Strategies for Aging and Declining Markets

Aging and declining markets experience permanent (rather than temporary) declines in demand, for various reasons. An obvious current example is the cigarette industry (due to changing consumer habits), as is the Japanese aluminum industry (due to the high cost of producing electricity, critical to aluminum production).

One of the leading authors in strategies for declining businesses is Kathryn Rudie Harrigan of Columbia University. She uses the term *endgame* to describe the strategies businesses use in coping with declining demand. It is helpful to think of endgame as having rules, situations, strategies, and consequences.[56] Of course, in the real world, endgame—a condition of declining demand—is no mere "*game*" to the participants.

---

[55]Kami, *Strategic Planning*.

[56]K. R. Harrigan, "Strategic Planning for Endgame," *Long-Range Planning,* December 1982, pp. 17–20.

Characteristics of Declining Demand.   Before declining demand can be studied, it must first be defined and differentiated from temporarily sagging demand. It is a market condition in which demand will drop to and remain at a reduced level, or drop even lower. Sagging demand is a temporary dip in demand that will return to previous levels as soon as the condition causing the dip is gone. Declining demand necessitates retrenchment strategies.

Another distinction should be made at this point: the difference between the endgame challenge and revitalization. Analysis of product revitalization stems from the idea that temporarily declining demand for a product might be reestablished by finding new markets or even new uses for the product. Analysis of endgame assumes that there is little hope of reestablishing consumption of product at previous levels.

Reasons for a product or business decline can be roughly divided into two categories: technological and demographic. A technological change makes product substitutes available, thus causing the previous product to be obsolete. Some technological breakthroughs are so revolutionary that they may completely eliminate the demand for another product. Usually, even if a technological breakthrough is revolutionary, some isolated pockets of residual demand for the earlier product will remain, and there will always be a demand for replacement parts, especially if switching costs are high. This was basically the case with the electronic receiving-tubes industry. The development of the transistor eliminated the need for vacuum tubes virtually overnight. But because of the high switching cost, demand for replacement tubes existed for some time.

The second reason for changing demand has to do with changes in consumer buying patterns. Changes caused by demographics can be vague and confusing. A firm must closely analyze the exact cause of the demand decline before it can formulate a strategy. Some demographic characteristics, such as few buyers caused by declining birthrates, may be permanent and represent absolute declining demand. Other demographic characteristics, however, may be related more to fads or styles, and no one can predict the peculiar patterns that trends will follow. Other factors, such as changing attitudes and values are harder to interpret, and the firm is faced with a difficult decision of whether or not to stay in the industry. One thing has been proved over the years; if demand is declining for technological reasons, the likelihood of successful revitalization will be lower than if demand declines for demographic reasons.

Possibly the most important and most misunderstood aspect of endgame is: when does it start? History is littered with the stories of firms that folded or nearly folded because they failed to realize soon enough that they were playing in endgame. It is much easier for a company to take corrective measures early and avoid or minimize the effects of declining demand than it is to pick up the pieces after things are falling apart. One reason big firms realize too late that they are in endgame is that they can survive a long time before they feel its effects. Also, whether it is out of stubbornness or wishful thinking, many firms simply do not want to recognize that they are in a declining industry. But once a business has identified itself as being in endgame, it must decide whether or not it wants to "play." If the environment appears hostile, the company may decide to exit as quickly as possible and minimize its potential losses. Most businesses do not simply "jump ship" when things get rough. They stay in the fight and do everything possible to survive. It is the decision to stay in business and recover profits that creates the need for endgame strategies. But, again, recognizing whether declines in demand are permanent or temporary is fraught with the risk of error. For example, are farm products, agricultural equipment, beer, and liquor in a state of temporary or permanent decline? Such questions are of vital importance to dominant businesses in those industries, such as Deere & Company and Anheuser-Busch.

Endgame Strategies.   As in other areas of business strategy, there is no one absolute rule to follow in endgame. Industries are not homogeneous, and it would be impossible to come up with a contingency theory to handle every possible situation. To further complicate matters, there may be several business strategies appropriate for a single firm experiencing declining demand. And what works for one firm may spell doom for another. In an attempt to conceptualize the strategies that firms seemed to follow in endgame, Harrigan has outlined five strategies.

1. Increase the investment (seek dominance).
2. Hold investment level.
3. Shrink selectively.
4. Milk the investment.
5. Divest now.[57]

Increase the Investment.   The underlying theme behind this strategy is the firm's belief that enduring pockets of demand will remain, so the firm must reposition itself to serve these pockets. By reinvesting, the company is hoping to gain market dominance, becoming the market leader when demand stabilizes. Because of the additional investment involved, this is one of the riskier strategies in endgame, but it also offers the biggest rewards if it pays off.

Hold Investment Level.   The hold-investment-level strategy means that a company is taking a defensive reinvestment position. It is interested in reinvesting only enough to maintain the level and tactics it has been following in the past. This strategy of matching competitors' price changes and marketing expenditures is a wait-and-see attitude designed to delay long enough to see whether the uncertainties of demand are resolved.[58]

A hold-investment-level strategy indicates that the firm in interested in remaining in the business, or that it is waiting for its exit barriers to lower so it can leave the industry in as orderly a manner as possible. The single-business

---

[57]K. R. Harrigan, "Strategies for Declining Businesses" (Lexington, Mass.: D.C. Heath, 1980), pp. 20–34.

[58]Ibid.

firm is much more likely to use this strategy than is a multibusiness firm, since the alternative for the single-business firm is completely closing its doors, instead of shutting down one or more unprofitable divisions.

Shrink Selectively.   A shrink selectively strategy is an attempt to reposition the firm within the industry. The objective is to identify the profitable market segments and then position the company and product to best serve this market niche. The firm is hoping to build a loyal customer relationship through some distinctive competence, either internal or external. Once a firm is serving this niche, it should try and raise barriers to entry, because, as the number of profitable niches decreases, there will be increased competition to serve the few profitable segments that remain.

The three strategies mentioned so far—increase the investment, hold the investment level, and shrink selectively—all assume that there are still acceptable returns to be earned in endgame. Firms in endgame can be assumed to pursue aggressive strategies, since their additional investments will motivate them to protect their commitment to continued performance. It is only when acceptable returns on assets cannot be earned by remaining invested in the endgame that a company may wish to exit.

Milk the Investment.   The idea behind a milk-the-investment strategy is to retrieve the value of earlier investments. This was commonly called a *harvest* strategy in the past.[59] Although participation in the industry still yields attractive cash flows, the firm has made a commitment to get out of the business as soon as: (1) the salvage value of its assets equals the expected value of cash flows generated, or (2) some other corporate criterion has been fulfilled.[60] Timing becomes critical with this strategy; the company drains its resources without regard for long-run positioning.

The objective of milking the investment is to either: (1) increase return on investment by surrendering market share; or (2) funnel as much cash as possible into other projects as quickly as possible.[61] The danger with this strategy comes from external or unforeseen forces inhibiting the planned actions of the company. An example of external factors would be customers or the government exerting pressure to keep the firm invested, even though the business is unprofitable.

Divest Now.   Divest now is simply a get out strategy. The idea behind this strategy is, as the earning power of the endgame business shrinks, to sell off assets as quickly as possible before their value shrinks too much. Divesting can either be through the sale or simply the abandonment of assets; the decision often comes down to the depreciated worth of the assets.[62] In any event, the crucial element in divesting is timing. The longer a firm waits to divest, the greater the likely loss on assets. The ability to get rid of assets quickly supports the practice of keeping a flexible position and having a realistic assessment of the assets' salvage value.

---

[59]Ibid.

[60]Harrigan, ''Strategic Planning,'' pp. 17–20.

[61]Ibid.

[62]Harrigan, *Strategies for Declining Businesses*, pp. 20–34.

Should a firm exit early? The advantage to early exit is that the firm will recover a substantial proportion of its cash, equivalent to the expected cash flows that would be realized from continued operation. An early exit often is motivated by fear and the belief that other strategies will not yield acceptable results. The disadvantage to early exit is that if the firm guessed wrong, it will have closed its doors to an industry that could yield very attractive profits in the future.

CONCLUSIONS

We have examined a number of business-level strategies, applicable primarily to single-business organizations or to an individual unit of a multibusiness or multimission organization. We grouped the strategic options into a framework consisting of several categories: strategies for positioning the business; distinguishing the business; increasing scope; redefining and reducing scope; and extending the core business (this latter category is discussed in Chapter 7 as part of multibusiness strategies). Having delineated all these strategies, the question becomes when and under what conditions to use each? Research in this area is sketchy and uneven, but the body of strategic knowledge is steadily developing.

Optimal strategies geared to the market's life-cycle stage depend on a number of factors, including the stage itself, the type of business and its competitive position, and the measure of performance used. In some instances, particularly in the growth stage, diametrically-opposed strategies may be recommended, depending on whether the goal is to improve market share or cash flow.

Other approaches may be warranted if other objectives are paramount, or if the primary strategies are not possible, warranted, or desirable. Typically in the later growth and maturity stages, a firm may take holding actions—steady-state strategies—designed to defend and maintain its position or allow it to pursue a profit or continuity approach. Here, the emphasis is on selectivity and critical review of strategic and operational decisions, ensuring that each expenditure and action is justified on a cost-benefit or adequate-return basis.

A note of caution is due, however, with regard to generic strategies. While a framework may help a firm see options more clearly, blind usage may put the business at a disadvantage vis-à-vis more creative competitors. If the use of generic approaches makes a firm's actions *predictable,* the strategy can be self-defeating. That is, predictable actions are easy to anticipate and relatively easy to defend against. For example, if a football team *always* runs the ball on "running downs"—such as 3rd and 2 yards to go—and *always* passes on "passing downs"—such as 3rd and 8 yards to go—the defending team has an easier task. Firms must have an element of unpredictability to their strategies, to keep the competition guessing and off guard. On the other hand, they need consistency to keep their strategic direction and focus.

Multibusiness Strategies: Coordination, Diversification, Venturing, and Restructuring

LEARNING OBJECTIVES

After completing Chapter 7, you should be able to:

Understand that organizations may be structured differently for strategic versus operational purposes.

Define strategic business units.

Understand the major strategic alternatives available for corporate-level decisions.

Understand the role of portfolio models in corporate-level strategy, as well as the strategies appropriate for each segment of the models.

Appreciate the role of mergers, acquisitions, and new ventures in diversifying and entering new businesses.

Understand how companies restructure their portfolios and exit from businesses, including divestitures.

Appreciate conditions under which the various strategic alternatives are appropriate.

In the previous chapter, we investigated strategies for individual businesses. Many organizations compete in essentially a single market, industry, or business. Others, however, have diversified or expanded into more than one business and are, therefore, "multibusiness" companies. Sometimes called *multimission* organizations, these firms are faced with corporate-level strategic decisions; that is, which businesses should the organization compete in, and what should be the relationship between the businesses?

In short, the major focus is on what to do *with* the business units, whereas what to do *within* the business unit—how to compete—is the focus of business-level strategies. Corporate-level performance is influenced by at least four general factors:

1. *Performance of existing business units.* A firm will grow if its business units grow (as a result of business-level strategies).
2. *The number of business units.* Corporate-level growth can occur by employing corporate resources to increase the number of business units. This can be done by acquiring existing businesses or by creating new ventures internally. The reverse is also true; corporate size can be reduced by divesting or liquidating business units.
3. *The mix of business units.* Corporate performance can be improved by divesting, retrenching, or liquidating poorly performing businesses, and by acquiring or starting better performers with the additional resources provided.
4. *A combination of actions.* The three actions listed above are not mutually exclusive. Firms can and often do use them in conjunction as part of their corporate-level strategies.

The focus in this chapter is on how multibusiness organizations organize and align their individual businesses, including how they decide to enter new businesses and retreat from existing businesses. Keep in mind, however, that diversified *companies* don't compete in individual markets; only their *businesses* do. Therefore, competition occurs at the business-unit level; unless a corporate-level strategy focuses on the success of each unit, the strategy will fail, no matter how clever or elegant.[1]

PROFILE   **ITT Corp.**

During the 60s and 70s, the legendary Harold S. Geneen turned the ailing International Telephone and Telegraph Co.—whose business was mainly overseas—into the world's foremost conglomerate, with some 2,000 units. In the late 70s, Geneen's star dimmed with revelations of bribery in Chile and Italy, "accounting gimmickry," declining profits, high debt, declining stock price, and low morale. Geneen retired in 1979, and was replaced by the current CEO, Rand V. Araskog.

---

[1] Zane N. Markowitz, "Hidden Sector Competitor Analysis," *Planning Review* 15, no. 5 (September/October 1987), p. 20.

Since 79, Araskog has sold off all or part of 100 companies in an attempt to focus and restructure the company, changing its sights from size and growth to earnings and return on equity. The sell-offs have changed ITT dramatically, reducing employees from 348,000 to 123,000. ITT today is a trimmer, more efficient, comprehensible collection of nine basic businesses, with profits up 65 percent on an 11 percent increase in sales in 1987 and 88.

In the early 80s, raiders were circling as the company's stock price fell below $22 per share, with some estimates of a breakup value of close to $100 per share. So, Araskog began selling off parts of the company, keeping the more promising, efficient businesses with synergy and which fit his new corporate focus. In the process, sales have increased from $12 billion in 83 to $19.4 billion in 88—all from internal growth—and the stock price rebounded to over $60 per share. Araskog isn't finished restructuring yet.

ITT's Rayonier, Inc., forest products division, with $1.3 billion in assets, has no synergy with the rest of ITT. "Its the kind of company that we could one day let go," says Araskog. But, not yet. "There's going to be an upsurge in interest rates and inflation again . . . when that happens, we're going to have Rayonier worth probably twice to three times what it is today. *Then* we can decide what to do with it."[2]

PROFILE   ### Coca-Cola Co.

Coca-Cola's "49 percent solution" strategy is reshaping the soft-drink giant into what may be the model for the post-80s conglomerate—a company that goes back to basics but retains big stakes in diversified businesses while assuming little risk. In the early 80s, Coca-Cola diversified into the entertainment business in a big way, buying Columbia Pictures, 40 percent of Tri-Star Pictures, Merv Griffin Enterprises ("Wheel of Fortune" and "Jeopardy"), and others.

While Coca-Cola liked the entertainment business, it didn't like the risks and capital investments it and some of its bottling company holdings entailed. Therefore, Coca-Cola spun off or sold majority ownership in several restructured businesses, resulting in the following framework:

	Debt	Equity	Capital
Coca-Cola Co. (Parent)	$ .45 B	$3.2 B	$3.65 B
Coca-Cola Enterprises, Inc.	2.1 B	1.65 B	3.75 B
Columbia Pictures Entertainment, Inc.	.63 B	1.01 B	1.64 B
T.C.C. Beverages Ltd. (Canada)	.14 B	.16 B	.3 B

---

[2]Leslie Eaton, "Getting the Message: Investors Start to Appreciate a New ITT," *Barron's,* August 31, 1987, p. 13.

Thus, Coca-Cola was able to sweep $3 billion of debt off its books, keeping effective control over the businesses while it concentrated on its soft-drink and foods operations. The move provided a degree of insulation between Coca-Cola and its entertainment businesses, making the parent company more of a pure soft-drink company once again, with much lower capital investments. This is where they want to be. Roberto C. Goizueta, CEO, says that the parent company's food and soft-drink businesses are high in profit margins and low in capital requirements, and lower in risk than the entertainment business. In fact, some employees describe the company's traditional business of making and selling its secret formula syrup as "a license to print money."[3]

MANAGING THE MULTIBUSINESS ORGANIZATION

Running a diversified company is different than managing an individual business company; the main difference arises from the need to manage diversity. As SCM Corporation's George Hall observes, three points need to be kept in mind:

1. In the diversified company, each separate unit has to carry its own weight, as if it were an independent business. To a large extent, such units should do their own planning (business-unit planning) and run themselves.

2. Some operational and staff functions, such as personnel matters, coordination of information networks, and external relations, are best left to the parent.

3. The parent must forge a sense of group identity in the units, judging their performance through review and budget processes and rewarding business-unit managers for good performance.[4]

But what kind of structure works best for diversified firms? Recent research has shown that the M-form structure (multidivisional) increases the rate of return for unrelated diversifiers—companies diversified into unrelated businesses. However, this structure decreases the rate of return for vertically integrated firms, and results in no significant change for related diversifiers (companies diversified into related businesses).

As shown in Table 7.1, unrelated diversifiers improve their performance by being able to take advantage of resource allocation efficiencies in the M-form structure. For vertically integrated firms, however, performance declines, possibly because interdependence between businesses now in separate divisions compromises the vertically integrated firm's ability to allocate resources. Although related diversified firms' performance also declined (again, possibly because of divisional interdependence), the drop was not statistically significant.

---

[3]Betsy Morris, "Coca-Cola's Corporate Strategy Is Divide and Conquer," *The Wall Street Journal,* October 8, 1987, p. 6.

[4]George E. Hall, "Reflections on Running a Diversified Company," *Harvard Business Review* 65, no. 1 (January–February 1987), p. 84.

TABLE 7.1   ROA before and after M-form Structure

Firm Type	Before M-form	After M-form
Unrelated diversified	4.11%	5.16%
Vertically integrated	6.85	5.86
Related diversified	7.60	7.11

Keep in mind that the related diversified firms outperformed the other two, regardless of the type of structure. The results indicate that unrelated diversifiers *should* adopt the M-form structure, bringing their performance closer to the others, while vertically integrated firms should not. Regardless of the corporate structure, however, related diversified firms are the top performers.[5]

Strategic versus Operational Structure

An organization's management makes two major types of decisions, strategic and operational. How a firm organizes its strategic functions and processes can be quite different from the way it organizes its operational functions and processes. In reality, a company can have *two* ways of structuring itself—one for strategic purposes and one for operations. The organization most of us "see" is operational—producing and delivering goods and services. This operational organization is comprised of divisions, functional departments, plants, sales regions, and other units on the firm's organization chart. But the strategic organization, consisting of business units, markets, and strategic levels, is seldom seen by outsiders.

While strategies are formulated and "made" in ways that may be separate from the operational organization, it is through the operational structure, systems, and processes that they are implemented and carried out. Strategies involve the future and directions for the firm, while operations deal with the present—achieving and fulfilling those strategies and objectives. Do not fall into the trap of trying to judge which is more important. Both strategies and operations are important for organizational success. Without effective operations, strategies will not yield results through the delivery of high-quality goods and services. Yet without good strategic direction, operations that are otherwise effective may be for naught. The strategic/operational linkage is critical to the successful achievement of future objectives.[6]

---

[5]R. E. Hoskisson, "Multidivision Structure and Performance: The Contingency of Diversification Strategy," *Academy of Management Journal* 30, no. 4 (December 1987), pp. 625–44.

[6]J. D. Romano, "Operations Strategy," in *The Strategic Management Handbook,* ed. K. J. Albert (New York: McGraw-Hill, 1983), p. 13–1.

Most students of management and business are familiar with the way organizations are structured for operating purposes. The operational organization reflects departmentation decisions implemented to produce and deliver goods and services. For example, a New York-based organization may decide to expand into West Coast markets. This strategy may require building a manufacturing plant in California and creating a West Coast sales district. Assume that this firm wants to produce three types of metal products—for example, aluminum siding and storm doors, electric power and distribution cable, and transportation components (such as panels for automotive and mass-transit assemblies). Since all of these products are aluminum, it is logical and efficient that they be produced in a single plant under the responsibility of a plant manager. It also is possible that all three types of products may be sold to customers by the same sales force. Therefore, the structure of this division might show the new plant and sales district as in Figure 7.1.

However, on closer inspection, the products the division manufactures may have little in common. For example, aluminum siding, electric transmisson cables, and transportation parts are used for very different purposes, are sold to different customers in different industries, compete with different suppliers, have different cyclical and seasonal influences, and are affected by different economic factors. Competing in three or four distinct markets, or businesses, may require very different strategies and subject the division to dissimilar environmental factors. In reality, aluminum siding may have more in common with masonite siding than with mass-transit panels.

FIGURE 7.1   Operational Organization Structure

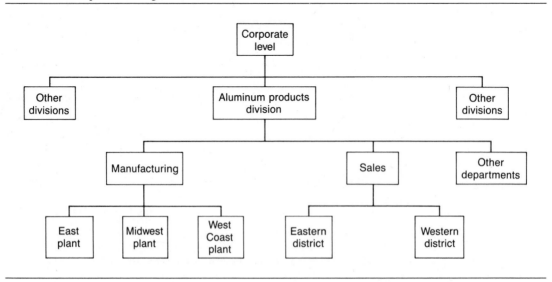

Strategic Business Units

For these and additional reasons, companies have created the strategic business unit (SBU) to describe the businesses or markets in which they compete and to provide the structure for their *strategic* decisions. Thus, while a single plant may at the same time be *operationally* producing products for different business units, one of the business units—say, building products—may be supplied by more than one plant (such as those manufacturing wood and aluminum products). One organization structure may exist for *strategic* purposes and another for *operational* purposes. Still, the organization structure should represent the simplest, easiest, and most effective means of accomplishing the operational and strategic tasks.

The ideal organizational arrangement obviously would be to have the strategic structure and the operational structure coincide with one another—but this is not always possible, as our example has shown. The key building block in organizing the firm's strategic planning activities is the *strategic business unit*. A strategic business unit can be defined as an operating unit or a focal point for planning that provides a distinct set of products or services to a distinct group of customers and competes within an identifiable group. It is the point at which business-level strategy is focused and developed.[7]

The strategic business unit concept was developed by General Electric in the 1970s as a solution to its previous "profitless growth" and other problems it was experiencing with its planning processes. GE is perhaps the most widely diversified nonconglomerate company in the world. (In the late 1970s, it consisted of 170 separate departments grouped into 49 divisions. The divisions, in turn, reported to 10 group executives, who reported to the CEO.) The basic unit of organization in GE was the department—the profit center within which goods and services are manufactured and distributed. As shown in Figure 7.2, the reason for the division and group levels in GE's hierarchy was to make the organization manageable; a span of control of 170 departments reporting to a single CEO obviously would be unworkable. To reduce the span of control, related departments were grouped into the 49 divisions, and related divisions were gathered into the 10 groups.

As suggested by Figure 7.2, GE's diversification put it into product lines ranging from toaster ovens to nuclear reactors, and from jet engines to construction equipment, chemicals, light bulbs, electric motors, transformers, turbines, space products, and more. While GE's organization in the early 1970s worked well in managing the diversified operations, it did little to facilitate effective planning. This was because, as you know, a strategic plan requires an analysis of the environment—competitive, technological, and so on—but widely divergent products are beset by very different environmental influences. There is

---

[7]A. C. Hax and N. S. Majluf, *Strategic Management* (Englewood Cliffs, N.J.: Prentice-Hall, 1984), p. 294.

FIGURE 7.2 GEs Operational Organization in the 1970s

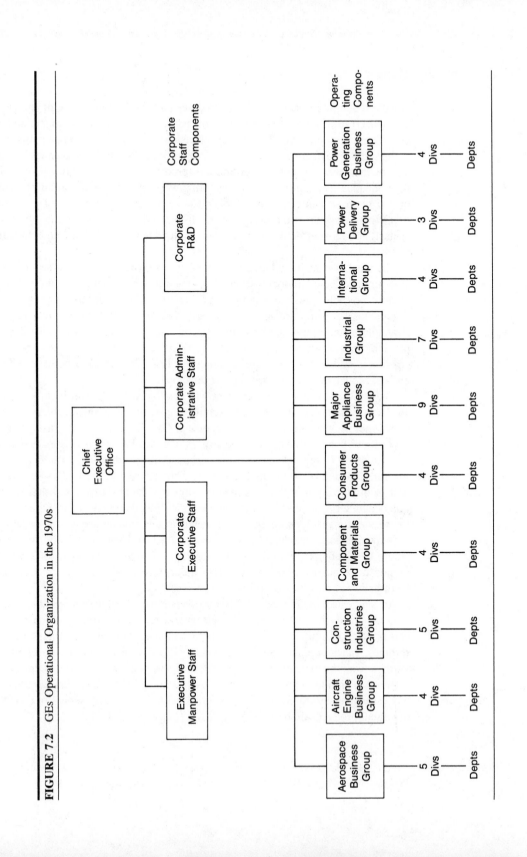

no *common* conclusion that can be drawn concerning the technological environment and competitive environment for refrigerators and jet engines, for example. Therefore, a single strategic plan for GE would be useless and 170 strategic plans would be unwieldy. Developing strategic plans for the 10 groups or 49 divisions would make more sense. But the departments comprising them were joined for *operational* effectiveness and efficiency, and typically included product lines in differing markets. For example, the consumer-products group encompassed home entertainment products as well as light bulbs. Obviously, such products are different in terms of many competitive, technological, and purchase-decision aspects.

So how does one plan in such a setting? If one plan is meaningless, 170 plans are unwieldy, and many of the 10 groups and 49 divisions did not share the homogeneous environments required to develop meaningful plans. GE's solution was to reorganize for planning purposes only, around the markets it serves rather than around production or other functions. In the process, GE created 43 strategic business units, one for each of the "businesses" it competed in, and for which a meaningful and separate strategic plan could be developed. Many of the SBUs cross traditional group, division, and departmental profit-center lines. For example, food preparation appliances had been located in three separate divisions for operational efficiency. For strategic-planning purposes, these appliances were merged into a single SBU serving the housewares market.[8]

SBU Criteria.

Most small and many medium-sized companies (particularly nondiversified firms) compete in only one business—in effect they have only one SBU. This is not the case for large, diversified, companies; GE saw itself as being in 43 different businesses.

What are the criteria for creating SBUs? What determines whether two product lines should be in the same or different SBUs? Try thinking of an SBU as the intersection of products and markets. Arthur D. Little has defined SBUs as "composed of a product or product lines with identifiable independence from other products or product lines in terms of competition, prices, substitutability of products, style, quality, and impact of product withdrawal."[9] In other words, boundaries for SBUs may be affected by environmental influences (such as technology, price factors, product similarities, type of competition, industry factors, and type of customers) and public policy influences (such as industry concentration or degree of regulation). The crucial issue in defining an SBU is finding the largest segment that allows for a proper assessment of internal strengths and environmental opportunities, and that can be treated as a separate entity during resource allocation. Of foremost importance is the ability of managers to operate an SBU with a high level of independence with respect to other business units in the firm. They must be free to respond in an effective way

---

[8]W. K. Hall, "SBUs: Hot, New Topic in the Management of Diversification," *Business Horizons,* February 1978, p. 17.

[9]*A System for Managing Diversity* (Cambridge, Mass.: Arthur D. Little, 1974), p. 9.

to competitive pressures. SBUs should possess strategic autonomy, and should not compete against each other.

The following criteria are useful for deciding whether products should be included in the same or separate SBUs:

1. *Price*. Does a price change in one product group require an examination of prices in other groups? If so, the products may be related sufficiently to warrant inclusion in the same SBU. For example, if IBM lowers the price of its microcomputer line, does this action require the company to reevaluate its prices for minicomputers, large-scale systems, and word processors so they will not be overpriced in relation to the personal computer line (ignoring corporate rules of thumb for pricing)? Would this affect sales of the other lines? Probably not, with the possible exception of the word processing line.

2. *Competitors*. Do the products share the same group of competitors? If two products compete largely against the same firms, this may indicate that they belong in the same SBU.

3. *Customers*. Are the products sold mainly to the same groups of customers? If they are, they are candidates for inclusion in one SBU.

4. *Shared R&D, manufacturing, and marketing*. Do the products share similar types and levels of technology? Are manufacturing processes similar and production facilities shared? Are similar distribution channels, as well as sales and advertising approaches, utilized?[10]

Other factors can be pertinent. Industry maturity, life-cycle stage of the products, competitive position, and the degree of freedom to implement strategies should be considered.

Obviously, some products may be very similar with regard to some factors and less similar with regard to others. Should they be placed in the same or different planning units (SBUs)? The question is one of judgment. The goal should be to create as few SBUs as possible, to reach the highest level of aggregation possible given the factors employed to analyze the product groups. Many companies fall into the trap of creating too many SBUs—carving out so many that each is too small and meaningless from a marketing and planning viewpoint. One guide is that each SBU should *require* a separate strategic plan. If several strategic plans are essentially similar, perhaps fewer SBUs are required. Remember, GE—one of the most diversified corporations in the world—created 43 SBUs. Union Carbide has 9, Westinghouse has 37 "basic business units," Olin has 30 "strategic planning units," IBM has 7 "independent business units," Intel has 24 "strategic business segments," and Oki Industries has 15 units. These companies are all diversified, and therefore require more SBUs than do less diversified firms. Many large but concentrated companies may have only one SBU. General Motors' North American passenger car operations has only two SBUs—one for small and large cars (the Buick–Oldsmobile–Cadillac group) and one for mid-sized cars (the

---

[10]Peter Patel and Michael Younger, "A Frame of Reference for Strategy Development," *Long-Range Planning* 11 (April 1978), p. 6.

Chevrolet–Pontiac–GM of Canada group). Thus, each car group is responsible for its types of car, and the six car divisions (Chevrolet, Pontiac, Oldsmobile, Buick, Cadillac, and Saturn) can market cars engineered and assembled by either group.[11]

GE Update. A company that is just starting a formal strategic planning process may find the identification of SBUs very taxing. Normally, a temporary definition of SBUs is suggested at an early stage; as the planning system evolves, major redefinitions may be required.[12] For example, in 1977, GE reorganized its SBUs into six sectors of the economy (consumer products and services, industrial products and components, technical systems and materials, international, power systems, and the since-sold Utah International Inc.). The sectors consisted of related groups and divisions. GE felt that one level of business-unit planning was not enough. In the early 80s, they used 49 SBUs with a plan developed for each. The strategies of each of its 6 to 10 businesses (SBUs) were reviewed and resources allocated to them at the sector (industry) level. This was then reviewed at the corporate level, where allocations were also approved. So, GE essentially created a two-level business-unit planning structure by grouping similar SBUs into sectors.[13]

In the past several years, GE has significantly restructured its portfolio, selling off several of its businesses (including consumer electronics) and sectors and adding several new businesses, notably RCA and its subsidiary, NBC. GE most recently replaced its sector-form of organization, dropping a layer of top management and effectively merging its strategic and operational organizations. Under CEO Jack Welch, GE now manages on the basis of three groups of 14 key businesses—technology businesses, services businesses, and core manufacturing businesses—aided by four support businesses,[14] as shown in Figure 7.3.

Therefore, GE now plans and operates on the basis of key ''businesses.'' It has gone to the ideal of having the planning structure the same as its operating structure, minimizing the differences between its planning and operating units to the point that the company plans by businesses, not separate SBUs. This decision on GE's part involves a trade-off; its ideal planning units do not *exactly* coincide with its ideal operating units, but merging the two creates fewer problems than having two structures. This is not the case for all organizations or situations.

Corporate-Level Processes

Again, the main goal of corporate-level strategies is to find and manage the right combination of business, so that the corporation can achieve its goals and objectives. In the past, growth has been a dominant corporate objective; more

---

[11]Joseph B. White, ''GM to Consolidate Big, Small Car Roles for Cost Savings, Reversing Revamp Goal,'' *The Wall Street Journal*, June 7, 1989, p. A8.

[12]*A System for Managing Diversity*, p. 10.

[13]R. F. Vancil, *Implementing Strategy: The Role of Top Management* (Boston: Harvard Business School, 1982), p. 83.

[14]*GE Annual Report*, 1987, p. 7.

FIGURE 7.3   GE's Current Structure

Corporate
Executive
Office

Corporate staff components

Technology businesses	Services businesses	Core manufacturing businesses	Support businesses
• Aircraft Engine	• GE Financial Services	• Major Appliances	• Semiconductors
• Aerospace	• National Broadcasting Company	• Lighting	• Ladd Petroleum
• Plastics	• Communications and Services	• Power Systems	• Corporate Trading
• Medical Systems		• Construction Equipment	• International
• Factory Automation		• Transportation Systems	
		• Motors	

recently, the balance has swung toward returns on investment. Equally important to having business units in which the company has a competitive advantage is the coordination of those businesses. For example, a number of functional strategies and actions may benefit the company, but are beyond the scope of and may not be presently feasible for any one business. Technology development and innovative activity is one such case, where the corporate level can coordinate business-level technology strategies and actions for the benefit of other businesses of the company. The corporate level can fund, for example, the development of an advanced technology by one business unit (or in a corporate laboratory) that may have application across several businesses, and would be too costly or risky for any one business to undertake on its own. Thus, coordination and funding of functional activities (technology, marketing, and the like) between businesses are responsibilities of corporate management in multibusiness firms.

CORPORATE PORTFOLIO MODELS

One tool many corporations use to aid in corporate-level strategic decision making is corporate portfolio models. These models illustrate the relationship between business units and highlight which should be retained or divested, and which types of businesses should be acquired or started. Four commonly used and related portfolio models will be examined: the growth/share matrix, the GE business screen, the business profile matrix, and the directional policy matrix.

These models were developed in the late 1960s because, understandably, corporate management usually didn't know as much as the division general managers did about the firm's operating divisions. Portfolio models provided

FIGURE 7.4 BCG Growth/Share Matrix

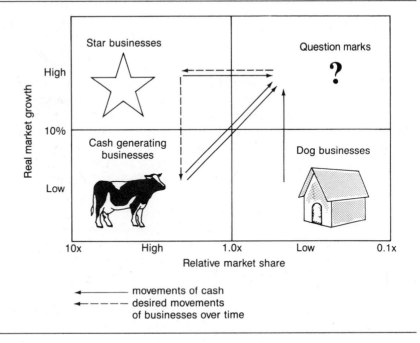

corporate management with a mechanism for comparing the *relative* strength and attractiveness of each SBU without being familiar with each in detail. The purpose of portfolio analysis, then, is to encourage a more rational allocation of corporate resources to SBUs based on their attractiveness and strength.[15]

The Growth/Share Matrix

The Boston Consulting Group (BCG) proposed a new way to visualize the role played by each SBU in a diversified organization, as well as the relationships of SBUs. The BCG matrix plots market growth rate on the vertical axis and the business's relative market share on the horizontal axis, as shown in Figure 7.4. Actually, market growth rate is used as a proxy to indicate the attractiveness of the industry in which the SBU competes, and the market share in relation to the leading competitor is used to indicate the competitive strength of the business. This matrix is divided into four cells, with some figure (an arbitrary 10 percent market growth, the firm's target growth rate, the inflation rate, or whatever is meaningful) used to

[15]R. F. Vancil, *Implementing Strategy: The Role of Top Management, Teacher's Manual* (Boston: Harvard Business School, 1982), p. 6.

distinguish between high and low industry attractiveness. High competitive strength, in turn, is typically indicated by a relative market share over 1.0, with low strength below that level. (Relative market share is the SBU's sales divided by those of the largest competitor in the market.) The growth/share matrix visually portrays a company's SBUs in relationship to one another on these two axes.

Cell Categories. Business units positioned in the upper-left cell of the grid are *stars,* and are strong competitors (they have the largest market share) in high-growth markets. Stars usually require large amounts of cash to sustain their growth, but their strong position in the market makes them highly profitable. Thus, their cash flow is typically close to being in balance and is usually positive.

Cash cows are SBUs in the lower-left cell, and usually are large net providers of cash for the firm. Their leading market position usually makes them highly profitable, and because their needs for cash are less than those of stars, the net result is a healthy positive cash flow.

Question marks—sometimes called wildcats, sweepstakes, or problem children— are those in the upper-right cell. They are in high-growth industries and therefore require large amounts of cash. However, because of their relatively weak position competitively, they tend not to be very profitable, meaning that they require cash from outside (borrowing from the corporation "bank" or from other SBUs).

Dogs are businesses in the lower right—those in low-growth industries and in a weak competitive position. They usually are not very profitable (if at all), but do not require a lot of cash because of the low growth of their industry. In fact, they are typically providers of small amounts of cash.

Matrix Observations. Several points concerning the matrix should be kept in mind. One is that the product life cycle indicates that growth declines with maturity. Thus, over time, stars can be expected to become cash cows (which is *not* undesirable) and question marks may turn into dogs (which *is* undesirable). The company should be continually striving to move its SBUs farther to the left, in effect turning question marks into stars and possibly dogs into cash cows. Remember from the discussion of the life cycle in Chapter 5, however, that it is difficult to gain market share in the maturity and decline stages. The best action may be to "spruce up" the dogs for the purpose of divesting them. (Keep in mind that a dog to one company may be a cash cow to a stronger competitor, and thus, an attractive purchase.) Ideally, question marks are in the preshakeout stage of the life cycle and market share possibly can be gained, so they may become stars. However, the risks may be high (hence, the term *wildcat*).

The largest amount of cash flow is from cash cows to question marks, so the company needs a balance of these types of SBUs. While a preponderance of stars may appear ideal, they typically do not produce enough cash to fund many future growth products, such as new stars. Thus, a few cash cows may be necessary to create new stars. Likewise, a predominance of cash cows may generate high profits and cash now, but what about the future as these businesses go into the decline stage? Too many question marks mean too much risk and the need for too much cash, and too many dogs may signify a company approaching serious trouble.

FIGURE 7.5   General Electric's Nine-Cell Business Screen

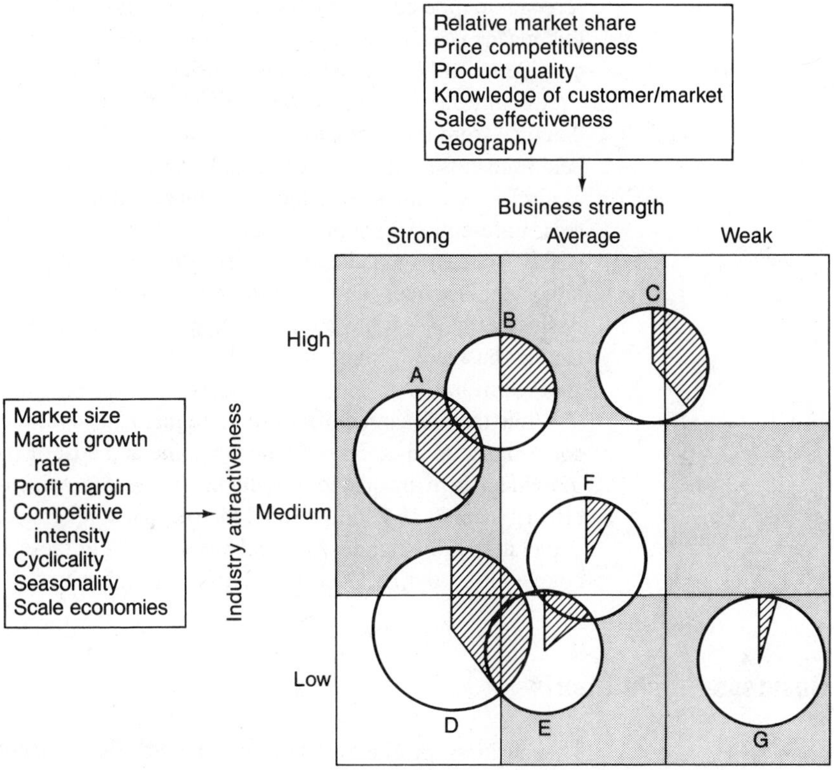

Source: Modified from Charles W. Hofer and Dan Schendel, *Strategy Formulation Analytical Concepts* (St. Paul, Minn.: West Publishing, 1978), p. 32.

GE's Business Screen

In the early 1970s, GE and McKinsey & Company, consultants, developed a nine-cell "business screen" that is more complex than the simple growth-share matrix. While the screen is conceptually similar to the matrix, it defines industry attractiveness and business strength in terms of composite measures, determined and weighted by the company. As Figure 7.5 suggests, a number of factors besides market growth may determine attractiveness. These factors can be weighted according to their relative importance to the company, assigned a relative value, and combined into an overall index of industry attractiveness.

The same approach can be used for business strength, which obviously depends on more than just relative market share, especially when the future is considered. Other factors beyond those in Figure 7.5 might include breadth of product line, patents and other proprietary factors, newness and efficiency of plants, level of capacity, and experience-curve effects.

Like the growth-share matrix, the business screen is a portrayal of a company's SBUs, providing a visual display of its portfolio. GE divides its screen into nine cells, which becomes the basis for its "stoplight strategy." What this means is that the three cells in the upper left get the "green light" and are considered to be "invest-grow" businesses. The three in the lower right get a "red light," and are slated for "harvest-divest" action. The middle three on the diagonal from upper right to lower left get a "yellow light," or caution, and are held for a closer, more selective look. SBUs are typically portrayed on the screen as circles, with the size of the circle representing the SBU's size, and the shaded area representing its market share.

GE's current goal is to compete only in those businesses where it can be either the number one or two competitor; in other words, only in those businesses where it has a clear competitive advantage. This would result in their having businesses only in the left third of the matrix, on anything but a short-term basis.

While the GE screen offers some refinements over the BCG matrix, it also has some shortcomings. Its refinements come at a cost of increased complexity. The individual firm must decide whether using the screen is worth the additional effort. Second, as with the BCG matrix, the business screen does not adequately depict new-growth industries and businesses. For these reasons, many companies couple either the BCG or GE matrix with a business profile matrix.

Business Profile Matrix

The business profile matrix plots the SBU's competitive position against its life-cycle stage. The purpose is to portray the relative strength of SBUs in the embryonic and growth stages. Plotting the SBUs on the matrix, using circles as in the business screen, provides several types of information:

1. The relative strength of the company's business portfolio.
2. The likely future prospects for the company, as indicated by where the SBUs fall on the life-cycle axis.
3. Which relatively weak SBUs are targets for actions to improve their position (since the embryonic, shakeout, and decline or aging stages are those in which major changes in competitive position can occur most easily).
4. What type of generic strategy is most appropriate for the businesses falling in each of the 20 cells of the matrix.

Suggested strategic guidelines for each of the cells are shown in Figure 7.6. (Some companies portray the turbulent shakeout stage separately, giving the matrix 25 cells.)[16]

---

[16]Peter Patel and Michael Younger, "A Frame of Reference," pp. 6–10.

FIGURE 7.6 Business Profile Matrix

Strength of Competitive Position	Life-Cycle Stage			
	Embryonic	Growth	Maturity	Aging
Dominant	Hold position All-out push for share	Hold position Hold share	Hold position Grow with industry	Hold position
Strong	Attempt to improve position All-out push for share	Attempt to improve position Push for share	Hold position Grow with industry	Hold position or Harvest
Favorable	Selectively attempt to improve position Selective or all-out push for share	Attempt to improve position Selective push for share	Custodial or maintenance Find niche and attempt to protect it	Harvest Phased withdrawal
Tentative	Selectively push for position	Find niche and protect it	Find niche and hang on Phased withdrawal	Phased withdrawal or abandon
Weak	Up or out	Turnaround or abandon	Turnaround or Phased withdrawal	Abandon

Source: Adapted from Peter Patel and Michael Younger, "A Frame of Reference for Strategy Development," *Long-Range Planning* 11 (April 1978), p. 8.

Directional Policy Matrix

Another strategic planning tool is the directional policy matrix (DPM), developed by Royal Dutch Shell. While it is similar to the GE business screen, the axes and their directions are reversed. In addition, the DPM focuses on a business sector of the economy rather than on a specific industry. Figure 7.7 shows the DPM and recommended strategies. The DPM also can be used to display all of the competitors an SBU faces in a particular sector, enabling the company to compare its SBU to the competition.

To illustrate how the DPM might be used to aid in corporate-level strategic decisions, consider Tenneco's J.I. Case Co. Case has been a consistent third in farm equipment, behind Deere and International Harvester (IH), which would make its rating no better than "average" (maybe even "weak") in terms of competitive capability. But what are the industry's prospects? Many say "average" or below for the foreseeable future. From the DPM, a generic strategy of "phased withdrawal" looks most appropriate for Tenneco's Case business unit, perhaps ranging from a pessimistic "disinvest" to an optimistic "custodial." But what did Tenneco do? It bought IH's farm equipment business, to combine it with Case's. Why? Evidently Tenneco's management feels that the industry's prospects are attractive in the long run, warranting a "double or quit" strategy. Should Tenneco have quit—withdrawn from the industry and used its cash from the proceeds for other purposes? Or should they have doubled (which they did) using their healthy $2 billion annual cash flow from energy, auto parts, and shipbuilding to try to forge a viable number-two supplier in a mature industry increasingly dominated by Deere? Whatever the outcome, the action reduces Tenneco's cash and makes it a less attractive takeover candidate.

After acquiring IH's businesses, Tenneco closed IH's Farmall tractor plant in Rock Island, Illinois, significantly reducing industry overcapacity and helping all firms in the industry—including Deere—in the long run.

FIGURE 7.7   Directional Policy Matrix

Company's Competitive Capabilities	Business Sector Prospects		
	Unattractive	*Average*	*Attractive*
Weak	Disinvest	Phased withdrawal Custodial	Double or quit
Average	Phased withdrawal	Custodial Growth	Try harder
Strong	Cash generation	Growth Leader	Leader

Source: Adapted from *The Directional Policy Matrix: A New Aid to Corporate Planning,* (New York: Royal Dutch Shell Co., 1975).

Portfolio Models: A Critique

Business portfolio models can be helpful in arraying the corporation's business units, and in showing the relative balance between them, or lack thereof. Using such tools helps the company decide on future corporate actions: which businesses should grow, which should be divested, where voids and overrepresentations exist, and the like. They also highlight the rationale for interbusiness-unit relationships, such as cash throw off and absorption.

Such models do have weaknesses, however. They are static and don't represent trends; they depict, at best, the present performance of business units. But strategic decisions relate to the future, so care must be taken to realistically estimate where SBUs are likely to be in the future. As an example, investment in a high-potential question mark should be continued, while one in low star potential should be dropped. Keep in mind, however, that such assessments (particularly the latter case) can become self-fulfilling prophecies as a result of the firm's subsequent actions.

In addition, the portfolio models say nothing about another important variable—the relationship between headquarters and the business unit. In reality, it takes more than portfolio-dictated actions to succeed; one of the corporation's key roles is establishing the proper intracompany environment for each of its SBUs. Factors such as the degree of autonomy of an SBU, including its responsibility for its own functional decisions, as well as how much of division management's compensation is based on the unit's performance, all weigh heavily on its success.[17]

There are mechanical problems with some of the models, particularly the growth/share matrix. First, any SBU with less than 1.0 relative market share is a dog or wildcat. In any given market, only one business can have a relative share of greater than 1.0—all the others are dogs or wildcats! Second, most SBUs are likely to fall closer to the middle of the matrix than to the ends; there is likely to be relatively little difference between SBUs falling close to the dividing lines, but on opposite sides. Blind use of the matrix prescriptions, however, would suggest very different treatment of these businesses. Finally, comparing *extreme* stars, cash cows, wildcats, and dogs (corner cells of the nine-cell matrix) indicates that *all* tend to have positive ROI, as shown in Table 7.2. However, wildcats have the least favorable cash flow, with even extreme dogs close to self-sufficiency.[18] Remember, portfolio planning can improve corporate strategy, but only when used with other techniques for analyzing industries and competitors.

---

[17]R. G. Hamermesh and R. E. White, "Manage beyond Portfolio Analysis," *Harvard Business Review* 62, no. 1, (January–February, 1984), p. 103.

[18]N. E. Swanson and L. A. Digman, "Organizational Performance Measures for Strategic Decisions: A PIMS-Based Investigation," in *Handbook of Business Strategy: 1986/1987 Yearbook,* ed. W. D. Guth (Boston: Warren, Gorham & Lamont, 1986), pp. 17–19.

TABLE 7.2   Performance of Corner Cell Businesses in a Nine-Cell Matrix

Measure	Wildcats	Stars	Cash Cows	Dogs
Return on investment	14.90	32.94	27.40	14.66
Cash flow on investment	−4.20	5.14	8.03	-0.69

ENTERING NEW BUSINESSES: DIVERSIFICATION STRATEGIES

Growth and profitability are goals of most, although not all, organizations, at least those in the private sector. While satisfying a need or performing a level of service may be the primary mission and even the number-one goal for most organizations, even those in the public and not-for-profit sectors most often want to grow—to offer more and better service, for example. However, in the private sector, some for-profit organizations make a conscious decision as to size and do not attempt growth beyond that. Typical examples are smaller firms, family-run businesses, and service firms (such as hospitals, schools, law firms, clinics, and the like).

Given that *whether* to grow is a basic decision, the majority of organizations doggedly pursue growth—in sales, market share, geographical area, and more. There are three generic strategies usually employed in the pursuit of growth, in this order:

1. *Horizontal growth of existing businesses,* including more volume, greater market share, geographical (even international) expansion, a broader product line, and the like.
2. *Vertical integration,* both forward and backward. This strategy is typically followed as additional horizontal growth becomes more difficult.
3. *Diversification.* After approaching the limit of vertical integration opportunities, firms typically seek out new business opportunities via diversification. Diversification can be into related products, markets, industries, or technologies, or into unrelated areas.

Diversification, the opposite of concentration, usually results from several pressures. One is that the business cannot grow beyond its present size, because either the market is not large enough, or gaining additional shares of the market is not feasible. Another is the emergence of new markets that the firm would like to take advantage of. New technologies or new applications of existing technologies may also lure the firm into new markets. Finally, firms may diversify for legal reasons, such as tax laws that reward the firm for reinvesting profits as opposed to distributing them to shareholders. But, whatever the reason for diversification, the firm must define the role of each business within the enterprise—successful diversification is not mere aggregation (which may come as a surprise to certain conglomerates).[19]

As Peter Drucker states, "attempts to diversify without either a foundation in common markets or in common technology are doomed to frustration." He further concludes that diversification to make a business "countercyclical"—balancing the cycles of one industry with those of another—rarely works, nor do attempts to marry businesses with high demands for capital with those having a high cash throw off; the balance tends to change with time, invalidating the reason for the diversification. There is one absolute requirement for successful diversification: unity of values. The business unit's climate and values must be compatible and there must be "respect" for the businesses.[20]

Entry Strategies

There are a variety of mechanisms for entering new businesses. Each is described briefly below, and the advantages and disadvantages of each are summarized in Table 7.3.

1. *Acquisitions.* Purchase of an existing business.
2. *Internal development.* Establishing a business new to the company, using internal resources, operating as an internal part of the company.
3. *Licensing.* Acquiring products or technology through licensing is an alternative to purchasing an entire company, and avoids the risks of product development.
4. *Internal ventures.* Entering markets different from the existing base businesses by setting up a separate entity within the existing corporate structure.
5. *Joint ventures or alliances.* Either formation of third corporations involving several or more companies, or "mutual pursuit" alliances between two companies (often a small company with new technology and a larger company with marketing capability).
6. *Venture capital and nurturing.* Securing closeness to (and possible later entry into) new technologies by making minority investments in young and growing enterprises.
7. *Educational acquisitions.* Acquisitions for the purpose of obtaining people familiar with a new business area, which can complement one of the other methods.[21]

The entry alternatives fall into two main types—acquisitions and internal developments and ventures—which are discussed in the following sections.

---

[19]Peter F. Drucker, *Management: Tasks, Responsibilities, Practices,* (New York: Harper & Row, 1974), pp. 683–97.

[20]Ibid., pp. 706–10.

[21]E. B. Roberts and C. A. Berry, "Entering New Businesses: Selecting Strategies for Growth," *Sloan Management Review,* Spring 1985, pp. 3–17.

TABLE 7.3   Entry Mechanisms: Advantages and Disadvantages

New Business Development Mechanisms	*Major Advantages*	*Major Disadvantages*
Acquisitions	Rapid market entry.	New business area may be unfamiliar to parent.
Internal developments	Use existing resources.	Time lag to break even tends to be long (on average eight years). Unfamiliarity with new markets may lead to errors.
Licensing	Rapid access to proven technology. Reduced financial exposure.	Not a substitute for internal technical competence. Not proprietary technology. Dependent upon licensor.
Internal ventures	Use existing resources. May enable a company to hold a talented entrepreneur.	Mixed record of success. Corporation's internal climate often unsuitable.
Joint ventures or alliances	Technological/marketing unions can exploit small/large company synergies. Distribute risk.	Potential for conflict between partners.
Venture capital and nurturing	Can provide window on new technology or market.	Unlikely alone to be a major stimulus of corporate growth.
Educational acquisitions	Provide window and initial staff.	Higher initial financial commitment than venture capital. Risk of departure of entrepreneurs.

Source: Adapted from E. B. Roberts and C. A. Berry, "Entering New Businesses: Selecting Strategies for Success," *Sloan Management Review*, Spring 1985, p. 8. Used with permission. All rights reserved.

Acquisition-Related Strategies

Acquisitions are one way a firm may attempt to grow in size and sales, to increase its economies of scale, or to spread its risks. Divestitures, in turn, are attempts by a firm to eliminate ''dogs'' or other businesses that do not fit the firm's portfolio for one reason or another. Here, acquisitions—types and reasons for acquiring businesses—are examined. Ways of making acquisitions, setting an appropriate price (applicable also to divestitures), the acquisition process, and antitrust implications are treated in Appendix D.

There are five basic reasons for acquiring businesses:

1. To strengthen or protect the base business. An acquisition may provide key personnel, assets, and purchasing power that aid an existing business. An acquisition may provide economies of scale or entry to additional markets (such as G. Heileman's acquisitions of various regional and local brewers), making the firm a stronger and more viable competitor.
2. To diversify, for the reasons discussed previously.
3. To avoid a takeover by acquiring a competitor of a company desiring to take over your business. For example, Ryder Systems (truck rental) intended to take over Frank B. Hall Company (insurance brokerage), which acquired Ryder's competitor Jartran as a defensive move. Thus, antitrust laws prevented Ryder from acquiring Frank B. Hall.
4. To improve financial returns by, for example, improving return on excess capital or purchasing tax credits owned by the acquired firm.[22]
5. To alter the company's business mix (perhaps coupled with divestitures). For example, Gould changed from an electrical equipment to an electronics company through acquisitions.

Types of Acquisitions.   There are four types of acquisitions: (1) vertical, (2) horizontal, (3) concentric diversification, and (4) unrelated diversification, as shown in Figure 7.8.

According to George Steiner, ''vertical acquisitions are those in the same product-line (or line of business) and involve integration from basic raw materials to the ultimate sale to consumers.''[23] For example, a producer of steel ingots may acquire an iron mine or a steel fabricating company. The company can proceed ''upstream'' toward the source of supply by acquiring supplies of raw materials, or components, or subcontractors, or ''downstream'' through the channels of distribution toward the final customer.[24] Vertical acquisitions can reduce costs and increase a firm's competitive market position.

---

[22]L. L. Fray, J. W. Down, and D. Gaylin, ''Acquisitions and Divestitures,'' in *Handbook of Business Strategy,* ed. W. D. Guth (Boston: Warren, Gorham & Lamont, 1985), p. 12–4.

[23]George Steiner, *Top Management Planning* (New York: Macmillan, 1969), p. 641.

[24]N. A. Stacey, *Mergers in Modern Business* (London: Hutchinson, 1970), p. 33.

FIGURE 7.8 Types of Acquisitons

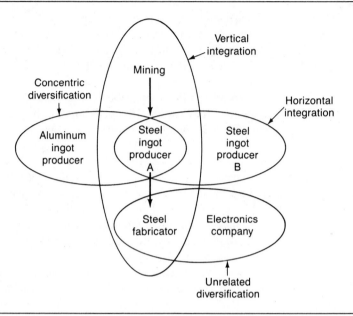

Although vertical acquisitions can improve a firm's market position, they have two major drawbacks. The first is that the firm is still dependent on its particular market and on the business fluctuations of its industry. The second is the possibility of social repercussions, primarily government intervention on antitrust grounds. A major example of government intervention in vertical-control firms was the antitrust decision that led to the breakup of AT&T.

In a horizontal acquisition, a competitor or a business in the same field of endeavor is purchased. Functional skills and resources are expanded and market share is increased. One example is the acquisition of Continental Airlines by Texas International. The same two drawbacks of vertical acquisitions—the firm is still confined to the same industry and the possibility of government antitrust intervention—also affect horizontal acquisitions.

A concentric acquisition occurs when two businesses in different industries have a common thread of interest. An example would be the acquisition of a cake mix producer by a shortening manufacturer. Another form is the acquisition of a business in a separate industry that uses the same marketing channels.

Another type of acquisition involves diversification into unrelated industries. The firm expands not into similar fields but into totally unrelated markets. This decreases the firm's dependence on a particular product or market.

These multi-industry firms are typically either diversified majors or conglomerates. The two styles of firms have dissimilar functions and strategies at the corporate level.[25] The diversified major attempts to bring a synergistic approach to the business units. A conglomerate treats each unit as a complete and independent, or even as a separate, company. In a diversified major, the corporate level is involved in R&D, marketing, manufacturing, and purchasing. A conglomerate, however, is rarely involved in these functional areas. Some examples of diversified majors are GE, Du Pont, and Union Carbide—firms that expanded internally and through acquisition of technologically and market-related businesses. Two examples of conglomerate firms are Textron and ITT. Textron expanded from the wool market into a wide range of consumer and industrial goods. ITT used cash from its communications business to acquire consumer, industrial electronics, and financial service industries.

Internal Development and Venture Strategies

In addition to acquisition strategies, internal actions are also a means of diversification. Business-unit strategies appropriate for the growth, maturity, and decline stages, as well as the judicious use of strategies pertaining to positioning, distinguishing, and determining the desired scope of the businesses can be employed to achieve corporate-level objectives. A corporate-level strategy, the creation of new business units either internally or by joint ventures, is discussed in the following paragraphs.

Internal/Joint-Venture Strategies.   There are two main types of new ventures: those intended to function as a separate company and those created *within* a larger company. The latter are often called *intracorporate ventures,* or *internal new ventures,* and function within a distinctly different environment than does the totally separate venture.

The internal venture is many times a "question mark" or "wildcat" in the corporate portfolio, and has the financial backing of the corporation. The price it pays for this backing, however, is often a lack of independence and an element of corporate "meddling" and control over its activities. Often, the internal new venture is unduly constrained by the parent, because corporate management may not fully appreciate the unique needs of the venture: for entrepreneurial people, flexibility, avoidance of conformity, and risk-taking behavior. Separate ventures do not have these potentially inhibiting constraints, but often possess inadequate financial backing, which inhibits their growth.

As Peter Drucker has said, "it is widely believed that large companies cannot innovate. That is simply not true: Merck, Citibank, and 3M are but three examples of highly innovative corporate giants. But it is true that to innovate successfully, a company has to be run differently from the typical 'well-

---

[25]Norman Berg and R. A. Pitts, "Strategic Management: The Multi-Business Corporation," in *Strategic Management,* ed. D.Schendel and C. W. Hofer (Boston: Little, Brown, 1979), p. 339.

managed' business, whether large or small.''[26] Innovative companies have a separate "innovation budget" to support potential new ventures; they do not expect returns in the short run; they closely control new ventures; and they do not hesitate to abandon obsolete products.

Venture Characteristics.   Inadequate capital remains an important source of failure for new ventures. Ralph Biggadike found this to be a problem even for internal ventures.[27] In his study, he found, for example, that the median ROI was minus 40 percent for the first two years of operation, and minus 14 percent for the next two years. According to Biggadike, it takes *8 years* on the average for new ventures to reach profitability, and *10 to 12 years* before their ROI equals that of mature businesses. Furthermore, the highest ROI tends to go to businesses with high market shares. So the strategic objective for the early years should be to build share, regardless of short-term profitability. In fact, the biggest risk is entering *too small*. Entering on a large scale leads to better financial results earlier than does entering on a small scale. From this it can be seen that the venture with a high chance of succeeding requires a large amount of capital—enough to enter on a large scale and enough to stand negative profits and cash flow for eight years or so. It is better not to enter at all than to enter without adequate backing and fail before the corner is turned. For larger firms, then, it is better to adequately finance fewer ventures than to "test the water" (and likely fail) with a larger number of ventures. Big losses are rare events; small losses are numerous and more likely. As a result, for a start-up, it is not uncommon for a provider of venture capital to give *more* money to the entrepreneur than was requested, to improve the likelihood of survival.

Venture Strategies.   Figure 7.9 displays the range of alternative strategies for launching new ventures, ranging from low to high corporate involvement. At the left, *venture capital* involves the investment of money in the stock of one company by another. The capital source may be an existing industrial firm, or a firm specializing in venture capital, which underwrites a stock issue.

In *venture nurturing,* the investing company contributes more than just capital, usually, managerial assistance in such areas as research, manufacturing, and marketing.

A *venture spin-off* is a new company created by a larger firm to capitalize on its R&D efforts. The new company can pursue an idea or technology that does not fit the developing firm's interests or risks or may be better developed in an outside "entrepreneurial" company. Exxon pursued this approach with its Solar Power Corp.

---

[26]Peter F. Drucker, "The Innovative Company," *The Wall Street Journal,* February 26, 1982, p. 22.

[27]Ralph Biggadike, "The Risky Business of Diversification," *Harvard Business Review,* May–June 1979, p. 103.

FIGURE 7.9   Spectrum of Venture Strategies

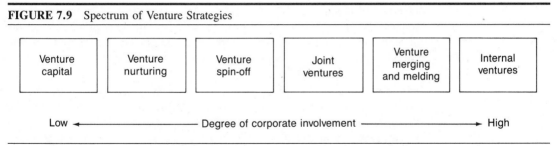

In a *joint venture,* two companies—typically, one large and one small—enter jointly into a new project or venture. The smaller company provides enthusiasm, vigor, flexibility, and technology, and the larger one provides capital and channels of distribution, marketing, and service. In this way, the benefits of both the large and small firm can be realized by the joint venture. IBM employed this approach in conjunction with Rolm and Intel in recent years. A current example of two large companies pursuing joint ventures is the New United Motors Manufacturing, Inc. (NUMMI), undertaken by General Motors/Toyota. Also, in 1988, Motorola and Toshiba entered into a 50–50 joint venture. Called Tohoku Semiconductor Corp., the venture was created to combine Motorola's advanced microprocessor designs with Toshiba's manufacturing knowhow.[28]

Venture merging and melding attempts to piece together similar ventures (e.g., having similar technologies) into a ''critical mass'' to increase their marketing and technological strengths. This improves the success rate of otherwise small ventures. The semiconductor industry's joint research consortiums—Sematech and Microelectronics and Computer Technology Corp. (located in Austin, Texas) are prime examples. Another, less successful, example is Exxon Enterprises.

Internal ventures, as discussed previously, are situations in which a firm sets up a separate internal group to develop a new product line or to enter a new market; 3M has been consistently successful using this approach. Additional examples include IBM's personal computer division and General Motors' Saturn Corp.[29]

Successful Internal Ventures.   A number of companies have begun to stress ''intrapreneurship''—encouraging entrepreneurial behavior within the corporate structure—with varying degrees of success. IBM, for example, recognized the personal computer market as a separate business, and set up independent engineering, marketing, and distribution for the product. Companies without

---

[28]Larry Armstrong, ''A Chipmaking Venture the Gods Smiled upon,'' *Business Week,* July 4, 1988, p. 109.

[29]E. E. Roberts, ''New Ventures for Corporate Growth,'' *Harvard Business Review,* July–August 1980, p. 130.

such an approach typically try to "find a home" for new products and technologies in existing business units. Most often, the new product represents a small market, and suffers accordingly in comparison to "bread and butter" products, or is poorly understood, or does poorly because it doesn't fit the existing structure and strategies.

Recent studies have shed some light on how internal entrepreneurial activities can succeed. Successes mainly occur in firms that are able to delicately balance the need for diversity and order; the diversity results from operational-level innovation and strategic initiatives, while order flows from imposing a strategy concept on the organization. Top management's critical task is to balance these conflicting demands for diversity and order, controlling the level and rate of change, rather than the specific content of entrepreneurial activity.[30] Typically, a few key people in an organization are the indispensable entrepreneurs and innovators. Management should know clearly who they are, and go to great pains to *keep* them by overriding seniority systems, and by providing big rewards, freedom, and responsibility.[31]

Strategic Alliances.   Joint ventures as a strategy option are not a new approach, but "alliances" forged for the purpose of expanding the business portfolio are relatively recent and becoming more prevalent. These strategies stress cooperative mutual gain through networking, rather than strict competition. These strategic alliances or sustaining networks seek "long-term, purposeful arrangements among distinct but related for-profit organizations that allow those firms in them to gain or sustain competitive advantage vis-à-vis their competitors outside the network."[32] They do this by trading resources, pooling similar resources and risks, expanding total demand, and increasing the number of firms committed to a particular strategy.[33] Examples are Microsoft® and IBM (software for PCs), Matsushita, and other producers sharing the VHS format for videocassette recorders, and others.

As an example, Apple and Digital Equipment Corporation announced a joint development agreement which will enable users to connect Macintoshes® and DEC VAX® computers. Called a *classic preemptive strike* and a strong marketing (rather than technology) strategy, the move will enable software developers to write applications using the companies' jointly developed communications foundation. Each company stands to gain. Apple gets access to DECnet's IBM SNA gateways and wide area network links as well as the VAX's computer performance; DEC gets help in its weakest area, the desktop—where IBM's PS/2

---

[30]R. A. Burgelman, "Corporate Entrepreneurship and Strategic Management: Insights from a Process Study," *Management Science* 29, no. 12 (December 1983), p. 1349.

[31]Michael Kami, *Strategic Planning for Changing Times* (Dayton: Cassette Recording Co., 1984).

[32]J. C. Jarillo and J. E. Ricart, "Sustaining Networks," *Interfaces* 17, no. 5 (September/October 1987), p. 83.

[33]R. P. Nielsen, "Cooperative Strategies," *Planning Review* 14, no. 2 (March 1986), p. 16.

threatens to encroach on the office and engineering workstation roles of both companies.[34]

Diversification and Performance

Under what conditions should a company employ the various methods of diversification to assure maximum success? In general, new business development should be constrained within areas related to a company's base (present) businesses in order to ensure highest performance and likelihood of success. Given this criterion, either internal developments *or* acquisitions may be successful diversification methods. But, there are degrees of familiarity a firm may have with both the market and the technology represented by the products and services of the new business. If the market or technologies (or both) are not part of the firm's present businesses, different entry strategies may be called for to maximize entry success, depending on the degree of familiarity. Figure 7.10 highlights strategies appropriate for various situations.

Diversification Results.   In a well-publicized study (1987), Michael Porter found that more than half of the diversification efforts by large companies since 1950 have ended in failure. Diversification—whether through acquisition, joint venture, or start-up—has not generally brought the competitive advantages or profitability sought by management. Why? Companies undertaking diversification typically fail one of three key tests: they overspend for the new business; they rationalize rather than analyze the attractiveness of the new industry; or they don't demonstrate how the new business will fit with the company's strategy and existing businesses. In contrast, successful companies transfer skills and share activities between businesses; this is the practical essence of effective corporate-level strategy.[35]

Other recent studies show somewhat inconsistent and even conflicting results. There seems to be some indication, however, that related diversifiers (e.g., horizontal and concentric expansions) earn higher returns than unrelated diversifiers.[36] Another study suggests that firms attempt related diversification in order to exploit operating synergies, and attempt unrelated diversification to increase leverage due to greater stability of cash flows. The study found that related diversification tends to yield higher profitability than does unrelated, but

---

[34]"Alliances: Users Are Applauding the Apple-DEC Pairing," *Datamation,* March 1, 1988, p. 19.

[35]M. E. Porter, "From Competitive Advantage to Corporate Strategy," *Harvard Business Review* 65, no. 3 (May–June 1987), pp. 43–60.

[36]R. M. Grant, A. P. Jammine, and H. Thomas, "Diversity, Diversification, and Profitability among British Manufacturing Companies, 1972–84," *Academy of Management Journal* 31, no. 4 (December 1988), p. 774.

FIGURE 7.10 Optimum Entry Strategies

Market Factors	*New Unfamiliar*	Joint ventures	Venture capital or venture nurturing or educational acquisitions	Venture capital or venture nurturing or educational acquisitions
	New Familiar	Internal market developments or acquisitions (or joint ventures)	Internal ventures or acquisitions or licensing	Venture capital or venture nurturing or educational acquisitions
	Base	Internal base developments (or acquisitions)	Internal product developments or acquisitions or licensing	Strategic alliances
		Base	*New Familiar*	*New Unfamiliar*

Technologies or Services Embodied in the Product

Source: Adapted from E. B. Roberts and C. A. Berry, "Entering New Businesses: Selecting Strategies for Success," *Sloan Management Review*, Spring 1985, p. 13. Used with permission.

pure financial diversification (unrelated) results in more stable cash flows, higher leverage, and lower profitability.[37]

Acquisition Results. In a late study of 64 Fortune 1,000 firms, it was found that conglomerate, technology-related, and marketing-related acquisition strategies *all* were associated with a decline in market position; however, the marketing-related strategy was superior to the other two. Therefore, managers may want to consider internal growth as an alternative to acquisitions.[38] On the other hand, some acquisitions create value—some more than others. A recent Harvard/Booz, Allen & Hamilton-sponsored study found that value is created by acquisitions in which the assets of either the target or the bidder are used more intensively (e.g., identical, vertical, or concentric). But those that permit acquisition into new markets (concentric) or within the same business (identical),

[37] R. Amit and J. Livnat, "Diversification Strategies, Business Cycles, and Economic Performance," *Strategic Management Journal* 9, no. 2 (March–April 1988), p. 99.

[38] H. D. Hopkins, "Acquisition Strategy and the Market Position of Acquiring Firms," *Strategic Management Journal* 8, no. 6 (November–December 1987), pp. 535–47.

create the *most* value.[39] Therefore, horizontal and concentric acquisitions are preferred over vertical moves, and unrelated acquisitions appear least desirable. Another study found that acquiring firms tend to outperform nonacquirers in the years *prior* to the acquisition, but underperform the others *after* the event. In addition, this study raised the point that firms may acquire others because of their prior superior performance, as an investment. Interestingly, the remuneration of the acquiring firms' managers significantly outpaced the others, indicating that firm performance may not be the only factor motivating acquisition behavior.[40]

Finally, in a study of 297 large mergers, it was found that *all* types of mergers—single business, vertical, related, and unrelated—were associated with *increases* in the risk (variance) resulting from the firm's individual businesses. Further, only related mergers significantly reduced the sensitivity (risk) of returns to variations in the aggregate returns of the marketplace.[41]

All in all, these studies seriously question the desirability of unrelated diversification strategies via acquisitions. Perhaps corporate managers should concentrate on building competitive advantage in each business rather than pursuing new markets to spread their risk. If diversification is desired, internally developed related businesses seem to be the superior choice.

CORPORATE CONCENTRATION AND RESTRUCTURING STRATEGIES

Given the pessimistic results concerning diversification strategies, it is understandable that many firms have undertaken restructuring actions, designed to *reduce* their diversification and focus their companies on a few key-related businesses. Sometimes companies are forced by the threat of takeover to divest and restructure, and some have done so at a loss. The French oil service company Schlumberger acquired Fairchild Semiconductor Corp. in 1979 for $425 million. In 1985, Fairchild had a $627 million loss, and Schlumberger sold Fairchild to National Semiconductor in 1987 for $122 million in stock and warrants.[42]

Recent studies support the trend toward more concentrated, restructured firms. Because different markets require different skills for success, firms which

---

[39]L. M. Shelton, ''Strategic Business Fits and Corporate Acquisition: Empirical Evidence,'' *Strategic Management Journal* 9, no. 3 (May–June 1988), p. 284.

[40]K. L. Fowler, D. E. Schmidt, and L. A. Digman, ''The Effect of Tender Offer Acquisitions on the Bidding Firm: Overall Performance, Managerial Gain, and Gains to Shareholders,'' *Proceedings of the 18th Annual Conference, Decision Sciences Institute,* November 1986.

[41]Michael Lubatkin and H. M. O'Neill, ''Merger Strategies and Capital Market Risk,'' *Academy of Management Journal* 30, no. 4 (December 1987), pp. 665–84.

[42]R. B. Schmitt, ''Schlumberger Reaches Accord to Sell Fairchild,'' *The Wall Street Journal,* September 1, 1987, p. 2.

concentrate in one market area (e.g., consumer or industrial), at a given level of diversification, achieve superior performance.[43]

Divestiture Strategies

Divestiture involves selling a business unit, subsidiary, division, or product line as a going business. In contrast to the situation in the 1960s when acquisitions and takeovers were the rage, in recent years there has been a growing desire on the part of many companies to go the other way; to divest themselves of unrelated, unprofitable, or unmanageable operations.[44] In fact, sometimes the two strategies are coupled; one company acquires or takes over another, and then divests the unwanted businesses, perhaps retaining the business units or assets it wanted at little cost.

Portfolio models can give an indication of business units that are potential candidates for divestment. In most cases, however, it is not clear that a unit should be divested immediately. Management usually must decide whether or not a business unit should be retained and possibly reduced in size or turned around, or whether it should be divested. In addition, even if the decision is to divest, timing the divestment is a major concern. An important aspect of the decision to divest is the amount and timing of the cash recovery from the divestiture. In addition, as is pointed out in Appendix D, the decision may entail appreciable costs.

In general, however, studies have shown that divestitures linked to corporate- or business-level strategies tend to be valued positively by the market; those perceived as the sale of unwanted units in the absence of defined strategic goals tend to be valued negatively.[45] A company can have several reasons for divesting itself of a division: unsatisfactory earnings performance, expansion needs that the parent company cannot afford, a need to diversify that the segment does not meet, receipt of an attractive offer, lack of synergy with the company's other businesses, government antitrust action, and debt reduction.

Exit Barriers. Kathy Harrigan has described problems associated with divesting an SBU. Once the decision is made, a company may find divestment is not easy, especially in the case of a failing business. Even trying to sell the assets, let alone the entire unit, may be impossible if there is no market. Paradoxically,

---

[43]N. Capon, J. M. Hulbert, J. U. Farley, and L. E. Martin, "Corporate Diversity and Economic Performance: The Impact of Market Specialization," *Strategic Management Journal* 9, no. 1 (January–February 1988), p. 61.

[44]Laurie Meisler, "Mergers and Divestitures: A Forbes Special Supplement," *Forbes,* November 5, 1984, p. 4.

[45]Cynthia Montgomery, A. R. Thomas, and R. Kamath, "Divestitures, Market Value, and Strategy," *Academy of Management Journal* 27, no. 4, (December 1984), p. 830.

entry barriers that the divesting company helped put in place to protect its own market niche from competition may now become barriers to exit. Exit barriers include:

1. *Economic*. These factors could induce the firm to continue operating a subsidiary even while earning a below-normal return from it. Exiting a business may be blocked by the high cost of dismantling assets, such as plant, or the lack of an adequate resale market. For relatively new businesses, it may be better to recapture the value of the assets through depreciation over several years than to sell them at a loss immediately. A simple formula can aid in making this decision: the discounted expected value of future operations is divided by the expected salvage value. A ratio greater than one would indicate that it is better to continue operations.

2. *Strategic*. If a synergy exists between the unattractive business and the company's other units, the firm may be reluctant to divest itself of the "lemon." These exit barriers include: customer service obligations; the possibility of hurting the quality image of the firm and its other products; physical facilities shared by businesses the corporation wants to keep; and the loss of strong customer industries that have relied on the products that will be discontinued. This last factor could damage the firm's competitive posture in other markets.

3. *Expectations*. If a company expects demand to pick up, it may decide to weather the storm instead of giving up on a failing business. Also, if one niche of the product market is still attractive, the firm may not want to lose the assets that serve that niche.[46]

It is suggested that companies plan their exit from a business at the time of entry. If a company keeps these exit barriers in mind, and realizes that any business's attractiveness can decline as fast as its profits, the company can be more prepared to hurdle these barriers.

Thus, divestitures are not always clear-cut or simple procedures. Barriers to exit and tax considerations easily can override decisions that appear straightforward up to that point. Some alternatives to divestiture or liquidation, including defense, renewal, retrenchment, or turnaround, were discussed in Chapter 6 as business-unit strategies.

Corporate Restructuring

Many companies—such as ITT, Allied-Signal, and others—have recently undertaken restructuring actions, at least partly to increase shareholder value. In fact, some experts see restructuring as "the biggest issue in corporate America

---

[46]K. R. Harrigan, "Deterrents to Divestiture," *Academy of Management Journal*, June 1981, p. 306.

today,'' downsizing and simplifying corporations to focus their businesses more clearly.[47] Many corporate restructurings have been undertaken because of the threat of a corporate takeover; the firm is valued by the stock market at less than its book value and its breakup value (the *parts* are worth more than the whole—a *negative* synergy exists). Raiders tend not to be interested in companies whose stock prices reflect their true value; therefore, a real takeover defense ''requires developing the perspective of a corporate raider and learning to act like a turnaround artist.''[48]

A 1988 study of top executives and financial professionals revealed that 97 percent saw restructuring as an *ongoing* process, rather than as a single event, and felt that either they or their clients were likely to execute major restructuring moves in the near future. Also of interest are the major reasons for restructuring, which the respondents ranked as follows:[49]

To increase shareholder value	83%
Change in corporate strategy	66
To meet increasing competition	33
Defense against hostile takeover threat	30
To redeploy funds more productively	30
Decline of important markets	26
Diversification	20
Loss of synergies	14

Studies bear out the trend toward restructuring. Even going back to the 1975–84 time period, managers of multibusiness firms were reducing the complexity of their enterprises by decreasing the number of businesses managed as well as by increasing the relatedness of their portfolio of businesses.[50]

How to Avoid Being Acquired. While mergers, acquisitions, and takeovers may be good or bad for the stockholders of the acquired company, they frequently are detrimental to the acquired's management. To reduce the likelihood of a takeover, management should reduce as many as possible of the factors favoring the action. Management has little control over the firm's desirability as

---

[47]W. B. Shaffir, ''Focus and Simplicity: Today's Strategic Priorities,'' *Planning Review* 15, no. 3 (May–June 1987), p. 44.

[48]B. C. Reimann, ''Realizing Shareholder Value,'' *Planning Review* 15, no. 4 (July–August 1987), p. 42.

[49]Martin Sikora, ''Corporate Restructuring,'' undated promotional material for *Corporate Restructuring* newsletter, Spring 1988.

[50]J. R. Williams, B. L. Paez, and L. Sanders, ''Conglomerates Revisited,'' *Strategic Management Journal* 9, no. 5 (September–October 1988), p. 403.

a target for horizontal or vertical integration or diversification. But it can reduce the firm's vulnerability through the following actions:

1. Remain as efficient and profitable as possible, contenting stockholders and reducing attractiveness to a firm looking to purchase turnaround situations.
2. Acquire a competitor of the acquirer.
3. Keep liquidity to low but safe levels to discourage cash-hungry firms.
4. Follow innovative, aggressive strategies and policies that—coupled with good earnings and growth—result in a high stock price/earnings ratio.
5. Broaden and splinter outside ownership of stock through timely splits.
6. Adopt antitakeover amendments.

Since all of these moves are not possible at all times, management should monitor stock ownership by pension and investment funds and potential arbitrageurs (third-party speculators hoping to profit from a takeover attempt), as well as by potential acquirers. In the event that a takeover attempt does occur, the company can denounce the offer and urge stockholders not to accept it, seek to block it through legal action or government intervention, or even acquire another firm in the interim. If all else fails, management can look for a ''white knight,'' or favorable acquiring company. A recent study of antitakeover amendments showed that they had no significant strategic, managerial, or organizational effects on firms adopting them. While the relationships may be complex, there is no evidence that the amendments affect a firm positively or negatively.[51]

Leveraged Buyouts. A practice currently attracting a lot of attention and some controversy is the leveraged buyout. In general, a leveraged buyout (LBO) is a financial transaction in which the buyer (either an individual or a group, management or outsiders) takes over the company by using its assets as collateral. In a typical LBO, management borrows against the firm's assets or issues junk bonds to buy all of its outstanding stock. Once the LBO has occurred, the new owners usually take bold actions to pare the resulting debt down to a more manageable, less-risky size.[52] One of the key questions concerning LBOs is why managers who can't maximize shareholder value while the company is publicly traded seem to be able to do so as soon as it goes private. Perhaps the main forces at work are those of corporate control and personal gain.[53]

---

[51]Paul Mallette, *An Empirical Examination of the Strategic, Managerial, and Organizational Consequences of Antitakeover Amendments,* Ph.D. dissertation, University of Nebraska, 1988.

[52]Joe Queenan, ''The ABCs of LBOs,'' *Barron's,* September 5, 1988, p. 58.

[53]Phillip D. Hall, *An Investigation of the Strategic Use of Leveraged Management Buyouts,* Ph.D. dissertation, University of Nebraska, 1988.

CONCLUSIONS

Multibusiness organizations often find the need to depart from their operational structures to accomplish their strategic planning tasks. Focusing on markets and strategic business units rather than on operational divisions or departments has facilitated this task in a number of companies. However, SBUs and operating units should be aligned as closely as possible.

Various portfolio models, if properly used, can aid in formulating corporate-level strategies, highlighting the portfolio of businesses and their interrelationships. Corporate-level growth strategies most often involve growth and diversification decisions, particularly after horizontal and vertical expansion options have been exhausted. At this stage, adjusting the mix of business units through acquisitions, divestitures, internal and joint ventures, and combination strategies takes center stage. Recently, studies and practice have found diversification results to be disappointing, forcing many companies to sharpen their focus by restructuring and divestitures. For some, these actions have been taken in self defense to avoid being taken over.

Chapter 8

Developing and Evaluating Strategic Options

LEARNING OBJECTIVES

After completing Chapter 8, you should be able to:

Describe the sources of comparative and competitive advantage and their relationship to corporate- and business-level strategies.

Understand the concept and importance of critical success factors to an organization's strategic decisions.

Appreciate the various methods of determining critical success factors.

Describe the PIMS project and understand its major findings.

Discuss the major corporate- and business-level strategies and options available to management.

Describe the major steps involved in evaluating alternatives and selecting a strategy.

Identify the major criteria strategic alternatives must meet.

To this point, the strategic situation has been assessed in terms of the general and competitive environments, the firm's resources, distinctive competencies, and vision, and the values and expectations of the stakeholders (discussed in Part II). Corporate-level and business-level strategic options (Chapters 6 and 7) have also been explored. At this point, we are ready to begin the process of selecting a strategy. As part of the process of making this strategic decision, the situation assessment based on critical success factors for the organization, development of final strategic alternatives, evaluation of those alternatives, and selection of a strategy will be dealt with.

The first section of this chapter will examine the strategic decision process, particularly in organizations facing rapidly changing environments, followed by ways to create sustainable advantages—a critical element of successful strategic decision making.

PROFILE	**Citibank**

In 1983, Citibank had assets of $128.3 billion, making it the largest U.S. bank, overtaking Bank of America through more aggressive growth. Its lead was short-lived, however, as Bank of America regained the top spot with its acquisition of the troubled SeaFirst Corp. of Seattle. However, the lead soon swung back to Citibank as it left Bank of America in the dust (it ended 1988 with $208 billion in assets, compared to Bank of America's $95 billion). Citi has clearly emerged as the dominant U.S. firm in international banking. This position is the result of a well-laid plan, building on a huge network of global branches and a corporate culture that rewards aggressive managers of its decentralized units.

Citi's approach has been to penetrate foreign markets, gradually building a major presence in a country's domestic market. The approach has been to quickly take advantage of all opportunities, not "analyzing it to death; don't worry about the first year's profits. Any time you can get a license, take it; almost any time you can get a relationship with a desired customer, take it," says former Vice Chairman Thomas Theobald. However, having led the charge into foreign countries, Citi began to change its strategy. It is now adjusting to the growing number of foreign customers who cannot come up with the cash to service their debts; the new emphasis is on quality, not quantity. As former Chairman Walter Wriston stated, "Our strategy is not one of making loans; our strategy is one of making money."

The company now is more willing to turn down a business that does not meet strict hurdle rates—criteria for profit potential. It also is careful about restricting itself to short-term risks. In sum, with its huge investment in systems, its competitive strength, its ability to respond quickly, its committed managers, and its bottom-line focus, the firm is well situated for continued selective growth in a competitive and turbulent environment.[1]

STRATEGIC DECISION MAKING

The process of strategic decision making was discussed and described in detail in Chapter 2, and depicted in Figure 2.2. To recap this model, the process begins with the vision of top management and the values and expectations of important

---

[1]"Citibank's Pervasive Influence on International Lending," *Business Week,* May 16, 1983, p. 124.

stakeholders. These factors affect the firm's mission, goals and objectives, policies and procedures, and—relevant to this chapter—strategy formulation. Remember, strategy formulation consists of developing strategy alternatives, evaluating those alternatives, and selecting a strategy for implementation and detailed planning. On the surface, the decision-making portion of the process (formulating, evaluating, and choosing from alternatives) appears similar to the making of other decisions. In actuality, however, it is more complex because the situations are often ill-structured, the decisions are often complex and momentous, and it occurs in an atmosphere of organizational politics.

It may be helpful to examine the process in one of its most demanding circumstances—that of a high-velocity environment. Such environments—where the rate of technological and competitive change is so extreme that market information is often unavailable or obsolete, where strategic windows (opportunities) are opening and shutting quickly, and where the cost of error may be involuntary exit from the industry—may describe the limiting case of strategic decision making; other situations may seem relatively simple by comparison. High-velocity environments are characterized by rapid, frequent, and discontinuous change, and may characterize today's microcomputer, airline, and banking industries. A recent study of microcomputer firms found that high performers make major decisions carefully, but decide quickly; they have both a powerful, decisive CEO *and* a powerful top-management team; and they seek bold, innovative strategies but follow safe, incremental implementation. These complex relationships are shown in Figure 8.1.

Several of the points may need further explanation. First, high performers deal with their extremely uncertain world by structuring it, using a thorough, analytic process similar to a "classic textbook strategic planning effort." Second, while the analytic approach provides order to their fast-moving world, they prevent premature commitments to irreversible actions by using "threshold-triggered execution decisions." Thus, they keep their implementation options open as long as possible. As more industries face high-velocity environments in the future, this model of decision making may take on increasing importance.[2]

CREATING SUSTAINABLE ADVANTAGES

From earlier discussions in Chapters 3 and 5, we learned that firms desire to create competitive advantages. We said that a competitive advantage is critically important to any strategy; in fact, firms should probably *not* compete in markets in which they do not have a competitive advantage. Competitive advantage relates to how well a business is able to conduct the activities along its value-added chain, and includes any number of factors, such as technological advantages, marketing superiority, productive efficiencies, brand images, customer loyalty, superior service, and the like.

---

[2]L. J. Bourgeois III and K. M. Eisenhardt, "Strategic Decision Making in High Velocity Environments," *Management Science* 34, no. 7 (July 1988), pp. 817–35.

FIGURE 8.1 Strategic Decision Making in High-Velocity Environments

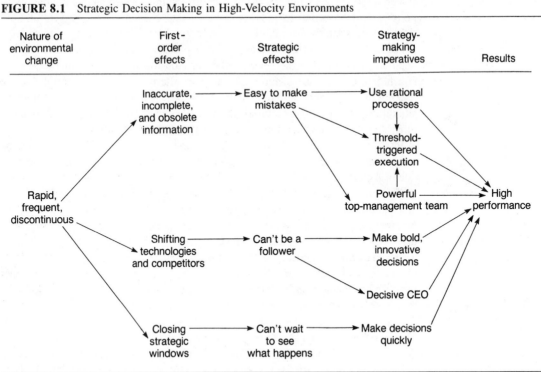

Source: Adapted from L. J. Bourgeois, III and K. M. Eisenhardt, "Strategic Decision Making in High Velocity Environments," *Management Science* 34, no. 7 (July 1988), p. 833.

Comparative advantage, on the other hand, depends upon the costs of inputs to the business. A firm with access to superior or lower cost inputs necessary to produce its goods or services is said to have a comparative advantage. These inputs can include labor, equipment, raw materials, management and other personnel, financing, and the like, and can depend upon and vary from region to region (e.g., between cities, areas, countries, and so on). Further, comparative advantages can be significant factors in determining the competitive advantages of a business, along with the firm's distinctive competencies and its resources.

Further, it is important that businesses possess *sustainable* competitive advantages; a temporary competitive advantage is of little value. For example, competitors secure detailed information on 70 percent of all new products within a year of their development, and can soon offer competing products. New production processes are even harder to protect than are new products. Competitors often can quickly respond to marketing strategies, such as prices and advertising. What steps can be taken to ensure that a competitive advantage can be sustained? The difference between advantages that will endure and those that won't is often a matter of degree, partly dependent upon the industry, the competitors, and the relative strength of the advantages. Four factors helping to create sustainable advantages include:

1. *Large-scale commitments.* Investing in larger scale and more diverse operations can preempt competitors and result in great power in a given market.
2. *Experience.* Use of superior knowledge and reputation to improve quality, reliability, superior service, and marketability can be difficult for competitors to overcome.
3. *Comparative advantages.* Access to resources, information, or markets on favorable terms—protected by contracts or other mechanisms—can provide a long-term advantage.
4. *Competitor restraints.* Anything which limits competitors' options and prevents or slows their response—such as government regulations, resource limitations, previous commitments, and other weaknesses—can provide your business with a head start which may be sustainable.[3]

As shown in Figure 8.2, a number of factors interact to determine the level of competitive advantage a business possesses—an important determinant of which business strategies it should pursue. For example, market/industry factors and environmental influences contribute to comparative advantages and factors critical for success in a particular market. Combined with an accurate and thorough analysis of competitors and distinctive competencies, these factors are important determinants of competitive advantages. Multibusiness firms have additional influences. For example, the corporate portfolio of businesses and corporate resources can add to comparative advantages, plus create the possibility of synergies with other businesses in the portfolio—another possible source of competitive advantage. Depending on the positions of competitive advantage that exist (or lack thereof) the firm may attempt to resegment the market or industry, or may take action to restructure its corporate portfolio to improve advantages and synergies.

EVALUATING THE STRATEGIC SITUATION

The first step in evaluating and choosing a strategy is to review the results of the strategic situation assessment (consisting of an analysis of the general and competitive environments, and the firm's distinctive competencies and resources as described in Chapters 3, 4, and 5) in terms of factors critical to the success of the business which create competitive advantages. Sometimes called the *strategic position* or *strategic profile,* the strategic situation involves an analysis of the firm's external opportunities and threats and its strengths and weaknesses.

---

[3]Pankaj Ghemawat, "Sustainable Advantage," *Harvard Business Review* 64, no. 5 (September–October 1986), pp. 53–59.

FIGURE 8.2   Competitive Advantage and Strategies

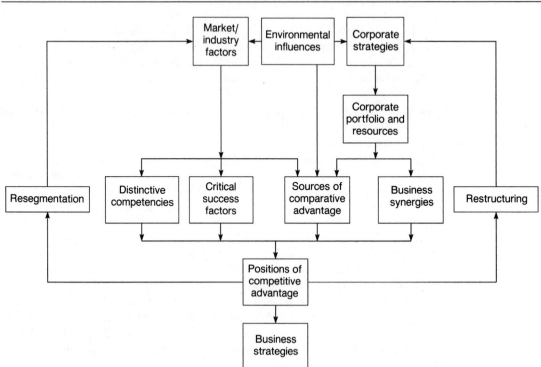

George Steiner stated that three types of data are required to perform a *situation audit* identifying opportunities, threats, strengths, and weaknesses:

1. Past performance of the firm.
2. Data about the current situation, including:
    a. Analysis of customers and markets.
    b. Resources of the company.
    c. Competition.
    d. Environmental setting.
    e. Other performance measures or areas of interest.
3. Forecasts of the future.[4]

Arnoldo Hax of MIT developed a chart showing eight steps useful in analyzing a firm's current and future situations, illustrated in Table 8.1, and described below.

---

[4]G. A. Steiner, *Strategic Planning* (New York: Macmillan, 1979), p. 129.

TABLE 8.1 Major Steps for the Implementation of the Attractiveness-Strength Matrix

Analysis of Current Situation	*Analysis of Future Situation*
Step 1 Definition of critical internal and external success factors	Step 5 Forecasting of trends for each external factor
Step 2 Assessment of external factors	Step 6 Developing the desired position for each internal factor
Step 3 Assessment of internal factors	
Step 4 Positioning of the business in the attractiveness-strength matrix	Step 7 Desired positioning of each business in the attractiveness-strength matrix
	Step 8 Formulation of strategies for each business

Source: Reprinted by permission of A. C. Hax and N. S. Majluf, "The Use of the Industry Attractiveness-Business Strength Matrix in Strategic Planning," *Interfaces* 13, no. 2 (April 1983), p. 56. Copyright 1983 The Institute of Management Sciences.

Defining Critical Success Factors

The first step in the situation audit is to identify the critical external factors, largely uncontrollable by the firm, that have an impact on effectiveness. Similarly, *critical success factors* (CSFs), typically pertaining to the industry and the firm, must be identified. Once these external and internal factors are identified, their impact can be assessed. Critical success factors for any business are the limited number of areas in which satisfactory results ensure successful competitive performance. Studies have shown that three to six factors are usually critical to success in most industries; these are the areas where things must go right if the firm is to flourish. If they do not, the firm's performance is likely to be disappointing, regardless of its performance on other factors.[5] Thus, these factors are of paramount importance in formulating and evaluating strategies.

Critical success factors can be examined at several levels; those relating to the firm, to the industry, and to the general environment. Obviously, all three levels are important.

More specifically, CSFs can be influenced by the *sector* of the economy of which the business is a part. For example, for-profit businesses would typically have different CSFs than not-for-profit businesses and public-sector organizations. Other factors could be influenced by the *industry;* for example, industry structure and type of market (whether perfectly competitive, or monopolistic, for example). Also, the *strategic group* would exert an influence, depending on the

---

[5]J. F. Rockart, "Chief Executives Define Their Own Data Needs," *Harvard Business Review,* March–April 1979, p. 81.

types of strategies and focus pursued by the group. Internally, the firm's distinctive competencies and competitive advantages would impact the relative importance of CSFs. As a final point, critical success factors are also likely to change with the stage of the product/market life cycle, as well as with changes in strategic group membership, competition, and focus.

Table 8.2 lists CSFs for several industries, while Table 8.3 takes a closer look at CSFs for four firms in the semiconductor industry. The point is that the industry factors would apply to all firms in the industry, but individual firms may have unique CSFs because of their relative position and thrust within the industry.

Looking at CSFs another way, as Table 8.4 shows, the degree of criticalness of certain factors varies by industry. And, as shown in Table 8.5, they also vary for firms within the same industry.

In general, at least five criteria tend to determine which factors are critical to the business and their relative importance:

1. Impact on performance measures, such as market share, profits, cash flow, and the like.
2. Relationship to strategic thrusts, such as differentiation, costs, segmentation, preemptive, turnaround, renewal, and the like.

TABLE 8.2 Critical Success Factors for Selected Industries

Automotive	*Semiconductor*	*Food Processing*	*Life Insurance*
Styling	Manufacturing process, cost efficient, innovative, cumulative experience	New-product development	Development of agency personnel
Perceived quality			
Strong dealer network		Good distribution	Effective control of clerical personnel
Manufacturing cost control	Technological competence, adequate technical product development	Effective advertising	Innovation in policy development
Ability to meet EPA standards	Capital availability		Innovative advertising Marketing strategy

Source: Adapted from *Long-Range Planning* 17 (February 1984), J. K. Leidecker and A. V. Bruno, "Identifying and Using Critical Success Factors," p. 24. Copyright 1984, Pergamon Press, Ltd. Reprinted with permission.

TABLE 8.3   Critical Success Factors for Selected Firms in the Semiconductor
Industry

National Semiconductor	*Intel*	*Advanced Micro Devices*	*Avantek*
Broad product line	Innovator and leader in technology	Proprietary innovative products	Strong transistor line
Large efficient production capacity	Strong product development and customer service capability	Does not compete in price-sensitive markets	Solid customer range High-yield manufacturing
Vertically integrated		Effective location of fabrication and assembly	
Innovative packaging and assembly operations	High-margin proprietary devices	Operations; strong technical marketing capabilities	

Source: Reprinted with permission from *Long-Range Planning* 17 (February 1984), J. K. Leidecker and A. V. Bruno, "Identifying and Using Critical Success Factors," p. 24. Copyright 1984, Pergamon Press, Ltd.

TABLE 8.4   Importance* of Selected CSFs for Four Industries

	Industry			
Factor	*Soft-drink Bottlers*	*Semiconductor Manufacturers*	*Ferrous Metals Distribution*	*Tax Preparation*
Basic R&D	Slight	Major	Unimportant	Unimportant
New-product development	Secondary	Major	Slight	Unimportant
Manufacturing	Major	Major	Secondary	Unimportant
Distribution	Major	Secondary	Major	Slight
Customer service	Major	Secondary	Major	Major
Advertising	Secondary	Unimportant	Unimportant	Secondary
Post-sales service	Secondary	Slight	Slight	Major

*Classifications are for purposes of discussion.

Source: Reprinted with permission from *Long-Range Planning* 17 (February 1984), J. K. Leidecker and A. V. Bruno, "Identifying and Using Critical Success Factors," p. 31. Copyright 1984, Pergamon Press, Ltd.

TABLE 8.5 Importance* of Selected CSFs for Four Semiconductor Manufacturers

	Firm			
Factor	*National Semiconductor*	*Intel*	*Signetics*	*Texas Instruments*
Basic R&D	Slight	Major	Slight	Secondary
New-product development	Secondary	Major	Secondary	Major
Manufacturing	Major	Major	Major	Major
Distribution	Major	Secondary	Secondary	Major
Customer service	Major	Secondary	Secondary	Major
Advertising	Slight	Slight	Slight	Secondary
Post-sales service	Unimportant	Unimportant	Unimportant	Secondary

*Classifications are for purposes of discussion.

Source: Reprinted with permission from *Long-Range Planning* 17 (February 1984), J. K. Leidecker and A. V. Bruno, "Identifying and Using Critical Success Factors," p. 31. Copyright 1984, Pergamon Press, Ltd.

3. Relationship to life-cycle stage; that is, introduction, growth, maturity, and aging and decline.
4. Relates to a major activity of the business, such as marketing at IBM.
5. Involves large amounts of money relative to other activities of the firm.

There are several techniques for identifying CSFs for a business, its industry, and its general environment. They include environmental scanning, industry structure analysis, opinions of experts in the industry, analysis of competitors, analysis of the industry's dominant firm, a specific assessment of the company, intuitive judgment or "feel" of insiders, and profit impact of market strategy (PIMS) data.[6] The focus, sources, advantages, and disadvantages of each of these techniques are listed in Table 8.6. Remember that these techniques are to be used in conjunction with one another, not in place of one another.

Finally, keep in mind that the way the dominant firm in an industry conducts business can provide insights into an industry's CSFs. Figure 8.3 is an illustration of this approach based upon the leading firm in the electronic components distribution industry. This figure also illustrates how the CSF concept fits in with the firm's goal structure. Expert input is required to judge those elements in the hierarchy that are critical, as well as unique relationships that may exist. Keep in mind, however, that blindly copying the leading firm in an industry may be counterproductive and a recipe for disaster; less-dominant firms may need to carve out their own niche, which, along with different competitive advantages, may produce a very different set of CSFs.

---

[6]J. K. Leidecker and A. V. Bruno, "Identifying and Using Critical Success Factors," *Long-Range Planning* 17 (February 1984), pp. 26–31.

TABLE 8.6 Techniques for Identifying Critical Success Factors

Technique	Focus	Sources	Advantages	Disadvantages
Environmental analysis	Macro	Environmental scanning (corporate staff) Econometric models Sociopolitical consulting services	Future orientation Macro orientation: analysis goes beyond industry/firm focus Can be linked to threats/opportunity evaluation	More difficult to operationalize into specific industry or firm CSFs Results may not lend themselves to incorporate usage in current time frame (today's CSFs)
Analysis of industry structure	Industry Macro	A variety of industry structure frameworks	Specific focus is on industry Frameworks allow user to understand interrelationships between industry structural components Can force more macro level focus (beyond industry boundaries)	While excellent source for industry wide CSFs, not as useful in determining firm specific CSFs
Industry/business experts	Industry Micro	Industry association executives Financial analysts specializing in industry Outsider familiar with firms in industry Knowledgeable insiders who work in industry	Means of soliciting conventional wisdom about industry and firms Subjective information very often not discovered with more objective, formal, and analytical approaches	Lack of objectivity often leads to questions of verifiability/justification
Analysis of competition (focus is limited to the competitive environment, how firms compete)	Industry Micro	Staff specialists Line managers Internal consultants External consultants	Narrowness of focus, offers advantage of detailed, specific data Depth of analysis leads to better means of justification	Narrowness of focus, CSF development limited to competitive arena (as opposed to industry structure approach)

TABLE 8.6 *(concluded)*

Technique	Focus	Sources	Advantages	Disadvantages
Analysis of the dominant firm in the industry	Industry Micro	Staff specialists Line managers Internal consultants External consultants	Dominant competitor may in fact set industry CSFs Understanding of number 1 may assist in corroborating firm specific CSFs	Narrow focus may preclude seeking alternative explanations of success May limit individual firm's strategic response and focus
Company assessment (comprehensive, firm specific)	Micro	Internal staff line organizations (detailed analyses by organization function—checklist approach)	A thorough functional area screening reveals internal/strengths and weaknesses that may assist CSF development	Narrow focus of analysis precludes inputs of more macro approaches Checklist approach can be very time-consuming and become data bound
Intuitive judgment (firm specific)	Micro	Internal staff Brainstorming CEO/General management observation	More subjective and not limited to functional analysis approach Leads to identification of important short-run CSFs that may go unnoticed in more formal reviews	Difficulty in justifying as CSF if of short-term duration Important factors may be overstated, if, in fact, a short-run phenomenon
PIMS data	Industry Micro	Articles of PIMS project results	Empirically based Excellent starting point	General nature Applicability to your specific firm or industry Determination of relative importance

Source: Reprinted with permission from *Long-Range Planning* 17 (February 1984). J. K. Leidecker and A. V. Bruno. "Identifying and Using Critical Success Factors." p. 26. Copyright 1984 The Pergamon Press, Ltd.

FIGURE 8.3   Electronic Component Distribution Industry CSFs

*Product penetration = all the sales and/or marketing activities that make the distributor the preferred supplier for the customer by creating awareness of the firm's product mix, depth, and potential to benefit the customer through dissemination of product knowledge, value-added, and purchase discounts.

Source: J. K. Leidecker and A. V. Bruno, "Critical Success Factor Analysis and the Strategy Development Process," in *Strategic Planning and Management Handbook*, ed. W. R. King and D. I. Cleland (New York: Van Nostrand Reinhold, 1987), p. 343.

PIMS Data

The profit impact of market strategy (PIMS) program began in 1960 as an internal project at GE in an attempt to discover the consequences of strategic business decisions. The goal was to discover the "laws of nature" that operate in the marketplace—the relationship between business-level decisions and their consequences. Using regression models, GE attempted to explain how return on investment (ROI) varied for their businesses in diverse markets and industries; in other words, which variables affect ROI, and what is their relative contribution?

The PIMS program was transferred to the Harvard Business School in 1972 and enlarged to include other companies, as well. In 1975, the member companies formed a nonprofit corporation—the Strategic Planning Institute (SPI)—to manage the PIMS project. Currently, the PIMS data base includes information on over 3,000 "businesses" (SBUs) from over 450 medium to large organizations in the United States and Europe. In return for submitting about 100 proprietary data items to SPI, the member firms receive feedback indicating how their strategic decisions and results compare with those of the other companies, and what strategic changes hold promise for improving their future performance.

Despite some criticism, the PIMS project has been a valuable source of concrete data on the results of strategic decisions, and has benefited the member companies. The fundamental PIMS concept is that there are certain strategic characteristics that companies and their markets have in common and that tend to determine profitability and cash flow. SPI has identified 37 key variables that together explain about 80 percent of the variance in ROI, for example. The following key findings summarize the PIMS results to date:

1. Business situations are generally regular and predictable. The performance of a business can be predicted with reasonable accuracy by the factors PIMS has identified.
2. Business situations obey common laws of the marketplace. This makes strategic management more of an applied science, and enables trained strategists to recommend strategies to the business.
3. Laws of the marketplace explain about 80 percent of the variance in business performance, as described above.
4. There are a number of important linkages between strategy and performance. For example:
   a. In the long run, the most important single factor affecting a business unit's performance is the *quality* of its products and services relative to those of its competitors. Higher quality boosts performance in two ways:
      (1) In the short run, superior quality yields increased profits via premium prices (on average, businesses with superior quality products have costs about equal to competitors').
      (2) In the long run, superior and/or improving quality is the most effective way for a business to grow, leading to market expansion and increasing market share.
   b. Market share and profitability are strongly related, since large-share businesses tend to have lower unit costs.[7]
   c. Investment intensity (investment as a percent of sales) is inversely related to profitability and cash flow. Investment is working capital plus fixed capital at book value.

[7]R. D. Buzzell, and B. T. Gale, *The PIMS Principles: Linking Strategy to Performance* (New York: Free Press 1987), pp. 1–15.

    d. Vertical integration (making rather than buying components, for example) favorably affects performance only in mature, stable markets; in growing, declining, or unstable markets, the opposite is true.

    e. Productivity is directly related to profitability and cash flow.

    f. Growth of served market is positively related to profitability in terms of dollars, indifferent to percent of profitability, and negatively related to cash flow.

    g. Innovation and/or differentiation activities produce positive effects on performance *if* the firm already has a strong market position; otherwise, they usually do not.

    h. Cost-push factors, such as wages, salaries, material costs, and the presence of unions depend on how the company is positioned—whether or not it can pass along the costs.

    i. Current strategic efforts may have effects opposite to those just described; for example, a high market share increases cash flow, but attempts to increase share drain cash.

5. Interaction of the factors is complex. Sometimes they offset, sometimes they reinforce one another, and sometimes they produce temporarily opposite effects.

6. Product characteristics do not matter; *business* characteristics, such as the nine described above, do matter.

7. The characteristics make their effects felt over time.

8. Business strategies tend to be successful if their fundamentals (the laws of the marketplace) are sound; unsuccessful if their fundamentals are not.

9. Most clear strategy signals are robust; that is, the above-mentioned effects usually override small-to medium-sized errors (such as in measuring one of the variables) and are therefore not sensitive to relatively minor errors or misinterpretations.[8]

The major PIMS findings are summarized in Tables 8.7 and 8.8. Keep in mind that the findings represent average or typical relationships; there are exceptions. For example, while market share correlates highly with return on investment (ROI) and return on sales (ROS), there are some very successful low-share businesses. While some confusion can creep in depending on how the market (and, therefore, its share) is defined, businesses that are not typical tend to have their own critical success factors that may differ from the average.

DEVELOPING STRATEGIC ALTERNATIVES

Strategy formulation is a complex task. It begins with the development of major strategic directions, sometimes called *generic strategies*. Within a given generic thrust, however, several options or alternative approaches may be possible. For

---

[8]Sidney Schoeffler, "The PIMS Program," in *The Strategic Management Handbook,* ed. K. J. Albert (New York: McGraw-Hill, 1983), chap. 23.

TABLE 8.7 PIMS Findings Regarding Competitive Position, Strategy, and Profitability

	Impact on	
	ROI	*ROS*
Competitive Position/Strategy Factors	+ = Positive	− = Negative
Share of served market	+	+
Relative product/service quality	+	+
New products, percent of sales	−	−
R&D expense, percent of sales	−	−
Marketing expense, percent of sales	−	−
Value added, percent of sales*	+	+
Fixed assets, percent of sales (at capacity)	−	−
Newness of plant and equipment	+	+
Labor productivity	+	+
Inventories, percent of sales	−	−
Capacity utilization rate	+	+
FIFO inventory valuation	+	+

*Value added is adjusted to remove above-average or compensate for below-average net profits.

Source: Adapted from R. D. Buzzell and B. T. Gale, *The PIMS Principles: Linking Strategy to Performance* (New York: Free Press, 1987), p. 46. Used with permission.

TABLE 8.8 PIMS Findings Regarding Market/Industry Influences on Profitability

	Impact on	
	ROI	*ROS*
Market/Industry Profit Influences	+ = Positive	− = Negative
Real market growth rate (annual %)	+	+
Stage of market evolution		
Growth stage	+	+
Decline stage	−	−
Rate of inflation in selling prices	+	+
Concentration of purchases with few suppliers	+	(+)*
Typical customer purchase amount		
Small	+	+
Large	−	−
Importance of product purchase to customer		
Low	+	+
High	−	−
Percent of employees unionized	−	−
Industry exports	+	+
Industry imports	−	−
Standardized products (versus custom produced)	+	+

*Relationship not statistically significant.

Source: Adapted from R. D. Buzzell, and B. T. Gale, *The PIMS Principles: Linking Strategy to Performance* (New York: Free Press, 1987), p. 47. Used with permission.

example, a company may embark on a high-profit strategy, only to find that this generic strategy can be pursued via three alternatives—focusing on high volume, high asset utilization, or aggressive financing. Thus, strategic alternatives exist not only at the broad generic level, but within major strategic directions, as well.

Strategy formulation is basically problem solving of a highly unstructured nature. The basis of any such problem-solving activity is to first recognize a changing situation. Whether the situation presents a threat or opportunity is the key question. Next, the situation must be clarified. How can it be classified, structured, or redefined in terms of more familiar subproblems?

The primary function of developing a strategic thrust is not to "solve" the situation in its entirety, but to structure the situation so that subproblems (or strategies) are solvable and manageable.[9] Solving the *right* problem is the most important task.

It is commonly felt that one set of generic strategies is not appropriate for all stages of the product/market life cycle. That is, different strategies may be called for as the market moves from the embryonic or introduction stage through the growth, maturity, and finally the aging or decline stage. Various authors have given a myriad of names to these prescribed strategic options. However, recent studies have shown that the options may not be appropriate for all types of businesses and industries, for all types of markets and competitive situations, and for all business objectives. What this means is that appropriate strategies are *contingent* on certain conditions, shown in Figure 8.4, and fall within the *range* of available strategic options.

Going beyond the general to the specific, certain studies have shown that appropriate strategies not only depend on the life-cycle stage, but are also influenced by the business's goals—whether long term (such as to increase market share) or short term (such as increasing cash flow—and depend on the type of business and industry/market conditions. In fact, there tends to be conflict between long- and short-term goals, suggesting a trade-off. As an example, market share tends to increase with increases in investment and assets. However, cash flow improves as investment and assets are cut. Thietart and Vivas found this to be true regardless of the life-cycle stage or type of business.[10] Their study looked at 1,100 industrial goods versus consumer-products businesses in the growth, maturity, and decline stages of the market. In general, their findings are as follows:

1. A trade-off *does exist* between long-term measures of performance (e.g., change in market share) and short-term measures (e.g., cash flow).
2. There is a set of strategic actions for each of these two performance measures that *does not* depend on the life-cycle stage, type of business, or market structure. These actions are:

---

[9]R. P. Rumelt, "Evaluation of Strategy: Theories and Models," in *Strategic Management,* ed. D. Schendel and C. W. Hofer (Boston: Little, Brown, 1979), p. 196.

[10]R. A. Thietart and R. Vivas, "An Empirical Investigation of Success Strategies for Businesses along the Product Life Cycle," *Management Science* 30, no. 12 (December 1984), p. 1405.

FIGURE 8.4 Strategic Options and the Life Cycle

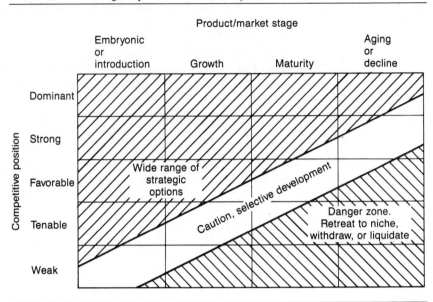

a. To increase market share, one should increase investment (but at a decreasing rate), increase capacity utilization, and increase assets.

b. To improve cash flow, one should decrease investment and decrease assets.

3. There are strategic actions that depend on life-cycle stage (growth, maturity, or decline).

4. There are strategic actions that depend on the type of business (generally, industrial versus consumer products).

5. The relative impact of strategic actions changes with life-cycle stage.[11]

Thus, although life-cycle stage is not the only determinant of business-level strategy, it is an important factor.

In Chapter 4, we observed that the financial services industry has been experiencing a high-velocity environment due to macroeconomic and technological changes, plus deregulation and globalization. We concluded in Chapter 5 that these environmental changes were affecting the industry's market structure, favoring superregional and foreign banks, plus nonbank competitors. But what should the strategies of commercial banks be, given these changes? What should they do to reposition themselves to survive and prosper? The banks need to make

---

[11]Ibid., p. 1421.

many changes, but perhaps two are primary: to lobby for relief from regulatory constraints which put them at a competitive disadvantage, and to seek expanded power in new fields (e.g., securities).[12] Thus, political/legal strategies discussed in Chapter 4 may be their most promising avenue.

The Process

James Quinn has pointed out that strategy is usually developed incrementally. That is, strategies are changed in small steps by modifying previous strategies.[13] Thus, the starting point in developing strategic alternatives is always the past and current strategies of the firm. Any modifications are reviewed as time goes on to see what new changes may be required or desirable. The process is one of continuous refinement and adjustment, with an occasional major change. In general, this process seeks answers to the questions listed in Table 8.9: what are we doing, what is happening externally, and what should we be doing?

Another step must be taken in the formation of strategy. It involves identification of major strategies, followed by an identification and later evaluation of substrategies. (All strategies must be broken down into substrategies for successful implementation.)

As Table 8.10 illustrates for eight common (or generic) strategic alternatives, adoption of given strategy alternative requires certain actions for its success. In addition, there is typically a desired outcome for each strategy alternative, but there is also a *required* outcome—an absolute accomplishment which must be achieved for the strategy to succeed.

Generic strategies often will be suggested by a business unit's position on the industry attractiveness/competitive position matrix shown in Figure 8.5. However, this is only the first phase of strategy formulation. The next stage is developing more specific competitive position objectives and investment strategies, as shown in Table 8.11. The generic strategies permit the development of broad internal and external action programs (substrategies) of the type shown in Table 8.12. At this stage, the broad action programs must be turned into very specific tactical plans, including detailed financial analyses. Here, specific quantitative projections of elements such as sales, prices, market share, costs, interest rates, and taxes are required to determine how attractive the proposed strategy might be.

In summary, remember that strategic options—whether corporate or business level—flow from the enterprise strategy (including the mission and societal-role) of the firm. The strategies are means to achieve the firm's goals and objectives,

---

[12]David Rogers, ''Environmental Change in the Financial Services Industry,'' in *Advances in Strategic Management,* ed. Robert Lamb and Paul Shrivastava 5 (Greenwich, Conn.: JAI Press) pp. 98–102.

[13]J. B. Quinn, *Strategies for Change* (Homewood, Ill.: Richard D. Irwin, 1980).

TABLE 8.9 Process for Formulating a Competitive Strategy

What is the business doing now?

Identification

What is the implicit or explicit current strategy?

Implied assumptions

What assumptions about the company's relative position, strengths and weaknesses, competitors, and industry trends must be made for the current strategy to make sense?

What is happening in the environment?

Industry analysis

What are the key factors for competitive success and the important industry opportunities and threats?

Competitor analysis

What are the capabilities and limitations and probable future moves of existing and potential competitors?

Societal analysis

What important government, social, and political factors will present opportunities or threats?

Strengths and weaknesses

Given an analysis of industry and competitors, what are the company's strengths and weaknesses *relative to present and future competitors*?

What should the business be doing?

Tests of assumptions and strategy

How do the assumptions embodied in the current strategy compare with the analysis above?

Strategic alternatives

What are the feasible strategic alternatives given the analysis above? (Is the current strategy one of these?)

Strategic choice

Which alternative best relates the company's situation to external opportunities and threats?

Source: Reprinted with permission of The Free Press, a Division of Macmillan, Inc., from *Competitive Strategy* by M. E. Porter, pp. 19–20. Coypright 1980.

within its chosen mission. At the corporate level, the primary strategic decision is whether to diversify or concentrate the firm, and to what degree. Diversification leads to acquisition, internal development, and venture-related decisions, while concentration points to divestiture and restructuring decisions.

At the business level, the basic strategies are related to positioning and distinguishing the business (including differentiation and scope). Other appropriate moves include increasing scope (penetration, product development, market development, and geographical expansion), or redefining and reducing scope (defense and renewal, retrenchment and turnaround, and endgame strategies).

TABLE 8.10   Strategic Alternatives, Actions, and Outcomes

Strategic Alternative	Action Required	Desired Outcomes	Required Outcomes
Build aggressively	Build share on all fronts as rapidly as possible.	Rapid growth in share—all markets. Leadership in technology, service.	Limits on losses and negative cash flow.
Build gradually	Steady sustained increase in share of entire market.	Sustained growth in share—all markets. Leadership in quality, service.	Limited losses. Sustained cost reductions.
Build selectively	Increased share in carefully selected markets.	Share growth in selected markets. Leadership in customer satisfaction. Superiority in market research.	Growth in profits and profitability. Growth in cash flow.
Maintain aggressively	Hold position in all markets and generate profits.	Hold market share in all markets. Relative cost leadership—fixed and variable. Technology leadership—in product and process.	Improve asset utilization. Growth in profitability and cash flow. Improve expense-to-revenue ratio. Reduce force levels.
Maintain selectively	Select high-profit markets and secure position.	Overall share reduction. Hold market share in selected markets. Improve relative profitability. Distribution, service leadership.	Minimum investment. Improve asset utilization and cash flow. Reduce fixed cost/sales.
Prove viability	If there are any viable segments, maintain selectively, divest rest.	In this exhibit, see the sections to the left called "Maintain Selectively" and "Divest or Liquidate."	Minimize drag/risk to organization. Growth in profits and cash flow.
Divest or liquidate	Seek exit and sell off at best price.	Reduce share except for highly selective segments. Enhance value added via technical leadership.	Minimize investment. Reduce fixed costs. Improve profitability. Maximize selling price. Reduce work force levels.
Competitively harass	Use as vehicle to deny revenues to competitors.	Attack competitor's high-share business but do not gain share. Relative price never above that of target competitors.	Minimize fixed costs. Sustained reduction of variable costs. Limits on losses and negative cash flows.

Source: Adapted from I. C. MacMillan and P. E. Jones, "Designing Organizations to Compete," *Journal of Business Strategy* 4 (1984), p. 13. Reprinted with permission.

FIGURE 8.5 Attractiveness/Competitive Position Strategies

Competitive Position

		Strong	Average	Weak
Industry Attractiveness	High	Grow Seek dominance Maximize investment	Evaluate potential for leadership via Segmentation Identify weaknesses Build strengths	Specialize Seek niches Consider acquisitions
	Medium	Identify growth segments Invest strongly Maintain position elsewhere	Identify growth segments Specialize Invest selectively	Specialize Seek niches Consider exit
	Low	Maintain overall position Seek cash flow Invest at maintenance levels	Prune lines Minimize investment Position to divest	Trust leader's statesmanship Sic on competitor's cash generators Time exit and divest

Source: C. W. Hofer and M. J. Davoust, *Successful Strategic Management* (Chicago: A. T. Kearney, 1977), p. 52. Reproduced by permission.

EVALUATING ALTERNATIVES AND SELECTING A STRATEGY

The development and evaluation of alternatives should be two separate and distinct steps. Separating the two seems to produce a broader range of alternatives. As our experience with the brainstorming technique suggests, evaluation during the generation stage appears to limit the development of alternatives.

Evaluation of Alternatives

Suppose that one objective of an organization's grand strategy is to achieve a 15 percent sustainable growth rate. This objective can be reached in three very

TABLE 8.11   Competitive Position Objectives and Investment Strategies

Generic Strategy	*Competitive Position Objective*	*Investment Strategy*
Share increasing		
Development stage	Increase position	Moderate investment
Shakeout stage	Increase position	High investment
Other stages	Increase position	Very high investment
Growth	Maintain position	High investment
Profit	Maintain position	Moderate investment
Market concentration and asset reduction	Reduce (shift) position to smaller defensible level (niche)	Moderate to negative investment*
Liquidation or divestiture	Decrease position to zero	Negative investment
Turnaround	Improve positions	Little to moderate investment*

*Usually, some new assets are required while others are sold off. The net level of investment depends on the relative proportion of these two activities in each specific case.

Source: Reprinted by permission of *Strategy Formulation: Analytical Concepts* by C. W. Hofer and D. Schendel, p. 160. Copyright © 1978 by West Publishing Company. All rights reserved.

different ways, as Table 8.13 illustrates. Each alternative is workable, but requires a very different way of operating the company. Which, if any, should the firm adopt? The answer can depend on a host of factors and criteria.

As the above suggests, in a large firm, evaluating and selecting a strategy usually involves a sequence of analyses and decisions, rather than a single decision. The requirements for an effective strategy will probably undergo frequent modification because change is continuous, both outside and inside the firm.

The evaluation should take place at the corporate, divisional, and business-unit levels, with close scrutiny of the policies and plans at each of these levels. Two basic questions must be asked during strategy evaluation: (1) Has the existing strategy been satisfactory? (2) Will the existing or proposed strategies be satisfactory in the future?

Evaluation of an existing strategy requires the following steps:

1. An identification of the existing strategy in terms of its components, including its underlying goal structure and environmental assumptions.
2. A comparison of the results achieved against goals that have been established.
3. A comparison of environmental assumptions included in the strategy with the changes currently expected, based on an analysis and forecast of the future environment.

TABLE 8.12   Example of Broad Action Programs

Broad action programs based on controllable internal factors
  Maintain R&D and technical standing above leading competitor level.
  Implement an automation program leading toward significant increases in labor
    productivity.
  Improve the distribution network worldwide, developing a sense of priorities
    according to the attractiveness of each individual market.
  Reduce manufacturing costs through proper rationalization in every stage of the
    production process.
  Increase number of qualified managers via proper hiring, developing, and
    promotional procedures.
  Maintain market positioning by the allocation of financial and human resources
    compatible with competitive challenges.

Broad action programs to deal with external environmental forces
  Profit from a possibly temporarily favorable currency situation by taking advantage
    of a strong purchasing power in terms of:
      Switching from national to foreign suppliers.
      Engaging in an active acquisition of manufacturing facilities abroad.
  Set up a task force to study the legal, financial, and sales implications of currency
    transfer.
  Use local manufacturing, distribution, and marketing facilities whenever possible,
    seeking partnerships to neutralize trends toward nationalization.
  Stockpile raw materials on critical items, and firm up long-term contracts for the
    procurement of those raw materials, taking advantage of the temporary strong
    currency situation.
  Address the issue of labor shortage by:
    Internal development of qualified labor at all levels.
    Seeking increased government support.
  Establish the base for a systematic information gathering conducive to a better
    understanding of competitors and market opportunities.

Source: A. C. Hax and N. S. Majluf, "The Use of the Industry Attractiveness–Business Strength Matrix in Strategic Planning," *Interfaces* 13, no. 2 (April 1983), p. 67. Copyright 1983 The Institute of Management Sciences.

4. A determination of whether the strategy appears capable of meeting its goals
   in light of the existing and expected environment.[14]

The firm's planning department, CEO, and other staff and division executives play important roles during evaluation. The planners review and critique strategy alternatives, while others involved typically are required to submit a one-page critique of the alternatives to the CEO, spelling out several strategic issues thought to be critical to the division's business. The CEO then must prepare a list

---

[14]Dan Schendel and C. W. Hofer, eds. *Strategic Management* (Boston: Little, Brown, 1979), p. 16.

TABLE 8.13   Three Alternatives Yielding 15 Percent Sustainable Growth

	Strategy Alternatives		
Growth Factor	*Efficiency*	*Balanced*	*Aggressive Financing*
After-tax return on assets (ROA)	18.7%	17.3%	12.0%
Debt/equity ratio (D/E)	0.5	0.4	1.5
After-tax interest on debt (i)	6.0%	7.0%	10.0%
Percentage of earnings retained (p)	60.0%	70.0%	100.0%
Sustainable growth*	15.0%	15.0%	15.0%

*Where sustainable growth $= p \left[\text{ROA} + \frac{D}{E} (\text{ROA} - i) \right]$.

---

of strategic issues for discussion, as well as chair the strategy review session.[15]

While strategy evaluation, like strategy formulation, is still very much an art, there are certain objective evaluation criteria or factors, including:

1. *Goal consistency.* Is the strategy an attempt to achieve goals or objectives that conflict with other goals, objectives, values, or even the mission of the firm? If so, the process should go no further until this inconsistency is resolved.
2. *Strategy content.* Does the strategy satisfy important criteria such as:
    a. Is it acceptable to the stakeholders of the firm in terms of their values, expectations, and goals?
    b. Does it support the organization's mission and comply with its policies?
    c. Will it achieve the goals and objectives of the firm, and to what degree?
    d. Is it consistent with the environmental assumptions within which the firm must operate?
    e. Does the firm have the necessary resources and competence to carry out the strategy?
    f. Is the strategy likely to be successful? That is, does it create or exploit an advantage for the firm?
3. *Implementation.* Can the strategy be implemented successfully by the firm? The considerations here include resource requirements and availability; the organization's systems, structure, and processes; and the skills, abilities, motivation, and dedication of the firm's people.

---

[15]Ram Charan, "How to Strengthen Your Strategy Review Process," *Journal of Business Strategy* 2, no. 3 (Winter 1982), p. 55.

Some additional questions that might be asked include: Does the strategy rely on areas in which the firm is weak or do anything to reduce weaknesses? Does it exploit major opportunities? Does it avoid, reduce, or mitigate major threats? If it does not, are there adequate contingency plans? Does it meet critical success factors for the industry and the business?

In addition to the above general criteria, more quantitative criteria and questions relating to the firm should be considered. Alfred Rappaport has suggested that the ultimate test of a strategy is whether or not it creates value for shareholders. Therefore, the following questions must be answered: (1) Will the corporate plan create value for shareholders? If so, how much? (2) Which business units are creating value and which are not? (3) How would alternative strategies affect shareholder value?[16]

Quantitative factors are important in evaluating strategies. They provide a solid basis for decision making. In analyzing quantitative data, the firm's results must be compared with those of its competitors or its own history. Often, profit is the starting point for many decisions in the strategic plan, but should not be the only criteria used in evaluation of strategic alternatives; degree of risk is also a critical factor. Nonetheless, the strategy chosen must be capable of meeting profit targets within a reasonable degree of likelihood.

Evaluation Techniques.   Several quantitative techniques have been proposed to aid in strategy evaluation. One, STRATPORT, developed by Jean-Claude Larreche of INSEAD in France and V. Srinivasan of Stanford, uses a decision support system to evaluate and formulate business portfolio strategies. Strategies are expressed in terms of market share objectives to be achieved in each of the business units in the corporate portfolio. STRATPORT evaluates a strategy in terms of the net present value of after-tax cash flows in the long as well as the short run.[17] Another, previously mentioned, technique is Rappaport's approach to calculating the shareholder value contributed by a strategy.[18] While such techniques may *assist* in evaluating alternative strategies, it should be obvious that while, at best, they can provide additional information to the strategic decision makers, such techniques will not *make* the decision.

Selecting a Strategy

In the final analysis, formulating, evaluating, and selecting strategies remains more an art than a science, and may continue to be so for the foreseeable future. Even after thorough evaluation of strategic alternatives, the ''best'' one still may

---

[16]Alfred Rappaport, ''Selecting Strategies that Create Shareholder Value,'' *Harvard Business Review* 59, no. 3 (May–June 1981), p. 139.

[17]J. C. Larreche and V. Srinivasan, ''STRATPORT: A Model for the Evaluation for Formulation of Business Portfolio Strategies,'' *Management Science* 28, no. 9 (September 1982), p. 979.

[18]Rappaport, ''Selecting Strategies,'' p. 149.

not be clear. The process will rule out alternatives that do not satisfy important criteria, but several alternatives may remain which are essentially equal. One may be favorable according to certain criteria, another may be favorable on other criteria, and so on. But, regardless, a decision must be made.

In deciding between the remaining alternatives, the decision maker should reexamine all major assumptions on which they are based. Care should be taken to ensure that participants in the formulation and evaluation process have been dealing with similar assumptions and speaking a common language. Then, in the final analysis, the decision may come down to the risks inherent in the alternatives as opposed to their potential return. Risks can be categorized as those you can expect to happen, those that you are willing to accept, those that you are *not* willing to accept, and those that you *must* accept.

For each major risk, the following questions should be answered:

1. What are the consequences?
2. Will the ''worst case'' scenario seriously hurt the company, the division, or finances?
3. What level of risk am I willing to accept?
4. What if I do not accept the risk? Will the competition accept it?
5. How can the risks be reduced?

In general, the firm must examine its attitude toward risk—is it a ''risk avoider'' or is it willing to gamble? The amount of risk versus the potential rewards must also be compared for each alternative. In no case should an alternative be selected that involves undue risk, regardless of the reward. The decision maker must determine how much of the company or division he or she is willing to bet on the outcome of the strategic decision.

CONCLUSIONS

Numerous factors affect both corporate- and business-level strategies. Consideration must be given to the external environment—the economy, the competition, the market, technology, social factors, and political/legal considerations—as well as to internal influences, including stakeholder values and expectations, management's vision, goals and objectives, and the firm's level and types of resources. Critical success factors *must* be included in the strategy, as well as whether or not the strategy is likely to create a sustainable competitive advantage. Strategy formulation, evaluation, and choice is no simple or easy task.

Part IV

Strategic Planning, Implementation, and Control

Chapter 9

Developing the
Strategic Plan

LEARNING OBJECTIVES

After completing Chapter 9, you should be able to:

Understand the roles of scanning and monitoring the environment in strategic decision making.

Appreciate the types and sources of information required for strategic decision making.

Relate the important characteristics of a strategic information system, especially in contrast to the MIS.

Describe the primary forecasting techniques and their features and applicability.

Understand the role of risk analysis in making strategic decisions.

Understand the strategic planning process, and what a strategic plan typically contains.

Realize the importance and roles of contingency and scenario-based planning, as well as issue and surprise management.

Appreciate the need for clear thinking, simplicity, and flexibility in planning.

In Part III, strategic decision making, including formulating, evaluating, and selecting strategies, was discussed. Various corporate and business-level options and alternatives were also dealt with as were factors critical to their evaluation and selection. In Part IV, the focus changes. Here, the systems and techniques for providing the information supporting those decisions, and then systems and techniques helpful in planning activities (Chapter 9) will be studied. Last, Chapter 10 discusses issues and concerns of strategy implementation and control.

This chapter also describes the systems managers need to help them make strategic decisions. It addresses how information and systems aid in strategy formulation and planning, and examines levels of planning, and how "formalized" planning systems and approaches tend to be in practice.

As was pointed out in Chapters 1 and 2, some organizations use formal systems that require strategies to be explicitly stated, while others follow less formal approaches, with more implicit strategies. Smaller organizations tend to use the latter. In contrast, leading large firms tend to use more extensive, formal systems. In addition, the larger firms tend to use more formalized systems and procedures for both strategy formulation and selection, as well as for strategy implementation planning.

Whether simple or complex, formal or informal, the process by which an organization develops its strategies is its *strategy formulation system*. Regardless of the degree of formality or complexity of the process, the strategy formulation system's purposes are the same: to help structure the unstructured problems the organization faces, and to assist in choosing the best strategies for the firm.

This chapter pays specific attention to techniques for coping with an unstable, dynamic, and rapidly changing environment. This is the environment many firms have faced in recent years and are likely to continue facing in the future. It has been difficult to use traditional planning processes to keep pace with the turbulent, discontinuous environment changes. As Ansoff points out, change has become more rapid and uncertain, making it increasingly difficult for firms to "forecast" the future.[1] Planning processes driven by forecasts of the future based on extrapolations of the past may be misleading at best and possibly dangerous. New tools and approaches for coping with a fast-changing environment include issues management, contingency planning, scenario development, and "surprise" matrixes. These techniques are now used in advanced firms, and will probably be widely used in coming years.

PROFILE

The President's Information System

Even when important information exists and is known by the organization, it may be misinterpreted or mishandled. Newspaper columnist Jack Anderson observed that the president of the United States has professionals who produce "stunningly accurate assessments" of world events of momentous importance, which seem to be routinely ignored because of system breakdowns. He cites the following examples:

- President Nixon could have prevented the 40-fold jump in oil prices.
- President Carter could have prevented the takeover of the U.S. embassy in Iran, the Soviet invasion of Afghanistan, and the deportation of Cuban criminals and undersirables to Florida.

---

[1]H. Igor Ansoff, "Strategic Issue Management," *Strategic Management Journal* 1 (1980), p. 131.

• President Reagan might have averted the Falkland Islands seizure, and could have dealt more effectively with the Lebanon crisis.[2]

According to Anderson, in each of these cases, the presidents had access to information *in advance* that would have enabled them to take preventive actions. Why didn't they? Because the information was misinterpreted and misrepresented at several steps along the way; in other words, the president's strategic information system malfunctioned due to human error. So, even a sophisticated, highly developed intelligence system does not guarantee success.

PROFILE

Johnson & Johnson

In 1982, several people died in Chicago after taking extra-strength Tylenol capsules that someone had laced with cyanide. Prior to the widely publicized deaths, Tylenol had built a 35 to 40 percent share of the $1.2 billion-a-year pain relief business. After the poisonings, many analysts predicted that sales of the Tylenol brand would be permanently, and perhaps terminally, harmed. Within three months, however, the brand had regained an astounding 95 percent of its prior market share. How? In large measure, the dramatic recovery was due to expert handling of the crisis. A plan was developed quickly to meet the problem head-on.

Historically, when a product has been involved in a calamity, the typical approach has been to pull back and lie low, waiting for the bad publicity to blow over and the public to forget the scare.

McNeil Labs (the Johnson & Johnson division that produces Tylenol) used a very different approach, however. McNeil took immediate action. Within four days after the poisoning, at a cost of $100 million, all extra-strength Tylenol capsules were removed from retailers' shelves. Johnson & Johnson management appeared on network television to state its case and describe its plans to prevent a future occurrence. These rapid moves prevented competitors from capitalizing on the situation. Then the company offered to replace the Tylenol capsules the public still had, free of charge. This helped head off the purchase of competing products. In the meantime, tamper-resistant packaging was introduced, and McNeil offered retailers a 25 percent discount on Tylenol purchases to ensure that valuable shelf space was not given to competitors. The public's distrust of Tylenol also eased after "copycat" poisonings occurred involving soft drinks and other products.

In short, McNeil reacted more quickly to the crisis than its competitors were able to. The Tylenol poisonings resulted in only a temporary, if extremely costly, setback. But the product was worth saving, management believed, in view of the cost of scrapping Tylenol and starting over with a new brand. An effective response to the crisis minimized the damage. An even better approach would

---

[2]Jack Anderson, "Why Presidents Stumble," *Parade,* March 13, 1983, p. 4.

have been to prevent the situation from happening. The use of scenarios and surprise matrixes (techniques discussed in this chapter) may have highlighted Tylenol's vulnerability to tampering, and caused the company to use protective packaging beforehand.

STRATEGIC DECISION SUPPORT SYSTEMS

Effective strategic decision making and planning require having access to vital information. This information includes: technological, social, economic, political, legal, and environmental facts; information on the market and competition; information on the firm's strengths and weaknesses; information on past performance; information on current opportunities, problems, and contingencies; and information on the risks and uncertainties of current and proposed strategies. *Strategic information,* then, is the information necessary to make strategic decisions at either the corporate or business level of the organization. This information can be an important resource to the company if it is used to achieve a strategic competitive advantage.[3] To do this requires analysis of critical information needs and acquisition, as well as proper storage and dissemination, of that information.

But how does the firm acquire and handle such diverse information? Some of it may be available within the organization, but a good share of it is not. Furthermore, much of it may be subjective, impressionistic, and possibly unreliable. Much information exists in unrelated, unevaluated "bits and pieces" that are difficult for the decision maker to use. As a result, much information goes unused.

Most companies have less sophisticated systems for handling strategic information than does the federal government. In fact, many try to rely on their management information systems (MIS). However, as information expert Stafford Beer has noted, the information top management really needs must be separately collected and processed and must follow separate pathways from information required for operations. In addition, top management cannot rely on lower levels of management to pick out and provide the information needed for strategic purposes.[4] King and Cleland point out that the MIS is almost exclusively concerned with the past, with the *control* function applied to the operational activities of the firm; few focus on the *planning* function or strategic decisions critical to the company's future.[5]

What is required is a separate strategic information system (SIS) designed to support the company's competitive strategies. Such systems are increasingly required for success and survival in the dynamic and turbulent environment of

---

[3]Charles Wiseman, *Strategic Information Systems* (Homewood, Ill.: Richard D. Irwin, 1988).

[4]"The Shorter Catechism of Stafford Beer," *Datamation,* February 1982, p. 146.

[5]W. R. King and D. I. Cleland, *Strategic Planning and Policy* (New York: Van Nostrand Reinhold, 1978), p. 221.

the 1990s.[6] The SIS should provide for "scanning" the business environment to pick up new signals, and "monitoring" to track previously identified trends singled out as important to the firm. An important part of an SIS is establishing responsibility for acquiring and handling such information within the firm, following systematic procedures. In doing so, it is necessary to specify the firm's information needs, the sources, and the systems necessary to handle the data and information.

Strategic Information Needs

What kinds of information do strategic decision makers need? Studies have shown that a number of environmental and organizational variables are of major importance in determining the content of specific business strategies, as listed in Table 9.1. Actually, there probably are additional important variables, such as stakeholder values and social responsibility of the firm, which have not been studied adequately by researchers. While the 54 variables in the table can be grouped logically, as shown, the fact remains that monitoring each of them constitutes a major task.

John Rockart of MIT proposed a way of making masses of information more manageable. He suggests that firms use critical success factors (CSFs) to define the *significant* information needs of the organization.[7] As we saw in Chapter 8, studies have shown that three to six factors usually are critical to success in most industries, and these key factors must be met exceedingly well if the firm is to be very successful. By starting with the CSFs and using them to determine our primary information needs, we will be specifying the *critical data set* needed to run the business.

Grayson Manufacturing Company, a British and U.S. textile firm with sales of about $500 million, uses the CSF method to determine the information it needs and who should receive it. As shown in Table 9.2, Grayson starts with its mission, then develops supporting goals, objectives, and strategies. Next, the strategic success factors are developed. As Table 9.3 illustrates for one of the strategic success factors, key performance indicators for each factor are developed, and the individuals critical to successful performance in terms of that factor are specified. The required information is provided to that individual on a priority basis, and is also provided to selected additional people.[8]

Rockart points out that although the information systems of organizations are capable of producing large amounts of information, very little of it helps managers perform their jobs better. The problem is to identify critical informa-

---

[6]N. E. Swanson and L. A. Digman, "Conceptual Framework for a Modular Data-Based Strategic Information System" Paper presented at 14th Annual Conference, American Institute for Decision Sciences, November 1982.

[7]John F. Rockart, "Chief Executives Define Their Own Data Needs," *Harvard Business Review* 57, no. 2 (March-April 1979), p. 85.

[8]V. E. Millar, "Decision-Oriented Information," *Datamation,* January 1984, p. 161.

TABLE 9.1 Some Strategically Significant Environmental and Organizational Variables

Broader environmental variables	*Industry structure variables*	*Market and consumer behavior variables*
Economic conditions	Type of product	Stage of the life cycle
GNP trend	Degree of product	Market size
Interest rates	differentiation	Seasonality
Money supply	Equal products	Cyclicality
Energy availability	Price/cost structure	Market segmentation
Demographic trends	Economies of scale	Buyer concentration
Growth rate of	Degree of automation	Buyer needs
population	Degree of integration	Buyer loyalty
Age distribution of	Experience curves	Elasticity of demand
population	Marginal plant size	Purchase frequency
Regional shifts in	Optimal plant size	
population	Rate of product	*Organizational*
Sociocultural trends	technological change	*characteristics and*
Lifestyle changes	Rate of process	*resources*
Consumer activism	technological change	Market share
Career expectations	Transportation and	Degree of customer
Political/legal factors	distribution costs	concentration
Antitrust regulations	Barriers to entry	Quality of products
Environmental	Critical mass for entry	Value added
protection laws	*Competitor variables*	Length of the
Supplier variables	Degree of seller	production cycle
Degree of supplier	concentration	Newness of plant and
concentration	Aggressiveness of	equipment
Major changes in	competition	Labor intensity
availability of raw	Degree of	Relative wage rate
materials	specialization in the	Marketing intensity
Major changes in	industry	Discretionary cash
conditions of trade	Degree of capacity	flow/gross capital
	utilization	investment

Source: C. W. Hofer, "Toward a Contingency Theory of Business Strategy," *Academy of Management Journal* 18, no. 4 (December 1975), p. 798. Reproduced by permission.

tion and separate it from the masses of data and less useful information. The CSF method highlights areas that should receive constant and careful attention from management; performance in these areas should be measured continually. In this way, the manager's information needs—both "hard" quantitative, factual data, and "soft" opinions, assumptions, and forecasts—can be identified and that information provided.[9] As Nobel laureate Herbert Simon of Carnegie-Mellon

---

[9]Rockart, "Chief Executives," p. 85.

TABLE 9.2   An Example of Strategic Success Factors

Mission	Goals	Objectives	Strategies	Strategic Success Factors
To be the dominant textile products supplier to the most profitable domestic market segments and to provide a high-quality employee work life	Compete in profitable market segments	Identify and enter five new market segments with high-profit potential by 1986	Upgrade market research function to identify high-profit potential market segments	Effective market intelligence
		Increase market share 15 percent in high-profit market segments where we are not the dominant supplier, by 1987	Develop a product line that fits the requirements and needs of the high-potential market segments	New products
			Expand product distribution network	Market segment dominance
			Product differentiation	
	Be the low-cost producer in our market segments	Reduce total manufacturing costs by 10 percent per unit by 1986 and achieve 15 percent ROI	Review and upgrade all labor standards	High labor productivity
			Negotiate lower prices for raw materials and tighten control over yields	Low material cost
		Achieve 3 percent return above the cost of capital, by 1986		

Source: Adapted from V. E. Millar, "Decision-Oriented Information," *Datamation,* January 1984, p. 161. Reprinted with permission of DATAMATION® magazine, © copyright 1984 by Cahners Publishing Company.

TABLE 9.3 Information and Recipients for One Strategic Success Factor

Strategic Success Factor: Low Material Cost

Key Performance Indicators	Information Recipients	
	Critical Individuals	Additional Recipients
Material costs versus long-term target	Vice president, production	CEO; vice president, R&D; vice president, purchasing
Grayson percent material costs versus industry		
Material price as percent of standard price	Vice president, purchasing (fabric group)	CEO; vice president, purchasing; vice president, R&D
Change in material price as percent of consumer price index		

Source: Adapted from V. E. Millar, "Decision-Oriented Information." *Datamation,* January 1984, p. 161. Reprinted with permission of DATAMATION® magazine, © copyright 1984 by Cahners Publishing Company.

observed, the scarce resource today is not information but the capacity to process it. The information system that brings *more* information to the desk of the executive does him or her a disservice; what is needed are mechanisms to *filter* information and make sure that only the most important data reach the executive. For top executives, this is largely information from outside the firm that enables them to answer the "what if" questions.[10]

It is information *needs* rather than information availability that drives the strategic information system. Information that is available but not related to the strategists' needs can be ignored; needed but unavailable information presents a problem that the firm may overcome by using judgment, outside sources of information, or competitor intelligence. Information needs specify the types of information to be included in the firm's planning data base, which "feeds" the company's planning system.

Strategic Information Sources

In general, strategic information needs relate to management's vision, viewpoint, and values; the organization's strengths and weaknesses; business and industry criteria for success; competitive information; and environmental oppor-

---

[10]"Simon Says," *Forbes,* December 20, 1982, p. 150.

tunities, threats, and risks. Basil Denning has categorized the major sources of environmental information, as shown in Table 9.4. Information on the economy is available primarily from government, industry, and private sources, as well as through market research. Technological information is gleaned from information service firms, market research, and intelligence activities directed toward competitors' developments. A number of sources are required to obtain sociological information; political information can be obtained from various services and government reports. Information about competitors' potential actions can be gotten largely from intelligence efforts and "market signals," actions by

TABLE 9.4   Environmental Information Sources

Type of Information	Sources	Techniques
Economic forecasts: national economy sector forecasts	Government and private forecasts Industry association, government, private forecasts Market research	Critical appreciation of published forecasts Development of models or relationships for sector forecasts Input-output analysis Large number of quantitative techniques
Technological forecasts	Technical intelligence service reports Technical market research Research into competitors' developments	Demand and conditional demand analyses Opportunity identification techniques Theoretical limits testing Parameter analysis Various systems analysis methods Discipline reviews Expert opinion
Sociological forecasts	Wide variety of sources of data, including government reports, educational forecasts, population forecasts, regional forecasts, skilled labor forecasts, institutional changes, etc.	National models such as built by Battelle (unlikely to be done in any one corporation) Expert opinion
Political forecasts	Political intelligence services and government reports	Expert opinion
Forecasting competitors' actions	Any intelligence about competitors	Any relevant technique to give information from intelligence

Source: Reprinted with permission from *Long-Range Planning*, March 1973, Basil W. Denning, "Strategic Environmental Appraisal," p. 22, Copyright 1973, Pergamon Press, Ltd.

competitors that indicate their intentions, motives, goals, strategies, or internal situation.[11]

Forecasts of the future environment are another important source of strategic information. One type of forecasting that may be helpful is an approach used by futurists. Graham Molitor, of Public Policy Forecasting and a futurist, has developed an unusual forecasting system to provide planning information. He uses certain leading events, authorities, organizations, and political jurisdictions as indicators of likely future events. For example, he has found that trends and issues tend to develop, grow, mature, and decline in a pattern similar to the product life-cycle curve. Information about a certain trend indicates its stage in the life cycle. The firm can use this information to forecast the likely future course of the trend. This approach applies to events occurring in certain countries and regions of a country, as is illustrated in Figure 9.1. Certain countries and regions tend to lead trends, and monitoring these areas can provide a source of information on developing, largely social, trends.

Environmental Scanning and Monitoring

Scanning techniques and methods are used to search the environment for early evidence of changes. This involves looking for signals that may precede significant changes, *before* the changes assume economic, social, or strategic importance. Perhaps scanning could be better described as a task rather than a technique, although the result is intended to be an early warning system of important events. As such, it is an attempt to detect the weak signals of new trends early enough so that the business has sufficient lead time to develop a response strategy. Scanning involves looking for weak signals, because by the time there are clear signals, the change is widely known, and the early warning advantage is lost. Unfortunately, weak signals are difficult to discern above the "noise" in the system, and many of the changes never materialize.

There are several steps in implementing a scanning system.

1. Formation of a scanning network.
2. Development of scanning guidelines (what to look for).
3. Determination of sources.
4. Establishment of a synthesis/analysis process.

In addition to scanning, it is necessary to monitor changes or trends that have already been identified. Monitoring is concerned more with the immediate and the known than with the future and weak signals.[12]

---

[11]B. W. Denning, "Strategic Environmental Appraisal," *Long-Range Planning,* March 1978, p. 22.

[12]Ian Wilson, "Evaluating the Environment: Social and Political Factors," in *Handbook of Business Strategy,* ed. W. D. Guth (Boston: Warren, Gorham & Lamont, 1985), pp. 3-17–3-20.

FIGURE 9.1 Leading Political Jurisdictions as a Forecasting Device

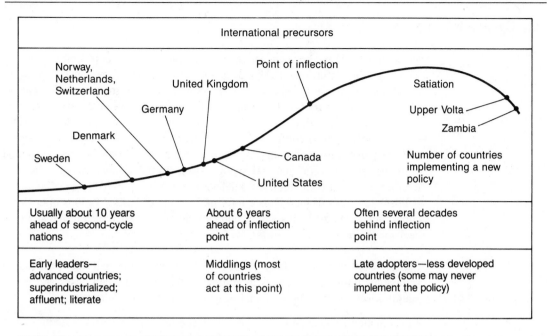

International precursors

Usually about 10 years ahead of second-cycle nations	About 6 years ahead of inflection point	Often several decades behind inflection point
Early leaders— advanced countries; superindustrialized; affluent; literate	Middlings (most of countries act at this point)	Late adopters—less developed countries (some may never implement the policy)

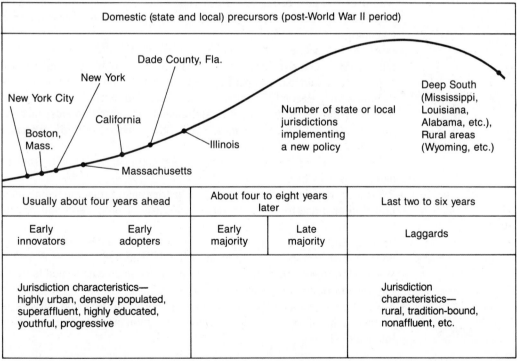

Domestic (state and local) precursors (post-World War II period)

Usually about four years ahead		About four to eight years later		Last two to six years
Early innovators	Early adopters	Early majority	Late majority	Laggards
Jurisdiction characteristics— highly urban, densely populated, superaffluent, highly educated, youthful, progressive				Jurisdiction characteristics— rural, tradition-bound, nonaffluent, etc.

Source: Graham Molitor. Reprinted with permission from the July 1977 issue of *Planning Review* 4, published by Robert J. Allio and Associates, Inc. for the North American Society for Corporate Planning, Copyright 1977.

Intelligence Information

Much information about the environment, particularly about competitors, is "intelligence" information. This does not mean that a firm must use "spies" or clandestine means to gather the information. In fact, a good deal of it can be gleaned from a variety of media, while market signals and other types of intelligence information can be gathered from a variety of other sources, including colleagues; conferences, meetings of trade groups, and professional societies; and informal contacts. Thus, "boundary people"—managers and particularly engineers and salespeople—are valuable sources of advanced intelligence about competitors.[13] Michael Porter has compiled a list of field and published sources of intelligence information, and describes various options for compiling, cataloging, analyzing, and communicating such data to the strategic decision maker, as shown in Figure 9.2

Public Sources and Data Bases. Much environmental data, including competitor information, exists in commercially available data bases and information services. A sample of such sources includes the following:

- Information on Demand: an information service company that maintains links with over 200 data banks which can yield facts and figures on topics ranging from the construction of steel pipeline in a given year to the latest silicon chip technology.
- DIALOG: a Lockheed service covering more than 120 data bases.
- DISCLOSURE: a data base of information on all publicly held companies required to file annual and periodic reports with the Securities and Exchange Commission. Recently available for microcomputers, the information includes balance sheets, quarterly and annual income statements, income by line of business, and the names, ages, titles, and salaries of officers and directors.
- COMPUSTAT: information on publicly held companies, available from Standard & Poor's Corp.
- Predicasts: detailed information on industries and firms, including market information, price trends, technology, forecasts of production and consumption, etc.
- Frost & Sullivan, Inc.: provides various industry studies, including assessments of risk factors on doing business in 70 countries.
- Washington Researchers, Inc.: provides information on data available from the government, much of which is free of charge.
- FINDEX: a directory of market research reports, studies, and surveys from sources such as Frost & Sullivan, Graham & Trotman, and Creative Strategies International.

---

[13]R. A. Thietart and R. Vivas, "Strategic Intelligence Activity: The Management of the Sales Force as a Source of Strategic Information," *Strategic Management Journal* 2 (1981), p. 15.

FIGURE 9.2   Intelligence Information System

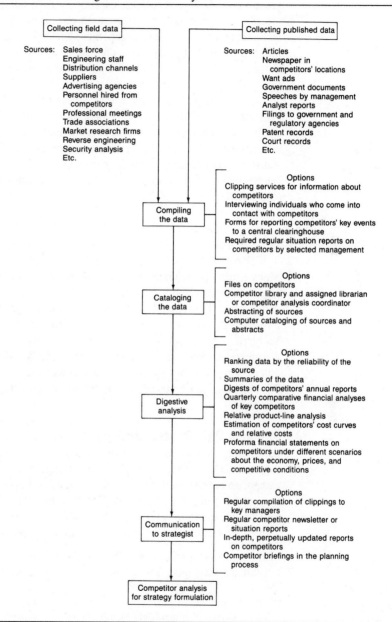

Source: Reprinted with permission of The Free Press, a Division of Macmillan, Inc., from *Competitive Strategy* by M. E. Porter, p. 73. Copyright 1980.

Numerous other sources, such as associations, trade groups, and data users' groups provide information at varying fees. In addition, a number of vendors offer systems that manage information once it has been acquired by the firm. In fact, there are over 200 companies currently supplying computer-readable information (data bases); these data bases are typically consulted more than 75 million times per year. The major services in this group are: The Source, CompuServe, Dow Jones News/Retrieval, DIALOG, and DRI/Visilink.[14] These are all secondary data bases in that access is controlled by the data service. A firm can also establish a primary data base, one that is assembled and accessed by the user. There are many packages available for forecasting that can use the information from data bases. In a recent article, 132 business forecasting, statistical, and financial planning packages were summarized, many of which can be run on a microcomputer,[15] some using Compact Disc-Read Only Memory (CD-ROM).[16]

Strategic Information Systems

Many firms—particularly large firms—of necessity employ systems for managing strategic data and information. This is where the strategic information system (SIS) comes into play. It is the SIS that incorporates the needs and sources of information: how information will be gathered, how and by whom it will be analyzed and interpreted, how and where it will be stored, and how it will be disseminated. Swanson and Digman have proposed designs for an SIS,[17] as have others. The work of King and Cleland is as advanced as any in this field, and is the basis for the material in the following paragraphs,[18] which examine the components of SIS.

Strategic Data Bases.   Strategic data bases group the most significant facts pertaining to a specific part of the strategic decision process. King and Cleland suggest that, to support strategic planning, a firm's information should be categorized in five such data bases, as shown in Figure 9.3. Drawing information from these data bases, and coupling it with assumptions and guidelines, plus forecasts of the future, provides the input for the strategic decision process. The data bases include the following types of information:

- *Strengths and weaknesses.* This is a candid and concise statement of the most significant strengths and weaknesses of the company. This data base would

---

[14]P. K. Coats, "Business Data Sources Grow with Personal Computer Usage," *Journal of Business Forecasting* 2, no. 1 (1983), pp. 22–24.

[15]G. Rice, E. Mahmoud, and S. M. P. Vadivel, "A Directory of 132 Packages for Forecasting and Planning," *Journal of Business Forecasting* 3, no. 1, pp. 11–23.

[16]Warren Briggs and James Coleman, "Compact Discs: New Tool for Competitive Analysis," *Planning Review* 15, no. 6 (November-December 1987), p. 32.

[17]Swanson and Digman, "Conceptual Framework," p. 15.

[18]King and Cleland, *Strategic Planning and Policy,* chap. 5.

FIGURE 9.3   Substantive Strategic Planning Process

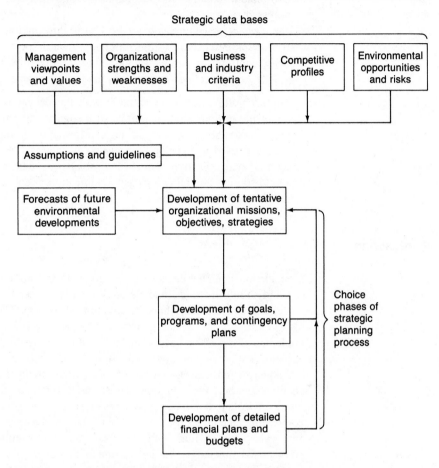

Note: This diagram draws on ideas from John H. Grant, ''Corporate Strategy: A Synthesizing Concept for General Management'' (University of Pittsburgh, 1975).

Source: Figure from *Strategic Planning and Policy* by W. R. King and D. I. Cleland, p. 76. Copyright © 1978 by Van Nostrand Reinhold Co. Inc. Reprinted by permission of the publisher.

probably include a summary listing of strengths and weaknesses plus data and exhibits elaborating on the summary.

• *Business and industry criteria*. Included here is information on what it takes to be successful in this business, including critical success factors.

• *Competitive profiles*. This data base includes analyses of competitors—their status, and present and likely strategies. In some ways, this information is a mirror image of the firm's strength and weaknesses.

• *Environmental opportunities and risks*. This data base contains specific questions and answers, including scenarios and issues, that can guide decision making and planning. Potential opportunities that may grow out of the environment should be included, and risks and their effects must be specifically addressed.

- *Management viewpoints and values.* Useful information would include aggressive versus defensive posture, attitudes toward social responsibility, preferences regarding government contracting, feelings toward diversification and growth, and guidelines for the firm in strategy evaluation and selection.

Any such SIS must be compatible with the decision-making processes and styles of the organization. It must also recognize the intersubjective nature of strategic information; that is, strategic information is interpreted subjectively, shared, and used to develop consensus. In contrast, MIS criteria are formal, structured, and objective. The SIS must also be flexible, providing personal access to sources and allowing easy modification of sources and perspectives as situations and managers change.[19]

Forecasting

Strategic management deals with the future. In attempting to decide what a firm can and should do to fit into its environment, three things are necessary: (1) strategic decision makers must be able to *forecast* what that environment will be like in the future (which is when strategic decisions made today will be implemented); (2) managers must be able to assess the firm's ability to implement strategic decisions in the future; and (3) the firm must be able to react and adapt to unforeseen or unpredictable environmental conditions which it is unable to predict. While all three are essential, the focus here is on predicting the future environment and being able to satisfactorily respond to the unpredictable. Forecasting techniques for the most predictable events, as well as techniques and approaches for dealing with the risks and uncertainties presented by less predictable happenings, will be examined. Techniques for contingency planning, possible future scenarios, and downright surprises are discussed in a later section of this chapter. Surprises, or sudden environmental changes, pose perhaps the greatest threats, but also offer the best opportunities for firms to change their relative position in the market.

Strategic forecasting primarily involves *predictions*—assumptions about the future—not projections. Projections are extensions of the past into the future, and may be appropriate for forecasting (or predicting) changes if the future does not radically or drastically depart from the present or the past. If changes occur suddenly, or if there are drastic breaks with the present and the past, change is discontinuous. With discontinuous change, projections do not make very good predictions, and most common forecasting techniques prove inadequate.

---

[19]Paul Shrivastava, "Variations in Strategic Decision Making Processes," in *Advances in Strategic Management*, vol. 2, ed. R. Lamb, (Greenwich, Conn.: JAI Press, 1983), p. 188.

Figure 9.4 shows that projection-based forecasting techniques fall short in predicting surprise events, and should be supplemented with approaches designed to predict discontinuities.

A forecasting technique that projects very precisely but misses surprise events is definitely of less value to a strategic decision maker than is a less precise approach that signals the likelihood of events that may result in discontinuities. It is better to be "roughly right" than "precisely wrong." Furthermore, it is more important for the strategist to correctly predict and assess the impact of major or broad changes than it is to predict specific changes that may be overridden by the broader trends. Predicting such trends, unfortunately, may be

FIGURE 9.4 Projection Techniques with Continuous and Discontinuous Change

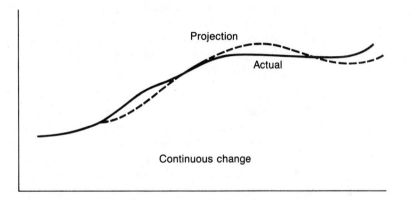

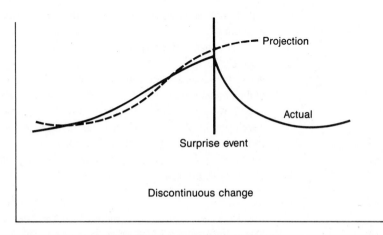

the easy part. The difficult task is predicting their *effects and timing*. For example, it may well be that the United States is in the process of restructuring itself from an industrial society to one based on information and knowledge, but what does this mean in terms of specifics? What effect will that phenomenon have on particular industries? And over what time frame and at what rate will changes take place?

Forecasting Techniques

Almost every strategic decision involves some sort of forecast. Therefore, the more the executive knows about forecasting techniques—including their strengths, weaknesses, and general applicability to specific types of forecasting situations—the better and more reliable his or her decisions will be. Selection of appropriate forecasting methods depends on a number of factors, including: the type of decision to be made, the availability of pertinent data, the required degree of accuracy, the length of the forecast period, the amount of time available for analysis, the importance of the forecast to the firm, and the stage of the product's life cycle. In general, four questions need to be answered *prior* to selecting a forecasting technique:

1. How is the forecast to be used? The purpose of the forecast determines its required accuracy and precision. A basic trade-off exists between the cost of producing the forecast and its accuracy. More accurate forecasting methods typically consume more resources, and less accurate methods cost less. Most strategic decisions do not require absolute accuracy. However, as accuracy declines, the cost of inaccuracy—the cost of making forecasting errors—increases, making a midrange level of accuracy the least-cost choice for many decisions.

2. What are the relationships between the variables to be forecast and the variables dependent on them? Specifically, what are the causal and interaction effects of the environmental variables to be forecast and company performance?

3. Can the past and present be reliably used to predict the future? To what degree?[20]

4. What decisions are the forecasts intended to support, and how do they relate to the product life cycle? Certain types of decisions tend to be made at various stages of the product life cycle (and before introduction, during the product development phase). Certain types of techniques support decision needs in each life-cycle stage. Further, it must be realized that no technique can accurately predict specific surprises, but it may predict average or aggregate events with precision.

---

[20]J. G. Chambers, S. K. Mullick, and D. D. Smith, "How to Choose the Right Forecasting Technique," *Harvard Business Review* 49, no. 4 (July-August 1971), p. 45.

Qualitative Techniques.   Qualitative techniques are likely to be used when data are scarce, such as prior to or during product introduction. These forecasts are based on opinion, judgment, and "feel" or personal experience, and generally represent the opinion or advice of some person or group knowledgeable in the area. Such forecasts are difficult to prove or disprove, and faith in them is largely a function of the reputation and track record of the forecaster. Sometimes, visionary forecasts, historical analogies, and panel consensus methods are classified as qualitative techniques. Many times, qualitative approaches are used in conjunction with more objective or quantitative approaches, with expert judgment (qualitative) used to interpret the results of the more formal methods.

Opinion Quantification Techniques.   These techniques attempt to quantify the qualitative forecasts of experts. Examples of such approaches are the Delphi method, the Nominal Group technique, and market research. In general, these techniques use rating schemes to turn qualitative information into quantitative estimates.

Extrapolation of Trends.   Most "traditional" forecasting methods attempt to project the past and present into the future in one way or another. Statistical techniques such as time-series analysis and projection are included here. Some specific approaches include moving averages, exponential smoothing, seasonal adjustments, trend projections, and Box-Jenkins techniques.

Simulation and Cause and Effect Techniques.   Simulation models attempt to relate environmental variables and constraints to end-result variables that affect the firm. Econometric models are examples; by "plugging" certain values for independent (environmental) variables into the models, a prediction of the effects on the firm is obtained. Related to simulation techniques are certain causal methods that can be used when historical data are available and enough analysis has been performed to specify the relationships between the dependent variable (the factor to be forecast) and the predictive factors. A causal model usually is the basis of a simulation model, although not all causal models are simulations.

STRATEGIC PLANNING SYSTEMS

One expert on strategic planning systems, Peter Lorange, has stated that far less is known about how to design formal planning systems than is known about effective strategies.[21] In other words, we know more about the strategies

---

[21]Peter Lorange, "Formal Planning Systems: Their Role in Strategy Formulation and Implementation," in *Strategic Management,* ed. D. Schendel and C. W. Hofer (Boston: Little, Brown, 1979), p. 237.

FIGURE 9.5   Phases in the Evolution of Strategic Planning

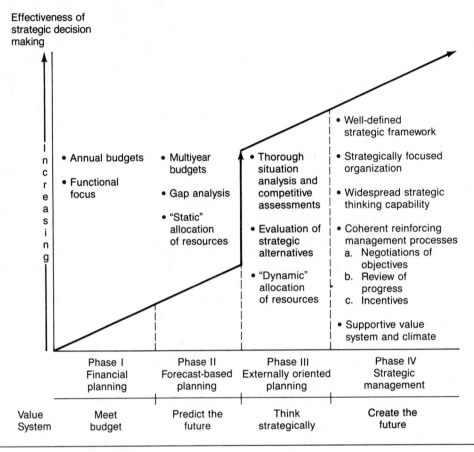

Source: Adapted from F. W. Gluck, S. P. Kaufman, A. S. Walleck, *The Evolution of Strategic Management* (New York: McKinsey & Co., 1978), p. 4.

themselves than we know about the processes of formulating and implementing them in organizations. Nonetheless, we *do* know that planning is a learning process, and organizations typically progress through several common stages in this learning or development process.

Planning System Stages

Gluck, Kaufman, and Walleck of McKinsey & Company found that firms are likely to be found in one of four evolutionary stages, as shown in Figure 9.5.

Phase I—Basic Financial Planning.   Most companies begin their formal planning with the annual budgeting process, where financial considerations dominate. The company's goal is to meet the budget, and a one-year time frame is usually used. Strategies are rarely formalized, but this does *not* mean that effective strategies are not employed.

Phase II—Forecast-Based Planning.   Most of what we know as long-range or strategic planning is in reality forecast-based planning. At this stage, firms try to foresee or predict the future impact of environmental forces, since basic financial planning on a yearly basis has proved inadequate. While more effective resource allocation plus portfolio analysis may be included here, Phase II primarily attempts to extend Phase I into the future; the company is still essentially *reacting* to the environment, rather than changing the organization to fit the environment more productively.

Phase III—Externally Oriented Planning.   This is the beginning of true *strategic* planning, where the firm focuses on changing its strategic thrusts to respond more effectively to markets and competition. In Phase I, the focus was operational control—attempting to control deviations from budgets. In Phase II, the emphasis was on more effective planning for growth by anticipating the environment. In this phase, strategic change, given *understanding* (rather than anticipation) of the causes of environmental changes, results in the firm looking for opportunities. Phase III employs the SBU concept, and represents a basic change in management style from those in Phases I and II. The planners are expected to offer strategic alternatives to management, including the risks and rewards associated with each.

Phase IV—Strategic Management.   Phase IV attempts to merge the scenario-based approach of Phase III with the management system of the firm. Strategic planning and operational decision making are linked for the first time. Not only does the firm think in terms of strategic alternatives and thrusts, but it also attempts to change its strategic *capabilities* by orchestrating its resources to *create* competitive advantages. In other words, the firm attempts to generate its own strategic alternatives. It does this through the use of: (1) a planning framework, which cuts across organizational units and levels, resulting in an integrated planning system; (2) a planning process that stimulates and rewards entrepreneurial thinking; and (3) a corporate value system that is geared to creating the firm's own future.[22]

Ansoff carries this progression to a "real-time" approach shown in Table 9.5. Ansoff feels that certain environmental changes occur too rapidly for manage-

---

[22]F. W. Gluck, S. P. Kaufman, and A. S. Walleck, "Strategic Management for Competitive Advantage," *Harvard Business Review* 58, no. 4 (July-August 1980), p. 154.

TABLE 9.5 Ansoff's Modern Management Systems

			Management Orientation			
	Control	*Long-Range Planning*	*Strategic Planning*	*Strategic Management*	*Strategic Issue Management*	*Surprise Management*
Purpose	Control deviations and manage complexity	Anticipate growth and manage complexity	Change strategic thrusts	Change strategic thrusts and change strategic capability	Prevent strategic surprises and respond to threats/opportunities	Minimize surprise damage
Basic assumption	The past repeats	Past trends continue into future	New trends and discontinuities	Expect resistance New thrusts demand new capabilities	Discontinuities faster than response	Strategic surprises will occur
Limiting assumption	Change is slower than response	The future will be "like" the past	Past strengths apply to future thrusts Strategic change is welcome	Future is predictable	Future trends are OK	Future trends are OK

⟵——— Periodic ———⟶   ⟵—⟶ ⟵——— Real time ———⟶

Source: H. Igor Ansoff, "Strategic Issue Management," *Strategic Management Journal* 1 (1980), p. 132. Copyright © 1980. Reprinted by permission of John Wiley & Sons, Ltd.

ment to either react to them or build them into the firm's plans. The firm may not have the luxury of waiting for the next annual planning cycle to respond, and it may not be possible to anticipate some of the changes, no matter how strategically oriented the firm's management may be. For these reasons, firms may need to think in terms of strategic issues (which may or may not arise) to prevent strategic surprises and to respond quickly to threats and opportunities. Even so, all issues or events are not forecastable. The firm will need a response mechanism *in place* to react to these unknown events as they occur (in real time) to minimize damage to the firm. (Techniques for treating such uncertain and risky events are discussed later in this chapter.)

A System of Plans

For planning to be effective, a firm must have a system of plans, a planning process, a decision subsystem, and a planning-management subsystem. A system of plans describes the interrelated ''subplans'' that include the mission, goals, objectives, strategies, and other planning aspects of the firm's divisions, functional departments, and projects. Using a school district as an example, King and Cleland show how such plans comprise a system, illustrated in Figure 9.6. The mission plan, sometimes referred to as the strategic plan, outlines the ''enterprise strategy'' of the organization, and how goals, objectives, and specific area strategies support the mission or role. The development plan determines the activities necessary for creation of a *new* generation of products or services, and guides formulation of divestment, diversification, and R&D plans. The operations plan, in turn, focuses on activities geared to the manufacture and delivery of current products and services, as well as other current operations of the firm. Program and project plans support higher-level plans and specify what is to be done in specific task or functional areas.

The result of the organization's planning processes at the strategic, tactical, and operational levels should be a system of interrelated and interdependent plans that serve as the basis for detailed scheduling and dispatching. As the figure shows, mission plans are the longest range, with development plans geared to a one-to-five-year future. Operations plans usually are one year in scope, though occasionally longer. All of these plans, however, are supported by program and project plans, which can have various time horizons.

A difference between the strategic and operational aspects of the organization involves the number of levels in the hierarchy. A large, diversified firm such as GE may have four or more operational levels, as Figure 9.7 shows. In addition to the corporate level, there may be 19 businesses, 150 departments, and 500 functional groups in a firm of this size. Four levels of plans are not required, however. As the figure shows, two to three levels of management are involved in planning reviews, and this reduction in levels often puts the CEO in contact with a department manager, for example. This streamlined planning hierarchy reinforces and emphasizes the importance of strategic planning throughout the organization.

FIGURE 9.6   A System of Plans

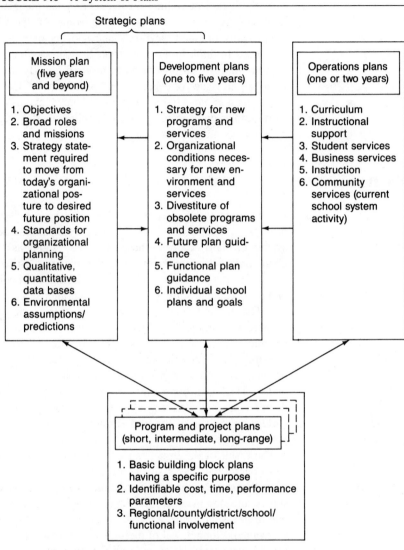

Source: Figure from *Strategic Planning and Policy* by W. R. King and D. I. Cleland, p. 62. Copyright © 1978 by Van Nostrand Reinhold Co., Inc. Reprinted by permission of the publishers.

Characteristics of Successful Systems

A successful planning system should encourage a congruence of people, rewards, information and decision processes, and structure. *Inc.* magazine, which is geared to new-venture managers, has suggested that successful business plans have five elements in common. They are, in order of importance:

FIGURE 9.7   Planning and Operational Levels

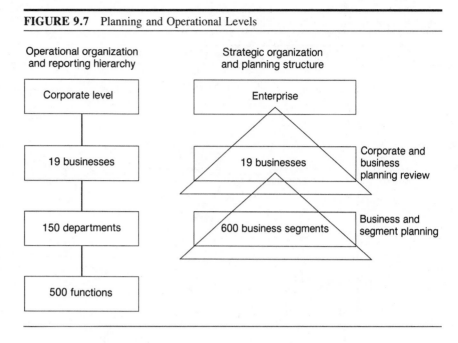

1. The president serves and is recognized as the top planning officer in the company. This responsibility cannot be delegated.
2. The plan is prepared with input from all departments.
3. The primary goal is to create concise, easy-to-follow guidelines.
4. Resources are concentrated on achieving a limited number of major, quantified objectives rather than many insignificant ones.
5. Objectives are tested for compatibility with each other.[23]

Don Harvey contends that the experiences of managers and consultants show that eight factors are important to successful planning systems: (1) Invent the future; do not merely try to project the present. (2) Stay flexible; update the plan periodically, via people-to-people contact, stressing fast response times. (3) Avoid getting into a numbers game; broad goals are more important than specific, detailed targets. (4) Involve top managers; the *real* planners should be the CEO and his or her team. (5) Utilize contingency planning; develop scenarios and ask "what if" questions. (6) Realize that the plan is not an end in itself; it is a guide and a means to an end. (7) Anticipate future problems; *reward*—don't punish—the person who alerts the firm about bad news. (8) Planning should flow from long-range goals.[24]

---

[23]Ivan C. Smith, "Management Strategy: Five Tips for Making Plans Tick," in *Strategy: A Report From Your Partner,* 1982, *Inc.* Magazine.

[24]D. F. Harvey, *Strategic Management* (Columbus: Charles E. Merrill, 1982), pp. 85–87.

FIGURE 9.8   Decreasing Predictability of the Future

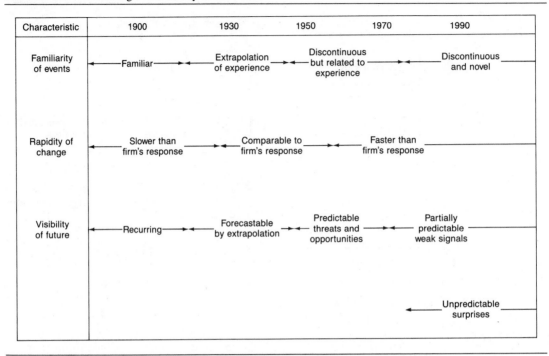

Source: Adapted from H. Igor Ansoff, "The Changing Shape of the Strategic Problem," in D. E. Schendel and C. W. Hofer, eds., *Strategic Management* (Boston: Little, Brown 1978), p. 39. Reprinted by permission.

PLANNING UNDER RISK AND UNCERTAINTY

Ansoff has repeatedly pointed out that predicting the future is becoming progressively more difficult for firms, since the future is becoming less and less predictable. As shown in Figure 9.8, events are becoming more discontinuous and novel, change is occurring faster than the firm's ability to respond, and the future contains more surprises. Prior to the mid-1970s, there was little need to anticipate crises such as inflation, materials shortages, and similar dilemmas. The current era, however, seems to be characterized by a nervous uncertainty. How to deal with this uncertainty causes uneasiness among strategic planners, and has led to a search for new methods to cope with unexpected events. Risk and uncertainty may be anticipated and responded to, and surprises avoided by increasing awareness of the environment and by preparing reactions to possible circumstances *in advance*. Multiple scenarios (which assume alternative sets of future conditions) and contingency planning are employed in some firms to mitigate the effect of future surprises.

In the past, managers were able to rely on judgment and intuition if analytical techniques were unavailable or in dealing with areas that the techniques were not

FIGURE 9.9   Risk Analysis

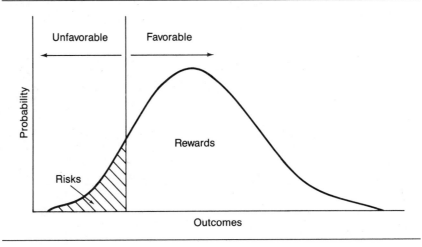

able to treat. Problems, situations, and decisions are becoming progressively more complex and interrelated, however, and a manager needs progressively more help in dealing with those problems, situations, and decisions. It is not that judgment and intuition are no longer necessary; they are no longer *sufficient*.

Risk Analysis.   The essence of managerial action today involves dealing with risks. Risk is inherent in any activity, because we live in a probabilistic world— one where nothing is absolutely certain. The successful decision maker is one who understands the existence of risk, is able to ascertain the degree of risk that exists, evaluates the potential desirable and undesirable outcomes and their ratio, limits assumed risks to tolerable levels (given the situation and resources), and is able to make decisions in this context. Much of the above is included in what we typically call *judgment,* knowing when and when not to pursue certain courses of action.

Simply stated, risk analysis involves determining the unfavorable outcomes possible as the result of a decision or action, and evaluating how likely it is that one or more of these undesirable events will occur. The likelihood that a venture will fail, and to what degree, is information every manager and planner needs to make decisions. If the needed information does not exist, it must be judged, guessed at, appraised by experts, or estimated by other means—but it cannot be ignored.

The prudent manager will weight the risk-to-reward ratio, ensuring that the favorable outcomes and their likelihood (return) clearly exceed the unfavorable and their likelihood (risk), as Figure 9.9 illustrates. Before proceeding, this manager will make sure that the organization can afford the worst possible case (the most unfavorable set of outcomes *does* sometimes occur).

FIGURE 9.10   Anticipatable and Unanticipatable Surprises

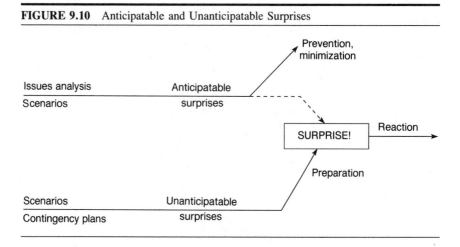

One of the major risks and uncertainties facing multinational firms today, for example, is that of political changes in the host country. Surveys of corporate executives, dating back to the 1960s, have found that managers rank political instability as one of their major considerations when making foreign investment decisions.

Regardless of whether the risk is foreign or domestic, predictable or unpredictable, however, logical processes can be followed to identify these risks and incorporate them into the strategic decision process.

Certain risks arise from the occurrence of surprise events, some of which may be anticipatable (such as strikes, wars, technological breakthroughs, and the like), while others may be unanticipatable (such as acts of God, fires, earthquakes, timing of stock market crashes, and plane crashes). By studying emerging issues and employing possible future scenarios, anticipatable surprises can be spotted and perhaps prevented or minimized by early action. On the other hand, the best we can do for unanticipatable surprises is to study them on a ''what if'' basis using future scenarios, and develop contingency plans to enable us to react as effectively as possible in the event the surprise scenario does occur. Figure 9.10 illustrates these relationships.

Contingency Planning

Contingency plans are alternative plans that can be put into place if events are not as expected. The more turbulent, discontinuous, and unpredictable the environment, the more likely this is to happen. Strategic plans are based on ''most likely'' events, those that have the highest probability of occurring. But because those events are most likely does not mean they are "certain"; other, less favorable, events *could* occur, creating serious problems for the firm. Interest rates could be higher than forecast, key executives could die or leave the firm, inflation could accelerate, prices could be frozen, imports of raw materials could be curtailed, a strike could occur, and a host of other events *could* materialize. Contingency plans are preparations to take certain actions when and if an event or situation that was not included in the strategic plan occurs.

There are four reasons for or advantages to contingency planning: (1) it helps the firm get into a better position to cope with unexpected developments; (2) indecision, uncertainty, and delays are reduced when something unusual happens; (3) the firm's responses are likely to be better thought out and more rational; and (4) managers are forced to think in terms of *possible* outcomes, rather than just the most likely outcome.

In general, the purpose of contingency planning is to prescribe *in advance* the actions a firm should take *if* some of the key assumptions or forecasts are not accurate. It provides alternatives, changing objectives, options, and strategy revisions to be implemented if the key assumptions and/or forecasts fail to hold. For example, *if* a firm's divestiture strategy is not successful, *then* the firm may opt (contingent on this unfavorable outcome) to: sell segments of the business; phase out unsold segments; close down certain segments; or withdraw from the business.[25] Thus, contingency plans can be a series of actions to be implemented in the event certain situations materialize.

The key elements in contingency planning include:

1. Identify contingent events. What less than likely events would cause serious damage to the firm? What is the "worst case" for interest rates, competitor actions, and the like? What events could render your plans ineffective? As an example, sales may be higher than planned, nullifying existing manufacturing schedules. While events can be negative *or* positive, in general, firms focus on the likelihood of unfavorable events. A company probably should focus on no more than 5 to 10 critical events, to keep the contingency planning process manageable.
2. What if? What if the critical event occurs? What strategies or actions can be put into place to deal with, offset, capitalize on, or neutralize the critical event? These actions should be specifically stated. The response is planned *in advance* should one or more critical events occur.
3. Trigger points. Specific "trigger points" should be specified in advance. These indicate *when* the contingency actions should be implemented. The question here is, what will trigger implementation of the plan? For example, a company may specify that a contingency plan is to be put into practice if sales are 10 percent below forecast for two consecutive months. The plan may

---

[25]King and Cleland, *Strategic Planning and Policy,* p. 55.

include a production slowdown, increased advertising, reduction of inventories, a cutback in raw material purchases, and other steps in response to the unexpected low sales.

Contingency plans, then, are reactions planned in advance if things do not go according to forecast. Most companies prepare such plans for a few critical events after the basic strategic plan has been completed.[26] During 1982, for example, many companies had prepared contingency plans in the event that the Reagan administration's "riverboat gamble"—Reaganomics—failed. In fact, automakers, among others, were forced to trigger their contingency plans, including postponing new models and new plants, and slashing the number of salaried employees.[27]

Scenario Analysis

Related to contingency planning is the concept of scenario analysis. Scenarios are "attempts to describe in detail a sequence of events which could plausibly lead to a prescribed end state, or alternately, to consider the possible outcomes of present choices."[28] Scenarios enable the firm to plan for specific situations, or scenarios, and attempt to answer two kinds of questions: (1) How might the situation (favorable or unfavorable) come about? (2) What alternatives exist for preventing, facilitating, or altering the process leading to the situation? Scenarios may be low-probability events with high impact, such as a plane crash, nuclear power station melt down, corporate takeover attempt, or new technological breakthrough.

Michael Naylor of General Motors has described seven steps firms should follow in a scenario analysis.

- Step 1: Develop a pair of scenarios—optimistic and pessimistic. This forces consideration of both outcomes (a "best case" and a "worst case" scenario). What are the key determinants and principal impact factors of each?
- Step 2: Write down the basic strategy options that can be pursued. Many times, strategy options fall into four categories: business as usual (no changes in present programs, organization, or personnel); reorganize the present business (regroup, transfer people, relocate plants, etc.); adjust the level of integration (more, or less, vertical or horizontal integration); or diversify into new businesses.
- Step 3: Evaluate the outcomes of the various strategies, assuming the optimistic scenario. Each strategy should be evaluated and ranked relative to the other

[26]G. A. Steiner, *Strategic Planning: What Every Manager Must Know* (New York: Free Press, 1979), p. 235.

[27]R. E. Winter, "Supply-Side Sighs: Business Leaders Begin to Express Skepticism about Reaganomics," *The Wall Street Journal*, January 29, 1982, p. 1.

[28]J. H. Grant and W. R. King, "Strategy Formulation: Analytical and Normative Models," in *Strategic Management*, ed. D. Schendel and C. W. Hofer (Boston: Little, Brown, 1979), p. 11.

TABLE 9.6   Scenario-Strategy Matrix

Optimistic scenario	+ +	+	+ +	−	+
Pessimistic scenario	− −	+	−	+	+ +
Strategy	Business as usual	Reorganize	More integration	Less integration	Diversify

Source: Adapted from M. E. Naylor, ''Planning for Uncertainty—The Scenario-Strategy Matrix,'' in K. J. Albert, ed., *The Strategic Management Handbook* (New York: McGraw-Hill, 1983), p. 22–9.

strategies. This ranking and evaluation should be in terms of how favorable the outcome will be to the firm.

- Step 4: Follow the same procedure for the pessimistic scenario.
- Step 5: Combine the two strategy evaluations into a scenario-strategy matrix such as the one shown in Table 9.6. The key here is to examine the spread in desirability for each strategy between the optimistic and pessimistic scenarios. For example, the business-as-usual strategy has the highest spread (+ + to − −) and thus the highest uncertainty. It also has the highest risk, since it has the most negative outcome if the pessimistic scenario occurs. Furthermore, the strategy of more integration dominates the business-as-usual strategy (it has the same optimistic results but a better pessimistic outcome), and reorganize dominates the less-integration strategy. If the firm is not willing to tolerate the moderately negative risk of the more-integration strategy, only reorganize or diversify remain. These are ''robust'' strategies, since the outcome is favorable under either scenario. However, the diversify strategy appears to dominate the reorganize approach, and appears to be the best option for the firm.
- Step 6: Evaluate the strategies against pairs of scenarios for other factors. The example in steps 1 to 5 represented one set of critical factors for the firm. The same approach should be used for several other critical factors or areas.
- Step 7: Compare results for each of the critical factors analyzed. Using decision rules (perhaps similar to those in step 5), strategies are progressively eliminated, and the remaining strategies are examined in closer detail. In summary, the scenario-strategy matrix approach is useful in strategic planning because it depends less on the accuracy of specific forecasts than do traditional methods. In addition, it forces people to think in terms of a *range* of outcomes and emphasizes flexibility.[29]

A scenario can be described as ''a slice of future history.'' It is also a model used to examine relationships between the environment and an organization. The scenario is a hypothetical sequence of events designed to draw attention to causal

---

[29]M. E. Naylor, ''Planning for Uncertainty—The Scenario-Strategy Matrix,'' in K. J. Albert, ed., *The Strategic Management Handbook* (New York: McGraw-Hill, 1983), p. 22–9.

processes and decision points.[30] Scenarios will probably be more widely applied in an increasingly more turbulent environment.

For example, the October 19, 1987, stock market crash caused some analysts to consider possible future scenarios. In reality, the Wall Street plunge should not have been totally unexpected, given the debtor status of the United States, the huge budget deficits brought on by tax cuts and military spending, high interest rates and strong dollar, and chronic trade deficit. Thinking in terms of three scenarios—the worst case, or "hard landing"; a less drastic outcome; and the most desirable, or "soft landing"—the market drop may have signaled that the United States was initially on the path toward the "hard landing" scenario.

The three plausible scenarios were as follows:

1. *The worst case.* A wave of selling of dollars occurs within a few weeks, dropping the value to about the 130 yen range. Interest rates skyrocket and inflation fears lead Japanese institutional investors to pull away from their U.S. investments. That sends the dollar lower and freezes consumer spending. The U.S. congress enacts a protectionist trade package.
2. *Less drastic.* In this case, the market, disappointed with inability of the United States to cut its deficit, puts more pressure on the dollar. Selling depresses the dollar even lower than 130 yen by mid-1988. Anxiety over creeping inflation and rising interest rates causes a worldwide recession in 1988.
3. *The most desirable, but the most complex.* Stock prices edge lower, but a tight money supply stabilizes the dollar, limiting the trade deficit. Reagan and Congress cooperate on an aggressive combination of budget-tightening cuts and higher taxes. The combination convinces central banks in Japan and West Germany that they should ease their own monetary policies. The effectiveness of such measures would depend upon the changes during the first six months, when the growth rate would be expected to be nearly zero.[31]

Thus, government policymakers need to determine in which direction the economy is headed, and try to steer it toward favorable outcomes and minimize the negative effects of worst case outcomes, if they materialize.

Another current example of scenario analysis is the approach used by research institutes and business firms to plan for possible impacts of the "greenhouse effect." Battelle Pacific Northwest Labs is developing a computer model to predict possible impacts on various regions of the United States, because the firm expects a demand for such information for business planning in the 1990s. In fact, companies such as Archer Daniels Midland (barge lines), Weyerhaeuser (lumber), and Travelers Corp. (insurance) are already developing "what-if" plans based upon the greenhouse scenario.[32]

---

[30]A. W. Smith, *Management Systems: Analyses and Applications* (Hinsdale, Ill.: Dryden Press, 1982), p. 193.

[31]Yoichi Funabashi, "Stock Plunge Hint of Hard Landing," *Sunday Journal-Star,* November 1, 1987, p. 1.

[32]"When the Rivers Go Dry and the Ice Caps Melt," *Business Week,* February 13, 1989, p. 95.

Issues Analysis

A more recent approach, called *issues analysis,* is related to contingency planning and scenario analysis. The purpose of issues analysis is to alert management to emerging political, social, and economic trends and controversies and to mobilize the company's resources to deal with them. An issue "is a condition or pressure, either internal or external to an organization, that, if it continues, will have a significant effect on the functioning of the organization or its future interests."[33]

Issues analysis supplements other forecasting approaches. Atlantic Richfield (ARCO), for example, felt that its planning was too numbers oriented, and created a team of issues managers. Their task is to spot trends, a job previously done somewhat haphazardly by top executives, government relations people, planners, and public relations staffs. Recently, ARCO was tracking 140 issues, including such government matters as state tax rates, the Clean Air Act review, natural gas decontrol, and state legislation on hazardous wastes.

Other companies with issues managers include S. C. Johnson & Company, Sears, and the Bank of America. Johnson removed fluorocarbons from its aerosol sprays three years before federal action forced others in the industry to do so. Sears became aware of the flammable-nightwear controversy and placed non-flammable goods on its shelves before it was required to do so. Sears also realized that a cancer issue was building over Tris (a flame retardant used in clothing) and removed affected garments from its shelves early. Issues managers alerted Bank of America about a likely controversy over redlining of loans (avoiding certain neighborhoods). Bank of America changed its lending policies two years before Congress required banks to do so.[34]

Today, over 70 companies have issues staffs and use varying techniques to rank issues. One way is to assign an "impact index" to each issue, reflecting its potential effect on the firm. Multiplying this index by its probability of occurrence gives an estimate of the expected effect, which can be used to rank the issue's importance.[35] An example of this procedure is shown in Table 9.7.

Surprise and Crisis Management

Issues analysis is designed to reduce the number of potential "surprises" facing a company. However, not all surprises can be forecast. Therefore, the firm must be able to react effectively to as well as anticipate such events. In addition, there

---

[33]J. K. Brown, *This Business of Issues: Coping with the Company's Environments* (New York: Conference Board, 1979), p. 1.

[34]E. C. Gottschalk, Jr., "Firms Hiring New Type of Manager to Study Issues, Emerging Troubles," *The Wall Street Journal,* June 10, 1982, p. 21.

[35]Brown, *This Business of Issues,* p. 32.

TABLE 9.7 Procedure for Ranking Issues

Issue	Impact*	Probability of Occurrence†	Expected Effect‡	Ranking of Issue
A	8.8	0.3	2.64	4
B	6.7	0.7	4.69	1
C	4.4	0.9	3.96	2
D	3.8	0.8	3.04	3
E	2.1	0.5	1.05	5

*Rated on a scale of 1 to 10, from least to greatest.
†From 0, improbable, to 1, certain.
‡Impact multiplied by probability.

are surprises that are not really issues, such as natural disasters, accidents, and wildcat strikes. Such events, including totally unpredictable chance events, are impossible to deal with effectively in the firm's planning cycles.[36] An example would be Union Carbide's December 1984 tragedy in Bhopal, India, where a leakage killed thousands of residents. Other examples would include the Exxon Valdez oil spill and the sudden unrest in China.

Unanticipated events may occur because management either

Did not make the necessary efforts to anticipate them, or because the events could not be forecast effectively on the basis of existing knowledge, intuition, and wisdom. Such surprises often lead to crisis situations, where the organization's objectives, plans, intentions, and assumptions are profoundly modified. . . . They also usually produce increased uncertainty, greater disorder, and higher costs. Over the last few years, there have been many such surprises in Western societies, including the rapid deterioration of the international monetary system, the inflationary wave, the oil crisis, and the explosion of political violence.[37]

The reason for such surprises is that most human situations involve both forces of changes and forces of continuity.

Surprises tend to occur when the forces of change move much faster and become stronger than the forces of continuity (which are themselves never completely stable). For instance, a currency might enjoy a solid position for a while because of adequate reserves and a favorable balance of payments. However, a sudden flow of capital in or out can completely alter the situation and create both surprise and crisis.

Such surprises and crisis can originate either within the organization (e.g., the sudden death of a general manager) or outside of it (e.g., a takeover bid). Because such crises are costly in all respects (money, morale, etc.), some effort should be made to locate the areas where surprises may occur. (Note: While it may be possible to identify the general areas in which a surprise may occur, it is seldom possible to identify the

---

[36]Ansoff, "Strategic Issue Management," p. 131.

[37]C. W. Hofer, *Instructor's Manual to Accompany Strategic Management* (St. Paul, Minn.: West Publishing, 1981), p. 191.

surprise itself, which by its nature can hardly be forecast, otherwise it would not be a surprise.) One way to identify such areas is by analyzing in as much detail as possible the circumstances in which surprises would seem most likely to take place. In this regard, it has become an important aspect of management, both in business and in the military, to build so-called surprise matrixes. In such matrixes, potentially destructive events are identified . . . according to the areas from which they originate and the strategy elements and/or functional activities of the firm that they may affect.[38]

Such a matrix could resemble the one shown in Table 9.8. Of course, different forms may be appropriate depending on the environment, the industry, and the firm involved.

> The exact construction will also depend on the perception and realism of the builder. Nevertheless, every firm should try to build such a surprise matrix, even if only in the most simplified way.
>
> Once a surprise matrix has been constructed, the next step in the surprise management process is to plan countermeasures (contingency plans) for the most probable [and most important surprises]. In some cases (e.g., fires or strikes), detailed plans can be set up. [For less precise events,] only relatively broad responses may be possible. However, in every area some individual should be assigned responsibility for dealing with such surprises should they occur.[39]

An example of effective scenario analysis and contingency planning relates to the October 19, 1987 stock market crash. Weeks before the crash, Federal Reserve Board Chairman Alan Greenspan asked his key aides to pinpoint weak spots in the U.S. economy and financial system, and to preplan responses, should the weaknesses develop into crises. They identified three areas: how to deal with major bank failures; how to respond to a free-fall of the dollar; and, most important, as it turned out, how to handle a stock market collapse. The team considered all of the "flash points" that could cause a breakdown, including scenarios of how each could occur. When the stock market actually did crash, Greenspan and his aides followed the contingency plan prepared weeks earlier which outlined the emergency actions to take.[40]

PUTTING IT ALL TOGETHER

Once the strategic decision has been made, detailed planning can begin. Now the chosen strategy is created in detail for each division or business unit, and specific time-phased actions required to support the strategy, including budgets, are developed. The result is the strategic, long-range master plan, typically covering five years or more. From this plan, more specific and shorter-range tactical and

---

[38]Ibid., pp. 191–93.

[39]Ibid., p. 193.

[40]Alan Murray, "Fed's New Chairman Wins a Lot of Praise on Handling the Crash," *The Wall Street Journal,* November 25, 1987, p. 1.

TABLE 9.8 Surprise Matrix

Sources of Surprise Events / Functional Areas of the Organization Affected by the Surprise	Outside the Organization					Within the Organization		
	Customers	Suppliers	Political Environments	Economic Environments	Technological Environments	Physical Events	Psychological Events	Social Events
Marketing	Boycotting of a customer	Become competitors	A revolution	Price controls	Product obsolescence through competitor's innovation	Fire in warehouse	Corruption in sales personnel	Strike of salespeople
Finance	Bankruptcy of a product	Take-over bid	Increased taxes	Rapid increase in interest rates	—	Errors in computer system	Stealing of cash	Organized falsification of data
Personnel	Corruption by customers	Stealing of trade secrets	Terrorist action for political reasons	General strike	Technological unemployment	Epidemics	Sabotage	Factory occupation
Production								
R&D								
etc.								
etc.								

Source: Reprinted by permission of C. W. Hofer, *Instructor's Manual to Accompany Strategic Management*, p. 192; Copyright © 1981 by West Publishing Company. All rights reserved.

operating plans are developed. But this chapter focuses on the longer-term strategic plan.

Many firms experience two problems in planning. They have difficulty in producing reasonably accurate forecasts, and they tend to misuse the strategic plan as an operating document. In fact, many strategic plans are little more than "financial hopes filled with 'nice' numbers." This is unfortunate, for a plan is of value only if it is realistic. However, specific ways to overcome planning problems have been proposed:

1. Emphasize the *process* of planning, not the financial details of the plan.
2. Differentiate between the more serious risks to the balance sheet and risks to the profit and loss statement.
3. Measure the total market and competitive market shares as accurately as possible.
4. Gear the plan, especially spending, to the occurrence of major *events,* rather than to time periods.
5. Plan to expend money step by step as events warrant, rather than up front.
6. Build a second plan based on time periods.
7. Decide *in advance* the criteria for abandoning a project.
8. Set up a monitoring system.
9. Make a new five-year plan every year.
10. Avoid excessive publicity about long-term financial goals. (They *may* not materialize.)[41]

Remember, the goal of planning should be to speed up the organization's process of learning about its environment, not just to make plans.[42] Also, do not expect perfection in planning immediately; treat the initial try as just that—a first draft. Planning is a skill; no one ever became an expert golfer, musician, public speaker—or planner—on their first few tries.

The Plan's Process and Content

After strategic decisions have been made, more detailed planning occurs. Specific statements of policies and procedures, strategies and programs, priorities and schedules, and budgets and resources are developed. Figure 9.11 shows the process as practiced by the General Telephone Company of Illinois (GTI). In the GTI example, managers establish and maintain an "information bank" which they can draw from when setting performance goals and planning in their own areas of responsibility. This information bank is contained in a planning

---

[41]R. N. Paul, N. B. Donavan, and J. W. Taylor, "The Reality Gap in Strategic Planning," *Harvard Business Review* 56, no. 3 (May-June 1978), p. 124.

[42]A. P. DeGeus, "Planning as Learning," *Harvard Business Review* 66, no. 2 (March-April 1988), p. 70.

FIGURE 9.11   GTI's Planning Process

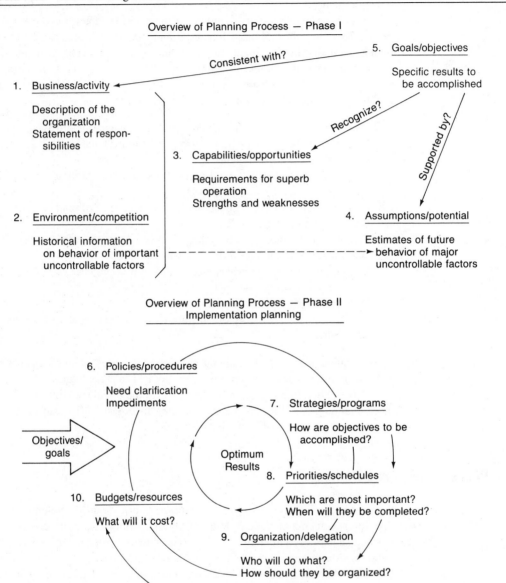

Source: Adapted from *MBO and the Planning Process in General Telephone Company of Illinois* (Bloomington, Ill.: GTC of Illinois, 1973), p. 4.

workbook with several interrelated sections so that individual planning efforts are coordinated and more supportive of the company's overall goals and objectives.[43]

Content and Format. There is no uniform format for a strategic plan; nearly every company has its own approach. As an example, strategic planning for a centralized company would differ from one that is decentralized. In the latter instance, each SBU may have its own strategic plans that would comprise the following elements:

- A statement of the SBU's mission.
- The key environmental assumptions summarizing the external environment and its opportunities and threats.
- Key competitor assumptions.
- A list of constraints imposed from either inside or outside the company.
- The desired future of the SBU—its *goals*.
- *Objectives*, stated as specific time-based measurements that will be met in pursuing the goals.
- The course of action to be followed to achieve goals and objectives—*strategy*.
- The programs, development and investment, critical to the strategy.
- Contingency plans, which recognize that things might go wrong, and what can be done to correct the situation.
- And finally, the financial components of the strategic plan in a form that will allow them to be integrated with the existing operational control system.[44]

An example of a strategic plan is included in Appendix C.

Keep It Simple, Flexible, and Workable

Unfortunately, many companies fall into the trap of allowing their strategic plans to become massive documents. Phillip Caldwell, former Ford CEO, cautions that "planning is basically a thought process. It is not a paper mill." Ford's final corporate plan may run only 30 to 35 pages, with key issues covered on a single page.[45] Michael Kami agrees, stating that the plan should be short and cover only a few really key areas, perhaps in six pages or so for a typical business unit. The emphasis should be on the thought process, not methodology. In fact, Kami

---

[43]*MBO and the Planning Process in General Telephone Company of Illinois* (Bloomington, Ill.: GTC of Illinois, 1973).

[44]Robert M. Donnelly, "Strategic Planning for Better Management," *Managerial Planning* 30, no. 3 (November-December 1981), pp. 3–6.

[45]"Some Better Ideas from Ford Motor's CEO," *Planning Review* 12, no. 5 (September 1984), p. 9.

feels that elaborate methodology plus "paralysis-by-analysis" kills effective planning.[46]

Another example of a less formal, flexible approach to planning was that used by Honda in entering the U.S. motorcycle market in 1959. Honda began by importing primarily heavyweight bikes to compete with the then-dominant Harley-Davidson. However, they had severe problems with clutches and oil leaks, and withdrew. They were forced to replace the big bikes with their lightweight 50cc Supercub, which they initially felt wouldn't do well here because of Americans' preference for "macho" cycles. To Honda's surprise, the smaller bikes became an immediate hit. The point is that a business should remain flexible and not overplan.[47]

Michael Kami suggests a simple, action-oriented approach to developing strategic plans:

1. Assemble a team of six or so people knowledgeable about the industry and the business, and put them in a conference room for two or three days.
2. Have them brainstorm 100 factors that will affect the organization in the next three years.
3. Categorize the factors by their level of importance (such as critical, very important, not so important, and so on).
4. Arrive at a consensus about the 10 most important factors, and assign priorities to them.
5. Brainstorm 50 to 100 alternative actions for dealing with each important factor.
6. Pare this list down to 5 to 10 clever, innovative actions.
7. Reconcile the actions and take steps to begin implementation right away.[48]

IBM uses a similar approach, called *process quality management* (PQM) for certain of its strategic planning activities, relying heavily on the critical success factor concept in determining what the company must accomplish to achieve its mission and what must be done to meet the critical success factors. PQM—like Kami's approach—demands an intensive one- or two-day session attended by *all* key managers and employing a brainstorming and consensus-building approach.[49]

Strategic planning does not have to be a complex, voluminous, methodologically threatening, time-consuming process. The emphasis should be on clear thinking, not on format and sophisticated analysis.

---

[46]Michael Kami, *Strategic Planning for Changing Times,* (Dayton, Ohio: Cassette Recording Co., 1984).

[47]Milton Moskowitz, "Honda's Market Conquest Not Entirely Planned," *The Media General Financial Weekly,* June 25, 1984, p. 6.

[48]Kami, *Strategic Planning for Changing Times.*

[49]M. Hardaker and B. K. Ward, "How to Make a Team Work," *Harvard Business Review* 65, no. 6 (November–December 1987), pp. 112–20.

CONCLUSIONS

Strategic information is essential to making strategic decisions. But what is strategic information? One approach to determining strategic information needs is to start with the critical success factors for the business, and specify the information required to judge how well the business is doing in terms of the CSFs. While there are numerous sources of strategic information, some items will probably not be available; in these areas, assumptions must be made. Also, it is necessary to scan the environment for weak early warning signals of trends and changes. In addition, existing changes must be monitored. It is advisable for firms to set up flexible strategic information systems around custom-designed guidelines to help them manage strategic information acquisition, analysis, dissemination, storage, and recall.

Again, management needs various types of external and internal information, available from a variety of sources. Management must ensure that important and essential information for strategic decisions is acquired through properly managed scanning and monitoring systems. The firm's MIS (which is internally and past-performance oriented) is not a sufficient source of such information. A present- and future-oriented strategic information system (SIS) is needed that incorporates the *pertinent* external and internal strategic decision information. In larger firms, the SIS may incorporate and draw from several data bases.

In formulating strategy, forecasting the future is important. It is not adequate to *project* the past and present into the future; an attempt must be made to *predict,* or assume, what will or can occur. Various qualitative and quantitative forecasting techniques exist. Most are based on past data. Some, however, attempt to discover cause-and-effect relationships and can be used to simulate future conditions, rather than using statistical techniques to *project* the future. Approaches based on past data are dangerous in turbulent, discontinuous environments. To help strategists anticipate and react more effectively and quickly, approaches such as scenarios, issue analysis, and surprise matrixes can be used, and can serve as the basis for the preparation of contingency plans.

Many formal planning systems utilized by companies deal more with actions required to implement strategies than they do with formulating those strategies. However, firms use various approaches (systems) in formulating strategies. Such systems should be of a contingent nature, designed to fit the specific organization in question.

Relatively simple, less formal strategic decision and planning systems can work well in many firms, particularly in the less complex, smaller company. Systems should be no more complex than required, yet larger firms many times require more formal planning systems because of the organization's complexity, not because more sophisticated systems are better.

Chapter 10

Strategy Implementation and Control

LEARNING OBJECTIVES

After completing Chapter 10, you should be able to:

Relate the steps involved in implementing a strategic planning process.

Describe the specific steps in implementing strategic decisions.

Realize the major factors required for successful implementation of strategic decisions.

Describe the types of managers appropriate for various types of strategic business units.

Appreciate the effects of organizational climate, culture, and other social/political influences.

Understand the elements and levels of strategic control.

Appreciate the roles and key elements of strategic audits.

In Part II assessing the strategic situation was discussed, and in Part III the focus was on formulating, evaluating, and selecting strategies—making the strategic decision. Building on the strategic planning systems and techniques presented in Chapter 9, we will now address the important areas of strategy implementation and control.

Experts have repeatedly cited strategy implementation, strategic performance evaluation, and international strategic management as being the ''most intractable problems'' of strategic management. This is the case because these problems are new, ill-defined, complex, and not amenable to study through traditional discipline-bound fields. In addition, these problems are among the most critical facing strategy practitioners.[1] What good is a brilliant strategy that can't be implemented; how can we evaluate strategic (versus operational) performance, both domestically and internationally?

Since the early 1970s, many companies have jumped on the strategic planning bandwagon, and have acquired substantial and sophisticated strategic planning capabilities. However, relatively little attention has been given to the processes required to effectively implement the strategies. And remember, the strategic management concept encompasses strategy formulation, implementation, and control.[2]

In fact, "implementation" is now one of *the* buzzwords in strategic planning, pulling ahead of "market share" and "competitive analysis."[3] Frederick Gluck of McKinsey & Company has stated: "Planning without equal emphasis on what must be done to make plans work, is in trouble."[4] A poorly *executed* strategy can produce unsatisfactory results just as easily as can a strategy that was poorly *formulated*. It is difficult to question the value of good planning, but a number of companies have learned that if equal (or greater) attention is not given to executing strategy, failure is likely.

Unfortunately, implementation is often ignored in studies of decision making, quantitative methods, economic analysis, behavioral techniques, and organizational changes. Yet the *way* a decision is implemented determines its ultimate effectiveness. *How* the decision is put into practice is of critical, if not primary, importance. As King and Cleland have observed, "the greatest difficulties in instituting change . . . do not lie in the design and development of the changes themselves. Rather, the greatest obstructions to positive change lie in the processes that are used to implement them."[5]

Implementation involves executing the strategic plan.[6] It is the process of:

- Designing the organization's structure and climate to match the strategy.
- Ensuring that divisional and functional managers have the right background, skills, and attributes to make the strategy work.
- Employing the right functional policies to make the strategy work.[7]

---

[1]Robert Lamb and Paul Shrivastava, eds., *Advances in Strategic Management,* vol. 4 (Greenwich, Conn.: JAI Press, 1986), p. xi.

[2]C. H. Roush, Jr., "Strategic Resource Allocation and Control," in *Handbook of Business Strategy,* ed. W. D. Guth (Boston: Warren, Gorham & Lamont, 1985), p. 20–2.

[3]D. R. Hykes, *"Planning for Plan Implementation,"* paper presented to Omaha Chapter, North American Society for Corporate Planning, November 7, 1984, p. 6.

[4]"Top Speakers Get Rave Reviews at Annual Conference," *The Planner,* May–June 1983, p. 1.

[5]W. R. King and D. I. Cleland, *Strategic Planning and Policy* (New York: Van Nostrand Reinhold, 1978), p. 325.

[6]D. F. Harvey, *Strategic Management* (Columbus: Charles E. Merrill, 1982), p. 236.

[7]W. F. Glueck and N. H. Snyder, eds., *Readings in Business Policy and Strategy from Business Week* (New York: McGraw-Hill, 1982), p. 22.

- Allocating resources to the operating units in support of the strategies approved for those units.

Every element of the company now comes into play—manufacturing, marketing, finance and accounting, purchasing, personnel, distribution, customer service, and so forth—to give life to the plan and accomplish the objectives.

Also, decision making and planning processes are important, not only in implementing decisions and plans, but in formulating them as well. Therefore, we will first look at implementing planning *processes* likely to facilitate quality strategic decision making. Next, we turn to implementing those *decisions,* which are described in terms of strategic *plans,* our final implementation topic.

Implementation is essentially an *administrative* and behavioral task, while strategy formulation is more analytical and intuitive. Implementation occurs through the operational functions of the organization, while formulation is a product of the strategic function.

Another area, *strategic control* (strategy analysis and corrective action after implementation), is also very important and perhaps even more neglected in studies. Strategic control focuses on two questions: Is the strategy being implemented as planned? and Is it producing the intended results?[8] The world (and the firm) are constantly changing, and it is not possible to forecast these changes with certainty. So the organization must be able to review the ongoing results of its strategic decisions and take corrective actions (modify the strategies, their implementation, and the firm's performance) as necessary.

PROFILE   *AM International, Inc.*

Addressograph-Multigraph Corp., headquartered in Cleveland, was a marginally profitable manufacturer of old-fashioned duplicators and addressing machines. The company was being beaten in the marketplace by Japanese competition and producers of more advanced xerographic copiers. In 1976, Roy Ash, cofounder of Litton Industries and budget director in the administration of President Richard M. Nixon, was brought in as chairman and CEO.

Ash arrived with new strategies and promises of a new future for the company. He planned to remake the firm into a major supplier of word processors, small computers, and other components to be used in the "office of the future." Renaming the company AM International, his strategy was to use AM's older products as cash cows and to find new ventures, acquiring young companies and technologies to bring the company's products up to the level of Xerox, IBM, Wang, and other leaders in office automation. The strategy was appropriate and well conceptualized; the basic direction was correct and the strategy workable.

---

[8]Dan Schendel and C. W. Hofer, *Strategic Management* (Boston, Little, Brown, 1979), p. 17.

However, in 1981, AM lost $245 million on sales of $857 million. In 1980, AM had equity of $232 million; in early 1982, the equity had fallen to $14 million. In February 1982, the board forced Ash to resign. What went wrong?

Under Ash, AM had a superb strategic plan that was poorly executed. Ash replaced 80 percent of the company's management and moved the headquarters from Cleveland to Los Angeles. He moved quickly into unfamiliar high-technology areas, buying a number of young companies that didn't have proven track records. Adequate financial controls to monitor performance of the divisions were not installed, nor were AM's older businesses—the cash cows—kept healthy enough to fund the new ventures. The changes in management caused too much instability in the company, and the skills of the new managers were not adequately matched to the needs of the divisions.

In short, investing in high-technology ventures can breathe new life into an old-line company when the investments are well thought out, experienced management is on board, and cash flow can support the ventures.

Unfortunately, that was not the case at AM, and the company had to fight for survival.[9]

PROFILE

Union Pacific Corp.

The Union Pacific Corp. (UP) undertook an ambitious diversification program in the late 1960s, positioning itself in energy (Champlin Petroleum Company), mining (Rocky Mountain Energy Company), and land development (Upland Industries Corp.), in addition to its Union Pacific railroad. The acquisitions provided synergy: the energy and land development businesses encouraged growth in areas serviced by the railroad. The railroad, in turn, transported much of the energy and mining output, and the railroad owned much of the territory Upland is developing and managing.

The railroad was a mature cash cow in a growing part of the country, the West. Consequently, the company focused on its diversification program. Recently, however, the company has turned its attention back to railroading by acquiring the Western Pacific and Missouri Pacific railroads. With these acquisitions, even more synergy was likely because more of Rocky Mountain's mining output would be transported all the way to California, Illinois, Washington, Texas, Louisiana, and Tennessee on Union Pacific.

To promote efficiency and productivity, UP more recently combined its Champlin Petroleum and Rocky Mountain Energy subsidiaries into a single operating company, the Union Pacific Resources Co. In September 1987, the Interstate Commerce Commission approved UP's $1.2 billion acquisition of

---

[9]"AM International: When Technology Was Not Enough," *Business Week,* January 15, 1982, p. 62.

Richmond-based Overnite Transportation Co., a trucking company. The move enabled Union Pacific to offer new choices in multimodal transportation, and to extend Union Pacific's reach into the eastern half of the United States.[10]

Further productivity-enhancing and restructuring moves may soon be in the offing, as the rail company under CEO Drew Lewis concentrates on "moving cargo for customers, not just shuffling trains." As a result of such efforts, UP probably now runs the most sophisticated "just-in-time" inventory contract service in the country, shipping auto parts from Detroit to the GM/Toyota NUMMI plant in California.[11]

IMPLEMENTING STRATEGIC PLANNING PROCESSES

As we observed earlier, effective implementation requires more than deftly turning strategic decisions into reality. Implementation also includes developing and using strategic planning processes and systems. These processes *aid* in the implementation of strategic decisions, as well as in strategy formulation, analysis, and choice.

Businesses need planning systems to help them cope with the increasing complexity and range of today's issues. Planning systems are vital to resource allocation, and they help integrate and coordinate activities between business units and across organizational levels.[12]

Unfortunately, firms frequently invest relatively little effort in training managers at all levels to accept, understand, and use strategic planning systems. Specifically, managers must understand:

1. What the strategic planning system is supposed to do. The ultimate purpose of any planning system is to influence the behavior of managers: it should assist, guide, and motivate their efforts.
2. How effectively the system can do what it is supposed to do. Many systems, such as growth/share matrixes and PIMS guidelines, focus on a narrow range of critical factors.
3. How planning systems can be better utilized by top management. Specifically, operating managers will take their cues from the way top managers use such systems.[13]

---

[10]Laurie McGinley and Daniel Machalaba, "ICC Clears Union Pacific's Plan to Buy Overnite Transportation for $1.2 Billion," *The Wall Street Journal*, September 16, 1987, p. 8.

[11]Jack Willoughby, "The Rebuilding of Uncle Pete," *Forbes*, November 14, 1988, pp. 182–90.

[12]Schendel and Hofer, *Strategic Management*, p. 221.

[13]S. R. Palesy, *Implementing Strategic Planning in Diversified Companies*, Case No. 9–580–049 (Boston: HBS Case Services, 1979).

Dale Hekhuis of GE has observed that CEO involvement is the key to effective planning systems. The most important contribution of the planning system may be that it *forces* time for thinking about the future into the executive's crowded calendar.[14]

Phases in System Implementation

Just as it is important to have a strategic plan, it also is important to have a plan for implementing the planning process. Consultants John Roach and Michael Allen have stated that implementation of planning systems occurs in six phases:

- Phase I: Assessment of the need for stronger planning, as evidenced by weak financial performance, eroding strategic performance, or mounting environmental challenges.
- Phase II: Making the strategic planning process (SPP) fit the company, reflecting company size, business type, structure, business elements, and environment.
- Phase III: Implementing the basic SPP.
- Phase IV: Integrating the SPP with the firm's basic strategies, such as production/technology resource strategies, budgeting strategies, and management selection strategies.
- Phase V: Auditing the SPP to keep the process "on course" and ensure that it operates effectively.
- Phase VI: Counseling on SPP problems to ensure that they do not render the system ineffective.[15]

Measures of System Effectiveness

But how does one measure the effectiveness of a planning system? Early studies of planning merely examined links between the degree of formality of planning and the firm's financial performance—a complex link at best. To evaluate planning systems, we need to think in terms of how well the system fulfills *its* objectives, how well it helps the organization perform, and the executives' satisfaction with the system. Planning system objectives include:

- Predicting future trends.
- Evaluating strategic alternatives.
- Avoiding problem areas.
- Enhancing management development.

---

[14]Schendel and Hofer, *Strategic Management,* p. 221.

[15]J. D. C. Roach and M. G. Allen, "Strengthening the Strategic Planning Process," in *The Strategic Management Handbook,* ed. K. J. Albert (New York: McGraw-Hill, 1983; pp. 7–22–7–44.

TABLE 10.1 Planning System Effectiveness

Effectiveness Measure	*Most Important Contributing Factors*
Meeting system objectives	1. System Capability 2. Overcoming resistance to planning
Organizational performance	1. Planning resources 2. System Capability
Planning system satisfaction	1. Overcoming resistance to planning 2. System capability

- Improving short-term performance.
- Improving long-term performance.

As shown in Table 10.1, the overall capability of the planning system is important in managers' perceptions of how well the system meets their planning objectives, how well the organization performs, and their satisfaction with the system. However, other factors—overcoming resistance to planning and resources available for planning—were judged more important factors for two of the effectiveness measures.[16]

Problems and Pitfalls

Successful implementation and use of strategic management systems require that firms be fully aware of the problems and pitfalls associated with the system's use. In general, a company implementing a strategic planning system must be prepared to modify it to fit the "administrative realities" within the firm. Specifically, portfolio planning, the creation of strategic business units, and generic strategies for units often conflict with the way the firm operates.

Creation of strategic business units may define a planning structure that conflicts with the operating structure already in place. The strategic business units (SBU) that exist only for planning purposes may be a meaningless concept offering little in the way of direction and motivation to employees of operating units. Further, management time demands often limit the number of units that can be reviewed adequately. Thus, many companies limit the number of SBUs to certainly no more than 30 or 40.

Management may not always have enough information to balance cash flows between SBUs. Also, problems of motivation may result when employees of a

---

[16]V. Ramanujam, N. Venkatraman, and J. C. Camillus, "Multi-objective Assessment of Effectiveness of Strategic Planning: A Discriminant Analysis Approach," *Academy of Management Journal* 29, no. 2 (June 1986), pp. 347–72.

TABLE 10.2   Strategic Planning Pitfalls

Rank	Description
1	Top management's assumption that it can delegate the planning function to a planner.
2	Top management becomes so engrossed in current problems that it spends insufficient time on long-range planning, and the process is discredited by other managers and staff.
3	Failure to develop company goals suitable as a basis for formulating long-range plans.
4	Failure to assume the necessary involvement in the planning process of major line personnel.
5	Failing to use plans as standards for measuring managerial performance.
6	Failure to create a climate that is congenial to and not resistant to planning.
7	Assuming that corporate comprehensive planning is something separate from the entire management process.
8	Injecting so much formality into the system that it lacks flexibility, looseness, and simplicity, and restrains creativity.
9	Failure of top management to review the long-range plans they have developed with departmental and divisional heads.
10	Top management's consistently rejecting formal planning mechanism by making intuitive decisions that conflict with the formal plans.

Source: Reprinted with permission of The Free Press, A Division of Macmillan, Inc. from *Strategic Planning: What Every Manager Must Know* by G. A. Steiner, p. 294. Copyright 1979.

unit perceive their sole function as generating cash for other divisions. The same goes if their unit is known as a dog. Labels may become self-fulfilling prophecies. In addition, such assumptions as "high growth necessitates sacrificing short-term profits" may be used to justify mediocre short-term performance.

Additionally, with candidates for divestiture, affected managers often suffer morale and commitment problems. In short, the impact of the planning system depends less on the analytical techniques utilized than on the style, objectives, and practices of the CEO. Thus, administrative considerations affect the implementation of a strategic planning system, and firms must be prepared to adjust their systems to fit administrative realities.[17]

George Steiner surveyed 215 companies on their experience with planning systems.[18] The study covered 50 pitfalls or mistakes related to the nature of strategic planning, implementing planning, doing the planning, and using the plans. The 10 highest-ranking pitfalls or mistakes are shown in Table 10.2. Note

---

[17]Richard Hamermesh, "Administrative Issues of Strategy," in *Implementing Strategy* (Cambridge, Mass.: Management Analysis Center, undated).

[18]G. A. Steiner, *Strategic Planning* (New York: Free Press, 1979), p. 294.

that those ranked first, second, fourth, and ninth deal with inadequate involvement in the planning process by the CEO and line management.

IMPLEMENTING STRATEGIC DECISIONS

The purpose of implementation is ensuring that the planned results of the strategic decisions are realized. Implementation involves carrying out the chosen strategy—doing what must be done to make the strategy successful. As Harvard's Kenneth Andrews has observed, the corporate strategy must dominate the design of organizational structure and processes. That is, successful implementation requires that management shape the formal structure of the organization, its informal relationships, and the processes of motivation and control (which provide incentives and measure results) to the particular needs of their strategy.[19] Stated another way, implementing strategy decisions results in the choice of organization structure, of information and measurement systems, and of reward-and-punishment systems; it also influences the style of management used to administer the organization.

The first step in implementation is identifying the activities, decisions, and relationships critical to accomplishing the strategy. For example, low-cost mass production may be critical to Ford, but ultra-high quality is the key to Rolls Royce. This phase of implementation requires that the strategy be broken down into specific and assignable tasks, usually according to specialized economic and technological factors. In addition, however, this series of specialized efforts must be reintegrated in a coherent fashion, which is largely a behavioral (as well as economic and technological) task. As a note of caution, unless consideration is given to reintegration of the tasks during the specialization step, it may be impossible to put the specialized tasks back together again—sort of like Humpty Dumpty.[20]

Key Implementation Tasks

Implementation of strategies is an administrative task performed by the operational organization. However, more is involved that just turning selected strategies over to those responsible for implementation and hoping for the best. The organization—its structure, processes, systems, and people—must be pointed toward what is needed to make the strategy work. Consequently, five

---

[19]Kenneth Andrews, *The Concept of Corporate Strategy,* rev. ed. (Homewood, Ill.: Richard D. Irwin, 1980), p. 109.

[20]J. L. Bower, "Solving the Problems of Business Planning," *The Journal of Business Strategy* 2, no. 3 (Winter 1982), p. 32.

critical administrative tasks emerge that are vital to successful implementation. These tasks are shown in Figure 10.1.[21]

1. Building an organization capable of carrying out the strategic plan. The organization must have the structure and skills necessary to turn the strategy into reality. As pointed out in Chapter 3, the appropriate structure depends on a number of factors—the stage of the firm's development, the degree of diversification, the sector of the economy, to name a few—in addition to the needs of the chosen strategy. Furthermore, the firm's personnel must possess the skills necessary to make the strategy work. Related to this is the need to assign the responsibility for accomplishing key implementation tasks and for making related decisions to the right individuals or groups.

2. Allocating and focusing resources on strategic objectives. If the firm is to accomplish strategic objectives, top management must provide the resources needed. Management shows where its priorities are by how it allocates its resources: budgets, people, and support. The first step is to develop a corporate financial strategy that defines the boundaries within which resource allocations eventually will be made. After proposed strategies have been approved and top management has decided on how resources are to be applied, budgets can be prepared. Budgets should include the new capital expenditures required to implement the strategy, as well the more difficult and less common estimation of the various incremental expenses associated with implementation. Further, once the strategy has been decided on, the key tasks to be performed and kinds of decisions required must be identified; plans must also be developed. The tasks should comprise a *formal plan*; they should be arranged in a sequence comprising a plan of action with targets to be achieved at specific dates. Formal provisions for coordinating the tasks and activities of the plan must be made. Included in this is the need to develop substrategies in the functional areas of the firm, such as marketing, R&D, finance, production, personnel, and the like.

3. Galvanizing organizationwide commitment to the chosen strategic plan. People and departments of the firm must be influenced, through incentives, constraints, controls, standards, and rewards, to accomplish the strategy. This requires measuring the contributions of people and departments to the strategic objectives, and linking the reward structure to their strategic performance. Also, policies and procedures must be established that encourage attention and commitment to the strategy.

4. Installing internal administrative support systems. The management process, the way the managers in an organization work together, is the critical element in successful implementation and performance. Internal systems must support this process, as well as monitor strategic progress. Actual performance must be measured against planned performance in meeting strategic objectives,

---

[21]A. A. Thompson, Jr. and A. J. Strickland III, *Strategy Formulation and Implementation: Tasks of the General Manager,* rev. ed. (Plano, Tex.: Business Publications, 1983), p. 314.

FIGURE 10.1 The Administrative Aspects of Strategy Implementation

Building an Organization Capable of Carrying Out the Strategic Plan	Allocating and Focusing Resources on Strategic Objectives	Galvanizing Organizationwide Commitment to the Chosen Strategic Plan	Installing Internal Administrative Support Systems	Exerting Strategic Leadership
Key Recurring Issues:	*Key Recurring Issues:*	*Key Recurring Issues:*	*Key Recurring Issues:*	*Key Recurring Issues:*
1. How to match organization structure to the needs of strategy.	1. What budgets and programs are needed by each organizational unit to carry out its part of the strategic plan.	1. How to motivate organizational units and individuals to accomplish strategy.	1. What kinds of strategy-facilitating policies and procedures to establish.	1. What leadership actions to take in shaping values, molding culture, and energizing strategy accomplishment.
2. How to build and nurture a distinctive competence and to staff positions with the right talent and technical expertise.	2. How to focus the performance of tasks on achieving organizational objectives rather than on just carrying out the assigned duties.	2. What kind of strategy-supportive work environment and corporate culture is called for.	2. How to get the right strategic information on a timely basis.	2. How to keep the organization innovative, responsive, and opportunistic.
3. What kind of core executive group is needed and who to select for each slot.		3. How to create a results orientation and a spirit of high performance.	3. What "controls" are needed to keep the organization on its strategic course.	3. How to deal with the politics of strategy, cope with power struggles, and build consensus.
		4. How to link the reward structure to strategic performance.	4. How to create all the helpful administrative fits.	4. When and how to initiate corrective actions to improve strategy execution.

Source: A. A. Thompson, Jr. and A. J. Strickland III, *Strategic Management: Concepts and Cases*, 3rd ed. (Plano, Tex.: Business Publications, 1984), p. 198.

and corrective action taken where necessary. To acquire information on actual performance (as well as on changes in the external environment), strategic information systems must be designed and installed. In short, management must monitor the results of the strategy, adapt the organization to environmental changes, and ensure that the organization (and its people) work to carry out the strategy.

5. Exerting strategic leadership. Essentially, strategic leadership consists of obtaining commitment to the strategy and its accomplishment. This includes creating a climate and culture that causes the organization to work hard (and intelligently) toward the accomplishment of the strategy. While this requires management's personal leadership, it also involves the constructive use of power and politics in building a consensus to support the strategy.

Critical Senior-Level Abilities

Effective performance at senior levels in organizations requires abilities beyond and different from those needed at nonexecutive levels. Six such abilities identified by a recent New York University study are: knowing the business and markets; managing subunit rivalry; finding and overcoming problems; staying on strategy; being an entrepreneurial force; and accommodating adversity.[22]

The NYU study, as well as one by Harvard's John Kotter,[23] found that effective senior executives know their businesses well. They understand where it has been and where it is going and what the customers want. They also allow *productive* rivalry between subunits (functions and divisions); they don't try to eliminate rivalry or competition but to *manage* it to improve performance. Effective executives are also adept at diagnosing issues before they become problems, as well as at assessing the implications of an issue. They tend to think several "moves" ahead in the competitive game.

A critical strategy-related skill is the ability to keep the organization focused on the strategy; the plan must be prominent in the thinking of management. For example, all too often managers "chase" ad hoc opportunities not related to the firm's strategy. Effective managers possess the ability to continually evaluate ideas, opportunities, and alternatives against the strategy.

Further, good executives possess an entrepreneurial spirit. Not only can they create a vision of what the company can be, but they are able to articulate that vision so others can understand it, share in it, and become excited about it—they are able to "build a dream" for people. Finally, they can deal with, learn from,

---

[22]S. A. Stumpf, "Leadership and Beyond: The Need for Strategic Management Skills," in *Advances in Strategic Management,* ed. Robert Lamb and Paul Shrivastava, vol. 5 (Greenwich, Conn.: JAI Press, 1988), pp. 245–55.

[23]John P. Kotter, *The General Managers* (New York: Free Press, 1982).

and build upon setbacks—adversities. They are resilient and they don't dwell on setbacks; they move forward.

Management Selection, Development, Succession

Since strategic planning provides the link between the past, the present, and the future, executive succession—particularly CEO succession—is a vitally important strategic decision. In fact, some say that CEO succession is *the* most important strategic decision, because it determines all other strategic decisions for years to come (during the CEO's tenure).[24]

But CEO selection is not the only personnel decision with strategic importance. Selecting the best people to implement strategies is important in achieving the firm's strategic objectives. Today, there may be as many different types of managers and managerial styles as there are different types of businesses. Further, different types of businesses (such as cash cows, stars, question marks, and dogs) may require very different actions and leadership approaches for their strategies to be effective. Important to business-unit performance, then, is finding the right kind of manager for each type of business.

The managerial specialist best suited to handle a particular business situation can be identified and selected using the business screen matrix shown in Figure 10.2. Use of the matrix allows the business situation to be compared to its relative strategic position in the industry, allowing a manager or particular managerial style to be chosen to match the strategic situation. In the figure, suggestions are made about the types of managers most likely to be successful in each situation represented.

Professional Liquidator. A business that is a weak competitor in an undesirable industry may need a professional liquidator to divest the business quickly and as painlessly as possible. Liquidation skills are unlikely to be found within existing management. Thus, such an individual likely would come from outside the company and specialize in rescuing the interests of stockholders who find themselves in a sinking boat. The object here is to concentrate on the immediate and spend little time and effort on the long-term operations of the business. The professional liquidator should be a person who can manage a fast-paced brushfire situation. Minimal skills in strategic, long-range planning are required.

Experienced Cost Cutter. The experienced cost cutter is the most desirable style of manager for low industry attractiveness/average competitive position. This individual may come from within the company or from outside. His or her

---

[24]T. E. Comte and W. F. McCanna, ''Progressive Differentiation: Improving the Strategic Act of CEO Selection,'' *The Academy of Management Executive* 2, no. 4 (November 1988), p. 303.

FIGURE 10.2   General Managers Needed to Strategically Manage Different Types of Businesses

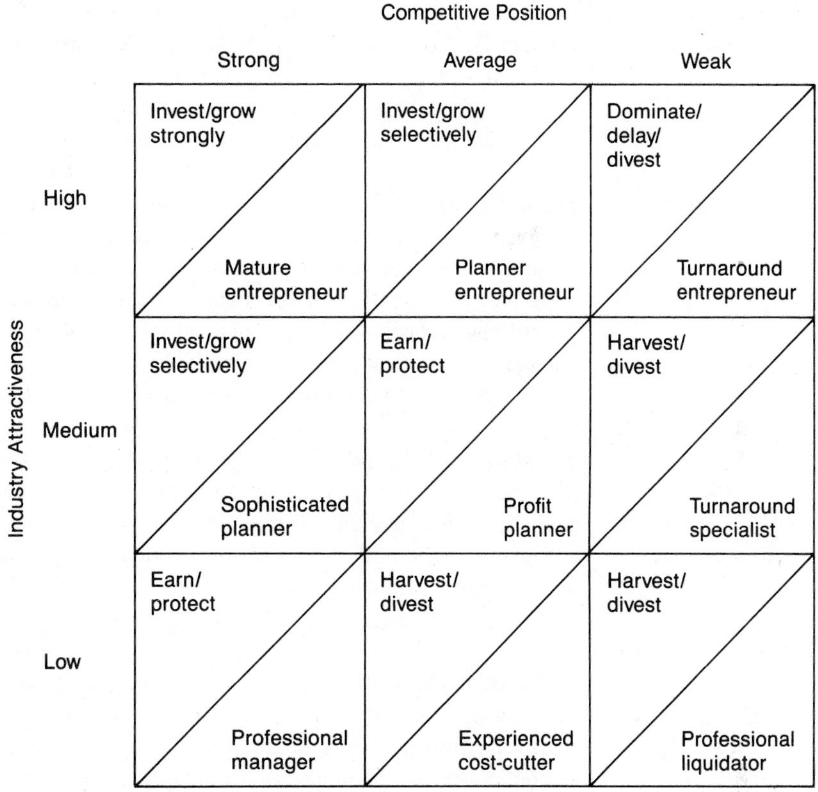

Competitive Position

	Strong	Average	Weak
High	Invest/grow strongly / Mature entrepreneur	Invest/grow selectively / Planner entrepreneur	Dominate/ delay/ divest / Turnaround entrepreneur
Medium	Invest/grow selectively / Sophisticated planner	Earn/ protect / Profit planner	Harvest/ divest / Turnaround specialist
Low	Earn/ protect / Professional manager	Harvest/ divest / Experienced cost-cutter	Harvest/ divest / Professional liquidator

Industry Attractiveness

Source: Adapted from C. W. Hofer and M. J. Davoust, *Successful Strategic Management* (Chicago: A. T. Kearney, Inc., 1977), p. 45 and 52. Copyright © 1977 by Charles W. Hofer and Merritt J. Davoust. Reproduced by permission.

objective is to take maximum advantage of every opportunity to succeed in the present, and to be less concerned about growth in the future. Profiting from existing capabilities is the goal. Eventual divestiture may follow this tactic, although more future planning is required than in the previous situation.

Professional Manager.   A professional manager is an absolute must in the low industry attractiveness/strong competitive position situation. This individual should not be a high flier, but an all-around, stable, experienced leader whose goal is to preserve the competitive strengths. A careful balancing act is necessary to prevent a slip into a weaker competitive position. This manager must be able to run hard and well just to keep things even. Careful short- and long-range planning is necessary.

Turnaround Specialist. A turnaround specialist seeks to improve the competitive position of the firm as quickly as possible and to milk the business if turnaround does not occur. A turnaround situation usually requires a fresh outlook, and a specialist in this area will probably be found outside the company. A great deal of risk will ride with the selection of this person. A turnaround specialist is likely to be strong and forceful, with an innovative mind and a penchant for challenge. Sound future-planning skills are required, but the preponderance of managerial activity should be focused on the present.

Profit Planner. The profit planner readily relies on and uses the talents of the organization. In the medium industry attractiveness/average competitive position situation, sound strategic planning is the key to maintaining profits or to increasing the position of the business within the industry. An ability to use quantitative decision-making tools and information systems is required. A profit planner could easily come from within the existing organization and characteristically is an individual trained specifically for the job.

Sophisticated Planner. A sophisticated planner is required when the company must worry more about growth than about immediate operations. Appropriate growth opportunities must be carefully weighed and planned for well in advance. This activity requires a very careful planner, a manager schooled in the contingency approach to management and keenly aware of the effect of the external environment.

Turnaround Entrepreneur. The turnaround entrepreneur is a very special manager and probably will come from outside the company. He or she is likely to be well known in the field and possess an established reputation for success in failing concerns. This person must score high in several areas, including knowledge, track record, ability to achieve, strategic planning skills, and forceful leadership. An example of such an individual is Lee Iacocca, chairman and chief executive officer of Chrysler Corp. The ultimate goal of the turnaround entrepreneur is to improve the competitive position of the business *before* it is pushed out of the industry entirely.

Planner Entrepreneur. The planner entrepreneur places emphasis on future planning. This type of manager is needed when the proper choices for growth are somewhat limited and must be made carefully.

Mature Entrepreneur. The mature entrepreneur can keep a going concern on an upward path. This person is as rare as the business that finds itself in the top slot of a "go-go" industry, because, in this situation, it is much easier to slip backward than to move forward. A strong concern for the present and future is necessary, in about a 50/50 balance. The personality of such a manager and the position and resources of such a company often allow the mature entrepreneur to take calculated risks to further the goals of the organization.

Michael A. Carpenter, GE's vice president for corporate planning, points out that a person rising through the ranks in a functional business typically has had no general management responsibility prior to becoming CEO. In a typical multibusiness company, the new CEO would have managed four or five business units—out of these, maybe one or two will have had serious strategic issues that needed to be addressed. Therefore, the new CEO will have had very little experience in dealing with strategy. On the other hand, GE's approach has been to make lots of general managers' jobs available; by the time someone makes CEO, he or she will have run 20 different businesses.[25]

Reward Systems

Managers, and people in general, tend to do what they are rewarded for doing. If the firm wants the professional liquidator employing a harvest/divest strategy to focus his or her efforts primarily on the present, the reward system (salary, bonus, promotions) must be so oriented. Likewise, reward systems for the turnaround and planner entrepreneur must be geared to future performance of the business unit, rather than to short-term results. Hofer and Davoust have suggested present- versus future-focused reward and bonus levels for each of the positions on the grid, as shown in Figure 10.3. In fact, General Electric has utilized such an approach in developing performance measurements, compensation, and promotion criteria for its SBU managers. As shown in Table 10.3, social responsibility comprises 12 percent of the measurement and compensation weights for all SBU managers. However, future performance factors constitute 48 percent of the weight for the manager of invest/grow SBUs, 28 percent for selectivity/earnings SBUs, and just 16 percent for harvest/divest SBUs. Current results count 40 percent for invest/grow SBU managers, 60 percent for selectivity/earnings SBU managers, and a high 72 percent for harvest/divest SBU managers. In this way, GE influences the actions of the SBU managers by gearing the reward system to the focus it wants them to adopt.[26]

Other companies use modified forms of this approach. For example, Emhart Corp., Combustion Engineering (CE), Borden, and Sears have adopted compensation plans that tie executive pay to long-term performance measures, such as stock price or return on equity. As an indication that such approaches are needed, at CE, prior to introduction of the new system, division general managers had been ignoring the company's strategic plans and focusing on what the bonus system rewarded them for doing—meeting short-term budget targets.[27, 28]

---

[25]"GE = Giant Entrepreneur?" *Planning Review* 13, no. 1 (January 1985), pp. 18–21.

[26]C. W. Hofer, *Instructor's Manual to Accompany Strategic Management* (St. Paul, Minn.: West Publishing, 1981), p. 332.

[27]"Rewarding Executives for Taking the Long View," *Business Week,* April 2, 1984, p. 99.

[28]See also M. R. Hurwich, "Strategic Compensation Designs that Link Pay to Performance," *The Journal of Business Strategy* 7, no. 2 (Fall 1986), pp. 79–81, and P. J. Stonich, "Using Rewards in Implementing Strategy," *Strategic Management Journal* 2, no. 3 (July–September 1981), pp. 345–52.

FIGURE 10.3   The Present/Future Focus of Compensation Bonuses for Business-Level General Managers

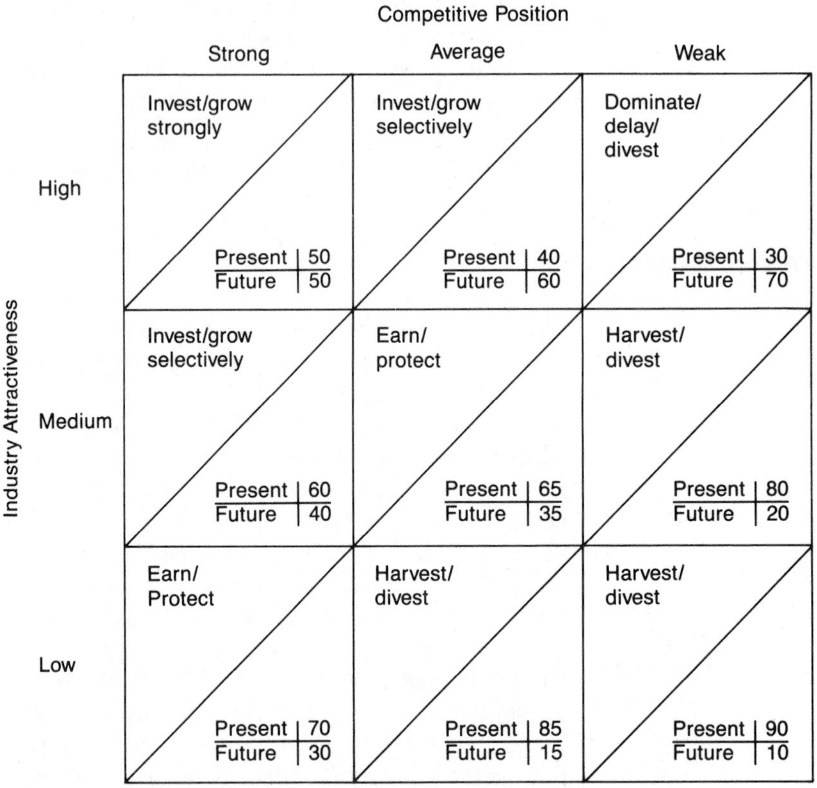

Competitive Position

	Strong	Average	Weak
High	Invest/grow strongly Present | 50 Future | 50	Invest/grow selectively Present | 40 Future | 60	Dominate/ delay/ divest Present | 30 Future | 70
Medium	Invest/grow selectively Present | 60 Future | 40	Earn/ protect Present | 65 Future | 35	Harvest/ divest Present | 80 Future | 20
Low	Earn/ Protect Present | 70 Future | 30	Harvest/ divest Present | 85 Future | 15	Harvest/ divest Present | 90 Future | 10

Industry Attractiveness

Source: Adapted from C. W. Hofer and M. J. Davoust, *Successful Strategic Management* (Chicago: A. T. Kearney, Inc., 1977), p. 46. Copyright © 1977 by Charles W. Hofer and Merritt J. Davoust. Reproduced by permission.

The Manager as an Organization Builder

The general manager is both a strategist and an ''organization builder.''[29] As a strategist, the general manager defines the corporate purpose and objectives, and the means to achieve them. As an organization builder, he or she must manage people as a cohesive unit in achieving the corporate mission and objectives through strategies. In this light, the *process* of carrying out the strategies takes on great importance. It is not enough that the manager has embarked the organiza-

---

[29]H. E. R. Uyterhoeven, R. W. Ackerman, and J. W. Rosenblum, *Strategy and Organization*, rev. ed. (Homewood, Ill: Richard D. Irwin, 1977).

TABLE 10.3   GE's Measurement, Compensation, and Promotion Criteria

		Measurement and Compensation Criteria and Weights		
Type of SBU	Manager's Key Characteristics	Future Performance Factors*	Current Financial Results†	Social Responsibility‡
Invest/grow	Entrepreneur	48%	40%	12%
Selectivity/earnings	Sophisticated/critical	28	60	12
Harvest/divest	Solid/experienced	16	72	12

*Strategy, programs, manpower, facilities; key checkpoints.
†Residual income (equals net income less a capital charge); last year versus this year.
‡Minority hiring, OSHA checks, environmental impact criteria, etc.

Source: Adapted from C. W. Hofer, *Instructor's Manual to Accompany Strategic Management* (St. Paul, Minn.: West Publishing, 1981), p. 332.

tion on the proper mission, toward the proper objectives, employing optimal strategies. *How* these activities are carried out is likewise important.

Effects on the Organization.   What does the manager really achieve if his or her objectives and strategies cause undue dissension in the organization, or if they—figuratively, if not literally—tear the organization apart? The goal of the general manger should be to strengthen—not weaken—the organization through the pursuit of objectives and strategies. What good are increased profits and market share and a better balance sheet if they result in a less conducive organizational climate and diminished human resources? The manager must consider not only what the strategies will do *for* the organization, but *to* the organization, as well. A less-than-optimal strategy that clearly strengthens the organization in terms of its climate, people, systems, and structure may be preferred over the "ideal" strategy.

In the final analysis, the policy-and-strategy job of the manager is to balance the relationships between the organization and its environment in such a way that the organization is strengthened. In fact, Sir Geoffrey Vickers sees the task as the "setting of governing relations or norms rather than the setting of goals, objectives, or ends."[30] The policymaker's job is to balance the desired relationships, consisting of setting directions for the firm "bounded by recognizable constraints which originate from desired and inevitable relationships between the organization and its environment, *and from the organization's past.*"[31]

---

[30]Sir Geoffrey Vickers, *The Art of Judgment: A Study of Policy Making* (New York: Basic Books, 1965).

[31]K. J. Hatten, "Quantitative Research Methods in Strategic Management," in *Strategic Management: A New View of Business Policy and Planning,* ed. D. Schendel and C. W. Hofer (Boston: Little, Brown, 1979), p. 461.

IMPLEMENTING STRATEGIC PLANS

Dennis Hykes, vice president of strategic planning services at Control Data Business Advisors, suggests that "implementable" strategic plans have, as a minimum, three characteristics:

1. They are linked to the appropriate control system within the organization.
2. They are "owned" by operating management.
3. They are perceived as being achievable by those responsible for implementation.

Concerning the first characteristic, the plans must be tied to the budgeting, operational planning, and incentive compensation systems. There must be a smooth transition from the planning cycle to the budget cycle, and close interaction between the strategic and operational planning systems. This link is accomplished through *strategic programs* that connect a strategy with a responsible member of operating management, and are an integral part of an operational plan.

Plans are likely to be "owned" by operating management when the following occurs:

1. Strategic planning must be in the management mainstream; that is, it should be a regular, continuous process, as other management processes tend to be.
2. Plans, and the process, must be easily digestible; that is, relatively uncomplicated planning systems, techniques, and forms should be used to produce relatively brief (20- to 30-page) plans.
3. The line managers are the planners, with the planning staff concentrating on process design, facilitation, troubleshooting, and review and analysis.

Hyke's final point is that the plans must be achievable—neither too difficult nor too easy. Finding the optimal level of difficulty can be aided by using an interactive, participative team approach in their development, coupled with a soundly constructed review program for the plan.[32]

STRATEGY AND STRUCTURE RELATIONSHIPS

Certain strategies are appropriate for certain types of organizations or stages of development. Likewise, the decision to compete in certain markets (e.g., to diversify into several product lines or to compete internationally) is a major one that requires an appropriate plan to implement the strategy successfully. But while an organization's strategy and structure are related and depend on one another, neither is an end in itself. Both are the *means* by which missions are fulfilled and goals and objectives are met. The strategy is the direction or route

---

[32]Hykes, "Planning for Plan Implementation," pp. 5–12.

chosen to meet the goals and objectives, and the structure is the vehicle through which the strategies will be implemented. Structure here is defined broadly, to include not only the type of departmentation employed, but the organization's systems, procedures, and processes, as well.

"Good" organization structure, systems, and processes do not necessarily produce successful performance, any more than a safe car produces safe driving. However, poor or inappropriate structure can make successful performance more difficult, perhaps even impossible. The proper structure can permit or facilitate the organization and its managers achieving their best performance. The ideal organization structure does not frustrate, thwart, or otherwise prevent the firm's managers from doing their work.

Alfred Chandler found that when organizations adopted a new strategy, such as diversification, they tended to change to a structure appropriate for the new strategy (in this case, a divisional M-form). He concluded from his studies that structure follows strategy, perhaps as "form follows function" in design.[33] Why this occurs is shown in Figure 10.4.

Assuming the firm has been pursuing a certain strategy such as related diversification, using an appropriate centralized-functional (U-form) structure, a mismatch can occur if the firm changes its strategy. Under competitive conditions, adoption of a strategy change, such as unrelated diversification, while retaining a U-form structure can result in a performance decline. Therefore, the organization will need to adopt a structure appropriate to this strategy (an M-form structure) to restore its performance and take advantage of the new strategy. It is possible, however, that the company will judge the new strategy a failure and return to its previous approach (related-business strategy), reachieving the strategy-structure match. Or attempts may be made to influence or negotiate with the environment, perhaps restoring performance in spite of the mismatch. It should be noted that performance declines may occur because of strategy-structure mismatches only under competitive conditions. If little competition exists, as in the case of a monopoly or where the organization can influence its environment sufficiently, a performance decline may not occur. Therefore, this type of organization may not feel sufficient pressure to change its structure, and may retain the strategy-structure mismatch with few apparent ill effects.

Others have suggested that a reverse relationship also exists; that the firm's structure and processes influence its choice of strategies. The important point is that strategy and structure must be consistent and congruent with one another. The firm should *match* its strategy and structure, and should match the strategy with the environment.

Recent studies have indicated that it is this match—or interaction effect—that is the most significant factor in explaining an organization's performance. That is, it is not just the strategy *or* the structure *or* the environment that is most

---

[33]Alfred Chandler, Jr., *Strategy and Structure* (Cambridge, Mass.: MIT Press, 1967).

FIGURE 10.4   Strategy and Structure Example

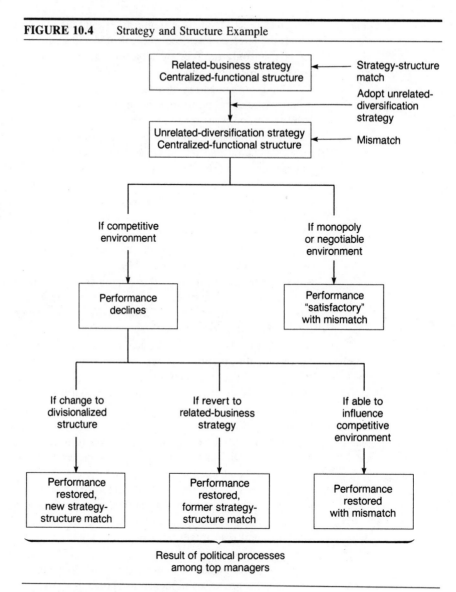

Source: Adapted from *Strategy Implementation: Structure Systems, and Process* by J. R. Galbraith and R. K. Kazanjian, p. 143; Copyright © 1986 by West Publishing Company.

important in explaining performance, but the interaction between the factors.[34] In short, the relationships between the variables are more complex than most researchers have acknowledged.[35]

SOCIAL AND POLITICAL INFLUENCES

The organization is a minisociety (or not so "mini" in the case of the old AT&T, which employed 1 percent of the total U.S. work force). An organization has assorted internal constituencies (departments, divisions) attempting to influence the direction of the organization and to achieve a favorable share of its resources. External stakeholders attempt to influence the organization, as well. It is not surprising, then, that power and influence play major roles in organizational decisions—strategic perhaps even more than operational. Nothing is inherently wrong or "bad" about this situation; politics are a fact of organizational life. As a result managers of today's large organizations may be less economic decision makers than they are "governors of a social and political strategic management process."

The management of power is an explicit CEO function; "in large, complex organizations we cannot talk about the process of strategy formulation *except* in social and political terms."[36] The task of the CEO in strategy formulation is twofold: he or she must develop a broad vision of what the firm's future position in its environment should be; the CEO must also manage a network of organizational forces to refine and implement the attainment of that vision. Strategy can be viewed as the outcome of cognitive, social and organizational, and political processes, and it is the CEO's task to *administer* these processes.

One of the CEO's key responsibilities is to forge a degree of agreement on the organization's goals (ends) and strategies (means), within the broad vision of the future of the organization. This is no easy task; in fact, it is sometimes easier to get parties in the organization to agree on means rather than ends. This is particularly true in the case of large organizations with multiple goals because not everyone will agree on all of them. The important thing is to find something to agree upon, such as means, that results in action toward the multiple goals. In fact, studies have shown that agreement on means is actually more important than agreement on goals. While agreement on both was associated positively with economic performance, agreement on means is significantly more impor-

[34]Soen Tjan and L. A. Digman, "The Interaction Effects of Environment, Structure, and Strategy on Firm Performance," *Proceedings of the Midwest Decision Sciences Institute,* April 1989.

[35]D. B. Jemison, "Risk and the Relationship among Strategy, Organizational Processes, and Performance," *Management Science* 33, no. 9 (September 1987), p. 1087.

[36]J. L. Bower and Yves Doz, "Strategy Formulation: A Social and Political Process," in *Strategic Management: A New View of Business Policy and Planning,* ed. D. Schendel and C. W. Hofer (Boston: Little, Brown, 1979), p. 165.

tant. In fact, agreement on goals without agreement on means was found to correlate with *poor* performance. Therefore, strategy makers should concentrate more strongly on reaching consensus concerning means than concerning ends. Agreement on means enables people to commit themselves to those strategies, while lack of such agreement (regardless of the end being pursued) reduces their commitment to action.[37]

Climate and Culture

All organizations must make changes continuously to resolve three basic dilemmas in dealing with their mission, objectives, policies and strategies. These dilemmas involve: (1) The technical design problem—in the face of environmental threats and opportunities, social, financial, and technical resources must be arranged to produce a desired output. (2) The political allocation problem—organizations must allocate power and resources. The uses to which the organization will be put, as well as the people who will reap the benefits, must be determined. (3) The cultural problem—organizations are in part held together by the normative glue that is called *culture*. Culture consists of the values, objectives, and beliefs shared by organization members.

These three dilemmas form three strands of a "strategic rope" in the sense that the strands must be interwoven and mutually supportive for an organization to be effective. And strategic management requires attention to all three strands. This is carried out by adjusting the organization's (1) mission and strategy, (2) structure, and (3) human resources to balance technical, political, and cultural concerns.[38]

There is not as yet a firm agreement on exactly what is meant by the culture of a business firm. Ansoff and Baker, however, offer a particularly attractive definition consisting of two aspects:

1. A shared *commitment* to norms and values. This common commitment to a set of behavior norms, for example, is an important contributor to the consistency of the firm's behavior. It also contributes to the energy and enthusiasm level of the individuals, plus the performance discipline within the firm. But culture can be more than values, beliefs, and norms; it also includes:
2. A shared *understanding* of what needs to be done to assure the firm's success. Participants must also know the success model and critical success factors for the firm, its niche, its industry, and environment.[39]

---

[37]L. J. Bourgeois III, "Performance and Consensus," *Strategic Management Journal* (1980), p. 227.

[38]Noel M. Tichy, "The Technical, Political, and Cultural Keys to Managing Change," *Organizational Dynamics*, Fall 1982.

[39]H. I. Ansoff and T. E. Baker, "Is Corporate Culture the Ultimate Answer," in *Advances in Strategic Management*, ed. Robert Lamb and Paul Shrivastava (Greenwich, Conn.: JAI Press, 1986), p. 83.

What a business is able to accomplish may be determined as much, if not more, by its culture than its strategic plan. Strategies are only as good as the culture that exists to encourage and support them. This culture is, in large measure, the product of the CEO's behavior over time. And, if there is no way of translating strategy moves into culture change, little change in subordinate behavior is likely, regardless of the strategy. Sophisticated planning and strategy changes don't, by themselves, produce performance changes. *Implementation* is what counts, and is profoundly influenced by the corporate culture.[40] In fact, a firm's culture can be a source of sustainable competitive advantage, *if* that culture has economic value, is rare, and is not easy to imitate. To the extent that a firm's culture is hard to describe (as is usually the case) and is valuable, it is difficult to describe what it is about some firms that makes them more successful than others.[41]

In a multifaceted business world, it becomes vital to match the internally held (cultural) model of success with the realities of the external environment and the organization's resources, strengths, and weaknesses. On the one hand, therefore, culture can be a powerful motivator and contributor to success—when the cultural model of success *matches* the realities of the marketplace. But a strongly entrenched culture can be a major deterrent to success if the external requirements for success change.[42]

STRATEGIC CONTROL

One of the key tasks in strategy implementation is strategic control: monitoring strategic progress and taking corrective action. Strategic control attempts to ensure that performance conforms to plans. Effective control requires the measurement of performance, an evaluation of that performance, an analysis of any deviations between planned and actual performance, and taking the appropriate corrective action to modify future performance, the plans, or both. Just as effective management depends on effective control, effective strategic management also requires strategic control.[43]

Effective strategic control involves two key areas: has the strategy been implemented as planned (or have the implementation process and detailed planning unintentionally modified the strategy that was selected)? And, once implemented, is the strategy producing the desired results?

---

[40]Leonard R. Sayles and R. V. L. Wright, "The Use of Culture in Strategic Management," *Issues and Observations* 5, no. 4 (November 1985), pp. 1–9.

[41]Jay B. Barney, "Organizational Culture: Can It Be a Source of Sustained Competitive Advantage?" *Academy of Management Review* 11, no. 3 (July 1986), pp. 656–65.

[42]Ansoff and Baker, "Is Corporate Culture the Ultimate Answer," p. 84.

[43]P. Lorange, M. F. Scott Morton, and S. Ghoshal, *Strategic Control* (St. Paul, Minn.: West Publishing, 1986).

As is true of any effective control system, strategic control is not performed after the strategic plan has been fully carried out; instead, the results are evaluated *while* the strategy is being followed. A pilot flying from New York to Los Angeles makes course corrections all along the way, allowing for winds and other forces. He does not wait until he is in San Francisco to determine that he somehow has gotten off course.

Basic Control Elements

Any control system consists of several basic elements:

- *Setting predetermined standards.* These are the desired states, goals, objectives, or results that you are attempting to achieve. In general, they are reflected in the plans—long, intermediate, and short range.
- *Measuring actual performance.* This includes sales, costs, profits, share of the market, and the like, that the firm experiences once the plan has been put into effect. Short-term performance indicates preliminary results in terms of longer-term plans.
- *Comparing planned versus actual performance.* Do the two differ and by how much? What is a significant or important deviation? What techniques of analysis should be used to make the determination?
- *Taking corrective action.* If there is a significant deviation between planned and actual performance, what should be done? Can changes be made to get future performance back on course? Or do the plans and objectives need to be changed? Or both? Also, performance equaling or exceeding that specified by the plan may indicate that the plan was not ambitious enough and so should be adjusted.

In general, the planning and control process is as shown in Figure 10.5.

Levels of Control

Three levels of control—organizational, internal, and strategic—are needed to fulfill a firm's mission and achieve its goals and objectives.

Organizational Control. This control over strategic matters is accomplished at the general management and functional levels and is assumed by the board of directors. Board members should periodically review an ongoing strategy, questioning its validity, modifying and recycling, and reconsidering critical strategic issues.[44] At the general management level, the CEO and the president

---

[44]Y. N. Chang and F. Campo-Flores, *Business Policy and Strategy* (Santa Monica, Calif.: Goodyear Publishing Co., 1980), p. 226.

FIGURE 10.5   Planning and Control Cycle

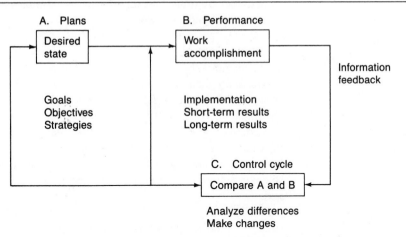

are responsible for overall strategic control, which includes establishing formats and criteria for a well-designed control system. However, they may designate the planning staff to act as the strategic control group for the organization.

Internal Control.   Internal controls expand into more specific operating and functional areas. Operating managers use these as guides, concentrating on the internal actions necessary to keep the organization functioning. Internal controls can be described as techniques for keeping in touch with the progress of the various parts of the plan, assessing information received, and responding to a variety of functional and operational information inputs. There are five basic internal areas any firm should consider. While these areas center more on tactical than on strategic control, they need to be established before the changes affecting the company's strategic assumptions can be monitored. The internal controls include:

1. *Overall performance.* General managers are responsible for gathering operating, financial, and resource data to measure and evaluate the performance of the firm and its operations.
2. *Organizational policies.* This type of control is maintained through additional policies established by the board of directors and policy executives.
3. *Financial activities.* Areas that should be strongly considered are assets management, cash budgets, tax planning, diagnostic surveys, interfirm comparisons, return on investment, and profitability.
4. *Budgetary control.* This involves departmental budgets and centrally prepared budgets relating to the total operation. Budgetary controls normally reflect costs and results.

5. *Operating*. Finally, line management can regulate departmental and program activities by using operating controls. Examples include: production, scheduling, and personnel control.[45]

Strategic Control. The final level of control complements the company's internal controls by instituting special controls over strategic activities. Strategic control is directed, first of all, at areas that must be visible to management. This ensures the flow of external and internal data and allows management to appraise environmental factors that may have an impact on the firm.

Also, management must specifically identify and assign responsibility for managing strategic programs and actions. These programs may be at any strategy level: R&D, new product/market, or acquisition and merger. Control over strategic activities is usually accomplished by periodic reporting or scheduled reviews.

Finally, strategic control provides a means of validating and adjusting strategies. The company's assumptions must be updated against evolving events, and its operations must be monitored to detect deviations. In any large organization, top management should be assured that each program can move efficiently toward its major goals.

The distinctive feature of strategic controls is that they are intended to *reassure* and allow those who are not close to the scene (such as top management) to see the strategic impact of functional and operating activities, and to evaluate them.[46]

A Contemporary View of Strategic Control

However, because of the uncertainty and complexity present in strategic management, the classic feedback model of control may be inadequate. Two West German scholars have recently proposed a new model of strategic control incorporating three elements: premise control, implementation control, and strategic surveillance. As shown in Figure 10.6, the three elements control both strategy formulation *and* implementation. In strategy formulation, a major consideration involves creating premises (assumptions, beliefs, scenarios) about the internal and external environments. *Premise control* has been designed to check systematically and continuously whether or not the premises set during the planning and implementation processes are still valid.

Not all important events and factors may be foreseen during strategy formulation; some of these may come to light during implementation. Thus, the implementation phase is an important course of additional information about the

---

[45]Ibid., p. 227.

[46]S. J. Carroll, F. T. Paine, and J. B. Miner, *The Management Process* (New York: Macmillan, 1977), p. 284.

FIGURE 10.6   Elements of Strategic Control

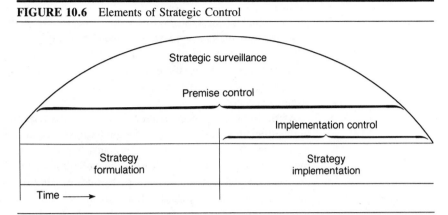

Source: Adapted from Georg Schreyogg and Horst Steinmann, ''Strategic Control: A New Perspective,'' *Academy of Management Review* 12, no. 1 (January 1987), p. 96

strategy and its likely results. Therefore, *implementation control* is used to assess whether or not the whole strategic course should be changed, given past, current, and likely future events which have come to light during implementation (note that implementation control is *not* designed to assure that implementation is proceeding as planned).

Finally, *strategic surveillance* is designed to monitor the full range of events, both inside and outside the firm, which could threaten the strategic action.[47] This type of control is more akin to scanning, whereas premise and implementation control are more focused, monitoring specific phases or elements of the strategy.

Strategic Control Processes

An important objective of strategic control is ensuring that performance is as near as practicable to the strategic plan. Four major steps can be identified in the strategic control process:

1. Evaluating the strategic plan and developing standard-of-performance criteria.
2. Measurement of actual performance.
3. Evaluating actual performance by comparing it to standards.
4. Taking corrective action and implementing contingency plans.

Step 1: Develop Performance Standards.   The first step in the strategic control process is evaluating the plan and developing standards of performance.

[47]Georg Schreyogg and Horst Steinmann, ''Strategic Control: A New Perspective,'' *Academy of Management Review* 12, no. 1 (January 1987), pp. 95–97.

Strategic performance should be evaluated in terms of whether it will yield the desired objectives established by management and whether the goals, plans, or standards are realistic and well defined. Strategy evaluation provides a broad view of the interaction of various operations and helps create a balance between goals and tasks. The focus of evaluation should be on what must be done in the areas of organization structure, people, culture, and control systems to make the strategy succeed.

As the strategic plan is evaluated, key success requirements must be defined with sufficient specificity that strategic performance criteria or indicators can be developed. These are standards against which actual performance can be measured. A means for monitoring the execution of plans should be developed concurrently with standards of performance. Helpful measures of strategic performance include: sales (total, and by division, product category, and region); sales growth; net profits; return on sales, assets, equity, and investment; cost of sales; cash flow; market share; value added; product quality; employee productivity.

Step 2: Measurement of Actual Performance.   Sensing (searching for and becoming aware of) and measuring actual conditions is the second step in the strategic control system. Data are collected and processed, functional controls are implemented, and environmental signals are monitored. The mechanism operates in a feedback network so that adjustments can be made to environmental changes.

Signals of change may be external or internal. External environmental signals are particularly significant since they are less predictable and their impact is more difficult to determine. Internal signals, on the other hand, tend to be more gradual, short term, and controllable. Knowledge of internal changes is more available and accessible than are details about external changes.

Environmental signals also can be classified as either strong or weak. Strong signals tend to have the following characteristics: (1) signal content is complete and clear; (2) response time is short; (3) response options are limited.

Strong signals, analogous to surprise, may appear without warning. It is urgent that management act on them, even though the situation is probably unfamiliar. Strong signals often reflect discontinuous changes, the sudden appearance of an opportunity or threat with a significant impact.

Sensing enables management to scan the environment for these signals of change and to detect weak signals. Since weak signals often precede strong signals, correct and early detection reduces surprises and increases response time. The firm can respond gradually and position itself to act decisively and directly when the signal becomes more clear and complete. Once weak signals are detected, they can be monitored and planned for so that response options can be carefully developed and chosen.

Methods should be developed and evaluated to make certain that performance measures assess what they are supposed to measure. Areas of performance for which standards have been set should be measured as the strategic plans are implemented and at times corresponding to scheduled accomplishment of goals and objectives.

Step 3: Evaluating Actual Performance.

The third step in strategic control is to evaluate actual performance, as measured in step 2, by comparing it to the standards of performance developed in step 1. In this way, deviations from the strategic plan can be determined.

Step 4: Corrective Action and Contingency Plans.

Corrective action and implementation of contingency plans is the final step in strategic control. Once external environmental threats or opportunities have progressed to the point that a particular outcome is likely, corrective action may be necessary. Corrective action must also be taken when there is an undesirable deviation between the standard and actual performance.

There are three choices of corrective action:

1. Normal mode—follow a routine, noncrisis approach; this takes more time.
2. Ad hoc crash mode—saves time by speeding up the response process, geared to the problem at hand.
3. Preplanned crisis mode—specifies a planned response in advance; this approach lowers the response time and increases the capacity for handling strategic surprises.

Contingency plans should be developed to help counter the effects of strategic surprises. These plans can be applied quickly and help management face unfamiliar events.

In summary, the strategic control process attempts to ensure that performance will be as close as practicable to the plan. The objective of control is to take corrective action when actual and planned performance differ. In practice, strategic reappraisals are routinely conducted on an annual or biannual basis. In many companies, each SBU manager must completely reassess the unit's competitive position and strategy during an annual presentation to corporate management. At the same time, a staff review group evaluates and presents alternatives for the corporation's total portfolio of SBUs.[48]

Measuring and Analyzing Performance

Measuring performance is critical to strategic control. But which measure of performance? Peter Drucker says five basic measures of performance are necessary and sufficient for the manager:

---

[48]W. K. Hall, "SBUs: Hot, New Topic in the Management of Diversification," *Business Horizons,* February 1978, p. 22.

1. Market standing—is share increasing? What is it doing in particular submarkets and niches?
2. Innovative performance—new products in growth areas.
3. Productivity—how much value has been added per resource input.
4. Liquidity and cash flow.
5. Profitability.

None of the measures is perfect, and none will give precise readings. However, the *trend*—not the absolute value—is most important.[49]

Benchmarking. It is not good enough to compare your performance—and practices—against the best in your industry, because it is unlikely that you will surpass a competing firm by trying to imitate it. In addition, the competitor may not be excellent across the board, as compared to the best from other industries. Therefore, a recommended approach for those seeking to better the competition is to "benchmark" one's activities against the best—firms known to be excellent in a particular functional area, regardless of their industry. (Noncompetitors are much more likely to cooperate and share information, too.)

As an example of successful benchmarking, Xerox Business Systems' Logistics and Distribution unit was looking for ways to further increase its productivity growth, which was 3 percent to 5 percent per year. Xerox found the best warehousing and materials handling organization to be L. L. Bean in Freeport, Maine. With Bean's cooperation, Xerox studied their operation, and was able to improve its productivity growth to 10 percent per year[50]—and was able to "breakthrough" to a higher standard of performance.

Evaluating Past Strategic Decisions. As part of the control process, reviewing the previous years' plans and their results before beginning a new planning cycle can be very informative. Often, plans include a degree of optimism or hope for the future that may fail to materialize. Looking at the results of past plans can determine whether or not planning has been unrealistic and whether the current plan is likely to follow suit. For example, Figure 10.7 shows a continuing pattern of overly optimistic "hockey stick" (because that is what each projection resembles) projections experienced by a top-50 U.S. multinational firm. Each year from 1984 to 1989, a turnaround in operating margin was forecast and never materialized. In reality, performance continued to decline. In view of this record, how much faith would you put in the firm's current projections? As the above indicates, the assumptions and strategic outcomes on which the projections were based need to be carefully examined and corrective action should be taken.

---

[49]Peter F. Drucker, "If Earnings Aren't the Dial to Read," *The Wall Street Journal*, October 30, 1986, p. 15.
[50]F. G. Tucker, S. M. Zivan, and R. C. Camp, "How to Measure Yourself against the Best," *Harvard Business Review*, 65, no. 1 (January–February 1987), pp. 8–10.

FIGURE 10.7   Performance versus Projections

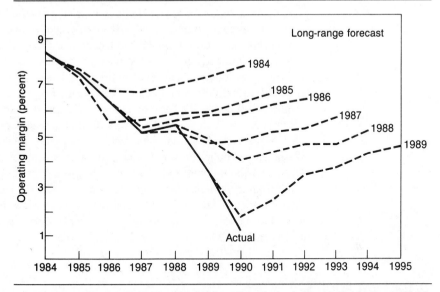

Source: Adapted from J. D. C. Roach and M. G. Allen, "Strengthening the Strategic Planning Process," in *The Strategic Management Handbook,* ed. K. J. Albert (New York: McGraw-Hill, 1983), p. 7–13. Copyright © 1983. Reprinted with permission.

Firms should also monitor short-term results and changes as closely as they do over the long term. Cordis Corp. is a manufacturer of pacemakers that thought being number one in research and development spending would make the company—a leader in its field—grow and prosper. Unfortunately, the company's long-range but narrow research focus prevented Cordis from noticing important changes in its markets. As a result, market share dropped from 20 to 13 percent in a three-year period, even though the firm was greatly outspending its main competitors on research and development. Preoccupation with the long term also led Cordis to ignore short-term changes in the kidney dialysis market (another product line), with disastrous results for its sales. Today, under new management and refocused on the fast-growing angiographic catheter business, the firm realizes that effective marketing, better quality, and the short term are equally as important as new technology and the long run.[51]

When to Pull the Plug.   Why do decisions fail? Recent research has shown that failed decisions tend to be associated with imposing ideas on the decision

---

[51]Thomas Jaffe, "Streetwalker: Heart Thumper," *Forbes,* June 27, 1988, p. 312.

process, using too limited a search for alternatives, and using power tactics to force implementation of the decision.[52]

A major source of decision failures is what some call *decisional quicksand,* where the organization is gradually drawn deeper and deeper into a losing project, hoping to turn it around and listening to pleas for additional resources to "save" the project, until it is too late and has become a major loss. Let's say your organization has spent several million dollars on a development project, and is already $500,000 over budget. This year, the project manager pleads that another $300,000 will "turn the corner" and result in success, whereas killing the project now will waste the several million already spent. What do you do? This is precisely how major projects (such as the Lockheed L-1011 and the Washington Public Power System) became major debacles—incrementally. Thus, decision failures are less likely to be gross miscalculations than they are to result from incremental decisions that seemed to be the lesser of two evils at the time; the trick is knowing when a particular project is going nowhere and when it should be terminated (versus those which *do* have a good chance of turnaround).[53]

STRATEGIC AUDITS

To aid in control, firms will occasionally perform audits to ensure that certain aspects of their operations are in order. It is a legal requirement, for example, that the financial books of a publicly held firm be audited by an outside CPA firm once each year. In addition, most larger firms have internal auditors who perform related audits for management. In recent years, periodic audits have been utilized by a number of firms to evaluate management activities, policies, systems, procedures, and performance. More recently, this concept has been extended to include operational audits (assessing the firm's operating health) and strategic audits (assessing the firm's strategic health). Such audits can be conducted regularly as needed when problems exist or significant changes have occurred either externally or internally.

Measures of Organizational Health

Measures or indicators of a firm's current operating and strategic health are shown in Tables 10.4 and 10.5. As the tables show, to assess a firm's current operating health, short-term financial, market, technological, and production

---

[52]Paul C. Nutt, "Why Decisions Fail," *Proceedings of Decision Sciences Institute Annual Meeting* (Atlanta: DSI, 1987), pp. 1127–29.

[53]B. M. Staw and Jerry Ross, "Knowing When to Pull the Plug," *Harvard Business Review* 65, no. 2 (March–April 1987), pp. 68–74.

TABLE 10.4 Assessing Current Operating Health

Criteria	Current Operating Health Weak	Current Operating Health Average	Current Operating Health Strong
Short-term financial position:			
Current ratio	< 1.0	1.5 to 3.0	> 4.0
Quick ratio	< 0.50	0.75 to 1.5	> 2.0
Pro forma breakeven	Volume < BE	BE < Volume < 1.2 BE	Volume > 1.4 BE
Altman's Z-score	< 1.8	2.0 to 3.0	> 3.5
Short-term market position:			
Σ Current product/market segments in relation to breakeven	PMS < BE volume	Be < PMS < twice BE	PMS > four times BE
Σ Volume all products in all markets	All < BE volume	BE < all < twice BE	All > four times BE
Short-term technological position:			
New or modified products available in less than one year	One or none	Two or three	Four or more
Relative product quality	Low	Average	High
Short-term production position:			
Variable costs versus competition's variable costs	Much higher	≈ Same	Much lower
Facilities replacement costs in next year	Substantially greater than depreciation	≈ Depreciation rate	Little or none
Facilities that could be sold in next year	None	Up to one fourth of fixed assets	More than one fourth of assets
Overall current operating health			

Source: Charles W. Hofer, "Designing Turnaround Strategies," (unpublished working paper, University of Georgia), 1986. Copyright © 1986 by Charles W. Hofer, used by permission.

TABLE 10.5 Assessing Current Strategic Health

Criteria	Current Strategic Health		
	Weak	*Average*	*Strong*
Strategic market position:			
Relative industry attractiveness	Low	Medium	High
Relative market share	Low	Average	High
Stage of product/market evolution	High cost to change position	Moderate cost to change position	Low cost to change position
Distribution systems	Changing rapidly	Changing slowly	Not changing
Strategic technological position:			
New product concepts	Follower	Average	Leader
Major product improvements	Follower	Average	Leader
Product modifications	Follower	Average	Leader
Process improvements	Follower	Average	Leader
Strategic production capabilities:			
Experience curve position	Follower	Average	Leader
Strategy versus experience curve position	Inconsistent	Partially consistent	Consistent
Newness of production assets and technology	Old	Middle age	New
Strategic financial health:			
Long-term investment needs versus long-term internal cash flow	Needs $>>$ flow $+ \uparrow$ debt	Needs $\simeq$ flow $+ \uparrow$ debt	Flow $>>>$ needs
Long-term growth rate versus desired objectives	Objectives $>>$ growth rate	Growth rate $\simeq$ objectives	Growth rate $>$ objectives
Overall current strategic health			

Source: Charles W. Hofer, ''Designing Turnaround Strategies,'' (unpublished working paper, University of Georgia), 1986. Copyright © 1986 by Charles W. Hofer. Used by permission.

position are used, while current strategic health is based on strategic market position, technological position, production capabilities, and financial health.

To determine a firm's vulnerability to financial trouble, some analysts use Altman's Z score (described in Table 10.6) or a refined but proprietary version, the Zeta score. The Zeta concept combines weighted key financial ratios to produce an indicator of financial vulnerability—the Zeta score. Ratios included are cumulative profitability (retained earnings and assets), leverage, earnings stability, return on total assets, fixed-charge coverage, liquidity, and total assets. A Zeta score of less than zero suggests that the company may have trouble meeting its financial obligations, while positive values indicate financial health.[54]

---

[54]''Corporate Finance: Companies that Face Financial Strain,'' *Business Week*, May 17, 1982, p. 110.

TABLE 10.6   Altman's Z Score

$$Z = 1.2x_1 + 1.4x_2 + 3.3x_3 + 0.6x_4 + 1.0x_5$$

where

x_1 = Working capital ÷ Total assets
x_2 = Retained earnings ÷ Total assets
x_3 = Earnings before interest and taxes ÷ Total assets
x_4 = Market value of equity ÷ Book value of total debt
x_5 = Sales ÷ Total assets

Z values range from -4 to $+8$; the higher the number, the healthier the company.
If Z exceeds 2.99, the company is financially healthy.
If Z is below 1.81, serious financial trouble exists.

Source: Adapted from J. R. Weston and E. F. Brigham, *Essentials of Managerial Finance*, 6th ed. (New York: Holt, Rinehart & Winston, 1982), p. 110.

Strategy Audits

A strategy audit may be needed under the following conditions: Performance indicators show that a strategy is not working or is producing negative side effects. High-priority items in the strategic plan are not being accomplished. A significant change occurs in the external environment. Management wishes to fine tune a successful strategy. To ensure that a strategy is in tune with external and/or internal changes.

Strategy audits should address the following key questions:

1. Is the strategy working?
2. Is the strategy practical?
3. Are objectives, goals, policies, and programs clear and consistent?
4. Are the assumptions valid?
5. Have contingencies been assessed?
6. Is the strategy still appropriate?
7. Is the strategy congruent with management's style, values, and preferences for risk?
8. Is the organization properly structured to implement the strategy?
9. Do systems and processes support the strategy and programs?
10. Does the information system monitor implementation?
11. Is there an appropriate balance between present and future performance?
12. Is there agreement regarding the strategy within the company?

In general, the audit concerns itself only with broad questions of competitive positioning and allocation of resources, and tries to uncover the reasons for past success or failure in strategy formulation and execution. Examples of the questions addressed in the audit are shown in Figure 10.8.

FIGURE 10.8 Strategy Audit Flow Chart

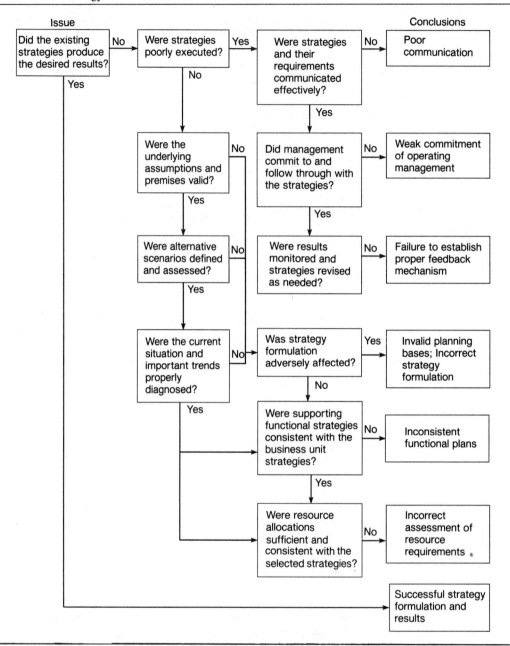

Source: Adapted from Jeffrey A. Schmidt, ''The Strategic Review,'' *Planning Review* 16, no. 4 (July/August 1988), p. 15.

CONCLUSIONS

Good strategic management requires effective strategy implementation and control as well as effective strategy formulation (including planning decisions and processes). Strategic decisions result from strategy evaluation and choice activities, after which strategy implementation and detailed planning occur. Control activities ensure that the strategy is implemented and performing as planned; if it is not, corrective actions are required.

While the process of formulating and selecting strategies requires solid, objective quantitative analysis, social and political processes play a major role, too. One of the key tasks of the CEO is to manage these processes. Effective strategic management is truly the lifeblood of all organizations, and is the critical determinant of eventual success or failure.

Part V

Contemporary Strategic Management

Chapter 11

Strategic Management in Varied Contexts

LEARNING OBJECTIVES

After completing Chapter 11, you should be able to:

Understand and describe the unique characteristics of start-up ventures.

Appreciate the strategy concerns and processes of small businesses.

Understand and describe the types and unique characteristics of not-for-profit organizations, including government, public service, and public-interest organizations.

Appreciate the unique characteristics of third-sector organizations and institutions.

Realize the important role in the economy and the strategic aspects of service organizations and functions.

The discussion of the process and content of strategic management, including the systems and techniques of strategic planning, is complete. Now several extensions, or special topics, will be explored. The primary perspective to this point has been that of the central type of organization in our economy, the medium-to-large, for-profit, well-established, private-sector corporation. While a good share of the material discussed is applicable not just to this typical corporation, but to organizations in general, certain organizations have unique characteristics. For this reason, attention in this chapter is devoted to several specific types of organization commonly found in our economy: the start-up venture, the small business, not-for-profit organizations, and service organizations. Such organizations have many unique characteristics and needs that may significantly affect strategic decisions and processes. These are given special attention in this chapter.

The unique features of an important type of for-profit organization—entrepreneurial start-up ventures—will be addressed first, followed by small businesses. Not-for-profit organizations, concentrating initially on public-sector organizations such as government, public-service, and public-interest organizations, will then be examined. Other not-for-profit groups, such as third-sector organizations (amalgams of private organizations with a public charter) and institutions (education, health care, religious, etc.), will also be dealt with. Finally attention will be directed toward the increasingly important service organization, including professional organizations (such as consulting firms, law firms, and professional practices).

There are important distinctions between for-profit firms and not-for-profit organizations. First, there is a basic difference in purpose. Different missions are likely to result in different goal structures, as well as in differences in the strategies formulated to reach those goals. Economic goals act as a powerful constraint on for-profit firms, while such constraints have much less immediacy in the not-for-profit organization and play less of a role in the selection of strategies. In addition, within the for-profit sector, significant differences exist between the small business, the start-up venture, and the larger, more established business. New ventures and small businesses have differing goals and objectives. Larger, established firms have more complex goal structures and goal- and strategy-formulation processes. Furthermore, the nature of the environments is different for each of the organizational types. However, all are similar in that the roles and responsibilities of general managers differ from those of functional managers. In short, the major differences are found in the areas of strategy substance and *content,* while the main similarities—and there are many—occur in the area of strategic *processes.* Nonetheless, this chapter's intent is to point out the unique features and concerns of each type of organization, stressing how they differ from the "typical" medium-to-large, for-profit business firm.

PROFILE   *Primerica*

For decades, the American Can Company was the nation's premier packaging company, as well as one of the blue chip stocks making up the Dow-Jones Industrial Average.

Over the years, the company pursued a diversification strategy, moving beyond packaging into other areas. In 1981, the company made a major corporate strategy change, deciding to fundamentally redirect its operations from manufacturing to the services sector of the economy. Consistent with that move, American Can announced the ultimate step in its new strategy; it divested itself of its capital-intensive packaging business—the original core business for American Can. Since the company was no longer in the can business, it needed a new corporate name and identity, and selected "Primerica."

Thus, under former CEO Gerry Tsai, a premier manufacturing company underwent a complete transformation to the growing services sector of the economy. Subsequently merged with Commerical Credit Corp. under former Shearson CEO Sandy Weill, the company is now focused primarily on financial services (A. L. Williams insurance, Commercial Credit loans, and Smith Barney brokerage).[1]

PROFILE

The HMO Industry

Health maintenance organizations (HMOs) provide health services to an enrolled group of patients for a fixed, prepaid fee. From its fees and any outside support, the HMO must cover all its patients' expenses, including hospital stays, when necessary.

While HMOs may appear to be a relatively recent phenomenon—and an attempt to hold down the rapidly rising costs of medical care—the first HMO began in 1929. Growth of the concept accelerated when Kaiser Industries began an HMO for its employees, opening enrollment to the public in 1945. Since that time, and largely in recent years, various forms of HMOs have arisen, ranging from not-for-profit to profitmaking concerns, to company-operated plans (to reduce the cost of company-paid health insurance premiums), to community-operated plans. Today, there are more than 300 HMO plans in operation in the United States with over 15 million members. Not all are successful, however; to date over 30 HMOs have failed.

Ideally, the HMO is supposed to save money by encouraging preventive medicine; that is, keeping their patients healthy and out of the hospital. In reality, there is little evidence to show that HMO patients are healthier. While HMOs do cut hospitalization rates by 15 to 30 percent, no one is sure just why. Some say they are more economical; others say that HMO physicians are pressured to skimp on medical care, that doctors have been overusing hospitals, or that HMOs tend to have younger members who need less medical care. In addition, some people balk at the HMO concept because of the loss of the patient's right to choose his or her own doctor.

Whatever its form or future, HMOs have proliferated recently as an attempt to reduce burgeoning health-care costs. To succeed, their overall concept and mission must be sound, they must provide quality medical care of the type demanded by the public, and their operating strategies must be sound. Whether operated privately or publicly, for profit or not for profit, in the long run their costs cannot exceed their revenues—a condition any organization must meet.

---

[1]Linda Sandler, "Creating Bountiful Primerica May Take Weill Awhile," *The Wall Street Journal,* April 10, 1989, p. C1.

ENTREPRENEURIAL VENTURES: START-UPS

Start-up (new) ventures and small business often are discussed together, as if they have similar characteristics. In the broad sense, starting a small business is certainly a new venture of sorts, and most new ventures are relatively small. The differences, however, outweigh the similarities. Many small businesses are not "new"; they are family-run operations that have been around for 20 years or more. While they may still be called *ventures,* they certainly are not new. Also, forming a new business is only one type of venture. Many new ventures are begun *within* large firms, for example, as was discussed in Chapter 7. (The focus here is on the *separate* start-up company.) In addition, most small businesses have a goal that is very different from the goal of even recently formed new-venture firms. The venture firm has no intention of remaining small for very long; small size is a very brief phase through which this well-financed firm hopes to pass on its way to becoming a much larger firm. Most small businesses, on the other hand, are poorly financed and concern themselves with growth only after survival seems assured (if ever). However, once survival is established, some small businesses can become new ventures in the true sense of the word, with additional outside financing and a clear concept and plan for growth.

Karl Vesper, an expert in the new-venture field, has pointed out that those who run small businesses and entrepreneurs (people who form new ventures) differ in significant ways. Vesper observed that entrepreneurship is concerned with the *creation* of new businesses, some of which turn into substantial enterprises. Small business, however, mainly involves *operating* established firms that do not have many employees. He believes that entrepreneurs (many of whom previously worked for large, technically oriented or marketing-oriented firms) work harder, more efficiently, "and generate more ideas and create more employment than established [managers of small businesses]."[2]

In addition, some of the claims made about smaller firms can be misleading. Dun & Bradstreet reports that 66 percent of the new jobs created in the United States in recent years came from concerns employing 20 or fewer people, and over 80 percent came from those with fewer than 100 employees.[3] This sounds impressive, but when you realize that 95 percent of all businesses have fewer than 20 employees, it becomes evident that 95 percent of the businesses create only 66 percent of the jobs. Put another way, 5 percent of businesses (i.e., those with over 20 employees) create 34 percent of the jobs. In addition, the 500 largest industrial firms alone contribute two thirds of U.S. output and three fourths of profits.[4]

---

[2]S. N. Charkravarty, "Bashful Entrepreneurs," *Forbes,* June 20, 1983, p. 66.

[3]F. C. Klein, "Manageable Size: Some Firms Fight Ills of Bigness by Keeping Employee Units Small," *The Wall Street Journal,* February 5, 1982, p. 1.

[4]Norman Berg and R. A. Pitts, "Strategic Management: The Multi-Business Corporation," in *Strategic Management,* ed. D. Schendel and C. W. Hofer (Boston: Little, Brown 1979), p. 339.

The point of the above is not to deride small business, which is important and essential to our economy. Growth and jobs, however, come largely from new ventures, both start-ups and those within larger firms. In contrast, most small firms are not particularly innovative; it is the *growth-oriented* small firms that are most likely to have this characteristic.[5]

Remember our earlier discussion which showed that the fastest growing 5 percent of companies created 83 percent of the new jobs, and 88 percent of these fastest growing companies employed fewer than 100 people.[6]

Types of Smaller Firms

Several researchers have attempted to categorize the major types of smaller firms found in the economy. The frameworks of Cooper,[7] Sussbauer,[8] and Vesper[9] can be combined in the following typology:

1. *Survival firms.* These are the typical "mom and pop" businesses particularly found in retailing and service industries. Survival firms represent the vast majority of all U.S. businesses and often have no hired employees. The founders frequently lack managerial training and use intuitive methods. The firms are usually undercapitalized, undermanaged, and have very limited potential. This type of firm succeeds by surviving.

2. *Underachieving firms.* This type of firm may have established a profitable market niche and may provide the entrepreneur with a good standard of living. However, the firm has additional growth potential that either intentionally or unintentionally, is not being realized. In the intentionally underachieving firm, the entrepreneur may choose to keep the company small because he or she realizes an inability to manage a larger firm; because he or she values the leisure time and lifestyle possible with a small, profitable firm; or because the entrepreneur does not want to trade control of the business for the external capital required for growth. This type of stable, high-payoff company is often a small manufacturing firm. The unintentionally underachieving firm may be experiencing a mismatch between the market, technology, finance, and management skills.

3. *Potential growth firms.* This type usually possesses competitive advantages that result from growing markets, innovative methods or products, or managerial ability. Survival usually is a temporary concern as the firm searches out proper capitalization to permit growth and more substantial profits. This growth puts

---

[5]A. C. Cooper, "Strategic Management: New Ventures and Small Business," in *Strategic Management,* ed. D. Schendel and C. W. Hofer (Boston: Little, Brown, 1979), p. 322.

[6]D. L. Birch, "The Booming Hidden Market," *Inc.,* October 1987, p. 15.

[7]Cooper, *Strategic Management,* p. 316.

[8]J. C. Sussbauer, "Commentary," in *Strategic Management,* ed. D. Schendel and C. W. Hofer (Boston: Little, Brown, 1979), p. 327.

[9]Karl H. Vesper, "Commentary," in *Strategic Management,* ed. D. Schendel and C. W. Hofer (Boston: Little, Brown, 1979), p. 332.

heavy demands on the founders, which they are willing to meet. They are also willing to take the personal and company risks necessary for future growth.

4. *Successful growth firms.* These firms have survived and are achieving their growth potential. They have capitalized on their distinctive competencies, have adequate financial backing, and are pursuing proper strategies in their markets. They have taken (and survived) the necessary risks, and typically have their sights set on becoming a much larger company. Their management team, while entrepreneurial, is capable of managing a larger company and is willing to make the personal sacrifices and organizational (including personnel) changes to continue the company's growth. These are the Apple Computers, ValComs, COMPAQ® Computers, ROLMs, Intels, Genentechs, Nikes, and so on that are likely to become the "darlings" of Wall Street.

The first two types—the survival firm and the underachieving firm—are the typical small businesses in our society. The latter two—the potential and successful growth firms—typify new ventures. Most small businesses are either unable or unwilling to reach these levels; most new ventures are not content to remain at the survival stage for long and have no intention of becoming underachievers. While any growing firm goes through several developmental stages—including start-up, early growth, and later growth—most start-ups do not progress through all three stages. In fact, most typical small businesses reach maturity *without* growth.

Characteristics of New Ventures

In some ways, start-up ventures and small businesses are similar. For example, the goal-formulation and strategy-formulation processes are largely in the hands of the entrepreneur/founder. This person also divides his or her time between strategic and operating tasks, usually without the benefit of formalized systems or procedures. For both, the key to effective strategy is creating a unique match of skills and resources at the individual product or market level by filling a niche (providing a unique service or product to a small or specialized group of customers). Nonetheless, many new ventures fail. The major reasons for this include:

1. Lack of well-rounded experience in sales, production, and management by the founder (remember, the entrepreneur is now a general manager and no longer a specialist).
2. Lack of adequate financial controls.
3. Inadequate capitalization.[10]

In contrast to small business start-ups, the new venture typically has a new-business plan that describes how the new firm plans to compete. This plan is

---

[10]D. Schendel and C. W. Hofer, eds. *Strategic Management* (Boston: Little, Brown, 1979), p. 310.

essential in seeking the relatively large amounts of outside capital that the venture requires. Still, inadequate capital remains an important source of failures.

New-Venture Problems

Many start-up ventures grow rapidly—even spectacularly—for a time and then level off and even decline or fail. The reason is that the capitalization and narrow product lines that permit spectacular growth also permit disasters, sometimes almost overnight. To *continue* to grow and prosper, the start-up company must extend its initial idea as it matures through add-ons and variations, and continue to come up with additional viable ideas. Some are not able to do this and fail. Others find that their great idea soon attracts large competitors into their niche, such as Minnetonka, Inc. (creator of ''Soft Soap''), leaving little profit for the innovator.

Many emerging growth companies peak and decline because their ''shallow pockets'' often force them to ''bet the company'' on the outcome of new moves. They don't always win the bet.[11]

New ventures, whether separate or internal, are a high-risk/high-reward strategy. While the entrepreneur is a critical element in the success of new ventures, appropriate strategies and financial backing are essential. The entrepreneur is a unique type of person, one with a high need for achievement, independence, confidence, and the ability to take calculated risks. It may not be true, however, that entrepreneurs are inherently risk-takers. What is more likely is that they have a different *perception* of risks than do nonentrepreneurs. For example, entrepreneurs see the risk of ''missing the boat''—letting an opportunity slip away—as a more threatening situation than the risk of failure, or ''sinking the boat.'' In this light, entrepreneurs may be as risk averse as anyone else; they perceive failure as missing an opportunity. In addition, certain areas of the country seem to spawn an unusually high percentage of new ventures: Santa Clara County in California, Boston, New York, New Jersey, Minneapolis, Boulder, Austin in Texas, and North Carolina's ''research triangle,'' to name a few. New ventures are the companies that have the potential to become the giants of the future, transforming whole industries in the process.

SMALL BUSINESSES

Here, the separate, already operating and established small firm is the subject. It is typically a survival firm (such as a ''mom and pop'' business) or an underachieving (either consciously or unintentionally) firm, although some small businesses may be potential growth or even high-growth firms.

---

[11]G. Smith and P. B. Brown, ''Emerging Growth Stocks—Why So Many Peak So Early,'' *Forbes*, January 28, 1985, p. 69.

Characteristics of Small Business

In discussing "small" business, it is inevitable that the question of size must be addressed. Size has been explored and defined in terms of many dimensions. Common descriptions of small business include firms with annual sales of less than $25 million or firms with fewer than 500 employees. However, firms with fewer than 1,000 employees are sometimes considered small. Whatever the definition, most firms in the United States can be called *small*. Statistics supplied by the U.S. Department of Commerce show that 99.7 percent of U.S. companies in all industries have fewer than 250 employees, as shown in Table 11.1. In addition, these figures seem to be relatively constant over time.

Given that most businesses in our economy are small, what types of firms are these? A helpful categorization of small businesses is as follows:

1. *Rare success:* Firms evolving from small beginnings to substantial size under the founder's leadership. H. Ross Perot established Electronic Data Systems in 1962 with a $1,000 investment. Other examples are Technican, Winnebago, and Dekalb Ag-Research.
2. *Firms in "small business industries":* Industries in which the optimal scale of the individual firms is small. Metalworking, ethnic food production, printing, design consulting, and land development are just a few.
3. *Firms based on successful specialization.* Firms based on a unique innovation or the holding of a patent. Research instruments, gold-refining operations, and independent producers of coffee and beer are examples.
4. *Satellite firms:* These are organizations linked to one or more large buyers. The industrial distributor who sells for a manufacturer on a commission basis is the classic example.
5. *Turnover firms:* These are firms whose activities consist of entry into a field followed by an exit from it in a few years or less. In the United States, a third of all small businesses are estimated to turn over every year.[12]

Small Business Strategy Formulation

Small businesses often experience scarcity of resources of every nature. To survive in the midst of significant problems, the manager of a small business has to stay in tune with the market and the environment. There is very little room for error. As Peter Drucker has pointed out,

In the first place, [the small business] needs strategy. The small business cannot afford to become marginal. Yet this is its perennial danger. It must, therefore, think through a strategy which gives it distinctions. It must, to speak in biological terms, find its

---

[12]Lee E. Preston, "The World of Small Business: A Suggested Typology," *American Journal of Small Business* 1, no. 4 (April 1977), p. 13.

TABLE 11.1 Distribution of U.S. Companies by Number of Employees and Size of Company

	Companies with Fewer than 20 Employees		Companies with 20 to 249 Employees		Companies with 250 Employees or More	
	Percent of All Companies	Percent of All Employees	Percent of All Companies	Percent of All Employees	Percent of All Companies	Percent of All Employees
All industries	94.7%	21.7%	5.0%	26.3%	0.3%	52.0%
Manufacturing	71.0	4.5	26.3	19.8	2.7	75.7
Wholesale trade	88.0	40.7	11.8	46.1	0.3	13.2
Retail trade	96.3	39.4	3.6	25.8	0.1	34.8
Services	97.8	41.7	2.1	33.4	0.1	24.9
Construction	96.2	38.9	3.7	41.7	0.1	19.3

Source: Adapted from J. Deeks, *The Small Firm Owner-Manager: Entrepreneurial Behavior and Management Practice* (New York: Praeger Publishers, 1976), p. 62.

specific ecological niche in which it has an advantage and can therefore withstand competition. This specific niche may be leadership in a distinct market, whether it is defined by geography, consumer needs, or consumer values. The strategy may lie in a specific excellence, such as a capacity to give service. Or it may lie in a specific technology. . . . For the typical small business has no strategy. The typical small business is not "opportunistic," it is "problematical"—it lives from problem to problem. But the typical small business is also, as a result, not a successful business. [13]

Drucker also has stated that it is more important for a small business to do the right things than to do things right. This stresses the need for effective tactics in a small business. With limited resources, the company has to be effective. If the firm is not effective, efficiency cannot even be considered. In a sense, the ineffective firm does not get the chance to be efficient. Rather, it becomes a business failure statistic.

Small firms are in a unique strategic situation compared to large firms. They must find a market niche and operate within this niche. Their distinct competitive advantage is often flexibility in production or service. Changes in demand that alter product or service properties are seen as an advantage because of the firm's flexibility. Specialization also can be a distinct advantage.

The strategy formulation process must fit the characteristic mold of small businesses and the manager of a small business. The process therefore must be simple, practical, and easy to use. It must be functional and be in line with the user's personality traits and decision processes.

How Small Businesses Plan

Large corporations typically start their strategic planning process with an examination of future economic and competitive conditions in relation to the company's existing businesses. Then they consider potential new businesses in terms of their companies' strengths, weaknesses, and needs. A strategic plan is developed from this analysis, followed by a projection of resources needed to accomplish the plan. Next, more specific plans and resource budgets are developed to implement the strategic plan.

This process is different in a smaller company. The large corporation can recruit people and raise money almost at will. The smaller company is much more restricted. Resources must be considered much earlier in the process, as must personal planning of the owner. While the larger firm often can *create* its own opportunities, the small firm cannot. It must plan to be able to *seize* opportunities if and when they arise. Thus, its strategies must be more flexible, adaptive, and opportunistic. [14] Small firms should strive to excel in *short-term,* not

[13]P. F. Drucker, *Management: Tasks, Responsibilities, Practices* (New York: Harper & Row, 1974), pp. 649 and 651.

[14]Neil C. Churchill, *Planning in Smaller Companies: An Argumentative View,* Case No. 9-179-014 (Boston: HBS Case Services, 1978).

long-term, planning, remaining as adaptable and flexible as possible. But the small firm does need a planning process and discipline, just as does its larger counterpart.

In spite of this, only one third of small businesses have a written strategic plan defining long-term objectives (about 50 percent of those over 50 employees had written plans, while one fourth of those with under 50 people did).[15] Table 11.2 contrasts strategic planning in small versus large companies, in terms of administration, procedures, and substance.

While executives of small firms are intimately familiar with their own operations, they are often too busy to update their knowledge of factors outside the company, such as: the prices charged by the major competitors; the *real* attitude of major customers toward the product and service; the market share of each product; the various ways customers use their products; or the potential impact of pending legislation.

The manager of a small company should realize that he or she cannot do all things for the firm. Planning may require the assistance of others, outsiders or insiders. In any case, survival is "job one" for the small firm, and nothing— including planning—should be permitted to detract from the small firm's primary advantages: customer service and product customization.[16]

Problems of Small Businesses

Many small businesses fail each year. Poor management has been cited most often as the reason for these failures, along with lack of resources (both financial and human). However, many observers postulate that a lack of strategic planning is also responsible for a growing number of small-business failures. Studies have shown that small firms with a higher level of formal planning tend to show better performance in terms of five-year annual growth rates. Other evidence indicates small firms that plan are more successful than those that do not.

The major strategic causes of small-business failure include:

1. *Faulty research.* Starting the business on a hunch or feeling instead of using market research.
2. *Wrong skills.* Running a small business requires more than just engineering, sales, manufacturing, or management experience obtained by working for a larger company.
3. *Undercapitalization.* Most new businesses are not profitable for several years, and significant cash is required to start and stock the business. Will the business be able to withstand early mistakes, operational problems, contingencies, or a possible recession?

---

[15]"Long-Range Plans," *The Wall Street Journal,* October 31, 1986, p. 29.

[16]R. B. Troxel, "How Small Companies Can Plan Effectively," *Management Focus,* September–October 1978, p. 13.

TABLE 11.2   Strategic Planning in Large and Small Companies

Strategic Factor	Typical Large Company	Typical Small Company
Company Administration and Strategic Decisions:		
Strategy, operations, and management	Complex	Relatively simple
Operations	Tactics (distinct from strategy)	Intertwined with strategy
Dealings with customers and vendors	Via lower-level employees	Personally by owner
Administration of company	Formal planning and delegation	Owner's personal overview
Organizational design	Based on tasks to be accomplished	Based on capabilities of incumbents
Desired qualification of employees	Specialized expertise	Mainly versatility
Attractiveness to employees	Maintenance factors exceed motivational incentives	Motivational incentives exceed maintenance factors
Regulations	Heavy	Though burdensome, enjoys many exemptions
Typical life span	Perpetual	Brief
Strategic Planning Procedures:		
Pervasiveness of strategic planning	In general use	Most firms abstain
Where used, plan's format	Written (formal)	Oral
Organization	Decentralized planning. Coordinator needed	Owner conducts centralized planning
Strategic subunits	Divisions or SBUs	Functions
Perceived financial burden	Almost negligible	Substantial
Specialized assistance	Board of directors and planning experts	None
Tools, techniques	Management information systems, sophisticated models, portfolio analyses, scenarios, and other planning routines	Much improvisation
Alignment of functions and projects	Numerous special meetings	Frequent routine contact
Financial analysis	In-depth cost accounting, adjustments for time differences, inflation, etc., many other techniques	Superficial
Beneficiary	All stockholders	Owner-manager
Strategic Planning Substance:		
Company mission	Formal statement	Not defined
Environment	Proactive	Passive
Environmental scanning	Formal efforts	Haphazard, mainly owner's chance contacts
Assessment of strengths and weaknesses	Realism (documented)	Optimism (opinion)
Forecasts	Causal methods	Extrapolation
Options	Analyses in depth	Few considered: little analysis
Feedback	Reports	Boss's inspection
Financial objective	Return on investment	Amount of profit
Financial planning	Main quest is quarterly growth in sales and profit	Main problem is insufficient cash
Type of strategy	Multiple approaches (differentiation strategies)	Concentration (focus strategy)
New products	Strong in marketing	Strong in development

Source: Harold N. Fox, ''Strategic Planning in Small Firms,'' in *Strategic Planning and Management Handbook,* ed. W. R. King and D. I. Cleland (New York: Van Nostrand Reinhold, 1987), pp. 576–77.

4. *Poor franchises.* Many franchises promise more than they can deliver and may be more interested in collecting the franchise fee than assisting the franchisee. Also, many franchises do not have well-developed criteria and guidelines to help the owner succeed.[17]

An additional problem for family-run businesses is management succession. The founder is often reluctant to relinquish control to his or her children. A successor should be trained in the same way executives are groomed in big corporations, by working his or her way through important areas such as marketing or sales, production, and finance. Children should work outside the family business first, making their mistakes away from their parent and learning how other businesses and managers operate. Ideally, children should enter the family business when they are in their 30s and the founder is close to retirement. However, the question of *which* members are to take over the top spots can be a source of family conflict and resentment. Individuals—family or otherwise—who are unable or unwilling to earn their keep should not be kept on the payroll. As indicated, the family firm has unique problems and concerns.[18] For example, when a company is operated largely as a vehicle for the family—to provide jobs, security, and goals geared as much to the family as to the market—then conventional financial rules don't always apply.[19]

In Conclusion

To summarize, most literature on strategic planning (indeed, most business literature in general) focuses on the large, multiproduct corporation and ignores the small business. For this reason, owners of small businesses may feel that they simply are not big enough to have to worry about strategic planning. But they need it, too. Many small firms have relatively few products, or rely heavily on a few major customers, so that demand shifts away from their products or loss of a major customer may be catastrophic. Small businesses face more risk than larger businesses due to their lack of diversification and smaller resource "cushion." Consequently, strategic planning is perhaps *more* critical to the success of a small firm than to that of a large one.

Yet, Sexton and Van Auken found that a minority of the small businesses they studied employed strategic planning.[20] Possible reasons for this include:

1. Lack of enough management expertise to do strategic planning.
2. Attitude: many owners of small businesses feel they must pay attention to the present, rather than worrying about the situation several years in the future.

---

[17]"How to Start a Sideline Business," *Business Week,* August 6, 1979, p. 94.

[18]S. L. Jacobs, "Small Business: It's Often Hard in a Family Firm to Let the Children Take Over," *The Wall Street Journal,* March 14, 1983, p. 23.

[19]R. I. Levin and V. R. Travis, "Small Company Finance: What the Books Don't Say," *Harvard Business Review* 65, no. 6 (November–December 1987), pp. 30–36.

[20]D. L. Sexton and P. M. Van Auken, "Prevalence of Strategic Planning in Small Business," *Journal of Small Business Management* 20, no. 3 (July 1982), pp. 20–26.

3. Limited resources: management in many small firms simply doesn't think it has the financial and/or human resources to develop a strategic planning process.
4. Lack of relevant information: a significant amount of data is available on the relevant environment facing large corporations; much less has been made available for small firms.

Basically, the study found that the small firm that planned was more dynamic, proactive, and successful (as measured by return on assets). The emphasis in the small firm is on simplicity and manageability. It is not necessary for the small firm to "burden itself with a detailed formal planning document, an extensive reporting system, or an avalanche of paperwork" to engage in strategic planning. If the basic steps are followed to the degree appropriate for the firm, the result will be the same benefit a more elaborate process provides for a larger firm—better control over the company's destiny.[21]

NOT-FOR-PROFIT ORGANIZATIONS

The not-for-profit (NFP) area includes a host of organizational types: publicly funded organizations (such as government, service, and public-interest organizations); institutions (such as most schools, hospitals, and charities); and "third-sector" organizations (research institutes, cooperatives, and government-chartered private organizations such as the Federal National Mortgage Association). A "fourth sector" could be discussed—the publicly chartered for-profit firm, such as COMSAT, CONRAIL and AMTRAK.

Many business students are likely to find themselves employed by NFPs. Some schools have colleges of business and public administration, others have departments of public administration, and some teach public administration in departments such as political science. In such schools, the student is exposed to the workings of "public organizations," primarily government. However, many NFPs are neither "business" nor "government," but institutions or third-sector organizations. Thus, the study of a large percentage of NFPs tends to be totally ignored in colleges and universities.

Types and Characteristics of Not for Profits

Max Wortman has written extensively on strategic management in NFPs. Table 11.3 is a modification of a typology of different NFPs that Wortman proposed. As can be seen from the table, the term NFP indicates much more than a simple public versus private dichotomy. There are types of NFPs in both sectors, and some private NFPs have more in common with certain types of public-sector organizations than they do with other private for-profit firms. Thus, the term *nonprofit* is not very descriptive; it tells only what an organization is *not*, not

---

[21]W. D. Jones, "Characteristics of Planning in Small Firms," *Journal of Small Business Management* 20, no. 3 (July 1982), pp. 15–19.

TABLE 11.3   A Typology of NFPs

Public organizations:
  A. Governmental executive agencies and departments at the federal, state, and local levels, including the military.
  B. Public-service organizations
    1. Urban services, such as law enforcement, fire, and public housing.
    2. Rural services, such as rural electrification, agricultural services, and county agents.
    3. General services, such as postal, transportation, social services and welfare, human resources, medicare and medicaid, and the FBI.
  C. Public-interest organizations, such as those involved with conservation, water resources, energy resources, and air pollution.

Institutions:
  Education (public and private)
  Hospitals and health care
  Labor unions
  Political parties
  Churches
  Libraries
  Performing arts
  Voluntary associations
  Organized charities
  Foundations

Third-sector organizations:
  Publicly chartered private firms (e.g., Federal National Mortgage Association and Government National Mortgage Association).
  Research institutes.
  Not-for-profit consultants, including American College Testing and Educational Testing Service.
  Consumer cooperatives.

Source: Modified from Max S. Wortman, Jr., "Strategic Management: Not-for-Profit Organizations," in *Strategic Management: A New View of Business Policy and Planning,* ed. D. Schendel and C. W. Hofer (Boston: Little, Brown 1979), p. 353. Reproduced by permission.

what it *is*. The NFP designation covers a whole spectrum of organizations, as different from each other in some cases as they are from for-profit firms.

Norman Waks, of the MITRE Corporation (a third-sector research institute), concluded that NFPs seem to be *services* enterprises (which are discussed later in this chapter), rather than producers of goods. In contrast, most enterprises that provide *goods* for sale seem to be for-profit enterprises. (Some services enterprises that require expensive capital equipment must also be profit making to provide a return on the capital.) In general, though, NFP means simply that no individual or group realizes profit or personal financial gain (other than salary) from the organization's operations.[22] NFPs, then, tend to be service oriented and people based, rather than product oriented and capital-equipment based.

---

[22]Norman Waks, *Strategic Planning in Private Non-Profit Organizations,* MTP-201 (Bedford, Mass.: The MITRE Corporation, 1979), p. 3.

Also, many organizations could be classified one of several ways. Hospitals, for example, can be either for profit or not for profit, and are considered to be service organizations. Colleges and universities are also service organizations, and can find themselves either in the public sector or private sector.

An enterprise will be likely to operate as an NFP for one or more of the following reasons:

1. *Cannot make profits.* By law or the nature of its services, the organization is not permitted to make a profit. This type of organization has no choice; it *must* be an NFP. (Others may have the option of being NFP or for profit.) Organizations required to be NFP include government agencies, voluntary organizations (religious, social welfare, and so on), stock exchanges, unions, and consumer cooperatives.
2. *Should not make profits.* These organizations are permitted to make a profit, but are involved in activities where it is considered improper to do so. Examples are most hospitals, schools, most institutions, and privately operated public-interest organizations.
3. *Should make but not retain profits.* These organizations try to make as much money as possible, but do not retain it. Their very purpose is to give such money away. Foundations and charitable organizations are obvious examples.
4. *Optional NFP.* These are firms that can and should make and retain profits, but have elected not to as an element in their strategy. They see themselves being significantly aided in their mission by choosing to be an NFP. Many research institutes fall into this category (such as Battelle, SRI, Brookings), as do federally funded R&D centers and organizations such as American College Testing (ACT) and the Educational Testing Service (ETS).

Differences between NFPs and For Profits

The basic difference between NFPs and for-profit firms is their missions. In addition, goals and objectives may differ considerably. For-profit firms tend to seek profits, by definition, whether or not you agree that they actually try to maximize profits. Thus, profit is a basic consideration in their need hierarchy, while it is not for the NFP. NFPs tend to focus on goals and objectives such as improving the quality and coverage of their service, increasing their reputation and influence, increasing their responsiveness and prestige, containing costs within budget, and increasing their budget. However, the use of planning in many NFPs is in its infancy, and goals frequently are short range and poorly defined. In addition, some types of NFPs pose particular problems.

Additional unique features of NFPs include:

1. *Governing boards.* Boards of NFPs are often made up of individuals with varying interests, backgrounds, and expertise, who frequently act as fund raisers or public relations people for the organization, rather than as true "directors."

2. *Measures of success.* The for profit can simply compare revenues and costs, and conclude that the market values its goods or services accordingly. But service is intangible and hard to measure. Also, outputs (services) are in different units than inputs (dollars), making it difficult to "prove" that the organization is efficient or effective.

3. *Planning initiatives.* NFPs tend to be skill based, and their degree of activity is a function of needs and problems that may (or may not) arise. Attempts to plan and forecast often take the form of simple extrapolations of the past. Marketing to "create" needs may be expressly forbidden for many NFPs.

4. *Weak customer influence.* The NFPs budget may be largely independent of customer or client need for the service.

5. *Commitment to cause or profession.* Employees may identify more with a movement, cause, or profession than with the NFP organization itself.

6. *Undue contributor influence.* Funding sources, private and public, may attempt to exert undue influence over goals, operations, and management, putting management in a compromising position.

7. *Charismatic leaders.* The organization may rise and fall with the fortunes and credibility of the founder or director.

8. *Reward constraints.* NFPs tend to have no "profit centers," but only cost centers. How, then, is service improvement rewarded as opposed to cost cutting? The tendency is to pay salaries that are independent of results and input resources employed.

9. *Culture and values.* Many NFP employees tend to discount any trade-off possibilities between resources (time and money) and performance. An attitude of spending whatever it costs to do the job, as well as doing whatever one's value system requires may predominate.

Strategic Management in NFPs

In sum, the primary goals of the NFP are noneconomic and difficult to measure. An NFP manager is primarily involved in operations, and is more of an "administrator" or implementer than an entrepreneur. Many NFPs have goal structures and policies to guide their operations, but no explicit strategies to tie the two together. They tend to be managed much more in terms of short-term operations than in a strategic sense. Management control is based on inputs, rather than on objectives or intended outcomes. This is not an indictment of NFP managers, however, because their task and environment is different from those in the for-profit firm, and perhaps more difficult, as well. Formulating and implementing long-term strategies and plans in such organizations may be difficult (and, in some instances, fruitless) because of the imposition of goals and objectives by a frequently changing group of outside stakeholders.

The quality of resources, particularly management and personnel, is frequently more varied in the NFP organization than in the for-profit organization. Also, financial resources tend to be more widely dispersed. In spite of such factors, consistent and effective strategy formulation *is* possible for the NFP, following a process similar to that used by the for profit—careful strategy assessment; evaluation of the fit between the environment, the organization, and the strategy; and changes in strategy if needed. While these tasks may be *more* complex for the NFP manager as he or she monitors the varied constituency and objectives, they are not impossible. Testing the consistency of the current strategy with the environment and the resources and values of the organization spotlights strengths and weaknesses. Comparing a proposed future strategy with the expected future situation helps to ensure that strategies are appropriate for the organization's upcoming needs.[23]

Also, NFPs are regulated organizations. The more regulated an organization (or even an industry in the for-profit sector), the less leeway or freedom the organization has. Therefore, fewer strategic options are open to regulated organizations. For highly regulated or constrained organizations (such as in the public sector), few true ''strategic decisions'' may exist, as compared to the typical unregulated, for-profit firm. By comparison, public-sector organizations' ''strategies'' are more akin to the for-profits' tactics or operating strategies.

Public-Sector Management

Management in the public sector is different from corporate management not just in degree; it is also qualitatively different. For example, in contrast to the case in the private sector, managers in the public sector must frequently accept goals that are set by groups or organizations other than their own. Also, the managers must often operate with structures designed by outside groups. Further, they must commonly work with, for, and manage people whose careers are in many respects outside of their control. As if these factors weren't enough, public-sector managers must often accomplish their goals and objectives in less time than is allowed to corporate managers.[24]

Government.   Management's task in managing governmental organizations differs from business organizations in many important ways. For example, businesses strive to make a profit, whereas governmental organizations are often left to provide services which cannot be provided profitably by the private market. Additional differences are as follows:

- Government administrators pursue goals and objectives which are more difficult to measure; the appearance of success may be as important as the reality.

---

[23]M. L. Hatten, ''Strategic Management in Not-for-Profit Organizations,'' *Strategic Management Journal* 3 (1982), p. 103.

[24]J. L. Bower, ''Effective Public Management,'' *Harvard Business Review* 55, no. 2 (March–April 1977), p. 134.

- A government agency's performance is often judged in terms of effort, or inputs, rather than results.
- Government managers typically receive little credit for effective administration, since its benefits are hard to measure.
- Because they are evaluated on the basis of effort rather than on results, government managers are often reluctant to delegate responsibility to subordinates.
- Government managers are often accused of being ''inconsistent'' if they change their positions, even if their response is a reasonable reaction to changing events.
- Actions of government top managers are exposed to intensive scrutiny by the media.
- While shareholders' interests are typically consistent with those of business managers, government managers must often report to hostile and varied constituencies.
- Government managers usually have less control over their subordinates and, because of the difficulty of measuring output, find it more difficult to set goals and evaluate the performance of subordinates than do private-sector managers.
- Political leaders and high-level government managers often have not been prepared for their responsibilities by either formal training or pertinent experience.[25]

Charitable Organizations. Certain charitable organizations, such as the United Way, utilize well-developed strategic planning and management by objectives approaches. In fact, their progress and sophistication may cause some resentment on the part of certain of their agencies and donors. As shown in Figure 11.1, United Way's long-range planning model is a logical modification of the basic strategic planning model, adapted to United Way's situation. In addition, United Way develops alternative scenarios of the future, based on predicted events in the environment. These predicted events are interpreted to determine the likely key implications for United Way. Thus, charitable organizations, as well as other NFPs, can make effective use of strategic management concepts.

The Process in the Public Sector. As noted above, United Way's strategic planning process looks startlingly similar to that used by businesses. On the other hand, public-sector organizations *are* different from businesses. It may be that United Way is independent enough to be able to operate more like a business than like a government agency. For an actual government agency, however, our business model may need to be modified. A modified model of the process for public organizations is shown in Figure 11.2.

The main difference between this model and other strategic management models is the modified model's increased emphasis on the identification

---

[25]P. E. Morrison and J. R. Fox, *How Management in Government Differs from Business,* 9-386-085 (Boston: HBS Case Services, 1985), pp. 1–2.

FIGURE 11.1 Long-Range Planning Model for United Way

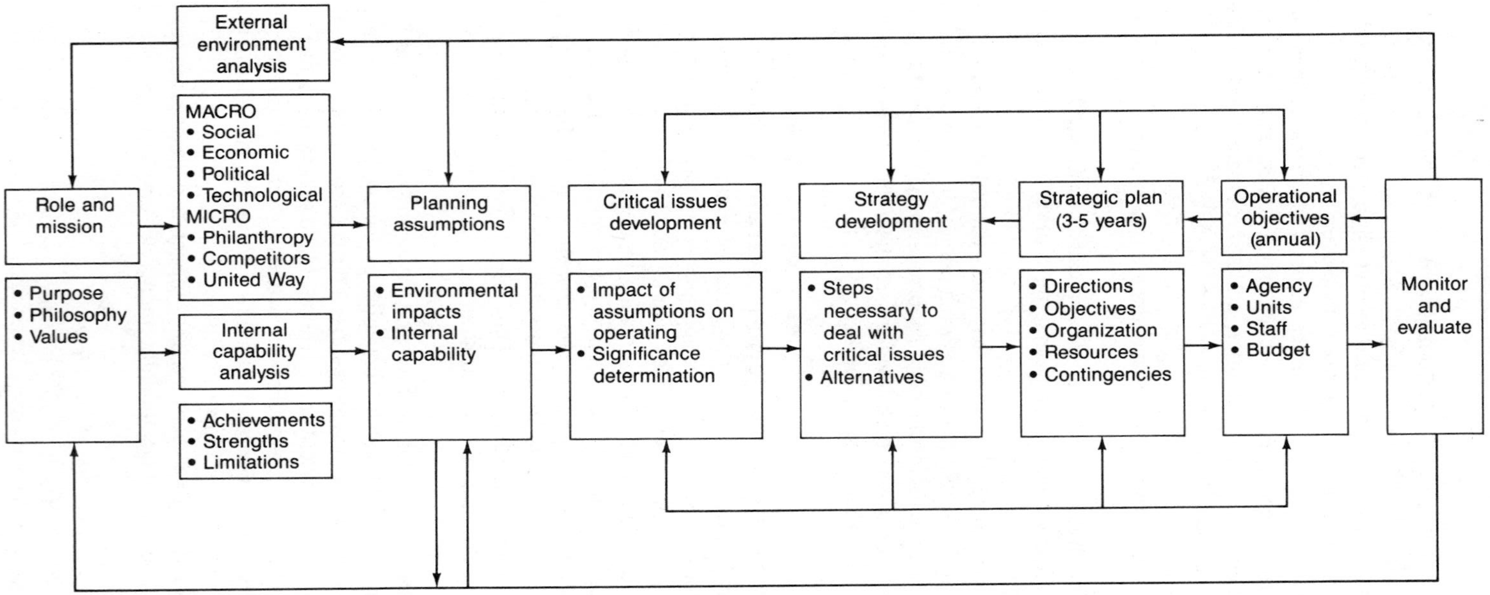

External environment analysis

MACRO
- Social
- Economic
- Political
- Technological

MICRO
- Philanthropy
- Competitors
- United Way

Role and mission
- Purpose
- Philosophy
- Values

Internal capability analysis
- Achievements
- Strengths
- Limitations

Planning assumptions
- Environmental impacts
- Internal capability

Critical issues development
- Impact of assumptions on operating
- Significance determination

Strategy development
- Steps necessary to deal with critical issues
- Alternatives

Strategic plan (3-5 years)
- Directions
- Objectives
- Organization
- Resources
- Contingencies

Operational objectives (annual)
- Agency
- Units
- Staff
- Budget

Monitor and evaluate

Source: Reprinted with permission of the United Way of America. *Environmental Scanning* (Alexandria, Va., 1980), p. 4.

FIGURE 11.2   Modified Strategic Management Model for Public Organizations

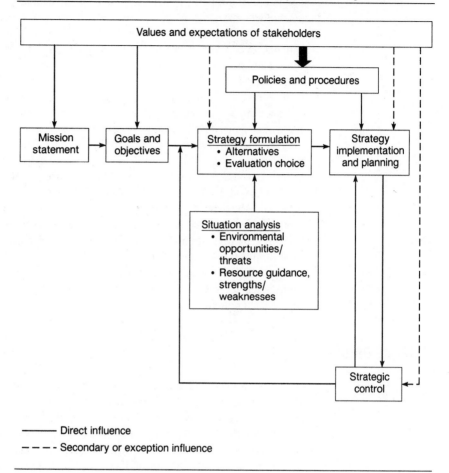

——— Direct influence

– – – – Secondary or exception influence

of important outside stakeholders and their role during the entire strategic planning process. In many ways, the strategic management process in public organizations revolves around the values, views, and expectations of the organization's most important outside stakeholders. To be successful at strategic management, top management must realize this and take action to at least indirectly include the outside stakeholders in virtually all stages of the strategic management process. This is why the stakeholders' value analysis stage of the strategic management process dominates or overshadows the other elements of the new model.

Additionally, policies and procedures take on a more important role in this model, flowing directly from and reflecting the stakeholders' values and expectations. The policies and procedures also function at least partially as proxies for the stakeholders. However, should the policies and procedures fail to adequately or properly influence their respective elements in the process, the stakeholders have the power to override them and exert direct influence, as shown by the dotted lines. Therefore, the stakeholders exert direct or indirect influence over virtually all of the elements in the process; some flow through policies and procedures, but the possibility of secondary or exception basis direct control exists.

Therefore, the more central role of stakeholders' values and expectations facilitates direct and indirect communication between important stakeholders and public managers during each stage of the strategic management process. This gives outside stakeholders the opportunity to give valuable input and feedback to public managers at each stage of the strategic management process. As stated earlier, top management's careful consideration of feedback from outside stakeholders at each stage of the planning process is generally crucial for the strategic management process to work in a public setting, due to the greater amount of power held by the outside stakeholders versus the for-profit setting. Other models that attempt to describe the strategic management process do not allow for this type of direct feedback at each stage of the process. But then again, this type of direct feedback is not as crucial for success in a for-profit setting where much more discretion is allowed its top management as compared to its outside stakeholders.[26]

SERVICE ORGANIZATIONS

Service industries and the providing of "service" by all organizations have become the buzzwords of the latter 80s. As part of this phenomenon, the service industries have become widely accepted as the future strength of advanced industrialized nations (or, for some, an example of their *lack* of strength). Yet most serious study in the areas of business strategy and practices has ignored the service industries and focused on the manufacturing sector.

This is unfortunate, because the production of services currently exceeds 68 percent of U.S. gross national product and employs over 72 percent of the work force.[27] Again, strategic management of service organizations has received limited attention in the business literature, and many misconceptions abound concerning services; for example, some have expressed fears that the United States is fast becoming a nation of people who are "serving each other hamburgers or taking in each other's laundry,"[28] with the real engines of

---

[26]J. J. Hoffman and L. A. Digman, "An Analysis of the Strategic Management Process for Public Organizations," *Proceedings of the Midwest Decision Sciences Institute Meeting*, 1988, pp. 184–97.

[27]Mack Ott, "The Growing Share of Services in the U.S. Economy—Degeneration or Evolution?," *Review*, Federal Reserve Bank of St. Louis 69, no. 6 (June/July 1987), p. 5.

[28]Alan Murray, "The Service Sector's Productivity Problem," *The Wall Street Journal*, February 2, 1987, p. 1.

economic growth moving offshore. We will take a look at the role of services in our economy, some characteristics and types of service organizations, including some suggestions for strategies and operations of service organizations.

Role in the Economy

The view that a move toward services signals a decline in our economy is not based in fact; it has been the strength of our manufacturing sector—not weakness—that has precipitated the shifts in employment and output toward services. In fact, high-productivity growth in manufacturing and agriculture, plus the long-term effects of American investment in education—have made faster growth of the service sector possible. What's more, these trends have been occurring for a century or more with no significant recent changes in the trends. Also, an appreciable share of these services aid in the production of goods, making their production more efficient.[29] Remember from an earlier chapter that the U.S. private sector is 167 percent as productive as Japan, including being 771 percent as productive in agriculture, 127 percent in manufacturing, and over 150 percent in services.

As Table 11.4 illustrates, most of the growth in services has occurred at the expense of other commodities, not manufacturing, with productivity increases in almost all areas. The biggest growth in services output has occurred in finance, insurance, and real estate; business services; and health services; with declines in a number of other areas (the segments containing hamburger cooks and laundry workers have not increased).

Types and Characteristics of Service Organizations

Service organizations (the types listed in Table 11.4) and the delivery of services in general have certain unique features. One is that service jobs (with certain notable exceptions, such as utilities and communications) tend to be located where and when the customer wants them, rather than centralized, as in manufacturing. This means more and decentralized workplaces, with fewer people at each. Also, in many services, the service is produced, marketed, and delivered at the same place and time, often by the same person; there is no "inventory" that can be accumulated for later delivery. Many are "information driven," beginning with familiarity between the server and the served.[30]

There is a tendency for service companies to view themselves as unique, and consequently they tend to not promote operations management and efficiency

---

[29]Ott, "The Growing Share of Services."

[30]J. L. Heskett, "Lessons in the Service Sector," *Harvard Business Review* 65, no. 2 (March–April 1987), pp. 118–26.

TABLE 11.4   Percent of U.S. Labor and Output by Various Sectors

	1948		1972		1985	
	Labor	GNP	Labor	GNP	Labor	GNP
Commodities (total):	46.2	41.2	33.9	35.8	28.1	32.4
Agriculture	11.4	5.5	3.9	2.7	2.9	2.6
Manufacturing	27.4	21.3	23.6	21.5	18.7	21.6
Mining	1.8	6.5	0.8	5.2	0.9	3.6
Construction	5.7	8.0	5.6	6.4	5.7	4.5
Services (total):	53.8	58.8	66.1	64.2	71.9	67.6
Transportation	5.2	6.8	3.5	4.2	3.1	3.5
Communications	1.3	0.8	1.4	1.8	1.2	2.6
Utilities	0.9	1.2	0.9	2.5	0.9	2.9
Wholesale trade	4.9	5.0	5.3	6.7	5.6	7.4
Retail trade	13.5	9.5	14.1	9.2	15.5	9.5
Finance, insurance, real estate	3.2	9.6	5.0	13.5	6.2	14.6
Government	11.7	13.8	18.3	13.1	16.3	11.1
Personal services	2.1	1.3	1.6	0.9	1.5	0.6
Business services	0.7	1.0	2.3	2.0	4.5	3.3
Auto repair	0.6	0.4	0.7	0.7	1.1	0.8
Health services	1.9	2.2	4.3	3.4	6.0	4.3
Legal services	0.4	1.0	0.5	0.9	0.9	1.0
Miscellaneous professional	0.4	0.7	1.0	1.1	1.6	1.5
Other	7.1	4.9	7.4	3.4	7.7	3.3

Source: Adapted from Mack Ott, "The Growing Share of Services in the U.S. Economy—Degeneration or Evolution?" *Review,* Federal Reserve Bank of St. Louis 69, no. 6 (June/July 1987).

techniques with the same vigor as the manufacturing sector; they need to realize that they are not merely unique entrepreneurial entities, but can learn from other industries (and other segments of the service sector). In addition, they are not necessarily labor intensive; many are quite capital intensive, such as utilities, communications, and even hospitals. In fact, the most labor intensive tend to be brokerage houses, insurance, and business services.[31]

Franchising seems to be a growing trend in services; not just for fast food and other outlets, but for *professional* services as well, such as optical, medical, legal, real estate, and other services.

A closer look at two types of service institutions—hospitals and higher education—sheds some light on their operations and strategies.

Hospitals.   As Drucker observed, managing a hospital is one of the most difficult managerial tasks. One reason is that major controllers of the use of the

---

[31]R. W. Schmenner, "How Can Service Businesses Survive and Prosper?," *Sloan Management Review,* Spring 1986, pp. 21–32.

hospital's facilities—the physicians—are typically not employees and are not under management's supervision or control. In addition, many of the hospital's employees, especially the nurses, are responsible both to the hospital *and* to the physician on an ad hoc basis. A hospital also involves very diverse functions that entail very different skill levels and types of operations, including:

1. Medical services, such as surgery, obstetrics, anesthesiology, radiology, and the like, which are performed by nonemployees often reporting to a nonemployee (the chief of medicine or surgery), but using the hospital's facilities.
2. Hospital services, such as pharmacy, nursing, laboratory, and the like.
3. The "hotel" function, including housekeeping, laundry, food service, and others.
4. Administrative services, such as records, accounting, and billing.

In addition, hospitals are forced to mix several types of production/operations approaches in the same facility, which is not an ideal situation. For example, patient care is typically of the "unique product" category, while many of the administrative services are "process production." On the other hand, hospital and hotel-services functions most often function as "flexible mass-production" units.

Hospitals also typically have very high fixed costs, with 40 to 50 percent of their budget going to salaries. For the NFP hospital, excess capacity *raises* its prices—the amount it must charge for use of its facilities (such as room rates)—since these charges must be set so that the hospital will break even.

Colleges and Universities.   Most colleges and universities have traditionally done very little strategic planning. Even when warned as long as 10 years ago that declining enrollments were imminent, most seemed to assume that the other institutions would be affected. Today, however, higher education is being forced to think in terms of distinctive competencies, niches, and missions, but their strategic decision processes still appear to be primarily ad hoc; most have not implemented a regular strategic management process.

Some schools—such as Carnegie-Mellon, Stanford, Houston, George Mason, and Miami—are exceptions. In 1981, Carnegie-Mellon developed a plan to seek academic excellence in selected areas of comparative advantage. This focus has catapulted departments such as computer science and cognitive psychology into national prominence, and has increased the applicant pool by 15 percent. Miami uses a modified portfolio model to focus its programs and allocate its resources.[32]

Professional Services Organizations

Another largely overlooked type of organization from a strategic perspective is the professional services firm, including legal, CPA, and management (and other) consulting firms, medical and dental practices, and advertising agencies.

---

[32]"How Academia Is Taking a Lesson from Business," *Business Week,* August 27, 1984, p. 58.

Many business school graduates find themselves employed by such firms. Professional service firms differ in important ways from the traditional corporation, and are also unlike most types of not-for-profit organizations.

Most professional service firms are relatively small, and are either incorporated or operate as partnerships. The choice of organizational form, however, has little to do with size. For example, many large law, CPA, and consulting firms operate as partnerships (the giant CPA firm, Peat, Marwick Main and Co., for example, operates as a partnership), while even very small medical and dental clinics tend to incorporate. An important strategic decision, then, concerns the form of organization.

A second key decision is scope of services—how specialized or general does the firm want to be? A management consulting firm may choose to specialize in manufacturing planning, or personnel selection, or executive development, for example.

A third consideration is how large does the firm want to become? For many, this is a function of available business, but some feel that it is better to remain small and busy (and able to select desirable clients and projects) than to grow and become concerned with searching for clients. In a way, the decisions concerning size and specialization are related. A firm could grow while remaining specialized, or grow by broadening its services.

A fourth strategic decision involves whether or not to advertise, and, if so, how. Recent legal changes have permitted certain types of professional services firms to advertise, something that is foreign to many professionals. Should a CPA firm advertise in the media or market its services through seminars and public service, as has been the traditional approach? This decision depends upon how well established the firm is, as well as the image (the degree of "professionalism") it wishes to project.

Another strategic decision involves financial and operational policies. How will the firm charge for its services? How will the profits be distributed among the members of the firm? And what will the pay scale be? What percentage of a firm member's time will be required to be "billable"? What arrangements exist if a member decides to leave the firm? Mistakes, miscalculations, or oversights in any of these areas can spell problems for an otherwise promising professional services firm.

Operations in a professional services firm tend to be very different from those in traditional organizations. Most professional firms operate as committees, with the partners or officers acting as a group of equals. For example, the president of a medical group is not a "superior" to the others in the practice. He or she is merely a firm member who acts as head of the firm for a specified period of time—usually one or two years. The other firm members have "delegated" speaking for the firm and handling administrative tasks for the specified period. Typical levels of practitioners in such firms are shown in Figure 11.3. A principal is typically a senior firm member responsible for obtaining projects or clients and supervising all work in his or her area of expertise. A senior associate is usually in charge of a particular project or case, whereas associates usually

FIGURE 11.3 Titles, Ranks, and Career Paths in Professional Services Firms

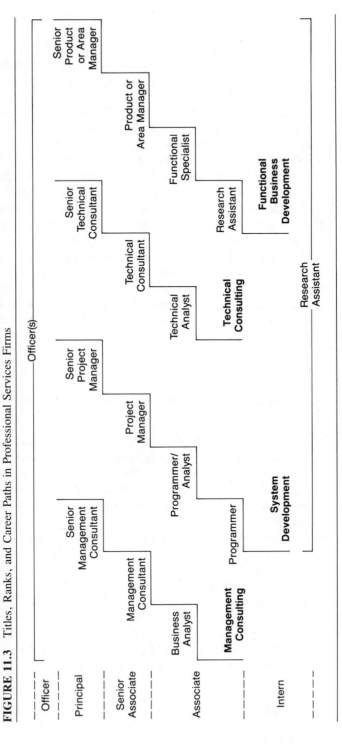

Source: David De Long, "Tell Employees Where They Stand," *Inc.* April 1982, p. 62. Reprinted with permission, *Inc.*. magazine, April 1982. Copyright © 1982 by Inc. Publishing Company, 38 Commercial Wharf, Boston, MA 02110.

work on a given project or case under the direction of a senior associate. Interns tend to be newer employees in a training and probationary period. If the firm is a partnership, senior associates *may* be elected to partner status, while principals are almost always partners. (A partner shares in the profits of the firm and has a vote in major decisions.)

The key resources in any professional firm are its specialists—the accountants, consultants, doctors, architects, lawyers, or engineers—who actually generate the client services and create a reputation for the firm. But how do you manage these people? If you pull the best into management, you lose your best producers; but the specialists won't accept less than the best producers as superiors. The solution is often the "producing manager"; that is a person responsible for *both* management activities and client services. With producing managers heading small business units as a "playing manager," the firm can stay productive and nonhierarchical, permitting it to grow and change while retaining its competitive edge.[33]

In short, professional services firms are distinctly different from most other types of organizations, both strategically and operationally. They tend to be less formal and more egalitarian, and depend on the knowledge, skills, abilities, and charisma of relatively few key people. In the final analysis, success lies in the ability of the key people to work as a team in acquiring jobs and satisfying the clients.

Service Sector Lessons

Successful service organizations tend to have several strategies in common. They include:

- Close coordination between marketing and operations, since marketing, production, and delivery of the service tend to occur together.
- Development of a *strategic service vision*—identification of a target market segment, development of service concepts geared to the targeted customers' needs, an operating strategy to support the service concepts, and an efficient and effective delivery system.
- Employee understanding of the service vision; because the employees are vital to productivity and quality of service, their internalization of the concept is vitally important.
- A stress on quality control of service, through generous incentives, pride, teamwork, and customer contact.
- A close look at economies of scale; service firms, particularly delivery points, can easily become too large to deliver superior service.
- Recognition that information about customers is important to providing service to existing customers as well as in attracting new ones.[34]

---

[33]J. W. Lorsch and P. F. Mathias, "When Professionals Have to Manage," *Harvard Business Review* 65, no. 4 (July–August 1987), pp. 78–84.

[34]Heskett, "Lessons in the Service Sector."

CONCLUSIONS

In earlier chapters, the characteristics of traditional, private-sector, medium-to-large business organizations were examined which affect their choice of strategies and policies. This chapter addresses the unique features of certain other organizations commonly found in our economy, for the purpose of identifying those characteristics that affect these organizations' choice of missions, goals and objectives, strategies, and policies. From our analysis, we saw that new ventures, small businesses, not-for-profit organizations, and service organizations are sufficiently different from the traditional organization to warrant special attention and unique approaches.

Chapter 12

Strategic Management: Trends and Directions

LEARNING OBJECTIVES

After completing Chapter 12, you should be able to:

Discuss the role of the board of directors in strategic management.

Understand the role of the consultant.

Summarize the entire strategic management process, including major findings and conclusions.

Assess the current state of the art of strategic management, including current developments.

Discuss emerging trends in the field.

Speculate on several likely future trends as the field matures.

Strategic management is maturing as a field. It has experienced embryonic and rapid growth over the past 15–20 years, and is currently in the throes of a shakeout and consolidation prior to entering its second generation—that of a more mature and defined field.

In this, the final chapter, several tasks will be attempted. First, the roles of two "quasi insiders" in the strategic management process—the board of directors and the hired consultant—will be examined. Second, some of the major findings and conclusions of the previous 11 chapters, representative of the state of the art as the field's first generation draws to a close, will be reviewed. Next, attention will be directed to current major transitional trends as the field undergoes a shakeout and consolidation. Finally, likely trends as the field matures and enters its second generation will be discussed.

THE ROLE OF QUASI INSIDERS

The board of directors plays an important role in the long-term strategic, operational, and policy-related activities of any organization. The board does not act as management, although certain inside officers may be members. However, for larger organizations in particular, the bulk of board members are outsiders, thus the term *quasi insiders* is used when referring to them. Consultants— outsiders who may play an important advisory role in strategic management processes and content—are another group of important quasi insiders.

The Role of the Board

What is the role of the board of directors of an organization? More specifically, what is the board's role in strategic management? The first role of any board is legal. Under corporate laws, the board represents the owners' (i.e., shareholders), interest in a firm, by choosing a chief executive officer, evaluating and rewarding the CEO, and replacing the CEO if necessary. The board's loyalty must be to the stockholders rather than to management. There is a problem inherent in performing this function: the CEO also often chairs the board of directors. This makes ambiguous the role of the board and especially the role of the chairman—when the chairman speaks, is he or she representing management or the board (thus indirectly the stockholders)? How can the board objectively evaluate the CEO's performance if he or she is, in fact, the chairman of the board?

Responsibilities of the Board.   William Boulton of the University of Georgia sees the board as progressing through a series of transitions from legitimizing to auditing to directing. Using a survey of 45 chief executives and directors, as well as in-depth investigations of boards in seven firms, Boulton attempted to trace the processes that boards had gone through in evolving to their current format. The first transition, from legitimizing to auditing, comes about partly due to increased legal pressures on directors, making them more insistent on being informed. As the board becomes more involved in decisions, it may then adopt a directing role in questioning the firm's long-term direction. At this point, the board develops a formalized statement of its role and function. Boulton considers providing continuity to be one of the most important functions of the board. Chief executive officers come and go, but the organization lives on; it is the role of the board to maintain a continuing philosophy of the firm. The board must ensure that management is carrying out the functions necessary for long-term viability.[1]

---

[1] W. R. Boulton, "The Evolving Board: A Look at the Board's Changing Roles and Information Needs," *Academy of Management Review* 3, no. 4 (October 1978), pp. 827–36.

Involvement in Strategic Planning. Courtney Brown of the Conference Board has discussed the various responsibilities of the board and identified four areas in which the board should be involved: policy, personnel, procedures, and performance. Brown has contended that the only area being adequately dealt with is performance. He has stated, ''the board of directors is the proper body for the establishment of broad policies and procedures . . . management personnel are selected by the chief executive officer in collaboration with the board and delegated to carry out these policies and procedures.'' The paradox seems to be that although boards are legally accountable for corporate affairs, they do not often involve themselves in the *planning* of such affairs. The two reasons most often cited for this noninvolvement are the directors' lack of time and of necessary expertise.[2]

Reasons for Involvement. Kenneth Andrews believes there are several reasons for the board of directors to become involved with corporate strategy. First, the involvement provides evidence that management has some process for evaluating alternatives. It also provides an understanding of the company's business and a means of evaluating management. Another, and perhaps the most important, reason for board involvement is that an understanding of corporate strategy provides a reference point for evaluating other decisions and their impact.[3] An effective board should require that management formulate a unique corporate strategy, should review it periodically, and should use it as the reference point for all other board decisions.

Another writer, Robert Mueller, has identified three areas in which he feels that the skills and objectivity of the board of directors would prove useful:

1. Determining new directions of growth.
2. Deciding when to make profound changes in the strategic approach to corporate objectives.
3. Choosing a philosophy and the timing for investments.[4]

If it is assumed that boards should be involved in strategic management in some way, the next question becomes: How involved? Should boards actually determine strategy or merely evaluate the strategy determined by management? Should the board examine the process by which the strategy has been formulated? Samuel Felton has identified three possible levels of board involvement.

1. Approve strategic recommendations; monitor the agreement between plans and performance.
2. Take part in the determination of objectives.

---

[2]Courtney Brown, *Putting the Corporate Board to Work* (New York: Macmillan, 1976), p. 30.

[3]Kenneth J. Andrews, ''From the Boardroom: Replaying the Board's Role in Formulating Strategy,'' *Harvard Business Review* 59, no. 3 (May-June 1981), p. 18.

[4]Robert Mueller, ''Criteria for the Appraisal of Directors,'' *Harvard Business Review* 57, no. 3 (May-June 1979), p. 48.

3. Become completely familiar with the plans of management. By doing this, the board will be able to discriminate between external and internal causes of performance and results.[5]

Felton has defined the role of the board to include deciding what business the firm is in (enterprise and corporate-level strategies), defining the principal quantitative and qualitative objectives of the firm, and reviewing the strategies the organization is going to employ.

Obviously, there are differences of opinion concerning board involvement. Some feel that if the board actually gets involved in planning, it would be a duplication of effort, since management would also be doing planning. This view holds that even if all the board did was approve plans, they would need to be experts to pass judgment. Thus, corporate boards should *not* be involved in the development and approval of business-level plans, but should rely on management. According to this view, the role of the director is to ensure that the premises for planning correspond to the board's shared views of the business. These premises should be audited when there are large discrepancies between planned outcomes and actual results, leading to conflicting assumptions about the causes. The board's role in this process is to synthesize the competing assumptions as well as to discuss diverging viewpoints. The board manages the discussion, commits the firm to a new direction, and ensures that those parties advocating defeated alternatives are not punished. It should be pointed out that this view does not explain how directors will gain the expertise for this task, but not the expertise to evaluate strategy.

It seems, then, that the board's responsibility is to evaluate strategy but not to formulate it. However, the level of strategy in question needs to be considered. For example, the board should be intimately involved in the formulation of and changes in enterprise strategy, as in the case of Primerica. In addition, it should probably be involved in any *major* changes in corporate-level strategy, such as the decisions to restructure ITT and Coca-Cola—at least in evaluating and approving the concept in advance. But business-level strategy is another matter, especially in multibusiness firms. When the board starts developing business-level strategy, it is usurping management's responsibility, which can lead to a disastrous relationship between management and the board.

Given that most board members have a great deal of business knowledge that can best be utilized by allowing them to analyze management problems and decisions, how does the board go about evaluating strategic alternatives? It must be remembered that board members are usually employed in high-level positions in other firms and cannot devote more than a small part of their time to board activities. In addition, they cannot wait to evaluate a strategy based on the results obtained. Strategic management involves crucial, long-term decisions; if mistakes are made, the firm's existence may be put in jeopardy.

---

[5]S. M. Felton, Jr., "Case of the Board and the Strategic Process," *Harvard Business Review* 57, no. 4 (July-August 1979), p. 20.

TABLE 12.1   Committees of the Board in a Sample of 16 Companies

Company	Audit	Compensation	Executive	Finance	Nominating	Public Policy	Other
Allied Chemical	X	X	X		X	X	XX
American Airlines	X	X	X	X	X		XX
AT&T	X	X	X	X	X	X	XX
Armstrong World	X	X					X
Bethlehem Steel	X	X	X				
Boeing	X	X		X	X		
Champion International	X	X					XXX
Dow Jones	X	X	X				
Du Pont	X	X	X	X			
Eastern Air	X	X	X				X
Exxon	X	X	X		X		X
Mobil	X	X	X		X	X	X
Pan Am	X	X	X	X	X	X	
Textron	X		X		X		X
UAL	X	X	X				
Union Carbide	X	X	X	X	X	X	

Source: Stanley C. Vance, *Corporate Leadership: Boards, Directors, and Strategy* (New York: McGraw-Hill, 1983), p. 62.

Felton has advocated evaluating strategy based on five criteria:

1. Does it exploit opportunity fully in terms of market share?
2. Is it internally consistent?
3. Is it feasible in terms of competence and resources?
4. Does it have the support of those who must carry it out?
5. Is it a clear stimulus to achievement?[6]

Committees of the Board.   How a board performs its functions is partially a result of its structure. While this structure is affected by the laws of the state in which the firm is incorporated, most firms tend to show some similarities in the committees that comprise the board. Table 12.1 lists the committees used by 16 typical major corporations.

---

[6]Ibid.

All of the firms included had an audit committee that serves as an intracompany watchdog to ensure that the affairs of the company are being handled competently and ethically. (Any company listed on the New York Stock Exchange *must* have an audit committee.) Another fairly universal committee is the executive committee. This is usually the most powerful, and typically is empowered to act for the total board between meetings. The compensation committee recommends compensation for senior management, while the nominating committee selects or evaluates candidates for the total board, for membership on board committees, for top corporate officers, and the like.[7]

Strategy Committees. Because of the importance of strategy and policy, some firms have created board committees to deal with these areas. Kenneth Andrews, for example, recommended formulation of a strategy committee that would be similar to an audit committee. The objective of the strategy committee is to encourage and strengthen the strategic planning process within the company. This committee first would become familiar with current strategy, then assess the current strategy's strengths and weaknesses and consider what measures would improve strategy. Another recommendation was the implementation of full-scale strategy reviews, which, at a minimum, should compare last year's results against planned performance. These reviews should also evaluate and modify long-range plans. The special skills and talents of directors can be fully utilized only by involving them in these critical issues.[8]

William Wommack also has suggested forming a corporate strategy committee composed of outside, independent directors. This would involve the board in the strategy of the company, something not done by many companies. If such a committee is formed, the chief executive officer should develop a set of objectives. Wommack suggested identifying someone in the organization as the chief strategic officer (CSO)—not to be confused with the chief staff officer— who would develop a strategic philosophy. The CSO should be at an organizational level at least equal to that of the chief operating officer (COO) and must have control over resources likely to affect change (i.e., capital funds). In this approach, the board reviews and approves corporate-level objectives (as determined by the chief executive officer) and broad strategic directions (as determined by the chief strategic officer). The chief strategic officer then provides the board objectives committee with strategic guidelines for each strategic business unit. With this information, board members can evaluate the soundness of decisions, such as capital allocations, by relating them to the strategic guidelines.

Wommack has provided some additional information on the job characteristics of the chief strategic officer. First, the job cannot be done by a group; if strategic change must occur, group consensus usually will not bring it about. In addition,

---

[7]Stanley C. Vance, *Corporate Leadership: Boards, Directors, and Strategy* (New York: McGraw-Hill, 1983), p. 62.

[8]Andrews, "From the Boardroom."

success in effecting strategic changes is in inverse proportion to the number of duties the chief strategic officer has. The chief strategic officer also must make direct contact with every level at which strategic choices are considered rather than waiting for these ideas to filter up.[9] In practice, however, the CSO role has not materialized in many companies. Working counter to Wommack's concept is the growing realization that the CEO and CSO are in reality one and the same. Thus, a separate CSO may not appear to exist on paper, but one *does* exist in the form of the CEO.

Additional Board Approaches. Another suggestion in terms of board involvement in strategic management is having outside directors conduct a performance audit. This would involve appraising the results of management performance so that the board can evaluate the success of strategy and objectives. The problem with this technique is that the results of strategic decisions may not be known for many years, and it is foolish to wait that long before evaluating strategy. This would, however, begin to involve the board in the consideration and evaluation of strategic alternatives. An alternative would be for the board to set standards of performance for management and then evaluate management based on achievement of these standards. This suggests placing some levels of strategic planning in the hands of the board and leaving only the decisions as to what means will be used to accomplish these plans in the hands of management. The prevailing opinion, however, is that business-level strategy formulation is properly the management's domain.

In Summary.   During the past 5–10 years, there has been strong interest in the United States in increasing the role of the board in strategy-related activities, for some of the reasons mentioned in the preceding paragraphs. In actuality, however, these expectations have not been realized.[10] What we have seen, however, is increased ''hands-on'' involvement in *select* areas of responsibility, such as corporate control. That is, the board must be intimately involved in actions affecting corporate ownership (mergers, takeovers, LBOs, and the like), and in decisions likely to have a major impact on corporate control. Examples would be enterprise and corporate-level actions involving the corporate purpose, the corporate portfolio of businesses, and restructuring actions. This is because the board is responsible to the stockholders and has an obligation to maximize their welfare. In recent years, we have seen boards take their powers—and responsibilities—much more seriously in these areas.[11]

There are no concrete answers as to how deeply the board of directors should be involved in strategic management. However, board members have no choice

---

[9]W. W. Wommack, ''The Board's Most Important Function,'' *Harvard Business Review* 57, no. 5 (September-October 1979), p. 58.

[10]Joseph Rosenstein, ''Why Don't U.S. Boards Get More Involved in Strategy?'' *Long-Range Planning* 20, no. 3 (March 1987), pp. 30–34.

[11]Arthur Fleischer, Jr., G. C. Hazard, Jr., and M. Z. Klipper, *Board Games: The Changing Shape of Corporate Power* (New York: Little, Brown, 1988).

but to get involved in some way in strategic management. They can no longer afford to act as a rubber stamp for managerial decisions when they should be protecting the interests of the owners. A challenge for the future may be to develop a means of involving directors in strategic management in such a way that the amount of time they devote to board matters is not increased.

Role of the Consultant

Outside consultants can be important in strategic management, as they perform their customary roles of defining, analyzing, and solving problems for their clients. Despite the old adage that ''a consultant is someone who borrows your watch to tell you what time it is, and then keeps the watch as payment,'' consultants *can* make a contribution in four areas of strategic management: corporate strategy formulation; business-unit strategy formulation; strategic planning system design; and general education and transfer of experience.[12]

Corporate Strategy Formulation.   Corporate strategy issues essentially involve resource allocation, such as allocation of cash among existing business units and the proportion of assets invested in the various businesses. The pattern of resource allocation can be examined and evaluated by consultants. Sometimes outsiders can see situations and simple theories more clearly and objectively than can insiders. Consultants can often perform objective analyses for the company and advise it on the practices and experiences of other companies.

Business-Unit Strategy Formulation.   The predominant use of strategy consultants is in the area of analyzing and recommending strategies for individual business units.

Strategic Planning System Design.   Another area in which consultants can be helpful is in the process area, recommending, establishing, or modifying the strategic planning systems and techniques used by the organization.

General Education and Transfer of Experience.   The body of strategic management is growing so rapidly that it is difficult for practitioners to keep up with it. Consultants—experts and specialists in the field—can brief and train practicing managers on the latest process and content knowledge in the field. Consultants are in a position to keep up with developing techniques, philosophies, and attitudes. It is especially important for top management to be aware of the latest philosophies and attitudes. Also, consultants can often act as facilitators, creating the consensus necessary for the formulation and implementation of strategic decisions.

---

[12]Peter Carroll, ''The Role of the Consultant,'' in *Handbook of Business Strategy,* ed. W. D. Guth (Boston: Warren, Gorham & Lamont, 1985), p. 28–11.

In the final analysis, consultants, no matter how knowledgeable, cannot (and should not) *make* strategic decisions for management. Management must make its own decisions, using the consultants only for advice, training, analysis, and temporary assistance.

CURRENT STATE OF THE ART

Chapters 1 through 11 represent a summary of the state of the art of the strategic management field, as it has developed over the past 15–20 years. As noted, strategic management is more than strategic planning; it includes formulation, implementation and planning, and control. In addition, an organization may be required to make strategic decisions at several levels: at the enterprise (or mission) level; at the corporate level, relating to its selection of businesses and their interrelationships; at the business-unit level; and at the functional and operations levels.

Strategic management is a logical—but creative—process. The process includes an assessment of the strategic situation facing the organization, including environmental analysis, resource analysis, management's vision, and consideration of the values and expectations of stakeholders. The environmental analysis involves diagnosing the general environment as well as the competitive environment, including a look at markets that can range from local, to regional, to national, to international, to global in scope.

Another important part of the process includes strategic decision making—formulating, evaluating, and selecting strategies. We saw that the manager may choose from certain generic business-level strategies, such as strategies for positioning the business, distinguishing the business (including differentiation and scope), plus those for increasing, redefining, and reducing scope. At the corporate level, general-purpose differentiation, concentration, and restructuring strategies exist. In contrast, certain strategies must be specific; the appropriate approach can vary by phase of the life cycle, type of business, and certain other factors.

Certain strategic planning systems and techniques are helpful. For example, determining a business's competitive advantages and critical success factors can greatly assist in formulating and evaluating strategies, as well as in determining management's information needs. Preparation of scenarios and contingency plans can help the manager deal with an uncertain and risk-laden environment.

Organizations often structure themselves differently for strategic decision purposes (using strategic business units) than for operational purposes. Also, strategy is implemented through the operational organization, which can sometimes result in a lack of continuity and puts a premium on strategic control activities.

Finally strategy processes and content are different and less developed in organizations other than the medium-to-large, for-profit corporation. These differences must be realized and taken into account when dealing with other increasingly common types of organizations.

A number of practices currently exist in leading organizations that represent the latest "best-business practices," or state of the art. These include the points described in the following paragraphs.

Creating a Vision

Strategic management is not a mechanistic, "by the numbers" exercise in analyzing forecasts and evaluating alternatives. It begins with the creation of a "vision" by top management of what *can* be, what the future can bring, and results in developing plans for how to get there. It is not enough to create a vision; management must "build a dream" for people in the organization by articulating that vision so that others can understand, appreciate, and commit to it. Forward thinking management teams today are beginning the process with "vision statements," so that key stakeholders and others can share the dream.

Greater Management Involvement

There is an increasing awareness that strategic management activities are the responsibility of line managers, not planners. The planner should function as an analyst and facilitator, managing the *process* and stimulating planning by the line. With this realization, and as managers became more comfortable in formulating and analyzing strategies, companies can reduce the number of staff planners in their employ. This does not suggest that the importance of the *function* is being reduced; rather, it is being assumed by line managers, which is as it should be. In reality, this is an increase in the function's central role in the management of organizations.

Shorter and Simpler Plans

Along with the trend toward greater management involvement has come a change in the type of plans organizations prepare. Managers are more interested in strategic plans that get to the point, plans that describe the strategies themselves rather than containing detailed analyses, budgets, and the like. General Electric's CEO, John Welch, goes so far as to assert that a strategy can be summarized in a page or two; it is different from appropriation requests, product development plans, detailed implementation plans, and the like.[13] As does GE, companies such as Ford and Control Data also put an upper limit on the length of their strategic plans—such as 20 to 30 pages—so that they focus on

---

[13]"The New Breed of Strategic Planner," *Business Week*, September 17, 1984, p. 66.

strategies, not analysis and detail. In addition to brevity, plans increasingly stress flexibility, simplicity, and workability.

Less-Structured Planning Processes

In line with the above processes, leading companies appear to be downplaying the highly formal, structured planning process in favor of more flexible, creative, qualitative, and intuitive processes. The emphasis is on creative strategic thinking, developing the vision of where the company should go and how it should get there.

Restructuring and Internal Growth

Diversified growth through acquisitions is on the decline, replaced by restructuring and internal growth. Many past acquisitions have been disappointing, and corporate raiders have forced many companies to refocus and concentrate their corporate portfolios. In addition, related-diversified firms have been shown to outperform others, and internal growth seems to avoid a number of merger-related problems.

An Emphasis on Functional Coordination

A recent study showed an increase in emphasis on marketing, R&D and technology, and computers and information systems in planning. This is a realization of the central importance of these functions to both the content of the strategies and the strategy-development process. Of additional interest was a relative decline in the importance of finance, reflecting a realization that corporate planning today is much broader in scope than conventional budgeting and control.[14]

A Look at High-Growth Companies

A recent study by the American Business Council of midsize corporations ($10 to 400 million in sales) with high-growth characteristics (typically 30 to 40 percent per year) revealed several interesting findings. First, these firms tend to be in rather ''dull'' industries, as mundane as hotel laundry, and not in high-tech

---

[14]V. Ramanujam, J. C. Camillus, and N. Venkatraman, ''Trends in Strategic Planning,'' in *Strategic Planning and Management Handbook*, ed. W. R. King and D. I. Cleland (New York: Van Nostrand Reinhold, 1987), p. 615.

and glamor areas. Second, the organizations tend to pursue niche markets. They also tend to stress value, not price, often charging premium prices for their products and services. They tend to be fast on their feet, moving into markets quickly and getting out when growth of the niche declines. Their employees tend to either have or look forward to ownership in the company. Their top executives tend to be hard drivers, with the CEO many times putting in 12 to 14 hour days. A primary concept in these companies is to "fix it *before* it breaks," relying on preventive actions and not waiting until the crisis stage. Further, they tend to act as disciplined, organized entrepreneurs. They are willing to experiment and try new approaches, and work to eliminate red tape, Finally, values tend to be clearly understood and shared throughout the organization.[15]

EMERGING TRENDS

A number of trends are currently evident, as strategic management progresses from its first generation to a more mature field. Many of these trends are confusing to some observers, but they need not be. While the majority of such trends were mentioned in the preceding chapters, they are highlighted here for perspective and emphasis.

Improved Strategy Frameworks

The generic strategy classifications of Derek Abell, Michael Porter, and others have contributed greatly to our understanding of the principal types of strategies available to and appropriate for business units and corporations. Analysis of these frameworks by notable scholar/experts such as Hofer and Mintzberg have pointed up deficiencies in the options, and improved classifications have been proposed. This evolutionary process is likely to continue until a commonly accepted "general theory" of basic strategies is developed and supported by research. The framework presented in this book (Chapters 6 and 7) represents an emerging view of generic strategies.

Better Information and Tools

Efforts such as the profit impact of market strategies (PIMS) project are making a definite contribution to the practice of strategic management. As relationships between decision variables and actual results are examined, specific decisions are becoming more objective and less dependent on rules of thumb, mythical

---

[15]Michael Kami, *Strategic Planning for Changing Times* (Dayton, Ohio: Cassette Recording Co., 1984).

relationships, and unproven hypotheses. Specific guidelines are being provided concerning the *content* of strategic decisions, rather than placing an overreliance on process-related suggestions. One problem with PIMS data in particular has been the proprietary nature of the research findings; however, the Strategic Planning Institute has been liberal in allowing publication of general findings. Better information is also becoming available to decision makers who utilize custom-designed strategic information systems geared to critical success factors for the organization and the industry.

Providers of goods and services are looking more to the ultimate consumer for feedback information and in designing their offerings for the marketplace. For example, Goodyear's ultimate customer is not Ford or General Motors, but the person who buys the automobile. However, some suppliers have tended to lose sight of the final customer. As an illustration, fireplace manufacturers have tended to consider lumber stores, home improvement centers, and the like as their customers, assuming that the public buys the product largely for fuel savings, energy saving, and related reasons. A study of the final customers revealed that nostalgia is the number one reason for purchase, and that Florida ranks high in the number of fireplace sales per capita.[16]

Many of the tools used for strategic management are being refined both in terms of their mechanics and their role in the process. There is less a reliance on simplistic portfolio models and a greater realization that the picture they provide is just one input to the decision process.

Rewarding Strategic Performance

Traditionally, managers have been rewarded primarily on the "bottom line," profit and cash-flow measures of an organization's performance. As seen in Chapter 10, reward systems that *do not* treat all business-unit managers equally are starting to be developed with the realization that different units can and do have very different goals and objectives. Also, measures and rewards are becoming more closely tied to the costs and results of implementing a particular strategy, rather than strictly to operational results.

Development of Strategic Managers

Companies have long indulged in transferring employees from one division, plant, function, or location to another to develop management. The emphasis has been on "learning the business" by gaining experience in various facets— usually operational entities—of the organization. But what of strategic experi-

---

[16]Ibid.

ence? Why not transfer future top strategic decision makers between business units possessing differing strategic characteristics? In this way the manager's on-the-job development would be specifically orchestrated to expose him or her to a preselected range of *strategic* situations, rather than to differing *operational* situations that may (or may not) result in optimum exposure to strategic learning. Further, we have come to realize that the skills required by top-level managers (including strategic management and general managers) are not the same as those required by managers in general. The abilities discussed in Chapter 10 are difficult to learn in the classroom as well as on the job, and may require special developmental techniques and approaches.

Fostering Organizational Learning

It is not only the individual manager who must develop; the organization must "learn" as well. In this light, the role of corporate planning departments and systems is becoming less one of "preparing plans" than it is one of enhancing the organization's ability to learn. That is, making the organization's managers aware and appreciative of significant environmental and competitive changes and trends early so that timely action can be taken. The key is management's "quick study" understanding of the trends and their implications. The realization that planning is more about fostering learning processes than it is about developing specific plans is beginning to take hold in leading corporations.

Interorganizational Strategies

Strategies involving joint ventures, or "strategic alliances," have started to become more common and may continue to grow more so in the future. Such arrangements can exist between two firms, such as Microsoft and IBM for personal computer software development, or between several firms. Actually, such strategies exist in organizations ranging from trade associations, lobbying groups, and industry committees to joint ventures and even collusions and cartels. OPEC is an example. Another, perhaps less threatening, is the sharing of automatic teller machine networks by banks, as is the creation of Sematech and the Microelectronics and Computer Technology Corp. to perform research for various firms in the semiconductor industry.

Systematic Board Involvement

As more strategic alliances form, as more merger, acquisition, diversification, concentration, and restructuring decisions are made, and as more enterprise-level strategic questions arise, we are seeing the need to more systematically involve the board in certain types of strategic decisions. Therefore, guidelines for involving boards in various levels and types of strategic decisions are evolving. A recent study found that virtually every board influences decisions regarding numerous strategy-related issues. Unfortunately, many do not recognize that they are involved in strategic decision making.[17] This is likely to change.

Considering Culture and Climate

It is being recognized that organizational culture can be a source of sustained competitive advantage for a firm. That is, what a firm is able to accomplish may be determined as much by its culture as by its strategic plan—strategies are only as good as the culture, climate, and structure that exist to implement them and carry them out. Therefore, the corporate culture and its role in successfully implementing proposed strategies is starting to be explicitly considered. For example, IBM pulled back from its acquisition strategy after experiencing culture clashes with its ROLM subsidiary.

Contingent Strategy Processes

It was shown that top-down strategies, determined by the corporate level, are best if coordination between business units is critical, and bottom-up (business determined) strategies are best if financial performance is most important. Corporations are beginning to employ approaches contingent on the needs of their particular situations, rather than "one size fits all" prescriptions. Likewise, planning systems contingent on the type of environment have been proposed. The use of structured processes in "high-velocity" environments has been found to be associated with high-performing firms, for example. Such advances in prescribed processes are likely to continue.

Strategic and Operational Harmony

The accepted approach of creating market-oriented strategic business units to serve as the structure for corporate- and business-level planning in multibusiness companies has some disadvantages. While it provided a common denominator for defining separate businesses for which separate plans had to be developed, the SBUs did not always coincide with operating divisions. Thus, this approach required two separate structures—one for strategic planning and one for

---

[17]J. W. Henke, Jr., "Involving the Board of Directors in Strategic Planning," *The Journal of Business Strategy* 7, no. 2 (Fall 1986), pp. 87–95.

operations. If the SBUs and operating divisions could not be reconciled, this dual structure may have been a necessary evil. Some organizations, however, are forcing a merger of the strategic and operating organizations—resulting in one set of "businesses"—and a single structure for both. To the extent that this harmony is possible, a more efficient process of planning *and* implementation can result.

THE COMING SECOND GENERATION

Strategic management is maturing. As is true of any adolescent, the field has had some growing pains, inconsistent behavior, and confusion in terms of the future, while showing potential and long-term promise. Future directions of the field may be speculated on.

Managing Global Integration

The term *global* has begun to appear so frequently that it has become a buzzword. Buzzword or not, the concept is likely to be one that strategic managers will have to live with (and pursue) for the foreseeable future. And global does not mean Japan, Europe, China, and a few other countries. In 1970, North America and Western Europe generated over 60 percent of the world's manufacturing output; by 2000 it will likely be less than 40 percent. Most of the growth will come from a host of newly industrialized countries (NICs).[18]

Managers will have to reorient their concepts of industry structure and strategic groups to incorporate relevant international variables; that is, a firm's "relevant environment" may contain global variables and intercultural dimensions. The firm's (particularly multibusiness firms) structure, systems, processes, and strategies will be affected. Specifically, strategic managers will likely be affected by European integration, Pacific Rim competitors, Russian *glasnost* (openness), and the emergence of 24-hour capital markets. Defensively, domestic (niche) suppliers will need to develop means of beating or neutralizing the global strategies of the multinationals.

Strategies for NFPs and Services

The not-for-profit sector has consistently lagged behind the for-profit sector in strategic thinking and the use of up-to-date approaches. It is in many of these organizations that planning is an ad-hoc process still in Phase I or II (financial planning or forecast-based planning), resulting in voluminous budget and operationally oriented

---

[18]R. Lamb and Paul Shrivastava, eds., *Advances in Strategic Management,* vol. 4 (Greenwich, Conn.: JAI Press, 1986), p. xvii.

documents. In the foreseeable future, many such organizations, including those in the service sector, will be forced to think strategically, bringing themselves into the modern-day world of flexible, externally oriented plans and processes.

The Long-Term Vision

An important realization on the part of management is that the organization may continue to exist long after current management has departed. In this light, a major goal of any management team should be to steadily build the organization toward some long-term future dream, rather than to impatiently focus on the here and now and current accomplishments. A major item in management succession activities should be a discussion and sharing of the organization's very long term—say 30, 50, even 100 years into the future—and what type of managers are needed for the next phase of this progression.

This is in line with the nature of strategic management, since significant strategic shifts in large enterprises can take years, if not decades, to accomplish. Thus, individual strategic moves have greater purpose and relevance if they are part of a continuum that has been building for years and is part of a *purposeful* evolutionary process. Major strategic decisions are not ad hoc but are formulalted and evaluated on the basis of their contribution to the long-term direction of the enterprise.[19]

Maximizing Stakeholder Value

It is likely that we will see a shift from the goal of maximizing short-term shareholder value to one of long-term growth of different measures of value to a broader range of stakeholders. Recent corporate restructurings have raised the question of whether portfolio managers of institutional shareholders are the proper constituents that top management and their strategies should attempt to satisfy. Should these groups (and other short-term investors) be in the "drivers seat"? There is a need for techniques and measures geared to the maximization of long-term stakeholder value, including means to assess and rationalize the values and expectations of various stakeholder groups. Pioneering efforts by firms such as NCR are already under way.

Improved Performance Measures

Along with the need to maximize stakeholder value (or returns) from the firm will come the need for improved performance measures. Such measures will

---

[19]J. B. Quinn, *Strategies for Change: Logical Incrementalism* (Homewood, Ill.: Richard D. Irwin, 1980), p. 145.

likely include yardsticks to best measure the welfare of each major stakeholder group, as well as means of assessing firm performance on a multistakeholder basis. The latter goal may require the development of completely new performance measures. Improved measures would also allow the firm to better assess the performance of diverse business units, building on the recent promise shown by value-added performance measures.[20] Finally, better measures would aid management in evaluating the results of strategic decisions and in other aspects of strategic control.

Practical, Contingent Research Data

Medical practitioners look to research-oriented medical schools for the latest findings in their field. The case of management is not yet similar. Hopefully, as strategic management matures, less time and effort will be spent studying the practitioner, and more will be spent on underlying disciplines and relationships. As we have seen, appropriate strategies depend on the measure of performance, type of industry, life-cycle stage, and other factors. Consequently, creation of a set of contingent relationships would appear to be a logical next step for research in the field. This would highlight the major areas where research voids exist. In addition, the practicing manager could use such contingent relationships and their research findings as a guide in the formulation of strategy alternatives.

For example, we have recently learned that in many instances, internal growth is preferable to growth by acquisition. Also, related diversification produces superior financial returns, as compared to unrelated diversification. However, the M-form of organization (divisionalized) works better for the unrelated-diversified firm than for the related (which performs best with the U-form). At the business-unit level, researchers are attempting to learn correlation and cause/effect relationships between an appropriate group of generic strategies and business performance. Additional studies are investigating the roles of environment, structure, and strategy on performance. Late results indicate that interactions between the variables are the dominant influences on performance.[21] This means that managers will need to consider the interaction, or fit, between the combination of variables when making strategic decisions. Thus, we are seeing the beginnings of a contingency-based set of research data and prescriptions, which will become increasingly valuable to strategic decision makers in the future.

---

[20]N. E. Swanson and L. A. Digman, "A Value-Added Management Support System," *International Journal on Policy and Information* 12, no. 2 (December 1988), pp. 1–15.

[21]S. E. Tjan and L. A. Digman, "The Interaction Effects of Environment, Structure, and Strategy on Performance," *Proceedings of the Midwest Decision Sciences Institute,* April 1989.

Contributions from DSS/AI/ES

Decision support systems (DSS) are making contributions to many management decisions, via the organization's management information system. Artificial intelligence (AI) and expert systems (ES) are also beginning to assist in certain decision tasks. As more strategic research data is gathered, analyzed, and structured into data bases and contingent relationships, computer-based tools and systems will gradually help the strategic decision maker as well. It is not likely, however, that major portions of strategic decisions will be "automated" through these approaches, but certain amenable analyses and subdecisions will likely lend themselves to this approach (e.g., multiple scenario analysis)[22], allowing the decision maker to focus on the more judgmental, intuitive, and creative aspects of the task.

Sustaining Networks and Cooperation

Competition has been a byword in the strategy field. However, there are numerous instances where cooperation may be beneficial to the "competitors." Interorganizational strategies, such as joint ventures and strategic alliances, are already a step in this direction. However, collective, cooperative strategies could be formulated to respond to environmental challenges and to influence, through an interorganizational network, the nature of the environment itself. In the future, we are likely to see more collective endeavors, whether at the national level in the form of an industrial policy or at the unit level between two or more businesses.[23]

CONCLUSIONS

In this, the final chapter, the role of two quasi-inside participants in the strategic management process—consultants and boards of directors—were examined. The main points in strategic management were summarized, with the conclusion that the end of the first generation of development in the field is approaching. Currently there is a transition to an emerging second generation offering more focus and maturity to the practitioner and the researcher. But the field is not diminishing in importance. While responsibility for strategic planning in company after company has been taken out of the hands of the planning

---

[22]Ruth S. Raubitschek, "Multiple Scenario Analysis and Business Planning," in *Advances in Strategic Management*, ed. Robert Lamb and Paul Shrivastava, vol. 5 (Greenwich, Conn.: JAI Press, 1988), pp. 181–205.

[23]Charles Fombrun and W. G. Astley, "Strategies of Collective Action," in *Advances in Strategic Management*, ed. R. Lamb, vol. 2, (Greenwich, Conn.: JAI Press, 1983), p. 125.

departments and given to the general managers, the role is growing. In short, the consensus among top executives in major corporations is overwhelming: "You won't become a top manager unless you learn to manage strategically."[24] You will also need to think strategically to work for and with such individuals. Strategic management is not primarily a set of concepts and models; it is a way of thinking and acting. A strategy, then, can be thought of as the firm's "vision in action."

---

[24]J. W. Patten, *How to Become a Strategic Manager,* Business Week Executive Program Brochure, 1985.

Appendix A

Financial Ratios

Liquidity Ratios

$$\text{Current ratio} = \frac{\text{Current assets}}{\text{Current liabilities}}$$

$$\text{Quick ratio} = \frac{\text{Current assets} - \text{Inventory}}{\text{Current liabilities}}$$

$$\text{Defensive interval} = \frac{\text{Cash} + \text{Short-term marketable securities} + \text{Accounts receivable}}{\text{Daily operating expenses}}$$
(days)

Leverage Ratios

$$\text{Debt ratio} = \frac{\text{Total debt}}{\text{Total assets}}$$

$$\text{Debt/equity ratio} = \frac{\text{Total debt}}{\text{Stockholders' equity}}$$

$$\text{Long-term debt/equity ratio} = \frac{\text{Long-term debt}}{\text{Stockholders' equity}}$$

$$\text{Times interest earned} = \frac{\text{Net income before taxes} + \text{Interest expense}}{\text{Interest expense}}$$

Profitability Ratios

$$\text{Profit margin} = \frac{\text{Net income}}{\text{Net sales}}$$

$$\text{Return on investment (ROI)} = \frac{\text{Net income}}{\text{Average stockholders' equity}}$$

$$\text{Return on assets (ROA)} = \frac{\text{Net income}}{\text{Average total assets}}$$

$$\text{Return on capital employed (ROCE)} = \frac{\text{Net income}}{\text{Average long-term debt} + \text{Stockholders' equity}}$$

$$\text{Return on value added (ROVA)} = \frac{\text{Net income}}{\text{Value added}}$$

Activity Ratios

$$\text{Accounts receivable turnover} = \frac{\text{Credit sales}}{\text{Average accounts receivable}}$$

$$\text{Average collection period} = \frac{\text{Average accounts receivable} \times 365}{\text{Credit sales}}$$

$$\text{Inventory turnover} = \frac{\text{Cost of goods sold}}{\text{Average inventory}}$$

$$\text{Days of inventory} = \frac{\text{Average inventory} \times 365}{\text{Cost of goods sold}}$$

$$\text{Working capital turnover} = \frac{\text{Sales}}{\text{Average working capital}}$$

$$\text{Fixed asset turnover} = \frac{\text{Sales}}{\text{Average net fixed assets}}$$

$$\text{Total asset turnover} = \frac{\text{Sales}}{\text{Average total assets}}$$

$$\text{Fixed assets per sales dollar} = \frac{\text{Average net fixed assets}}{\text{Sales}}$$

$$\text{Total assets per sales dollar} = \frac{\text{Average total asset}}{\text{Sales}}$$

Common Stock Ratios

$$\text{Earnings per share} = \frac{\text{Net income available for common}}{\text{Common shares outstanding}}$$

$$\text{Cash flow per share} = \frac{\text{After-tax profits} + \text{Depreciation}}{\text{Common shares outstanding}}$$

$$\text{Book value per share} = \frac{\text{Shareholders' equity}}{\text{Common shares outstanding}}$$

$$\text{Market to book value} = \frac{\text{Market price per share}}{\text{Book value per share}}$$

$$\text{Dividend yield} = \frac{\text{Annual dividends per share}}{\text{Market price per share}}$$

Coverage Ratios

$$\text{Cash flow coverage} = \frac{\text{Cash flow}}{\text{Interest} + \dfrac{\text{Principal payments}}{1 - \text{Tax rate}}}$$

$$\text{Fixed charge coverage} = \frac{\text{Earnings before interest and taxes} + \text{Lease obligations}}{\text{Interest} + \text{Lease obligations}}$$

Appendix B

Strategic Planning Worksheet

The strategic planning worksheet, shown as Figure 1, is designed to facilitate use of the simple, flexible planning process described in Chapter 9. It is particularly useful in organizing one's strategic thinking regarding a given business unit, and provides the basis for development of the complete strategic plan.

This completed form is the core of the strategic plan for the business. The form is self-explanatory, and forces management to think through the business unit's broad goals and specific objectives, as well as its critical success factors. Next, the five most critical environmental factors likely to affect the business over the next five years are listed, followed by the five most promising actions (strategies) to deal with each. Finally, implementation responsibility and schedule are listed for each of the actions.

FIGURE 1 Strategic Planning Worksheet

Business Unit	Critical Environmental Factors	Action Items	Implementation Responsibility	Implementation Schedule
Name _____				
Broad Goals	1.	1. 2. 3. 4. 5.		
1.				
2.	2.	1. 2. 3. 4. 5.		
3.				
4.	3.	1. 2. 3. 4. 5.		
5.				
Specific Objectives	4.	1. 2. 3. 4. 5.		
1.				
2.	5.	1. 2. 3. 4. 5.		
3.				
4.	6.	1. 2. 3. 4. 5.		
5.				
Critical Success Factors				
1.				
2.				
3.				
4.				
5.				
6.				

Appendix C

Strategic Plan Example

Companies use varying degrees of detail in preparing their strategic plans. Some use a one- or two-page summary form similar to the one used by Borg-Warner (Figure 1). Short summaries give corporate-level executives a "snapshot" of the strategic business unit (SBU), its business description, market attractiveness and business strengths, matrix position, strategies and action plans, environmental issues, and forecast and actual financial goals and capital requirements by year. But summaries give only parts of the plan, which can become quite lengthy. For this reason, many firms set an upper limit on the length of the total plan, for example, 40 pages or so. The detailed plan itself typically consists of the following segments:

- Executive summary.
- Statement of mission/charter.
- Appraisal/situation analysis:
    Corporate environmental assumptions and guidelines.
    Division environmental assumptions.
    External analysis: Market and competition, opportunities and threats.
    Internal analysis: Strengths and weaknesses:
        Product-line analysis.
        Evaluation of previous plan.
- Objectives and goals:
    Characteristics and criteria.
    Specific goals.
    Gap-closing actions.
- Strategies.
- Action programs.
- Contingency plans, alternatives, and scenarios.[1]

The Borg-Warner form typically would be part of the executive summary, a condensed version of the overall plan. Instructions for completing an executive summary are shown in Exhibit 1. Exhibit 2 shows the format of the appraisal, including the major

---

[1]Rochelle O'Connor, *Corporate Guides to Long-Range Planning*, Report No. 687 (New York: Conference Board, 1976), p. iii.

407

FIGURE 1   Borg-Warner Planning Form

Summary Form for Strategic Plan		
Strategic Plan Summary (19 ___ to ___) for _____		
I. Business description		

A. Nature and scope	B. Industry description	C. Markets served

II. Analysis	Strategic characteristics		
A. Market attractiveness factors	High	Medium	Low
B. Business strength factors			

assumptions, a breakdown of the economic assumptions, and market analysis and penetration for the firm. Exhibit 3 details a typical external analysis of competitors, while Exhibit 4 shows an action program summary, relating strategic objectives, strategies, tactical goals and actions, resource needs, schedule, and responsibility. Examples of optimistic and pessimistic contingency plans are illustrated in Exhibit 5.[2]

It should be evident that strategic plans are detailed, thorough, and require a significant amount of work to prepare. Many times, it is difficult to keep them within specified page limits, but it is their quality and consistency—not their length—that is important.

---

[2]Ibid., pp. 26, 33–36, 48, 81, 87–88.

FIGURE 1 (*concluded*)

III. Matrix position

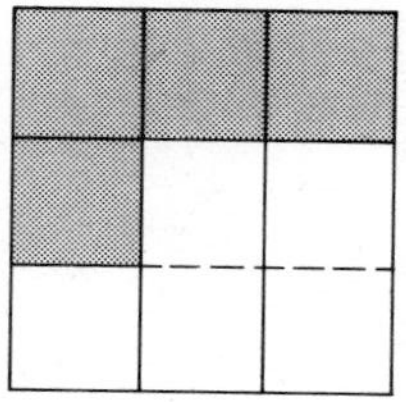

IV. Strategy
   A. Strategic objective
   B. Action plans

VI. Environmental issue
(thousands of dollars)

V. Sample financial goals	1990	Forecast 1991	Actual 1991	Forecast 1992	Actual 1992	Forecast 1993	Actual 1993	Forecast 1994	Actual 1994	1995	1996	1997	1998
Sales													
Returns													
Capital requirements													

EXHIBIT 1 Executive Summary Instructions—A Construction Equipment Company

---

Executive Summary—Overview

The purpose of this section is to summarize the results of the proposed plan. It includes a management summary letter, financial summary, and a brief description of where the division is going and how it expects to get there.

Executive Summary—Instructions

This is a cover letter from the division president to group vice president. While no specific format is dictated, certain items are suggested below that should probably be covered in the summary. It is intended that this summary should enable the division president to set the stage for the formal plan in his or her own words.

Items that should be incorporated in the executive summary may include:

Summary of profit and sales goals over the next five years including:

Sales
Profit before tax (PBT)
PBT as percent of sales
Percent ROA

Significant characteristics of the division:

Opportunities
Strengths
Weaknesses
Threats

Basic strategy of the division
Brief summary of the development plan
Brief summary of functional plans

Marketing
Engineering
Manufacturing
Purchasing/Material Control
M.I.S.
Personnel
Export
Financial

Complete financial summary
List of significant events

The summary letter can be of any length, but two or three pages with appropriate attachments should suffice if the letter is confined to significant points. Please refer to the Planning Guide for specific instructions on the [company's] planning process.

Source: Adapted from Rochelle O'Connor, *Corporate Guides to Long-Range Planning,* Report No. 687 (New York: Conference Board, 1976), p. 26.

EXHIBIT 2   The Appraisal—A Construction Equipment Company

Business Plan (1990–1994)

Section II

Appraisal—Overview

The selection and organization of information and analyses, in a form that is useful for planning, is the purpose of this section. This includes economic, environment, and performance assumptions, as well as other factors affecting business, including government regulations. Market analysis and company penetration for each business segment are also included.

Appraisal—Instructions

The appraisal is comprised of the following five sections:

I. *Environment*—This should include a brief description of external and internal environment factors and assumptions that underlie division sales and profit forecasts. Concise statements giving the assumption and outlining the resulting action are recommended. Divisions should not limit their assumptions to the list provided but add or substitute appropriate items. The major purpose of the assumptions list is to set the stage or present the environment in which division management feels it will be operating during the subsequent five years. Specific forecasts of division economic assumptions should be shown in the second exhibit. Business Planning will publish a series of five-year forecasts that can be used as guidelines in developing forecasts relating to your specific situations.

_____ Division   Date _____

Business Plan (1990–1994)

Major Assumptions of Division Business

Area/Item	Assumption	Action
Economic	No-growth economy in 1990 with gentle recovery thereafter peaking in 1992.	Improve margins through cost-reduction programs. Expand sales through increased market penetrations.
Inflation		
Market environment		
Competitive environment		
Government legislation		
Other external—energy, etc.		
Internal		
Other		

EXHIBIT 2 *(continued)*

_____ Division   Date _____

Business Plan (1990–1994)

Economic Assumptions

	Percent Change (1984/1989)	Percent Change					Percent Change (1989/1994)
		1990	1991	1992	1993	1994	
Economy—General Indicators							
A. Gross national product							
B. FRB index of industrial production							
C.							
Economic assumption related to division group activity							
A. Intercity truck tonnage							
B. Net farm income							
C.							
D.							
E.							
F.							

II. *Markets*—The initial step in analyzing the markets in which the division competes is to subdivide the business into meaningful segments. Market segments group potential customers according to the similarity of their needs, geographic location, and behavioral response to marketing strategy. In each market segment, it is necessary to obtain a measure of the current and potential markets in units and/or dollars and estimates of the market growth rate. This information for the division, the industry and the resulting market share will be supplied on the appropriate exhibit. Some of the questions and factors that might be considered in developing market segment analyses and in writing the text directed to the exhibit are listed below.

A. *Market Segment Analysis*

1. At what rate has the market been growing?
2. Historically, what are the external market indicators and how do they behave?
3. If industry volume is cyclical, will recovery cause volume to pick up faster than GNP? How cyclical is the industry in relation to GNP?
4. What external environmental factors might cause the industry to grow faster or slower than GNP? (Foreign competition? Competition from other industries? Government regulations and pressures?)
5. Are industry growth rates during the plan years consistent with historical trends? If not, why?

EXHIBIT 2   *(continued)*

_____ Division   Date _____

Business Plan (1990–1994)

Market Analysis and Company Penetration

Total Division Market	1989	1990	1991	1992	1993	1994	Percent Change (1989/1994)
Unit sales (by product group)							
A.							
B.							
C.							
D.							
Industry unit sales							
A.							
B.							
C.							
D.							
Market share							
A.							
B.							
C.							
D.							

B. *Market Penetration Analysis*
  1. Identify and discuss customers.
  2. What are customer needs? (e.g., service, financing, distribution, etc.)
  3. Is the product price sensitive or can brand loyalty be established? What is the impact for the company's share?
  4. Explain the competitive factors that account for the current trend of the company's share, irrespective of whether the trend is up or down.

C. *Impact of Market and Penetration Analyses on Division Long-Range Goals*
  1. Briefly define the division's planned penetration objectives.
  2. Discuss the critical "stumbling blocks" that are preventing goal achievement. Examples might include poor distribution systems, insufficient advertising, too little emphasis on product development, poor product positioning, not enough management depth, etc.
  3. Indicate steps the division will take to increase the company's market penetration; for example, more selling effort, strengthen distribution system, provide better service or more customer financing, etc.
  4. Relate steps that should be taken to achieve plan goals relating to customer needs. Why will steps we are taking to improve penetration satisfy customer needs better than the competition does?
  5. Evaluate competitive reaction to the company's moves to increase penetration.
  6. Are we doing enough to react to moves by competition?

EXHIBIT 2   *(concluded)*

III. *Competition*—This section should include an analysis of the following factors:

  A. *Competitive Product Lines*

  B. *Competitive Strengths and Weaknesses*—Analyze competition versus the company in these areas:

  1. Market share—current and projected
  2. Price position
  3. Product strengths
  4. Distribution systems
  5. Customer image
  6. Sales and income over last five years

  C. Evaluate competition in major international markets with specific reference to U.S.-sourced and foreign-sourced in at least the following areas:

  1. Market share
  2. Relative pricing versus the company
  3. Future marketing planning and product planning assumptions

  D. *Competitive Strategies*—Briefly outline price and product strategies of each major competitor.

IV. *Division Strengths, Weaknesses, Opportunities, Threats*—Evaluate current status of strengths and weaknesses of the division relative to advantageous or disadvantageous *internal* situations in the division. In a similar manner, evaluate advantageous or disadvantageous situations of the division relative to *external* actions by a competitor or in the environment.

V. *Analysis of Previous Strategies*—Finally, in the appraisal section, evaluate the impact of subsequent events on previous strategies. Indicate changes in current strategy to reflect these identified changes in the business environment.

Source: Adapted from Rochelle O'Connor, *Corporate Guides to Long-Range Planning*, Report No. 687 (New York: Conference Board, 1976) pp. 33–36.

EXHIBIT 3   External Analysis Form—A Container Company

Strategic Plan (1990–1994)

(Division)
Key Competitors and Their Strategies

Competition	A	B	C	D
Name				
Estimated sales volume and growth				
Product line				
Customer base				
Market size and growth				
Market share				
Technology				
Method chosen to compete				
Rank as most serious competition				
Now				
1994				

Internal evaluation
  What advantages do we have over competitors?
  What advantages does competition have over us?
  What can we do to counteract competitors'
    strengths or to take advantage of our strengths?

Source: Adapted from Rochelle O'Connor, *Corporate Guides to Long-Range Planning,* Report No. 687 (New York: Conference Board, 1976), p. 48.

EXHIBIT 4 Action Program Summary Form—A Paper Manufacturer

STRATEGIC ACTION PROGRAM SUMMARY

PROGRAM TITLE: *Earnings improvement of the Y—Supplies Business*
PROGRAM PURPOSE: *Strengthen the profitability and defensibility of our position in the Y—Supplies market*

Strategic Objectives	Strategies	Tactical Goals	Tactical Actions	Resources Required	Target Dates Begin	Target Dates End	Responsibility
Profitably commercialize new product YZ and achieve an annual sales rate of 1.5 million units by the end of 1993.	Introduce product YZ with a concentrated promotion campaign into the southeastern region at a premium price.	Annual sales rate of 400,000 units in southeastern region at a minimum price of $5 each by end of 1990.	Launch a four-month direct-mail campaign at city engineers of all cities with population of 5,000 or more.	$25,000 and two labor-months	June 1, 1990	September 30, 1990	Marketing manager of southeastern region
			Launch personal sales contact campaign at city engineers of all cities with 50,000 or more population.	$40,000 and eight labor-months	August 1, 1990	November 1, 1990	Same
			Develop indirect sales channel by adding one distributor in Alabama and Georgia and two in South Carolina.	$100,000 cash investment for capital and two labor-months	April 1990	August 1990	Same

Objective	Program	Strategy	Budget	Start	Completion	Responsible
Build a small initial plant in Birmingham with 1 million-unit capacity which can be doubled in capacity to 2 million units in 1992 if the market sustains a growth rate of 10 percent or more through 1991.	Construct original 1 million-unit plant within total cost budget of $1.3 million.	Use turnkey contract for speedy design and construction of the plant. Specify the X-11 vacuum-molding process in the design of equipment.	$1,300,000 and 20 labor-months	January 1, 1990	August 15, 1990	Project manager
	Start up initial new plant and achieve a direct unit cost under continuous operation of $1.50 per unit by the end of September, 1990.	Complete training program of key personnel prior to completion of construction. Other tactical actions, etc.	$50,000 and 15 labor-months	May 1, 1990	August 1, 1990	Plant manager
Upgrade quality of products Y9 through Y15 and their acceptance in the market while increasing our average Y-gross-margin to 35 percent by the end of 1991.	Reorganize the purchasing department, and so forth.	Use national account purchasing as leverage for, and so forth.				

Source: Adapted from Rochelle O'Connor, *Corporate Guides to Long-Range Planning*, Report No. 687 (New York: Conference Board, 1976), p. 81.

417

EXHIBIT 5 Contingency Plans

Occurrence	Chance (percent)	Trigger	Advance Actions Contingent Actions	Financial Impact	
				New Sales ($000)	Earnings ($000)
IPM Corp. has major prolonged strike starting about August 1.	25%	IPM's labor relations have not substantially improved by July 1.	Advance actions Increase inventory in matching and higher quality lines. (Invest $35,000). Develop promotion campaign and advertising literature aimed at competitive issues of reliable delivery and quality of product. Develop incentives for customer to sign new long-term contract.		
			Contingent actions Offer price concessions on matching lines. Launch promotion and advertising campaigns. Initiate biweekly sales meetings to coordinate new-accounts efforts.	$2,000	$500
The General Corp. will attempt new national accounts direct sales program.	33	They begin servicing their Imperial Food Chain and Ford accounts with direct sales.	Advance actions In February, launch advertising campaign in trade publications stressing long-term loyalty to independent distributors. In March, launch campaign at large accounts emphasizing rush-order service from local distributors. Finance inventory increases at our distributors under guise of economics in distribution. (Invest $20,000.)		
			Contingent actions Initiate missionary sales campaign at medium-sized accounts to assist in taking advantage of competing distributor's letdown. Allow distributor's price concessions to reduce inventory and gain new accounts. Introduce new product-V15 through distributors within two months rather than through direct sales.	$1,000	$200

			Advance actions / Contingent actions	
J.S. Seagull Corp. introduces YZ into Southeastern markets during spring.	20	Seagull issues contract for production of YZ prior to June 1.	**Advance actions** Build inventory of black dye materials required for production of Super-YZ. Complete by May 1. ($20,000 investment.) Develop standby promotion campaign for commercialization of Super-YZ. Complete plans by May 1. **Contingent actions** Drop commercialization of YZ. Accelerate commercialization of Super-YZ. Modify the vacuum-molding process to a vacuum-extrusion process. Launch standby promotion campaign in lieu of planned campaign.	(1,000) (150)
Fuel gas supply interrupted at Birmingham plant.	30	Notice from gas company	**Advance actions** Complete construction of reverse oil tanks by March 1 ($30,000 investment). Locate and contract for oil supply by Feb. 1. Fill tanks by April 1, ($45,000 investment). **Contingent actions** Switch to fuel oil from new reserve tanks.	
The small Lowline Corp. cuts prices at least 10 percent on Product Y5.	30	Lowline announces price cut on Y5.	**Advance actions** Increase our inventory of the higher quality Y8 to 25 percent above normal ($50,000 investment). Develop standby promotional literature designed to emphasize false economy of switching to lower quality and the availability advantages of buying from larger corporation. **Contingent actions** Immediately allow matching price reductions on our superior Y8 and launch promotion campaign.	(100)

Source: Adapted from Rochelle O'Connor, *Corporate Guides to Long-Range Planning*, Report No. 687 (New York: Conference Board, 1976), pp. 87–88.

Acquisition and Divestiture Processes and Methods

ACQUISITION METHODS

There are two basic approaches to gaining control over another firm's assets: buying the assets directly or obtaining an ownership interest in the company's common stock. These approaches can be further broken down into:

1. Acquisition of assets. This involves the purchase of a major portion of a company's assets, requiring approval by its board of directors and/or stockholders. No ownership rights in the actual company are attained by the buyer.
2. Acquisition of stock. There are four ways to attain an interest in a company using this method:
   a. Direct purchase of outstanding stock in the stock market.
   b. Negotiation with major stockholders to acquire part or all of their interests.
   c. Purchase of authorized but unissued shares from the company itself.
   d. A tender offer. For this latter method, the investor publicly announces his or her offer to the stockholders, stipulating the purchase price (which usually is at least 15 percent above market), the number of shares desired, the time period the offer will stand, and what will happen if more or fewer than the desired number of shares are tendered. The investor also must file information with the Securities and Exchange Commission before the announcement and furnish the target's management with the soliciting material.
3. Statutory mergers. These occur under the laws of the state(s) in which the involved companies obtained their charters. One or more of the combining companies give up their separate legal identities to the others, which maintain their own legal identity.
4. Statutory consolidations. All companies involved lose their separate identities and a new corporation is formed.

In these last two approaches, the boards of directors of each company and two thirds of the shareholders of each must approve the combination.

The first approach—acquisition of assets—is normally a "friendly" acquisition, since the target firm's approval is required. Mergers and consolidations are also friendly. Acquisitions via stock purchases, however, can be friendly acquisitions or hostile takeovers, depending on whether or not the target wants to be acquired.

The Acquisition Process

As Peter Drucker has observed, a firm should not begin the acquisition process by looking for a "bargain"; the beginning should involve looking for a good fit with the company's businesses. You do not *start* with the financial figures, you *end* with them. Whether or not the acquisition fits is not negotiable, but the price is. If the acquisition does not fit, price is irrelevant.[1]

Rochelle O'Connor of the Conference Board describes the roles of the inside and outside groups typically involved in the various steps in the acquisition and divestiture processes.[2] As can be seen in Table 1, division management takes the lead in planning and implementing the acquisition; identifying the need, performing the industry analyses, and implementing (postacquisition responsibilities). Corporate management sets the criteria and conducts the negotiations, while finance performs a detailed analysis of the company and works out the details of the deal. Investment bankers usually are key players in locating acquisition candidates for the firm.

In the planning phase, management should define desirable directions for growth and diversification, evaluating corporate strengths and weaknesses in relation to the environment. Specifically, it should determine criteria for such variables as projected market growth rate, market share, degree of regulation, ease of entry, degree of capital or labor intensity, quality of management, profitability, and size.[3]

Different guidelines are necessary for screening related or unrelated diversifiers. For related diversification, companies with functional skills and/or resources that enhance those of the acquiring firm and produce a strategic fit or synergy must be identified. The principles for unrelated diversifiers are improved corporate management of working capital, resource allocation, or capital financing that leads to an improved or less risky cash flow.

The screening process for an acquisition should examine industries, industry subgroups, and companies according to the specific criteria set down. Companies should be evaluated according to a scoring system on each important variable.

The financial evaluation phase should determine:

1. The maximum price that should be paid for the target.
2. The principal areas of financial risk.
3. The implications of the acquisition for earnings, cash flow, and the balance sheet.
4. The best way to finance the takeover.

---

[1]Peter Drucker, "Why Some Mergers Work and Many More Don't," *Forbes,* January 18, 1982, p. 34.

[2]Rochelle O'Connor, *Managing Corporate Development* (New York: Conference Board, 1980), p. 31.

[3]Alfred Rappaport, "Strategic Analysis for More Profitable Acquisitions," *Harvard Business Review* 79, no. 4 (July-August 1979), p. 99.

TABLE 1 Principal Participants in Acquisitions and Divestitures

Activity	Insiders				Outsiders	
	Top management	Division management	Finance	Legal	Consultant	Investment banker
Long-range planning process		✓✓			✓	
Acquisitions and mergers						
Identifying needs or opportunities	✓	✓✓				
Setting criteria	✓✓	✓✓	✓			
Industry analysis		✓✓			✓	
Locating candidates		✓				✓✓
Company analysis		✓	✓✓			✓
Approaching candidate	✓	✓				✓
Conducting negotiations	✓✓			✓		
Closing the deal (terms, methods of payment, etc.)	✓		✓✓	✓✓		
Postacquisition responsibilities		✓✓	✓✓			
Divestitures						
Recommending businesses to spin off	✓	✓				
Locating buyers	✓	✓				✓
Conducting negotiations	✓		✓			
Closing the deal (terms, methods of payment, etc.)	✓		✓✓			

Note: Not all the survey participants indicated the other organizational units or outside intermediaries involved in each aspect of acquisitions and divestitures. From the questionnaire responses where this information was given, ✓✓ indicates the unit or outsider with the greatest involvement in the activity, and ✓ indicates the unit or outsider that also participated to a large degree. In categories where no ✓✓ appears, participation is dispersed fairly equally among the units shown with a ✓.

Source: Adapted from Rochelle O'Connor, *Managing Corporate Development* (New York: Conference Board, 1980), p. 31.

The maximum price to be paid for a potential target should be determined using discounted cash flow to incoporate the time value of money. This requires estimates of:

1. The incremental cash flows expected from the target.
2. The maximum desired rate of return (or cost of capital).
3. The horizon date (beyond which cash flows cannot be reasonably projected).
4. The residual value (assumed market value of the acquisition) at the horizon date.

Above all, keep in mind that there is no fixed price for an acquisition. Book value or stock price may bear little relationship to what a firm is worth to the acquiring company. The acquiring firm should naturally try to buy at as low a price as possible, but never pay more than the target's worth to the firm, regardless of market or book values.

Antitrust Considerations

When making an acquisition, an everpresent concern is the effect the combined companies will have on competition in the industry—whether or not the merger will result in restraint of trade or lessening of competition.

In 1982, the Justice Department unveiled a new set of less restrictive guidelines to be used in scrutinizing mergers for antitrust problems. The new merger guidelines entail extensive economic analysis to determine the proper geographic and product *markets* to which the market concentration index, the Herfindahl Index, will be applied (as opposed to applying it to the industry as a whole).

The Herfindahl Index, a sum of the square of market shares of all the firms in a given market, is used to determine whether a merger should be challenged on the basis of the market concentration the merger would create. (See Table 2.) Industries with indexes below 1,000 (out of a maximum of 10,000) would be considered "unconcentrated," and mergers would not be challenged. If the Herfindahl Index falls between 1,000 and 1,800 after the merger, this would qualify as a "moderately concentrated" industry. In such a case, a Justice Department challenge would be unlikely if the increase resulting from the merger is less than 100 points. Increases of 1,000 points or more most likely would draw a challenge. Markets with an index over 1,800 would be considered "highly concentrated." Mergers in these cases, however, might not be challenged if the increase in the index is below 50 points. Increases between 50 to 100 points would be more likely to be challenged, though various economic factors will be considered by the Justice Department in making this determination. Mergers increasing the index by more than 100 points probably would be challenged.[4]

DIVESTMENT PROCESS

Bettauer described a three-stage analysis when considering a divestiture: deciding, planning, and making the sale.[5]

---

[4]Department of Justice Announces New Guidelines for Evaluating Mergers," *Executive Newsletter* 8, no. 7 (July 9, 1982), p. 2.

[5]Arthur Bettauer, "Strategy for Divestments," *Harvard Business Review,* March-April 1967, p. 116.

TABLE 2   Judging Industrial Concentration

The traditional way to measure concentration has been to add the market shares of the four largest companies, A, B, C, and D. Their combined 50 percent market share would make this a fairly concentrated industry. If D and F wanted to merge, creating the industry's largest producer with 17 percent of the market, the merger would be suspect.

Under the new guidelines, the Justice Department will insure that any merger that does not raise the Herfindahl index above 1,000 is legal. Antitrusters would look at the makeup of the industry after the merger. Combining D's 10 percent and F's 7 percent, and squaring them, raises the Index to 997 virtually assuring legality.

Companies	*Old Method (market share) percent*	*Herfindahl Index (share squared)*
A	16%	256
B	13	169
C	11	121
D	10	100
E	8	64
F	7	49
G	6	36
H	5	25
I	4	16
Others(24)	20	(Est.) 21
Total	100%	857

Industrial Areas with the Highest Herfindahl Indexes		*And the Lowest*	
Military tanks	5,823	Specialty dies and tools	11
Telephone and telegraph equipment	5,026	Concrete blocks	27
Sewing machines	4,047	Metal plating and polishing	31
Cellulosic synthetic fibers	3,189	Commercial lithography	32
Turbines	2,443	Ready-mix concrete	32

Source: "A Loosening of Merger Rules." Reprinted from the May 17, 1982 issue of *Business Week*, p. 120, by special permission, © 1982 by McGraw-Hill, Inc.

Deciding stage

In exploring whether to actually rid the company of an unprofitable or undesirable business, management may need to be somewhat circumspect. If the public, shareholders, competitors, or the employees of the subsidiary find out about a possible sale prematurely, the process could become muddled.

Once it is decided that divestiture is a possibility and the company's board has approved the decision, the division should be evaluated in terms of its future potential and capital requirements. The alternatives of investing more in the division and continuing the status quo should be compared to selling the division off, and opportunity costs should be considered, using discounted cash flow techniques. Possible costs of a divestiture include:

severance compensation, vacation accruals, and pension provisions; demands of key personnel whom purchasers may wish to retain; termination of leases and other commitments; tax obligations; accounting and legal fees; appraisals; finder's fees; executive time; and loss of initiative, momentum, and sales during the negotiation period.

Planning Stage

The approach taken in planning a divestiture is similar to that of a major marketing operation and should involve all functional skills and departments. There are several alternatives to consider, including:

1. *Selling the parts:* An analysis should be undertaken to determine whether parts of the division could be sold separately rather than sold with the entire segment. Extra assets, such as unused real estate or equipment, often can be sold to different parties at good profits instead of being thrown in free with the rest of the business. Disposal can also be facilitated by reducing the inventory in advance, financing receivables, transferring useful equipment to other subsidiaries, and mortgaging or arranging sale and lease back of properties. These actions basically separate earning power from asset value, and could make the business more attractive to smaller buyers.
2. *Varying forms of payment:* Since many acquisitions involve combinations of stock and/or property as well as cash, a willingness to be flexible may enhance the sale's chances.
3. *The spin-off method:* If circumstances permit, a spin-off may be advantageous. A spin-off involves creating a separate company out of the division and distributing some of its shares to the stockholders of the parent company. If the new corporation can attain enough market share on its own through managerial autonomy, despite higher administrative costs, the shareholder will benefit. This method is used when government antitrust settlements demand divestiture, but could also be used for any subsidiary of sufficient size and potential to exist on its own. The stockholders will be better off with shares in the new company if a high enough selling price is unattainable. In the past few years, a form of spin-off called the *leveraged buyout (LBO)* has become popular. The LBO is a sale to business unit management or outsiders, heavily financed by banks. The new owners typically pare the unit drastically to make it more efficient, and the selling company often finds a buyer willing to pay a relatively high price. With a renewed entrepreneurial spirit and some luck, the new owners may turn the unit around, as Victor Kiam did with his purchase of Remington Shaving Co.
4. *Liquidation:* When the possibility of a division's survival is too poor for a chance of a sale or spin-off, it simply must be liquidated. Losses usually occur, but are partially offset by income tax credits. The effects on communities and employees should be anticipated and steps taken to soften the blow.

Making the Sale

Once a plan is adopted, it must be pursued as fast as possible to avoid rumors, employee morale problems, inroads in the business by more aggressive competitors, and customer nervousness.

The search for a buyer can start by eliminating certain parties, such as competitors who could benefit from acquiring the division, companies that key personnel find unattractive, industry leaders with antitrust problems, or, if the seller desires a cash transaction, firms with insufficient funds.

If a candidate can be identified through the process of elimination, an offer should be made to the firm, detailing the proposal. If a buyer cannot be found, other sources may be consulted, such as investment bankers, industry associations, the company's own board of directors, the division's suppliers or customers, or business reference services. Any finder's fee should be agreed on in advance.

Once negotiations are underway, all parties involved (attorneys, bankers, accountants, planners, negotiators) must actively communicate about technical developments. The seller must remain very patient, open, and cooperative, as the buyer will try to uncover anything that could lead to surprises later on.

Part VI

Strategic Management: Cases

INTRODUCTION: LEARNING BY THE CASE METHOD

Courses in strategy and policy are typically taught by relying primarily on the case method of instruction. For many students, this may be a new experience, since most college courses are taught using the lecture and discussion method. In such courses, the student is exposed to concepts, principles, and theories via readings and lectures, and is tested over this substantive material. While this method of teaching is very good for acquiring knowledge and learning concepts and techniques, it is not very effective for developing skills in analyzing business problems, proposing realistic solutions, or developing mature judgment. For these purposes—developing the key skills required by managers—the case method is superior.

In fact, studies have shown that case teaching is clearly more effective than lecture teaching with regard to achieving both cognitive and motivational aims in the classroom. In other words, students learn more by using the case method, and they are more stimulated. Case teaching has been shown to be *especially* fruitful in advanced courses devoted to: (1) developing the ability to solve ill-structured problems, and (2) applying theories and techniques. The capstone policy and strategy course meets both of these criteria. Thus, not only is the case method more effective than lectures, it is ideally suited to this particular course.[1]

---

[1]Franz Böcker, "Is Case Teaching More Effective than Lecture Teaching in Business Administration? An Exploratory Analysis," *Interfaces* 17, no. 5 (September/October 1987), pp. 64–71.

What Is the Case Method?

The case method is not new. It originated years ago in law schools throughout the country, and over the years has found its way into professional business education as well. It has been used at the Harvard Business School since the early 1920s, and has been used widely at other business schools since the 50s and 60s. The case method focuses the probing and analytical thinking of students on actual business problems; the approach is much the same as that found in actual management situations. It emphasizes thinking, analyzing, questioning, recommending, and planning rather than the memorization or understanding of principles, facts, or concepts (although a knowledge of principles and concepts is essential to effectively analyze a case.)

In addition, case analysis requires a different student-professor relationship than do traditional methods of instruction. The student takes an active rather than passive role—learning by doing rather than by merely listening and reading. Learning by doing is effective; it is how we learn most skills in life.

How Does It Work?

Cases are typically records of actual business situations, rather than problems that are preformulated for students to solve. The organization, its history, and current situation are typically described, and it is left to the student to analyze what course of action the organization should pursue. Rather than handing problems to the students on a platter for their solution (perhaps using a specified technique), the students are put in the position of managers who must develop alternatives and propose specific actions for the firm.

The responsibility for analyzing, recommending, and convincing others lies with the *students,* not with the instructor. In some cases, there may be no "problem" as such; the issue may be one of maintaining and continuing successful performance into the future. There may be no single "right" answer to the case situation; there may be several plausible alternatives each with its own pros and cons. The student will need to support his or her analysis and recommendations against the critical questioning of the instructor and the rest of the class.

In summary, the case method is a learning approach which recognizes that people are most likely to retain and use what they learn through guided discovery—by *doing*. Case analysis requires the student to take risks, make judgments in uncertain situations, and to propose and select from multiple possible options, none of which may be "right" or "wrong." Memorization and "studying" are of little use in case analysis, as is true in real-world, on-the-job settings. The case method allows students with real expertise and understanding, as well as judgment, to excel.

However, there is no "free lunch." Even though cases motivate students to learn, and case teaching yields better results, it also requires more work. The case method requires more time and effort for students to get through a topic, and (to the surprise of many students who feel that the instructor is not "working" when not lecturing) case teaching requires significantly *more* preparation and evaluation on the part of the instructor.[2]

How to Analyze a Case

In analyzing a case, an orderly, step-by-step approach often is helpful. It is important to gain an appreciation of the overall situation initially, as well as to learn what information is contained in the case. Therefore, it is suggested that the case be skimmed first to gain this overall perspective. While or after doing so, jot down the key points and issues that come to mind, as well as your first impression of the problems, issues, and opportunities facing the company. Then read the case in detail, adding to and modifying your initial thoughts. Remember that not everything in the case is vitally important, nor is all the important information necessarily included. The case represents someone's (e.g., management's) description of the company and its situation—it is up to *you* to probe deeper, sort and sift things out, and acquire additional information. It is *your* responsibility to analyze and recommend alternatives and approaches to management.

The following guide may be helpful to you in your task:

1. Define the situation. What are the challenges, problems, potential problems, opportunities, and potential opportunities facing the company? Typically, the case will contain various *symptoms* you will have to diagnose. To do so, try and isolate the *major* issues facing the company and their causes. Keep in mind that there are likely to be sub and secondary issues, as well as related and perhaps extraneous issues described in the case. Your task is to assign priorities to the issues, focusing on the critical few.
2. Assemble and analyze the important facts (gleaned from the case) which bear on the situation.
3. Specify important information that is needed but not included in the case. Determine whether or not it is available elsewhere. If available, acquire it.
4. Make assumptions. For important information that is not available from the case or elsewhere, make logical assumptions as to what it might be. State these assumptions.
5. Draw conclusions based on your analysis, information, and assumptions.
6. Determine alternatives and their likely outcomes. What are the major alternative actions open to the company, and what is likely to happen if each is adopted? Evaluate each.
7. Make recommendations. Based on your analysis, what do you recommend to management and why? Be prepared to defend your recommendations under

---

[2]Ibid.

critical questioning by the instructor and the class (the types of questions which might be posed by the company's management and other stakeholders).

8. Prepare an implementation plan. How should your recommendation be implemented, by whom, in what sequence (short-term versus long-term actions), and the like. Where will the resources come from?

9. Prepare contingency plans. What do you recommend if your suggestions do not work as anticipated, or if certain external or internal conditions change?

It is recommended that you use the above sequence as a guide, but that your presentation of the case contain the following four sections:

I. *Background.* Describe the *pertinent* history of the organization, including its mission, goals and objectives, and strategies. Include only those points which affect the current situation, possible alternatives, or future performance of the company.

II. *Situation Analysis.* Describe the current and future threats and opportunities present in the general and competitive environments, as well as the organization's strengths and weaknesses. What is the firm's financial and other health, and what resources can they marshal? What are the critical success factors?

III. *Alternatives and Recommendations.* Propose and analyze alternatives for the company in terms of the four major components of any strategy—scope, distinctive competence, competitive advantage, and synergies. Discuss and defend your recommendations.

IV. *Implementation.* Present your implementation plan, including your contingency (what if) analysis.

CASES SELECTED FOR THIS BOOK

The cases included in this book were selected from a review of hundreds of cases, screened from a list of several thousand strategy-related cases. Careful consideration was given to the quality of the case, a balance of strategic issues and decisions, a wide representation of industries, varying sizes of companies, varying complexity and length of the case, geographical balance, how current the case is, and organizations that students are likely to recognize or have an interest in. Given these criteria, the list of potential cases was progressively narrowed to those included in the following sections of this book.

Strategic Issues and Decisions

The cases are grouped into eight sections representing the major strategic issue or decision faced by the organization described in each case (although each case contains other issues and decisions, as well). These issues/decisions include:

Section A: Defining the Business: Vision, Values, Mission, Policies

Section B: Start-up Strategies: New Ventures

Section C: Growth and Share-Building Strategies

Section D: Corporate Size and Focus: Diversification and Restructuring

Section E: Coping with Environmental Change and Turbulence

Section F: Strategy Change, Renewal, and Turnaround

Section G: Strategy Refinement and Control

Section H: Strategy Implementation and Planning

Organization Type

The cases reflect 11 major types of organizations, including the following: small firms, new ventures, not-for-profit organizations, single-product firms, dominant-product firms, diversified firms, multi-industry firms, business units, service organizations, associations, and cooperatives.

Industries

The cases directly represent the following 35 industries: aerospace, agricultural equipment, automotive products, broadcasting, cereal products, charitable foundations, clothing retailers, construction materials, consumer products, electric utilities, electronics retailers, entertainment, financial services, food products, food service, food stores, government, greeting cards, historic preservation, lodging, microcomputers, natural gas, offshore drilling, oil, pipelines, recreation, restaurants, retailing, rubber products manufacturing, software, software services, space, sports, tires, and welding equipment. In addition, many of the organizations are diversified and involved in a number of other industries in addition to those listed above. At least four of the cases have "industry pairs" for comparison purposes.

Primary Location

The cases selected closely approximate the relative population of the United States, divided into the following regions:

Pacific and Northwest.

Southern California and Hawaii.

Gulf and Southwest.

Plains and Rockies.

Great Lakes and Midwest.

New York and New England.

Mid-Atlantic and Southeast.

In addition, cases from Canada, Great Britain, and Sweden are included. Many of the cases, while headquartered in a given region, have national and international recognition, and operations.

A

Defining the Business: Vision, Values, Mission, Policies

1.   *The Farm Management System*

In late 1982, the management of Homestead Computers was considering the future of its primary proprietary product, the Farm Management System (FMS). Their early hopes for rapid market penetration had not been realized through their current corporate strategy. Management was also concerned about the way in which they were approaching the market for this product. In addition, they were also aware that they must consider the strengths, weaknesses, and positioning of the company as a whole in reaching a decision regarding how to proceed with the FMS.

THE MICROCOMPUTER SOFTWARE INDUSTRY

The commercial introduction of microcomputers in 1976 sparked a revolution in the field of information processing. A proliferation of hardware created tremendous opportunities for the creation and sale of integrated systems and applications software. These are the programs which enable microcomputers to perform particular jobs.

Perhaps, surprisingly, the demand for software for the new micros was not met by the established (mainframe computer) software producers. A new industry was born, largely spawned in the basements of numerous creative entrepreneurs.

HOMESTEAD COMPUTER SERVICES LTD.

Since its creation in 1979, Homestead's strategy had been to try to carve out specialized target markets for itself. The firm has concentrated on combining its expertise in microcomputers with applications within selected industries. Homestead was an outgrowth of

---

Prepared by John Fallows under the direction of Walter S. Good, The University of Manitoba as a basis for classroom discussion. This case is available in looseleaf form from Lord Publishing, Inc., One Apple Hill, Natick, Mass. 01760. Call (617) 651–9955 for information regarding this case. Copyright © 1986.

Westburn Development Consultants, an agricultural consulting firm with a number of years' experience in the grain industry and related fields such as transportation and information systems.

One of Homestead's target industries was agriculture. The company enjoyed excellent success in the area of custom software development, with its major achievement being the development and installation of a computer-assisted trading system for the Winnipeg Commodity Exchange. This led to a contract to develop a similar system for the London International Financial Futures Exchange. At the same time, the company also developed a number of proprietary products including an "Elevator Information System" and the "Farm Management System."

Homestead employed 15 people, most of whom had expertise in fields such as business administration, computer science, engineering, electronics, agricultural economics, and science. Sales were approaching $1 million annually, with the Westburn Division providing a steady $250,000. The company was seeking sales growth of 50 percent each year, and expected this growth to come mainly from the sale of customized and proprietary information systems. The financial condition of the company was good, with a debt : equity ratio of 0.3, a current ratio of 1.2, and a return on sales exceeding 10 percent.

THE FARM MANAGEMENT SYSTEM

Homestead's primary growth was expected to come through the sale of its proprietary Farm Management System. Sales revenue forecasts were based on the sale of 300 to 400 such systems each year for the following three years. However, early results were disappointing.

PRODUCT DESCRIPTION

The main features of the Farm Management System are described in Exhibit 1. While the system was normally sold on a turnkey basis, it was also available on a software-only basis. (Homestead enjoyed OEM status with Vector Graphics. With this status, it was able to buy the hardware as an "original equipment manufacturer" for a very low price per computer. Homestead then packaged its software into the Vector Graphics machine and sold a final product consisting of a "system" of both hardware and software.) The software was configured to run on any microcomputer which used the CP/M operating system. This included a broad range of equipment using an Intel 8080-type CPU (including the Z-80). However, it did *not* include other 8-bit CPUs, such as the Motorola 6500 types common to Apple® and Commodore® computers, or the newer 16-bit CPU machines, such as the IBM® personal computer.

The Farm Management System was customized to the specific needs of farmers and, therefore, enjoyed an advantage over generic accounting software packages available from other firms. It performed more functions than either the generic systems or those of other competitors that were also targeted towards the farm market. Furthermore, the accounting system operated on a cash as well as an accrual basis, as this approach is more meaningful to the farmer. The hardware was well built and reliable. The system operated on a stand-alone basis and could prepare reports at any time. This was a distinct advantage and provided much faster turnaround than competitors who offered a centralized "mail-in" accounting system (where delays of 10 to 14 days could occur). It was also superior to the time-shared remote computing systems, since telecommunications charges could be expensive. (Also, due to the fact that many farms were served by party-line telephone systems, the telephone companies would not allow computers to tie up these phone lines.) The type of competition faced by Homestead in this market segment is summarized in Exhibit 2.

PRICING

In many respects, the decision as to the price to charge for computer software was quite arbitrary. Regardless of the method used to allocate development costs, such

---

EXHIBIT 1 Farm Management System Specifications

SOFTWARE:

- Double-entry accounting system with nine profit centres.
- Comprehensive inventory control system.
- Fixed asset recording.
- Labor use and manpower planning.
- Simulation modules for cash flow and product planning in special fields such as feedlot management.

HARDWARE:

- Vector Graphics microcomputer with 56K RAM.
- Dual floppy disks (1.26M storage total).
- Centronics printer (dot matrix).

Note: The Vector Graphics computer contains the keyboard, computer and screen in one unit. It uses the Z-80 eight-bit central processing unit (CPU) and the CP/M operating system designed for such eight-bit CPUs.

EXHIBIT 2 Farm Management System Competitors

1. Other stand-alone, microcomputer-based systems.
2. On-line, remote access mainframe systems
3. Batch mail-in systems.
4. Accounting consulting services.
5. Manual accounting systems.
6. The "old shoe box."

outlays were "sunk" costs. The variable cost of production was, at most, a few dollars per unit. The sale of software to commercial microcomputer users was still quite new and little was known about the price elasticity of demand. The general approach taken to pricing most software products was competitive pricing, although some price-level positioning was starting to appear. General-purpose business packages sold at the $500 to $700 retail level, while specialized agricultural software was somewhat more expensive.

Homestead positioned itself with a premium price for a superior system (See Exhibit 3.) American selling prices were lower for two reasons. First, the hardware was cheaper since the company didn't have to pay duty on the equipment (Vector Graphics was an American manufacturer), as well as the exchange rate differential. Second, Homestead provided less support in the United States. On software sales, the dealer discount ranged from 25 percent to 30 percent in Canada and up to 50 percent in the United States. On the sale of a turnkey system in Canada, the contribution received by Homestead was about $5,500 of which $2,500 came from software. Competitive specialized agricultural software sold in the range of $500 to $1,300.

PRODUCT MARKET

In general, Homestead felt that its FMS was most appropriate for larger farms (i.e., with gross sales exceeding $100,000) operated by younger owners (i.e., between 20 and 50 years of age—see Exhibit 4). Aside from the increasing availability of lower cost computing hardware, Homestead saw three factors which contributed to the potential of the FMS. First, farmers were continuing to place more emphasis on high productivity and increased profitability as a key to their long-term survival. Farming was becoming more of a business and farmers were starting to perceive themselves as professional managers. Second, with higher costs and better education, modern farmers were less tied to the traditional ways of doing things and were more receptive to innovation. Third, the small rural communities were becoming less cohesive and farmers were prepared to look farther afield for their supplies and capital equipment. The younger, better-educated farmer and the larger, progressive farmer were likely to be the "principal innovators" who would try the FMS first. In general, the "opinion leaders" were those who would

---

EXHIBIT 3   Farm Management System Prices

	Canada (Can. $)	United States (U.S.$)
Turnkey*	$12,500	$8,000
Software only		
Accounting	2,500	1,500
Specialty planning modules†	1,000	500

*The turnkey system is comprised of the hardware, the accounting software, and one specialty module.
†There are three modules, each designed for a special type of agricultural activity, such as cattle feeding. Price listed is for one module.

EXHIBIT 4   Total Potential Farm Management System Market

	Total Farms	Target Market
Canada	300,000	6,000
United States	2,300,000	45,000
Total	2,600,000	51,000

try the FMS second. They were fairly progressive farmers and likely of above-average size; they would be willing to experiment with an innovation but not as the initial users. This type of adoption process tended to indicate that Homestead must be prepared to devote a number of years to market penetration, with substantial sales increases probably coming only after these opinion leaders have passed judgment on the acceptability of the product. There was a real danger, however, that a company like Homestead could devote a lot of money and effort to introducing the product (perhaps profitably, perhaps not) but other firms would reap the benefits after the market has been established.

PRODUCT DISTRIBUTION

Homestead's distribution objective was to have broad geographic coverage which was not too expensive to manage. Their initial coverage included western Canada, southern Ontario and the north central United States. The original distributor agreement established by Homestead specified that each distributor must sell 25 systems in the first six months and 100 in the first year. Ten distributors were established, including three in the United States. These were mainly computer businesses specializing in the sale of hardware and software. In Canada, first-year sales were only 24 units, with Alberta and Saskatchewan each accounting for one third of these sales. In the United States, three units were sold out of Dayton, Ohio, five units out of Fargo, North Dakota, and one unit out of Great Falls, Montana. Within Manitoba and Saskatchewan, Homestead marketed the system on a turnkey basis only. Outside this area, the company supplied its dealers with software only, and users were free to select whatever compatible hardware on which they wished to run the programs.

Due to its highly specialized nature and newness, the product required extensive demonstration and personal selling; distribution was very important.

PRODUCT PROMOTION

Homestead took the position that the product and its distribution must be well established before a major promotion effort was undertaken. One promotion technique used was the demonstration of the FMS at agricultural trade shows. Another was a small technical booklet which explained and outlined the various features of the system. A third technique was the generation of publicity in newspapers and specialized agricultural publications such as *Country Guide*.

PROBLEMS AND OPPORTUNITIES

Personal computer use was growing at between 50 percent and 100 percent a year and this trend was expected to continue into the near future. In addition, personal computer users stimulated an even greater growth in the software market. The question was, how could a company like Homestead best address the opportunities presented by this tremendous growth?

Up to 1982, Homestead had concentrated on turnkey sales combining both hardware and software and the results were disappointing. A major problem appeared to be the use of the Vector Graphics computer. The brand had a small following in the United States but was largely unknown in Canada. Indeed, given current trends, the very survival of the manufacturer over the next five years was uncertain. Apple, Tandy® (Radio Shack) and Commodore® emerged as household names and industry observers speculated that these major firms would dominate the market. IBM® had also entered the market with its personal computer, a move which early indications suggested would be very successful. Homestead's turnkey approach resulted in some consumer resistance due to the hardware being an "unknown brand." Perhaps the system should be redesigned around another computer, such as the Apple or IBM personal computer, or both, if Homestead were to continue selling on a turnkey basis. However, it is not clear, given their present level of sales, that Homestead could achieve OEM status with these other manufacturers.

Another alternative available to the company was to sell the software only. This would require modifying the software to run on other operating systems, especially that used by the IBM personal computer. The sale of software only would result in a lower per unit contribution margin than a turnkey sale, but this difference could be offset by greater volume. Preliminary industry surveys of pioneering farm computer users indicated market domination by the best-known "brand" names—Apple, IBM and Radio Shack. These machines had been successful due to heavy advertising, widespread availability and support, and low cost. Neither Radio Shack nor

Apple offered substantial support for the CP/M operating system. Industry experts expected the IBM personal computer to dominate the market within two years.

Homestead also had to revitalize its distribution strategy. Its alternatives included: (*a*) continued emphasis on developing a system of many small distributors: (*b*) an emphasis on developing a number of larger distributors; and (*c*) the development of a direct sales force. In addition, if it used distributors, what type of firms should they be? Yet another idea under consideration was to get out of downstream distribution altogether, and license the product to an established software distributor.

Parallel to these considerations, Homestead was also facing some critical decisions regarding possible areas for new-product development. These related to two areas. First, they already had several computer programs at various stages of development, which could extend

the Farm Management System. These included programs in the following areas:

1. Marketing information—buy/sell, trends, options.
2. Livestock breeding.
3. Tax preparation.
4. Lease versus buy analysis.

Some of these applications were already available to farmers on time-shared systems but not on a stand-alone basis.

The second area under consideration was the development of business software for firms operating in other segments of the agri-business sector. Homestead thought there might be an opportunity for synergy with the FMS by providing software products for businesses in other industries which served the farming community.

---

2. *The National Jazz Hall of Fame*

Mr. Robert Rutland, founder of the National Jazz Hall of Fame, poured himself another drink as he listened to some old jazz recordings and thought about the decisions facing him. Established about one year ago, the National Jazz Hall of Fame (NJHF) had achieved moderate success locally but had not yet attracted national recognition. Mr. Rutland wondered how much support existed nationally, what services the NJHF should provide and for whom, and what the NJHF should charge for those services. He also thought about other jazz halls of fame and their implications for the NJHF. Although he had engaged an independent consultant to find some answers, the questions still lingered.

This case was written by Professor Cornelis A. de Kluyver, with assistance of Jonathan Giuliano, MBA 1985, John Milford and Bruce Cauthen, MBAs 1984, as a basis for class discussion, rather than to illustrate effective or ineffective handling of an administrative situation. Copyright 1984 by the Sponsors of the Colgate Darden Graduate School of Business Administration of the University of Virginia. WP7191B.

JAZZ

The word *jazz,* according to Dr. David Pharies, a linguistics scholar at the University of Florida, originally meant copulation, but later identified a certain type of music. Amid the march of funeral bands, jazz music began in New Orleans in the early 1900s by combining black spirituals, African rhythms, and Cajun music; Dixieland jazz became the sound of New Orleans. Jazz traveled from New Orleans, a major trade center, on river boats and ships and reached St. Louis, Kansas City, Memphis, Chicago, and New York. Musicians in these cities developed local styles of jazz, all of which remained highly improvisational, personal, and rhythmically complex. Over the years, different sounds emerged—swing, big band, be bop, fusion, and others—indicating the fluidity and diversity of jazz. Jazz artists developed their own styles and competed with one another for recognition of their musical ability and compositions. Such diversity denied jazz a simple definition, and opinions still differed sharply on what exactly jazz was. It was difficult, however, to dispute Louis Armstrong's statement that "if you have to ask what jazz is, you'll never know."

ORIGINS OF THE NATIONAL JAZZ HALL OF FAME

Mr. Rutland, a history professor at the University of Virginia, which is in Charlottesville, discovered that renovation plans for the city's historic district excluded the Paramount Theatre, a local landmark. The Paramount was constructed in the 1930s and used as a performance center and later as a movie theatre. It was closed in the 1970s and now was in danger of becoming dilapidated. Alarmed by the apparent lack of interest in saving the Paramount, Mr. Rutland began to look for opportunities to restore and eventually use the theatre. The most attractive option to him was to establish a jazz hall of fame that would use the theatre as a museum and performance center; this would capitalize on the theatre's name, because the Paramount Theatre in New York City was a prominent jazz hall during the 1930s and 1940s. Mr. Rutland mentioned his idea—saving the theatre by establishing a jazz hall of fame—to several friends in Charlottesville. They shared his enthusiasm, and together they incorporated the National Jazz Hall of Fame and formed the board of directors in early 1983. A few prominent jazz musicians, such as Benny Goodman and Chick Corea, joined the NJHF National Advisory Board. The purpose of the NJHF was to establish and maintain a museum, archives, and concert center in Charlottesville to sponsor jazz festivals, workshops, and scholarships, and to promote other activities remembering great jazz artists, serving jazz enthusiasts, and educating the public on the importance of jazz in American culture and history.

THE FIRST YEAR'S EFFORTS

Immediately after incorporation, the directors began their search for funds to save the Paramount and to establish the NJHF, and soon encountered two difficulties. Philanthropic organizations refused to make grants because no one on the board of directors had experience in a project like the NJHF. In addition government agencies such as the National Endowment for the Arts and the National Endowment for the Humanities considered only organizations in operation for at least two years. However, some small contributions came from jazz enthusiasts who had read stories about the NJHF in *Billboard,* a music industry magazine, and in the Charlottesville and Richmond newspapers.

By mid-1983, the board of directors discovered that to save the Paramount at least $600,000 would be needed, a sum too large for them to consider. They decided, however, that out of their love for jazz they would continue to work to establish the NJHF in Charlottesville.

Despite these setbacks, Mr. Rutland and the other directors believed that the first year's activities showed promise. The NJHF sponsored three concerts at local high schools. The concerts featured such jazz greats as Maxine Sullivan, Buddy Rich, and Jon Hendricks and Company, and each concert attracted more than 500 people. Although the NJHF lost some money on each concert, the directors thought that the concerts succeeded in publicizing and promoting the NJHF. In addition, a fund-raiser at a Charlottesville country club brought $2,000 to the NJHF, and Mr. Rutland started the NJHF newsletter. The collection of objects for the museum was enlarged, and Louis Armstrong and Duke Ellington were posthumously inducted into the NJHF. At the end of the first year, enthusiasm among board members was still high, and they believed that the NJHF could survive indefinitely, albeit on a small scale.

BUT A HALL OF FAME IN CHARLOTTESVILLE . . .

Mr. Rutland believed that a hall of fame could succeed in Charlottesville, though other cities might at first seem more appropriate. More than 500,000 tourists annually were attracted to Charlottesville (1980 population: 40,000) to visit Thomas Jefferson's home at Monticello, James Monroe's home at Ash Lawn, and the Rotunda and the Lawn of the University of Virginia, where total enrollment was 16,000. Mr. Jefferson designed the Rotunda and the buildings on the Lawn and supervised their construction. The Virginia Office of Tourism promoted these national landmarks as well as the city's two convention centers. In addition, 13 million people lived within a three-hour drive of Charlottesville. If Charlottesville seemed illogical for a hall of fame, Mr. Rutland reasoned, so did Cooperstown, New York, home of the Baseball Hall of Fame and Canton, Ohio, location of the Professional Football Hall of Fame. He thought that successful jazz festivals in such different places as Newport, Rhode Island, and French Lick, Indiana, showed that location was relatively unimportant for jazz. Moreover, a Charlottesville radio station recently switched to a music format called "Memory Lane," which featured classics by Frank Sinatra, Patti Page, the Mills Brothers, the Glenn Miller Orchestra, and numerous others. The station played much jazz, and won the loyalty of many jazz enthusiasts in the Charlottesville area. The success of "Memory Lane" indicated to Mr. Rutland that the Charlottesville community could provide the NJHF with a base of interest and loyalty. Most important, Mr. Rutland believed that he and his friends possessed the commitment necessary to make a jazz hall of fame succeed.

... AND HALLS OF FAME IN OTHER CITIES?

Although no national organization operated successfully, several local groups claimed to be *the* Jazz Hall of Fame, as *Billboard* magazine reported.

Billboard, 4/28/84

HALL OF FAME IN HARLEM
by Sam Sutherland and Peter Keepnews

CBS Records and the Harlem YMCA have joined forces to establish a Jazz Hall of Fame. The first induction ceremony will take place on May 14 at Avery Fisher Hall, combined with a concert featuring such artists as Ramsey Lewis, Hubert Laws, Ron Carter, and an all-star Latin Jazz ensemble. Proceeds from the concert will benefit the Harlem YMCA.

Who will the initial inductees be, and how will they be chosen? What's being described in the official literature as "a prestigious group of jazz editorialists, critics, producers, and respected connoisseurs" (and, also, incidentally, musicians—among those on the panel are Miles

Davis, Dizzy Gillespie, Cab Calloway, Max Roach and the ubiquitous Dr. Billy Taylor) will do the actual selecting, but nominations are being solicited from the general public. Jazz lovers are invited to submit the names of six artists, three living and three dead, to: The Harlem YMCA Jazz Hall of Fame, New York, NY 10030. Deadline for nominations is May 1.

Billboard, 5/19/84

ONE, TWO, MANY HALLS OF FAME?
by Sam Sutherland and Peter Keepnews

Monday night marks the official launch of the Harlem YMCA Jazz Hall of Fame (*Billboard,* April 28), a project in which CBS Records is closely involved. The Hall's first inductees are being unveiled at an Avery Fisher Hall concert that also includes performances by, among others, Sarah Vaughan and Branford Marsalis.

The project is being touted as the first jazz hall of fame, a statement that discounts a number of similar projects in the past that never quite reached fruition. But first or not, the good people at CBS and the Harlem YMCA are apparently in for some competition.

According to a new publication known as *JAMA,* the Jazz Listeners/Musicians Newsletter, Dizzy Gillespie—who also is a member of the Harlem YMCA Jazz Hall of Fame committee—"promised in Kansas City, Mo. to ask musicians for help in establishing an International Jazz Hall of Fame" in that city. The newsletter quotes Gillespie, whom it describes as "honorary chairman of the proposed hall," as vowing to ask "those musicians who were inspired by jazz"—among them Stevie Wonder, Quincy Jones, and Paul McCartney (?)—to contribute financially to the Kansas City project, which, as envisioned by the great trumpeter, would also include a jazz museum, classrooms and performance areas.

Is there room for two Jazz Halls of Fame? Do the people involved in the New York City project know about the Kansas City project, and vice versa? (Obviously Gillespie does, but does anyone else?) Remember the New York Jazz Museum? Remember the plaques in the sidewalk on 52nd Street (another CBS Records brainchild)?

The notion of commemorating the contributions of the great jazz musicians is a noble one. It would be a shame to see the energies of the jazz community get diverted into too many different endeavors for accomplishing the same admirable goal—which, unfortunately, is what has tended to happen in the past.

Billboard, 5/26/84

Also noted: the first inductees in the Harlem YMCA Jazz Hall of Fame (*Billboard,* May 19) have been announced. The posthumous inductees are, to nobody's great surprise, Louis Armstrong, Duke Ellington, Count Basie, Charlie Parker, and—a slight surprise, perhaps—Mary Lou Williams. The living honorees are Roy Eldridge, Dizzy Gillespie, Miles Davis, Ella Fitzgerald and Art Blakey.

The New York Jazz museum (which the 5/19/84 article referred to) was established in the early 1970s but quickly ran out of money and was closed a few years later. In the early 1960s, a jazz museum was established in New Orleans and because of insufficient funds, all that remained was the Louis Armstrong Memorial Park, the site of an outdoor jazz festival each summer. Tulane and Rutgers universities each possessed extensive archives containing thousands of phonograph records, tape recordings, posters, books, magazines, journals, and other historic pieces and memorabilia. Neither university, however, considered its archives a hall of fame.

OTHER HALLS OF FAME

The more prominent halls of fame in the United States were the Baseball, the Professional Football, the College Football, and the Country Music Hall of Fame. These and many other halls of fame were primarily concerned with preserving history by collecting and displaying memorabilia, compiling records, and inducting new members annually.

Mr. Rutland visited most of the other halls of fame and learned that they were usually established by a significant contribution from an enthusiast. In the case of the Country Music Hall of Fame, some country music stars agreed to make a special recording of country hits and to donate the royalties to the organization.

Mr. Rutland was especially interested in the Country Music Hall of Fame because of similarities between country music and jazz. Country music, like jazz, had a rich cultural history in America, and neither type of music was the most popular in the United States.

The Country Music Hall of Fame (CMHF) was established in 1967 in Nashville after a cooperative fund-raising effort involving the city, artists, and sponsors. By 1976, the CMHF included a museum, an archives, a library, and a gift shop. More than one-half million people visited the CMHF in 1983, partly because of the nearby Grand Ole Opry, the premier concert hall for country music where the Grand Ole Opry cable radio broadcasts originated. Of the CMHF's $2.1 million annual budget, 85 percent came from admissions, 10 percent from sales at the gift shop and by mail, and 5 percent from donations. In the past two years, the CMHF had formed the Friends of Country Music, now more than 2,000 people who donated $25 each per year and who received a country music newsletter every three months and discounts on CMHF merchandise.

THE NATIONAL ASSOCIATION OF JAZZ EDUCATORS

Mr. Rutland was uncertain how much and what type of support he could get from the National Association of Jazz Educators. This organization, with 5,000 members, primarily coordinated and promoted jazz education programs.

Performance programs were normally offered through music departments. Most high schools and colleges had bands that played a variety of jazz arrangements as part of their repertoire. Band conductors usually had a music degree from a major university and belonged to the National Association of Jazz Educators.

Most of the jazz appreciation courses offered in schools throughout the United States treated jazz as a popular art form, as a barometer of society, rather than as a subject of interest in itself. Some educators believed that jazz greats such as Louis Armstrong and Duke Ellington should be honored not as jazz musicians, but as composers like George Gershwin and Richard Rogers. Indeed, a prominent jazz historian told Mr. Rutland that jazz might benefit more from breaking down this distinction between jazz artists and composers than from reinforcing it.

THE NATIONAL SURVEY

To get some of the answers to his many questions, Mr. Rutland engaged an independent consultant who conducted two surveys: the first was a national survey and the second a tourist survey. For the national survey (Appendix A), the consultant designed a questionnaire to gauge the respondent's level of interest in both jazz and the concept of a National Jazz Hall of Fame, and to determine the respondent's demographics. A sample size of 1,300 was used and the mailing covered the entire continental United States. The mailing list, obtained from the Smithsonian Institution in Washington, D.C., contained names and addresses of people who had purchased the "Classic Jazz Record Collection," as advertised in *Smithsonian* magazine. Of the 1,300 questionnaires, 440 were sent to Virginia residents and 860 to residents of other states in order to provide both statewide and national data. Of the questionnaires that went to other states, the majority was targeted toward major cities and apportioned according to the interest level for jazz in each city as indicated by the circulation statistics of *Downbeat*, a jazz magazine. Of the 860 questionnaires sent to the other states, 88 were sent to residents of Chicago, 88 to Detroit, 83 to New York City, 60 to San Francisco, 56 to Philadelphia, 56 to Washington, D.C., 52 to Los Angeles, 46 to Charlotte, 46 to Miami, 45 to Dallas, 42 to Atlanta, 42 to Houston, 30 to Denver, 28 to Kansas City, 28 to New Orleans, 28

to St. Louis, 27 to Boston, and 15 to Seattle. Of the 1,300 questionnaires, 165, or 12.7 percent, were returned.

As shown in Exhibit 1, 79 percent of the respondents were 35 years of age or older, 73 percent were male, and the majority were well-educated, professionals, and had an annual income of more than $50,000. Of interest also was that 75 percent of the respondents contributed $200 or more per year to different nonprofit organizations. Since the sample included a large number of record buyers of age 50 or older, the consultant weighted the survey results with age data obtained from the Recording Industry Association of America to make the survey results representative of all jazz-record buyers.

The survey also showed in Exhibit 2 that swing was the most popular form of jazz, followed by Dixieland, and then more traditional forms of jazz, from which the consultant concluded that a nostalgic emphasis should gather support from jazz enthusiasts of all ages, and that later, the National Jazz Hall of Fame could promote more contemporary forms of jazz.

As for services, the survey suggested in Exhibit 3 that respondents most wanted a performance center or concert hall. A museum and seminars were also popular choices. The consultant was surprised by the strong interest in information about jazz recordings because the average respondent did not buy many records. A newsletter was rated relatively unimportant by most respondents. Most gratifying for Mr. Rutland was that respon-

---

EXHIBIT 1   Survey Results: Demographics of Respondents

Demographics	Percentage of Respondents	Percentage of All Record Buyers*	Census Data†
Age—35+	79%	37%	43%
Sex—Male	73	82	49
Education—Grad. +	54	24‡	31
Job—Professional	57	26	22
Income—$50,000+	50	23	7
Nonprofit contributions $200 per year+	75		

Consumer Purchasing of Records and Pre-recorded Tapes in the U.S., 1979–1983, Recording Industry Association of America.
†U.S. Department of Commerce, Bureau of the Census, 1982.
‡Simmons Market Research Bureau, 1982

EXHIBIT 2 Survey Results: Preferences for Different Styles of Jazz

Type of Interest	Percentage of Respondents Answering with a 4 or 5 Rating	Weighted Percentage of Respondents answering with a 4 or 5 Rating
General interest in music	62%	71%
Dixieland	62	70
Swing	87	81
Traditional	63	66
Improvisational	41	48
Jazz rock	25	47
Fusion	15	9
Pop jazz	27	53
Classical	68	73

EXHIBIT 3 Survey Results: Preferences for Services Offered

Service	Percentage of Respondents Answering with a 4 or 5 Rating	Weighted Percentage of Respondents Answering with a 4 or 5 rating
Performance center	70%	83%
Concert hall	66	79
Artist seminars	50	62
Nightclub	52	57
Museum	57	57
Tourist center	42	48
Audiovisual exhibitions	57	55
Shrine	55	52
Educational programs	48	51
Record information	71	69
History seminars	38	54
Member workshops	25	34
Lounge	37	45
Financial support:		
$10 per year	17	13
$20 per year	30	26
$30 per year	15	25
Number of contributors	62%	64%

dents on average were willing to contribute between $20 and $30 per year to the National Jazz Hall of Fame, with a weighted-average contribution of $23.40.

THE TOURIST SURVEY

In addition to conducting the National Survey, the consultant developed a questionnarie (Appendix B) and interviewed approximately 100 tourists to the Charlottesville area at the Western Virginia Visitors Center near Monticello. About 140,000 tourists stopped at the center annually to collect information on attractions nearby and throughout the state. The respondents came from all areas of the country, and most were traveling for more than one day. Almost 70 percent said they liked jazz, mostly Dixieland and big band, and more than 60 percent indicated they would visit a jazz hall of fame. The average admission they suggested was $3.50 per person.

THE CONSULTANT'S RECOMMENDATIONS

The consultant limited his recommendations to the results of the two surveys. As a result, the question of whether the efforts in other cities to establish a National Jazz Hall of Fame would make the Charlottesville project infeasible was still unresolved. In a private discussion, however, the consultant intimated that "if the other efforts are as clumsily undertaken as many of the previous attempts, you will have nothing to worry about." He thought it was time that a professional approach was taken toward this project. Specifically, he made three recommendations:

1. Launch a direct-mail campaign to the 100,000 people on the Smithsonian jazz mailing list. The focus of the mailing should be an appeal by a jazz great such as Benny Goodman to become a Founding Sponsor of the National Jazz Hall of Fame. He estimated that the cost of the campaign would range between $25,000 and $30,000; however, with an average contribution of $25 per respondent, a response rate of only 2 percent would allow the National Jazz Hall of Fame to break even.

2. Appoint a full-time executive director with any funds exceeding the cost of the mailing. The principal responsibilities of the executive director would be to organize and coordinate fund-raising activities, to establish a performance center and museum, and to coordinate collection of memorabilia and other artifacts.

3. Promote the National Jazz Hall of Fame at strategic locations around Charlottesville to attract tourists and other visitors. The Western Virginia Visitors Center was a prime prospect in his view for this activity. He calculated that 50,000 tourists annually at $3 each would provide sufficient funds to operate and maintain the National Jazz Hall of Fame.

The consultant also identified what he considered the critical elements for his plan's success. First, the National Jazz Hall of Fame should be professional in all of its services and communications to jazz enthusiasts. Second, the executive director should have prior experience in both fund-raising and direct mail; he should have a commitment to and love for jazz, as well as administrative skill and creativity. Third, the National Jazz Hall of Fame should communicate frequently with Founding Sponsors to keep their interest and excitement alive. Finally, to ensure the enthusiastic cooperation of city officials, local merchants and the Charlottesville community, he thought that more local prominence for the National Jazz Hall of Fame would prove indispensable.

THE NATIONAL JAZZ HALL OF FAME—DREAM OR REALITY

As he paged through the consultant's report, Mr. Rutland wondered what to make of the recommendations. While he was encouraged by a national base of support for his idea, he was unsure how the board of directors would react to the consultant's proposals. With less than $2,500 in the bank, how would they get the necessary funds to implement the plan? Yet he knew he had to make some tough decisions, and quickly, if he wanted to make his dream a reality.

APPENDIX A   NATIONAL JAZZ HALL OF FAME SURVEY

1. How would you classify your interest in jazz? (Please circle)

    Not interested   Moderate interest   Very enthusiastic

       1   2   3   4   5

    1. _____

2. Rate your interest in the following categories of jazz. (Circle your answer)

	No Interest		Some Interest		Very Interested	
Dixieland/New Orleans (K. Oliver, P. Fountain)	1	2	3	4	5	2. _____
Big Band/Swing (B. Goodman, G. Miller)	1	2	3	4	5	3. _____
Traditional (A. Tatum, E. Garner)	1	2	3	4	5	4. _____
Improvisational (C. Parker, D. Gillespie)	1	2	3	4	5	5. _____
Jazz/Rock (M. Ferguson, P. Metheny)	1	2	3	4	5	6. _____
Fusion (M. Davis, S. Clarke)	1	2	3	4	5	7. _____
Pop Jazz (B. James, G. Benson)	1	2	3	4	5	8. _____

3. Besides Jazz, what other types of music do you usually like to listen to?   (Circle your answer)

	Never				Often	
Popular/Top 40	1	2	3	4	5	9. _____
Classical	1	2	3	4	5	10. _____
Easy Listening	1	2	3	4	5	11. _____
Rock and Roll	1	2	3	4	5	12. _____
Country	1	2	3	4	5	13. _____
Soul/Disco	1	2	3	4	5	14. _____
Nostalgia	1	2	3	4	5	15. _____

4. How many jazz albums have you bought in the last 3 months? ___

                                       in the past year? ___

    16. _____
    17. _____

5. Do you play a musical instrument?

    Yes ___   How many? ___   Hours per week ___   No ___

    18. _____
    19. _____
    20. _____

    Do you sing?   Yes ___   Hours per week ___   No ___

    21. _____
    22. _____
    23. _____

    Do you compose music?   Yes ___   Hours per week ___   No___

    24. _____

6. Are there any Jazz nightclubs/concert halls in your area?   Yes ___ No ___

    If yes, how many times have you been there in the last 3 months?

        0–1 ___   2–4 ___   5–9 ___   10 or more ___

    25. _____
    26. _____

7. How many hours per week do you listen to the radio?

    0–5 ___   5–10 ___   10–15 ___   15–20 ___   More than 20   27. _____

    What format(s) do you listen to most often?

Popular/Top 40 ___	Rock and Roll ___
Classical ___	Jazz ___
Easy Listening ___	Country ___
Talk Show ___	All Night ___
Soul/Disco___	Nostalgia___

8. Have you ever visited a Hall of Fame?   Yes ___   No ___   28. _____

9. The following section is an attempt to determine the services you would expect from a National Jazz Hall of Fame. Please circle the level of your interest in each of the following services.

	Low				High	
Performance center	1	2	3	4	5	29. _____
Concert Hall	1	2	3	4	5	30. _____
Seminars by Jazz artists	1	2	3	4	5	31. _____
Seminars by Jazz historians	1	2	3	4	5	32. _____
Student workshops	1	2	3	4	5	33. _____
Member workshops	1	2	3	4	5	34. _____
Jazz nightclub	1	2	3	4	5	35. _____
Museum with memorabilia	1	2	3	4	5	36. _____
Tourist center	1	2	3	4	5	37. _____
Audiovisual exhibits	1	2	3	4	5	38. _____
Recording studio	1	2	3	4	5	39. _____
Music chart library	1	2	3	4	5	40. _____
Shrine for Jazz greats	1	2	3	4	5	41. _____
Souvenir shop with mail order	1	2	3	4	5	42. _____
Jazz Lounge	1	2	3	4	5	43. _____
School education programs	1	2	3	4	5	44. _____
Newsletter	1	2	3	4	5	45. _____
Jazz journal/Magazine	1	2	3	4	5	46. _____
Concert update	1	2	3	4	5	47. _____
Record information	1	2	3	4	5	48. _____
Musician referral center	1	2	3	4	5	49. _____
Toll free jazz "hot line"	1	2	3	4	5	50. _____
Other (Describe below)	1	2	3	4	5	51. _____

10. We would now like to ask you how much you would be willing to pay for the services you feel are essential. Please check the box below for the annual contribution you would be willing to pay for the items you circled "4" or "5" above.

    $10 ___ $20 ___ $30 ___ $40 ___ $50 ___ $100 ___   52. _____

    Please check here if you would *NOT* be willing to financially contribute to a National Jazz Hall of Fame. ___

11. Would you consider donating any of your Jazz albums or memorabilia to the National Jazz Hall of Fame?

    Yes ___   No ___   Do not own any ___   53. _____

12. Please circle the number indicating how often you read each of the following magazines:

	Never				Often	
Time	1	2	3	4	5	54. _____
Barron's	1	2	3	4	5	55. _____
Esquire	1	2	3	4	5	56. _____
Harper's Bazaar	1	2	3	4	5	57. _____
Jet	1	2	3	4	5	58. _____
Inside Sports	1	2	3	4	5	59. _____
Money	1	2	3	4	5	60. _____
Omni	1	2	3	4	5	61. _____
New Republic	1	2	3	4	5	62. _____
Psychology Today	1	2	3	4	5	63. _____
Playboy	1	2	3	4	5	64. _____
Down Beat	1	2	3	4	5	65. _____
Rolling Stone	1	2	3	4	5	66. _____
Musician	1	2	3	4	5	67. _____
The New Yorker	1	2	3	4	5	68. _____
The National Enquirer	1	2	3	4	5	69. _____

13.   How many movies have you been to in the last 3 months?

    0–1 ___   2–4 ___   5–9 ___   10 or more ___   70. _____

14.   How many books have you read during the past year?

    0–2 ___   3–6 ___   7–10 ___   More than 10 ___   71. _____

What type of books do you like to read? (Answer below)

15.   What other hobbies/activities do you regularly engage in?

16.   Do you belong to any clubs or community organizations? If so, please list them in the space below.

17.   Our group is considering locating the National Jazz Hall of Fame in Charlottesville, Virginia. Some other attractions in the area are the home of Thomas Jefferson, Monticello, the University of Virginia, and the Blue Ridge Mountains. Would you plan a vacation to include a visit to Charlottesville and the Hall of Fame?

    Yes ___   No ___   72. _____

18.   What do you think about the idea of locating the Hall of Fame in Charlottesville?

19.   If the Hall of Fame were located in Charlottesville, and if it offered the services you felt were essential (Question 9), would you support it?

    Yes ___   No ___   73. _____

The following questions will enable us to better compare you to the nation at large. Your responses will help us very much, and will be kept STRICTLY CONFIDENTIAL.

20.   In what city and state do you live? _____   74.–75. _____

21.   What is your age?   76. _____

    Less than 20 ___   20 to 24 ___

    25 to 29 ___   30 to 34 ___

    35 to 39 ___   40 to 49 ___

        50 and older ___

22. What is your sex?   Male ___   Female ___   77. _____
23. What is your race?   Caucasian ___   Black ___   Hispanic ___   Other ___   78. _____
24. What is your marital status?   Married ___   Single ___   79. _____
25. How many people are in your household? ___   80. _____
26. What is your highest level of education?   81. _____
    Have not received high school diploma ___
    High school graduate ___
    Some post-high school education ___
    Associate's Degree ___
    College graduate___   What Degree? ___
    University work beyond Bachelor's degree ___   What Degree? ___
27. What type of job do you have?   82. _____
    Student ___   Sales/Clerical ___
    Semi/Unskilled Labor ___   Professional ___
    Skilled Labor ___   Managerial ___
    Technical ___   Retired ___
28. What is your total household income?   83. _____
    Under $5,000 ___ $5,000 to $15,000 ___
    $15,000 to $25,000 ___ $25,000 to $35,000 ___
    $35,000 to $50,000 ___ $50,000 and above ___
29. How much do you contribute to nonprofit organizations annually?   84. _____
    Under $25 ___ $25 to $50 ___
    $51 to $75 ___ $76 to $100 ___
    $101 to $200 ___ $200 and above ___
30. We would appreciate any other comments or suggestions.

    _____
    _____
    _____
    _____
    _____

31. Please write your name and address below if you wish to be added to our mailing list:

THANK YOU VERY MUCH!

APPENDIX B

Hello, My name is ___. I am a Graduate Student at the University of Virginia and am conducting a survey. Could I ask you a few questions?

We are conducting a survey for a group here in Charlottesville who are considering the establishment of a National Jazz Hall of Fame. We would like to get some information from you about your visit to Charlottesville and the tourist sites you plan to visit.

1. Where are you from?_____
   How far is that from Charlottesville?
       0–50 ___   50–150 ___   150–300 ___   300+ ___

2. Have you visited Charlottesville before?   yes ___   no ___

3. How long do you plan to stay here?
       one hour ___   ½ day ___   overnight ___   more ___

4. Are you stopping here on your way to another destination?
       yes ___   no ___

5. What places do you plan to visit in Charlottesville?
       Monticello ___   Ash Lawn ___   Michie Tavern ___
       U.Va. ___   Downtown ___   Castle Hill ___
       Mountains ___   Other _____

   Now, I'd like to ask you some questions about the music you like to listen to.

6. What is your favorite type of music?
       Popular/Top 40 ___   Classical ___   Easy Listening ___
       Rock and Roll ___   Country ___   Soul/Disco ___
       Nostalgia ___   Jazz ___   Other _____

7. Do you have an interest in Jazz music?   yes ___   no ___

8. If yes, how often do you listen to Jazz?
   Seldom   Always
      1   2   3   4   5

9. If yes, what is your favorite type of Jazz?
       Dixieland ___   Big Band ___   Traditional ___
       Improvisational ___   Jazz/Rock ___   Fusion ___   Pop/Jazz ___

10. Have you ever visited a Hall of Fame?   yes ___   no ___

11. The people who are considering opening a Jazz Hall of Fame in Charlottesville plan a building which would house a collection of memorabilia, audio/visual displays, a gift shop which would sell magazines, books and records, and perhaps a performing arts center. Would you be interested in visiting such an attraction?   yes ___   no ___

12. If YES, We are trying to determine what effect the location of the Hall of Fame would have on your decision to visit it. Would you visit the Hall of Fame if it was located
        More than 10 minutes from the Visitors Center?   yes ___   no ___
        5 to 10 minutes away from the Visitors Center?   yes ___   no ___
        Less than 5 minutes away from the Center?   yes ___   no ___

13. Finally, how much do you think you would be willing to pay (per person) to visit a National Jazz Hall of Fame as described above?   1 2 3 4 5 6 7 8 9 10

3.   Apple Computer, Inc. (1986)

INTRODUCTION

A computer-age version of the American dream became a reality when Apple Computer went public with an initial stock offering of five million shares at $22 per share in 1980. Incorporated in 1977, Apple Computer, Inc., designed, developed, produced, marketed, and serviced microcomputer-based personal computers (PC) and related software and peripheral products.

This famous "hacker-in-blue-jeans" computer company took less time to reach the Fortune 500 than any other start-up in the history of the index, and stands a good chance of falling among the 100 largest U.S. industrial corporations before its 10th birthday, according to Michael Moritz, author of *The Little Kingdom.*

INDUSTRY SITUATION

With the emergence of the microcomputer, American industry experienced an explosion in technology and business. Consumers were so caught up in the high-spirited "keep-up-with-the-Joneses" attitude that many were unsure of their specific needs, yet joined the masses. Likewise, computer manufacturers who were springing up on every street corner were not altogether sure of the consumers' specific needs. Before long, the industry was trying to convince the public that the PC was the latest necessity for the household, joining ranks with the likes of the microwave oven. By 1984, the dust had begun to settle and dealers and manufacturers alike found their shelves stocked full of inventory, which in turn led to an industry price slump.

The overzealous nature with which the industry had grown led many entrepreneurs to believe that the market was inexhaustible in size. As a result, the PC market was confused due to the numerous competitors. Businesses overpurchased microcomputers for which they were

unsure how to best utilize their capabilities and others purchased machines that were incompatible with other makers', thus inhibiting flexibility and expandability. In addition, many manufacturers specializing in the same area were facing an oversupply of computers and accessories because of the unanticipated low demand level. As a result, a survival-of-the-fittest situation existed and only those manufacturers who could effectively determine the needs of the marketplace and could provide them in time at a suitable price would prevail in this young industry. Market analysts agreed with Apple cofounder Steven Wozniak who believed the industry's problems to be the sign of a shrinking market.

HISTORY

Apple's origin began long before the famous 1976 graduation of the first Apple computer, designed and built in the garage of Apple's cofounder, Steven P. Jobs. Jobs and Steve Wozniak, Apple's other cofounder, had known each other since junior high school and both graduated from Homestead High School in Santa Clara, California.

Steve Wozniak was first introduced to computers by his father who was employed as an electronics engineer with Lockheed Corporation's Lockheed Missiles and Space Company. Wozniak's father began teaching Steve the workings of computers by helping him design logic circuits when Steve was in the fourth grade and continued to guide him through computer projects to the extent that by the eighth grade, the boy was building an entire computer.

After completing high school, he attended the University of Colorado where he developed an interest in minicomputers. But after just one year in attendance, Wozniak transferred to De Anza College in Cupertino, California, where he came close to building what he believed to be the first low-cost hobby computer.

Steve Jobs's experience with college was not as successful as Wozniak's. He dropped out of school after just one week and spent the next year in India. In 1975, the two were reunited and began meeting in Jobs's garage so as to build a circuit board that could be sold to hobbyists. With surprise as to their board's popularity,

This case was prepared by Rusty Crews, Cherie Lyon, Russell Neely, and John Williams under the supervision of Professor Sexton Adams, North Texas State University, and Adelaide Griffin, Texas Woman's University.

Jobs and Wozniak discovered that their board could be sold for twice what it cost them to make. By early 1976, they had obtained an order from one customer for 50 boards. This would be, in retrospect, the Apple® I computer.

In March 1976, Jobs and Wozniak formed a partnership, and in June the first of the ordered boards were shipped. Sensing that there was a great demand for their board, the two partners sold a Volkswagen and Wozniak's calculator to raise $1,300 and also obtained $10,000 in grants on credit. The money enabled them to produce 200 boards.

As the new venture continued to grow, the two young entrepreneurs discovered that their paramount problems were money and marketing. These problems were quickly solved by Mike Markkula of Intel Corporation, a semiconductor manufacturer. Markkula became interested in the new circuit board designed by Jobs and Wozniak that would later become the Apple II computer, to which the company would owe a great deal of its success. Convinced of its potential, Markkula invested $91,000 of his own money into the new venture, secured a $250,000 line of credit from Bank of America, and raised $600,000 from venture capitalists.

As Apple grew, more people became involved in the company and contributed to its formation. With this growth evolved the problem of deciding who would assume responsibility for the day-to-day operations. Neither of the two cofounders was interested in the position; therefore, Markkula was selected to be chairman of the board and Mike Scott, a director at National Semiconductor Corporation, was recommended by Markkula to be Apple's first president. With both in agreement, Steve Jobs then assumed the position of vice chairman and Steve Wozniak became vice president, research and development.

MANAGEMENT

John Sculley (age 46) joined Apple as president and chief executive officer in May 1983. Prior to joining Apple, Mr. Sculley was president and chief executive officer of Pepsi-Cola Company, a manufacturer and distributor of soft drink products, for five years. Pepsi-Cola is a division of PepsiCo, Inc., of which Mr. Sculley was also a senior vice president.

William V. Campbell (age 45) joined Apple as vice president of marketing in June 1983, was appointed executive vice president, sales, in September 1984, and became executive vice president, group executive of U.S. sales and marketing in June 1985. Before joining Apple, Mr. Campbell served as director of marketing for Eastman Kodak, a photographic equipment and supplies manufacturer, from June 1982 to July 1983, and as account director for J. Walter Thompson Advertising from January 1980 to June 1982.

Delbert W. Yocam (age 41) joined Apple in November 1979 as director of materials. In August 1981, he was promoted to vice president and general manager of operations, and in January 1984, was appointed executive vice president and general manager, Apple II Division. In June 1985, Mr. Yocam was named executive vice president, group executive of product operations.

Albert A. Eisenstat (age 55) joined Apple in July 1980 as vice president and general counsel; he has also served as secretary of Apple since September 1980. In November 1985, Mr. Eisenstat was promoted to senior vice president and was elected to the board of directors to fill the vacancy created by the resignation of Steven P. Jobs.

David J. Barram (age 41) joined Apple in April 1985 as vice president of finance and chief financial officer. Prior to his employment with Apple, he was the vice president of finance and administration and chief financial officer of Silicon Graphics, a manufacturer of high-performance engineering workstations, from April 1983 to April 1985. From January 1970 to April 1983, Mr. Barram was controller of the Computer Products Group of Hewlett-Packard, a diversified electronics measurement and computer equipment manufacturer.

Deborah A. Coleman (age 32) joined Apple in November 1981, initially as controller and subsequently as director of operations of the Macintosh Division. Prior to her promotion in November 1985 to vice president of manufacturing, Ms. Coleman had been director of manufacturing from June 1985 to November 1985. Before joining Apple, Ms. Coleman served as a financial manager and cost accounting supervisor at Hewlett-Packard.

Jay R. Elliot (age 46) joined Apple as senior human resources manager in May 1982, and became vice president, human resources, in September 1983. Before joining Apple, Mr. Elliot served as personnel manager for Intel Corporation, a semiconductor manufacturer, from August 1980 to May 1982.

Jean-Louis Gassee (age 41) joined Apple in February 1981 as general manager of Seedrin S.A.R.L., a wholly owned subsidiary of the company. In May 1985, Mr. Gassee became director of marketing for the Macintosh

Division in Cupertino, California, and in June 1985, he was named vice president, product development. Prior to joining Apple, Mr. Gassee was president of Exxon Office Systems from July 1979 to February 1981, in Paris, France.

Thomas Marano (age 35) joined Apple as vice president, U.S. sales, in January 1985. Before joining Apple, Mr. Marano served as director of business development for Pepsi-Cola Company from October 1978 to February 1985.

Michael Muller (age 46) joined Apple in September 1979 as president of The Keyboard Company, then a wholly owned subsidiary of Apple. In April 1982, The Keyboard Company became Apple's Accessory Products Division, and Mr. Muller was promoted to vice president and general manager of that division. In June 1985, Mr. Muller was appointed vice president in charge of special projects.

Michael Spindler (age 43) joined Apple as European marketing manager in September 1980, was promoted to vice president and general manager, Europe, in January 1984, and was named vice president, International, in February 1985.

Roy H. Weaver, Jr. (age 53) joined Apple in September 1980 as U.S. distribution manager. Beginning in April 1981, he was director of distribution and service operations, and in April 1982, was promoted to general manager of distribution and service. In September 1982, he was appointed vice president and general manager of the Distribution, Service and Support Division; in September 1983, vice president, field operations; and in June 1985, vice president, distribution.

Robert Saltmarsh (age 35) joined Apple as assistant treasurer in November 1982, and was promoted to treasurer in November 1985. Between February 1979 and November 1982, Mr. Saltmarsh worked for Data General, a minicomputer manufacturer, first as European treasury manager and then as corporate treasury manager.

JOHN SCULLEY

The man Steve Jobs and Apple's board of directors chose to help Apple Computer develop professional management was John Sculley, the mid-40-year-old president of the Pepsi-Cola Company, the domestic drink subsidiary of PepsiCo, Inc. John Sculley represented the opposite of Jobs who dropped out of college

and spent his youth experimenting with electronic gizmos, mystical religions, and fruitarian diets. Sculley was cool, disciplined, and orderly; a character developed through strict eastern boarding schools.

After Sculley earned a bachelor's degree in architecture from Brown University, he then pursued a M.B.A. degree at Wharton School, at the University of Pennsylvania, where he graduated in 1963. "He wasn't a particularly noteworthy academic at school, but people tended to follow him," said his younger brother, David. This quality followed Sculley to Pepsi where, by age 38, he had become president of PepsiCo, Inc.'s Pepsi-Cola subsidiary. Sculley's ambition and achievement at such a young age attracted Jobs who realized Apple was in need of headstrong leadership.

To lure Sculley away from a shot at becoming chairman of the $7.5 billion food conglomerate, Jobs promised Sculley a deal which included:

- $2 million in salary and bonuses for his first year.
- Help with the purchase of a $2 million home in Woodside, California, 14 miles from Apple headquarters.
- Options in 350,000 shares of Apple stock.

Upon joining Apple in May 1983, Sculley was faced with a company full of problems. Committed to turn Apple around in the microcomputer industry, Sculley established structure and discipline within Apple, unlike the free and unstructured organization followed by his predecessor. Sculley brought boot camp drill to Apple, classifying employees as A, B, or C players.

In the fall of 1983, Sculley invented a dismissal program designed by one Apple programmer:

> They've been telling people they've got two choices. They've got five days to resign or they're going to be put in a job for which they are unqualified, unsuited, and ill-equipped where they'll be allowed to fail and then be fired.

Less than one year after Sculley joined Apple, only 8 of the 14 senior executives who were present when Sculley joined, remained at Apple; eventually both cofounders departed.

"I am alone at the top now," declared Sculley, referring to the removal of Steve Jobs. Jobs had recruited Sculley to help Apple develop a professional management. Sculley saw it as his mission to teach Apple marketing and to improve its response to retailers and customers.

Sculley began his mission by merging the company's nine highly decentralized divisions, most of which had been responsible for one product line, into an organization structured according to business functions as demonstrated in Exhibit 1.

Transforming Apple became a tougher task than Sculley had first imagined. Under the leadership of Steve Jobs, Apple had acquired a near maniacal focus on products. Jobs talked of creating "insanely great" new computers, and made stars out of product designers. Sculley refocused Apple's direction through the consolidation of Apple's divisions into just three: a sales division for all products, a division for the Apple II family, and a division for Macintosh with Jobs as its general manager.

THE FALL OF JOBS

"They've cut the heart out of Apple and substituted an artificial one. We'll just have to see how long it pumps," said one Apple insider shocked at the announcement of Steve Jobs's departure from Apple Computer, Inc.

The decline of Steve Jobs began as the personal computer industry was experiencing a slump in demand, and Apple was experiencing disappointing sales in its Macintosh Division, headed by Jobs as its general manager. Urging John Sculley to assert his authority over the company in order for Apple to be spared any additional losses was Arthur Rock, a San Francisco venture capitalist and a member of Apple's board of directors. Sculley was reluctant to act as hastily as the board wished, putting off any confrontations with Jobs due to a cautious feeling about radical organizational changes and also out of concern for Jobs's feelings.

"I decided to change my life and come to Apple because of my admiration for Steve and what he had done. Our reorganization was all the more painful because we are such close friends," said the president. Sculley was forced to reorganize Apple and eliminate the company's cofounder when he learned that Jobs was plotting to dispose of him.

The Macintosh Division considered itself the company's elite due to the protective environment created by Jobs who publicized the members of the division as superstars. This attention was not to the liking of the Apple II Division whose president was responsible for 65 percent of Apple's total sales. Although the Apple II Division was producing more of the company's sales

and profits, the Macintosh Division was receiving all of the perks which included free fruit juice and a masseur on call.

Born out of the belief that new technology should supersede the old, Jobs once referred to the Apple II Division's marketing staff as members of the "dull and boring product division." So protective of the Macintosh Division was Jobs that whenever there was a complaint about the division, Jobs would confront the source on the telephone and, said a Macintosh staff member, "chew the guy out so fast your head would spin."

Falling short of its plan to sell 150,000 Macintoshes during the Christmas 1984 season by 50,000 computers, Apple's board began to develop concerns regarding its new product and how it was being perceived by the market as "a cutesy avocado machine for yuppies and their kids," not as a sophisticated and innovative office machine.

On April 11, 1985, at an Apple board meeting, the company's directors urged Sculley to assert himself as the chief executive officer, but Sculley stated it was difficult to act as CEO when he had to "boss a general manager who happened to be chairman of the board." With that situation in mind, Apple's directors resolved to have Jobs relinquish his position as general manager of the Macintosh Division; however, Jobs would remain as Apple's chairman. Jobs believed that his removal from the Macintosh Division was a cruel, surprise act.

No set schedule for Jobs's abdication was established, an error which lead Jobs to forget the meaning of the board's resolution. In Jobs's mind, the board's decision was a reprieve and not to be taken seriously, but in the minds of Sculley and Apple's other directors, it was a phaseout. This difference in perceptions concerning the removal of Jobs lead to the final eruption within Apple.

ENTER GASSEE

To strengthen the Macintosh Division, Jean-Louis Gassee, head of Apple France, was recruited as the eventual replacement for Steve Jobs as general manager. Gassee was a strong-willed and talented mathematician who was responsible for turning Apple France into the company's fastest growing and most profitable division.

Sculley's plan was to move Gassee into the Macintosh Division as its marketing director with the intent to move him to the position of general manager at some unspecified date. Gassee, however, insisted upon a written

EXHIBIT 1 Apple Organization

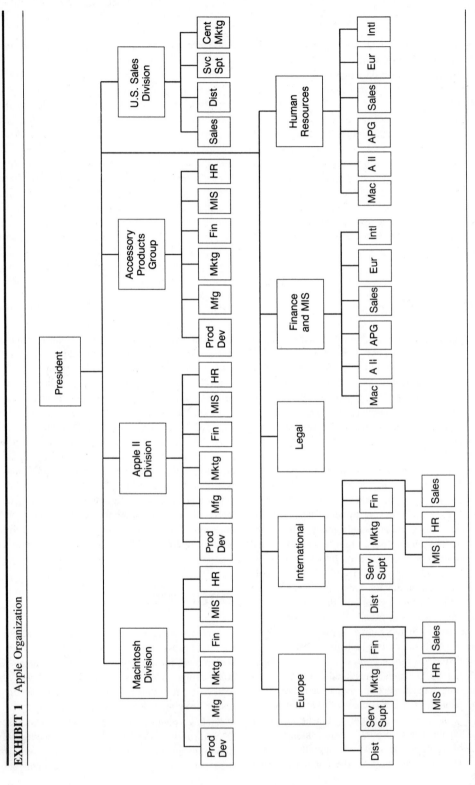

Source: 1985 Apple Annual Report.

guarantee stating an exact date for his promotion to general manager; a demand viewed as an outrage by Jobs who thought Gassee should earn his way to the position.

Reluctant to relinquish his authority, Jobs began suggesting to his friends at Apple that the company was too small for both Sculley and himself and that the board would have to choose between them. The day after Apple's board announced that Gassee would become the marketing manager for the Macintosh Division, Jobs called together his top aides and asked in a hypothetical vein whether they would support him if forced to make a choice. What Jobs had hoped to be a coup to dispose of Sculley turned out to be the catalyst that set off a company reorganization and his ultimate removal.

During the May 24, 1985 executive committee meeting attended by both Jobs and Sculley, the president of Apple firmly stated that he was the one calling the shots at Apple and the company would undergo a restructuring. As a result of the discussions in the meeting, the committee failed to find a future role for Jobs in the day-to-day operations of Apple. Jobs agreed to take a long vacation and return after the reorganization was complete. In two marathon meetings held on May 29 and 30, Apple was reorganized, structured entirely on a functional basis (as shown in Exhibit 2), with Jobs removed as chairman and left with no direct authority other than a role described as "global visionary."

FINAL SPLIT

During the September 12, 1985 board meeting, Steve Jobs declared that he wished to proceed with his life and he had a plan to start a new company that would design and produce products that would complement Apple. In order to avoid any more disruption at Apple, he offered to resign as chairman.

Jobs's idea for a business was to design and produce high-tech computers that could display lifelike simulations of laboratory experiments. The company he envisioned would have modest sales of $50 million annually, because he was not interested in another high-growth firm destined for public status. It would offer the heady environment Jobs had created for the development of Macintosh.

Several board members became alarmed when Jobs eluded to the possibility of hiring Apple personnel for his venture, although he assured them that the employees he might possibly hire would most probably be those who already had plans to leave Apple and that none would be important to the development of Apple products.

The following day, Jobs informed Sculley as to the identity of the five Apple employees he had hired. Sculley became enraged to learn that among the five, three of the employees were those whom Apple could ill afford to lose:

David Lewin—Head of Apple's marketing to schools and colleges.

Bud Tribble—Manager of software development for all of the company's computers.

George Crow—Apple's senior engineer for power circuitry.

The board decided to demand the resignation of Jobs and began discussing legal actions to take against him

---

EXHIBIT 2 Apple Reorganization

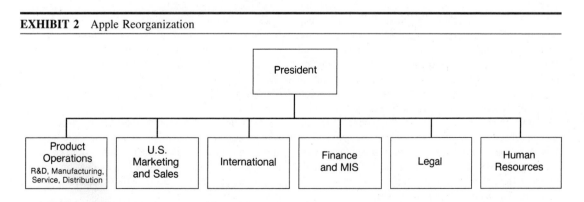

Source: 1985 Apple Annual Report.

due to his blunder in hiring Apple employees while still chairman.

On September 17, 1985, Jobs sent an elaborate letter of resignation to major newspapers before he submitted a formal resignation to Sculley and the board. In the letter, the "original employee" cast himself as a wronged innocent who held the belief that in a publicity battle he had the advantage because he felt the "folk hero" always would win. He continued a public fight with his former colleagues through press releases and public interviews.

PRODUCT MARKETING

Apple's product line was basically dependent upon two families of PCs comprising of four machines. The Apple IIc, the "everything-you-need-in-one-box" computer, was a portable version of the Apple II, first introduced in 1977. Although the Apple II was built with an "open architecture," the IIc was provided with a "closed" system because add-on capabilities were not considered to be necessary with a small portable model. The Apple IIe was the other member of this family of PCs with its own line of software and peripherals that would accommodate the IIc machine. The IIe was a 128k memory machine that could be expanded to hold a capacity of 256k of memory. The Apple II line was very popular in the educational sector and subsequently accounted for nearly 60 percent of Apple's sales and the majority of its profits. In addition to the Apple II line, the Macintosh had its own family. The original Macintosh was a powerful machine that offered 512k of memory. This PC, originally designed with a "closed architecture," was still offered to those consumers who were not interested in expandability or flexibility, yet needed powerful PC processing capabilities. To answer to the needs of those users who were interested in starting out simple or complex and growing into a near minicomputer machine, the Macintosh Plus was introduced in January 1986. Sculley's accommodation to the third-party developers provided users with the ability to "pick and choose among variables instead of having to accommodate absolutes." The new machine, referred to as "Modular Mac," had two megabytes of random-access memory (RAM), double-sided disks, and a read-only memory (ROM) with an operating system that would accommodate hard disks and file servers.

DISTRIBUTION

While trying to predict which computer would be the product most accepted by the business world, many dealers worried that Apple's management turmoil, as well as the company's subsequent restructuring and dismissal of 1,200 workers in a cost-cutting campaign, would hamper Apple's ability to form a marketing strategy.

Apple's principal method of distribution of its products was through independent retail dealers, national retail accounts, and direct sales; however, Apple's new sales strategy included a larger role for retailers. This followed a long period of strained relations between Apple and its independent dealers caused by the direct sales force's erosion of the profit margins of independent retail dealers. "Apple has been ripping us apart," said Billy Ladin, chairman of Computercraft, Inc. "I recently asked my dealers 'Who's your biggest competition with Apple?' and they said, 'Apple'." In marketing to business customers, the company took positive steps to reduce the conflict between dealers and Apple's sales force by reducing the size of its national account sales force and focusing their efforts on specific major corporate customers, thus allowing dealers to sell and support Apple's products to a larger business customer market.

OUTSIDE ACCESSORY DEALERS

For the Macintosh computer, Apple had worked to strengthen its relations with outside companies that produce and sell accessories, some of which complained they were disregarded by Steve Jobs in his pursuit of Mac's development within the company. Although Mac's innovative built-in software allowed a user to easily enter commands by pointing to symbols on the display, it made it difficult for accessory companies to design a wide range of well-tailored accessories for Macintosh as they were able to for the IBM personal computer.

Mac's unorthodox design could be attributed to Jobs who conceived the computer after he was shut out of the development of the Lisa model which was discontinued in April 1985. It was Jobs's approach in product development to always begin with a clean slate, starting from zero.

After Apple's reorganization under Sculley, the company promised a significant role for outside accessory companies through the adoption of a long overdue open architecture design for Macintosh as well as for all Apple products.

TARGET MARKETS

The Home-User Market

Because the Apple IIe had historically been a success in the educational sector, Apple was excited about its introduction of the extension of the Apple IIc in 1984. The Apple IIc was designed for the home-user market, an estimated market of more than 20 million potential customers with an expected purchasing power amounting to $5.7 million or 6 million units in 1985.

The 1984 Christmas season was a learning experience for most personal computer manufacturers. The market for PCs was believed to be moving away from lower priced computers, such as the Commodore C64, to more expensive and more powerful machines such as the IBM personal computer junior and the Apple II. As a result, IBM, Apple, and other PC manufacturers heavily invested in the promotions of their high-end machines, and the 4 percent drop in the home market took a toll on them. Wozniak, whose new venture post-Apple was in the development of microprocessor-based electronic home appliances, had been predicting a "permanent slide in computer sales, particularly for the home." He said, "All people really need is a $30 typewriter and a vacation to Hawaii." According to "Woz," there was "no market for the PCs as helpers with routine household chores like cooking, cleaning, and laundering," and that "PCs will sell at a level a lot lower than people think." Others agreed with the inventor of the first personal computer and said that until small machines were capable of accessorizing television sets, an area the Japanese had been exploring, or until more powerful machines could "drive home appliances that make life's little chores more palatable," PCs would be used predominately for in-home office work.

Apparently, there was much "finger pointing" going on in the industry as companies were looking at "disappointing sales and stock prices." Timothy Williams, a senior analyst at Future Computing, Inc., research company said, "It's our belief that a lot of uncertainty is from self-inflicted wounds caused by individual manufacturers' optimistic assumptions about their market growth."

"That segment of the market has not experienced growth as fast as we had hoped," said John Pope of IBM's Entry Systems Division. Pope said his company had inventory levels necessary to meet projected demand for the IBM personal computer junior, because although the company discontinued production of the super-small machine in 1985, it would still "market and fully support" the micro. IBM discovered with the IBM personal computer junior that the home market favored a machine priced under $1,000. Sales of the IBM personal computer junior were weak until its price was slashed to $900. However, IBM was unable to continue to sell "junior" due to its price's inability to support its manufacturing cost.

The Educational Market

The educational market and telecommunications industry were open avenues of use for PC owners at home. The educational market was application intensive, with the use of microcomputers for drill practices in the primary education field and program instruction in the secondary educational field. As this market expanded, parents could have purchased computer models that were used in the schools by their children for home use (homework). The telecommunications industry offered an even greater opportunity for home computer application with the vision of machines connected to telephone lines that could be used to gain access to data banks to allow home shopping and banking and to send electronic mail messages to others.

In 1984, the home-user market accounted for 4.8 million computers sold, and the Apple IIe and IIc claimed a 16 percent share of the market. Future Computing, Inc., a Dallas-based research firm, predicted the home computer market would grow at an average rate of 26 percent until 1989, as shown in Exhibit 3.

The growth in the educational market for personal computers was considered to be the possible savior of the home PC market due to the belief that those consumers who would be purchasing a personal computer for use in their home would choose the machine used in the schools by their children. Unlike the home

PC market, specific need applications had been identified by the educational sector. The Apple IIe had long been a popular tool with which to solve problems. The educational market had the opportunity to influence future sales of PCs with the brand awareness the school exposure provided to the student population. When students were ready to purchase their own PC, manufacturers who had entered the educational market would be positioned as quality producers that had played a role in the education of those students.

The combined enrollment for all U.S. public and private schools was 44,701,367 students in the 1984–85 school year. In 1985, the entire educational expenditures for instructional materials was an estimated $2,625,527,000 ($2.7 billion) for all U.S. schools (refer to Exhibit 4).

In small schools with an enrollment under 500 students, the principal had the greatest influence and approved procurement. Schools of this size represented 34 percent of all elementary and junior highs. In larger schools, the principal typically conferred with teachers and specialists. With 72,784 elementary school principals, 39,049 junior high school principals, and 23,286 senior high school principals, the possibilities for infiltration of PC makers into this sector seemed endless. In addition, with the influence teachers have had with the purchase of instructional material and equipment (including microcomputers), the 243,189 public junior high and 384,539 public senior high school teachers furthered the opportunities this target market could provide. Computers most commonly used in this sector are shown in Exhibit 5.

The Business Market

With the introduction of Macintosh in 1984, Apple had begun to focus on the estimated 5 million small- and medium-sized businesses in the United States as a target market. In companies consisting of 20 or less employees, one in four used PCs in the course of conducting business. In companies comprised of between 20 and 99 employees, 33 percent of those companies used PCs. As the size of the firms increased, so did the frequency of microcomputer use, as 47.1 percent of companies who

EXHIBIT 3 Home-Computer Market Sales Forecast

Year	Sales Forecast (billions)
1986	$7.18
1987	$9.05
1988	$11.4
1989	$14.4

Source: *Mini-Micro Systems,* June 1985, p. 123.

EXHIBIT 4 Number of Public and Private Schools in the United States

	Public	Private
Elementary	51,255	16,070
Junior high	9,841	—
Senior high	13,874	2,436 (Junior and senior high combined)
K-12	2,851	4,058
	77,821	22,564

Source: *Market Data Retrieval,* 1984–1985, pp. 15–16.

employed between 100 and 499 people used PCs and an astounding 71.8 percent of companies with 500 to 999 employees used PCs.

Expandability was a key necessity to the business user of a personal computer. A user could take advantage of the numerous third-party manufacturers' add-on hardware and software accessories for additional flexibility. Not only was technology vital, but service, advice, and training rated extremely high on the list of priorities a business user made in the purchase of a PC. With the increase in efficiency in the day-to-day performance of their jobs and more effectiveness in decision making that a microcomputer could offer to today's managers, a PC became a necessity. With an estimated 11 million managers in the United States, there was room for many PC makers with astute awareness, knowledge, and tools to be very profitable.

In 1984, the $6.6 billion spent by businesses for PC represented 2.7 million machines sold. Future Computing, Inc. projected that the average growth rate of the business market for PCs would be 26 percent until 1989.

COMPETITION

The market for the design, manufacture, sale, and servicing of personal computers and related software and peripheral products is highly competitive. It has been characterized by rapid technological advances in both hardware and software development advances that have substantially increased the capabilities and applications of personal computers. The principal competitive factors in this market are product quality and reliability, relative price/performance, marketing and distribution capability, service and support, availability of hardware and software accessories, corporate reputation, and ease of use.

Apple originally positioned itself as the alternative to IBM by adopting the company motto of "the computer for the rest of us." One former company executive said, "Jobs would on occasion respond to marketing suggestions with 'That's IBM talk,' whereas Sculley is far more conscious of what the market demands of PCs and how he thinks they should be sold." Marketing Vice President William Campbell had been as aware of Apple's failure to accurately recognize the effects of IBM-inism in the business PC market as Sculley—"We will be careful not to pose ourselves in an obvious confrontation with IBM."

IBM

IBM stated its company goal to be the leader in every market it entered. In August 1981, "Big Blue" introduced its PC, the IBM personal computer, and set in

EXHIBIT 5 Microcomputers Used in Education

Brand Used	Number of Schools			
	Public	*Private*	*Catholic*	*Total*
Primary education:				
Apple	23,107	2,410	2,462	27,979
Radio Shack	6,631	1,011	1,097	8,739
Commodore	6,030	1,242	890	8,162
IBM	420	94	36	550
Secondary education:				
Apple	14,236	1,204	672	16,112
Radio Shack	7,348	715	532	8,595
Commodore	3,851	563	270	4,684
IBM	694	100	61	855

Source: *Market Data Retrieval*, 1985, p. 17.

motion an avalanche of software products. By 1982, the company had claimed an 18.4 percent share of the $2.7 billion office PC market, but was still trailing Apple who led the industry with a 23.3 percent share. By 1983, IBM had taken over with a 30 percent share of the $4.2 billion in sales to which the business market had grown. Not only had the original PC company lost the market share leadership, but Apple found its share had dropped to 12.1 percent. IBM continued to devour the business market at such a rapid pace that by 1984, its share was four times that of Apple's dwindling 11 percent at 41.4 percent of the $6.6 billion office PC market. The industry giant continued to consume the office PC market and by 1985, owned 60 percent, along with a 34 percent share of the entire PC market.

The IBM personal computer had become the standard in the PC industry. Of the approximately 90 different machines aimed at the business market, 60 claimed to be compatible with the IBM personal computer. The IBM personal computer compatible market accounted for $5.5 billion in sales.

IBM employed an open architecture design that allowed a multitude of hardware accessories vendors to supply add-on features that greatly expanded the market for their personal computer. The computer was distributed through a combination of computer specialty stores, and by IBM direct sales representatives that also handled IBM mainframe computers. The IBM product line was carried by 80 percent of the computer specialty stores in the United States which accounted for 30 percent of all personal computer sales to businesses.

IBM's success in the home and educational markets had not been quite the fairy tale of the business sector. The failure of the personal computer junior (a smaller version of the personal computer discontinued in 1985) had undermined confidence in IBM which had benefited from the perception among its customers that the firm would never leave the business and abandon its customers as "computer orphans."

By promoting itself as the leader in the market and emphasizing its dedication to service, IBM priced its products above the market to maintain its quality image (although discounts were offered to retailers for large orders of IBM personal computers which allowed dealers to realize a larger margin of profit with every sale of an IBM personal computer.

IBM selectively distributed its products through computer/business equipment stores and mass merchandisers. A strong belief existed among competitors that they should build product image through the use of a selective distribution strategy which utilized only computer stores. This represented a unique characteristic of IBM in that the product was independently strong so as to allow the personal computer to obtain greater exposure through the use of nontraditional outlets for business-oriented customers.

COMPAQ ®

In 1983, COMPAQ offered its first line of personal computers aimed at the business sector. The young company's revenues were impressive in 1984, at $329 million while it had captured a 16 percent share of the office market with the Deskpro PC. The Deskpro was a microcomputer that could be enhanced for compatibility with both the personal computer XT and the personal computer AT.

The rapidly advancing firm boasted of the fact that they sold more micros in the IBM personal computer compatible market than any of their competitors. It was very costly for a retailer to provide shelf space for the estimated 60 microcomputers in this category, so due to COMPAQ's 100 percent IBM compatibility with all accessories carried for the PC, any retailer could well afford to carry the COMPAQ line. Through an exclusive distribution to specialty retailers, COMPAQ had successfully flooded 66 percent of all U.S. computer dealerships.

The "compact" computer company was committed to second-place status behind IBM in the business computer market through the use of an imitator strategy. In order to set the company apart, IBM-cloned machines of the highest level of quality and technology were produced and priced at a competitive level. Such a strategy was affordable to COMPAQ due to a two-level distribution system that simply consisted of middlemen and computer business equipment stores.

In order to allow for open comparison between computers, COMPAQ's desire was to find shelf space in every outlet that carried the IBM line of products—not necessarily a fantasy. COMPAQ had a very unique relationship with its dealers because of the absence of a competitive sales force. Through the use of incentive programs and exclusive dedication to dealers, it had been able to build one of the strongest company/dealer relationships in existence.

Commodore

Although not quite the "young pup" COMPAQ was, Commodore's experience in the business market had been launched. With the introduction of the Amiga®, the company had joined the mainswing of the personal computer market toward business. Unfortunately, the microcomputer was better suited for the home due to its low price and color graphics. In addition, the native operating system, Amiga DOS®, was incompatible with software for other computers.

To further the limitations, the development of application programs very vital to PC office use seemed to have been almost forgotten. Commodore had announced its line of software designed for the Amiga of which most were games, programming languages, and programming tools.

Historically, Commodore had relied on success in the home personal computer market. The C64 was a very popular 64k machine that the consumer could purchase at a very low price of approximately $100 and take home to hook up to the family television set. There was a wide range of game and home application software from which to choose that owners found very appealing. For those who outgrew the C64 and those modern high-tech-student types, a more powerful version, the C128 was introduced for the educational market.

Commodore distributed its low end home computer through an extensive infiltration of mass merchandisers, discount stores, and department stores. The C64 could be found in such popular stores as Sears, K mart, and Toys-"R"-Us. Plans for the C128 would follow the same strategy and also be priced competitively so as to encourage sales and increase volume. As for the Amiga, Commodore continued to follow an innovative strategy whereby product enhancements were aimed at successful competition against the Macintosh (which used the same microprocessor) and the IBM personal computer, which the Amiga offered to the consumer an accessory that allowed the machine to act as a PC clone.

OPERATIONS

Apple strove to use the most innovative manufacturing tools. The company believed that Japanese dominance in the electronics industry was due in large to their concentration on maintaining highly innovative factories, whereas the American companies had concentrated their efforts more in the laboratories. Apple's "goal is to be as good in manufacturing technology as the best Japanese electronics companies will be." The long-term goal was to achieve status as "one of the world's lowest cost, highest quality manufacturers." In order to achieve this status, Apple built six state-of-the-art facilities worldwide. A plant located in Fremont, California, occupied 160,000 square feet and was highly automated. In 1985, the company closed three manufacturing sites as part of the plan to restructure. Although it was an unpopular decision among plant employees, Debbie Coleman, head of worldwide manufacturing, felt it was necessary to keep the company competitive in the midst of the PC slump. A surprisingly young vice president at 32 years of age, the Stanford M.B.A. graduate said, "I had a concise and particular strategy about what I wanted to do. I had to choose which factories to shut down and which were crucial to our success." Her decision was based on which plants had the most flexible machinery. "It was a technical issue. Fremont was supposed to be a single-product factory, but in 1984 and 1985, we changed strategy. To be world-class, it would have to handle multiple production in varying volumes." So the Fremont plant became the primary facility for the assembly of the Macintosh and Apple IIc, and the Singapore plant was left with the responsibility for the Apple IIe. To accommodate the European market, Apple IIe and Apple IIc would continue to be assembled at Apple's Cork, Ireland, facility. The company also transferred the operations for peripherals at the recently closed Mill Street, Ireland, plant to the Cork facility. Operations at the Dallas plant (Apple IIc and Apple IIe factory) and the Garden Grove, California, plant (peripherals factory) were shut down, leaving the Fremont plant all alone on the home turf.

Coleman's expertise and experience in innovative manufacturing techniques, stemming from her days in production and quality control at Hewlett-Packard, had kept Apple's operations technologically superior. She switched the factories from a "hard" automation process system to one that was "flexible." Coleman said, "A hard system is right for a single product. In the late 70s it was state-of-the-art. We were tooled for high volume, to get process quality up, and get product costs down. I had gone for it, but was wrong. It was right in 1984, but things change. With flexible automation you have robotics with sensors you can reprogram, so you can produce 8 to 24 products on one line." The Fremont factory could produce 80,000 Macintoshes monthly, although demand was approximately 30,000 per month.

Coleman also switched the plants from the stockpiling of parts and inventory system to a "just-in-time" scheduling system. In an effort to reduce inventory, Apple would build machines to "keep up with demand rather than overshoot it." As a result, inventory decreased from $261 million to $107 million in 1985.

In her efforts to clean up the excessive plant operations, Coleman had to relieve 700 manufacturing employees of their jobs. In total, 1,200 employees were laid off as a result of the clean-up plan in the reorganization at Apple. Coleman said it was the most difficult part for her but that "it was a question of the long-term success of Apple versus these jobs."

TECHNOLOGY

Apple's claim to fame had always been that of the innovative leader in the personal computer industry. It began with Apple and although the company had been overpowered by IBM and found itself competing for the number two position in the market with an abundance of other hardware companies, it prided itself as an original, not a user of "off-the-shelf-tool-technology." This role that the company had assumed had been integral to its ability to differentiate itself from all the companies that had contributed to the explosion in the personal computer market and Apple historically felt the need to remain distinctive.

Apple also incorporated into its philosophy the idea of "user-friendliness." Jobs always stressed the importance of an easy-to-use, yet highly innovative and technologically superior machine. The realization that people who lacked technical knowledge and skill were not so eager to use a machine bogged down with complex procedures came to him long before the IBM personal computer was born. The incentive to use a computer was that it could simplify the complexity of a task.

Although Apple's drive to remain lead innovator distinguished it from other industry giants, the company had found itself alienated from the business community. Jobs's insistence on a closed architecture had thus far crippled Macintosh's ability to thrive in the business market. Michael Joseph, of Lomega Corporation, said "the good side is that he made computers that were easier for people to use. The bad side is that they were harder for people like me to build parts for." Joseph was referring to the Macintosh's "unorthodox" design. Because hard disk drives and other peripherals were becoming a necessity for PCs in order to store more data, buyers had turned to IBM and other makers who did provide such hardware in addition to a "wide variety of well-tailored accessories." Other competitors had seen the advantages to joining "Big Blue" rather than trying to beat the giant. William H. Bowman of Spinnaker Software Corporation said, "Jobs was totally dedicated to pushing the Macintosh against IBM in the business channel." Jobs felt the Macintosh was a superior machine to the IBM personal computer and "thought it would be slumming to support the PC," according to Charles Rubin, an Apple software book author. Since the reorganization in 1985, Sculley's job had been to redirect some of the technological energies that had historically driven the company to realistic marketing strategies.

The key to a realistic marketing strategy in Sculley's mind was to be "a more responsive market-driven firm" that would stay in tune with customers', dealers', and third-party software and hardware developers' needs. He firmly believed the Macintosh should be compatible with IBM in order "to achieve the primary goal we set for Macintosh at the beginning of 1985—a significant penetration in the business market." Sculley had developed a "customer-driven" strategy to focus in on two new growing market segments. One was called *desktop publishing*. It was a "solution to create reports, presentations, proposals, and newsletters of superb quality on a quick turnaround low-cost basis," that could be used by connecting the Macintosh with LaserWriter®. The other opportunity Sculley felt that was prevalent in the business market was communications. By the employment of data communication links between workstations, hosts, and local networking between workstations, information sharing "may launch a rejuvenation of the personal computer industry." Sculley felt that Apple could "be the leader in bringing together a superior human interface with real functionality in an IBM-defined systems world."

In 1985, sources outside of Apple said the reorganized company would soon announce new-product releases which included a Macintosh hard disk drive, file server, ImageWriter® II printer, new Apple II disk drives, new 800k Sony drives for Macintosh, and a revised Macintosh disk operating system. Yocam said, "I absolutely believe in open architecture.'' With his guidance, it was expected that Apple products would change and users would be able to increase memory as well as the number of peripherals used.

In January 1986, Sculley announced plans for a software link between the Macintosh and IBM mainframes, minis and micros (PCs), and Digital Equipment Corporation's VAX system. Sculley said ''the systems will not penalize the user with slower response time or other limitations and will provide not only terminal emulation or PC-like functions, but also access to completed office systems and distributed data processing functionality.'' Bill Krause, president and CEO of 3COM Corporation, said ''Apple recognizes that anyone who wants to exist in the computer market has to support IBM.'' He did not think the company made any compromises but was simply ''pragmatic.''

RESEARCH AND DEVELOPMENT

In order to continue the position of the innovative leader in the PC industry, Apple's research and development expenses had averaged 4.5 percent to 6.5 percent of net sales from 1982 to 1985. In 1985, the company spent $73 million compared to $71 million in 1984. There was an increase in product development centered around the Macintosh in 1984, and in 1985 several product projects were canceled due to the reorganization. In spite of the transitionary slowdown in research and development, Apple continued its commitment to a significant research and development budget to support new-product development in order to manufacture products of superior design and quality.

FINANCIAL

After the Christmas slump of 1984, Apple was off to a dismal start in 1985. The company had planned to sell 150,000 Macintoshes over the season, but reached only about two thirds of its goal. As a result, there was not the same stream of back orders as the 1983 season had produced, and dealers were deep in inventory stock. Sales of Macintoshes declined to 19,000 units monthly for the first quarter. Although Apple earned a record $46 million on sales of $698 million during the Christmas quarter, the figures were due to the strength of Apple II.

The picture became even more bleak as the reorganization rapidly progressed. Eugene G. Glazer, an analyst for Dean Witter Reynolds, Inc., felt that the industry slump was harder for Apple than competitors because of the company's narrow range of products. He predicted that in 1986, Apple would earn $1.55 per share and said, ''if there isn't an upturn in the computer market, there's no way they can make these numbers.'' By the end of the third quarter, Apple's stock had hit a four-year low of $14 compared to a high of $63 in 1983. Even more disillusioning was a $17.2 million loss for the quarter. This was a first for Apple since its incorporation in 1977. The loss was the result of a one-time charge against earnings of $40.3 million due to the reorganization of the company. On the bright side, Apple had lowered its break-even point considerably from $425 million at the beginning of the year to $350 to $370 million. This had been the direction management had hoped to move in by the layoff of 20 percent of personnel and the closings of three factories in addition to other costs incurred from redundancy under the old structure. Another positive stroke was that Apple's balance sheet was very strong as cash reserves had grown to $254.6 million.

As the year rolled on, Apple's situation improved. Net sales increased 27 percent to approximately $1.9 billion for the year. The gross profit margin remained stable at 42 percent of net sales, albeit the gross profit margin improved to 46 percent during the fourth quarter of 1985. The reduction in facilities and payroll costs and declining semiconductor prices were offset by competitive price pressures and expenses resulting in excess and obsolete inventories. Research and development expenditures increased approximately $1.4 million during 1985, but declined as a percentage of sales. Also Apple began to keep a closer eye on marketing expenditures which decreased as a percentage of net sales from 26 percent to 25 percent. Campbell said such measures as withdrawal from the National Computer Conference would help dramatically since the company typically spent $800,000 per show to participate. A decrease in advertising was the predominant factor in the decline in marketing expenditures. Also over the 1985 fiscal year, interest income decreased due to declining interest rates available on cash and temporary investments.

Coleman's ''as-needed'' basis for purchases of raw material realized a $97.6 million decrease in inventories. Others kept Apple moving—the board of directors authorized for issuance 5 million shares of preferred stock in one or more series. The effective income tax rate of the company had increased from 41 percent in 1984 to 48 percent in 1985. Apple had over 8 million shares in stock option plans, outstanding under various stock option plans, ranging in exercise prices of $19 to $59 per share. By the quarter ended September 27, 1985, the company had $337 million in cash and temporary cash investments and no long-term debt.

As time progressed, Apple continued slowly to recover costs since the consolidation of functions within the company. In January 1986, Apple's reported break-even point had been reduced further to $325 million. Although the first quarter of the 1986 fiscal year resulted in a sales decline of 23 percent, the cost-cutting measures that had improved margins to 52 percent of sales and produced higher inventory turnover allowed Apple's profits to grow 23 percent to a record 0.91 cents per share. The company also announced plans to increase research and development expenditures by 50 percent to an estimated $108 million.

The pattern had continued in the same direction for Apple as the firm focused on costs to survive the ongoing sales slump. Earnings increased for the quarter ended March 28, 1986, despite the 6 percent decline in sales from $435 million in 1985 to $409 million. Earnings jumped to $32 million compared to $22 million in the second quarter of 1985. Apple's rise in the quarter profit to $1.40 per share generally surprised Wall Street analysts who had been expecting a per-share net of $0.30 to $0.35 cents. The improved financial state of Apple was attributed to the deep cost-cutting measures, improved foreign sales, and higher than average sales of high margin printers, disk drives, and peripherals.

PATENTS AND TRADEMARKS

Apple held the rights to patents and copyrights relating to certain aspects of its computer and peripheral systems. In addition, Apple had registered trademarks in the United States and a number of foreign countries for "Apple," the Apple silhouette logo, the Apple color logo, and numerous product trademarks.

Apple had licensed rights for use of the trademark "Macintosh" that extended through May 1983, and were renewable thereafter. Although Apple believed that the ownership of such patents and trademarks was an important factor in its business and that success depended in part on the ownership thereof, Apple relied primarily on the innovative skills, technical competence, and marketing abilities of its personnel.

LITIGATION

"Apple's called me a thief in public, and that's simply not true," said Steve Jobs responding to a lawsuit filed by his former employer. The lawsuit alleged that Steve Jobs, by virtue of his position in Apple as its chairman, had access to confidential business information relating to Apple's future computer products, strategic business plans, and key personnel, and that he conspired to use such information to form a new company which would hire away Apple employees and compete with Apple.

"Steve is trying to turn this into a trial-by-press, and we're not going to do this," said Albert Eisenstat, indicating Apple's displeasure with the numerous comments made by Jobs to the press. Since Jobs still owned approximately 9 percent of Apple's stock, he had the financial means to fight a legal battle with Apple and also start a new venture.

Six class-action lawsuits had been filed against Apple and 14 of its officers and directors, alleging violations of state and federal securities laws relating primarily to allegations of fraud and inside trading based upon the company's alleged failure to make certain disclosures of material facts during the period from November 12, 1982, to September 23, 1983.

An $11 million lawsuit was filed against Apple by a distributor in Chile charging that Apple had improperly terminated the company in Chile as an Apple distributor. Six dealers filed suits against Apple seeking to restrain the company from implementing a prohibition of mail-order sales. Apple received a favorable summary judgment, but the case was appealed by the dealers.

Apple believed that the suits filed against them were without merit, and the company continued to litigate vigorously the asserted claims in these actions. In addition, Apple maintained liability insurance which would help to defray the legal expenses of any unfavorable outcome.

In January 1986, Apple Computer, Inc., reached an out-of-court settlement with its former chairman in which Jobs's new company, Next Inc., was prohibited from marketing its new computer, targeted at the university market, until July 1987. Under the settlement, Apple was given the right to inspect the new computer to determine if it used certain proprietary technology, and Jobs agreed not to use certain other undisclosed technologies. In the settlement, Apple was given the right to inspect the prototype of the new computer for 30 days to determine if any of Apple's proprietary technology was utilized. The 30-day limit agreement for Apple's inspection of Jobs's computer was regarded by industry experts as a coup for Jobs since disputes of this type often could drag on for several months and disrupt marketing and production plans.

OUTLOOK

As the computer slump continued, many companies were fighting to avoid becoming victims in an inevitable shakeout in the industry. Computer manufacturers were struggling to compete by offering lower prices and cutting production costs so as not to lose much profit margin. The American dollar remained stronger than foreign currency, such as the Japanese yen, and a large trade deficit continued to hamper American industry.

The future was left to tell who would be able to survive in the new personal computer world of IBM. For the first near-decade, Apple was successful as the personal computer ideal and could afford to thumb its nose at the computer mammoth. Could the company who was responsible for the creation of an industry of the personal computer's proportions thrive under the rule of "King" IBM? With the original "hackers in blue jeans" gone (Jobs and Wozniak), would the image so endearing to Apple computer disappear? And if so, how would the company set itself apart from the rest in an IBM-clone world? Jean Richardson, who headed Apple's marketing communications department for seven years, made this observation, "Can you think of one company that created the brand awareness, the innovation, that Apple did in seven years? There's an incredible amount of positive 'stuff' inside Apple. Apple won't be hurt dramatically by all the changes. The company still has so many dollars working for it that the public will not notice a lot of differences other than a stronger market presence."

Start-up Strategies: New Ventures

4. *The Douglasville Athletic Club Venture*

On a Sunday evening in 1984, John Quincy props his feet on the couch in his office as he contemplates progress on the Douglasville Athletic Club venture. He is scheduled to meet with a group of potential investors on Thursday afternoon, and Friday he is meeting with the commercial loan officer from a local bank. Early next week he has an appointment for initial discussions regarding a loan guarantee with a representative of the Small Business Administration.

He has been working on the venture for six months during spare hours, and almost full-time for the last two months. He wonders if all the major potential problems have been identified. He wonders what questions will be asked by potential investors, the commercial loan officer, and the Small Business Administration representative.

John was a senior executive with Wilcox Manufacturing Company until his resignation three months ago. While at Wilcox, John and a number of local sports enthusiasts formed a partnership to start a racquet club in their hometown of Carrollton. There were serious problems with the Carrollton Racquet Club during the first two years of operation, in part because they were unable to find a competent manager.

John felt that there were opportunities for fitness facilities in other regional towns if the clubs were well conceived and managed. Over the past two years he investigated opportunities and made some preliminary negotiations, but dropped them due to lack of sufficient business potential.

For the past six months, he has been looking into a new location in Douglasville, Georgia, located just 20 miles west of Atlanta on Interstate 20 (I-20). He believes that this could be the beginning of a chain of athletic clubs located in large rural and suburban markets. John would focus on developing and starting up the clubs, and Al Medina, the current manager of the Carrollton Racquet and Fitness Club, would establish and control the operations in each location. Al would recruit, hire, and train resident managers while overseeing operating

---

This case was written by Frank R. Hunsicker, Professor of Business, West Georgia College and Gordon E. Johnson III.

problems, budgets, and costs. With this arrangement, they hope to develop and manage three clubs within the next five years. The primary people involved in the venture are:

~ why did he resign?

- John Quincy (age 50) has a masters degree in electrical engineering and was with Wilcox for nearly 20 years, rising to group vice president for metal products and CEO of two subsidiaries.

- Al Medina (age 34) is working on his M.B.A. and is presently manager of the Carrollton Racquet and Fitness Club. He served in the Air Force for four years.

Potential Partners. The group consists of partners in the Carrollton Club and others from the area. Several of the group members acted as an informal advisory group for John as he investigated opportunities. The group consists of lawyers, an accountant, and several businessmen from Carrollton and Douglasville.

THE CONCEPT AND STRATEGY

The general concept is to establish a limited partnership of 10–15 members, with John and Al as general partners. As each partnership is established, local investors will be sought to link the community and the athletic club. Each club will be organized to meet the needs of its community with flexibility to take advantage of additional fitness activities as they develop. It is believed the market will not support single-use facilities. However, by skillfully planning the building, several closely related markets could be penetrated, thus attracting families who want physical activity but have varied interests.

John's experience at the Carrollton Club and at Wilcox helped him to realize that employee participation in profits is critical to success. Although it was easy to recruit employees who were skilled in the activities of a club, they often lacked interest in satisfying customers.

Linking an incentive plan to club success has proved to be an excellent motivator.

The growth of fitness facilities was phenomenal during the 1960s and 1970s compared to previous decades. This pattern has continued into the 1980s, and the outlook for long-term future growth is excellent. Although activities such as tennis and racquetball reached a mature stage of growth in the 1970s and early 1980s, respectively, many people still participate in these sports. People continue to demonstrate an interest in fitness, but the means of attaining and maintaining fitness has changed. The fitness market is dynamic, and a new variety of products must be provided to interest the consumer. This rationale was used as a basis for the concept of operations at the Douglasville development.

John's five-year strategy, which he mailed to potential investors last week, provides insight into how he intends to develop profitable ventures. It is presented here in a slightly abbreviated form:

> Although we don't use the words "human potential" in our descriptive literature, it is to those sets of human needs that the Carrollton Racquet and Fitness Club has appealed. People have always wanted to look better and be healthier, more successful, and better liked. Every level of Maslow's Hierarchy of Needs is embraced, particularly the security and affiliative needs. From Charles Atlas and Norman Vincent Peale to Richard Simmons and Robert Schuler, the multitude of human potentialists exhort us to be more successful with less stress and more fun. *Megatrends* identifies the High Touch (social) needs growing from the incursion of High Tech. The move from institutional help to self-help is also documented therein. Alvin Toffler, in *The Third Wave,* clearly points out the trend to destructuring lifestyles and the impact of the information age on diversification of interests. For over eight years, we have carefully observed the trend states of California, Connecticut, Colorado, and Florida for the effect on clubs of this nature, and we feel reasonably confident of follow-on trends in Georgia for the next three to five years. The Douglasville club will continue to build on the success of the Carrollton club as well as taking forward steps.

> He suggests the products are directed at their basic needs, categorized as "enhancement" (looking better),

"defensive" (preventing premature heart attack), and/or "social-recreational" (fun, affiliative). He further suggests that needs vary with age and social categories, the primary human potential-need categories.

John states the basic strategy is to: (1) be an early entrant in the Douglasville market in order to gain a majority share of the market for a strong referral base; (2) operate with a consistently high quality of courtesy, cleanliness, and reliability; and (3) build upon the Carrollton experience with a stream of proven product improvements, beginning with enhancement in a social-recreational environment for a 25–45-year age range and shifting to broader age appeals and defensive products (e.g., a Wellness Center). The strategy will be implemented in two phases.

Phase I—Initial Entry

The product array will consist of the elements that have been most successful in Carrollton. Expected participation percentages in Douglasville are summarized below (most people take advantage of more than one activity):

- 30 percent racquetball.
- 35 percent group exercise (aerobics, stretchicize, etc.).
- 40 percent swimming.
- 50 percent equipment-oriented physical conditioning.
- 75 percent amenities: nursery, whirlpool, sauna, tanning, television lounge, snack bar, pro shop.

The appeal is primarily to the 25–45-year age-group, but broader programming will be introduced after the start-up months for such things as weight control, group trips, and networking activities (joggers, campers). Children's activities will be added to encourage full family participation. Tennis, a low-cost addition, will be added for adults, and should result in a 15 percent–20 percent increase in membership potential.

Phase II—Wellness Center

The Wellness Center concept is being pioneered with success in a number of clubs throughout the United States, including the Wellness and Fitness Center owned

VERY DIFFUSE

by Riverside Hospital of Newport News, Virginia; Charter Medical at St. Simons Island, Georgia; and the YMCA of Colorado Springs, Colorado. The Center is medical supervised and deals with health promotion and sickness prevention in such areas as prenatal exercise, stress management, prescriptive programs, weight reduction, and rehabilitation areas such as postcardiac rehabilitation. The Douglasville location, near a hospital, would support this concept very well.

As a fall-back alternative, the location and style of the buildings are planned so they can be converted to professional offices such as a medical or legal center. Like a military attack, success is envisioned, but the possibility of retreat is not ignored.

DOUGLASVILLE MARKET STUDY

Using knowledge gained from construction and from five years of operation in Carrollton, combined with information on demographics and features of Carrollton and Douglasville, John projected membership sales in Douglasville. Subjective adjustments for competitive influences were required.

Members of the Carrollton club were typically white-collar or semiprofessional people, 25–45 years old, who lived within 12 minutes drive of the club. There was a 60/40 male to female ratio and a household income in excess of $15–20,000 per year. A similar member profile would be expected in the Douglasville club.

Initially, new members would come from the existing population base. People moving into the community or coming of age constitute a sustaining source of members. Net growth of an area indicates only the surface of market growth because in-migration is a major consideration. Federal Reserve Board data identifies the rate of in-migration, out-migration, and net growth of communities, with the average in-migration rate in the South being 2.4 times the net growth rate. For a transient community like Douglasville, the in-migration rate is probably higher than average, whereas Carrollton's is probably lower. Information on new meter hookups and reconnects obtained from electric utilities in both communities supports these findings. It is anticipated that members would be attracted from within a 12-minute driving range of the club. Douglasville is elongated by I-20, whereas Carrollton is a typical semirural town with a dispersed road network.

Carrollton, as a self-contained city, has excellent and definable communication networks. It has a widely read daily newspaper and two local radio stations with broad appeal. The community has strong informal networks through civic clubs, places of employment, and varied recreational activities. On the other hand, Douglasville is a "bedroom community" for Atlanta, so places of employment are not shared to a high degree. There are two biweekly newspapers, and the radio is dominated by Atlanta stations. Civic clubs and community recreational centers are not very active. Interstate 20 is well traveled by a high proportion of the community, so billboards will be a strategic communication means. Direct mail will probably be more effective than newspaper/radio advertising. Referrals through neighborhood associations will be relied upon more than employment-related organizations.

Competition derives from demands for time and dollars of prospective members, and it can be from either commercially or publicly owned facilities. John compared the competition in a note summarized in Table 1.

In an effort to quantify the competitive forces, John set up the following numerical rating system: 1—attracts fewer than 100 potential members; 2—attracts fewer than 250 potential members; 3—attracts 300–500 potential members; and 4—attracts more than 500 potential members. Table 2 summarizes the competitive forces. Therefore, in a qualitative sense, John expects competitive pressures to be less in Douglasville than in Carrollton on both a relative and an absolute basis.

The key demographic information for the two markets is summarized in Table 3. The higher household income level, in-migration rate, and population suggest a better market potential in Douglasville than in the successful Carrollton facility.

Against established competition, the Carrollton Club added 1,850 memberships over a four-year period, with 600 new members in the fourth year, 1983. John felt that the first two years had been learning years and that the last year was more representative of a well-marketed and managed club.

John developed three projections for membership in the Douglasville Club based on a 1984 base year and on the expected in-migration. He used the Carrollton membership experience as a basis for projecting the potential Douglasville membership sales of about 1,000 per year. He expected to sell memberships for $625, 20 percent more than the cost of a Carrollton Club membership.

TABLE 1   Comparison of Competition

Facility	Carrollton	Douglasville
Spa	On Bankhead Highway; open alternately to men and women; probably about 600–900 members, mainly older and less-active members; reasonably good reputation.	Off Highway 80; open alternately to men and women; probably a small membership due to limited facilities; past reputation poor; not a significant threat; wide age range.
Gym	Al's Gym near square attracts weight lifters, budget minded; monthly renewal; small operation, but probably has 200 or so members.	None known.
Lean-to operations	Several operating; tend to come and go; budget minded; little long-term commitment.	Similar.
College	Excellent facilities available to community including six tennis courts, track, pool, and adult education including physical exercise classes.	Not available.
Proximity to Atlanta	No impact on Carrollton.	Many people belong to Atlanta clubs; closest club is 15 miles away; limited by general tenet of being within 12–15 minutes away.
Public recreation	Excellent recreation program with adult recreation and exercise; well-organized gym, softball, tennis, swimming, and so on; a strong competing force.	Modest recreation program primarily for children; limited tennis, small pool, slight facilities.
Country clubs	18-hole Sunset Hills; 18-hole Fairfield Plantation.	9-hole St. Andrews; 18-hole Fairfield Plantation; 18-hole Douglasville.

Optimistically, he expected $650 per membership and pessimistically $575.

Three alternative projections were developed from the market data.

Case I: Conservative. Competition assumed to be as strong as Carrollton; evidence indicates less. Sales as projected above, less 12.5 percent for a conservative adjustment. Average sales of 900 member-ships per year at an average of $625 per membership.

Case II: Optimistic. Competition less than Carrollton, as evidence indicates. Membership sales as projected above, 1,014 memberships per year. Selling price averages $650.

Case III: Pessimistic. Competition increases and/or price pressure; maintain about 55 percent market

TABLE 2   Rating of Competition

Facility	Carrollton	Douglasville
Spa	4	3
Gym	2	—
Lean-to	2	2
College	2	—
Proximity to Atlanta	—	4 — *atlanta!*
Public recreation	3	— *dekalb.*
Country clubs	3	3
Total	16	12

TABLE 3   1984 Demographics of Carrollton and Douglasville

Demographic category	Carrollton	Douglasville
Approximate area	300 square miles	275 square miles
Driving time to club	12 minutes	12 minutes
1980 population (ages 20–54)	21,650	30,900
Average In-migration rate 1980–90 (ages 20–54)	1,765 per year	4,178 per year
Household incomes over $20,000 (1980)	5,850	10,878

share, which would be 825 membership sales per year, or about 20 percent less than projected and at an average selling price of $575.

Selection of an appropriate location in Douglasville requires additional research. John identified six factors critical to location: convenience, visibility, cost, ambience, synergy, and alternative uses of real estate.

Convenience is judged to be the ease of accessibility for the prospective member. Members use the club in the following circumstances:

30 percent–40 percent in the evening en-route from work to home.

20 percent–30 percent during the day in conjunction with shopping, dropping children at school, or other daily chores.

20 percent–30 percent from home and returning to home after exercise.

10 percent at lunch time, generally professionals.

10 percent–20 percent miscellaneous other circumstances.

To meet the convenience criteria, the club should be located (1) generally en-route from work to home (most Douglasville people work in Atlanta); (2) within 8–12 minutes driving time of home, preferably within 8; (3) convenient (less than 8 minutes) to grammar schools, nurseries, and shopping centers; and (4) generally within 8 minutes driving time of professional office complexes.

Visibility is judged to be the combination of factors that create a continuing presence of the club in the minds of members and prospective members so that when a person thinks of fitness or other club products, he or she automatically thinks of the club. This presence is created by visibility of the facilities to the using public along a thoroughfare, which is reinforced by advertising, network referrals, billboards, and sponsorships. All visibility factors have a cost associated with them. The single most important factor is the physical location of the club along a major route of travel for continuing visibility.

Because Douglasville is a bedroom community, the employment and civic club networks are less effective than in Carrollton. This extremely important referral network will have to be supplanted through neighborhood and other informal networks. Also, the radio and newspaper channels are more diffused in Douglasville. All of this means that physical visibility supplemented by billboard advertising is extremely important.

The ambience factor is comprised of environmental aspects that create a favorable impression conducive to making members want to use the club, while also appealing to prospective members. A particular site either has sufficient ambience or is unsatisfactory. If all other factors are equal, the site with the best appeal should be chosen.

The synergy factor is related to neighboring facilities encouraging more usage of the club, or providing a natural business-development opportunity including nearby shopping centers, schools, and colleges.

Although the project is strong and viable, it is prudent to plan a fail-safe position. Therefore, it is important to locate the facility where real estate can have alternative uses. The planned facility ideally should be adaptable to office space, so the location also should be able to support professional or general offices. The locations under consideration meet this criteria: one is in an office park, one is near the hospital, and the other two are high-visibility, high-traffic sites that could easily be converted to medical, legal, or professional offices.

FINANCING AND OPERATING PLAN

After reviewing the market projections, John developed a scenario reflecting membership, income, and cash-flow potential of the Douglasville Athletic Club. The three projections developed in the marketing study were used as a basis for financial and operating plans.

Using the conservative projection, a membership scenario was developed as follows using a 40 percent renewal rate:

Capacity of the club is planned for about 2,000–2,200 memberships. For this reason, sales projections are cut back to 800 in 1987. After three years, if capacity is restricted, a decision will have to be made to expand the facility or limit membership.

John's basic strategy is to become an early entrant, establishing 60 percent–70 percent market share and defending that share against competition with high quality, service, and adequate capacity. An early share establishes the basis for a referral network, the strongest sales tool.

The basic product is health and fitness in a social/recreational environment. As in any business, a continuous evolution of products must be based on these needs. The trends of self-reliance, health, and high touch are well documented in the book, *Megatrends*. The fitness-club customer requires a continuous stream of improvements and products to maintain interest and renew membership. These changes also become the basis for membership promotional efforts. For that reason, the initial establishment of the club should be considered over a three- to four-year period with facilities, staffing, and programs evolving over that period. A base plan should be established with enough flexibility to allow modification as needs dictate.

The real estate (building, land, and improvements) will be acquired and built within a budget of $668,000. All furnishings and equipment will be held within a budget of $153,000. The facility will have a large free-exercise area for aerobic activity, four racquetball courts, an enclosed pool, a Nautilus exercise area, lounge, pro shop, control desk, training and test rooms, nursery, ladies-only exercise area, and locker rooms with sauna, whirlpool, and tanning room. The main building will be 12,000 square feet, and the racquetball building will be about 7,000 square feet. Tennis courts will be built as needed after the first year, and expansion capabilities will be incorporated.

The form of organization will be a limited partnership. Pro forma statements are summarized in Table 4 (assuming a 6 percent inflation factor) using the conservative projections. Sensitivity for three market situations

Year	1984 (3 mos.)	1985	1986	1987
New membership sales	500	900	900	800
Memberships in force	500	1,328	1,868	2,100

was examined by comparing net income and cash flow, as summarized in Table 5.

The costs and sources of capital for the project are summarized in Table 6. John plans to sell 10 shares at 2 percent to limited partners, with two large shares at 15 percent. John and Al as general partners would invest 50 percent of the capital. It was contemplated that several partners would be from Douglasville, and additional financing would be obtained from a local bank.

TABLE 4 Pro Forma Statements of Douglasville Athletic Club (conservative projection in $000)

Year	1984 (3 mos.)	1985	1986	1987
Income—gross profit	$327	$620	$756	$803
Operating expenses	251	513 *83%*	532 *70%*	542 *67.5%*
Operating profits/losses	76	107	224	261
Other expenses	8	41	50	65
Net income	68	66	174	196
Cash flow—Positive	165	96	114	169
Cumulative cash flow	165	261	375	544

TABLE 5 Comparison of Net Income and Cash Flow ($000)

Net income	1984 (3 mos.)	1985	1986
Optimistic	$98	$184	$264
Conservative	68	66	174
Pessimistic	17	5	92

TABLE 6 Cost and Sources of Capital

Cost		Sources
Land	$ 90,000	$555,000 SBA guaranteed loan; 20 year (prime + 1½%).
Buildings; 3 racquetball courts	448,500	$110,000 (prime + 2%) commercial loan.
Contingency	30,000	$ 26,000 from preopening membership sales.
Equipment, furnishings, fixtures	153,000	$210,000 equity; general and limited partners; 20% equity general partners.
Pool; Bubble	55,000	
General contractor; architect's fee	19,500	
Developer's fee	30,000	
Design package	20,000	
Closing costs; construction of interior	55,000	
Total cost	901,000	

CONCLUSION

John has discussed the proposal with several members of the advisory group he formed over a year ago. They provided suggestions and were quite satisfied with the project. Several have indicated an interest in investing. He has an obligation to offer partners in the Carrollton Club an opportunity to invest, although he knows several do not have ready cash at this time.

Probably, John's most serious concern is the difference in the nature of the market. Because there is less informal communication in Douglasville, the marketing effort would have to be adjusted. He is satisfied that design changes for the new club would enhance management control and efficiency while improving customer service. The prospect of developing a Wellness Center in conjunction with the club will be an interesting new challenge after the first year of the club's operation.

John reviews his thoughts while taking one last look at the notes and statements that had gathered on his desk during the last year. He concludes that the project is ready to go. He needs to get the project under way so the club can open in the fall of 1984. He feels the risks have been well analyzed and once the start-up decision has been made and financed, marketing and management of the club will be the key to success. The team developed at Carrollton, and Al's experience, should provide sound management. Al and he will work the marketing effort together. John is ready to talk with investors, banks, and the Small Business Administration.

---

5. *Infosoft Inc.*

On January 6, 1986, Dr. L. L. Roos, academic and potential entrepreneur, entered his packed but well-organized University of Manitoba office, having just returned from health policy conferences in Washington, D.C., and Cophenhagen. His newly formed company Infosoft, faced six new buyer leads for HUMANS (Health and Utilization Monitoring Systems), the software package his research group had developed to facilitate analysis of local hospital and medical claims.

Development of HUMANS had been justified as a computer time/money saving strategy and was financed from government grants supporting Roos's advanced health-care research, using the large data base provided by the Manitoba Health Services Commission (MHSC).[1]

This case was prepared by C. Bhakar under supervision of Dr. L. L. Roos as a basis for classroom discussion rather than to illustrate either effective or ineffective handling of an administrative situation.

Copyright by The Case Development Program, Faculty of Management, University of Manitoba. Support for the development of this case was provided by the Canadian Studies Program, Secretary of State, Government of Canada.

[1]MHSC was the comprehensive medical and hospital insurer for the province of Manitoba.

In 1988, Dr. Roos's five-year Career Scientist Award from the National Health Research and Development Program (NHRDP) would be up for review. Dr. Roos was one of approximately 10 recipients of this prestigious federal grant, and over the years, competition had become more intense. This grant permitted him to spend most of his time on his health-care research. Maintenance of his primary salary source demanded a continuing heavy time commitment to research.

At this point Dr. Roos had some choices to confront. He wished to maintain support for his NHRDP career award, yet he firmly believed there was money to be made from marketing the HUMANS package. Perhaps such money might be funneled back to support more of his research. But that strategy would still demand ongoing planning and new product support. And if he made that choice, what marketing approach would be fair to the NHRDP? What approach would do justice to the university where his research group was located? What approach would allow him to make the most efficient use of scarce personal and staff time? What would allow him to generate adequate financial backing to sustain a new product in an ambiguously defined, emerging market?

THE PRODUCT

HUMANS possessed highly marketable features for health-care systems around the world. For example, the software directly addressed two major issues in the health-care industry (cost control and quality assurance). It promised to put analysis immediately at the fingertips of nonprogramming specialists. And it could read data from well-known, existing record forms such as hospital discharge abstracts, medical claims, cancer registries, and vital statistics files.

From a geographic perspective, product benefits were readily apparent in North America, Europe, Australia, and New Zealand where insurance systems were generating a large volume of claims data. For instance, in Canada claims data were widely collected by provincial health insurance commissions. And in the United States, federal legislation in the 1980s had mandated detailed scrutiny of the amount and kind of services provided to the over-65 population under the Medicare program.

According to promotional materials, HUMANS was a "generic information management system which offers health-care providers the capability of conducting state-of-the-art analysis in the area of finance, marketing management, and strategic planning." The software was comprised of three predesigned modules which could be used separately or linked together to form a single program stream:

1. The RATES module computed length of stay statistics and hospital utilization rates for different hospital market areas. This type of analysis could be used to study rate variations among providers of surgical procedures/diagnoses and to provide feedback on any hospital physician service that differed significantly from the norm (cost control).
2. The COMBINE module facilitated combining two patient records for further analysis. One use for this module was to look at hospital readmissions after discharge for a particular surgical procedure.
3. The HISTORY module compiled patient histories either for particular time periods or before and after any medical or surgical stay. It could be used to identify items such as other problems for which health care has been obtained (comorbidity), the progressive severity of a particular diagnosis, or the severity of cases (case mix) handled by a particular hospital. Such data could be used to adjust length of stay statistics for comparison of the RATES figures among different hospitals.

Technical Specifications

The HUMANS software was written in a fourth-generation program language known as SAS.[2] SAS was selected because of its relative ease of use by nonprogrammers and its capability to integrate smoothly with other data processing needs of sophisticated medical systems. SAS programs are relatively easy to read, modify, and maintain. One drawback was that SAS generally required longer run times than a language like FORTRAN or COBOL. On the other hand, SAS offered economies in input, output, and sorting capabilities; the professionally designed HUMANS modules ran about four times faster than SAS programs prepared by less-experienced users. SAS is widely used on mainframe and minicomputers; SAS products are in the process of being made available for IBM® personal computers and DEC Micro VAX® computers.

End User Benefits

The HUMANS-integrated software package grew directly out of Dr. Roos's research with the Manitoba Health Services Commission. Health analysts there were interested in routine applications of his latest research work published in major international health-care journals. Yet, despite high interest in timely evaluations for quality control and cost containment, no other generic software for the nonspecialist had been developed. Complicated computer runs on large databases generated from hospital claims were performed irregularly and only with heavy programmer input. The HUMANS product sought to remedy this situation. HUMANS streamlined and coordinated the specialized programs which had already been developed and tested at the University of Manitoba and made them applicable for general use. Analysts would be able to manipulate data, alter variables, update population statistics, and so forth, on the spot, without having to wait for the services of

---

[2]SAS stands for the Statistical Analysis System which was developed and marketed by the SAS Institute in Gary, North Carolina. This highly sophisticated programming language condensed complicated "machine" or "first-generation" programming steps into simplified routines which more closely resembled the logic found in normal English language structures.

EXHIBIT 1 Sample of RATES Program Output—Simulated Data

HEALTH CARE UTILIZATION STATISTICS PACKAGE VERSION 1.0. 1985

SUMMARY OF RATES

BY REGION

.... PROCDURE–HYSTERECTOMY ....

Region	Population at Risk	Frequency Observed	Frequency Expected	Standard Morbidity Ratio	Direct-adj Rate /Per 10,000/	Crude Rate /Per 10,000/	CHI-SQ	Prob of CHI-SQ	Systematic Variation Component
REGION 1	21161	5	23	22.02	2.5128	2.3628	13.8098	.0002	
REGION 2	11999	14	13	104.75	11.8330	11.6676	0.0301	.8622	
REGION 3	13831	12	15	77.79	8.6831	8.6762	0.7606	.3831	
REGION 4	10737	18	14	127.81	15.1452	16.7645	1.0891	.2967	
REGION 5	13955	6	15	40.67	4.4442	4.2995	5.1922	.0227	
REGION 6	34771	11	37	29.94	3.4627	3.1636	18.0391	.0000	
REGION 7	176852	252	201	125.42	14.0930	14.2492	12.9870	.0003	
	283306	318	318			11.2246	51.9080	.0000	0.6252

HEALTH CARE UTILIZATION STATISTICS PACKAGE VERSION 1.0. 1985

SUMMARY OF TOTDAYS

BY REGION

.... PROCDURE–HYSTERECTOMY ....

Region	Frequency Observed	Direct-adj Rate /Per 10,000/	Indirect-adj Rate /Per 10,000/	Mean	Std	Min	Max	Range	Mean Totdays /Per 10,000/
REGION 1	5	2.5128	2.4714	9.2000	3.9051	3	14	11	23.1179
REGION 2	14	11.8330	11.7574	14.5714	13.4756	7	60	53	172.4232
REGION 3	12	8.6831	8.7321	12.8333	8.4631	7	39	32	111.4336
REGION 4	18	15.1452	14.3459	11.8333	4.9484	8	31	23	179.2185
REGION 5	6	4.4442	4.5654	8.3333	1.2111	6	11	5	37.0354
REGION 6	11	3.4627	3.3601	9.4545	1.5124	7	12	5	32.7385
REGION 7	252	14.0930	14.0784	10.4444	4.1607	3	36	33	147.1940
	318			10.7013	5.0240	3	60	57	

heavily backlogged computer departments. Standard or custom-tailored reports could be generated at the discretion of each analyst.

Productivity of programmers and analysts was expected to at least double after the HUMANS software was implemented. However, Dr. Roos expected possible internal resistance from established programming departments within the organization. Historically, moves to put computing power in the hands of users have been resisted by some computer departments.

Feedback from the HUMANS program to administrers, regulators, and providers of medical services was estimated to yield a 10 percent potential savings of resources in "outlier" hospitals/physicians.[3] Thus HUMANS promised some pertinent answers to the question of highest priority within the health-care industry: "Where are we spending all that money?"

THE U.S. HOSPITAL MARKET

Recently, popular business magazines had reported a dramatic increase in the purchase of computers by hospitals in the United States. At one end of the spectrum, they were using computers to reduce expenses associated with manual charting in a clinical setting. At the other end, hospitals were using computers to improve cost accounting and strategic planning.

In 1985, sales of software packages that linked clinical information with financial data totalled just $15 million. But, in the next five years, according to hospital consultant Sheldon Dorenfest, such sales might grow to $100 million. Shared Data Research, a hospital information firm in Hudson, Ohio, reported that hospital spending on computer hardware and software grew at an average annual compound rate of 18 percent, from $1.5 billion in 1981 to $2.6 billion in 1984, the year mandated pricing for medicare patients became law. This same firm expected spending to rise to $4 billion in 1987 and to $6 billion by 1990.

Before 1984, U.S. medicare payments had been based on cost-reimbursement for individual procedures and services provided to a specific patient. Rand Corporation

researcher Kathleen Lohr observed that under the old system, concerns about overuse (such as excessive lengths of stay without improved patient outcomes) were a top priority with government regulators.

After 1984, reimbursement became "prospective." That is, payment was based on the average costs per case of treating patients classified into one of over 460 diagnosis-related groups (DRG). With the latter incentive system, government concerns about the underprovision of services (such as volume increases coupled with early release and a high rate of complications afterwards) became more prominent. As a result of this change, the Health Care Financing Administration set up local Peer Review Organizations and required hospitals to cite specific quantitative indicators justifying the quality and cost performance of physicians and facilities receiving medicare payments.

Pressure from Private Business

From 1980 to 1985, the amount of money U.S. business spent on health insurance doubled to almost $90 billion. As a result, companies began to exercise their economic clout with health providers both to improve the quality and price of care and to ration the use of experimental technology. For example, many corporations encouraged employees to enroll in prepaid health maintenance organizations that had a large incentive to limit treatment and avoid hospitalization. Corporations also negotiated with suppliers that wanted to become "preferred provider organizations" in which doctors and hospitals charged discounted fees in anticipation of quick payment and a stable volume of business.

The burden of these health policy decisions fell on American corporations because 69 percent of the U.S. population had employer-provided health insurance, with the employer typically paying 90 percent of the premium. Moreover, one popular way for doctors and hospitals to make up the short-fall from medicaid and medicare payments was to overcharge such privately insured patients. Finally, the cost of health care had soared in recent years—total spending on it climbed from 4.4 percent of the gross national product in 1955 to about 11 percent in 1985—until business spending on health almost equalled after-tax corporate profits.

As one executive described the magnitude of this responsibility:

---

[3]Outliers are those whose billed services greatly exceeded the norm.

Corporations are being asked to play God with money. . . . It's a brutal issue—the most sensitive thing companies have had to deal with in employee relations in years. Should the company pay for controversial and extraordinarily expensive procedures that may prolong life only for a short time? Should it pay for a liver transplant that costs up to $240,000 but keeps most adult recipients alive for less than a year?

CURRENT MARKETING EFFORTS

For the past six months, product promotion had been based primarily on informal contacts among Dr. Roos's academic peers at national and international conferences and on the reputation of his published research. The following activities were among Dr. Roos's more structured marketing efforts.

1. A review of health-care literature and responses to a product announcement had allowed him to identify four groups of potential high-interest prospects:
   a. Regulatory groups—such as the Canadian Hospital Association, the College of Physicians and Surgeons in Canada, and their international counterparts.
   b. Individual hospitals and physician groups (especially in the United States).
   c. Insurers—such as the Blue Cross/Blue Shield and medicare in the United States and the provincial insurers in Canada.
   d. Consulting and contract research firms.
2. A user's manual was available for the software. Brochures and professional presentation materials were being developed. Announcement of product availability appeared in the January 1986 issue of SAS Communications and generated about 20 requests for more information.
3. A Canadian copyright for the HUMANS prototype software was obtained on September 13, 1985. A U.S. copyright was not pursued because more information about the product had to be revealed, while the Canadian registration offered a precedent for applying for a U.S. version at a later date.
4. A summer Work/Study student developed a mailing list of prospects.

5. Plans had been confirmed for two test sites: one in Canada and one in the United States. Search was under way for a U.S. distributor/management consultant. The hope was to support continuing product development reflecting commercial market needs.
6. A test user at the Manitoba Health Services Commission ran the software in the fall of 1985 and was very pleased with it. One report was generated for internal MHSC use.
7. A "concept evaluation survey" was being considered for mass-mail distribution to potential buyers. This survey would be designed to identify high-potential customers and determine what features the market perceived as being most important.
8. Two training sessions were scheduled in conjunction with the Canadian Health Economics Research Association Meetings in Winnipeg, Manitoba, on May 31 and June 7, 1986.

Pricing and Distribution

Dr. Roos had considered a two-tiered pricing structure (Exhibit 2). He was not sure what price the market would bear, but he wanted to recognize the support for development he had received from the NHRDP. Moreover, he wished to encourage other Canadian and U.S. collaborators to install the product, generate word-of-mouth enthusiasm, and furnish ongoing feedback for future product updates.

At the high end of the competitive software market, SysteMetrics, a division of McGraw-Hill publishers, was installing and supporting a program supposedly like RATES for a total package said to cost $50,000 to $100,000, depending on the size of the installation. At the low end of the market, there was the possibility of "unbundling" the complete package and charging separate prices for each item provided (i.e., software tapes, manuals, on-site training, hot-line services, new-product developments, and so on). SAS charged as little as $2,000 per year to universities for one of its program modules.

The latter pricing strategy allowed sophisticated buyers to realize significant savings by eliminating expensive training components, but inexperienced users could find themselves spending considerable amounts on computer consultants, just to get the system operating. Infosoft's cost of duplicating and shipping the HUMANS package was approximately $100 per unit.

EXHIBIT 2

THE UNIVERSITY OF MANITOBA   FACULTY OF ADMINISTRATIVE STUDIES   Winnipeg, Manitoba
                                      Department of Business Administration   Canada R3T 2N2

(204) 474-9672

July 17, 1985

Dr. R.A. Heacock
Director General
Extramural Research Programs Directorate
Health Services and Promotion Branch
Health and Welfare Canada
Ottawa, Ontario
K1A 1B4

Dear Mr. Heacock:

I wanted to keep NHRDP up to date on the software we are developing for our own research purpose. We are hopeful that the software will be adopted by other organizations and research groups, but nothing is definite as yet.

If such interest does materialize, we think it appropriate to adopt a two level pricing policy vis-a-vis licensing the software:

    a - a low price for Canadian organizations which would reflect the NHRDP support which has gone into development of the software. Because of the collaboration of several American research groups, they would be included in this low price.

    b - a higher price for other organizations (most of these would presumably be American) which would be using the software.

I am currently discussing with the University administration, procedures which would enable funds received to offset expenses associated with development and distribution of the software.

It should be stressed that we are still in the planning stage. The enclosed paper provides an idea of what directions the information system might take. We have received federal funding for a summer work/study student to participate in determining markets for the software.

As always, we greatly appreciate NHRDP support for our research.

Sincerely,

Leslie L. Roos, Jr. Ph.D.,
National Health Scientist
Faculties of Administrative Studies
    and Medicine

U.S. Representative

Early in the development cycle Dr. Roos cultivated the interest of Second Opinion Consultants of Millwood, New York, in distributing HUMANS in the United States. Second Opinion argued in favor of a skimming strategy—charge a high price to generate high profits from initial sales while competitors in this software marketing niche were relatively scarce.

Second Opinion also warned Dr. Roos that marketing such innovative software often required a selling cycle of several months or even a year. Approaches had to be initiated directly with top decision makers who had the authority to overcome the possible resistance of mid-level specialists and get service to the designated end-user—health-care analysts with only a moderate degree of programming sophistication.

Finally, Second Opinion predicted a need for a heavy training component for nonspecialist users, a service information hot-line direct to program authors, continuing update requirements, and customization of user reports, especially in the first few installations.

COMPETITION

One observer has characterized the software industry by its ease of entry. Programming skills plus little more than pencil, paper, and access to hardware were all that were needed to set up a business; hence, many software houses were thinly capitalized. Also, there were few universally accepted standards for program design and virtually no way to ensure those standards were maintained.

Consultants and Marketers from Academia

The husband and wife team of Second Opinion Consultants had spent much time and money developing their marketing techniques. As a result, they had clearly expanded their contacts beyond their original academic setting, and offered Dr. Roos at least 25 regular customer prospects among U.S. health insurers and labor unions. Nevertheless, Dr. Roos had been counselled that such consultants might just as well wish to produce and sell their own reports to their client base as to market the

HUMANS package. Alternatively, they might develop a competing product of their own.

The other significant competition from an academic entrepreneur came from The Codman Group, originally founded by Dr. Jack Wennberg of Dartmouth. Wennberg had the entire summer 1984 issue of *Health Affairs* devoted to the study of medical practice variation. This national coverage promoted the importance of analyzing "the practice style factors of individual physicians which determine the demand for hospitalization in any particular market area." Normally an optimist who enjoyed the interpersonal aspects of the business, Dr. Wennberg had recently confided to Dr. Roos that marketing software was time and dollar consuming. The Codman Group has several full-time employees and markets a product for IBM Personal Computer ATs (with hard disks).

Major Institutions

Other U.S. competition offered basic length of stay calculations and approached the health-care market with an integrated financial/administrative package. Among the top contenders in this category were such major consulting firms such as Deloitte Haskins and Sells and Peat Marwick Mitchell & Co. Health Micro Systems Data and John Snow Inc., a subsidiary of Bell Laboratories, also offered financial management packages combined with rudimentary health-care analysis programs for medical and hospital environments.

Canadian Competition

In Canada, the Hospital Medical Records Institute of Ontario could become either a competitor or a purchaser. They have a number of contracts to produce summaries of hospital data.

THE ORGANIZATION

Dr. Roos heartily subscribed to the advice of software entrepreneur Philippe Khan: the environment most conducive to software excellence was one of a small development group of no more than three or four programmers. This was the setting for the development of LOTUS® software for the IBM® Personal Computer versus the larger numbers of developers involved with the complicated and less successful Symphony® project.

Adopting this mode for HUMANS, the Infosoft development group was comprised of four people: Dr. Roos, the group leader, workaholic and idea man; one programmer, specializing in writing efficient programs in using the SAS language; a second programmer concerned with software objectives and specializing large-scale database management; and health-care analyst who, in the spring of 1985, swiftly fleshed-out the original idea for the program on small data sets. A proposed organization chart is shown in Exhibit 3.

This group was fully occupied with product refinements and additional research projects. If any HUMANS software were sold, the future staffing arrangements would have to be reevaluated. There might be a heavy service component required for installation, for tailoring to an outside database, for linking with an existing system, for staff training, and for manning a telephone hot-line. Dr. Roos was not sure just how much effort it would take to launch this test market/prototype program.

Creation of the Company

The idea for the HUMANS product grew out of Jack Wennberg's visit to Manitoba in January 1985. At that time, Wennberg told Dr. Roos he thought generic software which analyzed hospital claims data "might be marketable," but he wanted something that ran on micros. As groundwork, Dr. Roos and analysts Andre Wadja and Pat Nicol prepared a conference paper for publication and presentation at the American Public Health Association meetings and the Canadian Health Economics Research Association.[4] By spring 1985, health analyst, Sally Cageorge, had the first version of the HUMANS program operating on local data. By August, SAS programmer Andre Wadja had a general version ready for formal documentation.

By early fall, Dr. Roos was conducting negotiations with the University Administration vis-à-vis royalties and possible sponsorship of the new commercial venture. An agreement was finally reached which provided for a royalty split of two thirds to Infosoft and one third to the University.

Entrepreneur

By January 1986, Dr. Roos was ready to try marketing his new software; he was willing to invest a modest

---

[4]The title of the paper was "Health Policy Information Systems: What Software Is Needed?"

EXHIBIT 3   Proposed Organization Chart, January 1986

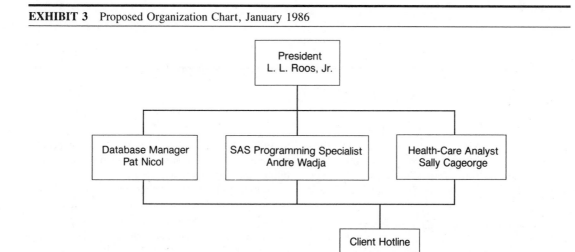

amount to see if the product might have potential. He planned to keep initial overhead expenses low by "donating" his time and working out of his home. As a start he had drawn up a projected income statement for the first year (Exhibit 4).

The idea of a private company appealed to Dr. Roos. Like other colleagues on the Faculty of Management he had some business experience. He felt that a start-up company operation would offer him maximum freedom and flexibility. Nevertheless, in the pit of his stomach there remained a gnawing contradiction between the promising enterprise at hand and the strenuous time

demands of top-notch research for someone who regularly puts in 60 to 70 hours a week on his normal academic work.

What should he do? Should he pull back from overextension of his resources of time, money, and research staff? Should he seek more extensive marketing, organizational, and financial advice? But what kind and at what cost? Should he run full throttle with his entrepreneurial impulse, or should he proceed at a more moderate pace? What goals should he plan to achieve and when?

EXHIBIT 4

INFOSOFT INC.
Pro-Forma Income Statement

	Year 1
Revenue from sales and/or leases	$10,000
Expenses:	
Incorporation costs and legal fees	1,000
Telephone hot-line expenses	2,400
Cost of producing software copies	1,000
Brochures and stationary	1,000
User manuals	1,000
Postage	500
Office supplies	100
Miscellaneous expenses	500
	$ 7,500
Gross profit	$ 2,500

---

6. *The NFL versus the USFL*

From his office window, Pete Rozelle, commissioner of the National Football League (NFL), looked down on Park Avenue in New York City. It was February, 1985—the off-season—and the Super Bowl had fetched

$1 million per minute for television commercials. Yet the number in the commissioner's mind was $1.32 billion, the amount of damages in an antitrust suit filed against the NFL by its fledgling competitor, the United

States Football League (USFL). The USFL had begun playing in 1983 and was planning to move its season into the fall, in direct competition with the NFL. Rozelle had to decide how, if at all, to respond.

PROFESSIONAL FOOTBALL

American football (hereafter referred to as football) was a spectator sport, played initially at the amateur level in the late 1800s. For a basic description of the sport, see Appendix.

As the dominant force in professional football in 1985, the NFL consisted of 28 teams that played a season of games in the fall and winter of each year. Each NFL team had an owner and received revenues by charging for attendance at games and obtaining fees for the right to broadcast games on television and radio. While NFL teams were profit-making companies, the league was a nonprofit organization that promoted professional football and fostered the primary business interests of league members. The league governed play by standardizing rules and establishing schedules.

HISTORY OF THE NFL

In the early part of the twentieth century, baseball, not football, enjoyed the distinction of the "Great American Pastime." Football was popular enough, however, to lead some to consider organizing it for profit. Although individual players had been paid to play as early as 1892 and professional teams had been assembled, no successful effort to organize a group of teams into a professional league was made until 1920. Meeting in an automobile showroom in Canton, Ohio, George Halas, A. F. Ranney, Stan Cofall, and Jim Thorpe organized the first professional league, called the American Professional Football Association. Eleven teams paid $100 each as a membership fee.

Without an organized schedule, the Association folded after one year. In 1921, however, 13 teams played the first organized season under the leadership of Joseph Carr. In the following year 18 teams competed, and the league took the name of the "National Football League" even though only seven states of the Great Lakes region were represented.

In the 1920s professional football stars such as Red Grange and Ernie Nevers gained wide publicity and drew crowds as large as 70,000. Because teams were associated with cities or states, team loyalties and regional rivalries developed and ticket demand increased. As the NFL grew in stature, demand increased to form new teams. In 1926 C. C. (Cash and Carry) Pyle, a small-town movie theater owner who was the agent for football star Red Grange, tried to acquire an NFL franchise in New York City. The NFL refused his request because it already had a team in New York City—the Giants. So Pyle formed the American Football League which included his own New York team that featured Red Grange. The league folded the next year, but Pyle's Yankees were invited to join the NFL due to Grange's immense drawing power.

As NFL attendance increased, so did ticket prices. By 1939, ticket prices had risen to $4.40 for the championship game—but the stadium was sold out in two days, pushing NFL attendance for the year above the one million mark for the first time.

In 1946 a rival league, called the All-American Conference (AAC), was formed with teams in Buffalo, Brooklyn, Los Angeles, Miami, Chicago, New York, San Francisco, and Cleveland. Paul Brown, owner and coach of the Cleveland franchise and a reputed football genius, was the new league's driving force. Five of the eight AAC teams were located in NFL cities, and the AAC season was in the fall with a championship game at the end of the season. The AAC bid for players both from colleges and existing NFL teams. The AAC struggled for three years and then merged with the NFL, although only three teams (Baltimore, Cleveland, and San Francisco) were invited to join.

The decade of the 1950s witnessed continued growth in the popularity of professional football. The league was divided into two conferences, the American and the National, with seven teams each. Only two new teams, Baltimore and Dallas, were admitted into the NFL during the 1950s, even though the demand for franchises had been much greater.

In 1959, 27-year-old Lamar Hunt of Dallas, Texas, who had been denied an NFL franchise by Commissioner Bert Bell, joined forces with seven businessmen to form a new league called the American Football League (AFL). The AFL plan was to play in the fall, with teams in cities that were not represented in the NFL but also teams in New York and Los Angeles, which already had an NFL team but could probably support another. Team ownership was limited to financially substantial individuals. The AFL structured its rules to encourage higher scoring games and attracted and signed college prospects with guaranteed bonus contracts. The league also lured veteran players away from NFL teams with bonuses and higher salaries. The new AFL signed a five-year TV contract with ABC in 1960 and started play in 1960 with teams in New York,[1] Dallas,[1] and Los Angeles,[1] Buffalo, Denver, Boston, Oakland, and Houston. The new league also filed an antitrust lawsuit in 1961 that charged the NFL with being a monopoly that unfairly restricted other teams from competing in the industry and deprived the public of more variety.

Legal controversy had long surrounded professional sports. In 1922 Justice Oliver Wendell Holmes had written for the U.S. Supreme Court that baseball was not a product and not commerce, and therefore did not fall within the scope of antitrust law. In 1953 the Court reluctantly upheld this verdict, but directed Congress to resolve disputed points with legislation. In 1957 the Court denied professional football and other professional sports the same blanket antitrust exemption given baseball. In response, Congress passed legislation in 1958 that exempted the NFL from antitrust concerns raised by its player draft and reserve clause. As television became more important to the NFL, the league returned to Congress in 1961 and won legislation that legalized the signing of a collective league contract with television. The AFL suit was lost in 1962 on the grounds that football did not fall under the antitrust laws.

The year 1964 proved to be a turning point for the AFL. After signing a new five-year, $36 million TV contract with NBC, Joe Foss, the AFL commissioner, remarked: "People have now stopped asking me if we're going to make it." That year the New York Jets also signed all-American quarterback Joe Namath to a reported $400,000, four-year contract, making him the highest paid player in pro football. With Namath in the lineup, the Jets set AFL attendance records.

Although peace feelers had reportedly been underway for several years, bidding between the two leagues for players intensified in 1966. For example, the AFL signed away NFL star John Brodie for a reported $1 million bonus. Secret meetings held in 1966 between Tex Schramm, NFL president, and Lamar Hunt, AFL president, resulted in an announcement on June 8, 1966, that the 15-team NFL and the 8-team AFL would merge. The agreement specified that the merger would take place in 1970 and that the new league would be called

the National Football League. Pete Rozelle, the reigning NFL commissioner, would continue in the post. Although the old leagues would continue playing separate schedules until 1970, they would meet for a championship game beginning in the 1966 season, hold a combined player draft beginning the following January, and play interleague preseason games starting in 1967. Television coverage by two networks would continue, and no existing franchises would be moved. The previously announced AFL expansion to Miami in 1967 would be followed by leaguewide expansion of two more teams by 1968 and an additional two by 1970, bringing the total number of teams in the postmerger NFL to 28 by 1970. The AFL agreed to pay a total of $18 million over a 20-year period to enter the league and not to share in the $7 million in franchise fees to be paid by the next two expansion teams. Because of pending suits challenging the merger, Rozelle went to Congress and received antitrust exemption for it. As a condition for the exemption, the NFL agreed to ban Friday night and Saturday games that might conflict with high school and college games.

The postmerger NFL continued to thrive, with rising attendance and TV ratings. Demand for professional football team franchises continued. In 1974, Gary Davidson, a successful sports entrepreneur, easily sold twelve $2 million franchises in a new pro football group named the World Football League (WFL).[2,3] Davidson's idea was to offer professional football to areas of the country not represented by an NFL team but with strong collegiate football interests. The games would start in the summer, before the NFL began its season, and end before December. The WFL sought to acquire a few name veteran players and fill out its rosters with second-tier players. NFL stars Larry Csonka, Jim Kiick, and Paul Warfield were signed to lucrative salaries which helped the WFL draw large regional crowds at its early games. No major television contracts were signed, and the coaches were not well known. Attendance declined throughout the season, and the league folded the next year when teams were unable to meet operating expenses.

By 1981 football had become the nation's number two spectator sport (behind horse racing) and arguably the

---

[2]This fee was in the form of pledges, backed by letters of credit.

[3]The last reported NFL sale price was $16 million in 1969 when the Philadelphia Eagles changed hands.

---

[1]There were also NFL teams in these cities.

national pastime. The success of the NFL with fans and viewers had been marred beginning in 1982 by a number of news stories disclosing the use and sale of drugs by professional football players.

THE NATIONAL FOOTBALL LEAGUE IN 1983

The 28 NFL teams all had the same general structure in 1983, the year in which the USFL entered. The owner served as president and delegated the daily operating assignments to a general manager. Typically, three areas reported to the general manager: the coaching staff, responsible for the players and their training; the administrative staff, responsible for general business operations; and the director of player development, in charge of scouting for new players and assessing veteran players for potential trades.

Exhibit 1 provides the average NFL team operating statements for the 1970–1984 seasons. NFL teams derived revenues from ticket sales, individual contracts with local radio stations and for the televising of preseason games, and the leaguewide national television and radio contracts. Additionally, teams obtained revenues from the sale of promotional items and from concessions such as food and beverages.

Home and visiting teams shared ticket revenues for each game according to a 60/40 formula, respectively. Total NFL attendance stood at 17 million in 1981. Fees for television rights were negotiated and collected by the league and distributed equally among the teams. The three TV networks had agreed to pay a combined $2 billion for the right to carry NFL games for five years commencing in 1982. The previous contract had been for $650 million for four years. Under the new agreement, each NFL team received $11.9 million per year in 1982 rising to $18.6 million in 1986.

Compared to the old contract, the new contract granted each network an extra preseason game and more commercial minutes. The new contract also provided that rights to the games would not be sold to any cable broadcasters. The CBS radio network negotiated a four-year, $12 million contract to broadcast 37 NFL games a year beginning in 1980. Local television rights for preseason games and local radio rights were sold to all games, generating an average of $0.5 million of revenue per team per year.

This operated at a loss, but satisfied CBS radio affiliates by enhancing their local prestige and improving their commercial appeal. In 1982, 14 million fans heard Super Bowl XVI on radio. For the 1982 Super Bowl, a 30-second advertisement on CBS radio cost $11,000 versus $345,000 on TV.

PLAYERS

Every NFL team consisted of 45 players, a number set through negotiation between owners and the players union. Due to the physical nature of the sport, the average player's career lasted only five years. Most players entered the league immediately after they left college. Veteran players faced intense competition from the rookies for most of the 45 slots on each of the 28 NFL teams.

Salaries were set by negotiation between a player (or his agent) and the individual club. The average player earned about $105,000 during the 1982 season, up from $55,000 in 1977. In 1982, the average quarterback—the most highly-paid position—earned $178,000/year. This contrasts with $92,000/year for defensive backs, the least-highly paid position. Exhibit 2 shows mean average player salaries over the 1977 to 1984 period.

The NFL used a draft to allocate college players among teams. NFL rules limited the draft to those college athletes who had completed their four-year collegiate eligibility. Rules and regulations covering the draft were negotiated by the players' union and the owners as part of the collective bargaining agreement. As of 1982, the NFL draft took place on May 1 each year. The league, through an agreement with the players' union, was allowed to change this to February 1 although it had not chosen to do so.

The potential draftees were well-known and highly scouted by each team. The order of selection in the draft was designed to allow the teams with the worst playing records during the season the opportunity to choose first from the available talent pool. Teams could trade their draft choices either for established players, negotiating rights to players, or money.

The team which drafted a player would, for one year, be the only NFL team which could negotiate or sign a contract with that player. If that player did not sign a contract, he was considered available for the next draft. In the event that a drafted player played for a non-NFL

EXHIBIT 1 The NFL vs. the USFL

Income Statements of Average NFL Team, 1970–1984
($000)

	1972	1973	1974	1975	1976	1977	1978	1979	1980	1981	1982	1983	1984*
I. Income													
Ticket sales (pre- and regular season)	$3,555	$3,880	$3,623	$4,282	$4,411	$4,753	$5,082	$5,345	$6,206	$6,814	$3,827	$7,300	
Television and radio	1,630	1,711	2,200	2,442	2,307	2,328	5,197	5,556	5,864	6,216	5,714	14,000	
Other income													
Postseason participation	179	200	212	230	209	252	339	362	422	464	260	406	
League receipts	194	216	230	249	227	273	366	391	457	501	148	438	
Programs, concessions, films, royalties	113	126	134	145	132	159	214	228	266	292	86	213	
Miscellaneous, including luxury box rental	103	115	122	132	120	144	194	207	242	266	149	275	
Total other income	588	657	698	755	688	828	1,113	1,189	1,347	1,523	855		
Total income	$6,362	$6,905	$7,219	$8,235	$8,094	$8,737	$12,505	$13,278	$14,804	$16,076	$11,039	$22,632	$25,000
II. Operating expenses:													
Player costs:													
Preseason	$ 71	$ 75	$ 92	$ 96	$ 114	$ 122	$ 139	$ 159	$ 181	$ 208	$ 242	$ 252	
Regular season salaries	1,871	1,988	2,427	2,543	3,024	3,228	3,688	4,208	4,802	5,502	3,847	6,948	
Postseason	86	92	112	117	139	149	170	194	221	254	296	321	
Player retirement, insurance trust	142	151	184	193	229	245	279	319	364	417	486	2,026	

	(1)	(2)	(3)	(4)	(5)	(6)	(7)	(8)	(9)	(10)	(11)	(12)	(13)
Medical compensation, worker's compensation	138	147	179	188	223	238	272	311	354	406	473	2,083	
Total player costs	$2,308	$2,453	$2,994	$3,140	$3,729	$3,982	$4,548	$5,191	$5,922	$6,787	$5,344	$11,630	$13,600
Team expenses (i.e., coaching, travel, etc.)	1,214	1,324	1,437	1,582	1,667	1,837	2,135	2,392	2,839	3,203	1,762	3,986	
Stadium rent and services	264	288	313	345	363	400	465	521	619	698	767	867	
League operations	176	192	200	229	242	266	309	347	411	452	483	546	
General and administrative	960	1,047	1,136	1,250	1,318	1,452	1,687	1,890	2,244	2,464	2,636	2,981	
Total other operating expenses	$2,614	$2,851	$3,086	$3,406	$3,590	$3,955	$4,596	$5,150	$6,113	$6,817	$5,648	$8,380	
Total operating expenses	$4,922	$5,304	$6,080	$6,546	$7,319	$7,937	$9,144	$10,341	$12,035	$13,604	$10,992	$20,010	$22,500
Total operating profit	$1,440	$1,601	$1,139	$1,689	$755	$800	$3,361	$2,937	$2,769	$2,472	$47	$2,622	$2,500
Other income:													
Interest income	$ −14	$ −15	$ −16	$ −18	$ −18	$ −19	$ −28	$ −30	$ −33	$ −36	$ −43	$ −51	
Net interest before taxes	1,426	1,586	1,123	1,671	757	781	3,333	2,907	2,736	2,436	4	2,571	
Provision for income taxes	713	793	562	836	379	391	1,667	1,454	1,368	1,218	2	1,286	
Net income	$713	$793	$562	$836	$379	$391	$1,667	$1,454	$1,368	$1,218	$2	$1,286	

*Unaudited estimates by NFL officials.

Source: National Football League.

EXHIBIT 2 Mean Average NFL Player Compensation, 1977–1984 ($000)

By Position*	1977	1978	1979	1980	1981	1982	1983	1984
Quarterback	$ 89.4	$102.6	$113.9	$131.2	$160.0	$177.8	$ 233.7	$ 301.1
Running back	60.4	66.5	74.2	83.5	94.9	113.2	142.4	169.8
Receiver	53.8	59.8	64.6	76.0	85.9	103.9	122.6	146.9
Offensive lineman	52.3	60.2	66.6	74.6	85.5	100.5	132.4	161.1
Defensive lineman	59.6	66.1	75.2	85.7	93.0	106.1	127.4	166.6
Linebacker	50.4	58.1	63.4	70.8	85.2	97.9	119.9	156.7
Defensive back	47.4	54.8	58.9	68.8	79.6	91.6	110.9	136.7
Kicker	41.5	48.4	53.0	60.9	65.8	80.3	94.0	114.9
Average	$ 55.3	$ 62.6	$ 68.9	$ 78.7	$ 90.1	$104.8	$ 130.0	$ 161.6
Contract Value By Draft Round†								
Round one	$320.6	$402.2	$473.7	$629.5	$695.6	$856.4	$1,396.1	$1,725.7
Round two	228.8	269.5	285.9	380.0	399.5	527.8	763.6	1,075.3
Round three							507.1	803.2

*Yearly data includes base salary, deferred compensation in reported year, prorated share of signing bonuses, reporting bonuses, and roster bonuses. Averages include all active, reserve/injured, reserve/physically unable to perform, and reserve/non-football injury categories.

†Complete package includes roster, reporting, and signing bonuses plus *four years'* salary. Averages include the 28 players chosen in each of the two rounds.

Source: National Football League.

team, the NFL team that drafted him retained exclusive rights over the player for four years.

Any player could be traded or sold to any other team at any time in his career. If a player desired to change teams at the end of his contract, he had to achieve free agent status. If the player had fewer than four years' experience, he had to play one additional year for his current team after contract expiration. This extra year was called the option year. Players with more than four years' league experience were not required to play an option year and could become free agents immediately upon contract expiration. Once a free agent, a player was permitted to receive offers from any team. However, his old team had the right of first refusal and received significant compensation from his new team.[4] These two provisions had resulted in few players using free agent status to change teams.

Since 1959, professional sports teams had been allowed to allocate a portion of the team's purchase price to player contracts and to depreciate those contracts. The depreciation applied to the cost of acquired teams and to the entry fee paid for a newly formed (expansion) team. Numerous disputes about the percentage of a team's purchase price allocable to player contracts had arisen between professional sports teams and the IRS, with over 100 tax cases litigated. The 1976 Tax Reform Act set 50% as the guideline maximum allocation to player contracts.

THE PLAYERS' UNION

The first attempt by the players to bargain collectively with the owners occurred in 1956 with the formation of the Players' Association, an effort summarily ignored by the owners. In the subsequent years through 1966, the players found little reason to organize. Salaries tripled and the NFL added lucrative fringe benefits such as insurance.

By the time the AFL and NFL drafts merged in 1967, however, the demand for collective bargaining had

---

[4]This provision had been termed the Rozelle Rule. If, for example, a team signed a five-year veteran to a $300,000/year contract, it would have had to compensate the player's prior team with two consecutive first-round draft choices. The rule was conceived by the commissioner and enforced by him as well. During the 1982 Collective Bargaining Agreement negotiations, the owners refused to discuss changes to this rule.

become great. After the players threatened to join the Teamsters, the players and owners agreed to their first contract. Two years later, after the contract expired, the owners stiffened and there was a two-day strike and lockout during the preseason. By 1971, the players' group had been certified as a union.

The first major confrontation between the new union (called the National Football League Players' Association or NFLPA) and the owners came in 1974 during negotiations on a new collective bargaining agreement. Dissatisfied with the owners' concessions, the players voted to strike during the preseason. The owners did not cancel games, but employed rookies, free agents, and nonstrikers. The players returned to work after missing 42 days and acquiesced to the owners' demands.

The negotiations for the most recent collective bargaining agreement had opened on February 16, 1982. The players' union proposed a revolutionary concept for the agreement: a specified percentage of gross revenues (55%) would be allocated to a central fund to compensate the players. Players would be paid on a seniority scale from this fund without regard to performance. Teams could pay additional amounts to players from the remaining 45% of their revenues. The owners flatly refused to consider the proposal.

The owners proposed a 43% increase in minimum salaries, a 60% increase in playoff monies, a 67% increase in life insurance, and a doubling of major medical coverage. After both sides filed a series of unfair labor practice charges with the NLRB, the union voted to strike on September 25, 1982. The union's solidarity was complete. The strike lasted 57 days and was timed to begin in the middle of the regular season. In all, half the regular season games were cancelled and cost the league about $200 million in television revenues.

In the end, the players abandoned their revenue-sharing demands and settled on a pact with a value of about $1.6 billion over five years. The players received bonuses immediately of up to $60,000, based on seniority, a lucrative minimum salary scale, severance pay, and an increase in postseason pay. The total package was similar to the one proposed by the owners before the strike commenced. The free agent rules were unchanged.

OWNERS

Owners of NFL teams in 1983 were a mixture of old and new. Some teams had a history of family ownership dating back to the early days of the NFL. Other owners had been involved in the NFL for a number of years and thought of their team as their primary business. Newer owners, part of the old AFL or owners of expansion teams, were often entrepreneurs whose primary business and source of wealth was not football.

NFL ownership carried with it a blend of celebrity and civic leadership. Any new owner, whether through expansion or sale of an existing team, had to be approved by 21 of 28 existing NFL owners. See Exhibit 3 for a profile of NFL owners. The table below lists franchise changes since 1969.

MUNICIPALITIES AND STADIUMS

All teams required a stadium in which to play their home games. Exhibit 4 shows the stadiums used by NFL teams, the owners of each stadium, original construction costs, the year of lease expiration, and lease-payment schedules for all 28 NFL teams. Many of the stadiums were used for both football and other professional sports or entertainment.

Relocating a team to a new city had been rare. The 1982 season saw the most publicized case in NFL

NFL Franchise Changes (1969–1982)

Year	Team	New Owner	Purchase Price
1969	Philadelphia Eagles	Leonard Tose	$16,100,000
1972	Los Angeles Rams	Carrol Rosenbloom	Unknown
1977	San Francisco 49ers	Edward DeBartolo	$21,000,000 (estimate)
1981	Denver Broncos	Edgar Kaiser	$50,000,000 (estimate)

Sources: National Economic Research Associates, *The Wall Street Journal.*

THE LEAGUE

The league was managed by a commissioner and a six-member executive committee, both elected by team owners. The Constitution and Bylaws of the league governed league procedures. Owners met twice annually to rule on major issues. During the remainder of the year, the commissioner and the committees made operating decisions.

The NFL had had five commissioners in its 51-year history. Pete Rozelle, the current commissioner, had served since 1960. By the 1970s, Rozelle was being referred to as the "Czar" of professional football. Rozelle exercised a great deal of power as well as influence. The Constitution and Bylaws of the NFL gave Rozelle broad authority over many aspects of the league including exclusive contract negotiating privileges with outside parties (networks), control over player contracts, and disputes among owners and teams. He also had the power to levy fines on individual owners, teams, players, and coaches. It took a 3/4 vote of those teams in the NFL prior to the AFL merger to remove Rozelle. The NFL Management Council was the labor bargaining unit for NFL owners, and a vote of 21 of 28 teams was needed to ratify a new labor agreement.

history. Oakland Raider owner Al Davis wanted to move his franchise to Los Angeles. The Raiders had been a successful team on and off the field in Oakland, but the economics were more attractive in Los Angeles, with its larger population and stadium package.

The NFL refused to approve the move. Davis challenged the league's decision in court on the basis that the league was violating certain antitrust laws. Davis argued that the other owners and the league were conspiring to limit competition in football, which constituted an illegal restraint of trade. A federal court jury agreed with Davis' arguments, and the Raiders moved to Los Angeles. Appeals and suits brought by the city of Oakland were filed and were pending as of January 1983.

TELEVISION

Professional football games were broadcast on the three major television networks: ABC, CBS, and NBC. Sports and television had become intertwined by 1983, exemplified by the degree to which the rules in many sports had been designed to maximize their broadcasting appeal and to allow advertisers ample opportunity to sell their products. One example was the predetermined number of time-outs in each football broadcast allocated to advertisers.

The fees that TV networks could pay for NFL broadcast rights were determined by advertising rates that NFL broadcasts could command, a function of the ratings of NFL games. The rating measured the percentage of all households with TVs that were tuned in to a given program. Another measure, called share, measured the percentage of TVs turned on at a given time that were watching a particular program. Therefore, if 60% of the TV households were watching TV at a particular time and all of them were watching the same program, the program would get a rating of 60 and a share of 100.

Televised sports had been a boon to the networks. According to one industry watcher, the networks knew within 10% how their sports broadcasts would do in the ratings, who would be watching, and when they would be watching. This high degree of predictability allowed the networks to target their advertising sales and to command premium rates. The networks also considered the high Sunday afternoon football ratings to be a desirable lead-in to their evening programming. The amount of sports programming on the networks had grown from 1,288 hours in 1979 to 1,352 in 1982. Exhibit 5 gives television ratings for professional sports including football.

In 1981, the NFL had the highest average audience of all TV network sports with an 18.3% rating, although the rating had fallen in 1982. Regular season average advertising rates on the NFL had risen from $58,700 for 30 seconds in 1978 to $103,000 in 1982.

The demographic segments targeted by football advertisers were males 18–49 years old and males aged 25–54. Advertisers believed that no other programming could deliver these segments in a more concentrated audience than professional football. According to a Simmons Market Research study, 20 million males aged 18–49, representing 45% of all homes with TV, watched the NFL in 1981. This was six times the number of males who watched the top primetime shows, and double the number who watched college football, the nearest competitor. The 18–49 male demographic was ideal for marketers of beer, cars, men's toiletries, and other male-oriented products. The degree of emotional involvement of the audience in the game made the NFL a very desirable advertising medium. Advertisers believed that this viewer involvement carried over to the ad message.

The largest TV sports advertisers were General Motors, Philip Morris (parent of Miller Beer), Anheuser-Busch, and Ford, who accounted for 25% of the advertising dollars spent on TV sports. When a large advertiser purchased sufficient time, it could be granted product exclusivity by the network, which ensured that its competitors would not be able to advertise on that program.

Historically, NFL advertisers tended to allocate a significant portion of their advertising dollars to sports programming. Cable TV, wired directly into the viewer's set, represented a growing source of TV programming. In 1982, 20 million homes (25% of TV homes) were hooked up to cable TV services. The number of cable hookups was expected to rise to 50 million by 1990. Sports programming had been used as a sales leader to gain viewers for cable TV. This led to active bidding among the cable networks for sporting events. When NCAA basketball was put up for bid, for example, Ted Turner bid $17 million versus other bids of $800,000 and $7 million. Some sports teams, such as the Chicago White Sox under new owner Eddie Einhorn (former owner of TVS), retained cable rights for themselves in order to obtain those profits and retain greater control over the broadcasts and the resultant image for the team.

Some of the major providers of sports programming for cable TV included the following:

Entertainment and Sports Programming Network (ESPN).

The stated goal of ESPN was to "provide the sports viewer with as many events and as much information about sports as we can." As of 1982, ESPN reached 17 million households and had agreements with the National Basketball Association, the Canadian Football League, and the North American Soccer League, as well as rights to broadcast various college football games, boxing, tennis, and golf. ESPN also had 200 national advertisers, including a five-year, $25 million contract with Anheuser-Busch conferring product exclusivity.

USA Cable.

Like ESPN, USA Cable was created to be a national cable network. In 1982, USA Cable signed a long-term agreement with CBS to provide coordinated coverage of many sporting events. In 1982, the company had 11 million subscribers and 100 national advertisers.

EXHIBIT 3   NFL Owners Profile

Team	Owner	Since	Education
AMERICAN FOOTBALL CONFERENCE:			
Miami Dolphins	Joseph Robbie	1967	U. of South Dakota Law
Buffalo Bills	Ralph C. Wilson, Jr.	1960	U. Virginia; U. Michigan Law
New England Patriots	William H. Sullivan, Jr.	1960	Boston College, 1937, B.A.
New York Jets	Leon Hess	1963	NA
Baltimore Colts	Robert Irsay	1972	U. of Illinois; Mech. Eng.
Cleveland Browns	Arthur B. Modell	1961	Hon. LLD, John Carroll U.
Cincinnati Bengals	John Sawyer	1968	NA
Houston Oilers	K. S. (Bud) Adams, Jr.	1960	U. of Kansas, Pet. Eng.
Pittsburgh Steelers	Arthur J. Rooney, Sr.	1933	Georgetown U.; Duquesne
Denver Broncos	Edgar Kaiser, Jr.	1981	Stanford, 1965; Harvard M.B.A., 1967
Kansas City Chiefs	Lamar Hunt	1960	Southern Methodist University
Los Angeles Raiders	Al Davis	1967	Syracuse U.
San Diego Chargers	Eugene V. Klein	1966	New York University
Seattle Seahawks	Herman Sarkosky	1976	Washington U.

Primary Business if Other Than Football	Biographical Data
	Former Miami legislator, gubernatorial candidate, and practicing attorney for 20 years. Involved with expansion Dolphins by default as an attorney for an investor. In 1970, hired away successful Baltimore coach Don Shula. Team has flourished.
President, Ralph Wilson, Ins. and Auto Transport	Founding member of AFL. Sole owner and key participant in opening merger talks with NFL. Also a racehorse breeder and considered a multimillionaire.
President, Metropolitan Petroleum Corp; Executive Vice President, Pittston Corp.	Self-made millionaire, joint owner of AFL Boston team. Gained 88% control in 1975. Moved team to Foxboro (45 miles S.W. of Boston). President of AFL from 1961–1964, a principal negotiator of AFL TV package and NFL/AFL merger.
Chairman, CEO, Amerada-Hess Petroleum Corp.	Joint owner, silent partner until 1981 purchase of Townsend Martin's interest brought Hess 75% control and installed his management team.
Construction company; former air conditioning co.	Sold multi-million dollar business built from $800 loan from wife in early 1970s. Bought Los Angeles Rams in 1972, then swapped franchises with Baltimore's Carroll Rosenbloom. Said to thrive on controversy.
	Self-made multimillionaire, made reputation and fortune in TV and advertising before purchasing Browns. Very active NFL owner, considered one of three most knowledgeable men in in NFL on television industry along with Pete Rozelle and Al Davis.
J. Sawyer Co., agricultural concern	Son of late Secretary of Commerce Charles Sawyer. President and majority owner of Bengals since founding in 1967. Legendary coach Paul Brown is part owner and general manager.
President, CEO of Adams Resources; other business ventures	Born in Oklahoma, son of a Phillips Oil Co. CEO. Launched many successful business ventures after military duty in WWII. One of founders of AFL.
Former brewery owner, boxing promoter	One of grandfathers of NFL. Has the rare distinction of holding a Hall of Fame ring (1964) as well as a Super Bowl ring.
Chairman and CEO of Kaiser Resource Ltd. of Canada	Heir to an aluminum fortune. Purchased Broncos from Phipps Brothers.
Oil and sports businesses	Son of billionaire H. L. Hunt, conceived the idea of the AFL in 1959. Also a principal investor in World Championship Tennis, NASL Soccer, and NBA. First AFL figure to be inducted in Pro Football Hall of Fame and win a Super Bowl.
23 years in pro football	Managing partner of Raiders, former coach, and AFL League Commissioner (prior to the merger). Possesses a wealth of knowledge concerning all aspects of pro football. Has reputation as a fierce competitor.
CEO of National General Corp., 1961–1973	Sold holdings in NSG in 1973 to become a full-time owner. At 6' 5'', 250 pounds, Klein is said to have become a very influential owner.
Real estate and home construction	Another thoroughbred racer and president of Portland Trail Blazers basketball team. Managing general partner but delegates operational.

EXHIBIT 3   *(concluded)*

Team	Owner	Since	Education
NATIONAL FOOTBALL CONFERENCE:			
Dallas Cowboys	Clint Murchison	1959	M.I.T.
New York Giants	Wellington T. and Timothy J. Mara	1925	Fordham; Iona
Philadelphia Eagles	Leonard Tose	1969	Notre Dame
St. Louis Cardinals	William V. Bidwill	1932	Georgetown U.
Washington Redskins	Jack Kent Cooke	1974	Malvern Collegiate
Chicago Bears	George Halas	1922	U. of Illinois, B.S.
Detroit Lions	William Clay Ford	1964	Detroit U., Yale
Green Bay Packers	City owned		
Minnesota Vikings	Max Winter	1961	Hamline U. (Minnesota)
Tampa Bay Buccaneers	Hugh F. Culverhouse	1974	U. of Alabama, B.S. and J.D.
Atlanta Falcons	Rankin M. Smith	1965	U. of Georgia
Los Angeles Rams	Georgia Frontiere	1972	NA
New Orleans Saints	John Mecom, Jr.	1967	U. of Oklahoma, U. of Texas
San Francisco 49ers	Edward J. DeBartolo, Jr.	1977	Notre Dame

Primary Business if Other Than Football	*Biographical Data*
Various	Heir to family oil and real estate fortune. Awarded the Dallas NFL franchise over Lamar Hunt. Long known for hands-off ownership, has left management of team to his general manager, Tex Schram.
	One of the early families of the NFL, this father/son duo has been associated with the Giants since 1925, and as such, has cultivated a great deal of influence over the years.
	Started in family trucking business and worked his way to the top. Culminated lifelong interest in sports with the purchase of the Eagles. Considered an influential member of the NFL.
	Charles Bidwill founded the Chicago Cardinals in 1932. His son Bill became sole owner in 1960 and moved the team to St. Louis.
Real estate	With a real estate and business fortune estimated at $600 million, Canadian-born Cooke, with prior ventures in pro sports (Los Angeles Lakers basketball, Los Angeles Kings hockey) assumed control of the Redskins in 1974 and has turned the management and team fortunes around.
	One of the founders of the NFL, Halas got his start as a player/coach in the first NFL season and has been in those positions as well as owner ever since. No one other individual has had either the longevity or impact that George Halas has.
Automobiles	The grandson of Henry Ford and current vice chairman of Ford Motor Co., sole owner Ford takes an active role in his team.
	Judge Robert J. Parins is president of the Packers and reports to a board of directors.
	Formerly a promoter for the Harlem Globetrotters, and then with the Minnesota Lakers pro basketball, Winter led a group of investors that received an expansion franchise in 1961.
Law	A practicing lawyer and real estate developer, Culverhouse has successfully developed his Bucs, the 27th NFL franchise, as well as his reputation within the NFL, where he sits on three of the NFL's most influential committees, the Executive, Financial, and Management Council.
	Retired as head of Life Insurance Co. of Georgia, Smith (an avid sportsman and hunter) delegates most of the operation of the Falcons to his executives.
	After taking over after husband Carroll Rosenbloom's death three years ago, Mrs. Frontiere has actively assumed her role as the only woman owner in the NFL. Named Headliner of the Year by the Los Angeles Press Club in 1981, she is also very active in civic affairs.
Oil	Native of Houston and heir to a family oil fortune of $150 million. Became an NFL owner at 27.
Real estate	From a family that pioneered the shopping mall concept into a real estate empire, overseas shipping, and race tracks estimated at $500 million, DeBartolo is the youngest of the NFL owners at 27.

EXHIBIT 4 NFL Team Stadium Data

Team	City[d]		Facility Name	Capacity
AMERICAN FOOTBALL CONFERENCE:				
Eastern Division:				
Dolphins	Miami	(13)	Orange Bowl	75,206
Bills	Buffalo	(32)	Rich Stadium	80,290
Patriots	New England[a]	(6)	Sullivan Stadium	60,606
Jets	New York[a]	(1)	Giants Stadium[b]	76,891
Colts	Baltimore	(20)	Memorial Stadium	60,586
Central Division:				
Browns	Cleveland	(9)	Cleveland Stadium	80,098
Bengals	Cincinnati	(27)	Riverfront Stadium	59,754
Oilers	Houston	(11)	Astrodome[c]	50,495
Steelers	Pittsburgh	(12)	Three Rivers	59,000
Western Division:				
Broncos	Denver[a]	(19)	Mile High[b]	75,100
Chiefs	Kansas City	(36)	Arrowhead	78,067
Raiders	Los Angeles[a]	(2)	Coliseum[b]	92,604
Chargers	San Diego	(25)	Jack Murphy	60,100
Sea Hawks	Seattle	(14)	Kingdome[c]	64,984

NATIONAL FOOTBALL CONFERENCE:

Eastern Division:			
Cowboys	Dallas	Texas Stadium	(10)	65,101
Giants	New York[a]	Giants Stadium[b]	(1)	76,891
Eagles	Philadelphia[a]	Veterans Stadium[b]	(4)	73,484
Cardinals	St. Louis	Busch Stadium	(18)	51,392
Redskins	Washington[a]	Robert F. Kennedy[b]	(8)	55,363

Central Division:			
Bears	Chicago[a]	Soldier Field[b]	(3)	65,793
Lions	Detroit[a]	Pontiac Silverdome[b,c]	(7)	80,638
Packers	Green Bay	Lambeau Field and Milwaukee City	(289)	56,155
Vikings	Minnesota	H. H. Humphrey Metrodome[c]	(16)	62,345
Bucs	Tampa Bay[a]	Tampa Stadium[b]	(17)	74,317

Western Division:			
Falcons	Atlanta	Fulton County	(15)	60,763
Rams	Los Angeles[a]	Anaheim Stadium	(2)	69,007
Saints	New Orleans	Louisiana Superdome[c]	(34)	71,330
49ers	San Francisco	Candlestick Park	(5)	61,413

[a]USFL cities.
[b]USFL stadiums.
[c]Domed stadiums.
[d]A. C. Neilson designated market area ranking is in parenthesis.

EXHIBIT 5   Ratings of Sports Programs in Television, 1977–1982

	1977	*1979*	*1980*	*1981*	*1982*
Football:					
Regular season:					
ABC Monday Night Football	21.2%	19.5%	20.3%	21.2%	19.4%
CBS NFL Broadcasts	16.1	15.0	15.3	17.5	16.5
NBC NFL Broadcasts	13.5	14.0	14.9	13.9	13.9
Post-Season:					
AFC Championship (NBC)	35.6	34.2	31.5	35.0	33.5
NFC Championship (CBS)	35.0	33.4	34.9	42.9	32.4
AFC-NFC Pro Bowl (ABC)	18.4	20.0	18.2	18.7	16.3
Super Bowl	44.4	47.1	46.3	44.4	49.1
College Football	13.2	11.4	11.5	12.0	10.9
Other sports:					
NBA Basketball	7.2	4.8	5.2	6.0	5.8
Baseball:					
Regular season (evening)	12.5	12.6	12.4	12.0	11.8
Regular season (Saturday)	6.7	6.9	7.2	6.3	6.3
World Series	29.8	28.5	32.8	30.0	27.9
Multi-Sports:					
ABC Wide World (Sunday)	12.4	10.0	10.2	9.7	8.0
NBC Sports World (Sunday)	NA	6.0	6.2	6.6	6.1

Source: A. C. Nielsen and Co.

Superstations.   The concept of a superstation was created by Ted Turner in Atlanta. The idea was to broadcast his station's local signals over a satellite to be delivered by cable networks in other areas. Turner's WTBS was by far the most prominent superstation and was the largest cable outlet in 1982 with 21.1 million homes served. In addition to broadcasting the games of the local Atlanta baseball and basketball teams, WTBS had an agreement to televise NCAA football and basketball games.

Regional Networks.   Regional networks developed programs of interest throughout a regional area and then marketed them through the cable operators in the communities within that region. For example, the Yankees baseball team had reportedly received $5 million a year for 15 years for the rights to a large part of their games.

   The question of whether fans would pay to watch their teams play on TV was still open. Benton & Bowles' viewer survey indicated that 30% of viewers were prepared to pay to see additional TV sports, but that 81% of the men polled would be either very or moderately angry if the Super Bowl or World Series were only available on pay TV. However, a majority said that they would be willing to pay to see these events. The Seattle Supersonics basketball team had netted close to $1 million in 1981 by charging $120 for a subscriber to see the entire schedule on pay TV. Dallas Cowboys President Tex Schramm said, ''I don't think that it is feasible for sponsors to continue paying the total load, when it has become obvious that viewers are prepared to pay for . . . a certain share.''

THE UNITED STATES FOOTBALL LEAGUE

The United States Football League began its first season in February 1983. USFL games were played in the spring, from February to July. David Dixon, the founder of the USFL, had decided in 1980 that the market was ripe for a new professional football league. Dixon was described by *Sports Illustrated* as follows:

[Dixon is] sort of a professional enthusiast, an effervescent and often successful jack of many, many trades, including plywood manufacturer, car dealer, co-founder (with Lamar Hunt) of World Championship Tennis, amateur art collector turned professional art dealer, executive director of the New Orleans Superdome, unsuccessful candidate for the U.S. Congress and amateur golfer good enough to qualify for the U.S. Open.

Dixon, an ardent booster of the city of New Orleans, actually began thinking about a spring football league in 1964 as a ploy for pressuring the NFL into granting New Orleans a franchise. Once Dixon's idea became public, he got some enthusiastic responses. Paul Brown, former coach of the NFL Cleveland Browns and present owner of the NFL Cincinnati Bengals, told Dixon ''never let anyone talk you out of this. It'll work, and I want the San Francisco franchise.'' Others interested reportedly included Gussie Busch of Anheuser-Busch and oilman Nelson Bunker Hunt.

The idea of a spring season created interest not only outside of the NFL but also within the league. According to New York Giant President Wellington Mara, ''The NFL once considered launching a spring-time league, but dropped the idea for fear that college players would thereby be induced to quit school in their senior year without waiting to get their degrees.'' Dixon's interest in the league diminished as New Orleans got closer to securing an NFL franchise. With the award of an NFL franchise to John Mecom in 1967, Dixon devoted his time to assisting in establishing that team, and he later played a critical role in the building of the Superdome.

During 1980, Dixon constantly read about the cable TV explosion, and concluded ''that this was going to break the NFL monopoly on pro football TV, and it also occurred to me that this was the time to bring the old 'spring season' idea out of mothballs.'' Dixon felt that the spring season idea was viable because football fans had nothing to do between January and August, the NFL's off-season. To explore this hunch, Dixon hired Frank N. Magid Associates, a Marion, Iowa, media research firm, who had also done work for ABC television. Magid conducted research in nine top metropolitan markets and found that 76% of those polled indicated an interest in watching televised football games during the spring and summer.

Armed with this information, Dixon began developing the new league's strategy for entering the industry.

He decided that the league would play under the same game rules as the NFL, the only exception being to allow either a one- or two-point conversion after a touchdown. It was also decided that the USFL would be made up of 12 teams with as many as possible playing in NFL cities. These teams would play their games in the same stadiums as NFL teams. The owners would be people who were financially capable and willing to lose money for several years during the league's infant stages.

Dixon adamantly opposed the idea of using players that were ''has-beens and never-weres.'' He also rejected the strategy of outbidding the NFL for college stars and superstar veterans with expired contracts. He said,

> We're going to create our own stars. We'll have troubles in the first and second round of the draft. But once we get to the third, fourth and fifth rounds—there we'll be real competitive. We'll offer things the NFL wouldn't think of giving, such as three-year, no-cut contracts to rookies and a promise that a player will stay in the territory where he was a college star.

Dixon searched for wealthy individuals who would be willing to purchase franchises. Going from state to state, he tried to persuade some of the wealthiest people in America that they could reap major profits and benefits from owning a professional football team. Dixon met with significant resistance and skepticism. For example, John Bassett, the owner of the defunct WFL's Memphis Southmen and future owner of the USFL's Tampa Bay Bandits, recalled his meeting with Dixon: ''I bought him lunch and told him he was crazy.''

By late 1981, Dixon had found enough prospective owners willing to risk millions of dollars on his idea. In May 1982, 15 owners and co-owners announced at a press conference in New York City's ''21'' Club that they were launching a new 12-team professional football league with play to begin in February 1983. Ten of the franchises—Boston, Chicago, Denver, Detroit, Los Angeles, New Jersey, Oakland, Philadelphia, Tampa Bay, and Washington—would be in established NFL cities. The other two—Arizona and Birmingham—would be in cities where fans had shown an insatiable appetite for local college football. Exhibit 6 gives a profile of USFL teams, cities and stadiums.

Dixon realized that he was not wealthy enough to be among the group of owners and sold his Chicago

EXHIBIT 6 USFL Team Profile

City	City's National Ranking as a Television Market	Team	1983 Average Attendance	1984 Average Attendance[a]
Arizona	24	Wranglers	25,780	25,621
Birmingham	40	Stallions	22,046	40,722
Chicago[c]	3	Blitz	18,090	7,975
Denver[c]	19	Gold	41,736	34,599
Los Angeles[c]	2	Express	22,357	17,040
Michigan[c]	7	Panthers	21,513	34,536
New Jersey[c]	1	Generals	33,933	41,059
New Orleans[d]	34	Breakers	12,735	31,723
Oakland	5	Invaders	30,622	22,747
Philadelphia[c]	4	Stars	18,794	28,238
Tampa Bay[c]	17	Bandits	45,255	45,830
Washington[c]	8	Federals	13,850	7,863
Houston[b]	11	Gamblers	—	29,330
Jacksonville[b]	65	Bulls	—	48,597
Memphis[b]	39	Showboats	—	25,132
Oklahoma [b]	43	Outlaws	—	17,125
Pittsburgh[b]	12	Maulers	—	24,529
San Antonio[b]	45	Gunslingers	—	9,002

[a]Teams played nine home games per season, with an average ticket price of about $9.
[b]Expansion team in 1984.
[c]NFL teams play in these cities.
[d]Moved from Boston.

franchise rights to Dr. Ted Diethrich, a Phoenix heart surgeon. Referring to the wealth of the owners, John Bassett remarked, ''In the WFL I was the league's richest guy. Here, I'm the poorest.'' (See Exhibit 7 for a profile of the USFL owners.) The new owners had various reasons for being in football. Alan Harmon, co-owner of the Los Angeles franchise, stated, ''My first reaction was to see pictures of myself sitting in the glass box, maybe drinking a scotch and water, picking up the telephone and maybe calling a play or two.'' His partner Bill Daniels responded, ''The older the boys, the more expensive the toys.''

Each franchisee was required to put up a $1.5 million letter of credit, held in escrow, to be used by the league to bail out failing franchises if necessary. Each of the owners verbally pledged his willingness to lose $3–$6 million over the next several years to ensure adequate time for the league to establish its position.

Each team would operate with a cumulative salary cap of $1.4 million for the 40 active players. This rule was later modified to allow each team to sign two players whose salaries would not count in their cap. The USFL draft would occur during the first week of January, following all of the college bowl games. In addition to the regular draft of college players, the USFL would have a territorial draft. This system would give each team exclusive rights to players from certain colleges, generally within the team's own region. For example, the Tampa Bay franchise would have exclusive rights to players from Florida State University and the University of Miami.

The USFL's next task was to pursue a network television contract. With Mike Trager, the former president of NBC Sports, as their television consultant, they approached all three major networks and several cable companies. ABC and NBC each offered approximately $18 million for the first two seasons with options for two years. It was unprecedented for the networks to bid for the rights to a league that would not even play its first game for another nine months. ABC's offer of $9

EXHIBIT 7   Profile of USFL Owners

DAVID F. DIXON, Founder, United States Football League
David F. Dixon, founder of the United States Football League, is a New Orleans art
  dealer with a unique background in sports.

MARVIN L. WARNER, Birmingham Franchise
Marvin L. Warner, owner of the Birmingham franchise, is a native of Birmingham,
  Alabama. He is chairman and chief executive officer of ComBanks Corp. and Great
  American Banks, Inc. of Orlando and Miami, Florida, respectively.

EDWARD DIETHRICH, M.D., Chicago Franchise
Dr. Diethrich is an internationally renowned cardiovascular surgeon and is the founder
  and medical director of the Arizona Heart Institute in Phoenix.

RON BLANDING, Denver Franchise
Ron Blanding is the owner of the Denver franchise. He is president of Blanding and
  Company, a leading Denver-based commercial real estate development and
  construction firm.

ALAN HARMON, Los Angeles Franchise
Alan Harmon, co-owner of the Los Angeles franchise is president of Harmon & Co., a
  Denver-based cable television operator with 20 systems in seven states.

BILL DANIELS, Los Angeles Franchise
Bill Daniels, co-owner of the Los Angeles franchise, is best known as "The Father of
  Cable Television." It has been said that Daniels is to cable TV what John D.
  Rockefeller was to oil and what J. P. Morgan was to railroads.

A. ALFRED TAUBMAN, Michigan Franchise
Mr. Taubman, co-owner of the Detroit franchise, is one of the nation's leading real
  estate developers. He is chairman and chief executive officer of the Taubman
  Company, Inc., which he founded in 1950. The firm is one of the foremost
  owner-builder-developers of regional shopping centers in urban and suburban
  locations throughout the United States.

JUDGE PETER B. SPIVAK, Michigan Franchise
Judge Spivak, co-owner of the Michigan franchise, was formerly a judge of the Third
  Judicial Circuit of Michigan from 1974 to July 1981. He is now of counsel to the
  law firm of Bushnell, Gage, Doctoroff & Reizen in Detroit.

RANDY VATAHA, New England Franchise
Randy Vataha, co-owner of the New England franchise, was a standout pass receiver
  in both the professional and college football ranks. An outstanding end at Stanford
  University, Vataha's National Football League playing career spanned seven years
  with the New England Patriots and Green Bay Packers.

GEORGE J. MATTHEWS, New England Franchise
George J. Matthews, co-owner of the New England franchise, is a General Partner of
  The Matthews Group, Boston. The company is a limited partnership holding
  company with diversified interests.

J. WALTER DUNCAN, JR., New York Franchise
J. Walter Duncan, Jr., owner of the New York franchise, is the founder and principal
  owner of Walter Duncan Oil Properties, a leading oil and gas producing company
  located in Oklahoma City, Oklahoma. The company's operations are involved in
  exploration, development and production.

EXHIBIT 7   *(concluded)*

THADDEUS N. TAUBE, Oakland Franchise

Thaddeus N. Taube, co-owner of the Oakland franchise, is Chairman of Taube
Associates, Inc., a diversified real estate investment, development, and management
company he formed in 1964. Taube Associates, Inc. is involved in major apartment,
industrial and commercial real estate operations throughout the western part of the
United States.

MYLES H. TANENBAUM, Philadelphia Franchise

Myles H. Tanenbaum, managing partner of the Philadelphia franchise, is executive
vice president of Kravco, Inc., a major developer and manager of shopping centers
and other commercial real estate.

JIM S. JOSEPH, Phoenix Franchise

Jim S. Joseph, co-owner of the Phoenix franchise, is president of Interland
Corporation, a real estate development, management and construction company in
San Mateo.

STEPHEN W. ARKY, Tampa Bay Franchise

Stephen W. Arky, a co-owner of the Tampa Bay franchise, is president of the law firm
of Arky, Freed, Stearns, Watson & Greer, P.A. with offices in Tampa, Miami and
Orlando, Florida.

JOHN F. BASSETT, Tampa Bay Franchise

John F. Bassett, co-owner of the Tampa Bay franchise, is a native of Canada and
currently resides in Toronto and Sarasota, Florida. He is president of Amulet
Pictures, Ltd., a producer of feature motion pictures and has numerous real estate
and business interests in both countries.

BERL BERNHARD, Washington, D.C. Franchise

Berl Bernhard, owner of the Washington, D.C. franchise, is senior partner and
president of Verner, Liipfert, Bernhard & McPherson, chartered, a prominent
Washington, D.C.-based law firm.

---

million each year for the first two years and $14 million
and $18 million, respectively, for the two option years
was accepted because of ABC's reputation as a premier
sports network. The USFL also signed a two-year deal
with ESPN for $11 million. The TV revenue would be
evenly split among the teams. The revenue from ticket
sales would be split, with 60% for the home team and
40% for the visitors.

Armed with two television contracts before any players had even been signed, the USFL owners searched for
a league commissioner. The owners first approached
NFL Commissioner Pete Rozelle, who refused the offer.
Chet Simmons, former president of ESPN, became the
first commissioner. In his efforts to promote and publi-
cize the league, he continually met criticism from
sportswriters who asserted that the league was not

legitimate because it was created for television. Simmons announced two significant league objectives regarding television and attendance. First, he indicated
that the league would seek to beat the 4.8 rating that
ABC television averaged in the same slot the previous
year with sports programs such as "Superstars" and
"The American Sportsman." The second objective was
to average 25,000 fans per game throughout the season.

The league began signing players and coaches who
were "gate attractions." George Allen, Chuck Fair-
banks, and Red Miller, all coaches of previous NFL
play-off teams, were signed. Several dozen college
stars, many projected first-round draft choices such as
Kelvin Bryant from the University of North Carolina,
Craig Jones from SMU, and Tim Spencer from Ohio
State, were signed to guaranteed multimillion dollar

contracts. These players were supported by other players who had contracts for as little as $25,000 per year. The major media coup for the USFL prior to its initial season was the signing by the New Jersey Generals of Georgia University's junior running back and Heisman Trophy winner Herschel Walker. His three-year, $3.9 million guaranteed contract included incentive bonuses that could push the total to $4.5 million. This contract, which also included a $1 million cash signing bonus, made Walker the highest paid athlete in professional football. This was the first time in professional football history that a college undergraduate had signed a professional contract before his class's graduation year. Thus, this incident was termed "the shot heard around college sports." The responses to the Walker signing varied. The Generals claimed that they sold 6,900 season tickets in the 72 hours after the signing. Emory Bellard, the coach of Mississippi State University, called Walker's signing "the single worst thing that has happened to college football since its inception."

Pete Rozelle chose not to make any comments about the USFL. Jim Finks, the general manager of the NFL Chicago Bears, commented, "They [the USFL] have to have the live gate. You don't make it as a studio show in this business. Nothing looks worse than a game played before empty stands." NFL owners also criticized Simmons for the Walker signing. An NFL official expressed the hope that the league wouldn't have to "stoop to the USFL's level and raid the campuses." But Al Davis, general partner of the NFL's Los Angeles Raiders, viewed the attitude of his fellow owners and Pete Rozelle about the USFL as a "country club mentality" and a "Rip Van Winkle approach."

THE USFL'S FIRST TWO SEASONS

Over 2.5 million fans attended USFL games during the first season (1983), with a season low of 4,200 for a game in Boston and a season high of 53,000 for a game in New Jersey. Average attendance per game was 25,276, and Exhibit 6 shows attendance per team. The first USFL championship game, between the Michigan Panthers and the Philadelphia Stars, attracted 50,906 fans. By comparison, the AFL's first championship game had drawn 32,183 fans and the first NFL Super Bowl drew 61,946 fans.

USFL ratings on ABC for 1983 were 6.2 versus the original projection of 5. This compares favorably with the first-year AFL rating of 5.8, and also with the 4.8 average rating for ABC's sports programming during the same period in the previous year. On ESPN, the average rating for the season as 3.3, quite solid for cable. Demographic analysis of USFL viewers showed an older than expected audience, with the 18- to 45-year-old males not as well represented as expected. There was some disappointment that only the season opener managed to break into the double-digit ratings, and that ratings dropped over the season.

In the inaugural USFL season, ABC grossed approximately $40 million in advertising sales, of which $10 million was profit. Sales were brisk, with 92% of all time sold out well before the first game. The list of advertisers was not very different from those on NFL broadcasts. ABC increased its rates for the 1984 USFL season by 10%, to $33,000 per 30 seconds for regular season games and $66,000 for 30 seconds on the championship game.

USFL teams ended their first season with total losses of approximately $40 million.[5] However, a high level of interest in the league was reflected in offers from investors from cities such as Pittsburgh, Memphis, and Jacksonville to establish new franchises. Groups in Japan and Hawaii also wanted to put teams in Tokyo and Honolulu. The equity value of existing franchises also increased. For example, the Denver Gold was sold for $10 million shortly after the first season.

The USFL decided to capitalize on interest from potential new owners by expanding 50% for its second season. Expansion offered the league the opportunity to enter additional major television markets such as Pittsburgh as well as cities of secondary size without NFL teams such as Jacksonville. Expansion was also viewed as a means to combat the threat of the start up of a competitive league, the International Football League.[6] Each of the six new USFL franchises cost $6 million of which $2.5 million would be payable in 1984. This entry fee would be equally divided among the 12 original owners. In return, the new owners would share equally in the league's television revenues and have the oppor-

---

[5]The Tampa Bay and Denver franchises made close to $1 million each; Oakland came close to breaking even. New Jersey, Birmingham, and Arizona each lost between $1–$1.5 million, while the other six franchises lost between $1.5 and $6 million each.

[6]The IFL never materialized.

tunity to build their teams by selecting from a pool of 20 unprotected players from each of the original teams.

The USFL continued to seek college stars as well as NFL veterans, which ultimately led to nearly every team violating the league's salary-cap rules. A primary focus was quarterbacks, but star players in all positions won lucrative, guaranteed contracts. For example, Mike Rozier, the second straight Heisman Trophy winner signed by a USFL team, agreed to play for the Pittsburgh Maulers for $3.2 million over three years. Donald Trump, the new owner of the New Jersey Generals, also made headlines by signing Lawrence Taylor, the star linebacker for the NFL's NY Giants, to a future contract for 1988 when Taylor's NFL contract was due to expire. In response, the Giants renegotiated Taylor's contract giving him $7.3 million through 1990.

The second USFL season ended with the league losing over $60 million. While data on all teams was not available, Tampa Bay broke even while New Orleans lost $3 million; Jacksonville, $3.6 million; and Philadelphia, $3 million. Most observers believed that the quality of play on the field improved. Average attendance per game was 28,675. The average TV rating on ABC for the 1984 season was 5.5, beginning at around 8 in February and ending at 3.7 in late June. The USFL's rating on ESPN was 2.9 in the second year.

In response to the USFL's second year ratings, Jim Spence, the head of ABC Sports Programming, said, "When we got involved with the USFL it was never our expectation that the ratings would be NFL type numbers of even approach NFL numbers. Or even college numbers." Another response to the USFL's second season came from Al Davis, General Partner of the NFL's Los Angeles Raiders.

> The USFL has undergone franchise changes. It has suffered attendance headaches. And its TV ratings have been thin. But, the AFL had its share of grief too—and those teams now are worth $70 million or so.

The ESPN contract was renewed after the second season, and called for the league to receive $70 million over three years. According to John Bassett, owner of the Tampa Bay USFL franchise and head of the USFL's Television Committee, the USFL turned down an offer from ABC in mid-1984 to renegotiate their contract for $150 million over four years. He also indicated that the USFL was negotiating to have all teams' away games televised to their home markets. However, further ne-

gotiations with ABC were unsuccessful in leading to an agreement.

USFL STRATEGIC REPOSITIONING

In August of 1984, led by Donald Trump and Eddie Einhorn, the USFL voted unanimously to compete directly with the NFL by moving its season to the fall in 1986. Explaining this decision, Einhorn said:

> Cheap football fits in the spring. The expensive football dollars are in the fall.

To strengthen the league in preparation for the switch to the fall, the USFL made a number of important decisions prior to the beginning of what was scheduled to be their final spring season in 1985. The first was to reduce the number of teams from 18 to 14 by consolidating some franchises together to husband resources.

The league also entered two new markets in the 1985 season with the Washington and New Orleans franchises moving to Orlando and Portland, respectively. The league also decided to play some games on Saturday in competition with college football. In October 1984, the Justice Department gave the USFL permission to do so.

Another major move by the USFL was the filing of a $1.32 billion antitrust suit against the NFL in October, 1984, charging the older league with conspiring to keep the USFL from securing television contracts and setting up a special committee to destroy the USFL. In addition to damages, the USFL was asking the courts to rule that the NFL's current relationship with the television networks be declared illegal. The USFL's attorney, Roy Cohn, commented:

> When they tie up the three networks, dictate when you can play, and then tie up all of the stadiums, that's when they are breaking the Sherman Antitrust laws.

NFL DEVELOPMENTS—1983–1984

Exhibit 1 shows the average NFL team income statement for 1983 and 1984. Total NFL attendance was 16.2 million in 1983 compared to 17.3 million in 1981, the last full season. The NFL's ratings on NBC were 12.2 in 1983, the lowest rating since the AFL merger and down

10% from 1981. Ratings on ABC fell to 18.1, down 17%, and CBS was down 4.6% to 16.7. Robert Blackmore, NBC's network sales head, said, "There's no question that football in 1983 wasn't quite the delivery vehicle that advertisers were counting on to spread their messages. But most people feel it's a temporary situation."

Advertisers were expressing concern about the NFL's TV contract, which was driving up ad costs. As one advertising executive said, "Advertisers' budgets are finite; they can make only so much available for sports." Anheuser-Busch (A-B) began an experiment in 1984 to advertise more heavily on prime time network programming.

Exhibit 2 displays 1983 and 1984 NFL player salaries by position for players drafted and subsequently signed in the May 1983 and 1984 college drafts. By the end of the 1983 NFL season, at least 18 established NFL players were planning to defect to the rival USFL. One NFL owner summarized his thoughts on player negotiations by saying, "This thing is going to turn into a blood bath."

In March 1984, Robert Irsay, owner of the NFL Baltimore franchise, moved his team to Indianapolis. Irsay did not seek league approval nor did he go to court, as Oakland's Al Davis had done in 1982. Instead, he claimed, "My franchise is mine to do as I see fit." One March night, all team equipment was loaded into moving vans, provided by the city of Indianapolis. The city of Baltimore attempted to stop the move legally but was unsuccessful. Speaking for the NFL, Pete Rozelle said simply, "We just weren't in a position to stop him (Irsay)." Instead, the commissioner called for, "Supreme Court clarification regarding antitrust matters in sports."

NFL ratings continued to decline in 1984. In the 1984 season, "ABC Monday Night Football's" ratings were 16.9%, CBS's NFL ratings were 14.3%, and NBC dropped to 11.8%. Ratings for almost all other televised sports had dropped as well, while the number of hours of sports programming continued to climb. Advertising during the 1984 season was reported to be selling at discounts of 25–30%, with many advertisers holding back and buying in the spot market. Chevrolet, the incumbent domestic auto sponsor, chose not to advertise in the 1985 Super Bowl in protest of the over $1 million per minute price tag. The gap was promptly filled by Ford, who chose to use the event as the cornerstone of its 1985 ad campaign. Chevy, meanwhile, took a 50% sponsorship on ESPN's college football programming.

A number of alternatives were discussed to spark renewed interest in the NFL. One was scheduling two games for Monday night, or changing the starting time for Monday night games so that they would end earlier. Other ideas included jazzing up the game via the rulebook, and reinstituting something like nationwide "punt, pass and kick" contests to generate enthusiasm for football among young people.

During the 1984 season, two more NFL owners threatened to move their franchises to new cities. In the middle of the season, the Philadelphia franchise negotiated with a group of Phoenix businessmen to buy and relocate the franchise. Before a deal had been consummated, however, the city of Philadelphia gave owner Leonard Tose special financial considerations on the lease of Veterans Stadium and convinced him to remain. At the end of the season, the St. Louis franchise cited lost revenues due to Busch Stadium's capacity as reason for considering a move. By the end of 1984, Al Davis had survived all appeals in lawsuits against his 1982 franchise move. Davis also won a $50 million judgment against the league in his antitrust suit. The amount of the award was under appeal as of April 1985.

During the 1983 and 1984 seasons, three NFL franchises were sold. In 1983, H. B. (Bum) Bright bought the Dallas Cowboys for an estimated $80 million. In 1984, Patrick Bohlen bought the Denver Broncos for an estimated $70 million. Also in 1984, Alex Spanos bought the San Diego Chargers for an estimated $70 million. Early in 1985, the Philadelphia franchise as sold to Norman Brahman, a Miami auto dealer, and the New England Patriots were also rumored to be for sale.

DEVELOPMENTS—1985–1986

In July 1986, the USFL-NFL lawsuit was decided largely in the NFL's favor. While the NFL was judged to be "guilty of antitrust violations," it was fined only $3, and no other damages, restrictions, or other relief was involved. The decision was currently under appeal by the USFL in the Federal courts. Meanwhile, the USFL decided not to operate in the Fall 1986-87 season, as previously announced. Star USFL players were quickly signed by NFL teams.

In January 1987, Rozelle was negotiating with the three major networks (ABC, NBC, and CBS) as well as ESPN and other cable networks. However, the current negotiations were characterized by a new cost-consciousness among all three networks. Advertising budget cutbacks by major advertisers, management and ownership changes in all three networks, and higher per-game production costs contributed to the perspective of network executives toward a new contract. Ratings for all three networks improved significantly in 1985 over 1984, but declined slightly in 1986. There were rumors that all three networks actually lost money on the NFL telecasts in 1986. Attendance was strong in both 1985 and 1986.

Finally, looming on the horizon in early 1987 were negotiations with the players' association, which league officials felt would be "difficult," since player salaries have come under significant pressure. Payroll costs in 1986 averaged $290,000 per player for each of the 55 team members, but there were significant variations around the average among the 28 NFL teams. Player salaries had continued to grow since the demise of the USFL, but at a slower pace.

OTHER DEVELOPMENTS

In the summer of 1983, the Supreme Court ruled that the NCAA's control of the negotiation of TV rights for college football was anticompetitive, thereby negating the previously negotiated contracts with ABC and CBS and opening up a free-for-all among various groups of schools, networks, and syndicators to establish new agreements. Ratings for college football were down in 1984.

In 1983, NBC and ABC reportedly paid $1.1 billion for a six-year contract with Major League Baseball. This would provide revenue of $7.7 million per team per year. According to Robert Mullholland, president of NBC, "The price we paid was to keep baseball, the crown jewel of sports, on free TV. The trend to cable is clear. It began with regional sports, but as cable gets more money, no one knows where the migration will stop." In 1984, ABC bought an 80% interest in ESPN for $167 million. CBS also agreed to buy a $57 million interest in four regional pay TV sports channels.

In 1986, the Boston Celtics announced the sale of 29% of their common stock to the public. The initial offering sold out, and the Los Angeles Lakers were reported to be considering a similar move.

APPENDIX: AMERICAN FOOTBALL

American football is an extremely physical, sometimes violent contact sport played between two teams of 11 players each. The sport traces its evolution to Harvard College in 1871, when the rules of rugby and soccer were altered to create the forerunner of today's game.

In 1983 the game is played on a field of grass or artificial turf that is 100 yards long from goal line to goal line and 53 ⅓ yards wide between side lines. Extending beyond the goal lines at each end is another area 10 yards deep and the same width called the end zone. Outside of the field is considered out of bounds. In the middle of each end zone line are goal posts, 24 feet apart, 20 feet high, with an attached crossbar 10 feet off the ground.

The game is played with a ball, a leather sphere. Fighting for possession and position of the ball and using it to score more points than the opposing team is the object of the game. Playing time is divided into four 15-minute periods or quarters with an intermission at the half mark. While game time is 60 minutes, actual playing time is about two to three hours because the clock stops when the ball goes out of bounds and at other times during the game.

Before each play begins, 11 players on each team line up on opposite sides of an imaginary line running from the front of the ball to each side line parallel to the goal line. Typically the offensive team has a center player who hands (snaps) the ball between his legs to another player, the quarterback, who will then either run with it, hand it to another player (one of 2 or 3 running backs), or throw (pass) it to one of 2 or 3 receivers. The other offensive players, 2 guards and 2 tackles, line up on opposite sides of the center and block the defensive players in their attempts to down the player with the ball.

On the defensive side, there are usually 4 or 5 players directly on the line, 2 or 3 one yard behind the line, and

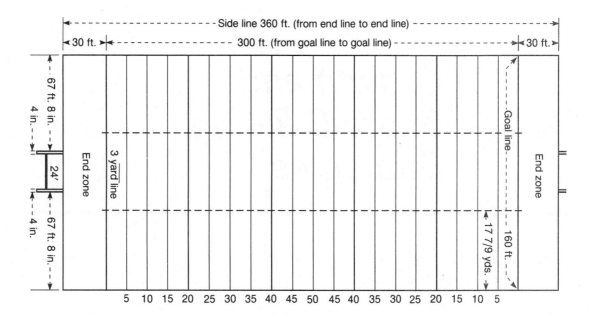

Side line 360 ft. (from end line to end line)

30 ft. — 300 ft. (from goal line to goal line) — 30 ft.

67 ft. 8 in. — 4 in. — 24' — 4 in. — 67 ft. 8 in.

End zone   3 yard line   Goal line   End zone

17 7/9 yds. — 160 ft.

5 10 15 20 25 30 35 40 45 50 45 40 35 30 25 20 15 10 5

4 players farther back (5 to 10 yards) who guard against passes and act as the last lines of defense if a ball carrier escapes the other players near the line. As one can imagine, the strategies employed by coaches and players on both offense and defense can be quite complex, leading some people to compare the playing, planning, training, and discipline of American football to intricate warfare.

To start a game, one team (determined by a coin flip) kicks to the other from its half of the field. After intermission the team that lost the coin flip at the start of the game now has the option of kicking or receiving. The other team catches the ball and tries to advance it across its opponent's goal line. If the offensive team can make at least 10 cumulative yards during the four downs, then it earns a new series of downs each time it makes 10 yards, whether in one play or four. If it fails on a fourth down try, then the other team gets the ball. The offense has the option to kick (punt) the ball away to its opponent's end of the field at any time, and will usually do so if it fails to make a first down (10 yards) before the fourth or last down. By punting, the offense relinquishes possession, but at a greater distance from the goal. Possession of the ball also changes if a defensive player recovers a dropped (fumbled) ball, takes it away, or intercepts it in the air. Otherwise the offensive team retains possession as long as it advances the ball or until it scores. After a scoring series the ball changes hands with a kick and the sequence begins again.

SCORING

If a team crosses its opponent's goal line with the ball, it scores 6 points, a touchdown, and earns the chance to score another point (or 2 in college and school football) by kicking the ball between the goal posts above the crossbar from two or three yards from the goal line.

The offense can also attempt, at any time and from any place on the field, a placement kick. If good, this is a field goal worth 3 points. If the kick fails, then the ball changes hands from the point of the ball before the kick. Typically, a team will not attempt a field goal unless it has a good kicker, is within his range (40–50 yards or less from the goal post), and does not think it can score a touchdown.

If the defensive team tackles the offense behind its own goal with the ball, provided that the offensive player entered the end zone on his own impetus, the defense scores 2 points and gets the ball back after the other team kicks from its own 20-yard line.

REFEREE

The rules and operation of the game are enforced by officials or referees (four to six people) who put the ball in play after each down, keep track of the official game time, and levy penalties (loss of yardage, repeat plays, etc.) for infractions of the rules.

C

Growth and Share-Building Strategies

---

7. *Burger King's Battle for the Burgers*

In 1985, J. Jeffrey Campbell, Burger King Corporation's Chief Executive Officer since 1983, was still trying to put together a winning formula. With four different CEOs since 1977, it was not surprising that Burger King had made a number of strategic changes in recent years. More changes were probably necessary as Burger King prepared itself for the rest of the 1980s and beyond. How should it position itself in the fast-food industry? What could it do to dethrone McDonald's, the number one firm in the industry? How could Burger King convince the public that its hamburgers were really superior to McDonald's? What could be done to hold off the challenge from Wendy's, Hardee's, and a number of other chains that were growing in size and competitive power? These and other questions came to mind as Burger King's Campbell tried to develop a winning strategy and bring stability to Burger King.

HISTORY

Burger King Corporation started when David R. Edgerton obtained the Miami-area rights to a fast-food concept called Insta/Burger King. He opened the first restaurant in March 1954. Three months later, James W. McLamore joined the venture, and the pair built three more Insta/Burger Kings. Hamburgers were sold for just 19 cents and french fries for 10 cents. Edgerton invented a chain broiler during 1956 that moved the hamburgers along a chain conveyor over the broiler until they were cooked. The restaurant name was changed to just Burger King, and they no longer used the broilers sold to them, but rather their own chain broilers.

In 1957, McLamore invented the Whopper and claimed it was the first fast-food jumbo hamburger. Although Burger King had expanded to just five restau-

rants by 1959, Edgerton and McLamore still envisioned someday becoming a chain of restaurants located throughout the United States. At that time, the fast-food industry was still very fragmented, and no national or significant regional chains existed. In 1961, Burger King made its first move outside of Florida when it opened a franchise in McLamore's hometown of Wilmington, Delaware.

Burger King's initial franchise agreements were relatively inexpensive and contained few restrictions. The franchisee paid only $25,000 for an exclusive franchise to a specified region, where he had a Burger King monopoly. The franchisee could decide how many Burger King restaurants, if any, could be opened and where to locate them. He could even decide to sell off part of his region to other people. Such an unencumbered franchise agreement attracted many franchisees, particularly as they paid only a modest 1 percent of sales to Burger King.

The year 1967 was a historic one for Burger King, which had already grown to 274 restaurants. In 1967 McLamore and Edgerton sold their chain to Pillsbury for $18,000,000. The two founders sold out to Pillsbury to obtain the financial resources Burger King needed to expand further and to increase its market share. McLamore agreed to continue on as Burger King's CEO.

Pillsbury bought Burger King primarily because of the high growth potential for the fast-food industry. As Paul S. Gerot, then President of Pillsbury, noted (*The Wall Street Journal*, 1967):

> We view Burger King as an opportunity to participate in the rising trend toward more away from home meals. Burger King has demonstrated the ability of a franchise operation to grow in the most rapidly expanding segment of the food business, where quality, convenience, and economy are important.

In 1970, Burger King had over 700 franchised and company-owned restaurants. In addition, it was opening new restaurants at the rate of 10 per month. To handle this rapid expansion, its marketing organization was

This case was written by Larry D. Alexander, Associate Professor of Strategic Management, and Thomas W. Ripp, MBA student in Management Science, both of the R. B. Pamplin College of Business, Virginia Polytechnic Institute and State University, Blacksburg, VA 24061. Copyright © 1985 by Larry D. Alexander and Thomas W. Ripp.

restructured. A new position of director of advertising and merchandising was created. Three advertising and merchandising coordinators, who reported to the director, handled advertising and sales promotional activities for seven newly established districts, each headed up by a district manager. Finally, a new position of advertising and merchandising planner was created to handle new products.

One of Burger King's franchisees, Chart House Inc., had been increasing its size and power over the years. Unlike many other franchisees, it owned the land and buildings itself for each restaurant. Chart House had grown so big, under Burger King's franchise agreement, that it began competing with Pillsbury for territorial expansion. For example, in 1970, Pillsbury wanted to buy out five franchisees who held 99-year rights to a territory that included Chicago. Chart House, however, beat them to it and by 1971 owned 100 Burger King restaurants. Later, in 1972, Chart House offered $100,000,000 to purchase Burger King, but Pillsbury turned it down. Chart House still continued to acquire smaller franchises. When it bought 9 restaurants in Boston and 13 in Houston, Pillsbury sued both Chart House and the Boston franchisee for disregarding Pillsbury's right of first refusal. Later, Pillsbury and Chart House reached a compromise whereby Chart House gave up its Boston franchise in exchange for keeping its Houston restaurants.

Pillsbury subsequently took action to make Burger King restaurants more profitable. In 1974, it required all new restaurants to be equipped with multiple order-taking lines and requested franchisees to shift to multiple lines in their existing restaurants. Chart House refused to change to multiple lines and claimed that the additional cash registers would cost more than the increased sales they would generate. Many smaller franchisees followed Chart House's lead by refusing to switch to multiple lines until sales increased enough to make the change profitable.

In 1977, Burger King began to remake its franchise system based on McDonald's model. New franchisees had to agree not to own any other fast-food business and had to live within an hour's drive of all their Burger King restaurants. This greatly reduced the potential size and power of future franchisees. An exception to this rule was made for Chart House. It was allowed to continue to build as many restaurants as it liked in its Illinois territory, but it had to agree not to expand elsewhere without Pillsbury's approval.

THE COMPANY'S CURRENT OPERATION

Burger King was an operating unit within Pillsbury's Restaurants Group. The other operating unit within this group was the S & A Restaurant Corporation, which was comprised of Steak and Ale, Bennigan's restaurants, and JJ. Muggs. Burger King had such a high priority, however, that its own CEOs reported directly to William H. Spoor, Pillsbury's CEO, rather than to a group vice president. Pillsbury had four other major groups: Agri-Products, Dry Grocery Products, Frozen and Refrigerated Products, and International.

Marketing/Sales

Burger King's name itself appropriately reflected the wide variety of hamburgers that were included in its menu. Its various hamburgers included a plain hamburger, cheeseburger, double hamburger, double cheeseburger, bacon double cheeseburger, the Whopper, the Whopper with cheese, Whopper Jr., and Whopper Jr. with cheese. Amazingly, more than 600,000,000 Whoppers were sold annually. Burger King's menu did not stop there, as Table 1 clearly shows. It also included various specialty sandwiches, soft drinks, french fries, and onion rings. A salad bar was added in 1983 following Wendy's tremendous success with this menu addition.

In 1979, Burger King restaurants started opening early for breakfast. By 1983, the breakfast menu included eggs, bacon, omelets, and pancakes. Its Croissan'wich, which was added later that same year, was a crescent-shaped flaky roll with eggs, cheese, and bacon, sausage, or ham inside. A "morning-topping" station was also added that same year.

Burger King relied heavily on a number of advertising campaigns in recent years, as shown in Table 2. One of its famous early campaigns was "Have It Your Way." The catchy words to the tune in this television advertisement stated:

Hold the pickles, hold the lettuce, special orders don't upset us. All we ask is that you let us serve it your way.

In early 1982, Burger King launched a new campaign with the slogan "Aren't You Hungry?" which again used a song to make its point. This theme was introduced because Burger King's CEO, Norman Brinker, wanted improved ads with more imagination. Brinker's new philosophy brought about Burger King's various "Battle of the Burgers" advertisements. In September 1982, Burger King launched an ad campaign that for the first time directly compared its hamburgers to McDonald's and Wendy's hamburgers. The attacking ads claimed that the Whopper won nationwide taste tests over McDonald's and Wendy's hamburgers. Burger King also claimed that its hamburgers were bigger and prepared better than its competitors' hamburgers.

Wendy's and McDonald's each filed suit against Burger King. When Burger King agreed to phase out its ads, Wendy's and McDonald's dropped their lawsuits. Still, the ads paid off for Burger King. Its fourth-quarter

---

TABLE 1   Burger King's Menu Items

Breakfast items only:
  Croissan'wich (bacon, egg and cheese; ham, egg, and cheese; or sausage, egg and cheese)
  French toast
  Scrambled egg platter with bacon or sausage
  Hash browns
  Danish pastry (cinnamon, apple, or raspberry)
  Orange juice

Hamburgers for lunch, dinner, or snack:
  Hamburger
  Cheeseburger
  Double hamburger
  Double cheeseburger
  Bacon double cheeseburger
  Bacon double cheeseburger deluxe
  Whopper junior
  Whopper junior with cheese
  Whopper
  Whopper with cheese

Specialty sandwiches and salads:
  Chicken
  Whaler
  Ham & cheese
  Salad bar

Side orders:
  French fries (small or large order)
  Onion rings

Beverage (served anytime, except for shakes):
  Soft drinks (Pepsi, Diet Pepsi, Mountain Dew, Dr Pepper, in small, medium, or large)
  Shakes
  Iced tea (small or large)
  Coffee (small or large)
  Milk

Desserts:
  Pies (apple, cherry, and pecan)

1982 sales increased by 10.8 percent, up 3.8 percent from a 7 percent sales growth rate before the ad campaign started. This was the first time that Burger King had achieved a double-digit growth rate, which was almost twice McDonald's 5.8 percent increase during 1982.

The 1982 settlement between Burger King, McDonald's, and Wendy's, according to Pillsbury's vice chairman, Winston Wallin, did not prohibit Burger King from launching future comparative advertisements. Burger King later undertook another round of comparative ads in 1983. This time, Burger King focused on its flame-broiled hamburgers versus its competitors' fried hamburgers. The ads stated that Burger King had won another taste test that found hamburger eaters preferred flame-broiled to fried hamburgers. Consumer comments on flame broiling being better were also included in the ads to drive the point home. This time, the ads mentioned only its arch rival McDonald's. Unlike the previous ads, these did not claim that Burger King served bigger hamburgers than its competitors.

Burger King has tried to link all of its ads to its ongoing "Aren't You Hungry?" theme since 1982.

During the summer of 1983, Burger King's ads concentrated on its new salad bar and emphasized that many of its drive-thru order windows were open until 4 A.M. That summer's campaign seemed aimed at countering Wendy's restaurants, which all had salad bars and drive-thru windows.

In the fall of 1983, Burger King's commercials reverted back to attacking McDonald's. A supposedly real-life family coincidentally named the MacDonald's talked about why they switched to Burger King. The entire family, plus their dog, masked their identities by wearing false glasses, noses, and mustaches. Burger King hoped this ad campaign would match the success of its earlier "Battle of the Burgers" theme.

Burger King took its "Battle of the Burgers" to Europe in the fall of 1984. The campaign first began in West Germany, where Burger King had 22 restaurants compared to McDonald's 200. The idea behind this campaign was to be as aggressive as possible without violating comparative advertising restrictions. West Germany's regulations state that ads (1) cannot be dishonest or misleading, (2) cannot degrade another product, and (3) must serve a consumer need. Burger King first used

---

TABLE 2 Some of Burger King's Major Advertising Campaigns

Advertising theme	Year(s)
"Have It Your Way" emphasized the fact that Burger King was willing to make special orders.	Late 1973
"Magical Burger King" aimed advertising at the kids; a Ronald McDonald-type costumed man magically made french fries and other Burger King products appear before a group of children.	Late 1978
"Aren't You Hungry?" moved Burger King away from its lifestyle themes to more aggressive advertising.	Early 1982
"Battle of the Burgers" launched the first round of ads that compared Burger King directly to McDonald's and Wendy's; later, Burger King agreed to stop ads and McDonald's dropped its lawsuit.	Late 1982
"Battle of the Burgers" launched another round of comparative advertising focusing on flame broiling versus frying, and which only mentioned competitor McDonald's.	1983
"Aren't You Hungry?" theme was returned to as its major theme, but Burger King also continued to compare flame broiling to frying.	Early 1984
"Battle of the Burgers" was used again to compare Burger King's hamburgers against both McDonald's and Wendy's.	Mid-1984
"Battle of the Burgers" was taken overseas by Burger King to Europe to try and educate Europeans about the difference between flame broiling and frying.	Late 1984
"Eight Simple Words that Can Change Your Life" showed hamburger eaters tasting their first flame-broiled hamburger and then stating, "I'll never eat another fried quarter pounder again."	Late 1984

outdoor billboards and newspaper ads to make German customers aware of the difference between flame broiling and frying. Later, television and radio commercials were used that featured female models eating a Whopper with the captions "All like it hot" or "Love at first bite." Burger King conducted similar campaigns later in the 10 other European countries where it operated.

In late 1984, Burger King launched another domestic advertising campaign that attacked fried hamburgers. Burger King's new ad said that it would like to introduce "Eight Simple Words that Can Change Your Life." In the ad, hamburger eaters tasted a flame-broiled Burger King hamburger for the first time and then uttered the eight key words, "I'll never eat another fried quarter pounder again."

Burger King used television as its chief advertising medium. It spent nearly $40,000,000 on its spring 1984 television ad campaign alone. This used up about 40 percent of its annual ad budget. Unfortunately, McDonald's outspent Burger King by about three to one on network advertising and had an annual ad budget of nearly $400,000,000. Because Burger King's advertising budget was much smaller, it felt that its television ads needed to be deliberately combative.

Burger King had opened restaurants in weak locations in recent years. As a result, Burger King's top management stated it would start concentrating on increasing its penetration in important metropolitan areas where it was already located. For example, in early 1984, Burger King bought 11 Arby's in Kansas City and St. Louis and indicated it planned to add more restaurants there as well as in other growth areas.

Burger King had also established a long-term objective of placing restaurants in new and unique locations. One such nontraditional location was military bases, which Burger King first entered when it won a bid to open a franchise at the Pearl Harbor naval base in 1982. That new Burger King restaurant was built by the Navy and leased to the franchisee, who also ran 11 other Burger Kings on the Hawaiian islands. Burger King later opened restaurants at a Navy base in Norfolk, Virginia, and a Coast Guard station at Governor's Island, New York. In May 1984, Burger King announced it had beat out McDonald's in competitive bidding to open fast-food restaurants at selected U.S. Army and Air Force bases in the United States, Germany, Korea, and selected Pacific islands. Under the terms of the agreement, Burger King could open as many as 185 military restaurants by 1989. All of the restaurants on U.S.

military bases would be operated by the Army and Air Force Exchange Service. Still, Burger King expected to earn more than $13,000,000 a year from the 6 percent royalties collected from the restaurants.

Later in 1984, Burger King linked itself with Woolworth's, a large national retailer. Under the agreement, Burger King would convert at least 50 in-store food-service units into Burger King restaurants over the next five years. Woolworth's would operate the restaurants itself, but with employees trained by Burger King. Some of the restaurants would serve a mix of Woolworth's old menu items and Burger King's fast-food items. The Burger King in-store restaurants could be entered from inside the Woolworth's stores and also by a separate street entrance. This would let the restaurants open earlier and close later than Woolworth's retail stores.

In 1983, Burger King switched from Coke to Pepsi soft drinks in its U.S. restaurants. Pepsi had been trying to get Burger King to serve its other soft drinks ever since Burger King added Diet Pepsi in 1979 and Mountain Dew in 1980 to its otherwise Coca-Cola soft-drink line. Burger King's switch to Pepsi made it Pepsi's number one fast-food account. This change was made in hopes that it would result in better service than being Coca-Cola's number two fast-food account behind McDonald's. Management felt that by bringing together its "Battle of the Burgers" ads with Pepsi's similar "Pepsi Challenge," they might help convince consumers to switch to their products. Burger King's top management also hoped that being Pepsi's number one account might give it first crack at any licensing rights for Pepsi products in the future. Despite Burger King's switch to Pepsi in the United States, it stayed with Coca-Cola products overseas because of their better customer recognition and more efficient foreign distribution.

Two Burger King franchises began experimenting with local delivery. In early 1984, a Burger King franchisee named Consumer Food Service announced that it would offer free delivery to the immediate area. Because all of its restaurants were located in downtown Manhattan, the cost of free delivery was minimized. Uniformed employees made the deliveries using hot-box equipment to keep the orders warm. Later that year, another Burger King franchisee in Columbus, Ohio, started offering local delivery. A five dollar minimum order was required for this service but only a five-cent delivery fee was added on. Deliveries were to any home, business, or other location within a three-mile radius of the restaurant. Top management at Burger King was closely watching both of these delivery attempts to evaluate their potential use at other Burger King restaurants.

Operations

Burger King operated 3,827 fast-food restaurants in all 50 states and 25 foreign countries by 1984. Only 301 of its restaurants, however, were located in foreign countries. Some 109 restaurants were in Canada, 49 in Puerto Rico, 37 in Australia, 22 in West Germany, 18 in Spain, 9 in England, 8 in Venezuela, and fewer restaurants in all the other foreign countries. Burger King opened 356 new restaurants in fiscal year 1984 and a similar number were scheduled to open the next year. Approximately 86 percent of all its restaurants worldwide were owned by independent franchise holders. These franchise holders still were required to follow Burger King's policies and procedures in running their restaurants.

The typical Burger King restaurant had a seating capacity for 86 customers and parking for 40 cars. A floor plan of one typical Burger King restaurant is shown in Figure 1. In recent years, Burger King had also opened smaller restaurants with a 60-seat capacity and larger ones with a 100-seat capacity.

All Burger King restaurants featured eat-in as well as carry-out service. In addition, 95% of its free-standing restaurants had a drive-thru service for customers who did not want to leave their cars. Some Burger King restaurants had even added an outdoor playground similar to what McDonald's had placed outside some of its restaurants.

Burger King painstakingly analyzed what effect new product introductions would have on operations in its restaurants. For example, it studied various data for more than two years before deciding to switch from Coke to Pepsi. Burger King even sent employees on undercover missions to Jack-in-the-Box restaurants to clock how much time was wasted on informing customers who asked for Coke that the chain only served Pepsi. Burger King even used a computer to predict how much labor a new product would require, what effect it would have on sales for other items, and how much total profits it would generate. Finally, Burger King considered the logistics of national distribution, supplier availability, and price stability for the new ingredients.

Burger King made a number of other changes to handle more customers in less time. It installed comput-erized french fry machines that sounded a warning when the french fries were done. Television terminals, linked to the cash register, were placed in the kitchen. This let the cooks read incoming orders on a screen, rather than relying on verbal orders that were sometimes misunderstood. Burger King also installed soft-drink dispensers that only required the push of a button to dispense the desired amount of drink. All of these improvements were first simulated on a computer, then tested at Burger King's research and development restaurants in the Miami area.

Top management encouraged individual restaurant managers to make productivity suggestions. If their suggestions proved useful, they were given a cash award. Management used this approach to tap the ideas of the restaurant managers who were right on the firing line.

Burger King franchisee John Diab developed the Whopper Express to meet the challenge of doing business in high-cost urban areas. Consumer Food Service, which Diab was a partner in, opened five Whopper Expresses in Manhattan in early 1984 and had two under construction in Philadelphia. The Whopper Express served a scaled-down menu in a smaller restaurant. For example, only one size of drink and fries were served. Although breakfast was still served at these restaurants, all specialty sandwiches and the small hamburger were eliminated. Consumer Food Service planned to open up to 10 Whopper Expresses per year through 1989.

The Whopper Express restaurant generated about twice the hourly sales of the larger, traditional Burger King restaurants. Some 900 customers per hour were served, which generated sales of up to $3,000 per hour. The Whopper Express had two complete service areas, each with its own broiler. The average Whopper Express was only 1,300 square feet. Its kitchen took up only 200 square feet of that space, versus 500 square feet for a traditional Burger King kitchen. Burger King was able to reduce the kitchen size by eliminating unnecessary equipment and scaling down most of the remaining equipment. Although a Whopper Express restaurant employed the same number of people, most of them worked just during the lunch hours. Whopper Expresses did not have tables and chairs for customers; instead, they had eating bars where the customers stood. As a result, most customers came for take-out food.

Burger King also had increased the efficiency of site development for its restaurants. Burger King's computers contained a software program to make site selections that included key decision-making criteria. This cut down the average site-approval time from two weeks to one day. Burger King also added a construction specialist in each of its 10 regional offices. These specialists knew the various building codes in their regions and were able to cut the average time spent on the design of each restaurant from six to two weeks. Regional staff people were also taught how to negotiate real estate deals to save both time and money.

When Jeffrey Campbell took over as Burger King's CEO in 1983, he launched ''Operation Shapeup.'' It was initiated to improve the efficiency of its restaurant employees up through all levels of management. A crash training program for restaurant managers and their employees was started to address the issue of uneven franchise performance. Campbell also started tackling the tough task of reining in the franchisees and convincing them that they had to follow policy and procedures developed by corporate headquarters.

Campbell tried to emphasize better communications throughout Burger King. He met with corporate employees in Miami. He held meetings with the regional staffs and then gave them 30 days to come up with three-year plans for their regions. He also relocated some corporate staff out into the field to be closer to the divisions and

---

FIGURE 1   Typical Floor Plan of a Burger King Restaurant.

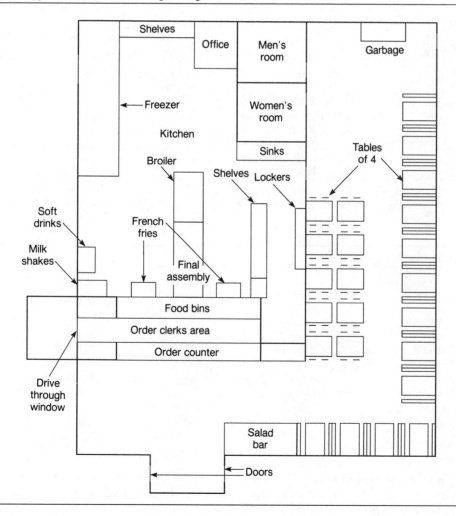

districts they served. He moved two regional managers out of Miami and placed more authority with the division managers.

Campbell also tried to get more media coverage for Burger King. He was personally interviewed by the *Washington Post, Chicago Tribune,* and *Business Week.* One reason for this effort to get more public attention was to boost the morale of Burger King employees and franchise holders.

Burger King had established DISTRON to serve its domestic restaurants. This independently operated supply and distribution division handled food, paper products, and other supplies utilized by its restaurants. DISTRON's operations in the United States were run through three decentralized divisions, overseeing 11 regions.

Finance

Burger King had gross sales of $3,430,000,000 for fiscal year 1984, which ended May 31, 1984. That amounted to over one and a half billion hamburgers for the year. Sales averaged $944,000 per restaurant, which was a 13 percent increase over the previous year. Company-operated restaurants had significantly higher yearly sales at $1,040,000, whereas domestic franchises averaged $928,000. Burger King's goal for 1985 was to get the

average domestic restaurant's sales near $1,000,000, with a 17.4 percent operating profit per restaurant.

Pillsbury's consolidated statement of earnings for fiscal years 1982–1984 are shown in Table 3. The consolidated sales for Pillsbury for 1984 amounted to $4,172,300,000. Net earnings after taxes were $169,800,000, which was a substantial increase over the previous two years. The consolidated balance sheets for Pillsbury for fiscal years 1983 and 1984 are shown in Table 4. It must be emphasized that Pillsbury does not report detailed financial reports for individual strategic business units such as Burger King. However, Pillsbury does provide a financial summary by industry segment, as shown in Table 5.

Innovation

Burger King has introduced a number of innovations to the fast-food industry. An early innovation by Burger King was the continuous chain broiler, which enabled Burger King to broil its burgers efficiently and evenly and gave fast-food customers an alternative to the typical fried hamburger.

Burger King also introduced several firsts in its restaurants' format. It was the first fast-food chain to offer inside sit-down eating for what had previously been all take-out food. In addition, the company also pioneered drive-thru window service.

TABLE 3   Pillsbury's Income Statement for Fiscal Years Ended May 31, 1982–1984*

	1984	*1983*	*1982*
Net sales	$4,172.3	$3,685.9	$3,385.1
Costs and expenses			
Costs of sales	2,952.5	2,589.5	2,389.7
Selling, general, and administrative expenses	871.9	826.8	728.1
Interest expense (net)	44.2	39.4	39.3
Subtotal	3,868.6	3,455.7	3,157.1
Earnings before taxes on income	303.7	230.2	228.0
Taxes on income	133.9	91.3	91.7
Net earnings	169.8	138.9	136.3
Average number of shares outstanding	43.5	43.5	43.3
Net earnings per share	3.91	3.20	3.14

*All figures in millions except per share amounts.

Source: *Pillsbury Annual Report 1984,* p. 35.

TABLE 4 Pillsbury's Balance Sheet for Fiscal Years Ended May 31, 1983 and 1984*

	1984	1983
Assets		
Current assets:		
Cash and equivalents..	$142.5	$129.6
Receivables, less allowance for doubtful accounts of $11.5 million and $12.9		
million, respectively...	355.8	350.6
Inventories:		
Grain...	75.5	52.9
Finished products..	214.1	204.1
Raw materials, containers, and supplies	150.6	133.7
Subtotal...	440.2	390.7
Advances on purchases..	107.7	128.4
Prepaid expenses	25.6	22.3
Total current assets	1,071.8	1,021.6
Property, plant, and equipment:		
Land and improvements..	199.2	179.2
Buildings and improvements..	885.1	788.2
Machinery and equipment	692.5	600.3
Subtotal...	1,776.8	1,567.8
Less accumulated depreciation..	583.8	514.6
Total...	1,193.0	1,053.2
Net investment in direct financing leases...........................	184.0	178.7
Intangibles	83.2	21.6
Investments and other assets	76.3	91.5
Total assets..	2,608.3	2,366.6
Liabilities and Stockholders' Equity		
Current liabilities:		
Notes payable	17.3	10.5
Current portion of long-term debt....................................	94.3	32.8
Trade accounts payable	369.2	279.6
Advances on sales	136.0	136.7
Employee compensation..	83.8	72.4
Taxes on income...	16.5	20.8
Other liabilities...	169.3	152.1
Total current liabilities	886.4	704.9
Long-term debt, noncurrent portion	503.1	572.4
Deferred taxes on income...	149.3	108.5
Other deferrals...	23.3	24.4
Stockholders' equity:		
Preferred stock, without par value, authorized 500,000 shares, no shares issued	—	—
Common stock, without par value, authorized 80,000,000 shares, issued		
43,516,019 shares and 43,462,156 shares, respectively..........................	306.2	284.1
Common stock in treasury at cost, 322,785 shares and 180,318 shares,		
respectively...	(11.7)	(4.6)
Accumulated earnings retained and used in the business	792.4	704.9
Accumulated foreign currency translation	(40.7)	(28.0)
Total stockholders' equity	1,046.2	956.4
Total liabilities and stockholders' equity	2,608.3	2,366.6

*All figures in millions.

Source: *Pillsbury Annual Report 1984*, p. 36–37.

TABLE 5 Pillsbury's Financial Summary by Industry Segment for Fiscal Years Ended May 31, 1982–1984*

	1984	*1983*	*1982*
Net sales:			
Consumer foods	$1,793.9	$1,652.1	$1,635.7
Restaurants	1,768.7	1,494.6	1,279.3
Agri-Products	694.8	627.5	568.6
Less Agri-Products intersegment sales	(85.1)	(88.3)	(98.5)
Total	4,172.3	3,685.9	3,385.1
Operating profit:			
Consumer foods	146.8	139.4	134.8
Restaurants	187.4	135.3	116.3
Agri-Products	34.5	16.4	28.6
Total	368.7	291.1	279.7
General corporate expense, net	(20.8)	(21.5)	(12.4)
Interest expense, net	(44.2)	(39.4)	(39.3)
Earnings before taxes on income	303.7	230.2	228.0
Identifiable assets:			
Consumer foods	836.3	725.4	747.9
Restaurants	1,191.2	1,025.7	993.3
Agri-Products	498.2	486.1	536.6
Corporate	82.6	129.4	150.5
Total	2,608.3	2,366.6	2,428.3
Capital expenditures:			
Consumer foods	59.4	48.7	50.0
Restaurants	197.4	164.0	126.8
Agri-Products	13.8	20.9	15.8
Corporate	11.8	10.3	15.9
Total	282.4	243.9	208.5
Depreciation expense:			
Consumer foods	36.1	33.0	30.3
Restaurants	59.5	54.7	48.6
Agri-Products	14.2	13.6	11.5
Corporate	4.8	4.2	2.4
Total	114.6	105.5	92.8
Foreign operations included in the above categories are as follows:			
Net sales	355.5	360.1	357.9
Operating profit	16.2	18.0	22.8
Identifiable assets	241.8	212.8	241.8
Capital expenditures	20.4	16.3	22.6
Depreciation expense	9.7	10.3	8.8

*All figures in millions.
Note: Pillsbury is a diversified international food company operating in three major segments of the food industry. Net sales by segment include both sales to unaffiliated customers, as reported in the consolidated statements of earnings, and intersegment sales made on the same basis as sales to unaffiliated customers. Operating profit of reportable segments is net sales less operating expenses. In computing operating profit, none of the following items has been included: interest income and expense; general corporate income and expenses; equity in net earnings (losses) of unconsolidated affiliates; and income taxes.

Source: *Pillsbury Annual Report 1984*, p. 32.

Burger King also made various menu innovations. In 1982, it introduced the bacon double cheeseburger, which was the first new hamburger from a major chain in 10 years. Later, it introduced the bacon double cheeseburger deluxe, with toppings including bacon, lettuce, tomato, and mayonnaise. In the fall of 1983, Burger King introduced a morning topping station in test markets in Miami, Florida; Hartford, Connecticut; and Savannah, Georgia. Cheese, tomatoes, and salsa sauce were available for customers to add to their omelets. Similarly, hot apple fruit topping, whipped cream, and various syrups could be added to customers' pancakes. Orange juice, sliced fruit, individual boxes of cereal, and freshly ground coffee were also available at its morning topping station and breakfast bar. Also in the fall of 1983, Burger King tested its new Croissan'wich, which was later made available at all of its restaurants that served breakfast.

Several of Burger King's new products were made in response to innovations by competitors. For example, in the spring of 1983, Burger King began to test a new one-third pound hamburger. This was done to compete more effectively against the growing number of gourmet hamburger chains that specialized in large hamburgers with fancy toppings. Burger King's new hamburger, however, soon had to be put on hold because of equipment problems that caused uneven broiling during the tests. Also in 1983, Burger King introduced a salad bar in response to Wendy's salad bar, which had done very well.

New menu innovations at Burger King were the result of its extensive ongoing research and development program at Burger King's Miami headquarters. For example, Burger King was testing new toppings in 1984 for its hamburgers in Milwaukee, Detroit, Pittsburgh, and Houston that were first developed at its research and development center. The toppings offered for its double hamburger included pizza sauce with mozzarella cheese, taco sauce with jalapeno and cheese, and a mushroom and Swiss cheese topping. Other new breakfast, lunch, dinner, and dessert items were being tested. If successful, they would become a part of each restaurant's menu offerings in the future.

Human Resources

Burger King employed approximately 38,500 people worldwide. An additional 161,000 people were employed in franchised restaurants; however, they were not considered Burger King employees. Burger King's corporate headquarters staff in Miami, made up of 550 people, ran a variety of functional areas such as finance, marketing, operations, and personnel.

Burger King conducted many training programs on an ongoing basis. It operated Burger King University, a $2,000,000 training center near its Miami corporate headquarters. In addition, it ran 10 regional training centers located throughout the United States known as Whopper Colleges. These 11 facilities provided initial training and ongoing educational classes for Burger King restaurant franchisees and managers.

Burger King, along with other fast-food restaurants, had been having problems with its work force. Burger King's average restaurant had a staff of 35 workers. Unfortunately, the average Burger King employee lasted only a couple of months, resulting in a very high employee turnover ratio. In addition, the declining number of youths in the United States made it difficult to attract and retain employees willing to work at or near minimum wage. Furthermore, it was estimated that the 37,000,000 young workers in 1980 would dwindle to only 24,000,000 by 1990. Burger King had already taken efforts to retain its employees by paying them up to $4.50 a hour, $1.15 above the minimum wage in 1984.

Burger King also took actions to increase the productivity of its employees and their equipment. This was particularly important during peak meal times. Every movement of the employees was studied, and changes were made to eliminate needless motion. For example, productivity experts found that it took Burger King order takers 11 seconds just to answer customers whose cars had tripped the bell hose at the drive-thru window. When they relocated the bell hose back 10 feet, the order taker was ready to serve the customer by the time the customer had stopped his car to place an order. This and other small changes allowed the drive-thru window to handle an extra 30 cars per hour.

Burger King's franchisees had also tried various programs to improve worker productivity and service. In 1982, Greyhound Food Management, a franchisee of Burger King, sponsored a promotion called "Beat the Clock." The employees of its Burger King restaurants competed in a service-time race. Cash prices of $1,500, $1,000, and $500 were to be awarded to the top three Burger King restaurants. Any customer who was not served in three minutes or less was entitled to a free meal on his next visit to the same restaurant. The rules of the competition were changed when only 26 out of 62,151 customers were awarded a free meal because they waited more than three minutes. The next competition cut the serving time to two and a half minutes, two minutes the following week, and to one and a half minutes the week after that. Even then, 10 of the 28 restaurants still had not awarded any free meals. According to Greyhound Food Management, the employees and their customers were enthusiastic about this promotion.

Another franchisee, Dennis C. Erwin, had been promoting "The Pride of Burger King" in his seven restaurants since 1979. At the start of each day, he had the employees sign stickers for their individual stations. As orders were prepared during the day, an employee would attach a sticker to the food item that he prepared. One typical sticker read as follows (*Restaurant Business*, 1982):

> The Pride of Burger King. Hello from the drink person. I check everything daily before we serve you. It's my job to serve you a quality drink. Thank you.

The goal of Erwin's program was to restore employee pride in their work and to let Burger King's customers know of that pride. The customers reacted favorably to the program, and employee mistakes were reduced by more than 90%.

Burger King hired an outsider to fill a newly created position of vice president of human resources in 1984. This was done because Burger King had not done much to make its key managers and hourly employees remain at Burger King. Career ladders were developed for senior managers, who were also given pay incentives and chances for personal development that it was hoped would make them want to stay.

Management

Burger King was organized on a geographic basis. A handful of restaurants reported to a district manager who visited each restaurant at least once a month. District managers in turn reported to an area manager, who reported to a regional manager. Regional managers reported to a division manager in Miami, New York, or

Denver. Finally, these three division managers reported directly to the CEO of Burger King.

Burger King's big advances against McDonald's started after Donald N. Smith became its CEO in 1977. To combat its number one foe, Pillsbury Chairman Spoor had hired away Smith, the number three man at McDonald's, to "McDonaldize" Burger King right down to the french fries. Despite being only 36 years old at the time, many of his actions were just what Burger King needed.

One of Smith's first actions was to decentralize the management structure. He established four major operating units: Burger King U.S.A., Burger King Canada, Burger King International, and Distribution. Smith also quickly broadened Burger King's menu to include more than just hamburgers. Unfortunately, he left Burger King in mid-1980 to head up Pizza Hut.

Pillsbury then had Louis P. Neeb head up Burger King. Neeb, age 43, had been head of another Pillsbury unit, Steak & Ale. He introduced breakfast at Burger King restaurants and opened approximately 500 new restaurants. Unfortunately, he also left, in mid-1982.

Pillsbury again went inside to find Burger King's next CEO, Norman E. Brinker. Brinker, age 50, was moved from the presidency of Pillsbury's Restaurant Group. Within his first two weeks as CEO, Brinker made several top-management changes. After the management changes, Brinker's strategy was to go back to the basics. He remarked (*Fortune*, 1982):

> We're going back to emphasizing the hamburger, back to being the home of the Whopper.

Brinker was openly critical of his predecessor Neeb and felt he had not been aggressive enough for the fast-food industry. Unfortunately, in June of the next year, Brinker announced that he was leaving Burger King to become chairman of Chili's Inc., a gourmet burger firm.

J. Jeffrey Campbell, age 39, was appointed the new chairman and CEO of Burger King in June of 1983. Campbell had worked his way up through the management ranks of Burger King. When Brinker was still CEO, he had promoted Campbell to president of Burger King U.S.A. As CEO, Campbell's early strategy was to focus on hamburgers and emphasize quality control. For his longer term strategy, Campbell said (Erickson and Baldwin, 1983):

We're not out to simply make plans or have a good year. We're out to change the competitive environment of the fast-food industry and that's a three to five year job.

To achieve this objective, Campbell launched an effort to improve operations, media coverage, market development, and management.

Campbell also wanted to restore the confidence that employees had in top management. Burger King had been plagued by top management turnover since 1977. Surprisingly, Campbell was the first CEO promoted from within Burger King. By early 1984, 8 of the top 10 executives had been with Burger King for at least five years. Campbell hoped that he could provide stability among the senior management ranks that would help calm the franchisees.

THE FAST-FOOD INDUSTRY

The fast-food industry is actually a segment of the food-service industry. Sales for just the hamburger part of this segment were growing so rapidly that its $24,600,000,000 total sales in 1979 were expected to rise to $42,000,000,000 in 1985. This phenomenal increase was facilitated by an annual 10% growth in the amount that Americans spent on meals away from home.

The fast-food industry is composed of numerous national and regional chains located throughout the United States. In addition to these chains, numerous independent fast-food type restaurants can be found many places. Table 6 shows a list of the top 30 franchise restaurants systems in the United States, ranked according to total sales. Figure 2 shows the market share and sales of the top six fast-food chains. Each firm's market share is calculated as a percent of the total sales for the 30 leading restaurant chains rather than as a percent of total industry sales.

McDonald's

McDonald's is clearly number one in the fast-food industry. It was started in 1949 by Maurice and Richard McDonald in San Bernardino, California, selling 15 cent hamburgers. It had net sales of $8,600,000,000 for 1983. McDonald's 1983 sales from only its company-owned restaurants plus licensing fees from the franchised restaurants were $3,062,922,000. McDonald's had a staggering 7,778 restaurants, of which 68% were franchised. Some 6,251 of its restaurants were located in the United States, 442 were located in Canada, and the remaining 1,085 were located in 30 other countries.

McDonald's product offerings focused on hamburgers, including a simple hamburger, cheeseburger, double cheeseburger, Big Mac, and Quarter Pounder. These main-dish items were complemented with french fries, soft drinks, milk shakes, ice cream cones, sundaes, and Danish pastries.

McDonald's had a history of introducing new products over the years. Filet-O-Fish sandwiches were added in 1962. Later, Egg McMuffin was introduced when its restaurants started opening early for breakfast in 1973. McDonald Cookies were added the next year. More recently, Chicken McNuggets were offered in 1982.

The four Ps of marketing—product, price, promotion, and place—were clearly emphasized at McDonald's. Its product was a standardized, reasonably priced array of hamburgers, drinks, french fries, etc. Service was so that its customers only had to wait a minute or two to place and pick up their orders. Its prices had always been kept low in order to stimulate customer demand. Although the Quarter Pounder and Big Mac were priced over a dollar in late 1984, its plain hamburgers cost only about half as much. McDonald's promotion of its product was one of its greatest strengths. It spent nearly $400,000,000 on advertising in 1983 alone, relying heavily on national television using its Ronald McDonald costume character. McDonald's spent heavily on major television events. For example, it spent about $35,000,000 for ads during two weeks of the 1984 Summer Olympics in Los Angeles alone. Finally, its restaurants seemed to be located virtually everywhere, with thousands of restaurants located in all 50 states and numerous foreign countries, and 500 new restaurants being opened each year.

Its overall marketing strengths helped McDonald's achieve a 28.2% market share of the total sales for the top 30 food franchise systems, whereas second place Burger King had only a 9.2% market share (*Restaurant Business*, 1984). Not surprisingly, the four Ps at McDonald's created a large fifth P called profit. Its profits after taxes for 1983 were a whopping $342,640,000, for an 11.1% return on sales ratio.

In recent years, McDonald's has been trying to expand into new and different market segments. In 1976, McDonald's opened its first restaurant in a high school cafeteria. In 1984, McDonald's experimented with restaurants in office buildings, and it also won a 10-year contract with the Navy to open as many as 300 restaurants at Navy bases throughout the world.

Kentucky Fried Chicken

Although Kentucky Fried Chicken (KFC) sold no hamburgers, it was still ranked third in the fast-food industry. KFC, a division of R. J. Reynolds Industries, had total sales of $2,623,000,000 in 1983, which was a 10% increase over the previous year. There were 4,471

TABLE 6 Sales of the Top 30 Franchise Restaurant Systems

Franchise System	1983 Sales	Percentage Increase over 1982
1. McDonald's	$8,600,000,000	10%
2. Burger King*	2,810,000,000	19
3. Kentucky Fried Chicken	2,623,000,000	10
4. Wendy's	1,800,000,000	10
5. Hardee's*	1,718,000,000	54
6. Pizza Hut	1,671,000,000	19
7. Dairy Queen*	1,288,000,000	8
8. Big Boy	1,000,000,000	6
9. Taco Bell	693,000,000	20
10. Arby's	650,000,000	12
11. Church's*	613,900,000	22
12. Long John Silver's*	554,500,000	7
13. Ponderosa*	554,000,000	7
14. Jack in the Box*	546,700,000	13
15. Dunkin' Donuts*	475,800,000	9
16. Western Sizzlin'*	473,800,000	5
17. Baskin Robbins*	455,000,000	8
18. Howard Johnson's (loss)	435,100,000	(4)
19. Godfather's Pizza	400,000,000	28
20. Bonanza*	389,000,000	6
21. Domino's Pizza	365,700,000	58
22. Sizzler*	353,700,000	9
23. Roy Rogers	341,700,000	33
24. Perkins Cake & Steak	287,900,000	6
25. Sonic Drive Ins*	262,600,000	4
26. Popeyes Famous Fried Chicken*	240,000,000	39
27. Pizza Inn*	236,600,000	3
28. International House of Pancakes	226,000,000	8
29. Captain D's*	215,700,000	10
30. Chi-Chi's*	198,500,000	72

*Indicates figures are for the firm's 1983 fiscal year. All other figures are for calendar year 1983.

Source: *Restaurant Business*, 1984.

domestic KFC restaurants, of which 998 were company owned. Internationally, KFC had already placed approximately 1,500 restaurants in 47 foreign countries. Its largest overseas market was Japan, which had 413 KFC restaurants alone.

KFC's principal product was fried chicken, prepared in accordance with methods first developed by Colonel Harland Sanders. Customers could choose from regular or extra-crispy chicken, which could be bought in 2-, 3-, or 5-piece dinners and 9-, 15-, or 21-piece bucket sizes. Although most KFC restaurants had some tables for customers to eat their meals at, most customers took their chicken dinners home.

Wendy's

Wendy's, which ranked fourth among fast-food restaurants, tried to appeal to a more discriminating customer. Its more expensive hamburgers, salad bar, chili, and stuffed baked potatoes were aimed at "Wendy's kind of

FIGURE 2   Fast-food Chains' Market Share by Sales and Percent Using Total Sales Data from the Top 30 Chains in 1983 ($ in millions).

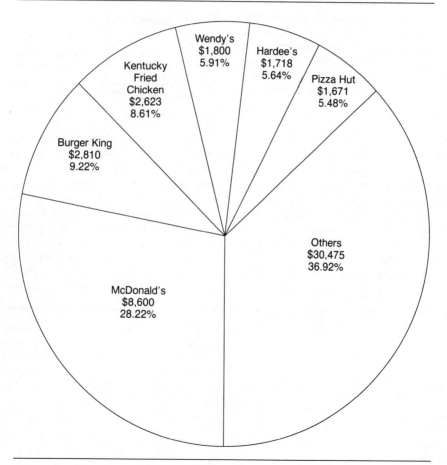

Source: *Restaurant Business*, 1984

people.'' Its customers had to pay more, but Wendy's felt its higher-quality products clearly justified somewhat higher prices.

Although considerably smaller than McDonald's, Wendy's had a net income after taxes of $55,220,000 on total sales of $1,800,000,000 for 1983. Its average restaurant volume was $754,000 per year; however, Wendy's hoped that it would top $1,000,000 by 1985. At a cost of approximately $75,000 per restaurant, Wendy's was installing glass-enclosed extensions to several hundred restaurants each year. In many respects, this made efficient use of earlier outdoor patios that were not used by very many customers.

In mid-1984, Wendy's launched its famous ''Where's the Beef'' commercials. These various commercials featured Clara, who could never find the beef in competitors' skimpy hamburgers. These humorous commercials were so popular that 1984 Democratic candidate Walter Mondale even asked ''Where's the beef'' of his opponent President Reagan and his campaign promises. Wendy's future commercials will undoubtedly emphasize the new upscale menu items it is continuing to develop.

Pizza Hut

In sixth place was Pizza Hut, a division of PepsiCo, Inc. Like its name suggests, its menu focused heavily on pizza, but it also had a salad bar. Like Kentucky Fried Chicken, however, Pizza Hut did not sell any hamburgers. It had some 1,900 company-owned restaurants and 2,090 franchises in 1983. For 1983, the total revenues for the overall parent corporation were $7,093,587,000

with a net income of $284,111,000. Pizza Hut sales for that same year were $1,671,000,000, which was a 19% increase over 1982.

Pizza Hut had become more competitive ever since Donald Smith was lured away from Burger King. Some industry analysts felt that Smith's prior experience at both McDonald's and Burger King might help to further strengthen Pizza Hut in coming years.

Pizza Hut's recent actions had substantially improved its position in the fast-food industry. It was trying to move away from being a fast-food chain to more of a family style restaurant. More private booths and wood decor were being used to give the restaurants a cozier atmosphere.

Other Competitors

In addition to these top national chains, Burger King also had to complete with a variety of other types of restaurants. The next largest segment was the steak and full menu segment. This included places such as Western Sizzlin, Ponderosa, and Bonanza. The third largest segment was the pizza segment. This segment was headed by Pizza Hut, Godfather's Pizza, and Domino's Pizza. In addition there was Long John Silver's, which catered to the fish segment. Some of the restaurants in these other segments were also fast-food restaurants. Finally, Burger King had to compete against restaurants such as Big Boy, Denny's, and Howard Johnson's, which straddled most of the different segments in family style restaurants. Table 7 shows a comparison of how Burger King's lunch and dinner menu compares with many of its major competitors.

TABLE 7   Lunch and Dinner Menu Comparison

	A	*B*	*C*	*D*	*E*	*F*	*G*	*H*
Main dish items:								
Hamburgers	X	X	X	X	X			
Chicken	X	X	X	X	X	X		X
Fish	X	X		X	X	X		
Pizza							X	
Turkey				X	X			
Ham and Cheese	X			X	X		X	
Roast beef				X	X			
Hot dog with chili				X				

TABLE 7 (concluded)

	A	B	C	D	E	F	G	H
Bacon, lettuce, and tomato			X					
Meatball							X	
Spaghetti							X	
Cavatini							X	
Ham, salami, and cheese							X	
Baked potato			X	X	X			
Scallops						X		
Shrimp						X		
Side orders:								
French fries	X	X	X	X	X	X		
Potato cakes					X			
Mashed potatoes								X
Onion rings	X							
Chili			X					
Cole slaw						X		X
Potato salad								X
Chicken livers								X
Gizzards								X
Baked beans								X
Hush puppies						X		
Corn on the cob						X		X
Clam chowder						X		
Salads:								
Garden salads	X		X	X		X	X	
Seafood salads				X		X		
Taco salads			X					
Desserts:								
Pies/turnovers	X	X	X	X	X	X		X
Cookies		X		X	X			
Sundae		X						
Cones/frosty		X	X					
Beverages:								
Soft drinks	X	X	X	X	X	X	X	X
Coffee	X	X	X	X	X	X	X	X
Milk shakes	X	X		X	X			
Iced tea	X	X	X	X		X	X	X
Hot tea		X	X			X		
Milk	X	X	X	X	X	X	X	X
Hot chocolate			X			X		
Orange juice	X	X		X	X			
Beer							X	X

Symbols: A = Burger King; B = McDonald's; C = Wendy's; D = Hardee's; E = Arby's; F = Long John Silver's; G = Pizza Hut; H = Kentucky Fried Chicken.

BURGER KING'S FUTURE BATTLE FOR THE BURGERS

One and a half years had passed since Jeffrey Campbell became CEO in mid-1983. A lot had been done in recent years to improve the firm's performance. Still, a lot more could be done. Shortly after becoming CEO, Campbell remarked (Kohn, 1984):

> Three to four years from now, I want a little more than half the restaurants of McDonald's, about half the market share, higher average sales, higher . . . [restaurant] operating profits, and as good if not better return on investment for the operator.

Burger King had been trying to tap new locations to continue growing in a saturated market. The Greyhound Food Management franchisee had even opened Burger King restaurants in some of its downtown bus terminals. In 1983, Burger King reached an agreement with Howard Johnson's to be its sole franchise at all of its turnpike service plazas. Clearly, Burger King's recent move onto military bases and in-store restaurants at Woolworth's retail stores were good moves. However, Burger King still needed to identify other nontraditional locations to counter the growing maturity of the fast-food industry.

Burger King had used new product offerings in recent years to increase its sales. Expanded menus had the potential to attract customers who were going elsewhere to get these offerings. New product introductions were also a key to maintaining market share and stealing customers from its competitors. Burger King had some success with new menu items such as the Croissan'-wich, the bacon double cheeseburger, and the salad bar. However, it also had been plagued by the failure of other new products in the past, such as the veal parmigiana specialty sandwich, pizza, and a one-third pound hamburger. Future new product items could be an asset to Burger King's sales growth if they were successful, but they would also be a costly drain on cash if a number of them failed.

Burger King's ad campaigns had been successful in stealing customers away from competitors in recent years. Its "Battle of the Burgers" theme was clearly appropriately named given the intense competition in the fast-food industry. As its flame broiling versus frying theme grew old and less effective, Burger King needed to develop new ad campaigns to draw customers away from its competitors. What form and theme they would use remained to be seen. Hopefully, future ads would help win more converts to Burger King while not turning off some customers who did not like the knocking-of-competitors nature of its ads. In addition, Burger King hopefully could find a way to counter a recent *Consumer Reports* survey (1984) that found more people preferred Burger King's hamburgers over McDonald's hamburgers, yet they were more likely to eat at McDonald's.

In another effort to maintain growth, Burger King had been considering new market concepts. Pillsbury had given Burger King the go ahead to shop for new alternative restaurant concepts. Burger King might possibly acquire one or more existing smaller restaurant chains that were not intensely focused on fast-food hamburgers. At the same time, totally new restaurant concepts had already been ruled out. Italian and other ethnic foods are distinct possibilities. Pillsbury's Totino's and Fox Deluxe lines of frozen pizza could represent a substantial resource for Burger King to draw upon if it decided to enter a Burger King owned pizza venture. A Mexican food chain was another possibility as Mexican food was enjoying the highest yearly increase in sales of any ethnic food.

Finally, Burger King needed to bring about more stability from its top management down to its hourly employees in its restaurants. Four different CEOs since 1977 had caused too many changes in Burger King's strategy. Similarly, the high turnover in its individual restaurants made any ongoing relationship between customers and Burger King employees almost impossible. Furthermore, new employees usually made more mistakes in handling customer orders and were less productive.

These and other strategic issues may need to be addressed as Burger King prepares for the rest of the 1980s. It was hoped that the decisions and actions made by Jeffrey Campbell would bring Burger King closer to challenging McDonald's and maybe even someday becoming the leader in the fast-food industry.

REFERENCES

Consumer Reports, "Fast foods," July 1984, p. 370.

Erickson, J. L., and Baldwin, M. F. "1983 Change maker: Burger King Corporation." *Restaurants and Institutions,* October 15, 1983.

Fortune, "Another Change at Burger King," June 14, 1982, p. 8.

Kohn, D. (1984). J. "Jeffrey Campbell, Burger King," *Restaurant Business,* April 10, p. 90.

Restaurant Business, "Restaurant Franchising in the Economy," March 20, 1984, p. 170.

Restaurant Business, "The Pride of Burger King." May 1, 1982, p. 62.

The Wall Street Journal, "Pillsbury Co. Says It Agreed 'in Principle' to Buy Burger King," January 20, 1967, p. 12.

8.   *The Limited, Inc.*

INTRODUCTION

Where are the hottest names in women's apparel today? Some would argue that they are not on Seventh Avenue, or in Paris, or in Milan. They are in Columbus, Ohio, where Leslie H. Wexner has built The Limited, Inc. into one of the nation's fastest-growing and most admired retailers. It offers apparel tailored to the tastes and lifestyles of fashion-conscious, contemporary women and provides fashion, quality, and value through multiple retail formats. The Limited, Inc., has positioned itself to penetrate the women's fashion apparel market through specialty stores and mail-order catalogs. Its portfolio in 1986 consisted of six retail divisions with nearly 2,400 stores and seven nationally distributed mail-order catalogs. In 1985 The Limited sold more than 200 million garments, three for every woman in the country between the ages of 15 and 55. Profits were $140 million on $2.4 billion in sales. The Limited may be the most misnomer company in America.

This case was prepared by Jeff Friant and Elsie Fletcher under the supervision of Professor Sexton Adams of North Texas State University and Professor Adelaide Griffin of Texas Woman's University as a basis for class discussion rather than to illustrate either effective or ineffective handling of an administrative situation.

BACKGROUND/HISTORY

Leslie Wexner left his parents' general apparel store in 1963, borrowed $10,000 from his aunt, and opened his first Limited Store in the Kingsdale Shopping Center near Columbus, Ohio. The store carried strictly sportswear for women in the 16- to 25-year-old range—hence the "Limited" name. Industry analysts reflected that this approach was distinctly ahead of its time considering that most women's apparel was marketed in department stores. In 1969, The Limited went public with a six-store chain.

In 1977, everything seemed to be going well for The Limited. Growth had been steadily remarkable; there were 188 stores with annual sales of $175 million and a respectable net income of $13.2 million. Suddenly in 1978, major problems seemed to be crawling out of the woodwork. The causes of these problems, however, had been brewing for some time.

In 1978, sales rose to a record $218 million; however, most of the gain was attributed to the opening of 70 new stores. Despite this record earnings net income actually fell to $5.9 million. Sean O'Leary, contributing editor for *Visual Merchandising & Store Design,* stated that this scenario was common when companies tried to grow too fast. The year 1978 was also marked by several major events for The Limited. The Limited moved into a new $20 million distribution warehouse/headquarters, a facility that was 10 times beyond the current needs of the company according to industry analysts, in the thick of a recession in one of the hardest hit areas of the country. A new computer system that would serve to computerize inventory and distribution was installed and inevitability was not working right. At the same time, management was devoting its attention to acquiring Mast Industries, Inc., an apparel supplier with worldwide manufacturing connections. This acquisition would give The Limited major supply side advantages over their competitors.

The Limited did survive these adversities of the late 70s. The way in which Wexner and his management responded to these problems played an integral part in the creation of The Limited legend. Mast Industries was purchased. This acquisition gave the Limited large worldwide advantages and options on the supply side. The distribution center, with its excess capacity, proved invaluable when The Limited began its series of acquisitions. Last, but not least, the computer was repro-

---

EXHIBIT 1   History of Growth

Retail Divisions	Date Started	Date Acquired	Number of Stores Fiscal Year-End					
			1982	1983	1984	1985	First Quarter 1986	Second Quarter 1986
Limited	1963		489	521	562	597	610	619
Limited Express	1980		30	70	133	218	233	244
Lane Bryant		1982	222	245	322	401	416	438
Victoria's Secret		1982	6	16	46	93	104	120
Sizes Unlimited (consolidated with Pic-A-Dilly)		1982	78	85	349	293	287	239
Roamans (merged into Sizes Unlimited)		1982						
Pic-A-Dilly (merged into Sizes Unlimited)		1984						
Lerner		1985				750	737	736
Henri Bendel		1985				1	1	1
Totals			825	937	1,412	2,353	2,388	2,397

Mail-Order Divisions	Date Acquired
Brylane	1982
Lane Bryant	
Roamans	
Lerner Woman	
Sue Brett	
Lerner Sport	
Tall Collection	
Victoria's Secret	1982

grammed. Company operations were tightened. Industry analysts noted that one significant event of this period was that Wexner backed off from the financial end of the company and allowed Vice Chairman Robert Morosky, a CPA, to fully assume responsibility.

In 1981, The Limited decided to try to recapture the 80s model of the young woman they had begun in the 60s. Limited Express was launched, specializing in popular-priced sportswear for the 15- to 25-year-olds. By the end of 1982, 30 stores were open nationwide.

The corporate name was changed to The Limited, Inc., in 1982 and the company was listed on the New York Stock Exchange. This was also the year of acquisitions—The Limited, Inc., acquired Lane Bryant, a $419 million volume, large-size apparel specialist; Brylane, the nation's largest catalog retailer of women's special size apparel and shoes; Victoria's Secret, a five-unit $5 million better lingerie chain plus catalog; Sizes Unlimited, which offers off-price, special size apparel for women; and Roamans, a $100 million chain of women's special size apparel store and mail-order operation that was merged into Sizes Unlimited. In the years to come, The Limited, Inc., would acquire three more women's apparel chains. In 1984, Pic-A-Dilly, which specialized in budget women's apparel was acquired and merged into Sizes Unlimited. The year 1985 brought the final two acquisitions—Lerner Stores, a $400 million chain that specialized in budget-priced women's apparel and Henri Bendel, the $2.4 million prestigious New York specialty store. These acquisi-

tions, financed largely by large debt issues, have given The Limited a niche in almost every segment of the women's clothing market. Exhibit 1 illustrates the growth and acquisition pattern of The Limited. Exhibit 2 illustrates the sales volumes for 1984 and 1985 of The Limited.

Art Carpenter of Goldman, Sachs & Co. stated, "It doesn't take a shrewd analyst to figure out that The Limited has specialized in specializing and that the sum total of the empire covers just about every segment of the women's apparel market—working contemporary women, trendy juniors, large sizes, fashion lingerie, and catalogs." In its 1984 Annual Report on American Industry, *Forbes* called The Limited the fastest-growing, most profitable specialty apparel retailer. Net sales have grown from $70,303,000 in 1975 to $2,387,110,000 in 1985 (Exhibit 3). Based on these simple facts, The Limited, Inc., could well be the world's largest specialty retailer of women's clothing.

THE STORE BASE

The Limited, Inc., had nearly 2,400 retail outlets throughout the United States. In 1985, The Limited, Inc., opened its flagship store on Manhattan's miracle mile amid designer boutiques like Yves Saint Laurent. Included in this complex were three stores: The Limited, Limited Express, and Victoria's Secret. The way Wex-

EXHIBIT 2   1985 Sales Rank ($000s)

Company	1984 Sales	1985 Sales	Percent Sales Change
Limited	$552,289	$637,825	+15.5
Lane Bryant	356,076	431,736	+21.2
Lerner Stores	—	521,988	—
Limited Express	46,963	69,406	+47.8
Victoria's Secret	30,814	51,677	+67.7
Sizes Unlimited	281,000	254,784	−9.0
Henri Bendel	—	8,500	—
Others	—	411,194	—

Source: *Apparel Merchandising,* June 1986.

EXHIBIT 3   The Limited's Growth ($000)

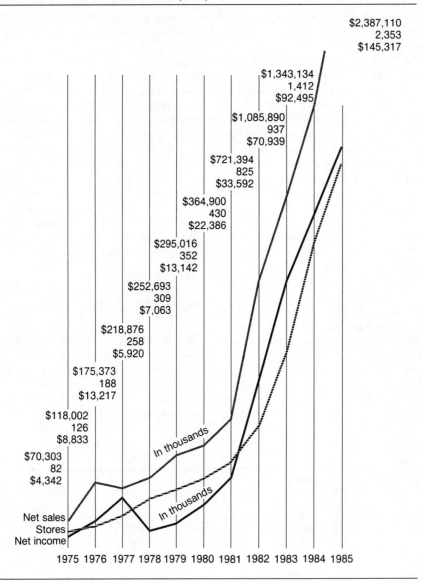

$2,387,110
2,353
$145,317

$1,343,134
1,412
$92,495

$1,085,890
937
$70,939

$721,394
825
$33,592

$364,900
430
$22,386

$295,016
352
$13,142

$252,693
309
$7,063

$218,876
258
$5,920

$175,373
188
$13,217

$118,002
126
$8,833

$70,303
82
$4,342

In thousands

In thousands

Net sales
Stores
Net income

1975 1976 1977 1978 1979 1980 1981 1982 1983 1984 1985

Source: The Limited, Inc., 1985 Annual Report.

EXHIBIT 4 The Store Base (number and type of stores)

Store	Type	Number
The Limited	Medium-priced women's sportswear	619
Limited Express	Popular-priced teen sportswear	244
Victoria's Secret	Lingerie	120
Lane Bryant	Women's large sizes	438
Sizes Unlimited	Large women's budget	239
Lerner	Women's budget sportswear	736
Henri Bendel	Upscale women's sportswear	1
Total Stores		2,397

Source: The Ohio Company: *Investment Research*, August 14, 1986.

ner saw it was "if you can make it everywhere, you can make it in New York." Exhibit 4 shows the store base in July of 1986.

Its distribution facility and corporate headquarters were in Columbus, Ohio. A secondary corporate headquarters was planned to open in New York City so that The Limited Inc.'s executives would be closer to the heart of the fashion industry.

INDUSTRY

The specialty apparel retail industry was one of the largest industries in the world. Over $60 billion were spent in 1985 for the purchase of specialty clothing in the United States. A wide variety of companies competed in the industry and were classified into a number of categories.

The first category was department stores which was furthered segmented into three groups: those that targeted upscale customers; companies that targeted the middle-income market; and the companies such as Mervyn's that competed in the popular-priced market. There were two groups in the specialty retailing category. The first was the narrowed focused chains such as The Limited and The Gap. The second group was the specialty department stores like Neiman-Marcus which competed for the upscale market. Discount stores, such as K mart and Target,

were in the third category and were subgrouped by the type, price, and quality of merchandise.

According to Aimee Stern, a retailing industry analyst for *Dun's Business Month,* a vast restructuring was changing the shape of retailing, creating new opportunities for the quick and resourceful, leaving the less-prepared companies behind. The winners were identified as the creative specialty chains that developed unusual merchandising and operational techniques; the innovative department stores that repositioned themselves with new consumer-driven marketing strategies; and the savvy discounters that have overturned the pricing structure of the industry by turning the country into a nation of bargain hunters. Industry analysts agreed that the key to success in the highly competitive specialty apparel business was a well-defined merchandising strategy or focus. According to *Barnard's Retail Marketing Report*, two factors were essential to the successful merchandising strategy of a specialty retailer. The factors were the ability to identify and fill high-growth niches and to provide superior customer service.

In order to develop a successful focus, retailers had to consider continually changing fashions as well as transitional and divergent consumer shopping habits and values. "The trick is to identify a lifestyle and demographic segment and create a store for them (the customers)," observed Joseph Ellis, vice president with Goldman, Sachs & Co. Through merchandise selection, price level, and ambiance, a focused store developed a distinctive and consistent identity that allowed shoppers to decide if it fit their preferences and budget.

To further develop a focus, retailers had to understand the consumers. This was no small task considering that the basic demographics of the United States were changing. In the 1960s, most people were in the 15 to 25 age-group. The population grew older in the 1970s and this trend was expected to continue throughout the rest of the century. Another demographic factor was the changing role of women. Many more women were working which increased their income, however, because of work they had less time to shop. According to the Greater Washington Research Center, many nine-to-five retailers were considering expanding business hours to snare the female labor force.

At the same time, retailers had to recognize the changing makeup and shopping patterns of their customers. For example, the previous success of many retailers was directly related to their dependence on the growth and evolution of the shopping mall. The shopping mall was becoming more of an entertainment center where people went to spend much of their time and money. However, shopping mall growth had flattened considerably since 1982 limiting one of the main avenues of growth.

Another limit to growth was that the United States was "overstored," especially with apparel retailers. According to *Dun's Business Month,* an industry survey showed that the country had ample retail space for that time as well as for the next four or five years. Apparel sales were expected to increase only 1 or 2 percent a year at least until 1990.

Because of these limits, retailers could no longer just add stores in order to grow. "If you're going to grow, you have to do it by taking someone else's market share and by literally killing off a competitor," said Cyrus Wilson, president of the retail consulting firm, Management Horizon.

Economic factors had also changed consumer shopping patterns. A larger share of wealth was being distributed among fewer people, increasing the significance of the upscale market. After two recessions, consumers were debt ridden and more willing to shop around at a number of stores because they wanted both quality and value. This pattern held true even though there was a lower inflation rate and a relatively attractive employment picture. This new attitude forced many stores to cut prices while their operating costs had been increasing.

The industry was also subject to fluctuations from changes in customer preferences which were dictated by both fashion and season. These fluctuations affected the inventory selection of apparel retailers, since merchandise usually was ordered a significant time in advance of the specific season and in some instances before the fashion trends were evidenced by customer purchases. It was the general practice to build up inventory levels prior to peak selling seasons. Companies usually had to enter into contracts for purchase of materials and manufacturing well in advance of the season. As a result retailers were vulnerable to demand pricing shifts.

Identifying the right merchandise selection was perhaps the most elusive part of developing a store's focus. "It is difficult to impossible for a store's product managers to design a fashion line; so what usually has ended up happening is that they study the season's fashions, find the things they like, and then have them knocked off," said Stan Schwartz, president and chief executive officer of Guy Laroche North America. "Knock off" meant to copy the popular styles of an established designer and was common among apparel retailers.

Schwartz added, "On the other hand, working with a designer on an exclusive licensing basis gives the store access to a true design house. Then the store is free to concentrate on details of coordination and marketing those designs."

Licensing was also used for knockoff lines that were endorsed by celebrities. Cheryl Teigs had such an agreement with Sears as did Jaclyn Smith with K mart. Commenting on the agreement with Smith, Joseph Antonini, senior vice president of K mart, said, "What our customers are asking for is a little better styling, and we think this line will fill that need." Such licenses are not limited to celebrities. Coca-Cola, Disney, and the American Ballet Theatre have all signed licensing agreements.

Each store had a need to set itself apart from the crowd. That was certainly what stimulated the growth of many department store private label programs in the 1950s. However, the private label programs in fashion are changing, Schwartz reported. Private labels were becoming associated with a designer name rather than a store name. Exclusive licensing agreements with designers were providing many stores with new private label merchandise. Consumers were causing this change because of their desire for a unique identity at an affordable price.

Licensing agreements were not without risk, however. "There is a certain aura to a designer name, but much depends on how it is packaged and marketed," said Richard Carty, fashion marketing manager for Bloomingdale's.

COMPETITOR PROFILES

Clothestime Inc.

According to *Business Week,* this California-based company was one of the fastest-growing companies in the United States. Started in 1974 by brothers, Michael and Ray DeAngelo, Clothestime had over 235 stores in the Sunbelt in August 1986. It tripled its 1985 profits to $10 million based on $127 million in sales.

The DeAngelos' ability to bargain had made Clothestime one of the few success stories in the popular-priced teen apparel business. Clothestime typically located its stores in strip malls where rent was lower rather than in large shopping centers. Also, much of its merchandise was purchased from manufacturers' closeouts or canceled orders. Both of these tactics were part of the overall strategy to keep the cost of overhead and goods low. Chairman Michael DeAngelo adamantly stated, "We don't pay full price for nothin'."

Because the strip malls did not get much traffic, heavy emphasis had been placed on advertising through direct mail and radio ads on rock and roll stations. Clothestime spent roughly 3 percent of sales on advertising, more than most other retailers.

The DeAngelos, who started in business together by selling odds and ends out of their van at flea markets, recognized the riskiness of their business. "Junior apparel is like dynamite. It can explode in your hand," remarked Ray DeAngelo. "Styles change so quickly that some chains have trouble keeping up."

Critics had questioned Clothestime's ability to become a national chain. Most of its growth came from opening new stores rather than increasing sales at current locations. Sales growth at existing locations dropped from 24 percent in 1983 to 7.2 percent in 1984, although sales growth had averaged 40.5 percent in 1982, 1983, and 1984. In response to their critics, Michael DeAngelo stated that they were "fine tuning" the Clothestime concept.

Petrie Stores Corporation

In 1986 Petrie Stores, a $1.2 billion women's specialty retailer, was headed by 83-year-old Milton Petrie, chairman and CEO. Petrie Stores was comprised of 14 chains with 1,400 stores in the United States, Puerto Rico, and the Virgin Islands. Petrie also owned 27 percent interest in Toys "R" Us and 26 percent of Paul Harris stores, an Indiana-based specialty retailer. In addition to the Petrie name, the Secaucus, New Jersey, retailer operated under different trade names such as Marianne, Stuarts, Rave, Jean Nicole, and Three Sisters.

The company had recently completed an electronic point of sale systems development program. This program included new merchandising and markdown systems through which the company was able to minimize its costs by enhancing communication between merchandising, stores, and distribution centers. Additionally, the company spent $74 million in 1984 and 1985 to renovate over 520 stores.

Milton Petrie and Leslie Wexner had long been acquainted. In 1965, Petrie offered Wexner a $75,000 a year job as his understudy. "Those numbers were like the GNP to me," Wexner recalled. "But I still said no. I wanted to run my own business." Wexner also turned down Petrie's offer to buy a 49.5 percent interest in The Limited, Inc., for $500,000 when total sales were only $400,000.

A few years ago Wexner almost took over Petrie Stores, but Milton Petrie backed out at the last minute. After The Limited, Inc., bought Lerner in 1985, Wexner and Petrie became direct competitors. About The Limited Inc.'s entry into the low-cost apparel business, Petrie said, "He (Wexner) won't find it as easy in our field."

Petrie Stores continued to be a target for takeovers. Petrie's strong financial performance, its interest in the profitable Toys "R" Us and Paul Harris, Milton Petrie's age, and no heir apparent to head the company were all contributing factors to its attractiveness as a takeover target.

The Gap Inc.

Until 1985, the 600 nationwide Gap stores focused on the jean and teenager clothing markets. With the growth of the traditional business slowing, Gap management, headed by President Donald E. Fisher, changed the Gap's merchandising mix and renovated "The Gap" stores and added the "Super Gap" stores. Although still the largest vendor of Levi Strauss jeans (27 percent of sales), the new emphasis was on fashion-oriented, medium-priced sportswear. The Gap, established in 1969, began to target 20 to 45 year olds with a quality look and up-to-date styling. Sixty percent of its merchandise was under its own private label.

The San Bueno, California-based company had also expanded into one of the newest areas of specialty retailing: travel and safari wear. The Banana Republic, which was expected to have 30 stores by the end of 1986, had about twice the average sales volume per store ($2 million) as the average Gap store.

The new merchandising strategy seemed to pay off. In the first nine months of fiscal 1985, the Gap's total sales increased 23 percent over the same period in the previous year to $423.8 million. Earnings jumped 143 percent to $1.46 a share.

Carter Hawley Hale Stores, Inc.

Carter Hawley Hale (CHH) was a Los Angeles-based holding company of five department store and three specialty retailing chains. The stores which had a wide selection of fashionable and competitively priced merchandise, targeted middle and upper income segments. The department store chains included: The Broadway Southern California, The Broadway Southwest, Emporium Capwell, Thalhimers, and Weinstock's. Bergdorff-Goodman, Neiman-Marcus, and Contempo Casual were the specialty units.

In the 1980s, the CHH divisions were producing marginal results. In the 1980 to 1985 time period, CHH's return on equity was 10.3 percent as opposed to 20 percent and 14.5 percent, respectively, for competitors R. H. Macy and Federated. In the same time period, net income as a percentage of sales was 1.9 percent for CHH while it was 4.5 percent for Macy's and 3.5 percent for Federated. Although 1985 saw a 77 percent increase in sales over 1984 to nearly $4 billion, CHH Chairman Philip Hawley said a greater customer service orientation was required for continued improvement.

Hawley, who started with The Broadway in 1958 as a

buyer, became president of CHH in 1972. Since 1980, Hawley has overseen the development and installation of a new computer system. This system aided in better management of inventories and buying and greater customer service by decreasing credit approval time and speeding sales transactions in the stores. Hawley also introduced more employee training programs to improve product and fashion knowledge and to enhance communication and selling skills.

In 1984, CHH faced one of its greatest challenges when it became a takeover target of The Limited, Inc. CHH fiercely resisted the takeover by selling 37 percent of its equity to the General Cinema Corporation in exchange for an agreement that restricted General Cinema's rights to sell its stock until 1991. Additionally, CHH sold its profitable Waldenbooks Division to K mart and changed its corporate bylaws to make a takeover more difficult. Later that year Limited Chairman, Leslie Wexner, who had been interested in CHH since 1980, halted the takeover attempt. Commenting on the failed takeover, Wexner said, "The war isn't over yet." Wexner was not kidding. In 1986, The Limited, Inc., in a joint venture with shopping center magnate Edward J. Debartolo, began a second takeover attempt by offering $1.7 billion for CHH.

MANAGEMENT

More than two decades after its founding in Columbus, Ohio, The Limited was something of a legend among retailers and so was Leslie Wexner, the man who originated it and who keeps it going. "The Limited's billionaire founder was regarded as a merchandising genius as well as one of retailing's most tough-minded managers," stated Richard Stevenson in *The New York Times.* Milton Petrie, president of Petrie Stores, called Wexner "the greatest merchandising talent in America."

Wexner served as chairman of the board of The Limited, Inc. His associates credited him with keeping an entrepreneurial spirit alive in the company, despite its mushroomlike growth. He and his family control 35.1 percent of company stock. Leslie Wexner studied business administration at Ohio State University. He enrolled in law school but dropped out to work in his father's store. His "Limited" creation has made him a billionaire and helped him acquire the tangible items that accompany this status—five residences, corporate jets, and rare automobiles. In addition to his passion for fashion, he is on the board of Sotheby's and the Whitney. His major philanthropies are The Ohio State University and the city of Columbus, Ohio. "Les Wexner belongs in with Watson of IBM, Ray Kroc of McDonald's," said Tom Peters who included The Limited in his book *A Passion for Excellence.*

The most well-known members of the board of directors in addition to Wexner, were Robert Morosky as vice chairman, and Bella Wexner, Leslie's mother, as secretary. Robert Morosky, who had been with The Limited since 1972, believed in Wexner so much that he sold his house to buy Limited stock. A CPA by trade, Morosky handled financial affairs. Through his association with The Limited, he became a millionaire.

The presidents of each of the nine divisions reported directly to Wexner and Morosky. According to Michael Weiss, head of Limited Express, each president was given a totally free hand in running their divisions. The country was divided geographically into regions. Regional managers reported directly to their respective president. Below regional managers were district managers and then individual store managers. An overview of management is represented in Exhibit 5.

LABOR RELATIONS/EMPLOYEES

The company has acknowledged that the number one incentive was not money, but self-realization and recognition. "We start with the fundamental premise that work is an uplifting experience that can be just as fun as the golf course," said Thomas Hopkins, vice president of organizational development. The Limited exemplified this philosophy in its employee relations. The philosophy contended that employees are part of the company and when they feel that way, they will be their most productive.

The corporate culture at The Limited was intense. There were no employees at The Limited, Inc., but "associates." These 33,000 full-time associates, about 50 of them millionaires, controlled roughly half the company's stock. Top managers were flown once a year to Vail to celebrate. Wexner held yearly dinners for the staff and gave awards for outstanding contributions. He freely admitted that he copied these employee awards

programs from IBM. On the staff of The Limited, Inc., was a full-time manager of nonmonetary compensation and incentives, Lynn Beckmaster-Irwin. One of her projects was to develop the company magazine, *Applause, Applause* to recognize employee and company achievement. Associates are warned not to talk to competitors or the press. Some critics said The Limited is more a corporate cult than a culture, that conformity was as important as creativity. Industry analysts noted that this conformity tended to induce some management turnover.

The style of The Limited was to promote from within. Store managers became vice presidents of distribution and merchandise clericals became executive vice presidents of merchandise. For example, Verna Gibson who was president of The Limited store's flagship division, started in 1971 as a trainee. Robert Grayson, the president of the Lerner stores division, started as a store manager. This was The Limited family. Wexner stated that "his executives are good people—they don't get divorced and are good to their parents." Most of them have worked for him from the beginning and were fiercely protective around him.

MERCHANDISING STRATEGY

When studying the success of The Limited, analysts first point to its merchandising ability. These analysts believed that The Limited's success had been due to its ability to identify what fashions American women were going to buy, just before American women knew it and just before their competitors knew it. It also had an uncanny knack for bailing out of a style before demand for it collapsed. The Limited's fashion strategy was to design a look. When asked what women want, Wexner answered, "Anything they don't have. Every woman already has enough clothes to last 100 years. You have to sell excitement."

Many of The Limited's most successful fashions were private-labeled "knockoffs" of more expensive designer labels. Buyers and executives reported from their perpetual shopping tours of markets at home and abroad. In 1983, on a trip through Italy, Verna Gibson noticed teenagers in Florence wearing bulky yachting sweaters. The sweater was copied under the division's private

EXHIBIT 5   The Limited, Inc.—Table of Organization

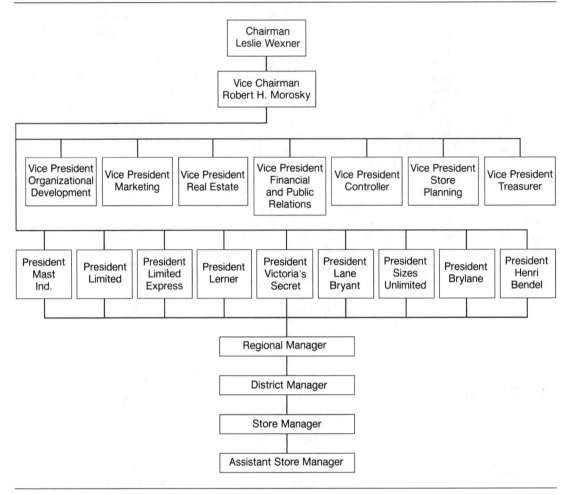

label, Forenza, and sold by the millions. "It was probably the most successful sweater to hit the American retailing market," said Gibson. Many stores attempted to clone the sweater but The Limited managed to sell more than 3 million at about $29 apiece. Wexner himself dreamed up the Italian sounding name "Forenza." *The Wall Street Journal* stated that Forenza was the number three best seller in sportswear in the world in 1986. The marketing approach created by The Limited led buyers to believe that the tuxedo-clad man on the Forenza ads was the designer Forenza himself. There was even an Italian address on the garment tags. But alas, a small amount of research would have shown that the fictitious Forenza was invented in 1984 by the marketing staff of The Limited.

These private-label goods carried large margins because they were produced at low cost and sold for whatever price the market would bear. This technique of selling private brands served to enhance The Limited's marketing strength.

In addition to its private-label merchandising, The Limited also entered into agreements with several European designers to design lines of apparel and accessories to be sold in their chains. The first designer label chosen by The Limited in 1985 was Kenzo, a Japanese designer well known in Europe but not in the United States. The Limited's "Album by Kenzo" line was distinctly different from his Paris collection. The designer chosen for 1986 was Krizia, an Italian designer.

Analysts questioned why a "knockoff" store such as The Limited would hire designers to create lines exclusively for them—the answer is simple—it sells. A spokesperson from The Limited's public relations department said, "American women are more sophisticated in their fashion taste than they are given credit for. The only thing stopping them is the price tag."

In late 1985, another new and vastly successful private-label brand was introduced. Outback Red was a new line of stylish safari clothing—basically a "knockoff" on the popular Banana Republic clothing store. Unlike most other retailers, The Limited routinely test-marketed its new clothing lines. This prevented bloated inventories which could ultimately lead to drastically marked down prices. The line was an instant success. So with four strong clothing lines leading into 1987—Forenza, Kenzo, Krizia, and Outback Red—could The Limited continue its success?

MARKETING

One thing that The Limited did extremely well was turnaround the ailing companies it acquired. Marketing in the other Limited retail divisions was very similar to the flagship stores. After acquisitions, major changes usually occurred. For example, when The Limited acquired Victoria's Secret their lingerie was priced to accommodate only about 12 to 15 percent of the market. The Limited kept the tasteful look of the lingerie but reduced the prices to attract a larger market. After the Lerner acquisition, The Limited shocked the business community by canceling an estimated $100 million worth of merchandise orders with various manufacturers and reestablishing its on-order inventory. A similar

process occurred in other Limited acquisitions; that is, replacing a large amount of inventory with lower cost, and in most cases private-label clothing.

The Limited, Inc., managed its marketing, production, and distribution from one central location in Columbus, Ohio. All retail stores were tightly controlled. The whole system was monitored by the POS (point of sale) computer. This computer tracked what items, sizes, and styles of merchandise were being sold so that replacements could be ordered and slow-moving items could be dropped. The computer system allowed a new item to be in the stores within six weeks after the original design approval. The industry average was 10 weeks.

The fact that all stores looked alike was no accident. Every other Tuesday the displays were torn apart and rearranged. Pictures were taken in the model stores and sent to the other stores. By the next Monday, they were all identical. No deviations were allowed. The stores were decorated in high-tech chrome and glass with plants and wicker furniture. Lifelike mannequins were dressed and accessorized in the latest fashions. Each week managers received a plan, developed by the marketing department at Limited headquarters in Columbus, that dictated changes in pricing, presentation, and merchandise mix.

MANUFACTURING AND DISTRIBUTION

Mast Industries, acquired in 1978, was The Limited's manufacturing and buying arm. Mast had interest in 12 factories in Asia and long-standing relationships with 190 others around the world. According to Milton Petrie, "Mast is The Limited's trump card." Most retailers depended on middlemen such as wholesalers, importer, and independent buying offices and waited considerably longer periods of time for their orders. According to Wexner, "You can't patent anything in the clothing business, so you've got to be the first to get your stuff to the consumer if you want to be successful." Mast had helped bail The Limited out of serious difficulties. For example, in 1984, The Limited stocked cotton career clothing that was not selling. It placed new orders with Mast and within months had new lines to offer.

In addition to Mast Industries, The Limited was vertically integrated. Most retailers relied on New York middleman suppliers along with the rest of the retail herd. Mast owned the steamers used to bring cotton fabric from China to factories in Hong Kong. It owned the planes that rushed the goods to the United States. After clearing customs, a fleet of tractor-trailers owned by The Limited and operated by Walsh Trucking, a New Jersey-based company, rushed the goods to the distribution center in Columbus, Ohio. There each style was sorted by size and color and assigned to containers destined for particular stores. They computer read the bar codes on the containers and directed them to the proper shipping location and again the company-owned truck fleet delivered the merchandise to the stores. It took an average of 48 hours for a garment to pass through the distribution center, whereas other less-automated warehouses took weeks to process a garment. The Limited fed fresh merchandise into its stores at the rate of two shipments a week.

One problem revealed by Bettye Benton, the manager of The Limited Prestonwood—Dallas store, was the delays associated with processing goods through customs. Ms. Benton sighted a recent example of a popular blouse, known as a "Ten Buttons" that buyers were demanding daily but she was unable to provide because the blouses were tied up in the red tape associated with customs. The Limited was addressing this problem by trying to obtain zoning approval for an airstrip near their distribution center so that goods could be flown directly to Columbus.

The Limited turns over its inventory 10 times a year compared to an industry average of 3 times a year. Mr. Morosky, vice chairman of The Limited, Inc., boasted that its chains had the highest sales per square foot of any stores in their market segments. They relied on high traffic locations to draw customers and were willing to pay in mall rent what others spend on advertising. The flagship Limited stores had sales of almost $300 a square foot, triple the industry average.

It was not The Limited's strategy to advertise. Their first advertising began in 1985. Advertisements appeared in youthful magazines such as *Glamour* and *Elle*. In the past, The Limited had depended on store display and choice, higher cost mall locations to secure business. The new advertisements promoted the designer lines.

FINANCE AND ACQUISITIONS

The Limited, Inc., had made spectacular use of leverage, the strategy whereby companies use borrowed money to finance acquisitions. The risk associated with this strategy was that the company must produce enough cash flow to cover interest charges and pay off the debt or face a financial crunch.

Leslie Wexner faced this crunch in 1978 when The Limited issued a $30.9 million debt to acquire Mast Industries, to install the computer network, and to build the distribution center. Cash flows slowed dramatically when sales started to slump and inventories piled up. At this point, Wexner halted the expansion program and tightened operations. By January 1981, the long-term debt was down to $16.6 million.

In July 1982, Wexner took on $97.2 million of debt, in the form of bank loans and debt issues, and went on an acquisition binge that doubled the size of the company. In 1982 The Limited, Inc., acquired Lane Bryant, Brylane, Victoria's Secret, Roamans, and Sizes Unlimited. Sales soared 100 percent and earnings rose 50 percent from 1981 figures. The entire loan was repaid in 18 months.

In April 1984, The Limited borrowed $515.4 million to finance a hostile takeover of the Carter Hawley Hale department store chain. The specialty-line department store would have completed The Limited, Inc.'s coverage of the women's clothing market. Wexner lost the battle and the debt was eventually trimmed to $92 million.

In April 1985, Wexner purchased Lerner Stores, leaving The Limited with a debt of $353.9 million. In addition, The Limited opened hundreds of new stores across the country. This debt was in the form of convertible debt issues. Many of these issues were called in so as to force conversion in mid-1986. This action brings Limited's debt-to-total capital ratio under 20 percent from nearly 50 percent.

On October 21, 1986, The Limited, Inc., increased its available bank credit lines to $1.4 billion from $700 million. Robert Morosky, vice chairman, said, "This move sends a signal to the investment community that we are a potential buyer of retail operations, however, there is nothing specific in way of a pending acquisition."

New sales have increased 37.5 percent in the first six

months of 1986 and net income has increased 52 percent. There are 119,946,441 shares of outstanding stock with a market value of $3,078,000.00.

FUTURE

The Limited believed its existing businesses had the potential to grow from about 2,400 stores to 5,000 and produce revenues of $5 billion in the next few years. Wexner wanted nothing less than to dominate the $50 billion-a-year women's clothing business. Industry experts reported that the future of retailing can be summed up in two key words: specialization and consolidation. Recognizing that the future of retailing was a battle over a largely stagnant market, future growth would be at the expense of competitors. The Limited, Inc., planned to continue to use its expertise to carve out unexploited niches in the women's clothing market. Wexner believed that a weakened major retailer or department store chain could become available as a merger partner. Although it appeared the company still had plenty of segments to expand into now, a saturation level would eventually occur. Where will the new growth come from then? Should The Limited, Inc., pursue the takeover of Carter Hawley Hale? Did the future hold limits for The Limited?

THE LIMITED, INC.
Consolidated Balance Sheet
(thousands)

	February 1, 1986	February 2, 1985
Assets		
Current assets:		
Cash and equivalents	$ 12,948	$ 7,494
Accounts Receivable	62,077	45,912
Inventories	320,305	190,014
Prepayments and Other	20,994	13,056
Total current assets	416,324	256,476
Property and equipment	648,314	267,528
Investment in and advances to finance subsidiaries	74,795	23,672
Other assets	72,077	19,476
Total assets	$1,211,510	$567,152
Liabilities and Shareholders' Equity		
Current liabilities:		
Accounts payable	$ 184,368	$103,010
Accrued expenses	103,381	47,719
Income taxes payable	9,253	9,378
Deferred income taxes	56,416	29,109
Total current liabilities	353,418	189,216
Senior long-term debt	213,744	60,139
Subordinated convertible debt	175,000	—
Deferred income taxes	44,506	42,394
Other long-term liabilities	20,767	—
Shareholders' equity:		
Common Stock	59,917	29,807
Paid-in capital	24,695	22,466
Retained earnings	319,463	223,130
Total shareholders' equity	404,075	275,403
Total liabilities and shareholders' equity	$1,211,510	$567,152

Source: 1985 Annual Report.

THE LIMITED, INC.
Consolidated Statement of Income
(thousands except per share amounts)

	1985	1984	1983
Net sales	$2,387,110	$1,343,134	$1,085,890
Costs of goods sold, occupancy and buying costs	1,668,267	938,813	758,274
Gross income	718,843	404,321	327,616
General, administrative and store operating expenses	442,631	231,219	192,239
Operating income	276,212	173,102	135,377
Interest expense	(41,230)	(16,662)	(10,248)
Other income, net	4,335	1,055	9,810
Income before income taxes	239,317	157,495	134,939
Provision for income taxes	94,000	65,000	64,000
Net income	$ 145,317	$ 92,495	$ 70,939
Net income per share	$ 1.20	$ 0.77	$ 0.59

Source: 1985 Annual Report.

THE LIMITED, INC.
Consolidated Statement of Changes in Financial Position
(thousands)

	1985	1984	1983
Cash was provided from:			
Operations:			
Net income	$145,317	$ 92,495	$ 70,939
Add expenses not requiring working capital:			
Depreciation and amortization	80,128	34,526	28,427
Deferred income taxes and other	(3,030)	7,587	12,511
Working capital from operations	222,415	134,608	111,877
Cash flow additions (requirements) resulting from:			
Inventories	(51,342)	(67,157)	(20,698)
Payables	62,567	36,240	2,147
Income taxes	11,082	16,326	8,779
Other current assets and liabilities	4,528	288	4,490
Cash provided from operations	249,250	120,305	106,595
Other sources of cash:			
Subordinated convertible debt	175,000	—	—
Other long-term debt	346,590	38,290	—
Disposal of assets	8,323	2,716	25,252
Total cash provided	779,163	161,311	131,847
Cash was used for:			
Net cash to acquire subsidiaries and retire debt	331,462	14,142	24,493
Reduction of long-term debt	196,398	—	52,648
Investment in property and equipment	180,269	117,684	52,016
Investment in and advances to finance subsidiaries	47,456	8,000	—
Cash dividends	19,118	14,263	7,056
Other, net	(994)	1,010	(159)
Total cash used	773,709	155,099	136,054
Increase (decrease) in cash and equivalents	5,454	6,212	(4,207)
Cash and equivalents, beginning of year	7,494	1,282	5,489
Cash and equivalents, end of year	$12,948	$ 7,494	$ 1,282

Source: 1985 Annual Report.

THE LIMITED, INC.
Consolidated Statement of Shareholders' Equity
(thousands)

		Common Stock		
	Shares Outstanding	Par Value	Paid-in Capital	Retained Earnings
Balance, January 29, 1983	29,216	$14,608	$12,267	$ 95,703
Net income				70,939
Cash dividends				(7,056)
Exercise of stock options and other	588	294	5,821	—
Two-for-one stock split	29,376	14,688	—	(14,688)
Balance, January 28, 1984	59,180	29,590	18,088	144,898
Net income				92,495
Cash dividends				(14,263)
Exercise of stock options and other	434	217	4,378	—
Balance, February 2, 1985	59,614	29,807	22,466	223,130
Net income				145,317
Cash dividends				(19,118)
Exercise of stock options and other	488	244	2,229	—
Two-for-one stock split	59,732	29,866	—	(29,866)
Balance, February 1, 1986	119,834	$59,917	$24,695	$319,463

Source: 1985 Annual Report.

9.   *Circuit City Stores, Inc.*

Ed Kopf, director of planning for Circuit City Stores Inc., had just finished reviewing a consultant's report, which concluded that Circuit City should once again offer products through mail order. More specifically, the consultant recommended that Circuit City introduce a high-gloss, mail-order catalog containing top-of-the-line, high-margin consumer electronic items.

The potential benefits of mail-order sales were attractive. Mail order seemed to offer a quick and inexpensive means of expanding geographically as well as increasing Circuit City's penetration in its existing markets. Mail-order sales also would allow Circuit City to extend its product lines to include high-margin but low-volume items that were not feasible to carry in all stores. In addition, there would be promotional synergies between mail-order and retail store operations.

The consultant believed that this was an opportune time for Circuit City to reintroduce mail-order selling. There were currently no dominant mail-order catalogs specializing in Circuit City's merchandise lines. Furthermore, Circuit City had demonstrated an ability to satisfy diverse consumer markets. Circuit City's advanced point-of-sale (POS) system, which supplied on-line communications between all Circuit City operations and its corporate offices in Richmond, could give the company a competitive advantage in processing orders. Also, no existing consumer electronics mail-order firm could match Circuit City's buying power. Strategically, catalog sales would allow Circuit City to take advantage of growing consumer acceptance of in-home shopping. And, it would put the company in a position to test new technologies in in-home shopping that many experts believed would significantly affect retailing in the near future.

Despite the consultant's enthusiasm, Ed had more than a few misgivings. If Circuit City were to offer a "high-end" catalog, as the consultant recommended, how would a high-price product offering affect Circuit City's "Low-Price" image and promotion strategy? How would a "skim" marketing strategy fit with one of Circuit City's greatest competitive strengths, its ability to underprice and outpromote the competition by concentrating on volume? Circuit City had succeeded by mass marketing products with a broad-based appeal. Would the company know how to promote more exclusive products to the electronics buff?

On the other hand, if Circuit City were to offer a catalog featuring items comparable to current in-store offerings, would it generate new business or would it cannibalize the existing customer base? Would the catalog prices have to match in-store prices? What would the catalog offer that other local retailers didn't?

Regardless of the type of product offered, other issues would have to be resolved before deciding whether to enter the mail-order business. How would mail order fit into the volatile consumer electronics market? Today's prices and technology might be hopelessly outdated before the completion of the catalog's life. Would consumers buy high-ticket consumer electronics without having the opportunity to test the product or at least to see it? Would they be confused by differences between the product and service offered by the retail stores and those available through the catalog? How would the product be serviced? An important question for Circuit City was whether there were better opportunities in areas other than mail order. Should the company get involved in what could be presumed to be a sideline, during a time of very rapid growth?

COMPANY BACKGROUND

Circuit City was the largest specialty retailer of name-brand consumer electronics and appliances in the United States. Through its outlets centered in the Southeast, Circuit City sold large and small appliances, audio and video equipment, and advanced consumer electronics (ACE). Circuit City sought to dominate the markets it entered, and often achieved more than a 35 percent share of market in consumer electronics sales. Circuit City was the largest-volume member of NATM (National Appliance and Television Merchants), the industry's

This case was prepared by James Olver under the supervision of Eleanor G. May, Professor of Business Administration. Copyright © 1985 by The Colgate Darden Graduate School Sponsors, Charlottesville, Virginia. WP1616a

largest-buying group. Tremendous buying power, coupled with what the company's chairman, Alan Wurtzel, called a "critical mass" of convenient local outlets, allowed Circuit City to offer broad selections and low prices, as well as local repairs and optional extended warranties on most products.

Circuit City's promotional activities were well suited to its guaranteed-lowest-price strategy (within 30 days of purchase a customer received a refund of the difference if another retailer in the market area offered the identical merchandise for a lower price than that paid at Circuit City). Frequent storewide sales with names like "Midnight Madness," "Price Slasher," and "The Thing" contributed to Circuit City's tremendous sales volume, which averaged around $5.6 million per store—about 10 times that of the typical consumer electronics specialty store, by Circuit City estimates. Promotions were backed by full-page newspaper ads and inserts packed with sale-priced items, primarily at the lower-price end of each product category. In most markets, promotions were supported also by television and radio advertising that the smaller local specialty stores typically could not afford to match. Circuit City's gross advertising expenditures in 1984 were 5.9 percent of sales.

Until 1979, Circuit City Stores Inc., then operating under the name Wards Company, Inc., had offered consumer electronics through mail order, first under the name Dixie Hi-Fi (which was the name used by Wards in its discount audio outlets located in the southeastern states). Fair trade laws had allowed Dixie Hi-Fi to sell audio equipment through the mail at prices significantly lower than those at the retail stores in most areas, resulting in roughly $5,000,000 in annual mail-order sales. The layout of the Dixie catalog emphasized a "low cost, no nonsense" approach: black-and-white sketches of the items were accompanied by detailed descriptions of the product and its technical specifications.

In the early 1970s, Wards operated several retail consumer electronics and appliance chains of its own, plus the Dixie mail-order/discount outlet business, and leased departments in several discount department stores. During the recession of the mid-1970s, Wards suffered severe losses when several of the department store chains from which it leased went bankrupt. Between 1977 and 1981, the Dixie Hi-Fi discount audio stores and Custom Hi-Fi and Sight and Sound consumer electronics stores were consolidated as Circuit City. The resulting entity offered consumer electronics at Dixie's low prices, with the superior service, selection, convenience, and aesthetic appeal of Custom Hi-Fi and Sight and Sound. In addition, the chain of discount appliance stores, Wards Loading Dock ("name brand appliances at forklift prices"), was revamped, consumer electronics product lines available in the Circuit City stores were added, and the stores were renamed Circuit City Superstores. With the demise of the fair trade laws and the tremendous success of the Circuit City format, mail order was abandoned in favor of vigorous expansion of retail outlets. In 1984, the corporate name was changed from Wards to Circuit City Inc., to diminish confusion and more clearly to describe the firm.

The strategy paid off handsomely. Sales revenues had grown at a compound annual rate of 43 percent between 1982 and 1985, while profits had increased almost sevenfold in the same period. (See Exhibits 1, 2, and 3.)

Circuit City's retail operations in late 1984 included 35 Circuit City stores, 13 Superstores, 12 Lafayette stores on the East Coast, and 33 leased departments in Zody's Department Stores on the West Coast. (See Exhibit 4.) The company had nearly 3,800 employees and 377,000 square feet of selling space. (See Exhibit 5.) In 1985, Circuit City was involved in a program of upgrading the Circuit City stores (to Superstores if there was sufficient space, to "mini" Supers if there was a space limitation) and opening free-standing Superstores to replace the Zody's units.

CIRCUIT CITY STORES

Whether in Superstore or regular format, the Circuit City store layout emphasized an expansion of "The Four Ss" to five: the fifth "S" was for "Speed." As the 1985 Annual Report noted "Circuit City has long recognized that retailing is part theater. The Superstore has been carefully designed to dramatize and efficiently to deliver to the customer exceptional *Savings,* outstanding *Selections,* and high-quality *Service* before and after the sale—all with *Speed* and guaranteed *Satisfaction.*" The effect of this combination was particularly dramatic in the 30,000- to 40,000-square-feet Superstores, which had up to 14,000 square feet of showroom space, 15,000 square feet of warehouse, plus space for service and sales support. (Other Circuit City stores and the Lafayette stores had a minimum of 4,000 square feet of selling space and 1,500 square feet of storage.)

Upon entering a typical Superstore building, the customers walked by large picture windows behind which repairmen could be viewed working on Circuit City products. Adjacent was "Kiddie City," a playroom to occupy children while parents shopped. Inside the showroom, the customer was confronted by an impressive array of television and video equipment, appliances, and consumer electronics grouped by product category, each featuring a wide variety of price/performance choices. The TV and appliance areas occupied 5,000 to 10,000 square feet. Appliances included washers and dryers, refrigerators, freezers, dishwashers, and microwave ovens. One wall in the television area was lined from floor to ceiling with sets of various sizes and descriptions. In front of these were aisles of shelves stocked with other television and video equipment and accessories such as VCRs, cameras, and videodisc players. A vast assortment of tape decks, phonographs, receivers, tuners, amplifiers, and speakers, sorted by price/performance characteristics, were displayed. A

EXHIBIT 1

CIRCUIT CITY INC.
Balance Sheet
Years Ended February 28 or 29
(in thousands)

	1985	1984	1983
Assets			
Cash	$ 5,124	$ 45,230	$ 21,761
Accounts and notes receivable	9,615	10,544	8,318
Merchandise inventory	116,775	73,688	47,346
Other current assets	4,425	1,749	1,642
Total current assets	135,939	131,211	79,067
Property and equipment, net	83,331	43,984	21,566
Deferred income taxes	1,637	1,531	1,568
Other assets	23,029	14,647	7,701
Total assets	$243,936	$191,373	$109,902
Liabilities and Stockholders' Equity			
Current installments of long-term debt	$ 2,014	$ 1,477	$ 277
Accounts payable	57,209	37,016	25,545
Accrued expenses and other liabilities	14,492	8,160	6,550
Accrued income taxes	8,570	13,432	621
Total current liabilities	82,285	60,085	32,993
Long-term debt	40,005	27,885	15,187
Other liabilities	0	1,652	1,297
Deferred revenue	9,874	5,733	4,141
Excess of value received over cost of assets acquired, net	0	6,843	7,707
Stockholders' equity:			
Preferred stock of $20 par value	589	590	591
Common stock of $1 par value	10,945	10,861	9,882
Capital in excess of par value	28,651	27,064	6,826
Retained earnings	71,587	50,660	31,278
Total stockholders' equity	111,772	89,175	48,577
Total liabilities and stockholders' equity	$243,936	$191,373	$109,902

listening room was available where the audiophile could test the stereo equipment; an adjacent, separate area contained car stereos. The advanced consumer electronics products and accessories included tape recorders, radios, handheld TVs, telephones and other communication devices, and portable stereo equipment. A limited line of home computer hardware and software had been carried, but by 1985 this merchandise had been discontinued.

All models of most products were set up for the shopper to try out. But, in contrast to most catalog showrooms, a knowledgeable and eager sales force was

---

EXHIBIT 2

CIRCUIT CITY INC.
Statements of Earnings
Years Ended February 28 or 29
(in thousands)

	1985	1984	1983
Net sales and operating revenues	$705,490	$519,214	$356,708
Cost of sales, buying, and warehousing	505,691	370,765	253,887
Gross profit	199,799	148,449	102,821
Selling, general, and administrative expenses	157,521	109,031	79,140
Interest expense	2,257	1,409	1,372
Total expenses	159,778	110,440	80,512
Earnings before income taxes	40,421	38,009	22,309
Provision for income taxes	18,000	17,775	10,300
Net earnings	$ 22,021	$ 20,234	$ 12,009
Earnings per common share (in dollars)	$ 1.98	$ 1.94	$ 1.23

EXHIBIT 3

CIRCUIT CITY STORES INC.
Sales and Earnings
Years Ending February 28 or 29

	Net Sales	After-Tax Earnings
1985	$705,500,000	$22,021,000
1984	519,214,000	20,234,000
1983	356,708,000	12,009,000
1982	245,914,000	5,507,000
1981	176,169,000	2,935,000
1980	131,881,000	2,701,000
1979	119,609,000	2,286,000
1978	111,534,000	2,570,000
1977	90,799,000	2,052,000
1976	72,360,000	1,250,000

available to answer questions and offer advice both about the product and about the sales terms. Once a purchase decision was made, the salesman entered the order on a POS computer terminal on the showroom floor, which simultaneously placed the order to the warehouse, updated the inventory, recorded the name and phone number of the customer, the size and type of his order, and the name of the salesman, and computed the salesman's commission.[1] Daily summary reports allowed store managers to evaluate sales and profit performance both of salesmen and of product categories. (See Exhibit 6.)

After the salesman placed the order, the customer took the order slip to the cashier where payment was made or credit was arranged for. Small accessories, such as tapes and batteries, were available next to the cashier. After the sale was consummated, the customer walked to the warehouse to pick up the order.

[1]According to *Mart* magazine (June 1985) the median salary for a floor salesperson selling this type of merchandise in appliance/TV stores, home electronics stores, specialty stores (i.e., telephone, computer, video, hi-fi), or department stores and mass merchandisers was $18,061 in 1984. Of the respondents that pay commissions, 40 percent pay between 1 percent and 3 percent, 13 percent between 4 percent and 9 percent, and 47 percent, 10 percent or over.

EXHIBIT 4 Number of Retail Units

Fiscal Year, Ending February	Superstore	Circuit City	Lafayette	West Coast	Total
1984	13	35	12	33	93
1983	8	38	11	41	98
1982	7	36	8	50	101
1981	7	31	8	51	97
1980	4	37	0	41	82
1979	4	36	0	35	75
1978					70
1977					70
1976					61

EXHIBIT 5 Space and Employee Data

	Square Feet Selling Space	Sales per Square Foot	Number of Employees
1984	376,607	$1,371	3,796
1983	360,792	989	2,057
1982	349,389	704	1,664
1981	308,754	571	1,323
1980	230,936	571	1,052
1979	215,570	555	957
1978			943
1977			824
1976			610

Although Circuit City often did not carry top-of-the-line models because of the company's reliance on volume, most departments had something for the vast majority of consumer electronics customers. Overall, Circuit City merchandise sales were about 50 percent video, 30 percent audio, 10 percent appliances, and 10 percent ACE. In addition to the merchandise sales, less than 10 percent of the revenues come from sales of services, including delivery, extended warranty, and repair services.

Offering a selection of ACE products, particularly home computers and accessories, was difficult, how-

---

EXHIBIT 6 Example of "Daily Processed Sales Summary" Store: 0817

Salesman	TIC (no.)	Merchandise ($)	Gross Margin (%)	Exended Service Plans ($)	Exended Service Plans (%)	SPIFF ($)
A	15	$ 1,412.41	33.7%	$ 97.88	6.9%	$ 38.25
B	17	3,098.32	18.8	0	0	24.00
C	9	265.44	10.6−	169.97−	64.0−	8.50
D	11	2,377.64	22.1	0	0	44.00
E	1	24.00−	100.0−	0	0	0
F	1	64.29	0	0	0	0
G	2	357.00	11.5	0	0	1.00
H	14	1,044.75	27.3	88.94	20.0	38.25
I	16	1,490.54	32.5	83.26	6.1	60.25
J	2	118.88	0	0	0	6.00
K	1	599.00	28.9	0	0	20.00
L	7	141.16	20.2	0	0	0.75
M	19	1,363.61	31.6	89.79	7.2	24.50
N	2	140.65−	70.8−	0	0	2.00−
O	13	3,452.89	21.0	229.91	6.7	47.00
P	1	0	0	69.97	0	0
Q	2	298.00	23.2	0	0	2.50
R	8	95.33	27.9	0	0	1.50
S	9	125.72	18.6	0	0	1.25
T	16	172.83	10.3	2.50	1.5	1.00
U	13	3,823.67	21.4	0	0	27.00
V	7	218.07	31.1	1.00	.5	4.50
W	10	135.92	15.4	17.66	13.0	2.50
X	18	4,302.56	19.4	225.88	5.3	34.75
Y	8	138.49	15.9	0	0	3.50
Z	2	21.18−	100.0−	29.97	141.5−	0
AA	10	1,420.51	29.0	27.94	2.4	24.50
BB	15	3,124.98	21.7	129.88	4.2	36.50
CC	23	1,713.63	29.8	38.03	2.2	25.75
DD	13	29.31	14.4	0	0	5.25
EE	20	1,558.40	27.9	91.73	5.9	25.00
FF	21	2,388.33	19.8	0	0	10.25
Total	326	$35,145.85	22.7%	$1,054.37	3.0%	$516.25

EXHIBIT 6   *(continued)*

Category of Sales	Sales ($)	Cost of Sales ($)	GM (%)	ESP ($)	ESP (%)
Merchandise:					
Video	$13,215.58	$10,602.86	19.8%	$ 413.55	3.1%
Major	8,765.57	7,209.69	17.7	204.73	2.3
Audio	8,236.33	5,594.88	32.1	121.22	1.5
ACE	5,088.34	3,879.57	23.8	211.26	4.2
Other	159.97–	127.98–	20.0–	103.50	64.7–
Subtotal	$35,145.85	$27,159.02	22.7%	$1,054.26	3.0%
Delivery	$ 41.97				
Installation	0				
Service parts	0				
Service labor	0				
VCR membership	0				
VCR rental	56.50				
Service charges	12.00				
Grand total	$35,256.32	$27,159.02		$1,054.26	

ever. Circuit City stores and Superstores had carried in prior years some of the more popular lines, such as the Commodore®, Texas Instruments, and ATARI® home computers and video systems. Rapid technological innovation in these products made demand and prices particularly unstable, and the wide range of options and accessories available (e.g., computer software) made it difficult to stock an adequate inventory. As a result, these ACE products had not been backed by Circuit City's 30-day lowest-price guarantee. One attempt by Circuit City to cope with product proliferation and obsolescence was an in-store "catalog" through which customers could order software and accessories that were not stocked in the stores. The catalog, actually a computer printout of product names and prices without any descriptive information, had to be updated weekly.

MAIL-ORDER FEASIBILITY STUDY

In the summer of 1984, Circuit City decided to reexamine the issue of mail-order catalog sales. A consulting firm was employed to examine trends in mail-order merchandising and in attitudes toward mail order of consumer electronics, and to recommend a course of action based on Circuit City's competitive strengths,

broad strategic considerations, and a cost/benefit analysis. If the mail order looked promising, the consultant was asked to develop an implementation plan that would include recommended product offerings, positioning of the catalog, development of a customer base, and the relationship between store and mail-order operations.

THE MAIL-ORDER MARKET

For purposes of the analysis, "mail order" was limited to mail, telephone, or catalog-desk orders of merchandise, and excluded telephone solicitation; it also excluded types of transactions in which the product ordered was immediately available to the customer. For example, store sales by catalog showrooms such as Best Products would not be included, while sales at Sears and Penney catalog order desks would be. By this definition, mail-order sales had been increasing nationally at an average annual rate of about 10 percent for the prior five years, roughly twice the growth rate of traditional retail outlets. The Direct Marketing Association estimated that Americans purchased about $40 billion worth of merchandise through the mail in 1983; other estimates ranged from $25 to $100 billion, depending on the definition of "mail order."

There were in 1983 between 4,000 and 5,000 mail-order catalogs for consumer goods; about 6,700,000,000 catalogs were mailed both by mail-order firms and by other retail firms. The market segments most relevant to Circuit City were classified as "Audio-Video" and "Consumer Electronics/Scientific," with approximately 230 catalogs in Audio-Video and 190 in Consumer Electronics/Scientific. Mail-order sales in 1982 for these two categories were estimated at $515 million, roughly 22 percent higher than in 1981.[2] The consultant's report noted that the largest competitors in these areas had roughly 10 percent of the sales share of their market segment, and no major U.S. retailer had entered either segment.

Marketing strategies in both of the segments relevant to Circuit City varied widely from firm to firm. Some firms, such as 47th Street Photo, were discount operations targeting a fairly broad-based audience. Others, such as Sharper Image and Markline, featured list-price specialty products that would appeal to a select clientele. Copy and layouts reflected the theme of the catalog and the characteristics of the target audience.

Mail-order merchandisers were able to target audiences with desired demographic, psychographic, and purchase-pattern profiles, through specialized mailing lists. As a result, some catalogs projected the image of an exclusive specialty shop yet generated large sales volumes. There was little evidence that a mass-appeal approach necessarily resulted in greater sales.

CONSUMER TRENDS

The consultant noted four broad consumer trends that had been credited with contributing significantly to the overall growth in mail order. These highlighted a growing demand for more specialized mail-order services:

- As a result of increased emphasis on developing and maintaining personal individuality, consumers were demanding more choices than stores could display or stock.

- A higher proportion of women in the work force meant less time for shopping but increased household disposable income.
- Awareness of and demand for hard-to-find items had increased consumers' interest in alternatives to in-store retailing.
- Consumers' desire for more leisure time for self-development and creative expression was leaving less time to search for a particular item or service.

TECHNOLOGICAL DEVELOPMENTS AND FUTURE TRENDS

Technological developments had complemented, and perhaps accelerated, the movement toward greater acceptance of in-home shopping. For example, passive direct-response systems, such as toll-free 800 phone numbers, contributed to the growth in mail-order sales. An experimental cable TV channel, offered "infomercials"—5- to 10-minute descriptions of particular products. Catalogia, Inc., consolidated a national network of 3,000 electronic multicatalog retail shopping systems into a central data base, through which consumers could obtain the names of catalogs where a desired product was available. Sears and J. C. Penney had experimented with videodisc catalogs.

Teletext data transmission systems offered information varying from stock prices to weather reports; retailers could use teletext to present products to consumers. The Source, CompuServe, and Dow Jones Information/Retrieval were all examples of teletext services available in the United States. All three national television networks had competing teletext systems in test market. Unlike other commercial teletext systems, which used computer terminals as vehicles, the network systems embedded a digital signal in the television vertical blanking interval (the technology used in captioning for the deaf). The signal could be read using a relatively inexpensive decoder, allowing the user to access, on the television, "pages" of information at will. When coupled with an 800 number for ordering, placing an order simply involved turning on the TV and dialing the phone.

One of the most promising and controversial technologies under development was videotex, a two-way interactive system that could operate through either home computers or cable TV. Unlike teletext, videotex

---

[2]Total sales in 1984 of major appliances were reported by *Merchandising* magazine to be nearly $17 billion; for video equipment, $12 billion; for audio, $7 billion; and for ACE (including personal computers), $5 billion.

subscribers could transmit as well as receive information. Videotex applications already included in-home financial transactions, electronic mail, reservation bookings, and retail sales transactions. Videotex, in use in Europe since 1976, was available commercially or publicly in several European countries and in Canada. In the United States, many of the largest communications, retailing, banking, and computer companies had been attempting to determine how to develop a dominant position in the business and/or consumer end of the videotex market. The list of firms involved in individual or joint ventures included CBS, Knight-Ridder, Times-Mirror, Time Inc., Cox Cable, Warner/AMEX, AT&T, Honeywell, Digital, IBM, and Chemical Bank, as well as Sears, Dayton Hudson, J. C. Penney, Melvin Simon, and Federated Department Stores.

Industry observers differed widely concerning time horizons for videotex development and adoption, as well as concerning its eventual impact on retailing. There were several barriers to widespread consumer adoption, such as the cost of videotex terminals and user mistrust of the technology, as well as technological problems that needed to be resolved. Nonetheless, the consultant believed that videotex and related technologies had potentially significant ramifications for retailing, and it was important that Circuit City be prepared to adopt these technologies as they developed.

FURTHER CONSUMER RESEARCH

It was clear that some consumers were willing to order some types of consumer electronics through the mail. In order to learn more about this market segment, the consultant had conducted a focus group interview to determine the issues deemed important by mail-order customers.

These issues were then addressed in more detail in a survey of consumer electronics mail-order customers. A questionnaire was mailed to 1,500 subjects chosen at random from the mailing list of a prominent consumer electronics mail-order firm. About a 30 percent response was received.

FOCUS GROUP FINDINGS

Most of the 10 focus group participants had had some experience with mail order. Two of the attendees reported poor experiences—slow delivery or defective

products—but this had not prejudiced them against using mail order.

There were three frequently cited advantages of store purchases over mail order:

- The opportunity to see, hear, and touch the merchandise.
- The opportunity to take the purchase home immediately.
- Greater confidence in warranty and repair availability.

For the most part, participants saw little or no value in the information and recommendations provided by in-store salespeople. Salespeople were described variously as:

- Order-takers only.
- Unpleasant to deal with.
- Low paid and low skilled.
- Not well versed in the characteristics of their own and their competitors' products.
- Insensitive to the consumer's needs.

Focus group participants seemed most likely to consider mail order if the following conditions were met:

- Merchandise could be returned unconditionally.
- The company offering the catalog was known to the consumer.
- The catalog offered brand-name products.
- The desired product was unlikely to be damaged in shipping.
- The product had a relatively low markup.

Participants reported that generally they researched products prior to purchase, particularly in the case of expensive items. They were likely to seek recommendations from friends and family, *Consumer Reports,* and in-store demonstrations, and they were likely to compare prices among catalogs. Many indicated that they often visited specialty shops in the evaluation process, but would purchase the item wherever they could secure the lowest price.

MAIL SURVEY FINDINGS

The demographic profile of the questionnaire respondents corresponded closely to that found among other consumers who used mail order. When compared with the general population, however, respondents tended to be:

- Concentrated between 25 and 54 years of age.
- Largely male.
- Surburban.
- College graduates.
- More likely to be employed in professional/managerial positions.
- From households with incomes over $25,000.

Demographics varied by product purchase category. Younger, less affluent subjects had bought proportionally more stereo components and portable stereos. ACE purchases, such as computer accessories, on the other hand, were concentrated among the more educated, affluent, professional respondents. Homeowners were more likely than nonhomeowners to have purchased appliances, but were less likely to have purchased a home stereo.

Respondents who reported using mail order for their most recent consumer electronics purchase had also ordered proportionally more mail-order products in the prior two years, and had ordered through more different catalogs than had other respondents. It appeared that consumers were most familiar with catalogs with an image or product offering similar to that of catalogs they had purchased from in the past. For example, in general, respondents who were most familiar with *Lands End* (a catalog including a wide assortment of active sportswear) were also familiar with *L.L. Bean,* and to a lesser extent with *Sharper Image,* but were less familiar with Circuit City. Circuit City customers, on the other hand, were generally quite familiar with Radio Shack, and somewhat with Sharper Image, but were less familiar with L.L. Bean. Reported familiarity with Lubin & Sons, a fictitious name included to check reliability of the answers, was very low.

The percentage of respondents who had used mail order was highest among the better educated consumers, aged 35 to 54 years. This held across a variety of catalogs as well as for mail order in general, although Sears mail orderers were more middle income, and Lands End and L.L. Bean had sales concentrated at both the high and low ends of the income scale. With the exception of Spencer Gifts, purchase experience increased with education.

Preferences for certain sources of product information varied according to respondents by age and education. Younger respondents relied more on friends, salesmen, and hands-on experience in purchase decisions. Those aged between 35 and 54 years were less inclined to shop around, either by visiting stores, checking ads, or asking advice. They were more likely to buy through catalogs,

and more often sight unseen, than those either younger or older. Better-educated consumers were most likely to use catalogs as a means of comparison, and were less concerned with helpful salesmen, familiarity with the store, or store reputation. They placed proportionally more orders by phone, and asked for additional information when placing orders.

In deciding where to purchase a product, in-store shoppers placed more importance on convenient location and availability of repairs than did mail-order shoppers. They also relied more on past experience with the retailer than did those who purchased through catalogs. Mail-order purchasers, on the other hand, were relatively more concerned than were in-store shoppers with the retailer's reputation, return policies, price, breadth of product line, and ease of purchase.

The consultant compared the relative importance of several purchase criteria across various types of consumer electronics and appliance purchases. (See Exhibits 7, 8, and 9.) It appeared that stereos and peripherals were deemed suitable for mail order, but only after first examining the product in a store. Telephones, portable stereos, and computer software seemed to be considered ''safe'' mail-order categories, even if the product had not been pre-tested in a store. Other products, such as televisions, video games, and microwave ovens, were not often purchased through the mail. The consultant believed the results indicated particular concern about dealer reliability and service when purchasing TV's and microwaves. Purchasers of video games, on the other hand, apparently were more interested in convenience, which was interpreted to mean getting the product quickly.

CONSULTANT RECOMMENDATIONS

The following are excerpts from the consultant's report:

We see a clear opportunity for Circuit City to build a prominent position in the consumer electronics segment of mail-order catalogs. There are, however, two basic strategies the Circuit City catalog could pursue.

First, Circuit City could develop a catalog with a similar format to its store operations; namely, guaranteed lowest price, low- to middle-line products across a wide spectrum of product categories, and high-volume sales with modest profit margins. The primary advantage to this approach is that it matches the strengths that Circuit City has built and demonstrated successfully. However, we believe that the following disadvantages make this strategy unattractive for implementation:

- This strategy has the greatest potential for cannibalizing current Circuit City sales, rather than adding incremental sales.
- The guaranteed lowest price would be extremely difficult to administer because the catalog would face price competition in virtually every part of the United States.
- There is a strong possibility that this strategy would fail to take full advantage of the higher margins mail order makes available through low overhead.
- If Circuit City wanted to modify the catalog's product mix in the future, it would be difficult to try to

upgrade the quality and prices of a catalog that has already built a discount image and reputation.

Conversely, a catalog that carried a top-of-the-line group of products not only avoids the disadvantages described above, but also offers several advantages to Circuit City:

- Circuit City would be able to build purchasing power in top-end products by expanding its base of sales for those items (this would allow Circuit City to offer some of these items in their high volume retail stores as well as in the catalog).
- Circuit City would have an opportunity to try new and different products on a limited basis without having to

EXHIBIT 7   Consultant's Report—Most Recent Consumer Electronics/Appliance Purchase

Most Recent Purchase	Percentage, Who Bought It through Mail Order	Percentage Who Had Considered Buying It through Mail Order	Percentage Who Had Owned/Tried the Product before Buying	Percentage Who Had Never Seen the Product before Buying
Stereo	72%	11%	30%	28%
Software	61	23	13	42
Telephone	46	23	32	39
Portable stereo	38	23	38	29
VCR	37	26	29	25
Peripherals	36	40	34	15
TV	9	44	36	26
Video games	9	46	64	0
Microwave	6	38	41	0

EXHIBIT 8   Consultant's Report—Consumer Electronics/Appliance Purchases in the Past Three Years

Product Category	Percentage Who Had Bought	
	Through Mail Order	Not Through Mail Order
Stereo component system	34%	32%
Telephone	24	44
Computer software	21	14
Computer peripherals	15	36
Portable stereo	9	27
VCR	6	18
Video game system	5	21
Television	3	36
Microwave oven	1	34

bump existing store products in favor of more uncertain items.

- This approach would place Circuit City in a market segment where the number one catalog (Sharper Image) has sales only a fraction of Circuit City's and where Circuit City could price lower than its major competitors without having to offer "rock bottom" prices.

To pursue this aggressive strategy in the top-of-the-line catalog market, we suggest that Circuit City develop their catalog along the following lines:

A. Products.
   1. The catalog should contain a select number of consumer electronics products from the top-end of Circuit City's current audio, video, telephonic, computer, and recording product categories. These products might not be available in Circuit City stores, and as such would supplement rather than compete with existing Circuit City sales. These products would represent approximately 90 percent of the catalog's contents.
   2. The catalog would also contain a few specialty, "one-of-a-kind" or "gadget" electronic items (video watches, for example). These would be high-margin, gift/impulse items and would compose 10 percent of the catalog. However, at Christmas time, a larger proportion of such items should be included in the catalog.

   3. At least 20 percent of the products in each issue of the catalog should be new items. This approach assures that the catalog remains interesting to the consumer.
B. Prices.
   1. Catalog prices should be slightly lower than competing specialty electronics/audio stores and catalogs. This should be feasible because of Circuit City's tremendous buying power. While top-of-the-line products can command price premiums, if consumers find identical products in different catalogs, lowest price determines which catalog gets their order.
   2. The catalog should not pursue a lowest-price guarantee, thus allowing margins well above those in the Circuit City stores, and avoiding the disadvantage discussed above.
   3. Catalog prices should include shipping costs, to insure that the face value of the Circuit City catalog price is the actual price paid by the consumer.
C. Layout.
   1. The name of the catalog should suggest exclusivity and high technology, with only a small reference to its association with Circuit City. This approach takes advantage of potential Circuit City name recognition without confusing the catalog with Circuit City's discount image. Examples of appropriate types of names are as follows:

EXHIBIT 9   Consultant's Report—Purchase Decision Criteria by Product

Product Purchased	Decision Criteria			
	Informative Salesperson	*Convenient Location*	*Outlet Reputation*	*Availability of Repairs*
Microwave oven	44*	31	44	69
Stereo	31	10	58	32
VCR	31	24	31	23
Peripherals	28	9	17	30
Television	21	21	37	33
Telephone	19	26	34	34
Video games	18	64	27	18
Software	17	20	30	20
Portable stereo	10	15	25	14

*To be read: "Of the respondents whose most recent consumer electronics/appliance purchase was a microwave oven, 44 percent rated 'informative salespeople' as 'extremely important' in their purchase decision."

a. The Cutting Edge, a division of Circuit City.

b. Uptown Electronics, a subdivision of Circuit City.

c. Select Customer Electronics, a subsidiary of Circuit City.

2. The outside dimensions of the catalog should be somewhat smaller than most catalogs (approximately 7'' × 10'' overall) because when catalogs are stacked on the consumer's coffee table, this smaller catalog will be placed on top of the larger 8½'' × 11'' catalogs published by Sharper Image, Markline, and so on.

3. The cover design should be uncluttered and clever. It should promote general interest rather than specific products. These covers will encourage the customer to open the catalog (clearly a critical step) and will help distinguish the catalog from other electronics catalogs which tend to print simply a barrage of products on their catalog covers.

4. The catalog should be relatively brief (between 24 and 48 pages), with four-color, high-gloss print, and with no more than two or three items per page. This format strongly supports an image of top quality and exclusivity.

5. The descriptions of each item should be as brief as possible for easy browsing, but appropriate to the price and complexity of the specific item.

D. Distribution.

1. The catalog should be mailed to a select number of Circuit City customers, based on their past history of buying top-end items or having spent a certain amount of money in the store, perhaps $500. This will limit the number of catalogs that will be sent, and more importantly, ensure that they are sent to segments of Circuit City customers that are most likely to purchase from the catalog.

2. The catalog should also be sent to people nationwide who have previous experience with consumer electronics through the mail, or who meet certain demographic characteristics as determined by our research. These people can be reached through one or more of the following methods:

a. Renting mailing lists from companies such as American Express, Crutchfield, or Sharper Image.

b. Placing advertisements with clip-out coupons for a free catalog in select national and/or regional magazines and newspapers.

c. Producing television ads that promote one product, but which include an opportunity to call in for a free catalog.

3. The initial mailing should be at least one million pieces, sent in late September/early October on a staggered basis (200,000 each week for five weeks). One million catalogs must be printed to achieve economies of scale in printing costs. The staggered mailing will help Circuit City administer the flow of orders since most of them will come soon after the catalog arrives in the customer's home.

4. The catalog should be updated on a quarterly basis, again with staggered mailings, to allow product-line changes and replace catalogs that have been discarded or forgotten.

E. Services.

1. Customers should be able to order items via mail, through a toll-free 800 number, or through a store. The first two are conveniences that catalog customers will expect. Use of the POS system would be an added convenience that Circuit City can provide as well, allowing store salespeople to sell catalog items not available in the stores.

2. Telephone salespeople should be trained to provide additional product information, encourage sale of related items, and promote extended warranty plans, in addition to taking orders. These talents will encourage consumers to purchase technical items that cannot be described fully in a few paragraphs; they will also allow Circuit City to achieve some of the trade-up and warranty sales often precluded by catalogs.

3. A 60-day, "no questions asked," return policy should be provided. A strong return policy is a major selling point for catalogs.

This strategy is highly aggressive and would entail significant start-up and operating costs. It will also provide significant returns to Circuit City. Based on only a 2 percent response rate on 1 million catalogs at an average of $120 per order (as seen in comparable catalogs), Circuit City would realize sales of $2.4 million.

We feel that Circuit City is particularly well suited to succeed with this aggressive approach for the following reasons:

a. Circuit City is substantially larger than the major players in the consumer electronics end of the mail-order industry (compare Circuit City's sales of $246 million to Sharper Image's sales of only $35 million).

b. Circuit City has the buying power to allow higher margins than other competitors in this segment. Thus, even if pricing becomes the major form of competition, Circuit City should be able to win out.

c. Circuit City already has some experience with catalogs and substantial experience in consumer electronics sales. Besides being a substantial plus in and of itself, its retail stores also give Circuit City immediate access to a substantial list of potential catalog customers.

CONCLUSIONS

Ed Kopf, who had been director of marketing when the study of mail order was commissioned, realized that this subject was one of important concern for long-range planning. He saw the need to watch developments in in-home shopping, but was unsure of their economic implications for Circuit City.

He knew that some firms whose business was primarily mail order, reported significantly higher profit ratios than did the average retailers. Firms that distributed principally through stores and that had treated mail order as an add-on usually were not able to develop detailed cost data to determine the bottom line profitability of mail order. Indications were, however, that the profit results were not so successful for retail store firms that added mail-order operations as for the firms that had always concentrated on mail order.

The costs to develop and distribute a mail-order catalog were reported from one source to be 40 cents per copy, with 1,500,000 mailed. The return (number of orders) ranged from below 2 percent to 5 percent of the mailings. A rule of thumb had been established in the business that a 2 percent return was needed to break even. To obtain a high number of returns as well as when a firm began a catalog operation, it was necessary to "rent" names from other mail-order firms through list brokers. The cost of names printed on pressure-sensitive labels ranged from $2.50 to $10.00 per thousand, depending usually on the quality of the list.

Ed wondered whether the Circuit City warehouse system could handle the mail orders, or whether it would be necessary to set up a separate warehouse for fulfillment of mail orders. But his biggest concern was when the time would be right for Circuit City to enter the rapidly growing mail-order market. And, if the firm were to decide to embark on this venture, what should be the extent of the merchandise offered and where should responsibility for the project lie in the Circuit City organization?

10.   *American Greetings*

"We're in touch" and the corporate rose logo identify the world's largest publicly owned manufacturer of greeting cards and related social-expression merchandise, American Greetings (AG). In 1981, President

---

This case was prepared by Dan Kopp and Lois Shufeldt of Southwest Missouri State University as a basis for class discussion rather than to illustrate either effective or ineffective administrative practices. The authors would like to acknowledge the cooperation and assistance of American Greetings. It was presented at the North American Case Research Association's annual meeting in November, 1987.

Morry Weiss announced the formulation of a corporate growth objective to achieve $1 billion in annual sales by 1985, which would represent a 60 percent increase over 1982 sales of $623.6 million. The battle for market share dominance between the two industry leaders, Hallmark and American Greetings, had escalated and intensified. Previously, the two leading firms peacefully coexisted by having mutually exclusive niches. Hallmark offered higher-priced, quality cards in department stores and card shops, and American Greetings offered inexpensive cards in mass-merchandise outlets. However, in 1977 American Greetings formulated a growth strategy to attack the industry leader and its niche.

THE GREETING CARD INDUSTRY

In 1985, Americans exchanged more than 7 billion cards—around 30 per person, marking the highest per capita card consumption ever. And with the average retail price per card of a dollar, that made "social expression" a $3.4 billion business. According to the Greeting Card Association, card senders gave 2.2 billion Christmas cards, 1.5 billion birthday cards, 850 million valentines, 180 million Easter cards, 140 million Mother's Day cards, 85 million Father's Day cards, 80 million graduation cards, 40 million Thanksgiving cards, 26 million Halloween cards, 16 million St. Patrick's Day cards, and about 10 million Grandparent's Day cards. Everyday, nonoccasion cards now account for more than half of all industry sales, and they're on the rise. People living in the northeast and north-central parts of the country buy more cards than average, and southerners 30 percent fewer. People who buy the majority of them tend to be between 35 and 54 years of age, come from large families, live in their own homes in the suburbs, and have an average household income of $30,000. Changes in society—demographic and social—are fueling the growth of alternative cards. These changes have included increases in the numbers of:

Blended families.

Single-parent households.

Working women.

Divorces and remarriages.

Population segments which traditionally have included the heaviest greeting card users—35 to 65 year olds (baby-boom generation approaching the peak card purchasing age).

Women purchase over 90 percent of all greeting cards. Women enjoy browsing and shopping for cards, and tend to purchase a card only if it is appropriate, when the card's verse and design combine to convey the sentiment she wishes to express. However, because an increasing number of women are working, these women are shopping less frequently and buying less impulse merchandise.

The growth rate for the industry has been 5 to 6 percent annually over the past several years. Sales of unorthodox cards aimed at 18 to 35-year-old baby-boomers have grown 25 percent a year. However, sales of greeting cards for the past few quarters have been lackluster. The industry is mature; sales are stagnant at about 7 billion units. According to *Chain Store Age,* the channels of distribution have been moving away from speciality stores to mass merchants. Now, department stores are cutting back square footage and dropping cards altogether. Mass market appeal now has growth—one-stop shopping. Hallmark has been pushing its Ambassador line through mass merchants such as Wal-Mart and Target, in addition to diversifying into other areas.

AG is concentrating on the social expressions business; it has launched a massive national television advertising campaign to firmly position itself in all aspects of the greeting card industry. On the other hand, Hallmark, whose recent acquisitions are unrelated to the social expressions industry, is shifting its emphasis. Irvine O. Hockaday, Hallmark's CEO, said recently that he prefers outside businesses to contribute 40 percent of total Hallmark revenues, instead of the 10 percent it now contributes. Cards accounted for 64 percent of AG's 1985 sales. According to some industry experts, Hallmark is now playing follow the leader in card innovations and character licensing.

Overall slowdown in retail. traffic has resulted in reduced sales. Generally, there is a soft retailing environment. The retailing industry is overstored and promotion oriented, which may result in retailers asking greeting card suppliers for lower prices to assist them in keeping their margins from shrinking. Retailers are losing their loyalty to manufacturers that supply a full line of products—cards, gift wrap, and so on, and are looking instead for the lowest cost supplier of each, according to Kidder, Peabody & Company. The competition in the industry has become and will continue to be intensified, especially in the areas of price, sales promotion, distribution, and selling.

More new cards have been introduced in 1986 than in any other previous year, according to the Greeting Card Association. More "feelings" type of cards, such as the In Touch line by AG, have been introduced. Since men buy only 10 percent of all cards sold, they are the prime target for many of the new types of cards.

Hallmark and AG are experimenting with different styles, fabricating novel reasons for people to buy their wares and using new technology that enables cards to play tunes or talk. According to *Time,* Hallmark offers 1,200 varieties of cards for Mother's Day, while AG boasts of 1,300. The product ranges from a traditional card with a picture of flowers and syrupy poetry for $1 or less to a $7 electronic version which plays the tune, "You Are the Sunshine of My Life."

Hallmark has introduced several lines of personal relationship-oriented cards, commemorating such milestones as the wedding anniversary of a parent and a stepparent. In 1984, Hallmark introduced its Honesty Collection, which has been discontinued, with messages that reflected the nature of modern-day relationships. In May of 1985, AG's primary competitor brought out its Personal Touch line of cards, with intimate, conversational prose displayed on the front and with no message inside. The Greeting Card Association found that 83 percent of all card senders do something—add a snapshot or a newspaper clipping or jot a note—to personalize a card, and Hallmark has been quick to supply a vehicle to take advantage of this opportunity.

Forbes has reported that there are more than 400 firms in the greeting card industry, but the two major ones, Hallmark and American Greetings, control approximately 75 percent of the market. Gibson Greetings is the third major firm in the industry. Approximate market shares for the three industry leaders have been:

Company	1985	1984	1977
Hallmark	40–45%	45%	50%
AG	30–35	33	24
Gibson	8–10	NA	5

Analysts expect AG to keep increasing its market share. Over the last five years, unit growth rate at AG has been 4 to 5 percent a year, against industrywide growth rate of 1 to 2 percent. Industry expert, E. Gray Glass III, of Kidder, Peabody & Company, has indicated that AG has been showing good growth at 15 percent or better annually. Furthermore, *Chain Store Age* has projected that AG will continue to take some of Hallmark's market share, but that it will take a long time for AG to pass it.

The New York Times has reported that Hallmark has been successful in freestanding card shops, which account for about 40 percent of all greeting cards sold. Fastest growth for AG has been big drugstores and supermarket chains. Growth has been slower at variety stores, traditional department stores, and gift shops, which account for about 30 percent of AG sales.

According to *Investor's Daily,* AG and Hallmark have been increasing their market shares at the expense of smaller card companies, which have been forced out of the market due to the high costs of selling, distributing, and marketing, as well as the lack of extensive computerized inventory monitoring systems that only large companies can afford. Industry analysts, however have predicted that small firms, with a focus niche and geographic area, will continue to enter the industry and can be profitable.

Richard H. Connor, AG executive vice president, stated that AG has been gaining ground on Hallmark, although he wouldn't say by how much:

> If you compare the businesses that are similar with both companies, we are closing the gap. Between the both of us, we have 75 percent of the market, and some of our growth must be at their expense.

Both Hallmark and AG are being challenged by Gibson, which is the fastest-growing company in the industry. Gibson scored a coup with Walt Disney Productions when they secured the rights to use Mickey Mouse and his friends, who previously had been featured by Hallmark. Gibson also has licensed Garfield the Cat and Sesame Street characters, but Hallmark's line of Peanuts cards remains one of the industry's most successful.

HISTORY OF AMERICAN GREETINGS

The story of American Greetings is one of the "American Dream" of an immigrant from Poland who came to the land of promised opportunity to seek his fortune. Jacob Sapirstein was born in 1884 in Wasosz, Poland, and because of the Russian-Japanese war of 1904, was sent by his widowed mother, along with his seven brothers and one sister to live in America.

Jacob, also known as J. S., began his one-man business buying postcards made in Germany from wholesalers and selling them to candy, novelty, and drugstores in Cleveland in 1906. From a horse-drawn card wagon, the small venture steadily flourished.

J. S. and his wife, Jennie, also a Polish immigrant, had three sons and a daughter; all three sons became active in their father's business. At the age of nine, Irving, the oldest, kept the family business afloat while

J. S. was recovering from the flu during the great epidemic of 1918. The business had out-grown the family living room and was moved to a garage at this time.

J. S. had a basic philosophy of service to the retailer and a quality product for the consumer. He developed the first wire wall rack as well as rotating floor stands to make more attractive, convenient displays. In the 1930s the Sapirstein Card Company began to print its own cards to ensure the quality of its product. The name of the company was changed to American Greeting Publishers to reflect the national stature and functioning of the company. Their first published line of cards under the American Greetings name, the Forget Me Not Line, went on sale in 1939 for a nickel. One card, which remains the company's all time best seller, was designed by Irving.

The company saw great expansion throughout the 1940s, as loved ones found the need to communicate with World War II soldiers. The most significant effect of this was the widespread use of greeting cards by the soldiers. In the past, cards had been primarily a product utilized by women, thus the expansion to the male market was a significant breakthrough for the card industry.

The 1950s marked the first public offering of stock and the name change to American Greetings Corporation. Ground was broken for a new world headquarters, which led the way for expansion to world markets. The company made connections with several foreign markets and acquired a Canadian plant.

In 1960, J. S. stepped down at the age of 76. His son, Irving, succeeded him as president. Under Irving's leadership and with the assistance of his brothers, Morris and Harry Stone (all three brothers had changed their names from Sapirstein, meaning sapphire, to Stone in 1940 for business reasons), the company has continued to expand into gift wrapping, party goods, calendars, stationery, candles, ceramics and perhaps, most importantly, the creation of licensed characters.

Expansion into these related items has somewhat diminished AG's recession proof profits. Greeting card sales typically increase during recessions as people refrain from gift buying and instead remember others with a less expensive card. The supplemental items now constitute one third of the company's sales, not enough to seriously jeopardize AG during down economies, but greatly augment the company's sales during good economic times.

AG's world expansion became a major pursuit throughout the 1960s and 1970s. Morry Weiss, a grandson-in-law of J. S., became the new president of AG in 1978 with Irving continuing to act as the CEO and chairman of the board of directors. Morris Stone continues to serve as vice chairman of the board, and Harry Stone remains as an active board member.

OBJECTIVES

In 1981 at the first national sales meeting ever held by AG, President Morry Weiss announced the formulation of a major corporate objective: to achieve $1 billion in annual sales by 1985. During fiscal 1985, AG strengthened its position as a leader in the industry; that year marked the 79th consecutive year of increased revenue—total revenue increased to $945.7 million, while net income increased to $74.4 million. This record of success represented:

A 300% increase in total revenue during the past 10 years.

A 613% increase in net income during the past 10 years.

A 315% increase in dividends per share in the past 10 years, with two increases in fiscal 1985.

According to Morry Weiss, president and chief operating officer:

AG today is positioning itself for transition from a greeting company to a total communications company. For years, AG was thought of only as a greeting card maker. That narrow description no longer applies to the world's largest, publicly-owned manufacturer of greeting cards and related social-expression merchandise. Today we are diversified into other major product lines, including gift wrap, candles, stationery, ceramics, party goods, and calendars. In addition, we lead the industry in licensing characters, such as Holly Hobbie, Ziggy, Strawberry Shortcake, Care Bears and Care Bear Cousins, which are featured on thousands of retail products and on television and in motion pictures.

Irving Stone, chairman of the board and chief executive officer added:

AG is aggressively pursuing growth in their core business, concentrating specifically on increasing market share and unit volume, and continued margin. We'll grow through our retailers by providing the programs that will generate sales and make the greeting card department the most profitable area in their store. We'll grow through our consumers by understanding their needs and providing them with products they want and enjoy buying. We'll grow by constantly improving our operations and productivity through creativity, innovation, and technology.

He further added:

We expect growth and are planning for it throughout the corporation. In the past four years we have invested heavily in increased capacity, plant expansion, new equipment, and new technology. Almost two years ago, we completed an equity offering that substantially strengthened our financial position; an additional offering is not expected in the near future. Today we see no problem financing our growth while at the same time increasing our dividends.

A flurry of acquisitions occurred in the 1980s. A full list of subsidiaries, as well as AG's international operations is displayed in Exhibit 1.

MARKETING STRATEGIES

Product

AG produces a wide product line including greeting cards, gift wrap, party goods, toys and gift items. Greeting cards accounted for 66 percent of the company's 1986 fiscal sales. The breakdown of sales by major product categories is as follows:

Everyday greeting cards	37%
Holiday greeting cards	29
Gift wrap and party goods	18
Consumer products (toys, etc.)	7
Stationary	9

It is the belief of AG that one of the keys to increased sales is to have a product line that offers a wide variety and selection of cards, such that a consumer can always find the right card for that special person. Each year AG offers more new products than ever before. The creative department produces over 20,000 different designs to ensure the wide selection.

AG's creative staff is one of largest assemblages of artistic talent in the world. The department has over 400 designers, artists, and writers who are guided by the latest research data available from computer analysis, consumer testing, and information from AG's sales and merchandising departments. Careful monitoring of societal changes, fashion and color trends, and consumer preferences provides further guidance to product development. AG also gives uncompromising adherence to quality—in papers, inks, and printing procedures.

AG pioneered licensing and now dominates the industry of character licensing. Their strategy has been to maximize the potential of their creative and marketing expertise. Holly Hobbie was the first licensed character in 1968; Ziggy in 1971, and Strawberry Shortcake in 1980. When introduced, Strawberry Shortcake was the most popular new character in licensing history. Sales for Strawberry Shortcake will soon exceed $1 billion in retail sales, a revenue larger than that of any other character. In 1983 AG introduced Care Bears and Herself the Elf. The product was launched with General Mills and 23 licensees supported by an $8 million advertising and promotional campaign, including a half-hour animated television special. The Care Bears license identifies 10 adorable cuddlies, each with a sentiment message on its tummy.

Another licensing creation, Popples, added a new dimension to a field crowded with look-alikes. Popples literally "pops-out" from a plush ball to a lovable, furry, playmate. A plush toy that folds into its own pouch, Popples enables children to make its arms, legs, and fluffy tail appear and disappear at will. Two new toys from AmToy are reaching another new and undercultivated market: My Pet Monster and Madballs. They were the hits of 1986s Toy Fair show. These creatures are designed to delight the millions of young boys who prefer the bizarre to the cuddly. Forty companies initially signed up to manufacture other products such as clothing, knapsacks, and books featuring the characters. AG and Mattel spent about $10 million promoting the characters, including a half hour Popples television special. The licensed product industry is $50 billion strong.

EXHIBIT 1   Corporate Directory

Board of Directors	*Corporate Officers*	*American Greetings Division*
Jacob Sapirstein, Founder	**Irving I. Stone,** Chairman, Chief Executive Officer	**Richard H. Connor,** Executive Vice President
Irving I. Stone,* Chairman, Chief Executive Officer	**Morris S. Stone,** Vice Chairman	**William E. Schmitt,** Group Vice President–Marketing
Morris S. Stone,* Vice Chairman	**Morry Weiss,** President, Chief Operating Officer	**Robert C. Swilik,** Group Vice President Manufacturing
Morry Weiss,* President, Chief Operating Officer	**Richard H. Connor,** Executive Vice President American Greetings Division	**James Van Arsdale,** Group Vice President–Operations
Hugh Calkins† Partner, Jones, Day, Reavis & Pogue (attorneys-at-law)	**Morton Wyman,** Executive Vice President	**H. David Bender,** Vice President Information Services
Herbert H. Jacobs, (personal investments and consultant)	**Rubin Feldman,** Senior Vice President	**Edward F. Doherty,** Vice President–Manufacturing/ Everyday Division
Frank E. Joseph,† Attorney and Secretary. Kulas Foundation (philanthropic foundation)	**Henry Lowenthal,** Senior Vice President Chief Financial Officer	**James H. Edler,** Vice President Materials Management
Millard B. Opper† Retired Chairman of Canadian Operations	**Packy Nespeca,** Senior Vice President Corporate Trade Development	**John T. Fortner,** Vice President–Manufacturing/ Seasonal Division
Albert B. Ratner,† President, Forest City Enterprises, Inc., (real estate, construction and retail operations)	**Al J. Stenger,** Senior Vice President International & Subsidiary Operations	**Edward Fruchtenbaum,** Vice President Marketing Administration
Harry H. Stone,† President Courtland Management, Inc. (personal investments), Chairman Barks Williams Oil	**Dale J. Beinker,** Vice President International	**David J. Gamble,** Vice President Inventory and Quality Control
Milton A. Wolf, Former U.S. Ambassador to Austria (personal investments)	**Raymond P. Kenny,** Vice President Strategic Planning	**Gary E. Johnston,** Vice President–Creative
Morton Wyman* Executive Vice President	**Ralph L. White,** Vice President Chief Human Resource Officer	**David R. Ledvina,** Vice President Computer Operations
	Allan J. Goodfellow, General Counsel and Secretary	**William R. Mason,** Vice President General Sales Manager
	John M. Klipfell, Controller	**William R. Parsons,** Vice President–Chain Sales
	Eugene B. Scherry, Treasurer	**Ronald J. Peer,** Vice President–Field Sales
		Joy E. Sweeney Vice President–Primary, Product Management
		Kenneth J. Valore, Vice President–Finance
		Gordon Van Over, Vice President–Consumer Product Management
		George A. Wenz, Vice President National Accounts

*Member of Executive Committee.
†Member of Audit Committee.

EXHIBIT 1 (*concluded*)

International and Subsidiary Operations

United States:

A. G. Industries, Inc.
Cleveland, Ohio
Charles H. Nervig, President
AmToy, Inc.
New York, New York
Larry Freiberg, President
Drawing Board Greeting Cards, Inc.
Dallas, Texas
Selwin Belofsky, President
Plus Mark, Inc.
Greeneville, Tennessee
Ronald E. Clouse, President
The Summit Corporation
Berlin, Connecticut
Robert P. Chase, President
Those Characters From Cleveland, Inc.
Cleveland, Ohio
John S. Chojnacki, Thomas A. Wilson, Co-Presidents
Tower Products Company, Inc.
Chicago, Illinois
Melvin Mertz, President

Canada:

Carlton Cards Ltd.
Toronto, Ontario
William L. Powell, President and Chairman of Canadian Operations
Plus Mark Canada
Toronto, Ontario
Richard L. Krelstein, President
Rust Craft Canada, Inc.
Scarborough, Ontario
Gary Toporoski, Vice President, Managing Director

Continental Euorpe:

Richard C. Schulte
Director of Operations
Grako Oy
Helsinki, Finland
Risto Pitkanen, Managing Director
A/S Muva Grafiske Produkter
Oslo, Norway
Aage Dahl, Managing Director
Muva Greetings B.V.
Heerlen, The Netherlands
Huub Robroeks, General Manager
Susy Card
Hamburg, West Germany
Charles Wightman, Managing Director

Mexico:

Felicitaciones Nacionales S.A. de C.V.
Mexico City, Mexico
Antonio Felix G., President

Monaco:

Rust Craft International S.A.
Michel Bourda, Managing Director

United Kingdom:

Rust Craft Greeting Cards (U.K.) Ltd.
Dewsbury, England
David M. Beards, Managing Director and Chairman of U.K. Operations
Andrew Valentine Holdings Ltd.
Dundee, Scotland
Alistair R. L. Mackay, Managing Director
Celebration Arts Group Ltd.
Corby, England
W. George Pomphrett, Managing Director
Denison Colour Ltd.
Guiseley, England
Brian Holliday, Managing Director

Source: American Greetings.

According to *Forbes,* all of AG licensed characters have not been successful. One flop, Herself the Elf, was perceived by retailers as being too much like Strawberry Shortcake; it also missed the Christmas season because of production problems. Another failure was Get Along Gang, which tried to appeal to both little girls and boys.

Distribution

AG distributes its products through 90,000 retail outlets located throughout the free world, which has increased from 80,000 in 1983. Additionally, there has been growth in the channels of distribution where AG is dominant. Consumers have been seeking greater convenience and one-stop shopping, channels in which AG is strong—chain drugstores, chain supermarkets, and mass merchandise retailers. Thirty-nine percent of AG sales went to drug stores, with the remaining sales (in order of rank) going to mass merchandisers, supermarkets, stationery and gift shops, variety stores, military post exchanges, combo stores (food, general merchandise, and gift items), and department stores. During the last five years, sales to drug, variety, and department stores as a percent of total revenue have declined, while sales to supermarkets, mass merchandisers, combo store, and military post exchange units have increased, while stationery and gift shops have remained constant.

Promotion

In 1982, AG became recognized nationwide, first through television commercials and then through a new corporate identity program. The new logo is now featured prominently at retail outlets; the updated corporate rose logo is now a standard and highly recognizable feature greeting AG customers on all product packaging, store signage, point of purchase displays, and even their truck fleet. The year-round advertising campaign included the promotion of the major card-sending holidays and nonseasonal occasions during daytime and prime-time programming.

Supporting marketing is a promotional generator out of which flows seasonal and special displays, special signs, sales catalogs, national television advertising, media and trade journal exposure, television programming and special events featuring AG's exclusive characters. Results can be seen in increased support for AG's sales personnel, greater consumer awareness, improved relations with retail dealers, greater visibility within the financial community and improved relations with employees and communities where plant facilities are operating.

The aim of AG's national consumer advertising and public relations programs is to remind people to send cards, in that one of AG's chief competitors is consumer forgetfulness. AG is the only company in the industry to sponsor national consumer retail promotions. These consumer-directed programs serve to establish brand identity and generate retail store traffic.

In 1983 AG employed 1,600 full-time salespeople, in addition to 7,000 part-timers, all of whom have been directed through 15 regional and 66 district sales offices

in the United States, the United Kingdom, Canada, Mexico, and France. AG employs a large force of retail store merchandisers who visit each department at regular intervals to ensure that every pocket in every display is kept filled with appropriate merchandise.

The AG sales force is meeting the unique and challenging needs of their customers; no other company in the industry has sales and marketing personnel assigned to specific channels of distribution to give retailers the advantage of working with specialists who understand their markets, their customers, and their specific marketing needs.

The success of AG's aggressive marketing programs is explained by William E. Schmitt, group vice president, marketing:

> First we have the creativity to develop the best products in the industry. Every year we prove this with new characters, new card lines, and other products and programs that attract consumers and increase sales for our customers and ourselves. Second, we have a close relationship with our customers. The retailer support programs we offer—including terms, display fixtures, advertising and merchandising programs, promotion support and inventory controls—are unsurpassed in the industry.

Programs are tailored for individual retailers to help plan their greeting card locations, department sizes, and displays. AG shows the retailers how to merchandise innovative ideas and enhance visibility by means of proven promotional programs.

Computer technology is helping AG's salespeople to project retailers' needs better, which has resulted in improved sell-through of the product at retail. MIS, the data processing unit for the AG Division, is playing a vital role in increasing sales for AG's products at the retail level. In 1984, AG began implementing a computer-to-computer reordering system which allows retail accounts to control inventories and turnaround time by electronic transfer of data to AG's headquarters data center.

Good retail presentation is a key to card sales; AG has created a unique identification for the greeting cards department. It is called the Total Retail Environment, and it uses a completely planned and coordinated approach to integrate display cabinets, signage, lighting, product packaging, and even products to create a stunning new AG look. The purposes of this new system are to establish greater consumer awareness of the AG card department, to provide a distinctive look and appeal, and to provide an attractive and enjoyable place to shop.

AG also possesses the most favorable terms-of-sale program in the industry. To improve the retailer's return on inventory investment, AG has successful merchandising plans, retail store merchandisers, and computerized inventory controls. AG also sports a direct product profitability (DPP) concept to evaluate productivity and space allocation for products in stores. DPP takes gross margin and return on inventory investment analysis a step further by reflecting revenue after allowances and discounts and subtracting all costs attributable to the product, including labor and freight. AG's salespeople can then demonstrate to retailers that their greeting card department returns a high rate of profit for the space allocated.

Richard H. Connor, AG executive vice president recently announced:

> To increase market share, AG revamped its sales force and created one sales department that specializes in independent retail accounts and another sales department that specializes in selling to retail chains. A third department will stock and service all types of accounts. This will give greater selling strength where it's needed and lowers our selling costs.

AG has created a New Retail Communications Network (RCTN) which conducts research that will better enable AG to identify for accounts the appropriate products to meet the needs of their customers. Data are compiled by monitoring product sales and space productivity from a chain of nationwide test stores that encompasses all demographic and geographic variables and represents all channels of distribution. The RCTN then interprets data as it would apply to an account's specifications, including type of store, size, location, and consumer profile. This total merchandising approach to achieving maximum sales and space potential is unique in the industry.

PRODUCTION STRATEGIES

AG has 49 plants and facilities in the United States, Canada, Continental Europe, Mexico, Monaco, and the United Kingdom.

AG has been concerned with reducing production costs in order to remain the industry's lowest cost producer through efficient manufacturing operations while maintaining quality and service to their customers. According to Robert C. Swilik, group vice president, manufacturing:

> Improved control of our manufacturing process through planning and scheduling enable us to improve productivity, reduce manufacturing costs and reduce inventory. Increased productivity is the result of our growing sense of shared responsibility. The relationship between management and the work force is excellent.

Quality improvements have been consistently made. Some of the major improvements have been:

1. Upgraded die cutting and embossing capabilities with the purchase of nine high-speed Bobst presses costing $1 million each.
2. Added capacity to the hot stamping and thermography operations.
3. Streamlined order filling in both everyday and seasonal operations.
4. Completed a 200,000-square-foot warehouse addition to the Osceola, Arkansas, plant and began operations on an addition to the Ripley, Tennessee, plant, which increased its capacity by 20 percent.
5. Installed a Scitex system that will dramatically improve product quality and increase productivity; new electronic pre-press system enables the creative department to interact with manufacturing at the creatively crucial pre-press stage.
6. Installed additional high-speed and more powerful presses to further improve quality of die cutting and embossing at the Bardstown, Kentucky, plant; a 300,000-square-foot addition is also planned.
7. Installed new computer graphics system called Via Video for design and layout functions for a variety of in-house publications and brochures (this gives the artist freedom to create while quickly and inexpensively exploring options and alternatives, thus increasing productivity).

PERSONNEL STRATEGIES

American Greetings currently employs over 20,000 people in the United States, Canada, Mexico, and Europe.

According to Morry Weiss, AG is deeply concerned about management succession:

Our young executives are being developed to succeed retiring senior officers. Last year, more managment movement occurred than in any of the preceding five years. The Stone family built and developed the company. However, managing this dynamic business today presents challenges beyond the capability of any one or two persons. Thus, over the past 10 years, the management of AG has been changing from a singular head to a broad-based management group. We have broadened decision-making authority. Each business unit has been given stretch goals and responsibility for achieving those goals. Units are preparing strategic plans and are vying for corporate resources based upon projections of growth and profitability.

According to Robert C. Swilik, group vice president:

Relationship between management and the work force is excellent. We have never had a strike in any of our plants, and we plan to work on keeping that harmonious spirit alive. We will expand an employee involvement program that brings all levels of employees into greater participation.

MANAGEMENT

In 1983, AG underwent a major management restructuring to permit top officers of the company more time to concentrate on strategic planning. The company was reorganized from a centralized structure to a divisional profit center basis. Each division has its own budget committee, while an executive management committee comprised of five senior executives approves the strategic plans for all the divisions. Strategic plans are established in 1-, 3-, 10-, and 20-year time frames. Corporate AG maintains strict budgetary and accounting controls.

The basic domestic greeting card business was placed under the AG Division. Foreign and U.S. subsidiaries and the licensing division have become a second unit, with corporate management a third. Restructuring has allowed corporate management to step back from day-to-day operations and focus on the growth of American Greetings beyond the $1 billion annual revenue.

According to Irving Stone:

The prime function of corporate managment is to plan and manage the growth of the entire corporation, developing capable management and allocating corporate resources to those units offering the greatest potential return on investment. Greeting cards has been our basic business for 78 years and remains today our largest business unit; there are smaller business units, which complement the greeting card business and are deserving of our attention.

American Greetings is composed of the following divisions:

American Greetings Division. Encompasses core business of greeting cards and related products, including manufacturing, sales, merchandising, research, and administrative services. Produces and distributes greeting cards and related products domestically. Same products are distributed throughout the world by international subsidiaries and licensees.

Foreign and Domestic Subsidiaries. Two wholly owned companies in Canada, four in the United Kingdom, six in Continental Europe, and one in Mexico. Licensees use AG designs and verses in almost every free country in the world. Subdivisions include:

Canadian Operations. Carlton Cards and Rust Craft, two companies.

United Kingdom Operations. British are largest per capita senders of greeting cards in the world. Three AG companies in the UK—Rust Craft, Celebration Arts, and Andrew Valentine.

Continental European Operations. Five companies wholly owned.

Those Characters from Cleveland. Licensing division of AG. Characters and new television series, The Get Along Gang.

Plus Mark. Began producing Christmas promotional products such as gift wrap, ribbon, bows, and boxed Christmas cards in an industry selling primarily to mass merchandisers.

AmToy. Sells novelties, dolls, and plush toys.

AG Industries. Produces display cabinet fixtures in wood, metal, or plastic for all AG retail accounts and growing list of external clients.

Exhibit 1 provides a corporate directory of management personnel and their divisional assignments.

FINANCE STRATEGIES

Exhibits 2–4 contain relevant financial information of American Greetings. The financial condition of AG has been exemplary over the years. However, AG's financial

EXHIBIT 2

AMERICAN GREETINGS
Consolidated Statements of Financial Position
As of February 28
(in thousands)

	1986	1985	1984	1983	1982
Assets					
Current assets:					
Cash and equivalents	$ 26,853	$ 66,363	$ 62,551	$ 19,950	$ 3,367
Trade accounts receivable, less allowances for sales returns of $57,382 ($42,198 in 1985) and for doubtful accounts of $3,378 ($2,900 in 1985)	240,471	173,637	146,896	148,018	131,996
Inventories:					
Raw material	59,343	59,197	48,738	47,636	53,515
Work in process	60,179	53,728	43,929	54,756	52,214
Finished products	181,237	152,543	139,275	122,167	97,221
	300,759	265,468	231,942	224,559	202,950
Less LIFO reserve	76,552	71,828	63,455	59,345	55,051
	224,207	193,640	168,487	165,214	147,899
Display material and factory supplies	26,826	20,809	11,532	12,245	11,724
Total inventories	251,033	214,449	180,019	177,459	159,623
Deferred income taxes	36,669	33,016	26,517	24,847	18,014
Prepaid expenses and other	6,228	4,795	4,187	3,524	2,057
Total current assets	561,254	492,260	420,170	373,798	315,057
Other assets	47,085	31,634	34,820	32,866	22,063
Property, plant and equipment:					
Land	7,523	6,822	6,621	5,427	3,380
Buildings	165,241	143,671	133,868	118,598	110,479
Equipment and fixtures	222,718	182,101	158,507	133,731	115,927
	395,482	332,594	298,996	257,756	229,786
Less accumulated depreciation and amortization	130,519	108,591	95,092	83,745	75,052
Property, plant and equipment—net	264,963	224,003	203,904	174,011	154,734
	$873,302	$747,897	$658,894	$580,675	$491,854

(continued)

EXHIBIT 2 *(concluded)*

AMERICAN GREETINGS
Consolidated Statements of Financial Position
As of February 28
(in thousands)

	1986	1985	1984	1983	1982
Liabilities and Shareholders' Equity					
Current liabilities:					
Notes payable to banks	$ 15,921	$ 4,574	$ 4,647	$ 29,836	$ 4,564
Accounts payable	66,685	56,840	52,302	40,568	39,016
Payroll and payroll taxes	28,675	26,761	23,160	16,914	17,224
Retirement plans	11,697	12,612	10,362	7,405	5,696
State and local taxes	2,763	2,796	2,811	2,448	3,278
Dividends payable	5,317	4,622	3,304	2,641	1,918
Income taxes	18,988	27,465	23,672	8,841	12,177
Sales returns	23,889	21,822	17,795	16,423	9,241
Current maturities of long-term debt	4,786	4,359	6,432	6,998	6,531
Total current liabilities	178,721	161,851	144,485	132,074	99,645
Long-term debt	147,592	112,876	119,941	111,066	148,895
Deferred income taxes	64,025	47,422	28,972	21,167	15,530
Shareholders' equity					
Common shares— par value $1:					
Class A	29,203	28,835	28,397	27,996	12,293
Class B	2,982	3,046	3,070	3,080	1,413
Capital in excess of par value	93,055	87,545	80,428	76,851	37,690
Cumulative translation adjustment	(16,801)	(13,688)	(9,158)	(7,179)	(3,829)
Retained earnings	374,525	320,010	262,759	215,620	180,217
Total shareholders' equity	482,964	425,748	365,496	316,368	227,784
	$873,302	$747,897	$658,894	$580,675	$491,854

Source: American Greetings.

EXHIBIT 3

AMERICAN GREETINGS
Consolidated Statements of Income
Years ended February 28 or 29
(in thousands of dollars except per share amounts)

	1986	1985	1984	1983	1982	1981
Net sales	$1,012,451	$919,371	$817,329	$722,431	$605,970	$489,213
Other income	23,200	26,287	22,585	20,252	17,634	9,059
Total revenue	1,035,651	945,658	839,914	742,683	623,604	498,272
Costs and expenses:						
Material, labor and other production costs	416,322	377,755	339,988	310,022	276,071	222,993
Selling, distribution and marketing	308,745	274,095	246,456	217,022	179,021	140,733
Administrative and general	131,928	123,750	112,363	96,012	76,494	61,033
Depreciation and amortization	23,471	18,799	15,507	13,890	12,752	10,863
Interest	19,125	15,556	16,135	24,086	21,647	13,548
	899,591	809,955	730,449	661,032	565,985	449,170
Income before income taxes	136,060	135,703	109,465	81,651	57,619	49,102
Income taxes	61,635	61,338	49,807	37,069	24,776	22,587
Net income	$ 74,425	$ 74,365	$ 59,658	$ 44,582	$ 32,843	$ 26,515
Net income per share	$ 2.32	$ 2.35	$ 1.91	$ 1.54	$ 1.20	$ .97

Source: American Greetings.

EXHIBIT 4

AMERICAN GREETINGS
Selected Financial Data
Years ended February 28 or 29
(in thousands of dollars except per share amounts)

	1986	1985	1984	1983	1982
Summary of operations:					
Total revenue:					
As reported	$ 1,035,651	$ 945,658	$ 839,914	$ 742,683	$ 623,604
Adjusted for general inflation*	1,035,651	979,399	906,904	827,715	737,611
Material, labor and other production					
costs	416,322	377,755	339,988	310,022	276,071
Depreciation and amortization	23,471	18,799	15,507	13,890	12,752
Interest expense	19,125	15,556	16,135	24,086	21,647
Net income:					
As reported	74,425	74,365	59,658	44,582	32,843
Adjusted for specific inflation*	63,630	63,860	52,298	34,817	21,349
Net income per share:					
As reported	2.32	2.35	1.91	1.54	1.20
Adjusted for specific inflation*	1.98	2.02	1.67	1.20	.78
Cash dividends per share:					
As reported	.62	.54	.40	.31	.27
Adjusted for general inflation*	.62	.56	.43	.35	.32
Fiscal year end market price per share:					
As reported	35.62	33.06	23.69	18.69	9.63
Adjusted for general inflation*	35.05	33.75	25.16	20.60	11.03
Purchasing power gain from holding net					
monetary liabilities*	1,843	1,438	1,784	4,739	9,366
Increase (decrease) in value of assets					
adjusted for specific inflation					
compared to general inflation*	(5,642)	(16,067)	(10,605)	2,693	(4,981)
Translation adjustment*	(3,653)	(5,881)	(2,289)	(4,701)	(3,867)
Average number of shares outstanding...	32,059,851	31,629,418	31,240,455	28,967,092	27,352,342
Average consumer price index	322.2	311.1	298.4	289.1	272.4
Financial position:					
Accounts receivable:	$ 240,471	$ 173,637	$ 146,896	$ 148,018	$ 131,996
Inventories	251,033	214,449	180,019	177,459	159,623
Working capital	382,533	330,409	275,685	241,724	215,412
Total assets......................	873,302	747,897	685,894	580,675	491,854
Capital additions	61,799	43,575	46,418	33,967	26,720
Long-term debt	147,592	112,876	119,941	111,066	148,895
Shareholders' equity:					
As reported	482,964	425,748	365,496	316,368	227,784
Adjusted for specific inflation*	642,767	602,350	559,395	518,955	432,781
Shareholders' equity per share	15.01	13.35	11.62	10.18	8.31
Net return on average					
shareholders' equity..............	16.5%	19.2%	17.8%	17.1%	15.4%
Pre-tax return on total revenue	13.1%	14.4%	13.0%	11.0%	9.2%

*In average fiscal 1986 dollars.

Source: American Greetings.

1981	1980	1979	1978	1977	1976
$ 498,272	$ 427,469	$ 373,487	$ 315,644	$ 277,985	$ 255,770
650,499	633,535	615,852	560,333	525,318	511,223
222,993	190,135	161,654	131,769	118,252	114,190
10,863	10,070	8,453	7,544	6,982	6,328
13,548	9,716	5,911	3,935	5,423	4,970
26,515	25,638	22,911	19,926	16,787	14,601
17,495	23,024				
.97	.94	.84	.73	.62	.53
.64	.84				
.26	.25	.22	.19	.15	.13
.34	.37	.36	.34	.28	.26
5.50	5.69	5.75	5.25	4.69	5.07
6.87	7.99	9.12	9.08	8.68	9.83
9,391	9,750				
(15,935)	9,625				
27,314,594	27,302,686	27,293,376	27,292,036	27,292,484	27,292,484
246.8	217.4	195.4	181.5	170.5	161.2
$ 114,051	$ 76,629	$ 67,651	$ 54,634	$ 48,920	$ 53,258
133,836	112,279	98,075	71,581	53,741	52,581
167,772	135,443	119,421	98,188	90,308	99,643
433,204	344,395	305,746	256,297	247,503	233,572
22,768	34,516	25,205	20,586	7,630	15,150
113,486	75,994	54,845	45,929	41,855	66,048
205,550	186,043	167,168	150,242	135,370	122,608
422,991	421,248				
7.52	6.81	6.12	5.51	4.96	4.49
13.7%	14.6%	14.5%	14.0%	13.0%	12.5%
9.9%	11.2%	12.0%	13.3%	11.7%	10.2%

performance in 1986 was disappointing, with revenue growth estimated to be at 7 percent and earnings to be similar to those of 1985. AG's revenue and earnings growth rate for the previous five years increased at compound annual rates of 17 percent and 29 percent, respectively. AG's stock declined sharply after the disappointing financial report.

According to the research department of the Ohio Company, the reasons for the change in sales and revenues were attributed to:

1. Weak retail environment—decline in retail traffic.
2. Heavy investment in display fixtures—intense competition has forced larger investment than anticipated.
3. Reduced licensing revenues—short life cycle of products and greater competitive pressures reduced licensing revenues.
4. Increased accounts receivables and inventory due to slower collections and weak ordering by retailers.
5. Increased interest expense due to increased accounts receivable and inventory levels.

Irving Stone remarked about the company's finances:

> In Fiscal 1986, the retailing picture was a rapidly changing mosaic, featuring a generally poor environment marked by a substantial drop-off in store traffic. As a result, sales of many of our products, which are dependent upon store traffic and impulse buying, fell below our expectations. Nevertheless, total revenue increased for the eightieth consecutive year, primarily due to increased greeting card sales. This is a proud record which few business enterprises can match. While this increase established a new corporate revenue milestone, it did not meet our performance goals, and earnings were flat for the first time in ten years.

FUTURE OF AG

Although AG has had significant growth in the past, events in its external environment are clouding the long term picture.

Again, from Irving Stone:

> We foresee opportunities to expand our business and profitability. Recent management restructuring

provides key officers with the time necessary to concentrate on long-term strategic planning in order to identify specific opportunities, seize upon them, and transform them into bottom-line results. Much growth potential lies ahead in our basic greeting card business, both domestically and internationally. We will strengthen our growing number of subsidiaries, improve efficiency, and increase productivity. Sales increases and expanded distribution in all channels of trade are key objectives. Licensing will continue to flourish, extending our horizons further and further.

Morry Weiss further added:

> Our future growth plans: aggressively pursuing growth in our core business, concentrating specifically on increasing market share and unit volume, and continued margin improvement.

However, according to William Blair and Company, AG's earnings growth will moderate significantly from the high earning growth rate over the past five years. This is due in part to cyclical factors in the economy, but also because of slowdowns in expansion of market share, licensing revenues, and more intense competition. Furthermore, there are two conflicting trends for AG's operating margins: gains should be made from increased productivity, but the increasing competitive nature of the industry with increased promotion might well erode such productivity increases.

Furthermore, according to industry expert, E. Gray Glass III, of Kidder, Peabody, & Company, there are some positives in the industry such as demograhics and promising Christmas sales. However, major concerns exist, which include:

> Aggressive price competition which was only modest in the past (mark up for greetings cards is 100 percent between factory and retail outlet).

> High account turnover as retailers look for most profitable lines and card companies fight intensely for large chain retail accounts (AG recently acquired the Sears' account while Hallmark secured Penney's).

> Increased cost pressures due to increasing advertising and distribution costs (racks, point of purchase, etc.). Hallmark will spend in excess of $40 million in television and magazine ads for Hall-

mark merchandise and benefits of sending cards. AG will spend $33 million.

Market share gains at the expense of other firms which come at high cost to the winner.

Growth rate of past five years will not be matched over the next five years.

New, viable, and growing competitors will emerge.

Investment decisions will have to be made more carefully.

Speculation exists that Hallmark may be formulating some counterattack strategies.

Merrill Lynch recently reduced AG's earnings estimates for fiscal 1987 and 1988 because of the above conditions, as well as difficulties in production and shipment of the Christmas line to retailers, in addition to higher than expected new business expenses. Needless to say, the Executive Committee of AG is concerned about the future growth potential and is in the process of formulating long-term objectives and strategies.

D

Corporate Size and Focus: Diversification and Restructuring

11.   Hallmark Cards, Inc.

"When You Care Enough to Send the Very Best" beneath a gold crown identifies the leader in the greeting card industry, Hallmark Cards. The slogan and logo have become synonymous with quality and excellence in the minds of the American public.

THE GREETING CARD INDUSTRY

The demand for greeting cards is currently growing at about 4–5 percent a year (*Forbes,* July 30, 1984). Approximately 7 billion cards are purchased annually, generating sales of around $3.5 billion. According to market studies, greeting card market growth will increase as the baby-boom generation enters the 35–54 years age-group because this population group includes the most frequent buyers of greeting cards (*The New York Times,* December 25, 1983). Almost 90 percent of all greeting cards are purchased by women (*The Wall Street Journal,* March 17, 1982). The demand for greeting cards is seasonal. Almost half of the cards purchased are Christmas cards; it is estimated that 3 billion of the 7 billion purchased annually are exchanged at Christmas. Boxed cards make up the majority of cards sold at Christmas. The average person purchases 50 boxed cards, and the trend is growing to add about a dozen individual counter cards (*TWA Ambassador,* 1979). Besides Christmas, the most popular card-sending holidays are Valentine's Day, Easter, Mother's Day, Father's Day and graduation.

Half the cards sold are everyday cards. Sales of everyday cards, such as nonoccasion cards, is on the

This case was prepared by Daniel G. Kopp, Lois M. Shufeldt, and Kim L. Stoops, as a basis for class discussion rather than to illustrate either effective or ineffective administrative practices. It was presented at the Southern Case Writers Association Workshop in November 1985.

Copyright © 1986 by Elsevier Science Publishing Co., Inc. Reprinted by permission of the publisher.

The authors would like to acknowledge the cooperation and assistance of Hallmark Cards, Inc., and the Greeting Card Association.

increase. The retail price for cards ranges from $0.35 to $7.50, with an average price of $1.00. The more expensive cards feature new technologies and special techniques (music, holography).

Industry officials are concerned about the impact of postage increases. Historically, postage expenses have caused fluctuations in overall demand for greeting cards. The Greeting Card Association, based in Washington, D.C., actively lobbies against postage hikes.

Inflation affects the greeting card industry, causing labor and material costs to rise. Advertising expenses for the industry were around $60 million in 1983. The two largest firms, Hallmark Cards, Inc. and American Greetings Corp., are the only firms that advertise extensively, probably due to the fact that a card is basically self-selling, and advertising that is done usually results in stimulating sales industrywide. However, advertising is also done to build and maintain the image of a company.

For the most part, greeting cards are in the maturity stage. New cards are being introduced, and there is heavy advertising. Hallmark Cards and American Greetings spend $60 million a year on advertising to keep the market growing at its present rate (*Forbes,* July 30, 1984). New lines of cards are being introduced that are aimed at the new and changing lifestyles of the population. Because there is an increasing number of single parents, working mothers, divorcees, and couples living together, Hallmark introduced its "new relationship" cards in January 1984. American Greetings soon followed with a similar line to accommodate new lifestyles. These new cards are nontraditional messages to appeal to the new and developing segments of the population.

Hallmark and Ambassador (a division of Hallmark) publish more than 11 million greeting cards and manufacture 1.5 million related items each day. Greeting cards are marketed through various channels. Hallmark sells through 22,000 retail outlets, all of which are independently owned, except for 100 company-owned specialty shops. Hallmark also sells through department stores. The Ambassador brand supplies the mass-distribution markets such as supermarkets, chain drugstores, and discount stores, which comprise 15,000 outlets. American Greetings cards are sold in about 50,000 stores such as large drugstores and supermarket chains; this represents 25 percent more outlets than those selling Hallmark/Ambassador lines.

There are more than 400 firms in the greeting card industry, but the two major firms dominate this social-expression business by controlling approximately 75 percent of the market (*Forbes,* July 30, 1984). Gibson Greetings, Inc. is the third major firm in the industry. Approximate 1984 market shares were: Hallmark Cards (including Ambassador), 40–45 percent; American Greetings, 30–35 percent; Gibson Greetings, 8–10 percent; these three firms together garner 78–85% of the market. This is in contrast to the 1955 scenario, when the three major firms, plus Norcross Greeting Cards and Rust Craft Greeting Cards, accounted for a mere one-third (approximate) of the U.S. card sales (*Kansas City Times,* November 28, 1985).

The fastest growing company is Gibson Greetings, which has more than doubled its revenue in the past five years to about $302.5 million in 1984. Gibson's success is largely due to "paying attention to its customers" by making use of their floor space more efficiently and developing very competitive products, especially their gift wrapping paper. Gibson's products are sold through mass merchandisers such as drugstores, supermarkets, and discount stores (*Kansas City Times,* November 28, 1985).

The remaining firms in the industry are small firms that have very select niches and are capable of responding and adapting to trends and fads very quickly. There are specific market segments that small companies can reach relatively easily with creative cards, such as off-color humor cards or those intended for gays. It is relatively easy to enter the greeting card industry.

The Greeting Card Association (GCA) is the trade association representing greeting card publishers and their suppliers. Its primary objectives include: (1) serving as a communication exchange forum for its members, (2) promoting the tradition of greeting cards on a national level, and (3) encouraging close cooperation between the greeting card industry and the federal government. Its primary effort is lobbying.

The GCA has more than 100 members, who represent approximately 80 percent of the greeting card market in the United States. Three GCA committees provide the focal direction: Public Relations, Legislative, and Small Business. The Legislative committee emphasizes close working relationships with the U.S. Postal Service. The Small Business committee has been formed recently and will attempt to create an industry directory and conduct workshops. The Public Relations committee attempts to stimulate the demand for greeting cards.

Hallmark is being challenged for supremacy in the greeting card industry for the first time in its 75-year life. In fact, one observer, Michael E. Porter, a professor of competitive business strategy at Harvard University, has identified Hallmark as one of seven U.S. companies whose industry leadership is in jeopardy (*Kansas City Times,* November 28, 1985).

Analysts expect the smaller companies to be squeezed out of business by Hallmark, American Greetings, and Gibson Greetings. The three big firms have been increasing their market shares at the expense of the smaller firms (*The New York Times,* December 25, 1983). Hallmark is the undisputed leader in the greeting card industry and boasts that its Hallmark line is the country's largest greeting card operation, while its Ambassador line is the third largest.

Competition is increasing in all areas of marketing—product, price, place, and promotion—between the two industry leaders. Historically, the two leading firms peacefully coexisted by each serving an existing and mutually exclusive clientele: Hallmark offered higher-priced, quality cards in department stores and card shops, and American Greetings offered inexpensive cards in mass-merchandise outlets. However, around 1977, American Greetings began formulating a plan to make a serious run at Hallmark. The number two firm realized that as smaller firms were squeezed out, further growth in market share would have to come from Hallmark, so the firm decided it would aggressively pursue its competitor. American Greetings realized that Hallmark does have a perceived quality advantage. To counter this advantage, American Greetings has increased its advertising; it spent between $10 and $15 million in 1984, which is about half of what Hallmark spent. Further, American Greetings plans to widen its penetration of Hallmark's upscale retail business by creating its own brand identity and improving the quality of its cards. Additionally, American Greetings has begun a corporate-identification program to identify outlets carrying American Greetings cards with the company name and newly designed logo of a rose. For many years, Hallmark stores have prominently displayed the Hallmark name and crown logo. Finally, American Greetings has increased prices by about 10 percent to match those of Hallmark cards.

American Greetings signed an agreement with Sears in early 1984 to sell its products exclusively. To compete against American Greetings moving into its higher-priced department, Hallmark is expanding their Ambassador line of mass-merchandise cards to be sold in supermarkets, drug, and discount stores such as Kroger, Safeway, Target, and Wal-Mart, which are segments of the market share where American Greetings and Gibson Greetings are the dominant forces. The Ambassador line was created in 1959; due to increased marketing efforts, the company (Ambassador) has doubled in size between 1980 and 1984 and is forecasted to double again by 1988. Annual retail sales for Ambassador are over $250 million.

American Greetings offers services such as free shipment and return of unsold seasonal cards to its retailers. They are now trying to lure retails from Hallmark by promising topnotch services. The majority of retailers carry only one brand, not lines from both Hallmark and American Greetings.

American Greetings has a definite edge over Hallmark in the licensing of characters; some of their very successful characters include Ziggy, Holly Hobby, Strawberry Shortcake, and Care Bears. The success in licensing has served to increase the company's visibility with the general public and has improved its image. In 1983 American Greetings earned 2.2 percent of its revenues from licensing, which amounted to $16.1 million (*Industry Week*, December 12, 1983).

Hallmark entered the licensing business in the mid-1970s. Since then Hallmark has been trying to create some successful characters of their own to license as licensing arrangements are quite profitable; the company can earn 5–10 percent of the wholesale value of each item sold. Hallmark created the Shirt Tales in 1981 and purchased Pac Man characters in 1982, which are marketed under the Ambassador line. Hallmark's entry into the licensing business—the Shirt Tales line—did not prove as productive as was hoped, given the very successful Strawberry Shortcake character of its competitor. Then in 1984 Hallmark introduced Rose Petal Place and Rainbow Bright, and, in 1985, Hugga Bunch. Rainbow Bright was the most successful first-year toy line in the history of the toy industry, surpassing even Cabbage Patch dolls; manufactured by Mattel, wholesale shipments are expected to total $110 million. Over $20 million in national advertising and promotions were spent to assure its success. Hallmark also has exclusive

rights to use Peanuts and Muppets characters, but does not own them.

Gibson Greetings also has licensed characters, although they are not its own creations. Garfield, as well as characters from Sesame Street, Looney Tunes, and D.C. comic books are licensed by Gibson. In February, 1985, Gibson Greetings was awarded exclusive rights for the Walt Disney characters, rights that Hallmark had held previously since the 1930s (*Kansas City Times*, November 28, 1985).

Hallmark has the edge in technological advances in the greeting card industry. The company markets musical greeting cards. In 1983, after spending $20 million for research and development, Hallmark produced a talking card utilizing microchips to imitate voice sounds. However, Hallmark removed the "talkies" from the market after low retail sales, probably due to the high retail price of $10 per card. Hallmark hopes to successfully reintroduce the product as the price of microchips falls (*The Wall Street Journal*, March 27, 1984).

Another area Hallmark is entering is holography. This is a laser-based technology used to create graphics and images that appear to be three dimensional. Commercial use of holograms has only recently been made possible because of a new method of embossing that makes it possible to mass-produce holograms. Hallmark produced a new card line of holographic greeting cards in 1984 (*The New York Times*, February 20, 1984).

With the aid of computers, Hallmark has identified 54 characteristics found in a successful card. The characteristics of successful cards are on computer files and are utilized to determine the best style, message, and sentiment for a new card design. The visual design and editorial characteristics are also considered. Although it is essential to provide a wide selection of cards, the individual performance of a card is analyzed to determine what makes a successful card. Inventory control is also facilitated by computer technology. Because cards are designed and developed two years before they are in the market, it is essential to determine any flaw that would cause the card not to be successful as early as possible so it can be corrected.

The environment is changing mainly because of lifestyles and demographic factors. This change is beneficial for the greeting card companies because the baby-boom generation is moving into the 35–54-years age-group, which includes the most frequent buyers of greeting cards. This movement will create a larger market for the industry. Annual greeting card sales have grown 8.8 percent in dollars and 2.7 percent in units between 1965 and 1982. The industry is expected to experience accelerated growth for the rest of the 1980s due to the demographic trends (*The New York Times,* December 25, 1983).

Changing lifestyles and values are affecting the greeting card industry. There are increasing numbers of single parents, working mothers, and live-in partners. These new emerging markets are quite large; there are 2.4 million new divorces per year, 1.2 divorced women for every 10 married women, and 1.6 million households with two unrelated adults of the opposite sex, one quarter of which are children under 15. These new

relationships present a market segment with potential for increasing sales volume. American Greetings expected to get 10 percent of its market from new-relationship cards in 1984, and up to 25 percent by 1986 (*Forbes,* July 30, 1984). However, greeting card firms will be faced with the challenge of creating nontraditional cards and messages that will appeal to this new market.

Because 90 percent of all greeting cards are purchased by women, the changes in women's lifestyle are significant to the industry. The major changes affecting women are presented in Table 1. The increase in the number of working women is extremely significant. These women are more likely to purchase cards and related items in more convenient outlets such as mass

---

TABLE 1 Lifestyle Changes in Women

Delayed marriages
  Women marry two years later than previously
  Average marrying age in 1950, 20.3 in 1981; 22.3 years
  One half of women 20–24 years have never married compared to one third previously
Rise of divorce
  Divorce rate doubled in past 20 years
  One half of all marriages from early 1970s will end in divorce
Delayed births
  1960s—women delayed having children until after age 25
  1980s—women delayed having children until after age 30
  In 30–34 years age-group proportion of women childless is 21 percent
  In 35–39 years age-group only 12 percent of married women are childless
Smaller families
  1957—average woman had four children
  1984—typical family has two children
  Approximatley 20 percent of professional career women do not plan to have children
Rise in education levels
  13 percent of women over age 25 have completed college
  In 1984, for first time, more women were in college than men
  Women business majors increased 300 percent from 1966 to 1978
Change in households
  25 percent of children live in no-parent or one-parent households
  40 percent of all children live in one-parent households before age of 18
  1982—women maintained 90 percent of all single-parent families
Rise in numbers of working mothers
  1950—12 percent of married women with children under six were in the labor force
  1982—50 percent of married women with children under six were in the labor force

---

Source: *American Demographics.* May 1983; *Ladies Home Journal,* October 1984.

merchandisers rather than in card shops, according to industry researchers (*Kansas City Times,* November 28, 1985).

Based upon the 1985 National Stationery Show (the trade show for the greeting card industry), the GCA identified some major card trends for the industry. These trends include the following:

- More designs and licensed characters typifying the working woman.
- More cards for the men of the 1980s—sensitive, sentimental, yet strong.
- More licensed properties for all ages from young children to yuppies.
- Bolder, brighter cards with direct sentiments, off-beat humor, and unusual photography.
- Cards emphasizing the modern, youth-oriented, trend-conscious, and urban consumer.
- More fashion-oriented cards using fabric textures, bright pastels, lines, and patterns reflecting the latest Paris fashion designs.
- More traditional cards bringing back the ''good old days'' theme.
- More ethnic, cultural cards.

HISTORY

Greeting Cards

Greeting cards as we know them are relatively recent phenomena—dating back to approximately 150 years. But the traditions that led to greeting cards go back thousands of years. Egyptians, for example, celebrated the New Year as a time of nature's reawakening. Early Romans observed the Feast of Lupercalia, which evolved into our Valentine's Day.

Until the mid-1800s, the only people who sent personal messages to their friends to wish them a Merry Christmas or Happy Birthday were those who could read and write and could afford to pay a messenger to deliver their sentiments. With the advent of the Industrial Revolution, many people were earning money on jobs provided by the invention of machines and learning to read and write through free public education. The printing press was being perfected, which allowed for machine-made cards.

The first commercially printed Christmas card dates to 1843; it was designed by artist John Calcott Horsley for a London businessman, Henry Cole. The card was divided into three panels with the main illustration showing adults at a family party raising wine glasses in a toast. The panels on either side showed two of the oldest traditions of Christmas—feeding the hungry and clothing the needy. The card bore the now classic greeting, ''A Merry Christmas and a Happy New Year to You.''

Louis Prang was the U.S. greeting card leader; his first Christmas cards were published in 1875, and he is often called the Father of the American Christmas Card. He also refined the printing of Valentines, but Esther Howland of Holyoke, Massachusetts, was the first successful maker of Valentines in America. Her ornate, beautiful Valentines often sold for as much as $35 each during the 1850s and 1860s.

In the 1890s, the penny postcard craze hit America, which drove Prang and other publishers of more expensive greeting cards out of business. Thus ended the first phase of the greeting card industry!

In January of 1910, 18-year-old Joyce Clyde Hall stepped off a train in Kansas City, Missouri, carrying a battered suitcase and two shoeboxes full of picture postcards. He rented a room at the YMCA. He had come from Norfolk, Nebraska, where he and his two older brothers, Rollie and Bill, owned a little store specializing in small gifts and postcards. There was not much of a market in Norfolk, so Joyce, who had a natural flair for salesmanship, sought out the most dynamic city in the Midwest. Hall wanted to create personalized cards.

Business was sufficiently promising that Rollie joined him the following year and the young men soon opened a specialty store in downtown Kansas City dealing in postcards, gifts, books, and stationery. Joyce Hall then called on merchants in Kansas City and other towns he could reach by train in Kansas, Oklahoma, Missouri, and Nebraska. That was the beginning of Hall Brothers, Inc., as Hallmark was known officially until 1954.

Joyce Hall believed in working hard and thought that good taste is good business. He developed Hallmark along a conservative stance. Middle-of-the-road cards were emphasized, and cards of questionable taste were avoided. Hallmark does not use off-color sentiments or produce products that feature celebrities. Joyce C. Hall served as Hallmark's chief executive for 56 years, until 1966 when his only son, Donald Joyce Hall, took over.

When Joyce Hall stepped aside as president in favor of his son, Donald J. Hall, the company had yet to experience its greatest period of growth. The founder of Hallmark died in late 1982.

Management

Donald J. Hall, 57, is chairman of the board and chief executive officer of the company. He is the second board chairman in the history of Hallmark Cards, Inc., succeeding his father.

Donald Hall started working with the company at age 17 as an assistant salesman in the Midwest. He attended Dartmouth College majoring in economics. While at Dartmouth he worked the local sales territory. Graduating in 1950, Hall joined the U.S. Army as an officer and served in Japan.

Donald Hall formally joined Hallmark in 1953, becoming assistant to the president in 1954, and being elected to the board of directors in 1956. He became administrative vice president in 1958 and was elected president and chief executive officer in 1966. He became chairman of the board in 1983.

David H. Hughes, 57, has been president of Hallmark Cards, Inc., since 1983. He joined Hallmark in 1958 as executive assistant to the executive vice president and was named vice president of product management in 1967, being responsible for the planning, creating, producing, and marketing functions of Hallmark products. Hughes became senior vice president in 1971, at which time he was elected to the board. He served as executive vice president of marketing from 1973 to 1979.

Before joining Hallmark Cards, Hughes' prior experience included a position at Midwest Research Institute as assistant to the president. He was also employed by Herbert V. Jones and Company in the commercial lease and sales department. Hughes was graduated from Princeton University with a degree in engineering and holds an M.B.A. degree from the Harvard Business School. Hughes is actively involved in the operational aspects of the company. The senior vice president, who is responsible for the functional departments, reports to Hughes.

Irvine O. Hockaday, Jr., 49, has been executive vice president of Hallmark Cards since joining the firm in 1983. He was elected to the board of directors in 1978. He was graduated from Princeton University in 1958 and

holds a J.D. degree from the University of Michigan Law School. He practiced law in Kansas City before working for Kansas City Southern Industries, Inc., a diversified New York stock exchange company. He served as president and chief executive officer of that firm from 1971 to 1983. Hockaday became Hallmark's president and chief executive officer on January 1, 1986.

Hockaday was the first member of top management selected from outside the company's rank. His principal task is to expand and diversify Hallmark's operations. The vice president of corporate planning reports to Hockaday. Strategic planning is receiving more attention because of Hallmark's desire to diversify. Multifaceted planning documents including short- and long-range plans are being prepared. Hockaday feels that Hallmark is financially strong and has substantial borrowing capacity. Hockaday, a close friend of Donald Hall, was selected to help map Hallmark's future course.

Hockaday is leading Hallmark on a diversification drive into specialty publishing, broadcasting, computer software, and crayons. He maintains, however, that the diversification strategy will not come at the expense of its traditional business. Currently, Hallmark receives less than 10 percent of its profits from nongreeting card businesses; Hockaday hopes that eventually 40 percent of Hallmark's profits will come from businesses outside its maturing greeting card business (*Business Week,* November 12, 1984). Hallmark has spent more than $250 million in outside diversification since Hockaday joined the firm.

Diversification must take place, according to Webster Scott, Gibson's vice president of marketing:

Hallmark's simply prudently using their funds. They've still got such a big share of the (social expression) market, and they've got to do something with their money. (*Kansas City Times,* November 28, 1985)

How prudent Hallmark's use of their funds is remains to be seen. Binney and Smith, the first company purchased by Hallmark that was clearly outside the card business, produced a modest income for several years before the takeover by Hallmark. Earnings fell 29 percent in 1983, and in the first quarter of 1984 Binney and Smith reported a loss of $435,000 (*The New York Times,* October 13, 1984).

Table 2 identifies Hallmark's acquisitions, start-ups, and investments. Table 3 provides information regarding Hallmark's 30 percent interest in SFN Holding Com-

TABLE 2   Hallmark's Acquisitions, Start-Ups, and Investments

1910   Hallmark's founding (first corporate name: Hall Brothers Co.), greeting cards.
1922   First departure from greeting cards, gift wrap.
1957   Henri Fayette* (sold in 1971), specialty cards.
1958   William E. Coutts, Ltd,* Canadian card maker.
1959   Ambassador Cards, mass-merchandise outlet cards.
1961   Seelman Printing Co.,* printer.
1966   Hallmark International.
1967   Springbok Editions,* jigsaw puzzles; Crown Center Redevelopment Corp., real estate.
1968   Nob Hill,* candles.
1975   Trifari, Krussman & Fishel,* jewelry.
1978   Tandem Jewelry, jewelry.
1979   Speciality Greetings,* Australian card maker; Dawnson Printing,* New Zealand card maker; Burnes of Boston, picture frames; Litho-Krome of Columbus, Ga.,* lithographer; Felicity Cards (N.Z)* (phased out immediately), New Zealand card maker.
1980   Evanson Card Shops, Inc.,* U.S. cardshop chain; Valentines of Dundee,* United Kingdom Card maker.
1982   Hallmark Properties, licensing of character properties; Marvella,* jewelry.
1983   Heartline (division of Graphics International subsidiary), nonpaper gifts.
1984   Information Technology Design Associates Inc.† (80 percent interest), computer software; W.N. Sharp Holdings,* United Kingdom card maker; Binney & Smith Inc.,* crayons, art products.
1985   SFN Cos. Inc.‡ (30 percent interest), textbooks, publishing, broadcasting, etc.

*Acquisition.
†Investment was announced in October 1984 but not completed until later.
‡Investment.

Source: *Kansas City Times*, November 28, 1985.

TABLE 3   SFN Holding Company

Company	*Product Area*
Scott, Foresman & Company	Publisher of textbooks and educational material.
Mindscape, Inc.	Publisher of educational, entertaining, personal computer software for children and adults.
South-Western Publishing Company	Publisher of textbooks and related materials.
Silver Burdette Company	Publisher of elementary and secondary textbooks, puzzles, and games for preschoolers.
Broadcast Advertisers Reports, Inc.	Publisher of database of national and local information about commercial activity and estimated advertising expenditures in radio and television.
Biomedical Information Corporation	Publisher of medical and scientific related journals.
Data Acquisition Services, Inc.	Develops, manufactures, and markets telecommunications equipment.
Broadcast Properties	Five television and three radio stations.

Source: Hallmark Cards, Inc.

pany. Hallmark has recently announced its participation in a bid for the $2 billion Group W Cable systems of the Westinghouse Corporation (*Kansas City Times,* November 28, 1985).

Current Objectives

Hallmark seeks to provide quality products that are attuned to the changing emotion of their customers and to create a pleasant atmosphere in which consumers may shop. It has marketing and store-design specialists who create showplaces that attract the consumer's interest and utilize the latest advances in retailing concepts. It has created new and expanded product lines under both the Hallmark and Ambassador names. Hallmark was founded upon the idea that good taste is good business, and quality has always been emphasized; Hallmark has become known for offering quality products. The atmosphere at Hallmark is of friendly, caring service. It enjoys a unique relationship with its customers. The Consumer Affairs Department receives more than 30,000 positive letters a year, which is indicative of the feeling of warmth and trust that exists between shoppers and their favorite greeting card maker.

Hallmark strives to go beyond what is expected and use their corporate resources to benefit society. This social opportunity is simply a recognition that the health of our communities, our schools, our government, and our other institutions bears directly on the health of the corporation. Since Hallmark was founded, it has worked to develop a social conscience. For example, Hallmark has opened training centers for the disadvantaged and started a creative-art workshop for children.

Hallmark also has undertaken an urban redevelopment project in Kansas City, Missouri. It created the Crown Center Redevelopment Corporation, which is a wholly owned subsidiary, in order to redevelop 85 acres of a downtown Kansas City slum area. When completed, the Crown Center will represent an investment of $500 million. Fifty buildings will have been added to the city's skyline near the heart of the city to complement the downtown area.

The original cost estimate of the Crown Center project was $115 million for 50,000 square feet of space. By 1980, Hallmark had lost $65.7 million on the project, half of which was taken as tax write-offs for the company, and its own share of the center's debt amounts

to $80.3 million. Kansas City allowed the new buildings to be 100 percent tax-free for 10 years following the acquisition of the property and 50 percent tax-free for another 15 years. The tax-free advantage is coming to a close (*Forbes,* August 4, 1980).

Hallmark's philosophy toward social responsibility is reflected in the following quote from Donald Hall:

> When Hallmark speaks of social responsibility we don't mean truth in advertising, job safety, or equal opportunity. These are legal and moral obligations that are accepted and expected. . . . Rather, I like to think in terms of a higher standard which defines social responsibility as social opportunity: the opportunity to bring the resources and skill of business people to bear on community problems. It is a standard which encourages Hallmarkers to be involved in community activities . . . that the company should use its talents and resources to benefit its communities. (*Crown Magazine,* December 1984)

Hallmark is very conscious of and places a great value on their employees. Hallmark is very people oriented. According to David Hughes:

> . . . for employees to be productive, they must gain personal satisfaction and self-fulfillment from their jobs. One way we achieve this is to provide them security and genuine participation—the knowledge that every individual's opinion and contribution makes a real difference. It is a principle that good families employ, and we have found that it works equally well at Hallmark. (*Personnel,* October 1984)

Besides the traditional fringe-benefit packages (they were one of the first companies to have a cafeteria), Hallmark has "caring benefits." These benefits include short-term, interest-free loans to employees, adoption assistance, alcohol and mental health assistance, college loans, scholarships, product discounts, and physical fitness facilities. Hallmark also has an employee profit-sharing plan, which was started in 1956 (*Personnel,* October 1984).

Hallmark has expanded its operations internationally. Its International Division serves more than 122 countries, and Hallmark cards are distributed in 20 languages. These operations range from wholly owned subsidiaries and branches to license agreements. In 1984 Hallmark agreed to buy a majority stake in WN:Sharpe Holdings, a 114-year-old British greeting card company. The company will operate as a separate unit under Hallmark.

Stan Hamilton, president of Hallmark International, acknowledges that operating in foreign companies does present unique challenges. He stated:

> Every country has its own way of celebrating holidays and special occasions, many of which don't occur outside the boundaries of that country. For example, in France the New Year is a bigger card sending holiday than Christmas. Canadians celebrate Thanksgiving in October, and without the symbols of Pilgrims and Indians with which Americans are so familiar. Because Christmas is a summer holiday in Australia, wintry scenes are out of place on yuletide cards. (Unpublished press release of Hallmark Cards, Inc.)

Hallmark International operates several wholly owned subsidiaries in Canada, England, Germany, and Ireland. In turn, it distributes Hallmark products to other areas and countries such as North Africa, Saudi Arabia, Nigeria, the Mediterranean, Belgium, Austria, Holland, Italy and Scandinavia. There are also Hallmark licenses that manufacture and distribute Hallmark products in Australia, Brazil, Japan, Mexico, New Zealand, Trinidad, Philippines, South Africa, and Venezuela. Hallmark International sells directly to Hong Kong, Central America, Taiwan, and Indonesia.

Strategies

Marketing. Hallmark has a wide product line. This line is necessary to maintain their position in the specialized card shop business. The firm seeks to continue providing items consumers might expect to find in stores that carry Hallmark products. Some of the products offered are greeting cards, Hallmark Keepsake ornaments, stickers, partyware, gift wrap, stationery, mugs, jewelry, Springbok jigsaw puzzles, photo frames, and crystal gift items. Its greeting cards come in a variety of styles and messages to appeal to a variety of consumers—traditional, nontraditional, religious, contemporary, and humorous cards. Hallmark has a card for

almost all occasions, holidays, weddings, births, sympathy, thinking of you, and "personal expression" cards (which allow the consumers to select the cover and insert of their choice). In 1983 greeting cards represented 50 percent of revenues, whereas in the 1960s they made up 90 percent (*The New York Times,* December 25, 1983). More than 14,000 greeting cards and 6,300 related product designs are created by Hallmark and Ambassador creative staff annually.

Hallmark has traditionally offered high-quality, high-priced products. Hallmark has been successful by marketing products in the carriage trade, or free-standing card shops. These shops account for 40 percent of all greeting cards sold in the United States and represent a strength for Hallmark, because its closest competitor did not enter this type of distribution until recently. However, Hallmark is expanding card sales from traditional department store and gift shops to drugstores and discount stores in an effort to be more competitive. A new line of display fixtures was developed to create the most effective presentation of social expression products. Hallmark and Ambassador stores have signs and decorations in the store that identify the brand to increase name recognition. A Retail Enhancement Program was started in 1982 to create a more effective card shop design. For consumer convenience, merchandise was placed in shopping zones, innovative graphics and photographs were used to give a seasonal look, cashiering and showcase islands were centrally located, plus new fixtures and state-of-the-art focused lighting were used to highlight the product.

Creativity is extremely important at Hallmark. Emphasis is placed on providing a pleasant working environment as well as opportunities to be creative and innovative. The company provides educational programs to excite and stimulate ideas that will result in new products and lines. These programs include trips to foreign countries to observe the latest trends in color, fabric, and design. The company also presents Creative Thinking Awards as an incentive for new ideas and better ways of performing; the data (*Hallmark 1984 Corporate Report*) regarding these awards for the past five years are listed in Table 4.

In sales, Hallmark rewards creative suggestions through their Marketing Ideas Programs. In 1984, 32 field salespeople won awards. Employee suggestions have resulted in better ways of tracking the retail performance of products by adding a five-digit supple-

TABLE 4   Creative Thinking Awards 1980–1984

Year	Number of Awards	First-Year Savings
1980	61	$158,226
1981	159	160,990
1982	241	124,770
1983	509	486,130
1984	124	403,119

ment to the U.P.C. bar code on the back of Ambassador cards.

The Hallmark name and crown logo have come to represent quality, which has been achieved primarily through advertising. Hallmark has sponsored the "Hallmark Hall of Fame" television series for over 30 years. This sponsorship has enabled the company to provide entertaining and enriching programs while simultaneously creating a positive image. The "Hallmark Hall of Fame" has been hailed by public and critics alike as the most consistently outstanding dramatic series in television. It has won 49 Emmys, more than any other show on television, including the first Emmy ever accorded a sponsor.

Advertising is also used to stimulate sending of cards for other than the usual holidays, which accounts for half of the nation's card sending. "When you care enough to send the very best" has been the theme line for Hallmark for many years. The firm sees its product as emotion and communications. The fundamental motivation for sending cards is the need to maintain relationships. Therefore, Hallmark uses commericals that "'tug at the heartstrings" through the use of flashbacks. You see the receiver while hearing the thoughts of the sender. Hallmark wants advertising to stimulate category growth and protect its brand share position. The advertising agency of Ogilvy and Mather currently handles the Hallmark account, which represents $35–40 million in annual billings. Hallmark spends about twice what American Greetings does on advertising. In contrast to Hallmark, American Greetings uses humor in its television ads.

Hallmark has sponsored seasonal promotions such as sweepstakes and ornament promotions. It also advertises in women's magazines, such as *Good Housekeeping, Redbook, People,* and *Glamour,* to increase traffic and sales. Hallmark date books and pocket calendars continue

to win friends and generate sales for Hallmark retailers. The company also uses promotions to introduce new products, such as the press luncheon that was held to introduce a new line of paper plates. The guests were served on paper plates that were promoted as offering a combination of convenience and style. Hallmark uses advertising effectively to promote its products and image.

Hallmark has responded to its changing environment with the following developments.

Modern Women Line.   A 99-card line about the concerns of women in a changing world. The cards cover topics such as marriage, divorce, pregnancy, diet, exercise, work, career, dating, men, aging, and loneliness. The designs range from bold graphics to muted pastels, photographs to cartoons. The cards are directed toward women in the 20–40 years age category.

Lovetalk Line.   The 92-card line is for all stages of love relationships. The cards are appropriate for married and single men and women of all ages, and messages range from light and teasing to the very serious.

More Convenient Party Line.   Research has indicated that Americans are giving more informal parties than ever before. Paper plates are now being used for one half of all parties given. Consequently, Hallmark has redesigned its paper party line.

Nontraditional Cards.   Hallmark has created anniversary and wedding cards for second marriages. Birthday cards suitable for stepparents and stepchildren are also being offered.

Stickers.   Hallmark has begun to offer some of the most innovative sticker designs (scented, glow-in-the-dark, etc.). It also introduced skin decals and sticker collection books.

New Retail Boutiques.   Hallmark has and will continue to open small specialty stores such as Heartbeeps, Portfolio, and Celebrate to appeal to teenagers, party givers, and shoppers with sophisticated tastes.

Finance. Hallmark is one of the largest privately held companies in the world.[1] The company has set guidelines for acquisitions; it seeks companies that are in businesses compatible with Hallmark's current product lines. Hallmark intends to remain a private corporation; therefore, it does not plan acquisitions that would necessitate equity financing. Hallmark's revenues and profits are probably twice those of American Greetings, the second leading firm in the industry. Hallmark admits that the company ranks midway among the nation's top 500 public companies in sales and book assets and would be ranked even higher if income is computed as a percent of sales. From this disclosure, experts estimate Hallmark would have $40.1 million in net income, $1.05 billion in assets, and a 10.9 percent return on equity. Surprisingly, Donald Hall announced that Hallmark's revenues for 1983 were at $1.5 billion, which was up from $1.25 billion the previous year (*The New York Times,* December 25, 1983). The Hall family owns two thirds of the Hallmark shares, and employees hold about one-third of the company through profit sharing.

Production. Hallmark has large-scale, efficient operations. These operations enable the company to respond extremely quickly in manufacturing cards; for example, the company was the only manufacturer ready with two million cards in 30 designs for Grandparent's Day, just six weeks after it was declared a national holiday. It employs 700 talented and creative people who are allowed to work in a free atmosphere. Hallmark's research and creative team is the largest in the industry and is estimated to be almost twice as large as that of American Greetings.

For Christmas 1983, approximately 2.3 billion cards were sold to retailers, and of this amount Hallmark reported shipping 1 billion. This figure represents a 13 percent increase over the previous year and can be compared to a 7 percent increase registered by the industry as a whole (*The New York Times,* December 25, 1983).

Hallmark has six production centers located in five cities and two distribution centers. Table 5 provides a summary of these data.

David Hughes strongly feels that quality from both an operations and employee perspective is one of the keys to Hallmark's success:

One of our strengths for 75 years is our unswerving commitment to quality and to being first with the best. As we expand our product offerings, we will continue to preserve our heritage of quality. . . . While Hallmark has a far-reaching quality control program that touches everyone from artist to pressman, what really makes a difference here is the personal involvement each employee feels with the quality of our products. The familiar advertising slogan, ''When You Care Enough to Send the Very Best,'' creates a very personal responsibility for every Hallmark employee. (*Executive Excellence,* June 1985)

According to corporate officials, Hallmark's plants are the most modern in the industry. An extensive expansion program was begun five years ago; Hallmark has substantial production capacity. Additional space has been added to the Lawrence, Leavenworth, Osage, Topeka, and Kansas City production centers. A second Enfield distribution center began operations in 1981.

To ensure that Hallmark stays ahead of the competition, a Technical and Innovative Center will be completed in late 1985. The 170,000 square foot facility will be located in Kansas City, Missouri. David H. Hughes reports:

. . . the center will be a hub of the company's product development activity. . . . designed to stimulate creative interaction among artists, craftsmen, technicians, engineers, and scientists. . . . As an industry increasingly involved in new technology, we are taking the steps necessary to keep Hallmark in the lead. (Unpublished press release of Hallmark Cards, Inc.)

The facility will be designed to utilize ''open areas'' to provide for a free flow of information among the 200 permanent employees. Each floor will have vast open areas (the size of two football fields). Conversation lounges and a food service area will facilitate employee interaction.

Hallmark is recognized as a leader in the materials handling and distribution facilities. The Liberty Distribution Center was opened in 1973. This facility has a real-time automated storage system combined with mechanical and computer-directed devices to form a very efficient material-handling system. The Enfield facility was completed in 1981. It has been cited as the best-designed distribution center in the United States, and perhaps the world.

---

[1]Because Hallmark is privately held, it does not release its financial statements.

TABLE 5   Production and Distribution Centers

Location	Size (sq. ft.)	Number of Employees	Speciality
		Production Centers	
Lawrence, Kansas	700,000	980	Greeting cards, ribbon, bows, puzzles, invitations, tallies, place cards.
Leavenworth, Kansas	710,000	657	Candles, plaques, pens, pencils, plastic items, labels, gift wrap.
Leavenworth, Kansas	255,066	247	Merchandise bags, date books, gift wrap, paper partyware, and Christmas ornaments.
Osage, Kansas	210,000	213	Paper plates and cups, paper table covers, and napkins.
Topeka, Kansas	715,000	875	Greeting cards, stationery and notes, party centerpieces, and envelopes.
Kansas City, Missouri	650,000	1,064	Greeting cards, books, albums, invitations, tallies, place cards, calendars, and ornaments.
		Distribution Centers	
Liberty, Missouri	1,500,000	1,133	Receipt, storage and shipment of Hallmark and Ambassador products to Midwestern, Western and Southern regions of United States.
Enfield, Connecticut	1,650,000	723	Receipt, storage and shipment of Hallmark and Ambassador products to Eastern and Midwestern United States.

Source: Hallmark Cards, Inc.

Personnel.   Hallmark is a Kansas City institution and one of the city's major employers. As of June 1985 Hallmark employs 20,100 full-time and 5,800 part-time employees worldwide. There are 6,000 employees in Kansas City. In 1984, there were 6,300 full-time male employees and 7,100 female employees in domestic Hallmark operations. The five largest divisions in 1984 are listed in Table 6. The occupations of permanent, full-time, domestic Hallmark employees in August 1984 are given in Table 7.

TABLE 6   Hallmark Cards, Inc., Five Largest Divisions

Division	Number of Employees
Manufacturing	3,700
Order distribution	1,900
Technical development graphic production	1,400
Marketing	1,100
Speciality production	1,100

TABLE 7   Occupations of Permanent, Full-Time, Domestic Hallmark Employees in August 1984

Occupation	Number of Employees
Managers and supervisors	1,600
Professional	1,700
Technicians	500
Sales workers	1,200
Office workers	2,000
Production, distribution and warehouse workers	6,050
Service workers	300
Trainees	50

According to company officials, the average Hallmark employee is a woman 35 years old with 10 years of company service. She works in the Operations Area, has a high school education, is married with children, and lives in Kansas City (*Crown Magazine,* December 1984).

Hallmark is very family oriented in its personnel policies. David H. Hughes believes security and creativity can coexist. The company policy is:

> Job security establishes a positive environment that releases creativity. We've avoided layoffs historically because through the years our company has experienced substantial growth. . . . I think most people familiar with the creative process will tell you the roots of a creative staff more often rest in ''insecurity'' than security. That insecurity is not, we hope, generated by management, but comes from the creative individual's knowledge that his or her creative work must find acceptance in the market place. (Unpublished press release of Hallmark Cards, Inc.)

Hallmark has avoided layoffs in three ways. First, it offers individuals time off without pay. This is voluntary time off and many see this as a benefit. Second, individuals are assigned meaningful work in other areas. The company has found this to be an effective method. When necessary, training classes are provided. Third, Hallmark maintains an on-call, part-time work force to cover peak production periods. This program has also been successful.

Hallmark does not tolerate poor performance, however. Dismissals do take place. Hallmark attempts to identify the reasons for people not being successful and then tries to correct them. If it cannot correct the situation, people do leave (*Executive Excellence,* June 1985).

FUTURE OF HALLMARK, INC.

According to Don Hall:

> The future looks exceptionally bright to me, largely because . . . of the people of Hallmark. Perhaps I should use the plural and say futures. Since both the immediate and long range futures appear to be promising. . . . The time ahead will be different and filled with change. We see it throughout our past, from counting to computers, from air brush and hard press to licensing and lasers. But change comes with growth, it is necessary and welcome. It comes from our own internal momentum and from outside influence. (*Crown Magazine,* December 1984)

In 1984, more than anytime in recent history, Hallmark Cards, Inc. concentrated on positioning itself for the immediate and long-range future.

Robert L. Stark, senior vice president, noted:

> To continue our enviable position as one of this nation's premier companies, to remain an

outstanding example of excellence among other top firms, we will have to continue our emphasis on sales. The sales success of our products is of concern to all of us; we need to understand what is selling and where, what today's woman is buying and why. (*Crown Magazine*, Summer 1985)

Success comes from the basics—an excellent product, sound selling, and dedication to marketing. According to Glenn Davis, corporate vice president, order distribution:

As Hallmark responds to new markets, we can anticipate a host of new products. This will undoubtedly promulgate some major challenges to distribution: that is, bulky items consume more space in storage and selecting activity; fragile items require special handling, expensive items demand security; short shelf-life items involve first-in first-out control. (*Crown Magazine*, Spring 1985)

Bob Payne, vice president of manufacturing observed:

The jobs of tomorrow will be different. Jobs, products, process—many will be different, but it is the acceleration of those changes that will be most amazing. (*Crown Magazine*, December 1984)

Jeannette Lee, former vice president, corporate design, asserted:

Ours is a woman's business. Women are our buyers and more than half our employees are women. We need more women in decision-making roles to top levels, and perhaps the future will bring that. (*Crown Magazine*, December 1984)

Stan Hamilton, president of Hallmark International summarized:

There are many areas where the custom of sending greeting cards is still in its infancy. As social expression needs evolve worldwide, Hallmark and its affiliates will be there to help consumers in any way we can. (Unpublished press release of Hallmark Cards, Inc.)

REFERENCES

Business Week, May 19, 1975, pp. 57–58.

Business Week, November 12, 1984, pp. 73–74.

Cosmopolitan, February 1981, pp. 31–35.

Crown Magazine, December 1984, pp. 10, 11, 15, 21.

Crown Magazine, Spring 1985, foreward.

Crown Magazine, Summer 1985, pp. 8, 9, 15.

Executive Excellence, June 1985, pp. 6–7.

Forbes, August 4, 1980, p. 63.

Forbes, July 30, 1984, p. 102.

Hallmark Cards, Inc., Corporate Report, 1984.

Industry Week, December 12, 1983, pp. 21–23.

Kansas City Times, November 28, 1985, pp. 1, 16–19.

The New York Times, March 3, 1982, p. 15.

The New York Times, October 30, 1982, p. 35.

The New York Times, December 9, 1982, p. 8.

The New York Times, December 25, 1983, p. 1.

The New York Times, January 8, 1984, p. 14.

The New York Times, February 20, 1984, p. 1.

The New York Times, May 4, 1984, p. 16.

The New York Times, June 18, 1984, p. 6.

The New York Times, June 27, 1984, p. 23.

The New York Times, October 13, 1984, p. 36.

Personnel, October 1984, pp. 7–9.

TWA Ambassador, 1979, pp. 1–3.

The Wall Street Journal, August 6, 1981, p. 25.

The Wall Street Journal, March 17, 1982, p. 1.

The Wall Street Journal, April 13, 1983, p. 8.

The Wall Street Journal, March 27, 1984, p. 33.

The Wall Street Journal April 16, 1984, p. 26.

The Wall Street Journal, April 26, 1984, p. 28.

The Wall Street Journal, May 23, 1984, p. 7.

The Wall Street Journal, June 12, 1984, p. 11.

The Wall Street Journal, June 18, 1984, p. 39.

12. *Mesa Petroleum Company (C)*

T. Boone Pickens, Jr., chairman of Mesa Petroleum, didn't seem to agree with the way major companies in America were being run.

"People talk about fiefdoms in the Middle East, in these Arab countries. What do you think you have in these chief executive offices in these companies in the United States? I mean they've got everything in their command. I do. Hell, I could order this airplane down and load it up with girls and go to Las Vegas," commented Pickens. . . . "But you've got to have discipline to run it like it should be run, and it should be run for the stockholders," continued Pickens. "These people are caught up in their empire. Look at a guy like Lee [Gulf's CEO]. Where do you think a guy like Lee can get another job for $800,000 a year? He's not articulate. He's not knowledgeable. Hell, he's about as attractive as yesterday's toast."[1]

Certain of Pickens' contemporaries had definite opinions on his takeover ploys and his claims to be working in the shareholders' interests.

"He's only after the almighty buck, he's nothing but a pirate," said G. C. Richardson, formerly of Cities Service.[2]

"My only objection to Pickens is the aura he tries to create when he says he is for the small shareholder. That's just a lot of crap," remarked Harold Hammer, head of Gulf Oil's defense effort.[3]

Senator Howard Metzenbaum (D–Ohio) commented, "Pickens makes a crusade out of what he is doing because he can make a lot of money."[4]

Pickens' critics regularly hurled invectives, calling him a raider, a greenmailer, and a waster of corporate assets. These criticisms, however, rarely came from Mesa Petroleum's shareholders and partners.

PETROLEUM INDUSTRY IN THE EARLY 1980s

The oil and gas industry entered the 1980s riding a boom of at least a half dozen years of immense prosperity. The boom quickly, and surprisingly to many, turned sour in late 1981. By 1982, the industry found itself heading into a severe recession. Oil and gas firms in 1985 were still deeply mired in this recession and showed few signs of a near-term recovery.

The Boom. After the OPEC oil embargo in 1973, world crude oil prices rose steadily through the 70s, peaking at $35 per barrel in 1981 (Exhibit 1). Expectations by many in the industry were for crude prices to reach $60–$100 per barrel in the next decade.

As the "boom" fever spread, investors poured literally billions of dollars into oil and gas deals. Oil company stock prices became "hot" plays as their prices pushed upward. Oil and gas syndicates also became popular among investors seeking tax benefits and earnings potential. Bankers competed fiercely to loan money for both oil and gas production and oil field equipment.

This case was written by Mark Rich and Francis C. Stiff, research assistants, and Robert R. Gardner, associate director of the Maguire Oil and Gas Institute, under the direction of Professor M. Edgar Barrett, director of the same institute. It is designed to serve as the basis for class discussion and is not intended to illustrate either effective or ineffective handling of an administrative situation.

Copyright © 1985 by M. Edgar Barrett. Reproduced with permission.

This case is available in looseleaf form from Lord Publishing, Inc., One Apple Hill, Natick, Mass. 01760.

[1]"Playing for Keeps," *Westward Magazine, Dallas Times Herald,* March 25, 1984.

[2]"High Times for T. Boone Pickens," *Time,* March 4, 1985, pp. 52–64.

[3]Ibid.

[4]Ibid.

EXHIBIT 1   Refiner Acquisition Price per Barrel of Crude

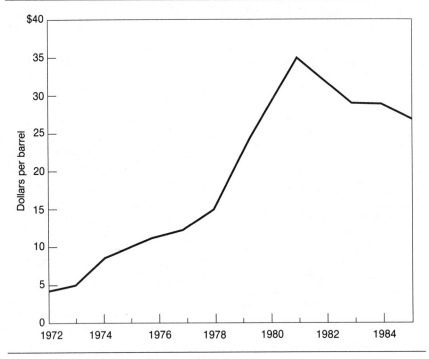

Source: "Big Oil Starts Thinking Smaller," *The New York Times*, March 17, 1985, p. 1, sec. 3.

Within the industry itself, drilling activity began to rise dramatically as exploration and production companies spent the dollars flowing in from increased production revenues and from new investors. Increased activity by established drilling contractors was complemented by a substantial number of new drilling companies attracted by the profits to be earned. According to *Reeds Rig Census,* there were 3,100 rigs capable of drilling to 3,000 feet or better in operation as of December 1979. By December 1981, the same count had grown to 4,800 rigs. The number of working rigs at the peak of demand was 4,530 at the end of 1981. At that time new rigs were coming on-line at the rate of 2.5 rigs per day.[5]

As drilling activity increased, so did the demand for oil field equipment. Prices on rigs, pipe, and related products moved up sharply. Increasing costs, rather than

discouraging drilling, seemed only to add to the frenzy, as investors and bankers viewed the oil field equipment industry as another "hot" play.

The Bust.   Meanwhile, in the face of the boom, demand for refined products was slowing. Gasoline consumption was down due to the switch to more fuel-efficient cars (average mpg had risen from 13.2 in 1973 to 24.6 in 1982), and reduced driving in general (down 10% between 1978 and 1982).[6] The combined effects led to a decrease in gasoline consumption by 1 million barrels per day between 1978 and 1983.[7]

In addition to gasoline, the demand for middle distillates was also down. In the industrial and utility sectors,

---

[5]*Reeds Rig Census.*

[6]"Energy," *Forbes*, January 2, 1984, p. 74.
[7]Ibid.

EXHIBIT 2   Oil Use per Dollar of GNP

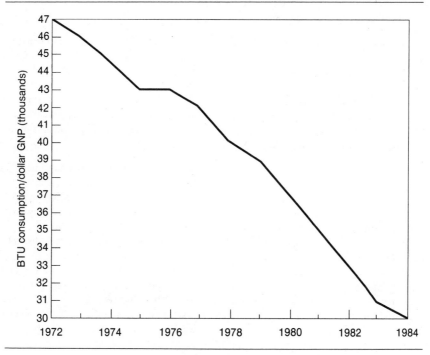

Source: "Big Oil Starts Thinking Smaller," *The New York Times,* March 17, 1985, p. 1, sec. 3.

a massive effort at conservation and fuel substitution was paying off. Oil consumption per dollar of GNP was falling steadily throughout this period (Exhibit 2). Heavy industries led this trend, with oil consumption in the steel industry down 80% from 1979–84 and oil use by the pulp and paper industry falling 50% during the same period.[8] Contributing to the decrease in oil consumption by industrial users was the economic recession that also began in 1981.

While demand was falling, production had been continuing at a record pace. OPEC countries had reached a peak in production of 32 million barrels of oil per day (bopd) in 1979 and were still producing at very high levels.[9]

The turn from boom to bust in the industry became apparent on the order books of drilling contractors by late 1981. Land-based contractors were booked solid through the end of the year, but had little or no backlog of orders for 1982. By April of 1983, the number of rigs in operation had fallen to 1,807.[10]

At the same time, investors began to cool toward oil and gas plays. A major factor was the Income Tax Reform Act of 1981. This act reduced the top tax bracket from 70% to 50%, thus reducing the value of immediate tax reductions and, hence, the appeal of many drilling ventures.

Decreased demand for oil ultimately led to falling prices. As E&P companies had borrowed heavily to finance their operations, the fall in prices placed these

[8]"Scorecard for the OPEC Meeting," *The Wall Street Journal,* July 5, 1985, p. 6.

[9]"Energy," p. 75.

[10]"Oilfield Drillers and Services," *Forbes,* January 2, 1984, p. 84.

companies in a severe cash bind. With a loss of revenues due to falling prices, and a decline in investor interest in oil and gas plays, hundreds of operating companies were forced into bankruptcy.

The refining and marketing segment of the industry was also hard hit. The fall in demand left the industry with significant overcapacity. Competition at the gas pump combined with already low refinery utilization rates led to very poor profitability throughout the refining and marketing industry. Despite closure of more than a hundred refineries, the industry in 1985 was still saddled with overcapacity and thus, poor profitability (Exhibit 3).

Outlook.   The near-term outlook for the oil industry as of 1985 was not encouraging. With the control of much of the world's oil production in the hands of foreign-exchange-hungry governments, the prospect of reducing the oversupply of oil through production cuts appeared unlikely. OPEC's production had fallen to 16 million bopd and many members of the cartel were either cheating on their production quotas or selling oil below set prices.[11] Saudi Arabia, in turn, threatened cheating OPEC countries with a price war that could flood world markets with oil and drive prices below $20 per barrel.[12]

Analysts did not look to demand increases to bolster prices, even with a strong economy. Said Raymond Mason, Charter Co. president,

Even if the economy keeps expanding, pressures will continue to push oil prices down.[13]

Fred Singer, of George Mason University, remarked,

Consumption in the transportation sector may increase slightly if gasoline prices fall; for other sectors, gas and coal prices will adjust downward and provide competition. The big item in demand (short run) may be inventories; will oil stocks be built up at $24 (per barrel of oil)? I don't think so.[14]

Boone Pickens summed up the outlook for the industry as follows:

Of all the wells that have been drilled in the world, 80 percent of them have been drilled in the Lower Forty-eight. . . . So, while you've got a limited number of good prospects in the U.S., you still have more rigs running than the rest of the world does. You also have natural gas markets that are weak, and oil markets that are uncertain. That's a very sobering set of fundamentals the industry is facing.[15]

Adding to the dilemma of many major oil companies was the current trend in the financial markets of low valuation of conglomerates. Many major oil companies found themselves "undervalued" by the market, both because of the poor outlook of the oil industry and because of Wall Street's current disenchantment with multibusiness firms.[16]

Development of spot markets for both crude and refined products was a new addition to the industry in the 1980s. This new feature served to establish a world market for oil and refined products, and reduced some of the advantages of integration in the oil industry. The long-term effects of this addition were still unclear.

MESA PETROLEUM COMPANY: 1981–1985[17]

By early 1981, Mesa was a reasonably good-sized oil and gas exploration company. Based in Amarillo, Texas, it had reported revenues in 1980 of $200 million and net income of $95 million. Mesa was primarily a domestic E&P firm with approximately 90% of its revenues generated by its exploration and production operations. Its oil and gas reserves in 1980 were estimated at 25 million barrels of oil and 858 billion cubic feet (bcf) of

---

[11]"Scorecard for the OPEC Meeting."
[12]Ibid.
[13]"Energy," p. 74.
[14]"Scorecard for the OPEC Meeting."

---

[15]"Interview: T. Boone Pickens, Wildcats on Wall Street," *Planning Review,* July 1985, p. 6.
[16]"Splitting Up," *Business Week,* July 1, 1985, p. 50.
[17]For background data on the firm from its inception until 1980, see *Mesa Petroleum Company (A)* and *(B),* [not included in this publication].

EXHIBIT 3   Number of U.S. Refineries*

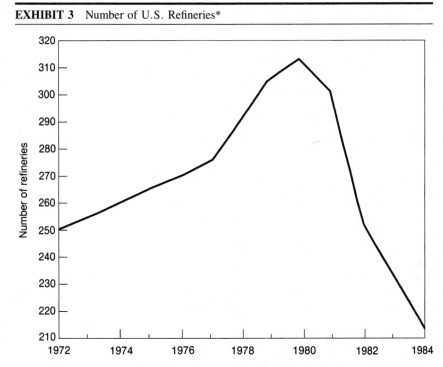

*Many of the refinery closures illustrated here were the result of the Reagan administration's elimination of entitlement cross-subsidies in 1981. The majority of these closed refineries were small, "teakettle" operations.

Source: "Big Oil Starts Thinking Smaller," *The New York Times*, March 17, 1985, p. 1, sec. 3.

gas, with production of 3 million barrels of oil and 106 bcf of gas during the year.

Mesa's finding costs had risen fairly dramatically since 1979. According to *Petroleum Outlook*, it cost Mesa $15.06 to find a barrel of oil in the United States in 1981. By comparison, Mesa's finding costs were $13.80 a barrel in 1980 and $5.43 a barrel in 1979.[18]

Though Mesa had exhibited a healthy earnings growth rate through 1981, this was partially a function of the firm's accounting practices. A 1979 FASB ruling had allowed the capitalization of certain interest costs related to developing properties. Since 1979, Mesa had been capitalizing an increasing percentage of its interest costs. In 1979, Mesa had capitalized $6.2 million, or 11% of its interest costs. By 1981, the firm was capitalizing $70 million, or 70%. Had that interest been expensed, 1981 earnings would have been reduced by some $38 million.[19]

Mesa's capital expenditures during the early 80s peaked in 1981 (during the industry boom) and thereafter declined steadily. Expenditures in 1985 were projected to be $85 million. Recent reductions in capital spending were due in part to the general slowdown in the industry and in part to a change in strategy at Mesa. Sid

---

[18]"A Nicely Coppered Bet," *Forbes*, July 5, 1982, p. 40.   [19]Ibid.

Tassin, assistant to Mesa's financial Vice President David Batchelder, recalled when the initiative to change strategy began:

> Pickens said it wasn't enough to just hunker down like a bunch of groundhogs; get rid of a little fat; accept a little less cash flow, lower reserves and less net income, and next winter come out of the hole. . . . He said it was time to take a fresh look at our own business.[20]

The "fresh look" that Pickens took resulted in a change in strategy and a restructuring of Mesa's operations. The changes included reducing the work force by one third, selling overseas interests, halting the issue of company cars, and holding exploration costs at less than $10 per barrel.[21] Early in 1984, Mesa reduced the number of its vice preidents from 10 to 3. Mesa's employees in 1985 averaged 36 years of age, with all of Pickens' closest advisers being below 35 years of age.[22]

Despite Mesa's leaner operations, the firm continued to perform well. Oil and gas revenues rose steadily through the 80s, reaching record levels. Total assets and shareholder's equity of the company, after a fall in 1982, grew strongly through 1984. The net amount of Mesa's debt also declined from 1982 to 1984 by about $60 million. In addition, Mesa was able to remain at or above the industry average (excluding acquisitions) of replacement percentage (Table 1).[23] Including acquisitions, the replacement percentage was higher in later years. Mesa also continued to introduce innovations into its operations. Examples of these included running wells by wind chargers and reducing obsolete inventory by trading with other companies.[24] Exhibits 4–6 summarize Mesa's recent financial and operating history.

Mesa continued its policy of spinning off oil and gas properties into tax shelters for its shareholders. In 1982, Mesa transferred a 90% net overriding interest in 10 offshore, partially developed properties into the Mesa Offshore Royalty Trust. The trust was somewhat unique

TABLE 1   Reserve Replacement Percentage

Year	Percent of Mesa Replaced (excluding acquisitions)	Percent of Industry Replaced (excluding acquisitions)
1980	145%	80%
1981	154	87
1982	117	70
1983	80	81
1984	65	64

Source: "Mesa's Style Is Lean and Unorthodox," *Los Angeles Times,* April 22, 1985.

TABLE 2   Mesa's Capital Expenditures

Year	Amount (millions)
1980	$397
1981	420
1982	332
1983	223
1984	105
1985	85 est.

Source: "Mesa's Style Is Lean and Unorthodox," *Los Angeles Times,* April 22, 1985.

in that the properties transferred were only *partially* developed and would require significant expenditures to complete development. The development expenditures meant that no distributions from the trust would take place in 1983, and only a minimal distribution was likely in 1984.

---

[20]"Mesa's Style Is Lean and Unorthodox," *Los Angeles Times,* April 22, 1985.

[21]Ibid.

[22]Ibid.

[23]Replacement percentage is the amount of new reserves discovered divided by the amount of production in the period. It should be noted that Mesa tended to book its reserves just

before they were brought into production. Therefore, reserve increases shown in a given year in the 1980s could, in fact, reflect discoveries made in the mid- to late-1970s.

[24]"Mesa's Style Is Lean and Unorthodox."

Citing a lack of economically drillable prospects, Pickens, during this period, diverted a portion of Mesa's resources away from oil and into other opportunities. One activity was the purchase of undervalued reserves from other oil companies. Generally, this meant attempting to take over companies with assets valued below appraised value. The details of Mesa's ventures in this area, specifically the attempted takeovers of Cities Service, General American Oil, Superior Oil, Gulf Oil, Phillips Petroleum, and Unocal, are presented in the

---

EXHIBIT 4

MESA PETROLEUM COMPANY
Income Statement
Years Ended December 31
($ in thousands)

	1984	1983	1982
Revenues:			
Natural gas	$ 279,317	$262,620	$264,776
Oil and condensate	115,807	112,618	96,342
Natural gas liquids	14,829	13,084	13,766
Other	3,536	2,812	1,497
	413,489	391,134	376,381
Costs and expenses:			
Lease operating	51,628	48,850	50,353
General and administrative	21,476	20,235	19,440
Production, federal excise and other taxes	30,516	26,472	29,798
Depreciation, depletion and amortization	155,137	137,070	124,226
	258,757	232,627	223,817
Operating income	154,732	158,507	152,564
Other income (expense):			
Gain on sale of securities and assets	403,549	89,221	63,967
Interest income	87,748	19,524	23,942
Interest expense, net of amounts capitalized	(184,192)	(77,513)	(40,299)
Dividend income	22,403	10,108	4,943
Other	(8,649)	(102)	(9,613)
	320,859	41,238	42,940
Income before income taxes	475,591	199,745	195,504
Provision for income taxes	(205,407)	(73,835)	(65,600)
Net income	270,184	125,910	129,904
Preferred stock dividends	(16,333)	(11,019)	(13,959)
Net income available for common shares	$ 253,851	$114,891	$115,945
Net income per common share	$ 3.75	$ 1.72	$ 1.72
Weighted-average shares outstanding	67,657	66,987	67,462

Source: Mesa Petroleum Company, Annual Reports.

EXHIBIT 5

MESA PETROLEUM COMPANY
Balance Sheet
as of December 31
($ in thousands)

	1984	1983
Assets		
Current assets:		
Cash and short-term investments	$ 550,946	$ 22,722
Accounts and notes receivable	136,926	126,630
Marketable securities	338,507	—
Inventories	12,524	31,644
Prepaid expenses and other	18,325	2,885
Total current assets	1,057,228	183,881
Long-term receivables:		
Secured installment note	796,007	—
Term royalty	185,273	222,232
Other	22,274	22,248
	1,003,554	244,480
Marketable securities	249,051	637,220
Property, plant and equipment (using full cost accounting):		
Oil and gas properties, wells and equipment	2,191,833	1,599,888
Oil and gas properties not yet evaluated	45,582	64,074
Transportation, office and other properties	53,896	54,425
	2,291,311	1,718,387
Less—Accumulated depreciation, depletion and amortization	664,116	491,706
	1,627,195	1,226,681
Deferred charges and other assets	18,923	13,383
	$3,955,951	$2,305,645
Liabilities and Stockholders' Equity		
Current liabilities:		
Current maturities on long-term debt	$ 27,670	$ 54,745
Revolving credit debt repaid in 1985	350,000	—
Accounts payable	58,561	80,375
Accrued liabilities:		
Interest	21,935	17,619
Other	8,790	5,217
Total current liabilities	466,956	157,956
Long-term debt, net	1,625,009	1,248,878
Subordinated variable rate notes	500,000	—
Deferred revenue and other	115,478	42,532
Deferred income taxes	422,914	227,774
Contingencies		
7% redeemable preferred stock	84,000	126,000
Stockholders' equity:		
Common stock, $1 par value; authorized 100,000,000 shares;		
outstanding 66,959,000 and 66,904,000 shares, respectively	66,959	66,904
Capital surplus	163,412	162,852
Reinvested earnings	530,500	290,032
Unrealized loss on marketable securities	(19,277)	(17,283)
Total stockholders' equity	741,594	502,505
Total liabilities and stockholders' equity	$3,955,951	$2,305,645

Source: Mesa Petroleum Company, Annual Reports.

EXHIBIT 6

MESA PETROLEUM COMPANY
Statement of Changes in Financial Position
Years Ended December 31
($ in thousands)

	1984	1983	1982
Funds provided by operations:			
Net income..	$ 270,184	$ 125,910	$ 129,904
Depreciation, depletion and amortization......................	155,137	137,070	124,226
Deferred income taxes.......................................	194,971	66,753	59,432
Gain on sale of securities and assets	(403,549)	(89,221)	(63,967)
Interest capitalized	(7,263)	(10,831)	(57,323)
Unrealized foreign exchange loss............................	11,298	1,659	10,255
Funds provided by operations..........................	220,778	231,340	202,527
Other funds provided:			
Proceeds from sale of securities and assets, net................	1,099,451	284,383	330,839
Marketable securities classified as current assets	338,507	—	—
Increase in deferred revenue and other liabilities...............	72,946	23,121	—
Other	(4,627)	5,525	(7,003)
Other funds provided	1,506,277	313,029	323,836
Funds provided by (utilized in) financing:			
Long-term borrowings.......................................	1,789,470	631,544	305,864
Issuance of subordinated notes	500,000	—	—
Retirements of long-term debt...............................	(1,386,909)	(104,765)	(430,832)
Decrease (increase) in long-term receivables..................	(770,372)	25,044	(6,002)
Redemption of preferred stock	(42,000)	(42,000)	(42,000)
Funds provided by (utilized in) financing	90,189	509,823	(172,970)
Funds utilized:			
Capital expenditures—			
Purchase of Mesa Royalty Trust units	507,068	—	—
Oil and gas properties and other, net	109,278	235,989	314,495
Purchases of marketable securities...........................	606,835	801,192	62,225
Cash dividends...	29,716	24,385	27,315
	1,252,897	1,061,566	404,035
Resulting in an increase (decrease) in working capital of..........	$ 564,347	$ (7,374)	$ (50,642)
Changes in working capital:			
Cash and short-term investments	$ 528,224	$ 8,603	$ (978)
Accounts and notes receivable..............................	10,296	(10,609)	(60,572)
Marketable securities	338,507	—	—
Inventories, prepaid expenses and other......................	(3,680)	(26,644)	(5,455)
Current maturities on long-term debt.........................	27,075	(20,730)	3,698
Revolving credit debt repaid in 1985........................	(350,000)	—	—
Accounts payable and accrued liabilities	13,925	42,006	12,665
	$ 564,347	$ (7,374)	$ (50,642)

Source: Mesa Petroleum Company, Annual Reports.

following sections. Although a great deal of Mesa's net income was attributable to these activities, Mesa's oil and gas operations also remained relatively profitable during the 1981 to 1984 period.

MESA'S ATTEMPTED ACQUISITIONS AND MERGERS: 1982 AND 1983

In early 1982, Pickens offered his assessment of the market for oil and gas securities, an appraisal that foreshadowed a series of mergers and attempted mergers that he would initiate over the next two years. Stated Pickens,

> The company remains committed to the replacement and enhancement of its reserves, the depletable assets of the shareholders. . . . Oil and gas assets are currently undervalued in the security markets. . . . [Mesa] will actively evaluate and pursue opportunities to enhance its shareholders' investment through acquisitions and financial innovations.[25]

Cities Service Co. Pickens did not delay in moving actively and aggressively to capitalize upon apparent opportunities. In May of 1982, Pickens lined up partners to help finance a tender offer for 51% of Cities Service Co. at $45 per share. The stock of Cities Service, the nation's 20th largest oil company, was then selling at approximately $35 per share. Cities Service was a much larger company than Mesa, with 1981 revenues of $8.56 billion versus Mesa's $407.7 million.

Learning of the proposed offer, Cities Service's management surprised Wall Street by making a preemptive offer of $17 per share for 51% of Mesa's 73.8 million outstanding shares. Mesa responded by offering $50 per share for 51% of Cities' 80.7 million shares outstanding. Pickens made the offer to Cities Service's board as a proposed "friendly" merger. Explaining his reason for wanting to merge with Cities Service, Pickens voiced a theme he would return to often, "We had a feeling we needed to do something about our invest-

---

TABLE 3 Gains on Takeover Attempts (in millions, pre-tax gain)

Supron (1982)	$ 22.3
Cities Service (1982)	31.5
General American Oil (1983)	43.6
Superior Oil (1983)	31.6
Gulf Oil (1984)	760.0
Phillips Petroleum (1985)	89.0
Unocal (1985)	83.0*
Total	$1,061.0

*Estimated after-tax gain from *The Wall Street Journal*, July 3, 1985.

Source: "High Times for T. Boone Pickens," *Time Magazine*, March 4, 1985, p. 55.

---

ment, because Cities Service management was depleting the company's reserves and not replacing them."[26]

Many industry analysts felt there was good reason to take Mesa's offer seriously despite the disparity in the companies' sizes. As one executive stated, "This man is definitely who Cities fears most. He is a cool and calculating gambler, the arch stereotype of the West Texas poker player."[27] Pickens' uncanny financial abilities had earned the respect of much of the investment community. "He has made a lot of people a lot of money by doing what he says he is going to do," said a Houston-based analyst. "I suspect that 99 percent of the world loves Boone Pickens."[28]

When Cities' board did not respond to his merger offer, Pickens made a tender offer directly to the shareholders. The offer was for 12.1 million shares at $45 per share. Pickens' apparent objective was to strengthen his bargaining position by proving that Cities' shareholders were eager to sell.

On June 8, after rejecting Mesa's offer, Cities' board made its second offer—a "friendly" bid to purchase all

---

[25]*Mesa Petroleum Company 1981 Annual Report*, p. 5.

[26]"Cities Service Heats up Battle with Mesa via Fraud Suit, Legal Pressure on a Bank," *The Wall Street Journal*, June 3, 1982.

[27]" The Man Cities Service Fears," *Dallas Times Herald*, June 6, 1982, p. 2.

[28]"Mesa's Founder Takes on Big Foe," *The New York Times*, June 7, 1982, p. D–1.

of Mesa for $21 per share. This offer was, in turn, rejected by Mesa's board.

During the following week, Mesa and Cities were each tendered approximately 45% of the other's shares.

Attempting to thwart Cities Service's takeover, Mesa's board voted for two antitakeover measures. The first measure was a "super-majority" provision, requiring a 75% shareholder vote to approve a change in the control of Mesa. The second measure removed from Mesa's bylaws a provision that gave anyone holding at least one third of the shares the right to convene a special shareholders meeting.

On June 17, Gulf Oil Corp. announced a $63 per share bid for Cities Service, a total purchase price of $5 billion. Gulf's chairman, James E. Lee, acknowledged that the large jump in bidding (from Mesa's $45-a-share offer to Gulf's $63-a-share offer) was designed to prevent a bidding contest with any other potential suitors.

Three-way negotiations involving Mesa, Cities, and Gulf ensued, eventually resulting in Mesa selling its 4.1 million shares of Cities back to Cities for $55 a share. As part of the peace agreement, Mesa agreed that for a period of five years it would not purchase Cities stock or seek to influence the affairs of Cities. The total pre-tax gain to Mesa was said to exceed $30 million.

With Mesa out of the way, the road seemed to be paved for Gulf to proceed with its bid for Cities. The potential for antitrust objections still threatened to derail the acquisition, however. [Cities Service ultimately merged with Occidental Petroleum in a $4.05 billion transaction.]

Just days after accepting the Gulf deal, Pickens made it clear he was not through dealing in the securities market. "We've got to come up with some other deals, because this industry is in for some rough sledding. . . . As long as the costs of finding oil and gas reserves stay high, 1982 will be a shakeout year in this industry, especially if companies keep depleting their reserves."[29]

General American Oil (GAO).

In an effort to take control of Dallas-based General American Oil Co. of Texas, Mesa, in December of 1982, offered $40 a share for a majority of GAO's stock. GAO was primarily an exploration and production firm operating in Canada, the United States, the Gulf of Mexico and the North Sea. Mesa and GAO were roughly of equal size in terms of reserves and undeveloped acreage.

Mesa had purchased 7.5% of GAO's stock in 1976. Subsequently, Mesa issued debentures exchangeable for most of the GAO shares it had accumulated.[30]

In a surprise reaction to Mesa's hostile bid, GAO made a $50-a-share offer for nearly a third of its own outstanding shares. The strategy behind the move appeared to center on GAO management's control of a large block of its shares held in a foundation and two trusts set up by GAO's late founder. Should a third of GAO's shares be repurchased and retired, the management-controlled block of shares which remained would constitute a clear majority.

At the proration deadline several days later, Mesa's hostile tender offer for control of GAO was heavily oversubscribed.

In a move similar to the ending of the Cities Service deal, Phillips Petroleum Co. stepped in and purchased GAO for $1.14 billion. As a part of the deal, Mesa dropped its hostile bid; in return, GAO paid Mesa $15 million for tender offer expenses. Mesa further agreed not to purchase GAO securities for five years.

Mesa's pre-tax gain on its holdings of GAO stock amounted to $43.6 million.

Superior Oil Co.

In early March, 1983, Pickens spoke in Dallas. "You've got to replace your reserves or you are liquidating the assets," said Pickens. "We have to replace those reserves because we're on record for five years now saying that if we have back-to-back years of down reserves we'll sell out."[31]

Within a week, Mesa's latest play for oil became public. On March 14, the financial press announced that Mesa had purchased 2.5 million shares (or nearly 2%) of Superior Oil Co., the nation's largest independent oil company. Like Cities Service, Superior was a much larger company than Mesa. In 1982, Superior earned $223.4 million on revenues of $2.04 billion. At the time

---

[29]"Mesa's T. B. Pickens Is 'Delighted' in Spite of Failure of Offer," *The Wall Street Journal*, June 21, 1982.

[30]An earlier case, *Mesa Petroleum Company (B)*, describes this transaction in greater detail.

[31]" Speculation focuses on Mesa," *Dallas Morning News*, March 14, 1983, p. 3-D.

of Mesa's purchases, Superior's stock was selling for about $35 per share. Analysts placed the company's liquidation value at $57 per share.

Many oil industry analysts quickly stated that they doubted whether Mesa intended to actually take over Superior. "I don't believe Mesa Petroleum wants to acquire Superior," said one analyst. "I think Pickens sees a company that's undervalued and the majors might want to get in there and do a deal. He's just an opportunist."[32]

Mesa's purchases helped give visibility to a resolution that was scheduled to come before Superior's annual meeting. The resolution was sponsored by Wilametta Keck Day, daughter of the company founder and sister of retired chairman Howard M. Keck. The resolution called for certain above-market offers for at least 45% of Superior's shares to be submitted to a committee of three independent directors. Unless the committee found the offer unfair it was to recommend that the full board approve it. Mrs. Day's spokesman stated that she had submitted the resolution because "if an offer is submitted, she thinks the shareholders ought to know about it."[33]

Mesa raised its stake in Superior to 3% over the summer. In September, Superior and Mesa reached an agreement, with Mesa selling its 3.98 million shares back to Superior for $42 a share, a 10% premium over its market value. The buyback resulted in a $32 million profit for Mesa.

Criticism was immediately directed at Superior. One industry observer derided the buyback as "the ultimate bailout." He continued, "To bail out a 3 percent small stockholder for a 10 percent premium above the market is going to get a lot of criticism from stockholders."[34]

Added another analyst,

It's been a no-lose proposition for him. He takes a position in a company, the speculation takes over from that point and the company bails him out or a white knight comes in. He's making more money that way than turning the [drill] bit.[35]

Big institutional investors were also incensed. Portfolio managers were angry that Superior did not offer to buy them out at the same premium. In the weeks following the buyback, Superior officials admitted they had received many calls from upset investors. Many of the big institutions showed signs of worry. "Major institutions are increasingly anxious to sell, and might not hold out for top dollar," warned one portfolio manager.[36]

In March 1984, Mobil Corp. announced it had agreed to acquire Superior for $45 a share, a total of $5.7 billion. It would be the fifth largest takeover in history.

KN Energy Inc.   Mesa's attempt in the fall of 1983 to take over KN Energy Inc. was short lived. KN Energy operated a 16,000 mile natural gas pipeline system and held various oil and gas interests. Mesa, it was said, was primarily interested in the firm's natural gas reserves.

In September, Mesa had offered to purchase all of KN's outstanding shares at a price of $54.25 per share. A month later, Mesa backed down, declining to press for an unfriendly takeover after KN directors rejected Mesa's earlier bid.

Mesa's reticence to persevere in the takeover attempt fueled speculation that Pickens was considering bigger plays.

STALKING BIG GAME: MESA VERSUS GULF

In August of 1983, a Mesa-led group of investors had, in fact, begun quietly to purchase shares of Gulf Oil Corporation. The increased trading was soon noticed in Pittsburgh by Gulf executives who had been worried about what they perceived to be the low market valuation of the firm's common shares.

Problems at Gulf.   When James E. Lee became Gulf's chairman in 1981, he took over a company that many considered to be the weakest of the Seven Sisters. Gulf had been shaken by political payoff scandals in the mid-1970s, and had not appeared to move decisively

---

[32]Ibid.

[33]"Mesa Buys Stake in Superior Oil; Intent Is Unclear," *The Wall Street Journal*, March 14, 1983.

[34]"Mesa Will Sell Stake in Superior Oil Co.," *Dallas Morning News*, September 2, 1983, p. 6E.

[35]"Mesa Petroleum to Sell 3% Stake in Superior Oil," *The Wall Street Journal*, September 2, 1983, p. 4.

[36] "The Takeover Game Isn't over at Superior Oil," *Business Week*, September 19, 1983, p. 103.

since. This apparent passivity was accompanied by a steep decline in proven reserves.

Lee moved rapidly to implement a plan to return Gulf to long-term health. His program had four major thrusts: (1) reduction of Gulf's work force, (2) repurchase of Gulf shares, (3) consolidation and elimination of many downstream operations, and (4) refocusing Gulf's exploration efforts on domestic, high-risk, frontier (arctic, offshore, etc.) ventures.

Gulf began the implementation of Lee's strategy with a repurchase of 10 million Gulf shares (out of 195 million shares then outstanding) in the latter half of 1981. Despite the repurchase, Gulf's share price fell 19% during 1981. Moreover, although Gulf had significantly increased new project spending in 1981, the firm's domestic reserves continued to fall. Gulf had, in fact, been unable to replace its reserves since 1972.

In an effort to improve the profitability of its marketing operations, Gulf concentrated on increasing market share on the East Coast, where it was the second-largest marketer with an 8% share. While Gulf's gasoline sales still decreased 3% that year, the drop was less than the 4.5% decline seen industrywide.

During 1982, Gulf continued to emphasize domestic oil and gas exploration and production. The company widthdrew many of its refining, marketing and chemicals operations overseas. Write-offs during 1982 totaled $200 million. The remaining worldwide refining, marketing and chemical operations produced an operating loss of more than $250 million during the year. As part of the employee reduction program, Gulf in 1982 removed some 12% of its work force from the payroll. Though the firm's total revenues in 1982 remained at about the previous year's level, earnings fell by 27%.

Gulf's net margin improved somewhat in 1983, a fact management attributed to its recent cost-cutting moves. Throughout 1983, Gulf had stepped up the pace of its restructuring by closing all European refining and marketing operations, closing domestic retail outlets, reducing companywide employment by another 17%, and repurchasing more of its outstanding shares.

With both prices and demand for oil products falling, however, Gulf's strategy by mid-1983 was not impressing the markets. By August, Gulf's market capitalization[37]

had fallen to $6 billion on 166 million shares outstanding— a drop of almost 50% since 1980.

Mesa Closes In.   As heavy trading in Gulf stock continued into the early fall, Gulf's board began to consider possible antitakeover provisions. On October 11, the board, spurred by the trading of almost 2 million Gulf shares the previous Friday, proposed abolishing cumulative voting for directors and other charter amendments designed to reduce the threat of a takeover. A shareholders meeting to vote on the proposals was set for December.

On Monday, October 17, a Mesa-led investor group revealed that it held 14.5 million shares of Gulf (8.75% of the then outstanding shares). Mesa itself held 9.6 million of the total. The partners joining Mesa were Canada's Belzberg family, Wagner & Brown (a Midland, Texas independent), Harbert International Inc. (a privately held Birmingham, Alabama construction and real estate firm), and Sunshine Mining Co. of Dallas. The announcement stated that the group had spent $630 million to purchase the stake. The group had decided that Mesa would coordinate future purchases and have exclusive power to vote the group's shares through September 30, 1984.

In its SEC filing, the investor group intimated that it would like to restructure Gulf to increase returns to shareholders. The filing stated, "significant recapitalization transactions and assets restructurings" could be used to increase shareholders' returns. Possible methods described included, "repurchases of shares and distributions of assets to shareholders in the form of independent operating entities, royalty trusts or limited partnerships."[38]

Gulf's senior management responded with criticism of the restructuring idea, and a defense of company policies. "We've looked at royalty trusts . . . and all the ideas that are included in the filing." The royalty trust concept had been rejected because it would mean increased tax expenses for owners. "We've been doing many of these things over the past two years," said a Gulf official. "All our actions are directed at . . . returning value to our shareholders."[39]

---

[37]*Market Capitalization* is defined here as the number of shares outstanding times the price of the firm's stock.

[38]"Mesa Petroleum Group Discloses Gulf Oil Holding," *The Wall Street Journal,* October 18, 1983, p. 3.

[39]Ibid.

Vertical Integration, Cash Returns and Market Valuation. In the fall of 1983, large oil companies' vertical integration strategies were under attack by the investment community. Integrated companies were being valued at 40% or less of their asset value, while small E&P companies were valued at an average of 90%.[40]

Many analysts and oil industry consultants were advocating the breakup of integrated companies to allow earnings from oil and gas production to flow directly to shareholders. "There is a fundamental restructuring taking place," said one consultant. "You're going to see more and more of the traditional integrated companies broken up."[41] An investment banker stated, "Certainly there are efficiencies with integration. But that doesn't mean we need 20 integrated oils."[42]

Arguing against breakups and concepts such as the royalty trust, many majors contended that they needed to retain their cash flow to search for future supplies of oil and gas. In the past, the high cost of exploration had often been cited as a reason for high oil prices. Many oil executives felt that distributing profits from high-priced oil, rather than reinvesting to assure future energy supplies for America, would anger consumers and bring on new government regulations. As a government energy analyst put it, "Corporate strategy in cash-rich oil companies is a public policy matter."[43]

In November 1983, Gulf's chairman, James E. Lee, defended the integrated companies' strategies in an interview. Answering a question concerning Pickens' philosophy he stated, "I see a mutual interest in increasing shareholder value. We may have a difference of opinion as to how best to do that." . . . Articulating his disagreement with the royalty trust concept, Lee stated, "If you're going to be an oil and gas company, everything still indicates that it's the natural resource base that really determines the value the market places on the company . . . we decided to focus our technology, our capital, toward the U.S., the frontier areas, because that's where we think we have the best probability of

successfully replacing our reserves . . . and the only way we can continue even to hold the level of oil production is to reinvest to replace reserves." [44]

Countered Pickens,

> Over the period 1978 to 1983 Gulf Oil only replaced about 43 percent of the oil and gas produced. . . . Over that five-year period, they actually lost 634 million [equivalent] barrels off their reserve base. Do you think the stockholders knew anything about that?[45]

Pickens and his supporters argued that cash flow was being wasted on increasingly risky exploration projects that wouldn't pay off and on unprofitable downstream operations. Therefore, they wanted to force oil company managements to return more cash to investors. Pickens contended that this would force managers to abandon marginal exploration. In support of this viewpoint, an oil analyst remarked, "Full replacement of domestic reserves by domestic companies has become an all but unrealistic and impossible objective."[46]

Pickens often asserted that oil companies could therefore "liquidate efficiently" by sending cash flow directly to shareholders. Spinning off assets to shareholders, according to Pickens, would both make it easier for a company to replace remaining reserves and force the market to value the company at closer to its true value.

Gulf Defense Mechanisms. Immediately after the Mesa group's announcement that it was behind the activity in Gulf's shares, Gulf officials began to analyze possible defenses. To prepare for any contingency, Gulf lined up a $5 billion line of credit with 38 banks. At the same time, four of the banks backing the Mesa group withdrew. Pickens charged that Gulf pressured the institutions, a charge Gulf denied.

Gulf had numerous possible defenses, each with its own perils. The first defense was simply to convince Gulf shareholders that Gulf's long-term strategy would provide a better return than Pickens' short-term plans. Unfortunately for Gulf, approximately one third of its shares were held by institutions who might not only find

---

[40]"Boone Pickens, Company Hunter," *Fortune,* December 26, 1983.

[41]"Restructuring Big Oil," *Business Week,* November 14, 1983, p. 139.

[42]Ibid.

[43]Ibid., p. 146.

[44]Ibid., p. 143.

[45]"Interview: T. Boone Pickens," p. 8.

[46]Ibid., p. 139.

the idea of a quick pay-off appealing, but whose fiduciary responsibility might lead to a decision to sell.

The second possible defense was attacking Pickens personally—the "low road" approach. Gulf had already run ads attacking Pickens' record of attempted takeovers, portraying him as a hit-and-run artist, an opportunist unconcerned with shareholders.

Other plausible defenses were financially oriented. Gulf could buy back the investor groups' shares. This move risked provoking other shareholders who were not offered the same opportunity.

Gulf could also buy Mesa Petroleum and depose Pickens. Pickens had foreseen this possibility, however. His investors had agreed that in this event, voting control of the entire block would pass to the private firm, Harbert International. In addition, as pointed out by a Texan close to the investor group, this option would "make Boone several hundred million dollars richer, (with his options on millions of Mesa shares), and he'd still be around advising the group."[47]

A further option for Gulf was to purchase reserves in the market, an approach advocated by Pickens himself. This would have defused Pickens' liquidation argument. But, there was no guarantee Pickens would not then argue for a bigger royalty trust.

October: Mesa's Growing Stake. By the end of October, the Mesa investor group had increased its share of Gulf to 17.9 million shares. The investors also made a filing under the Hart-Scott-Rodino Act. This act required a filing if a securities purchaser may have intentions other than investment. This filing barred the Mesa group from making further purchases until the government determined that there were no antitrust problems. On the final day of October, Mesa filed with the SEC for permission to seek proxies at Gulf's December meeting and named Lehman Brothers Kuhn Loeb Inc., as their financial advisor.

November: The Royalty Trust. By November, the battle had begun to focus on the possible shareholder value of a Gulf royalty trust. Mesa disseminated a book detailing possible Gulf trusts which would distribute

from 10% to 75% of Gulf's U.S. oil and gas production revenues. The report predicted that the trust units would have a significantly higher market valuation than equivalent Gulf shares. It contended that the trust units would trade at 8 to 10 times cash flow, versus Gulf's current stock price of 2 to 3 times.

As expected, Gulf officials took issue with Mesa's report. "Contrary to the proponents' assertions, the capital markets are sufficiently sophisticated to know that one plus one equals two," asserted a Gulf spokesman. "Thus, except for an initial flurry of excitement . . . the distribution of [units] has resulted in a drop in the distributing company's stock price that reflects the value attributed to the royalty trust units."[48]

Gulf's management also rebutted the traditional argument for tax savings due to the elimination of double taxation by creating a royalty trust. They claimed that tax credits and deferments gave Gulf approximately an 8% effective tax rate.[49] In addition, they pointed out that Gulf shareholders would have to pay taxes on the initial distribution of trust units. This distribution would be treated as a dividend. Gulf officials stated that many individual shareholders would have to sell shares to pay the tax bill.

James Lee hit hard on this last point: "It's certainly clear Mr. Pickens doesn't care a hoot about the huge unnecessary tax bite that would hit most of our shareholders."[50] Pickens responded to this issue by stating that when shareholders make money they should expect to pay taxes.

On November 22, Mesa was cleared by the SEC to purchase more Gulf shares. The investor group immediately began to increase its holdings. By the December 2 meeting, the investors had purchased another 1,963,200 shares for $87.1 million.

Attempted Takeover. In the first round of Pickens' bid to restructure Gulf, Pickens was soundly beaten. Gulf's management won a December proxy fight that

---

[47] "Future of Gulf Oil Hinges on Proxy Fight Led by Mesa Chairman," *The Wall Street Journal*, November 2, 1983, p. 18.

[48] "Gulf Oil Royalty Trust Plans Are Outlined by Mesa and Partners, Raising Questions," *The Wall Street Journal*, November 9, 1983.

[49] "Future of Gulf Oil."

[50] "Pickens Says He Wouldn't Break up Gulf, Pledges Not to Sell Stake Back to Oil Firm," *The Wall Street Journal*, November 11, 1983, p. 10.

allowed the firm to reincorporate in Delaware. Delaware laws would make it much more difficult for Pickens to elect directors to Gulf's board.

After Gulf's reincorporation, T. Boone Pickens began looking for additional financing to fund a Gulf takeover. Previously, Pickens had insisted that the investment group's goal was to force Gulf to return earnings to shareholders. Now, Pickens contended that Gulf had pushed his group into a corner, forcing a tender offer.

In early February, 1984, the investor group released a study by Drexel Burnham Lambert Inc., detailing a possible Gulf purchase plan. The plan called for purchasing Gulf at $55 per share in a two-step takeover.[51] The first step involved raising $3.66 billion to purchase 61.3 million shares of Gulf, giving the investors greater than 50% ownership.

To raise the money, a new company would be formed. The company would sell $1.73 billion worth of investment units consisting of common and senior preferred stock. The new company would also issue $450 million of senior notes. The Pickens investor group would contribute another $482 million, and the final $1 billion would come from new bank borrowings.

The second step of the takeover plan involved the remaining Gulf shares. After Gulf and the new company were merged, the remaining Gulf shares would be swapped for additional securities worth $55 a share. These securities would include $3.07 billion of 20-year, 16% junior debentures, and $1.5 billion worth of preferred stock with a 15% dividend rate.

The terms of the $450 million of senior notes used in the first step specified that they would be paid off within 30 days of the merger. Gulf would then be liquidated over a period of up to three years with the proceeds going to the shareholders of the new company. Independent estimates of the disposal value of Gulf's assets ranged as high as $15 billion.

Gulf's response was immediate—it filed suit in a Delaware federal court, charging the investment group with "market manipulation and other violations of securities laws." Gulf also increased its credit lines to $6 billion. A Gulf official described the Pickens group's plans as an effort "to seize the future potential of Gulf

for the benefit of [the Pickens] investors with money borrowed on the strength of Gulf's assets."[52]

The announcement of Mesa's acquisition plan had another effect. Numerous potential Gulf suitors began to approach Gulf's management. One of the more ardent was Robert O. Anderson, chairman of Atlantic Richfield Co. Talking with Lee over the phone, Anderson proposed a $70 per share purchase.[53]

Learning of the offer, Pickens moved quickly and made an offer for 13.5 million shares at $65 per share. Pickens was said to be hoping the offer would be heavily oversubscribed. He apparently felt banks would lend the money needed to purchase any additional shares offered, knowing they could be sold to Arco for $70.

Worried that Pickens might be offered enough shares of Gulf to obtain effective control, Gulf's management suddenly found themselves on the defensive. Gulf's board met, and, on February 29, announced that Gulf was looking for a purchaser. The board members directed its investment bankers to pursue "all alternatives."

In other moves to prepare for the sale of the company, Gulf's board awarded $7,158,900 in bonuses to Gulf employees, set aside $7,203,100 for "additional grants contingent upon a change in control of the company," and raised the investment bankers' combined fees to 0.35% of Gulf's final sale price.[54]

To help speed the sale, and to prevent Pickens from gaining control, Gulf allowed possible purchasers to study internal company records. Some of these potential suitors included Standard Oil of California (Socal), Atlantic Richfield, Standard Oil (Ohio), Union Oil of California, and Allied Chemical.

On Monday, March 5, Gulf's board announced the sale of the company to Socal (Chevron) for $80 per share, a total purchase price of $13.4 billion. Gulf's announcement stated that Socal "will begin shortly a cash tender offer for all of the outstanding shares of Gulf common stock."[55]

---

[51]"Gulf Oil Unveils Moves to Block Pickens Group," *The Wall Street Journal*, February 13, 1984.

[52]Ibid.

[53]"Why Gulf Lost Its Fight for Life," *Business Week*, March 19, 1984, p. 84.

[54]Ibid.

[55]"Gulf Agrees to Be Acquired by Socal," *The Wall Street Journal*, March 6, 1984, p. 3.

Onboard a Mesa corporate jet headed for New York, Pickens received the news from an aide in Amarillo. "Shucks," he said, "I guess we lost another one."[56]

It was later reported that Mesa's investor group would report a pre-tax gain of $760 million on the purchase of Gulf by Socal. Mesa Petroleum's share of the investor group's profit was said to be about $500 million.[57] Pickens personally received a cash bonus of $18.6 million for his performance in 1984 as Mesa's CEO. The bonus was to be drawn from a $20 million pool set up to reward certain Mesa executives for their roles in the battle to acquire Gulf Oil. Pickens' bonus was thought to be the largest ever given to an executive of a public company.[58]

BUY-BACK OF THE MESA ROYALTY TRUST

In a move that took most industry observers by surprise, Mesa, in May of 1984, made a $570 million cash tender offer for the 16.3 million outstanding units of its own Mesa Royalty Trust. The buy-back offer for the trust Mesa had established in 1979 marked the first time an oil company had sought to repurchase oil and gas interests it had earlier spun-off to shareholders.

According to Pickens, his main objective in making this unusual move was to acquire high-quality producing oil and gas properties at a reasonable price. "We're buying gas in the ground for 92 cents [per thousand cubic feet]," said Pickens, "and that's cheaper than we can find it. . . . Gosh. Just think. We didn't make anyone angry on this deal."[59]

Mesa's offer of $35 per unit represented a 25% premium over market price. Throughout the year, the stock price for the trust had ranged from a high of $29.875 to a low of $24.625 and had closed at $27.5 the day before the announcement was made.

Analysts were quick to ascribe motives to Pickens' surprise move. The most plausible explanation concerned certain political moves being made by the Kansas legislature. The majority of the Mesa Royalty Trust properties were located in Kansas' Hugoton Field. Kansas officials, said analysts, were on the verge of reducing the spacing between gas wells. If such infill drilling were allowed, the underlying asset value of the Mesa Royalty Trust could rise to as high as $60 to $70 a unit.[60] It was the apparent belief of Mesa officials that investors would be willing to tender to receive a sure price immediately rather than speculate on the future.

Other observers suggested that the buy-back offer was designed to quickly bolster the firm's reserve position. It seemed likely that Mesa would fail to replace all of its reserves for the second year in a row. Still others viewed the offer as an easy way for Mesa to boost its own value—just in case Mesa should become the target of a hostile raid.

The buy-back offer was ultimately an unqualified success. By the end of June, approximately 88% of the outstanding units had been tendered and accepted for payment.

MESA VERSUS PHILLIPS

In December of 1984, Pickens announced that Mesa and its partners had acquired a 5.7% interest in Phillips Petroleum and that they intended to acquire a controlling interest in the company. Their first step in the acquisition was a tender offer for an additional 15% of the company at $60 per share. At $60 per share, the total value of Phillips would be $9.3 billion. Pickens made it clear in the early going that his group was opposed to "greenmail" and would not sell their stock unless all shareholders got the same price.[61]

At the time, Phillips Petroleum was the nation's 11th largest oil and gas firm, with total assets in 1983 of $13 billion, revenues of $15 billion, and net income of $721 million. The company's significant reserves of crude oil and natural gas are shown in Table 4. Although the

---

[56] "Why Gulf Lost Its Fight for Life," p. 76.

[57] "Mesa Chief Pickens Is Awarded Bonus of $18.6 Million," *The Wall Street Journal,* March 21, 1985.

[58] Ibid.

[59] "Raiding Mesa Discovers Target Right at Home," *Dallas Morning News,* May 16, 1984, p. 1D.

[60] Ibid.

[61] "Phillips Novel Solution," *The New York Times,* December 26, 1984.

TABLE 4 Phillips Petroleum Reserve Base

Year	Crude (millions of barrels)	Natural Gas (billions of cubic feet)
1979	1,023	7,741
1980	834	6,778
1981	749	6,776
1982	737	6,677
1983	969*	7,646*

*Includes reserves from the purchase of 119 million barrels of oil and 487 billion cubic feet of gas from Aminoil.

Source: "The Attractions of Phillips," *The New York Times*, December 6, 1984.

appraised value of Phillips stock was $76 per share, it had only been trading in the mid-40s prior to the bid. Said George Baker, energy analyst for Smith Barney, "At $60 per share, Phillips Petroleum is a bargain."[62] According to analysts, Phillips met almost all of Pickens' requirements for restructuring—it had "an above average dividend, managers that were not pushing to maximize shareholder wealth, and a lackluster record at replacing oil and gas reserves."[63]

Phillips quickly rejected Mesa's offer and sought to block the takeover bid. Their most effective tactic was a suit against Mesa citing a breach of a non-takeover contract with General American Oil (GAO). The GAO standstill agreement called for Mesa not to try to acquire GAO "directly or indirectly" for five years. Phillips claimed that Mesa's attempted acquisition of Phillips, as it was an indirect attempt to acquire GAO, violated this earlier contract. Despite the opinion of many analysts that Mesa would eventually win the suit, Mesa was forced to postpone the beginning of its tender offer due to legal uncertainties.

On Sunday, December 22, after a weekend of tough negotiations, Phillips and Mesa came to an agreement ending Mesa's takeover bid and adopting a plan to "put more value" in Phillips stock. The agreement was a part of a recapitalization plan for Phillips. Under this plan Phillips would:

1. Repurchase 38% of Phillips' 154 million outstanding shares using debt with an intended market value of $60 per share. This would amount to approximately $3.5 billion for 58.8 million shares. The recapitalization would raise Phillips' debt/equity ratio (defined as long-term debt to total stockholders' equity) from 35% to approximately 70%.
2. Spend an additional $1 billion buying stock on the open market, approximately 20 million shares.
3. Issuance of 32 million shares to the Phillips employee stock ownership plan (ESOP). The ESOP could borrow money for these shares at low rates due to favorable tax laws. The ESOP would end up owning approximately 38% of Phillips.
4. Arrange for Mesa to sell its shares of Phillips for a minimum of $53 per share.
5. Phillips would sell approximately $2 billion in assets.[64]

Although many of the individual actions in the recapitalization plan were relatively common ones, the packaging of them was somewhat unique. Sources involved in the negotiations said that each part of the plan was designed to please individual groups without hurting the company.[65] Alan Edgar, analyst for Schneider, Bernet and Hickman Inc., remarked on the significance of the plan:

It's a lot more important than just a partial success for Boone Pickens. It has some far-reaching ramifications. There are other companies out there that are going to get exposed to this blueprint, either voluntarily or involuntarily.[66]

Pickens later boasted that Mesa had, over time, developed an in-house financial group that could compete with anyone. "Look at the Gulf and Phillips deals," said Pickens. "Gulf and Chevron paid $64 million to investment bankers. We paid $8.5 million. In the Phillips deal—they paid $35 million to investment bankers; we paid zero."[67]

---

[62]"The Attractions of Phillips," *The New York Times*, December 6, 1984, p. 33.

[63]Ibid.

---

[64]"Phillips Novel Solution," *The New York Times*, December 26, 1984.

[65]Ibid.

[66]Ibid.

[67]"Interview: T. Boone Pickens," p. 11.

MESA VERSUS UNOCAL

The Mesa-Unocal battle began in February of 1985 when Pickens announced that Mesa and its partners had acquired a 7.9% stake in Union Oil of California. Mesa announced the purchase was for investment purposes. Fred Hartley, chairman of Unocal, commended Mesa on making a good investment. It was not until the end of March that Pickens, now with 13.6% or 23.7 million shares of Unocal, announced that Mesa was considering a takeover or restructuring of Unocal. Shortly thereafter, Mesa announced a cash tender offer of $54 per share for just over 50% of Unocal. The other 50% would be purchased later for an equivalent $54 per share in notes, bringing the total offer to approximately $8.1 billion.[68] After the bid, Pickens announced that close to $4 billion in financing had already been arranged. A Unocal adviser commented on this announcement,

> All of us were just shocked when Boone came up with that money. . . . Think of it! That's green for half the company.[69]

Unocal was the nation's 12th largest oil company. It had the sixth lowest finding costs in the industry, and ranked second in terms of reserve replacement.[70]

Excluding the rash of name-calling in the press, the takeover battle was being fought over two basic issues. The first of these was over the date of the Unocal annual meeting. The Mesa group sought to delay the meeting so that it would have a chance to put together a slate of directors to run against the Unocal directors. Unocal strongly opposed this proposal in an effort to deprive Mesa of the opportunity to gain control of the board of directors. As Unocal had recently added several anti-takeover provisions to its charter, attempting a takeover at any time other than an annual meeting was very difficult. Due to an intense effort, Unocal was able to win the proxy fight and block Mesa's bid to delay the meeting.

A second major battle, meanwhile, was being fought in the Delaware courts. Unocal had initially counterat-

tacked the Mesa offer with a defensive tactic designed to shake Mesa's financing. Under this plan, Unocal would tender for its own stock for $72 per share. The offer would commence only when the Mesa group got 51% of the company. Mesa would then acquire a company with a long-term debt to the total shareholders' equity ratio of 60%, as opposed to 16%. Unocal later changed this strategy, instead offering a straight repurchase of 29% of the company's securities for $72 per share. Under the new offer, Unocal would not accept any of the Mesa shares for repurchase. It was this issue which caused Mesa to seek redress in the Delaware courts. The courts initially ruled in favor of Mesa on two occasions, but later reversed themselves. The Delaware Supreme Court overruled the lower courts and allowed the targeted repurchase to continue. Analysts expected the SEC would move quickly to block future repurchases of this type.

The two sides got together for the first time the day after the Unocal annual meeting. Although the results of the proxy fight to delay the annual meeting were not official, it was believed that Mesa had lost. At the time of the meeting, Mesa had won the initial decision in the Delaware courts and analysts expected the Delaware Supreme Court to rule in Mesa's favor. The meeting itself seemed to go well, with Pickens commenting at the end of the day,

> Fred, I think we did pretty damn good today. I didn't call you arrogant, and you didn't call me an idiot once.[71]

Despite having made progress toward a solution, the next day the two sides found themselves far apart. Sources said that the Unocal team had decided that there was no reason to make any concessions. The Unocal draft of the solution worked out the previous day was, according to a Pickens aide, " . . . the most ridiculous deal you ever saw. . . . It went backwards from where we were the day before."[72] Pickens and his staff walked out of the meeting and returned to Amarillo.

After losing their bid to postpone the annual meeting, the Mesa Group's primary hope of success hinged on the tender offer. Assuming Unocal lost in the Delaware courts, Mesa planned to tender its shares in the Unocal

---

[68]"How Mesa's Boone Pickens Finally Met Match in Unocal's Fred Hartley," *The Wall Street Journal,* May 24, 1985, p. 1.

[69]Ibid.

[70]"Unocal Chairman Digs in," *The New York Times,* April 16, 1985.

[71]"How Mesa's Boone Pickens Finally Met Match."

[72]Ibid.

$72 offer and use the proceeds to finance the rest of the takeover bid. Shortly after the surprise ruling by the Delaware Supreme Court, Mesa lawyers contacted Unocal and the negotiations for a final settlement began. Hartley was said to be anxious to end the battle, due to worries about what the Pickens group would do next. Pickens' advisers, meanwhile, were concerned that further attempts to make cash tender offers for Unocal could be stymied if Unocal continually outbid the Mesa group while saddling the company with more debt.[73]

The final agreement called for Unocal to include 7.7 million of Mesa's shares in the repurchase and to spin off a large proportion of its domestic oil and gas reserves into master limited partnerships (MLPs) (MLPs are larger, more complex versions of the more traditional limited partnership arrangement. The shares, or "depository receipts," of an MLP are publicly traded and therefore liquid). Despite Pickens' claims that the Mesa shareholders would not lose any money, analysts predicted that the settlement would cost Mesa from $80 to $110 million.

On June 2, Mesa reported an $83 million *gain* as a result of the Unocal takeover bid. The gain came from an income tax rule that allowed Mesa to report the gains it received from the settlement as dividends and not

capital gains. Mesa was also able to take a write-down of $305 million on the Unocal shares it had to hold as a part of the settlement agreement. This write-down offset gains from previous takeover attempts.

STOCK REPURCHASE

In July of 1985, Mesa's board approved a plan to purchase up to $100 million worth of Mesa's own 67 million outstanding shares.

"We believe that our shares represent an attractive reinvestment opportunity," explained Pickens. "Mesa constantly evaluates alternatives to maximize values for Mesa shareholders, and we believe that share repurchases meet the criteria at this time."[74]

Company officials stressed that the offer should not be interpreted as an antitakeover effort. "It's not of the size that would have any antitakeover type intent," said Mesa Vice President David Batchelder. "It's really a matter of having undervalued assets in the form of Mesa common stock, which we find an attractive investment. We're able to buy reserves for $4 a barrel."[75]

---

[73]Ibid.

[74]"Mesa Approves Plan to Buy Back $100 Million Worth of Shares," *Dallas Morning News*, July 9, 1985, p. 1D.
[75]Ibid.

EXHIBIT 7   Domestic Finding Costs (dollars per barrel)

	1979	1980	1981	1982	1983	1984
Mesa	$ 5.43	$13.80	$15.06	$17.13	$12.89	$ 6.06
Phillips	9.04	9.85	12.56	6.12	7.77	6.72
Unocal	8.87	10.64	13.43	12.86	6.38	10.09
Gulf	16.47	15.84	19.23	16.00	9.11	—
Superior	43.92	10.75	14.52	15.69	—	—
Industry average	11.74	10.07	12.18	11.93	8.97	7.73

Source: *Petroleum Outlook*, June 1985, *Petroleum Outlook*, June 1984.

EXHIBIT 8   Mesa Petroleum Reserve Recognition Accounting (in thousands)

	Years Ended December 31		
	1984	1983	1982
Standardized Measure of Future Net Cash Flows of Proved Reserves (unaudited):			
Future cash inflows......................................	$ 4,594,130	$ 3,629,048	$ 3,439,222
Future development and production costs:			
Operating costs and production taxes	(924,386)	(984,801)	(826,489)
Federal excise tax on oil and condensate....................	(34,345)	(57,278)	(96,338)
Development and abandonment costs	(129,836)	(151,349)	(177,052)
Future net cash flows before income taxes....................	3,505,563	2,435,620	2,339,343
Discount at 10% per annum	(1,755,174)	(1,160,910)	(1,041,935)
Discounted future net cash flows before income taxes	1,750,389	1,274,710	1,297,408
Future income taxes, net of discount at 10% per annum.......	(319,999)	(265,461)	(252,879)
Standardized measure of future net cash flows of proved oil and gas reserves	$ 1,430,390	$ 1,009,249	$ 1,044,529
Changes in the Standardized Measure (unaudited):			
Standardized measure at beginning of year	$ 1,009,249	$ 1,044,529	$ 1,036,113
Revisions of reserves proved in prior years:			
Net changes in prices and production costs...................	(33,387)	25,454	46,868
Net changes due to revisions in quantity estimates............	105,656	11,618	(10,577)
Net changes in estimates of future development costs	483	(205)	(22,816)
Accretion of discount	127,471	129,741	129,032
Other, primarily timing of production......................	13,917	(73,984)	(54,401)
Total revisions..	214,140	92,624	88,106
Extensions, discoveries and other additions, net of future production and development costs	81,942	119,508	310,581
Purchases of producing properties	515,532	34,801	—
Sales of oil and gas produced, net of production costs...........	(332,152)	(316,411)	(298,497)
Sales of producing properties	(27,628)	—	—
Previously estimated development and abandonment costs incurred during the period	23,845	46,780	31,892
Distribution to Mesa Offshore Royalty Partnership..............	—	—	(124,991)
Net change in income taxes..................................	(54,538)	(12,582)	1,325
Net changes in standardized measure	421,141	(35,280)	8,416
Standardized measure at end of year.........................	$ 1,430,390	$ 1,009,249	$ 1,044,529

Note:

Discounted future net cash flows before income taxes are calculated by discounting such cash flows at 10% per year, compounded monthly, over the expected period of realization.

Future income taxes are computed by applying the statutory tax rate to future net cash flows less the tax basis of the properties and net operating loss and investment credit carryforwards as of each year end; permanent differences and tax credits applicable to future oil and gas producing activities are also considered in the income tax computation.

Canadian reserves have an insignificant effect (less than 3%) on either the standardized measure or the results of operations.

Undiscounted future income taxes totaled $1.1 billion in 1984, $746 million in 1983, and $668 million in 1982.

Source: Mesa Petroleum Company, Annual Reports.

EXHIBIT 9 Mesa Petroleum Marketable Securities

	1984				1983	1982
	Current	Non-current	Number of shares	Percent of class	Non-current	Non-current
			($ in thousands)			
Phillips Petroleum Company (Phillips)	$338,507	—	7,910,044	5.1%	—	—
Unocal Corporation (Unocal)	—	$253,662	6,393,060	3.7	—	—
KN Energy, Inc. (KNE)	—	14,666	431,300	4.8	$ 9,448	—
Gulf Corporation (Gulf)	—	—	—	—	639,425	—
Midlands Energy Corporation (Midlands)	—	—	—	—	5,548	—
General American Oil Company of Texas (GAO)	—	—	—	—	—	$ 24,138
Louisiana Land and Exploration Company (LL&E)	—	—	—	—	—	9,454
Other	—	—	—	—	82	100
Total cost	338,507	268,328			654,503	33,692
Unrealized gain (loss)	15,467	(19,277)			(17,283)	29,299
Total market value	$353,974	$249,051			$637,220	$ 62,991

Income attributable to the company's investment in marketable securities for the three years ended December 31, 1984, was comprised of the following ($ in millions):

	1984	1983	1982
Gains on sales	$ 403.5	$ 62.7	$ 64.0
Dividend income	22.4	10.1	4.9
Interest expense	(40.6)	(24.1)	(18.6)
	385.3	48.7	50.3
Income taxes	(172.6)	(13.0)	(7.5)
Income from securities	$ 212.7	$ 35.7	$ 42.8

Source: Mesa Petroleum Company, Annual Reports.

EXHIBIT 10 Ten-Year Summary of Mesa Petroleum's Financial Data (in thousands except per share data)

Years ended December 31 (not covered by auditors' report)

	1984	1983	1982	1981	1980	1979	1978	1977	1976	1975
Oil and gas revenues	$ 413,489	$ 391,134	$ 376,381	$ 367,552	$ 332,193	$ 266,941	$ 164,748	$139,257	$ 96,527	$ 63,426
Operating income	154,732	158,507	152,564	171,633	143,900	122,545	$ 84,568	$ 79,439	$ 53,677	$ 31,714
Other income (expense) and taxes:										
Gain on sale of securities and assets	403,549	89,221	63,967	1,730	15,931	346,012	—	—	—	—
Interest income	87,748	19,524	23,942	33,075	40,608	14,519	781	—	—	—
Interest expense, net	(184,192)	(77,513)	(40,299)	(29,332)	(32,655)	(49,601)	(18,301)	(8,840)	(3,384)	(3,708)
Dividend income and other	13,754	10,006	(4,670)	8,683	(7,359)	1,710	988	800	541	539
Provision for income taxes	(205,407)	(73,835)	(65,600)	(70,740)	(65,189)	(149,563)	(26,270)	(30,100)	(20,100)	(9,375)
Net income	270,184	125,910	129,904	115,049	95,236	285,622	41,766	41,299	30,734	19,170
Preferred stock dividends	(16,333)	(11,019)	(13,959)	(8,670)	—	—	—	(2,394)	(4,899)	(3,288)
Net income available for common	$ 253,851	$ 114,891	$ 115,945	$ 106,379	$ 95,236	$ 285,622	$ 41,766	$ 38,905	$ 25,835	$ 15,882
Net income per common share	$ 3.75	$ 1.72	$ 1.72	$ 1.54	$ 1.38	$ 4.43	$ .66	$ .64	$ .48	$ .31
Cash dividends per common share	$ .20	$ .20	$ .20	$ .12	$ .0525	$ .0975	$ .11	$ .0625	$ .025	$ .0125
Cash and short-term investments, marketable securities and interest-bearing receivables	$2,119,835	$ 882,426	$ 294,506	$ 556,072	$ 418,688	$ 398,951	$ 87,204	$ 71,876	$ 48,247	$ 12,498
Long-term debt, including current maturities, subordinated notes and redeemable preferred stock	$2,586,679	$1,429,623	$ 924,114	$1,094,780	$ 661,968	$ 626,551	$451,233	$321,453	$224,571	$150,730
Total assets at year end	$3,955,951	$2,305,645	$1,667,230	$2,069,355	$1,426,850	$1,268,459	$974,963	$800,210	$614,627	$496,897
Stockholders' equity	$ 741,594	$ 502,505	$ 416,901	$ 595,445	$ 509,775	$ 400,181	$315,044	$337,223	$300,483	$276,476

Source: Mesa Petroleum Company, Annual Reports.

13.   *Turner Broadcasting System, Inc.*

TED TURNER: ENTREPRENEUR

In 1962, at age 24, Ted Turner faced some very difficult decisions—more difficult, in fact, than most people, including businesspeople, ever face. His father committed suicide and left an outdoor (billboard) advertising business that was $6 million in debt and short of cash. Rejecting the advice of the company's bankers who believed Turner was too inexperienced to run the company, he chose not to sell the firm, but instead, to build it. Immediately, he sold some of the company's assets to improve its cash position, refinanced its debt, renegotiated contracts with customers, hired new salespeople, and literally turned the company around. By 1969, the company's debt was paid off, and in 1970, having secured the future of Turner Advertising, Ted Turner purchased Channel 17, an Atlanta independent/UHF television station. Although Channel 17 is widely recognized today as a profitable business, in 1970 it was two years old, losing $50,000 per month, and competing in a market dominated by three firmly-rooted network stations in Atlanta.

Recently, due in large measure to his phenomenal financial success, journalists have begun to explore Ted Turner, the man. Below are excerpts from *The Wall Street Journal* article:

> Associates of broadcaster Ted Turner like to retell the story of his victory in a 1979 yachting race because they think it says it all about the man.
>
> Mr. Turner's boat, *Tenacious,* battled 40-foot waves whipped by 65-knot winds in the Irish Sea to win the Fastnet race. Of the 306 boats that started the race, only 87 finished, and in one of ocean racing's greatest tragedies, 19 sailors drowned.

This case was prepared by Neil H. Snyder, Donna Biemiller, Kerrie Morrison, Diane Reiff, and Laura Weiss of the McIntire School of Commerce University of Virginia; Melanie D. Sheip of Morgan Guaranty Trust. This case is designed to be used as a basis for discussion rather than to illustrate either effective or ineffective handling of an administrative situation.

> After his extraordinary display of skill and courage, Mr. Turner at dockside callously reminded his somber British hosts that in the 16th century the Spanish Armada ran into similar trouble. "You ought to be thankful there are storms like that," he said, "or you'd all be speaking Spanish.". . .

The flamboyant Southerner, called a visionary by some and a buffoon by others, seems a bit of both. Widely referred to as "Terrible Ted" and "The Mouth of the South," he has been charged with hypocrisy for preaching family values and then appearing drunk in public, and for criticizing the networks' TV "garbage" while boasting to *Playboy* magazine that he has photographed nude women. . . .

Friends and colleagues attribute both Mr. Turner's successes and his excesses to a personality riddled with contradictions. "Ted is a brilliant person," says Irwin Mazo, a former Turner accountant, "but he also borders on egomania." Although he often talks hard-line conservatism, Mr. Turner seems genuinely concerned about pet liberal issues like overpopulation, world hunger and nuclear proliferation. He presides over a major news organization but says he limits his newspaper reading to glances at *USA Today* and the Atlanta papers' sports section. He professes to admire the courtly values of the Old South yet often treats his senior executives like servants.

The conflicting sides are cemented by an overwhelming tenacity. "He competes in everything he does," says Jim Roddey, a former Turner executive and sailing buddy who has known him for 25 years. "He sails like he conducts business—it's all or nothing." Indeed, when he saw an Atlanta Braves game-night promotion threatened by lack of participants, he jumped into the contest: He rolled a baseball around the infield with his nose and emerged with blood streaming from forehead to chin.

That incident, his friends say, demonstrates both Mr. Turner's love of publicity and his willingness to sacrifice his dignity in his drive to win. . . .

Mr. Turner was thrust into the business world more than 20 years ago, when his father committed suicide immediately after selling most of the family billboard business. Then 24 years old, Mr. Turner challenged the would-be buyers and regained control of the company. "He could have lost it all," recalls Mr. Mazo, the accountant. But then as apparently now, says Mr. Mazo, "Ted is willing to put all his chips on the table and roll the dice."

In 1970, with the billboard business reestablished, Mr. Turner gambled next on buying a floundering Atlanta UHF television station. In 1976, he transformed it into one of the nation's most profitable stations by having its signal bounced off a satellite and into the nation's cable-TV systems. He channeled Turner Broadcasting's profits from the superstation into a round-the-clock news service dubbed Cable News Network. Five years later, as CNN approaches profitability, Mr. Turner is looking for a new challenge.

Throughout, Mr. Turner's revolutionary moves have been scoffed at by the broadcasting establishment, just as brokers now are scoffing at his CBS takeover bid. Even Turner confidants have been skeptical about his moves. "He's made about $500 million and at least $400 million of that was on deals I told him not to do," chuckles Mr. Roddey, the former Turner executive who admits to advising the company to stick with billboards. . . .

Mr. Turner's management technique isn't any more conventional. "He's not a manager," says Mr. Roddey. "He's not hands-on. He always used to tell me I was getting bogged down in the details, like making the payroll."

But the volatile executive is "a very tough guy to work for," says Reese Schonfeld, the first president of CNN, who left after a dispute with Mr. Turner over hiring and firing. "I've seen him abuse a lot of people. Once you let him humiliate you, he'll walk all over you." Mr. Schonfeld says Mr. Turner has a habit of ordering his senior executives to fetch drinks for him.

Not all Turner employees have such gripes. Lower-level workers at CNN, housed in the basement of Turner Broadcasting's Atlanta headquarters, say their encounters with Mr. Turner are infrequent and non-confrontational. But life in Turner's executive suite looks stressful: In June 1983, for example, when

Mr. Bevins was 36, he was struck by a heart attack while in Mr. Turner's office. Mr. Bevins declines to discuss the incident. . . .

In recent years, however, both Mr. Turner and his company have toned down. Aides say the change began when Mr. Turner began to realize that obtaining control of a network might someday be within his grasp. He began to position himself for an eventual combination, they say.

For Mr. Turner, that meant dropping off the interview trail and scaling down his public excesses. He repeatedly declined to be interviewed for this story, for instance. While hardly prim these days, "he's become more discreet," says one longtime Turner employee. And with age, his friends say, has come a dose of maturity. "Lately he talks a lot about world peace, nuclear war, improving the environment," says Gary Jobson, tactician aboard many of Mr. Turner's winning yachts (*The Wall Street Journal;* April 19, 1985; pages 1 and 6).

Turner's perspective on business is interesting to say the least. He is quoted as saying,

I don't think winning is everything. It's a big mistake when you say that I think trying to win is what counts. Be kind and fair and make the world a better place to live, that's what's important. . . . I think the saddest people I've ever met were people with a lot of wealth. If you polled 90 percent of the people and asked them what they want most, most would want to be millionaires. I'll tell you, you've got to be one to know how unimportant it is. . . . I'm blessed with some talents. I've made a lot of money, more than I ever thought I would. . . . But if I continue to be successful, I would like to serve my fellow man in some way other than doing flips at third base. . . . People want leadership, somebody to rally around, and I want to be a leader (*Atlanta Constitution,* January 8, 1977).

CREATING A NETWORK: WTBS, THE SUPERSTATION

WTBS is the pioneer of the superstation concept. Owned and operated by the Turner Broadcasting System Inc., it is an independent UHF television station, Channel 17 in

Atlanta, Georgia, whose signal is beamed via satellite to television households nationwide. Ted Turner, TBS president and chairman of the board, purchased Channel 17 in January 1970. By merging the then Turner Communications Corporation with Rice Broadcasting, he gained control of the television outlet, which became WTCG, flagship station of the Turner Communications Group.

Realizing that WTCG's programming could be made available by satellite to millions of television viewers throughout the country, Turner originated the superstation concept. In short, the superstation is a reworking of the traditional television network concept, in which one station acts as original programming supplier for a multiplicity of distant cable markets. On December 16, 1976, WTCG made history, as its signal was beamed to cable systems nationwide via a transponder on RCA's Satcom I satellite. Satcom I was replaced by Satcom III–R in January 1982, and by Galaxy I in January 1985.

In 1979, the Turner Communications Group was renamed Turner Broadcasting System Inc., and, to reflect this change, the WTCG call letters became WTBS. The company estimates that, as of February 29, 1984, WTBS was beamed into approximately 75 percent of U.S. cable homes and 35 percent of U.S. television homes.

WTBS broadcasts 24 hours per day, acquiring its programming primarily from film companies, syndicators of programs that have run successfully on television networks, and its sports affiliates. WTBS currently has available 4,100 film titles for its programming needs, the majority of which are available for multiple runs. In addition, approximately 500 titles are under contract and will become available for programming purposes in the future. Approximately 23 percent of the purchased programming has been obtained from Viacom International, Inc., and 17 percent from MCA. WTBS has not obtained more than 10 percent of its purchased programming needs from any other single supplier, and approximately 1,900 hours of programming broadcast on WTBS during 1983 were produced internally, or under contract. WTBS plans to produce more programs internally in the future.

WTBS derives revenue from the sale of advertising time, and advertising prices depend on the size of WTBS' viewing audience and the amount of available time sold. Since February 1981, the A. C. Nielsen Company has been measuring the audience level of

WTBS for use by the company and its advertisers. The demand for advertising time on cable television is significantly lower than that for advertising time on the three major networks because of the relatively small size of the cable network audiences and the fact that cable has not penetrated significantly in many of the major urban markets. The board of directors of TBS anticipates that the continued growth of the cable television (CATV) industry, particularly in the major urban markets, will result in increased demand on the part of advertisers.

The revenues of WTBS also include amounts obtained from "direct response" advertising, which represent fees received by the company for the sale of products it promotes by advertisement. The company broadcasts advertisements for the products during unsold advertising time, and the products are ordered directly by viewers through the company by mail or telephone. WTBS collects a fee for each order. In 1983, these fees amounted to 6.6 percent of total advertising revenues for WTBS.

Advertising time for WTBS as well as the company's cable news services is marketed and sold by the company's own advertising sales force consisting of approximately 101 persons located in sales offices in New York, Chicago, Detroit, Los Angeles, and Atlanta.

According to *The Wall Street Journal* (April 19, 1985):

> It's hard to laugh at Mr. Turner's operations now, or at least the WTBS operation. His superstation, one of the nation's most popular cable services, now beams a steady diet of sports, movies and reruns into almost 34 million U.S. households, or about 84% of all homes equipped for cable.
>
> It has revolutionized the cable-television business, says Ira Tumpowsky, a Young & Rubicam Inc. senior vice president who oversees the agency's cable-TV buying. "He's the person who moved cable from a reception industry to a marketing industry," the advertising executive says.

TBS Sports

In January 1976, TBS acquired the Atlanta Braves professional baseball club, and on December 29, 1976, the Atlanta Hawks professional basketball club was acquired. Although both teams have consistently lost money, they have provided TBS with excellent sports programming, and the Atlanta Braves, "America's Team," have a national following. TBS aired 150 Braves games and 41 Hawks games in 1984.

Along with a full schedule of Atlanta Braves baseball and Atlanta Hawks basketball, TBS Sports offers NCAA basketball, NBA basketball, NCAA football, Southeastern Conference football, and a variety of special sports presentations. For example, TBS Sports telecast the NASCAR circuit's Richmond 400, college football's Hall of Fame Bowl, and World Championship Wrestling during 1984.

Recently, baseball Commissioner Peter Ueberroth persuaded Ted Turner to make annual payments to other major-league teams if he continued to broadcast Braves games across the nation over his cable station. Turner has agreed to make these payments, totaling more than $25 million according to *The Wall Street Journal* (April 19, 1985), into a central fund for five years. This agreement is a compromise. Ueberroth had wanted to end nationwide cable broadcasts of baseball games, since they were hurting the profits of teams in other cities. Ueberroth is reported to have said that superstations are the most serious problem facing professional baseball (*Richmond Time Dispatch,* January 28, 1985).

Ted Turner is said to be as creative with his sports franchises as he is with TBS. For example, *The Wall Street Journal* (April 19, 1985) concluded that:

Even in the stodgy game of baseball, Mr. Turner has displayed some business acumen. The Atlanta Braves franchise that he bought in 1976 was mired in mediocrity. Mr. Turner beefed up its farm system, paid top dollar to lure stars from elsewhere, and transmitted across the nation practically every game the team played. Average attendance at Braves' home games last year was 21,834, triple the figure for 1975. The Braves are widely considered pennant contenders this season.

In baseball, as in his other businesses, Mr. Turner has managed to outrage both his employees and his peers. Mr. Turner once tried to demote a slumping star to the minor leagues. At another point, he named himself manager of the team. Such antics led to a collision with the then-commissioner of baseball, Bowie Kuhn, and to Mr. Turner's temporary suspension from the game. According to

one biography, Mr. Turner pleaded with Mr. Kuhn: "I am very contrite. I would bend over and let you paddle my behind, hit me over the head with a Fresca bottle."

CNN

Through its subsidiary Cable News Network, Inc. (CNN), which began broadcasting on June 1, 1980, TBS provides a 24-hour news programming service which is available to CATV systems throughout the United States and in some foreign countries. The programming includes comprehensive reporting of domestic and international news, sports, business and weather, plus analysis, commentary and reports by its staff of experts and investigative reporters. CNN obtains news reports from its bureaus in various U.S. and foreign cities. Each of these bureaus is equipped to provide live reports to CNN's transmission facility in Atlanta thereby providing the capability for live coverage of news events around the world. In addition, news is obtained through wire services, television news services by agreement with television stations in various locations worldwide, and from free-lance reporters and camera crews.

CNN employs over 160 journalists, executives, and technicians. The news channel was initially received by 193 CATV systems serving approximately 1.7 million subscribers. As of December 31, 1983, 4,278 CATV systems serving approximately 25.1 million subscribers received CNN's programming.

According to *The Wall Street Journal* (April 19, 1985):

During its five years of losses, CNN has grown to become the nation's most popular cable service, available in some 32 million homes. And this year, the company indicates, CNN should move into the black. Though still not an equal of the high-powered network news operations, CNN is nipping at their heels, and doing it on a bargain-basement budget.

CNN is weak on features says Jim Snyder. News vice president of Post-Newsweek Stations Inc., the broadcasting division of the Washington Post Co., but it covers breaking news "as well as anybody." A recent Washington Journalism Review assessment of the channel carried the headline "CNN Takes Its Place Beside the Networks."

CNN Headline News

CNN offered another 24-hour news service to cable operators effective December 31, 1981. Referred to as CNN Headline News (CNN HN), this service utilizes a concise, fast-paced format, programming in half-hour cycles throughout the day. CNN HN employs approximately 225 people, and its start-up required the construction and furnishing of a studio facility and additional transmitting facilities. The resources and expertise of CNN is utilized by CNN HN for accumulation of news material. Its revenues are derived from the sale of advertising on CNN HN and from fees charged for the syndication of CNN HN directly to over-the-air television and radio stations.

The number of cable homes receiving the CNN HN signal increased from approximately 5,400,000 in October 1983 to approximately 9,100,000 as a direct result of TBS' agreement to acquire CNN HN's major cable news competitor (The Satellite News Channel). Despite this increase in cable homes, TBS executives do not expect CNN HN to be profitable in 1984.

Cable Music Channel

On October 26, 1984, TBS launched its own brand of video-clip programming to compete with MTV. The Cable Music Channel started with 2.5 million households, about half the expected subscriber count company executives had predicted. However, by November 30, 1984, the Cable Music Channel's title and affiliate list was sold to MTV Networks Inc. for $1.5 million in cash and advertising commitments at a loss of $2.2 million. Cable Music Channel President/TBS Executive Vice President Robert Wussler acknowledges that operator resistance was largely responsible. "We didn't get the homes and we weren't about to get 3 or 5 million homes. We surveyed the field, felt we had a good product, but the industry obviously embraced MTV, the future in terms of acquiring subs was bleak and we felt strongly that this was our best course of action" (*CableVision*, December 10, 1984).

KEY EXECUTIVES AND OWNERSHIP

Ted Turner is aided by highly qualified, experienced men. Robert J. Wussler, executive vice president, had 21 years' experience with CBS, including his appointment as president of the CBS Sports Division, before joining TBS in August 1981.

William C. Bevins, Jr., is vice president of finance, secretary and treasurer as well as a director of the company. Previously, he was affiliated with Price Waterhouse for 10 years, most recently as senior manager.

Henry L. (Hank) Aaron has been vice president–director of player development for the Atlanta Braves since 1976, and the vice president of community relations and a director of the company since 1980. He was previously a professional baseball player with a total of 28 years of experience in professional sports, and he holds the world's record for the most home runs hit by a professional baseball player.

Burt Reinhardt became president of CNN in 1982 and a director of CNN in 1983. He was employed by the company in 1979 and was instrumental in organizing CNN. Previously, he served as executive vice president of UPI Television News and executive vice president of the Non-Theatrical and Educational Division of Paramount Pictures.

Gerald Hogan joined the company in 1971 and served as general sales manager of WTBS from 1979 until 1981. He became senior vice president of Turner Broadcasting Sales, Inc., in 1982.

Henry Gillespie joined TBS in 1982 as chairman of the board of Turner Program Services, Inc. Prior to that, he served as president of Columbia Pictures Television Distribution and president of Viacom Enterprises.

J. Michael Gearon has been a director of the company, president of Hawks Management Company, and general partner of Atlanta Hawks, Ltd., operator of the Atlanta Hawks professional basketball team, since 1979. He previously owned a real estate brokerage and development firm in Atlanta, Georgia.

OWNERSHIP PHILOSOPHY

Currently, Ted Turner owns 86 percent of the common shares outstanding. Exhibit 1 presents TBS common stock ownership of selected individuals. Most of the

EXHIBIT 1 Common Stock Ownership

Name of Beneficial Owner	Amount	Percent of Class
R. E. TURNER	17,579,922	86.2%
William C. Bevins, Jr.	20,000	0.1
Peter A. Dames	98,910	0.5
Karl Eller	1,000	—
Tench C. Coxe	128,285	0.6
J. Michael Gearon	31,500	0.2
Martin B. Seretean	20,800	0.1
William C. Bartholomay	210,700	1.0
Allison Thornwell, Jr.	215,912	1.1
All directors and officers as a group (27 persons)	18,421,489	90.4%

Source: From 1984 Annual 10-K Report.

stockholders besides Turner and his family are either directors or executive officers of TBS.

FINANCIAL ISSUES

Debt Philosophy

TBS is a highly leveraged company that emphasizes the building of asset values. Presently, the company has a $190 million revolving credit agreement extending until 1987, and $133 million of this credit line has been borrowed. Concerning long-term debt, the company has incurred debt restructuring fees which it expenses as interest based on the weighted average of the principal balance outstanding throughout the term of the agreement. The company paid restructuring fees of $3,650,000 during 1983, and the balance due at year-end is classified as current and long term in accordance with the payment terms of the agreements.

Under terms of its 1983 debt agreement, the company is limited with regard to additional borrowings, cash dividends, and acquisition of the company's common stock. TBS is also required, among other things, to maintain minimum levels of working capital and to meet specified current ratio requirements. It is important to note that the company was not in compliance with certain restrictive covenants of its loan agreement on December 31, 1983. TBS received waivers of these restrictions from lenders; accordingly, the amounts due have been classified in accordance with the original terms of the agreement.

Owner's Equity

Characteristic of firms in the growth stage of the business life cycle, TBS has experienced mostly negative earnings since its inception (see Exhibit 2). Most of its losses have resulted from the high start-up costs associated with the divisions that have been created in the past 10 years. Exhibit 3 shows balance sheet information for the years 1977 to 1983.

Working Capital

During 1983, the company was unable to generate sufficient cash flow from operations to meet its needs. Working capital deficits were primarily funded through short-term credit lines and financing agreements with vendors, program suppliers, and others during the first three quarters of the year. A large percentage of cash outflow resulted from the debt restructuring fees.

TBS faces several uncertainties that could arise out of normal operations that might require additional cash. However, management feels that the current financing program will be adequate to meet the company's antic-

EXHIBIT 2

TURNER BROADCASTING COMPANY
Historical Common-Size Income Statement
($ in thousands)

	1977		1978		1979	
Revenue:						
Broadcasting	$ 19,573	51.9%	$ 23,434	62.1%	$ 27,789	73.7%
Cable production	0	0.0	0	0.0	0	0.0
Sports	6,706	17.8	8,181	21.7	7,395	19.6
Management fees	1,782	4.7	2,094	5.6	2,285	6.1
Other	738	2.0	134	0.4	252	0.7
Total revenue	$ 28,799	76.3%	$ 33,843	89.7%	$ 37,721	100.0%
Cost of expenses:						
Cost of operation	$ 12,767	33.8%	$ 13,219	35.0%	$ 16,997	45.1%
S, G, & Admin.	10,729	28.4	12,736	33.8	14,460	38.3
Amortization film contracts	1,178	3.1	1,571	4.2	2,290	6.1
Amort Player/other contracts	1,556	4.1	1,599	4.2	1,508	4.0
Depreciation of P, P, & E	934	2.5	1,037	2.7	1,222	3.2
Interest expense/amort debt	1,291	3.4	1,323	3.5	2,098	5.6
Other	1,251	3.3	0	0.0	0	0.0
Total costs and expenses	$ 29,706	78.8%	$ 31,485	83.5%	$ 38,575	102.3%
Income (loss) from operation	− 907	− 2.4%	$ 2,358	6.3%	$ − 854	− 2.3%
Equity loss-limited partners	− 1,053	− 2.8	− 1,225	− 3.2	− 2,014	− 5.3
Income before gains or dispos.	− 1,960	− 5.2	1,133	3.0	− 2,868	− 7.6
Gain on disposition of prop.	0	0.0	395	1.0	312	0.8
Income bef. tax and extra. items	− 1,960	− 5.2	1,528	4.1	− 2,556	− 6.8
Provision (benefit) for taxes	− 728	− 1.9	669	1.8	− 1,060	− 2.8
Income bef. extra. items	− 1,232	− 3.3	860	2.3	− 1,496	− 4.0
Gain on prepayment of debt	0	0.0	343	0.9	0	0.0
Net income (loss)	$− 1,232	− 3.3%	$ 1,203	3.2%	$− 1,496	− 4.0%

ipated needs. In the unlikely event that these uncertainties do materialize and require cash in excess of the anticipated amounts, because of limitations in existing loan agreements, there is no assurance that the company can obtain additional borrowings which might be needed to meet these excess needs.

Dividend Policy

TBS has not paid a cash dividend since 1975. In view of the unavailability of funds to the company and restrictions in its loan agreements against any dividend pay-

ments, it is not anticipated that dividends will be paid to holders of its common stock in the foreseeable future.

Capital Structure

Presently, 97 percent of TBS' capital structure consists of long-term debt. In the fourth quarter of 1984, TBS was considering a public offering to raise $125 million to pay off its bank debt. The company planned to use a combination of 10-year notes, stocks, and warrants to raise the capital. Based on preliminary plans, the offering would boost the number of shares outstanding from

	1980		1981		1982		1983	
$	35,495	65.0%	$ 55,329	58.2%	$ 96,647	58.3%	$136,217	60.7%
	7,201	13.2	27,738	29.2	49,708	30.0	65,169	29.0
	9,211	16.9	8,840	9.3	16,263	9.8	21,401	9.5
	2,473	4.5	2,835	3.0	2,717	1.6	1,462	0.7
	230	0.4	305	0.3	306	0.2	283	0.1
	54,610	100.0%	$ 95,047	100.0%	$165,641	100.0%	$224,532	100.0%
$	35,124	64.3%	$ 49,036	51.6%	$ 81,187	49.0%	$105,695	47.1%
	25,218	46.2	37,067	39.0	60,343	36.4	80,722	36.0
	2,803	5.1	4,010	4.2	7,497	4.5	8,674	3.9
	1,210	2.2	0	0.0		0.0		0.0
	2,172	4.0	3,469	3.6	4,182	2.5	4,706	2.1
	4,437	8.1	9,673	10.2	13,084	7.9	14,383	6.4
	0	0.0	0	0.0	0	0.0	0	0.0
$	70,964	129.9%	$ 103,255	108.6%	$166,293	100.4%	$214,170	95.4%
$ −	16,354	−29.9%	$ −8,208	−8.6%	$ −652	−0.4%	$ 10,362	4.6%
	−2,905	−5.3	−5,215	−5.5	−2,698	−1.6	−3,350	−1.5
	−19,259	−35.3	−13,423	−14.1	−3,350	−2.0	7,012	3.1
	15,694	28.7	0	0.0		0.0		0.0
	−3,575	−6.5	−13,423	−14.1	−3,350	−2.0	7,012	3.1
	200	0.4	0	0.0		0.0		0.0
	−3,775	−6.9	−13,423	−14.1	−3,350	−2.0	7,012	3.1
	0	0.0	0	0.0		0.0		0.0
$	−3,775	−6.9%	$− 13,423	−14.1%	$−3,350	−2.0%	$ 7,012	3.1%

the current 20.3 million to 22.2 million, reducing the percentage of shares held by Turner from 87 percent to 79 percent.

INDUSTRY AND COMPETITION

The dramatic increase in the number of alternative sources of television broadcasting has led to a measurable drop in the audience shares of the three major networks. Consequently, there is a great deal of pressure for change in the television industry. Pay and ad-supported cable, independent broadcast stations and videocassettes are all seen as contributing to the decline. In the next decade, it is believed that television entertainment may shift toward a broader range of outlets including ad hoc and regional networks, pay-per-view networks, and more reasonably priced videocassette recorders.

Networks

Although television audience viewing is growing, the big three networks are concerned about the decline in their audience shares and about when the decline will

EXHIBIT 3

TURNER BROADCASTING COMPANY
Historical Common-Size Balance Sheet
($ in thousands)

	1977		1978		1979	
Current assets:						
Cash	$ 1,351	3.6%	$ 154	0.4%	$ 342	0.9%
Accounts receivable	3,537	9.4	4,951	13.1	6,322	16.8
Less: allow for doubt. accts.	431	1.1	547	1.5	415	1.1
Net accounts receivable	3,106	8.2	4,404	11.7	5,907	15.7
Prepaid expenses	1,250	3.3	563	1.5	585	1.6
Notes payable—S-T	0	0.0	0	0.0	0	0.0
Curr. port. def. prog. prod. cost		0.0		0.0		0.0
Film contract rights—current	1,128	3.0	2,055	5.4	2,570	6.8
Other current assets	1,359	3.6	528	1.4	644	1.7
Total current assets	$ 8,194	21.7%	$ 7,704	20.4%	$10,048	26.6%
Film contract rights	$ 3,193	8.5%	$ 5,632	14.9%	$ 7,537	20.0%
Inv. in limited partnerships	1,000	2.7	2,578	6.8	2,480	6.6
Net prop., plant, & equipment	6,543	17.3	7,784	20.6	13,381	35.5
Notes receivable—L-T	1,146	3.0	404	1.1	514	1.4
Deferred program prod costs		0.0		0.0		0.0
Deferred charges	0	0.0	0	0.0	0	0.0
Net contract rights	6,165	16.3	4,947	13.1	3,628	9.6
Intangible assets	0	0.0	0	0.0	0	0.0
Other assets	1,624	4.3	1,349	3.6	1,696	4.5
Total assets	$27,865	73.9%	$30,398	80.6%	$39,284	104.1%
Current liabilities:						
Accounts payable	$ 2,043	5.4%	$ 2,615	6.9%	$ 1,351	3.6%
Accrued expenses	0	0.0	0	0.0	1,752	4.6
Deferred income	0	0.0	0	0.0	216	0.6
Short-term borrowings	0	0.0	0	0.0	6,642	17.6
Long-term debt—current	5,411	14.3	4,910	13.0	2,704	7.2
Obligation-film RTS (current)	0	0.0	0	0.0	3,344	8.9
Debt restructure fees (current)	0	0.0	0	0.0	0	0.0
Income taxes payable	0	0.0	0	0.0	0	0.0
Total current liabilities	$ 7,454	19.8%	$ 7,525	19.9%	$16,009	42.4%
Long-term debt	15,968	42.3%	16,329	43.3%	14,158	37.5%
Unfunded pension cost	283	0.8	283	0.8	283	0.8
Deferred income taxes	1,076	2.9	1,980	5.2	918	2.4
Deferred income	0	0.0	0	0.0	0	0.0
Debt restructure fees payable	0	0.0	0	0.0	0	0.0
Obligations— Emp. contracts	0	0.0	0	0.0	1,410	3.7
Obligations—Film rights	0	0.0	0	0.0	3,631	9.6
Other liabilities		0.0		0.0		0.0
Total liabilities	$24,781	65.7%	$26,117	69.2%	$36,409	96.5%
Common stock, par 0.125	1,024	2.7	1,024	2.7	2,663	7.1
Capital in excess	1,541	4.1	1,572	4.2	291	0.8
Retained earnings (deficit)	1,095	2.9	2,298	6.1	802	2.1
	3,660	9.7%	4,894	13.0%	3,756	10.0%
Less shares of stock—treasury		0.0		0.0		0.0
Notes rec.—Sales of CS-treas.		0.0		0.0		0.0
Treasury stock	−576	−1.5%	−613	−1.6%	−881	−2.3%
Total stockholders' equity	6,744	17.9%	9,175	24.3%	6,631	17.6%
Total liabilities and stockholders' equity	31,525	83.6%	35,292	93.6%	43,040	114.1%

	1980		1981		1982		1983	
	$ 489	0.9%	$ 504	0.5%	$ 538	0.3%	$ 594	0.3%
	10,662	19.5	18,868	19.9	25,728	15.5	34,186	15.2
	793	1.5	1,164	1.2	1,997	1.2	2,418	1.1
	9,869	18.1	17,704	18.6	23,731	14.3	31,768	14.1
	552	1.0	1,086	1.1	1,378	0.8	2,177	1.0
	0	0.0	0	0.0	0	0.0	0	0.0
		0.0		0.0	2,490	1.5	2,660	1.2
	2,521	4.6	3,495	3.7	4,516	2.7	12,163	5.4
	$ 1,591	2.9	1,433	1.5	2,585	1.6	2,305	1.0
	$ 15,022	27.5%	$ 24,222	25.5%	$ 35,238	21.3%	$ 51,667	23.0%
	$ 5,660	10.4%	$ 9,464	10.0%	$ 15,633	9.4%	$ 26,057	11.6%
	2,027	3.7	900	0.9	1,900	1.1	1,633	0.7
	26,647	48.8	28,698	30.2	67,555	40.8	71,505	31.8
	920	1.7	0	0.0	0	0.0	0	0.0
		0.0		0.0	4,460	2.7	11,432	5.1
	0	0.0	9,623	10.1	6,585	4.0	13,926	6.2
	2,784	5.1	2,084	2.2	1,583	1.0	1,246	0.6
	0	0.0	0	0.0	0	0.0	25,567	11.4
	958	1.8	1,970	2.1	2,232	1.3	2,805	1.2
	$ 54,018	98.9%	$ 76,961	81.0%	$ 135,186	81.6%	$ 205,838	91.7%
	$ 2,079	3.8%	$ 3,926	4.1%	$ 7,548	4.6%	$ 6,954	3.1%
	7,196	13.2	11,152	11.7	16,750	10.1	22,551	10.0
	700	1.3	2,226	2.3	7,220	4.4	7,083	3.2
	17,907	32.8	42,783	45.0	49,924	30.1	0	0.0
	8,430	15.4	3,005	3.2	4,266	2.6	14,473	6.4
	2,456	4.5	3,465	3.6	5,613	3.4	11,317	5.0
	0	0.0	2,253	2.4	3,000	1.8	3,650	1.6
	163	0.3	0	0.0	0	0.0	0	0.0
	$ 38,931	71.3%	$ 68,810	72.4%	$ 94,321	56.9%	$ 66,028	29.4%
	9,825	18.0%	7,165	7.5%	42,802	25.8%	122,404	54.5%
	283	0.5	283	0.3		0.0		0.0
	918	1.7	2,834	3.0		0.0		0.0
	0	0.0	1,313	1.4	646	0.4	562	0.3
	0	0.0	4,207	4.4	3,000	1.8	650	0.3
	2,221	4.1	2,560	2.7	3,442	2.1	5,201	2.3
	2,662	4.9	3,943	4.1	7,379	4.5	13,959	6.2
		0.0		0.0	1,097	0.7	7,507	3.3
	$ 54,840	100.4%	$ 91,115	95.9%	$ 152,687	92.2%	$ 216,311	96.3%
	2,663	4.9	2,663	2.8	2,663	1.6	2,663	1.2
	602	1.1	1,508	1.6	1,508	0.9	1,508	0.7
	− 2,973	− 5.4	− 16,396	− 17.3	− 19,746	− 11.9	− 12,734	− 5.7
	292	0.5%	− 12,225	− 12.9%	− 15,575	− 9.4%	− 8,563	− 3.8%
		0.0		0.0	− 474	− 0.3	− 754	− 0.3
		0.0		0.0	− 1,452	− 0.9	− 1,156	− 0.5
	− 1,114	− 2.0%	− 1,929	− 2.0%	− 1,926	− 1.2%	− 1,910	− 0.9%
	− 530	− 1.0%	− 26,379	− 27.8%	− 17,501	− 10.6%	− 10,473	− 4.7%
	54,310	99.5%	64,736	68.1%	135,186	81.6%	205,838	91.7%

stop. The availability of syndicated programs is becoming scarce as new broadcasters race to buy up existing shows. However, networks have an advantage in this competition because of their programming expertise and facilities. Exhibit 4 shows how precipitous the decline in network television audience share was between 1975–76 and 1981–82.

Independents

Independent television stations have experienced phenomenal growth in the past 15 years. In 1971, there were 65 independent broadcasters serving 30 markets in the United States with losses of $24 million. In 1980, 179 independent stations served 86 markets with profits of $158 million. This growth can be largely attributed to the FCC's financial interest rule which prohibits the big three networks from syndicating programs that they originally aired and from owning any financial interest in programming produced by others. The independents thus have been able to compete against the networks by airing former network hit shows at key times during the day, including prime time.

Cable

The cable industry is in the midst of a gigantic building boom which can be attributed to two advances. First, there was an increase in the number of channels picked up by cable operators from 12 to 54. Second, in 1975, Home Box Office (HBO) started sending its signal via satellite and other stations, including WTBS, followed and were able to easily attain national distribution for their cable programming.

The Fall 1984 Cable Study Report conducted by Mediamark Research, Inc., found that the median age of pay television subscribers was 35.2 years with an average yearly income of $29,879. *Cablevision,* the trade magazine of the cable industry, projects that the percentage of pay television subscribers will jump from 23 percent of the population in 1984 to 27 percent in 1986. Most of the cable industry's profits will be

EXHIBIT 4   Decline in Network TV Audience

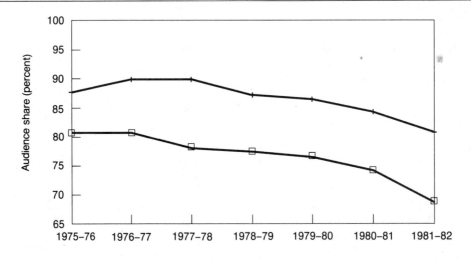

Source: Needham Harper Steers, based on data from A. C. Nielsen.

invested in the wiring of additional homes, particularly those in major urban areas. The high costs associated with wiring these areas had kept cable operators out previously. Now, cities represent more than four fifths of the potential market.

Ad-Supported Cable

With the emergence of cable television as a national delivery system, many media people became excited about a concept called *narrowcasting*. Narrowcasting consists of the programming of one particular type of entertainment (i.e., ESPN—a sports channel) that enables a programmer to target his audience and thus attract specific advertisers at higher rates. Although several narrowcasting networks exist, their success has been very limited because of the lack of quality programming. Dave Martin, vice president for broadcasting at Campbell-Ewall said, "Narrowcasting allows an advertiser to take advantage of a specific opportunity. . . . If it works, though, there is nothing on the mass level that will parallel the opportunity of true narrowcasting to a target audience." Another good example of successful narrowcasting is Music Television (MTV). Narrowcasting is not the only form of ad-supported cable. Stations such as WTBS in Atlanta, WGN in Chicago, and WOR in New York have been successful with their broad-based programming.

Pay Television

Pay television has been the leader in the cable industry, and it is currently experiencing significant change. Most of the change is being introduced by motion-picture companies who are trying to become more directly involved in pay television. For example, Columbia Pictures teamed up with Time, Inc., parent of HBO, and CBS in an attempt to grab a large share of the pay TV market and to become involved in pay-per-view (PPV) television. PPV requires a subscriber to pay an additional fee to view certain major programs. Thus far, most PPV has not been profitable because of the high prices viewers must pay for the programs.

A major threat to large pay television systems comes from smaller private delivery systems. For example, SMATV is a private system that picks up cable signals using a satellite disk and sends the signal via cable to a group of apartment houses, hotels, or clusters of private homes. SMATV has been extremely effective in urban areas previously ignored by other cable systems. This system does not offer the potential, however, of other systems such as MDS (multipoint distribution system) or DBS (direct broadcast satellite).

FCC Rulings

Television broadcasting is subject to the jurisdiction of the Federal Communications Commission (FCC) under the Communications Act of 1934, as amended. Among other things, FCC regulations govern the issuance, term, renewal, and transfer of licenses which must be obtained by persons to operate any television station. The FCC's recent proposal to repeal its network syndication and financial interest rules is strongly supported by the three major networks. Currently, the networks cannot syndicate their own programs, nor can they have a financial interest in programs produced by others. This rule prevents the networks from making money from their shows in syndication. Independent television stations, on the other hand, have grown substantially under this rule because of their ability to air former hit shows.

Independent broadcasters argue that repeal of the financial interest rule will increase the possibility of the networks' monopolizing and withholding off-network, syndicated, prime time entertainment programming. However, CBS, NBC, and ABC contend that this possibility would not materialize, since the networks have neither the incentive nor the opportunity to discriminate against the independents.

To make the television industry more competitive, the FCC is preparing to adopt a plan to expand the 7-7-7 rule to the 12-12-12 rule. Currently, television station owners are allowed to own only seven AM and seven FM radio stations in addition to seven television stations. This limitation was adopted in the 1950s to encourage program diversity in the marketplace. Under the new plan, media companies would be allowed to own as many as 12 television stations only if the audience reach of the stations does not exceed 25 percent of the national viewing audience. This plan would eventually result in an increase in the number of television station owners capable of competing with the three major broadcast networks.

Another important issue facing the FCC concerns the reexamination of the fairness doctrine, the 35-year-old requirement that broadcasters cover "controversial issues'' and air contrasting views. FCC Chairman Mark S. Fowler says that ''the government shouldn't be the one to decide what's fair and what isn't'' (*Business Week,* May 7, 1984). However, defenders of the fairness doctrine counter that the airwaves are a scarce public resource that must be protected from abuse. Under Fowler's administration, the FCC has continued to expand its deregulatory efforts by abolishing regulations and relaxing rules that restrict regional concentration and multiple ownership of broadcast stations. ''These are the areas where the agency must regulate, but in the choice between competition and regulation, competition is far better for the consumer,'' says Fowler (*Business Week,* May 7, 1984).

The Changing Landscape of Competition

Clearly, competition in the home entertainment industry, in general, and television, in particular, are changing. VCRs are the hottest items going. Exhibit 5 shows how rapidly factory sales of VCRs have risen since 1982. Exhibit 6 shows that firms competing in the cable

EXHIBIT 5 VCR Factory Sales (in $ billions)

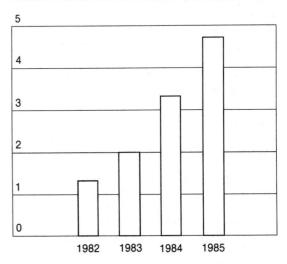

Figures for 1985 are projected.

Source: Electronic Industries Association. (Appeared in the *Richmond Times-Dispatch,* July 5, 1985.)

EXHIBIT 6 Homes with Cable TV (in millions, rounded)

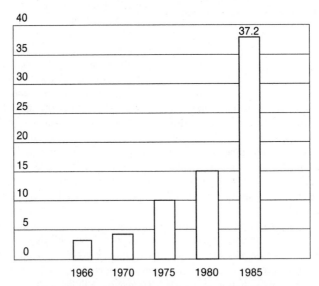

Figures are as of January 1 except for 1985, when May statistics were used.

Source: National Cable Television Association using Arbitron estimates for 1985. (Appeared in the *Richmond Times-Dispatch,* July 4, 1985.)

EXHIBIT 7 Tape Sales to dealers (in millions of units)

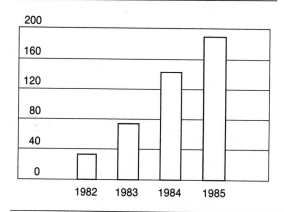

Source: Electronic Industries Association. Figures for 1985 are projected. (Appeared in the *Richmond Times-Dispatch*, July 5, 1985.)

industry have made significant progress over the last 20 years "wiring" homes in our nation. Finally, Exhibit 7 shows how rapidly sales of videocassette tapes have increased. There can be no doubt that the landscape of competition is changing.

OUTLOOK FOR THE FUTURE

The future of the cable industry is still bright. According to Robert J. Wussler, executive vice president of TBS, "I don't think the momentum is out of the game, although I certainly think the bloom is off the rose. But all you have to do is come to a couple of cable conventions and see that there's still enough money around and there are still enough young people around to execute all the ideas people can dream up. No, there's still a lot of momentum around, even if it's not the gold rush" (*Broadcasting*, December 12, 1983). Wussler believes broadcasting in general has hit a plateau or is shrinking. Due to the rise of independents, cable, direct broadcast satellites, videocassette recorders, and our various lifestyles, he does not believe broadcasting is becoming more powerful. According to Wussler, broadcasters do not need to worry about getting bigger again, but instead they must worry about getting smaller and about how they are going to manage being smaller. As for cable industry growth, Wussler does not see many

limitations. Although it is a tough business to get into today because it requires a lot of capital and there are channel capacity problems, the future is bright.

If the cable industry continues to grow and superstations proliferate, TBS will face more competition. According to *The Wall Street Journal* (April 19, 1985), some industry observers have questioned whether Turner Broadcasting could hold up if superstation imitators proliferated beyond the handful now operating. But Bonnie Cook, an analyst for J. C. Bradford & Co. in Nashville, dismisses that notion. She believes that anybody can transform a television station into a superstation, but cable systems can carry only a limited number of channels. Thus, it is unlikely that the number of superstations will increase dramatically.

Television broadcasting is changing. In early 1985, Capital Cities Communications, Inc., purchased ABC, and in April 1985 Ted Turner made a move to acquire CBS for $5.4 billion including no cash. This acquisition attempt attracted praise, criticism, and ridicule. According to *The Wall Street Journal* (April 19, 1985),

Mr. Turner has long broadcast his drive to run a network. Some associates contend that this desire became almost an obsession after Capital Cities Communications Inc. last month agreed to acquire American Broadcasting Cos. CBS thus was seen as Mr. Turner's last chance, because RCA, the parent of NBC. was probably too big to be taken over.

William C. Bevins Jr., the financial vice president of Turner Broadcasting, denies that the ABC acquisition move forced Mr. Turner's hand. But he concedes that the transaction "certainly crystallized where the various regulatory agencies stood and that the timing was propitious."

The package offered by Turner, which is reputed to be made up primarily of junk bonds, is presented below.

CBS rejected Turner's offer as inadequate and took steps to prevent a takeover. Andy Rooney, a regular on the television program "60 Minutes," had this to say about Turner's offer,

Ted Turner, the Atlanta, Ga., money operator, yachtsman and baseball team owner, has applied to the Federal Communications Commission for its approval of his scheme to take CBS away from its present owners. He has offered CBS stockholders a grabbag of what are known on Wall Street as "junk bonds" for their shares in CBS. . . .

Turner Broadcasting System Inc.'s Package for CBS

For each of CBS's 30 million shares, Turner offers the following package:

Type of Security	Face Value
$46 of 15% 7-year senior note	$ 46.00
$46 of 15½% 15-year, senior debenture	46.00
$10.31 of 5-year Series A, Zero coupon note	5.00
$11.91 of 6-year Series B Zero coupon note	5.00
$15.90 of 8-year Series C Zero coupon note	5.00
$18.38 of 9-year Series D Zero coupon note	5.00
$30.00 of 16¼% 20-year senior subordinated debenture	30.00
1 share of $2.80 preferred	16.50
0.75 share of Class B common	16.50*
Total	$175.00

*This is the face value of the offer for each CBS share. Analysts say there isn't any way of currently evaluating the market value of the package because the issues don't yet exist.

Source: *The Wall Street Journal*, April 19, 1985.

I offer my services in trying to locate a new anchorman for the "CBS Evening News" and someone else to do pieces at the end of "60 Minutes" because if Ted Turner takes over CBS, I doubt very much that Dan Rather will want his job and I know darn well I won't (*Richmond Times-Dispatch*, April 25, 1985).

On May 7, 1985, TBS announced a first quarter loss of $741,000, compared with a $5.3 million loss a year earlier.

MGM

Turner Develops an Interest in MGM

On March 25, 1986, Ted Turner completed the $1.5 billion acquisition of MGM-UA and immediately sold UA to Kirk Kerkorian for $480 million. MGM-UA shareholders received "$20 in cash and one share of new TBS preferred stock . . . " for each MGM-UA share they owned (*Atlanta Constitution*, March 26, 1986). The cash portion of the acquisition was financed with junk

bonds yielding returns to investors ranging from 12.5 percent to 14.5 percent.

Turner became interested in acquiring MGM in the early 1980s when the cost of leasing movies for WTBS began to increase rapidly. According to the *New York Times* (March 30, 1986):

Mr. Turner had begun to have problems buying movies for the Atlanta superstation. . . . In many cases, he was still paying the low rates for films that he had been charged in the 70s, when WTBS was just beginning to develop a national audience. That irritated Hollywood, and MGM even refused to lease films to WTBS. By 1985, Mr. Turner was worried that profit margins were beginning to erode as ad revenues failed to keep pace with costs at the superstation, which accounts for 80 percent of the operating profits of Turner Broadcasting's core businesses. "There was no question that movie fees were rising," Mr. Turner said. "I mean every time we signed a new contract, it was more, more, more." So when he read last summer that MGM-UA was for sale, Mr. Turner jumped.

But there are at least two other reasons why Turner wanted to make a deal to increase his stake in the entertainment industry, and they help explain why he moved so quickly to acquire MGM after his earlier attempt to acquire CBS failed. First, according to William Bevins, "The way the (entertainment) business was consolidating, to be a factor long-term, we either had to increase the distribution base—that would have been the CBS transaction—or acquire some software. That was the MGM deal" (*New York Times,* March 30, 1986).

Second, "Mr. Turner was also betting on 'one factor that nobody considers' . . . what he calls *colorization,* a technical process that he believes will enhance the value of old black and white movies. When a color version of *Miracle on 34th Street* was shown on WTBS, its ratings tripled (*New York Times,* March 30, 1986).

Mr. Turner's ego played a part as well. According to Turner, "Without MGM, there was a question mark with advertisers about our long-term viability. They used to throw that up at me. Early on, there was a certain group of people in the New York establishment: the same sort of thinking that gave me such a hard time at one time in the New York Yacht Club. You know: 'He's from Georgia, we don't need him around here. Here is a quarter, go shine my shoes.' You know: Stepin Fetchit" (*New York Times,* March 30, 1986).

In Turner's opinion, buying MGM was the natural thing to do after the CBS deal fell through. But the risk involved in this acquisition was great, and the outcome of the decision will not be known for several years.

The Effects of the MGM Deal on TBS

TBS is now more leveraged than most analysts think is reasonable. "Many industry observers say the enormous debt leaves Turner with a house of cards that could collapse with the slightest downturn in the economy" (*Atlanta Constitution,* March 30, 1986).

But Turner is accustomed to having his ideas criticized, and he seems to thrive on proving the experts wrong. In fact, some experts suggest that "Turner has fortified his cable empire for an inevitable battle with the major broadcasting networks. . . . When the dust settles in a few months, it will be clear to more people that

Turner, sooner than anyone else, is capable of taking on the TV networks he has tried to buy or beat" (*Atlanta Constitution,* March 30, 1986).

Competing with the networks will not be easy, because the operating costs are very high. John Malone, president of Denver-based Tele-Communications, Inc., said, "it will take a program budget of about $500 million annually to make TBS competitive with the networks in prime time. . . . TBS currently spends about $100 million on programming" (*Atlanta Constitution,* March 30, 1986).

Turner believes the acquisition of MGM will not affect the operation of TBS. "Our ongoing operations have not been and will not be affected in any way, shape, or form," he claimed. "In the financing package we obtained to complete the deal, we got $200 million in overfunding that is earmarked for operations. It allows us to go ahead with a full slate of motion pictures in Los Angeles, and we have the capital to go ahead with all of the other projects at WTBS and CNN" (*Atlanta Constitution,* March 30, 1986).

In response to comments by industry analysts that Turner paid too much for MGM, Turner had this to say:

> We'll just have to wait and see. . . . Those are the same people who said that WTBS wouldn't work on a satellite, and that CNN wouldn't work and that we paid too much for the Braves, etc.,
> etc. . . . Only we know what we plan to do, and they don't have a basis to comment (*Atlanta Constitution,* March 30, 1986).

It was reported that Turner considered selling stock in TBS to reduce the firm's debt. Since he owns 81 percent of the company, he could sell 31 percent and raise about $120 million without giving up control. However, industry experts say that the overall company is not worth as much as the individual parts because the firm is so heavily in debt. They doubt Turner will choose this course of action.

Selling TBS assets to help reduce the debt is being explored actively. In late October 1985, TBS announced its intention to put 20 percent to 50 percent of CNN on the market to raise cash. CNN is valued at $600 million. As one would expect, before any deal can be finalized the proposed buyer's goals must be consistent with those of CNN and Turner must remain in control. An offer from NBC was rejected earlier because Turner refused to relinquish editorial control to a rival.

What Did Turner Buy When He Acquired MGM?

Turner's deal with MGM-UA puts him at the helm of a large, vertically integrated motion picture and television business. Turner acquired the MGM film library, which contains 3,650 films including such classics as *Singing in the Rain, Gone with the Wind, Ben Hur,* and *The Wizard of Oz.* Along with this library, Turner acquired the rights to a broad variety of television shows. Shows produced under the MGM-UA banner will be the property of both Turner's TBS and Kerkorian's new United Artists. Each will have half-ownership in the newly formed MGM-UA Distribution Co., which will continue to distribute the shows to major networks, as well as to other broadcasters. The MGM package also includes a 44-acre studio complex in Culver City, California, with 24 sound stages and a film processing laboratory that handled 532 million feet of film in fiscal year 1984.

MGM and Movie Production

Despite its successful history, MGM-UA has been struggling with financial difficulties for the past few years. As with any major studio, the company's fortunes depend on its ability to release successful motion pictures. Lately, the box office results of MGM movies have not been good. For the fiscal year ending August 1985, MGM-UA lost $116 million.

It is no secret that Turner wants MGM to continue its movie production operation. "Of course, I want MGM to stay involved in the production of motion pictures if we can figure out a way to raise the money and do it. We would have to have a partner or a joint venture of some sort. So we've got to find someone that thinks the way we do in order to do that. But we're not ruling out new movie projects by any means" (*Atlanta Constitution,* March 30, 1986). According to Alan Ladd, Jr., chairman and chief executive officer of MGM, it is Turner's "desire to provide MGM with every available resource

to sustain the studio's growth as a leading supplier of worldwide entertainment product" (*Atlanta Constitution,* March 26, 1986).

MGM and Television Production

MGM-UA Entertainment Co., the division in charge of television broadcast material, released only one television series in 1985—"Lady Blue" on ABC. In 1984, two MGM-UA series were canceled not long after introduction—"Jessie" and "Paper Dolls," both on ABC. In contrast, other major studios such as Universal Television, Columbia, Paramount, Warner Brothers and 20th-Century Fox produced 12, 7, 5, 3, and 4 television series, respectively.

NEW OPTIONS FOR TURNER AND TBS

Before the MGM acquisition was completed, there was a great deal of speculation about what Ted Turner might do with the people and the assets of his new firm. Frank Rothman, chairman and chief executive officer of MGM-UA at the time of the acquisition, agreed to stay on until the deal was completed, and he characterized negotiations with Turner as "harmonious and pleasant" (*Atlanta Journal and Constitution,* August 11, 1985).

But MGM has not performed well lately, and some movie industry insiders say that changes must be made if the firm is going to be turned around. One unidentified MGM studio executive believes that Turner may have difficulty engineering the needed changes. "Turner may know television," he said, "but he's just another amateur when it comes to making films. His best hope is to put together a good team of seasoned people and let them have their head" (*Dun's Business Month,* September 1985).

The MGM acquisition gives Turner options he has not had in the past. He can differentiate his superstation from the major networks and from independent television stations by offering "the best of both worlds"—old movies and television programs and new releases. Reruns shown on the superstation have gained new popularity, especially with the baby boomers. Broadcast industry executives say these shows embody traditional values. ''The formerly hokey and corny is now heartwarming and refreshing,'' says Dan Greenblatt, president of distribution at LBS Communications, Inc., a distributor of television programs (*The Wall Street Journal,* August 20, 1985).

Turner can now produce his own movies to compete with major network programming. In addition, it has been suggested that Turner is considering launching a new pay-cable movie service that utilizes the MGM library to compete with HBO, Showtime, and The Movie Channel (*Atlanta Journal and Constitution,* October 10, 1985).

There has been further speculation that Turner might attempt to turn Atlanta into the ''Hollywood of the East.'' Film makers say that low labor and production costs and beautiful scenery make Georgia an ideal location for shooting pictures. Georgia has already been the site for a wide variety of major motion pictures that have turned out to be box office bonanzas.

There is also speculation that Turner has aspirations beyond building a media empire. ''Hollywood hands (are) welcoming the wild man of Dixie as a kindred spirit. . . . Those who know him say Ted Turner desperately wants to be the next William Paley,the founder of CBS, and ultimately president of the United States.'' (*Newsweek,* April 29, 1985).

THE DEAL OF A LIFETIME MAY HAVE TURNED SOUR

According to *The Wall Street Journal* (June 5, 1987), Ted Turner ''in effect, gave up contol of his life's work. In exchange for the money to stabilize his debt problems, he granted a group of cable television operators, including Time Inc., broad authority to oversee—and if necessary to veto—the management decisions of Turner Broadcasting System, Inc. . . . ''

The article went on to say that the MGM-UA deal was like

> a bomb, with a slow-burning fuse. The bomb was the preferred stock that was to pay dividends in common shares beginning this month; unless redeemed, it could eventually have reduced Mr. Turner's common-stock holdings from 80 percent

currently to a minority. To prevent that, Turner Broadcasting on Wednesday sold two new classes of preferred shares, amounting to 37 percent of the company's voting stock, to the cable companies for $562.5 million. The company will use the money to redeem the original preferred shares. . . .

Mr. Turner still owns 51 percent of his company's voting stock, and he remains chairman. But the board has been expanded to 15 members, and the cable operators have elected 7 of them. A supermajority of 12 directors will be required to approve each item of the annual budget. The supermajority will also be required to approve acquisitions, asset sales, borrowings, refinancings, amendments to bylaws, dividends, top-level executive changes, and anything that isn't in the budget and costs more than $2 million.

Furthermore, if Turner Broadcasting doesn't bring its remaining debt problems under contol within a year, the cable companies get an outright majority of the board. And if Mr. Turner decides to sell his stake, they have the right of first refusal to buy it. . . .

'It's clear from the transaction as it's structured—and I think it's an economic fact of life—that Ted no longer owns the company,' says William Bevins, Turner Broadcasting's chief financial officer.

WHAT NEXT FOR TED TURNER?

This turn of events raises some obvious questions. First among them is whether Ted Turner will be satisfied with his new, much less powerful role. Can he serve as leader of TBS now that he can be prevented from pursuing his goals if he cannot persuade 12 of 15 TBS directors that what he wants to do is also what is best for the company? The key word to consider is persuade. Ted Turner has not had to concern himself with persuading people in his company. In the past when he decided what he wanted to do, he simply did it.

Those who know him best suggest that Turner will not want to play this role. If they are correct, then what is next for Ted Turner? He is a very wealthy man who is about 50 years old and who has an enormous amount of talent and energy. Will he be a politician? Will he be a manager? Will he be a humanitarian who is willing to devote the rest of his life to pursuing world peace? Will he be an empire builder?

Exhibit 8 presents summary data about TBS as of May 1987.

EXHIBIT 8

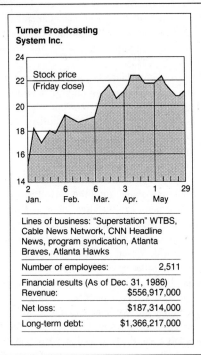

Lines of business: "Superstation" WTBS, Cable News Network, CNN Headline News, program syndication, Atlanta Braves, Atlanta Hawks	
Number of employees:	2,511
Financial results (As of Dec. 31, 1986) Revenue:	$556,917,000
Net loss:	$187,314,000
Long-term debt:	$1,366,217,000

Source: *The Wall Street Journal*, June 5, 1987, p. 11. Reprinted by permission of *The Wall Street Journal*, © Dow Jones & Company, Inc., 1987. All rights reserved.

14. Goodyear Tire and the Goldsmith Challenge

GOODYEAR IN 1985

Goodyear in 1985[1] was the world's largest manufacturer of tires and rubber products. Consolidated net sales in 1985 were $10.9 billion with consolidated income of $445 million. Worldwide employment averaged 133,271

This case was prepared by Bernard A. Deitzer, Alan G. Krigline, and Thomas C. Peterson of the University of Akron. This case represents neither effective or ineffective management in administrative situations. Rather, it is intended for use in classroom discussions of business strategic management.

Copyright © by Bernard A. Deitzer, 1989.

[1]Bernard A. Deitzer, Alan G. Krigline, Karl A. Shilliff, and John P. Wojnar, "Goodyear Tire and Rubber Company," ap-

persons, including 8,300 in Akron, Ohio. Goodyear manufactured its products in 57 plants in the United States and 45 plants in 27 foreign countries. Operations include over 2,250 facilities around the globe for the distribution and sale of its products; seven rubber plantations in Brazil, Guatemala, Indonesia, and the Philippines; a resort hotel in Litchfield, Arizona; and a government-owned uranium enrichment plant. Future growth potential for Goodyear appeared to be most likely in the areas of tires and related products, general products, high technology aerospace, and in defense and energy.

pearing in *Strategic Management* ed. J. M. Higgins and J. W. Vincze (Hinsdale, Ill.: Dryden Press, 1989).

GOODYEAR'S PRODUCT LINES

As in previous years, Goodyear's principal business was in the development, manufacture, distribution, and sale of tires for most applications. A broad line of tires is offered with emphasis on the high-performance, high-quality segment of the market. Goodyear also manufactures metal, rubber, and plastic products for the transportation industry and various industrial and consumer markets, synthetic rubber, several lines of chemicals, oil and gas, and high technology products for aerospace, defense, and nuclear energy application.

MANUFACTURING STRATEGY

As the rubber industry matured, competition consequently became more intense. Recognizing that the key to lower costs lay in improved production methods, Goodyear invested heavily in plant modernization to lower its costs. Conversely, its closest U.S. competitor chose to reduce costs (and reduce capacity) by closing older less efficient plants. Thus, Goodyear's modernized plants were able to compete successfully with foreign plants that had only two thirds of Goodyear's labor costs.

MARKETING STRATEGY

Management at Goodyear in 1985 coordinated worldwide facilities and efforts to put competition on a global basis rather than tailor competition to local markets as a multinational firm. Goodyear's share of the U.S. tire market was one third of the total and its share of the foreign tire market was one fifth of that total market. With one third of all autos in the United States and two thirds in foreign countries, the tire market shares translate into Goodyear having approximately one fourth of the world's market for auto tires.

FINANCIAL STRATEGY

Corporate financial goals were to reach sales of $15 billion in five year's time with a 5 percent return on sales and a 15 percent return on shareholder's equity. To achieve these goals, it was recognized that Goodyear's

heavy dependency on the slower growing and cyclical tire business would have to be reduced. Downturns in the auto manufacturing industry depressed original equipment tire demand; and technological improvements in tires, leading to increased mileage, lessened the demand for replacement tires.

GOODYEAR'S GRAND STRATEGY

Goodyear's overall strategy in 1985 was to have tire sales and general products bringing in one half of total sales volume while one fourth of total sales volume was to come from improved performance from Goodyear Aerospace Corporation (evolved from the Goodyear Aircraft Corporation). Originally established in 1939, it was renamed in 1963 to reflect its expanding role in space and defense programs.

The remaining one fourth of total sales volume was to come from the Celeron Corporation. Celeron was purchased in 1983 for $825 million of Goodyear stock, and was primarily involved in the transmission of natural gas through its extensive pipeline network. It also has plentiful gas and oil reserves. Celeron, moreover, was in the process of building an oil pipeline to move oil from the West Coast of California to the Gulf Coast oil refineries of Texas at a cost competitive with shipment by oil tankers through the Panama Canal.

IMPLEMENTING THE STRATEGY

As Goodyear proceeded to operationalize its grand strategy, a few dark clouds appeared on the horizon. At the time of the Celeron purchase, crude oil had been selling at a level near $30 per barrel. Crude oil was now in the $15 to $18 per barrel price range and had even dipped below $10 per barrel for a short time. This had the effect of reducing the value of Goodyear's oil reserves.

More significantly, the low oil price gave foreign oil an advantage over domestically produced oil. The low price depressed domestic production and this would reduce the amount of oil on the West Coast of California needing transport to the Texas Gulf Coast. Goodyear management recognized this as being only a short-term development in the oil market and proceeded with the construction of the hot-oil pipeline. It was uncertain at this time when Celeron's contribution to sales volume and contribution to profits would be able to reach the goal established in overall corporate planning.

PIPELINE RESISTANCE

On Wednesday, March 19, 1986, a full-page advertisement appeared in the *Akron Beacon Journal,* the major paper where Goodyear's corporate headquarters are located. It consisted of an open letter to Robert Mercer, chief executive officer and chairman of the board of Goodyear Tire and Rubber Company. The full-page letter was paid for by the Centex Water Preservation Fund and was signed by the Honorable Gonzalo Barrientos, Texas state senator, the Honorable Mike Renfro, Texas Travis County Judge, and the Honorable Walter Burnett, Texas Hays County Judge. The letter was a plea for Goodyear to add 20 to 60 miles to its pipeline and change its route to divert it from the Edwards Aquifer. The hot-oil, pressurized, pipeline was called a threat to the water supply of over a million Texans. In addition, the letter also requested that an Environmental Impact Study (EIS) be conducted. This action consequently would temporarily halt construction of the pipeline until the EIS was completed.[2] Goodyear quickly acknowledged the complaint and, as a socially responsible corporate citizen, promised to investigate and alleviate the aquifer problem as soon as possible.

CORPORATE RAIDER ACTIVITY

Goodyear's management, while working to resolve the unexpected downturn of events at Celeron, had also been aware that Goodyear itself might be an attractive target for a takeover attempt. Over a four-year period, it had witnessed four attacks on the rubber industry by corporate raiders. In 1981, for example, Loew's Corp. announced an intention to purchase up to 15 percent of Firestone stock. As Firestone's shares rose from $10 to $13 on the market, the company purchased large blocks of shares on the market including Loew's shares. Carl Icahn purchased Firestone shares in 1982 and was bought out by Firestone at the market price, which had risen by about $2 per share.

Icahn then proceeded to purchase 1.2 million shares of Goodrich stock which was subsequently repurchased by Goodrich in 1984 at a premium of 25 percent over market price. The profit, now referred to as "greenmail," was about $7 million. The next target for Icahn in the rubber industry was Uniroyal in 1985. A tender offer was made for two thirds of Uniroyal's stock at $18 per share. Uniroyal management was able to arrange a stock buyback for $22 a share. Icahn and his investment group subsequently made a profit of about $18 million.[3]

GOODYEAR'S PREEMPTIVE STRIKE

With the knowledge that it was a potential target for a raid, Goodyear management had taken some steps to reduce its attractiveness to corporate raiders. They had conferred with investment analysts in an effort aimed at boosting its stock price to make Goodyear less of a target by making any acquisition attempt more costly. Goodyear's board of directors in July of 1986 approved a shareholder rights plan, a "poison pill" tactic, that would also make any acquisition attempt prohibitively expensive.

Under this arrangement, shareholders could exercise their rights by converting them into additional shares during a takeover attempt, raising the purchase price of the company. Also in July 1986, William Newkirk, the vice president for public relations, directed his public relations staff to a takeover preparedness camp in Maryland for four days of preemptive tactical training. These steps were taken calmly with no sense of urgency at the corporate office. At this time, Goodyear's shares were trading, as they had for several years, in the low $30 per share range.[4]

TAKEOVER SPECULATION

At the end of September 1986, Goodyear's share price started to rise in active trading on the New York Stock Exchange. The share price continued to rise until by the week of October 20–24, 1986, it closed the week at 44⅛ a share, up 2⅝ for the week. More than 16 million

---

[2]*Akron Beacon Journal,* March 19, 1986, p. A9.

[3]D. Oplinger, "Raiding the Rubber Industry," *Akron Beacon Journal,* December 1, 1986, p. C2.

[4]"The Goodyear War," *Akron Beacon Journal,* November 30, 1986, pp. B1–B10.

shares or nearly 15 percent of Goodyear's outstanding shares had changed hands during the week. Rumors and takeover speculation intensified, particularly since a Form 13-D had not yet been filed with the Securities and Exchange Commission by the close of business on Friday, October 24, 1986. Form 13-D is required when any one investor accumulates 5 percent or more of the shares in a company.[5]

The steady increase in volume and share price for Goodyear shares on the floor of the New York Stock Exchange was viewed with some alarm by Goodyear's management. Adding to their alarm was the difficulty of sorting out and identifying one buyer or group of buyers as a potential corporate raider.

THE RISK ARBITRAGEURS

Concurrently, anonymous risk arbitrageurs accounted for much of the trading as Goodyear shares became the most actively traded on the NYSE. The arbitrageurs would buy Goodyear shares or the shares of any potential takeover target that was being rumored on Wall Street in the hopes that the shares would quickly rise in value and make large short-term profits possible. It was not clear at this time whether a raider was accumulating stock to gain control of Goodyear or whether a Wall Street "shark" might be using timely rumor to drive up share price and later sell out at a much greater profit.

In response to rumors, Robert Mercer, chairman of the board, pointed out the company's situation in a letter to Goodyear's employees. Apparently, a large block of stock, 1.7 million shares, was sold by an institutional investor through a Merrill Lynch broker to another Merrill Lynch broker acting for Merrill Lynch Capital Markets. When Goodyear contacted their local Merrill Lynch office to inquire about the transaction, the local analyst replied that he wasn't permitted to comment on the transaction.

THE GOLDSMITH CHALLENGE

On November 3, 1986, *The Wall Street Journal* broke the news by reporting on a Securities and Exchange Commission filing. A group led by Sir James Gold-

smith, a global financier holding both French and English citizenship, disclosed that it had acquired an 11.5 percent stake or nearly 12.5 million of Goodyear's approximately 109 million outstanding shares. In the filing, it was disclosed that the group's ultimate goal was to obtain control of or make a business combination with Goodyear. The group had purchased 1.7 million Goodyear shares on September 25, 1986, at $33 a share. Most of the group's shares apparently were purchased at $40 to $44 a share. Between October 27 and 29, 1986, nearly 1.5 million shares were purchased at $48 a share, evidently the highest price paid by the group.

GOLDSMITH'S "WAR CHEST"

In a separate SEC filing, Goldsmith indicated that he would receive $246.6 million from the sale of a container company he acquired when Crown Zellerbach Corp. was taken over by him earlier in 1986. In October 1986, Goldsmith raised an additional $213 million by having another company, also acquired from Crown Zellerbach, issue an unusual special dividend. These two moves would give Goldsmith about $460 million in cash for his "war chest" if he should decide to make a tender offer for Goodyear.

In a letter to Mercer, Goldsmith explained his delay in making a bid for Goodyear by saying, "It seemed to us that the market had overreacted and that both the volume and price of Goodyear's shares have reached unexpected levels." In this same letter, he expressed a desire to discuss "possible ways to advance the interests of Goodyear's shareholders and employees" and he believed "a greater concentration on the core business would be more beneficial than major diversification efforts."[6]

A detailed look at the SEC filing for the acquisition of Goodyear shares subsequently revealed that Goldsmith reported a total of $3.1 billion available to gain control of Goodyear. After the purchase of 11.5 percent of the company's stock altogether $2.6 billion in financing remained. Some of the financing was to come from Wells Fargo Bank in San Francisco, First National Bank of Chicago, and Bank of Nova Scotia in Canada.

---

[5]"Regional Stock Report," *Akron Beacon Journal,* October 27, 1986, p. B5.

[6]G. Stricharchuk and P. Miller, "Goldsmith Goodyear Stake Put at 11.5%," *The Wall Street Journal,* November 3, 1986, p. 8.

Goldsmith's first purchase of Goodyear's shares was for 33,000 shares at 31⅞.

An additional block of 1.7 million shares was purchased on September 25, 1986, at $33 a share. (Most of the initial purchases were financed by foreign banks.) The combined 12.5 million shares held represented a total investment of $530 million. Based on the closing price of 48⅝ on October 31, Goldsmith's holding now had appreciated to $610 million. At this same price, Goldsmith would need an astounding $1.14 billion more to acquire a 35 percent interest in Goodyear, the minimum amount regarded as necessary to have controlling interest in a company.

GOLDSMITH'S FINANCIAL EMPIRE

Goldsmith had paid Merrill Lynch Capital Markets $5 million to assist in the purchases of Goodyear's shares and had contracted to pay from $7.5 million to $15 million more for continued assistance. The stock was held by General Oriental Ltd. Partnership of Bermuda, incorporated September 19, 1986, shortly before Goldsmith's first purchase, and by General Oriental Partnership of Delaware, incorporated October 27, 1986. The two newly incorporated partnerships are the latest in the maze of Goldsmith's financial empire (Exhibit 1). The structure and locations of Goldsmith's conglomerate were obviously designed to take advantage of tax laws which would maximize earnings.[7]

GOODYEAR'S DEFENSE

In October 1986, Representative John Seiberling, the Democratic congressman for Akron and a former 17-year employee of Goodyear, as well as the grandson of Goodyear's founder, requested that the Judiciary Committee hold hearings on the Goodyear takeover. The hearings would most likely take place before the monopolies and commercial law subcommittee. The hearings were to be held in an effort to encourage the administration to enforce antitrust laws in order to stop

---

[7]G. Gardner and L. Pantages, "Goldsmith Would Sell Off Non-Tire Operations," *Akron Beacon Journal*, November 2, 1986, pp. A1, A16.

the Goodyear takeover. Under the Clayton Antitrust Act, the administration has very broad powers to prohibit any takeover that would weaken competition. Its competitive position, Goodyear argued, would be weakened if it were forced to cut spending for research and development or if it were forced to sell valuable assets.

SEIBERLING'S EFFORTS

Seiberling was also considering that a request be made of the House Energy and Commerce Committee to hold hearings to ensure that the Securities and Exchange Commission properly monitor the trading of Goodyear stock. Seiberling, a senior member of the Judiciary Committee and its subcommittee, had grown up with the knowledge and remembrance that Wall Street and similar financiers had forced Goodyear out of his grandfather's hands in the 1921 reorganization of Goodyear. He also felt that Congress should pass a law to prohibit the takeover of Goodyear by a foreign investor because of Goodyear's defense work. Since Congress had already adjourned, no such legislation could be passed.

COMMUNITY SUPPORT EFFORTS

The citizens of Akron gradually rallied to voice their support for Goodyear by sending letters to the local newspaper, the *Akron Beacon Journal*. The newspaper joined in support by writing in its editorial for Sunday, November 2, 1986:

> What Goodyear has going for it in this fight is that, as analysts note, it is a very well-managed company. That such a company should be targeted for a hostile takeover makes a mockery of the argument that such corporate raids are a part of capitalism's natural sorting-out process. If so, it is certainly not the best use of the capitalist system.
>
> Corporate raiders are the most extreme manifestations of one common criticism of American corporations: that they focus too much on short-term profits.
>
> But, Goodyear has been playing the game the right way. To combat foreign and domestic competition, Goodyear has taken the long-range view, investing in productivity and improving its

EXHIBIT 1   Goldsmith Financial Empire

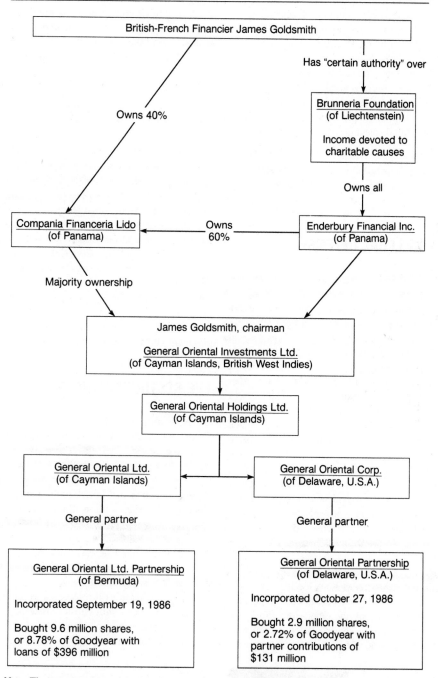

Note: These companies represent only a portion of Goldsmith's holdings.

Source: *Akron Beacon Journal*, November 2, 1986, p. A16, Ref. 11, p. 284.

international market position, at the expense of short-run profits. These expenditures, say some analysts, may have made Goodyear an appealing takeover target, even though its plan is one that should be followed by other corporations.

As U.S. Rep. John Seiberling said, ''What kind of message does this send to managements across the country?'' . . . More general standards would be welcome that might prevent any corporation from being in danger, simply for making the right moves toward future planning.

Goodyear encouraged all such public efforts for its support and proceeded to lobby the Ohio legislature to enact laws preventing such unwanted takeovers for any corporation.

GOODYEAR'S LEGAL DEFENSE

Sometime in October 1986, and after learning the identity and interest of the raider, Goodyear decided the best defense would be a good offense. The investment banking firm of Goldman Sachs & Co. was consequently hired as a primary adviser. The New York law firm of Cahill Gordon & Reindel also was enlisted to assist Goodyear's own legal talent. The Carter Organization, a proxy solicitation firm, hired more often than any other company of its kind for corporate-control battles, was commissioned to identify the corporate raider. Its success would depend on the company's extensive back office contacts in Wall Street, as well as on its access to official records.

Another investment banking firm, Drexel Burnham Lambert Inc., which had pioneered the use of high-risk ''junk bonds'' as a tool for raiders in takeovers, was hired to advise Goodyear on a possible restructuring to maximize shareholder value. Moreover, their key executive, Martin Siegel, specialized in mergers and acquisitions.

Drexel, in turn, brought in Joe Flom, one of Wall Street's best-known takeover artists. Goodyear management felt that if Siegel and Flom were not on Goodyear's side, they might be hired by the other side. Ironically, many of the outsiders on Goodyear's defense team were more accustomed to working for raiders than for acquisition targets.

Goodyear's Mercer said, ''Whoever the raider was, we didn't want him to have Drexel and Flom. They

knew what to say. They knew the language [in meetings]. Whether or not it was worth the money to pay them, I don't know. But I do know this: You'd be severely criticized if you went into this kind of battle without hiring the best people in the business to advise you.'' The best people would eventually cost Goodyear several million dollars.[8]

GOODYEAR'S OPTIONS

Goodyear's advisers presented three options. Goodyear could (1) repurchase the stock that Goldsmith had garnered, (2) sell off subsidiaries, trim operations, take on enormous debt and thus elevate the stock price beyond Goldsmith's war chest, or (3) find a ''white knight'' who possibly might take the same actions, but in a much less brutal fashion. Whatever, it was clear that a Goodyear recovering from the trauma of takeover conflict would emerge a smaller and more debt-ridden company. Moreover, the costs of buying back stock and paying investment bankers, lawyers, and public relations firms, in addition to interest payments on a mammoth debt, would almost certainly mean that significant employment cutbacks would be necessary.

THE RESTRUCTURING PROCESS

On November 3, 1986, the first business day after Goldsmith announced his intentions for embattled Goodyear, Mercer initiated Goodyear's takeover defense by announcing a dramatic restructuring plan. The restructuring was to include selling its oil and gas subsidiary Celeron. Celeron had been acquired earlier in 1983 by Goodyear for $825 million. Simultaneously, its Louisiana pipelines and processing plants were sold by Goodyear for $447 million. Later on, oil and gas reserves were acquired from Chevron Corp. for $395 million and in subsequent years Goodyear invested $900 million in Celeron's All-America pipeline.

In 1986, Celeron's oil reserves were estimated at 100 million barrels and with current crude oil prices at $14 per barrel, the reserves alone would be worth $1.4 billion. The sale of these reserves would allow Goodyear

---

[8]''The Goodyear War,'' pp. B1–B10.

to repurchase about 30 percent of its outstanding shares while leaving in place the debt of $600 million borrowed for the pipeline. With a total debt of $1.9 billion, Goodyear would be a more highly leveraged company and a less desirable target.

Another result would be that with fewer shares outstanding, the current earnings of $3 per share would increase to $4.50 or $5 per share. With Goodyear's stock selling at 10 to 11 times earnings just before Goldsmith began buying, and if that multiple were applied to the earnings estimate, Goodyear's stock could be selling for $50 a share, a price higher than Goldsmith was willing to pay. [9, 10, 11]

Goodyear's gas and oil holdings possibly may have been the primary attraction for Goldsmith who might keep them for himself while selling off Goodyear's core tire business. In two earlier takeovers, Diamond International in 1982 and Crown Zellerbach in early 1986, Goldsmith had sold off the acquired companies to repay his borrowings for the acquisitions, while keeping the timber holdings from each. From Diamond International, he had received 1.9 million acres of timberland, and from Crown Zellerbach he had acquired 1.6 million acres of timberland, all located in the United States. Other natural resources included large oil reserves in Guatemala, estimated at nearly 200 million barrels, that Goldsmith controlled as chairman of Basic Resources International (Bahamas) Limited. [12]

MARKET REACTIONS

At noon on this same day, November 3, 1986, Goodyear's stock was off 1¼ at 47⅜ on a volume of 1.59 million shares. It closed off ⅜ at 48¼ on a volume of 3.9 million shares, at the time the second most actively traded stock in the history of the New York Stock Exchange.

THE GOLDSMITH LINEAGE

James Goldsmith traces his family ties back some 500 years to Frankfurt, Germany. The family name appropriately was taken from the craft it practiced—goldsmithing. Over the years, along with their cousins, the eminent Bischoffsheims and the much storied Rothschilds, the family solidly established themselves throughout Europe in banking and finance. [13]

Frank Goldsmith, his father, came to England by way of France; studied law at Oxford and was elected to the House of Commons. Although commissioned in the British army, rising to the rank of major, and ultimately a member of Parliament, Frank Goldsmith was nonetheless persecuted and forced to leave England at the time of the First World War because of his German ancestry. Returning to France, he eventually entered the hotel industry where he became one of the most powerful and popular hoteliers in Europe. The company he founded controlled 48 hotels, and Frank Goldsmith and his family regularly traveled from Paris to Monte Carlo to Cannes to Trouville on the Channel then to London and Paris. [14, 15]

THE EARLY GOLDSMITH

On February 26, 1933, James Michael Goldsmith was born into this affluent lifestyle. He spent his early years in some of the grandest hotel suites in Europe. Uninterested and largely unsuccessful in his formal education, as well as being nonconforming in behavior, he also acquired a reputation as a playboy with a fondness for the gaming tables. His interest in business developed when he discovered that it was as exciting as gambling. [16, 17, 18]

[9]G. Gardner and L. Pantages, "Goodyear Seeks a Buyer for Celeron," *Akron Beacon Journal,* November 3, 1986, pp. A1, A14.

[10]T. Gerdel, "Goodyear to Sell Unit," *Cleveland Plain Dealer,* November 4, 1986, p. 2C.

[11]R. Winter and G. Stricharchuk, "Goodyear, Responding to Takeover Bid, Seeks Buyer for Its Oil and Gas Unit," *The Wall Street Journal,* November 4, 1986, p. 3.

[12]G. Wansell, *Tycoon—The Life of James Goldsmith* (New York: Macmillan, 1987), pp. 315, 317.

[13]Ibid., chap. 1, pp. 22, 26–31.
[14]Ibid.
[15]Ibid., chap. 2, pp. 34–35, 38.
[16]Ibid., chap. 3, pp. 39, 43–44, 45–48.
[17]Ibid., chap. 4, pp. 53–57.
[18]Ibid., chap. 7, pp. 86, 93.

THE GOLDSMITH GENIUS

James Goldsmith's genius for financing was aided by both timing and amazingly good fortune. As a child in 1939, he had escaped from France with his family on the last boat departing from Bayonne, France, for England, just before the arrival of the German army. The boat, incidentally, designed for 400 carried 5,000 passengers, and was fired upon by a German U-boat. Fortunately for Goldsmith, only one torpedo was fired and after it missed, the submarine departed. In his first business venture, he was saved from certain bankruptcy when the staff of every bank in France went on strike for the first time in 20 years. In England, and in the United States, he was successful in his two most critical business takeovers because he had expected the stock markets to rise while they had been falling. When the markets quickly rebounded, he was able to sell stock at high enough prices to pay off his borrowings for the acquisitions.[19, 20]

EARLY GOLDSMITH DYNASTY

The foundations for James Goldsmith's business empire were laid by acquiring failing companies, selling off unprofitable operations or closing them, and installing management teams capable of running the companies at above-average profits. The assets of the company were then parlayed for the next acquisition. Goldsmith encountered little opposition until his takeover of Bovril, an old establishment company in England that was operating profitably. Even though this change in tactics made him somewhat unpopular in the business world, he was nonetheless recognized for his contributions to the economies of England and France with a knighthood by the English government and the Légion d'honneur by the French.[21]

The Goldsmith business empire eventually crystallized with his U.S. acquisitions of Diamond International and Crown Zellerbach. Up to this point, Goldsmith, the penultimate gambler, had always risked all in "double or nothing" fashion; afterwards he would not have to risk everything to make an acquisition.[22]

GOLDSMITH PHILOSOPHY

Goldsmith viewed himself as a change agent, an undiluted capitalist, who steadfastly maintained that the control of major U.S. corporations which began as capitalist enterprises is bound to evolve from traditional entrepreneurial founders to professional managers, and eventually and finally, to institutional investors and savers. And corporate raiders, catalysts of that change, he avowed, are really breaking the vice of the managing class.[23] Concurrently, with this dramatic change is the opportunity to advance one's own interest and those of others just as the "invisible hand" of Adam Smith guaranteed that the pursuit of individual interests resulted in an overall good.

> He [Goldsmith] was more convinced than ever that the United States offered him a unique opportunity to make a considerable fortune for himself—and to improve the basis of the American economy. For, just as he had condemned the suffocation of England and the bureaucracy of France in the past, now he was attacking the stuffy "corporatism" of the United States.[24]

The very epicenter of the controversy, according to Goldsmith, was the relationship between the shareholder and the corporation:

> Although corporations belong to their shareholders, . . . corporate managements sometimes believe that the business that employs them has become an institution and that they are the trustees of that institution. Some believe that they have developed some sort of proprietorial rights. Shareholders then become no more than an inconvenience. . . . The principal difference between a friendly merger and a hostile takeover is that management agrees to a merger. A hostile takeover is only hostile to established management.

---

[19]Ibid., chap. 11, pp. 147–50.
[20]Ibid., chap. 21, pp. 303–5.
[21]Ibid., chap. 11, pp. 147–50.

[22]Ibid. chap. 24, pp. 368, 370, 375–76.
[23]Ibid., chap. 23, pp. 354–55, 357.
[24]Ibid., chap. 22, pp. 314–15.

. . . The management of large, tired companies, fearful of the free market, plead with the government bureaucracy for special protection to protect the status quo and avoid change. . . . Corporate raiders don't perform their useful function altruistically. But their self-interest usually leads to a collective good. . . . In a free economy, the inefficient are eliminated and the efficient—as long as they remain so—grow for the benefit of all.[25]

GOLDSMITH'S EARLIER SENATE TESTIMONY

On June 12, 1985, more than a year before the Goodyear challenge, and because of the successful takeover of Diamond International, Goldsmith testified before the U.S. Senate subcommittee on corporate takeovers. An excerpt follows:

Who would have believed a few years ago, . . . that conglomerates, created at the time by freewheeling entrepreneurs, today are described by some as sacrosanct institutions which should be protected from the marketplace by special legislation. . . . All that has changed in many of these companies is that the flame of the founder has been replaced by the complacency of the bureaucrat. And because the members of such bureaucracies control the disposition of vast amounts of other people's money and the power and patronage that accompany it, they feel they are part of the establishment and therefore deserve special privileges. . . .

I would only like to make one obvious point. . . . Corporations are owned by their shareholders. Management is employed by shareholders to look after shareholder interests. Devices like poison pills, paying greenmail, defensive acquisitions, super majority voting, staggered boards, et cetera, should all be subject to a prior and free vote by shareholders and should not be imposed unilaterally by management. . . . When management acts unilaterally, without consulting shareholders, it is seeking protection not for their shareholders but from their shareholders. . . .

There's nothing hostile about a hostile bid. There's no difference between a raid and a merger except that the established bureaucrat loses his job, not the owners and not the business. . . . The word hostile is merely a bureaucratic term to try and create a nobility to entrenchment. . . . Raiders shouldn't put on a halo. They are doing it for personal gain. The important thing is whether their action is generally beneficial or generally detrimental, not why they are doing it. . . . The dead hand of the bureaucrat does not produce growth. It does not produce innovation. It produces complacency, ossification and decline.[26]

COMMUNITY REACTION

In the fall of 1986, as the price of Goodyear's stock rose, some employees and Akron residents sold their shares to cash in on the dramatic increase. However, within a few days, the local selling of Goodyear stock almost stopped as the workers and citizenry came to realize the consequences of such a change in Goodyear's ownership. The prevailing mood then became defensive and placards and posters appeared in front of homes reading "Don't turn your back on family! Save Akron! Buy Goodyear stock!" As part of its defensive strategy, Goodyear welcomed and encouraged this community support. The momentum was growing.

Some 50 mayors from surrounding communities met with township trustees and county officials to discuss the threatening situation. Goodyear's public relations staff lobbied the state legislature urging the passage of laws that would hinder unwanted takeovers of companies. Akron's Mayor Tom Sawyer was to arrange a two-way teleconference linked by satellite with 33 cities across the country having Goodyear plants in them. Plant officials citing danger to their communities, were to call for state and federal legislation to block unwanted takeovers. It was time for legislators and the SEC to examine America's hands-off policy on hostile takeovers and the question of what speculators are doing to America's industrial base.[27]

---

[25]Ibid.

[26]Ibid., chap. 23, pp. 354–55, 357.

[27]M. Gleisser, "Rallying for Goodyear," *Cleveland Plain Dealer,* November 14, 1986, p. 25-B.

Goodyear Earnings Model (dollars in millions)

	1985R	1986R	1987	1988E	1989E	Percent Change from Prior Year		
						1987	1988E	1989E
		5%	7%	1%	1%	7%	1%	1%
Unit tire sales —est. change	−2%	5%	7%	1%	1%	7%	1%	1%
Sales:								
Tires	$6,190	$6,630	$7,305	$7,750	$8,125	10	6	5
Related	986	1,214	1,262	1,300	1,325	4	3	2
Tires and related	$7,176	$7,844	$8,567	$9,050	$9,450	9	6	4
Ind. rub., chem., plast.	1,102	1,136	1,246	1,300	1,300	10	4	0
Other	64	60	93	150	150	55	62	0
Total	$8,341	$9,040	$9,905	$10,500	$10,900	10	6	4
Variable costs	5,905	6,224	6,682	7,185	7,530	7	8	5
Variable profit	$2,437	$2,816	$3,223	$3,315	$3,370	14	3	2
Depreciation	$ 268	$ 349	$ 350	$ 360	$ 370	0	3	3
Research	264	290	267	275	285	(8)	3	4
Pensions	57	15	3	15	15	(79)	384	0
Retiree health care	57	63	73	80	90	15	10	13
Cost of goods	$6,550	$6,942	$7,375	$7,915	$8,290	6	7	5
Gross profit	1,791	2,098	2,531	2,585	2,610	21	2	1
Selling + admin.	1,381	1,597	1,635	1,720	1,775	2	5	3
Operating profit	$ 410	$ 502	$ 896	$ 865	$ 835	78	(3)	(3)
Interest expense	102	122	283	260	255	132	(8)	(2)
Currency loss	34	19	39	40	35	104	3	(13)

Other income	114	121	180	180	180	49	0	0
Pretax income	$ 389	$ 482	$ 754	$ 745	$ 725	57	(1)	(3)
Income taxes	138	193	297	268	263	54	(10)	(2)
Minority interests	7	10	17	20	20	75	19	0
Income—continuing operations	$ 244	$ 279	$ 440	$ 457	$ 442	58	4	(3)
Discontinued operations	185	(93)	257	0	0			
Nonrecurring gains—net	(17)	(63)	74	0	0			
Net income	$ 412	$ 124	$ 771	$ 457	$ 442	521	(41)	(3)
Shares	107	107	61	57	57	(43)	(6)	0
E.P.S.								
Continuing operations	$ 2.27	$ 2.61	$ 7.27	$ 6.00	$ 7.75	179	10	(3)
Discontinued operations	1.73	(0.86)	4.24	0.00	0.00			
Nonrecurring gains—net	(0.16)	(0.59)	1.22	0.00	0.00			
Net	$ 3.84	$ 1.16	$12.73	$ 8.00	$ 7.75	999	(37)	(3)
Percent of Sales:								
Variable profit	29.2%	31.2%	32.5%	31.6%	30.9%			
Gross profit	21.5	23.2	25.5	24.6	23.9			
Operating profit	4.9	5.6	9.0	8.2	7.7			
Pretax profit	4.7	5.3	7.6	7.1	6.7			
Net profit—continuing operations	2.9	3.1	4.4	4.4	4.1			
Tax rate	35.6	40.0	39.4	36.0	36.2			

(R) Restated to classify Motor Wheel, Goodyear Aerospace and Celeron Oil and Gas Co. as discontinued operations.

1986 earnings from continued operations exclude after-tax restructuring costs of $223 million ($2.08 per share), a gain on pension fund settlement of $152 million ($1.42), and a gain on the sale of facilities of $8 million ($0.07). The net charge was $63 million ($0.59).

Source: Harvey E. Heimback, CFA, *Tire Industry Quarterly Review*, April 1988, Merrill Lynch, Pierce, Fenner and Smith, Inc., with permission.

MERRILL LYNCH CONNECTION

When it became known that Merrill Lynch Capital Markets was supporting Goldsmith with $1.9 billion of its own funds, Akronites threw up a picket line at the local Merrill Lynch office. Clients with ties to Goodyear withdrew their funds from Merrill Lynch to demonstrate their displeasure for its part in the takeover. United Auto Workers' Local 856 at Goodyear Aerospace withdrew $70,000 in union funds held by Merrill Lynch. Ohio Machine & Mold, a small Goodyear supplier, withdrew $130,000, while the Akron Police Department withdrew $272,000 in insurance money from the brokerage giant.

The local protest continued in other ways. Radio station WNIR sent tapes of calls from irate listeners to Goldsmith. A petition drive was launched to collect 100,000 signatures to be ultimately forwarded to President Ronald Reagan.

THE GOLDSMITH INTERVIEW

The *Akron Beacon Journal* which normally prints part of one editorial page with letters from readers, twice printed two double pages of letters from angered readers, mostly in favor of Goodyear. The letters poured in after the newspaper published the following interview with Goldsmith. Excerpts follow:

Q. How did you become aware of Goodyear as a good company for investment?

A. Well, we felt that the tire company, the core business, is a great business. And, we felt the company—and I emphasize without inside knowledge, but from the outside—had weakened its position somewhat by losing its focus. And, that the diversification had weakened the company, and this had been the perception in the marketplace, and it was therefore a company which we think could be improved by refocusing it and working exclusively on developing the core business to make it the best in the world, even better than it now is. And releasing assets which are used in peripheral activities and concentrating on the core business.

Q. What did you consider attractive about Goodyear as a company to operate?

A. Well, first I wouldn't operate it. Let me make that quite clear. I'm not a manager. And I certainly don't pretend to know the tire business. The only input that I can have is input in strategic terms—to avoid, for instance, diversification, which is sometimes good, sometimes not. I don't say that I have all the knowledge in the world, or that I'm the fount of all wisdom, but I think I can participate in the strategic thinking of a company and creating an environment in which the management can get on and develop the business they're supposed to be developing. . . . Goodyear is clearly the best tire company in the world. It shows it by its market leadership, by its brand leadership. I'm not saying that there are certain things that shouldn't be looked at and assessed because that's a continuing process which any management team—new or old—has to continue to do.

The Goodyear Tire & Rubber core business is a very fine business, which is number one in the world.

* * * * *

Q. Do you and your partners plan to maintain their interest in Goodyear or any of its subsidiaries?

A. Oh, absolutely. . . . If we were to gain control, we would intend to stay . . . to invest in the long term, for the long term in improving Goodyear's core business.

* * * * *

Q. You've indicated you are not a manager. Do you know whether Hanson [Trust, a British holding company] plans to have a management role in Goodyear?

A. I did say, we call the shots on this. They are limited partners. We are the general partner. We would want to work with management. It would be ridiculously, grotesquely arrogant of us, and stupid, to believe that we could supply better tire management—a core business management—than Goodyear. It's got the best.

Q. Does that mean you would plan to keep current management?

A. That means that we would plan to work with current management, ask the questions, work out plans with them. We have no alternative, no alternative management team or any of that stuff.

Q. What brought you to Goodyear? There's been some speculation in *The Wall Street Journal* that Merrill

Lynch played a major role in actually putting the whole plan together and you said that they did. Are they the ones that actually brought Goodyear to you?

A. I'll tell you, we've been looking at a number of companies to invest in, and we studied Goodyear, and we studied it with Merrill. But I can't say they actually brought the deal to us—because we constantly study things. But they did develop it, study it, analyze it and work on the financing structure.

* * * * *

Q. According to the 13-D, it appears that you laid out about $5.7 billion or so in financing, roughly $52 a share, available in equity and loan commitments if you were to acquire all the shares. Is that a correct assessment?

A. I haven't got the exact figure in my mind, but it sounds about right.

Q. *The New York Times* is saying that Hanson Trust has $5.5 billion in cash. Do you know how much of that cash they are willing to contribute to this endeavor?

A. I do not. At the moment they have contributed $200 million.

Q. If we could ask one question on a lighter note . . . do you prefer one line of tires over another?

A. (Laughs) I'm of immense ignorance, I'm afraid. One of the strengths that I've got is that I'm ignorant.[28]

* * * * *

EARLY RESTRUCTURING EFFORTS

As the battle for Goodyear progressed, the first steps were taken in the restructuring that Mercer had announced in his second meeting with Goldsmith on November 5. Goodyear said it was retiring its blimp "Europa" based near Rome. The annual cost to keep its four blimps afloat is $10 million. Also in Europe, the company closed its advanced tire building group at Howdins Ltd., in Britain, transferring the technology to technical centers in Luxembourg and Akron. A 26-year participation in Formula One Grand Prix auto racing was ended. This first restructuring move was to cost jobs in Akron. An unspecified number of engineers would lose their jobs and an expanded early retirement program for salaried employees was detailed.[29, 30]

THE COUNTERATTACK CONTINUES

The battle to save Goodyear during the early weeks of November 1986 was being carried on outside of the company itself. Members of the United Rubber Workers' Local 2 in Akron approved a plan calling for workers to voluntarily give up some pay and buy Goodyear stock. The URW represents about 23,000 Goodyear tire employees through 29 locals.[31]

Akron Mayor Tom Sawyer was to moderate a closed-circuit television satellite linkup with phone hookups in each of 33 cities having Goodyear plants or offices. Its purpose was to gather data about the impact the takeover would have on the involved cities. The data, consisting of possible disastrous effects on finances, employment and taxes if plants were to close, would be used for the testimony to be given to the monopolies subcommittee of the U.S. House Judiciary Committee. Goldsmith, Mercer, Sawyer, and President Milan Stone of the URW were to testify on the takeover attempt.[32] On November 10, Goodyear stock closed at 47⅝, up ⅛. More than 6.2 million shares were traded, making it the most active stock on the NYSE.

U.S. HOUSE JUDICIARY COMMITTEE TESTIMONY

The U.S. House Judiciary Committee's subcommittee on monopolies convened on Tuesday, November 18, 1986. Both Goldsmith and Mercer were ordered to testify. Goldsmith prefaced his testimony with the following opening statement. Excerpts follow:

---

[28]D. Oplinger, et al., "Transcript of *Beacon Journal,* Interview with Goldsmith," *Akron Beacon Journal,* November 6, 1986, p. A14.

[29]T. Gerdel, "Goodyear Deflates European Blimp, Tire Works," *Cleveland Plain Dealer,* November 11, 1986, p. 1-A.

[30]L. Pantages and K. Byard, "Goodyear Will Lower Its Profile in Racing," *Akron Beacon Journal,* November 12, 1986, p. A1.

[31]Gerdel, "Goodyear Deflates European Blimp," p. 1-A.

[32]C. Nevada, "Video Hookup to Gather Data for Hearing," *Akron Beacon Journal,* November 12, 1986, p. A8.

Paul W. Litchfield was chief executive officer of Goodyear during the 30 years of its greatest prosperity and growth. He defined Goodyear's job quite clearly. It was, he said, "to build better tires, cheaper, and sell them harder."

The current management of Goodyear forgot Mr. Litchfield's lesson. It strayed into industries [Celeron] about which it knew nothing, jeopardizing the very heart of Goodyear's business and the security of all those associated with it.

* * * * *

The approximately $2 billion spent in the oil and gas business should have been invested to build the most modern, state-of-the-art, frontier-breaking industrial infrastructure to produce better tires, cheaper, and to ensure that Goodyear's operations could compete with anything, including imports, no matter their origin.

* * * * *

After giving his testimony, Goldsmith was questioned by the House subcommittee members. The following pointed questions were asked by Representative John F. Seiberling, Democratic representative from Akron, Ohio:

Q. Mr. Goldsmith, . . . you stated, "I certainly don't pretend to know the tire business." Now you are saying that you do know more about the tire business than those who have been in it for many years because you're deciding how Goodyear ought to operate. My question is: Who the hell are you?

A. . . . I made it quite clear to the stockholders that I was an active investor. And I'm happy to define what is an active investor and what is the role of an active investor.

An active investor is not a manager. He is not a particularist. He is not a man who thinks that he can double guess management. He is not a man who thinks that he can do the job better than management he has hired. . . . Number one; the right manager has to be properly rotated. Number two; and the right manager properly motivated and run the company according to reasonable strategy. And not go and chase after all sorts of decisions he knows nothing about.

Q. Now, I presume that the purpose of your acquisition of this company [an earlier Goldsmith takeover] was to end up with a profit for yourself.

A. There's no other reason for doing business.

Q. Do you recognize any obligation to the communities, employees, and people of the United States?

A. Not only do I reconize it, I have delivered.

MERCER'S TESTIMONY

Mercer's remarks preceding his testimony before the subcommittee were as follows:

Mr. Chairman and members of the subcommittee, I am Robert E. Mercer, chairman and chief executive officer of the Goodyear Tire and Rubber Co., a corporation which is known to James Goldsmith and his partners, Merrill Lynch and the Hanson Trust of Great Britain, by the code name "Patience."

I won't quibble over their choice of "Patience" as a code for a project to take over control of Goodyear. But I can tell you that our classic shareholders, our employees, our customers, our suppliers, and the communities in which we operate are running out of patience—and pretty darned fast.

Look at it from their view: They have supported a corporation which for 88 years has made money the old-fashioned way—we've earned it through a strong work ethic and solid commitment to our shareholders and all of our constituencies.

And what we have earned, we have shared with our shareholders. In the last six years, for instance, our stock has appreciated 250 percent, and we have maintained a yield of 5 percent.

* * * * *

When you look at the move on Goodyear, it's apparent that one group left out are the shareholders that invested in Goodyear for its stability, its growth, and its yield. They were not left in on the fact that those looking on us as a code name on a hit list were planning a run which they knew would push our stock to new price highs.

* * * * *

It's high time that the administration, Congress, and the appropriate regulatory bodies face up to what this unrestrained takeover activity is doing to the nation's economy, its industrial base, and the prospect of being any real force in the markets in the years ahead, not only overseas but right here at home.

While there is still time for our nation, I urge you to put some reasonable curbs on the activity that is sapping more and more of America's industrial strength.

In my opinion, it is reasonable to require an individual, group, or partnership seeking to acquire control of a company to reveal that intent at the onset, rather than only after a significant position has been achieved in a company's shares.

I consider it reasonable to ask such an individual, group, or partnership to file a pre-merger notification under the Hart-Scott-Rodino Antitrust Improvements Act.

I consider it reasonable to require anyone who gets 5 percent or more of a company's shares to keep that position for at least one year.

And I consider it reasonable to require that anyone who considers control of a company discusses in advance his detailed description of his plans—including hard estimates on how he is going to cut employment, whether he plans to extract a lot of cash from the company's operations and force it to operate in a rundown and declining condition, and whether he will maintain the level of research and development that will enable the company to survive in its markets.

American industry deserves no less, in my opinion; the public will settle for nothing less.[33]

GOLDSMITH-MERCER NEGOTIATIONS

Goodyear Chairman Mercer was pessimistic about the likely outcome of the takeover after the subcommittee hearings. "If this guy has got the ability to buy the whole company, there is little we can do to stop him, I'm not sure where we go from here."[34] It was Goldsmith who made the next move by inviting Mercer to a luncheon meeting, Tuesday, November 18th at the Hay-Adams Hotel. Goldsmith informed Mercer he had to proceed with his tender offer for Goodyear by Wednesday, November 19th. Goldsmith, it seemed, was also concerned about the imminent passage of new laws by the Ohio state legislature that would hinder takeovers. Mercer asked Goldsmith if he still had an open mind on the takeover and when Goldsmith replied he was still open, Mercer suggested Goodyear buy back Goldsmith's holdings.

Representatives for both sides then met during the night and reached an agreement by Wednesday morning. In addition to the new laws pending in Ohio, Goldsmith cited the changing climate of opinion on Wall Street and in Washington for terminating his efforts to take over Goodyear. "The Boesky scandal altered the environment, and at the same time, Congress went back to the Democrats. Things were different. It was also not a good time for Europeans in America."[35]

THE NEGOTIATED AGREEMENT

In the agreement reached by the two sides, Goodyear was to buy all of Goldsmith's 12.5 million Goodyear shares for 49½ each, or a total of about $619 million. In addition, Goldsmith would receive $37 million to cover his expenses. This last payment was referred to as "greenmail" by some observers. It was estimated that Goldsmith's group netted a profit of $94 million for their two-month effort. Goldsmith, moreover, agreed not to buy Goodyear stock for a period of at least five years.

THE AFTERMATH

Goodyear also announced that it would continue its restructuring and planned to spend $2.0 billion to buy 40.4 million of its shares, or about 41.5 percent of the

---

[33]M. Calvey, "Excerpts of Goldsmith, Mercer Testimony," *Akron Beacon Journal*, November 19, 1986, p. A16.

[34]L. Pantages, et al., "Board Meets as Goodyear Stock Falls," *Akron Beacon Journal*, November 19, 1986, p. A17.
[35]Wansell, *Tycoon*, pp. 385–86.

total remaining shares, for $50 per share. It was this buyback of shares at a price higher than that paid to Goldsmith that circumvented the greenmail charge. The settlement would add $2.6 billion to Goodyear's total debt and double its debt-equity ratio to about 72 percent.[36] One year after the takeover, the gambling Goldsmith had liquidated his position in the American stock market, after generating a reported $300 million and emerged unscathed from the stock market crash of October 1987.

On Friday, November 21, 1986, Goodyear stock closed at 42⅛ on a volume of 2.9 million shares, down 5⅛ for the week.[37] On Thursday, November 20, the stock had closed at 43, on a volume of 7.6 million shares, the most active on the NYSE despite a freeze on its trading for some of the session.[38]

RESTRUCTURING

Goodyear, to generate enough funds needed for its tender offer to shareholders, began to both discontinue and downsize aspects of its business. On July 24, 1987, the company sold approximately 6.50 percent of its oil and gas reserves to a subsidiary of International Paper for $70 million. On December 4, 1987, the company sold substantially all of its remaining oil and gas reserves in the sale of all the shares of Celeron Oil and Gas Company to an Exxon subsidiary for $615 million.

Celeron, the oil pipeline, went on the block for $1.3 billion with the expectation that a consortium of oil companies would come forward in a partnership arrangement. The pipeline begins at Santa Barbara, and its last leg from central Texas to the Gulf Coast is still under construction. Goodyear does not plan to sell until the line is a completely finished unit. A sale is expected in 1989 with the proceeds slated to reducing the mammoth corporate debt of $3.62 billion, as of September 30, 1988, which requires massive interest payments of about $1 million each working day.[39]

ASSET DISPOSITION

In December 1986, the company sold the assets of two Arizona subsidiaries involved in agricultural products, real estate development, and a resort hotel for a total price of $220.1 million to the SunCor Development Company, a subsidiary of AZP Group Inc., of Phoenix, Arizona, an electric utility with diversified operations.

On March 13, 1987, the company sold substantially all of the assets of Goodyear Aerospace Corporation and certain related assets to Loral Corporation, an international, high technology company, ironically an earlier Goodyear takeover possibility, for $588 million. Earlier, on December 30, 1986, the company sold the capital stock of Motor Wheel Corporation for an aggregate selling price of $175 million, and on April 1, 1987, sold the capital stock of Motor Wheel Canada and certain other assets, including three manufacturing plants to MWC Inc.

During the summer of 1988, Goodyear endured additional downsizing. In an effort to eliminate overhead expenses, avoid job redundancies, and expendable support staff, it reorganized the firm into two major divisions—tire and nontire products. Formerly separated geographic business segments were combined in global divisions. Furthermore, the company reduced R&D expenditures, shuttered plants in Cumberland, Maryland, and Toronto, Canada, and overall cut 6,000 jobs with direct terminations and early retirement incentive plans. Additional cutbacks were gloomily predicted.[40]

THE POST-GOLDSMITH CHALLENGE

In the climactic aftermath of hostile raider Sir James Goldsmith's takeover attempt, Chairman Robert E. Mercer found himself at several critical junctures. And, the challenges beyond Goldsmith were almost over-

---

[36]T. Gerdel, "Goodyear Tire Wins Takeover Fight," *Cleveland Plain Dealer,* November 21, 1986, p. 1-A.

[37]K. Byard and L. Pantages, "Goodyear Closings to Cost 3,200 Jobs," *Akron Beacon Journal,* November 22, 1986, p. A1.

[38]R. Reiff and G. Gardner, "Market Reaction Negative, Shareholders May Be Losers," *Akron Beacon Journal,* November 21, 1986, p. A1.

[39]Goodyear Annual Report, 1987, 89th Annual Report for the Year Ended December 31, 1987.

[40]"Goodyear's New Boss Faces a Rough Road Test," *Business Week,* December 12, 1988, p. 90.

whelming. After drastic organizational restructuring and downsizing to accommodate debt, the company was now in full circle shift in its corporate direction and grand strategy from one of intended de-emphasis on the tire business to one of almost total dependency. Mercer's original plan had been to eventually reduce tire manufacturing to about 50 percent of Goodyear's overall business. Goodyear is now approximately 85 percent concentrated in tires—certainly a dramatic turnaround for a diversified conglomerate aspiring to worldwide greatness. And, all because of one man's aggressive and successful efforts in targeting Goodyear. Finally, there was the need to bequeath his newly appointed successor a once-again solidly established firm in the increasingly intensive global tire business.

THE GOODYEAR 1987 ANNUAL REPORT

In the Goodyear 1987 Annual Report, Chairman Mercer reported:

> This 1987 annual report contains striking confirmation of the fighting spirit of Goodyear's organization throughout the world.

Fewer in number, working under the constraints and stress of restructuring, the people of all walks of Goodyear seized the opportunities that exist in the global marketplace and achieved outstanding returns on the prior investments that built our strength and durability. For that, I commend them and thank them. . . .

Income from continuing operations reached an all-time high in 1987, as did sales and net income. . . .

As the year closed, we were ahead of schedule in our program to reduce the added debt resulting from the restructuring. [Debt reached a peak of $5.61 billion in February 1987 and was $3.62 billion at year's end]. We will endeavor to maintain this momentum in 1988. To this end, our plans for our business segments include special emphasis on cash flow. We will continue our strides in cost reduction while maintaining research and development and other investments at levels designed to maximize the cost/benefit equation and maintain our technological edge in the future.[41]

---

[41]Goodyear Annual Report, 1987.

THE GOODYEAR TIRE & RUBBER COMPANY AND SUBSIDIARIES
Consolidated Statement of Income
Year Ended December 31
(in millions, except per share)

	1987	1986	1985
Net sales	$ 9,905.2	$9,040.0	$8,341.1
Other income	179.9	121.0	114.2
	10,085.1	9,161.0	8,455.3
Cost and expenses:			
Cost of goods sold	7,374.6	6,941.5	6,550.4
Selling, administrative, and general expense	1,634.9	1,596.6	1,380.9
Interest and amortization of debt discount and expense	282.5	121.9	101.5
Unusual items	(135.0)	10.1	21.3
Foreign currency exchange	38.9	19.1	33.8
Minority interest in net income of subsidiaries	16.8	9.6	6.6
	9,212.7	8,698.8	8,094.5

THE GOODYEAR TIRE & RUBBER COMPANY AND SUBSIDIARIES
Consolidated Statement of Income (*concluded*)

	1987	1986	1985
Income from continuing operations before income taxes	$ 872.4	$ 462.2	$ 360.8
U.S. and foreign taxes on income	358.5	245.4	133.7
Income from continuing operations	513.9	216.8	227.1
Discontinued operations	257.0	(92.7)	185.3
Net income	$ 770.9	$ 124.1	$ 412.4
Per share of common stock:			
Income from continuing operations	$ 8.49	$ 2.02	$ 2.11
Discontinued operations	4.24	(.86)	1.73
Net income	$ 12.73	$ 1.16	$ 3.84

THE GOODYEAR TIRE & RUBBER COMPANY AND SUBSIDIARIES
Consolidated Balance Sheet
For Year Ended December 31
($ in millions)

	1987	1986	1985
Assets			
Current assets:			
Cash and short-term securities	$ 200.5	$ 130.5	$ 139.0
Accounts and notes receivable	1,501.3	1,986.5	957.4
Inventories	1,501.4	1,352.2	1,378.5
Prepaid expenses	101.3	82.7	83.3
Net assets held for sale	—	107.8	—
Total current assets	3,304.5	3,659.7	2,558.2
Other assets:			
Investments in nonconsolidated subsidiaries and affiliates, at equity ...	107.6	32.9	181.3
Long-term accounts and notes receivable	354.0	240.0	126.8
Investments and miscellaneous assets, at cost	53.8	34.4	30.6
Deferred pension plan cost	373.1	320.2	—
Deferred charges	74.6	72.1	31.6
Net assets held for sale	—	96.6	—
	963.1	796.2	370.3
Properties and plants	4,128.3	4,583.4	4,025.0
	$8,395.9	$9,039.3	$6,953.5

THE GOODYEAR TIRE & RUBBER COMPANY AND SUBSIDIARIES
Consolidated Balance Sheet (*concluded*)

	1987	1986	1985
Liabilities and Shareholders' Equity			
Current liabilities:			
Accounts payable—trade	$ 821.9	$ 749.5	$ 657.4
Accrued payrolls and other compensation	322.9	337.1	347.4
Other current liabilities	375.9	406.9	219.1
U.S. and foreign taxes:			
Current	268.7	168.5	173.2
Deferred	16.0	—	58.8
Notes payable to banks and overdrafts	244.0	304.2	116.3
Long-term debt due within one year	90.2	44.4	35.2
Deferred gain on sale of assets	—	134.7	—
Total current liabilities	2,139.6	2,145.3	1,607.4
Long-term debt and capital leases	3,282.4	2,914.9	997.5
Other long-term liabilities	376.7	317.5	301.6
Deferred income taxes	679.3	586.4	475.3
Minority equity in subsidiaries	83.5	72.6	64.3
Shareholders' equity:			
Preferred stock, nopar value:			
Authorized, 50,000,000 shares			
Outstanding shares, none	—	—	—
Common stock, nopar value:			
Authorized, 150,000,000 shares			
Outstanding shares, 56,986,579 (97,080,482 in 1986) (108,110,085 in 1985)	57.0	97.1	94.1
Capital surplus	11.2	104.2	655.4
Retained earnings	1,922.6	3,122.2	3,172.2
	1,990.8	3,323.5	3,921.7
Foreign currency translation adjustment	(156.4)	(320.9)	(414.3)
Total shareholders' equity	1,834.4	3,002.6	3,507.4
Total liabilities and shareholders' equity	$8,395.9	$9,039.3	$6,953.5

THE GOODYEAR TIRE & RUBBER COMPANY AND SUBSIDIARIES
Consolidated Statement of Changes in Financial Position
Year Ended December 31
($ in millions)

	1987	1986	1985
Funds provided from operations:			
Income from continuing operations:	$ 513.9	$ 216.8	$ 227.1
Noncash items:			
Depreciation	349.9	349.0	268.3
Unusual items	4.1	(45.5)	28.5
Accounts and notes receivable reduction (increase)	485.2	(295.2)	—
Inventories (increase) reduction	(149.2)	26.3	(45.1)
Long-term accounts and notes receivable (increase)	(114.0	(113.2)	(87.2)
U.S and foreign taxes increase (reduction)	116.2	(64.2)	(59.3)
Deferred income taxes increase	92.9	111.1	26.4
Other items	118.7	170.7	138.6
Income (loss) from discontinued operations	257.0	(92.7)	185.3
	1,674.7	263.1	682.6
Funds (used for) provided from financing:			
Notes payable to banks and overdrafts (reduction) increase	(60.2)	187.9	(41.1)
Long-term debt and capital lease reduction	(2,846.2)	(109.6)	(234.7)
Long-term debt and capital lease increase	3,259.5	1,455.7	982.4
Common stock issued	14.6	66.0	43.4
Common stock acquired	(2,027.2)	(614.2)	—
	(1,659.5)	985.8	750.0
Funds used for investment:			
Capital expenditures	(665.6)	(1,130.8)	(1,098.2)
Property and plant dispositions	925.0	254.3	405.6
Discontinued operations—capital expenditures	(92.2)	(256.8)	(577.7)
Other transactions	(185.9)	(43.4)	(47.0)
	(18.7)	(1,176.7)	(1,317.3)
Dividends paid	(91.0)	(174.1)	(171.3)
Foreign currency translation adjustment reduction	164.5	93.4	51.6
Cash and short term securities increase (reduction)	$ 70.0	$ (8.5)	$ (4.4)

THE GOODYEAR TIRE & RUBBER COMPANY AND SUBSIDIARIES
Consolidated Statement of Shareholders' Equity
(in millions)

	Common Stock		Capital Surplus	Retained Earnings	Foreign Currency Translation Adjustment
	Shares	Amount			
Balance at December 31, 1984					
after deducting 1,423,479 treasury shares	106.5	$ 92.5	$ 613.6	$ 2,931.1	$(465.9)
Net income for 1985				412.4	
Cash dividends paid in 1985—$1.60 per share				(171.3)	
Common stock issued (including 102,750 treasury shares)	1.6	1.6	41.8		
Foreign currency translation adjustment					51.6
Balance at December 31, 1985					
after deducting 1,320,729 treasury shares	108.1	94.1	655.4	3,172.2	(414.3)
Net income for 1986				124.1	
Cash dividends paid in 1986—$1.60 per share				(174.1)	
Common stock purchased for treasury	(13.1)	(13.1)	(601.1)		
Adjustment of stated capital to $1.00 per share		14.0	(14.0)		
Common stock issued (including 547,196 treasury shares)	2.1	2.1	63.9		
Foreign currency translation adjustment					93.4
Balance at December 31, 1986					
after deducting 13,904,338 treasury shares	97.1	97.1	104.2	3,122.2	(320.9)
Net income for 1987				770.9	
Cash dividends paid in 1987—$1.60 per share				(91.0)	
Common stock purchased for treasury	(40.5)	(40.5)	(107.2)	(1,879.5)	
Common stock issued (including 383,800 treasury shares)	.4	.4	14.2		
Foreign currency translation adjustment					164.5
Balance at December 31, 1987					
after deducting 54,005,825 treasury shares	57.0	$ 57.0	$ 11.2	$ 1,922.6	$(156.4)

Timetable

1986 late August to early September	Goldsmith selects Goodyear as the target company for takeover from his list of target companies.
Friday, September 19	First purchase of Goodyear shares, 66,000.
Thursday, September 25	116,000 shares of Goodyear stock accumulated by Merrill Lynch. 1.7 million shares purchased for $56.3 million ($33 per share) by Merrill Lynch.
Tuesday, October 7	Goodyear rumored as takeover target. Stock reaches $37 per share—a 15-year high.
Friday, October 17	2.1 million shares purchased. $41 per share, closing price.
Saturday, October 18	Goodyear notifies their investment banker Goldman Sachs and starts defense against possible raider.
Friday, October 24	Goodyear contacts identify Goldsmith as raider. 4.1 million shares trade, second most active stock on NYSE, closes at $44—another 15-year high. Mercer sends letter to 13,000 Akron employees promising "We are not sitting idly by."
Monday, October 27	First meeting to "introduce" Goldsmith to Goodyear. Held in New York. 12.7 million shares traded, ninth highest volume day for any individual stock on NYSE. Closes at $48½.
October 27–29	1.5 million shares purchased by Goldsmith at $48 per share.
Wednesday, October 29	Mercer's letter to Goodyear employees naming Goldsmith as raider and pledging to use all of company's resources "to stave off a hostile takeover." Condemns flaws in free enterprise system that allows foreigners to usurp America's industrial base.
Thursday, October 30	Mercer's first meeting with Goldsmith at Goldsmith's New York home. Goldsmith attacks Goodyear's lack of focus on core tire business. Mercer defends diversification. Agree takeover bid is unsolicited, not hostile; no greenmail to be offered or accepted.
Friday, October 31	Goldsmith files 13-D with SEC detailing financing and plans for restructuring Goodyear. Discloses 11.5 percent stake acquired for $530 million. Goodyear stock closes at $48⅝.
Monday, November 3	Goodyear announces Goodyear Aerospace to be sold, proceeds used to battle takeover.
Wednesday, November 5	Mercer's second meeting with Goldsmith in New York at Goodyear's site. Asks Goldsmith delay $49 per share tender offer for two weeks while restructuring plan is developed by Goodyear.
Thursday, November 6	Goldsmith accepts two-week standstill. Goodyear announces restructuring.
Friday, November 7	Mercer's third letter to employees stating need for layoffs as part of restructuring.

	Timetable (*concluded*)
Tuesday, November 18	Congressional subcommittee hearing on takeover. Mercer and Goldsmith give testimony. Hay-Adams Hotel meeting between Mercer and Goldsmith. Agree to meet overnight to negotiate possible buyback of Goldsmith's Goodyear stock.
Wednesday, November 19	Settlement announced. Stock closes at $42.
Thursday, November 20	Goodyear buys Goldsmith's stock for $49½ per share and offers to buy 40 percent of shareholders stock for $50 per share.
Friday, November 21	Expiration date for Merrill Lynch's offer of $1.9 billion financing for Goldsmith's tender offer. Could extend the offer.

E

Coping with Environmental Change and Turbulence

15. *Global Marine, Inc.*

"You would not want to stay in this business if you expected the price of oil to drop," asserted David Herasimchuk, vice president for market development, Global Marine, Inc. Saudi Arabia's decision in the fall of 1985 to increase crude oil production caused oil prices to drop dramatically and led to widespread unprofitability and disarray within the international offshore oil and gas drilling industry. However, optimism is endemic to the industry, and most independent offshore oil and gas drilling contractors at the beginning of 1986 believed the worst was over.

CORPORATE ORGANIZATION

Global Marine, Inc. (GMI), a member of the international offshore oil and gas drilling industry, has three subsidiaries: Global Marine Drilling Company, Challenger Minerals, Inc., and Applied Drilling Technology. The corporate headquarters and the headquarters of subsidiaries are located in Houston, Texas. The corporate organization of Global Marine, Inc., is shown in Figure 1.

THE 1977 SEVEN-YEAR STRATEGIC PLAN

C. Russell Luigs became CEO of Global Marine, Inc. in 1977. GMI's offshore drilling capability at that time was limited entirely to eight oceangoing drillships that were becoming technologically obsolete. The choice facing Luigs and GMI was either to maintain an existing conservative philosophy of bidding for drilling contracts with obsolete and, therefore, inferior equipment, or take the high-risk option and develop a worldwide capability

This case was prepared by James W. Clinton of the University of Northern Colorado and is intended to be used as a basis for class discussion. Presented and accepted by the refereed Midwest Case Writers Association Workshop, 1986. All rights reserved to the authors and the Midwest Case Writers Association.

to drill in any offshore environmental conditions and be a major factor in the industry. Russ Luigs, with the consent and encouragement of the board, embarked upon the high-risk alternative. Global Marine's expansion strategy for the 1980s locked the company into large capital commitments with high penalties if rig construction contracts were canceled.

GMI diversified at first into semi-submersibles and then into jackups (See next section for a description of drilling equipment.) GMI's 1981 budget provided for an inventory of 52 offshore drilling rigs. In 1981, however, David Herasimchuk, GMI's director of market development, noted that: (1) rigs were being delivered to contractors at three times the rate of 1978, (2) shipyards were able to deliver two jackups a month, and (3) delivery rates of jackups implied a 27 percent increase in jackups for 1981 and a 29 percent increase in jackup inventories in 1982. Herasimchuk concluded that any change in year-to-year demand of less than 25 percent could create a serious oversupply of jackup rigs and reduce day rates charged for offshore drilling as much as 50 percent. At the time, however, there was a lack of unanimity within the industry concerning the outlook for offshore oil drilling since industry rig utilization rates averaged above 95 percent between mid-1979 and mid-1982, and within the industry the rule is that new rig construction is justified when the utilization rate is above 95 percent.

(Note: Construction lead times for jackups normally was about two years and as little as 18 months. At the height of the rig construction boom in 1981, lead times were three years. By adding together existing inventories of offshore drilling rigs and anticipated additions to inventory, the supply of rigs is known. Industry analysts can then forecast what demand is necessary for day rates to stay within a profitable range.)

In April 1982, GMI's management concluded that the industry's expansion plans were overly ambitious and reduced the company's offshore drilling rig construction program by about one third, setting a target of 35 rigs. GMI decided also not to order any more 250 foot jackups and to order a 300 foot jackup only if the company had a firm contract for its use. GMI thus canceled delivery of all jackups that it was possible to cancel, and deferred delivery of some jackups until

---

FIGURE 1   Organization Chart, 1986

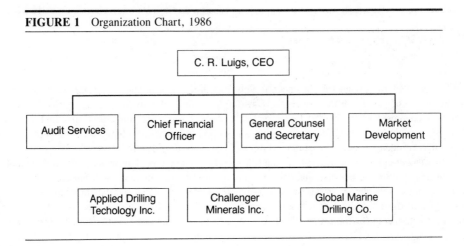

1984, anticipating that the industry cycle would peak once again, as it had in the past, at a later date.

GLOBAL MARINE DRILLING COMPANY (GMDC)

GMDC, Global Marine's largest subsidiary, is engaged in offshore oil drilling operations throughout the world. GMDC, as of the end of 1985, operated 34 offshore drilling rigs capable of operating in a variety of marine environments. The entire fleet possessed the capability to drill in any ocean—from shallow water in the Gulf of Mexico to 2,500-foot depths off the coast of Spain to the icecaps of the Arctic. The fleet consisted of 21 jackups, seven drill ships, five semi-submersibles, and one arctic submersible.

Drilling Equipment.   Rigs used to drill offshore for oil and gas are sturdier than land-based rigs because the former are subject to greater stresses. GMDC uses a variety of rigs in offshore drilling operations. The most frequently used rigs (and the sequence in which they generally are utilized) are: (*a*) jackup rigs, (*b*) drillships, (*c*) semi-submersibles, and (*d*) fixed platforms.

Jackups.   The jackup rig is so named because of steel legs located at the three corners of the rig that are extended (jacked) down to the ocean floor to provide a stable drilling platform or raised up above the main

platform of the rig to allow the rig to be towed to another drilling site. Jackups generally drill in water depths of 15–375 feet and can drill to a depth of up to 25,000 feet. Jackups are used both for exploration and field development drilling.

Some jackups are cantilevered so that they can drill over a fixed ocean platform without putting weight on the platform—thus permitting the fixed platform to be lighter and, therefore, less costly.

Drillships.   Drillships are oceangoing vessels which, unlike most jackups and semi-submersibles, do not require towing. Drillships typically operate in water depths up to 1,500 feet and can drill to a depth of about 25,000 feet. Drillships are self-contained rigs configured to the shape of a ship. Drillships are used for deep-water exploration in moderate environments and in remote areas. They possess the advantage of mobility and are able to carry large loads necessary for remote drilling operations.

Most moored ships and semi-submersibles are limited to drilling in water depths between 600 and 1,500 feet. Dynamically positioned ships and semi-submersibles operating without a mooring system are generally capable of drilling in water depths of 3,000 to 6,000 feet.

Semi-submersibles.   Semi-submersible ocean drilling rigs are mobile and float in the water on very large pontoons submerged below the ocean surface to provide stability to the platform floating on the pontoons above the water. Semi-submersibles drill in water depths up to about 1,500 feet and can drill to a depth of 25,000 feet. Semi-submersible rigs operate in most of the same areas in which drillships are used and are preferable for deep-water drilling in more hostile seas.

Fixed Platforms.

If an offshore operator drills a successful exploratory well, a platform rig may next be used to drill additional, developmental wells in the oil field. The platform can only be justified economically, however, if the oil field is large.

GMDC Drill Rig Inventory and Utilization.

GMDC owns all of its rigs now in service except for one jackup rig, the Glomar Main Pass II, and the Concrete Island Drilling System (CIDS), which are under long-term lease. All rigs owned by GMDC are subject to mortgages except for the Glomar Platform I, the Glomar Biscay I, and the Glomar Adriatic VIII.

The average age of GMDC's fleet of rigs is six years, compared to an industry average of nine years. GMDC operates a modern rig training and drilling simulation center in Houston, Texas. Drilling crews receive periodic refresher training as part of the company's objective of developing the most highly skilled crews in the industry.

Global Marine recognized in 1982 that offshore oil and gas drilling was below earlier forecasts. The company, as a result, delayed delivery of three semi-submersible rigs and one drillship and canceled orders for four jackup rigs. The company also agreed to reduce drilling rates charged customers if customers agreed either to use Global Marine rigs in the future or extend existing drilling contracts.

During 1985 the company concluded 71 drilling contracts and contract extensions. As of January 1, 1986, drilling contracts for 31 of the company's 34 rigs were due to expire during 1986. For 1987, rigs were presently contracted for drilling for only 3 percent of their availability. Utilization rates of the company's rigs

for the last eight years and the rate estimated for 1986 are shown below. Utilization rate is computed by dividing number of days a rig earned revenues by total days the rig was available for work.

Arctic Exploration.

Global Marine also designs and develops the latest in state-of-the-art offshore oil drilling technology and other oil service equipment. The company has developed a new concept to replace arctic drilling platforms used only one time. There is great interest in a mobile drilling platform for arctic operations because a $140 million dry hole in the Arctic involved a platform costing about $85 million which had to be abandoned since it was permanently constructed on the drilling site. This costly approach was labeled the "gravel island" concept. Global Marine's concept involves the use of a concrete and steel island capable of operating in water depths of 35 to 52 feet with a maximum drilling depth of 25,000 feet. The island can be ballasted (temporarily seated on the ocean floor), deballasted (prepared for towing), moved, and used again.

Global's portable island, labeled the Concrete Island Drilling System (CIDS), was first used by Exxon in November 1984 to explore an area near Prudhoe Bay. CIDS is 300 by 300 feet, and was constructed in Japan. CIDS is intended to replace gravel islands constructed in shallow waters in the Arctic that cannot be moved. The company presently is researching a more advanced concept that can operate in deeper arctic waters. Approximately 20 U.S. and Canadian oil companies are potential customers for Global Marine's arctic drilling equipment.

THE OFFSHORE OIL AND GAS DRILLING INDUSTRY

Current Situation.

At the beginning of 1986, international oil and gas drilling contractors were engaged in offshore drilling operations around the world in the

	1986E	1985	1984	1983	1982	1981	1980	1979	1978
Rigs in fleet at end of year	32	34	35	32	28	28	18	14	11
Percent of utilization	30%	91%	92%	92%	93%	100%	100%	98%	91%

North Sea, the Mediterranean Sea, Southeast Asia, South America, and the Gulf of Mexico. Contractors were experiencing reduced demand for their offshore drilling rigs and profit margins were narrowing or nonexistent. The entire industry was exceedingly competitive.

Offshore, a publication about the offshore oil and gas industry, reported in June 1985 that worldwide rig usage showed 550 rigs of a total 742 were working, 8 were enroute to drill sites, and 184 were idle. This was compared to 1984 figures of 539 working, 170 idle, and 8 enroute. In addition to these 742 mobile offshore drilling rigs, approximately 100 other drilling rigs were located in Eastern-bloc communist countries or positioned in Lake Maracaibo, Venezuela (an unusually placid body of water not subject to stresses encountered in the open sea).

Most offshore oil and gas drilling rigs are owned by independent contractors. Some foreign governments that control nationalized oil companies operate their own rigs, and several major international oil companies maintain equity positions in offshore drilling rigs to influence rig design related to specialized needs.

Historical Background.   The offshore oil and gas drilling service industry was born out of the desire by international oil companies to concentrate on those areas they knew best and expected the greatest profit— purchase or lease of oil and gas properties, transporting, refining, and marketing of petroleum and petroleum by-products. Independent offshore drilling contractors provided and operated drilling rigs at locations selected by the international oil companies' own geologists. Contractors absorbed the risk of low rig utilization in exchange for rates that returned a satisfactory profit— when and if most drilling rigs were under contract.

Post-World War II.   Since the end of World War II, the offshore oil drilling industry has experienced a succession of boom and bust cycles that led contractors to conclude that if demand for rigs was depressed, recovery and future prosperity were not far off. The fortunes of the offshore oil and gas industry are inextricably tied to the international oil and gas industry. When demand for oil and gas is high, and prices paid for oil and gas are similarly high, the world's major oil companies exert strong demand for offshore mobile drilling rigs. The reverse is also true—low oil and gas demand

coupled with low prices reduces the demand for drilling rigs.

1970–1979.   Some major oil producers anticipated a constant increase in oil prices because of expected steady growth in consumer demand. Natural gas was in short supply during the 1970s, culminating in 1978 in widespread media publicity about aged widows freezing to death because they were unable to pay large utility heating bills. This unacceptable human suffering led the federal government to halt construction of new utility plants using natural gas and effectively limit new construction to nuclear and electricity-generating facilities.

1979–1981.   Between 1979 and 1981, demand for offshore drilling rigs drove daily rental rates (day rates) up to record levels and encouraged substantial increases in construction of new drilling rigs.

1983

Declining Demand for Natural Gas.   A combination of factors led to a major decline in demand for natural gas in 1983. In addition to federal restrictions on natural gas utility plants, the United States experienced a recession. American consumers also proved more adept at conserving gas and oil than anticipated. Meanwhile, the United States was shifting from a production to a service economy, requiring less energy per employee, and the traditionally high consumers of energy, "the smokestack industries," were depressed as a result of increased low-priced foreign competition.

Gas pipeline companies had commonly committed themselves to 15–20-year long-term contracts for gas deliveries when both demand and prices were high, and demand was expected to increase steadily. The decline in demand for gas forced many pipeline companies to renege on long-term contracts because they could not sell the gas at the prices or volumes at which they had agreed to buy. Many of these canceled contracts are still under litigation.

Expanded Availability of Federal Offshore Leases.   James Watt, secretary of the interior, further complicated the nature of the natural gas industry and its economics. Secretary Watt eliminated the previous practice of major oil and gas companies proposing certain tracts of acreage for drilling and negotiating a price directly with the government. Secretary Watt introduced an areawide leasing system in 1983 that opened offshore areas to competitive bidding. Watt's more liberal attitude toward the development of America's energy resources produced a fivefold increase in acreage leased for a five-year period for oil and gas exploration.

New Drilling Rig Construction. Addition of new rigs to the worldwide inventory lowered ultilization rates for mobile offshore drilling units from approximately 100 percent in 1981 to a low of 74 percent in August 1983. At the same time, day rates declined as much as 75 percent.

Buying versus Exploring for Oil and Gas Reserves. Oil and gas exploration in the United States, both on and offshore, declined 23 percent during 1983. Forty percent of oil companies surveyed in 1983 increased reserves by acquiring producing oil and gas properties or companies, reflecting a belief that oil obtained through purchase was cheaper than oil obtained through exploration and development.

1983–1984.   Offshore oil and gas drilling rose late in 1983 and the signals were that a recovery was under way. However, at about this time, T. Boone Pickens, president of Mesa Petroleum, threatened a takeover of several oil companies. Other major oil companies followed his lead and several giant mergers took place. Many oil companies became apprehensive that they too might be takeover targets. Their managements acted to avoid takeover by increasing financial leverage, thus becoming less attractive to raiders, but also reducing funds available for oil and gas exploration and drilling. To placate shareholders considering sale of their stock to unfriendly raiders, managements increased cash flow to shareholders through formation of royalty trusts, further curtailing drilling plans.

1985.   By February 1985, utilization rates for all types of offshore drilling rigs had risen to 84 percent. Along with the increase in utilization rates, day rates also rose by about 50 percent during the same period. Major oil companies, however, reduced worldwide exploration so that offshore rig utilization declined steadily through the year to 81 percent at year-end. Rig utilization in the Gulf of Mexico declined even further to 75 percent, as of January 1, 1986. The decline in rig utilization caused a concurrent decrease in day rates.

Despite the declining demand for offshore drilling rigs, as of May 1985, there were a total of 53 new offshore drilling units under construction worldwide: 18 jackups, 32 semisubmersibles, two drillships, and one submersible (The characteristics of these rigs were discussed earlier.)

In December 1985, George Gaspar, an oil and gas industry analyst, forecast oil prices in 1986 to decline $1–2 a barrel from 1985's average price of $27.50 per barrel. Oil prices were forecast to continue to fall $1–2 a barrel through 1988 before reversing direction.

A positive factor for the domestic offshore drilling industry was that about 2,000 leases of offshore drilling tracts bought by oil companies for $6.4 billion are due to expire between 1986 and 1988. The oil companies must drill before the leases expire or lose the leases.

INFLUENCES ON OIL AND GAS EXPLORATION AND PRODUCTION

Oil and gas exploration and production are influenced by a variety of factors that include: (*a*) governmental regulation of production, (*b*) availability of government offshore lands for drilling, (*c*) prices for competitive fuels, (*d*) seasonal variations in demand, (*e*) investment tax credits and other regulations that either encourage or discourage oil exploration and production, (*f*) attempts by the Organization of Petroleum Exporting Countries (OPEC) to administer prices and establish a single worldwide price, and (*g*) efforts by individual nations to increase market share of total oil production, regardless of price.

Oil Supply.   The world supply of oil is generated by OPEC and non-OPEC countries. OPEC is an international cartel that attempts to control supply, and thus the price of oil. However, OPEC's members squabble among themselves concerning their fair share of oil production and some secretly sell more than their allotted share, thus increasing supply and tending to reduce the price of oil. As non-OPEC countries compete to sell their supply and acquire larger market share, OPEC becomes less influential. Up to 90 percent of the increase in non-OPEC oil production since 1978 is derived from offshore wells. Offshore oil production represents 28 percent of total world production. Non-OPEC oil production was two thirds of worldwide oil production in 1985, compared to only one third of worldwide production in 1975. If both OPEC and non-OPEC countries reduce supply, however, prices will rise and offshore drilling outside of the Persian Gulf becomes attractive. Low-priced oil makes many offshore drilling areas uneconomical to drill.

Oil Demand.

Demand for oil is related to price and alternative forms of energy, the price of these alternatives, and the latter's compatibility with environmental laws and regulations. Oil is the more popular energy alternative since it burns cleaner than coal. When consumers conserve use of petroleum, demand for oil routinely declines.

Supply of Drilling Rigs.

The number of offshore drilling rigs available in the industry and their ability to drill in the specific environment for which needed is a major factor affecting day rates for offshore rigs. When demand for drilling rigs falls below the supply of rigs, day rates fall rapidly and drilling contractors compete to keep their rigs busy.

The Cost of Money.

The offshore drilling industry is capital intensive because of the high cost of drilling rigs. If drilling contractors borrow money at high interest rates, they are committed to long-term debt repayment of interest and principal, possible only if owned drilling rigs are leased to achieve high utilization rates. When day rates decline, contractors are squeezed and profitability is difficult. The more modern the drilling fleet, the higher the company's fixed payments and the greater its vulnerability to a decline in day rates.

Foreign Tax Rates.

Offshore oil exploration budgets of the major oil companies typically followed increases in oil prices. Higher oil prices, however, led foreign governments hosting drilling rigs to raise taxes on recovered oil and several years thereafter, oil exploration decreased.

The Federal Debt.

Some industry analysts suggest that the ballooning size of the federal debt soon would lead to a new tax on oil, lead to additional consumer conservation, and reduce the need for offshore oil exploration.

Costs of Exploration Vary.

Exploration, drilling, and development costs for offshore oil vary widely throughout the world. In the Persian Gulf, the total cost to find and develop a barrel of oil was $1 a barrel in 1984.

United States major oil companies at other foreign offshore locations incurred a $7 a barrel cost, up to and including development of the drill site location. In the continental United States, onshore drilling costs were $12 a barrel. Offshore drilling in the North Sea near the United Kingdom was $14 a barrel. Additional costs depend upon the tax structure of the country or state in which the drilling takes place. One industry expert estimates that a drop from $30 to $20 a barrel would decrease the number of drillable offshore prospects by about 25 percent.

RISKS AND ENVIRONMENTAL HAZARDS

Offshore drillers experience hazards and difficulties their land-based competitors do not have to contend with. Offshore oil spills near resort areas can inflict substantial damage upon beaches, the tourist trade, sealife, and cause major environmental harm. The spill of oil from a well being drilled from an offshore drilling platform in the Santa Barbara Channel off the California coast in 1969 led to a 10-year moratorium on all drilling off the California coast and stricter state regulation of subsequent offshore drilling operations. Owners and operators of offshore facilities on the Outer Continental Shelf of North America, moreover, are liable for damages and for the cost of removing oil spills for which they are responsible.

Since 1970, only one oil spill has released more than 10,000 barrels of oil into the environment. That spill was the result of a ship's anchor being dragged across a seabed and rupturing an oil pipeline. Between 1975 and 1982, the U.S. Department of the Interior reports that total oil spillage related to offshore drilling in federally leased waters amounted to about 17,000 barrels of oil—only 0.07 of 1 percent of total oil produced.

When drilling for oil, ''mud'' is pumped to the bottom of the well bore to raise rock chips cut by the drill bit up from the well and control well pressure and avoid ''blowouts.'' Mud is a mixture of clay, barite, water, and several concentrated chemicals. Most mud does not pose a threat to the environment. According to the National Academy of Sciences, natural seepage from the earth accounts for 15 percent of the oil that reaches the world's water surfaces. Runoff from industry onshore generates additional oil pollution. In contrast, offshore drilling operations in U.S. waters account for 5/100 of 1 percent of oil pollution of the world's oceans.

Drilling for oil and gas involves the hazard of a blowout, an uncontrolled high-pressure flow of oil or gas from a well bore, that can catch fire and destroy a rig. Offshore rigs are also susceptible to collisions while being towed or positioned for drilling. Rigs under tow have sometimes run aground and some rigs have been destroyed or severely damaged by hurricanes, storms, tidal waves, and typhoons.

Global Marine, Inc., experienced a major maritime disaster on October 25, 1983 when its drillship, the *Glomar Java Sea,* capsized and sank during Typhoon Lex in the South China Sea. All 81 persons aboard the drillship are presumed dead. The *Glomar Java Sea* was valued at $35 million. The National Transportation Safety Board (NTSB) determined that the ship sank due to a structural failure. The NTSB also stated:

> Contributing to the structural failure was the decision that the drillship would remain anchored with all nine anchors, which subjected the vessel to the full force of the storm. Contributing to the large loss of life was the failure of the master and Atlantic Richfield Company and Global Marine management personnel to remove nonessential personnel from the *Glomar Java Sea.*

Oil drilling contractors who operate in foreign locations encounter additional risks that include: (*a*) expropriation, (*b*) nationalization, (*c*) foreign exchange restrictions, (*d*) foreign taxation, (*e*) changing political conditions, (*f*) foreign and domestic monetary policies, and (*g*) foreign government regulations that give preferential treatment to local contractors or require foreign contractors to employ local citizens or purchase supplies locally.

CHALLENGER MINERALS, INC. (CMI)

Global Marine's second major subsidiary, CMI, is engaged in both onshore and offshore oil and gas exploration. The company's primary exploration and development areas are in the Gulf of Mexico and onshore within four states in the United States.

A CMI customer for natural gas has refused delivery of a minimum quantity of gas previously contracted for. Gas intended for such delivery is produced at CMI's Weatherford properties in Oklahoma. The Weatherford

properties were the source of slightly over one half of CMI's oil and gas revenues for 1984. Because of this customer's refusal to accept delivery, CMI has been forced to reduce or close down approximately one half of the company's current production capacity. Global Marine has filed suit against Southern Natural Gas Company (SONAT) for failure to honor its gas purchase contract and is attempting to require SONAT to accept delivery of such gas. CMI is claiming damages of about $99 million.

Another major CMI customer also has refused to accept future delivery of gas previously contracted for. During 1984, CMI evaluated 17 of the company's leased drilling areas and determined that declining oil prices and a reduction in the properties' production potential lowered the properties' value. Consequently, CMI charged $73 million against 1984 income. In 1983, CMI made a similar charge of $26.9 million.

APPLIED DRILLING TECHNOLOGY, INC. (ADTI)

ADTI, Global Marine's third major subsidiary, provides offshore turnkey drilling services; that is, ADTI guarantees a customer a specified fixed cost for drilling a well that includes all supervision and management, necessary equipment, material and personnel. ADTI drilled 4 turnkey wells in 1985 compared to 10 drilled during 1984, and has completed a total of 41 turnkey wells since 1980. Through 1984, ADTI performed 75 percent of all offshore turnkey drilling in the Gulf of Mexico.

MARKETING

Global Marine maintains sales offices at nine overseas locations: Aberdeen, Scotland; Anchorage, Alaska; Cairo, Egypt; Calgary, Alberta; Jakarta, Indonesia; London, England; Port Gentil, Gabon (west-central Africa); Singapore; and Siracusa, Sicily. Global Marine also operates offices in Bakersfield and Los Angeles, California, and Lafayette and New Orleans, Louisiana.

GMI's potential customers are relatively few, numbering about 57 major oil and gas companies, and include affiliates of major oil companies. Customer buying decisions vary from total control at the company's headquarters to delegated decision making in the field. In between, the field manager makes his recommendation to headquarters and usually his choice is confirmed.

GMI's field representatives are expected to develop a relationship with each potential customer, assuring them that GMI is capable of performing a wide range of drilling requirements, and thus establish customer trust and confidence in GMI. Since many of the drilling contractors have similar capabilities, the difference between winning and losing a contract can depend upon the nature of the relationship between GMI's representatives and their customer contacts.

GMI develops a profile of each customer, noting customer concerns and preferences, which are incorporated within the bid the company makes to secure a drilling contract. GMI develops similar information about competitors, accumulating information about what they paid for their rigs, the length of existing contracts, availability of rigs for bidding, and what competitors bid on contracts either awarded or lost.

Bidding of contracts varies among competitors; some bid low to keep their rigs busy; others insist upon a minimum return on investment and will not contract for less; still others bid to maintain a target market share. Some bidders, prior to 1985, might even bid at a higher than expected price, anticipating the low bidders to drop out because of other jobs.

The first step toward obtaining a contract is to get on the qualified bidders list maintained by customers. Usually each company identifies about a dozen or so drilling contractors as qualified to drill for offshore oil and gas.

FINANCE

Global Marine lost $220 million in 1985 on revenues of $360.7 million, compared to a loss of $91.2 million in 1984 on revenues of $385.8 (see Table 1). Contributing to the 1985 loss was a charge of $102 million, made because of a lowered revaluation of the company's oil and gas properties—associated with a major decline in oil and gas prices (see Table 2). The previous six years, Global Marine earned a profit.

To conserve cash, Global Marine reduced 1985 capital expenditures to $36 million, a decline of $348 million from the previous year's $384 million capital expenditures.

Global Marine suspended dividend payments on both common and preferred stock in May 1985. On July 1, 1985, Global Marine suspended interest and principal payments (which amounted to approximately $240 million per year) on substantially all long-term debt and is, therefore, in default on most of its long-term debt. As a result, debt formerly identified as long-term has been reclassified as current debt.

Between 1980 and 1983, Global Marine spent approximately $1.3 billion on capital expenditures. Expenditures were financed from a variety of sources, which were: (*a*) current operations, (*b*) two stock issues that raised $178 million, (*c*) a convertible subordinated debenture issue of $100 million, (*d*) two subordinated debenture issues of $201 million, (*e*) $361 million received from subsidized or government guaranteed financing in support of shipyard deliveries, (*f*) a special lease transaction, (*g*) $168 million from the sale of tax benefits, (*h*) secured and unsecured loans from banks, and (*i*) $100 million from the United States Title XI government-guaranteed bonds secured by three of the company's previously unencumbered drilling rigs (see Table 3 for a summary of key 1981–85 data).

Some Global Marine creditors require their approval before the company can borrow additional funds. Another creditor restriction requires the company to maintain a minimum of $428.7 million in shareholders' equity.

The company's ability to pay maturing debt obligations depends largely upon the extent to which rigs are contracted out and the rates obtained for these contracts. Because most of the company's drilling contracts are short term in nature, annual cash flow is difficult to project. The decline in Global Marine's 1985 drilling revenues was attributed to lower rates at which the company's drilling rigs were leased to customers under new contracts.

Global Marine currently has 68 claims, totaling $208.5 million, pending in connection with the loss of the *Glomar Java Sea* (discussed earlier under "Risks and Environmental Hazards"). Five other claims have been settled by Global Marine. An additional five lawsuits have been filed against the company, seeking $240 million in damages. Global Marine is confident that existing insurance covers pending lawsuits and claims against the company.

TABLE 1

GLOBAL MARINE
Consolidated Statement of Changes in Financial Position
($ in millions)

	1985	*1984*	*1983*
Cash from operations:			
Net income (loss)	$(220.0)	$ (91.2)	$ 49.3
Noncash charges	192.2	111.5	109.2
Cash from operations	(27.8)	20.3	158.5
Changes in working capital:*			
Accounts receivable	5.2	(13.3)	26.7
Materials and supplies	1.5	12.9	(5.7)
Other current assets	1.9	(0.3)	(3.1)
Current maturity of long-term debt	—	—	—
Accounts payable	(18.0)	12.4	(8.2)
Accrued liabilities	56.0	1.4	16.9
Change in working capital	46.6	13.1	26.6
Net cash from operations	18.8	33.4	185.1
Cash required to expand operations:			
Capital expenditures	(35.9)	(384.0)	(332.1)
Disposal of properties	4.6	3.3	23.2
Equity investment	—	—	(17.5)
Other, net	(12.3)	0.1	(8.2)
Total	(43.6)	(380.6)	(334.6)
Cash before financing	(24.8)	(347.2)	(149.5)
Financing activities:			
Long-term borrowing	7.3	241.6	393.6
Reduction in long-term debt	(63.8)	(110.5)	(130.3)
Sale-leaseback of drilling rig	—	77.8	—
Preferred and common stock dividends	(6.6)	(23.9)	(8.6)
Sale of preferred stock	—	—	107.6
Other	(3.4)	4.5	79.3
Cash from financing	$ (66.5)	$ 189.5	$ 441.6
Increase (decrease) in cash	$ (91.3)	$(157.7)	$ 292.1

*Excludes cash, short-term investments, and current maturities of long-term debt.

COMPETITIVE FINANCIAL PERFORMANCE

The financial performance of major competitors in the offshore drilling industry for the period 1980–85 appears in Table 4 (page 561).

Mr. David Herasimchuk of Global Marine offered the following comments about several offshore drilling contractors:

Rowan Drilling Company and the Offshore Drilling and Exploration Company (ODECO) are

TABLE 2

GLOBAL MARINE
Consolidated Balance Sheet
As of December 31
($ in millions)

	1985	1984	1983
Assets			
Cash	$ 11.1	$ 4.3	$ 3.3
Short-term investments	78.7	176.8	335.5
Accounts receivable	59.5	64.7	51.4
Materials and supplies	24.3	25.8	38.7
Prepaid expenses	10.6	4.9	6.9
Deferred income taxes	—	7.6	5.3
Total current assets	$ 184.2	$ 284.1	$ 441.1
Rigs and drilling equipment (less accumulated depreciation)	$1,260.3	$1,324.6	972.0
Rigs under construction	—	—	80.3
Oil and gas properties:			
Subject to amortization	90.2	168.7	222.5
Not subject to amortization	—	15.1	85.7
Net properties	1,350.5	1,508.4	1,360.5
Other assets	38.3	54.3	42.5
Total assets	$1,573.0	$1,846.8	$1,844.1
Liabilities			
Current maturity of long-term debt	$ —	$ 97.8	$ 83.5
Accounts payable	30.6	48.6	36.2
Accrued liabilities	30.2	71.5	70.1
Long-term debt reclassified due to default	1,087.7	—	—
Related accrued interest	97.3	—	—
Total current liabilities	$1,245.8	$ 217.9	$ 189.8
Long-term debt	—	$1,035.0	902.9
Other long-term liabilities	25.5	22.6	18.7
Deferred income taxes	—	21.6	76.2
Deferred credits	11.1	34.6	28.3
Total long-term debt	$ 36.6	$1,113.8	$1,026.1
Shareholders' Equity			
Cumulative convertible preferred stock	$ 115.0	$ 115.0	$ 115.0
Common stock	4.1	4.0	3.9
Additional paid-in capital	211.8	209.8	207.9
Retained earnings	(40.3)	186.3	301.4
Total shareholders' equity	$ 290.6	$ 515.1	$ 628.2
Total liabilities and shareholders' equity	$1,573.0	$1,846.8	$1,844.1

TABLE 3   Five-Year Review, 1981–1985, Global Marine ($ in millions)

	Year Ended				
	1985	*1984*	*1983*	*1982*	*1981*
Summary of operations:					
Revenues:					
Marine drilling	$ 360.7	$385.8	$421.2	$421.0	$324.2
Oil and gas	17.9	20.6	22.3	24.4	16.3
Other energy services	—	.2	3.5	10.3	11.9
Total revenues	$ 378.6	$406.6	$447.0	$455.7	$352.4
Net income (loss)	(220.0)	(91.2)	49.3	85.0	79.8
Shareholders' equity	290.6	$515.0	$628.0	$476.0	$394.0
Net income (loss) per common share	($ 7.27)	($ 3.35)	$ 1.52	$ 2.71	$ 2.61
Dividends paid per common share	$ 0.06	$ 0.24	$ 0.24	$ 0.23	$ 0.175

TABLE 4   Financial Performance, Selected Offshore Drilling Contractors, 1981–1985

	1985	*1984*	*1983*	*1982*	*1981*
Global Marine, Inc.					
Revenues (mil.)	$ 378.6	406.6	447.0	455.7	352.4
Net income (mil.)	(220.0	(94.9)	49.3	85.0	79.8
Book value: Common	$ 5.34	12.86	16.13	15.15	12.81
Ocean Drilling and Exploration Company (ODECO):					
Revenues	$ 633.8	698.6	811.7	979.6	892.2
Net income	33.7	65.8	119.4	191.9	175.0
Book value: Common	$ 16.30	16.34	16.31	15.05	12.09
Reading & Bates Corporation:					
Revenues	$ 236.7	329.2	431.1	516.8	530.5
Net income	(83.2)	18.7	38.2	73.3	93.4
Book value: Common	$ 7.87	15.36	15.21	14.80	13.07
Rowan Companies, Inc.:					
Revenues	$ 272.5	198.4	206.5	400.4	369.0
Net income	3.8	4.2	21.9	119.4	111.8
Book value: Common	$ 10.61	10.66	10.66	10.54	8.23
Zapata Corporation:					
Revenues	$ 288.7	421.3	443.0	537.1	413.0
Net income	(63.9)	26.1	52.5	103.9	81.7
Book value: Common	$ 19.05	23.21	22.65	20.90	18.30
Helmerich and Payne:					
Revenues	$ 192.0	192.6	208.1	338.2	287.6
Net income	18.5	21.4	47.8	75.7	75.3
Book value: Common	$ 17.01	16.63	16.12	14.54	12.04

Source: *Value Line*, June 13, 1986, pp. 1868–78.

financially conservative. Rowan finances capital investments primarily from operations.

Atwood Oceanics, 41% of which is owned by Helmerich and Payne, is conservatively managed and does not order offshore drilling rigs constructed on speculation. The company has equipment that tends to be obsolete. The company's financial condition, however, is excellent. Atwood has accumulated cash while using older rigs and invested profits in major oil companies—its customers—rather than purchase high technology offshore drilling equipment.

MANAGEMENT

Corporate Officers.   C. Russell Luigs, 52, is chairman of the board, president, and chief executive officer. Luigs was elected president and CEO in May 1977. He has served as chairman since 1982. Luigs previously was president and a director of U.S. Industries, a diversified manufacturing and service company, from 1974 to 1976.

Jerry C. Martin, 53, senior vice president and chief financial officer, joined Global Marine in 1979 and was elected to his present position in May 1985. Other officers include:

James T. Goodwyn, Jr., 57, president, Challenger Minerals, Inc. (joined Global Marine in February 1985).

Gary L. Kott, 43, president, Global Marine Drilling Company (joined Global Marine in 1978 and appointed to present position in 1979).

Thomas E. Short, 57, president, Applied Drilling Technology, Inc. (1979).

Robert E. Sleet, 39, vice president and treasurer (joined Global Marine in April 1985).

David A. Herasimchuk, 43, vice president, market development (August 1980).

John G. Ryan, 33, senior vice president, secretary and general counsel.

James C. Schmitz, 37, vice president, tax and government affairs.

Board of Directors.   The board of directors includes Chairman Luigs and:

Retired (1985) Senior Vice President William R. Thomas.

Donald B. Brown, 58, an oil and gas consultant (elected to the board in 1982).

Edward J. Campbell, 56, president and chief executive officer, Newport News Shipbuilding, a Tenneco subsidiary (elected in 1981).

Hubert Faure, 65, senior executive vice president, United Technologies Corporation (elected in 1984).

John M. Galvin, 52, senior vice president, Aetna Life and Casualty (joined the board in 1979).

Warren F. Kane, 61, private consultant and recently retired president of Baker Drilling Equipment Company, a subsidiary of Baker International Corporation (elected in 1982).

Lynn L. Leigh, 59, chairman, president, and chief executive officer, Summit Oilfield Corporation (elected to the board in 1981).

William C. Walker, consultant to the petroleum industry (1985).

Anti-takeover Actions in 1985.   The board of directors was concerned in 1985 about the possibility that Global Marine was vulnerable to takeover by a larger company. Therefore, several anti-takeover provisions were proposed for inclusion in the company's certificate of incorporation. These proposals would: (1) divide the board of directors into three classes serving staggered three-year terms; (2) allow board size to range from a minimum of 3 to a maximum of 15 directors; (3) require stockholder actions to be initiated only at a stockholders' meeting to which all stockholders were invited; (4) permit incumbent directors to fill any vacancies on the board; (5) increase the stockholder vote required to change, amend, or repeal company bylaws from a majority to 80 percent of the stock available for voting.

REEVALUATING GMI'S FUTURE DIRECTIONS

Russ Luigs joined Global Marine in 1977 and shortly thereafter introduced a seven-year plan intended to place the company in a position of preeminence within the industry. During most of those years, Global Marine experienced profitability and record growth in assets and revenues. The year 1985 was a watershed year for Global Marine, however. The company's $1 billion investment in state-of-the-art technology had indeed brought Global Marine to a leadership position among offshore oil and gas drilling contractors but cash flow was insufficient to pay off the company's indebtedness.

Luigs might well reflect on those factors critical to success and survival in the offshore drilling industry. He had driven Global Marine to the cutting edge of offshore drilling technology and assembled a fleet of rigs capable of meeting any customer's needs, no matter what the environment. His organization personified the concept, "The Customer Is King."

In an industry renowned for risk, Russ Luigs had taken no more than a conventional approach and pursued a strategic course of action that neither he, his board of directors, nor his creditors perceived as excessively risky. Was the price of industry leadership too high? Should he and could he have acted differently? What basis was there to indicate that an alternative course of action would have led to a more favorable set of circumstances?

Global Marine, Inc., as of January 1, 1986, had no seven-year strategic plan for the future. The company's primary objective was survival, as stated by Mr. Luigs in the company's 1985 Annual Report. Although hindsight indicated that the company could have pursued less ambitious objectives, Global Marine's current concerns were what actions and circumstance might combine to preserve the company as an independent entity in the international offshore oil and gas drilling industry.

16. *Gotham Utilities Co.*

The north wind blew daggers early that Sunday morning as the ragged band of nuclear power protestors took up their vigil outside the comfortable home on a quiet Tonawanda, New York street. Their voices cracked with cold as they chanted slogans while freezing hands pumped placards in the falling sleet. Suddenly the door to the house opened and there, in his bathrobe and slippers, bleary-eyed, stood the rural New York boy who'd grown up to be the chairman and CEO of one of the Northeast's largest utility holding companies. Douglas DeLong ran his hand through his wiry, pewter gray burr-cut hair and gazed balefully at the dedicated few charging him and his company with mismanagement, negligence, polluting the environment, and covering up major construction flaws at the Delta Nuclear Plant, under construction near Fredonia, New York.

This case was prepared by Holly Feder and Linda McKee under the supervision of Professor Adelaide Griffin, Texas Woman's University and Professor Sexton Adams, North Texas State University.

Doug turned back into the house, closing the door. The protestors lit a small fire in an oil drum in the street, trying to keep warm as they settled down for what looked like a long, bone-chilling day. Soon though, the door to the house opened again. Tanya DeLong, coat thrown over her robe, came down the steps carrying freshly brewed coffee to the dissenters. Right behind her was Doug, carrying homemade doughnuts by the tray-full. The DeLongs and the protestors chatted over coffee and doughnuts until Doug, who was coatless, invited the entire group into the house to get warm while Tanya brewed another pot of coffee for everyone.

Slowly, a bit nervously, the people who thought he'd never acknowledge their existence filed into the warmth of the top man's house. Still in his pajamas and robe, Doug listened patiently to their concerns for several hours.

As Doug and the protestors talked, the electric utility parts of Doug's company, Erie Electric Company (EEC), just across the state line in Pennsylvania; Tonawanda Lighting Company (TLC); and Amherst Power Company (APCo) worked to keep up with the winter peak demand for electricity set that frigid day. (See Exhibit 1.) About 3:30 A.M. that morning the system dispatcher at Gotham Generating Company (GoGen, another Gotham Utilities subsidiary) had ordered all the peaking units to be ready to go on-line at 7:30 A.M. Tepid boilers several stories tall had to be fired to make 1,000° F. steam. The plant superintendents had kept the turbine rotors on turning gear all night, anticipating the dispatcher's call. They had all been watching the temperature drop steadily throughout the night, and knew another Canadian storm was on the way. When the public awoke that icy morning and wanted to be warm and fed before setting out for church, the dispatcher wanted the peaking units ready to go on-line to meet the surging demand.

The other parts of Gotham Utilities were doing their jobs to keep up with the winter peak too. Gotham Gas Company, the subsidiary which owns 1,975 miles of gas pipeline, was pushing thousands of cubic feet of fuel gas to the hungry boilers, in addition to acquiring and storing more gas. Allegheny Coal Company, the mining subsidiary, had produced the coal the generation and weather forecasts specified, and was busily digging to keep pace with future needs.

A-G Transportation Company was delivering coal and other fuels to the system by the trainloads. Monday morning, the employees at Gotham Services, Inc., the financial, accounting, and administrative arm of Gotham, would have their hands full processing all the paperwork required with intracompany transactions worth millions of dollars. The company's simple credo: "Our first commitment is serving the needs of people who depend on us for reliable, economical electricity"[1] is considered the 11th Commandment by employees throughout the organization.

About the only people working for one of the subsidiary companies who were taking it easy that frigid morning were the folks at Partners Development Company. They were home all snug in their beds, while visions of lucrative, unregulated, cogeneration deals danced in their heads.

Only Partners is allowed such visions. All the other subsidiaries, as well as the holding company itself, are regulated by a dizzying array of politicians or political appointees. At the national level regulation begins with the Utility Holding Company Act of 1935; the Federal Power Act; the Public Utility Regulatory Policies Act

(PURPA); the Environmental Protection Agency (EPA); the Resource Conservation and Recovery Act of 1976; the Fuels Use Act of 1978; the EPA's division called the National Pollutant Discharge Elimination System; and for the Delta Plant, the Nuclear Regulatory Commission (NRC); and the Atomic Safety and Licensing Board (ASLB), which has been holding hearings on the Delta Plant since October 1981.[2]

Because Gotham wheels (transmits electricity over lines for sale to utilities in other states) their excess power through the Northeast power grid, they are also subject to the Federal Energy Regulatory Commission (FERC). FERC has specific criteria for what, in their minds, constitutes a utility in interstate commerce.

At the state level, Gotham is regulated by the New York Clean Air Act; the Air Control Board of New York; the New York Water Commission; the New York Railroad Commission; the New York Solid Waste Disposal Act; the Northeast Power Coordinating Council (NPCC), a power pool which shares power among themselves and establishes minimum reserve margins for capacity; and last but certainly not least, the New York Public Utility Commission (PUC).[3] In New York, utilities are also regulated at the municipal level by every town which does not cede original jurisdiction to the state PUC. Since Gotham is an investor-owned utility, and traded on the New York, Midwest, and Pacific Stock Exchanges, they are also subject to the Securities and Exchange Commission.

It wasn't always such a regulatory maze, though. When Gotham was formed by EEC, TLC, and APCo in June 1940, they only had to worry about 415,000 customers using 2 billion kilowatts (kw) of power annually. Each of those separate utility companies has roots in the electric service industry over 90 years old. They haven't missed a dividend since 1917.[4]

In many ways, the story of what we now know as Gotham Utility Company is the story of our nation and the electric utility industry in the years after World War II. The civilian soldiers came home from the war, went to work, and produced an unprecedented economic growth rate in addition to the "baby-boom" generation. Because a utility is a natural and legal monopoly[5] they

[1]Gotham Utilities, Annual Report, 1984.

[2]Gotham Utilities, *1985 SEC Form 10K*, 1985.
[3]Gotham Utilities, *1985 SEC Form 10K*.
[4]"Gotham Utilities," *Standard NYSE Stock Reports*, August 20, 1986.
[5]Milton H. Spencer, *Contemporary Economics*, chap. 23.

EXHIBIT 1   Subsidiaries' Operating Units

Unit	Fuel	Number of Units	1983 Net Generation (kwhr.)
Genesee	Virginia coal	2	7,125,566,000
Tonawanda	Virginia coal	3	13,668,990,000
Niagara	Virginia coal	3	12,724,977,000
Perth #4	Virginia coal	4	3,456,619,000
Dunkirk	Hydro	1	160,698,000
Pendleton	Gas/fuel/oil	1	2,616,741,000
Suny	Gas	2	316,861,000
Silver Creek	Hydro	1	107,449,000
Wattsburg	Gas	2	2,655,583,000
Allegheny	Gas	2	4,317,799,000
Lakeview	Hydro	6	292,196,000
Findley Lake	Gas	3	1,949,428,000
Corry	Gas	3	891,334,000
Erie	Gas	2	2,620,958,000
Cuba Lake	Gas	5	2,804,361,000
Cayuga	Gas/fuel/oil	8	3,203,859,000
4 Mile Creek	Hydro	1	114,617,000
North Warren	Gas/fuel/oil	7	2,303,115,000
Batavia	Hydro	9	57,695,000
Lime Lake	Gas	8	1,868,535,000
Oak Orchard	Hydro	3	280,737,000
Iroquois	Gas	3	1,903,467,000
Stillwater	Gas	2	2,265,139,000

Note: Kwhr is a measure of energy delivered to customers in kilowatt-hours.

Source: *Directory of Electric Utilities.*

have what is called a *mandate* to serve any and every customer who requests service. Demand for electricity was skyrocketing.

Trouble was, there were still quite a few small utility companies trying to keep up with demand in their areas on scanty construction budgets. Power generation was becoming an even more capital-intensive process. Basically, there are two ways for a utility to make money. They can add customers and sell additional kws; or they can add equipment to the system and incorporate the costs into a higher rate base. The nation's growth was producing a Catch 22 for some utilities. Gradually, the utilities formed holding companies and pooled their construction dollars to build larger and larger generating facilities.

In the 1950s and 1960s electricity rates declined, and utilities could count on a demand growth of 7–8 percent per year.[6] There was little trouble raising capital at 4.88 percent in the late 1950s.[7] About the only competition was the increasing use of then-cheap natural gas as an alternate fuel source. Electric utilities countered with the well-known Reddy Kilowatt and "Live Better Electrically" campaigns. Power companies sponsored cooking classes (on electric stoves, of course), and engaged magicians and raconteurs to entertain and instruct schoolchildren on the values of electricity. Builders were encouraged to build all-electric homes for the burgeoning population.

---

[6]"Utilities in Trouble," *Newsweek,* May 7, 1979, p. 81.

[7]"Public Utility Manual," *Moody's Investors Service,* vol. 2, 1986.

One of the better known companies of this era, General Electric Company (which also manufactures large power generation equipment), helped demand along as well as the busy housewife by producing and touting consumer goods such as roasters, coffee makers, air conditioning, dishwashers, blenders, and garbage disposals. Industry was thriving because the power to operate their ever more efficient machines was available in quantity at a low price. A cheap and plentiful power source is one of the basic building blocks of a strong national economy. Without such reliable, low cost energy, industries as diverse as steel and microchips can't run machines, operate computers, hire labor, or build factories to produce the goods and services demanded by the public. Without energy, Adam Smith's economic model breaks down faster than it does with government intervention; in fact our national GNP closely parallels our national energy consumption.

The utilities, meanwhile, were thinking in terms of larger economies of scale. Power plants and turbines are measured by their output in kw or megawatts (mw, or 1,000 kilowatts). Technology dictated small machines at first, but machines in the 300–500 mw and up range were becoming more and more attractive and feasible. Some corporate egos became involved with plant size

and pride of maintenance as though turbines, generators, rotors, and exciters were expensive sports machines.

Once the engineering and technological barriers had fallen, utility managements built more and larger units and plants to meet the still-growing demand of the 1950s, 1960s, and the early 1970s. Commonwealth Edison had the first small nuclear unit, 300 mw or so, which was closely watched by other utilities for its performance, reliability, and economy of production. Nuclear power production looked like it could be an efficient alternative to costly fuel oil, hydropower, or coal plants. When many of the nuclear plants operating today were on the drawing boards, nuclear power was seen as being a lower cost fuel than coal. Even today, the cost of electricity generated by the commercial "nukes" costs only 4.3 cents per kilowatt-hour, compared to 3.4 cents for coal and 7.3 cents for oil.[8]

There was no question in utility managements' minds that demand was still growing, and with their necessarily long-planning horizons (10 to 20 years), it was time to think about even larger plants and economies of scale (see Exhibit 2). The boys on the various state PUCs

---

[8]Atomic Industrial Forum, "News Release," September 25, 1986.

EXHIBIT 2 Capacity, Demand, and Reserve in Megawatts (mw) (August 1985)

Year	Added Capacity	Total Capacity	Firm Demand	Percent Reserve
1985	0	17,914	15,595	14.87%
1986	1,235	19,149	15,820	21.04
1987	1,140	20,289	16,285	24.59
1988	295	20,584	16,860	22.09
1989	260	20,844	17,340	20.21
1990	615	21,459	17,840	20.29
1991	629	22,088	18,305	20.67
1992	618	22,706	18,855	20.42
1993	847	23,553	19,515	20.69
1994	715	24,268	20,090	20.80
1995	1,020	25,288	20,775	21.72
1996	550	25,838	21,360	20.96
1997	680	26,518	21,945	20.84
1998	970	27,488	22,530	22.01
1999	550	28,038	23,215	20.78

Note: Firm demand does not include interruptible loads.

Source: Public Utility Commission.

hadn't given anyone any trouble in a long time. Being political animals, the PUCs certainly didn't want to put themselves in the position of appearing to stand in the way of progress. As utilities saw it, the only problems with building their first nuke were finding the money, and the perennial gadflies who didn't want transmission lines, transformers, or atoms in their backyards.

The 1970s were an era of heightened environmental and civil unrest throughout the country. The Delta Plant, begun in 1971, was only one of many nukes planned or under construction during those years. Much to their consternation and amazement, utilities around the country began to discover that they were vulnerable to Flower Children and fanatics alike who hurled verbal, if not actual, charges against an industry which they saw as the archtypical barons of Big Business. Even well-meaning citizens were brought onto the protest bandwagon through misinformed and sensationalist media coverage of any and all power protests both in the United States and Europe. The complexities of nonnuclear power production are intimidating enough, and the general public was not well informed about the most basic technicalities of nuclear power production.

The electric power industry didn't bother to educate their customers about the technology involved with power production from nuclear plants, or hydro or gas, for that matter. Their stoic, "trust us" attitude played right into extremists' hands as they conjured up pictures of an Hiroshima in every backyard, and people who glowed in the dark from radiation. During this era authority of all sorts was considered untrustworthy by many Americans, and since utilities, like banks and the government, had access to the corridors of power, utility managers were lumped together (as much by their silence as anything else) with politicians, financiers, and Big Business as unreliable sources of information at the very least.

To make matters worse, the price of oil used to fire many utility boilers began causing dramatic rate increases due to an oil embargo by the OPEC nations. Then, just when utility management across the country was thinking of retreating to the storm cellar and licking their wounds, along came the disaster known as Three Mile Island. The year was 1979, and the president was Jimmy Carter.

The NRC immediately announced a ban on the construction of new nukes after Three Mile Island. The ban was to last a minimum of six months to two years. At that time, there were 92 plants under construction, with 72 more in commercial operation. By contrast,

there are 86 commercial plants on-line today.[9] Exhibit 3 shows the fate of just some of the post-TMI reactors.

Additionally, the NRC announced that it would quickly establish more stringent safety and reporting regulations. The Kemeny Commission, charged with detailing those tougher rules, recommended among other things (1) more difficult and comprehensive operator training, and (2) state governor-approved evacuation plans for everyone within a 10-mile radius of any nuke plant. There were other requirements, too. NRC Chairman Hendrie told a House Subcommittee on Energy and Power that some existing nukes "may be unable to meet the new safety rules," and would be required to reduce their power output. He also said he was "considering ordering the shut down" of nuclear reactors "in heavily populated areas."[10]

Gotham Power's Delta Plant has been required to reinforce its control room foundations at least three separate times (plant gossip has it that a fleet of semis can park on the floor without damaging it). Gotham's also been required to replace every one of more than 41,500 pipe joints in both units in the plant, and to change all of the tens of thousands of components bearing the nameplates Gotham has used for years, and which are instantly recognized by any Gotham plant employee, and replace them with nameplates demanded by the NRC. (See Exhibits 4 through 6.)

There were many other hurdles, of course, for Gotham and the nation's electric companies. One of the most devastating nonfinancial aspects was reported by *Newsweek* on May 7, 1979, three months after TMI. The magazine told its readers that, "Three Mile Island is hurting another way; it has fed the growing suspicion among consumers and government officials alike that the managers of many power companies are simply not up to the complex task facing them." It added that, "with government policies unclear, fuel supplies uncertain, and public resistance to new plants on the rise, many utility managers are reluctant to make long-term plans."[11] For Doug DeLong, Gotham Power, and its partners, Long Island Lighting, Metropolitan Edison Company, and Delaware Electric Cooperative, the Delta Plant was to be their first nuke.

---

[9]Association of Edison Illuminating Companies, "Report of the Committee on Power Generation, 1984–1985," New York, N.Y.

[10]"Three Mile Island," *Time*, November 19, 1979.

[11]"Utilities in Trouble," *Newsweek*, May 7, 1979.

EXHIBIT 3 Two-Year Summary—Post-TMI Nuclear Power Reactors

Unit	Location	Power (MW)	Status
North Anna Unit 3	Virginia	907	Canceled
South Texas Project #1, #2	Texas	2,500	1989
Grand Gulf #2	Mississippi	1,250	Canceled
Zimmer Station #1	Ohio	810	Canceled
Delta Plant #1, #2	New York	2,300	Political
Watts Bar #1, #2 (TVA)	Tennessee	2,354	1986, 1987
Bellefonte #1, #2 (TVA)	Alabama	2,426	1989, 1991
Midland #2	Michigan	808	Converting to gas
Seabrook #1, #2	New Hampshire	2,400	Political
WPSS Project #1, #3	Washington	2,490	1991
Hartsville A-1, A-2, B-2 (TVA)	Tennessee	3,699	Canceled
Midland #1	Michigan	537	Canceled
Cherokee #1, #2, #3	South Carolina	3,817	Canceled
River Bend #2	Louisiana	934	Canceled
Clinton #2	Illinois	933	Canceled
Marble Hill #1, #2	Indiana	3,425	Canceled
Phipps Bend #1, #2 (TVA)	Tennessee	3,579	Canceled
Yellow Creek #1, #2	Mississippi	3,817	Canceled
Pebble Springs #1, #2	Oregon	3,621	Canceled
Clinch River (experimental)	Tennessee	975	Canceled
Allens Creek #1	Texas	3,579	Canceled
Skagit County #1, #2	Washington	3,833	Canceled
Shoreham Plant	New York	819	Political

Total Projected MW: 10,578

Total MW Canceled or Political: 41,235

Note: The TVA (Tennessee Valley Authority) has no nuclear units generating power due to political scandals. They have canceled all nuclear construction.

Source: Association of Edison Illuminating Companies.

In October 1982, Gotham routinely applied to the ASLB for various licenses for Delta, and the agency began their reviews and hearings on the applications. During that election year, gubernatorial candidate Mario Cuomo told voters he would reorganize the PUC to be more consumer oriented, and put a housewife on the PUC. He further promised to do away with the automatic fuel adjustment enacted by the PUC to grant relief to utilities suffering from the skyrocketing costs of oil. New York utilities were allowed to pass along their increased cost of fuel to the customer on a monthly basis. As fuel costs rose, so did the charge per kilowatt used. If fuel costs ever came down, so would the monthly bills.

The higher energy costs didn't seem to bother Gotham's customers overmuch. The winter, 1981 peak demand rose to 75 percent of summer demand. Gotham was in a strong financial position, and funded 58.8 percent of their total construction budget internally. They paid dividends of $1.88 per share on over 105.8 million outstanding shares.[12]

The ASLB questioned Gotham's quality assurance-quality control program (QA/QC) for the design of the plant, and demanded additional proof that the design was indeed adequate. Hearings continued throughout

---

[12]Gotham Utilities, Annual Report, 1984.

EXHIBIT 4   Comparison of Construction Costs and Times for Selected Operating Nuclear Power Plants, 1968 to 1985

Plant	Construction Cost (in millions)		Date of Commerical Operation	
	Est.	Actual	Est.	Actual
Nine Mile Point	$101.0	$ 150.5	11/68	12/69
Palisades	87.0	118.0	5/70	11/70
Monticello	74.2	88.8	5/70	5/71
Quad Cities #1	90.4	159.7	3/70	12/72
Zion #1	164.0	276.4	4/72	12/73
Arkansas Nuclear One #1	132.0	245.4	12/72	12/74
Millstone #2	150.2	416.3	4/74	12/75
Beaver Valley #1	150.0	605.6	7/73	10/76
Davis-Besse #1	179.8	649.0	12/74	12/77
D. C. Cook #2	235.0	439.0	4/72	7/78
Arkansas Nuclear One #2	182.7	577.5	10/75	9/79
North Anna #2	184.0	542.0	3/75	11/80
McGuire #1	358.4	919.0	11/75	12/81
La Salle #1	360.0	1,377.0	10/75	10/82
Susquehanna #1	150.1	1,941.0	12/75	6/83
WPPSS #2	187.4	3,200.9	9/77	12/84
Diablo Canyon #1	153.6	3,315.5	12/72	5/85

Source: U.S. Department of Energy.

1982 and 1983. Allegations were raised in the press, and heard by a special ASLB subcommittee, that clerks had been harassed and intimidated into falsifying documents pertaining to quality and safety checks. Over 18 months later, the NRC concluded that a climate of harassment and intimidation had never existed at the plant, but damage to Gotham's public image had already been done by the time the NRC cleared them of wrongdoing.

Under Governor Cuomo the PUC also began to take a very dim view of granting any utility rate requests in a timely fashion. More often than not, top management and supporting documentation and experts were tied up for months in Albany testifying about the necessity to raise rates to get a modicum of return on Gotham's investment in future generating capacity. On more than one occasion, Gotham was told to reduce their rates at the conclusion of the hearings.

The summer of 1983 saw a new record peak demand of 15,035,000 kilowatts, up 8.8 percent from the previous year. Gotham's management was worried that if peak demand increases continued in the 8 percent or larger range, they would be woefully short of capacity in the next 5 to 10 years, and that brownouts could easily result during peak demand hours. The PUC wasn't worried, however. In December 1983, Gotham again applied for an 8 percent rate increase. On June 27, 1984, the PUC issued its final order requiring Gotham to decrease their rates by 0.5 percent. The order was placed into effect in July of that year, and meant a 6.2 percent revenue shortfall for EEC; a 6.7 percent shortfall for TLC; and a 5.8 percent deficiency for APCo.[13]

New Year's Eve, 1983, saw Gotham's total 12-year investment in the Delta Plant reach $3,500,000,000, for an 85 percent stake in the plant. The cost of contracts for cooling water for the entire system decreased $18,000, to $5,344,000 for the year.[14]

The operating companies, EEC, TLC, and APCo merged on January 6, 1984, to form Gotham Utilities

---

[13]Gotham Utilities, *SEC Form 10K.*
[14]Ibid.

EXHIBIT 5   Average Construction Costs for Nuclear Plants 1968 through Projected 1996 (in dollars per kilowatt)

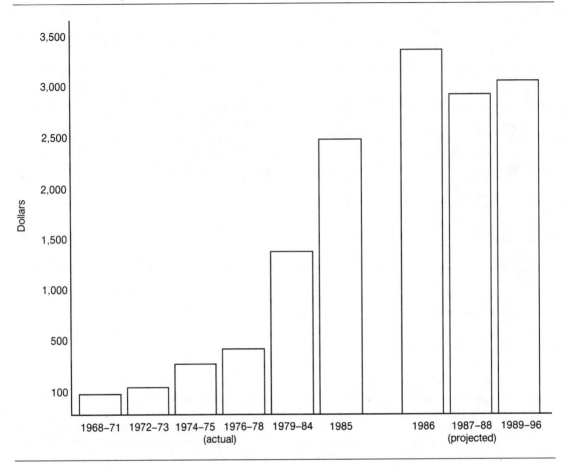

Source: U.S. Atomic Energy Commission and U.S. Department of Energy.

Company. GoGen was the fourth party in the merger. The Utility Company, in turn, became the principal subsidiary of the Gotham Companies. This merger eliminated considerable rate, paperwork, and administrative duplication. They now serve 56 counties in New York and Pennsylvania, and had 4,850,000 customers that year, or one third of the population of the western New York/Pennsylvania area. The winter peak was 87 percent of the summer peak, another record, of 16,501,000 kilowatts achieved on July 26th, 1984.

A report issued by the NRC's investigation team in February 1985, declared that Gotham had demonstrated that they lacked commitment to aggressively implement and follow through with an effective QA/QC program in several areas at the Delta Plant. The team told the press that they'd found evidence of faulty construction (all in noncritical areas), and deficiencies in such areas a paperflow and documentation control, and problems with the as-built drawings. The team recommended that Gotham give serious consideration to obtaining management personnel with a fresh perspective. Additionally, the team recommended that Gotham hire an independent, outside consultant to oversee the now-mandated corrective action program to fix all the alleged deficiencies.

Gotham then found a 1976 report in their files which, in hindsight, they believed should have been provided during one of the initial licensing proceedings in 1982.

EXHIBIT 6   Average Construction Time for Nuclear Power Plants (historical and projected time in years)

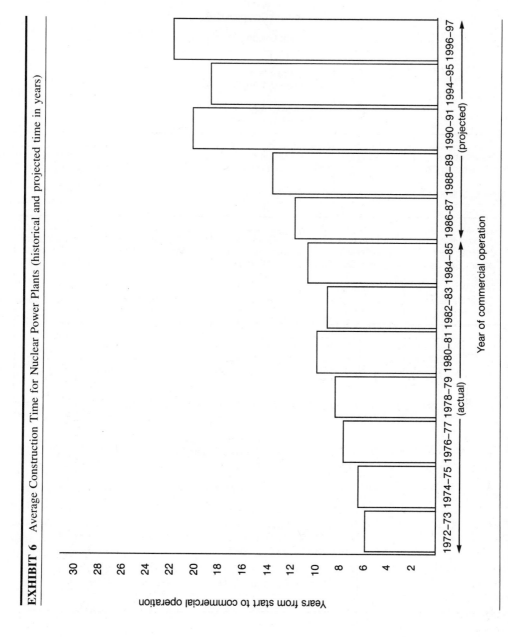

Source: U.S. Department of Energy and Atomic Energy Commission.

EXHIBIT 7   Organization Chart for the Gotham Companies

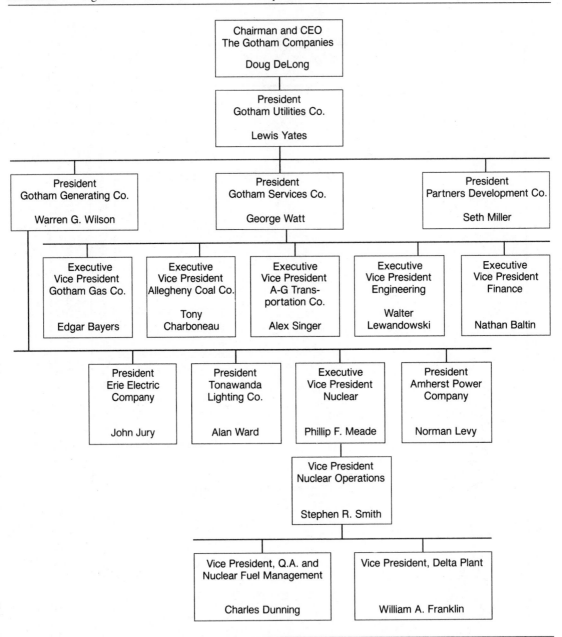

They immediately forwarded it to the ASLB amid editorial criticism in the media. During 1985, Gotham announced a reorganization and management changes in the nuclear side of their management and operations.[15] (See Exhibit 7.)

The top two construction managers for the plant general contractor at Delta were replaced on March 1. A new office of director of QA was created by Gotham. Charles Dunning, 46, was promoted to vice president, QA and nuclear fuel management. Joe Bob Burns, a 25-year company veteran, was reassigned to nonnuclear duties which required his presence at headquarters rather than at the plant site. Gotham followed a growing industry trend with their next appointment. A nuclear Navy protégé of Admiral Hyman Rickover's, retired Rear Admiral Stephen R. Smith, 51, was hired to replace Burns. Smith had been the commander of the U.S. Mediterranean Fleet. He believes, like Rickover, in attention to details and that excellence is as much a function of perspiration and dedication as it is a state of mind. Smith assumed the new title of vice president of nuclear operations.

William A. Franklin, 61, was promoted to vice president with both technical and administrative responsibilities at the Delta Plant. He had been the manager of operations at Delta since 1972. Franklin began his career with Gothham when he joined APCo in 1948. Among his new responsibilities are budgeting and security at Delta.

In late May, Phillip F. Meade, 47, was recruited from Consolidated Edison Service Company to become executive vice president, nuclear, for Gotham. He has over 20 years' experience with commercial nuclear power generation, and is a West Point graduate with a Harvard M.B.A. The new management team has been charged with the responsibility for, and oversight of, the reinspection and corrective action program. Gotham's spokesman, Bud Perkins, said the changes represented the creation of a permanent, separate organization wholly devoted to nuclear power. Meade is slated to gradually assume responsibility for all daily nuclear activities from Warren G. Wilson, GoGen president. Gotham maintains publicly that the management changes were not prompted by the NRC's investigation and report.[16] The continuing difficulties with Delta and

EXHIBIT 8   Planned Construction Schedule

Location and Unit	Net MW	Service Date
Delta Plant #1	1,010	1987
Delta Plant #2	1,010	1988
Indian Falls #1	750	1991
Indian Falls #2	750	1992
Sugartown #1	750	1993
Iroquois #4	750	1994
(Planned Peaking Units)		
Cuba Lake #6	320	1988
Findley Lake #4	320	1989
Wattsburg #3	320	1989
Cuba Lake #7	320	1990
Findley Lake #5	320	1991
Wattsburg #4	320	1992

Source: Gotham Utilities and Public Utility Commission.

Gotham's management changes did, however, prompt Moody's to lower Gotham's bond rating from AAA to AA.

Gotham then filed a comprehensive plan to correct all recognized and alleged deficiencies at the Delta Plant. The ASLB denied Gotham's motion to either adopt the plan outright, or proceed with further licensing hearings. The ASLB said it would be difficult to predict when the entire case might be concluded, and that the plant's operation would be delayed, upsetting the construction schedule shown in Exhibit 8. They wanted further proof of Gotham's commitment to aggressive implementation of the mandated programs. Further, the ASLB said that additional substantial proceedings would be necessary. Some financial analysts predict the Delta Plant will be delayed beyond December 1989.[17]

The total cost of the Delta Plant is now estimated at $5.8 billion, of which $5.1 billion represents Gotham's share of the costs. Stated another way, if the cost projections are accurate, the plant would cost a total of $2,325 for each kilowatt of capacity. Fifty-one percent of Gotham's total construction for all plants was financed internally in 1985, compared to 28.5 percent in 1975. Gotham's operating companies now serve more than 2.5 million customers who demand more than 81

[15]"Politics and Policy," *The Wall Street Journal*, September 19, 1986.

[16]Gotham Company, "News Release," July 8, 1985.

[17]Standard & Poor's Corporation, "Standard NYSE Stock Reports."

billion kilowatt-hours of electricity per year. They continue to see new summer peak records, but total demand has been declining recently. On August 10, 1985, the new record was 15,260,525 kilowatts used, and a record 1.8 billion cubic feet of gas for the system was delivered by the Fuel Company. In September their bond rating was lowered to Single A by Moody's.

Meanwhile, one of the Fortune 500 industrials decided it wanted to build a new plant in Gotham's area. The plant would provide close to 3,000 new jobs for the area, help the tax base in the rural country close to the Canadian border where the site had been purchased, and improve the local sagging economy by several million dollars in payroll alone. During the planning phase of the plant, Gotham's top management had several meetings with the industrial's top management. The industrial men wanted Gotham to grant them a substantially lower, uninterruptible, power contract for 10 years. Gotham's power rates are too high, the industrial men said, and if Gotham wouldn't do business with them, they would search elsewhere for power; or make their own.[18]

The industrial team revealed that they had studied the situation, and found they could import cheaper, Canadian government-subsidized power and save money even though they would have to invest in transmission lines and transformers. This was an unprecedented situation in the history of American power.

Power utilities are granted monopoly rights in return for regulation, over well-defined geographic territories. No one else is allowed to sell power in these protected areas, while the utility is obligated to serve every customer. Due to this large customer base, the cost of power is kept fairly low. If a major industrial pulled out of the rate base it would shrink, and rates for remaining customers would rise. The industrial said that if Gotham wouldn't provide power as cheaply as Canada, they'd forget the plant and move to the South. Gotham would then be seen as having been responsible for the loss of 3,000 jobs, higher electric rates, and as an impediment to the progress of a region beginning to recover from a recession.

The industrial's other option was to make the power themselves. The New York PUC, in concert with PURPA, had ruled that all New York utilities had to buy cogenerated power, even if they didn't need it, at higher rates than the utility could make it themselves.[19] Cogeneration is the simultaneous production of steam for industrial and utility use. The action taken by the New York PUC is not unusual among PUCs, and troubles utilities because they are no longer in control of the production or generation of the power. This means an industrial could interrupt (turn off) some of the utility's power supply at will, leaving customers literally in the dark. Until the passage of the 1986 Tax Reform Act, cogeneration facilities received very favorable treatment.[20] The power plant is generally smaller than an average utility power plant, and energy developers (cogeneration is unregulated) were quick to discover that an investment in the $20 to $40 million range could be repaid in as few as two to three years with savings and tax breaks generated by the plant.[21]

Governor Cuomo then stepped into the picture and began exerting pressure privately and in the media for Gotham to meet or beat the subsidized Canadian rates. He was unwilling, however, to similarly twist the PUC's arm to grant rate relief to Gotham. While this contest of wills continued, the Pennsylvania governor got wind of the industrial's stance and began wooing them to move to Pennsylvania. He promised to locate them outside Gotham's service territory, ram through enabling legislation so they would have favorable zoning, tax rates, and cheap power. He also promised state aid to build highways and connecting roads around and up to the new plant. The Pennsylvania governor induced another large utility to promise power to the industrial at a combined cost of their hydro and gas costs on a kilowatt-hour basis. The utility figured that, with the price of natural gas dropping, they could still break even.

Doug DeLong and his people were busy renegotiating lower natural gas contracts themselves. Utilities often contract for fuel for five or more years in advance, and buy limited quantities on the spot markets. With their volume buying power, Gotham was in a good position to nearly dictate the terms of contracts with whatever outside suppliers were necessary. Thus far in 1986, Gotham has seen another summer peak in spite of mild weather. They have refunded over $200 million to their customers because of overrecovery of fuel costs.

---

[18]"Rise in Residential Rates as Big Users Get Cuts," *The Wall Street Journal,* September 30, 1986.

[19]"Cogeneration is Booming," *Kiplinger Texas Letter,* October 10, 1986, p. 2.

[20]American Cogeneration Association, "Memorandum," September 26, 1986.

[21]Public Utility Commission, "Cogeneration and Small Power Producers," May 1986.

EXHIBIT 9   1983 Corporate Income—Averages of All Investor-Owned Utilities (in thousands)

Operating income:	
Operating revenues	$10,490,803
Operating and maintenance expense	7,449,610
Depreciation	771,472
Taxes	249,737
Total operating revenue deduction	8,470,816
Electric utility operating income	2,019,987
Other income	1,118,285
Gross income	3,138,272
Income deductions:	
Interest on long-term debt	1,676,031
Other income deductions	132,204
Net income	1,543,827
Electric utility plant	34,550,343
Reserves for depreciation and amortization	7,228,492
Other utility plant	2,162,047
Total utility plant	36,712,390
Long-term debt	24,632,187
Current and accrued liabilities	2,622,963
Total liabilities and other credit	39,766,744

Source: *Moody's Public Utility Manual.*

When Governor Cuomo changed the automatic fuel adjustment, higher fuel costs were charged to customers even though the price of fuel had dropped. The PUC passed an emergency action early in 1986 allowing the utilities to refund the difference to their customers on a quarterly basis. So, instead of a lower bill on a monthly basis, customers had to wait for a quarter to pass before realizing the fuel savings. Since 1986 was an election year, both candidates for governor took credit for lowering the public's utility bills. Governor Cuomo won the November elections for another term in office.

Perhaps the best news of 1986 for Gotham was the receipt, on April 15, of a favorable report from both the NRC and the ASLB. They were pleased with Gotham's plans to resolve all outstanding design, construction, and documentation issues. Parts of the plan have been in action since 1983, and the regulatory authorities went so far as to say that if the plan continued to be properly implemented at the Delta Plant, it would provide important evidence of Gotham's commitment to quality at the plant.[22] Gotham has recently begun submitting completed reports to both regulatory agencies.

Operating revenues declined thus far in 1986 by 5 percent, according to Gotham's midyear report to shareholders. Total income rose 6.5 percent during the same period. There were no further unfavorable actions upon Gotham's credit ratings, and they stand now at Single A. They have reduced over $200 million of high interest debt, and sold more than $250 million of 9½ percent bonds, as well as filed a shelf registration for about $170 million worth of cumulative preferred stock. Gotham still has about 50,000,000 authorized but unissued shares of serial preferred stock with a par value of about $25. They are expected to fund nearly 53 percent of their total construction budget internally this year.[23] (See Exhibits 9 through 12.)

---

[22]Gotham Utilities, "Quarterly Report to Shareholders," July 1, 1986.

[23]Merrill Lynch Research, "Quotron," September 15, 1986.

EXHIBIT 10   Dividends per share

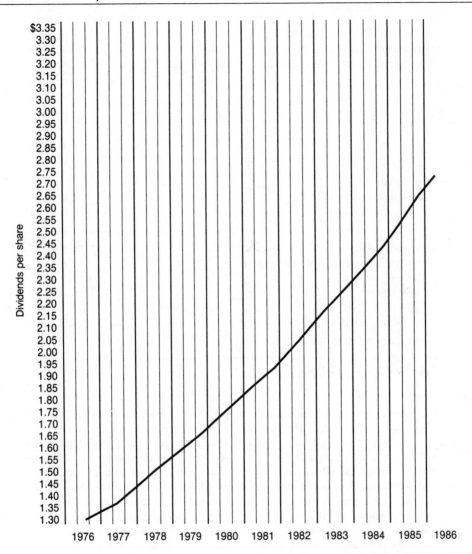

EXHIBIT 11   Cost Per Share in Dollars versus Range of Yield in Percent of High and Low Prices

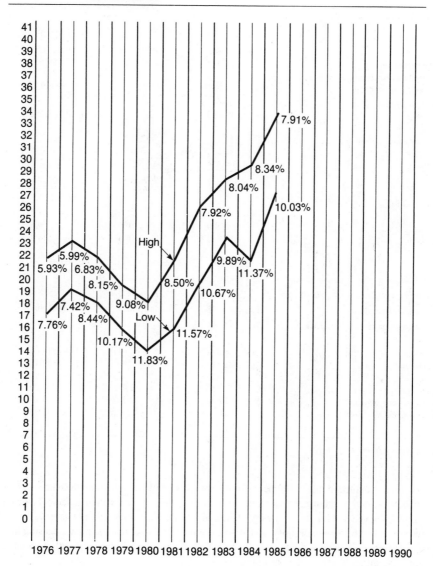

EXHIBIT 12 Financial Statistics

	1985	1984	1983	1982
Total assets end of year (thousands)...................	$ 10,867,022	$ 9,759,148	$ 8,780,954	$ 8,021,407
Utility plant end of year (thousands)	$ 12,144,563	$ 11,031,699	$ 9,967,653	$ 9,051,442
Accumulated depreciation end of year	2,331,783	2,143,863	1,958,103	1,758,156
Construction expenditures (including allowance for funds used during construction)	1,108,861	951,323	906,930	891,560
Capitalization end of year (thousands):				
Long-term debt	$ 3,615,669	$ 3,322,925	$ 3,103,452	$ 2,973,253
Preferred stock:				
Not subject to mandatory redemption	811,418	727,911	629,779	600,109
Subject to mandatory redemption..................	34,696	34,696	34,696	—
Common stock equity	4,066,664	3,573,103	3,235,375	2,810,195
Total	$ 8,528,447	$ 7,658,635	$ 7,003,302	$ 6,383,557
Capitalization ratios end of year:				
Long-term debt	42.4%	43.4%	44.3%	46.6%
Preferred stock......................................	9.9	10.0	9.5	9.4
Common stock equity	47.7	46.6	46.2	44.0
Total	100.0%	100.0%	100.0%	100.0%
Embedded interest cost on long-term debt, end of year ...	10.3%	10.1%	9.7%	9.5%
Embedded dividend cost on preferred stock, end of year..	8.2%	8.3%	8.0%	7.7%
Consolidated net income (thousands)...................	$ 587,758	$ 526,041	$ 461,468	$ 428,646
Dividends declared on common stock (thousands)........	$ 343,364	$ 298,878	$ 262,659	$ 227,076
Common stock data:				
Shares outstanding—average	135,266,534	126,626,241	118,454,666	111,356,815
Shares outstanding—end of year	138,043,162	128,585,669	123,685,058	114,182,319
Earnings per average share..........................	$ 4.35	$ 4.15	$ 3.90	$ 3.85
Dividends declared per share........................	$ 2.52	$ 2.36	$ 2.20	$ 2.04
Book value per share— end of year	$ 29.46	$ 27.79	$ 26.16	$ 24.61
Return on average common stock equity	15.4%	15.5%	15.3%	16.4%

Source: Gotham, Annual Report.

Doug DeLong has announced his retirement from Gotham, effective at the end of the fiscal year, June 30. He has seen nearly 40 years with the company. His successor, Lewis Yates, 56, will call upon his own nearly 30 years of experience with the company as he guides it through the difficult and time-consuming licensing hearings that remain. It's highly likely that Governor Cuomo will not only insist on prudency audits conducted by the New York PUC, but that he will also block Delta's last licensing hurdle by refusing to approve the required evacuation plan for the plant in case of an accident. In fact, he has so stated his intention to block the plan, believing the state has more right to decide these matters than a federal agency. He is not alone. At least three other state governors are trying to gain control over nuclear plant licensing in their states.[24] Cuomo says he will proceed with a state takeover of the utility.[25]

---

[24]"Potpourri," *Public Power Weekly*, November 3, 1986.
[25]"Politics & Policy," *The Wall Street Journal*, October 10, 1986.

1981	1980	1979	1978	1977	1976	1975
$ 7,306,658	$ 6,552,972	$ 5,821,933	$ 5,161,808	$ 4,563,806	$ 3,878,180	$ 3,245,663
$ 8,194,803	$ 7,438,877	$ 6,631,618	$ 5,862,096	$ 5,111,037	$ 4,398,695	$ 3,736,126
1,560,754	1,378,654	1,213,927	1,057,068	917,637	813,837	716,726
792,268	807,008	872,916	737,353	734,282	671,708	570,016
$ 2,713,863	$ 2,527,716	$ 2,368,612	$ 2,038,654	$ 1,859,057	$ 1,627,403	$ 1,334,881
600,109	600,109	535,824	506,233	476,578	446,923	417,373
—	—	—	—	—	—	—
2,421,864	2,090,520	1,830,472	1,624,298	1,432,830	1,266,086	1,024,491
$ 5,735,836	$ 5,218,345	$ 4,734,908	$ 4,169,185	$ 3,768,465	$ 3,340,412	$ 2,776,745
47.3%	48.4%	50.0%	48.9%	49.3%	48.7%	48.1%
10.5	11.5	11.3	12.1	12.7	13.4	15.0
42.2	40.1	38.7	39.0	38.0	37.9	36.9
100.0%	100.0%	100.0%	100.0%	100.0%	100.0%	100.0%
9.0%	8.3%	7.9%	7.5%	7.3%	7.2%	6.9%
7.7%	7.7%	7.4%	7.3%	7.2%	7.1%	7.0%
$ 359,398	$ 297,844	$ 211,151	$ 200,738	$ 175,919	$ 147,920	$ 120,976
$ 192,306	$ 164,527	$ 142,262	$ 119,945	$ 103,250	$ 85,800	$ 74,400
102,292,239	93,719,257	86,319,396	79,026,787	73,194,444	64,625,000	60,000,000
105,236,301	96,088,645	87,985,098	80,665,889	75,000,000	70,000,000	60,000,000
$ 3.51	$ 3.18	$ 2.45	$ 2.54	$ 2.40	$ 2.29	$ 2.02
$ 1.88	$ 1.76	$ 1.64	$ 1.52	$ 1.40	$ 1.32	$ 1.24
$ 23.01	$ 21.76	$ 20.80	$ 20.14	$ 19.10	$ 18.09	$ 17.07
15.9%	15.2%	12.2%	13.1%	13.0%	12.9%	12.1%

Yates will also have to ponder the fate of over a billion dollars worth of 15-year-old generation equipment rusting away at the Delta Plant. Even though every effort has been made to preserve the machinery, what was once state-of-the-art technology is now obsolete equipment which has never produced a megawatt.

If that weren't enough, Lewis Yates will have another worry. The Financial Accounting Standards Board has proposed write-offs of any PUC-disallowed plant costs. Phase-in deferrals would have to be fully recoverable in 10 years. Should any PUC delay or deny investment or operating cost recovery, it could result in a charge to expense in the period incurred. One Arizona utility has been forced to "eat" over $1.126 billion so far in 1986 as a result of state PUC actions. Similar indigestible meals are in the offing for other utilities around the country in the coming months.[26] Events throughout the country could well make Yates' tenure at the top a lively one indeed.

And then, along came Chernobyl.

---

[26]*Nucleonics Week* 27, no. 41 (October 9, 1986).

17. Manville Corporation (1988)

Perhaps no other mineral is so woven into the fabric of American life as is asbestos. Impervious to heat and fibrous—it is the only mineral that can be woven into cloth—asbestos is spun into fireproof clothing and theater curtains, as well as into such household items as noncombustible drapes, rugs, pot holders, and ironing-board covers. Mixed into slurry, asbestos is sprayed onto girders and walls to provide new buildings with fireproof insulation. It is used in floor tiles, roofing felts, and in most plasterboards and wallboards. Asbestos is also an ingredient of plaster and stucco and of many paints and putties. This "mineral of a thousand uses"—an obsolete nickname: the present count stands at around 3,000 uses—is probably present in some form or other in every home, school, office buildings, and factory in this country. Used in brake linings and clutch facings, in mufflers and gaskets, in sealants and caulking, and extensively used in ships, asbestos is also a component of every modern vehicle, including space ships.

This was written by columnist Bruce Porter in 1973, just as the dangers of breathing asbestos dust were becoming widely recognized by the general public. The box insert below describes certain health effects of breathing asbestos dust.

U.S. consumption of asbestos rose from around 200,000 metric tons per year during the 1930s to a plateau of about 700,000 metric tons a year in the 1950s, 1960s, and early 1970s. U.S. asbestos use dropped sharply after 1972, to just over 100,000 metric tons in 1985.[1] World asbestos production continued to expand rapidly until about the mid-1970s, when it abruptly

plateaued at about 4.6 million metric tons a year. Through 1976 world production barely dropped, apparently because increased shipments to developing countries offset declining usage elsewhere.[2]

From about the turn of the century, Johns-Manville Corporation (renamed Manville Corporation in 1981) was the world's leading asbestos company, involved in mining and sale of the raw fibers as well as development, manufacture, and marketing of intermediate and finished asbestos products. Manville was the main target of a trickle of asbestos-health (A-H) lawsuits in the 1920s and early 1930s which would become a flood by the 1980s.

On the evening of August 25, 1982, the Manville board of directors was provided a briefing on bankruptcy

---

Asbestos Diseases

Ingested asbestos causes mechanical injury to moving tissue, especially the lungs. The microscopic fibers are impervious to body fluids and oxygen and are almost impossible to filter out of air. The constant motion of the lungs causes tissue to be penetrated and cut by the fibers. This leads to progressive and irreversible scarring, thickening, and calcification of the lungs and their linings, a condition called asbestosis. A rare and always-fatal pleural cancer, mesothelioma, is strongly connected with asbestos exposure as are increased incidence and severity of lung cancer and many other respiratory ailments. The first outward symptoms of asbestos disease typically appear 10 to 30 years after exposure begins. But early damage is easily detectable by x rays and some cancers and respiratory deficiencies show up after only a year or two.

This case was prepared by Arthur Sharplin, McNeesse State University, Lake Charles, Louisiana. The assistance and encouragement of the Center for Business Ethics at Bentley College in Waltham, Massachusetts, of which the author is a fellow, is gratefully acknowledged as is the research assistance provided by Cam Leach and Jeanette Savoie.

[1]Barry I. Castleman, *Asbestos: Medical and Legal Aspects* (Clifton, N.J.: Prentice-Hall Law and Business, 1987), p. 614.

[2]Ibid., pp. 636–37.

reorganization. A petition for protection from creditors under Chapter 11 of the U.S. Bankruptcy Code had already been prepared. It was approved by the board that night and was filed the next day. It would be more than six years before a plan to emerge from court protection would be final. Many of the asbestos victims would die in the meantime. And the tens of thousands who had been held off during those years by the bankruptcy court would find their claims subordinated to those of commercial creditors as well as to other interests.

COMPANY BACKGROUND

Until the seventies, Manville was a success by the usual standards. Incorporated in 1901, the company saw consistent growth in sales and profits. Dividends were paid every year except for the war years of 1915–16 and the depths of the depression in 1933–34. Manville was one of the "Dow Jones Industrial Thirty" for many years.

In the decades before 1970, Manville's sales grew somewhat slower than the gross national product. But the company benefited from relatively low fixed costs, due to a largely depleted and depreciated capital base and the total absence of long-term debt in the capital structure. With low operating and financial leverage, the firm was able to adapt to sales downturns in 1957, 1960, 1967, and 1970 and still earn profits in each of those years. By 1970, Manville had about $400 million ($1.1 billion in 1986 dollars) in book value net worth garnered almost entirely from the mining, manufacture, and sale of asbestos products, for which it still held a dominant market position. Appendix A describes selected pre-1970s events concerning asbestos and health.

During the 1960s, a number of the senior officials who had been with Manville since the 1930s died or retired. Compared to just the 1966 board of directors, the 1970 board had a majority of new members. In 1970, departing from a tradition of promoting from within, the board of directors installed an outsider, psychologist Richard Goodwin, as president. Thus began a prolonged effort to diversify Manville away from asbestos and to change its image.

Goodwin arranged to move the corporate headquarters from its old Madison Avenue brick building to the Denver countryside. There, he purchased the 10,000 acre Ken Caryl Ranch and planned a luxurious "world headquarters," the first phase of which was to cost $60 million.

Goodwin also led the company through more than 20 small acquisitions—in lighting systems, golf carts, irrigation sprinklers, and other products. In the process, Manville's long-term debt went from zero to $196 million and fixed costs increased severalfold. A short, steep recession in 1975 cut Manville's profits in half, back to 1970 levels. U.S. asbestos consumption had begun a rapid decline, which was to accelerate and total more than 50 percent by 1982.

And Manville was suffering reverses in its fight against the asbestos tort lawsuits. In 1972, Manville and five other asbestos companies had lost the landmark Clarence Borel asbestos tort lawsuit. The appeals court in that case wrote, "The evidence . . . tended to establish that none of the defendants ever tested its product to determine its effect on industrial insulation workers. . . . The unpalatable facts are that in the twenties and thirties the hazards of working with asbestos were recognized."[3]

In an April 1976 deposition, Dr. Kenneth Smith, former Manville medical director, told of his knowledge of asbestos dangers during the 1940s. He also revealed his 1950 finding that the lungs of 704 of the 708 Manville asbestos workers he studied showed asbestos damage. He went on to describe his unsuccessful efforts to get caution labels put on Manville asbestos products.[4]

Then, in April 1977, the "Raybestos-Manhattan Correspondence" was discovered by asbestos plaintiff attorneys. Included were many letters and memoranda among Manville officials and other asbestos industry executives. Most were written during the 1930s. After reading the papers, a South Carolina judge wrote, "The Raybestos-Manhattan Correspondence very arguably shows a pattern of denial of disease and attempts at suppression of information which is highly probative [and] reflects a conscious effort by the industry in the 1930s to downplay, or arguably suppress, the dissemi-

---

[3]*Clarence Borel* v. *Fibreboard Paper Products Corporation, et al.,* 493 F. 2d. 1076–1109 (5th Cir. 1973).

[4]Dr. Kenneth W. Smith, Discovery deposition, *Louisville Trust Company, Administrator of the Estate of William Virgil Sampson* v. *Johns-Manville Corporation,* File no. 164-122 (Court of Common Pleas, Jefferson County, Kentucky, April 21, 1987). A Manville attorney later claimed Smith was an alcoholic.

nation of information to employees and the public. . . ."[5]

Confronted with the new and damning evidence, a growing number of juries awarded punitive damages against Manville during 1981 and 1982, as much as a million dollars per claimant. And many suits named current and former Manville executives as defendants.[6] When Manville sought bankruptcy court protection in August of 1982, asbestos-health claims against the company numbered 20,000 and new suits were being filed at the rate of three an hour every business day.[7] The average cost per case, the company said, was "sharply higher" than in prior years, averaging $40,000 per claim.[8]

The managers at Manville were particularly vulnerable to charges of conspiring to hide past sins of the company, if not for committing them. The top five executives had each been with the firm since 1952 or before. All had been senior officials since at least the early seventies.[9]

The outside directors were eminent in their respective fields, but they too could hardly claim noninvolvement. Among them were the dean of the School of Architecture at Princeton and the dean of the Graduate School of Business Administration at New York University. The latter had previously been chief executive of American Can Company. Also included were the chief executive of Ideal Basic Industries, Inc., who had earlier been elected

three times as governor of Colorado, the head of Phelps Dodge Corporation, and the top manager of three other companies.[10] All but 2 of the 11 directors in 1982 had over 10 years tenure, averaging 17 years on the board. Six had joined the board in the sixties and two others, the inside directors, had worked for Manville since about 1950.[11]

Five months after the Smith deposition, the nine outside directors of Manville demanded the resignation of Richard Goodwin. According to Goodwin, the three directors who transmitted the demand refused to explain their action.[12] A later Manville chief executive would claim Goodwin had been a womanizer and an alcoholic.[13]

John A. McKinney, Manville's lawyer—who had joined the company before 1950—took over as chief executive. McKinney divested many of the Goodwin acquisitions and turned his attention to what he called *aggressive defense* of the asbestos lawsuits and the search for a "substantial acquisition." He also made plans for a $200 million expansion in the company's fiberglass operations. In his 1977 "Presidents Review," McKinney wrote, "we do not expect asbestos fiber to dominate J-M earnings to the extent it has in the past."[14]

Ideal Basic Industries (IBI), a major producer of potash and portland cement, spurned a Manville buyout initiative in early 1978. It may have been important that the chief executive of IBI, John A. Love, was on the Manville board of directors. Next, Manville began a takeover battle (with Texas Eastern Corporation) for Olinkraft Corporation, a wood products company concentrated in paperboard and paper. Olinkraft's main assets were about 600,000 acres of prime southern timberland and several paper mills.

Manville won the contest and closed the deal in the last half of 1978. The purchase price was $595 million, 2.24 times book value and over twice recent market value. About half was paid in cash and the rest was represented by a new issue of cumulative preferred stock

---

[5]Amended Order (Survival and Wrongful Death Actions), *Bennie M. Barnett, Administrator, for Gordon Luther Barnett, decreased* v. *Owens-Corning Fiberglass Corp. et al.* (Court of Common Pleas, Greenville County, South Carolina, August 23, 1978), 10 and 5.

[6]Ronald L. Motley (leading asbestos plaintiff attorney), telephone conversation with author, October 9, 1987, Charleston, South Carolina. Also see Manville Corporation, *Quarterly Report on U.S. Securities and Exchange Commission Form 10-0,* for quarter ended June 30, 1982, p. II-8 (discussion of Louisiana cases).

[7]G. Earl Parker, "The Manville Decision," paper presented at the symposium "Bankruptcy Proceedings—The Effect on Product Liability," conducted by Andrews Publications, Inc., Miami, March 1983, p. 3.

[8]Manville Corporation, "Manville Files for Reorganization," media release, August 26, 1982, p. 2.

[9]Manville Corporation, *1982 Proxy Statement,* March 25, 1982, p. 12; *Moody's Industrial Manual,* p. 2 (New York: Moody's Investor Service, 1971), p. 1424; (1972), p. 3222; (1973), p. 2907–8; and (1974), 2040.

[10]Manville Corporation, *1982 Proxy Statement,* March 25, 1982, pp. 4–7.

[11]Ibid., pp. 4–7.

[12]Herbert E. Meyer, "Shootout at the Johns-Manville Corral," *Fortune,* October 1976, pp. 146–54.

[13]W. Thomas Stephens, conversation with author at Seventh National Conference on Business Ethics, Waltham, Massachusetts, October 16, 1987.

[14]Manville Corporation, 1977 Annual Report, p. 2.

which was required to be repurchased beginning in 1987.

The directors and officers were guaranteed indemnification by Manville, a contract they had the company reaffirm in 1981.[15] The importance of such protection is illustrated by attacks by asbestos victims against the estate of Vandiver Brown, Manville vice president and secretary during the 1930s, attacks which would continue into the mid-1980s.[16]

But ordinary business problems after 1978 imperiled the managers' indemnity and rendered even their jobs insecure, not to mention the professional embarrassment failure might bring such illustrious directors and executives. That year, the company began what seemed an irreversible downward slide financially. Revenues (in 1986 dollars) fell from $2.74 billion in 1978 to a $2.18 billion annual rate for the first half of 1982. And earnings available to common stock (also in 1986 dollars) simply evaporated, going from $198 million to an $85 million annual-rate *loss*.[17] Earnings available to common stock does not include dividends on the debt-equivalent preferred stock issued in the Olinkraft acquisition. Despite its acquisitions, Manville remained intensely concentrated in construction-dependent businesses, which all suffered from the construction industry recession that began in 1979. Appendix B provides financial summaries for 1978 through the first half of 1982.

Manville's auditors, Coopers and Lybrand, qualified its opinion on the company's 1980 and 1981 annual reports.[18] Of course, Standard and Poor's and Moody's downgraded the company's debt.[19] And Manville's

insurers gave the executives little solace; they stopped paying for most of the asbestos claims by 1981,[20] and generally could not pay punitive damages anyway.

The small amounts actually paid for "asbestos health costs," $13 million in 1981 and $16 million in 1982,[21] could hardly be blamed for the financial collapse. Those costs never amounted to even 1 percent of sales. But loss of asbestos profits was clearly a major factor. Until at least 1978, the immensely profitable asbestos trade was the company's mainstay. Sales of the raw fiber alone produced 41 percent of Manville's operating profit as late as 1976, though accounting for only 12 percent of revenues that year.[22] Further, many of the company's manufactured products were asbestos based, including asbestos felts, papers, textiles, asbestos-cement shingles, asbestos-cement water and sewer pipe, and asbestos paper and millboard.[23]

Public awareness of asbestos-health dangers continued to increase and U.S. purchases of the substance fell after 1976, by 36 percent in 1980 alone.[24] From a 1974 peak of over 750,000 metric tons, U.S. asbestos consumption would fall to under 200,000 metric tons in 1985.[25] Led by lawyer McKinney, the directors voted to reorganize the company in 1981, placing the nonasbestos operations in separate corporations under the parent Manville.

By 1982, Manville's asbestos-fiber revenues were half the 1976 level. An estimated 60 percent of the fiber was sold internationally, mainly in Western Europe.[26]

---

[15]Manville Corporation, *1981 Proxy Statement,* September 11, 1981, Ex. 2, pp. 5–7.

[16]"Stay Sought for Lawsuits against Estate of Vandiver Brown," *Stockholders & Creditors News Service Re. Johns-Manville Corp. et. al.* (Edgemont, Pa: Andrews Publications, November 5, 1984), p. 3082

[17]Manville Corporation, 1982 Annual Report and Form 10-K, p. 7; and *U.S. Securities and Exchange Commission Form 10-Q,* for quarter ended June 30, 1982, p. I-2. Also, Johns-Manville Corporation, 1978 Annual Report, p. 36. U.S. Consumer Price Index figures were obtained from Ibbotson Associates, *Stocks, Bonds, Bills, and Inflation: 1987 Yearbook* (Chicago: Ibbotson Associates, 1987), p. 30.

[18]Manville Corporation, 1980 Annual Report, p. 21, and 1981 Annual Report, p. 15.

[19]See, for example, "Manville Ratings Cut by Standard and Poor's" *The Wall Street Journal,* June 11, 1982, p. 36.

[20]Manville Corporation, *U.S. Securities and Exchange Commission Form 10-Q,* for quarter ended June 30, 1982, pp. II-11–II-14.

[21]Manville Corporation, 1982 Annual Report and Form 10-K, p. 7.

[22]Manville Corporation, 1977 Annual Report, p. 1.

[23]Johns-Manville Corporation, 1977 Annual Report, pp. 8, 10, and 13.

[24]Raymond A. Joseph, "Problems Have Long Plagued Asbestos Firms," *The Wall Street Journal,* August 30, 1982, p. 15 (U.S. Interior Department figures in thousands of metric tons for 1976–81 are given as 659, 610, 619, 561, 359, and 350, respectively).

[25]Barry I. Castlemen, *Asbestos: Medical and Legal Aspects,* 2nd ed. (Clifton, N.J.: Prentice-Hall Law & Business, 1986), p. 614.

[26]Manville Corporation, 1982 Annual Report and Form 10-K, pp. 18 and 30, and Johns-Manville Corporation, 1977 Annual Report, p. 1.

And each dollar of fiber sales produced markedly less operating profit, 18 cents versus 33 cents in 1976.[27]

The stock market reflected Manville's deteriorating financial condition. By mid-August 1982, the company's common stock price had dropped below $8, less than one fourth its 1977 high.

IN FULL READINESS FOR CHAPTER 11

The company was well-prepared for a Chapter 11 filing. Manville was still able to pay its bills. But the 1978 bankruptcy amendments had removed insolvency as a requirement for filing. The Olinkraft purchase had been structured so half the cost would not come due until 1987 and later. Filing would void that obligation. The 1981 reorganization had segregated the asbestos assets in separate corporations. Each corporation could file its own Chapter 11 petition. They could submit separate or joint reorganization plans. Management could decide which.

Manville had ready access to the best consultants and attorneys. For 50 years, the firm had been close to Morgan Stanley and Company and Davis Polk and Wardwell. Morgan Stanley was the nation's leading investment banker. Davis Polk was a top New York law firm.

And there were no rebels on the management team. Eight of the eleven directors had been with Manville since the fifties and sixties. After Goodwin took over in 1970, no senior manager came in from outside. In fact, the top five executives in 1982 each had at least 30 years' tenure.

Best yet, almost none of the company's $1.1 billion debt was secured. McKinney would soon boast of "nearly $2 billion in unencumbered assets." That would prove to be a real advantage in bankruptcy. Unsecured creditors have no claim on or control over any particular assets. Their claims can be discharged under a reorganization plan.

THE BANKRUPTCY REORGANIZATION

On August 26 that year, Manville filed its bankruptcy petition. The common stock fell from $7.875 the day before the filing to $4.625 a few days later. All legal

actions against the company, including the asbestos tort lawsuits, were automatically stayed under provisions of the bankruptcy law. Appendix C summarizes the Chapter 11 process.

The company's largest division, Manville Forest Products Corporation, emerged from Chapter 11 protection in 1983. Under the court order, it was obligated to pay its commercial debt, but was free of asbestos claims.[28] Various other units, notably the main asbestos fiber subsidiaries and certain asbestos-cement pipe operations, were sold that year, also free of Manville's asbestos liabilities.[29] Appendix D provides financial summaries for several years following Manville's bankruptcy filing.

A reorganization plan for the remaining divisions was filed by Manville management in 1986. The bankruptcy judge in the case issued a confirmation order December 22, 1986. But full implementation of the plan was held up pending the outcome of two appeals from the order.[30]

The plan provided for essentially full payment of $472 million of unsecured commercial creditor claims which had not been paid earlier. Secured obligations were to be either paid in full or reinstated with payment of accrued interest. Common stockholders were to be practically dispossessed through issuance of additional shares and rights. Preferred stockholders were to receive a mixture of common and "preference" shares worth an estimated 15 percent of the face value of their preferred shares.

A trust (the A-H trust) set up to pay asbestos-health claims was to receive the following assets: (1) $615 million in expected insurance settlement proceeds, partly deferred and all contingent on the plan surviving all appeals; (2) $111 million estimated confirmation-date value in cash and receivables; (3) a zero-coupon bond worth an estimated $249 million[31]—in an October 1987 debate at the National Conference on Business Ethics, Manville chief executive, W. Thomas Stephens, said the value of the bond was $350 million; (4) other debt

---

[27]Ibid.

[28]Manville Corporation, 1983 Annual Report and Form 10K, p. 13.

[29]Ibid., p. 15

[30]See, for example, "Appeals Consolidated in 2nd Circuit (sic), Possible Hearing in October," *Stockholders & Creditors News Service* (Edgemont, Pa.: Andrews Publications, September 21, 1987), p. 6953.

[31]Arthur Sharplin, "Liquidation versus 'The Plan.'" *The Asbestos Litigation Reporter* (Edgemont, Pa.: Andrews Publications, November 21, 1986), pp. 13636–40.

securities valued at about $45 million; (5) 50 percent of Manville's common stock, which was to be required to be voted for management's choices for directors for at least four years after plan consummation—sale of the stock was to be restricted for at least five years after consummation; (6) contingent claims on 20 percent of corporate earnings beginning the fourth fiscal year after consummation and on a new issue of convertible preferred stock.[32]

After the publicity surrounding the Manville bankruptcy, hundreds of property damage (PD) claims began to be filed. They were mainly claims for estimated costs of cleaning asbestos out of the thousands of schools and government and commercial buildings where it had been used as insulation or fire proofing. By 1986 the PD claims totaled over $70 billion. Manville's plan provided that a PD trust would be set up to pay these claims. It would be initially funded with $100 million from Manville and $25 million from the A-H trust. The PD trust was also supposed to get certain extra funds the A-H might have.

The A-H claimants committee, consisting of 19 lawyers and one asbestos victim, endorsed the Manville plan, emphasizing the $2.5 billion nominal value of the A-H trust. However one expert used discounted cash flow analysis to calculate the value of the proposed trust assets at $572 million.[33]

HOW THE MANAGERS FARED

Compared to the chaos which imperiled the executives' fortunes and jobs in the months before August 1982, the situation which existed thereafter must have seemed sublime. For the executives and directors, Chapter 11 brought a lightened management load, improved pay and benefits, munificent retirement for those who desired it, and bonuses and "golden parachutes" for others. The prefiling managers and directors even arranged to continue their power over the corporation after its possible emergence from bankruptcy court protection. Finally, some of the prefiling managers were able to control, or even own, company assets freed of asbestos claims.

---

[32]Ibid.
[33]Ibid.

Lightened Management Load

When Manville filed its Chapter 11 petition, the management burden was lightened by a surplus of cash and the ability to generate income out of avoided interest. The company's receivables flowed in and $627 million in unsecured liabilities were frozen, most to be paid only after conclusion of the Chapter 11 proceedings.[34] The company was not required to pay this debt, or even accrue interest on it after the filing. Consequently, Manville's cash and marketable securities balance varied from a little over $200 million in December 1982 to over $440 million December 31, 1986—compared to $27 million on June 30, 1982, shortly before the filing.[35] The prefiling unsecured debt, including accounts payable and other accrued liabilities, was down to $490 million by December 1986.[36] But if the avoided interest on even that amount had been accrued yearly, Manville would have suffered an overall loss for the five years 1982–86 instead of the reported $92 million total net profit it reported.

Further, the managers were undoubtedly more comfortable in the legal/administrative milieu of the bankruptcy court than in the economic one of competitive business. Chairman/chief executive/president, John A. McKinney, and 4 more of the 11 directors in 1982 were attorneys (although one, William D. Tucker, Jr. had just joined the board that year). The company had been involved in asbestos-tort litigation since the 1920s. The litigation and related public affairs matters had been a dominant concern since the early 1970s. The company's success in staving off the asbestos-health claims until the 1980s contrasted with its inability to reverse the economic downslide which began in 1979.

Improved Pay and Benefits

The directors and top executives of Manville, mostly unchanged after the sixties, increased their pay and

---

[34]Manville Corporation, 1982 Annual Report and Form 10-K, December 31, 1982, pp. 6 and 11.
[35]Manville Corporation, 1982 Annual Report and Form 10-K, p. 6, 1986 Annual Report and Form 10-K, p. 39; and *U.S. Securities and Exchange Commission Form 10-Q,* for the quarter ended June 30, 1982, p. I-3.
[36]Manville Corporation, 1986 Annual Report and Form 10-K, December 31, 1986, p. 45.

improved their benefits while in bankruptcy. For example, Chief Executive John McKinney's reported cash compensation went from $408,750 in early 1982 to $638,005 in 1985, his last full year of employment. Senior Vice President Chester Sulewski's increased by 88 percent from 1982 to 1986. The cash compensation of W. Thomas Stephens, who became president in September 1986, was 39 percent higher that year than in 1985, the first year he appeared in the company's Compensation Table.[37]

The cash compensation of the 32 officers and directors of Manville was shown as $3.9 million in the March 25, *1982 Proxy Statement* (p. 10). The *1986 Annual Report and Form 10-K* (p. 63) reported cash compensation of $5.5 million for just the 25 executive officers during 1986.

Secure Retirement, "Golden Parachutes," and Bonuses

And the most senior prefiling managers were able to retire in economic security, shielded by the bankruptcy court and indemnified by Manville against the asbestos victims. The Manville reorganization plan provided that the A-H Trust would be responsible for defending and paying any future asbestos claims against the company, its insurers, or the executives and directors. McKinney's severance agreement, effective September 1, 1986, granted him cash payments totaling $1.3 million, two extra years of fringe benefits, and two extra years of longevity for retirement purposes. Two other managers were given severance agreements at the same time providing for payments totaling $1,030,000 and certain other benefits.

By December 1986, four of the five most highly paid executives shown in the *1982 Proxy Statement* had left the company. J. T. Hulce resigned as president in 1986, allegedly under pressure from the asbestos victims' committee, and was authorized $530,000 in severance pay.[38] G. Earl Parker, Manville's legal chief under

McKinney, retired in March 1987. His severance agreement, approved by the bankruptcy court in September 1987, provided for payments of $430,000 a year through 1989, a total of $1.2 million, counting from March 1987, when he stepped down.[39] But the board of directors remained mostly unchanged from the 1982 board, with only one of the nine outside directors having departed.

The executives left behind were also reassured of large termination payments upon choosing or being asked to leave and probable bonuses in the meantime. At a special board meeting in New York held on October 11, 1985, McKinney discussed "Confidential Minute Number 13," which was said to address severance pay of up to two times annual salary for officers and other "key managerial personnel" upon any termination of employment. It was agreed that the special pay would even apply to persons terminated after any assignment of a trustee in the bankruptcy case.[40]

In mid-July 1987 Manville obtained court approval for a new executive bonus plan for that year increasing the possible bonuses for certain managers from 57.5 percent of annual salaries to 97.1 percent. The allowable bonuses for achieving less than 80 percent of goals were reduced.[41]

Post-Consummation Power

The power of the prefiling directors and replacement senior managers promised to remain firm for at least four years after plan consummation, if and when that was to occur. Two new directors were appointed at the insis-

---

[37]Manville Corporation, *1982 Proxy Statement,* p. 10; 1985 Annual Report and Form 10-K, p. 79; and 1986 Annual Report and Form 10-K, p. 63.

[38]Cynthia F. Mitchell, "Manville to Pay Large Severance to 2 Executives," *The Wall Street Journal,* June 24, 1986, pp. 3 and 5. Also see Cynthia F. Mitchell, "Manville President Quits after Dispute with Asbestos Plaintiff over Top Posts," *The Wall Street Journal,* April 30, 1986, p. 34.

[39]Arthur Sharplin, "Liquidation versus 'The Plan' " *The Asbestos Litigation Reporter,* November 21, 1986, pp. 13636–40. Also see Johns-Manville Corporation et al., "Application for an Order Approving Severance Pay Agreements," *Stockholders & Creditors News Service* (Edgemont, Pa.: Andrews Publications, September 8, 1986), pp. 5569–72; and "Judge Approves Severance Pay for G. Earl Parker," *Stockholders & Creditors News Service* (Edgemont, Pa.: Andrews Publications, October 5, 1987), pp. 6988–89.

[40]"Key Manville Officers Allowed Severance in Event of Termination by Trustee," *Stockholders and Creditors News Service* (Edgemont, Pa.: Andrews Publications, April 7, 1986), p. 4495.

[41]"New Bonus Plan for Executives Approved by Court," *Stockholders and Creditors News Service* (Edgemont, Pa.: Andrews Publications, August 10, 1987) pp. 6778–79.

tence of a group of preferred shareholders in 1984,[42] but no other new outside director appeared on the 1987 board.[43] A third director, Randall Smith, a limited partner in Bear Stearns & Co., had served briefly. Smith was appointed after Bear Sterns accumulated a large holding of Manville common stock.[44] Smith resigned his directorship in late 1985. No annual or special meetings of common shareholders, at which new directors might have been elected, were permitted after the bankruptcy filing.[45]

Further, the Manville reorganization plan provided that at least half of all common shares, those held by the A-H Trust, would be voted for mangement's nominees to the board of directors for four years after the consummation date.[46] While the initial post-consummation board of directors was to include seven new outside members, six of the prefiling directors were to remain on the board, as was Chief Executive W. Thomas Stephens.[47]

Control of Assets Free of Asbestos Claims

Some of the executives who left the company were able to remain in control of substantial assets, assets then free and clear of asbestos claims against Manville. For example, the group which bought Manville's Canadian asbestos division on July 1, 1983 was headed by the chief executive officer of Johns-Manville Canada.[48] Manville even continued to get most of the profits from those divisions' asbestos sales. Aside from about $47 million apparently borrowed on the asbestos assets and remitted to Manville, the $117 million to $150 million (Canadian) selling price was payable "out of 85.5% of available future cash flows from asbestos fiber operations."[49] The other divisions sold that year, notably certain asbestos-cement pipe operations, were presumably transferred with management in place.[50]

After leaving Manville in 1986, former President Hulce and another former Manville executive helped form a company, BMZ Materials, Inc., which purchased several Manville plants with annual sales of $17.5 million. The purchase price was $5.5 million in cash and a $1.5 million promissory note.[51]

Several other sales of Manville assets were approved by the bankruptcy court at about the same time.[52] In all these cases, the assets involved were legally placed out of reach of the asbestos victims.

Even some of the managers who stayed with Manville, those in Manville Forest Products Corporation, controlled assets not subject to asbestos claims. That subsidiary accounted for more than a third of Manville's assets in 1986.[53] As previously mentioned, it emerged from bankruptcy court protection in 1983.

BENEFITS FOR ATTORNEYS AND CONSULTANTS

The Manville executives and directors found themselves able to distribute much of the largess produced by decades of asbestos production to a host of consultants and attorneys. For example, Davis Polk and Wardwell, a New York law firm which had represented Manville

---

42"Manville Adds 3 to Board to Increase Shareholder Input," *The Wall Street Journal*, August 3, 1984, p. 4.

43Manville Corporation, 1986 Annual Report and Form 10-K, pp. 56–59.

44See Dean Rotbart and Jonathan Dahl, "Manville's Common Stockholders May Have Potent Ally as Bear Stearns Bolsters Holdings," *The Wall Street Journal*, July 25, 1984, p. 51.

45See, for example, Manville Corporation, 1986 Annual Report and Form 10-K, p. 33.

46Manville Corporation, *First Amended Disclosure Statement, Second Amended and Restated Plan of Reorganization, and Related Documents*, August 22, 1986, p. 41

47Manville Corporation, 1986 Annual Report and Form 10-K, pp. 56–61.

48"Hearing on Sale of J-M Canada Scheduled for August 30," *Stockholders and Creditors News Service* (Edgemont, Pa.: Andrews Publications, August 15, 1983), p. 1315.

49Ibid.

50Ibid.

51"3 Manville Manufacturing Plants Sold to Former President Hulce," *The Denver Post*, January 5, 1988, p. 2C; and "Manville Sells Three Plants for $7 million," *Stockholders and Creditors News Service* (Edgemont, Pa.: Andrews Publications, January 11, 1988), pp. 7, 261–62.

52See, for example, "Court Approves Sale by Manville of 100 Acres for $22 Million," "Court Approves Sale of 14 Acres to Manville Joint Venture," and "Order Authorizing Sale of Manville, NJ Property," *Stockholders and Creditors News Service* (Edgemont, Pa.: Andrews Publications, January 11, 1988), pp. 7261, 7262, and 7264, respectively.

53Manville Corporation, 1986 Annual Report and Form 10K, p. 53.

since 1928, was cocounsel for the Chapter 11 proceedings and charged over $200,000 a month early in the
proceedings.[54] First Boston Corporation was authorized
$100,000 a month in late 1984 to serve as financial
adviser to certain creditor groups.[55] Through 1986,
Manville had dispensesd $64 million in Chapter 11
costs.[56] By October 1987, Manville Chief Stephens said
the number had exceeded $100 million.[57]

Leo Silverman, the "Legal Representative for Future
Claimants" appointed by the bankruptcy court, submitted bills for $2.3 million for August 1, 1984 through
December 31, 1986.[58] Dr. Frederick W. Kilbourne was
paid $73,550 for work as Manville's actuarial expert
during November 1983 through April 1984.[59] The executive director of the Association of Trial Lawyers of
America, Marianna S. Smith, was hired as chief executive officer of the A-H Trust, at $250,000 a year.

The pattern continued into 1988. For the first six
months of 1987, 22 law firms submitted bills in the
Manville Chapter 11 proceeding for $5,733,983.[60] The

"Provisional" trust budget for January–August 1987
provided $4.6 million to administer the A-H trust,
including $194,000 for executive searches, $840,000 to
pay Smith and three assistants, and $257,000 for the six
trustees who were scheduled to meet only seven times.[61]
The trust rented 32,038 square feet of office space in
Washington, D.C., at an annual cost of $849,007.[62] In
addition to their $30,000 annual compensation, each
trustee was to get $1,000 a day for meetings, intercon-
tinental travel, and other work performed for the trust.

The managing trustee was authorized $1,500 for each
day his part-time trust duties were to occupy over half
his time. The trust budget for the 10 months September
1987 through June 1988 was $9.6 million, including
$2.9 million for salaries and benefits. Adequate funding
for such expenses was assured by the transfer of $150
million from Manville to the trust and was approved by
the bankruptcy judge November 25, 1987.[63]

BENEFITS FOR THE ASBESTOS VICTIMS

By 1988, an estimated 41,500 new A-H claims were
waiting to be filed against Manville[64] and, of course,
many of the 20,000 1982 claimants had died. Total A-H
claims filed in the United States by mid-1987 against all
companies were estimated at 70,000.[65] No prefiling A-H
claim had been paid by Manville or the trust. In July
1987, the A-H trustees estimated payments from the

[54]"Four Law Firms Submit Bills Totaling $1.8 Million as of
December 31, 1982," *Stockholders and Creditors News Service*
(Edgemont, Pa.: Andrews Publications, March 14, 1983), p. 794.

[55]*In Re Johns-Manville Corporation et al., Debtors,* Third
Supplemental Order Approving Expanded Retention and Reduced Compensation of Investment Banker, 82 B 11656-76
(BRL) (SD NY November 16, 1984) reprinted in *Stockholders
and Creditors News Service* (Edgemont, Pa.: Andrews Publications, December 10, 1984), p. 3184.

[56]Manville Corporation, 1986 Annual Report and Form
10-K, p. 40; and 1983 Annual Report and Form 10-K, p. 6.

[57]Debate at the National Conference on Business Ethics,
Waltham, Massachusetts, October 16, 1987.

[58]*In Re Johns-Manville Corporation et al., Debtors,* State-
ment of Compensation of the Legal Representative for Future
Claimants and His Counsel, 82 B 11656-62 and 82 B 11664-76
(BRL) (SD NY August 14, 1987) reprinted in *Stockholders and
Creditors News Service* (Edgemont, Pa.: Andrews Publications,
September 7, 1987), p. 6945.

[59]"Affidavit of J. Thomas Beckett in Support of the Motion
of the Committee of Unsecured Creditors for an Order Autho-
rizing and Directing Final Payment to Actuarial Experts, 82 B
11656-76 (HCB) (SD NY August 3, 1987)," in *Stockholders
and Creditors News Service* (Edgemont, Pa.; Andrews Publications, August 24, 1987), p. 6819.

[60]"Firms Seek $5.7 Million in Legal Fees for Six Months
Ending June 30," *Stockholders and Creditors News Service*
(Edgemont, Pa.: Andrews Publications, September 7, 1987),
p. 6905.

[61]"Manville Personal Injury Settlement Trust Provisional
Budget/Expense Estimates (January through August 1987),"
Stockholders and Creditors News Service (Edgemont, Pa.:
Andrews Publications, August 10, 1987), p. 6800.

[62]"Terms of Lease for Personal Injury Trust Quarters Approved," *Stockholders and Creditors News Service* (Edgemont,
Pa.: Andrews Publications, December 7, 1987), p. 7193.

[63]Manville Trust Forms Being Printed; $9.2 million (sic)
Interim Budget," *Stockholders and Creditors News Service*
(Edgemont, Pa,: Andrews Publications, January 25, 1988),
p. 7295.

[64]"Plan Protects Manville, Shortchanges Victims," *Asbestos
Watch* 4, no. 1 (Fall 1986), p. 1.

[65]"JM Trust to Accept Claims in January, Negotiate Even
before Consummation," *Stockholders and Creditors News Service* (Edgemont, Pa.: Andrews Publications, July 6, 1987),
p. 6681.

trust could begin during the spring of 1988,[66] nearly six years after Manville's bankruptcy filing. By January 1988, it seemed clear the bankruptcy judge's confirmation order would be appealed to the U.S. Supreme Court unless overturned by the court of appeals.[67] The estimate of when payments could begin was moved back to "April to November 1988."[68] But in March 1988 the Second Circuit U.S. Court of Appeals was still mulling one of the appeals.[69] So the consummation date seemed likely to slip into 1989, if not beyond.

In addition to the delay, the asbestos victims had six other reasons to despair. First, consummation of the Manville plan might not occur at all, or might be reversed if it did. Second, A-H representatives in the bankruptcy court had been effectively preempted. Third, the victims were to have little control over Manville or the A-H trust for years after consummation, if and when that was to occur. Fourth, the Manville plan provided for effective subordination of A-H claims to commercial debt, even that which was unsecured. Fifth, many of Manville's prefiling assets had already been irrevocably insulated from potential claims against them by A-H victims. Sixth, the prospective payments to the A-H trust provided for in the plan were to be substantially uncertain.

Consummation Might Not Occur or Might Be Reversed

Some A-H victims were convinced the Manville plan offered their best hope for compensation. But there were at least two reasons to think consummation might not occur at all—or might be reversed if it did. First, there

was evidence the A-H trustees were concerned Manville had made inadequate disclosure of incriminating evidence during reorganization. In March 1988, Manville and the A-H trust urgently began setting up a repository to hold 44 million pages of documents produced in two major lawsuits. The repository was to be ready in six weeks and was to be open to "those involved in resolving health claims against the comnpany."[70]

Second, court rulings in late 1987 and early 1988 seemed to suggest criminal indictments of Manville or its officials were possible. Such indictments could void Judge Lifland's ability to protect the company and its managers. In two Delaware cases Raymark Corporation (formerly Raybestos-Manhattan Corporation) was found liable for civil conspiracy with Manville to conceal or misrepresent the health hazards of asbestos. And a court in Washington state ruled Manville and Raymark engaged in "concert of action" to each market asbestos-containing products without warning of their potential dangers.[71]

Concerning the Delaware cases, the court later ruled the standard of proof required in civil conspiracy was "preponderance of evidence," not the "clear and convincing" test Raymark wished to impose. The court did not address whether the stronger test had been met, only that it was not required. The judge wrote, "I find no basis for singling out this type of intentional tort, or intentional torts in general, which involve a greater level of culpability than that involved in negligent conduct, for favored treatment in the proof of the wrongdoing.[72]

---

[66]"JM Trust to Accept Claims in January, Negotiate Even before Consummation," *Stockholders and Creditors News Service* (Edgemont, Pa.: Andrews Publications, July 6, 1987), p. 6680.

[67]Marianna S. Smith, Executive Director, Manville Personal Injury Settlement Trust, "Memorandum to Attorneys with Pre-petition Cases," January 27, 1988, in *Asbestos Litigation Reporter* (Edgemont, Pa.: Andrews Publications, February 5, 1988), p. 16503.

[68]Ibid.

[69]"2nd Circuit's Delay in Kane Appeal Causes Speculation," *Stockholders and Creditors News Service* (Edgemont, Pa.: Andrews Publications, March 7, 1988), p. 7417.

---

[70]"All Manville Documents to Be Available at Repository in Denver," *Stockholders and Creditors News Service* (Edgemont, Pa.: Andrews Publications, March 7, 1988), p. 7415.

[71]"Delaware Jury Awards $75 Million in Punitive Damages against Raymark," *Stockholders and Creditors News Service* (Edgemont, Pa.: Andrews Publications, November 23, 1987), pp. 7171-72; "Delaware Jury Awards $22 Million in Punitive Damages against Raymark," *Asbestos Litigation Reporter* (Edgemont, Pa.: Andrews Publications, March 18, 1988), p. 16723; and "Washington Judge Finds Concert of Action by Raymark and J-M," *Asbestos Litigation Reporter* (Edgemont, Pa.: Andrews Publications, March 18, 1988), p. 16724.

[72]"DE Judge: Conspiracy Requires Only 'Preponderance of Evidence' Proof," *Asbestos Litigation Reporter* (Edgemont, Pa.: Andrews Publications, March 4, 1988), p. 16665.

A-H Representatives Preempted in Bankruptcy Court

After 1984, the asbestos victims were essentially powerless to affect the outcome of the Chapter 11 process, mainly because Manville management was able to neutralize their committee in the bankruptcy court. The committee consisted of 19 contingent-fee attorneys and one asbestos victim. Until early 1984, the committee had aggressively confronted Manville management. For example, during September 1983 through January 1984, the committee asked the bankruptcy court to dismiss the bankruptcy filing,[73] rejected management's proposed reorganization plan,[74] requested that Manville's top management be replaced with a trustee,[75] and even petitioned the court to cut the managers' salaries.[76] But in January 1984, Manville obtained a hearing date on its motion to void the A-H attorneys' contingent-fee agreements, which generally gave the attorneys one-third of any settlement or judgment proceeds.[77] Manville had called the fee arrangements "completely unconscionable."[78]

In March 1984, the A-H committee withdrew its motion to decrease management salaries.[79] For the ensuing two years, the, *Asbestos Litigation Reporter*,

which reported legal news and filings in asbestos cases,[80] revealed no actions by the A-H committee to contest the authority or benefits of Manville management or to remove the company from bankruptcy court protection.[81] And Manville management relaxed its effort to void the contingent-fee arrangements. By July 1984, Manville was predicting quick agreement to its reorganization plan by all parties, including the A-H committee.[82] Leading asbestos attorney, and member of the A-H committee, Ronald Motley later wrote, "[The] intimation that there is some relationship between Manville's withdrawal of its objection to contingency fees in exchange for the A-H Committee's not opposing certain management decisions is both false and insulting."[83]

The A-H committee became a strong management ally in seeking approval of the plan. For example, the committee sponsored promotional brochures for inclusion in the 100,000 information packets and ballots on the plan mailed in September 1986 to persons who provided evidence they had asbestos-related disease.[84] The brochures stated, "The Asbestos Victims Committee urges you to vote in favor of the Plan. . . . Vote yes on the Manville Reorganization Plan."[85] Despite the promotional activity, including a nationwide multimedia campaign, one of the two national organizations of asbestos victims opposed the plan and the other refused to endorse it.[86] But the A-H attorneys throughout America apparently acted en masse in voting the asbes-

---

[73]"Committee of Asbestos-Related Litigants again Asks Bankruptcy Court to Dismiss Johns-Manville Bankruptcy," *Asbestos Litigation Reporter* (Edgemont, Pa.: Andrews Publications, September 23, 1983), p. 7148.

[74]"Asbestos Claimants Committee Rejects Plan," *Asbestos Litigation Reporter* (Edgemont, Pa.: Andrews Publications, November 25, 1983), p. 7416.

[75]"Asbestos-Related Litigants Move to Have Bankruptcy Court Appoint Trustee," *Asbestos Litigation Reporter* (Edgemont, Pa.: Andrews Publications, January 6, 1984), p. 7625.

[76]"Committee of Asbestos-Related Litigants and/or Creditors Withdraws Its Motion to Reduce Salaries of Manville Officers," *Asbestos Litigation Reporter* (Edgemont, Pa.: Andrews Publications, March 16, 1984), p. 7999.

[77]"Hearing Set on Replacement for Plaintiff Contingency Fee Arrangements," *Asbestos Litigation Reporter* (Edgemont, Pa.: Andrews Publications, February 3, 1984), p. 7785.

[78]"Johns-Manville Asks Court to Void Asbestos-Claimants Attorney Fees," *Asbestos Litigation Reporter* (Edgemont, Pa.: Andrews Publications, November 25, 1983), p. 7411.

[79]"Committee of Asbestos-Related Litigants and/or Creditors Withdraws Its Motion to Reduce Salaries of Manville Officers," *Asbestos Litigation Reporter* (Edgemont, Pa.: Andrews Publications, March 16, 1984), p. 7999.

---

[80]Published by Andrews Publications, Edgemont, Pa. 19028.

[81]"In Re Johns-Manville Corp.," *Asbestos Litigation Reporter: Eight-Year Cumulative Index, February 1979–July 1987*, (Edgemont, Pa.: Andrews Publications, August 1987), pp. 37–8.

[82]"Essentials of Consensual Plan Should Be Soon," *Asbestos Litigation Reporter* (Edgemont, Pa.: Andrews Publications, July 20, 1984), p. 8687.

[83]Letter to author, April 1, 1988.

[84]"100,000 Ballots and Information Packets Being Mailed This Week," *Stockholders and Creditors News Service* (Edgemont, Pa.: Andrews Publication, September 8, 1986), p. 5513.

[85]The Committee of Asbestos-Related Litigants and/or Creditors Representing Asbestos-Health Claimants of Manville Corporation, "Questions and Answers on Asbestor-Health Claims and the Manville Reorganization Plan" and "A Very Important Message for People with Asbestos-Related Diseases," n.d., distributed in August–October 1986.

[86]Continuing personal correspondence with the top official of each organization, 1984–88.

tos victims' proxies for the plan. And tens of thousands of persons were allowed to vote as asbestos victims though they had never submitted an actual claim. In any case, Manville claimed its plan received 96 percent of the 52,440 A-H votes cast.[87]

The bankruptcy judge further weakened any active opposition to the Manville plan by asbestos victims in late 1987, when he approved the transfer of $150 million into the A-H trust. Victims' hopes were undoubtedly raised because the money was not excluded from eventually being used to pay A-H claims. But the court order approving the transfer provided that if the plan failed to survive all appeals, unspent funds would go first to pay property damage claims and then to "charitable purposes."[88] So if opposition to the Manville plan from any quarter were to prove successful, an additional $150 million of Manville's assets, in this case cash, would be unavailable to pay A-H claims. Besides, much of the money would be consumed by trust administrative expenses, then running about $1 million a month.[89]

Little Control over Manville after Consummation

Even after plan consummation, if and when that were to occur, the A-H claimants would have little power over Manville or the A-H trust. As previously mentioned, six of the prefiling directors were to remain on the post-consummation board, as was chief executive, W. Thomas Stephens. The trust would own 50 percent of Manville's common stock. But sale of the stock was to be restricted for five years and the stock was to be required to be voted for management's choices for directors for at least four years after consummation.[90]

The A-H trustees, including an investment banker, four lawyers, and a business consultant, were to have lifetime tenure. Vacancies were to be filled by the remaining trustees, after consultation with Manville and selected asbestos counsel.[91]

A-H Claims Subordinated to Those of Commercial Creditors

The plan would effectively subordinate the A-H claims to those of commercial creditors, even unsecured ones. For example, an estimated $473 million in cash would be distributed by Manville if the plan were to go into effect.[92] *But only $55 million of this would go to the victims' trust* (technically, the trust would get $80 million but would have to give $25 million of that to the property damage trust).[93] In contrast, the general unsecured creditors would get $248 million in cash.[94] The rest of the general unsecured creditors' principal, with interest, would be paid within four and one-half years.[95]

And much of Manville's pre-filing commercial debt had already been reinstated or paid as divisions were reorganized or sold free and clear of asbestos claims during the lengthy Chapter 11 process. As a result, the liabilities subject to Chapter 11 proceedings reported on Manville's balance sheet declined by $161 million from 1982–86.[96]

The plan would prohibit interest on asbestos-health claims.[97] But unsecured creditors would receive 12 percent interest.[98] They would even get $114 million in debentures for interest while Manville was in

---

[87]"Manville Says Overwhelming Majority of Voters Accepted Plan," *Asbestos Litigation Reporter* (Edgemont, Pa.: Andrews Publications, December 5, 1986), p. 13677.

[88]"Manville Pays First $150 Million to Settlement Trust Mostly for Claims," *Stockholders and Creditors News Service* (Edgemont, Pa.: Andrews Publications, December 21, 1987), p. 7231.

[89]"Manville Trust Claims Forms Being Printed; $9.2 Million (sic) Interim Budget," *Stockholders and Creditors News Service* (Edgemont, Pa.: Andrews Publications, January 25, 1988), p. 7295. The budget authorized $9.6 million for the 10 months September 1987 through June 1988.

[90]Manville Corporation, *First Amended Disclosure Statement, Second Amended and Restated Plan of Reorganization, and Related Documents.*, August 22, 1986, p. M-41.

[91]Ibid., M-65.

[92]Ibid., pp. M-402 and M-407.

[93]Ibid., pp. M-72 and M-180.

[94]Ibid., p. 47.

[95]Ibid., p. M-60.

[96]Annual reports, respective years.

[97]Manville Corporation, *First Amended Disclosure Statement, Second Amended and Restated Plan of Reorganization, and Related Documents,* August 22, 1986, p. M-46.

[98]Ibid., pp. M-46 and M-47.

bankruptcy.[99] Further, the plan provided that Manville's ability to pledge assets to the victims' trust would be limited until the unsecured creditors were paid in full.[100]

Finally, as discussed below, most payments to the A-H trust would be made from future earnings of the company, earnings which were far from certain. In contrast, general unsecured creditors would be paid from the pool of liquid assets available upon plan confirmation and within four and one-half years thereafter.

Manville Assets Shielded from A-H Claims

The reorganization of Manville Forest Products Corporation in 1983 forever insulated that division's $870 million in assets[101] from victims' claims. Another $301 million in pre-filing assets were shielded from the asbestos liabilities through the sale of Manville's U.S. pipe operations in 1982 and the asbestos fiber operations in 1983.[102] In each case, commercial creditors of the affected divisions were either paid in full or had their claims reinstated. Manville's Denver headquarters and a number of other assets were sold in 1987 and 1988, all protected from asbestos claims by the bankruptcy court. In fact, Manville retained responsibility for cleaning up asbestos residue on certain of the transferred property, further decreasing the company's potential profitability.[103]

Payments to A-H Trust Uncertain

As indicated earlier, appeals from the Manville reorganization plan appeared headed for the U.S. Supreme Court in 1988. Of course, all payments to asbestos victims contemplated under the plan were contingent upon it surviving the appeals. In addition, payments under the insurance settlement agreements, which were to constitute the preponderance of A-H trust assets during the decade after consummation, were not to be paid until after the plan became final.[104]

But even if the plan were to be put into effect, little reason was given to expect the A-H trust would have the resources needed to compensate asbestos victims. The major promised source of long-term funding for the A-H trust would be an unsecured, zero-interest Manville bond. The bond would provide for semiannual payments of $37.5 million in the 4th through the 25th fiscal years after consummation.[105]

Aside from Manville's ability to pay the bond installments, reason was present for concern about the purchasing power they would represent. Using Manville's inflation assumption of 5.2 percent,[106] those payments would each be worth $29 million (consummation-year dollars) in the 5th year, $23 million in the 10th year, $17.5 million in the 15th year, and $14 million in the 20th year. If inflation were to average, say 3 percent higher than Manville anticipated, the installments in the 20th year would each only be worth $8 million. Further, the payments could be reduced after the 13th fiscal year.[107]

But, Manville's ability to pay its obligations to the A-H trust seemed problematical at best. The company estimated a $473 million payout under its plan upon consummation, most to commercial creditors, and another $546 million during the ensuing five years. A capital spending program would consume another $800 million over those five years.[108] These amounts total $1.8 billion, compared to Manville's estimated liquidation value for all its assets of $2-2.4 billion.[109] So after paying out over 80 percent of its asset value—over twice its reported net worth[110]—in just five years, Manville promised to honor its further obligations under the plan. These further payments would average $108 million a

---

[99]Ibid., p. M-48.

[100]Ibid., pp. M-300 and M-343.

[101]Ibid., p. M-431.

[102]Manville Corporation, 1983 Annual Report and Form 10-K, pp. 17 and 18.

[103]For example, see "Court Approves Sale by Manville of 100 Acres for $22 million," *Stockholders & Creditors News Service* (Edgemont, Pa.: Andrews Publications, January 11, 1988), p. 7261.

[104]Manville Corporation, *First Amended Disclosure Statement, Second Amended and Restated Plan of Reorganization, and Related Documents.*, August 22, 1986, pp. M-55 and M-149.

[105]Ibid., pp. M-67, M-68, and M-278.

[106]Ibid., p. M-76.

[107]Ibid., pp. M-67 and M-68.

[108]Ibid., p. M-519.

[109]Ibid., p. M-399.

[110]Ibid., p. M-418.

TABLE 1   Manville Actual and Projected Sales, Earnings, and Interest

	Year	*Net Sales*	*Net Earnings*	*Interest*
Actual:	1978	$1,648	$121	$ 22
	1979	2,276	115	62
	1980	2,267	81	65
	1981	1,895	60	72
	1982	1,685	(98)	52
	1983	1,729	67	26
	1984	1,814	77	21
	1985	1,880	(45)	23
	1986	1,920	81	20
Projected:	1987	2,043	108	112
	1988	2,239	86	114
	1989	2,411	108	116
	1990	2,636	118	115
	1991	2,480	47	106

year for years six, seven, and eight, including the two annual payments of $37.5 million to the A-H trust.[111]

In proving feasibility of the plan, Manville and its investment banker, Morgan Stanley and Company, "projected" the company's cash flows forward through 1991.[112] These figures were then "extrapolated" through 2011.[113] Table 1 shows Manville's actual sales and net earnings for 1978–86[114] and the projections for 1987–91. Also listed are the interest expense amounts for each of those years. As the table illustrates, Manville's net earnings declined from $121 million in 1978 to $60 million in 1981. Then, from 1982–86 net earnings averaged only $16 million a year. Manville would have lost money for the 1982–86 period except for two nonrecurring advantages. First, the company avoided at least $50 million a year in average interest charges on liabilities subject to Chapter 11 proceedings.[115] The unsecured portions of these liabilities varied from $627 million in 1982 to $490 million in 1986. Interest expense was projected to average $85 million a year more in 1987–91 than in 1982–86. Second, other income averaged $52 million in 1982–

86.[116] It was put at only $14 million a year for 1987–91.[117]

The projections and extrapolations promised an annual average of $93 million in net earnings for the five years after 1986. This despite the payment of $85 million a year more interest than in 1982–1986 and the loss of $38 million a year in other income.

Manville and Morgan Stanley claimed income from operations would reach $370 million in 1990. They estimated it would *average* $283.4 million annually for the five years 1987–91.[118] That is almost exactly double the $145 million average for the preceding five years and more than Manville had ever earned in any single year.[119]

Manville issued extensive disclaimers for itself and Morgan Stanley concerning the projections. For example, the company reported, "NO REPRESENTATIONS CAN BE MADE WITH RESPECT TO THE ACCURACY OF THE PROJECTIONS OR THE ABILITY TO ACHIEVE THE PROJECTED RESULTS . . . the above pro forma and projected financial statements are unaudited . . . Morgan Stanley did not independently verify

---

[111]Ibid., p. M-519.

[112]Ibid., p. M-405.

[113]Ibid., pp. M-86 and M-87.

[114]Annual reports for respective years.

[115]Annual reports for respective years.

[116]Annual reports for respective years.

[117]*First Amended Disclosure Statement*, p. M-405.

[118]*First Amended Disclosure Statement*, p. M-405.

[119]Annual reports for respective years.

the information considered in its reviews of [the assumptions upon which the projections were based] and for purposes of its reviews relied upon the accuracy and completeness of all such information . . . [Under certain] PESSIMISTIC ASSUMPTIONS MANVILLE WOULD NOT GENERATE THROUGH ITS OPERATIONS SUFFICIENT CASH TO MEET ALL OF ITS OBLIGATIONS UNDER THE PLAN DURING THE PERIODS ANALYZED."[120] The presentations were accepted by the bankruptcy court as proving plan feasibility.

CONCLUSION

On October 16, 1987, Manville chief Executive W. Thomas Stephens appeared in a debate before the National Conference on Business Ethics. He generally described past company managers as well intentioned but misinformed. He mentioned certain lessons he had learned: (1) Chapter 11 was the right decision; (2) "Today, it's 'Let the seller beware' and it's as it should be,"; (3) the industry did not tell employees and customers enough about the dangers of asbestos.[121]

On the broad question of toxic waste, Stephens said, "I think the companies and the officers of those companies should be held totally accountable for their actions. . . . Some horrible mistakes have been made in the past. . . . But I think the emphasis should be on solving the problem, learning the lessons from the past, and not bashing the guys that screwed up."[122]

Later Stephens said the advantage of the asbestos victims owning stock through the A-H trust was that they would be long-term investors looking for long-term results, not just a boost in one quarter's earnings. He expressed his hope that Manville would experience a rebirth, "like the Phoenix," when it emerged from Chapter 11. He said, knowing Manville's assets and liabilities gave Manville a competitive advantage.

The cover story in the November 1987 magazine *Corporate Finance* was entitled "Miracle at Manville: How Tom Stephens Raised the Bread to Overcome Bankruptcy." The article said many considered the Manville bankruptcy "the ultimate management copout of all time." It continued, "Soon these critics will have to eat their words."[123]

In a January 1988 *Financier* article, Stephens wrote, "We have set a goal: That the new Manville will be the model of ethical corporate behavior. We have demonstrated what we can and will do. I'm proud of our record."[124]

In March 1988, Stephens took questions from a University of Montana business ethics class. He said he thought Manville's bankruptcy choice was "the most courageous and most ethical decision ever made by a Fortune 500 company."[125]

In March 1988, Manville and the A-H trust announced the creation of a depository for asbestos-related documents, mainly those produced from 1983–87 in Manville's California lawsuit against its insurance carriers and a Washington, D.C., claims court case the company had filed against the government. That lawsuit had led to the insurance settlements which were to provide most early funding to the A-H trust. The depository, located near Manville's Denver headquarters, was opened in April 1988 and, according to Manville, was to contain over 44 million pages.

A news service reported some attorneys believed Manville and the A-H trust were anxious to avoid later claims that the full extent of the company's knowledge was hidden during the reorganization. And a person familiar with the case said certain A-H trustees became concerned about such concealment after reading a court-ordered summary of evidence in the Washington claims

---

[120]*First Amended Disclosure Statement.*, pp. M-75 and M-77.

[121]"Ethical Dilemmas of Chapter 11 Reorganization," transcript of session at the Seventh National Conference on Business Ethics, October 16, 1987. Reprinted in *Stockholders and Creditors News Service Re. Johns-Manville Corp. et al.* (Edgemont, Pa.: Andrews Publications), December 7, 1987, pp. 7196–7216.

[122]Ibid., p. 7215.

---

[123]Stephen W. Quickel, "Miracle at Manville: How Tom Stephens Raised the Bread to Overcome Bankruptcy," *Corporate Finance,* November 1987 (no page numbers; reprint of article provided by Manville Corporation).

[124]W. Thomas Stephens, "Manville-Asbestos Ethical Issues Shaping Business Practice," *Financier,* January 1988, pp. 33–36.

[125]Patricia Sullivan, "The High Cost of Ethics: Manville Chief Defends Bankruptcy Decision," *The Missoulan* (Missoula, Montana, newspaper), March 10, 1988, p. 2.

court case mentioned above. Some attorneys had advised the head of the Asbestos Victims of America that the inadequate disclosure which concerned the A-H trustees might necessitate a new vote by stockholders, creditors, and claimants on the Manville reorganization. One of Manville's attorneys wrote Judge Lifland that questions had been raised about the "breadth of the restraining provisions" which protected the A-H trustees and others involved in the trust from legal attack. Judge Lifland issued a new order on March 18, 1987 barring any action concerning "administration, enforcement or settlement of accounts" related to the trust in any court except the bankruptcy court.[126]

---

[126]"Judge Lifland Bars Any Actions Relating to Administration of PI Trust, " *Asbestos Litigation Reporter* (Edgemont, Pa.: Andrews Publications, April 8, 1988), p. 16798.

On March 30, 1988 the Second Circuit U.S. Court of Appeals issued its long-awaited decision on the remaining appeal from the Manville confirmation order. The other appeal had been rejected earlier and a petition for a rehearing was also rejected, setting the stage for a further appeal to the U.S. Supreme Court. Ninety days were allowed to seek review by the Supreme Court. A spokesperson for the A-H trust said if the Supreme Court refused to hear either of the appeals, consummation of the plan could occur sometime in the fall and payments to victims could begin by year-end. Otherwise, consummation would slip into 1989, the seventh year after Manville's bankruptcy filing.

Appendix E contains comments on the Manville bankruptcy by executives and other principals in the case.

APPENDIX A: PRE-1970 EVENTS CONCERNING ASBESTOS AND HEALTH

1898. Manville founder and inventor of uses for asbestos, Henry Ward Johns, dies of "dust phthisis pneumonitis," assumedly asbestosis.

1929. Manville defending early lawsuits for asbestos deaths. The company claims employees assumed the risks of employment, knew or should have known the dangers, and were contributorily negligent. Legal documents in these cases bear signatures of senior Manville officials who would remain with the company until the 1960s.

1930. Dr. A. J. Lanza, of Metropolitan Life Insurance Company (Manville's insurer), begins a four-year study on the "Effects of Inhalation of Asbestos Dust upon the Lungs of Asbestos Workers."

1933. Based on interim results of his study, Dr. Lanza suggests Manville engage an outside consultant to do dust counts at company plants. A decision is made to train an insider to do this rather than bring in someone from outside the company.

1934. Asbestosis is considered for classification as a disease for workmen's compensation purposes. Manville's chief attorney writes to the company:

In particular we have urged that asbestosis should not at the present time be included in the list of compensation diseases, for the reason that it is only within a comparatively recent time that asbestosis has been recognized by the medical and scientific professions as a disease—in fact one of our principal defenses in actions against the company on the common law theory of negligence has been that the scientific and medical knowledge has been insufficient until a very recent period to place on the owners of plants or factories the burden or duty of taking special precautions against the possible onset of the disease in their employees.

After reviewing a draft of Dr. Lanza's report (see 1930), Manville vice president and corporate secretary, Vandiver Brown, writes Dr. Lanza requesting changes. His letter states, "All we ask is that all of the favorable aspects of the survey be included and that none of the unfavorable be unintentionally pictured in darker terms than the circumstances justify. I feel confident that we can depend upon you and Dr. McConnel to give us this 'break.' "

1935. Brown writes another industry executive, Sumner Simpson, "I quite agree that our interests are best served by having asbestosis receive the minimum of publicity." He is commenting on Simpson's response to a letter by Anne Rossiter (editor of the industry journal *Asbestos*) in which she has written, "You may recall that we have written you on several occasions concerning the publishing of information, or discussion of, asbestosis. . . . Always you have requested that for obvious reasons, we publish nothing, and, naturally your wishes have been respected."

1936.   Messrs. Brown and Simpson convince nine other asbestos companies to provide a total of $417 per month for the industry's own three-year study of the effects of asbestos dust on guinea pigs and rabbits by Dr. LeRoy U. Gardner. Simpson writes Gardner, "we could determine from time to time after the findings were made, whether we wish any publication or not." In a separate letter, Brown states, "the manuscript of your study will be submitted to us for approval prior to publication." Gardner will tell the companies of "significant changes in guinea pigs' lungs within a period of one year" and "fibrosis" produced by long fibers and "chronic inflammation" caused by short fibers. He will make several requests for additional funding but will die in 1946 without reporting final results.

1940.   Lawsuits have increased in number through the 1930s, but Manville continues to successfully defend or settle them, using the same defenses as in the 1920s but adding a statute-of-limitations defense, made possible by the long latency period of asbestos diseases. The companies continue to be able to prevent significant publicity about asbestos and health.

The war will bring spiralling sales and profits, as thousands of tons of asbestos are used in building war machines, mainly ships—resulting in exposure of tens of thousands of shipyard workers and seamen, thousands of whom will die of asbestos diseases decades later. Manville will later sue the U.S. government, claiming government had "superior knowledge" of the asbestos dangers to shipyard workers. The federal judge will rule against Manville in 1987.

1947.   A study by the Industrial Hygiene Foundation of America finds that from 3 to 20 percent of asbestos plant workers already have asbestosis and a Manville plant employing 300 is producing "5 or 6 cases annually that the physician believes show early changes due to asbestos."

1950.   Dr. Kenneth W. Smith, Manville chief physician, has given superiors his report that of 708 workers he studied only 4 were free of asbestos disease. Concerning the more serious cases he has written, "The fibrosis of this disease is irreversible and permanent so that eventually compensation will be paid to each of these men but as long as the man is not disabled it is felt that he should not be told of his condition so that he can live and work in peace and the company can benefit from his many years of experience."

1952.   John A. McKinney, Fred L. Pundsack, Chester E. Shepperly, Monroe Harris, and Chester J. Sulewski, who will be Manville's top five officers as it prepares to seek bankruptcy court protection in 1982, have all joined the company in various capacities.

1953.   Dr. Smith tries to convince senior Manville managers to authorize caution labeling for asbestos. In a 1976 deposition he will characterize their responses: "We recognize the potential hazard that you mentioned, the suggested use of a caution label. We will discuss it among ourselves and make a decision." Asked why he was overruled, Smith will say, "application of a caution label identifying a product as hazardous would cut out sales."

1956.   The Board of Governors of the Asbestos Textile Institute (made up of Manville and other asbestos companies) meet to discuss the increasing publicity about asbestos and cancer and agree that "every effort should be made to disassociate this relationship until such a time that there is sufficient and authoritative information to substantiate such to be a fact."

1957.   The Asbestos Textile Institute rejects a proposal by the Industrial Health Foundation that asbestos companies fund a study on asbestos and cancer. Institute minutes report, "There is a feeling among certain members that such an investigation would stir up a hornet's nest and put the whole industry under suspicion."

1959.   An increasing number of articles connecting asbestos with various diseases have appeared in scholarly medical journals over the last few years.

1963. Dr. I. J. Selikoff, of Mt. Sinai Medical Center in New York, reads a report of his study of asbestos workers before the American Medical Association meeting. Like the earlier research, the Selikoff study implicates asbestos ingestion as the causal factor in many thousands of deaths and injuries. Selikoff will soon estimate that at least 100,000 more Americans will die of asbestos diseases this century. The study and the articles, news stories, and academic papers which follow will focus public attention on the asbestos and health issue. An estimated 100 articles on asbestos-related diseases will appear in 1964 alone.

1964. For the first time, Manville agrees to place caution labels on asbestos products. The labels say, "Inhalation of asbestos in excessive quantities over long periods of time may be harmful" and suggests that users avoid breathing the dust and wear masks if "adequate ventilation control is not possible." The company's most profitable— and deadly—product, bags of asbestos fiber for distribution to other manufacturers and insulators throughout the world, will not be caution labeled for another five years.

APPENDIX B: MANVILLE FINANCIAL SUMMARIES, BEFORE AUGUST 26, 1982

	Income Statements ($ in millions)*				
	1982 6 mos.	*1981*	*1980*	*1979*	*1978*
Sales	$949	$2,186	$2,267	$2,276	$1,649
Cost of sales	784	1,731	1,771	1,747	1,190
Selling, G & A exp.	143	271	263	239	193
R&D and eng. exp.	16	34	35	31	33
Operating income	6	151	197	259	232
Other income, net	1	35	26	21	28
Interest expense	35	73	65	62	22
Income before inc. taxes	(28)	112	157	218	238
Income taxes	2	53	77	103	116
Net income	(25)	60	81	115	122
Div. on preferred stock	12	25	25	24	0
Net income for C.S.	$(37)	$ 35	$ 55	$ 91	$ 122

*Totals may not check, due to rounding.

**Business Segment Information
($ in millions)***

	1981	1980	1979	1978	1977	1976
Revenues:						
Fiberglass products	$ 625	$ 610	$ 573	$ 514	$ 407	$ 358
Forest products	555	508	497	0	0	0
Nonfiberglass insulation	258	279	268	231	195	159
Roofing products	209	250	273	254	204	171
Pipe products and systems	199	220	305	303	274	218
Asbestos fiber	138	159	168	157	161	155
Industrial and special products	320	341	309	291	301	390
Corporate revenues, net	12	9	11	20	12	(22)
Intersegment sales	(95)	(84)	(106)	(94)	(74)	(56)
Total	$2,221	$2,292	$2,297	$1,677	$1,480	$1,291
Income from operations:						
Fiberglass products	$ 90	$ 91	$ 96	$ 107	$ 82	$ 60
Forest products	39	37	50	0	0	0
Nonfiberglass insulation	20	27	27	35	28	18
Roofing products	(17)	9	14	23	14	8
Pipe products and systems	0	(5)	18	26	24	(3)
Asbestos fiber	37	35	56	55	60	60
Industrial and special products	50	55	43	36	25	19
Corporate expense, net	(23)	(38)	(23)	(23)	(24)	(49)
Eliminations and adjustments	3	11	(2)	1	3	2
Total	$ 198	$ 223	$ 280	$ 260	$ 212	$ 116

*Totals may not check, due to rounding.

**Balance Sheets
($ in millions)***

	June 30	December 31			
	1982	*1981*	*1980*	*1979*	*1978*
Assets					
Cash	$ 10	$ 14	$ 20	$ 19	$ 28
Marketable securities	17	12	12	10	38
Accounts and notes receivable	348	327	350	362	328
Inventories	182	211	217	229	219
Prepaid expenses	19	19	20	31	32
Total current assets	$ 576	$ 583	$ 619	$ 650	$ 645
Property, plant and equipment:					
Land and land improvements		119	118	114	99
Buildings		363	357	352	321
Machinery and equipment		1,202	1,204	1,161	1,043
		$1,685	$1,679	$1,627	$1,462
Less: Accumulated depreciation and depletion		(525)	(484)	(430)	(374)
		$1,160	$1,195	$1,197	$1,088
Timber and timberland, net		406	407	368	372
	$1,523	$1,566	$1,602	$1,565	$1,460
Other assets	148	149	117	110	113
	$2,247	$2,298	$2,338	$2,324	$2,217
Liabilities					
Short-term debt	$	$ 29	$ 22	$ 32	$ 23
Accounts payable	191	120	126	143	114
Employee compensation and benefits		77	80	54	45
Income taxes		30	22	51	84
Other liabilities	149	58	61	50	63
Total current liabilities	$ 340	$ 316	$ 310	$ 329	$ 329
Long-term debt	499	508	519	532	543
Other noncurrent liabilities	93	86	75	73	60
Deferred income taxes	186	185	211	195	150
	$1,116	$1,095	$1,116	$1,129	$1,083
Stockholders' Equity					
Preferred	$ 301	$ 301	$ 300	$ 299	$ 299
Common	60	59	58	208	197
Capital in excess of par	178	174	164	0	0
Retained earnings	642	695	705	692	643
Cumulative currency translation adjustment	(47)	(22)	0	0	0
Less: Cost of treasury stock	(3)	(3)	(4)	(4)	(6)
	$1,131	$1,203	$1,222	$1,196	$1,134
	$2,247	$2,298	$2,338	$2,324	$2,217

*Totals may not check, due to rounding.

APPENDIX C: HOW CHAPTER 11 WORKS

Chapter 11 of the U.S. Bankruptcy Code was passed by Congress in 1978 with an effective date of October 1, 1979. This law replaced various business reorganization provisions in earlier law. The new act was amended in 1984 and 1986. An apparent premise of Chapter 11 is the pleasing idea that most businesses are worth at least as much as going concerns as in liquidation.[127] If this supposition is true, stockholders and creditors may get more out of a troubled company by allowing it to continue operating than by shutting the company down. A societal benefit is that employees keep their jobs and the community keeps the tax base and economic and social activity related to the debtor firm. Practically any company or individual may seek Chapter 11 protection. Insolvency is not a requirement.

Administration of the Debtor Firm

A U.S. bankruptcy court assumes oversight of any firm which desires to "reorganize" under Chapter 11. Upon filing, the firm becomes the "debtor in possession" (DIP) with the powers and obligations of a trustee in bankruptcy. The prefiling managers continue to operate the company in "the ordinary course of business" while a plan to emerge from court protection is being formulated, approved, and confirmed.

U.S. bankruptcy judges serve 14- year terms. Because these judges do not have the lifetime tenures and salary protection of other federal judges, they are limited to ruling on "noncontroversial" matters. Since many of the issues in bankruptcy are highly controversial, each bankruptcy court operates under the supervision of a federal district court. A U.S. trustee helps in the administration of cases under the bankruptcy court's jurisdiction.

A committee of unsecured creditors is appointed by the U.S. trustee. A committee of equity security holders may also be appointed, and usually is. Other committees or advocates may be established if necessary to represent interests which diverge from those of shareholders and unsecured creditors. In the *Manville Corporation* case, for example, a committee was set up for present asbestos tort claimants and an individual was appointed as an advocate for future claimants. In the *A. H. Robins* case, a committee was formed to represent women who had used the company's Dalkon Shield intrauterine device. The committees are charged with representing their respective claimant groups and participating in the formulation of a plan of reorganization.

For the first 120 days after filing, only the DIP can submit a reorganization plan. If a plan is not submitted within 120 days and accepted by "impaired" claimant groups within 180 days, any party in interest, even an individual shareholder or creditor, may file a plan. Both time limits may be extended or shortened for cause by the bankruptcy court. For example, Manville Corporation was given more than four years to prepare its plan and seek approval of it. On the other hand, Worlds of Wonder, Inc., filed for Chapter 11 protection in December 1987. The company's banks and unsecured creditors were allowed to submit a plan, which was approved by the bankruptcy court in March 1988.

The bankruptcy judge is authorized to confirm a plan if the following requirements, among others, are met. The plan must be proposed in good faith and the proponent must disclose certain specified information. Each holder of a claim or interest who has not accepted the plan must be allowed at least as much value, as of the plan's effective date, as Chapter 7 liquidation would provide. Each class of claims or interest which is "impaired" under the plan must have accepted the plan—unless the judge rules the plan does not discriminate unfairly and is fair and equitable with respect to the class.[128] In general, a plan is considered fair and equitable with respect to nonapproving impaired classes if it treats them equally in comparison to other classes of equal rank and if their allowed claims will be fully

---

[127]The popularity of leveraged buyouts and takeovers, after which acquisitions are dismembered and sold, suggests this may not be an entirely valid assumption.

[128]A class of claims or interests is unimpaired if reinstated and the holders compensated for damages or if paid in cash. Acceptance of a plan by a creditor class requires approval by over half in number and at least two thirds in amount of allowed claims in the class. Classes of interests, such as shareholders, must approve by at least two thirds in amount of such interests.

satisfied under the plan before more junior classes receive any distribution at all. Approval of a plan under this provision is called a *cramdown*. Finally, confirmation of the plan must not be likely to be followed by the need for further financial reorganization or liquidation.

While the plan is being negotiated, approved, and confirmed, all prefiling claims are automatically stayed and executory contracts may be unilaterally canceled by the debtor. The court has authority to lift the automatic stay with regard to particular claims. Also, the cancellation of executory contracts may create allowable claims against the debtor estate.

Ideally, the plan will provide that the value of the going concern as of the effective date of the plan will be allocated first to the administrative costs of the proceeding and any postfiling obligations of the debtor and then to the claimant groups in order of their "absolute priority in liquidation." Thus, the allowed prefiling claims on the debtor estate may be satisfied in this sequence: (1) secured debt (up to the value of respective collateral as of the effective date of the plan), (2) unsecured debt (including nominally secured debt above the value of respective collateral), and (3) equity claims in order of preference (e.g., preferred, then common). The "value" may be in the form of cash, securities, or other real or personal property and should be at least equivalent to what each party would have gotten if the company had been liquidated. Any claim not provided for in the final reorganization plan is discharged.

Managerial Incentives in Chapter 11

After filing for reorganization, management is bombarded with powerful conflicting demands. Employees want their jobs assured at the same or higher pay levels. Stockholders want share price to be propped up and dividends to be reinstated at the earliest possible time. Creditors demand payment or special considerations such as extra collateral or higher interest rates. The typical bankruptcy judge wants decorum and consensus to prevail and rapid progress to be made toward consummation of a workable plan.

Managers are forestalled from their traditional role of representing only shareholder interests. Shareholders have a committee to look out for them and putting management on their side would prejudice the interests of other claimants. Besides, little or no shareholder equity may be left in the debtor firm, so the court may rule there is no shareholder interest to protect. To prevent shareholders from extracting undue consideration from managers or voting in new ones, shareholders may be disenfranchised during the reorganization process. For example, the judge in the five-years-long *Manville* case turned down several petitions to require management to conduct annual and special stockholder meetings. He even disbanded the shareholders' committee in the bankruptcy court.

A common premise is that filing for chapter 11 protection stigmatizes management.[129] But unlike most fiduciaries, management of a Chapter 11 debtor has strong financial interests in its truster. As compared to outright liquidation or austere survival without court protection, bankruptcy reorganization can lead to improved pay and benefits, lengthened careers, lowered job demands, and heightened respectability for the managers. So burdened with profound self-interest and faced with an ambiguous charter, managers may seek to turn the reorganization process to personal ends.

_____

[129]See, for example, Robert I. Sutton and Anita L. Callahan, "The Stigma of Bankruptcy: Spoiled Organizational Image and Its Management," *Academy of Management Journal* (1987), pp. 405–436.

APPENDIX D: MANVILLE FINANCIAL SUMMARIES, AFTER AUGUST 26, 1982

Income Statements
($ in millions)*

	1987†	1986	1985	1984	1983	1982
Sales	$1,541	$1,920	$1,880	$1,814	$1,729	$1,772
Other income, net	31	39	62	59	61	34
	1,572	1,959	1,942	1,873	1,791	1,806
Cost of sales	1,136	1,452	1,473	1,400	1,370	1,391
Selling, G & A expenses	166	235	246	238	224	222
R&D and eng. exp.	27	39	35	36	35	28
Operating income	243	233	188	200	161	163
Loss on disp. of assets	(21)	47	151	0	(3)	110
Empl. sep. and ret. costs						39
Asbestos health costs	6	11	52	26	20	16
Interest expense	17	20	23	21	26	52
Chapter 11 costs	8	17	9	17	18	2
Income—cont. oper.	233	138	(47)	135	100	(56)
Income taxes	100	57	(2)	58	40	32
Net inc.—cont. ops.	133	81	(45)	77	60	(88)
Net inc.—discont. oper.	0	0	0	0	7	(10)
Net income	$ 133	$ 81	$ (45)	$ 77	$ 67	$ (98)

*Totals may not check, due to rounding.
†Nine months ended September 30. Sales for the year totaled $2.063 billion. Net income for 1987 was $73 million, after an extraordinary charge due to payment of $150 million to the A-H trust.

Business Segment Information
($ in millions)*

	1987†	1986	1985	1984	1983	1982
Revenues:						
Fiberglass products	$ 652	$ 809	$ 803	$ 781	$ 718	$ 609
Forest products	450	541	459	451	415	436
Specialty products	469	611	674	645	683	829
Corporate revenues—net	26	31	43	38	36	15
Intersegment sales	(25)	(33)	(37)	(42)	(61)	(82)
Total	$1,572	$1,959	$1,942	$1,873	$1,791	$1,806
Income from operations:						
Fiberglass products	$ 113	$ 133	$ 106	$ 115	$ 97	$ 75
Forest products	84	68	43	63	52	48
Specialty products	45	46	33	28	19	51
Corporate expense—net	(4)	(18)	(1)	(6)	(6)	(18)
Eliminations and adjmts	5	4	7	0	0	7
Total	$ 243	$ 233	$ 188	$ 200	$ 161	$ 164

*Totals may not check, due to rounding.
†Nine months ended September 30. Sales for the year totaled $2.063 billion. Net income for 1987 was $73 million, after an extraordinary charge due to payment of $150 million to the A-H trust.

**Balance Sheets
($ in millions)***

	1986	*1985*	*1984*	*1983*	*1982*
			December 31		
Assets					
Cash	$ 8	$ 7	$ 9	$ 19	$ 11
Mkt securities—at cost	437	314	276	240	206
Accounts and notes receivable	292	314	285	277	310
Inventories	153	153	164	141	152
Prepaid expenses	24	29	17	22	17
Total current assets	914	817	752	700	696
Property, plant & equip					
Land and improvements	99	95	96	97	108
Buildings	312	299	308	303	332
Machinery and equip	1,234	1,160	1,121	1,036	1,090
Less acc dpr & depl	586	538	513	472	547
	1,059	1,017	1,013	984	983
Timber and tbrland—net	376	385	392	395	402
PP&E—net	1,434	1,402	1,405	1,379	1,385
Other assets	165	174	182	174	154
	$2,513	$2,393	$2,339	$2,253	$2,236
Liabilities and Stockholders' Equity					
Short-term debt	$ 30	$ 26	$ 20	$ 94	$ 12
Accounts payable	93	84	102	65	86
Accrued employee compensation and benefits	103	94	81	14	63
Income taxes	16	12	18	9	32
Other accrued liabilities	62	69	35	26	29
Total current liabilities	304	286	256	209	221
Long-term debt	80	92	84	713	736
Liabilities—Chap. 11 proceedings	575	578	574	5	12
Other noncurrent liabilities	118	115	67	61	60
Deferred income taxes	161	144	162	136	140
	1,239	1,214	1,142	1,122	1,170
Preferred stock	$ 301	$ 301	$ 301	$ 301	$ 301
Common Stock	60	60	60	60	60
Capital in excess of par	178	178	178	178	178
Retained earnings	749	667	713	635	568
Cum. curr. transl. adj.	(11)	(26)	(53)	(41)	(39)
Cost of treas. stock	(2)	(2)	(2)	(2)	(2)
	974	878	896	831	765
	$2,513	$2,393	$2,339	$2,253	$2,236

*Totals may not check, due to rounding.

APPENDIX E: COMMENTS BY MANVILLE EXECUTIVES AND OTHER PRINCIPALS

John A. McKinney (letter to author): "The suggestion that the Chapter 11 filing was for the benefit of Manville Officers is laughable. . . . The filing preserved the position of the victims as equal creditors (virtually all unsecured) in the event of a financial calamity."

W. Thomas Stephens (letters to author): "There are really only two questions. First: How do we compensate for the mistakes already made? And, second: How do we prevent another problem like that from ever arising in our society again. . . . Nothing worse could happen to the asbestos health claimants than to initiate a liquidation process. . . . There are a lot of us in this case who didn't cause this problem. As professionals, however, we were brought in to solve it. . . . Personally, I am proud that we have found a solution to a very, very complex legal, social and financial problem."

Leading A-H Attorney Ronald L. Motley (letters to author): "After four years of discussions, negotiations and consultations with our committees and investment consultants, the overwhelming majority of the AH Committee, including the representative of the Asbestos Victims of America, voted in favor of the Plan of Reorganization which was largely shaped by Leon Silverman, in consultation with myself, Stan Levy, and our counsel, Elihu Inselbuch . . . the addition of the property damage weight to the scales led many of us to view the settlement as being in the best interest of the personal injury claimants. . . .

[The] intimation that there is some relationship between Manville's withdrawal of its objection to contingency fees in exchange for the AH Committee's not opposing certain management decisions is both false and insulting."

F

Strategy Change, Renewal, and Turnaround

18.   *The New Chrysler Corporation: Fall and Rise*

The key figure associated with the beginnings of the auto industry was Henry Ford. The second major figure to move the industry was Walter P. Chrysler. Chrysler was the head of the Buick Division of General Motors, but left the company in 1920 after a dispute with the chairman, William Durant. In 1923, Chrysler came out of retirement to reorganize the dying Maxwell and Chalmers Motor Car Companies. He was successful at this venture and later formed the Chrysler Corporation. In 1928, the Chrysler Corporation bought out Dodge and Plymouth, and by 1940 it had captured 25% of the domestic auto market. From the days of the innovations of Walter Chrysler, the Chrysler Corporation has always had a dominating prowess in the field of engineering. Their engineers were the first to alleviate the vibrations in cars and to design electronic ignitions, modern electronic voltage regulators, hydraulic brakes, and under-the-hood computers. These past successful accomplishments convinced Lee Iacocca, the present chairman, that the Chrysler Corporation still had a chance for future success. Thus began Chrysler's fight for survival, driven by Iacocca, in the late 1970s and early 1980s.

THE SITUATION IN 1978

After beginning his career at Ford in August 1946, Lee Iacocca rose to the presidency of Ford, second only to Henry Ford himself. However, on July 13, 1978, Iacocca was fired by a ''threatened'' Henry Ford. During the summer of that year, Iacocca was offered top-management positions at several corporations. The offer he finally accepted was the one made by the severely ailing Chrysler Corporation. When he accepted the position as Chrysler's president, Chrysler announced a third-quarter loss of almost $160 million, its worse

This case was prepared by Richard E. Miller and M. Reza Vaghefi.

deficit ever. At Chrysler, Iacocca found many seemingly insurmountable problems.

The first problem was the lack of a solid organization structure. There was no cooperation between individual departments, even for those departments that should have naturally formed a close relationship, such as engineering and manufacturing, and manufacturing and sales. Chrysler was a group of miniempires, with no one paying attention to what anyone else was doing. One possible contributing factor to this apathy was the fact that vice presidents were often transferred from one division to another. If top management felt a vice president had performed well in his particular field, they would not hesitate to move him to another area in the organization, the assumption being that if he could run one division efficiently, he must be able to manage another just as well.

The second problem at Chrysler was the lack of financial controls. There was no financial plan or projection of financial condition; consequently, top management was not aware that the company was running out of cash. John Ricardo, the chairman of Chrysler, and Bill McCagh, the treasurer, were spending the majority of their time dealing with the day-to-day concerns of keeping the outstanding Chrysler loans intact. Therefore they were limited in their effectiveness to plan long-term strategy and manage the company's overall operations.

A third problem brought to Iacocca's attention was the fact that over 50,000 automobiles had been taken out of the production schedule for the first quarter of 1979 alone because there were no dealer orders for the cars rolling off the production line. Chrysler regularly amassed a huge inventory of cars, known as the sales bank. The company would then deplete the inventory by offering lower prices for the cars to the dealers at the end of each month. The lack of organizational plan and marketing strategy was stated succinctly by Lee Iacocca in his autobiography (Iacocca, 1984, p. 163).

In the summer of 1979, when Chrysler first approached the government for help, the sales bank contained eighty thousand unsold vehicles. At one point the number reached as high as a hundred thousand units, representing about $600 million in finished inventory. At a time when our cash was dwindling anyway and interest rates were high, the costs of carrying this inventory were astronomical. But even worse, the cars were just sitting there in the great outdoors and slowly deteriorating.

Another situation that existed was the lack of attractive, innovative, and unique products among Chrysler offerings. Chrysler Corporation had lost the innovative image that it had enjoyed for many years. Chrysler's strategy was now one of playing catch-up to Ford and General Motors. In 1978, Chrysler's two divisions, Chrysler-Plymouth and Dodge, had a total of 15 models to offer and an 11.05% market share compared to Ford's 23.54% and GM's 47.70%.

Each of the three problems demanded Lee Iacocca's attention, and their alleviation depended on Iacocca having a homogeneous, competent, and totally familiar team who could project confidence and a unique capability in the automotive industry. So the first step was put in effect: a survival strategy.

SURVIVAL

During a three-year period, Iacocca had to fire 33 of Chrysler's 35 vice presidents. Iacocca was not daunted by their lack of ability to adapt to his system of management. With his Ford notebooks in hand, he began contacting competent executives he was familiar with and put together a new management team. Iacocca now felt confident that he and his new team could turn the ailing company around. One mistake they made, however, was not anticipating the Shah of Iran's departure or a lengthy recession. On January 16, 1979, the Shah left Iran, and within a few weeks, due to the shutdown of the Iranian oil industry and a chaotic world oil market, oil companies followed OPEC's lead and increased the price of oil from $12 a barrel to $36. The entire auto industry was shaken, and Chrysler, being the weakest auto company, was devastated. Just as Chrysler was taking expensive measures to retool and begin producing more small cars, the economy plunged into the worst recession in 50 years. Annual sales of cars sold were cut almost in half. Chrysler had to close plants and fire and lay off both salaried and hourly workers. In April 1980 alone, Chrysler cut their white-collar ranks by 7,000 people. Lee Iacocca, in an interview with Tom Brokaw, said "The ultimate price (for Chrysler's suc-

cess) was paid by the 20,000 white-collar people we laid off, probably forever, and the 40,000 blue-collar workers in the cutbacks and closing of plants and the thousand or so dealers. They paid the ultimate price" (NBC News Special Report, 1984). However, all the cutting and slashing could not counter what the government and economy were doing to Chrysler.

CONSOLIDATION

The Loan Guarantee Act was passed at the end of 1979, and it gave Chrysler a possible chance to hold their ground. The loan by itself was not enough to save Chrysler; other measures had to be taken. Iacocca began by taking a self-imposed cut in salary from $360,000 annually down to $1 a year. Then he started in on the executives by tossing out their stock-incentive plan and cutting salaries by 10%, which had never before been done in the auto industry. The third cut was suffered by the unions and their members. In Iacocca's own words (Iacocca, 1984, p. 233):

> I had to lay it on the line. I talked tough to them. "Hey boys," I said, "I've got a shotgun at your head. I've got thousands of jobs available at seventeen bucks an hour. I've got none at twenty so you better come to your senses." A year later when things got even worse, I had to go back to them a second time. One bitter winter night at ten o'clock I spoke to the union negotiating committee. It was one of the shortest speeches I've ever given; "You've got until morning to make a decision. If you don't help me out, I'm going to blow your brains out. I'll declare bankruptcy in the morning and you'll all be out of work. You've got eight hours to make up your minds. It's up to you."

Concessions had to be made by all the people from executives to suppliers all the way down to the workers in order for Chrysler to survive. "And that's how Chrysler pulled through. It wasn't the loans that saved us, although we needed them badly. It was the hundreds of millions of dollars that were given up by everybody involved. I called this equality of sacrifice" (Iacocca, 1984, p. 230).

In addition to across-the-board cuts from unions, employees, and executives, the New Chrysler Corporation embarked on a massive rebate campaign that was controversial to say the least. Chrysler had to resort to drastic measures to clear the lots of thousands of cars sitting there and rusting. The rebate campaign has now become an integral part of pricing policy not only of the automotive industry, but of whoever has a commodity to sell from a bottle of Italian wine to an expensive car.

The most extraordinary feature of this period was election of Douglas Fraser, president of the United Auto Workers of America, to the board of directors of Chrysler. This was yet another unconventional way that Iacocca dealt with the issue of consolidation of the car company.

COUNTERATTACK

"Net income for 1984 for $2.38 billion, $240 million better than our previous profit record, set just last year. This produced earnings of $18.88 per common share in 1984, compared with $5.79 per common share in 1983. At the end of the year, total debt was 19.7 percent of the total debt plus equity—down from 52.7 percent in 1983 and 69.8 percent in 1982, and our best ratio in 17 years" (Chrysler Corporation, 1984, p. 6). These words are from Lee Iacocca to the stockholders, as reported in Chrysler's 1984 Report to the Shareholders. From 1980, when Chrysler received loans backed by U.S. government guarantees, to 1984, Chrysler Corporation has traveled a long road, with many highlights. In 1980, Chrysler launched its most successful line of products led by the K-cars, Dodge Aries, and Plymouth Reliant. Aires and Reliant both received the *Motor Trend* Car of the Year award, and Chrysler products achieved the best corporate average fuel economy in the industry.

In 1981, Chrysler was the only U.S. automobile company to increase both its unit sales and its market share, and once again it had the best corporate fuel economy in the industry—28.4 miles per gallon, up from 25.5 miles in 1980. With the success of the Dodge Aries and Plymouth Reliant, the highest mileage six-passenger cars on the market, Chrysler sales accounted for 22% of the compact-car market segment. In 1981, Chrysler introduced the Dodge Power Ram 50 from Mitsubishi, a four-wheel-drive pickup that was named "Four Wheeler of the Year" by *Four Wheeler* magazine.

In 1982, Chrysler recorded its first third-quarter profit in five years; this was aided by two important developments. Chrysler sold its defense subsidiary, Chrysler

Defense Incorporated, which increased their cash flow. And, most importantly, between 1980 and 1982 Chrysler has reduced its fixed costs by $1 billion and cut its break-even point in half. Chrysler introduced the first U.S.-built convertible in six years, which proved very popular with the car-buying public. During 1982, Chrysler launched a record $6.6 billion program to develop and design products capable of capturing special segments of the market. This program is enabling Chrysler to establish itself as a company that produces innovative and attractive products—exactly the opposite of the image they had projected for years.

The year 1983 was a banner one for Chrysler, highlighted by their excellent financial position. This position was attributed to four factors. The first factor was the repayment of $1.2 billion in government-guaranteed loans, seven years early, which saved $392 million in interest and government fees. The second factor was the classifying of $1.1 billion of preferred stock into common stock. The third factor was the placing of the winning bid of $311 million for the 14.4 million Chrysler warrants held by the U.S. government. These warrants were retired, and the danger of their potential dilution and stock price effect was alleviated. Fourth, Chrysler resumed dividend payments on 10 million shares of preferred stock. This year also saw Chrysler launch the first American-built, front-wheel-drive sport cars, the Dodge Daytona and Chrysler Laser. Once again, Chrysler received a prestigious commendation for the Dodge Daytona Turbo Z from *Car and Driver* as one of the 10 best cars of the year. The company boosted its product-investment plan from $6.6 million to $8 billion. Chrysler's commitment to quality was evidenced by the facts: 7,403 Chrysler cars were recalled because of defects, compared to 1.6 million Fords, 1.2 million GM cars, and 1.2 million Japanese imports.

During 1984, Chrysler opened the first new auto plant in 20 years, the Sterling Heights Assembly Plant in Missouri. It is one of the most advanced and automated assembly plants in the world, with 57 welding robots, 32 material-handling robots, and 162 lasers and cameras that inspect more than 350 points on the car body. Chrysler renewed their financial strength even further by retiring their preferred stock and buying back close to 20% of their outstanding common stock. The two minivans, Plymouth Voyager and Dodge Caravan, received the *Consumer's Digest* Consumer Hall of Fame award and were listed by *Car and Driver* the best minivans of 1984. In October 1984, Chrysler Corporation announced its plan to increase capital spending to $9.5 billion over the next five years, including an accelerated new-car program that called for introducing a new car every six months. This is the attitude that has helped Chrysler reach its heights of success and will help continue the growth and prosperity begun by its chairman, Lee Iacocca.

GLOBALIZATION

During the summer of 1978, while Iacocca was semiretired, he entertained the concept of a venture called Global Motors, based on his product-market mix. According to this vision, a combination of German engineering, Japanese production, and American marketing could be most efficient in this global industry. His idea called for an international arrangement between car companies of Europe, Japan, and the United States. "The partners I had in mind for Global Motors were Volkswagen, Mitsubishi, and Chrysler, although the plan could also work with a different partner such as Fiat, Renault, Nissan, or Honda. But Chrysler was the logical American choice," (Iacocca, 1984, p. 142). Iacocca dismissed the idea after he was advised that the plan would run counter to American antitrust laws. Since that time, a new attitude has prevailed that might possibly have allowed such an arrangement. Evidence that gives support to this notion is provided by the joint-venture agreement between two of the largest automakers in the world, General Motors and Toyota, signed in February 1983. The formal dedication of the New United Motor Manufacturing Incorporated (NUMMI) plant occurred at Fremont, California, in March 1985. "I believe what we're doing in this plant will help the balance of trade," Smith [GM Chairman] said, noting that the cars are "being produced here rather than being imported" (*Automotive News,* April 8, 1985). The Toyota chairman, Toyoda, said NUMMI "will continue to better relationships between Japan and the U.S. and will help the automotive industry prosper in both countries" (*Automotive News,* April 8, 1985). Japan's ambassador to the United States, Nobuo Matsunage, said the joint venture "demonstrates that Japan and the U.S. are their largest trading partners and confident investors in each other's economic growth and strength (*Automotive News,* April 8, 1985)." At the same ceremonies Smith also said that GM will continue to pursue joint-venture activities aggressively around the world wherever

it is in the interest of the corporation. This attitude seems to be quite prevalent at other U.S. auto manufacturers. At first mention of the agreement between GM and Toyota, Chrysler filed a lawsuit to block the joint venture. However, in April 1985, Chrysler dropped the lawsuit after a settlement was reached between the companies. The agreement calls for an eight-year active cooperation between GM and Toyota instead of the original 12 years. "Active cooperation" refers to the GM employees who are part of the venture. The agreement also restricts GM to buying no more than 250,000 units annually from either Toyota or NUMMI for sale or distribution in the United States and Canada. Chrysler had alleged the joint venture would have a devastating effect on competition because GM and Toyota are the price leaders in their respective markets. The increased realization of interdependence between countries of the world has sent other automobile manufacturers scurrying for partners, as exemplified by the joint-venture agreement between Chrysler and Mitsubishi. The dropping of the lawsuit was viewed by many as a prelude to Chrysler's announcement of the Mitsubishi joint venture. However, Baron Bates, Chrysler's vice president for public relations, said "It has nothing to do with it. Our basic argument had to do with the size of the venture. Chrysler and Mitsubishi are smaller companies. If GM were to do something with Isuzu or Suzuki, we would have no objection. Bigness was the issue" (*Automotive News,* April 15, 1985, p. 2). Presently, GM is importing Isuzu-built Spectrums and Suzuki-built Sprints for sale through their Chevrolet dealers. General Manager Robert D. Burger said, "the nine states where Sprint was launched account for 19 percent of total U.S. small-car sales. The sixteen Eastern states where Spectrum is being launched account for 43 percent (*Automotive News,* April 15, 1985, p. 2).

In 1983, before the GM-Toyota plan was given the go-ahead by the Federal Trade Commission, Iacocca said, "If GM carries out its Japanese strategy, car imports from Japan will climb to 4 million because Chrysler and Ford will import them too, instead of making them here, and the U.S. will be out of the small car business" (*Forbes,* November 7, 1983, p. 43). How prophetic! Chrysler and Mitsubishi began their relationship in 1971 when Chrysler purchased 15% of Mitsubishi Motors Corporation (MMC) and began selling its products through Chrysler dealerships. Chrysler currently sells three Mitsubishi cars, the Conquest, Vista Horizon, and Colt, and a Mitsubishi truck, the Ram 50. In April 1985, amid many rumors, Chrysler finally announced a joint-venture agreement between Mitsubishi and Chrysler. The new car will, in effect, be the replacement for the existing Dodge Colt and Plymouth Horizon. Chrysler is also increasing its ownership share of MMC from 15% to 24%. The joint venture, called Diamond Star, will begin production in 1988 and will be located in Bloomington-Normal, Illinois. Production is expected to reach 180,000 cars a year, with half being sold by Chrysler and half by Mitsubishi Motors Sales of America, the Mitsubishi independent distribution arm in the United States. Iacocca hailed the deal as good for the United States. "The new plant will directly employ 2,500 people, and another 9,000 jobs will be created for suppliers" (*Automotive News,* April 22, 1985, p. 49). Further, Chrysler in May 1985 revised its contract with Mitsubishi to import a three-liter V-6 engine that will be used in the 1987 minivans, the new A-car in 1988, the C-car in 1987 or 1988, and the Imperial in 1988 (*Automotive News,* April 8, 1985). Because of Chrysler's healthy cash reserves and marketable securities of nearly $3 billion, they are looking to diversify even further. Chrysler currently has an agreement with Lotus Cars, Ltd. concerning the development of a new engine and use of Lotus' electronically controlled suspension. A Chrysler executive stated the company soon would announce it is purchasing 5–10% of Lotus as part of Chrysler's new global business strategy (*Automotive News,* May 13, 1985, p. 8). Chrysler has also contracted with the Italian automaker Maserati S.P.A. to develop and build a two-seater sports car for the U.S. market. Production will amount to 5,000 to 10,000 cars annually. The car will sell for at least $25,000 and will be introduced in the spring of 1987. Chrysler, in turn, paid $2.3 million for a 5% stake in Maserati. Chrysler also signed a deal with the Korean electronics firm, Samsung Group, for parts and components. Chrysler also holds 14% of French automaker Peugot, and is looking at the possibility of a joint venture in the labor-rich People's Republic of China. Chrysler has diversified further by purchasing Gulfstream, which makes corporate jets, for $641 million, and E.F. Hutton Credit Corporation for $125 million. "We're not going out on an acquisition binge, but Chrysler and its management represents attractive partners today to a lot of companies in a lot of businesses around the world" (*Automotive* News, May 27, 1985, p. 2). However, recently Chrysler announced that "it agreed to buy Regie Nationale de Usines Renault's controlling interest in ailing American Motors Corporation paving the way for Chrysler to acquire AMC'' (*The Wall Street Journal,* March 11, 1987, p. 24). The acquisition will combine the third and fourth largest American car manufacturers' capabilities (see Table 1).

General Motors and Chrysler are not alone in their efforts to globalize. Although talks between Ford of Europe and Fiat concerning a possible merger have broken off, the two companies have emerged from the discussions with a stronger relationship. Currently, Ford of Europe and Fiat are partners in the development of the CVT automatic transmission. The two companies are still looking at a truck venture between Fiat's Iveco and Ford in Great Britain. Back in the United States, Ford and Mazda have come close to signing an agreement whereby Mazda would sell part of its Flat Rock, Michigan passenger-car output to Ford. Louis Ross, Ford executive vice president for North American Automotive Operations, said Ford will probably buy between 40% and 60% of Mazda's 240,000 production capacity. After Ford lost out to GM in the bidding for Hughes Aircraft, it announced in August 1985 it would buy First Nationwide Financial, parent company of the nation's ninth largest savings and loan, for $493 million. Ford also purchased, in 1985, the New Holland farm equipment division of Sperry, for $463 million.

Other global movements include the Japanese shifting into European assembly and manufacturing with alliances between Honda and Austin Rover and Nissan and Alfa Romeo. The shifting patterns of globalization and diversification by major auto manufacturers show not only a closer interdependence between countries of the world, but a desire by manufacturers to strengthen their defense against the volatile auto industry. Joint ventures help ensure against one company's suffering huge losses, and diversification helps a company to "ride out" lags in the number of automobiles purchased. General Motors also stated one reason for the GM-Toyota joint venture was to gain technologic knowledge from the Japanese. So it appears for the time being and the near future that the globalization that Iacocca envisioned will continue to prosper.

THE MAN BEHIND THE TURNAROUND

"It seemed as if the company might join Studebaker and Hudson—out of automaking. Now look what's happening" (*U.S. News and World Report,* February 14, 1982,

TABLE 1 Chrysler and American Motors Corporation Compared (1986 data)

	Chrysler	American Motors Corporation
Number of assembly plants	7	4
Capacity (vehicles per year)	1,854,764	796,000
Employees	120,900	19,500
Car market share	11.9%	0.7%
Share of total U.S. light-truck market (including utility vehicles)	12.8%	4.5%
Net income (loss)	$1.40 billion	($81.3 million)
Number of dealers	4,026	1,300

Source: *The Wall Street Journal*, March 11, 1987.

p. 68). The miraculous turnaround of the headlong, falling, failing Chrysler Corporation surprised everybody. One person who was not surprised, however, was the man who engineered the amazing feat, Lee Iacocca.

In an age of media heroes drawn largely from the ephemeral world of sports and entertainment, Lee Iacocca is a real-world Rocky. The son of Italian immigrants, he swiftly climbed the corporate ladder at Ford Motor Company, built one of the best-selling cars in U.S. history—the Mustang—got thrown out by Henry Ford II himself, then went on to save the failing Chrysler Corporation and 600,000 American jobs. (*Newsweek*, October 8, 1984, p. 50)

He's become the nation's foremost symbol for "hanging tough," for "toughing it out" under high-pressure nerve-wearing situations. He came out of nowhere to become the executive-apparent of Ford Motor Company—he was named to the key vice presidency at the age of 36. He became the "industry genius" who conceived the Ford Mustang—which had the highest first-year sales in automobile history—and who later led Ford Motor Company to net profits of $1.8 billion in each of two successive years. It hadn't been done before. It hasn't been done since. So he was fired. (*Saturday Evening Post*, March 1982, p. 72).

He is a hard-nosed, direct man who demands the absolute most from his underlings and who has virtually no patience for their delinquencies, however minor: When one of his senior vice

presidents was two minutes late for the takeoff of a company plane on one occasion, Iacocca ordered the plane to leave without him. His underlings at Chrysler reacted to the change from "easy rider" to "snap-to" leadership in the expected way: Some of them began calling him "Lee Ayatollah." (*Saturday Evening Post*, March 1982, p. 72).

Mr. Iacocca also is a product man supreme and marketing man genius. When he puts all that together with his people skills from common decency to a tremendous computer-type mind he's just a helleva fun guy to work under if you can take the beating (NBC News Special Report, 1984).

Indeed, Iacocca was the type of leader that Chrysler needed in order to survive. Further comments on the turnaround include:

Iacocca is absolutely the worst loser in the world. There's no way the guy can lose because he simply will not let it happen. (NBC News Special Report, 1984)

This image of Iacocca has helped him to not only provide leadership for Chrysler Corporation, but also provide leadership for the country:

After saving and then rebuilding Chrysler Corporation against all odds, Lido Anthony Iacocca, 60, is now achieving another, more ephemeral sort of American miracle: he has become an industrial folk hero in a supposedly post-industrial age, and more improbably still, a corporate capitalist with populist appeal, an eminence terrible admired by working class and ruling class alike. (*Time,* April 1, 1985)

"I owe it all to Iacocca," says Sarah Haynes, a Chrysler assembly-line worker now back at work after a five-year layoff. "If the workers are saying he's great, it ain't no jive." (*Time,* April 1, 1985)

"He went out and did exactly what he said he was going to do," says Gordon North of Rochester, Minnesota. "He's probably the most honest man in America." (*Time,* April 1, 1985)

Economist Robert Lekachman wrote, "Above all, the juices of humanity course through his veins." (*Time,* April 1, 1985)

"He's real," say attorney Joseph Califano, formerly a member of the Carter Administration Cabinet and now of Chrysler's board. "And he cares—I think that comes through. He takes on fights he doesn't have to. He's like the hero of Raiders of the Lost Ark: he's been down, on the edge, picked himself up, came to the top again." (*Time,* April 1, 1985)

"He tapped into America's frustrations," says Ron DeLuca, the Kenyon and Eckhardt advertising agency executive in charge of Chrysler's ads. He said, "It doesn't have to be this way. You can create your own destiny," says Leo Arthur Kelmerson, president of Kenyon and Eckhardt. "The country was starved for leadership and charisma. Lee talked directly to the American people." (*Time,* April 1, 1985)

Gil MacDougald of Atlanta thinks Iacocca is great, and has a plausible sociological exploration to boot. "In America, people pull for underdogs and they just love a winner. Iacocca was both." (*Time,* April 1, 1985)

Certainly these few comments made by those infatuated with him do not show the complete Lee Iacocca, but they at least give one a glance at the super businessman. In the last few years, Iacocca has been very involved with the Statue of Liberty-Ellis Island Centennial Commission. His father and mother both passed through Ellis Island, and this might explain his preoccupation with the project. "The Statue of Liberty is just that—a beautiful symbol of what it means to be free. The reality is Ellis Island," Iacocca writes, "Freedom is just the ticket of admission, but if you want to survive and prosper, there's a price to pay . . . What the last fifty years taught us was the difference between right and wrong, that only hard work succeeds, that there are no free lunches, that you've got to be productive. Those are the values that made this country great (NBC News Special Report, 1984).

John Morrissey of Kenyon and Eckhardt Advertising said, "I don't know anybody else in Detroit who could have done what he did. I don't know anybody else who has the same kind of feeling for cars, toughness in doing what has to be done, as far as people, situations, and products are concerned. There may be somebody else who could have gotten it done, but I'll be damned if I know who it is" (NBC News Special Report, 1984).

With a 13.2% market share and massive personal promotion to widen his home base, it remains to be seen if Iacocca's charismatic leadership can increase Chrysler's market share at home and abroad in view of unrestrained Japanese imports and the entry of Hyundai (from South Korea), and a close to $1 billion investment by Honda, Toyota and Suzuki to produce over 200,000 units of small cars in U.S. assembly plants. Iacocca passed the first test with an A +. There are many unknowns and determined players in the second contest that Iacocca is faced with. How he will handle it remains to be seen.

REFERENCES

Automotive News, April 8, 1985.

Automotive News, April 15, 1985.

Automotive News, April 22, 1985.

Automotive News, May 13, 1985.

Automotive News, May 27, 1985.

Chrysler Corporation (1984). Annual Report.

Forbes, November 7, 1983.

Iacocca, Lee (1984). *Iacocca, An Autobiography,* New York, Bantam Books.

NBC News Special Report (1984) "Iacocca: An American Profile," January, with Tom Brokaw.

Newsweek, "Behind the Wheels," October 8, 1984.

Saturday Evening Post, March 1982.

Time, "A Spunky Tycoon Turned Superstar," April 1, 1985.

U.S. News and World Report, February 14, 1983.

The Wall Street Journal, March 11, 1987.

EXHIBIT 1   Chrysler Corporation's Full Product Lines (New Car Sales), 1977–1984

	1984		1983		1982		1981	
	Units	Market share	Units	Market share	Units	Market share	Units	Market share
Chrysler	—	—	—	—	—	—	15,071	0.2
Valiant	—	—	—	—	—	—	—	—
Turismo	46,013	0.6	37,079	0.6	38,776	0.7	—	—
Horizon	75,560	1.0	50,861	0.8	48,045	0.9	75,377	1.2
Reliant	141,377	1.7	161,757	2.5	151,279	2.7	190,158	3.2
TC3	—	—	—	—	—	—	51,815	0.8
Caravelle (FWD)	1,012	0.0	—	—	—	—	—	—
Grand Fury	14,221	0.2	15,867	0.2	17,792	0.3	9,311	0.1
Volare	—	—	—	—	—	—	6,839	0.1
Laser	52,073	0.7	925	0.0	—	—	—	—
LeBaron	96,256	1.2	80,566	1.2	81,599	1.5	46,992	0.8
Voyager	—	—	—	—	—	—	—	—
E.class	31,040	0.4	36,610	0.6	—	—	—	—
Cordoba	567	0.0	13,569	0.2	16,273	0.3	23,904	0.3
New Yorker	56,019	0.7	33,494	0.5	—	—	—	—
Fifth Avenue	78,399	1.0	77,700	1.2	51,757	0.9	—	—
Imperial	84	0.0	1,725	0.0	2,807	0.1	4,649	0.1
Fury	—	—	—	—	—	—	—	—
Total Chrysler-Plymouth	592,621	7.5	510,153	7.9	408,328	7.4	424,116	12.3
Charger	51,799	0.7	45,238	0.7	41,534	0.8	—	—
Omni	65,675	0.8	45,843	0.7	40,006	0.7	56,051	0.9
024	—	—	—	—	—	—	51,730	0.8
Daytona	42,596	0.5	802	0.0	—	—	—	—
Aries	110,939	1.4	124,650	1.9	112,761	2.1	143,619	2.3
400 (600 2 dr)	23,443	0.3	32,052	0.5	24,090	0.4	3,150	0.1
600 (4 dr)	36,864	0.5	30,042	0.5	—	—	—	—
Diplomat	21,932	0.3	24,966	0.4	23,928	0.4	25,598	0.4
Mirada	706	0.0	5,463	0.1	8,073	0.1	13,947	0.2
Dart	—	—	—	—	—	—	—	—
Aspen	—	—	—	—	—	—	6,034	0.1
Sportsman	—	—	—	—	—	—	—	—
Monaco	—	—	—	—	—	—	—	—
St. Regis	—	—	—	—	—	—	5,628	0.1
Total Dodge	353,954	4.5	309,056	4.8	250,392	4.5	305,757	4.9
Total Chrysler corporate	946,575	12.0	819,209	12.7	658,720	11.9	729,873	11.8

(*continued*)

Source: Chrysler Corporation and *Automotive Spring Yearbook 1985*.

EXHIBIT 1   *(concluded)*

	1980		1979		1978		1977	
	Units	*Market share*	*Units*	*Market share*	*Units*	*Market share*	*Units*	*Market share*
Chrysler	29,321	0.4	87,451	1.1	67,892	0.7	104,356	1.1
Valiant	—	—	—	—	—	—	2,243	0.2
Turismo	—	—	—	—	—	—	—	—
Horizon	78,823	1.2	146,740	1.7	118,993	1.3	—	—
Reliant	32,720	0.5	—	—	—	—	—	—
TC3	53,971	0.8	—	—	—	—	—	—
Caravelle (FWD)	—	—	—	—	—	—	—	—
Grand Fury	13,682	0.2	746	0.0	980	0.1	31,692	0.3
Volare	72,116	1.1	167,091	2.1	210,125	2.4	304,305	3.3
Laser	—	—	—	—	—	—	—	—
LeBaron	65,519	0.1	99,588	1.2	125,558	1.3	70,037	0.8
Voyager	—	—	8,265	0.1	13,895	0.1	13,767	0.2
E.class	—		—	—	—	—	—	—
Cordoba	44,908	0.7	61,801	0.7	105,442	1.1	142,619	1.6
New Yorker	—	—	—	—	—	—	—	—
Fifth Avenue	—	—	—	—	—	—	—	—
Imperial	2,497	0.0	—	—	—	—	—	—
Fury	—	—	2,681	0.0	60,378	0.6	92,056	1.0
Total Chrysler-Plymouth	393,557	9.7	574,363	3.9	703,263	12.1	761,075	8.5
Charger	—	—	—	—	—	—	29,099	0.3
Omni	61,240	1.0	124,378	1.5	89,497	1.0	—	—
O24	46,658	0.7	—	—	—	—	—	—
Daytona	—	—	—	—	—	—	—	—
Aries	25,784	0.4	—	—	—	—	—	—
400 (600 2 dr)	—	—	—	—	—	—	—	—
600 (4 dr)	—	—	—	—	—	—	—	—
Diplomat	33,157	0.5	45,129	0.5	60,656	0.6	40,072	0.4
Mirada	27,595	0.4	24,784	0.3	48,326	0.5	8,310	0.1
Dart	—	—	—	—	—	—	1,898	0.1
Aspen	55,092	0.8	117,777	1.5	157,308	1.6	242,111	2.6
Sportsman	—	—	24,917	0.3	44,376	0.5	45,380	0.5
Monaco	—	—	2,554	0.0	37,594	0.4	59,559	0.6
St. Regis	16,934	0.3	28,303	0.3	5,238	0.2	32,248	0.4
Total Dodge	266,460	4.1	367,842	4.4	442,995	4.8	458,677	5.0
Total Chrysler corporate	660,017	10.0	942,205	11.3	1,146,258	12.4	1,219,752	13.5

EXHIBIT 2   Comparison of Market Share*

Year	Chrysler	AMC	Ford	GM	Imports
1974	14.08	3.79	25.88	42.41	13.84
1975	12.25	3.73	23.61	43.83	16.58
1976	13.67	2.45	22.62	47.61	13.65
1977	12.00	1.65	23.40	46.31	16.64
1978	11.05	1.51	23.54	47.79	16.11
1979	10.13	1.52	20.81	46.26	21.28
1980	8.77	1.98	17.20	45.86	26.19
1981	9.85	1.97	16.56	44.49	27.13
1982	9.95	1.88	16.87	44.06	27.24
1983	10.36	2.47	17.11	44.15	25.91
1984	10.39	1.95	19.07	44.33	24.35
1985	10.32	1.18	18.75	41.72	28.08
1986	13.21	0.84	21.45	50.07	14.44
1987 (forecast)	10.72	0.75	19.27	48.62	19.98

*All figures are percentages.

Source: *1985 Ward's Automotive Yearbook; Automotive News* (1984 figures); and *Ward's Auto World* (1985 figures).

EXHIBIT 3   Chrysler's Revenue and Earnings

Year	Gross Revenue ($000)	Net Income ($000)	Earnings per Share
1974	10,977,800	− 52,094	− 1.30
1975	11,598,400	− 259,535	− 4.33
1976	15,537,800	422,600	7.02
1977	16,744,600	163,200	2.71
1978	13,669,800	− 200,600	− 3.54
1979	12,004,300	− 1,097,300	− 17.18
1980	9,225,300	− 1,709,700	− 26.00
1981	10,821,600	− 475,600	− 7.18
1982	10,044,900	− 68,900	− 1.28
1983	13,240,400	301,900	2.35
1984	19,572,700	1,496,100	11.75
1985	21,255,000	1,635,200	9.38
1986	22,590,000	1,400,000	9.47

Source: *Moody's Handbook of Common Stocks,* Spring 1985 Edition; and Fall 1986 *Moody's Industrial Stock Report,* 1987.

EXHIBIT 4

CHRYSLER CORPORATION
Consolidated Financial Statement
($ in millions)

	1984	1983	1982	1981	1980
Assets					
Cash and cash equivalents	$ 99.2	$ 114.7	$ 133.4	$ 121.3	$ 103.7
Short-term investment-at cost which approximates market ...	—	—	216.3	—	—
Marketable securities..............................	103.8	88.5	84.4	283.1	193.6
Inventories..	—	—	—	1,600.4	1,916.0
Finance receivables: 81 nets.......................	—	—	—	429.7	476.2
Retails and lease	4,696.5	2,310.6	1,957.5	—	—
Wholesale	2,738.9	1,276.0	1,292.6	—	—
Commercial and other..........................	103.8	108.0	126.1	—	—
Accounts receivable	47.7	38.8	45.6	—	—
Amounts receivable upon sale of overseas operations..	—	—	—	—	—
Less unearned income.............................	738.1	340.4	315.5	—	—
Allowances for credit losses.......................	55.5	33.2	26.7	—	—
Finance receivables—net	6,793.3	3,359.8	3,079.6		
Revenue vehicles at cost less valuation allowance..	—	—	—	—	—
Revenue vehicle held for resale	—	—	—	—	—
Restricted cash....................................	—	—	—	71.7	50.3
Investment in associated companies outside the United States...............................	—	—	—	352.4	353.3
Investment in and advances to 20% to 50% owned companies	—	—	—	35.2	30.5
Investment in and advances to unconsolidated subsidiaries	—	—	—	671.7	702.3
Investments in and amounts due from affiliated companies.............................	—	—	—	—	—
Other noncurrent assets............................	—	—	—	90.8	100.2
Property, plant, and equipment	—	—	—	3,886.8	3,877.9
Land, building, machinery, and equipment...........	—	—	—	2,237.5	2,158.7
Less accumulated depreciation.....................	—	—	—	1,649.3	1,719.2
Unamortized special tools.........................	—	—	—	797.6	800.8
Net property, plant, and equipment	—	—	—	2,446.9	2,520.0
Repossessed collateral, at estimated realizable value	—	—	—	—	—
Amounts due and deferred from receivable sales, net	100.9	689.7	214.5	—	—
Prepaid insurance and taxes	—	—	—	98.8	101.6
Prepaid expense and other assets	20.2	15.6	12.3	—	—
Income tax allocable to the following year	—	—	—	68.0	70.1
Unamortized debt expenses	23.5	7.2	4.1	—	—
Amounts due from affiliated companies	0.9	—	—	—	—
Property and equipment, at cost less accumulated depreciation of $3.7 (1984), $3.8 (1983), and $3.1 (1982)...................	6.8	6.7	6.7	—	—
Total other assets.............................	—	—	23.1	—	—
Total assets.......................................	$7,148.6	$4,282.2	$3,751.3	$6,270.0	$6,717.8

Source: Chrysler Corporation Annual Reports.

1979	1978	1977	1976	1975	1974
$ 127.4	$ 193.4	$ 161.6	$ 169.5	$ 207.8	$ 244.7
—	—	—	—	—	—
83.0	73.6	63.7	54.4	46.9	50.1
—	—	—	—	—	—
—	—	—	—	—	—
1,910.9	2,136.1	2,017.0	1,669.9	1,272.3	1,456.2
1,380.6	1,666.0	2,331.7	1,849.6	1,508.9	1,434.3
134.6	131.8	138.9	119.8	124.6	112.4
72.9	53.1	52.3	43.5	70.2	28.8
27.9	82.8	—	—	—	—
224.6	239.9	244.3	200.2	144.8	141.8
23.2	23.5	30.2	30.2	30.0	29.9
3,178.4	3,670.5	4,213.3	3,408.9	2,731.0	2,831.3
65.2	212.7	185.0	178.9	125.2	110.5
155.0	175.4	115.3	88.2	81.3	95.6
—	—	—	—	—	—
—	—	18.8	20.7	20.5	19.5
—	—	—	—	—	—
—	—	—	—	—	—
—	—	—	—	2.68	4.77
—	—	—	—	—	—
—	—	—	—	—	—
—	—	—	—	—	—
—	—	—	—	—	—
—	—	—	—	—	—
0.444	0.20	0.87	0.85	0.198	0.208
248.4	67.5	14.9	17.4	—	—
—	—	—	—	—	—
18.6	16.6	17.8	14.5	9.92	6.3
—	—	—	—	—	—
—	—	—	—	4.3	4.81
5.8	4.5	0.81	3.1	—	—
16.8	17.7	19.6	21.7	21.2	14.3
51.9	51.8	71.3	70.9	—	—
$4,010.0	$4,581.0	$4,877.0	$4,032.0	$3,322.0	$3,411.0

EXHIBIT 5

CHRYSLER CORPORATION
Liabilities and Shareholder's Investment
($ in millions)

	1984	1983	1982
Liabilities			
Notes payable, unsecured short-term..........................	—	—	—
Notes and debentures payable within one year.................	$2,994.4	$ 575.3	$ 199.9
Accounts payable	—	—	—
Short-term debt..	—	—	—
Accounts payable and accrued expenses......................	151.6	61.1	147.7
Current portion of restructured debt	—	—	—
Amounts due to affiliated companies	15.3	—	—
Payment due within one year on long-term debt	—	—	—
Deferred employee benefit plan accruals.....................	—	—	—
Reserve for insurance claims and adjustment expenses	12.8	6.6	7.0
Employee compensation benefits............................	—	—	—
Deferred taxes on income	—	—	—
Unearned insurance premiums..............................	40.2	31.0	28.1
Taxes on income...	—	—	—
Other taxes	—	—	—
Income tax payable.......................................	5.7	10.7	28.3
Interest payable..	—	—	—
Accrued expenses	—	—	—
Income tax deferred	92.7	40.6	46.5
Senior notes and debentures payable after one year...........	—	2,378.5	2,140.9
Subordinated notes and debentures payable after one year	—	225.2	235.4
Reserves withheld..	—	—	—
Dealers	44.5	35.4	32.0
Affiliates	12.7	12.7	19.4
12% subordinated debentures..............................	—	—	—
Amounts due to affiliated companies	—	197.2	201.8
Convertible sending fund debentures	—	—	—
Notes and debentures payable after one year	2,784.2	—	—
Other noncurrent liabilities................................	—	—	—
Total liabilities	6,154.1	3,574.3	3,087.0
Shareholder's Investment			
Preferred stock-no par value, authorized 20,000,000 shares 10,000,000 $2.75 cumulative shares issued and outstanding redemption value $250 million less unauthorized issue	—	—	—
Cost and value of warrants to purchase common stock 342,951 8 1/2% shares issued and outstanding at December 31, 1981, 171,473 at December 31, 1980 (redemption values at December 31, 1981, $1,097.4 million).....................	—	—	—
Common stock—no par value Authorized 170,000 shares; issued and outstanding 73,132,671 at December 31, 1981 and 66,972,683 shares at December 31, 1980.	—	—	—
Additional paid-in capital..................................	—	—	—
Accumulated deficit	—	—	—
Common stock—par value $100 a share Authorized, issued, and outstanding 250,000 shares	25.0	25.0	25.0
Additional paid-in capital..................................	485.9	282.4	282.4
Net earning retained for use in the business..................	483.6	400.5	356.9
Total shareholder's investment.....................	994.5	707.9	664.3
Total liabilities and shareholder's investment	$7,148.6	$4,282.2	$3,751.3

Source: Chrysler Corporation Annual Reports.

1981	1980	1979	1978	1977	1976	1975	1974
—	—	$1,253.9	$1,790.2	$2,329.8	$2,114.7	$1,871.3	$2,076.2
—	—	269.3	195.5	53.9	22.9	121.3	10.9
$1,022.8	$1,405.1	—	—	—	—	—	—
163.8	150.5	—	—	—	—	—	—
—	—	101.7	63.1	80.5	64.2	69.8	57.1
47.5	140.4	—	—	—	—	—	—
—	—	—	—	—	—	—	38.0
14.1	25.8	—	—	—	—	—	—
666.4	353.0	—	—	—	—	—	—
—	—	10.2	8.9	6.5	5.2	3.0	2.9
329.2	391.1	—	—	—	—	—	—
68.3	71.6	—	—	—	—	—	—
—	—	49.1	44.2	39.1	32.5	23.0	17.5
5.9	12.3	—	—	—	—	—	—
81.0	113.3	—	—	—	—	—	—
—	—	5.5	4.9	15.6	6.99	4.2	5.1
56.6	44.6	—	—	—	—	—	—
698.1	746.2	—	—	—	—	—	—
—	—	78.2	53.3	48.3	37.2	25.9	14.1
—	—	220.8	253.9	254.9	174.1	182.9	185.0
—	—	1,257.0	1,421.0	1,339.0	919.0	407.0	483.0
—	—	78.9	59.3	50.1	52.3	50.0	28.1
—	—	—	—	—	—	—	—
—	—	—	—	—	—	—	—
78.0	78.0	—	—	—	—	—	—
—	—	40.2	38.6	60.1	46.2	52.7	—
72.0	83.9	—	—	—	—	—	—
1,909.1	2,321.4	—	—	—	—	—	—
277.4	221.4	—	—	—	—	—	—
5,490.2	6,158.6	3,365.0	3,933.0	4,277.0	3,475.0	2,811.0	2,917.9
221.9	220.3	—	—	—	—	—	—
1,097.4	342.9	—	—	—	—	—	—
460.2	418.6	—	—	—	—	—	—
692.5	692.4	—	—	—	—	—	—
(1,692.2)	(1,215.0)	—	—	—	—	—	—
—	—	25.0	25.0	25.0	25.0	25.0	25.0
—	—	282.4	282.4	282.4	282.4	282.4	282.4
—	—	338.4	340.8	292.4	249.4	221.1	186.2
—	—	645.8	648.2	599.8	556.8	528.5	493.6
$6,270.0	$6,617.8	$4,010.0	$4,581.0	$4,877.0	$4,031.8	$3,339.6	$3,411.0

19.   *Deere and Company*

The past year [1982] has proved another disappointment to farmers. . . . farmers experienced the third year in a row of depressed farm income and, more recently, declining asset values. . . . [There is] the prospect of modest improvement in farm income in 1983. . . . (M. Duncan and M. Drabenstott, "Outlook for Agriculture: Is the Recovery on the Way?" *Economic Review: Kansas City Federal Reserve Bank,* December 1982, pp. 16–17.)

Prospects for a North American farm equipment recovery are clouded. . . . (Deere & Co. Annual Report, 1982.)

Now as the U.S. is about to propel the world into an economic recovery, it is becoming abundantly clear that the rebound will bypass agriculture. . . . Sales prospects are grim for farm suppliers. ("Why Recovery May Skip the Farm Belt," *Business Week,* March 21, 1983, pp. 106–14.)

The U.S. Farm sector began its climb back to health in 1983. . . . Farm income will likely post future gains in 1984. (M. Duncan and M. Drabenstott, "Better Times Ahead for Agriculture," *Economic Review: Kansas City Federal Reserve Bank,* December 1983, pp. 22–35.)

No one can predict with assurance at this time whether the recovery in the world economy will endure long enough to restore equipment demand to levels experienced in the 1970s. (Deere & Co. Annual Report, 1983.)

U.S. agriculture began 1984 with renewed hopes for a stronger farm recovery, and the record will show farm income did rebound sharply.

This case was prepared by Peter G. Goulet and Lynda L. Goulet, of the University of Northern Iowa, Cedar Falls, Iowa 50614, and is intended to be used as a basis for class discussion. Presented and accepted by the refereed Midwest Case Writers Association Workshop, 1986.

But . . . farm liquidations and declining asset values are visible symptoms of ongoing adjustments to market forces. (M. Drabenstott and M. Duncan, "Another Troubled Year for American Agriculture," *Economic Review: Kansas City Federal Reserve Bank,* December 1984, pp. 30–43.)

Once again, I must report to you that Deere & Company has completed a very difficult year. . . . Although 1985 will be another challenging year, we are determined to make it a year of constructive progress. (Deere & Company, Annual Report, 1984.)

The big question for the battered farm machinery makers is no longer when the recovery will arrive but whether it ever will. (F. Rice, "Cruel Days in Tractorville," *Fortune, October 29, 1984, pp. 30–36.)*

. . . in 1985. . . . Farm income dropped and farmland values fell further. *Another difficult year lies ahead in 1986* [emphasis added]. (M. Drabenstott, *Economic Review: Kansas City Federal Reserve Bank,* December 1985, pp. 35–49.)

The economic environment surrounding our industries remains difficult and uncertain. . . . Nonetheless, we are determined to make the most of these challenging times. (Deere & Co, Annual Report, 1985.)

*****

Like Tantalus in Dante's *Divine Comedy,* farm equipment makers have spent the years since 1981 pushing their rock up the hill only to see it poised to roll back over them. Even the largest and most efficient of these manufacturers, Deere and Company, has failed to generate an operating profit since 1981. The other large equipment maker, International Harvester (now Navistar), has maintained its identity only by selling its IH farm equipment business to Tenneco. White Farm Equipment and Massey-Ferguson (now Varity) have also suffered the ravages of bankruptcy.

BACKGROUND AND OPERATIONS[1]

Deere and Company, like its other large counterpart, International Harvester, began as the result of an invention. John Deere, a blacksmith originally from Vermont, developed one of the first plows which could effectively turn the sticky, rich, black soil of the giant prairies of the midwestern United States. In 1868, John Deere formed his company to make and distribute these plows. The distribution system and the founder's philosophy of emphasizing service and quality was developed in these early years and were critical factors in the firm's continued growth and success.

The next major turning point for the firm came in 1911, when six noncompeting farm equipment companies were consolidated into the company to form a full-line manufacturer of farm equipment. In 1918, this expansion continued with the purchase of the Waterloo Gasoline Engine Company, based in Waterloo, Iowa. This purchase brought the company into the mainstream of the conversion from animal to machine power on the farm.

Deere and Company has, for most of its existence, had unusually stable leadership, having only two CEOs during the period 1928–82. During this period the firm became the leading manufacturer of farm equipment in the world, developed its extensive and valuable dealer network, became a major supplier of construction machinery, and established facilities or affiliates throughout the world.

PRODUCT LINES

The main engine of agriculture is the tractor. By standard industry practice farm tractors are categorized in four major subgroups: utility tractors under 40 HP and from 40 to 100 HP, row crop tractors over 100 HP, and large four-wheel drive tractors. Though Deere supplies tractors in all of these categories, the majority of its sales come in the two groups of large machines. In recent years, the vast majority of the output in the smaller categories, those under 100 HP, has been manufactured overseas and imported to the United States. By 1985,

100 percent of the under 40 HP utility tractors were made offshore, with 89 percent of Japanese origin. Further, 95 percent of the 40–100 HP models came from Europe (70 percent) or Japan (25 percent).[2]

Farm implements drawn behind tractors make up several equipment categories. These include: soil preparation, tillage, and planting equipment (often combined for low-tillage applications); harvesting machinery; and crop handling equipment. In addition, some harvesting and crop handling functions are combined in self-propelled machines called *combines*. Self-propelled combines can be used to harvest corn, soybeans, cotton, tomatoes, grapes, and wheat. There are literally hundreds of items in these categories, each suited for particular soil conditions and crop needs. Deere and the other large full-line supplier, the Case-International Harvester Division of Tenneco, sell most, if not all, of the implement types in these categories. Other producers provide a selected subset of these items.

Another important line of products manufactured and sold by Deere and Company is industrial equipment. This includes machines involved in earth moving, forestry, and construction. Typical products include: bulldozers, backhoes, loaders, graders, scrapers, excavating equipment, and tree harvesting and log handling equipment. Though Deere does not provide as broad a line of construction equipment as its large competitors such as Caterpillar, it has entered the market in a variety of segments and sold nearly a billion dollars worth of these products in 1985.

The fastest growing product line for Deere in the 1980s is the lawn and garden implement line. The company makes and sells a variety of small lawn and garden tractors, mowing implements, snowblowers, riding mowers, and other outdoor power equipment. Some estimates place the size of the lawn and garden equipment market at $3 billion in 1985, growing at roughly 6.8 percent annually since 1976. The outdoor power products line is complemented by a number of minor items manufactured for the firm by others, including tools, clothing, and accessories.

In addition to those products the firm sells which are designed for end-users, the firm has begun to use its facilities and engineering expertise to develop a growing line of components and other products for other produc-

---

[1] The authors wish to thank Ashwani Bansal of Deere & Co. for his help in the preparation of this section of the case.

[2] Standard & Poor's Corporation, *Industry Surveys, Steel and Heavy Machinery,* February 13, 1986, p. S40.

ers of heavy equipment and vehicles. These products are called OEM components and include such items as castings, shock absorbers, steering gear, and so forth. Also, in 1984, Deere bought the U.S. rights to the manufacture and sale of the rotary engine from Curtiss-Wright Corporation. This engine has a number of possible applications in products both related and unrelated to Deere's current business.

Finally, another source of income for Deere, as for many firms making durable goods, is its financial subsidiary. Besides providing equipment financing for its dealers and loans to farmers, the firm also has an insurance division. These operations, currently holding around $3.7 billion in assets, have often helped offset operating losses in the 1980s, providing the firm's profits in several of those years.

FACILITIES AND OPERATIONS

Deere and Company has 12 factories in the United States Canada, with a total of more than 33 million square feet. In addition, the firm also owns and operates tractor manufacturing plants in Mexico, Germany, and Spain; farm implement facilities in France, Germany, and South Africa; and an engine factory in Spain. Other facilities and affiliated companies are operated in South America and Australia.

Since 1976, the firm has spent about $2 billion expanding or upgrading its facilities. Much of this capital investment was intended to make Deere the technological leader in its industry. According to some analysts, the operations in Blackhawk County, Iowa, include some of the most modern and efficient manufacturing plants to be found anywhere in the world. In the Waterloo tractor factory 10 minicomputers direct the facility's many functions including materials management, scheduling, painting, and various other manufacturing operations. Rubbish is even recycled to provide energy for the computer-controlled environment of the plant.

The Waterloo engine manufacturing facility is also highly automated, its heart being a 900-foot long automatic engine-block machining line. This plant will be instrumental in a new joint venture planned with the Detroit-Allison Division of GM. Under this planned venture Deere will help develop and produce diesel engines for the leading automaker.

Although Deere uses parts from a number of outside suppliers, it is a highly integrated manufacturer, making its own engines, hydraulic components, transmissions, castings, and other components such as steering mechanisms. The expertise developed by the firm through this integration provides the firm with a number of possible original equipment (OEM) products which could become an increasing source of sales for the firm in the latter half of the 1980s and beyond.

In addition to its manufacturing facilities, the company maintains major research and development facilities in Waterloo (Product Engineering Center) and Moline, Illinois (Combine Research Center). These facilities have been expanded at a cost of over $40 million since 1980, greatly increasing the firm's ability to develop the technologies it needs to maintain its position of industry leadership. The firm has also worked with NASA to develop improved metal alloys. The acquisition of the rotary engine technology is intended to provide the firm with opportunities for a variety of product applications and improvements, including a new generation, fuel-efficient aircraft engine. The diesel engine venture is also intended to advance the state of the art in this area, putting Deere in a position to be a leading designer and builder of a variety of engines.

Though Deere possesses some of the finest facilities of any industrial firm in America, it has been unable to utilize them to the fullest extent in the middle 1980s. The entire agricultural equipment industry has been operating with excess capacity throughout the decade. Standard & Poor's estimates that since 1979, the industry has cut production capacity by 50 percent.[3] In that year the industry had its sales peak and still operated at only 70–75 percent of capacity. In spite of the capacity contraction, operating rates stood at only about 30 percent in 1985. By mid-1986, S&P expects capacity to be cut an additional 15–20 percent, raising operating rates somewhat.

MARKETING AND DISTRIBUTION

Even the most efficient manufacturer of a durable good such as farm equipment cannot hope to control a significant portion of the market without a strong dealer

---

[3]Ibid., p. S41.

network. The customer needs to have ready access to the product, the means to finance it, and the ability to have it repaired. It is especially critical for field crop farmers to have access to emergency repairs when the narrow "windows" for certain operations such as planting and harvesting are open. Over the years, Deere has taken great pains to develop its dealer network into the strongest in the industry.

Regardless of its strength the dealer network has been under great stress. Slow sales at the retail level have left the dealers scrambling for income to stay in business. Because of the high value of farm equipment—large tractors and combines often sell for more than $100,000—it is difficult for equipment dealers to finance their inventories, often running to several million dollars. From 1980–1985 the National Farm and Power Equipment Association reports that it has lost 20 percent of its members.[4] Most of the approximately 3,500 Deere dealers who remain are hanging on through a combination of service and parts sales and interest concessions from the company.

Since 1979, Deere has seen accounts receivable grow from $1.4 to $2.75 billion while sales of equipment have gone from $5 billion down to $4.1 billion. In 1984 and 1985 Deere made special interest and payment concessions on as much as $600 million of its receivables. This cost the firm as much as $50 million in lost interest income in 1985. Further, up to 23 months of interest-free credit can be obtained under the current "normal" credit arrangements available from the company. As of October 1985, 15 percent of the firm's outstanding receivables were not due for over one year. It is clear that Deere is spending a great deal of its resources to support its dealers, giving some indication of how critical they are to the firm's success. The firm's marketing policy manual says, "Our dealers are our greatest assets. "If they do not succeed, any success we have is bound to be short-lived."

Historically, the typical Deere dealer has generated annual revenues of about $3 million. About 380 dealers sell only industrial equipment, with revenues of $10 million being achieved by some of these dealers. Overseas sales are generated through sales branches in Europe, South America, Australia, South Africa, and Mexico. These branches supply 1,300 overseas retail

dealers. Four export branches supply products to over 100 countries through 160 distributors.

The financial function of the dealer network is supported by the John Deere Credit Company which also helps finance retail sales of farm and industrial equipment. However, a great portion of the retail sales is supported by outside lenders. Through its purchase of Farm Plan in 1984, Deere Credit will also supply credit services to farmers for the purchase of seed, feed, planting supplies, and other needs.

The company's image is fostered by specialized forms of advertising. The company publishes technical support material and a farm magazine called the *Furrow*. The *Furrow*, published worldwide in 10 languages and 27 editions, is estimated to have a circulation of 2,000,000 readers. The company's marketing philosophy is perhaps best embodied by the following comments of the advertising planning manager. "We decided to position our tractors in the customers' minds as the most productive tractors on the market. Perhaps, just as important, our competitors in their advertising had left this position open to us."

It is hard to gauge Deere's market success precisely. Market share figures for various products are not generally published. However, it is estimated that Deere has over 40 percent of the North American market, which makes it the leading supplier. As late as 1984, it was estimated that Deere led worldwide sales with 32.4 percent, with the rest of the firms having the estimated shares shown in Table 1.[5]

AGRICULTURAL ENVIRONMENT

Agriculture is perhaps the oldest organized activity in which humankind participates. It is responsible not only for the production of food, but also for the fiber from which clothing and industrial goods are made. Though there are very few places on the globe where agriculture is not practiced in some form, the effort differs greatly, depending on climate, culture, resources, and other

---

[4]M. Thompson, "Implement Dealers Find Tough Going," *Waterloo Courier*, February 16, 1986, p. G7.

---

[5]J. Risen, "Dominant Deere Views Case-International Harvester Combination," *Waterloo Courier*, December 2, 1984, p. A12; T. Petzinger, Jr. and B. Morris, "Tenneco to Buy Farm-Gear Unit from Harvester," *The Wall Street Journal*, November 27, 1984, p. 2.

TABLE 1 Agricultural Equipment Market Shares, 1984

Firm	World Share
Deere & Co.	32.4%
Case-International Harvester	19.8*
Ford-New Holland	15.0*
Massey-Ferguson	11.1
Kubota	9.0
Fiat	8.7
Allis-Chalmers	4.0

Note: The Case-IH share for 1985 and beyond is lower because of subsequent capacity reductions and product rationalization, making Ford number two.
*Estimated by the authors based on subsequent mergers.

Source: Wertheim & Co.

important variables. One important factor varies little across much of the agricultural sector, however—the role of the markets for these goods. Even planned economies with state-managed distribution systems participate in the world markets for agricultural commodities.

Role of Commodity Markets

Agriculture is a highly fragmented activity with large numbers of producers, each wishing to market their largely undifferentiated products. The number of buyers of agricultural commodities is also large. When a market has these characteristics, the prices in the market tend to be volatile and cannot be controlled by individual buyers or sellers. This situation is further exacerbated by the fact that it is relatively easy for new producers to enter the market.

Many of the critical inputs to agriculture, especially in more developed economies, are not commodities. The chemicals and mechanical implements used in planting, cultivating, and harvesting are produced and sold by concentrated groups of manufacturers with sufficient bargaining power to control prices. Even the critical inputs of land and money, though traded in competitive markets, result in fixed costs which must be met regardless of the quantity of output produced by the farmer or the price at which it may be sold.

As a result of this market structure agricultural producers face output prices that vary greatly, while inputs like chemicals, tractors and land become more and more expensive. This leaves the farmer with very few options for protecting or improving profits. Any individual farmer cannot control the number of producers, what they choose to plant, or how much they produce. This means that each farmer must employ an approach that is essentially a self-sufficient solution to the problem. One option is to produce a crop in short supply which could be sold at a premium price. The main difficulty with such a strategy in the long run is that every other farmer is trying to do the same thing, given suitable climate and land, reducing the time available to exploit the advantage.

The most obvious option of any particular farm producer is to simply produce more output per unit of input than the competitors, thus raising productivity. Since so many of the costs of farming are fixed in relation to the farm operation as a unit, or per acre, for example, the more output per acre the farmer produces, the lower the cost per unit of crop produced. This strategy, too, has long-run ramifications. The more farmers generally increase productivity, the more they produce relative to effective world demand, with the result that commodity prices, in general, tend to trend lower.

Though Deere's agricultural equipment products are directed primarily at the production of coarse grains such as wheat, corn, and soybeans and this context is of the most immediate impact on the firm, all mechanized farmers face the general environmental structure described above. Domestically agriculture produces output in four main segments: coarse grains, livestock, fruits and vegetables, and fibers. The main impact on Deere is in the first segment, though grain production is also indirectly linked to livestock production and market behavior.

Impact of Environmental Trends

The drive to increase productivity initially created a strong demand for more effective tools needed to accomplish the task. Though the entire post-World War II period has been characterized by increasing farm productivity, in the decade of the seventies, especially, a number of forces combined to drive the demand for increasingly expensive and productive farm implements to record levels. Technological advances, dramatic rises in the rate of increase in the prices of all farm inputs, and the ready availability of cash supported by increases in land values all encouraged the trend toward increased equipment purchases. In addition to using improved equipment, farmers can also improve productivity improvement through the use of improved chemical and cultivation techniques. Innovations in biotechnology have also begun to contribute to productivity gains, with even more promised for the future.

The movement toward the use of chemicals and capital equipment to increase productivity was well on its way when the activities of OPEC began to influence the environment. The rising price of oil had an impact in two vital areas. Most farm chemicals, including fertilizer are produced from inputs based on petroleum or natural gas. This caused a rise in the cost of these important aids to productivity improvement. Oil price increases also caused all fuels to rise in price, making the operation of farm equipment more expensive. Farmers in developed countries, especially, began to trade in old equipment for newer, more efficient tractors and harvesters.

Rising fuel prices had an even greater impact outside the agricultural sector. Higher prices for oil and its derivatives dramatically changed world capital flows and forced many developed nations to scramble for exports that could be exchanged for oil. The most efficient food-producing nations naturally tried to raise exports of farm products to pay for their much needed oil. Rising fuel prices also helped touch off a general inflation across all sectors of the major developed economies, making it that much more imperative for farmers to increase productivity to offset generally rising input costs. Finally, interest rates also rose dramatically as a result of the general inflation, eventually making the purchase of expensive agricultural inputs such as equipment and land more risky.

Land values in the seventies proved to be something of a paradox. Prices rose steadily, helping to add value to an important source of wealth for farmers. Land is the critical foundation for the collateral farmers need for seasonal borrowing. However, rising land prices, combined with rising interest rates and increasing equipment purchases, greatly increased the amount of cash flow needed by farmers who purchased land during the last decade. Early in the decade price increases in farm commodities supported the increased cash flow require-

ments of farmers and encouraged expansion. The size of the typical farm in the United States increased, reflecting consolidation and land purchases. Farmers who did not expand during the period have not been affected by these land-associated costs. (See Tables 2 and 3 for summary data reflecting these trends.)

Eventually, rising productivity and a recession induced in part by monetary policy designed to reduce inflation and interest rates, put an end to the inflationary prosperity. Farmers were left with shrinking land values and high-fixed costs. Productivity improvements raised production quantities above demand causing surpluses and falling prices for crops. The resulting spiral put tremendous pressure on the agricultural sector. The more cash the farmers needed the more they had to try to produce. The more they produced, the lower farm prices became. Evidence of this set of interlocking trends can be seen in Tables 2, 3, and 4. Note especially the behavior of interest rates, land values, farm debt as a proportion of farm assets, commodity prices, and general inflation.

Other Agricultural Environment Issues

The attempts by farmers to improve productivity are not solely responsible for crop surpluses and falling prices. Government intervention and high exit barriers are also key culprits. Overproduction produces "carryover" stocks which depress prices, often to levels below the unit cost of production. Even the presence of a billion hungry people around the globe does little to reduce this problem. Most of these potential customers cannot afford to buy what they need. The critical political importance of food to all nations is a key factor encouraging the intervention of many governments in the agricultural marketplace. The magnitude of the overproduction issue is illustrated in Table 5.

In the developed nations farmers producing surpluses have had sufficient political clout to force their governments to subsidize overproduction, eliminating the negative market action that would normally force many producers from the industry. One style of program encourages reduced planting, while paying the farmers not to produce. Another typical program involves government purchases of surplus stocks, increasing prices and reducing farmer-owned carryovers. Once in posses-

TABLE 2   Selected Farm Production Data (all but index = million metric tons; for Index 1977 = 100)

(2.1)	(2.2)	(2.3)	(2.4)	(2.5)	(2.6)	(2.7)
			Less:			Index of Farm
	Starting	Plus: Production +	Domestic		Ending	Produc-
Year	Stocks	Imports*	Use	Exports	Stocks	tivity
1976	43.3	257.0	153.6	78.1	68.6	98.0
1977	68.6	264.8	161.7	88.4	83.3	100.0
1978	83.3	275.0	179.7	94.5	84.1	101.0
1979	84.1	301.2	184.6	111.2	89.5	105.0
1980	89.5	268.2	171.0	114.9	71.8	101.0
1981	71.8	328.8	178.6	110.8	111.2	116.0
1982	111.2	331.4	193.1	96.3	153.2	116.0
1983	153.2	206.9	183.0	97.7	79.4	98.0
1984	79.4	313.7	197.0	97.3	98.8	115.0
1985	98.8	345.7	300.8	62.8	80.9	127.0

*Import amounts in all years less than 1.0 million metric tons.

Source: U.S. Department of Agriculture.

TABLE 3   Selected Farm Financial Data

(3.1)	(3.2)	(3.3)	(3.4)	(3.5)	(3.6)	(3.7)
	Net Farm	Direct Government	Value of Land and	All Farm	Debt/	Average
	Income	Payments	Buildings	Debt	Assets	Farm Size
Year	($ bil.)	($ bil.)	1977 = 100	($ bil.)	(%)	(acres)
1976	$20.1	$0.7	86.0	$ 91.5	15.9%	422.0
1977	19.8	1.8	100.0	103.9	15.6	427.0
1978	27.7	3.0	109.0	122.7	16.7	429.0
1979	32.3	1.4	125.0	140.8	16.1	428.0
1980	21.2	1.3	145.0	165.8	16.5	427.0
1981	31.0	1.9	158.0	182.0	18.2	425.0
1982	22.3	3.5	157.0	201.7	20.1	428.0
1983	17.8	9.3	148.0	216.3	20.4	432.0
1984	34.5	8.4	146.0	212.6	22.2	437.0
1985	27.0	9.0	134.3	212.1	23.7	440.0

Source: U.S. Department of Agriculture.

sion of this surplus food the government is free to sell it or give it away as foreign aid. Such programs are not limited to U.S. farming. Nations in the European Economic Community (Common Market) also provide heavy subsidies to farmers in every sector.

Farming is a key source of trade receipts for many countries. Increased production in Brazil, Canada, Australia, Argentina, and other nations has served to improve the trade positions of all these countries. Though this increased activity has been helpful to equipment and

TABLE 4   Critical Price Levels (Index nos.—1977 = 100)

(4.1) Year	(4.2) CPI	(4.3) All Farm Inputs	(4.4) All Farm Receipts	(4.5) Agricultural Equipment	(4.6) Land Prices	(4.7) Interest Paid
1976	93.9	95.0	102.0	92.5	86.0	88.0
1977	100.0	100.0	100.0	100.0	100.0	100.0
1978	107.7	108.0	115.0	107.7	109.0	117.0
1979	119.8	123.0	132.0	117.3	125.0	143.0
1980	136.0	138.0	134.0	131.0	145.0	174.0
1981	150.1	150.0	139.0	147.7	158.0	211.0
1982	159.3	157.0	133.0	157.2	157.0	241.0
1983	164.4	160.0	134.0	164.9	148.0	250.0
1984	171.4	163.0	142.0	169.8	146.0	251.0
1985	179.6	163.0	128.0	170.5	134.3	205.0

Source: U.S. Department of Agriculture; Bureau of Labor Statistics.

TABLE 5   Current and Constant Dollar Sales, Agricultural Equipment (Index 1977 = 100)

(5.1) Year‡	(5.2) Equipment Expenses* ($ billions)	Industry (5.3) Price Index 1977=100 (4.5)	Industry (5.4) Expense Index 1977=100 (from 5.2)	Industry (5.5) Real Expense 1977=100 (5.4/5.3)	(5.6) Agriculture Equipment Sales† $ billions	Deere (5.7) Sales Index 1977=100 (from 5.6)	Deere (5.8) Real Sales 1977=100 (5.7/5.3)
1976	$ 8.05	92.5	95.4	103.1	$2.68	91.4	98.8
1977	8.43	100.0	100.0	100.0	2.93	100.0	100.0
1978	10.44	107.7	123.8	115.0	3.30	112.4	104.3
1979	11.75	117.3	139.3	118.8	3.94	134.2	114.4
1980	10.64	131.0	126.2	96.3	4.49	153.0	116.8
1981	10.22	145.7	121.2	83.2	4.67	159.0	109.1
1982	7.98	157.2	94.6	60.2	4.03	137.5	87.4
1983	7.58	164.9	89.8	54.5	3.31	113.0	68.5
1984	7.28	169.8	86.3	50.8	3.51	119.5	70.4
1985	7.25	170.5	86.0	50.4	3.12	106.3	62.3

*Equipment expenditure data represents USDA figure for actual equipment purchases.
†Excludes industrial equipment.
‡Reference to columns used in calculations.

Sources: Agriculture Department, Deere and Company Annual Reports.

other farm sector suppliers, the rise in world output has generally depressed world farm commodity prices. Outside the United States productivity is not as high as it is here but labor and land costs are lower. This leaves the United States with a number of tough competitors worldwide. Further, the governments of these competitor countries are not committed to the political issues which have recently plagued U.S. farmers in the form of trade embargoes to the USSR and South Africa, for example.

In the United States government intervention has also taken place in the credit markets, through the manipulation of federal lands—especially forest land, with insurance programs, and through numerous other less ambitious programs. Though the Reagan administration has vowed to reduce government intervention in farming, the political forces in the Congress, especially the Senate, and the depth of the farm recession in the eighties will make such a withdrawal difficult. Farm payments in 1986 reached record levels and the 1987 Federal Budget asking for agriculture exceeded $50 billion.

Normally when a particular business entity is unable to meet its obligations it should be forced to leave its industry. It is generally agreed that farm capacity in the United States is 25–30 percent higher than it should be. However, who should leave? Two farmers producing identical crops with identical productivity levels could find themselves in very different financial positions depending on when they purchased their land. It is difficult for any farmer whose troubles seem to stem from timing to feel it is fair to be forced out of business. Food production and land ownership are also emotional issues in our society—supported by much mythology and historic cultural connections. Finally, realistically, the disposal of 25–30 percent of our farm assets is probably impossible in the short-run. All of these exit barriers encourage political pressure and farm surpluses.

Finally, productivity improvement is not a strategy with unlimited capability. There is a point at which the scale economies deriving from larger farm sizes and more powerful equipment no longer have a significant impact. As tractors become larger they become more difficult to use on hilly ground. They also tend to compact the soil, making it more difficult to cultivate. High-yield agriculture based on heavy equipment works best on wide-open ground which subjects the farm to erosion. The loss of vital topsoil through erosion by wind and water has become a critical issue in agriculture.

To avoid loss of soil by erosion and to save fuel some farmers have begun to utilize reduced-tillage farming techniques. Reduced tillage methods eliminate post-harvest plowing and disking operations, leaving crop residue to hold loose soil. In its most efficient form, reduced tillage planting takes place in only one or two passes through the field. Seeds are planted in crop residue, with the soil being loosened by chisel plows

mounted with the planting equipment. Weeds and pests are controlled by the heavy use of chemicals, sometimes applied with the seeds. However, the multiple operations of reduced-tillage require more technologically complex tractors. The cost of the equipment required for reduced-tillage farming has reduced the rate of diffusion, despite its multiple benefits. Yields are also lower with reduced tillage, offsetting some of the cost savings from the smaller number of operations required.

CONSTRUCTION AND CONSUMER ENVIRONMENTS

Though Deere & Company was founded as a producer of agricultural equipment, and though this is still the firm's primary activity, declines in the market for these products have forced the firm to increasingly rely on other markets. The fastest growing segment of the business is the consumer and industrial market for lawn and garden implements and tractors. It has been estimated that lawn tractors and implements made up $650 million of Deere's sales in 1985. (This data is apparently included in the agricultural product line data shown in Tables 6 and 7.)[6]

The demand for these consumer product lines is directly affected primarily by levels of personal disposable income and construction of single-family housing.[7] Because the engine component makes up 50–70 percent of the value of the typical unit of outdoor power equipment, engine producers are important contributors to the industry. Domestic small gasoline engine production for these applications is dominated by two firms, Briggs and Stratton and Tecumseh. Kawasaki, Honda, and other Japanese firms are also involved, both in engines and equipment production. Kawasaki provides engines for some Deere lawn tractors, for example.

---

[6]J. Flint, "Root, Hog! Or Die," *Forbes,* November 4, 1985, pp. 170–78.

[7]Department of Commerce, *1986 U.S. Industrial Outlook,* Washington, D.C.: U.S. Government Printing Office, 1986), pp. 47.8–47.10.

Construction Equipment

The production of construction equipment resembles the agricultural equipment market in many ways. It is cyclical, heavily dependent on dealer networks and the availability of financing, and influenced heavily by developments in power-train technology. The structure and dynamics of the industry, however, are much different. Customers of this industry are primarily contractors, industrial buyers, and specialized users, such as mining and logging companies, for example, whose demand derives from a variety of forces. A major segment of the market is involved with lift trucks and other heavy material handling equipment. Further, 40 percent of the value of shipments in the industry is exported. As in the agricultural equipment market, overseas producers are growing and overcapacity generally plagues the industry. Also, as in the agricultural market, many domestic suppliers are importing components or moving the production of some small equipment offshore.

Deere and Company is a relative newcomer in the construction equipment market. Caterpillar Tractor Company is the world's leading producer of construction equipment, followed by Komatsu in Japan. Other firms are important producers, specializing in a narrow segment of the market. Clark Equipment is a major producer of material handling equipment, while Joy Manufacturing dominates underground mining equipment production, with Bucyrus-Erie and Koehring being important producers of surface mining equipment and cranes, respectively. Overall, with $943 million of sales in 1985, Deere appears to have about 6 percent of the total market.[8] Six U.S. producers account for roughly three quarters of the value of worldwide shipments and 69 percent of U.S. exports. The total number of U.S. producers is about 700.

AGRICULTURAL EQUIPMENT INDUSTRY

During the 1980s the agricultural equipment industry has undergone considerable consolidation with the result that only two producers of farm tractors remain in the

---

[8]Standard & Poor's Corporation, *Industry Surveys,* pp. S42–S45.

United States, Deere and Tenneco's J.I. Case-International Harvester unit. Massey-Ferguson (Varity), reorganizing after bankruptcy, has closed all U.S. production. IH tractor production has been absorbed by Case, eliminating much of the firm's capacity and overlapping product lines. White has been unable to reopen after entering reorganization. Allis-Chalmers has sold the bulk of its assets to Klockner-Humboldt-Deutz of West Germany. Ford has moved its tractor production overseas after purchasing Sperry-New Holland in 1985.

Unit tractors sales under 100 HP make up about 80–85 percent of the total, while accounting for only 50 percent of the tractor revenues of the industry. The $1.5 billion trade surplus in farm equipment experienced in 1981 largely disappeared by 1986, because of flagging demand and the transfer of most small tractor production overseas. Tractors account for roughly half of all international trade in farm machinery, with harvesters and implements accounting for the remainder.

One factor influencing the change in trade patterns has been the loss of the traditional technological advantage enjoyed by U.S. firms. European tractors now embody many features not yet found on U.S. models. Further, where European and Japanese firms (Kubota is the primary Japanese producer) have traditionally limited production to small (under 100 HP) units, European producers are now producing many of the larger models as well.

Though tractors are the biggest single revenue source for the farm equipment industry and few producers remain, there are hundreds of niche market firms producing a variety of specialized equipment lines. These small firms have not escaped the problems of the industry and several such as Hesston and Steiger have been acquired or forced into bankruptcy.

Tenneco

Tenneco entered the farm equipment business in 1967 when it acquired J.I. Case. The current chief executive of Tenneco, Jim Ketelsen started as president of the Case subsidiary just after the acquisition. With the IH acquisition in late 1984, Tenneco became the third largest producer in the industry, broadened its product line, and strengthened its dealer network. As a result of the Tenneco acquisition 30–40 percent of total U.S. tractor production capacity was eliminated and Ford was bumped up to second place in the market in terms of sales (though Ford no longer produces tractors in the United States).

RECENT DEVELOPMENTS AND STRATEGY

Deere and Company has become the leader in the farm equipment industry in recent years because it has recognized a number of important requirements of the environment. Recognizing that the key to selling its products is close contact with the customer, the firm has consistently supported its strong dealer network. This group not only sells the product but is also responsible for the service that maintains the firm's reputation for quality.

Deere has also recognized that to keep the goodwill of the customer an equipment maker must make a product that will do the work it was designed to do without breaking down. Weather conditions are very important to the farmer, especially when the growing season is limited. There are only a few days when fields are dry enough for fieldwork in the spring, for example. If the farmer does not complete needed soil preparation and planting in those days, the very least that will happen is that yields will be significantly reduced. At worst, the farmer may not be able to plant any profitable crop. An equipment breakdown in one of the critical periods could cause serious delays and a great deal of ill will for the company.

In the last 15 years a number of changes have taken place in farming. These changes became especially pronounced after oil prices and general price levels began to squeeze the farmer's profits and farmers began to recognize the importance of productivity. To improve per-acre yields in relation to costs it became essential to have equipment which could plant and harvest to very critical tolerances. An error of even a foot in the width of a row during planting process multiplies over a large field to such a degree that hundreds or even thousands of dollars in revenue can be lost. Many farmers and industry leaders also feel that the larger the farm, the lower the average production cost of the crop. Large farms require more powerful, sophisticated equipment.

In this context Deere made a strong commitment to the production of large, powerful, sophisticated tractors and implements. George Stickler of Deere's Technical Center has said, "We've never found a way to refute the economies of scale of larger farms." "I think the whole idea about going back to the old ways of agriculture is just a lot of baloney."[9] Accordingly, in recent years over 50 percent of Deere's farm equipment sales come from high horsepower row-crop and four-wheel-drive tractors and combines serving primarily coarse grain farmers.

Not all the most efficient and prosperous farms are large, however. A recent Agriculture Department report says that though only 1 out of every 250 farms (0.4 percent of the total number) has revenues over $1,000,000, these "superfarms" account for more than 20 percent of total farm revenue. In spite of this monopoly on revenues, however, one third of these farms are less than the average size. In fact, 10 percent of the richest farms have fewer than 50 acres.[10] Obviously, these relatively small, superfarms are not generating that much revenue from planting soybeans. Rather, they are involved in high revenue, specialty outputs such as vegetables and herbs; costly nuts such as pistachios and cashews; and exotic livestock such as buffalo and deer.

As the agricultural equipment industry has become more and more mature in recent years Deere has also seen the need to improve the productivity of its manufacturing operations. The massive capital investments of the last decade have created increased capacity and helped the firm become a leader in industry productivity. Sales per employee for the firm have nearly doubled from about $56,700 in 1976, to just over $100,000 in 1985. Labor costs have also been reduced as a result of these kinds of improvements. For example, at 4 percent of unit cost, labor costs on the firm's latest industrial equipment product line are proportionally only half of what they were in the mid-1970s.

These productivity improvements are not achieved without cost, however. Reducing labor costs through the use of capital equipment creates fixed costs which tend to raise a firm's break-even point. Sales declines, such as those which have been experienced by Deere can cause great losses or force huge price increases. To avoid both of these undesirable outcomes a firm must develop more efficient schedules, reduce waste,

---

[9]A. Anderson Jr., "Future Farming," *Omni*, June 1979, pp. 90–94 ff.

[10]D. Kendall, " 'Superfarm' Numbers Have Grown Rapidly in Past Decade," *Waterloo Courier*, February 16, 1986.

reduce white-collar personnel, and otherwise operate with the minimum possible cost. Throughout the slump in agricultural equipment sales Deere has worked hard to control costs and drive down its break-even point. In fact, the manager of the firm's Component Works—the division that produces major component parts for the firm—has set a goal of reducing the break-even point of the division by 33 percent in 1986, to an astonishing 22 percent of capacity.[11] There are limits to such activities, however. In the long run the firm may have to consolidate its facilities, closing some of its older plants as Case-IH has done, to reduce fixed costs.

Financial Results

The results of Deere's strategies in the last decade have been mixed at best. Until the deterioration of the farm situation in the 1980s the firm had achieved steady growth in sales, averaging 11.7 percent per year from 1976 through 1981. Since then sales have declined an average of 7.1 percent per year. Profits have not displayed such a clear trend. From 1976–81 profits grew at only 0.75 percent per year, declining at the rate of 41 percent a year since then. Financial results for selected years are shown in Tables 6 and 7. A context for these financial results is provided by Table 5, highlighting the influence of price inflation on the sales growth for both the firm and by the industry as a whole.

A significant part of the assets and income controlled by Deere and Company is not shown in the company's regular financial statements. The firm's two large financial subsidiaries and its interest in its partially owned foreign affiliates are reported only in the notes to the financial statements. These data are shown in Tables 8 and 9. The total income from the two finance subsidiaries is about half of the "other income" shown on the income statement for 1985 (Table 6), for example.

Table 10 reports the sales, operating income, and identifiable assets reported for each of the firm's two major segments of business, agricultural equipment and

industrial equipment. (The sum of the operating income figures in Table 10 and those in Table 6 do not match because the latter has been recast to a more conventional form to better reflect company operations as separated from the impact of the affiliates.)

Reorganization

In the years since 1980, Deere and Company has undergone at least two major periods of reorganization. In the early part of the decade the firm undertook a major physical reorganization of its Blackhawk County, Iowa, facilities. The completion of the Engine Works and Waterloo Tractor Works facilities in 1980 added a large chunk of capacity and permitted the firm to consolidate much of its internal supply operation in the former tractor assembly facilities. This new consolidated supply operation was designated as the Component Works. There are four major operations consolidated in the Component Works: the foundry, hydraulics production, drive train production, and a miscellaneous group to make gears and other machined parts. The total Component Works operation occupies 6.5 million square feet, producing 70 percent of the finished parts used in the firm's tractors.

More recently, the Component Works was again reorganized to implement a concept the firm calls the *focused factory.* Under this notion the four operational component units were given operational autonomy within the overall divisional structure, becoming "factories within a factory." The purpose of this action was to focus the energy of the four group managers on a narrower product line. It is intended that through this focus flexibility and efficiency could be developed in management and engineering. Management feels this change will enhance skill development consistent with its need to produce high-quality, complex components at a lower cost.

The primary purpose of the "factory within a factory" structure is designed to facilitate flexibility, problem-solving, communication, and a number of related management processes. In addition, however, it also facilitates the development of salable products which can be used to fill excess capacity in the various components divisions, thus reducing the cost burden on the parent organization.

---

[11]E. Adcock, "Testing, 'Seeding' of Diesels for OEM Business Begins in '86," *Waterloo Courier,* January 19, 1986, p. I1.

TABLE 6

DEERE AND COMPANY
Income Statements
For Selected Years Ending October 31
(in millions)

Item	1976	Percent	1981	Percent	1984	Percent	1985	Percent	Average Growth per Year
Farm Equipment	$ 2,682	85.6%	$ 4,665	85.6%	$ 3,505	79.7%	$ 3,118	76.8%	1.7%
Industrial Equipment	452	14.4	782	14.4	894	20.3	943	23.2	8.5
Net sales	3,134	100.0	5,447	100.0	4,399	100.0	4,061	100.0	2.9
Less: cost of sales	2,316	73.9	4,274	78.5	3,598	81.8	3,355	82.6	4.2
Gross Profit	818	26.1	1,173	21.5	801	18.2	706	17.4	−1.6
Less:									
General and Administrative expenses	316	10.1	515	9.5	501	11.4	508	12.5	5.4
Other operating expenses	47	1.5	142	2.6	42	1.0	54	1.3	1.5
Depreciation	66	2.1	177	3.3	192	4.4	184	4.5	12.2
Total operating expenses	429	13.7	834	15.3	735	16.7	746	18.4	6.4
Operating profit	389	12.4	338	6.2	66	1.5	−40	−1.0	N/A
+ Other income	75	2.4	265	4.9	237	5.4	206	5.1	11.8
− Interest and Other	57	1.8	232	4.3	235	5.3	199	4.9	15.0
Income before tax	408	13.0	371	6.8	69	1.6	−34	−0.8	N/A
Less: income tax	165	5.3	120	2.2	−36	−0.8	−65	−1.6	N/A
Net income	$ 242	7.7	$ 251	4.6	$ 105	2.4	$ 31	0.8	−20.4
Dividends	$ 62		$ 133		$ 68		$ 68		
Percent of net income	25.6%		53.0%		64.8%		218.0%		1.0
Current cash flow	$ 308	9.8	$ 428	7.9	$ 296	6.7	$ 215	5.3	−3.9
Number of common shares	60		66		68		68		
E.P.S.	$ 4.05		$ 3.79		$ 1.54		$ 0.46		−21.5
Capital Investment	$ 126		$ 303		$ 89		$ 144		
Number of employees (actual)	55,242		60,857		43,011		40,509		
Sales/employee (actual)	$56,728		$89,500		$102,280		$100,240		−3.4

Source: Deere and Company Annual Reports.

TABLE 7

DEERE AND COMPANY
Balance Sheet
As of October 31
(in millions)

Year	1976	Percent	1981	Percent	1984	Percent	1985	Percent	Average Growth per Year
Assets									
Current Assets:									
Cash	$ 173	5.9%	$ 68	1.2%	$ 41	0.7%	$ 88	1.6%	−7.3%
Accounts receivable	1,048	35.6	2,374	41.8	2,847	50.0	2,749	50.3	11.3
Inventory	623	21.2	872	15.3	540	9.5	447	8.2	−3.6
Other	253	8.6	250	4.4	246	4.3	150	2.7	−5.6
Total current assets	2,096	71.2	3,564	62.7	3,675	64.5	3,435	62.9	5.6
Fixed assets:									
Plant and equipment	1,066	36.2	2,446	43.0	2,484	43.6	2,629	48.1	10.6
Less: accumulated depreciation	495	−16.8	1,038	−18.3	1,452	−25.5	1,613	−29.5	14.0
Other fixed assets—net	277	9.4	711	12.5	990	17.4	1,012	18.5	15.5
Total fixed assets	848	28.8	2,119	37.3	2,023	35.5	2,028	37.1	10.2
Total assets	$2,944	100.0	$5,684	100.0	$5,697	100.0	$5,462	100.0	7.1%
Liabilities and Equity									
Current Liabilities:									
Accounts payable	$ 646	21.9	$1,320	23.2	$1,143	20.1	$1,044	19.1	5.5
Notes payable	112	3.8	679	11.9	568	10.0	521	9.5	18.7
Current payable, long-term debt	23	0.8	15	0.3	158	2.8	16	0.3	−3.6
Taxes payable	238	8.1	291	5.1	350	6.1	333	6.1	3.8
Total current liabilities	1,018	34.6	2,304	40.5	2,219	38.9	1,914	35.0	7.3
Long-term debt									
Bonds and notes	539	18.3	760	13.4	1,080	19.0	1,239	22.7	9.7
Deferred taxes	17	0.6	170	3.0	108	1.9	51	0.9	13.2
Total long-term debt	555	18.9	930	16.4	1,188	20.8	1,290	23.6	9.8
Owners' equity:									
Common stock	214	7.3	482	8.5	490	8.6	491	9.0	9.7
Retained earnings	1,157	39.3	1,967	34.6	1,801	31.6	1,767	32.4	4.8
Total equity	1,371	46.6	2,450	43.1	2,291	40.2	2,259	41.4	5.7
Total liabilities and owners' equity	$2,944	100.0	$5,684	100.0	$5,697	100.0	$5,462	100.0	7.1%

Source: Deere and Company Annual Reports.

TABLE 8

DEERE AND COMPANY
Financial Results—Nonconsolidated Subsidiaries
Selected Years Ending October 31
(in millions)

Income Statements

	Retail Finance Subsidiary			Insurance Subsidiary		
	1985	1984	1981	1985	1984	1981
Net revenues	$ 335.4	$ 333.9	$ 360.0	$260.2	$250.5	$266.0
Less: Expenses						
General and administrative	28.4	19.1	2.0	35.1	31.9	35.5
Depreciation / Claim costs	10.2	12.4		192.1	188.5	203.3
Insurance	24.2	22.8	12.1			
Operating Income	272.6	279.6	345.9	33.0	30.1	27.2
Less: Interest	172.5	183.0	238.3			
Income before tax	100.1	96.6	107.6	33.0	30.1	27.2
Less: income tax	40.1	39.3	49.9	7.1	4.6	
Net income	$ 60.0	$ 57.3	$ 57.7	$ 25.9	$ 25.5	$ 27.2

Balance Sheets

	Retail Finance Subsidiary			Insurance Subsidiary		
	1985	1984	1981	1985	1984	1981
Assets:						
Retail net receivables / Cash	$2,623.5	$2,586.6	$2,300.9	$ 39.9	$ 45.1	$ 59.2
Lease investment / Securities investment	442.8	396.8		410.6	365.5	213.1
Deferred assets	1.0	5.1				
Other assets	94.1	32.4	53.3	70.8	70.8	17.4
Total Assets	$3,161.4	$3,020.9	$2,354.2	$521.3	$481.4	$289.7
Liabilities:						
Notes payable / Policy reserves	$1,287.9	$1,344.5	$1,133.4	$218.0	$199.1	$ 87.7
Due JD & Co. / Unearned premiums	76.1	155.7	232.6	56.7	50.1	46.7
Other	370.4	387.8	280.3	32.5	32.8	23.2
Long term-debt	817.6	559.4	324.6			
Total liabilities	2,552.0	2,447.4	1,970.9	307.2	282.0	157.6
Owner's equity	609.4	573.5	383.3	214.1	199.4	132.1
	$3,161.4	$3,020.9	$2,354.2	$521.3	$481.4	$289.7

Source: Deere and Company Annual Reports.

TABLE 9

Financial Results of
Affiliates—Deere & Company for
Selected Years Ending October 31
(in millions)

	1985	1984
Position in affiliated companies:		
Net revenues	$ 407.7	$ 307.2
Less: expenses	377.6	311.7
Net income (loss)	$ 30.1	$ (4.5)
Deere's share	9.3	0.8
Total assets	$ 277.2	$ 245.9
Less: liabilities	147.8	146.5
Net assets	$ 129.4	$ 99.4
Deere's share	43.3	35.6

Source: Deere and Company Annual Reports.

TABLE 10 Segment Sales—for Selected Years Ending October 31 (in millions)

	1985	1984	1981
Sales			
Agricultural equipment	$3,118	$3,505	$4,665
Industrial equipment	943	894	782
	4,061	4,399	5,447
Operating income and equity investments:			
Agricultural equipment	$ 65	$ 181	$ 560
Industrial equipment	22	5	(38)
	87	186	522
Identifiable assets:			
Agricultural equipment	$3,625	$3,838	$3,868
Industrial equipment	732	726	890
Corporate	1,105	1,133	926
	5,462	5,697	5,684

Source: Deere and Company Annual Reports.

New Ventures

Though exact capacity utilization figures are not available, in 1985, the firm certainly operated far below its capacity. As a result of this continued difficulty the firm has sought to identify a number of areas in which to diversify to create additional revenues.

- *Chinese Sale:* In 1984, Deere signed a $25 million contract to provide a limited number of products and the technology to develop several models of tractors.

Presumably, as the technological development continues the firm will play a further role in the process, generating additional revenues.

- *Rotary Engine:* Also in 1984, Curtiss-Wright sold its patents and other interests in the rotary engine technology to Deere. Subsequent development of this technology is being directed toward a number of possible products. The chief focus, however, is on the joint development of a rotary aircraft engine under a contract with Avco-Lycoming. The agreement with Avco gives that firm world rights to aircraft uses of the engine in exchange for royalties. Deere is then free to develop other uses for the engine. As much as $50 million in research money may be allocated to the development of this engine in the near future.

- *Purchase of Farm Plan:* In July, 1984, Deere took another step in the diversification of its financing unit with the acquisition of a Wisconsin-based financial services firm called *Farm Plan.* This firm joins with local banks in 23 states to make loans to farmers for the purchase of equipment, seed, fertilizer, feed, and other necessary inputs. This gives Deere a range of financial services to aid the farmer in addition to its current retail equipment financing and its insurance.

- *Articulated Truck:* In early 1985, Deere announced the introduction of a new heavy dump truck based on a number of components supplied by various divisions of the firm. The engine, transmission, other power train parts, steering, hydraulic components, and other key parts are made by the Engine and Component Works divisions of the firm. The truck itself is built by Kress Corporation.

- *Diesel Engine Development:* Deere is in the process of developing a number of outlets for its sophisticated diesel engine technology. In 1986 it began to set up a joint venture with GM's Allison Division involving the joint development of a line of diesel engines for a wide range of powered vehicles. Deere is expected to contribute manufacturing and engineering facilities in Waterloo, Dubuque, and France, involving about 1,500 enployees. GM is expected to contribute its Detroit Diesel Allison Division with about 4,500 employees. The new venture will produce a broad range of engines. Annual sales for the venture have been estimated at $1.5–2 billion.[12]

- *Other Engine Developments:* The company has also begun to bid actively for contracts for military applications of its engines. A new program to be undertaken in 1986 is aimed at "seeding" engines to key customers in the replacement diesel engine market, with 1987 to be the first year for a primary thrust into this market segment. Ultimately, the firm has a goal of 40,000 to 50,000 extra diesel engines annually.

- *Engine Blocks:* In addition to producing complete engines for the original equipment (OEM) and replacement markets, Deere is also beginning the production of engine parts for other firms. In 1986, the firm will begin significant production of engine blocks for the Pontiac Division of GM. The ultimate goal of this product line is 50,000 to 70,000 tons of outside foundry business per year, with the initial contract placed at 18,000 tons.[13]

- *Motor Home Chassis:* Another major project for the firm in 1986, is the production of chassis for motor homes. The amount of production expected under this agreement with Winnebago is unknown, though it has been estimated that production could be in the range of 2,000–3,000 units. This project could also pave the way for the production of similar products such as truck chassis.

FUTURE GOALS AND DIRECTIONS

Since 1984, Deere has made a initial broad commitment to diversify its activities into a number of OEM products in order to utilize its excess capacity and expertise. In addition, many of these projects could foster the development of even more expertise, leading to a further strengthening of the firm's position in a variety of heavy equipment market segments. The management of the Component Works has set a goal of having $100 million in OEM sales by 1991. Though precise figures are not available, the fastest growing division of the firm in 1986 is the home lawn care and lawn tractor line, marketed with full exploitation of the company logo and color scheme to carry the firm's quality image into this market segment. In 1986, the marketing effort for these products has been increased and includes a significant price cut in the marketing mix.

---

[12]E. Adcock. "Deere, GM Plan to Form Diesel Engine Firm," *Waterloo Courier.* July 21, 1986. p. 1.

[13]Flint, "Root, Hog! Or Die."

TABLE 11   Historical Price Behavior—Deere and Company Common Stock

| Year | Price Range | | E.P.S. | Price Earnings Ratio | |
	High	Low		High	Low
1978	37	22½	$ 4.38	8.45x	5.14x
1979	41½	31¾	5.12	8.11	6.20
1980	49¾	28½	3.72	13.37	7.66
1981	49¾	32⅛	3.79	13.13	8.48
1982	36⅞	22	.78	47.27	28.21
1983	42⅜	28½	.34	124.62	83.82
1984	40⅜	24⅝	1.54	26.22	16.00
1985	33⅛	24¼	.46	72.00	52.71
1986	35⅛	27¼	− .60*	N/A	N/A

Note: P/E in early 1986 based on last full year's earnings = 75x.
*Consensus estimate.

The exact future of Deere's main business is still subject to question. In late 1984, CEO Hanson said he expected to see significant growth back to the historical sales levels—though he doesn't say when. Others disagree, saying that sales may never rise to more than 10–15 percent above the levels achieved in 1984–85.[14]

---

[14]F. Rice, "Cruel Days in Tractorville."

In spite of the problems in the industry and the sliding sales and profits in the firm, however, Deere's common stock was selling for around 70 times current earnings in March 1986! Such a high multiple might offer the firm a golden opportunity for making acquisitions designed for further diversification. At the very least such a multiple would seem to show a high degree of investor confidence in the firm's future. Table 11 shows the historical price behavior of the firm's stock, as well as accompanying data on E.P.S.

---

20.   Strategic Management at the Amherst H. Wilder Foundation

A tough-minded man of vision and opportunity, Amherst H. Wilder belonged to a select group of frontier tycoons who masterminded the early economic growth of the American Midwest. In the late 1800s Wilder amassed a fortune in transportation, government contracting, banking, insurance, real estate, manufacturing, and municipal utilities. He became one of the most prominent citizens of St. Paul, Minnesota, in the 35 years (1859–94) he lived there.

Amherst H. Wilder's vision and concern were embodied in his last will and testament, which stipulated that a charity should be founded "to aid and assist the worthy poor, sick, aged, and otherwise needy people of

---

This case was prepared by John M. Bryson, Paula J. King, William D. Roering, and Andrew H. Van de Ven of the University of Minnesota.

Copyright © J. M. Bryson. P. J. King, W. D. Roering, and A. H. Van de Ven, 1986.

St. Paul.'' Fanny, his wife, and Cornelia Day Wilder Appleby, their only daughter, specified the same charitable intent in their wills when both died a few years after Amherst. The charitable monies from all three wills were consolidated in 1910 into the Wilder Charity, which was incorporated as a nonprofit corporation under the laws of the state of Minnesota. A tradition of serving those in need began.

Today the Wilder Foundation's service area includes the four contiguous counties that comprise the eastern half of the Twin Cities (Minneapolis and St. Paul) metropolitan area of Minnesota. In 1984 the Foundation spent $5,372,000.00 of trust income, had 950 employees, and served 38,000 people in the greater St. Paul metropolitan area.

This case will recount the history of strategic management at the Wilder Foundation. The case ends in 1984 with the president and chief executive officer of the Foundation, Leonard Wilkening, pondering the future of the Foundation. The Appendix that details several environmental trends is attached.

A PUBLIC OPERATING FOUNDATION

An important contribution to the Wilder Foundation's ability to do what it does is its tax-exempt status under Section 501(A) of the Internal Revenue Code of 1954. In order to qualify for federal tax-exempt status an organization must be operated exclusively for certain charitable, religious, educational, or scientific purposes. In practice, this has meant that a ''substantial'' portion of the organization's activities must be devoted to these purposes. The Wilder Foundation's tax-exempt status is based on its charitable activities as stipulated in Amherst Wilder's last will and testament.

The federal tax code specifies two types of tax-exempt organizations: public and private. Wilder was a private charitable agency until 1982, when it became a public 501(C) charitable organization.

In 1982, the board of directors applied to the IRS for designation as a public tax-exempt foundation (publicly supported organization), as the foundation by this date derived at least one third of its support from public sources. The IRS made an advance ruling to permit the change in 1982 and will make a final ruling in 1987.

The federal tax code establishes different requirements for private and public tax-exempt organizations.

A private tax-exempt organization receives its support from private sources such as endowments, trust funds, or private gifts. The net income earned is subject to a 2 percent annual excise tax. In contrast, a public tax-exempt organization derives its support from public sources such as membership fees, public donations, government grants and contracts, or gifts from other charitable organizations. Different categories of public tax-exempt organizations face different support tests in order to keep their tax-exempt status. The Wilder Foundation must demonstrate that at lease one third of its total financial support derives from the public sources cited above. In addition, the IRS also requires that the organization's governing body include public representatives and that the organization's services be available to the public. It should be noted that a publicly supported organization may receive income from sources other than those listed above, including endowments, as in the case of the Wilder Foundation.

The two advantages of public tax-exempt status are: (1) the elimination of the 2 percent excise tax payment requirement on net investment income, and (2) the broader base of financial support available to the organization. It is estimated that the change from private to public status has saved the Foundation an average of $500,000 annually in taxes. A public tax-exempt organization also offers tax advantages to donors. A donor can deduct in full the value of a charitable contribution to a public tax-exempt organization and also may make gifts of appreciated property to the organization. These advantages provide an incentive to potential donors to give money or real property to the public tax-exempt organization.

Unlike a grant-making foundation, Wilder directly manages the programs and services it initiates—as opposed to funding programs initiated by others.

FOUNDATION OVERVIEW

A Profile

Over the years the Wilder Foundation's resources and activities have expanded greatly. From its start in 1910 to June 30, 1984, the market value of the family endowment increased from $2,602,000 to $105,037,000; the number of buildings the Foundation owns increased to 24, with an original book value of approximately $28,000,000;

and total assets equaled $173,516,712. The Foundation employs 950 people, and in 1984 served 38,000 people living in the greater St. Paul metropolitan area. Since 1910 the Foundation has spent $85 million of its endowment and investment income to carry out the intent of the Wilder wills.

The Foundation provides direct human services to people in need (e.g., services for children, adolescents, young adults, families, elderly) as well as indirect services (e.g., consultation, training) and cooperative ventures with other public and private organizations that focus more on the cause of needs than on the needs themselves or that seek to increase the Foundation's impact in some way. Over the years, these activities have expanded and contracted in response to changing needs of the community.

Purpose

The original intent of the Wilder wills was twofold. First, to establish a permanent trust that would "relieve, aid, and assist the poor, sick, and needy people of the city of St. Paul without regard to or discrimination for any person by reason of their nationality, sex, color, or religious scruples or prejudices." Second, the trust was established to perpetuate the name of Amherst H. Wilder. He died without a son to carry forth the family name.

One limitation was placed on the trustees: no part of the trust fund could be used to construct a church building or any building belonging to or used for the benefit of "any particular religious denomination, church or sect, nor for any public or private educational institution belonging to the city, county or state, nor to any secret or benevolent order, society or organization."

Organization

As a charitable organization Wilder is required to spend a substantial portion of its adjusted net income for the active conduct of its charitable activities. For the fiscal year ending June 30, 1984, the amount spent totaled $5,372,000 out of a trust income of $8,158,000. Wilder either manages or exercises substantial control over the programs it funds. Currently the Foundation operates 39

human-service programs and is organized into three major groups, as outlined below.

Services to Individuals and Families. This group includes three operating divisions: Services to Children and Families; Services to the Elderly; Housing Management Services. The Services to Individuals and Families group contains all the Foundation programs that provide direct service, on a one-to-one basis and in groups, to children, families, young adults, and elderly persons. These persons are clients of the Foundation and participate directly in Wilder programs. Services provided by this group of programs focus on the primary purpose of the Foundation—to directly help persons in need; for example, emotionally disturbed children, elderly persons with physical and social needs, and persons who need housing arrangements.

Services to Organizations. This group includes four programs that assist other nonprofit organizations and groups by providing training, management and program consultation, technical assistance, education, and special conference and retreat facilities. The Foundation has developed expertise in these areas and acts as a resource in the community.

Community Partnerships. This group consists of partnerships the Foundation has with other entities in the community, including: a wholly owned subsidiary of the Foundation formed to develop housing and retail and office space; a for-profit corporation organized to manage limited partnerships; a home for convalescing and chronically ill women; a venture between the Foundation and General Mills to explore alternative ways for caring for and delivering services to the elderly; and a partnership with two major health organizations to establish a health-maintenance organization plan designed for primarily the frail elderly.

Moreover, the Foundation provides internal administrative, technical, and support services to assist and complement staff. These services include accounting, data processing, personnel, building maintenance, and purchasing functions. The Office of Research and Statistics maintains computer-based record systems of Foundation service programs, surveys and studies the needs of various age and socioeconomic groups of the greater metropolitan St. Paul area, and conducts demonstration projects and client follow-up studies of Foundation programs.

From the date of incorporation in 1910 to the present, the Foundation has used a program-review process in deciding which programs will be added, modified, or deleted. The board of directors decides whether to change the status of a program based on an assessment of Wilder's strategy and the program's fit with that strategy.

FOUNDATION HISTORY

The Early Years

In the early days, the trustees (now called directors) of the charity were prominent St. Paul businessmen who approached their task with caution. Because the Wilder wills charted only a general course for the charity, the trustees sought advice from leading theorists of the era in the fields of social work and philanthropy. These experts warned the trustees against giving handouts lest they create a "dynasty of beggars." The trustees, said the experts, should "go slowly, adhere to no set plan, make a survey of conditions in St. Paul, and concentrate aid on mothers and children." The Foundation's early operations were based on these suggestions.

As the Foundation grew, the directors and staff developed a more sophisticated approach embracing program analysis, community-needs assessment, budgeting, and development of alternative sources of revenue in order to protect the value of the endowment and to have a significant impact on the problems they chose to address. By the late 1960s programs were supported by a variety of revenue sources (in addition to trust income) including: fees for services; third-party reimbursement (health insurance), medicare; medicaid; federal, state, and county fees for service and grants; and gifts.

The period from 1910 to 1971 was a time of program growth and capital expansion for Wilder. By 1970, endowment income had risen to $3,406,000, but expenses had risen farther, to $3,488,000. Large sums of money supported the Infirmary ($839,000), the Day Care Centers ($621,000), the Child Guidance Clinic ($370,500), and were used to make payments on land, buildings, and equipment ($308,200).

The growth of programs and the rise in costs and inflation strained the trust income badly. The real value of the endowment was not keeping pace. From 1963 to 1970 the real value of the endowment increased by 7.4 percent per year, or only 0.75 percent per year after inflation. One approach to this problem was to change the Foundation's investment policy. In 1969 the board, led by its chair, Julian Baird, sold large blocks of stock holdings in St. Paul Fire and Marine Insurance Company and reinvested the proceeds in higher-yielding assets. This policy change yielded the portfolio mix and return on investment shown in Table 1.

TABLE 1   Portfolio Mix and Return on Investment

Before		After	
Stocks	94%	Stocks	77%
Bonds	6%	Bonds	23%
Avg. ROI 1963–1970 7.4%*		Avg. ROI 1971–1983 10.9%*	
Avg. ROI 1963–1970 0.75%†		Avg. ROI 1971–1983 0%†	

Value of the Trust in 1983 dollars	
1910	28 million
1960	117 million
1970	126 million
1983	126 million

*Actual.
†Discounted for inflation.

Executive Succession

Since its creation, the Wilder Foundation has had three executive directors: Charles Spencer (1910–1940); Frank Rarig (1940–1971); and Leonard Wilkening (1971 to present). Wilkening's title has been changed to president and CEO.

In early 1968, Frank Rarig announced his plan to retire in 1971. He had joined Wilder in 1940 when the operation was relatively small, consisting of a dispensary, a child-guidance clinic, the Wilder baths, day-care centers, a visiting-nurse program, and direct relief. When Rarig announced his plan to retire, the board instructed Rarig to hire an executive assistant who was to be his successor. The extensive search process resulted in the selection of Mr. Leonard Wilkening, who was then executive director of United Community Services, Incorporated, of Racine, Wisconsin. Upon joining Wilder in June 1968 as assistant executive director, Wilkening took over many of the day-to-day operating responsibilities. During the next three years, he also met several times a week with Mr. Rarig to discuss the Foundation and its future.

Wilkening was appointed executive director on July 1, 1971, after the directors agreed to his conditions: first, that he be allowed to undertake up to three management studies each year to analyze crucial aspects of Wilder's operation; and second, that he be allowed to replace anyone. (Mr. Rarig stayed for one year to head the Minnesota Foundation, a grant-making foundation associated with the Wilder Foundation, and to train a successor to run that foundation.)

A Turning Point

When Leonard Wilkening assumed the post of executive director, the Wilder Foundation was at a turning point. On the one hand, the Foundation had a number of strengths. As Wilkening saw it:

> We had a stable, well-connected board of directors, a history of leadership in the human services area in St. Paul, high-quality programs, a professional staff, an ability to evaluate, expand, and delete programs, and the use of endowment income.

On the other hand, Wilkening believed the Foundation had some major problems: the real value of the endowment was declining; employee pension fund liabilities were unfunded; depreciation on land, buildings, and equipment was unfunded; and budgeted monies unspent in one year were carried over to the next year. During the first several years in his new position, Wilkening worked for the adoption of policies to correct all four problems, which will be discussed briefly below.

Declining Value of the Endowment. Wilkening observed that, "When I became executive director in 1971, the trust income was $1.7 million and we spent $2.9 million, including property additions. The real value of the endowment was declining for two reasons: we were spending beyond the yearly earnings and inflation was high." Wilkening concluded that "something had to be done, particularly when one asks 'How can we make an impact?' If we kept on as we were, the time would come when the real value of the endowment would be zero."

The problem was exacerbated by the slowing of federal funding for human services when Richard Nixon's presidency replaced Lyndon Johnson's "Great Society."

Wilkening decided that the Foundation income should be leveraged to increase its impact. The leveraging ratio was 1:3; that is, every one dollar of trust income spent was to be matched by $3 of income from other sources (such as fees, grants, or contract income). Although the leveraging policy has been used since 1972, it was not officially adopted until 1978. The policy is a goal or guideline, not a rigid rule, and applies to all programs as a group, not to each program itself.

The leveraging policy, of course, was not without precedent in the Foundation's history. Fees, grants, and reimbursements of various sorts had supplemented expenditures of endowment earnings in the past. Nevertheless, there was opposition to the policy, particularly by groups (e.g., the Ramsey County Board of Commissioners) that would be expected to share more of the costs of programs. The Wilder staff also found the concept difficult to understand at first. Ultimately the board supported the policy, although, as Wilkening observed:

> The board agreed with the policy on a philosophical level but had a hard time with it when it got down to the program level. For example, we had a very popular program called Motivational Tutorial to help

disadvantaged kids. Probably 200 volunteers were involved. But we cut it out in 1978 because none of the schools or colleges would give it any financial support.

Look, I believe if a product is good someone should buy it. If no one will pay or contribute anything, then we shouldn't be spending our resources either.

Unfunded Pension Liabilities. In 1971, Wilder's unfunded pension liabilities amounted to $1.3 million. Wilkening argued that if the practice continued the time might come when all of the endowment income, and perhaps some of the principal itself, might be needed to cover the liabilities. The policy of fully funding pension liabilities began in 1973.

Unfunded Depreciation. Because depreciation was not being charged to operating budgets, the Foundation was accruing no reserve to purchase or maintain land, buildings, and equipment. Instead, noted Wilkening, "When the Foundation wanted to purchase a major capital item, the board would just sell stock no matter what the market was. It just didn't make sense to me."

Wilkening proposed creating a land, building, and equipment fund equal to depreciation expenses each year. The board agreed to this policy in 1972, and also agreed to a policy of spending approximately 75 percent of the depreciation amount in any given year.

Budget Carryovers. Wilkening also opposed the Foundation's practice of carrying over unexpended program funds to the program's budget for the following year, instead of having them revert to the endowment. The problem, according to Wilkening, was that "no real expense budget or accountability could be established. You never *really* knew what things cost." He proposed the "no carry-over" policy, which began in 1972.

The Board of Directors

Unlike the directors of many boards, Wilder's directors serve for "life" ("life" being age 70). When Wilkening became executive director, the average length of board service was 17 years. It was obvious to him that this was no rubber-stamp board and equally obvious that they would not support changes without careful study. None-

theless, Wilkening believed the board recognized there might be problems with the Foundation and was open to persuasion:

They knew what was going on when I asked to be allowed to do three studies each year. And they knew what was going on when we started to have annual board/staff conferences in 1972, with each conference organized around a different theme. The board has always been a very active board composed of very bright people. They know changes are often needed. But they want to be careful and they want to exercise their responsibilities as board members. They're an excellent policy board.

Since Wilkening joined the Foundation in 1968, there has been an almost complete turnover on the board. The board also has expanded from seven to ten members. Wilkening was elected a member of the board and president of the corporation in 1980.

A Change in Purpose

In 1974, the Foundation changed its purpose statement. According to the original articles framed in 1910, the Foundation's aim was, briefly:

to aid and assist and to furnish relief and charity for the worthy poor, sick, aged, or otherwise needy who are legitimate objects of charity.

The 1974 version (the current version) states that the Foundation's purpose is:

to promote the social welfare of persons resident or located in the greater Saint Paul metropolitan area by all appropriate means, including relief of the poor, care of the sick and aged, care and nurture of children, aid to the disadvantaged and otherwise needy, promotion of physical and mental health, support of rehabilitation and corrections, provision of needed housing and social services, operation of residences and facilities for the aged, the infirm and those requiring special care, and in general the conservation of human resources by the provision of human services responsive to the welfare needs of the community, all without regard to or discrimination on account of nationality, sex, color, religious scruples, or prejudices.

According to Wilkening, two changes are noteworthy in the current purpose statement: (1) the service area was expanded from the city of St. Paul to include Ramsey, Anoka, Washington, and Dakota counties; and (2) the ''by all appropriate means'' phrase legitimized pursuit of the mission in the specified areas and also opened up the possibility of using unconventional vehicles for doing so, including cooperative ventures with other organizations.

Other changes were occurring in the areas of program emphasis and staff skills. In recent years, the Foundation had become involved with a number of products or services new to the Foundation, including corrections (which took the Foundation somewhat away from its traditional focus on children and the elderly), additional children's needs (such as a program for teenage mothers and their infants and a rapid expansion of a community mutual help and improvement program), and low- and moderate-income housing. In each case, Wilkening argued the Foundation was ''pushed by needs'' to respond. In addition, staff were added as the Foundation moved into new areas. Norrine Bohman, assistant to the president, noted that many new staff combined a care-giving background with strong management skills, experience, and education.

THE DEVELOPMENT OF STRATEGY

The Right Time

The broadened program focus, coupled with continued decline in the real value of the endowment and the addition of staff trained in management led Wilkening to believe in the mid-to late 1970s that the time was right to move to a more formalized strategic planning process. The leveraging strategy had successfully expanded the Foundation's impact but had not stopped the decline in the real value of the endowment (see Figure 1). Increased staff capabilities, however, augured well for the future: ''For the first time, in 1976–1978, we had the internal management skill to do real strategy formulation,'' Wilkening said.

Annual Board/Staff Conferences

Annual board/staff conferences were begun in 1972 as a team-building mechanism and as part of a rudimentary strategic planning process. The 1975 board/staff task force looked at the Foundation's role in the future. Marketing was the theme of the 1976 conference. It was determined that better demographic data were needed to support the sound financial information available for planning purposes. In 1977 it was determined that a sophisticated management information system was needed. This would ensure that client's records were linked to a computerized billing system and would thus improve collections of accounts receivable. Finally, in 1978, the first formal strategy statement for the Foundation was developed. The strategy statement is summarized in Exhibit 1.

Reflection on the Strategic Plan

Wilkening argues that the 1978 strategy ''all came true.'' In reflecting upon this fact Wilkening noted:

> At Wilder we probably shouldn't discuss something unless we want to do it. If we say it, it probably will happen. It seems like every five-year objective of the Foundation takes three years to accomplish.

During the period from 1979 to 1982, a number of programs were established or expanded, and new staff was added. These programs indicated a small but gradual trend toward indirect service, as opposed to direct service, for example: (1) the Office of Statistics and Research (actually created in 1976) grew in size; (2) the Management Support Services program was created in 1982 in order to expand the foundation's external and internal consultation services; (3) internal training increased; and (4) housing development (which began in 1974 with Wilder Square) continued with the completion of Wilder Park and the creation of the subsidiary AHW Corporation (in 1980) for the purpose of developing 49 acres and 950 housing units in the Energy Park area of St. Paul.

By 1982 the successful experience with strategic planning in 1978 was somewhat dated. New programs and new staff, continuing decline in the real value of the

FIGURE 1   Wilder Foundation Endowment: Nominal and Inflation-Adjusted Market Values from 1972 to 1981 ($ in millions)

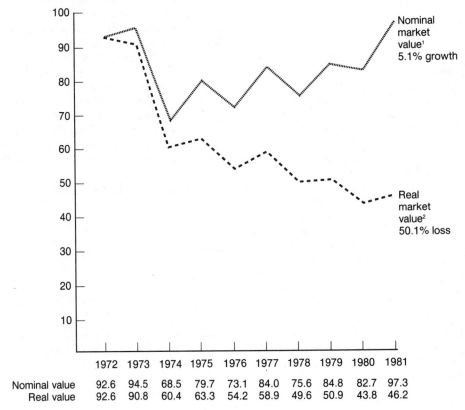

	1972	1973	1974	1975	1976	1977	1978	1979	1980	1981
Nominal value	92.6	94.5	68.5	79.7	73.1	84.0	75.6	84.8	82.7	97.3
Real value	92.6	90.8	60.4	63.3	54.2	58.9	49.6	50.9	43.8	46.2

[1]Market values of investments and operating cash as reported in the financial statements as of June 30 of each year.
[2]Real market values are reported in constant 1972 dollars adjusted by the C.P.I.

endowment (see Figure 1), and a changed administration in Washington, along with attendant changes in the national, state, and local human-services picture, led Wilkening to believe that it was time for a new round of strategic planning. An important step in the strategic planning process was a study of Foundation spending policies by an outside consulting firm. Included were simulations of what would happen to trust income and spending under different spending rules. This was the first time that such an outside analysis of Foundation spending had been prepared to inform board decision making.

The result of the second round of strategic planning was the 1982–1986 strategy statement and supporting documentation. Materials summarizing the statement and some of the analyses going into its preparation may be found in Exhibits 2, 3 and 4.

REPOSITIONING THE FOUNDATION

In 1983, the policy of leveraging endowment income continued. Also, cooperative activities with other orga-

---

EXHIBIT 1   The Wilder Foundation 1978 Strategy Statement

The Amherst H. Wilder Foundation is an old, $100 million, private 501(C)3, nonprofit, charitable, health and welfare operating foundation that will provide social services to two out of ten poor, sick, aged, and needy persons resident or living in Ramsey, Washington, Dakota, and Anoka counties, in cooperation with other public and private agencies, through the use of professional staff and income from trust, fees, contracts and grants by 6/30/84.

Major program goal emphasis is to be in Health, Housing, Social Functioning and Support. Minor program goal emphasis is to be in Income Security, Knowledge and Skills, and Collective Safety.

Present social service programs in each goal area are to be maintained and expanded as outlined in the 1979–84 guideline objectives.

1. Within the goal areas the Foundation will focus on the following needs:
   a. Problems of the 19–35-year-old age-group.
   b. Residential care of emotionally disturbed children.
   c. Elderly outreach, hospice, and geriatric center.
   d. Development of Camp Wilder.
   e. Needs assessments in various areas.
   f. Consultation.
   g. Training.
2. All new programs are to be:
   a. Started as demonstration models.
   b. Based on adequate research and study of community need.
   c. Include an evaluation component.
   d. Where possible, be in cooperation with other public and private groups.
   e. Time limited.
3. The Foundation will focus on those programs that:
   a. Influence rather than respond to environmental pressures.
   b. Are flexible and responsive to change but do not necessarily require purchase or construction of buildings and real estate.
   c. Have potential community impact, meet a known need, have a potential for standard setting, and have little or no alternative involvement.
4. Program, Financial, Building, and Board Relationship policies define how the Foundation is to conduct its business.

---

nizations increased. Two projects in particular demonstrate one or both of these policies in action: (1) AHW Corporation, and (2) Altcare, a joint venture with General Mills.

AHW Corporation

AHW Corporation is a wholly owned, nonprofit subsidiary of the Foundation formed in December 1980 to develop, construct, and market three interrelated projects in Energy Park. Energy Park is a cooperative undertaking of the Wilder Foundation, the city of St. Paul, the St. Paul Port Authority, Control Data Corporation, and the federal government "to combat deterioration and underutilization of a certain portion of the St. Paul community by providing a compatible energy-efficient environment for residential housing and commercial and industrial development."

To continue its involvement in Energy Park while limiting its financial liability, Wilder formed a separate

---

EXHIBIT 2   Wilder Foundation 1982–1986 Strategy Statement

As a board and staff, for the next five years the Foundation will:

1. *Continue as an operating, direct service, health and welfare agency,* 90 percent in the greater St. Paul metropolitan area with minor emphasis on support services such as: consultation, training, and communitywide cooperative approaches.

2. *Provide direct services for primary areas:* (*a*) outpatient and residential psychiatric services to children; (*b*) residential and home services to elderly; (*c*) correction services to children and adults; (*d*) administration of housing. In addition, special emphasis will be placed on training, education, consultation, and research through Wilder Forest, Office of Research and Statistics, and Management Support Services to other agencies.

3. *Within direct services for primary area:*
   a. Direct service to members of low-and moderate-income families.
   b. A gradual change to working with groups in comparison to one-to-one relationships.
   c. Direct service to a large range of persons: clients, members, participants, residents, attendees.
   d. Increased use of volunteers.
   e. Programs funded through: (1) leveraging income ($3 of outside funds for $1 of trust income) to increase impact, and (2) investing in comparison to direct use (grants) of trust income.
   f. Cooperation with other organizations.

4. *General policies will include:* annual funding of liabilities, balancing budgets, and perpetuity of trust.

---

corporation, the AHW Corporation. AHW Corporation's initial capitalization was a $6 million demand promissory note from the Wilder Foundation. These financial resources, and the good reputation of the Wilder Foundation, gave the AHW Corporation a credibility sufficient to leverage much greater public and private investment in Energy Park.

AHW Corporation is developing:

1. An owner-constructed housing project to consist of approximately 570 townhouses and condominium units.

2. A rental housing project to consist of approximately 380 units constructed in two phases on two sites within Energy Park.

3. Rehabilitation improvements to Energy Park, including the development of space in historically significant former railroad shop buildings for use as retail space and as the headquarters and a clinic for SHARE, a major Twin Cities health-maintenance organization.

Twenty percent of both the owner-occupied and rental units are reserved for low- and moderate-income families.

Construction financing for the housing development is provided by conventional construction loans from local lenders and by proceeds from tax-exempt St. Paul Port Authority housing-development bonds. Mortgage financing for condominiums and townhouse buyers has been provided from homeownership revenue bonds issued by the St. Paul Housing and Redevelopment Authority. Improvements to historic facilities are financed by the sale of tax-exempt St. Paul Port Authority industrial-development bonds.

By the end of 1983, 212 units of housing were complete, along with 150,000 square feet of the 350,000 square feet of historic preservation to be done. The venture has not been without problems. Ray Cunningham, vice-president for finance of AHW Corporation, said:

Considering what we're doing and considering how bad the economy has been in recent years, the

EXHIBIT 3 Analysis of Organization's Strengths and Weaknesses in Order to Determine Corporate
Competencies and Limitations

Strengths	Weaknesses	Opportunities
Committed and knowledgeable board	Time of staff	Emphasis on choosing impact areas that best use resources, structure, research
Intellectual skills and capacities	Money not available to do innovative things	Diversification
Flexibility of staff	Heavy dependency on public funds	Protective prevention of minorities, children, adults
Good corporate management team	Inability to harness skills of board/staff	*Horizontally:*
Climate of inquiry	Limited service area	Add nursing homes for elderly
Multiple lines of service	Growing reliance on narrow cost-based reimbursement	Secure additional managed housing agreements
Good local image and reputation	Small market composed of poor, sick, aged, and needy	Complete Energy Park
Financial strength and financial flexibility	Public relations activity is limited	Build additional 202 housing units
History of the organization	Lack of formal planning instrument with major funding organizations	Add volunteers: all areas
Evolving position in management-support market, consultation, housing, elderly services	No adopted operating policies	*Vertically:*
Constraints of the Wilder wills	Special-purpose program buildings	Aging demo/General Mills
Moderate growth in net worth	Inexperience in and lack of funding for aggressive marketing	Group home: aftercare corrections
Clear purpose	A give-away operating background	Group independent living: elderly
Value-added relationship of subsidy	Employees are caregivers, not for-profit minded	New joint-planning organization
	No incentive program to increase efficiency	Establish new working relationship with business and industry and national foundations
		Corporate restructuring

project has gone quite well. Considering current
market conditions, there are questions of feasibility,
mix, density of development, and so on. They're
problems, but they're solvable.

You know, this is a tough site to work with. You
have to build your presence all at once and then sell
it. You can't build a little, sell a little, build a little,
sell a little. It's real gutsy development. Your
typical for-profit developer wouldn't look at it. It
takes someone like Wilder with deep pockets and a
long vision.

Cunningham also notes that there have been some
problems linking the Foundation with the corporation.
He says:

It's sometimes hard to link an innovative, risky new
venture with an established, stable, structured
operating foundation.

If AHW Corporation is successful, it will produce
several payoffs. "Among those payoffs," said Wilkening, "will be long-term quality development in an area

---

EXHIBIT 4   Trends in Wilder Foundation Strategy

As a board and staff, for the past 10 years we have emphasized:

1. *Direct service versus indirect service,* such as research, consultation, training, communitywide cooperative approaches, grants. There has been a small but gradual trend toward:
    a. *Research*—with the start-up of a Statistics and Research Office: 1976–82/$400,000 annually
    b. *Consultation*—much individual response. Formal response with start-up of Management Support Services: 1982/$250,000
    c. *Training*—internal, not external or community/$40,000
    d. *Community-cooperation* —beginning in 1974 with Wilder Square, housing has been primary quasiindirect service and response to community. Housing as of this date does not have much of a social service component.
    e. *Grants*—the Foundation has made some small grants: homemakers, food bank, write-off to Oneida, and recently a loan fund.
2. *Direct services to low- and moderate-income families versus middle- and upper-income families.* There have been exceptions to this, primarily in those programs where illness or disabilities are not based on income.
3. *Direct services to children, elderly versus young adults, adults.* Only formal exceptions are in Corrections through Bremer House, Community Assistance Program, and children's programs such as Community Care and recently some movement toward recognizing parents of children at the Child Guidance Clinic.
4. *A gradual change toward working with groups versus one-to-one client relationship.* The Foundation still spends the majority of its funds and professional effort in one-to-one direct client relationships.
5. *A gradual change from a client orientation to members, participants, residents, attendees.*
6. *Perpetuity versus going out of business.*
7. *Leveraging income to increase impact versus use of only trust income to provide service.*
8. *Stretcher-bearer activities versus prevention.*
9. *Responding to need versus determining focus.*
10. *Involvement in multiple need areas versus single area of need.*
11. *Primarily relying on use of professional staff versus use of volunteers.*
12. *Use of research base, consultants versus acquired knowledge and in-house expertise.*
13. *Direct use of trust income for services versus investing in services.* This has gradually changed. Housing has been more of an investment than a direct-use approach.
14. *3:1 financing by outside funds.*
15. *Funding liabilities: retirement, depreciation.*
16. *Balancing annual budgets.*
17. *Four-county service area versus state/regional/national.*

---

that really needed it, housing and jobs, and, if a profit is turned, which appears likely, money that can be put to similar uses or to other purposes."

Altcare

Altcare (for alternative care) is a corporate joint venture begun in 1983 by the Wilder Foundation and General Mills. The purpose of Altcare is to help health and social service providers develop and finance alternative care for chronically ill and functionally impaired persons, many of whom are elderly. The goal is to make it possible for these persons to have a choice in selecting services and care givers to meet their needs.

Altcare services include:

1. Technical-assistance activities such as: consultation services to governmental agencies; planning assistance to health organizations; development of urban and rural alternative delivery networks; and development of housing alternatives with health and social components; Altcare executives hope these activities will be self-supporting;
2. Low-interest loans to organizations involved in alternative care programs; although these are considered high-risk loans, Altcare executives hope to minimize losses;
3. Development of products for use by other organizations, such as a management-information software system; there is a possibility that a considerable profit might be made on this software if an efficient and effective proprietary system can be developed.

The financial investment in Altcare will be shared equally by General Mills and the Wilder Foundation. The combined investment could exceed $5 million over a five-year period, when the two partners will make a final decision on the project's future.

The joint venture evolved out of a "felt need" at General Mills to be involved in a socially responsible program that could yield a profit and out of the Wilder Foundation's vast expertise in this area. Moreover, the Foundation was interested in collaborating with corporations to pursue its objective of multiplying the impact it can make on the provision of health and welfare services for persons in the community.

At an initial meeting, staff from the Wilder Foundation and staff from General Mills discussed their common goals and the possibilities of finding a significant social project that the two organizations could jointly sponsor. While General Mills continued its nationwide search for an appropriate project, Foundation staff searched for ideas that would match General Mills' criteria, namely:

1. The venture should be a unique demonstration in an area of high social priority that, if successful, would produce a substantial multiplier effect.
2. The venture should preferably be at least in embryonic form and be led by capable and experienced management to which General Mills would add its financial and managerial resources and be an active partner.
3. The venture should offer the potential of being financially self-sustaining over the long term; it need not meet normal commercial return on investment requirements.
4. The demonstration should produce a significant impact for the social area involved.

After considering a number of programs, Foundation staff narrowed their focus to a project that would help improve the method of care delivery and financing of services for the elderly. This project was selected because the current long-term care system was moving into a period of major crisis due to rapid increases in cost, impending radical changes in the availability of public resources, and significant increases in the number of aged and functionally impaired adults.

In January 1983 General Mills chose the Wilder project, which already had begun taking shape, as the project to which it would direct its resources. Altcare was then established and cosponsored by the Wilder Foundation and General Mills on a 50–50 basis.

The organization is, of course, still in the relatively early stages of development. In a recent interview, Verne Johnson, Altcare's president and CEO, was asked if there had been any problems with the joint venture over its short history. He said:

Not really, beyond those expected in establishing any new organization. We even went through a change in presidents (I was a General Mills employee and took over from a former Wilder Foundation employee) and we didn't have any problems. The purpose of the change was to get someone who had greater access to community organizations and it went quite smoothly.

There have been some minor differences. Wilder thinks you should cost everything, including contributed executive time, for example. But there really have been no problems of meshing a for-profit corporation and a nonprofit foundation. Wilder is as close to a for-profit, not-for-profit as you will find. They're very able, tough, and committed.

According to Wilkening, if Altcare succeeds, there will be several payoffs to the Foundation, including: (1) expansion of creative program options for the elderly; (2) changes in the health-care financing system (e.g., through gaining medicaid waivers or through holding down medicaid costs); (3) experience in working with a corporation; and (4) expansion of general knowledge in the field of health care for the elderly. According to Johnson, payoffs to General Mills will include: (1) making an impact in a critical area of need (care of the frail elderly); (2) getting the company's money back to invest in another project; and (3) substantial public relations gains.

A New Policy

While AHW Corporation and Altcare were under way, the Wilder Board chose as one of its top priorities for fiscal year 1985 (July 1984 to June 1985) the preservation of the endowment's purchasing power. The following assumptions were used by the board for purposes of planning the 1985 budget:

1. The Foundation intends to prevent the erosion of its trust, resources, and program quality.
2. On the average, the market returns 5 percent more than inflation over time.
3. The Foundation is attempting to adjust its annual spending for programs to an amount that is 5 percent of the market value of the trust.
4. A budget-stabilization fund has been established that is composed of previous years' unspent budgeted subsidy dollars. The present balance is $1,000,000. The purpose of this fund is to facilitate the transition of moving the annual use of subsidy down to 5 percent of the market value of the trust.
5. The beginning market value of the trust for 1985 will be $125,000,000.
6. For operations-planning purposes, the market return of the trust is projected at 11 percent per year.

7. Inflation is estimated at 6 percent per year over the next five years.

Sticking to the policy of preserving the value of the endowment will require cutting $350,000 worth of programs. If the board chooses to increase the value of the endowment, it will have to make more substantial budget cuts or authorize fundraising efforts.

LEONARD WILKENING REFLECTS

In an interview in 1984, Wilkening reflected on the changes at the Foundation since 1971, and also considered the future of the Foundation. Concerning the changes, Wilkening observed:

> I guess we've been involved in a ten-to-twelve-year process of change. We needed to change some of the value systems of the Foundation. We've changed the way we think about the trust. We've altered our service strategy to include more indirect service and services to groups, more efforts at changing the system instead of simply responding to it, and more cooperation with other organizations to pursue shared goals.

In the same interview session, Norrine Bohman, Wilkening's assistant, argued that most of the redirection had come at the prompting of Wilkening. Wilkening deferred judgment on the point but did go on to speculate on the process of strategy change at Wilder:

> In some ways people have led to changes in organizational structure that have led to changes in strategy, or at least, to the formal recognition of changes in strategy. We've always hired as key staff people individuals who are risk takers. We've placed them in existing divisions or into new operations and then let the risks be taken. The result often has been growth and new activities in those areas. When we reflect on what's happened, we sometimes alter our strategy to recognize and promote more of what we've been doing that needs done.

As for the future, Wilkening commented on executive succession and his belief that the time had come again for the Foundation to reposition itself:

You know, I'm 60 years old, and I might want to retire at age 62. I certainly think the Foundation ought to act as if I might retire at age 62.

But beyond that, I think we're at a major repositioning point, the same way we were at one in the early 1970s. The age distribution of the population as a whole is changing, and new needs and opportunities of various sorts are emerging across the board, in the areas of aging, housing, criminal justice, and so on (see Appendix). At the same time, the role of government—particularly the federal government—is changing. It's becoming harder for state and local governments and nonprofits to serve the needs of the poor, sick, disadvantaged, and needy—at least in traditional ways. In the meantime, we have a lot of young, bright, highly motivated, well-trained staff with their own ideas about what Wilder ought to be doing. I've been farming out some of my executive functions to prepare the Foundation for any leadership changes and to take advantage of some key staff.

In other words, a lot of things are coming together to make me think it's now time to reposition ourselves again.

APPENDIX: SOME ENVIRONMENTAL TRENDS, 1970–1980

POPULATION

The Wilder Foundation's service area includes the four contiguous Minnesota counties (Anoka, Dakota, Washington, and Ramsey) that comprise the eastern half of the Twin Cities (Minneapolis and St. Paul) metropolitan areas. The service area population has increased by 13 percent from 853,567 persons in 1970 to 963,632 persons in 1980. Ramsey County, the largest, contains St. Paul and declined in population by 3 percent between 1970 and 1980; Dakota County had the highest rate of growth (39%). In rank order, the 1980 county population totals are: Ramsey, 459,784; Anoka, 195,998; Dakota, 194,279; and Washington, 113,571.

AGE AND RACE

In all four counties, the age-group with the largest rate of growth from 1970 to 1980 was the group of 19–34 year olds. The number of preschool children (0–4 years) decreased substantially in Ramsey County during the 1970s although no major changes in the number of preschoolers occurred in the other counties. In Ramsey, the number of school-aged children (5–18 years) also declined, but it increased slightly in the other counties. The number of middle-aged residents (35–59 years) increased in Anoka, Dakota, and Washington counties but decreased in Ramsey County. The elderly population increased slightly in every county. Ramsey County has, by far, the largest number of elderly.

The racial composition of each of the four counties is predominantly White. Ramsey County has the largest non-White population; 7 percent of its population is non-White. The county has 14,720 black residents, 2,993 American Indian residents, and 14,918 residents of other races.

MARRIAGE AND FAMILY

The majority of adults in every county are married. Ramsey County has the lowest proportion of married adults (54 percent) and the highest of residents who are widowed (8 percent).

The number of marriages and the marriage rate in every county remained relatively stable from 1970 to 1979. However, the number of divorces increased in every county, and the divorce rates in Anoka, Dakota, and Washington increased substantially during the 1970s.

The proportion of children under age 18 who live with both parents declined in every county during the 1970s. By 1980, this proportion dropped to 77 percent in Ramsey County and to 85–87 percent in the other three counties. In Ramsey County, 18 percent (21,064) of all children lived with one parent in 1980. In Ramsey County in 1980, 79 percent of all families with children were two-parent families: 18 percent were families with mother only; and three percent were families with a father only. The proportions of two-parent families with children in Anoka, Dakota, and Washington counties ranged from 86 to 89 percent.

HOUSING

The number of housing units in each of the four counties increased during the 1970s. Ramsey County had the lowest rate of increase.

Approximately three out of every five housing units in Ramsey County are owner occupied whereas almost four out of five units in each of the other counties are owner occupied. The vacancy rate in the four counties is 3–4 percent. Tenure and vacancy status of housing units remained very stable during the 1970s.

One half of all housing units in the four counties have at least five rooms. The proportion of units with only one to two rooms is small, although Ramsey County has 9,046 such dwellings. Virtually all housing units in the four-county area now have complete plumbing facilities.

The number of persons per occupied housing unit in each of the four counties has decreased. In Ramsey County, 58 percent of all units have only one or two occupants. In 1980, the proportion of housing units with one person or less per room was greater than 92 percent in each of the four counties—a statistic that also reflects the trend toward fewer persons per household.

The median value of owner-occupied housing units increased dramatically during the 1970s from a range of $20,000–24,000 in the four counties in 1970 to a range of $60,000–68,000 in the four counties in 1980. In Ramsey County, 72 percent of all housing units were valued at less than $25,000 in 1970, whereas only 3 percent of all units were valued at less than $25,000 in 1980. Washington County and Dakota County have the largest proportion of housing units valued at $80,000 or more. The cost of rental housing also increased from 1970 to 1980: the median rent paid in the four counties rose from a range of $106–139 in 1970 to a range of $225–266 in 1980.

BIRTHS AND DEATHS

The birthrate declined in each of the four counties during the 1970s. The total number of births declined in Ramsey and Anoka counties and increased in Dakota and Washington counties. Each county reported decreases in high-risk births, inadequate prenatal care, and infant mortality. During the 1970s, out-of-wedlock births increased in each of the four counties.

The most frequent cause of death in each of the four counties in both 1970 and 1979 was cardiovascular disease. Cancer was the second most frequent cause of death. The proportion of deaths attributed to cancer increased substantially in Anoka, Dakota, and Washington counties during the 1970s. Accidents and respiratory illnesses were the third and fourth most frequent causes of death.

INCOME

Family income in each of the four counties rose from a median level of $11,000–12,000 in 1970, to a median of $23,000–26,000 in 1980. In 1980, Ramsey County had the largest percentage of families with an annual income of less than $10,000 (14 percent). Dakota County had the largest proportion of families with incomes of $25,000 or more (55 percent).

In Ramsey County, 35,876 persons (8 percent of the total population) live below the poverty level. Four to 5 percent of the residents of the other three counties live below the poverty level. In Ramsey County, 23,076 residents—or one out of every 20—have incomes below 75 percent of the poverty level. Three percent of the residents of the other three counties live below 75 percent of the poverty level. The proportion of persons living in poverty within the four-county area changed very little during the decade of the 1970s although the actual number of such persons increased.

The percentage and number of older people who live in poverty declined dramatically in each of the four counties during the 1970s. In Ramsey County, the elderly (i.e., persons 65 or older) are no more likely to be living below the poverty level than are persons younger than age 55. In Anoka, Dakota, and Washington counties older people are more likely to live in poverty than are younger people, but the proportion living in poverty does not exceed 9 percent. The number of Aid for Dependent Children (AFDC) cases and the number of children in AFDC families have increased in each of the four counties since 1970. The proportion of all persons under 18 who live in AFDC families increased in Ramsey County from 7 percent to 12 percent;

in Anoka County from 3 percent to 7 percent; and in Dakota and Washington counties from 2 percent to 5 percent.

EDUCATION

Educational attainment among persons aged 25 years and older increased in the four counties during the decade of the 1970s. By 1980, one person out of every five in Ramsey, Dakota, and Washington counties had completed four or more years of college. In 1980, 23 percent of Ramsey County's adults did not have a high school education, in contrast with 37 percent without a high school education in 1970. There was a similar trend toward a greater proportion of people with at least a high school diploma in Anoka, Dakota, and Washington counties.

The area's nursery school enrollment increased from 1970 to 1980. Kindergarten and elementary school enrollment combined, however, declined by 33 percent in Ramsey County, though it remained relatively stable in the other three counties. High school enrollment dropped in Ramsey County but increased in the other three counties. The number of residents enrolled in college increased in all four counties during the 1970s. Data for the 1980–1981 school year show that 7.4 percent of Ramsey County's students drop out of school. (In St. Paul, 12.2 percent of the students drop out.) In the other counties approximately 4–6 percent of the students drop out.

EMPLOYMENT

The total labor force increased in each of the four counties from 1970 to 1980. About two thirds of Ramsey County's residents and about three fourths of the other counties' residents were in the labor force in 1980. Men were more likely than women to be in the labor force. However, in Anoka, Dakota, and Washington counties the proportion of women in the labor force increased from less than one half in 1970 to almost two thirds in 1980.

Among women with children under six years of age, approximately 50 percent are in the labor force. Approximately 70 percent of women with school-age children only are in the labor force.

CRIME

The number and rate of violent crimes and of property crimes increased in all four counties from 1970 to 1980. Of the 1,480 felony convictions between September 1980 and September 1981, most were for burglary (397) and major theft (309).

G

Strategy Refinement and Control

21.   *The Kellogg Company and the Ready-to-Eat Cereal Industry*

You take care of the outside.
We'll help take care of the inside.

1985 ad for Kellogg's All Bran

Advertising campaigns for Kellogg products in the 1980s stress the healthy, nutritious quality of cereal flakes—corn, bran, wheat, oats—a Kellogg theme that began almost a century ago. Dr. John H. Kellogg and W. K. Kellogg sought to develop a cereal that could replace meat in the diets of the patients at the Battle Creek sanitarium that the Kelloggs managed. The product of their efforts, Corn Flakes, became popular enough with the patients that the Kelloggs formed two companies that became the Kellogg Company in 1899.

Eighty-six years later Kellogg is one of the largest food companies in the world, with annual sales exceeding $2.5 billion and earnings greater than $250 million. Kellogg has established a position in the ready-to-eat (RTE) cereal market almost twice as large as either of the two nearest competitors, General Mills and General Foods. "Kellogg knows the cereal business better than anyone else" said William Wason of Brown Brothers Harriman & Co., "and the management has had the wisdom to stick with what they know." In December 1985, Kellogg was named one of the five best managed companies in the United States by *Dun's Business Month* (December 1985). Kellogg won this acclaim because of its performance throughout the 1970s and early 1980s, the darkest time in the industry's history, and the progress Kellogg made in recovering during 1984 and 1985.

THE READY-TO-EAT CEREAL INDUSTRY

The RTE cereal industry is composed of firms that are engaged in the manufacture and sale of prepackaged, processed foodstuffs made primarily of grain products.

This case was prepared by Joseph A. Schenk, Dan S. Prickett, and Stanley J. Stough, University of Dayton.
Copyright © Joseph A. Schenk, 1986.

The user does not have to prepare the product prior to use, and it can be eaten in dry form or with the addition of other substances, such as milk and sugar. Advantages of the products from a consumer perspective include convenience of use and easy satisfaction of nutritional requirements. Consumption of the products takes place primarily at breakfast, but they are also used as between-meal snacks. The first products in the market were introduced by W. K. Kellogg, Wheat Flakes in 1894 and Corn Flakes in 1898.

The $4 billion RTE cereal industry is composed of several large companies that dominate the market. Led by Kellogg, the industry includes General Mills, General Foods, Quaker Oats, Ralston Purina, and Nabisco. Table 1 lists the market share performance of the major competitors as of 1984.

The significance of cereals within the product lines of the competitors changes as a result of competition and developments within the companies themselves. Although cereals represent more than 75 percent of Kellogg sales, cereals are estimated to constitute no more than 13 percent of General Foods sales and 7 percent of General Mills sales. Kellogg sales and estimated operating profits by division are listed in Table 2.

Vigorous competition in the RTE cereal industry requires intensive and decisive actions to expand investments in research, in the development of new products, and in marketing. Marketing plans generally center on facing the competition squarely and forcefully. Budgets for advertising and promotions have increased substantially in recent years, both to give additional support to established products and to successfully support new product introductions. Market shares for the top 10 products in the industry are listed in Table 3. Selected information regarding each major competitor is presented below.

General Mills

General Mills managed to increase its market share significantly during the 1976–1981 period. Since then

TABLE 1   The Ready-to-Eat Cereal Industry: Market Share Data*

Company	1976	1977	1978	1979	1980	1981	1982	1983	1984
Kellogg	42.6%	42.5%	42.0%	41.5%	40.9%	39.3%	38.5%	38.5%	40.3%
General Mills	20.8	20.5	20.4	22.2	22.4	23.0	23.1	23.2	23.1
General Foods	15.7	16.8	16.0	15.4	15.0	15.0	16.0	16.1	13.3
Quaker Oats	8.9	8.9	8.7	8.6	8.6	8.6	8.9	8.9	8.6
Ralston Purina	4.9	3.4	5.7	5.6	6.2	6.1	5.6	6.1	6.3
Nabisco	4.0	4.2	4.2	4.1	3.8	3.9	3.8	3.8	4.2
All others	3.1	3.7	3.0	2.6	3.1	4.1	4.1	3.4	4.2

*All figures are percentages.

Source: *Advertising Age:* August 5, 1985, p. 42; June 14, 1982, p. 62; May 25, 1981, p. 62; August 28, 1978, p. 217.

TABLE 2   Kellogg Company: Operating Profit at Year-End December Estimated by Division ($ in millions)

	1982	1983	1984	1985	1986 (estimated)
Net sales	$2,367	$2,381	$2,602	$2,930	$3,250
Operating profits					
Domestic RTE Cereals	238.0	255.0	311.0	395.0	450.0
Mrs. Smith's	29.0	28.5	31.5	36.9	43.0
Salada	9.0	10.0	11.0	12.5	14.0
Fearn	13.8	15.5	17.0	19.0	21.0
International	107.9	105.4	96.7	95.0	110.0
Total operating income	397.7	414.4	467.2	558.4	638.0
Net income	227.8	242.7	250.5	281.3	320.5

Source: Prudential-Bache Securities, Inc., April 2, 1986.

market share has stabilized, and General Mills has been able to maintain a share position in the industry at about 23 percent. Recent new product activity included the national rollout of E.T.'s, which failed to produce significant sales, reflecting a decline of consumer interest in licensed properties. Cinnamon Toast Crunch, Fiber One, Bran Muffin Crunch, and S'More's Crunch are all expected to perform well after national rollout in early 1986. General Mills' brands and the market share performance of each brand for the period 1982–1984 are shown in Table 4.

General Mills has concentrated its efforts on its snack food, yogurt, and restaurant businesses. It has divested some toy operations and repurchased 7 million shares of its own stock (44 million shares outstanding). General Mills net sales and operating profit by segment are listed in Table 5.

General Foods

Throughout the 1970s, General Foods relied on coffee—Maxwell House, Sanka, Yuban, and Brim—for approximately 40 percent of its total revenue (*The New York Times*, September 15, 1985). Since then, it has made major acquisitions. Currently, the company gets 40 percent of its revenues from packaged groceries, 28 percent from coffee products, and 18 percent from processed meats (*The Economist*, 1985). Coffee is still

TABLE 3   Cold Cereal's Top 10 in Market Share*

Brand (company)	1983		1984	
	Pounds	*Dollars*	*Pounds*	*Dollars*
Corn Flakes (K)	6.8%	4.7%	6.8%	4.7%
Frosted Flakes (K)	5.2	4.8	5.6	5.2
Cheerios (GM)	5.5	5.8	5.2	5.5
Raisin Bran (K)	4.6	4.1	4.5	4.0
Chex (RP)	4.3	4.4	4.3	4.6
Shredded Wheat (N)	4.0	3.1	4.0	3.3
Rice Krispies (K)	3.6	3.9	3.5	3.8
Raisin Bran (GF)	3.0	2.5	2.7	2.1
Cap'n Crunch (Q)	2.9	3.5	2.7	3.2
Honey-Nut Cheerios (GM)	2.3	2.6	2.6	2.9
Total	42.2%	39.4%	41.9%	39.3%

Abbreviations: K = Kellogg; GM = General Mills; GF = General Foods; Q = Quaker Oats; N = Nabisco; RP = Ralston Purina.
*All figures are percentages.

Source: *Advertising Age,* August 5, 1985, p. 42.

TABLE 4   General Mills' Ready-to-Eat Cereals: Market Share Data*

Brand	1982		1983		1984	
	Pounds	*Dollars*	*Pounds*	*Dollars*	*Pounds*	*Dollars*
Cheerios	5.6%	5.9%	5.5%	5.8%	5.2%	5.5%
Honey-Nut Cheerios	2.1	2.4	2.3	2.6	2.6	2.9
Total	1.7	2.4	1.9	2.6	2.1	2.8
Lucky Charms	1.7	2.2	1.6	2.1	1.7	2.1
Trix	1.5	1.9	1.5	1.9	1.5	1.9
Wheaties	2.5	1.9	2.3	1.7	2.0	1.4
Golden Grahams	1.3	1.3	1.3	1.3	1.3	1.3
Crispy Wheats 'n Raisins	1.1	1.3	1.1	1.3	1.0	1.1
Licensed Products	0.4	0.5	1.1	1.3	0.7	1.0
Monsters, etc.	0.7	1.0	0.6	0.9	0.5	0.8
Cinnamon Toast Crunch	—	—	—	—	0.6	0.7
Cocoa Puffs	0.7	1.8	0.7	0.8	0.6	0.7
Buc Wheats	0.5	0.6	0.4	0.5	0.3	0.4
Others	0.3	0.2	0.5	0.4	0.6	0.5
Total	20.7%	23.1%	20.8%	23.2%	20.7%	23.1%

*All figures are percentages.

Source: *Advertising Age,* August 5, 1985, p. 42.

TABLE 5   General Mills: Operating Profit at Year-End May, by Segment ($ in millions)

	1983	1984	1985	1986 (estimated)
Net sales	$4,082	$4,118	$4,285	$4,550
Operating profits				
Consumer foods	269.4	275.3	265.6	300.0
Restaurants	80.0	70.0	91.5	97.0
Specialty retailing and other (loss)	10.4	19.8	(1.7)	23.0
Total operating profit	359.8	365.1	355.4	420.0
Net income (loss)	245.1	233.4	(72.9)	182.9

Source: Prudential-Bache Securities, Inc., April 2, 1986.

TABLE 6   General Foods' Ready-to-Eat Cereals: Market Share Data*

Brand	1982		1983		1984	
	Pounds	Dollars	Pounds	Dollars	Pounds	Dollars
Post Raisin Bran	3.1%	2.8%	3.0%	2.5%	2.7%	2.1%
Grape-Nuts	2.9	2.4	2.5	1.9	2.2	1.5
Super Sugar Crisp	1.4	1.6	1.5	1.6	1.4	1.4
Honeycombs	1.1	1.5	1.2	1.5	1.1	1.3
Post Fruit & Fibre	1.5	1.7	1.3	1.4	1.3	1.4
Pebbles	1.2	1.4	1.2	1.4	1.1	1.3
Smurf Berry Crunch	—	—	1.0	1.1	0.5	0.6
Post Toasties	1.3	0.9	1.2	0.9	1.0	0.8
Alpha-Bits	0.8	0.9	0.8	0.9	0.7	0.8
Bran Flakes	0.8	0.8	0.8	0.8	0.8	0.8
Honey-Nut Crunch Raisin Bran	0.3	0.3	0.7	0.7	0.2	0.2
Raisin Grape-Nuts	0.8	0.8	0.6	0.6	0.4	0.4
Fortified Oat Flakes	0.6	0.5	0.6	0.5	0.5	0.4
C.W. Post Hearty Granola	0.2	0.2	—	0.1	0.1	0.1
Others	0.4	0.2	0.1	0.2	0.3	0.2
Total	16.4%	16.0%	16.6%	16.1%	14.3%	13.3%

*All figures are percentages.

Source: *Advertising Age*, August 5, 1985, p. 42.

General Foods' largest single product, and it holds a 38 percent share of the coffee market (Philip Morris, 1986). In fiscal year 1985, General Foods achieved total revenues of $9 billion and the RTE cereal sales accounted for $512 million of total sales (Drexel, Burnham, & Lambert, May 20, 1985).

Sales of Post Toasties and Grape-Nuts are eroding. Sales of Raisin Bran and Honey-Nut Crunch are reported to be performing well in the health-conscious market segment (*The New York Times*, September 15, 1985). Table 6 lists General Foods' RTE cereal products and market share performance for the 1982–1984 period.

Most of General Foods' development in the 1980s has consisted of creating or acquiring product lines to enter new markets, particularly convenience, low-calorie foods. Acquisitions include Oscar Meyer, Entenmann's bakery, Ronzoni, and Orowheat. New products developments include Crystal Light, Pudding Pops, Sun Apple, Lean Strips, and Crispy Cookin' French Fries, of which only Crystal Light and Pudding Pops had met with success as of the end of 1985.

Simultaneously, General Foods has divested its pet foods division and the Burger Chef restaurant chain and repurchased 11 percent of its stock. In 1985, Philip Morris acquired General Foods to integrate its food operations into the tobacco products company. General Foods sales and operating profits by segment are listed in Table 7.

Quaker Oats

In the 1960s, Quaker Oats acquired many diverse businesses. By the 1980s, Quaker Oats had divested its restaurants and chemical products units and was concentrating on acquiring packaged foods and specialty companies including Brookstone (tools), Jos. A. Bank (clothiers), Eyelab (eyeware retailing), and Stokely Van Camp (pork and beans, Gatorade). In addition, Quaker Oats repurchased 5 percent of its own shares in March 1985. The 1980s witnessed an aggressive Quaker Oats expanding its operations throughout its product lines.

Quaker Oats has bundled its product development (20 new products and line extensions since 1983) under the Quaker umbrella and has pushed those lines in which it has a leadership position: hot cereals, granola bars, and Gatorade. Spending $200 million in 1985 for advertising, Quaker Oats has shown a 16 percent growth in

advertising expenditures and a 31 percent growth in merchandising expenditures since 1984.

As a result of this strategy and increasing new product development at Kellogg, General Mills, and Ralston Purina, Quaker Oats has allowed its share of the RTE cereal market to erode from 8.9 percent in 1983 to 8.6 percent in 1984. Halfsies and Cap'n Crunch have lost market share, whereas Life and 100% Natural have maintained their sales levels. Quaker Oats RTE cereal brands and market share performance are listed in Table 8, and Quaker Oats net sales and operating profits by segment are shown in Table 9.

Ralston Purina

Ralston Purina led the RTE cereal industry in restructuring through the use of share repurchase. Ralston Purina has acquired almost 40 million shares of its own stock, and, through divestiture of its Foodmaker division, can acquire more. Ralston Purina acquired Continental Baking in 1984, which added the Hostess brands to the Ralston Purina product lines.

Ralston Purina is expected to focus on its pet food operations and the Hostess lines for the foreseeable future. New product activity in 1985, greatest in company history, brought extension of the Chuck Wagon line with three new dog food products, expansion of the dog treats line with Waggles and T-Bonz, and new cat foods. New products in cereals include Sun Flakes, Rainbow Brite, and Cabbage Patch. Ralston Purina's RTE cereal products and market share performance for the 1982–84 pe-

---

TABLE 7 General Foods: Operating Profit at Year-End March, by Segment ($ in millions)

	1983	*1984*	*1985*	*1986 (estimated)*
Net sales	$8,256	$8,599	$9,022	$9,500
Operating profits				
Packaged groceries	427.8	470.5	419.3	451.0
Coffee	131.1	107.9	127.2	135.0
Processed meats	90.1	96.9	104.2	115.1
Food services and other	38.4	39.9	51.2	55.0
Total operating income	686.6	715.2	701.9	756.1
Net income	288.5	317.1	302.8	316.4

Source: Prudential-Bache Securities, Inc., October 1, 1985.

TABLE 8   Quaker Oats' Ready-to-Eat Cereals: Market Share Data*

| | 1982 | | 1983 | | 1984 | |
Brand	Pounds	Dollars	Pounds	Dollars	Pounds	Dollars
Cap'n Crunch	3.2%	3.8%	2.9%	3.5%	2.7%	3.2%
Life	2.5	2.3	2.4	2.2	2.4	2.2
100% Natural	1.6	1.5	1.6	1.5	1.5	1.4
Halfsies	—	—	0.7	0.7	0.2	0.3
Corn Bran	0.7	0.6	0.7	0.6	0.6	0.6
Others	0.9	0.7	0.6	0.4	0.9	0.9
Total	8.9%	8.9%	8.9%	8.9%	8.3%	8.6%

*All figures are percentages.

Source: *Advertising Age*, August 5, 1985, p. 42.

TABLE 9   Quaker Oats: Operating Profit at Year-End June, by Segment ($ in millions)

	1983	1984	1985	1986 (estimated)
Net Sales	$2,611	$3,344	$3,520	$3,650
Operating profits				
U.S. and Canadian grocery	193.8	219.5	250.0	272.0
International grocery	49.1	32.9	49.7	60.0
Fisher-Price	29.6	43.6	47.1	50.0
Specialty retailing	15.8	12.7	15.2	18.0
Total	288.3	308.7	362.0	400.0
Net income	119.3	138.7	156.6	174.2

Source: Prudential-Bache Securities, Inc., April 2, 1986.

riod are presented in Table 10. Ralston Purina's net sales and operating profits by segment are listed in Table 11.

Nabisco

Since 1983, Nabisco has introduced 140 new products and line extensions globally. This aggressive posture indicated a recognition by Nabisco of the importance of the international market, which accounts for 40 percent of its normalized operating income.

In 1985, Nabisco was acquired by R. J. Reynolds, a tobacco products company. The combined R. J. Reynolds and Nabisco advertising budget weighs in at $1 billion. This financial strength is to be applied, among other things, to joint product marketing. For example, Del Monte coupons may come with Shredded Wheat. It is hoped that this mixed marketing approach will boost sales of product lines throughout the combined companies.

Nabisco's major product in the RTE cereals market is Shredded Wheat. Shredded Wheat held a 3.3 percent dollar market share in 1984 (4.0 percent in pounds). All Nabisco RTE cereal products held a total market share of 4.2 percent on a dollar basis (4.9 percent on a poundage basis) (*Advertising Age*, August 5, 1985).

INDUSTRY CHALLENGES

The RTE cereal industry emerged from the 1970s facing continuing challenges from the Federal Trade Commission (FTC). Founded in 1914 to combat monopolies, the FTC is charged with preventing unfair methods of competition and unfair or deceptive acts or practices that affect commerce. For almost a decade, the FTC had pursued the RTE industry leaders on two issues: children's television programming and advertising, and the operation of an oligopolistic "shared monopoly."

Children's Television and Advertising

As early as 1970, consumer groups pressed for greater regulation of children's television and advertising (*Federal Register,* vol. 49). A group called Action for Children's Television (ACT) prodded the FTC to establish minimum requirements for age-specific programming for children. In 1971, ACT petitioned the FTC to ban all vitamin advertising on programs intended for children. (One third of advertising on TV programs for children had been for vitamin products.) To avoid further

TABLE 10   Ralston Purina's Ready-to-Eat Cereals: Market Share Data*

	1982		1983		1984	
Brand	*Pounds*	*Dollars*	*Pounds*	*Dollars*	*Pounds*	*Dollars*
Chex	4.2%	4.0%	4.3%	4.4%	4.3%	4.6%
Donkey Kong	—	—	0.7	0.7	0.6	0.6
Cookie Crisp	0.6	0.6	0.5	0.7	0.4	0.7
Others	0.3	0.2	0.3	0.2	0.6	0.4
Total	5.9%	5.6%	5.9%	6.1%	5.9%	6.3%

*All figures are percentages.

Source: *Advertising Age,* August 5, 1985, p. 42.

TABLE 11   Ralston Purina: Operating Profit at Year-End September, by Segment ($ in millions)

	1982	*1983*	*1984*	*1985*	*1986 (estimated)*
Net sales	$4,803	$4,872	$4,980	$5,864	$5,350
Operating profits					
Pet food	227.0	263.5	303.0	350.0	399.0
Seafood	(11.0)	14.5	9.5	10.0	11.5
Cereals	38.5	43.5	41.5	45.5	50.0
Continental baking	—	—	—	84.0	94.0
Other consumer goods	3.7	5.5	1.6	6.6	8.0
Agriculture	96.6	105.6	92.5	74.9	82.0
Restaurant	46.7	58.5	61.4	47.2	0.0
Diversified operations	27.1	33.6	35.9	24.2	30.0
Total operating income	428.6	524.7	545.7	642.4	674.5
Net income	69.1	256.0	242.7	256.4	371.0

Source: Prudential-Bache Securities, Inc., April 2, 1986.

pressure, the manufacturers voluntarily compiled with the petition (Ward, 1978).

From 1971 through 1974, the Children's Television Task Force studied the state of children's television and recommended that licensees increase the amount of television programming created for children, particularly programs of educational and informational content. The task force recommended that selling, promotion, or endorsement of a product by the host of the program be prohibited, and that program content be clearly distinguished from commercial messages.

The ACT and other watchdog groups increased their efforts to influence the FTC in the late 1970s, with the result that the FTC introduced proposals for regulations to limit advertising on programs whose primary audience was children. Despite efforts toward self-regulation by industry groups such as the Children's Advertising Review unit of the National Council of Broadcasters and the Codes of the National Association of Broadcasters (Ward, 1978), the FTC banned all commercials on shows aimed at children of a very young age and commercials for highly sugared foods on programs directed at older children. The regulation also required advertisers to devote money to public service announcements to promote good dental and nutritional habits.

In 1980, Congress limited the scope of the FTC's attempts to regulate children's advertising to matters of deception and "unfair" or misleading advertising (Dewar, 1980). By October 1981, the FTC dropped its pursuit of the broadcasters and advertisers with respect to "Kid Vid" issues (*Federal Register,* vol. 46). The ACT continues to monitor television and file complaints to the FTC on those companies that ACT believes exploit the innocence of youth. The ACT has filed against Quaker Oats (1982), General Mills (1983), and General Foods (1983), charging unfair or deceptive advertising by each company (*Associated Press,* July 18, 1983).

In 1983, Kellogg was brought to court in Canada to force the company to cease advertising to children. Kellogg claimed that such a ban would limit the company's ability to release new products and thus freeze competitors' present market shares. The availability of U.S. television in Canada obscures any verification of Kellogg's claim. However, Kellogg and other companies marketing products aimed at children, including games, toys, and foods, were restricted from advertising to children on Canadian television. The Canadian court stated that ads are presumed to be intended for children

if they include "themes related to fantasy, magic, mystery, suspense or adventure," if they depict authority figures, role models, heroes, animals, or "imaginary of fanciful creatures," or if they rely on cartoons, children's music, or attention-getting technical devices (Lippman, 1983). Products of interest to children can be presented on Canadian television only if addressed to adults in a mature fashion.

Shared Monopoly

In the 10 years that followed the FTC's initial complaint against Kellogg, General Mills, General Foods, and Quaker Oats, 243 days of testimony produced more than 36,000 pages of transcript and 60,000 pages of documents. The FTC charged the industry leaders with operating a "shared monopoly" that resulted not from conspiracy or collusion but from the collective power of the few firms (Kiechel, 1978).

The concept of shared monopoly arose from a study by a Massachusetts Institute of Technology economist, Richard L. Schmalensee. He argued that the cereal companies crowded the supermarket shelves with a large number of brands that left little space for new entrants. The flood of products into the market invited competition among those brands with similar characteristics—crunchiness, flavor, sweetness—but not competition between all brands on the market. The profusion of brands ensured that only existing firms could afford to compete; a new entrant would be required to invest $150 million in development with little assurance that it could gain the 3–5 percent share necessary to gain scale economy in production (Sebastian, 1979).

Specifically, the FTC charged the companies with the following practices (*FTC* v. *Lonning & Kellogg*).

Brand Proliferation.   "The four companies introduce a profusion of ready-to-eat cereal brands into the market," that fill the "perceptual space" of the consumer with over 200 brands on the supermarket shelves.

Aggressive Marketing.   "The brands are promoted by intensive advertising aimed primarily at children, which . . . conceals the true nature of these cereals." For example, Honey and Nut Corn Flakes implies significant sweetening by honey; in fact the flakes contain more brown sugar, white refined sugar, vegetable oil, salt, and malt flavoring than honey (Sebastian, 1979).

Product Differentiation.

The four companies produce "basically similar" ready-to-eat cereals that are artificially differentiated through trivial differences.

In addition to creating barriers to entry into the RTE cereal market, the companies were also accused of other unfair methods of competition in advertising and product promotion. The charges included:

1. Cereal advertising is false and misleading. This issue, also raised by ACT, pits the claims of nutrition and health against the high sugar content of many cereals. The sugar content has been blamed for health and dental problems.
2. Kellogg's program of shelf-space allocation, a program emulated by other cereal manufacturers, controls the exposure of breakfast food products. Kellogg records the sales of cereals in the supermarket and recommends brand selection and shelfspace allocation to the supermarket manager.
3. The companies made numerous acquisitions to eliminate competition in the RTE cereal market. These acquisitions have enhanced the shared monopoly structure of the industry.
4. The companies have exercised monopoly power by refusing to engage in price competition or other consumer-directed promotions.

The FTC claimed that the results of these acts were artificially inflated prices, excessive profits, and an absence of price competition. Government economists used the concept of shared monopoly to explain the reluctance of large consumer-products companies, such as Procter and Gamble, to enter the lucrative, albeit competitive, cereal market.

The FTC hoped to apply shared monopoly or oligopolistic behavior restrictions to other industries after establishing the validity of the concept in a landmark decision with references to the RTE cereals industry case. Any industry in which relatively few companies hold 90 percent market share (examples include telecommunications, oil, automobiles, and computers) would then be vulnerable to FTC action (Cowan, 1981; *Time,* October 5, 1981).

Demographic Changes

Another basic challenge facing the industry has been a slowdown in the rate of growth of cereal consumption, brought about, in part, by the aging of the U.S. population. The U.S. median age is now 30 and is forecasted to reach 35 by the year 2000. The total population is expected to grow by less than 1 percent per year during the 1980s, primarily because of a slowdown in the U.S. birthrate.

Age-group populations do show different growth rates. Several changes expected in the 1980–1990 decade are listed below.

● The 15–24 year age-group will decrease by 17 percent or 7.1 million.
● The 25–34 year age-group will undergo a strong 14 percent increase.
● The 35–54 year age-group will undergo the largest increase of all age-groups, 25 percent.
● The 55–64 year age-group will shrink by 2 percent.
● The over–65 age-group will show the second largest increase, up by 20 percent (*Newsweek,* January 17, 1983).

These demographic trends pose a threat to companies that sell a significant portion of their production to the youth market. The greatest consumers of RTE cereals are children under the age of 13. In the 1970s, the industry had experienced a decline in the population of this group. Tables 12–15 provide additional data on demographic changes facing the industry and on consumption of RTE cereal products.

Despite the challenges faced by the industry, the 1980s held some promise for the RTE cereal makers. Grain prices were weakening, with strong gains in production continuing through mid-decade. Moreover, cereal companies were able to levy 5 percent and 6 percent price increases while maintaining cereal at the lowest cost-per-serving of any breakfast food.

KELLOGG'S BUSINESS SITUATION

For Kellogg, the end of the 1970s and the beginning of the 1980s was an era of severe problems. The company retained its market leadership position, but their erosion of market share in the United States was a growing concern.

TABLE 12 Age Distribution Changes and Composite Percentage Change

Age (years)	1970–1980	1980–1985	1985–1990 (estimated)
<5	−8.7%	32.1%	7.6%
5–13	−16.3	1.2	25.6
14–17	2.3	−11.6	−11.3
18–21	16.6	−9.9	−6.1
22–24	21.6	2.3	−14.3
25–34	38.5	13.8	3.1
35–44	8.6	24.8	16.6
45–54	−1.5	−2.2	12.7
55–64	12.3	3.7	−4.4
65+	22.8	10.7	9.2
Total	8.1%	7.4%	6.6%

Source: U.S. Bureau of Census.

TABLE 13 Ready-to-Eat Cereal Consumption: Percent of Total Consumption by Age-Group

Age (yr)	1984	1983	1982	1981	1980	1979	1976	1972
<13	31.0%	31.5%	31.5%	31.6%	31.8%	31.9%	32.2%	36.1%
13–18	13.9	13.9	13.8	13.8	13.8	13.9	14.0	12.9
19–49	28.9	28.1	28.0	28.2	28.1	28.0	27.9	25.7
50+	26.2	26.5	26.7	26.4	26.3	26.2	25.9	25.3
Total	100.0%	100.0%	100.0%	100.0%	100.0%	100.0%	100.0%	100.0%

Source: Drexel, Burnham, & Lambert Brokerage House Report, "Kellogg Co.," April 8, 1985.

TABLE 14 Pounds per Capita Ready-to-Eat Cereal Consumption by Age-Group

Age (years)	Pounds
<6	11.5
6–11	14.3
12–17	13.4
18–24	7.0
25–34	5.6
35–49	5.8
50–64	7.7
65+	11.3

Source: Kellogg Company publication.

TABLE 15   Ready-to-Eat Cereals: Consumption and Tonnage Shipped

Year	Pounds consumed per capita	Percent Change in Year-to-Year Tonnage
1971	6.76	3.00%
1972	7.75	9.30
1973	8.30	15.20
1974	8.62	7.20
1975	9.03	5.40
1976	9.06	5.80
1977	8.89	1.00
1978	9.07	0.20
1979	9.07	1.30
1980	9.13	2.80
1981	9.26	2.40
1982	9.30	2.10
1983	9.41	2.30
1984	9.74	4.20

Source: Drexel, Burnham & Lambert Brokerage House Report, ''Kellogg Co.,'' April 8, 1985.

Domestic Sales

The introduction of generic and private-label brands contributed to a loss of Kellogg market share. Kellogg's position in the industry weakened as its market share dropped from a high of 43 percent in 1972 to a low of 38.5 percent in 1983. Consumers appeared to switch to the less-expensive generic brands as the rate of inflation grew to double digits in the 1970s. The cost of this share erosion was substantial: each percent of the RTE cereal market is valued at approximately $40 million.

Kellogg executive Arnold Langbo stated that Kellogg was particularly vulnerable to the generic and private-label inroads in the RTE cereal market. He observed, ''The whole philosophy or principle of the private label is to copy the leading products in the market'' (Johnson, 1983).

Kellogg fought the invasion of generic and private-label cereals with aggressive price decreases, recovering 1.8 percent of market share in 1984 as generic goods dropped 10 percent in tonnage shipped. Kellogg's two primary competitors held 36.4 percent of the market, considerably less than Kellogg's 40.3 percent share. In

1984, General Foods market share dropped 2.8 percent to 13.3 percent, General Mills held constant at a 23 percent share. Sales trends for several of Kellogg's products are presented in Table 16. Market share performance of the Kellogg brands for the years 1982–84 is presented in Table 17.

Research and Development

In addition to price decreases, Kellogg increased its efforts in research and development (R&D), advertising, and new product introduction. With an R&D budget of $6.5 million in 1978, Kellogg began to develop cereals to appeal to different segments of the cereal market. By 1981, Kellogg was investing $20 million a year in research. Kellogg built two advanced research centers and acquired Agrigentics, a research company exploring improvements in grain development. Kellogg's efforts in research produced the first flaked cereal with no sugar or preservatives, Nutri-Grain in 1981, the first cereal to combine two grains with identity separation, Crispix in 1983, and the first cereals to fully

TABLE 16 Kellogg's Principal Products' Sales Trends ($ in millions)

Product	1983	1984	Change (%)
Corn Flakes	$141.3	$162.5	15.0%
Rice Krispies	144.1	141	−2.2
Raisin Bran	134.3	151.9	13.1
Special K	70.3	82.9	17.8
Fruit Loops	88.9	103.6	16.5
Frosted Flakes	188.8	217.9	15.4
Total	$767.5	$859.7	12.0%

Source: Drexel, Burnham, & Lambert, Inc.

TABLE 17 Kellogg's Ready-to-Eat Cereals: Market Share Data*

Brand	1982		1983		1984	
	Pounds	Dollars	Pounds	Dollars	Pounds	Dollars
Frosted Flakes	5.2%	4.8%	5.2%	4.8%	5.6%	5.2%
Corn Flakes	6.8	4.7	6.8	4.7	6.8	4.7
Raisin Bran	4.7	4.2	4.6	4.1	4.5	4.0
Rice Krispies	3.9	4.2	3.6	3.9	3.5	3.8
Fruit Loops	2.2	2.8	2.2	2.8	2.3	2.9
Special K	1.5	2.1	1.7	2.3	1.9	2.5
Bran Products	2.7	2.0	2.8	2.1	3.1	2.3
Frosted Mini-Wheats	1.8	1.8	1.8	1.8	1.9	1.9
Apple Jacks	1.0	1.5	1.0	1.5	1.0	1.5
Sugar Smacks	1.3	1.3	1.3	1.3	1.2	1.3
Sugar Pops	1.1	1.3	1.0	1.2	1.1	1.2
Product 19	0.8	1.1	0.8	1.1	0.9	1.1
Nutri-Grain	1.0	1.0	1.0	1.0	1.2	1.1
Crispix	—	—	0.7	0.7	0.5	0.5
Honey & Nut Corn Flakes	0.6	0.7	0.6	0.7	0.5	0.6
Marshmallow Krispies	0.5	0.7	0.5	0.7	0.4	0.6
Cocoa Krispies	0.5	0.7	0.5	0.7	0.6	0.8
Frosted Rice	0.6	0.8	0.5	0.6	0.4	0.4
Fruitful Bran	—	—	—	—	0.7	0.6
C-3PO	—	—	—	—	0.5	0.6
Apple Raisin Crisp	—	—	—	—	0.5	0.6
Raisin Squares	—	—	—	—	0.3	0.3
Most	0.3	0.4	0.3	0.4	0.2	0.3
Raisins Rice & Rye	0.5	0.6	0.3	0.4	0.1	0.1
Others	1.2	1.4	1.0	1.3	0.8	1.4
Total	38.5%	38.5%	38.5%	38.5%	40.5%	40.3%

*All figures are percentages.

Source: *Advertising Age,* August 5, 1985, p. 42.

enrobe fruit, Raisin Squares and OJ's in 1984 (Patent numbers: 4,178,392, 4,103,035, and 3,952,112).

Advertising

In 1984, Kellogg increased its advertising budget by 49 percent to $160 million, an aggressive move when compared to the 16 percent increase (to $52 million) of General Foods, and the 1 percent decrease in advertising by Post. As General Foods limited its primary advertising on its top 5 (of 14) leading brands, Kellogg was able to devote considerable push to its new products (*Forbes,* October 7, 1985). Kellogg advertising themes for selected products are presented in Table 18.

Kellogg was able to take advantage of reports connecting a high-fiber diet with a reduced risk of colon cancer and they positioned their new All Bran cereal as a cancer-preventative tool. Kellogg advertised, "At last, some news about cancer you can live with." By the end of 1984, $250 million of Kellogg's sales came from bran

cereals: All Bran, Bran Buds, Cracklin' Oat Bran, Fruitful Bran, Kellogg's Bran Flakes, Kellogg's Raisin Bran, and, in 1985, All Bran with Extra Fiber (Tracy, 1985).

The advertising campaign sparked controversy among industry, medical, and government groups. Officials at the FTC hailed the campaign as "the type of advertisement that we believe should be encouraged" (Kronhelm, 1985; Wollenberg, 1985). The Food and Drug Administration, however, protested that Kellogg was making medical claims for its product and considered seizing all boxes of All Bran from the shelves (Marwick, 1985). The National Food Processors Association petitioned the FDA to allow its member manufacturers to tout the health benefits of their products as long as the labeling was truthful and could be substantiated.

"Everyone has his opinions of advertising, but we didn't think anyone would misinterpret our commercials," explained Kellogg vice president of public affairs, Peggy Wollerman. "Our goal is to communicate recommendations of the National Cancer Institute's findings that maintaining a high-fiber diet is a direct

TABLE 18   Kellogg's Cereal: Products and Advertising Themes

Product	*Themes*
Special K	Thanks to the K, Staying in Shape Never Tasted so Good—Can't Pinch an Inch
Product 19	Flaky, Bumpy, Crispy, Crunchy *Vitamins*—100% of Your Daily Allowance of 10 Vitamins
Fruitful Bran	Bushels of Taste!—Fiber Rich
Nutri-Grain	Whole Grain Goodness . . . No Sugar Added—Dedicated to the Ones We Love
Apple Raisin Crisp	New Great Taste—New, Big, Juicy Chunks of Real Apple
Frosted Flakes	Gr-r-reat Taste—Tony the Tiger—The Taste Adults Have Grown to Love
Raisin Bran	Two Scoops of Raisins—Fiber Rich—Here is the Goodness of Fiber
All Bran	High Fiber—The Highest Fiber Cereal Ever
Rice Krispies	More Vitamin Nutrition than Old Fashioned Oatmeal—Snap! Crackle! and Pop!—The Talking Cereal Talks about Nutrition
Corn Flakes	The Original and Best—Provides 8 Essential Vitamins and Iron—How 'bout these Kellogg's Corn Flakes Now?—The Surprise is the People Who Eat Them
Just Right	High Nutrition . . . Uncompromising Taste—Kellogg's Just Right Cereal
Bran Flakes	Fiber-rich *Bran Flakes*—We'll Help Take Care of the Inside, You take Care of the Outside
Fruit Loops	Natural Fruit Flavors with 100% U.S. RDA of Vitamin C—All Natural Flavors: Orange, Lemon, Cherry—Delicious Natural Fruit Flavors with a Full Day's Supply of Vitamin C

Source: Kellogg advertisements.

means of reducing the risk of cancer'' (Rotenberk, 1984). The Kellogg advertisement had been cleared by Kellogg and National Cancer Institute scientists and lawyers for accuracy, and it had been passed by lawyers for the three television networks.

Until 1970, the FDA prohibited manufacturers from making any health claims on behalf of food products. In the following years, the FDA relaxed its standard for claims of ''low-calorie'' and ''low cholesterol.'' If a product is claimed to be useful in the treatment of a disease, it is considered a drug and the manufacturer must prove the efficacy of its claims (Cowart, 1985).

New Marketing Developments

Kellogg's move into the adult market in the late 1970s and early 1980s signaled a new direction for the cereal industry. Kellogg's strategy included promoting vitamin-enriched, whole grain, and sugarless cereals to the 25–49 year age-group, high fiber to the 65+ age-group, and C-3POs and OJs to the under 17 market (*Business Week,* January 8, 1977).

Recognizing sociological changes in the United States, Kellogg introduced all-family cereals to enhance the convenience of shopping. Kellogg also introduced Smart Start, a cereal aimed at the working woman (*Business Week,* November 26, 1979). Key to Kellogg's development and marketing were the themes of health, diet, convenience, and taste (Brody, 1985). Numerous surveys and surveying organizations, including the Bureau of Labor Statistics, have recorded significant social demographic changes in the last 15 years. A few of the changes that Kellogg and the other cereal companies had to address are listed below.

- In 1985, the numbers of families with school-age or preschool-age children increased by 460,000; the number of employed mothers increased by 765,000 to 18.2 million.

- In 1985, the median family wage and salary earnings increased 4.6 percent. Since 1982, the median family earnings increased 16 percent compared to a consumer price increase of 11 percent over the same period (*The New York Times,* February 19, 1986).

In the 1980s, breakfast has become a more significant part of the American diet, with 89 percent of the populace eating breakfast each day. Frozen breakfast foods were also becoming an important part of the breakfast food industry. In 1985, sales of all frozen foods totaled $849.3 million, 15 percent more than in 1984. In part, this increase was caused by the fact that more than 44 percent of American homes now had a microwave oven, making cooking at home easier. Sales of frozen breakfast entrees tripled from 1979 to 1985: sales of frozen pancakes increased 390 percent; frozen toaster items increased 1,000 percent. Moreover, between 1978 and 1984, the number of Americans eating breakfast at a restaurant increased 45.7 percent compared to the overall restaurant increase of only 6.3 percent (Callahan, 1986).

Despite the decline in the population of children under 13 years of age, competition in breakfast food market segment continued without any slackening of intensity. As consumers of the greatest per capita amounts of cereal, children have long been the focus of cereal company advertising. Although Tony the Tiger has represented Kellogg's Sugar Frosted Flakes for many years, General Mills broke new ground in products for children with the first licensed character, Strawberry Shortcake. This was a move to link the cereal with other commercial media. Other RTE cereal companies followed quickly. The RTE cereal companies' licensed character products now include General Mills' ET, General Foods' Smurf Berry Crunch, Ralston Purina's Donkey Kong, Rainbow Brite, and Gremlins, and Kellogg's C-3POs.

The benefit of tying a cereal to an established figure from television, movies, comics, or toys (character licensing) is a quick gain in market share through exposure in a good trial period. Although traditional cereal products have existed for more than 30 years, the licensed-character cereals may have a life cycle of only 6–18 months. ''The first licensed characters did well for about a year. Now their life span is about six months,'' said Nomi Ghez of Goldman Sachs & Co. (Spillman, 1985). The editor of *New Products News,* Martin Friedman, stated, ''the characters that have been created by cereal companies go on forever, and the others don't'' (Hollie, 1985). To seek a license for a character, Kellogg depended on assurances that the character would continue, that the character had personality and integrity, and that the character would not alienate adults.

By 1986, the cereal companies had less interest in developing licensed-character products because of a general decrease in the popularity of the characters with consumers (Friedman, 1986).

International Operations

By 1980, Kellogg measured sales in 130 countries from 19 manufacturing locations (Kellogg Annual Report, 1982). Kellogg International was divided into four divisions: Canada; United Kingdom and Europe; Latin America; and Africa, Australia, and Asia. International sales accounted for 30 percent of Kellogg's total sales. In France, Kellogg planned to target all segments of the population in hopes of replacing the croissant with cereal. In Japan, Kellogg has targeted children to establish the habit of eating cereal (*Dun's Business Month,* December, 1985). Financial results for several geographic operating segments are detailed in Table 19.

Federal Trade Commission Case Revisited

In addition to the problems created by the introduction of generic and private-label brands, Kellogg management also attributed the previously mentioned loss of market share to the inability of top management to concentrate on operating the business. The chairman of the board, William E. Lamothe, estimated in 1982 that 40 percent of top-management time had been spent on the FTC litigation (*Business Week,* December 6, 1982).

For Kellogg, losing the FTC case would have been significant. If the FTC had won the case, it would have divided Kellogg into five separate operating companies organized around its major product lines. Additionally, the FTC would have required Kellogg to license its brands to smaller, regional manufacturers. Kellogg argued that such actions would place Kellogg at a competitive disadvantage in the RTE market and would produce inconsistent quality within Kellogg's brands.

As the trial entered the 1980s, Kellogg changed its passive strategy of litigation, becoming an aggressive champion of the industry's positions. Kellogg sponsored intense letter-writing campaigns to congressional representatives from districts in which Kellogg maintained facilities. As a result, the FTC received numerous inquiries from congressional representatives regarding

TABLE 19   Kellogg Company: Geographic Operating Segments ($ in millions)

	1985	1984	1983	1982	1981
Sales:					
United States	$2,074.9	$1,789.6	$1,560.0	$1,514.3	$1,454.0
Canada	177.6	178.9	176.0	169.0	170.2
Europe	474.9	425.9	437.8	453.0	435.9
Other	202.7	208.0	207.3	230.8	261.2
Total	2,930.1	2,602.4	2,381.1	2,367.1	2,321.3
Net earnings:					
United States	222.7	194.7	170.5	163.0	150.7
Canada	11.7	11.6	27.6	15.2	13.1
Europe	38.8	35.0	38.6	36.9	34.0
Other	7.9	9.2	6.0	12.7	7.6
Total	281.1	250.5	242.7	227.8	205.4
Assets:					
United States	833.6	731.6	677.1	639.0	606.9
Canada	262.7	247.5	192.3	143.4	130.2
Europe	337.9	223.3	195.4	199.0	197.5
Other	158.9	148.6	139.8	153.7	178.0
Corporate	133.0	316.1	262.6	162.3	166.5
Total	1,726.1	1,667.1	1,467.2	1,297.4	1,279.11

Source: Kellogg Annual Reports.

the efficacy of continuing the case further (*Business Week*, November 26, 1979).

In 1981, Kellogg created Project Nutrition, a teaching unit for secondary grade school children, as well as nutrition inserts for children's television. Kellogg also provided cereals in 33,000 school breakfast programs. In 1982, Kellogg introduced Fitness Focus, a physical education program for high schools. Kellogg believed that the program would enhance its image as a producer of health-related foods, an image that could benefit Kellogg in its case against the FTC as well as in its position in the market.

Procedural errors in the handling of the case by the administrative judge and the FTC raised challenges from Kellogg and the other cereal companies. Judge Harry R. Hinkes decided in 1978 to retire from the judiciary in order to gain full pension benefits, some of which he would lose if he postponed his retirement. The FTC, fearing a considerable delay and possible dismissal of the case, offered the judge a salary to stay on the case. The impropriety of such an arrangement, alleging a possible conflict of interest, was raised by Kellogg as grounds for dismissal. A new judge was appointed to continue the suit in 1981. Later, in 1982, the FTC dropped its suit (*Federal Register,* vol. 47).

Following the collapse of the FTC lawsuit against its four largest companies, the RTE industry witnessed increased competitive rivalry. This increased rivalry manifested itself in new product releases and advertising, and in corporate-development activities including acquisitions, divestitures, and share repurchases.

Diversification. The slowing growth rate in the cereal industry compelled Kellogg to look toward diversification for continued growth and comparable rates of returns for reinvestment of its retained earnings. In 1970, Kellogg entered the frozen food industry with the acquisition of Fearn International. In 1976, Kellogg acquired Mrs. Smith's Pie Co. and in 1977, it acquired Pure Packed Foods. Products such as Eggo waffles, salad dressings, LeGout soups, Salada Tea, Whitney Yogurt, Mrs. Smith's Pies, and pickles entered Kellogg's lines. Kellogg consolidated its frozen food operations under the Mrs. Smith's label in 1980 to gain greater efficiencies in manufacturing, warehousing, transportation, and marketing as well as a stronger prooduct identity in the marketplace (Prokesch, 1985). By 1984, 25 percent of Kellogg's sales were noncereal

(Blyskal, 1984). Table 20 presents net income contributions of several elements of Kellogg, and Table 21 presents sales and operating income for several segments of the company.

Despite LaMothe's declaration that Kellogg was "gung ho" on diversification, Kellogg lost in three attempts to acquire Tropicana and in attempts to acquire Binney and Smith, manufacturers of Crayola crayons, and Seven-Up. Kellogg believed in each case that the price was too high for the company. "Today we are kind of glad we did [lose]," said LaMothe, "There is no embarrassment in losing. The big embarrassment is to win by paying too much and then never being able to make a return to your shareholders" (*Dun's Business Month,* December, 1985).

Capital Projects. Productivity improvements were made at many Kellogg manufacturing facilities in the late 1970s and 1980s, culminating in a $100 million expansion and improvement in the Battle Creek plant in 1985, the largest single capital expenditure in the company's history. Kellogg's ability to improve productivity is demonstrated by the 50 percent increase in revenues per employee that the company enjoyed between 1979 and 1985 (Drexel, Burnham, & Lambert, October 7, 1985). Early in 1986, Kellogg ended a long practice of public tours of the Battle Creek facility because of a desire to protect proprietary information. Several Kellogg capital projects for the years 1980–83 are listed in Table 22.

Preventing Takeover. Matching Kellogg's rates of return in an acquisition candidate is difficult. Moreover, the consumer-products companies such as Kellogg are attractive takeover targets themselves because of their high returns. To reduce the risk of a takeover, Kellogg purchased 20 percent of its own stock in 1984, an "investment in our own business," said LaMothe. The effect of the stock repurchase added $500 million of debt to the Kellogg balance sheet. Before the transaction, Kellogg enjoyed only $19 million of debt against $1 billion in equity. The 20 percent block of stock had been held by the Kellogg Foundation. Any potential sale of the stock, said LaMothe, was a "cloud we didn't think was good to leave hanging out there in today's time" (Willoughby, 1985).

TABLE 20 Kellogg Company: Net Income Contributions

Product/division	1981	1982	1983	1984	1985 (estimated)	1986 (estimated)
Domestic cereals	$121.0	$135.7	$138.0	$169.9	$206.0	$231.0
Canadian operations	11.0	13.0	13.8	9.4	10.0	12.0
Salada	12.1	13.0	14.0	15.0	16.0	18.0
Fearn International	9.0	9.5	10.5	11.6	12.0	14.0
Mrs. Smith's Pie Co.	8.7	7.0	8.0	8.9	10.0	11.0
Kellogg International	41.6	49.6	44.6	39.2	42.0	50.0
Total	$203.4	$227.8	$228.9	$254.0	$296.0	$336.0

Source: Drexel, Burnham, & Lambert, Inc., October 7, 1985.

TABLE 21 Kellogg Company: Estimated Sales and Operating Income ($ in millions)

	1979	1980	1981	1982	1983	1984	1985
Sales:							
RTE cereals	$1,426	$1,687	$1,802	$1,792	$1,755	$2,000	$2,260
Salada	128	140	154	165	182	180	190
Fearn International	118	132	145	165	177	165	180
Mrs. Smith's Pie Co.	157	172	200	218	239	222	235
Other	18	19	20	27	50	35	35
Total	1,847	2,150	2,321	2,367	2,381	2,602	2,900
Operating income:							
RTE Cereals	240	297	331	343.7	370	408.2	510
Salada	12	12	13	14	16	14	15
Fearn International	8	9	10	11	12.5	11.5	13
Mrs. Smith's Pie Co.	19	20	22	24	27.5	25	28
Other	2	2	2	3	4	4.5	5
Total	281	340	378	395.7	430	463.2	571

Source: Merrill, Lynch, Pearce, Fenner, & Smith brokerage house report: "Kellogg Co.," October 31, 1985.

Kellogg's competitors employed a range of strategies in response to the same takeover challenge. Ralston Purina also acquired blocks of its own stock, continuing this strategy through mid-decade. In 1985, R. J. Reynolds acquired Nabisco Brands, itself a result of a merger between Nabisco and Standard Brands. Philip Morris acquired General Foods. Table 23 lists several recent acquisitions of established brands.

Some of the largest companies in the food industry have been built through a series of acquisitions; Beatrice and Sara Lee Corporation are both the products of acquisitions. Traditionally, regional brands were acquired to take advantage of a larger, national sales force, as well as the financial strength of the parent company. When product lines of the two companies overlapped, the strength of the broader product line commanded greater influence in attracting shelf space in the supermarket, and greater discounts in advertising rates (Brown et al., 1985).

For Reynolds and Philip Morris, acquisition of food products carried other benefits. Slower sales of cigarettes and pending lawsuits and legislation about smok-

TABLE 22 Kellogg Company: Capital Projects

Year	Location	Project
1980	Rexdale, Ontario	Frozen food manufacturing facility
	Wrexham, England	Expanded capacity for Super Noodles
	Valls, Spain	New cereal plant
	Rooty Hill, Australia	Expansion of frozen food plant
	Queretro, Mexico	New corn milling operation
	Sao Paolo, Brazil	Expansion of cereal plant
	Maracay, Venezuela	New office building, processing, and packing
	Guatemala	Expansion of grain storage
	Arlington, TN	Pure Packed dry materials warehouse
	McMinnville, OR	Expansion of Mrs. Smith's plants
	San Jose, CA	Expansion of plant
	Blue Anchor, NJ	Mrs. Smith's facility
	Milpitas, CA	Eggo salad dressing plant
1981	Battle Creek, MI	Expanded for Nutri-Grain cereal
	Lancaster, PA	Increase capacity for cereal
	Battle Creek, MI	Advanced technology facility for research and development
	South Korea	New processing plants
	London, Ontario	Advanced technology center
	Manchester, England	Expansion of packing facility
	Bremen, West Germany	Purchased land
1982	London, Ontario	Expansion of plant
	Seoul, South Korea	Plant completed
	Manchester, England	Conversion of packing line
	Sao Paolo, Brazil	Expansion of facilities
1983	Pottstown, PA	Expansion of office space, storage Warehouse

Source: Kellogg Annual Reports.

TABLE 23 Recent Acquisitions of Established Brands

Buyer	Acquisition	Brands
Procter & Gamble	Richardson-Vicks	NyQuil, Vidal Sassoon, Clearasil
Philip Morris	General Foods	Jell-O, Maxwell House
Monsanto	G. D. Searle	Nutrasweet, Metamusil
Brown-Forman	California Cooler	California Cooler
Greyhound	Purex Cleaning	Purex Bleach, Brillo
Sara Lee	Nicholas Kiwi	Kiwi shoe polish
Nestle'	Carnation	Carnation Milk, Friskies pet food
Ralston Purina	Continental Baking	Hostess Twinkies, Wonder Bread
R. J. Reynolds	Nabisco Foods	Oreo cookies, Life Savers, Ritz Crackers, Shredded Wheat
Beatrice Foods	Esmark	Wesson Oil, Playtex
R. J. Reynolds	Canada Dry	Canada Dry soft drinks
Quaker Oats	Stokely-Van Camp	Gatorade, canned goods

Source: Paul B. Brown et al., "NEW? IMPROVED? The Brand Name Mergers," *Business Week,* October 21, 1985, p. 108

TABLE 24

KELLOGG COMPANY
Consolidated Balance Sheet
(in millions)

	1985	1984	1983	1982	1981
Current assets:					
Cash and temporary investments	$ 127.8	$ 308.9	$ 248.8	$ 159.8	$ 163.7
Accounts receivable.	203.9	182.5	157.1	140.7	158.9
Inventory					
Raw materials.	135.6	119.7	115.7	128.8	129.4
Finished goods and work in progress.	110.3	101.4	101.1	98.9	101.8
Prepaid expenses	40.5	39.0	40.4	35.9	28.4
Total current assets.	618.1	751.5	663.1	564.1	582.2
Property					
Land	25.6	25.6	26.3	25.1	24.0
Buildings	321.2	277.7	274.1	263.4	263.8
Machinery and equipment.	903.2	762.4	692.7	677.6	620.6
Construction in progress	280.4	215.7	143.7	83.5	90.0
Total property	1,503.4	1,281.4	1,136.8	1,049.6	998.4
Less accumulated depreciation	494.5	425.4	393.6	367.4	340.0
Net property	1,035.9	856.0	743.2	682.2	658.4
Intangible assets	28.3	30.5	29.0	33.6	32.2
Other assets	43.8	29.1	31.9	17.5	6.3
Total assets.	$1,726.1	$1,667.1	$1,467.2	$1,297.4	$1,279.1
Current liabilities:					
Current maturities of debt	34.8	340.6	20.0	6.5	16.5
Accounts payable.	189.7	127.4	116.8	99.1	104.5
Accrued liabilities					
Income tax.	29.4	51.4	85.0	81.9	77.4
Salaries and wages	41.8	38.7	36.2	31.4	29.9
Promotion	71.3	60.2	66.4	45.0	30.9
Other.	46.4	45.8	36.3	43.7	41.7
Total current liabilities.	444.3	664.1	360.7	307.6	300.9
Long-term debt.	392.6	364.1	18.6	11.8	88.2
Other liabilities.	12.3	9.5	9.2	11.0	9.8
Deferred income tax	193.9	142.2	100.8	82.3	69.9
Shareholders' equity:					
Common stock	38.4	38.4	38.2	38.2	38.2
Capital in excess of par value.	44.5	40.8	34.4	32.9	32.5
Retained earnings.	1,288.5	1,118.4	991.5	872.8	761.6
Treasury stock.	−576.8	−577.8			
Currency translation adjustment	−111.6	−132.6	−86.2	−59.2	−22.0
Total Equity	683.0	487.2	977.9	884.7	810.3
Total liabilities and equity	$1,726.1	$1,667.1	$1,467.2	$1,297.4	$1,279.1

Source: Kellogg Annual Reports.

ing are expected to eventually erode profitability in the cigarette industry. The higher than average returns of the cereal and food companies, with a strong brand image of health and nutrition, is an attractive inducement for investment.

According to Marc C. Patricelli of Booz Allen & Hamilton Inc., 19 of 24 RTE cereal brands retained their leadership position from 1923 to 1983. "So if a company buys a leader, and if they run it correctly, they are buying an annuity, because brand leadership is sustainable" (Brown et al., 1985). Kellogg's financial performance and dominance in the cereal industry makes it an appealing target for merger or acquisition. Tables 24–26 give financial information on Kellogg.

CONCLUSION

"The question is not whether this is a mature market," said LaMothe, "it's whether we can be inventive

enough. . . . [Americans now have] the highest level of per capita [cereal] consumption in U.S. history. A lot of areas are close to 13 pounds. Why not make the whole country average 13?'' (Willoughby, 1985). Kellogg's challenge is to increase the market for cereals, both domestic and foreign, by increasing consumption. In the United States, middle-aged and older Americans are the target segments. According to LaMothe (*Dun's Business Month,* December 1985):

Dr. Kellogg and Mr. Kellogg were going on either intuition or their basic beliefs coming out of a Seventh Day Adventist background, where they believed that meats were not healthful for the diet . . . We think that it (cereal) has a tremendous future . . . The whole grains . . . healthy lifestyle . . . avoidance of major disease in the Western World . . . more grains, fruit and vegetables. Where else can you get such nutrition for 20 cents a serving? There will be 6 billion people on the face

TABLE 25

KELLOGG COMPANY
Consolidated Earnings and Retained Earnings
(in millions)

	1985	1984	1983	1982	1981	1980
Net sales	$2,930.1	$2,602.4	$2,381.1	$2,367.1	$2,331.3	$2,150.9
Interest revenue	7.2	27.7	18.6	21.3	18.2	18.7
Other, net	−2.8	3.9	18.1	2.1	0.0	0.0
Total revenue	2,934.5	2,634.0	2,417.8	2,390.5	2,339.5	2,169.6
C.O.G.S.	1,605.0	1,488.4	1,412.3	1,442.2	1,447.8	1,385.2
S, G, & A expenses	766.7	650.8	554.4	529.2	501.1	435.7
Interest expenses	35.4	18.7	7.1	8.2	12.0	10.4
Total	$2,407.1	$2,157.9	$1,973.8	$1,979.6	$1,960.9	$1,831.3
EBT	527.4	476.1	444.0	410.9	378.6	338.3
Income taxes	246.3	225.6	201.3	183.1	173.2	154.3
Net earnings	281.1	250.5	242.7	227.8	205.4	184.0
Retained earnings, January 1	1,118.4	991.5	872.8	761.6	665.1	583.5
Dividends	−111.0	−123.6	−124.0	−116.6	−108.9	−102.4
Retained earnings, December 31	1,288.5	1,184.4	991.5	872.5	761.6	665.1

Source: Kellogg Annual Reports.

TABLE 26

KELLOGG COMPANY
Changes in Consolidated Financial Position
(in millions)

	1985	1984	1983	1982	1981	1980
Source of funds:						
Net earnings	$ 281.1	$ 250.5	$ 242.7	$ 227.7	$ 205.4	$ 184.0
Depreciation	75.4	63.9	62.8	55.9	49.1	44.7
Deferred tax/other	54.9	62.6	12.0	27.1	10.4	12.0
Total funds provided by operations	411.4	377.0	317.5	310.7	264.9	240.7
Changes in working capital components:						
Accounts receivable	−21.4	−25.4	−16.4	18.2	−9.2	−17.0
Inventory	−24.8	−4.3	10.9	3.5	26.1	−19.2
Prepaid expenses	−1.5	1.4	−4.5	−7.5	−3.7	−7.1
Current debt maturity	−305.8	320.6	13.5	−10.0	−10.0	5.7
Accounts payable	62.3	10.6	17.7	−5.4	−1.5	−9.8
Accrued liability	23.7	−27.9	21.9	22.1	25.2	46.2
Net change	−267.5	275.1	43.1	20.9	26.9	−1.2
Funds provided by operations and changes in working capital	143.9	652.1	360.6	331.6	291.8	239.5
Long-term debt	31.5	348.1	1.5	0.0	7.9	0.4
Common stock	3.7	6.7	1.1	0.4	0.0	0.0
Property disposal	4.3	12.0	38.0	5.3	2.9	5.0
Tax-lease benefits	1.2	3.1	6.2	12.0	0.0	0.0
Other	7.9	0.9	0.5	3.1	0.5	1.4
Total source of funds	192.1	1,022.9	407.9	352.4	303.1	246.3
Use of funds:						
Property	245.6	228.9	156.7	121.1	146.4	122.9
Cash dividends	111.0	123.6	124.0	116.0	108.9	102.4
Treasury stock purchases	0.0	577.9	0.0	0.0	0.0	
Investment in tax leases	0.0	0.0	11.6	14.2	0.0	0.0
Long-term debt reduction	2.8	2.7	3.6	75.7	0.4	2.8
Other	23.8	14.7	10.5	13.9	6.4	1.1
Total use of funds	383.2	947.7	306.4	341.5	262.1	229.2
Exchange rate effect on working capital	10.0	−15.1	−12.5	−14.9	−9.1	0.0
Increase in cash and temporary investments	−181.1	60.1	89.0	−4.0	31.9	17.1

Source: Kellogg Annual Reports.

of the earth by the year 2000 and grains will continue to be the most efficient way for most people to get their calories and nutrition. We are going to help feed them, that's what Kellogg is all about.

REFERENCES

Advertising Age, August 5, 1985, p. 42.

Associated Press, "FTC Accused of Sanctioning Bad Advertising Practice," July 18, 1983.

Blyskal, Jeff, "Branded Foods," *Forbes,* January 2, 1984, p. 208.

Brody, Jane E., "America Leans to a Healthier Diet," *The New York Times,* October 13, 1985, p. 32, sec. 6.

Brown, Paul B., et al. "NEW? IMPROVED? The Brand Name Mergers," *Business Week,* October 21, 1985, p. 108.

Business Week, Industrial Edition, January 8, 1977, p. 46.

Business Week, Industrial Edition, November 26, 1977, p. 80.

Business Week, "Too Many Cereals for the FTC," March 20, 1978, p. 166+.

Business Week, "Still the Cereal People," November 26, 1979, p. 80+.

Business Week, "Kellogg Looks beyond Breakfast," December 6, 1982, p. 66+.

Callahan, Tom, "What's New with Breakfast; Morning Meals, Fresh from the Freezer," *The New York Times,* February 16, 1986, p. 17, sec. 3.

Cowan, Edward, "F.T.C. Staff Is Rebuffed on Cereals," *The New York Times,* September 11, 1981, p. D1.

Cowart, V., "Keeping Foods Safe and Labels Honest; Food Safety and Applied Nutrition," *Journal of the American Medical Association,* 254, 2228–2229.

Dewar, Helen, "FTC Curbs Are Adopted by Senate," *Washington Post,* February 8, 1980, p. A1.

Drexel, Burnham, & Lambert, Brokerage House Report, "Kellogg Co.," April 8, 1985.

Drexel, Burnham, & Lambert, Brokerage House Report, "General Foods," May 20, 1985.

Drexel, Burnham, & Lambert, Kellogg Company, Research Abstracts; Food Processors, October 7, 1985.

Dun's Business Month, "Kellogg: Snap, Crackle, Profits," December 1985, p. 32+.

The Economist, "Philip Morris/General Foods: Chow Time for the Marlboro Cowboy", October 5, 1985.

Federal Register, Federal Trade Commission, "Children's Advertising", 46 FR 48710.

Federal Register, Federal Trade Commission, "Kellogg Company, et al; Prohibitive Trade Practices, and Affirmative Correction Actions," 47 FR 6817.

Federal Register, "Children's Television Programming and Advertising Practices," 49 FR 1704.

Federal Trade Commission v. J. E. Lonning, President, and Kellogg Company, a Corporation, Appellants, 539 F2nd 202.

Forbes, October 7, 1985, p. 126.

Friedman, Martin, "Cereal Bowls Spill over with Nuttiness," *ADWEEK,* February 10, 1986.

Hollie, Pamela G., "New Cereal Pitch at Children," *The New York Times,* March 27, 1985, p. D1.

Johnson, Greg, "Who's Afraid of Generic Cereals?" *Industry Week,* May 16, 1983, p. 33.

Kellogg Company Annual Reports, 1981, 1982, 1983, 1984, 1985.

Kiechel, Walter III. "The Soggy Case against the Cereal Industry," *Fortune,* April 10, 1978, p. 49.

Kronhelm, William, "Should Food Labels Carry Health Claims, FDA's Policy Challenged," *Associated Press,* May 15, 1985.

Lippman, Thomas W. "Quebec's Ad Ban No Child's Game; Advertisers, TV Try to Adjust," *Washington Post,* April 17, 1983, p. G1.

Marwick, C., "FDA Prepares to Meet Regulatory Challenges of 21st Century," *Journey of the American Medical Association,* 254 (1985) pp. 2189–2201.

Meadows, Edward, "Bold Departures in Antitrust," *Fortune,* October 5, 1981, p. 180.

Newsweek, "A Portrait of America," January 17, 1983, pp. 20–33.

The New York Times, September 15, 1985, sec. 3, p. 1.

The New York Times, "More Mothers Are Working," February 19, 1986, p. C4+.

Patent Number 3,952,112, "Method for Treating Dried Fruits to Improve Softenss Retention Characteristics," Fulger et al., April 20, 1976.

Patent Number 4,103,035, "Method for Retaining Softness in Raisins," Fulger et al., July 25, 1978.

Patent Number 4,178,392, "Method of Making a Ready-to-Eat Breakfast Cereal," Gobble et al., December 11, 1979.

Philip Morris Co., Press Release, April 24, 1986.

Prokesch, Steven, "Food Industry's Big Mergers," *The New York Times*, October 14, 1985, p. D1.

Prudential-Bache Securities, Inc., October 1, 1985.

Prudential-Bache Securities, Inc., April 2, 1986.

Rotenberk, Lori, "Ad Exec Blasts JWT's All-Bran Ad," *ADWEEK* (Eastern edition), October 29, 1984.

Sebastian, John V. "A Slight Taste of Honey," *Business Week*, Reader's Report, December 17, 1979, p. 10.

Spillman, Susan, "It's a Kid's Market," *USA Today*, October 7, 1985.

Time, October 5, 1981.

Tracy, Eleanor Johnson, "Madison Avenue's Cancer Sell Spreads," *Fortune*, August 19, 1985, p. 77.

Ward, S., "Compromise in Commercials for Children," *Harvard Business Review*, November 1978, p. 128 + .

Willoughby, Jack, "The Snap, Crackle, Pop Defense," *Forbes*, March 25, 1985, p. 82.

Wollenberg, Skip, "Reagan's Cancer Diagnosis Sparks Prevention Ads," *Associated Press*, July 29, 1985.

22. *The Lincoln Electric Company (1985)*

The Lincoln Electric Company is the world's largest manufacturer of welding machines and electrodes. Lincoln employs 2,400 workers in two U.S. factories near Cleveland and approximately 600 in three factories located in other countries. This does not include the field sales force of more than 200 persons. It has been estimated that Lincoln's market share (for arc-welding equipment and supplies) is more than 40 percent.

The Lincoln incentive management plan has been well known for many years. Many college management texts make reference to the Lincoln plan as a model for achieving high worker productivity. Certainly, Lincoln has been a successful company according to the usual measures of success.

James F. Lincoln died in 1965 and there was some concern, even among employees, that the Lincoln system would fall into disarray, that profits would decline, and that year-end bonuses might be discontinued. Quite the contrary, 20 years after Lincoln's death, the company appears as strong as ever. Each year, except the recession years 1982 and 1983, has seen higher profits and bonuses. Employee morale and productivity remain high. Employee turnover is almost nonexistent except for retirements. Lincoln's market share is stable. Consistently high dividends continue on Lincoln's stock.

A HISTORICAL SKETCH

In 1895, after being "frozen out" of the depression-ravaged Elliott-Lincoln Company, a maker of Lincoln-designed electric motors, John C. Lincoln took out his second patent and began to manufacture his improved motor. He opened his new business, unincorporated, with $200 he had earned redesigning a motor for young Herbert Henry Dow, who later founded the Dow Chemical Company.

Started during an economic depression and cursed by a major fire after only one year in business, Lincoln's company grew, but hardly prospered, through its first-quarter century. In 1906, John C. Lincoln incorporated his company and moved from his one-room, fourth-floor

---

This case prepared by Arthur Sharplin, McNeese State University, Lake Charles, Louisiana.

factory to a new three-story building he erected in east Cleveland. In his new factory, he expanded his work force to 30 and sales grew to over $50,000 a year. John Lincoln preferred being an engineer and inventor rather than a manager, though, and it was to be left to another Lincoln to manage the company through its years of success.

In 1907, after a bout with typhoid fever forced him from Ohio State University in his senior year, James F. Lincoln, John's younger brother, joined the fledgling company. In 1914 he became the active head of the firm, with the titles of general manager and vice president. John Lincoln, while he remained president of the company for some years, became more involved in other business ventures and in his work as an inventor.

One of James Lincoln's early actions as head of the firm was to ask the employees to elect representatives to a committee which would advise him on company operations. The Advisory Board has met with the chief executive officer twice monthly since that time. This was only the first of a series of innovative personnel policies which have, over the years, distinguished Lincoln Electric from its contemporaries.

The first year the Advisory Board was in existence, working hours were reduced from 55 per week, then standard, to 50 hours a week. In 1915, the company gave each employee a paid-up life insurance policy. A welding school, which continues today, was begun in 1917. In 1918, an employee bonus plan was attempted. It was not continued, but the idea was to resurface and become the backbone of the Lincoln Management System.

The Lincoln Electric Employees' Association was formed in 1919 to provide health benefits and social activities. This organization continues today and has assumed several additional functions over the years. In 1923, a piecework pay system was in effect, employees got two-week paid vacations each year, and wages were adjusted for changes in the consumer price index. Approximately 30 percent of Lincoln's stock was set aside for key employees in 1914 when James F. Lincoln became general manager and a stock purchase plan for all employees was begun in 1925.

The board of directors voted to start a suggestion system in 1929. The program is still in effect, but cash awards, a part of the early program, were discontinued several years ago. Now, suggestions are rewarded by additional "points," which affect year-end bonuses.

The legendary Lincoln bonus plan was proposed by the Advisory Board and accepted on a trial basis by James Lincoln in 1934. The first annual bonus amounted to about 25 percent of wages. There has been a bonus every year since then. The bonus plan has been a cornerstone of the Lincoln Management System and recent bonuses have approximated annual wages.

By 1944, Lincoln employees enjoyed a pension plan, a policy of promotion from within, and continuous employment. Base pay rates were determined by formal job evaluation and a merit rating system was in effect.

In the prologue of James F. Lincoln's last book, Charles G. Herbruck writes regarding the foregoing personnel innovations,

> They were not to buy good behavior. They were not efforts to increase profits. They were not antidotes to labor difficulties. They did not constitute a "do-gooder" program. They were expression of mutual respect for each person's importance to the job to be done. All of them reflect the leadership of James Lincoln, under whom they were nurtured and propagated.

By the start of World War II, Lincoln Electric was the world's largest manufacturer of arc-welding products. Sales of about $4,000,000 in 1934 had grown to $24,000,000 by 1941. Productivity per employee more than doubled during the same period.

During the war, Lincoln Electric prospered as never before. Despite challenges to Lincoln's profitability by the Navy's Price Review Board and to the tax deductibility of employee bonuses by the Internal Revenue Service, the company increased its profits and paid huge bonuses.

Certainly since 1935 and probably for several years before that, Lincoln productivity has been well above the average for similar companies. Lincoln claims levels of productivity more than twice those for other manufacturers from 1945 onward. Information available from outside sources tends to support these claims.

COMPANY PHILOSOPHY

James F. Lincoln was the son of a Congregational minister, and Christian principles were at the center of his business philosophy. The confidence that he had in the efficacy of Christ's teachings is illustrated by the following remark taken from one of his books:

> The Christian ethic should control our acts. If it did control our acts, the savings in cost of distribution would be tremendous. Advertising would be a contact of the expert consultant with the customer, in order to give the customer the best product available when all of the customer's needs are considered. Competition then would be in improving the quality of products and increasing efficiency in producing and distributing them; not in deception, as is now too customary. Pricing would reflect efficiency of production; it would not be a selling dodge that the customer may well be sorry he accepted. It would be proper for all concerned and rewarding for the ability used in producing the product.

There is no indication that Lincoln attempted to evangelize his employees or customers—or the general public for that matter. The current board chairman, Mr. Irrgang, and the president, Mr. Willis, do not even mention the Christian gospel in their recent speeches and interviews. The company motto, "The actual is limited, the possible is immense," is prominently displayed, but there is no display of religious slogans, and there is no company chapel.

Attitude toward the Customer

James Lincoln saw the customer's needs as the raison d'être for every company. "When any company has achieved success so that it is attractive as an investment," he wrote, "all money usually needed for expansion is supplied by the customer in retained earnings. It is obvious that the customer's interests, not the stockholder's, should come first." In 1947 he said, "Care should be taken . . . not to rivet attention on profit. Between 'How much do I get?' and 'How do I make this better, cheaper, more useful?' the difference is fundamental and decisive." Mr. Willis still ranks the customer as Lincoln's most important constituency. This is reflected in Lincoln's policy to "at all times price on the basis of cost and at all times keep pressure on our cost. . . ." Lincoln's goal, often stated, is "to build a better and better product at a lower and lower price." "It is

obvious," James Lincoln said, "that the customer's interests should be the first goal of industry."

Attitude toward Stockholders

Stockholders are given last priority at Lincoln. This is a continuation of James Lincoln's philosophy: "The last group to be considered is the stockholders who own stock because they think it will be more profitable than investing money in any other way." Concerning division of the largess produced by incentive management, Lincoln wrote, "The absentee stockholder also will get his share, even if undeserved, out of the greatly increased profit that the efficiency produces."

Attitude toward Unionism

There has never been a serious effort to organize Lincoln employees. While James Lincoln criticized the labor movement for "selfishly attempting to better its position at the expense of the people it must serve," he still had kind words for union members. He excused abuses of union power as "the natural reactions of human beings to the abuses to which management has subjected them." Lincoln's idea of the correct relationship between workers and managers is shown by this comment: "Labor and management are properly not warring camps; they are parts of one organization in which they must and should cooperate fully and happily."

Beliefs and Assumptions about Employees

If fulfilling customer needs is the desired goal of business, then employee performance and productivity are the means by which this goal can best be achieved. It is the Lincoln attitude toward employees, reflected in the following comments by James Lincoln, which is credited by many with creating the record of success the company has experienced:

> The greatest fear of the worker, which is the same as the greatest fear of the industrialist in operating a

company, is the lack of income. . . . The industrial manager is very conscious of his company's need of uninterrupted income. He is completely oblivious, evidently, of the fact that the worker has the same need.

*****

He is just as eager as any manager is to be part of a team that is properly organized and working for the advancement of our economy. . . . He has no desire to make profits for those who do not hold up their end in production, as is true of absentee stockholders and inactive people in the company.

*****

If money is to be used as an incentive, the program must provide that what is paid to the worker is what he has earned. The earnings of each must be in accordance with accomplishment.

*****

Status is of great importance in all human relationships. The greatest incentive that money has, usually, is that it is a symbol of success. . . . The resulting status is the real incentive. . . . Money alone can be an incentive to the miser only.

*****

There must be complete honesty and understanding between the hourly worker and management if high efficiency is to be obtained.

LINCOLN'S BUSINESS

Arc welding has been the standard joining method in the shipbuilding industry for decades. It is the predominant way of joining steel in the construction industry. Most industrial plants have their own welding shops for maintenance and construction. Manufacturers of tractors and all kinds of heavy equipment use arc welding extensively in the manufacturing process. Many hobbyists have their own welding machines and use them for making metal items such as patio furniture and barbeque pits. The popularity of welded sculpture as an art form is growing.

While advances in welding technology have been frequent, arc-welding products, in the main, have hardly changed except for Lincoln's Innershield process. This process, utilizing a self-shielded, flux cored electrode, has established new cost-saving opportunities for con-

struction and equipment fabrication. The most popular Lincoln electrode, the Fleetweld 5P, has been virtually the same since the 1930s. The most popular engine-driven welder in the world, the Lincoln SA-200, has been a gray-colored assembly including a four-cylinder continental "Red Seal" engine and a 200 ampere direct-current generator with two current-control knobs for at least three decades. A 1980 model SA-200 even weighs almost the same as the 1950 model, and it certainly is little changed in appearance.

Lincoln and its competitors now market a wide range of general purpose and specialty electrodes for welding mild steel, aluminum, cast iron, and stainless and special steels. Most of these electrodes are designed to meet the standards of the American Welding Society, a trade association. They are thus essentially the same as to size and composition from one manufacturer to another. Every electrode manufacturer has a limited number of unique products, but these typically constitute only a small percentage of total sales.

Lincoln's research and development expenditures have recently been less than 1.50 percent of sales. There is evidence that others spend several times as much as a percentage of sales.

Lincoln's share of the arc-welding products market appears to have been about 40 percent for many years, and the welding products market has grown somewhat faster than the level of industry in general. The market is highly price competitive, with variations in prices of standard products normally amounting to only 1 percent or 2 percent. Lincoln's products are sold directly by its engineering-oriented sales force and indirectly through its distributor organization. Advertising expenditures amount to less than one fourth of 1 percent of sales, one third as much as a major Lincoln competitor with whom the casewriter checked.

The other major welding process, flame welding, has not been competitive with arc welding since the 1930s. However, plasma arc welding, a relatively new process which uses a conducting stream of super heated gas (plasma) to confine the welding current to a small area, has made some inroads, especially in metal tubing manufacturing, in recent years. Major advances in technology which will produce an alternative superior to arc welding within the next decade or so appear unlikely. Also, it seems likely that changes in the machines and techniques used in arc welding will be evolutionary rather than revolutionary.

Products

The company is primarily engaged in the manufacture and sale of arc-welding products—electric welding machines and metal electrodes. Lincoln also produces electric motors ranging from ½ horsepower to 200 horsepower. Motors constitute about 8 percent to 10 percent of total sales.

The electric welding machines, some consisting of a transformer or motor and generator arrangement powered by commercial electricity and others consisting of an internal combustion engine and generator, are designed to produce from 30 to 1,000 amperes of electrical power. This electrical current is used to melt a consumable metal electrode with the molten metal being transferred in a super hot spray to the metal joint being welded. Very high temperatures and hot sparks are produced, and operators usually must wear special eye and face protection and leather gloves, often along with leather aprons and sleeves.

Welding electrodes are of two basic types: (1) Coated "stick" electrodes, usually 14 inches long and smaller than a pencil in diameter, which are held in a special insulated holder by the operator, who must manipulate the electrode in order to maintain a proper arc width and pattern of deposition of the metal being transferred. Stick electrodes are packaged in 6- to 50-pound boxes. (2) Coiled wire, ranging in diameter from 0.035 inch to 0.219 inch, which is designed to be fed continuously to the welding arc through a "gun" held by the operator or positioned by automatic positioning equipment. The wire is packaged in coils, reels, and drums weighing from 14 to 1,000 pounds.

MANUFACTURING OPERATIONS

The main plant is in Euclid, Ohio, a suburb on Cleveland's east side. The layout of this plant is shown in Figure 1. There are no warehouses. Materials flow from the half-mile long dock on the north side of the plant through the production lines to a very limited storage and loading area on the south side. Materials used on each workstation are stored as close as possible to the workstation. The administrative offices, near the center of the factory, are entirely functional. Not even the president's office is carpeted. A corridor below the main level provides access to the factory floor from the main entrance near the center of the plant. A new plant, just opened in Mentor, Ohio, houses some of the electrode production operations, which were moved from the main plant.

Manufacturing Processes

Electrode manufacturing is highly capital intensive. Metal rods purchased from steel producers are drawn or extruded down to smaller diameters, cut to length and coated with pressed-powder flux for stick electrodes or plated with copper (for conductivity) and spun into coils or spools for wire. Some of Lincoln's wire, called *Innershield,* is hollow and filled with a material similar to that used to coat stick electrodes. Lincoln is highly secretive about its electrode production processes, and the casewriter was not given access to the details of those processes.

Welding machines and electric motors are made on a series of assembly lines. Gasoline and diesel engines are purchased partially assembled but practically all other components are made from basic industrial products; for example, steel bars and sheets and bare copper conductor wire, in the Lincoln factory.

Individual components, such as gasoline tanks for engine-driven welders and steel shafts for motors and generators, are made by numerous small "factories within a factory." The shaft for a certain generator, for example, is made from a raw steel bar by one operator who uses five large machines, all running continuously. A saw cuts the bar to length, a digital lathe machines different sections to varying diameters, a special milling machine cuts a slot for a keyway, and so forth, until a finished shaft is produced. The operator moves the shafts from machine to machine and makes necessary adjustments.

Another operator punches, shapes, and paints sheet metal cowling parts. One assembles steel liminations onto a rotor shaft, then winds, insulates and tests the rotors. Finished components are moved by crane operators to the nearby assembly lines.

Worker Performance and Attitudes

Exceptional worker performance at Lincoln is a matter of record. The typical Lincoln employee earns about

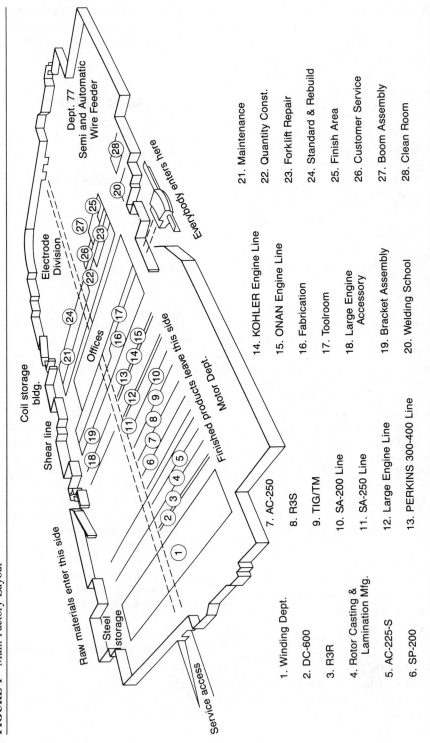

FIGURE 1 Main Factory Layout

1. Winding Dept.
2. DC-600
3. R3R
4. Rotor Casting & Lamination Mfg.
5. AC-225-S
6. SP-200
7. AC-250
8. R3S
9. TIG/TM
10. SA-200 Line
11. SA-250 Line
12. Large Engine Line
13. PERKINS 300-400 Line
14. KOHLER Engine Line
15. ONAN Engine Line
16. Fabrication
17. Toolroom
18. Large Engine Accessory
19. Bracket Assembly
20. Welding School
21. Maintenance
22. Quantity Const.
23. Forklift Repair
24. Standard & Rebuild
25. Finish Area
26. Customer Service
27. Boom Assembly
28. Clean Room

twice as much as other factory workers in the Cleveland area. Yet the labor cost per sales dollar at Lincoln, currently 23.5 cents, is well below industry averages.

Sales per Lincoln factory employee currently exceed $157,000. An observer at the factory quickly sees why this figure is so high. Each worker is proceeding busily and thoughtfully about the task at hand. This is no idle chatter. Most workers take no coffee breaks. Many operate several machines and make a substantial component unaided. The supervisors, some with as many as 100 subordinates, are busy with planning and record-keeping duties and hardly glance at the people they supervise. The manufacturing procedures appear efficient—no unnecessary steps, no wasted motions, no wasted materials. Finished components move smoothly to subsequent workstations.

Worker turnover at Lincoln is practically nonexistent except for retirements and departures by new employees. The Appendix includes summaries of interviews with Lincoln employees.

ORGANIZATION STRUCTURE

Lincoln has never had a formal organization chart. The objective of this policy is to ensure maximum flexibility. An open-door policy is practiced throughout the company, and personnel are encouraged to take problems to the persons most capable of resolving them. Once, Harvard Business School researchers prepared an organization chart reflecting the below-mentioned implied relationships. The chart became available within the Lincoln organization, and present Lincoln management feels that it had a disruptive effect. Therefore, the casewriter was asked not to include any kind of organizational chart in this report.

Perhaps because of the quality and enthusiasm of the Lincoln work force, routine supervision is almost nonexistent. A typical production foreman, for example, supervises as many as 100 workers, a span of control which does not allow more than infrequent worker-supervisor interaction. Position titles and traditional flows of authority do imply something of an organizational structure, however. For example, the vice president, Sales, and the vice president, Electrode Division, report to the president, as do various staff assistants such as the personnel director and the director of purchasing. Using such implied relationships, it has been determined

that production workers have two or, at most, three levels of supervision between themselves and the president.

PERSONNEL POLICIES

Recruitment and Selection

Every job opening at Lincoln is advertised internally on company bulletin boards and any employee can apply for any job so advertised. External hiring is done only for entry level positions. Selection for these jobs is done on the basis of personal interviews—there is no aptitude or psychological testing. Not even a high school diploma is required except for engineering and sales positions, which are filled by graduate engineers. A committee consisting of vice presidents and superintendents interviews candidates initially cleared by the personnel department. Final selection is made by the supervisor who has a job opening. Out of over 3,500 applicants interviewed by the personnel department during a recent period fewer than 300 were hired.

Job Security

In 1958 Lincoln formalized its lifetime employment policy, which had already been in effect for many years. There have been no layoffs at Lincoln since World War II. Since 1958, every Lincoln worker with over one year's longevity has been guaranteed at least 30 hours per week, 49 weeks per year.

The policy has never been so severely tested as during the 1981–83 recession. As a manufacturer of capital goods, Lincoln's business is highly cyclical. In previous recessions Lincoln has been able to avoid major sales declines. However, sales plummeted 32 percent in 1982 and another 16 percent the next year. Few companies could withstand such a sales decline and remain profitable. Yet, Lincoln not only earned profits, but no employee was laid off and year-end incentive bonuses were paid. To weather the storm, Lincoln cut most of the nonsalaried workers back to 30 hours a week for varying periods of time. Many employees were reassigned and the total work force was slightly reduced through normal attrition and restricted hiring. Many employees grumbled at their unexpected misfortune, probably to the surprise and dismay of some Lincoln managers. However, a modest sales resurgence in 1984 and 1985 seemed to portend brighter days.

Performance Evaluations

Each supervisor formally evaluates subordinates twice a year using the cards shown in Figure 2. The employee performance criteria, "quality," "dependability," "ideas and cooperation," and "output," are considered to be independent of each other. Marks on the cards are converted to numerical scores which are forced to average 100 for each evaluating supervisor. Individual merit-rating scores normally range from 80 to 110. Any score over 110 requires a special letter to top management. These scores (over 110) are not considered in computing the required 100 point average for each evaluating supervisor. Suggestions for improvements often result in recommendations for exceptionally high-performance scores. Supervisors discuss individual performance marks with the employees concerned. Each warranty claim on a Lincoln product is traced to the individual employee whose work caused the defect. The employee's performance score may be reduced or the worker may be required to repay the cost of servicing the warranty claim by working without pay.

Compensation

Basic wage levels for jobs at Lincoln are determined by a wage survey of similar jobs in the Cleveland area. These rates are adjusted quarterly in accordance with changes in the Cleveland Area consumer price index. Insofar as possible, base wage rates are translated into piece rates. Practically all production workers and many others—for example, some forklift operators—are paid by piece rate. Once established, piece rates are never changed unless a substantive change in the way a job is done results from a source other than the worker doing the job. In December of each year, a portion of annual profits is distributed to employees as bonuses. Incentive bonuses since 1934 have averaged about the same as annual wages and somewhat more than after-tax profits. The average bonus for 1981 was $20,759. Bonuses averaged $13,998 and $8,557, respectively, for the

recession years 1982 and 1983. Individual bonuses are proportional to merit-rating scores. For example, assume the amount set aside for bonuses is 80 percent of total wages paid to eligible employees. A person whose performance score is 95 will receive a bonus of 76 percent (0.80×0.95) of annual wages.

Vacations

The company is shut down for two weeks in August and two weeks during the Christmas season. Vacations are taken during these periods. For employees with over 25 years of service, a fifth week of vacation may be taken at a time acceptable to superiors.

Work Assignment

Management has authority to transfer workers and to switch between overtime and short time as required. Supervisors have undisputed authority to assign specific parts to individual workmen, who may have their own preferences due to variations in piece rates. During the 1982–83 recession, 50 factory workers volunteered to join sales teams and fanned out across the country to sell a new Lincoln welder designed for automobile body shops and small machine shops. The result—$10 million in sales and a hot new product.

Employee Participation in Decision Making

When a manager speaks of participative management, he usually thinks of a relaxed, nonauthoritarian atmosphere. This is not the case at Lincoln. Formal authority is quite strong. "We're very authoritarian around here," says Mr. Willis. James F. Lincoln placed a good deal of stress on protecting management's authority. "Management in all successful departments of industry must have complete power," he said, ". . . Management is the coach who must be obeyed. The men, however, are the players who alone can win the game." Despite this attitude, there are several ways in which employees participate in management at Lincoln.

FIGURE 2   Merit-Rating Cards

Increasing Quality ⇒

This card rates the QUALITY of work you do.

It also reflects your success in eliminating errors and in reducing scrap and waste.

QUALITY
This rating has been done jointly by your department head and the Inspection Department in the shop and with other department heads in the office and engineering.

Increasing Dependability ⇒

This card rates how well your supervisors have been able to depend upon you to do those things that have been expected of you without supervision.

It also rates your ability to supervise yourself including your work safety performance, your orderliness, care of equipment, and the effective use you make of your skills.

DEPENDABILITY
This rating has been done by your department head.

Increasing Ideas & Cooperation ⇒

This card rates your Cooperation, Ideas and Initiative.

IDEAS & COOPERATION
This rating has been done jointly by your department head and the Time Study Department in the shop and with other department heads in the office and engineering.

Increasing Output ⇒   Days Absent ○

This car rates HOW MUCH PRODUCTIVE WORK you actually turn out.

It also reflects your willingness not to hold back and recognizes your attendance record.

New ideas and new methods are important to your company in our continuing effort to reduce costs, increase output, improve quality-work safety and improve our relationship with our customers. This card credits you for your ideas and initiative used to help in this direction.

It also rates your cooperation—how to work with others as a team. Such factors as your attitude towards supervision, co-workers, and the company; your efforts to share your expert knowledge with others; and your cooperation in installing new methods smoothly, are considered here.

OUTPUT
This rating has been done jointly by your department head and the Production Control Department in the shop and with other department heads in the office and engineering.

Richard Sabo, manager of public relations, relates job enlargement/enrichment to participation. He said, "The most important participative technique that we use is giving more responsibility to employees. We give a high school graduate more responsibility than other companies give their foremen." Lincoln puts limits on the degree of participation which is allowed, however. In Mr. Sabo's words,

> When you use "participation," put quotes around it. Because we believe that each person should participate only in those decisions he is most knowledgeable about. I don't think production employees should control the decisions of Bill Irrgang. They don't know as much as he does about the decisions he is involved in.

The Advisory Board, elected by the workers, meets with the chairman and the president every two weeks to discuss ways of improving operations. This board has been in existence since 1914 and has contributed to many innovations. The incentive bonuses, for example, were first recommended by this committee. Every Lincoln employee has access to Advisory Board members, and answers to all Advisory Board suggestions are promised by the following meeting. Both Mr. Irrgang and Mr. Willis are quick to point out, though, that the Advisory Board only recommends actions. "They do not have direct authority." Mr. Irrgang says, "And when they bring up something that management thinks is not to the benefit of the company, it will be rejected."

A suggestion program was instituted in 1929. At first, employees were awarded one half of the first year's savings attributable to their suggestions. Now, however, the value of suggestions is reflected in performance evaluation scores, which determine individual incentive bonus amounts.

Training and Education

Production workers are given a short period of on-the-job training and then placed on a piecework pay system. Lincoln does not pay for off-site education. The idea behind this latter policy is that everyone cannot take advantage of such a program, and it is unfair to expend company funds for an advantage to which there is unequal access. Recruits for sales jobs, already college graduates, are given on-the-job training in the plant followed by a period of work and training at one of the regional sales offices.

Fringe Benefits and Executive Perquisites

A medical plan and a company-paid retirement program have been in effect for many years. A plant cafeteria, operated on a break-even basis, serves meals at about 60 percent of usual costs. An employee association, to which the company does not contribute, provides disability insurance and social and athletic activities. An employee stock ownership program, instituted in about 1925, has resulted in employee ownership of about 50 percent of Lincoln's stock. Under this program, each employee with more than one year of service may purchase stock in the corporation. The price of these shares is established at book value. Stock purchased through this plan may be held by employees only, and must be offered back to the company upon termination of employment. Dividends and voting rights are the same as for stock which is owned outside the plan. Approximately 75 percent of the employees own Lincoln stock.

As to executive perquisites, there are none—crowded, austere offices, no executive washrooms or lunchrooms, and no reserved parking spaces. Even the company president pays for his own meals and eats in the cafeteria.

FINANCIAL POLICIES

James F. Lincoln felt strongly that financing for company growth should come from within the company—through initial cash investment by the founders, through retention of earnings, and through stock purchases by those who work in the business. He saw the following advantages of this approach:

1. Ownership of stock by employees strengthens team spirit. "If they are mutually anxious to make it succeed, the future of the company is bright."
2. Ownership of stock provides individual incentive because employees feel that they will benefit from company profitability.

3. "Ownership is educational." Owners-employees "will know how profits are made and lost; how success is won and lost. . . . There are few socialists in the list of stockholders of the nation's industries."
4. "Capital available from within controls expansion." Unwarranted expansion will not occur, Lincoln believed, under his financing plan.
5. "The greatest advantage would be the development of the individual worker. Under the incentive of ownership, he would become a greater man."
6. "Stock ownership is one of the steps that can be taken that will make the worker feel that there is less of a gulf between him and the boss. . . . Stock ownership will help the worker to recognize his responsibility in the game and the importance of victory."

Lincoln Electric Company uses a minimum of debt in its capital structure. There is no borrowing at all, with the debt being limited to current payables. Even the new $20 million plant in Mentor, Ohio, was financed totally from earnings.

The unusual pricing policy at Lincoln is succinctly stated by President Willis: "At all times price on the basis of cost and at all times keep pressure on our cost." This policy resulted in Lincoln's price for the most popular welding electrode then in use going from 16 cents a pound in 1929 to 4.7 cents in 1938. More recently, the SA-200 Welder, Lincoln's largest selling portable machine, decreased in price from 1958 through 1965. According to Dr. C. Jackson Grayson of the American Productivity Center in Houston, Texas, Lincoln's prices in general have increased only one fifth as fast as the consumer price index from 1934 to about 1970. This has resulted in a welding products market in which Lincoln is the undisputed price leader for the products it manufactures. Not even the major Japanese manufacturers, such as Nippon Steel for welding electrodes and Asaka Transformer for welding machines, have been able to penetrate this market.

Huge cash balances are accumulated each year preparatory to paying the year-end bonuses. The bonuses totaled $32,718,000 for 1984. This money is invested in short-term U.S. government securities and bank certificates of deposit until needed. Financial statements are shown in Tables 1 and 2. Figure 3 shows how Lincoln's revenue has been distributed.

HOW WELL DOES LINCOLN SERVE ITS PUBLIC?

Lincoln Electric differs from most other companies in the importance it assigns to each of the groups it serves. Mr. Willis identifies these groups, in the order of priority Lincoln ascribes to them, as (1) customers, (2) employees, and (3) stockholders.

Certainly Lincoln customers have fared well over the years. Lincoln prices for welding machines and welding electrodes are acknowledged to be the lowest in the marketplace. Lincoln quality has consistently been so high that Lincoln Fleetweld electrodes and Lincoln SA-200 welders have been the standard in the pipeline and refinery construction industry, where price is hardly a criterion, for decades. The cost of field failures for Lincoln products was an amazing four one-hundreths of one percent in 1979. A Lincoln distributor in Monroe, Louisiana, says that he has sold several hundred of the popular AC-225 welders, and, though the machine is warranted for one year, he has never handled a warranty claim.

Perhaps the best served of all Lincoln constituencies have been the employees. Not the least of their benefits, of course, are the year-end bonuses, which effectively double an already average compensation level. The foregoing description of the personnel program and the comments in the Appendix further illustrate the desirability of a Lincoln job.

While stockholders were relegated to an inferior status by James F. Lincoln, they have done very well indeed. Recent dividends have exceeded $7 a share and earnings per share have exceeded $20. In January 1980, the price of restricted stock committed by Lincoln to employees was $117 a share. By February 4, 1983, the stated value, at which Lincoln will repurchase the stock if tendered, was $166. A check with the New York office of Merrill, Lynch, Pierce, Fenner and Smith on February 4, 1983 revealed an estimated price on Lincoln stock of $240 a share, with none being offered for sale. Technically, this price applies only to the unrestricted stock owned by the Lincoln family, a few other major holders, and employees who have purchased it on the open market, but it gives some idea of the value of Lincoln stock in general. The risk associated with Lincoln stock, a major determinant of stock value, is minimal because of the absence of debt in Lincoln's capital structure, because of an extremely stable earnings record, and because of Lin-

TABLE 1

THE LINCOLN ELECTRIC COMPANY
Balance Sheets
($ in thousands)

	1980	1981	1982	1983	1984
Assets					
Cash	$ 1,307	$ 3,603	$ 1,318	$ 1,774	$ 3,580
Bonds and CDs	46,503	62,671	72,485	77,872	57,212
Notes and accounts receivable	42,424	41,521	26,239	31,114	34,469
Inventories (LIFO basis)	35,533	45,541	38,157	30,773	37,433
Deferred taxes and prepaid expenses ..	2,749	3,658	4,635	4,704	5,095
	$128,516	$156,994	$142,834	$146,237	$137,789
Other assets.......................	$ 19,723	$ 21,424	$ 22,116	$ 21,421	$ 20,216
Investment in foreign divisions	4,695	4,695	7,696	8,696	8,696
	$ 24,418	$ 26,119	$ 29,812	$ 30,117	28,912
Property, plant, equipment:					
Land	$ 913	$ 928	$ 925	$ 925	$ 926
Buildings (net)...................	22,982	24,696	23,330	22,378	20,860
Machinery and equipment (net).....	25,339	27;104	26,949	27,146	28,106
	$ 49,234	$ 52,728	$ 51,204	$ 50,449	$ 49,892
Total assets	$202,168	$235,841	$223,850	$226,803	$216,593
Claims on Assets					
Accounts payable..................	$ 15,608	$ 14,868	$ 11,936	$ 16,228	$ 15,233
Accrued wages....................	1,504	4,940	3,633	3,224	4,358
Taxes payable	5,622	14,755	5,233	6,675	4,203
Dividends payable.................	5,800	7,070	6,957	6,675	6,207
	$ 28,534	$ 41,633	$ 27,759	$ 32,802	$ 30,001
Other long-term debt	$ 3,807	$ 4,557	$ 5,870	$ 7,805	$ 10,313
Shareholders' equity:					
Common stock....................	$ 276	$ 272	$ 268	$ 257	$ 239
Additional paid-in capital	2,641	501	1,862	0	0
Retained earnings	166,910	188,878	188,392	186,318	176,569
Foreign currency adjustment			(301)	(379)	(529)
	$169,827	$189,651	$190,221	$186,196	$176,279
Total claims on assets..............	$202,168	$235,841	$223,850	$226,803	$216,593

TABLE 2

THE LINCOLN ELECTRIC COMPANY
Income Statements
($ in thousands)

	1980	1981	1982	1983	1984
Revenue:					
Net sales	$387,374	$450,387	$310,862	$263,129	$321,759
Other income	13,817	18,454	18,049	13,387	11,814
	$401,191	$468,841	$328,911	$276,516	$333,573
Costs and expenses:					
Cost of products sold.................	$260,671	$293,332	$212,674	$179,851	$222,985
Selling and G&A expenses............	37,753	42,656	37,128	36,348	40,164
Year-end incentive bonus	43,249	55,718	36,870	21,914	32,718
Payroll taxes related to bonus	1,251	1,544	1,847	1,186	1,874
Pension expense	6,810	6,874	5,888	5,151	5,139
Interest on tax assessments...........	0	0	0	1,946	99
	$349,734	$400,124	$294,407	$246,396	$302,979
Income:					
Income before income taxes...........	$ 51,457	$ 68,717	$ 34,504	$ 30,120	$ 30,594
Federal income tax	20,300	27,400	13,227	14,246	12,429
State and local income taxes	3,072	3,885	2,497	(989)	1,443
	$ 23,372	$ 31,285	$ 15,724	$ 13,257	$ 13,852
Net income	$ 28,085	$ 37,432	$ 18,780	$ 16,863	$ 16,742
Employees eligible for bonus...........	2,637	2,684	2,634	2,561	2,469

coln's practice of purchasing the restricted stock whenever employees offer it for sale.

A CONCLUDING COMMENT

It is easy to believe that the reason for Lincoln's success is the excellent attitude of Lincoln employees and their willingness to work harder, faster, and more intelligently than other industrial workers. However, Mr. Richard Sabo, manager of publicity and educational services at Lincoln, suggests that appropriate credit be given to Lincoln executives, whom he credits with carrying out the following policies:

I. Management has limited research, development and manufacturing to a standard product line designed to meet the major needs of the welding industry.

II. New products must be reviewed by manufacturing and all production costs verified before being approved by management.

III. Purchasing is challenged to not only procure materials at the lowest cost, but also to work closely with engineering and manufacturing to assure that the latest innovations are implemented.

IV. Manufacturing supervision and all personnel are held accountable for reduction of scrap, energy conservation, and maintenance of product quality.

V. Production control, material handling, and methods engineering are closely supervised by top management.

VI. Material and finished goods inventory control, accurate cost accounting and attention to sales cost, credit, and other financial areas have constantly reduced overhead and led to excellent profitability.

FIGURE 3   How Lincoln's Revenue Dollar Was Disbursed, 1974–1983

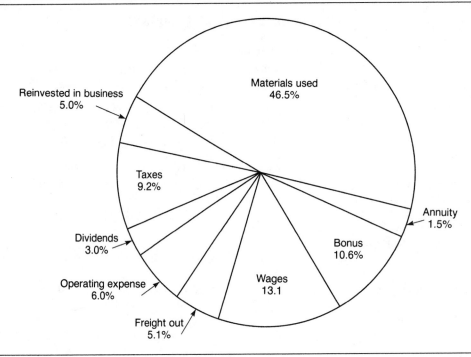

VII. Management has made cost reduction a way of life at Lincoln, and definite programs are established in many areas, including traffic and shipping, where tremendous savings can result.

VIII. Management has established a sales department that is technically trained to reduce customer welding costs. This sales technique and other real customer services have eliminated nonessential frills and resulted in long-term benefits to all concerned.

IX. Management has encouraged education, technical publishing, and long-range programs that have resulted in industry growth, thereby assuring market potential for the Lincoln Electric Company.

Mr. Sabo writes, "It is in a very real sense a personal and group experience in faith—a belief that together we can achieve results which alone would not be possible. It is not a perfect system and it is not 'easy.' It requires tremendous dedication and hard work. However, it does work and the results are worth the effort."

APPENDIX: EMPLOYEE INTERVIEWS

Typical questions and answers from employee interviews are presented below. In order to maintain each employee's personal privacy, fictitious names are given to the interviewees.

I

Interview with Betty Stewart, a 52-year-old high school graduate who had been with Lincoln 13 years and who was working as a cost accounting clerk at the time of the interview.

Q: What jobs have you held here besides the one you have now?

A: I worked in payroll for a while, and then this job came open and I took it.

Q: How much money did you make last year, including your bonus?

A: I would say roughly around $20,000, but I was off for back surgery for a while.

Q: You weren't paid while you were off for back surgery?

A: No.

Q: Did the Employees Association help out?

A: Yes. The company doesn't furnish that, though. We pay $6 a month into the Employee Association. I think my check from them was $105.00 a week.

Q: How was your performance rating last year?

A: It was around 100 points, but I lost some points for attendance with my back problem.

Q: How did you get your job at Lincoln?

A: I was bored silly where I was working, and I had heard that Lincoln kept their people busy. So I applied and got the job the next day.

Q: Do you think you make more money than similar workers in Cleveland?

A: I know I do.

Q: What have you done with your money?

A: We have purchased a better home. Also, my son is going to the University of Chicago, which costs $10,000 a year. I buy the Lincoln stock which is offered each year, and I have a little bit of gold.

Q: Have you ever visited with any of the senior executives, like Mr. Willis or Mr. Irrgang?

A: I have known Mr. Willis for a long time.

Q: Does he call you by name?

A: Yes. In fact he was very instrumental in my going to the doctor that I am going to with my back. He knows the director of the clinic.

Q: Do you know Mr. Irrgang?

A: I know him to speak to him, and he always speaks, always. But I have known Mr. Willis for a good many years. When I did Plant Two accounting I did not understand how the plant operated. Of course

you are not allowed in Plant Two, because that's the Electrode Division. I told my boss about the problem one day and the next thing I knew Mr. Willis came by and said, "Come on, Betty, we're going to Plant Two." He spent an hour and a half showing me the plant.

Q: Do you think Lincoln employees produce more than those in other companies?

A: I think with the incentive program the way that it is, if you want to work and achieve, then you will do it. If you don't want to work and achieve, you will not do it no matter where you are. Just because you are merit rated and have a bonus, if you really don't want to work hard, then you're not going to. You will accept your 90 points or 92 or 85 because, even with that, you make more money than people on the outside.

Q: Do you think Lincoln employees will ever join a union?

A: I don't know why they would.

Q: What is the most important advantage of working for Lincoln Electric?

A: You have an incentive, and you can push and get something for pushing. That's not true in a lot of companies.

Q: So you say that money is a very major advantage?

A: Money is a major advantage, but it's not just the money. It's the fact that having the incentive, you do wish to work a little harder. I'm sure that there are a lot of men here who, if they worked some other place, would not work as hard as they do here. Not that they are overworked—I don't mean that—but I'm sure they wouldn't push.

Q: Is there anything that you would like to add?

A: I do like working here. I am better off being pushed mentally. In another company if you pushed too hard you would feel a little bit of pressure, and someone might say, "Hey, slow down; don't try so hard." But here you are encouraged, not discouraged.

II

Interview with Ed Sanderson, 23-year-old high school graduate who had been with Lincoln four years and who was a machine operator in the Electrode Division at the time of the interview.

Q: How did you happen to get this job?

A: My wife was pregnant, and I was making three bucks an hour and one day I came here and applied. That was it. I kept calling to let them know I was still interested.

Q: Roughly what were your earnings last year including your bonus?

A: $37,000.00

Q: What have you done with your money since you have been here?

A: Well, we've lived pretty well and we bought a condominium.

Q: Have you paid for the condominium?

A: No, but I could.

Q: Have you bought your Lincoln stock this year?

A: No I haven't bought any Lincoln stock yet.

Q: Do you get the feeling that the executives here are pretty well thought of?

A: I think they are. To get where they are today, they had to really work.

Q: Wouldn't that be true anywhere?

A: I think more so here because seniority really doesn't mean anything. If you work with a guy who has 20 years here, and you have two months and you're doing a better job, you will get advanced before he will.

Q: Are you paid on a piece rate basis?

A: My gang does. There are nine of us who make the bare electrode, and the whole group gets paid based on how much electrode we make.

Q: Do you think you work harder than workers in other factories in the Cleveland area?

A: Yes, I would say I probably work harder.

Q: Do you think it hurts anybody?

A: No, a little hard work never hurts anybody.

Q: If you could choose, do you think you would be as happy earning a little less money and being able to slow down a little?

A: No, it doesn't bother me. If it bothered me, I wouldn't do it.

Q: What would you say is the biggest disadvantage of working at Lincoln, as opposed to working somewhere else?

A: Probably having to work shift work.

Q: Why do you think Lincoln employees produce more than workers in other plants?

A: That's the way the company is set up. The more you put out, the more you're going to make.

Q: Do you think it's the piece rate and bonus together?

A: I don't think people would work here if they didn't know that they would be rewarded at the end of the year.

Q: Do you think Lincoln employees will ever join a union?

A: No.

Q: What are the major advantages of working for Lincoln?

A: Money.

Q: Are there any other advantages?

A: Yes, we don't have a union shop. I don't think I could work in a union shop.

Q: Do you think you are a career man with Lincoln at this time?

A: Yes.

III

Interview with Roger Lewis, 23-year-old Purdue graduate in mechanical engineering who had been in the Lincoln sales program for 15 months and who was working in the Cleveland sales office at the time of the interview.

Q: How did you get your job at Lincoln?

A: I saw that Lincoln was interviewing on campus at Purdue, and I went by. I later came to Cleveland for a plant tour and was offered a job.

Q: Do you know any of the senior executives? Would they know you by name?

A: Yes, I know all of them—Mr. Irrgang, Mr. Willis, Mr. Manross.

Q: Do you think Lincoln salesmen work harder than those in other companies?

A: Yes. I don't think there are many salesmen for other companies who are putting in 50 to 60-hour weeks. Everybody here works harder. You can go out in the plant, or you can go upstairs, and there's nobody sitting around.

Q: Do you see any real disadvantage of working at Lincoln?

A: I don't know if it's a disadvantage but Lincoln is a spartan company, a very thrifty company. I like that. The sales offices are functional, not fancy.

Q: Why do you think Lincoln employees have such high productivity?

A: Piecework has a lot to do with it. Lincoln is smaller than many plants, too; you can stand in one place and see the materials come in one side and the product go out the other. You feel a part of the company. The chance to get ahead is important, too. They have a strict policy of promoting from within, so you know you have a chance. I think in a lot of other places you may not get as fair a shake as you do here. The sales offices are on a smaller scale, too. I like that. I tell someone that we have two people in the Baltimore office, and they say "You've got to be kidding." It's smaller and more personal. Pay is the most important thing. I have heard that this is the highest paying factory in the world.

IV

Interview with Jimmy Roberts, a 47-year-old high school graduate, who had been with Lincoln 17 years and who was working as a multiple-drill press operator at the time of the interview.

Q: What jobs have you had at Lincoln?

A: I started out cleaning the men's locker room in 1963. After about a year I got a job in the flux department, where we make the coating for welding rods. I worked there for seven or eight years and then got my present job.

Q: Do you make one particular part?

A: No, there are a variety of parts I make—at least 25.

Q: Each one has a different piece rate attached to it?

A: Yes.

Q: Are some piece rates better than others?

A: Yes.

Q: How do you determine which ones you are going to do?

A: You don't. Your supervisor assigns them.

Q: How much money did you make last year?

A: $47,000.

Q: Have you ever received any kind of award or citation?

A: No.

Q: Was your rating ever over 110?

A: Yes. For the past five years, probably, I made over 110 points.

Q: Is there any attempt to let others know . . .?

A: The kind of points I get? No.

Q: Do you know what they are making?

A: No. There are some who might not be too happy with their points and they might make it known. The majority, though, do not make it a point of telling other employees.

Q: Would you be just as happy earning a little less money and working a little slower?

A: I don't think I would—not at this point. I have done piecework all these years, and the fast pace doesn't really bother me.

Q: Why do you think Lincoln productivity is so high?

A: The incentive thing—the bonus distribution. I think that would be the main reason. The paycheck you get every two weeks is important too.

Q: Do you think Lincoln employees would ever join a union?

A: I don't think so. I have never heard anyone mention it.

Q: What is the most important advantage of working here?

A: Amount of money you make. I don't think I could make this type of money anywhere else, especially with only a high school education.

Q: As a black person, do you feel that Lincoln discriminates in any way against blacks?

A: No. I don't think any more so than any other job. Naturally, there is a certain amount of discrimination, regardless of where you are.

V

Interview with Joe Trahan, 58-year-old high school graduate who had been with Lincoln 39 years and who was employed as a working supervisor in the toolroom at the time of the interview.

Q: Roughly what was your pay last year?

A: Over $50,000; salary, bonus, stock dividends.

Q: How much was your bonus?

A: About $23,000.

Q: Have you ever gotten a special award of any kind?

A: Not really.

Q: What have you done with your money?

A: My house is paid for—and my two cars. I also have some bonds and the Lincoln stock.

Q: What do you think of the executives at Lincoln?

A: They're really top notch.

Q: What is the major disadvantage of working at Lincoln Electric?

A: I don't know of any disadvantage at all.

Q: Do you think you produce more than most people in similar jobs with other companies?

A: I do believe that.

Q: Why is that? Why do you believe that?

A: We are on the incentive system. Everything we do, we try to improve to make a better product with a minimum of outlay. We try to improve the bonus.

Q: Would you be just as happy making a little less money and not working quite so hard?

A: I don't think so.

Q: You know that Lincoln productivity is higher than that at most other plants. Why is that?

A: Money.

Q: Do you think Lincoln employees would ever join a union?

A: I don't think they would ever consider it.

Q: What is the most important advantage of working at Lincoln?

A: Compensation.

Q: Tell me something about Mr. James Lincoln, who died in 1965.

A: You are talking about Jimmy Sr. He always strolled through the shop in his shirt sleeves. Big fellow. Always looked distinguished. Gray hair. Friendly sort of guy. I was a member of the advisory board one year. He was there each time.

Q: Did he strike you as really caring?

A: I think he always cared for people.

Q: Did you get any sensation of a religious nature from him?

A: No, not really.

Q: And religion is not part of the program now?

A: No.

Q: Do you think Mr. Lincoln was a very intelligent man, or was he just a nice guy?

A: I would say he was pretty well educated. A great talker—always right off the top of his head. He knew what he was talking about all the time.

Q: When were bonuses for beneficial suggestions done away with?

A: About 15 years ago.

Q: Did that hurt very much?

A: I don't think so, because suggestions are still rewarded through the merit-rating system.

Q: Is there anything you would like to add?

A: It's a good place to work. The union kind of ties other places down. At other places, electricians only do electrical work, carpenters only do carpenter work. At Lincoln Electric we all pitch in and do whatever needs to be done.

Q: So a major advantage is not having a union?

A: That's right.

23.   *Food Lion, Inc.*

HISTORY OF THE FIRM

In 1957, three Winn-Dixie employees opened their first supermarket in Salisbury, North Carolina, under the name Food Town. Cofounders Ralph Ketner, Brown Ketner, and Wilson Smith all had considerable retail experience in the grocery industry, however, Food Town struggled in its early years. Various marketing gimmicks were implemented (the company gave away trading stamps and even free automobiles), but the stores failed to win the loyalty of customers. In fact, Ralph Ketner had to close 9 of the 16 stores during the first 10 years of operation. He blamed much of this failure on the underpricing techniques of Winn-Dixie. By 1966, only seven Food Town stores remained.

In response to the problem, Ketner adopted the idea of slashing prices on all items sold in the stores. He realized that a drastic increase in volume would be necessary to make this approach work and keep the company afloat. The company theme of LFPINC or "Lowest Food Prices in North Carolina" became popular as both customers and sales increased greatly. Sales rose 54 percent to $8.9 million, and profits rose 165 percent to $95,000 in the first year under the new policy.[1]

In 1970, the company went public. Établissements Delhaize Frères et Cie, a Belgium grocery chain, purchased 47.6 percent of the stock in 1974. Today, Delhaize controls 50.6 percent of the voting stock and has 5 of the 10 seats on the board of directors.[2] The company changed its name to Food Lion in 1983, to avoid confusion with another similarly named chain. Also, the company began implementing its expansion program.

Today, Food Lion has expanded into eight states, from Delaware to Florida, and is considered to be one of the fastest-growing retail grocers in the country. Food Lion President and CEO Tom E. Smith explains, "Our goal is to bring extra low grocery prices to as many people in the Southeast as possible."[3]

Food Lion has 27,000 employees, and continues to operate conventional size stores (21,000–29,000 square feet) and to offer discount prices. The company remains committed to expansion throughout the Southeast and has avoided moving into the sales of general merchandise in its stores. A food consultant's comments highlight the company's success in the aforementioned areas. He states that Food Lion is "probably the best example of commitment to a format and operating style in the industry today. And although it is a conventional store operator, it also stands as an excellent practitioner of niche marketing. The stores aren't fancy, but beat everyone on price, and the company doesn't make many mistakes."[4]

Ralph Ketner

Since cofounding Food Lion, Ralph Ketner has continued to be a force behind its success. In 1968, it was his idea to adopt the strategy of discount pricing and his LFPINC theme which promoted the company. He acted as chief executive officer until 1986, when he passed the reins to President Tom Smith. Despite resigning as CEO, Mr. Ketner still exerts considerable influence over the operation of Food Lion. He remains chairman of the board of directors, and plans to retain this position until 1991. In addition, Delhaize signed an agreement in 1974 to vote with Ketner for 10 years. This agreement was later extended and will be in effect until 1989.[5]

---

[1] Richard Anderson, "That Roar You Hear Is Food Lion," *Business Week,* August 24, 1987, p. 66.

[2] Ibid., p. 66.

[3] 1987 Food Lion, Inc., Annual Report., p. 1.

[4] Richard DeSanta, "Formats: Growing Apart, Coming Together," *Progressive Grocer,* January 1987, p. 37.

[5] "Ketner Gives up Food Lion Reins," *Supermarket News,* January 6, 1986, p. 18.

EXHIBIT 1   Store Distribution

Location	No. of Stores	Percent of Total
North Carolina	233	49.1%
Virginia	112	23.5
South Carolina	74	15.6
Tennessee	29	6.1
Georgia	19	4.0
Florida	6	1.3
Delaware	1	0.2
Maryland	1	0.2
Total	475	100.0%

Source: Standard & Poor's Stock Report, p. 3905.

Tom E. Smith

President and CEO Tom E. Smith is very much responsible for Food Lion's growth and success. This is largely attributed to his involvement with the company since his youth. At age 17, Smith began as a bag boy at Food Lion's first store. He attended night school at Catawba College and graduated in 1964 with an A.B. degree in Business Administration. He spent the next six years working for Del Monte, when he was hired as Food Lion's sole buyer. Smith developed the successful strategy of stocking fewer brands and sizes than his competitors. He also took advantage of wholesaler specials by purchasing large volumes at discount prices. He was named vice president for distribution in 1974, and later became executive vice president in 1977. His continued success in these areas led to his promotion to president in 1981, at the age of 39. In 1986, he was named CEO.

Smith views himself as a planner who carefully molds the company's growth while keeping a close eye on the operations. This style has enabled him to react to and resolve any problems quickly and effectively. He has been a primary reason for Food Lion's constant commitment to its overall strategy of discount pricing and cost reduction. Smith has also become well known through his participation in over 50 percent of the Food Lion commercials. This media exposure has brought him recognition not only in the Southeast, but as far away as San Francisco and even Scotland from visiting customers.[6] These commercials

portray Smith as a hardworking and very trustworthy manager.

FOOD LION'S ATTITUDE TOWARD SOCIAL RESPONSIBILITY

Food Lion is recognized as a corporate neighbor, and it takes pride in performing charitable acts. In 1986, the company received the Martin Luther King Award in recognition of its humanitarian efforts. Food Lion received the award after providing a series of commendable projects. Most notable was the donation of trucks to aid the southeastern farmers during the drought last year. These trucks enabled the farmers to transport hay from Indiana. Also, the company was cited for providing equal opportunity employment and establishing express lanes for handicapped customers.[7]

INDUSTRY

Several trends in the supermarket industry may be cause for concern for many retail grocers. During 1987, there was a decline in the percentage of disposable income

---

[6]Anderson, "That Roar You Hear Is Food Lion," p. 65.
[7]1986 Food Lion, Inc., Annual Report., p. 4.

EXHIBIT 2   Division of U.S. Retail Sales

Division of Sales	1983	1984	1985	1986	1987*
Food stores	22.0%	21.1%	20.6%	20.4%	20.3%
Eating and drinking	9.9	9.6	9.7	10.0	10.1
Drug and proprietary	3.5	3.4	3.4	3.4	3.6
General merchandise	11.1	11.0	10.9	10.7	11.0
Furniture and appliances	4.6	4.8	5.0	5.4	5.5
Auto dealers	19.8	21.6	22.6	22.9	22.2
Hardware and lumber	4.4	4.7	4.8	5.2	4.7
Clothing	5.3	5.3	5.4	5.5	5.8
Gas stations	8.5	7.8	7.3	6.1	5.7
All others	10.9	10.7	10.4	10.4	11.2

*First six months.

Source: Bureau of the Census (revised) 1987.

spent for food at home. After discounting inflation, real sales did not increase from 1986. As Exhibit 2 shows, food-at-home spending accounted for more retail sales than any other category in 1983. However, slow growth has caused a reduction in this percentage, leaving food stores in second place behind auto dealers. Another interesting trend has been the growth in sales of eating and drinking establishments during this same period.

The grocery industry is also experiencing competition from other types of stores. Discount department and drugstores are starting to sell more packaged foods. Many fast-food restaurants continue to sell a larger variety of prepared foods for takeout. Sales from specialty shops, which concentrate on one particular type of food, have increased as well. Wholesale clubs have also been of concern to retail grocers. These clubs have been effective at luring many customers away from conventional supermarkets. Supermarkets stressing discount prices have been hurt most by the emergence of the wholesale clubs.

In response to the trends, most grocery chains are stressing the idea of one-stop shopping. New store formats and product offerings are abundant. These ideas are an attempt to obtain a product mix which stresses higher margined items and services, as well as creating an atmosphere which causes consumers to view the supermarket as more than a place to buy groceries. Items such as flowers, greeting cards, videocasettes, and drugs are appearing more frequently in many supermarkets.

There has also been a greater emphasis on stocking perishables.

Clearly, the biggest trend in the industry is the use of bigger stores. Several experts believe that the increased size is necessary to provide the variety that many consumers desire. One chain president expressed this sentiment. "Customer satisfaction starts with the store design: one-stop shopping, complete service departments and integrating a drugstore and pharmacy into the store."[8] Much of this trend is a result of the massive increase in working women. The greater number of dual-income families, single parents, and singles living alone also contribute to the growth in one-stop shopping. Time and convenience are two characteristics that consumers fitting into the groups above often desire.

The one-stop shopping concept has resulted in several new store formats. Combination stores offer consumers a variety of nonfood items. These stores can be as large as 35,000 square feet, and 25 percent of the space is devoted to nonfood and pharmacy items. Superstores are similar to the combination stores in that they offer a wide selection of general merchandise items. These stores are all greater than 40,000 square feet, and are thought to be the strongest format for the near future. Exhibit 3 shows

---

[8]"Retail Operations: The New Basics," *Progressive Grocer,* September 1987, p. 56.

EXHIBIT 3   Chain Executives' Opinions on Prospects for New Formats

	Excellent	*Good*	*Fair/Poor*
Superstores	56%	36%	8%
Combination	38	53	9
Convenience stores	26	39	35
Super warehouse	22	39	39
Hypermarkets	10	33	57
Specialty	8	37	55
Wholesale clubs	6	30	62
Conventional	4	35	59
Warehouse stores	1	17	79

Source: *Progressive Grocer*, April 1988.

EXHIBIT 4   Store Attributes Desired by Consumers

Rank	*Characteristic*
1	Cleanliness
2	All prices labeled
3	Low Prices
4	Good produce department
5	Accurate, pleasant clerks
6	Freshness date marked on products
7	Good meat department
8	Shelves kept well stocked
9	Short wait for checkout
10	Convenient store location

Source: *Progressive Grocer*, April 1988.

chain executives' views on the prospects for the various formats that exist today.

The newest and largest of the formats is the hypermarket. Currently, 55 of these stores exist in the United States. The typical hypermarket ranges in size from 125,000 to 330,000 square feet and requires $25 to $50 million in sales per year just to break even.[9] Normally, 40 percent of the floor space in hypermarkets is devoted to grocery items and the remaining 60 percent is used for general merchandise. Their success depends on a variety of factors.

Freeway access, population density, and visibility are all key variables which contribute to a hypermarket's success. A majority of the stores are run by companies which are not U.S. food retailers. For example, Wal-Mart has opened several stores under the Hypermarket USA name. Also, Bruno's, a retail grocery chain, is teaming up with K mart to build a store in Atlanta.[10]

Because of the trend to expand store size, the number of stores declined for the first time in years. However, the larger store sizes resulted in an increase in actual square footage. Many small units have been closed due to the

[9]David Rogers, "Hypermarkets Need Something Special to Succeed," *Supermarket Business*. May 1988, p. 26.

[10]Ibid.

openings of larger stores. In many market areas, there continues to be too many stores and too few customers to support them. This is going to be an even bigger concern given the advent of the combination stores and hypermarkets, since they tend to attract customers from a wider area than the conventional stores.

Although the majority of retailers believe that the bigger stores are necessary to be successful in the future, there is a large group that believes the industry is going overboard in its attempt to provide one-stop shopping. Chain executive, Carole Bitter, believes that the emphasis on size is unfounded. "There has been an ego problem in the industry that has led to overbuilding and has driven up store sizes and has increased the number of formats."[11] Proponents of conventionals claim that the larger stores are too impersonal to be attractive to everyone. They also believe that many consumers desire the conventional type of store, and that this format will continue to be successful. Although many consumers claim that they want more service departments, studies have shown that the shoppers are not willing to pay enough for such departments in order to make them profitable. Exhibit 4 reveals what the average shopper desires. One-stop shopping capabilities rates only 26th on the list.

COMPETITION

In recent years, competition in the Southeast has become quite intense. Previously, this area was characterized by predominantly conventional stores. Combination and superstores were scarce. However, many retailers realized that the Southeast was a prime location for the newer formats. (See Exhibit 5.) In 1984, Cub Foods opened three large, modern stores in the Atlanta area in an attempt to challenge Kroger's dominance in the Southeast. This move marked the beginning of several competitive shakeups in the South.

Kroger

Kroger operates 1,317 supermarkets and 889 convenience stores in the South and Midwest. In 1987, sales

were nearly $18 billion. More than 95 percent of the floor space is either new or has been remodeled during the past 10 years.[12] This is a result of the chain's move to larger combination and superstore formats. Kroger has not been as successful as it would like. The company realizes a net profit margin of approximately 1 percent. This is partly due to its new outlets cannibalizing its existing stores and has caused some store sales comparisons to be relatively flat.[13]

In response to the disappointing profit margins, Kroger is planning to decrease its capital spending plans by about $300 million. It is hoped that this will reduce interest costs as well as keep start-up expenses down. Also, the firm is cutting corporate overhead 20 percent. As for future store designs, Kroger is considering the curtailment of the new super-warehouse stores. These stores combine low grocery prices with high-priced service departments and have not appealed to a large segment of the market. Furthermore, the company is planning to reduce store remodeling in mature market areas.[14]

Winn-Dixie

Winn-Dixie is the fourth largest food retailer in the country with sales of nearly $9 billion. The chain operates 1,271 stores in the Sunbelt area, with the heaviest concentration of stores located in Florida, North Carolina, and Georgia. During the past few years, Winn-Dixie has been hurt by the influx of competition in the Southeast. As a result, profit margins have dipped to just over 1 percent. Net income also declined in 1987. Management points to a lack of investment in new stores and a rather slow response to competitors' underpricing methods as the main reasons for the decline in profits.[15]

Management has adopted several new strategies to combat the competition. Foremost is the move to larger store formats. In the past, the chain operated mostly conventional stores and depended on operating efficiencies to realize sizable profits. However, management believes that it is now necessary to alter the stores in

---

[11]"Retail Operations," p. 62.

[12]*Standard & Poor's Standard Stock Reports*, p. 1318.
[13]*Value Line Investment Survey*, 1987, p. 1511.
[14]Ibid., p. 1511.
[15]*Standard & Poor's*, p. 2491.

EXHIBIT 5

	Kroger	Lucky	Winn-Dixie	Bruno's	Food Lion
Number of Stores	2,206	481	1,271	111	475
Employees	170,000	44,000	80,000	10,655	27,033
Sales ($ Million)	$ 17,660	$ 6,925	$ 8,804	$ 1,143	$ 2,954
Sales/employee	103,881	157,386	110,049	107,265	109,267
Net profit ($ Million)	$ 246.6	$ 151	$ 105.4	$ 31	$ 85.8
Net profit margin	1.4 %	2.2 %	1.2 %	2.7 %	2.9 %
Gross margin	22.4	25	22	20.8	19.2
Current ratio	1.1	.83	1.65	1.63	1.41
Return on equity	24.5	46.3	15.2	15.4	25.3
Return on assets	5.5	11.8	7.9	10.3	10.6
Long-term debt/equity	.69	.38	.03	.04	.26
Earnings per share	3.14	3.92	2.72	.79	.27
Average P/E ratio	15.1	10.2	13.9	23.1	35.3

response to changing consumer needs. At the end of 1987, the average supermarket was 27,700 square feet. There are approximately 250 new stores in the 35,000–45,000 square foot range, and they are expected to account for nearly half of all sales in the next five years.[16] The units in the 35,000 square feet category are combination stores which are operated under the Winn-Dixie name. The 45,000 square foot stores employ the superstore format and use the name Marketplace. Emphasis is being placed on service departments as well as price-sensitivity.

Other changes involve management. Last year, the company eliminated a layer of management that resulted in 60 layoffs. The firm is also adopting a decentralized strategy which divides the company into 12 operating units. Each division is allowed to develop its own procedures and image. It is hoped that this will help the stores cater to the consumers in each market area more effectively.

Lucky Stores

Lucky operates nearly 500 supermarkets throughout the country. The majority of these are located in California, however, the chain does operate 90 stores in Florida. In 1986, Lucky began a major restructuring. This resulted in the sale of all the nonfood businesses. Also, the company has concentrated on increasing the store size to enable the sale of more service and nonfood items. The average size of the stores at the end of 1986 was 31,000 square feet.[17]

At the end of the year, there was much speculation that American Stores Company would begin to pursue an unsolicited tender offer for all outstanding shares of Lucky common stock. American is a leading retailer in the country and operates mostly combination food and drug stores.

Bruno's

Bruno's operates approximately 100 supermarkets and combination food and drugstores in the Southeast. This chain pursues a strategy of high-volume sales at low prices. Another strategy involves the use of four different formats under various names. "Consumer Warehouse Foods" stores are relatively small warehouse-type stores which emphasize lower prices and reduced operating costs. "Food World" stores are large supermarkets which offer a variety of supermarket items at low prices. "Bruno's Food and Pharmacy" stores promote the idea

---

[16]"Winn-Dixie Strategy," *Supermarket News*, March 3, 1987, p. 12.

[17]*Standard & Poor's*, p. 1387.

of one-stop shopping through the combination store format. Finally, "FoodMax" stores are superwarehouses which offer generic and bulk foods in addition to the national labels.[18]

The company is also well known for its innovative forward-buying program. Bruno's is able to purchase goods at low prices because of its 900,000 square foot distribution center which houses excess inventory. This strategy has been very successful as the company boasts one of the highest operating (4.8 percent) and net profit margins (2.7 percent).[19]

EXPANSION AT FOOD LION

Food Lion has continued to grow and expand in the Southeast. During 1987, the chain opened 95 new stores while closing only 8, bringing the total to 475. (See Exhibit 6.) With the exception of four supermarkets, Food Lion operates its stores under various leasing arrangements. The number of stores has grown at a 10-year compound rate of 24.1 percent.[20] With this expansion has come impressive growth in both sales and earnings over the same period. The firm has attained 29.7 percent sales and 30.9 percent earnings compounded over the past 10 years.[21]

The existence and further development of distribution centers serve as the core for continued expansion. At the end of 1987, four such centers had been completed. These are located in Salisbury and Dunn, North Carolina, Orangeburg County, South Carolina, and Prince George County, Virginia. Two additional centers are planned for Tennessee and Jacksonville, Florida. These distribution centers enable Food Lion to pursue expansion using its "ink blot" formula. Using this strategy, new stores are added to an existing market area in order to saturate the market. "If anyone wants to go to a competitor, they'll have to drive by one of our stores," explains CFO Brian Woolf.[22] Despite the emergence of new stores, cannibalization has not been a problem. In fact, same-store sales increase approximately 8 percent

annually. When Food Lion enters a new area, the strategy of underpricing the competitors is employed. Such a strategy has caused average food prices to decline 10–20 percent in some parts of the country.[23] Every new store is constructed no further than 200 miles from a distribution center. With continued expansion, new distribution centers whose radii overlap an existing distribution territory are erected in order to keep warehouse and transportation costs down.

Moreover, Food Lion continues to employ a "cookie-cutter" approach to its new stores. Rather than purchase existing stores, the firm much prefers to build new ones from scratch. All the stores fall into the conventional store category. The majority are 25,000 square feet and cost only $650,000 to complete. These stores emphasize the fruit and vegetable departments. Approximately 40 percent of the new stores are 29,000 square feet and contain a bakery/delicatessen. These are placed after careful consideration is given to the demographics and psychographics of the area. Normally, new stores turn a profit within the first six months of operation. In comparison, most competitors construct slightly larger stores which cost over $1 million to complete.[24]

The standard size of the stores has allowed the company to keep costs down while sticking to basics. Aside from the bakery departments, Food Lion has stayed away from service departments such as seafood counters and flower shops. Such departments are often costly due to the increase in required labor. Also, Food Lion has remained a retail grocery chain, shunning the idea of moving into the general merchandise area. This structure has prompted Food Lion to be compared to both Wal-Mart and McDonald's.

With the steady increase in stores over the past 10 years comes an increase in the need for quality employees. In an interview last March, Smith expressed concern over the high dropout rate of high school students.[25] Food Lion relies heavily upon recent graduates, and the current trend may signal a decline in the quality of the average worker. Food Lion has responded to the labor problem by setting up an extensive training program for its 27,000 employees. These programs range from in-store training at the operational level to

[18]Ibid., p. 3358M.

[19]John Liscio, "Beefing up Profits," *Barron's,* May 25, 1987, p. 18.

[20]1987 Food Lion, Inc., Annual Report, p. 9.

[21]Ibid., p. 9.

[22]"Beefing up Profits," p. 19.

[23]"Food Lion's Roar Changes Marketplace," *Tampa Tribune,* April 5, 1988, p. 1.

[24]"That Roar You Hear Is Food Lion," p. 65.

[25]"Food Lion, Inc.," *The Wall Street Transcript.* March 28, 1988, p. 88890.

EXHIBIT 6 Growth and Expansion ($ in thousands)

Year	No. of Stores	Sales	Net Income
1987	475	$2,953,807	$85,802
1986	388	2,406,582	61,823
1985	317	1,865,632	47,585
1984	251	1,469,564	37,305
1983	226	1,172,459	27,718
1982	182	947,074	21,855
1981	141	666,848	19,317
1980	106	543,883	15,287
1979	85	415,974	13,171
1978	69	299,267	9,481

Source: Food Lion Annual Reports.

comprehensive training programs for potential managers. In addition, the firm continues to offer programs at headquarters in order to upgrade the work of the upper staff. Management is also attempting to increase the use of computers within the company. More specifically, Smith is hoping to utilize computer systems to handle much of the financial reporting aspects in the individual stores in an attempt to lessen the need for more employees.

ADVERTISING

Rather than employ costly advertising gimmicks, such as double coupon offers, Food Lion's advertising strategy combines cost-saving techniques with an awareness of consumer sentiment. Smith is the company's main spokesman, appearing in over half of the television commercials. Not only has this method kept advertising expenses down, but has also made the public aware of both Smith and his discount pricing policy. By producing most of the ads in-house and using only a few paid actors, the cost of an average TV spot is only $6,000. Also, the company policy of keeping newspaper ads relatively small results in annual savings of $8 million. Food Lion's advertising costs are a mere 0.5 percent of sales, one fourth of the industry average.[26]

The content of the ads is another reason for Food Lion's success. Many of the TV spots feature some of the cost-cutting techniques used by the firm. One theme often mentioned at the end of an ad states "When we save, you save." Another commonly used theme states "Food Lion is coming to town, and food prices will be coming down." Before moving into the Jacksonville, Florida area, Food Lion launched a nine-month advertising campaign. Many of these ads focused on innovative management methods which permit lower prices to be offered in the stores. For example, one ad demonstrates how a central computer is used to help control freezer temperatures. Other ads attempt to characterize Food Lion as a responsible community member. One such spot describes the importance that management places on the preventive maintenance of its forklifts and tractor-trailers.

Smith has also used the media to react to potential problems. For instance, Winn-Dixie launched an advertising attack against Food Lion reminding customers how competitors have come and gone. The company countered with an ad featuring Tom Smith in his office reassuring consumers. "Winn-Dixie would have you believe that Food Lion's low prices are going to crumble and blow away. Let me assure you that as long as you keep shopping at Food Lion, our lower prices are going to stay right where they belong—in Jacksonville."[27]

---

[26]"That Roar You Hear Is Food Lion," p. 65.

[27]"Food Lion, Winn-Dixie in Animated Squabble," *Supermarket News*, September 14, 1987, p. 9.

Smith also reacted quickly to a possible conflict in eastern Tennessee in 1984. Several rumors circulated which linked the Food Lion logo to Satanic worship. In response, Smith hired Grand Ole Opry star Minnie Pearl to appear in the Tennessee advertisements until the stories disappeared.[28]

INNOVATIONS

The grocery industry is characterized by razor-thin margins. While most retail grocery chains have failed to introduce new innovations in the industry, Food Lion has employed several techniques which enable the firm to offer greater discounts on nearly all its products. These innovations help Food Lion to realize a profit margin of nearly 2.9 percent, twice the industry average. Many of the innovations are ingenious cost-cutting ideas. CFO Woolf explains the company credo of doing "1,000 things 1 percent better".[29] Such a philosophy has resulted in keeping expenses at 14 percent of sales. This represents only 66 percent of the industry average.

Examples of the ideas are abundant. Rather than purchase expensive plastic bins to store cosmetics, Food Lion recycles old banana crates. These banana boxes are also used for storing groceries in warehouses. These innovations save the company approximately $200,000 a year.[30] Furthermore, the firm utilizes waste heat from the refrigerator units to warm part of the stores. Also, motion sensors automatically turn off lights in unoccupied rooms. Costs are further reduced by Food Lion's practice of repairing old grocery carts rather than purchasing newer, more expensive models. Perhaps the greatest savings can be attributed to the carefully planned distribution system. This system allows management to take advantage of wholesalers' specials. The centralized buyout-and-distribution technique allows products for all stores to be purchased at one volume price.

Moreover, labor costs remain lower than those of many competitors. Smith is vehemently opposed to the use of unionized labor. Despite protests from the United Food and Commercial Workers International Union claiming that Food Lion's wages are well below union standards, management has continued to please its workers and avoid unionization. In fact, Smith believes its employee benefit package is unequaled in the industry. A profit sharing plan linking an employee's efforts in making Food Lion profitable with wealth accumulation for the future is already in use. Plans to improve long-term disability insurance benefits are under way.[31] In contrast, several other chains have experienced problems solving labor union problems. For example, a month-long strike by Kroger's Denver-area employees resulted in concessions on wages, benefits, and work rules. Safeway employees were also given quick concessions after threatening to close down several stores.[32]

Other innovations are designed to increase sales. Food Lion often sells popular items such as pet food and cereal at cost in an attempt to draw more customers into the stores. The company makes $1 million a year selling fertilizer made up of discarded ground-up bones and fat. Lower prices are also feasible due to the policy of offering fewer brands and sizes than competitors. The company has increased its private label stock, which now includes at least one unit in every category. These two methods allow the company to price its national brand products below many competitors' private brands. As mentioned earlier, the smaller store size and sale of mostly food items have contributed to the high profit margin realized by the company.

FINANCE

Food Lion's sound financial structure has enabled the company to continue expanding without becoming overextended or burdened with heavy debt repayments. The firm's capital structure consists of 26 percent long-term debt and 74 percent equity. The majority of growth has been financed through internally generated funds. (See Exhibit 7.) The company does not want to grow at the expense of profits. With careful planning, Food Lion has been very successful in this area, and has been able to

---

[28]"That Roar You Hear Is Food Lion," p. 66.

[29]Ibid., p. 65.

[30]"Ad Series Heralds First Florida Food Lion," *Supermarket News,* March 2, 1987, p. 12.

[31]1986 Food Lion, Inc., Annual Report.

[32]*Value Line Investment Survey,* August 28, 1987, p. 1501.

EXHIBIT 7   Financial Ratios

Year	Operating Margin	Net Profit Margin	Return on Assets	Return on Equity	Long-Term Debt as Percent of Capital
1987	6.8%	2.9%	14.2%	32.4%	26.0%
1986	6.9	2.6	14.1	29.8	24.0
1985	6.3	2.6	14.4	29.1	20.5
1984	6.3	2.5	13.6	30.2	22.8
1983	5.9	2.4	13.0	28.3	25.9
1982	5.6	2.3	15.7	28.1	18.0
1981	6.7	2.9	18.1	32.3	12.4
1980	5.9	2.8	17.7	33.4	15.5
1979	6.7	3.2	20.0	39.0	19.0
1978	6.9	3.2	19.5	38.3	22.8

Source: 1987 Food Lion Annual Report.

EXHIBIT 8   Adjusted Stock Prices

	Class A		Class B	
	High	Low	High	Low
1983				
IV	2⅛	1⅝	2⅛	2
1984				
I	1⅝	1⅜	1¾	1⅜
II	1⅝	1⅜	1⅝	1½
III	1⅞	1⅜	1⅞	1½
IV	2¼	1⅞	2⅜	1⅞
1985				
I	2⅝	2⅛	2⅞	2¼
II	3⅛	2¼	3⅛	2¾
III	3	2¾	3	2⅞
IV	3¾	2¾	3¾	2⅞
1986				
I	4½	3⅜	4⅞	3⅜
II	6⅛	4⅛	7⅛	4⅝
III	7¼	5½	9	6⅞
IV	6⅛	5	7⅜	5⅞
1987				
I	7⅝	6⅛	8½	6⅜
II	8⅛	6⅞	8½	7
III	12¼	7¾	13	8¼
IV	13⅜	7¾	14¼	8

Source: Food Lion Annual Reports.

maintain very impressive margins throughout the expansion period.

The growth in Food Lion's stock prices also reflects the sound financial position of the company. This growth illustrates the continued confidence of investors in the future productivity of the firm. In response to the rapid rise of stock prices, management has declared two stock splits since late 1983, when the two separate classes of stock were formed from the previous single class. These splits are designed to keep the price of the stock low enough to be attractive and affordable to all investors. Exhibit 8 shows the adjusted stock prices beginning in 1983, when the two classes were formed.

Furthermore, the per share data reveals the success Food Lion has achieved over the past decade. (See Exhibit 9.) These figures also illustrate investors' desire for Food Lion stock. More specifically, the price/earnings ratio indicates how much investors are willing to pay for a dollar of the company's earnings. In 1987, Food Lion's P/E ratio was the 83rd highest of all the companies listed in the *Value Line Investment Survey.*

FUTURE

Next week, Tom Smith is meeting with the board of directors to discuss and present his ideas for the next few years. Given the recent troublesome trends in the grocery industry as well as the increasing competition in the Southeast, he is reviewing the future strategy of Food Lion. Foremost in his mind is the extent to which Food Lion should continue to expand operations of its conventional stores in this area. He is also pondering movement into other market areas. Smith wants to be sure that the company will be able to finance future growth without greatly changing its current capital structure. Although the current success of Food Lion is quite impressive, Mr. Smith realizes that other grocery chains have experienced problems by not responding to the changing environment. He wants to be certain that this does not happen to Food Lion.

EXHIBIT 9   Per Share Data

Year	EPS	P/E Range	Dividends	Payout Ratio
1987	.27	54–22	.04⅛	15%
1986	.19	47–17	.01⅞	9
1985	.15	25–15	.01¼	8
1984	.12	20–12	.00¾	6
1983	.09	28–19	.00¾	8
1982	.07	32–12	.00¾	9
1981	.06	17–10	.00⅝	9
1980	.05	13–9	.00½	9
1979	.05	17–8	.00½	9
1978	.03	11–5	.00⅛	4

Source: *1988 Standard & Poor's Corp.* p. 3906

EXHIBIT 10

FOOD LION INC.
Balance Sheet

	1987	1986	1985	1984	1983
Assets					
Cash and equivalents	$ 15.5	$ 22.0	$ 2.7	$ 24.4	$ 5.2
Receivables....................................	39.8	27.2	21.8	15.6	11.6
Inventories....................................	385.3	258.9	193.9	136.7	118.3
Other current assets............................	3.3	3.3	2.4	1.4	0.9
Total current assets	$443.9	$311.4	$220.8	$178.0	$135.9
Plant—gross	498.6	400.4	303.2	218.8	189.2
Less: Accumulated depreciation	136.7	106.9	84.3	65.7	50.9
Plant—net	$361.9	$293.5	$218.9	$153.1	$138.3
Construction in progress	0.7	6.4	13.1	0.0	0.1
Land..	4.1	6.2	3.5	1.7	1.7
Buildings....................................	85.5	58.6	34.8	32.2	20.2
Equip. and machines—net	207.4	159.5	122.1	81.6	73.4
Natural resources............................	0.0	0.0	0.0	0.0	0.0
Leases	64.1	62.7	45.4	37.7	32.9
Unconsolidated subsidiaries	0.0	0.0	0.0	0.0	0.0
Other investments	0.0	0.0	0.0	0.0	0.0
Intangibles...................................	0.0	0.0	0.0	0.0	0.0
Other assets..................................	0.0	0.0	0.0	0.0	0.0
Deffered charges	0.0	0.0	0.0	0.0	0.0
Total assets	$805.8	$604.9	$439.7	$331.2	$274.2

EXHIBIT 10 *(concluded)*

FOOD LION INC.
Balance Sheet

	1987	1986	1985	1984	1983
Liabilities and Net Worth					
Debt in current liabilities.........................	$ 96.1	$ 54.4	$ 28.1	$ 2.0	$ 22.3
Income taxes payable...........................	14.7	13.5	2.5	7.5	4.9
Accounts payable...............................	144.3	106.4	79.3	57.4	44.3
Other current Liabilities.........................	60.7	48.6	45.0	37.7	23.4
Total current liabilities	$315.8	$222.9	$154.9	$104.7	$ 94.8
Debt structure:					
Convertible...................................	0.0	0.0	0.0	0.0	0.0
Subordinated.................................	0.0	0.0	0.0	0.0	0.0
Notes	60.0	0.0	0.0	0.0	0.0
Debentures	5.8	6.9	18.0	17.3	18.4
Other long-term debt	5.0	35.2	5.1	2.5	1.5
Capital lease obligation........................	53.6	52.6	37.8	33.5	28.7
Less: Debt (1 year)............................	3.3	3.3	2.9	2.0	2.4
Total long-term debt	$121.0	$ 91.4	$ 58.0	$ 51.3	$ 46.2
Other liabilities................................	1.4	1.2	1.1	1.2	0.8
Deferred taxes and ITC	28.3	24.5	18.2	10.6	8.7
Minority Interest	0.0	0.0	0.0	0.0	0.0
Total liabilities	$466.6	$340.0	$232.3	$167.8	$150.6
Equity structure:					
Preferred stock................................	0.0	0.0	0.0	0.0	0.0
Redeemable preferred stock..................	0.0	0.0	0.0	0.0	0.0
Common stock.................................	160.9	80.3	26.6	26.5	26.2
Capital surplus................................	0.1	0.5	6.1	5.3	0.0
Retained earnings	173.3	184.1	174.7	131.6	97.4
Common equity................................	339.2	264.9	207.4	163.4	123.6
Total stockholders' equity	$339.2	$264.9	$207.4	$163.4	$123.6
Total liabilities and net worth....................	$805.8	$604.9	$439.7	$331.2	$274.2

Source: Lotus® One Source Databases Compustat Tapes.

EXHIBIT 11

FOOD LION INC.
Income Statement

	1987	1986	1985	1984	1983
Sales........	$2,953.8	$2,406.6	$1,865.6	$1,469.6	$1,172.5
Cost of goods sold....	2,385.3	1,948.8	1,521.3	1,206.9	968.9
Selling, gen. and admin.	366.6	296.1	226.6	169.5	134.4
Operating income	$ 201.9	$ 161.7	$ 117.8	$ 93.2	$ 69.1
Depreciation and amort.	(37.4)	(29.6)	(21.4)	(16.7)	(14.1)
Interest expense....	(13.8)	(9.2)	(7.2)	(5.1)	(4.6)
Interest capitalized	0.0	0.0	0.0	0.0	0.0
Non-operating income (exp.)....	0.0	0.0	0.0	0.0	0.0
Special items	0.0	0.0	0.0	0.0	0.0
Pre-tax income	$ 150.7	$ 122.9	$ 89.2	$ 71.4	$ 50.5
Income taxes:					
Income tax (fed.)	51.9	48.1	29.3	28.1	17.5
Income tax (st.)	9.2	6.7	4.7	4.1	2.7
Income tax (frn.)	0.0	0.0	0.0	0.0	0.0
Deferred taxes....	3.8	6.3	7.6	1.9	2.5
Minority interest....	0.0	0.0	0.0	0.0	0.0
Income before extra. items and disc. opns....	$ 85.8	$ 61.8	$ 47.6	$ 37.3	$ 27.7
Extraordinary items	0.0	0.0	0.0	0.0	0.0
Discontinued ops....	0.0	0.0	0.0	0.0	0.0
Net income	$ 85.8	$ 61.8	$ 47.6	$ 37.3	$ 27.7
Preferred dividends	0.0	0.0	0.0	0.0	0.0

Available for common:					
Before adjustments	$ 27.7	$ 37.3	$ 47.6	$ 61.8	$ 85.8
After adjustments	$ 27.7	$ 37.3	$ 47.6	$ 61.8	$ 85.8
Per share:					
EPS (primary)					
Excluding extraord. and discontinued items	$ 0.09	$ 0.12	$ 0.15	$ 0.20	$ 0.27
Including extraord. and discontinued items	$ 0.09	$ 0.12	$ 0.15	$ 0.20	$ 0.27
EPS (fully diluted)					
Excluding extraord. and discontinued items	$ 0.09	$ 0.12	$ 0.15	$ 0.20	$ 0.27
Including extraord. and discontinued items	$ 0.09	$ 0.12	$ 0.15	$ 0.20	$ 0.27
Dividends per share	$ 0.01	$ 0.01	$ 0.01	$ 0.02	$ 0.05
Comm. sh out (primary)	314.2	315.5	318.8	320.2	321.4
Comm. sh out (diluted)	NA	NA	NA	320.2	321.4
Supplementary items:					
Advertising expend.	NA	NA	NA	NA	NA
Amortization of intang.	0.0	0.0	0.0	0.0	0.0
Capital expenditures	46.8	42.8	91.1	107.6	113.6
Depletion expenses	0.0	0.0	0.0	0.0	0.0
Depreciation expenses	14.1	16.7	21.4	29.6	37.4
Excise taxes	0.0	0.0	0.0	0.0	0.0
Foreign currency adj.	NA	NA	NA	NA	NA
Intrst exp. on LT debt	NA	NA	NA	NA	NA
Interest income	0.0	0.0	0.0	0.0	0.0
Labor expense	NA	NA	NA	NA	NA
Pens. and retirement exp.	NA	NA	NA	NA	NA
Research & development	0.0	0.0	0.0	0.0	0.0
Unconsol. subsids. (EQ)	0.0	0.0	0.0	0.0	0.0

Source: Lotus® One Source Databases Compustat Tapes.

EXHIBIT 12 Food Lion Inc., Ratio Report.

	Fiscal Year End									
	1987	1986	1985	1984	1983	1982	1981	1980	1979	1978
Sales performance:										
Dollars of sales	2,953.8	2,406.6	1,865.6	1,469.6	1,172.5	947.1	666.9	543.9	416.0	299.3
$ change from prior year	547.2	540.9	396.1	297.1	225.4	280.2	123.0	127.9	116.7	80.8
% change from prior year	22.74%	29.00%	26.95%	25.34%	23.80%	42.02%	22.61%	30.75%	39.00%	38.66%
Sales per employee (thous)	109.27	115.31	109.17	114.95	116.44	109.19	108.05	112.88	101.29	88.49
Profitability performance:										
Income before extraordinary items and discount. opns.	85.8	61.8	47.6	37.3	27.7	21.9	19.3	15.3	13.2	9.5
$ change from prior year	24.0	14.2	10.3	9.6	5.9	2.5	4.0	2.1	3.7	3.0
% change from prior year	38.79%	29.92%	27.56%	34.59%	26.83%	13.14%	26.36%	16.07%	38.94%	60.04%
Return on sales %	2.90%	2.57%	2.55%	2.54%	2.36%	2.31%	2.90%	2.81%	3.17%	3.17%
Return on equity %	28.41%	26.18%	25.67%	25.99%	25.03%	24.89%	28.07%	28.96%	33.12%	32.18%
Interest expense after tax	7.83	4.64	3.86	2.65	2.53	1.27	0.85	0.98	0.83	0.70
Minority interest	0.00	0.00	0.00	0.00	0.00	0.00	0.00	0.00	0.00	0.00
Return on assets %	12.16%	11.84%	12.35%	12.32%	11.38%	12.41%	15.72%	15.85%	17.80%	17.87%
Return on invested capital %	21.02%	19.89%	19.82%	19.40%	19.08%	20.79%	23.98%	23.79%	26.00%	27.31%
Gross profit to sales %	19.25%	19.02%	18.46%	17.88%	17.36%	16.92%	17.20%	16.87%	17.36%	17.13%
SG and A expense to sales %	12.41%	12.30%	12.14%	11.53%	11.47%	11.34%	10.47%	10.95%	10.69%	10.27%
Asset management:										
Sales to assets	3.67	3.98	4.24	4.44	4.28	4.45	4.78	5.11	4.81	4.55
Sales to current assets	6.65	7.73	8.45	8.25	8.63	8.99	10.13	12.30	11.08	10.55

Sales to net plant	8.16	8.20	8.52	9.60	8.48	8.80	9.07	8.74	8.50	7.99
Inventory turnover—COGS	6.19	7.53	7.85	8.83	8.19	8.77	10.30	12.25	11.69	11.43
Inventory turnover—Sales	7.67	9.30	9.62	10.75	9.91	10.56	12.44	14.74	14.15	13.79
Days COGS in inventory	58.95	48.48	46.52	41.33	44.55	41.60	35.44	29.79	31.22	31.94
Sales to accounts rec.	74.22	88.56	85.62	94.40	100.92	93.92	89.85	112.82	135.10	129.11
Average collection period	4.92	4.12	4.26	3.87	3.62	3.89	4.06	3.24	2.70	2.83
Financial management:										
Total liab. to equity	1.38	1.28	1.12	1.03	1.22	1.18	0.79	0.78	0.89	0.95
Total assets to equity	2.38	2.28	2.12	2.03	2.22	2.18	1.79	1.78	1.89	1.95
Current liabilities to equity	0.93	0.84	0.75	0.64	0.77	0.88	0.57	0.52	0.59	0.59
Long-term debt to equity	0.36	0.35	0.28	0.31	0.37	0.23	0.15	0.19	0.25	0.31
Sales to equity	8.71	9.09	9.00	8.99	9.48	9.68	8.57	9.10	9.09	8.86
Net plant to equity	1.07	1.11	1.06	0.94	1.12	1.10	0.94	1.04	1.07	1.11
Interest expense to sales %	0.47%	0.38%	0.39%	0.35%	0.39%	0.24%	0.23%	0.32%	0.36%	0.43%
Times interest earned	11.95	14.33	13.32	15.06	11.96	18.23	23.81	16.52	16.94	14.59
Liquidity management:										
Current ratio	1.41	1.40	1.43	1.70	1.43	1.22	1.48	1.41	1.40	1.42
Quick ratio	0.19	0.24	0.17	0.40	0.19	0.18	0.28	0.23	0.30	0.33
Sales to cash	190.15	109.27	694.58	60.14	227.57	196.90	155.30	294.79	91.14	NA
Capital expenditures $	105.84	104.20	68.16	41.56	55.50	45.67	19.02	19.50	16.03	12.11
Advertising expense to sales %	NA	NA	NA	NA	NA	NA	NA	NA	NA	NA
R&D cost to sales %	0.00	0.00	0.00	0.00	0.00	0.00	0.00	NA	NA	NA
Rental expense to sales %	1.31	1.18	1.02	0.92	0.90	0.90	0.86	0.69	0.64	NA

Source: Lotus® One Source Databases Compustat Tapes.

Strategy Implementation and Planning

24.   *The American Food Corporation*

"The cooperative type of organization is our greatest strength and our greatest weakness," observed the chairman of the American Food Corporation. Few members of American, the largest retailer-owned food-merchandising cooperative in the United States, would disagree with his assessment. Since its founding 30 years ago, there has been persistent conflict among members and tension between member needs and the requirements of the corporation. Nevertheless, because of adroit management and the economies of large scale, the cooperative has been successful. Recently, however, novel organizational problems have developed, and the cooperative is confronting the most turbulent competitive environment in its history.

ISSUES IN THIS CASE

The central issue at the present time for the American Food Corporation is its structure: Is the cooperative form of organization capable of adapting to multiple internal strains and competitive challenges? To examine this global question, in addition to describing the formal structure of the cooperative, information will be presented on six variables—corporate culture, decision making, technology, leadership, strategy, and the competitive environment—that are influenced by the cooperative structure and are in various stages of change.

Corporate Culture.   To what extent does the corporate culture—a mixture of entrepreneurism, cooperative

This case study was prepared by Barry Allen Gold, based on data collected during four years of participant observation. In addition to observation of meetings, extensive informal interviews were conducted with members of the corporation including the chairman of the board, directors, the president, executive vice president, division directors, buyers, and lower-level participants in the distribution and retail levels of the organization. Company documents and trade journal articles were also consulted. Except for national companies pseudonyms are used in this report.

ideology, bureaucratic politics, and occasional intense conflict—affect management and strategy? In what ways can management either capitalize on or reduce the negative features of the culture?

Decision Making.   The decision-making process is not merely a product of rational business practice but also of the corporate culture. Can decision making reflect corporate philosophy, be equitable to members, and be responsive to rapidly changing business conditions?

Technology.   In recent years the technology available for use in the food-distribution industry has increased. What are the implications of new technologies for the organizational structure of the cooperative and the member firms?

Leadership.   Will the cooperative generate executive leadership that can maintain its entrepreneurial spirit while evolving toward a management style and organizational structure capable of sustained growth? More generally, what type of leadership is required for a successful merchandising cooperative? What are the leadership requirements for managing a transitional phase in an organizational life cycle?

Strategy.   How do corporate constraints and opportunities, as perceived by members of the cooperative, influence goals and strategy formulation?

Competitive Environment.   Finally, this case describes the competitive environment that the American Food Corporation confronts. What, if any, changes in strategy and structure are required for managing in a turbulent environment when the organization is loosely coupled?

The objective of this case is to present a holistic view of a particular type of complex organization and the changes occurring in it, rather than a detailed examination of a single management issue. The central *analytical* question is: Are the variables involved in the change process interconnected—does a change in one variable affect others—or do the variables act independently? The key *action* question is: How can the changes be managed within the context of the cooperative organizational structure?

A brief history of the company is presented; this is followed by a description of the structure and operation of member firms and the warehouse, with particular attention given to the way members of the cooperative make corporate decisions. The final section focuses on the competitive environment in the mid-1980s.

HISTORY

Early Years

Founded in 1955 by men whose business experience was family-owned butcher shops, wholesale produce companies, and diverse small businesses, American began as a grocery-buying cooperative. Members of the cooperative benefited from volume discounts from grocery manufacturers, which enabled them to be more competitive in their small neighborhood stores. Along with low grocery prices, the featured department in this easy-entry, labor-intensive business was the service meat department, which was operated by the butcher-buyer-manager-owner.

In 1958 a Buy-Mart logo was formulated to identify the retailers to customers as members of a cooperative. At this time joint advertising programs were also initiated and a private-label grocery product line was introduced.

In the early years growth was rapid. New members were admitted into the cooperative, and the original members either opened new stores or relocated to larger ones. In 1958 the annual sales volume of the American warehouse was $450,000. By 1962 sales volume was over $1 billion, and in 1969 it approached $2 billion annually and served 29 member firms.

During this period the variety of products available from the American warehouse increased and expanded to include meat, dairy, produce, frozen foods, health and beauty aids, general merchandise, tobacco products, prescription drugs, alcoholic beverages, and a full line of private-label products.

The Formation of NewKirk Operators

The year 1969 was pivotal for the American Food Corporation. The largest member firm, whose president was credited with being the creative force in American, withdrew from the cooperative. The reason for the departure was chronic conflict with other members over retail store locations. In retail food merchandising location is critical for success; approval of sites by the American Board of Directors became a political, time-consuming process. By leaving the cooperative NewKirk could open stores in any location including those in direct competition with Buy-Marts.

NewKirk merged with several other Buy-Mart members, and today NewKirk operates 120 supermarkets in the same trading area as Buy-Mart (Buy-Mart operates 179 stores) and has surpassed Buy-Mart in average weekly store sales. NewKirk also owns 30 home-improvement centers and 15 department stores. It is recognized nationally as a well-managed, growth-oriented industry leader.

The departure of NewKirk, which reduced the American warehouse volume by 32 percent, caused many remaining members to fear that the cooperative could not survive. Although the initial impact was severe, after three years of retrenchment that included modernization of warehouse management and the addition of stores, American regained a significant share of lost volume. Aiding this recovery was the strategic withdrawal from the market of two nationwide chains—Safeway and Acme—on the rationale that competition was too severe. At the same time A&P began its long decline as a major competitor. Nevertheless, despite the rapid recovery, the departure of NewKirk affected American over the long term as it has continued to be its most aggressive competitor. In addition, NewKirk's withdrawal set the stage for a 10-year conflict between factions of American's membership.

The Intensification of the Conflict Culture

Upon leaving American, NewKirk relinquished its stock, thereby creating an opportunity for the redistribution of this stock among remaining members. American's officers redistributed the stock, with the result of increasing the power of smaller member firms as stock ownership determines election of members to the board of directors.

After the redistribution, the largest member firm initiated a lawsuit claiming that the redistribution violated American's bylaws, was illegal under state corporate law, and was "a blatant attempt to usurp control of the corporation." After 10 years of legal maneuvering and personal and corporate conflict a United States Appellate Court found for the defendants.

As the lawsuit dragged on growth was sharply curtailed because of uncertainty over the outcome and the possibility that the cooperative might again lose its largest member. Also, the conflict diverted energy from the operating business; its resolution became an obsession for many members.

A lasting product of the protracted legal battle was intensification of the already conflict-prone organizational culture. Although there was rapprochement between the former litigants, a pervasive atmosphere of distrust and factionalism was embedded in the culture; today it is not uncommon for members to threaten litigation against each other.

A positive element of the corporate culture from American's founding until the present is the entrepreneurial character of its members. The founders and members are pragmatic, aggressive, tough, and essentially optimistic. Thus, despite their diverse personal styles, interpersonal intrigues, and corporate conflicts the entrepreneurial Weltanschauung, combined with the benefits of economies of large size, held the cooperative together.

To reaffirm the cooperative philosophy and the goals of the corporation, in 1980, shortly after the resolution of the lawsuit, American restated its purpose in a "Credo." The Credo is:

American/Buy-Mart is a retailer-owned cooperative. Its members consist of entrepreneurial families who have banded together to secure merchandise and services that they could not obtain economically or retail competitively if they acted individually.

They have accepted the creed of the cooperative movement because they recognize the value of people working together for their mutual benefit.

They assume the sacrifice of time and effort in order to achieve common goals.

They accept these burdens because they believe in the far-reaching benefits through cooperative methods.

The social purpose of American Food Corporation and the Buy-Mart stores, shall be to raise the standard of living of the consumers served by our stores by providing better merchandise at lower prices.

The next two sections describe the organizational structure, operations and social processes that were designed to manage the company, and, in several instances, have evolved to regulate the tension between the entrepreneurial goals of the members and the system requirements of the cooperative.

THE MEMBER FIRMS

Twenty-six companies are currently members of the cooperative (see Figure 1). Member firms vary in size from 1 to 38 stores. Eleven members operate one store each, and 9 members operate between two and eight stores each. These companies are closely held, with management primarily the responsibility of family members. The four largest member firms each have between 20 and 38 stores. Stock in these companies is traded on the American Stock Exchange, but ownership and control are retained by the founding families, who remain active in management.

Retail store sales volume ranges from $200,000 to $900,000 weekly with the average store at $365,000. Average gross profit is currently 22 percent and net profit less than 1 percent. In its primary trading area Buy-Mart currently has 14 percent of the market.[1]

---

[1] Detailed financial data are not included in this case for several reasons. First, of the 26 member firms only the 4 with stock on the American Stock Exchange provide public financial information. Second, the nature of the business is that profitability can vary greatly from one quarter to another and from one year to the next. Third, American does not publish public financial data.

FIGURE 1 Organization of the American Food Corporation

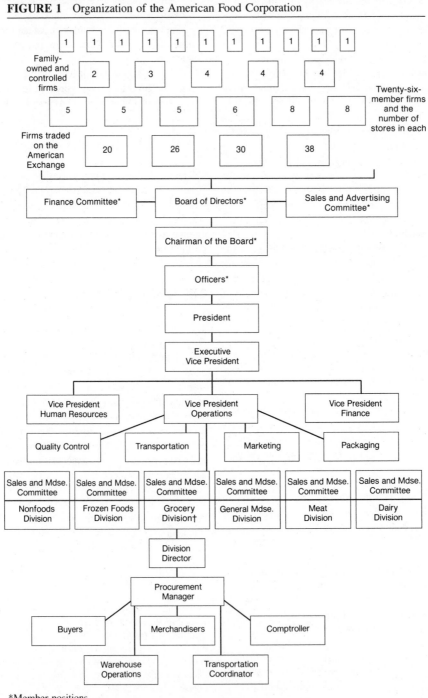

*Member positions.
†Each division is organized the same way as the Grocery Division.

Member Philosophy and Retail Strategy

Since its founding, in addition to the ideology of the cooperative movement, two principles have guided American's business philosophy: competitive pricing and extensive variety of merchandise.

In its price structure Buy-Mart has consistently attempted either to match or beat the prices of competitors. It usually succeeds; it is the low-price leader in its market. One result of this strategy has been reduced profit margins; to compensate for low margins continuous increase of sales volume is required.

Extensive product variety has been implemented successfully, surpassed in the last five years only by NewKirk.[2] Extensive merchandise variety requires large sales areas, raising operating expenses and, once again, increasing the necessity of high sales volume.

Although the merchandising strategy is adhered to by members—joint advertising programs limit opportunities for deviation—there is no prototype Buy-Mart store. Each owner is permitted to set his own prices on nonsale merchandise and to arrange departments and store decor as he desires; the only uniformity among the stores is some display material and logos. At present, a merchandising strategy that is accelerating the historical trend in food retailing, inclusion of specialty departments within each store, is being introduced.

Management Styles of Member Companies

The leadership styles of members vary considerably and are reflected in the management of their companies. Representative of the sophisticated management style is a continuously profitable 30-store company that is organized in what the owner-president calls a *matrix* structure. There are distinct authority structures for both operations and merchandising, decision making is decentralized to the level of the retail store, and staff positions are designed to facilitate the store manager, who is the focal point of the organization. In this company there is substantial investment of time and personnel in employee training and motivation. A management-by-objectives program integrates and guides the organization. Finally, there is a strategic plan for the growth of the company and a plan for the evolution of management techniques. Several other companies have developed similar approaches to management.

The most prevalent management style is found in firms that range in size from three to 38 stores. Despite recurrent attempts to improve, these companies alternate between autocratic and laissez-faire approaches to management. Which style is used depends on the issue involved, the nature and immediacy of the competition, and the short-term profitability of the business. The result of this ambivalent management style is uneven operations and erratic long-term profitability.

Finally, about one-third of the firms improvise operations and tactics to meet the daily demands confronting their businesses. These members, primarily single store owners but also several medium-size firms, frequently operate in a "crisis" atmosphere. To some extent this is cause by the nature of the business ("NewKirk lowered the price of milk. How should we respond?") and the personalities of the owner-managers. Although several of these members are unable to systematize their businesses and are only marginally profitable, others appear to benefit from anarchistic organization; it permits instantaneous adaptation to local competition.[3]

There is minimal diffusion of management philosophy and style from the sophisticated, consistently profitable companies to the less successful, crisis-oriented companies even though the characteristics of the retail stores are similar.

Retail Store Structure

The management of a supermarket typically consists of one general manager, three assistant managers, and

---

[2]NewKirk's merchandising philosophy is similar to Buy-Mart's, with the critical difference that NewKirk stores have high-profit, expanded general-merchandise departments. This fact permits price reduction of food items yet creates a high overall profit structure.

[3]Of course, despite periodic operating losses—even losses for several consecutive quarters—annual member compensation averages $150,000. One source of income for many members in addition to the retail business is rent from ownership of the real estate occupied by the operating business.

department managers.[4] Also part of the management structure are supervisors and merchandising specialists.

Each store has two unions: retail clerks and meatcutters. A store employs between 15 and 20 members of the meatcutter's union (including delicatessen workers) and between 50 and 70 retail clerks, two thirds of whom are cashiers. Hourly wages average $12.50 for meatcutters and $10.50 for retail clerks. Extensive employee benefits increase payrolls by 25 percent of wages.

Store Operations: Labor and Technology

Despite the gradual introduction of technological innovations, the retail food store is a labor-intensive workplace. In addition to scheduling workers, interacting with customers, and handling merchandising and security, store management must deal with replenishment of the 15,000 different products carried in the store.[5] Daily store volumes range from $30,000 to $200,000, creating a continuous need for restocking, which is done at night. Each worker unpacks several hundred containers; technological advances have had no impact on this critical function.

An area where technology has had significant effect on retail operations is "box" beef. Box beef is cattle that is fabricated on assembly lines in Midwestern factories instead of being cut in the retail store from hanging quarters of cattle.

Technological innovation has had the greatest impact on point-of-purchase procedures. "Scanning," the use of lasers to decode Universal Product Codes, has increased the accuracy and speed of customer transactions. Continuous inventory and reorder functions available with scanning have not been implemented by American.

Along with reduction of operating costs, a result of technological changes has been union attempts to reduce the impact on workers of new technologies by negotiating manpower clauses in contracts.[6] Technological innovations have also decreased worker morale and strained relations between management and labor. For example, two consequences of technology are deskilling and the nondifferentiation of skills; opportunities for either more satisfying jobs or meaningful advancement are reduced; under these conditions there are limited organizational methods for motivating employees.

With few exceptions, the introduction of technologies into the stores is dependent on either manufacturers, as with box beef, or, more often, the committee process of American, which is described in the next section.

THE AMERICAN WAREHOUSE

Corporate Philosophy

The cornerstone of American's management philosophy is to decentralize warehouse operations. Another goal is to promote professionalism through employee participation in decision making; a management-by-objectives program was established to achieve this along with an attempt to create a "Theory Y" corporate culture. Finally, in the past five years there has been a shift in management philosophy from a narrow focus on the operation of the distribution center to active concern with the problems of the retail stores.

Organization Structure

At the top of American's management hierarchy is the board of directors (see Figure 1). The chairman of the board of directors, with the officers, formulates policy and strategy for the corporation. Board members also serve as chairmen of corporate committees. Board members spend considerable time acting as brokers and buffers for member factions.

---

[4]Department managers are union members. They differ from other union members because they are responsible for ordering products from the warehouse.

[5]Store-level management does not set prices or select items to be advertised; American management in consultation with members performs these tasks.

[6]An example of union action to delay the impact of technology and protect jobs is a local meatcutter union's contractual redefinition of meat products to include frozen dinners and pet food. The union claim is that its members should handle all meat products, not only fresh meat.

Below the directors is the executive committee, composed of the president, executive vice president, vice president for operations, vice president for finance, and vice president for human resources. Along with performing their technical roles, this group formulates policy and strategy in consultation with the board of directors and is a liaison between members and the product divisions of the warehouse.

At the next organizational level decentralization was implemented by organizing each product division—meat, dairy, frozen food, etc.—into its own company with the division director serving as "president." The tasks of each division are to procure merchandise, select sale items, formulate advertisements, and operate the warehouse effectively.

The Role of Members

Relationships between members and professional managers are complex. Generally, directors, who are elected from the membership, support the president and executive committee. However, the director's and other members' entrepreneurial frame of mind is frequently uncomfortable with the "bureaucratic" style of the executive committee. The members are pragmatic, impatient, action oriented, and more informed and concerned with the retail aspect of the business than with warehouse operations. In addition, they are occasionally embroiled in disputes—for example, the lawsuit discussed above—and are continuously maneuvering for individual short- and long-term advantages.

Another influence on the behavior of the members and board of directors is variation in their perceptions of the type of management appropriate for American, its competitive position, and their vision of the corporate future. These multiple conflicting perspectives reflect the diverse management styles of their own firms. Because of this, board consensus—either on an internal problem or in response to competition—is infrequent and, when achieved, is often the product of reluctant compromise.

The role of the board of directors and members is diffuse—the boundaries for the use of influence are unclear—and this creates tension within the organization. After interviewing key personnel a consultant observed that:

The executive committee is seen as a unit of management which is at the beck and call of the ownership. Alarming in this instance is the lack of understanding on the part of the division directors and managers with regard to the necessary liaison activities between the ownership and the rest of American which are fulfilled at the executive level. Therefore, the executive director's role *vis à vis* the ownership remains unclarified.

In many ways the diffuse member roles and conflict affect the professional managers' interpretation of events and actions. The managers spend considerable effort avoiding conflicts and positioning within the separate power structures of the members and the corporate hierarchy. Another result is that many managers complain that their expertise is underutilized and their decision-making authority diminished because of member intervention.

Warehouse Operations and Technology

Before describing the objectives, structure, and decision-making process of the division committees an account of warehouse operations and technology is required.

In 1985 American's annual sales to its member firms was $3 billion. It operates three warehouses that ship daily to 179 retail stores supplying 90 percent of the products required to merchandise a supermarket (the remaining products are supplied through direct delivery by local and national vendors).

The work process at the distribution centers involves two sets of routine, repetitive tasks. The first task is receiving weekly deliveries of several hundred railcars and tractor trailers from manufacturers throughout the country. Once received, these shipments are allocated space in the warehouse. The second task is selection of orders placed by the retail stores. Forklifts are used to pick merchandise from the warehouse shelves and load it onto trucks (American operates a fleet of 1,500 tractor trailers).

This flow of products is created by a stream of orders between the stores and the warehouse and the warehouse and manufacturers. A bureaucratic structure coordinates and controls warehouse operations (see Figure 1). However, major merchandising and policy decisions are made by committees chaired by members.

Committee Purpose and Structure

Product divisions conduct weekly sales and merchandising meetings. The objectives of these meetings are to review the previous weeks' sales, pricing, write advertisements for the following weeks, and give advice and direction to the division director. These meetings are chaired by a member appointed by the chairman of the board and are attended by members, the division director, buyers, and merchandising, marketing, quality assurance, and advertising personnel.

Committee Processes

The decision-making processes used in sales and merchandising committees vary. Several chairmen encourage debate and try to achieve consensus, or, in some situations, resort to a formal vote. In other committees the chairman autocratically decides all major issues. Independent of each chairman's style, there is a pervasive tension that affects corporate decision making. Three competing sets of concerns shape the tension; the magnitude of tension varies with the importance of the topic.

The first tension is created by the dual role of members. Members are, of course, concerned about their own corporate problems and goals. The other concern a member has is to advance American's goals, which, on occasion, may not be in his firms' interest (e.g., technological innovations that would improve operations but require a capital investment that would burden an individual firms' finances). A second concern is the division director's sales objectives and profit projections (warehouse profit is distributed as an annual rebate to members). Finally, the participants in meetings—managers and members—often champion particular merchandising philosophies.

To illustrate this tension, a complex debate can arise over a mundane product like hot dogs. The dairy division director's goal is to increase the tonnage of hot dogs shipped from the warehouse; the member's concern is that refrigerated shelf space is limited and hot dogs are low-profit items; the merchandiser's desire adhering to

the philosophy of extensive variety, is to have many types of hot dogs available to customers. To resolve these tensions the decision is to stock 60 varieties of hot dogs in the warehouse and put 10 brands on sale in each advertisement.

Similar dynamics can be activated over any issue; these committees often become mired in trivia, ritualism, the idiosyncratic needs or views of a member, and, on occasion, the expression of power by groups within the cooperative. Although detailed records of product movement and advertisement effectiveness are referred to during meetings, the use of information and expertise is often subordinated to other considerations.

However, when a major decision approaches, or a member or director has a strong view on an issue, an attempt is made to structure the debate and control the committee assigned to the issue. The control method is extensive telephone conversations among members prior to the meeting. Support is sought on the basis of friendship, previous political alignments, common competitive situations, or a shared understanding of corporate goals, opportunities, and constraints. Implicit or explicit exchanges for support on future issues are part of the negotiations, creating a pattern that reinforces member allegiances. When this tactic succeeds, rather than acting as decision-making structures, the committees function as forums for members to "sell" their decisions, refine concepts, and formulate implementation plans.

When a telephone campaign is either impractical or unsuccessful, it is common for members to circumvent the committee process by directly approaching a division director, the president, or the chairman.

In sum, the diversity of interests represented by members and managers are axes on which temporary disagreements can develop, and enduring conflicts thrive. This structural feature of the cooperative coexists with and contributes to the conflict corporate culture. How these structurally generated tensions are managed determines the quality of corporate decisions. Presented below are examples of decision making in the areas of marketing strategy, technological innovation, and store location.

Decision Making I—Marketing Strategy

A competitive tool introduced and featured in advertisements by American's major competitors is generic, no-frill products. These products are staple consumer items—

peanut butter, peas, facial tissue—that are nongraded, but nutritionally standard, products packaged with plain labels and priced below national and private-label products.

Shortly after competitors introduced generic merchandise, debate among American members focused on the possible negative effects on Buy-Mart of stocking no-frills products, including lower gross profit and erosion of private-label sales. But market research indicated that competitors were successful with generic items. In addition, manufacturers offered attractive costs on generic products and needed little advance notice to start production.

Because of key member resistance, generic products were available to Buy-Mart stores two years after they were introduced by competitors. Implementation of the generic program within Buy-Mart varied; some companies installed full-scale displays of the merchandise to emulate competitors, some located it next to national brands, and others minimized its sale by stocking limited quantities of advertised items.

Members of the executive committee viewed the member decision-making process as too lengthy, cumbersome, and as a missed opportunity for a rapid response to competition on a major issue.

Decision Making II—Technological Innovation

Another example of decision making is the change from electronic cash registers to computerized, scanning, point-of-purchase equipment. Aside from the cost for each member ($250,000 for each store) the major barrier to introducing scanning was the ongoing cost of a staff of computer experts to support it. Nevertheless, the advantages of scanning included inventory control and reduction of operator error, resulting in higher gross profit.

The earliest user of scanning was the chairman of the board. After initial technical problems, his experience with IBM equipment and service was successful. Eventually, other members selected machines manufactured by National Cash Register, Monroe-Sweda, and Digital Equipment. Because each manufacturer required different support systems, American had to select one. Guidelines for the decision were ease of operation, service, and innovativeness of the manufacturer.

Judgments on the available equipment from the committees with responsibility for store operations varied substantially. The board of directors was requested to intervene. The board authorized American to supply computer support for equipment manufactured by four companies.

Decision Making III—Site Location

The location of a retail store is a critical decision; location determines sales volume, and, independent of management skill, volume can determine the success or failure of a store. Throughout American's history approval of member applications for retail locations was an area of conflict. Site approval was the domain of a subcommittee of the board of directors with an appeal process to the entire board. Politics, power, and friendship permeated the site-location process.

In 1980 a quasi-autonomous site-location committee was established to evaluate member applications. To depoliticize the process the committee was composed of a professor of retailing, a retired supermarket executive from another chain, and a bank president. This committee's recommendations are seldom reversed.

Decision Making and Leadership in the Future

Many of the original members of the cooperative are either semiretired or retired. In several instances sons and daughters have assumed leadership roles successfully; in other firms the transition is taking place slowly with uneven results.

The second generation is composed of people with diverse educational backgrounds and interests. They view the future of American with cautious optimism and plan to manage it by emphasizing technical expertise rather than the entrepreneurial instincts of their fathers. At present, many members feel constrained by their fathers and are impatient to assume roles with greater responsibility. They are also experienced in and concerned about the tradition of political intrigue and conflict that form American's culture; some evidence suggests that the younger members view the conflict culture as detrimental and desire a change toward a more rational corporation.

Compounding the complex dynamics of succession in a family business—in this case a multifamily business—key members of the executive committee are considering retirement. Selecting successors satisfactory to members could be a treacherous and possibly divisive process.

These leadership changes are occurring at a time when many American members and managers view the food-distribution industry and American as entering a transitional phase. One member of the executive committee expressed a sense of ennui and pessimism about the future. In his opinion, compared with other forms of business organization, cooperatives have truncated life cycles; American has plateaued and is entering a period of organizational decline. Other managers and members are more optimistic but acknowledge that to prevent deterioration changes in American may be needed. The ambitions of the emerging leadership, together with influential senior member's views, will influence not only American's decision-making process but also its strategy for the future.

THE COMPETITIVE ENVIRONMENT

Strategic Competitive Changes

The competitive environment of the supermarket industry since World War II has been turbulent. In the American trading area, the most dynamic in the nation, strategic changes in the marketing practices of retail food chains occur every few years.

One recent strategic change made by an American competitor was A&P's introduction of limited variety stores under the "Plus" logo. These stores offer a limited variety of grocery items—no meat or produce—and limited customer services in exchange for reduced prices.

Currently, in another strategic change, A&P is closing conventional stores, expanding the variety and quality of products, and modernizing and reopening under the name "Superfresh." The competitive advantage, aside from emulating the Buy-Mart merchandising format, is that these stores have a union contract requiring considerably lower wages than competitors.

Grand Union, until recently a minor Buy-Mart competitor because of a higher price structure, has also developed limited-variety or "warehouse" stores. More important, however, Grand Union has remodeled its conventional stores and installed a price structure equal to Buy-Mart and NewKirk. To emphasize this, Grand Union television commercials end with the phrase: "We are going to meet or beat your prices, Buy-Mart and NewKirk—FOREVER."

NewKirk has remained the chief Buy-Mart competitor in its primary trading area. NewKirk, with 120 supermarkets, has sustained a program of new store development and remodeling and expansion of existing units. An increasing number of NewKirk stores are 50,000 square feet, full-line stores, with highly competitive prices and often superior locations compared with competing Buy-Marts.

An important redirection of New Kirk's strategy was signaled by its recent acquisition of a 40-store chain in a trading area contiguous to its concentration of stores. Fifteen of these new stores are 60,000 square foot warehouse stores that could serve as pilots for development of a prototype of future NewKirks that would be developed in the Buy-Mart trading area.

Finally, other chains have made progress with new formats, particularly large warehouse stores. The impact of these chains has been minimal because they have been prevented from penetrating Buy-Mart's primary trading area because of lack of locations.

A significant difference in the current competitive environment, compared with previous changes such as A&P's Warehouse Economy Outlets (WEO), which lasted two years, is that it appears that A&P's Superfresh and Grand Union's low-price strategy will be sustained. These companies are now owned by foreign-headquartered multinational corporations; long periods of losses in the retail food industry can be offset by profits in other industries until a market niche is established.[7]

Buy-Mart's Competitive Strategies

The aggressiveness, cohesiveness, and scope of Buy-Mart's competitive strategy varies with the perceived threat of competition. In the case of the A&P Plus stores

---

[7]The trend toward multinationalism and diversification is exemplified by Sir James Goldsmith, who controls Grand Union and recently acquired Crown Zellerback, a forest products company.

key members felt that the new format had to be stopped; if it was not, chains outside the region would be encouraged to enter the market as limited-variety stores require little investment because of the small sales area and the absence of expensive refrigerated equipment. The cooperative acted as a unit with the advertising slogan "Price-PLUS." "Price" indicated that Buy-Mart's prices were competitive with A&P's and the "PLUS" reinforced its commitment to full customer service. The result of the concerted effort was that within one year all Plus stores in the Buy-Mart trading area were closed.

In the case of Grand Union and its low-price, full-service strategy, the threat is perceived as not affecting the majority of stores, and the Buy-Mart response is localized. As in other instances of regionally concentrated competitors, member preference is to subsidize sale merchandise for stores directly in competition. How readily and for how long a member is supported in his attempt to thwart competition depends on the potential competitive threat other members feel as well as the political connections of the member.

Generally, Buy-Mart's response to competition, including NewKirk, is that chances for success are increased by being all things to all customers; competition would be warded off because Buy-Mart would absorb or buffer their challenges by incorporating all of the innovations and promotions in the marketplace. This strategy has accelerated recently with the inclusion in stores of specialty departments such as custom meat shops, service gourmet cheese departments, fresh pizza departments, video departments, travel agencies, 24-hour photo development, banks, salad bars, and other attractions. These departments and services, which often require capital investment and additional labor expenses, offer customers convenience and low prices.

Within the strategy outlined above, to facilitate responsiveness to everyday, nonextraordinary competition American provides each member with a price structure geared to his primary competitor. In addition, each member has available stronger competitive devices ranging from special promotions to "double coupons."

Along with the strategy of comprehensiveness, targeted price zones, and devices such as double coupons, there is a stream of print and television advertisements emphasizing the low-price image. There are also several major promotions each year with a particular theme such as merchandise freshness, double-money-back guarantees on fresh meat, and "super" coupons.

Occasionally, a radical reinforcement of the low-price theme is launched. An example of this was the promotion of turkeys for Thanksgiving 1984. Store volumes suffered dramatically as the result of a five-week meatcutter strike that ended in mid-September. When the strike was over, despite the liberal use of coupons in addition to regular advertising, customer counts and store volumes remained lower than during the same quarter the previous year. Members were alarmed by the situation; money had been lost because of the strike, volume was not returning, the new contract increased labor costs, and profitable fall and winter quarters are essential.

After exhaustive discussion the directors decided that a potentially costly solution, but one that would have the greatest impact, would be to give a free turkey to customers who collected $350 of Buy-Mart register tapes during the four weeks preceeding Thanksgiving. The program was implemented and competition was unprepared for the unprecedented offer of free turkeys. Eventually, several chains developed a similar giveaway and others reduced turkey prices from 89 cents to 29 cents a pound.

The immediate result of the turkey promotion for Buy-Mart was significant increases in store volumes, reestablishment of its low-price image, and an average loss for each store of $60,000. The long-term effect on volume depended on the particular store and the follow-up promotions used by the owner. Overall, however, volume gains were not as enduring as anticipated; customer-survey data indicate that shoppers are no longer loyal to a particular store but frequently switch to the store with the lowest advertised prices.

Because of the relative success of these competitive strategies Buy-Mart has decided not to experiment with new formats such as warehouse or limited-variety stores. They have also decided not to diversify. Other factors influencing these decisions are the sunk costs of existing facilities and lack of the financial and organizational resources necessary to initiate and sustain changes similar to those undertaken by A&P, NewKirk, and Grand Union. Nevertheless, for the past five years American/Buy-Mart sales volumes have been stagnant.

Barriers to Growth

Several factors besides the turbulent environment have contributed to American's stagnation. First, there are few locations available for stores in its traditional trading area.

area. Several members have opened stores in nearby states but, despite sales volumes at projected levels, the high cost of advertising in a new market has resulted in financial losses and discouraged further expansion. Second, the cost of expansion has increased because of high interest rates and real estate, building, and equipment expenses. Start-up expenses for a 50,000 square foot supermarket are approximately $5 million, with a break-even sales volume of $500,000 weekly. Third, because competition is severe, resulting in depressed sales volumes and low profit margins, alternative investments are attractive.

Compounding the inability to expand, in recent years several member firms have experienced financial difficulty. A six-store company, facing extensive losses and internal conflict after an unsuccessful attempt to expand, liquidated its assets. Another multiunit company has been operating nonprofitably for several years and survives only because of American's reluctant extension of credit. A third company (which operates the highest-volume supermarkets in the nation) currently perches on the brink of bankruptcy after it opened two new stores near NewKirks, which started a price war. The largest publicly traded company has become the possible target of a takeover and liquidation by a real estate company. Finally, even though profitable, to avoid becoming embroiled in the protracted politics of American, one member surreptitiously sold his four stores to NewKirk.

An unintended result of member business failures is American's absorption of members of another food retail cooperative. This process began when a member of the competing cooperative purchased the assets of a near-bankrupt American member. Because of his positive experience with American he encouraged members of his former cooperative to switch. However, many of these stores are substandard in either size or location; they are not permitted to display the Buy-Mart logo but do purchase inventory from American.

Corporate Culture and the Future

Member financial problems have exacerbated the corporate culture of distrust and conflict. The primary cause of the renewed conflict is unequal treatment of members. For example, a member who opened his second store requested financial relief from the chairman of the board after six weeks of operation. Without consulting other members, the chairman authorized American to purchase the store; today American operates it with substantial losses. Another firm is permitted to purchase inventory from American even though its payments are continuously delinquent. However, in other cases, modest requests, for example, extension of credit to alleviate cash flow problems, are denied. At present one member is demanding that American purchase a new but unprofitable store that is threatening the solvency of his company. There is strong member opposition to the request.

A related factor contributing to member conflict is competition over the acquisition of stores that are for sale. Because suitable sites are scarce, several different members often want to purchase the same store; political and philosophical factions clash until a single candidate emerges.

Resolving the complex issue of member equity— which is at the core of member conflict—has major implications for American's future as a cooperative.

---

25. *The NASA Space Shuttle Disaster*

In retropsect, Thiokol Inc.'s perfunctory green light unwittingly reads like a death warrant. For a breathless moment the reader is transfixed with the thought that the shuttle accident might have been avoided (Figure 1). But the lethal calculus of limited O-ring tolerances and subnormal Florida temperatures served not only as the

This case was prepared by Robert Marx, Charles Stubbart, Virginia Traub, and Michael Cavanaugh of the University of Massachusetts.

FIGURE 1   Copy of Telefax Sent to Kennedy and Marshall Centers by Thiokol

---

MTI Assessment of Temperature Concern on SRM-25 (51L) Launch
- Calculations show that SRM-25 o-rings will be 20° colder than SRM-15 o-rings
- Temperature data not conclusive on predicting primary o-ring blow-by
- Engineering assessment is that:
  - Colder o-rings will have increased effective durometer ("harder")
  - "Harder" o-rings will take longer to "seat"
    - More gas may pass primary o-ring before the primary seal seats (relative to SRM-15)
      - Demonstrated sealing threshold is 3 times greater than 0.038° erosion experienced on SRM-15
  - If the primary seal does not seat, the secondary seal will seat
    - O-ring pressure leak check places secondary seal in outboard position which minimizes sealing time
- MTI recommends STS-51L launch proceed on 28 January 1986
  - SRM-25 will not be significantly different from SRM-15

Joe C. Kilminster

Joe C. Kilminster, Vice President
Space Booster Programs

MORTON THIOKOL, INC.
WASATCH DIVISION

Source: *Rogers Commission Report* (1986), p. 79.

---

immediate mechanical cause of the *Challenger* tragedy but also as a symptom of long-unresolved organizational issues. For example, besides advertising America's technological (and, derivatively, political) superiority, what, specifically, was the agency's actual scientific purpose? Was it reasonable to assume that a 14-year-old bureaucracy, driven by an exploratory ethos inspired by the futurology of H. G. Wells, could be readily adapted to a commercial schedule without creating serious organizational tensions? (From "Apollo" to "Shuttle"—the choice of project logos captures the essence of this radical reorientation.) Given the institution-wide appropriation of the original astronauts' style (i.e., "Right Stuff"—an unflinching mix of high-tech, high-macho, and high-risk drama) and the virgin technology employed, did NASA and its galaxy of subcontractors operate with an attention to safety? Who and what defined the margin of error? What kind of adverse data interrupted

a final countdown? How was it that after 25 elaborate countdowns and with onboard computers that routinely monitored 2,000 vital functions before every launch, the suspect integrity of the critical rocket joints was left un-"sensored"? Or did the collision of pioneering technology and unknown environmental factors make chance error inevitable? Risk could not be eliminated altogether and still allow spacecraft to be launched.

With the full backing of Presidents Kennedy and Johnson, James Webb, NASA's first and last entrepreneur, dreamed of fashioning an enlightened alliance between science and democratic tradition. Indeed, in light of the agency's dramatic accomplishments, it seemed that Webb's technocratic vision had been fulfilled. No order was too large, and on the surface at least, the agency's partnership with the private sector produced spectacular results. NASA evoked a public image of detached reason; it was a beacon of order, competence, and hope for Americans jaded by generalized institutional decline. NASA appeared to stand outside the malignant politics, inefficiency, and crossed lines of responsibility that sabotaged the efforts of other major agencies both public and private.

Of course, image and reality do not always correspond. Recent revelations surrounding the decision and communication processes affecting the *Challenger* launch demonstrate that NASA was foremost a human institution with all the imperfection that this implies. And perhaps because of this rude shock, we harbor an ongoing sense of institutional loss in addition to the human loss of the seven crew members. Ultimately, beyond all its advances to American rocketry, NASA's most enduring legacy may be to organizational and managerial science.

NASA: A NARRATIVE HISTORY

The ongoing saga of America's space program and, particularly, the events surrounding the January 1986 loss of the shuttle *Challenger* can be better undersood if divided into four successive periods: (1) a preliminary period of ad hoc and idiosyncratic research dating from Robert Goddard's pioneering experiments and ending abruptly with the Russian launch of *Sputnik 1;* (2) a second period of public-funded and directed "command technology" commencing with the passage of the National Aeronautics and Space Act of 1958 and closing with the 1968 retirement of James Webb, NASA's first and only "big operator" (McDougall, 1985); (3) a subsequent chapter of organizational decline culminating in the January 1986 explosion of the ill-fated *Challenger,* a patronless period characterized by mounting national indifference to NASA, shrinking congressional appropriations, and the unresolved organizational conflicts fueled by the agency's attempt to shift from an exploratory mode to a routine operation; and (4) following the *Challenger* loss, a self-searching period of mandated change and mission definition.

Period 1—Foundations

The interplanetary designs of Jules Verne and H. G. Wells served as principal inspiration for an entire generation of American and European backyard rocketeers. Yet, in every sense of the phrase, American rocketry was slow to get off the ground. Until World War II, the state remained disinterested. Invention and application of knowledge were generally acknowledged as the proper domain of private individuals and institutions. Indeed, dating from Robert Goddard's early experiments with liquid-fuel rockets in 1926 until the surprise attack on Pearl Harbor 15 years later, U.S. rocketry was relegated to an orphaned status. With the singular exception of the National Advisory Committee for Aeronautics (NACA), conceived at the end of World War I by Charles D. Walcott of the Smithsonian Institution to keep America abreast of advances in European aviation, large-scale government involvement in rocket (or most any other form of scientific) research languished.

World War II permanently altered this laissez-faire philosophy. Traditionally opposed to state assistance, America's political and scientific leadership closed ranks in recognizing the essential role of state-directed R&D in the conduct of modern warfare. Public funds, for instance, underwrote jet-assisted takeoffs and the development of antitank rockets (the bazooka). The war left its own special legacy to American rocket science, a fledgling aerospace industry. Ironically, the first private firm devoted to rocketry, Reaction Motors, Inc., founded in 1941, later became a division of Thiokol Chemical. Residual concerns about mixing politics and science swept aside, the war also facilitated public acceptance of a vast research consortium composed of government, industry, and university, thereby closing a long chapter in amateur invention. The efficacy of government-mobilized R&D was epitomized by the Manhattan Project and (exploiting the experience of captured German rocket scientists) a growing investment in the miltary applications of jet and rocket propulsion systems.

Although the war had served to resurrect and transform American rocketry, postwar rocket research lacked direction. Following demobilization, congressional and presidential interest waned. Constrained by parsimonious budgets, scientists tinkered with advanced versions of Von Braun's V-2 rocket. And satellite development, despite the promptings of the Rand Corporation, received low priority. Further developments awaited a crisis.

Period 2—Technocracy Achieved

In a 1954 report, Werner von Braun asked for $100,000 to build a space satellite because "a man-made satellite, no matter how humble (five pounds) would be a scientific achievement of tremendous impact.'' He prophesized that ''it would be a blow to U.S. prestige if we did not do it first'' (McDougall, 1985, p. 119). In a single stroke, the October 4, 1957 launch of *Sputnik I* overturned American assumptions about a U.S. technological monopoly and ignited a domestic political crisis. The U.S. response was rapid, however, and was waged along several fronts. The Congress promptly passed the National Defense Education Act to facilitate the recruitment of scientific and engineering talent. New and stricter criteria were promulgated for high school science curricula, backed by across-the-board increases in funding for basic science. On October 1, 1958, less than a full year after the first Soviet launch, the National Aeronautics and Space Act was signed into law creating a civilian bureaucracy to serve as the nation's foremost aeronautical contractor. (NASA performed only a small fraction of actual design and construction. Reviving cottage industry on an unprecedented scale, NASA contracted 80–90 percent of its work to private subcontractors.) Later, in 1961, impressed by the orbital flight of the Soviet cosmonaut, Yuri Gagarin, and in need of political ammunition to offset setbacks in Laos, the Congo, and the Bay of Pigs debacle, the new Kennedy administration declared its commitment to place Americans on the moon within the decade: ''This is the new ocean, and I believe the United States must sail on it and be in a position second to none'' (John Kennedy, *Time*, February 10, 1986). The young president would marshal American technology to extend America's landlocked frontier. Moreover, the Cold War now included outer space. Space science and the state were inextricably linked. Henceforth, space R&D budgets would be subject to the vicissitudes of superpower rivalry.

Under the energetic stewardship of James Webb, NASA underwrote the Mercury, Gemini, and Apollo programs, culminating in the *Apollo II* moon landing in July 1969. But even at the apex of its power—1964–1965—when the agency received money for the asking (1964 funding totaled $5.1 billion, nearly five times its 1961 budget), the program's long-term objectives remained unclear. Even the NASA field centers failed to reach agreement on charting their own post-Apollo course. Moreover, in the face of the Johnson government's escalating commitments to the Great Society and Vietnam, Webb feared to press for new projects (a manned mission to Mars, a permanent moon base, orbiting space stations) that promised high and unpredictable costs. Not unlike the boom-or-bust revenues of

the extractive economies within which it operated (the Gulf states), NASA funding began to evaporate in the second half of the decade. More pressing domestic problems and the relaxation of Cold War tensions undermined vital political support. And many had come to believe ''that Apollo was the space program. Once the race was over and won, Americans could turn back to their selfish pursuits'' (McDougall, 1985, p. 422).

Finally, in September 1969, the White House unveiled a new charter. A Space Task Group chaired by Spiro Agnew presented the president with three alternatives in descending order of cost. Nixon selected the least expensive—a space station with a shuttle. He later shelved the space station pending development of the shuttle. The message was clear. NASA, for all its technical achievements, was an institution without a coherent mission and was therefore expendable. Another Soviet first could have revived NASA. But having lost the race to the moon, Moscow seemed content to maintain a low profile.

Period 3—The Twilight Zone

''Apollo was a matter of going to the moon and building whatever technology would get us there: the Space Shuttle was a matter of building a technology and going wherever it could take us'' (McDougall, 1985, p. 423). After *Apollo II*, the agency and the aerospace industry languished. The agency's principal patrons had retired or died. Kennedy was dead. Both LBJ and Webb stepped down in 1968. (NASA chief administrators were replaced with every change in the White House). This was the situation until 1972, when the Nixon administration, convinced of the electoral fallout sure to result from an aerospace depression, agreed to fund the Space Shuttle (or Space Transportation System—STS).

The STS, however, represented a pyrrhic gain for the agency. Most of the original design was bargained away trying to accommodate competing military, commercial, and scientific interests. For instance, to meet Pentagon specifications, the orbiter's payload was increased. The vehicle's fully reusable technology was jettisoned. Furthermore, a zealous Office of Management and Budget trimmed original cost estimates by half. But perhaps most significantly, NASA bowed to congressional pressure to transform the shuttle operation into a government version of Federal Express (Wilford, 1986, p. 102):

To satisfy Congress, the system had to pay for itself, which meant that NASA, charted as a research and development agency, was put in the unaccustomed position of hustling business and running an orbital freight operation. The conflicting goals and pressures, as well as the complexity of the machines themselves, virtually assured that America's Space Transportation—as the shuttle is officially known—would not operate with the efficiency its original designers had planned.

The product of these compromises turned out to be an improvisational instrument useful for ferrying heavy (military) payloads into low earth orbit. But its technical limitations and the cost overruns associated with the preflight preparations forfeited the high ground to foreign competition (comsats require higher earth orbits) and pushed the agency into chronic budget overruns.

There was another matter. For James Webb, space conquest was only a spinoff. NASA represented nothing less than a "revolution from above" (McDougall, 1985), an extraordinary opportunity to demonstrate the power of the technological revolution including projected advances in quantitative management. Modeled after the grand patterns of the Tennessee Valley Authority and Manhattan projects, NASA would serve as the prototypic administrative instrument for large-scale social and political change. Like McNamara's efforts to rationalize the Pentagon, Webb aimed to pioneer a new era in management science.

Period 4—Crossroads

Intermittent shuttle launchings notwithstanding, NASA has existed in a suspended state of animation since the spectacular voyage of *Apollo II* in 1969. The agency's most vital period was remarkably brief (1962–1968). In an odd turnabout of events, the American space program is viewed in much the same terms as in its formative, pre–World War II years—an exotic novelty, peripheral to mainstream national concerns.

Such is the power of television that recent American generations distinguish themselves by the media events they recollect. For some it was the Kennedy assassination, for others the Iranian hostage crisis. The haunting TV image of the disintegrating *Challenger* represents another generation's indelible memory. Measured

against previous exploits, the "shuttle chapter" tells the story of an organization in decline. Fourteen years of development and 30 billion invested have produced only 25 flights since 1981. Sponsors were promised 30–60 profit-generating flights annually. NASA's romantic technology was inherently ill-suited for routine operations and commercial (cost-conscious) venture. The disappointment expressed by Dr. Alex Roland, a historian of technology at Duke University, seems almost mean-spirited at this stage: "The shuttle was an economic bust before the accident. It's just crazy to think, as some people in NASA do, that we can return to business as usual" *(The New York Times,* March 16, 1986). In the interim, with the shuttle program indefinitely grounded, the Pentagon's STS launch-dependent satellite program is stranded while foreign competitors eagerly vie for American commercial launch contracts.

NASA: A FUNCTIONAL ANALYSIS

NASA—The Organization

Officially, NASA is an agency of the executive branch, under the control of the president, who directs space policy and appoints NASA's head administrator. Congress sets spending limits and can specify projects to be undertaken. The head administrator has several important tasks, including drawing up proposals and making decisions on future programs, resolving high-level personnel problems, and selling NASA to Congress and the U.S. public. Assistant administrators head various support functions and programs. During the Apollo program, and in the early days of the shuttle, astronauts, who had an appreciation of operations and flight safety, were regularly promoted to management. By the 1980s, this had stopped. NASA has nine field centers, each with its own special mission in support of the overall NASA effort. Private contractors work with, and report to, the field centers.

NASA has undergone several reorganizations in order to meet changing goals. A 1961 reorganization was made to develop a stronger headquarters team that could coordinate efforts among the field centers. In 1963, NASA decentralized to better meet the "man-on-the-moon" goal. After a tragic fire took the lives of three astronauts, organizational changes in 1967 created a centralized structure that could integrate decision making and increase emphasis on safety. Another reorganization occurred in 1983 when the shuttle program was reclassifed from "developmental" to "operational." Figure 2 shows how NASA was organized as of January 1986.

Constituencies. From the very beginning, many people feared that NASA would become more political and less scientific. Although it still has a highly scientific orientation, the goals and policies of the agency have been dictated by political considerations. Whether NASA must answer primarily to the executive branch, Congress, or some other constituency is always a matter of debate. According to veteran observers of NASA, "NASA is a child of Congress, rather than that of the executive branch" (Hirsch and Trento, 1973, p. 126). On the other hand, former NASA Administrator James Beggs saw space-program support as a matter of "the mood of the country and a question of priorities" *(Sky and Telescope,* 1982, p. 333).

Without a doubt, each president set the tone for much of NASA's activities. It was during the Kennedy-Johnson administrations that NASA received its greatest support. In the post-Apollo days, NASA, fueled by the overwhelming technological success of its moon landings, pushed for manned space flight to Mars. One observer described NASA as "an organism that was more responsive to its own internal technological momentum than to externally developed objectives" (Logsdon, 1983, p. 86). The Nixon administration favored more practical goals. And politicians, who controlled matters of budget and set policy, pushed for a program with tangible benefits to science, the economy, and national security.

President Reagan's 1982 policy consisted of two priorities: maintaining U.S. leadership in space, and expanding private-sector involvement and investment. A less publicized policy was the increasing involvement of the Department of Defense and use of the space program for national defense. After three years of lobbying on the part of those supporting a space station, Reagan, in his 1984 State of the Union address, set a goal of an orbiting space station within 10 years. Administrator Beggs' push to make the shuttle "operational" may have been in part politically motivated; he recognized this was a necessary step in garnering support for the permanent,

manned space station. Many people in NASA supported this goal. So did commercial, private enterprise.

Furthermore, the contracting companies who performed 80–90 percent of NASA's design and development work had active trade associations and lobbying efforts to promote their interests. With the shuttle in an "operational" state and the potential development of the manned space station, NASA was no longer its own customer. It now had to serve the needs of private industry. In short, there was a close-knit network between NASA, Congress, the Department of Defense, and private industry.

Public Relations. With so many different constituencies, NASA had always been acutely aware of the value of public relations and image. In its earliest days, NASA was particularly concerned with maintaining secrecy. The Kennedy administration felt that openness was a better approach to provide a counterattack to Soviet propaganda and secrecy. It was also a way of getting the most mileage out of the image of the United States as the underdog, steadily maintaining its effort to "catch up." The press was eager for involvement in the space program. They knew it made good copy—spaceships, astronaut heroes, patriotism, and American know-how. Engineers were "scientists" and words like "enhance" and "uprate" replaced the verb "improve." "Integrity" now described machines, and the press became members of an exclusive space-age fraternity.

The merits of manned versus unmanned space flight had been a continuing debate within and outside of NASA. Manned flights were criticized for being expensive, dangerous, and largely unnecessary, particularly in light of improving robotics and computer capabilities. Proponents countered that the intelligence and versatility that on-board humans brought to space missions could not be duplicated by any machine. Even more important was the use of manned missions to win support and bolster enthusiasm of both NASA personnel and the general public.

If anything represented the public's pride in the national space program, it was the original seven *Mercury* astronauts. They were the nation's "champions" at the same time they were the All-American boys next door. But as the number of astronauts and the size of missions increased, it became harder for the public to keep track of and identify with astronauts. Until the first

FIGURE 2   NASA Organization

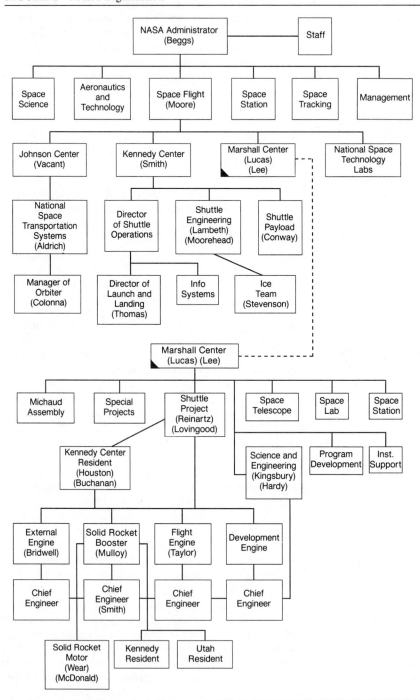

Source: *Rogers Commission Report* (1986).

manned moon flights, a rigid pecking order among the astronauts kept scientist and engineer astronauts on the ground while former fighter and test pilots were selected for moon missions.

Post-*Apollo* astronauts were selected for their capabilities as scientists. Racial and gender barriers were broken with the selection of female, black, and Asian astronauts. As NASA's programs became increasingly commercialized, it was difficult to retain the astronaut's pioneering and heroic image. Christa McAuliffe, selected as the first teacher in space, represented a new orientation toward the astronaut. The image of the fearless daredevil was no longer appropriate. Instead, outer space belonged to all and now the astronaut was Everyman and Everywoman.

Successes and Failures.   Even some of the most disastrous events in the agency's history were viewed as at least partial successes by NASA personnel. Prior to 1961, there were many rocket failures. In 1959, seven out of 17 launches failed. NASA saw these as necessary learning experiences, but there was much public criticism of their cost and delay.

By many accounts, however, the 1967 *Apollo* tragedy was an accident that should not have happened. In January 1967, during "routine" testing, a flash fire broke out in the command module, killing the three astronauts on board. The NASA review board acknowledged insufficient attention to crew safety. Some aspects of the investigation were suppressed by NASA and later revealed by a congressional inquiry. Among the congressional findings were "overconfidence" and "complacency" on the part of NASA and a lack of concern on the part of the prime contractor. A more critical review of the incident characterized congressional findings as "ambiguous" and asserted that because of its close ties with NASA, Congress was reluctant to do anything that would implicate itself. The critique alleged that "sloppy workmanship and slipshod quality" had been with the program all along.

Despite "official" stringent safety standards, the agency was more concerned with meeting deadlines than with safety issues. NASA used this tragedy to its best advantage. Invoking the memory of the dead, they stressed the importance of getting on with the program because that's what the astronauts would have wanted. In spite of this setback, Kennedy's challenge to land a man on the moon was met.

The lives of three other astronauts were seriously endangered during the *Apollo 13* mission. While enroute to the moon, the capsule's main oxygen tank exploded. Anderson, NASA's official biographer, believed that technology saved the day. The system contained sufficient flexibility and depth to permit the astronauts to ride safely back to earth. A review board investigating the incident had another perspective. They attributed the accident to a number of human errors and lack of proper monitoring and testing by NASA personnel and concluded that "the lessons of the *Apollo* 204 (fire) had not been fully applied" (Hirsch and Trento, 1973, p. 121).

Technical problems and failures with various *Skylab* and *Shuttle* missions called forth massive round-the-clock efforts by ground personnel and astronauts. Once again, failures became successes where problems were solved with "human ingenuity and courage" (Anderson, 1981, p. 83).

Finances and Budget.   NASA's budget and employment figures are listed in Table 1. In terms of both budget and employment, NASA enjoyed its greatest power in the mid-1960s with the buildup of the man-on-the-moon effort. Funding decreased steadily over the next 10 years, as the nation turned its attention and priorities to other matters. Although funding improved with the shuttle, inflation-adjusted figures show little increase, and the watchword has been fiscal restraint.

NASA—Life on the Inside

Decision Making.   Decisions had to be made about the agency's overall goals. But NASA could not be a good decision maker because "government policy is based on partisan and interest group politics instead of on business or technological grounds" (Goldman, 1985, pp. 48–49).

Decision making and problem solving around technical issues were accomplished by creating consensus. For example, one of *Apollo's* early tasks was to plan the mechanics of putting a man on the moon. A number of options were possible. A group of engineers came up with the idea of a lunar orbiter-lander combination. They spent two years refining the idea, arguing their case before various NASA groups, and they even went "out of channels" directly to NASA's general manager. Their idea gradually won adherents and was adopted.

TABLE 1   NASA's Budget and Employment

Fiscal Year	Budget (in billions)		Employment	
	Nominal	Real*	Government	Contractor
1959	0.33	0.37	9,325	31,000
1960	0.51	0.57	10,286	36,500
1961	0.96	1.07	17,077	57,500
1962	1.83	2.02	22,156	115,000
1963	3.76	4.00	27,904	218,400
1964	5.10	5.49	31,984	347,100
1965	5.25	5.56	33,200	376,700
1966	5.18	5.33	33,924	360,000
1967	4.97	4.97	33,726	273,200
1968	4.59	4.40	32,471	235,400
1969	4.00	3.64	31,745	186,600
1970	3.75	3.22	31,223	136,580
1971	3.31	2.73	29,479	121,130
1972	3.36	2.68	27,428	117,540
1973	3.43	2.58	25,955	108,100
1974	3.04	2.06	24,854	100,200
1975	3.23	2.00	24,333	103,400
1976	3.51	2.06	24,039	108,000
1977	3.82	2.10	23,569	100,500
1978	4.06	2.08	23,237	102,800
1979	4.35	2.00	23,237	104,300
1980	5.24	2.12	22,563	101,800
1981	5.52	2.03	21,873	110,000
1982	6.02	2.08	21,652	105,000
1983	6.84	2.29	21,219	107,000

*Adjusted for inflation using the 1967 consumer price index.

In mid-1968, with the Apollo program seriously behind schedule, the head of the Manned Space Flight Center, George Low, decided that the scope of each mission should be broadened. Specifically, he believed the *Apollo 8* mission should orbit the moon rather than the earth, as originally planned. This represented a bold new step in the Apollo program. He presented his idea to Robert Gilruth, the head of the space task group, who responded enthusiastically. Next they polled the senior project managers, who agreed that all current problems appeared to be solvable in time for the launch deadline. Within just a few months, the mission was reconfigurerd for its newly established goal.

By the mid-1980s, NASA administrators and engineers made a distinction between engineering and program management decisions. This represented a change from years past. An engineer who had been with NASA since 1960 said (Bazell, 1986, p. 12):

At the beginning, all the decisions were made at the lowest possible level. We worked together toward one goal. It was simply inconceivable that one person could have thought something was wrong—particularly if it was dangerous—and everyone else not know about it.

Another engineer echoed this perspective: "People making the decisions are getting farther and farther away from the people who get their hands dirty" (Bazell, 1986, p. 14).

A Changing Organization.

What was clear was that NASA had changed in many ways over the past 25 years; in other ways it remained the same.

NASA at the start faced many challenges on many fronts dealing with rapid expansion and coordination of activities: leapfrogging the Soviets, dealing with the executive branch and Congress, creating an environment good for scientific and technological creativity. The task was not merely to provide technical resources but also technical management so that a government-industry-university team could be built. The entire organization had to be geared toward flexibility to improve quality and reliability as the problems of space exploration were better understood. The emphasis was on avoiding "quick fixes" so that many small changes did not eventually add up to serious problems. The crash-program atmosphere of intense effort demanded by the program and by Kennedy's end-of-the-decade deadline was not without personal costs (divorces, heart attacks, and suicides) among NASA personnel.

At its 25th anniversary in 1983, NASA was facing a variety of issues, some of them new to the agency: commercialization of space activity; competition with Europe, Japan, and the Soviet Union; working closely with government military and civilian agencies as well as developing private-sector space activities; and meeting customer commitments. While the shuttle program had changed NASA's mandate, its field organizations retained their scientific and engineering orientations. Although this was appropriate for the *Apollo* era, observers felt this was currently causing problems for the agency.

Even before this time, NASA had shown resistance to certain changes. In 1973, one observer noted that there were difficulties associated with increasing the professional female and nonwhite staff and that the "overwhelming white domination of NASA is making it an increasingly conspicuous and embarrassing anomaly among government agencies" (Holden, 1973). Although NASA had hired a black woman for a top post in the agency's affirmative action department, the political realities of the Nixon administration made it a token gesture. She was dismissed for not fitting into the bureaucracy, but some felt her dismissal was precipitated by her refusal to play Nixon-era politics. It is not clear how much had changed by the mid-1980s, for in 1986 Robert Bazell described NASA insiders as a homogeneous group—white males in their 50s, career men with NASA or its contractors.

A 1979 shuttle management review team, headed by USAF General James Abrahmson, called for changes in management structure and philosophy. Some of the team's findings included the following:

The near-term potential for unanticipated technical problems, schedule slippage and cost growth is high and appropriate reserves should be included in all aspects of program planning.

There has been a lack of adequate long-range planning. . . . Emphasis has been on the current fiscal year, with only secondary attention to succeeding years. . . . Long-range planning has not been performed to the extent required for a program as complex as the shuttle.

. . . The successive program changes and associated up and down expenditure rates have resulted in experienced contractor and subcontractor personnel being terminated. Recent and current aerospace industry demand for such personnel is such that experienced people do not remain available, resulting in the employment of inexperienced personnel at a cost to overall efficient performance. This constitutes a major cause for concern, especially for the production phase of the program.

. . . The space transportation system associate administrator (or Level 1 management) has, through an ever increasing personal participation in program activities, become the de facto program director . . . during the course of the fact finding, it became apparent that there was a broad and detailed involvement of Level 1 on technical issues with lesser attention given to cost and schedule.

In the effort to live with funding limitations while still progressing acceptably toward completion, shuttle management has generally set up work schedules that demanded more performance than could be delivered.

Members of the shuttle management review team also mentioned that NASA managers felt the way to keep shuttle costs down was to set up high work performance goals. One NASA manager said (Covault, 1979, pp. 20–21):

> If we hadn't done it this way we could never have converted this thundering herd of Apolloites to more reasonable people. This program would have cost $10-$12 billion with the same philosophies we had in Apollo, and then there wouldn't have been any shuttle program.

A concern for costs persisted as the shuttle project progressed. Hans M. Mark, a NASA deputy administrator, reported that, "It is very unlikely that it will be possible to control costs of operations if the developmental attitudes that prevail at Johnson Space Center dominate after the shuttle becomes operational" (Covault, 1981, p. 13).

Despite a changing orientation toward the space program by the administration, many at NASA viewed the shuttle as another Apollo program. Therefore certain considerations, such as technical simplicity, minimizing operational costs, and meeting development schedules were seen by NASA people as less important than the technological development of the shuttle.

Heretofore, NASA had run with a single-flight focus. But because of the pressures of military needs and commercialization of shuttle flights, the program began to include several flights at various stages of readiness. It was becoming difficult to meet the flight schedule and maintain the overall efficiency of the system. By 1986, the schedule allowed for less than one month between flights. Furthermore, certain attitudes persisted from the resource-rich days of Apollo. There was still an inclination toward "can do" spontaneity in responding to crises and technological challenges and a very positive approach to problem solving. This type of enthusiasm was very costly at a time when the shuttle program required nurturing resources. The agency had an established tradition of flexibility, frequently changing shuttle plans as different needs and priorities of its commercial customers arose. These frequent and sometimes last-minute changes were a further drain on resources.

Tight schedules had to be balanced with cost constraints, and NASA contractors had rules governing employee overtime. Some required clearance for overtime in excess of 20 hours per week. Approval was frequently granted. For example, two contractors with employees working at Kennedy Space Center reported the 20-hour limit was exceeded about 5,000 times from October 1985 through January 1986.

During this era of multiple launches, it was necessary for key NASA and contractor personnel-skilled technicians and managers to log 72-hour work weeks and 12-hour days for weeks on end. One team leader worked consecutive work weeks of 60 hours, 96.5 hours, 94 hours, and 81 hours in January 1986. Given this unrelenting pace, it is not surprising that the likelihood for human error increased in early January 1986, when a group of technicians at Kennedy Space Center, working 12-hour shifts, repeatedly misinterpreted fuel-system error messages and made faulty decisions during previous shuttle launch preparations. The mission was scrubbed just 31 seconds before takeoff when an insufficient supply of liquid oxygen in the shuttle's fuel tank triggered alarms. A subsequent investigation attributed the launch abort to human error produced by fatigue. Human safety issues may have taken a back seat to cost considerations, as key personnel were pushed beyond their limits of endurance.

Much of NASA's current staff joined the organization in the *Apollo* build-up days of the early 1960s. Some were still in mid-career and interested in taking on technological challenges. The changed emphasis to cost and schedule constraints prompted these talented and motivated individuals to leave the organization. However, according to John Pennington, NASA's director of human resources, surveys indicated high motivation and morale and low turnover in the organization (Pennington, 1986).

Nevertheless, the motivation for many of NASA's personnel was still the excitement and challenge of manned missions, large space systems, and interplanetary exploration. Despite the inbred staff of the space program, there was no consensus on what the program's goals should be. For many who remembered the effort and accomplishments of Apollo, there was a growing "return to the moon" movement; others favored focus on a suborbital manned space station. Some people in NASA believed it should become an operational organization, others felt it should remain an R&D agency.

Overall, the lack of a clear mission and the seemingly conflicting roles created difficulties for the agency. There was a tendency at some of the field centers to solve problems in-house rather than pass them up the hierarchy. NASA project managers at some of the centers felt isolated from headquarters and more accountable to their field centers. Conflicting goals, roles, and expectations produced an almost schizoid character. There was difficulty transferring an Apollo-era mood to shuttle realities, in switching from shuttle to routine operations, and in moving from an organization dominated by scientists and engineers to one dominated by bureaucrats and administrators.

Flight Readiness and Safety.   Much of NASA's decision making was structured around flight readiness and safety issues. Planning for a shuttle flight began 12–18 months before a shuttle lifted off the pad. Figure 3 shows the steps that each flight had to clear. The Shuttle Flight Readiness Review was a complicated process. Flights required careful coordination among thousands of contractors, subcontractors, and three space centers (Kennedy, Marshall, and Johnson). Besides obvious concerns about the ability of the rocket to fly, officials allocated cargo space, trained the crew, designed a flight plan, scheduled space activities and experiments, and programmed dozens of computers. Literally hundreds of decisions were involved in a shuttle launch. Therefore, NASA had evolved a "Japanese" style of management: disagreements "bubbled up" the hierarchy until somebody resolved them.

The flight design process was the central concern in flight preparation. In this process, NASA officials and scientists set the flight objectives and laid out a detailed schedule of flight activities from launch until landing. Four field centers reported the Space Flight Program: Kennedy (launches), Johnson, Marshall (vehicle design and development), and the National Space Technology Laboratories. The planning went through several steps, as outlined below.

Level 4.   Level 4 was initiated by a formal directive from the NASA associate director of space flight. The burden was on contractors at the various space centers (who performed the bulk of the design and development and all of the manufacturing) to certify in writing that their components met the necessary standards.

Level 3.   After all certifications were received, the decision making moved down to Level 3. At Level 3, the project managers for the Orbiter, solid rocket booster, and external tank and main engines at Johnson, Kennedy, and Marshall made official presentations to their respective center directors. Each review verified the readiness of launch support elements.

Level 2.   Next came the Preflight Readiness Review at Level 2 at Johnson Space Center. In the Level 2 review, each shuttle program element certified that it had satisfactorily completed the manufacture, assembly, tests, and checks on shuttle equipment. The manager of the National Space Transportation Program presided.

Level 1.   The reviews culminated with Level 1. Under the direction of the associate administrator for space flight, the Flight Readiness Review at Level 1 checked previous planning activities, and a Mission Management Team was established.

Mission Management Team.   This team takes over management 48 hours before the launch and continues until the shuttle has landed and been secured. This team met 24 hours before the planned launch to take care of unsatisfied requirements, to assess weather forecasts, and to discuss any anomalies. The Mission Management Team encouraged officials at lower levels to report any new problems or difficulties.

The director of the Shuttle Project Office reported to the director of the Marshall Space Center. But the readiness review process mainly took place outside the normal chain of command. The levels of the Readiness Review paralleled and overlapped the levels of the formal management structure.

NASA's Safety, Reliability, and Quality Assurance Program came under the duties of the chief engineer at NASA headquarters. Out of a staff of 20, one person spent 25 percent of his time, and another spent 10 percent, on safety. At the various centers, the personnel who developed the shuttle hardware were also responsible for related safety issues. Components were engineered to meet stringent specifications, and they were tested. In 1980, NASA appointed a special committee to study the flight worthiness of the entire shuttle system.

Safety issues often cropped up at various levels of the Readiness Review. Flights had to meet 28 specific criteria before the countdown could begin. Participants mulled over technical specifications, interpretation of test results, and what constituted an adequate margin for safety. Those systems that had no back-up and which might bring about the loss of the vehicle and life were called "critical" and received special attention. In addition, the Flight Readiness Review procedure included official procedures for waiving nonconforming components or systems in the interests of flexibility, expendience, or extenuating circumstances.

FIGURE 3 Flight Readiness Review Process

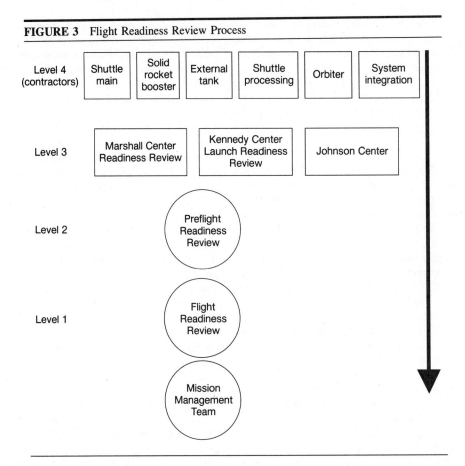

SHUTTLE FLIGHT PROCEDURES: *CHALLENGER* FLIGHT 51-L

May 1985. Crew training begins.

August 20, 1985. NASA conducts a Preflight Readiness Review. They discuss the crew, storage, engineering status, photo and TV requirements, the Teacher-in-Space program and the launch window.

December 13, 1985. Associate Administrator for Space Flight (Moore) schedules Flight Readiness Review for January 15, 1986.

January 9, 1986. Morton Thiokol (MTI) certifies solid rocket booster flight readiness (Level 4). This is the first stage where equipment problems can delay a launch. The O-rings are a known problem, but MTI and

NASA personnel do not believe they are serious enough to stop launch.

January 14, 1986. After weeks of intensive preparation, including a dress rehearsal and a mock firing of the main engines, Kennedy Center Director Richard Smith convenes the Preflight Readiness Review meeting (Level 2) and sets the schedule for Level 1/Mission Management Team meetings. Over 100 participants from Kennedy, Marshall, Johnson, Lockheed, and various subcontractors discuss what time of day to launch, conditions for viewing Halley's comet, excessive cargo weight, and the schedule of crew activitites. No problems with the solid rocket booster were identified. Kennedy Center Director Smith signs launch-readiness certificate.

January 15, 1986. NASA Associate Administrator Moore chairs Flight Readiness Review Meeting (Level

1). A video teleconference links NASA flight centers to Cape Kennedy. All systems are reviewed in detail, from engineering through flight responsibilities. They decide, "Go."

January 22, 1986. NASA officials are worried about dust storms in Dakar, the main emergency landing site. A shuttle can't go up unless it has a safe place to land if something goes wrong. Countdown is reset for January 26 at 9:36 A.M.

January 25, 1986. 11 A.M. EST. Level 1 team meets again. All unresolved flight readiness review items were reported closed. But rainstorms prompt officials to postpone until the 27th.

January 27, 1986. 12:36 P.M. Mission Management Team scrubs launch because of high winds and overcast at launch site. Rain can damage the shuttle's heat-resistant tiles. Problems with a sticky bolt cause a 90-minute dalay in the astronauts' disembarking from the orbiter. Team resets launch for 9:38 A.M., January 28.

2:00 P.M. Mission Management Team meets again. Because weather forecasts predict temperatures in low 20s, someone raises concerns about cold weather effects on launch facility water drains, fire suppression system, and water trays. They decide to activate heaters on the shuttle.

2:30 P.M. in Utah. Morton Thiokol engineers in Wasatch, Utah, hearing about forecast cold temperatures discuss possible effects of cold weather predicted for January 28 on solid rocket booster (see Figure 4 for MTI organization).

5:45 P.M. First teleconference between NASA Level 3 personnel at Kennedy (Lovingood) and Marshall (Reinartz) and Thiokol personnel in Utah. Morton Thiokol officials express reservations about effects of temperatures on O-rings. They postpone launch until noon or afternoon of 28th. Lovingood proposes going to Level 2 (Aldrich) if MTI stands by no-launch recommendation at second teleconference set for 8:15.

8:45 P.M. Second teleconference between MTI Utah (six members), Kennedy (Reinartz, Mulloy, McDonald—MTI liaison), and Marshall (Hardy, Lovingood, et al.). A technical discussion of O-ring problems and tests. Problems with the O-rings had a long history. One MTI vice president of engineering (Lund) says not to fly 51-L until temperature exceeds 53°F. Another MTI engineer (Boisjoly) presents charts and tables about problem. Mulloy

asks MTI Vice President Kilminster for recommendation. Kilminster says he cannot recommend launch. Reinartz, Mulloy, and Hardy challenge MTI conclusions, asking for hard data to support Boisjoly's conjectures. Hardy says he is "appalled" by the recommendation. Mulloy says, "Do you want us to wait until April to launch?" Kilminster asks for time to caucus. Later, Mr. Boisjoly remarks, "This was a meeting where the determination was to launch, and it was up to us to prove beyond a shadow of a doubt that it was not safe to do so . . . usually it is exactly opposite that." Mulloy says, "There was no violation of launch commit criteria . . . [there] were 27 full-scale tests of the O-rings damage tolerances . . . we had experience with this problem" (see Figure 5).

10:30 P.M. to 11:00 P.M. in Utah. MTI personnel discuss O-rings. Two engineers (Boisjoly and Thompson) continue to voice strong objections to launch. Mason asks Lund to "put on his management hat." The MTI top managers decide that objections are not serious enough to justify canceling 51-L. The MTI officials later characterize the discussion as "unemotional, rational discussion of the facts as they knew them . . . a judgment call."

10:30 P.M. to 11:00 P.M. at Kennedy. McDonald, Mulloy, Reinartz, Buchanan, and Houston discuss whether to delay. Mulloy says that none of MTI's data change the rationale from previous successful flights.

11:00 P.M. Second teleconference continues. The MTI officials say that O-rings are a concern but data are not conclusive against launch. Kilminster recommends launching. NASA asks MTI to put recommendation in writing.

11:15 P.M. to 11:30 P.M. at Kennedy. McDonald strongly argues for delay, says he would not like to answer to board of inquiry. Mulloy says that the temperature of the fuel in the booster will still meet the Minimum Launch Criteria. Reinartz and Mulloy tell McDonald that it is not his decision, that his concerns are noted and will be passed on. (See Figure 5 for summary of disputants.)

11:30 P.M. to 12:00 A.M. Teleconference at Kennedy. Mulloy, Reinartz, and Aldrich discuss icing in launch area and recovery ships' activities. The O-rings are not mentioned.

January 28, 1986. 1:30 A.M. to 3:00 A.M. at Kennedy. The Ice crew reports large quantities of ice on pad B. The spacecraft can be damaged by chunks of ice that can be hurled about during the turbulent rocket ignition.

5:00 A.M. at Kennedy. Mulloy tells Lucas of MTI concerns over temperature and resolution and shows the recommendation written by MTI.

FIGURE 4 Morton Thiokol Management Structure

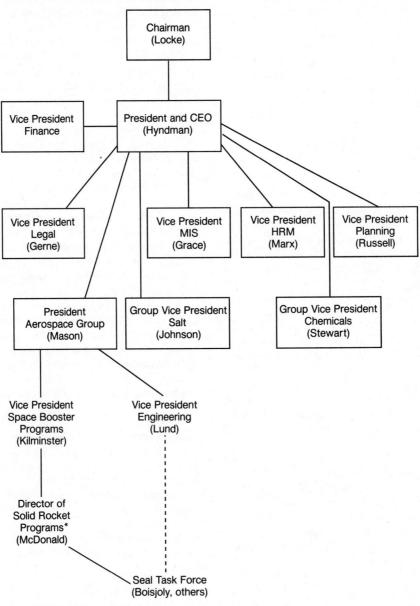

*At Kennedy Space Center.

FIGURE 5   Main Players at NASA, Marshall Center, and Morton Thiokol

NASA Top Management	Position	Action (Inaction)
1. Jesse Moore	Associate Administrator for space flight	Made decision to launch 51L, did not know of no-go recommendations
2. Arnold Aldrich	Shuttle Manager at Johnson	Knew only Rockwell reservations
Marshall Center		
1. William Lucas	Director	Outside launch chain of command
2. Stanley Reinartz	Manager, Shuttle Projects	Did not tell superiors about Thiokol reservations
3. Lawrence Mulloy	Chief of Solid Rockets	Did not accept Thiokol engineer's doubts
4. George Hardy	Deputy Director of Space Engineering	Did not accept Thiokol engineer's doubts
Morton Thiokol		
1. Jerald Mason	Senior Vice President	Asked for decision
2. Joseph Kilminster	V.P. for Boosters	Signed "go" memo
3. Robert Lund	V.P. For Engineering	Persuaded to OK launch recommendation
4. Allan McDonald	Director of Solid Rockets	At Kennedy—opposed launch
5. Rogert Boisjoly	Head of Seals Task Force	Worried about low temperature
6. Arnold Thompson	Engineer	Opposed launch
7. Brian Russell	Engineer	Opposed launch

Source: *Rogers Commission Report* (1986).

7:00 A.M. to 9:00 A.M. at Kennedy. The clear morning sky formed what glider pilots call a "blue bowl." Winds dwindled to 9 MPH. During the night temperatures fell to 27°F. The ice crew measures temperatures at 25°F on the right-hand solid rocket booster, 8°F on the left. They are not concerned as there are no Launch Commit Criteria relating to temperatures on rocket surfaces.

8:00 A.M. at Kennedy. Lovingood tells deputy director of Marshall (Lee) about previous discussions with MTI.

9:00 A.M. at Kennedy. Mission Management Team meets with Level 1 and 2 managers, project managers, and others. The ice conditions on launch pad are discussed, but not the O-ring issue.

10:30 A.M. at Kennedy. The ice crew reports to the Mission Management Team that ice is still left on booster.

11:18 A.M. A Rockwell engineer in California watching the ice team over closed-circuit television telephones the Cape to advise a delay because of the ice. Kennedy Center Director Smith, advised by the ice team that there is little risk, permits the countdown to continue.

11:28 A.M. Inside *Challenger's* flight deck (about the size of that of a 747), Commander Scobee and pilot Smith run through their elaborate checklists. The orbiter's main computer, supported by four backup computers, scans data from 2,000 sensors. If it detects a problem, it will shut down the entire system. In June 1984, the computer aborted four seconds before the rocket ignition. This time, it doesn't.

11:30 A.M. Thousands of motorists pull off highways to face toward the ocean.

11:37 A.M. The launch platform is flooded by powerful streams of water from 7-foot pipes to dampen the lift-off sound levels, which could damage the craft's underside.

11:38 A.M Flight 51-L is launched. Two rust-colored external fuel tanks, each 154 feet high, carrying 143,351 gallons of liquid oxygen and 385,265 gallons of liquid hydrogen power the rocket. They will burn until the fuel runs out.

11:39 A.M. Everything looked like it was supposed to look. As one MTI engineer watched the rocket lift off the pad into a bright Florida sky he thought, "Gee, it's gonna be all right. It's a piece of cake . . . we made it."

REFERENCES

Anderson, F. W. (1981) *Orders of Magnitude: A History of NACA and NASA, 1915–1980.* Washington, D.C.: NASA.

Bazell, R. (1986) "NASA's Mid-LIfe Crisis." *The New Republic,* March 24, pp. 12–15.

Beatty, J. K. (1982) "The Space Age" (25 Years and Counting)." *Sky and Telescope,* 64, pp. 310–13.

Becker, J. (1985) "NASA's Projects Reflect a New Attitude as Agency Competes for Launch Services." *EDN,* August 22, pp. 307–11.

Berry, R. (1986) "A Busy Year for the Shuttle." *Astronomy,* 14, pp. 8–22.

Brooks, H. (1983) "Managing the Enterprise in Space." *Technology Review,* 86, pp. 39–46.

Covault, C. (1979) "Changes Expected in Shuttle Management Philosophy." *Aviation Week and Space Technology,* September 24, pp. 20–21.

Covault, C. (1984) "NASA Formulates Policy to Spur Private Investment." *Aviation Week and Space Technology,* November 26, pp. 18–19.

Goldman, N. C. (1985) *Space Commerce: Free Enterprise on the High Frontier.* Cambridge, Mass.: Ballinger.

Guterl, F., and Truxal, C. (1983) "Militarization: Peace or War? *IEEE Spectrum,* September, pp. 35–39.

Hirsch, R., and Trento, J. J. (1973) *The National Aeronautics and Space Administration.* New York: Praeger.

Holden, C. (1973) "NASA: Sacking Top Black Woman Stirs Concern for Equal Employment." *Science,* 183, pp. 804–07.

Kennan, E. A., and Harvey, E. H. Jr. (1969) *Mission to the Moon: A Critical Examination of NASA and the Space Program.* New York: William Morrow.

Levine, A. L. (1975) *The Future of the U.S. Space Program.* New York: Praeger.

Levine, A. S. (1982) *Managing NASA in the Apollo Era.* Washington, D.C.: NASA

Logsdon, J. M. (1983) NASA's Dual Challenge: Serving Yet Striving." *IEEE Spectrum,* September, pp. 86–89.

McDougall, W. A. (1985) *The Heavens and the Earth: A Political History of the Space Age.* New York: Basic Books.

Murray, B. (1986) "In Search of Presidential Goals." *Issues in Science and Technology,* Spring.

Pennington, J. (NASA Director of Human Resources). (1986) Personal Communication, July.

Reichhardt, T. (1985) "Twelve Years From the Moon." *Space World,* July, pp. 13–14.

Rogers Commission Report. (1986) Washington D.C.: U.S. Government Printing Office.

Sidey, H. (1986) "Pioneers in Love with the Frontier." *Time,* February 10.

Sietzen, F. Jr. (1984) "Perspectives on the Apollo Era." *Space World,* July, pp. 4–9.

Sky and Telescope. (1982) "An Interview with James Beggs." October, pp. 332–33.

Space World. (1983) "NASA's First 25 Years." October, pp. 25–32.

Space World. (1984) "NASA Reorganizations." January, pp. 34–35.

Wilford, J. N. (1986) "After the Challenger: America's Future in Space." *The New York Times,* March 16.

Wolfe, T. (1986) "Everyman vs. Astropower." *Newsweek,* February 10, pp. 40–41.

Wolfe, T. (1979) *The Right Stuff.* New York: Farrar, Straus, Giroux.

26. AB Volvo (Sweden)

On March 26, 1986, Pehr G. Gyllenhammar, the CEO and chairman of Sweden's largest company, AB Volvo, gave a last minute glance to the statement he was going to make to the press releasing Volvo's 1985 annual report. He knew that the press will be eager to ask him questions about the recent resignations of the president of Volvo Group Haken Frisinger and some other top officials of Volvo; questions will be raised about the increased dividends for the Volvo stockholders for 1986 when the labor unions are asked to hold their demands for increased wages; and also concerns will be raised about the impact of the recent assassination of Swedish Prime Minister Olof Palme on Volvo's future plans. Gyllenhammar mentally prepared himself for all the probing questions he was about to face in the afternoon's conference. He wondered that, in search for not so bright aspects of the company's operations, probably most of the people would not notice that AB Volvo, which employed over 67,000 people and generated 13 percent of Sweden's GNP, had earned a record profit equivalent to about U.S. $1 billion in 1985.

HISTORY OF AB VOLVO

Volvo, incorporated in 1915 as a subsidiary of AB Svenska Kullagerfabriken, SKF, commenced business in 1926, assembling cars and trucks; and became an

---

This case was prepared by Jyoti N. Prasad, Hans J. Bocker, Megan E. Sutton, and Fazal J. Seyyed, of Western Illinois University and is intended to be used for class discussion. It was presented at the Midwest Case Writers' Association Workshop, 1986. It also appears in *Annual Advances in Business Cases*, 1986, pp. 1–25, edited by Philip C. Fisher. Reprinted by permission.

Note: Throughout the text and in the exhibits which follow, various financial information has been presented either in U.S. dollars or in Swedish kronor. Due to basic differences in U.S. and Swedish accounting principles, one has to be careful when computing and interpreting ratios or attempting to convert them into one single currency. However, for the advantage of U.S. analysts, AB Volvo recently has started the practice of reporting its financial information based on U.S. accounting principles.

independent company in 1935. From the late 1930s there has been steady development of the company's automotive business, and Volvo has grown into a diversified group with integrated manufacturing operations.

The Volvo company was founded by Gustaf Larson, an engineer, and Assar Gabrielsson, an economist, who rose so quickly within the Swedish ball-bearing company SKF that by the age of 32 he was the company's international sales manager. As a young fellow working in England, Larson got to know William Morris who at the time was designing a small car. Returning to Sweden, Larson earned his engineering degree and went to work for SKF. But it was not until after he left the firm that he met Gabrielsson in 1924. The two began work on a test series of 10 cars—1 sedan and the rest touring cars. The prototypes were finished under Larson's direction in 1926, and Gabrielsson convinced SKF to set up a new automotive company named Volvo. Gabrielsson remained at the helm of Volvo until 1956.

The first Volvo rolled off the line at a plant on the island of Hisingen, Gothenberg, April 14, 1927. That year Volvo's 66 workers built 297 cars, more American in style than European. The first series OV 4, featured long leaf springs front and rear, a four-cylinder engine that developed 28 horsepower and was capable of taking the car to 55 MPH. However, Volvo quickly discovered that its market lay in selling covered sedans, and in 1929 it introduced a new model, PV 651, equipped with a six-cylinder engine. The company sold 1,383 cars that year, enough to generate its first profit.

The company expanded its product line in the 1930s to include trucks and seven-passenger taxis. In the middle of the decade a revolutionary Volvo was introduced: The PV 36 with smoother, more aerodynamic lines and the first Volvo body made completely of steel. However, the car did not gain popularity and it took a long time to sell the 500 units of the limited series that the company had built.

In late 1936 the company introduced a smaller, inexpensive car with similar styling, the PV 51, and it proved a big hit. The little car still couldn't compete in price with some of the imports of the day, but Swedish buyers had come to trust Volvo's quality, and the new model helped propel the company to nearly double its sales in 1937.

During World War II Volvo became Sweden's number one defense contractor. It built special vehicles for the Swedish Army despite widespread parts shortages. Volvo remains in the defense business to this day, supplying engines built by its Volvo Flygmotor unit for Saab airplanes for both civilian and military use. Other Volvo Flygmotor engines, developed independently and in conjunction with General Electric, are also designed for military and civilian craft.

In the fall of 1944 about 150,000 people showed up for the Volvo Exhibition in Stockholm to see the PV 444 prototype, Volvo's postwar model. Nearly 2,300 signed orders for the car. Those who held orders for the first shipment were able to sell them, shortly afterward, for twice what they had paid originally.

Mainly, because of the eventual success of the little PV 444, Volvo auto production topped truck and bus output for the first time in 1949. By 1953 the PV 444 was Sweden's top-selling car. It was about this time that Volvo introduced fixed repair prices and five-year guarantees against auto damage in Sweden. In 1960 Volvo set up its own Swedish insurance company and issued all Volvo owners the guarantees.

The first Volvo sports car, a roadster called P 1900, went into production in 1956 with a fiberglass-reinforced plastic body. It failed completely. Only 67 were sold. The next—and last—time Volvo ventured into the sports-car market was in 1961 when the P 1800 two-seat coupe was introduced.

Although a handful of cars had been exported to California in 1955, Volvo's real push into the U.S. markets came in 1957. Its directors decided the company's need for growth was more compelling than their reservations about entering the highly competitive U.S. market. By 1960, however, 20 percent of Volvo's production was going to the United States. Today, the United States is Volvo's largest market—even bigger than Sweden. Volvo has the second-highest European brand sales in the United States, close behind Volkswagen. Only one tenth of all Volvos manufactured today are destined for the Swedish market.

Canada also proved to be a good market. In 1963, to satisfy local-content rules, Volvo started manufacturing in Nova Scotia. It was Volvo's first fully owned plant outside Sweden, and was soon followed by opening of a plant in Belgium.

The first U.S.-bound cars were the trusty PV 444. The PV was thoroughly updated in 1958, and remained in production until the end of 1965. When the last PV sedan rolled off the Gothenberg line, 440,000 units had

been built over its lifetime. PV station wagons stayed in production until 1969. The 121/122 model enjoyed a similarly long lifespan. The series was in production from 1956 until 1970, almost 15 years. But it was the 144 series, introduced in 1966 as the PV replacement, that gave Volvo its reputation for safety. The company had been the first to introduce: three-point seat-belts (1959), laminated windshields in the 1950s, front disc brakes, and orthopedically designed seats in the 1960s.

The company further enhanced its safety reputation by developing the Volvo Experimental Safety Car in 1972. This was a very favorable year for the company in other respects. Volvo bought 33 percent of The Netherlands' DAF Car Division, and opened the Volvo technical center. The DAF car was redesigned, the Holland company renamed Volvo Car BV, and its new model called the Volvo 66, which once more brought the Volvo name to a small car. Meanwhile, the Swedish cars were moving upscale; the 144 had evolved into the 200 series, combining safety with greater luxury. To celebrate its 50th birthday Volvo commissioned the 262, a luxury coupe, designed by Bertone. But the company's real drive into the luxury segment came in 1982 with the introduction of the 760 GLE. But Volvo hasn't abandoned its once successful niche. As of mid-1986 a replacement for the Dutch small car is in the works, and is expected to be headed for Volvo's top market, the United States.

In the 1970s Volvo undertook decentralization of its management's responsibility and expansion of its marketing organization. During this period, the company also introduced and implemented new production technologies, built plants in key market areas and developed further the quality, reliability, and safety of its products. In addition, Volvo has also identified the heavy vehicle industry as an area of increased strategic importance. Toward the end of the period, Volvo entered into a number of cooperation agreements with other companies and, in 1980, formed Volvo Energy Corporation to engage in hydrocarbon exploration, development, investment, and related activities, which the company had also identified as an area of strategic importance.

The transport equipment area dominated the Group's business up to 1981. In 1981 AB Volvo acquired all of the capital stock of Beijerinvest AB, a publicly traded Swedish holding company with interests in energy, industrial, food, trading and financial businesses. However, in recent years, Volvo has disposed of some Beijerinvest interests which had no immediate connection with the company's major business lines and has regrouped others into distinct business segments. Volvo has also made a number of strategic acquisitions of, and investments in, companies that complement the Volvo Group's industrial base and others that implement its developing emphasis of the energy business. Certain investments in shares of Swedish companies held by Volvo have been disposed of and other major investments acquired.

Volvo's international growth has been substantial. Production facilities abroad have been established and expanded through a joint venture truck and bus assembly plant in Brazil in the late 1970s, and the acquisition in 1981 of most of the truck manufacturing assets of White Motor Corporation in the United States. North America and Western Europe, especially the Nordic Area, are the Group's most important markets. Marine engines, oil rigs, factory automation equipment—even beer—now fall under the Volvo umbrella. The offshoot of a ball-bearing company is today Sweden's largest company employing 67,857 people and among the world's largest 50 companies in terms of business operations and profitability.

AB VOLVO: BUSINESS OPERATIONS

Volvo as an industrial group has operations in three principal areas: transport equipment, energy, and food. Volvo products are sold throughout the world and 84 percent of the Group's sales are to customers outside Sweden. As a part of its concentration on foreign markets, Volvo has established wholly or partially owned plants in the following countries, among others: Denmark, Belgium, The Netherlands, France, Austria, Great Britain, the United States, Canada, Peru, Brazil, Iran, Thailand, Malaysia, and Australia.

Volvo's growth and development have occurred primarily in the transport vehicle field, which continues to form the base of the Group's operations. The activities include the production of cars, of commercial vehicles such as trucks, buses and construction equipment, and of marine, industrial, and aircraft engines.

In the energy business, Volvo is active in oil trading as well as prospecting and recovery of oil and gas through associated companies.

The food companies are coordinated through Provendor Food AB. These firms produce and market frozen and preserved foods based on farm products and fish, as well as cured meat products, butchered meat, and

mineral water. Industrial operations are supplemented by strategic shareholdings in listed companies.

Volvo Cars

The cars operating sector comprises the activities of Volvo Car Corporation, the production of components within Volvo Components Corporation, marketing handled by Volvo's sales subsidiaries, and the spare parts business.

Development and manufacture of Volvo cars in the 200 and 700 series are parts of this sector. Most of the cars are assembled in Sweden, and Belgium, but assembly also takes place in Canada, Thailand, Malaysia, Australia, and other countries. The largest market areas of Volvo cars are in North America, the Nordic countries, and the other countries of Western Europe. The Volvo 300 series is produced at Volvo Car BV in The Netherlands, of which Volvo Car Corporation owns 30 percent.

Sixty years ago Volvo was not building cars but was manufacturing ball bearings. A decade ago the company's cars were considered means of solid transportation, but were far from being deemed luxury items. But, today Volvo builds some of the most sophisticated luxury automobiles in the world.

Volvo Trucks

Within its trucks operating sector, Volvo designs, manufactures and markets forward-control and normal-control heavy trucks for long-distance and forest transport, construction work, tanker and bulk transport. It also makes medium-sized trucks for local distribution service and light, long-distance traffic.

Assembly takes place mainly in Sweden, Belgium, Great Britain, the United States, Brazil, and Australia. There is a substantial market potential for Volvo trucks in all parts of the world.

On August 15, 1986 Volvo and GM announced their plans to merge their heavy truck operations in the United States. The joint venture with 65 percent of ownership by Volvo will be called the Volvo GM Heavy Truck Corporation, will be based on Volvo's wholly owned U.S. subsidiary, Volvo White Truck Corporation, in Greensboro, North Carolina, and the heavy-duty truck operations of GM's Truck and Bus Group in Pontiac,

Michigan. General Motors has agreed to pay an estimated $50 to $75 million for its stake in the venture which is expected to become fully operational in two years. Under the joint venture, the manufacturing operations would be based at Volvo/White's three existing plants in Virginia, Ohio, and Utah. The estimated U.S. market for heavy trucks in 1986 was 115,000 units, against 140,000 units in 1985.

Volvo Buses

Within its buses operating sector, Volvo develops, manufactures and markets bus chassis, components and complete buses. Volvo is one of the leading bus manufacturers in the Organization for Economic Cooperation and Development (OECD) countries. Assembly and production takes place in 12 countries, with most of the production occurring in Sweden. Volvo manufactures approximately 8 percent of all buses of more than 12 tons gross weight produced in the OECD.

Construction Equipment

Volvo BM designs, manufactures and markets wheel loaders, articulated dump trucks, rigid dump trucks and excavator loaders, and is one of Europe's leading construction equipment companies. Volvo BM has a substantial share of the world market for articulated dumpers and is further increasing its percentage of the market for wheel loaders.

An arrangement has been reached to merge with the Clark Michigan Company in the United States with a view to obtaining benefits in the areas of product development, production, and marketing of construction equipment.

Marine and Industrial Engines

The Marine and Industrial Engines operating sector comprises the development, design, manufacture and conversion of diesel and gasoline engines as well as marine transmissions and industrial components. The products are used in leisure and commercial craft, in materials handling vehicles, construction equipment, and so on, or as power sources for generators and pumps. Volvo Penta engines are sold in most markets throughout the world.

Aircraft Engines, etc.

Volvo Flygmotor's operations comprise the development and production of jet engines and components for military and civil aircraft and space projects, as well as the manufacture of hydraulic machinery, transmission systems, and heaters. The long-term objective is to replace a diminishing military workload with civil projects. The focus is on creating balance among the three large areas of operation: products for defense, civil aviation, and other civil applications.

Energy

STC Scandinavian Trading Company AB is one of the larger independent oil trading companies in the world. In recent years its operations have been broadened to include other types of international trading.

Volvo Energy has concessions in the North Sea and owns interests in Saga Petroleum a.s. (recovery of oil and gas in the North Sea), and in accommodation and service platforms. Volvo also has, through its subsidiary Volvo North America Corporation, substantial interests in the Hamilton Oil Corporation.

Food

This product group comprises a number of manufacturers who are well known in Sweden for such food products as preserved and frozen vegetables, meat and potato products, preserved fish products, processed meat and sandwich foods, chopped meat and mineral water. The operations of various companies are coordinated through Provendor Food AB.

TROUBLE IN PARADISE

Pehr Gyllenhammar Story

Pehr G. Gyllenhammar became head of Volvo in 1971 at the age of 36 after marrying the daughter of the carmaker's boss. Before that he was chief of Sweden's largest insurer, Skandia, where he succeeded his father.

But Gyllenhammar is more than a rich man's son and another rich man's son-in-law. Volvo has thrived under his stewardship. On sales of just $3.5 billion, its car business pulled out about $700 million in operating earnings in 1984. That's a 20 percent return on sales. Using U.S. accounting principles, about $400 million dropped to the bottom line, almost a 100 percent profit gain over 1983. AB Volvo as a group earned record profits of $860 million in 1984, and a staggering $1 billion in 1985. In 1985, Volvo sales increased to a record 392,600 cars, including the Dutch-built Volvo 340-360 series (which, in fact, has produced less than expected results). Sales totals in 1985 surpassed 1984 figures by 6,600 units.

However, trouble for Gyllenhammar began popping up starting in late 1982. Gyllenhammar was seen as the man most likely to succeed Swedish billionnaire, Marcus Wallenberg, as head of the Wallenberg empire. The Wallenberg financial empire controls major financial institutions and Saab-Scania cars and airplane manufacturing operations in Sweden. The Swedish billionnaire wanted Gyllenhammar as his heir rather than his own son Peter Wallenberg. But after the death of Marcus Wallenberg in September 1982, Peter Wallenberg made his move to take revenge. The power struggle was compounded when Volvo bought 25 percent shareholdings in two Wallenberg companies: Atlas Copco, the engineering group of which Peter Wallenberg is the chairman; and Stora Kopparberg, the paper manufacturer. Peter Wallenberg retaliated by buying into Volvo. Furthermore, the animosity between the two men was intensified by a fight over the chairmanship of Skandinaviska-Enskilda Bank, Sweden's biggest commercial bank. Its chairmanship was traditionally seen as the Wallenberg's throne. The position went to bank insider Curt Olsson, although both Wallenberg and Gyllenhammar were candidates. They blamed each other for allowing the chairmanship to slip into the hands of a third party.

Finally a settlement was arranged: Peter would sell off his Volvo stock, and Volvo would sell shares it held in divisions of the Wallenberg empire. Volvo made $190 million in that exchange. With that and auto profits, Volvo found itself to have accumulated $1.6 billion in cash and securities at its disposal in 1984.

Gyllenhammar has successfully run Volvo for over 15 years, and turned it into Sweden's biggest company. Sales in 1983 of Skr 99.46 billion and a pretax profit of

Skr 3.8 billion, represent a dramatic increase from sales of Skr 19.2 billion in 1978 (1984 sales were down to Skr 87.05 billion). Gyllenhammar is a respected industrialist in Europe as well as in his home country. Nobody doubts that he is a man of vision, but many of those visions have spurred criticism lately. For example, in recent years some of the moves by Gyllenhammar were obstructed or undermined because of his different way of thinking and his leadership style.

In 1983 Volvo's board successfully blocked Gyllenhammar's plan to issue $100 million equity in America late in 1984. However, Gyllenhammar asked the Swedish government for permission to change Volvo's restricting articles of association to enable the company to raise more foreign capital. In December 1984, in spite of Volvo board opposition Gyllenhammar was able to list Volvo shares on the Paris Bourse, and on the over-the-counter market in the United States via the NASDAQ system.

In retaliation of Volvo board's refusal to sell stock in the United States in 1984–85 Gyllenhammar replaced three outside directors with Volvo executives of his own choice. Rebellious stockholders struck back by thwarting his extraordinary proposal to sell 40 percent of Volvo's share capital to the Norwegian government in exchange for a share of Norway's oil fields in the North Sea. But Volvo later bought into North Sea and U.S. oil properties. These investments ultimately led to losses totaling $143.5 million.

The investment in the Dutch carmaker, DAF, intended to give Volvo a cheap entry to the market for small cars, also proved a failure.

A proposed merger between Volvo and its main competitor Saab-Scania, the other Swedish car and truck manufacturer, fell through when it was blocked by the Saab-Scania management.

There are signs of growing discontent within and outside the company that employs 10 percent of the Swedish work force and accounts for 13 percent of the country's gross national product. Some stockholders and analysts are increasingly wary of Gyllenhammar's management style. Stockholm's stock exchange is hitting new highs, but in the month of February 1986 the price of Volvo B shares—the restricted voting shares available to foreigners—had dropped from $50 to $42.

In early 1986, Volvo was tarnished by its close association with Egyptian-born Refaat El-Sayed, who controlled Fermenta, a Swedish biotech and chemical company. In January of 1986 Volvo and Fermenta agreed to a $556 million joint venture that would have made them the undisputed leaders of biotech in Sweden. But in February 1986, El-Sayed admitted that he had lied about holding a doctoral degree in biochemistry from the University of California at Davis, and he resigned as Fermenta's chairman. In March 1986 Volvo canceled its venture with Fermenta and admitted that it had lent an estimated $35 million to El-Sayed to finance purchases of Fermenta stock. Meanwhile heavy trading in Fermenta stock prompted an investigation on behalf of the 22 bankers and industrialists governing the Stockholm Stock Exchange. In May of 1986 they voted unanimously to fine Volvo $267,000 and Fermenta $152,777. Pehr Gyllenhammar denounced the action by the Swedish Exchange and called exchange president Bengt Ryden "meddlesome." He also said that he had broken no rules and threatened to sue the exchange's governing body. The Fermenta affair, however, made Gyllenhammar suffer a setback of prestige.

Gyllenhammar suffered another blow in early 1986. That happened when along with Volvo president, Haken Frisinger, and 28 other top Swedish executives, he became embroiled in a political and media controversy over a stock market investment that netted them large gains. The government subsequently launched an investigation into the practice—quite common by Swedish standards—whereby executives are given a chance to buy stock of their own company while denying it to small stockholders. Three years ago, a Volvo subsidiary, Sonesson, acquired a privately held medical company, Leo. When Sonesson decided two years ago to issue a separate and private stock for Leo, it offered the 30 executives shares at the same favorable price it paid for them. In 1985 the stock was then listed on the exchange for the first time. Sales of the shares opened at considerably higher prices, allowing the executives gains that in some cases reached millions of dollars. The transaction was revealed in the press the day before the traditional annual Volvo press conference to announce the results of the first nine months of 1985. Reporters centered their questions more on Gyllenhammar's business ethics than on the financial results of Volvo. The questions angered Gyllenhammar, who declared his honor was worth more to him than any private profit. He said he would sell his shares at their original price to the cancer research fund set up in the name of the Volvo founder, Assar Gabrielsson. The massive press coverage that followed snowballed into a political dispute concerning the so-called pilot practice that allows executives to make such profits while small stockholders in a company do not have such an opportunity. In the wake

of the *Leo Affair* as it was called, the Sonesson chairman resigned, and an executive of the bank that financed the executives' stock purchases—and who had bought stock for himself—was fired. The press also reported a rift between Gyllenhammar and Frisinger because Frisinger refused to forsake his profits, which were substantially larger than Gyllenhammar's. The affair got so hot that the late Socialist prime minister, Mr. Palme, subsequently ordered an official investigation into what occurred and how a similar situation could be avoided in the future. A three-person commission was quickly set up to start its official investigation beginning in early 1986. Among other things, the findings may result in tax implications for Gyllenhammar when the question will be addressed as to whether Gyllenhammar's donation of his share would be tax-exempt.

In wake of the above incident another shock came when both Volvo President Haken Frisinger and Executive Vice President Ulf Linden resigned effective in 1987. It came as a hard blow to Volvo because the 60-year-old Frisinger gets the credit for turning the car division around. From declining sales and a reputation for poor quality 10 years ago, Volvo has jumped to leadership in the U.S. market for imported luxury cars. Linden, 37, was Gyllenhammar's troubleshooter and responsible for Volvo's recent diversification into biotech. Frisinger agreed to take early retirement but will continue to advise Volvo on international matters. He wishes to be based outside Sweden. Linden will remain a director of AB Volvo and work part-time with issues related to financial development and strategic projects. Their respective replacements will be Gunnar Johansson, currently in charge of the Aerospace Engine Division, Volvo Flygmotor, and Lennart Jeansson, Volvo Car Corporation's director of purchasing.

In April 1986 Volvo experienced labor trouble. It occurred when Volvo raised dividends in the wake of its record profits for 1985. The action resulted in protests from labor unions, which had been told to be more moderate in their wage requests than ever before in order to help the government fight inflation. Volvo's profits in 1985 amounted to approximately $1 billion, compared with the former record profit of roughly $860 million in 1984. Dividends, which were stipulated to be frozen at around 76 cents per share, were raised to about $1.12, which led analysts to believe that if other important industries follow Volvo's lead, the annual round of labor negotiations in 1986 could be one of the toughest ever.

In spite of all the commotion, Gyllenhammar has proven that he can make things work. Although in 1984

European analysts were skeptical about his continuation as Volvo chief, Gyllenhammar is holding on and pursuing his goals. The Volvo insiders call him "the Emperor." He has been called "colorful," "ambitious," a "master builder" who is "a law unto himself," with "remarkable instinct for survival," and who will "recover and remain." A debonair and impeccable dresser, Gyllenhammar seems to enjoy his celebrity status. He is well known and is an essential figure within the international directors' circuit, including United Technologies, (Henry) Kissinger Associates and Chase Manhattan Bank's International Advisory Committee.

Gyllenhammar's Grand Strategy

Gyllenhammar has used the Volvo Group's successes to acquire businesses in and diversify into areas unrelated to automobiles, such as pharmaceuticals and biotechnology. After his skirmish with Wallenberg, from which Gyllenhammar emerged unscathed, he announced: "For the first time in our history, we have not only reached a size but also have the equity position where we have real freedom." And, Gyllenhammar plans to use this affluence and freedom by active diversification in the years to come.

Gyllenhammar figures that Volvo's car business has peaked and now it will serve only as a cash cow. The worldwide car business is going to grow only 2 percent a year, and the big Volvo-like cars aren't as popular in Europe as they used to be. Volvo builds only 390,000 cars a year, and 100,000 of them are low-profit runabouts picked up in acquisitions at times when it looked as if oil prices were headed through the roof. That leaves Volvo's car profits dangerously dependent on the U.S. market situations. Here Volvo sales are pushing 100,000, and Americans are willing to pay $20,000 for top models. The strong dollar made the profits even better than the unit sales gains. Besides, Gyllenhammar knows that European governments will continue subsidizing companies like Renault and Fiat, Japanese manufacturers will remain unbeatable, and Americans eventually will come back with a vengeance in the auto market should the dollar recover. The answer to such a complex situation, Gyllenhammar thinks, lies in "diversification." Gyllenhammar says that he does not have any ambition to push the auto division in faster growth and expanding capacity, except through Volvo's own moderate "natural" growth rates.

THE ACQUISITIONS BY VOLVO

Alarmed by the devastating effects of the oil crisis of the early 1970s and its threat to the world auto industry, Gyllenhammar has been intent on hedging Volvo's bets by buying into industries unrelated to autos. Even so, vehicles and engines still accounted for two thirds of Volvo's sales in 1985, as well as more than 90 percent of its profits of $1 billion.

In 1981 Volvo acquired Sweden's giant investment outfit Beijerinvest and its sizable oil-trading unit, Scandinavian Trading Company. Overnight this almost doubled Volvo's revenue. Gyllenhammar planned on entering a business countercyclical to the auto industry which also offered more growth potential.

But oil was just one of Gyllenhammar targets. With the Beijerinvest merger, Volvo also acquired, and plans to expand in, a group of Scandinavian food companies—herring, pickles, and mineral water. Gyllenhammar believes that although it is not a dramatic enterprise, it has a safe cash flow and is a good balance against Volvo's other businesses that tend to fluctuate rather widely with economic upturns and recessions.

According to a report in April 1986, Volvo finally succeeded in taking over the widely diversified Sonesson concern after a tough struggle. Sonesson is heavily involved in machines, communications, pumps, drugs, and biotechnology. Because of this acquisition, Volvo will now be able to regroup its biotech holdings on an international scale. Since Volvo is already a 40 percent shareholder with the firm "Pharmacia" (drugs, pharmaceuticals, diagnosis equipment) those divisions of Sonesson which do not fit into the new restructuring concept of the biotech area will most likely be sold off by Volvo. This will happen primarily because Volvo's top management had already developed a concept of how to structure and develop its own biotech empire, after a takeover attempt on Fermenta failed in January of 1986. In bidding for Sonesson, Volvo had gradually expanded its offer from the original 30 percent to eventually 80 percent of all shares. But to reach the critical limit of 90 percent at which according to Swedish laws, the remaining shareholders can be forced to turn their shares in and accept a reasonable offer—and the company thus acquired could officially run as a full subsidiary of the parent company—Volvo had to convince the South Swedish firm Crafoord to sell its 12.9 percent of Sonesson shares. This seemed to fail because of tax reasons, because Crafoord owned the Sonesson shares for a period shorter than two years.

In Sweden, any share sale within two years of its purchase is subject to a massive speculation tax, and in this case, Crafoord would have suffered a total loss of 70 million Skr after everything was settled.

In any case, to circumvent the tax dilemma a two-tier strategy was chosen in April 1986. First: the tax-free Crafoord foundation which is a member of the Crafoord concern, sells its Sonesson shares first to Volvo, tax-free of course. With that, Volvo just passes the critical 90 percent share limit. The remaining Sonesson shares, normally heavily taxable, could be obtained by the legal handover order. But if anyone is legally forced to sell his shares to the 90 percent holder, the two-year waiting period is not applicable. This is because "force" is not considered "speculation" in which case the shareholder has no choice. In the event of such a forced sale only a small tax will be applicable.

ATTITUDE OF SWEDISH GOVERNMENT TOWARD VOLVO

Although acquisitions are getting tougher for Gyllenhammar in socialist-ruled Sweden, the realistic Socialists know that free enterprise lays the golden eggs. As a result they avoid total strangulation of business but still place endless restrictions on industry in general. For example, exchange controls prohibit Volvo from using any of its domestic earnings for investments abroad; those funds must stay home. So overseas activities have to be financed with capital raised overseas. Volvo could acquire more Swedish companies, but it is so big in Sweden already that this might be politically unwise. Moreover, after the tragic assassination of Swedish Prime Minister Olof Palme, Swedish industry will need to monitor the future trends with extra caution.

For Gyllenhammar it has been a difficult ball game, however. He and Volvo have always been favorites of the Swedish government. In fact, Volvo is receiving massive government support for building an auto assembly plant in Uddevalla, a city 55 miles north of Gothenburg with a struck shipyard. Critics have accused the government of eating out of Pehr Gyllenhammar's hands, but neither of the parties has admitted to any complicity in making a deal that pours millions of public dollars into the project at a time when Volvo has achieved record profits. Apart from that, Volvo has already been promised it can use about $1.38 billion of set aside profits without taxation for different plant projects around Gothenberg.

THE VOLVO IMAGE

Recently, serious-minded readers of such publications as *The Wall Street Journal, The Financial Times* of London, *Le Monde,* and *Institutional Investor* have been looking at Volvo's heavily allegorical fairy tales, written and illustrated in children's book fashion appearing as dramatic three-page spreads in 14 countries. The moral of each tale was lent a concrete dimension by the real-life facts and figures on the diversified automaker. One senior Volvo official commented: "We wanted to expose our values, our philosophy, our way of doing business, not just facts. We asked ourselves, 'What is the oldest form to communicate wishes and values? Fairy tales.''

The ads, early in 1985, were the centerpiece of a broader international investor relations campaign meant to convey the message that Europe's 19th largest company has become much more than merely a carmaker. One senior official of Volvo North America observed that a few years ago in the United States over half of the general population didn't recognize that Volvo was a Swedish company or that it was also a large truck and marine-power manufacturer. Some thought that Volvo made motorcycles, while others believed that it was a Japanese or German company. In fact, autos account for only 40 percent of Volvo's worldwide revenues.

Investor image building, both domestic and foreign, has become an urgent priority for Volvo because of its push to diversify internationally. Early in 1985 Volvo announced a joint venture to manufacture off-road trucks and other types of heavy construction equipment with Clark Equipment Company of the United States.

Although fully 90 percent of Volvo's sales are generated outside Sweden, roughly the same proportion of its shares are held within the country, mostly by insurance companies and other institutions that are all but saturated with Volvo stock. Under Swedish law a foreign investor may hold only up to 40 percent of a Swedish company's capital. Adding extra impetus to the desire to broaden the shareholder base was Gyllenhammar's run-in with Peter Wallenberg in 1984.

Volvo has already had a headstart in raising its profile among foreign investors. Its shares have long been listed abroad—on both the West German Börse (bourse) and the London Stock Exchange since 1974, and on Norway's exchange since 1979. But despite deriving 40 percent of its revenues from the United States, Volvo waited until late 1983 to offer its shares directly to American investors in the form of unsponsored over-the-counter American depositary receipts (ADRs). The company followed up with sponsored shares in 1984, the same year Volvo obtained a listing on the Paris Bourse.

Although the late 1984 ADRs weren't exactly snapped up by the market, by early 1985 Volvo had some 3 million shares outstanding in the United States (compared with 78 million in Sweden), with further plans to cultivate U.S. investors. The company had scheduled a series of high-powered road shows in 1985 to introduce the company's senior management to U.S. analysts. The first of these—timed to follow the Volvo Masters Tennis Tournament in New York's Madison Square Garden in January of 1985—featured five top executives, including Volvo Chief Pehr Gyllenhammar.

In 1984 Volvo had budgeted just under $1 million for advertising each of the three fairy tales featured in the initial three-month campaign. Volvo Group Treasurer Holmstrom commented that he was aware that the U.S. investment community was familiar with Volvo. But, in addition to that he wanted them to know: the company's finances, its aims, its philosophy; and that it is not only successful, profitable, and international but is also a social laboratory.

Volvo's Marketing in the United States

Out of total 11,042,658 cars (which includes domestics, foreign-based domestics, and foreigns) sold in the United States in 1985, Volvo had a share of 104,267 units, a meager 0.94 percent. But, in 1985, out of a total of 2,837,963 imports sold in the United States Volvo had an impressive share of 3.7 percent. It also shows that Volvo has plenty of elbow room yet, to position its autos in U.S. markets.

In 1986, it appears that in the United States Volvo has positioned itself squarely in the center of the family-car segment in spite of heavy and increasing competition. Volvo anticipates better results in 1986, compared to 1985 sales. It recently introduced an entry into the over $30,000 luxury segment—the 780 series. While it won't be available until the fall of 1986 for marketing as a 1987 model, the 780 will give the company a full range of cars from the base 240DL, priced at $14,615 to the plus $30,000 level.

The decision to offer the 780 also gives Volvo one of the broadest model ranges, in terms of market price. It is apparent the company is pursuing repeat buyers and trying to keep them climbing into Volvos as they rise through income brackets.

REFERENCES

Automotive News. (1985). "Sweden Helps Volvo Build Plant," February 25, p. 20.

————. (1985). "Volvo: A Company on a Fast Roll—Upward," October 30, p. 404.

————. (1986). "Two Volvo Chiefs to Leave in 1987; Successors Named," January 27, p. 6.

————. (1986). "Volvo Moving Ahead with Product Plans," February 24, p. 12.

————. (1986). "Higher Dividend at Volvo Stirs Labor Protests," April 21, p. 30.

Bayless, P. (1985). "Volvo Draws a Moral for Investors," *Institutional Investor*, May, pp. 133–34.

Berss, M. (1984). "The Master Builder," *Forbes*, November 19, pp. 242–43.

Bjorklund, S. (1986). "Volvo Brass Embroiled in Stock Fray," *Automotive News*, January 13, p. 7.

Borsen-Zietung. (1986). Frankfurt, W. Germany. Vol. 80, April 26, p. 5.

Done, Kevin. (1986). "Volvo GM to Link Truck Operations in North America," *Financial Times*, London, August 16, p. 1.

The Economist. (1984). "A Wrench of the Wheel," April 14, p. 76.

Feast, R. (1984). "Volvo Becomes European High Roller," *Automotive World News*, May 21.

Kaja, J. (1985). "How Solid Is Sweden's Prosperity?" *Institutional Investor*, March, pp. 224–31.

Kapstein, J. (1986). "Volvo's Emperor Faces Rebellion in the Ranks," *Business Week*, March 31, p. 45.

————. (1986). "A Slap on the Wrist Leaves Volvo Smarting," *Business Week*, June 16, p. 52.

Krebs, M. (1986). "The Doomsayers," *Automotive News*, January 13, p. E4.

Moody's International Manual. (1985). vol. 2.

Russell, J. (1986). "Uncommon Market," *Automotive News*, March 10, pp. E20–E23.

EXHIBIT 1

AB VOLVO
Balance Sheets
As of December 31
(in Swedish kronor 1,000)

	1985	1984	1983	1982*	1981	1980	1979†	1978
Assets								
Cash in banks	4,202,000	5,713,000	6,000,000	3,583,000	785,000	503,400	683,700	498,800
Temporary investments	10,192,000	6,187,000	5,625,000	3,667,000	4,691,000	3,088,400	2,831,500	1,886,200
Accounts receivable	11,244,000	13,265,000	10,706,000	10,528,000	8,546,000	4,617,700	4,450,100	3,888,100
Inventories	16,044,000	15,462,000	15,415,000	14,341,000	11,580,000	8,783,400	7,920,500	6,902,900
Total current assets	41,682,000	40,627,000	37,746,000	32,119,000	25,602,000	16,992,900	15,885,800	13,176,000
Restricted deposits in Bank of Sweden	2,823,000	1,762,000	264,000	221,000	208,000	38,100	64,300	53,800
Long-term receivables and loans	1,209,000	1,213,000	1,670,000	996,000	618,000	183,500	162,100	177,300
Intangibles	620,000	419,000	576,000	523,000	1,832,000	243,100	129,600	80,700
Property, plant and equipment, net	9,565,000	8,199,000	10,056,000	8,960,000	8,385,000	5,661,600	4,750,400	4,224,100
Investments	6,894,000	5,409,000	3,194,000	3,456,000	—	—	—	—
Total	62,793,000	57,629,000	53,506,000	46,275,000	36,645,000	23,119,200	20,992,200	17,711,900
Liabilities								
Accounts payable	6,340,000	6,510,000	6,100,000	5,701,000	4,708,000	2,169,500	2,196,400	1,714,800
Advances from customers	1,024,000	1,015,000	1,052,000	1,101,000	1,070,000	1,091,800	747,300	594,200

854

Bank loans	6,595,000	7,553,000	5,768,000	4,088,000	2,214,200	1,439,500
Other loans	3,674,000	3,263,000	2,109,000	1,967,000	925,700	741,700
Other current liabilities	9,223,000	8,663,000	6,805,000	5,333,000	3,336,200	2,804,900
Total current liabilities	26,856,000	26,631,000	21,484,000	17,388,000	9,737,400	7,295,100
Notes payable, mortgage loans	4,032,000	4,932,000	6,577,000	4,333,500	2,323,500	2,056,000
Subordinated loans	677,000	764,000	802,000	862,000	130,000	140,000
Bond loans	2,710,000	2,016,000	1,287,000	1,227,000	1,006,600	1,050,500
Provision for pension	1,866,000	1,974,000	1,790,000	1,644,000	1,037,800	760,800
Deferred taxes	—	—	448,000	449	888,000	—
Untaxed reserves	17,738,000	14,973,000	7,846,000	6,458,000	5,716,500	4,193,800
Minority interests	116,000	229,000	732,000	451,000	327,200	198,700
Share capital (Kr. 50)	1,940,000	4,940,000	1,698,000	1,394,000	1,039,100	882,600
Reserves	2,585,000	2,854,000	2,257,000	1,389,000	1,149,400	717,000
Retained earnings including years net income	4,273,000	2,362,000	1,354,000	1,030,000	631,700	557,400
Shareholders' equity	8,798,000	7,356,000	5,309,000	3,813,000	2,846,200	2,157,000
Total	62,793,000	53,506,000	46,275,000	36,643,000	23,119,200	17,711,900
Net current assets‡	14,826,000	11,115,000	10,635,000	8,214,000	7,233,300	5,880,900

*Adjusted to reflect effective from 1980, change in accounting principles for translating the financial statements of foreign subsidiaries to Swedish kronor.
†Restated for comparative purposes.
‡Reflects total current assets — total current liabilities.

Sources: *Moody's International Manual*, vol. 2 (1985); and AB Volvo Annual Report, 1985.

EXHIBIT 2

AB VOLVO
INCOME ACCOUNTS YEAR ENDING DECEMBER 31
(in Swedish Kronor 1,000)

	1985	1984	1983	1982	1981	1980	1979	1978
Sales	86,196,000	87,052,000	99,460,000	75,624,000	48,017,000	23,803,200	23,471,500	19,132,900
Cost of sales	70,388,000	72,062,000	85,774,000	70,992,000	45,039,000	22,081,200	21,520,200	17,625,400
Selling, general and administration expenses	7,608,000	6,960,000	7,611,000					
Depreciation	1,725,000	1,402,000	1,573,000	1,297,000	1,012,000	676,000	649,500	658,100
Operating income	6,475,000	6,628,000	4,502,000	3,335,000	1,966,000	1,046,000	1,301,800	849,400
Divs. rec. & sale of secur. net	110,000	138,000	86,000	195,000	132,000	822,500	558,000	373,600
Foreign exchange gain (loss)	759,000	(551,000)	(226,000)	(721,000)	(246,000)			
Interest income	2,223,000	2,052,000	1,768,000	1,333,000	1,040,000			
Interest expense	1,802,000	1,803,000	2,185,000	1,897,000	1,467,000	861,300	615,400	577,100
Inc. after financial inc. & exp.	7,765,000	6,464,000	3,945,000	2,245,000	1,425,000	1,007,200	1,244,400	645,900
Extraordinary income	—	1,363,000	—	235,000	—	—	—	—
Provision for employee bonus	(163,000)	(180,000)	(166,000)	(40,000)				
Inc. bef. alloca. taxes & min. int.	7,602,000	7,647,000	3,779,000	2,440,000	1,425,000	1,007,200	1,244,400	645,900
Allocation to untaxed reserves	3,330,000	(4,384,000)	(2,981,000)	(1,348,000)	(704,000)	(873,900)	(575,000)	(170,900)
Inc. bef. taxes & min. int.	4,272,000	3,263,000	798,000	1,092,000	721,000	133,300	669,400	475,000
Provision for taxes	1,713,000	1,624,000	752,000	508,000	222,000	83,200	240,100	151,600
Minority interests	(13,000)	(74,000)	158,000	(88,000)	(46,000)	(11,600)	(12,800)	(11,600)
Net income	2,546,000	1,565,000	204,000	496,000	453,000	38,500	416,500	311,800

Sources: *Moody's International Manual*, 1985, vol. 2.; AB Volvo Annual Report, 1985.

EXHIBIT 3

AB VOLVO
Balance Sheets
(In Skr millions)

Under Swedish accounting principles: adjusted to conform with
U.S. GAAP (generally accepted accounting principles)

	Under Swedish Accounting Principles			Under U.S. GAAP		
	1985	1984	1983	1985	1984	1983
Current assets.........................	41,682	40,627	37,746	41,575	40,451	37,626
Restricted deposits in Bank of Sweden	2,823	1,762	264	2,823	1,762	264
Property, plant and equipment (net) ...	9,565	8,199	10,056	10,171	9,019	9,887
Investments...........................	6,894	5,409	3,194	7,358	5,479	3,250
Other assets...........................	1,829	1,632	2,246	2,306	1,632	2,246
Total assets	62,793	57,629	53,506	64,233	58,343	53,273
Current liabilities.....................	26,856	26,066	26,631	26,783	26,102	26,128
Long-term liabilities	9,285	9,005	9,706	9,285	9,005	9,706
Deferred taxes	—	—	—	10,245	9,147	6,758
Untaxed reserves	17,738	14,973	10,832	—	—	—
Minority interests....................	116	229	757	116	593	810
Shareholders' equity	8,798	7,356	5,580	17,804	13,496	9,871
Total liabilities and shareholders' equity...........................	62,793	57,629	53,506	64,233	58,343	53,273

Sources: AB Volvo Annual Report, 1985; and *Moody's International Manual*, 1985, vol. 2.

EXHIBIT 4   AB Volvo: Management Team

Chairman of the board of AB Volvo and CEO of the Volvo Group:
Pehr G. Gyllenhammar

Vice chairman of the Volvo board:
Tore Browaidh
Lennart Johansson

Members of the Volvo board:

Ulf Laurin	Goran Johansson
Sven Hulterstrom	Curt Nicolin
Mats Israelsson	Stig A. L. Svensson
Sven Agrup	Haken Frisinger
Nils Holgersson	

Deputy members of the board:

Egon Kajsjo	Ulf G. Linden
Olle Ludvigsson	Hans-Eric Ovin

Secretary to the board:
Claes Beyer

Group Executive Committee:

Pehr G. Gyllenhammar	Chairman and CEO
Haken Frisinger	Vice chairman
U. G. Linden	Executive vice president
Gosta Renell	Executive vice president
Bo Ekman	Senior vice president
E. G. Knappe	Senior vice president

Source: Annual Report, 1985.

EXHIBIT 5   Sales by Products (in Skr millions)

	1985	1984	1983	1982	1981
Cars	34,549	30,304	26,262	18,109	13,569
Trucks	16,642	15,219	11,576	10,793	8,209
Buses	1,672	1,336	1,131	1,028	1,030
Marine and industrial engines	2,262	2,238	2,011	1,508	1,308
Construction equipment	—	2,851	2,664	2,203	2,277
Aircraft engines, etc.	1,426	1,152	957	919	590
Industrial equipment	—	—	3,625	2,967	2,118
Energy and trading	21,514	27,737	46,030	33,512	14,638
Food	5,393	4,947	4,429	3,171	1,889
Other operations	2,738*	1,268	775	1,414	2,389
Total	86,196	87,052	99,460	75,624	48,017

*Includes Construction equipment sales of Skr 887 million.

Source: AB Volvo Annual Report, 1985, p. 5.

EXHIBIT 6   Sales by Market (in Skr millions)

	1985	1984	1983	1982	1981
Sweden	12,023	10,958	12,233	10,728	9,341
Nordic area (excluding Sweden)	6,211	5,418	5,025	4,207	3,835
Europe (excluding Nordic area)	16,789	16,258	15,849	12,206	9,298
North America	24,102	20,513	15,380	9,817	5,560
Other markets	6,573	6,988	6,146	5,959	5,678
Total (excluding oil trading)	65,698	60,135	54,633	42,917	33,712
Oil trading	20,498	26,917	44,827	32,707	14,305
Total	86,196	87,052	99,460	75,624	48,017

Source: AB Volvo Annual Report, 1985, p. 5.

EXHIBIT 7   Operating Income by Sector (in Skr millions)

	1985	1984	1983	1982	1981
Cars	6,138	5,737	4,805	1,801	736
Trucks and buses	981	1,236	437	1,260	1,075
Construction equipment	—	190	164	158	136
Marine and industrial engines	330	351	316	187	118
Aircraft engines, etc.	187	133	99	113	139
Industrial equipment	—	—	233	226	188
Energy	(146)	(22)	(1,175)	3	(15)
Food	167	152	174	128	89
Discounted operations	(364)	(202)	—	—	—
Other operations	170	(39)	(111)	(81)	(15)
Total	7,463	7,536	4,942	3,795	2,457
Corporate expenses	(988)	(908)	(440)	(460)	(491)
Total operating income	6,475	6,628	4,502	3,335	1,966

Source: AB Volvo Annual Report, 1985, p. 8.

EXHIBIT 8 Income before Allocations, Taxes and Minority Interests by Geographical Area (in Skr millions)

	1985	1984	1983	1982
Sweden	5,820	6,260	4,015	1,945
Nordic area (excluding Sweden)	139	117	72	76
Other Europe	313	208	270	281
North America	1,077	877	(591)*	102
Other countries	253	185	13	36
Total	7,602	7,647	3,779	2,440

*Includes losses of Skr 1,067 million on energy operations.

Source: AB Volvo Annual Report, 1985, p. 8.

EXHIBIT 9 Assets by Sector (in Skr millions)

	1985	1984	1983	1982
Cars	14,267	11,795	11,493	10,255
Trucks and buses	9,687	8,679	8,705	8,898
Construction equipment	—	2,377	2,353	2,355
Marine and industrial engines	1,378	1,569	1,322	1,182
Aircraft engines, etc.	2,034	1,672	1,585	1,562
Industrial equipment	—	—	3,409	2,586
Energy and trading	2,152	4,818	5,337	4,906
Food	2,047	1,842	1,788	1,529
Other	6,696	2,759	2,695	2,286
Discontinued operations	420	—	—	—
Corporate assets*	24,112	22,118	14,819	10,706
Total	62,793	57,629	53,506	46,265

*Consists of investments, restricted deposits in the banks and receivables.

Source: AB Volvo Annual Report, 1985, p. 10.

EXHIBIT 10   Assets by Geographical Area (in Skr millions)

	1985	1984	1983	1982
Sweden	39,657	37,370	33,900	30,169
Nordic area (excluding Sweden)	2,106	1,866	1,980	2,012
Europe excluding Nordic area	8,610	6,673	8,232	6,010
North America	10,507	10,336	7,921	6,455
Other countries	1,913	1,384	1,473	1,629
Total	62,793	57,629	53,506	46,275

Source: AB Volvo Annual Report, 1985, p. 8.

EXHIBIT 11   AB Volvo Acquisitions since 1983*

1. STC Scandinavian Trading Company AB
2. STC Venture AB
3. Hamilton Oil Corporation
4. Investment AB Beijer
5. Volvo Car Corporation
6. Saga Petroleum a.s.
7. AB Catena, Wilh Sonesson AB, Atlas Copco AB, and Stora Kopparbergs Bergslags AB
8. Consafe AB
9. Protorp Forvatnings AB and AB Cardo
10. Volvo BM AB
11. AB Custos
12. Pharmacia AB

*For details of each acquisition and its implications please refer to *Moody's International Manual*, 1985, vol. 2, p. 3311.

5 %

EXHIBIT 12   Automotive Production (absolute number of cars, trucks and buses including chassis, produced)

	1985	1984	1983
Cars: 200/700 series etc.	288,100	270,600	266,800
Cars: 300 series	109,000	108,900	105,600
Trucks	41,200	40,800	34,300
Buses and bus chassis	3,220	3,240	3,410
Total units	441,520	423,540	410,110

Sources: *Moody's International Manual*, 1985, vol. 2. AB Volvo Annual Report, 1985.

+ 4.25 %

EXHIBIT 13   1985 Top Selling Imports in the United States (units sold)

1.	Toyota	620,047
2.	Nissan	575,166
3.	Honda	552,389
4.	Mazda	211,093
5.	Subaru	178,175
6.	Volvo	104,267
7.	BMW	87,857
8.	Mercedes-Benz	86,903
9.	Audi	74,061
10.	Mitsubishi	49,734
11.	Saab	39,264
12.	Isuzu	26,953
13.	Porsche	25,306
14.	Jaguar	20,528

Source: *Automotive News*, January 13, 1986, p. 1.

2,651,743.
4 %

Volvo 104267
Bmw   87857   1.2
Audi   74061
Saab   39264
305,449
90us = 34 %

EXHIBIT 14 New Car Sales in Europe (in thousands)

	1985	1986*
Austria	227	250
Belgium	350	360
Denmark	139	131
Finland	132	133
France	1,810	1,902
Greece	71	74
Ireland	58	66
Italy	1,672	1,658
Netherlands	476	461
Norway	128	126
Portugal	96	91
Spain	528	570
Sweden	249	225
Switzerland	253	266
United Kingdom	1,770	1,732
West Germany	2,295	2,546
Total	10,254	10,591

*Projected figures

Source: DRI Europe, in *Automotive News*, January 13, 1986, p. E8.

$+ 3\%$

6m
$= 10 \% \ O/A$

11.04
10.25
21.29 $\cdot 10^6$ Cars US + Europ

Volvo Share = 1.9%

If GM = Leader @ 40%
then 8.5×10^6 cars

$V/_{GM} = \dfrac{400,000}{8.4 \times 10^6}$

11.1

Name Index

U–V

T

Subject Index

Q–R

Quaker Oats, 48–49, 759
Qualitative forecasting techniques, 289
Quality differentiation, 167
Quality improvement, 195
Question mark industries, 218
R. J. Reynolds Company, 116, 522, 760, 771
Radar detectors, 91–92
Radio Shack, 155, 437
Ralston Purina, 759–70
Ramsey County, Minnesota, 751–53
Raybestos-Manhattan Correspondence, 681
Raymark Corporation, 689
Rayonier, Inc., 207
RCA (Radio Corporation of America), 215
Reaction Motors, Inc., 826
Real-time approach to planning, 291–93
Recessions, 105, 177–78
Recombining strategies, 193
Redefinition strategies, 193
Reinvestment strategy, 202
Relocation strategy, 193–94
Renewal Factor (Waterman), 31
Renewal strategies, 194–95
Research and development, 108
Resource audit, 88–89
Resources, organizational, 87–88
Response action, 53
Rest-of-the-world strategy, 195
Restructuring, 237–39
   cases, 574–649
Retrenchment strategies, 195–98
Return on equity, 138
Return on investment, 23, 230
Revenue-increasing strategies, 199
Reward systems, 327–28
Rice Broadcasting, 614
Ringi system, 55–56
Risk
   analysis, 297–98
   in foreign competition, 184–92
Rivalry, 123
   among existing firms, 125
Riverside Hospital (Newport News, Va.), 469
Roamans, 528, 537
Rocky Mountain Energy Company, 315
Rolls-Royce, 169
Royal Dutch Shell, 222
Rust Craft Greeting Cards, 576
Ryder Systems, 227

S

Saab-Scandia, 845
Saint Laurent, Yves, 528

St. Paul, Minnesota, 738–53
Sandoz, Inc., 182
Santa Barbara Channel oil spill, 656
Sara Lee Corporation, 771
SAS programming language, 475, 481
Saturn Corporation, 231
SBU; *see* Strategic business units
Scanning techniques, 280
Scenario analysis, 300–302
Scheduling, 57
Schlitz Brewing Company, 194
Scope; *see* Focus strategies
SeaFirst Corporation, 242
Seagram Company Ltd., 182
Sears Roebuck, 303, 577
   financial services, 143
Second Opinion Consultants, 480
Second to market strategy, 172
Segmentation strategy, 168–69, 194
Selective segmentation, 168
Sematech, 231, 395
Semiconductor industry, 163
Service differentiation, 165
Service mobility, 137
Service organizations, 397–98
   colleges and universities, 377
   franchising, 376
   hospitals, 376–77
   professional, 377–80
   role in economy, 375
   segment of economy, 374–75
   successful strategies, 380
   types and characteristics, 375–77
Service technology, 109
Sewell Village Cadillac (Dallas), 165
SFN Holding Company, 580–82
Shakeout stage of products, 144–45
Share-building strategies, 174–75
Shared Research Data, 477
Shell Oil, 34
Shrink selectively strategy, 203
Sight and Sound stores, 545
Simmons Market Research, 491
Simulation forcasting techniques, 289
Single-product business, 79
Situation audit, 246–47
   critical success factors, 247–53
Sizes Unlimited, 528, 537
Slow-growth (dog) industries, 218
Small business
   characteristics, 360
   family-run, 365
   new ventures, 358–59
   number of employees, 356
   planning, 362–63
   problems, 363–65
   startup ventures, 356–59
   strategy formulation, 360–62
   types, 357–58
SMATV, 623
Smirnoff vodka, 167

Smoking, 116
Socal, 604
Social changes, 116
Social factors, 112–18
Solar Power Corporation, 230
Sonesson Corporation, 846, 847–48
Sophisticated planner, 326
Source, The, 284
Space program, 826–28
Space shuttle disaster, 825–40
Space Task Group, 827
Space Transportation System, 827
Spin-offs, 425
Sports Illustrated, 498–99
Sputnik I, 826
Stakeholders, 49
   components, 36
   definition, 67–68
   external and internal, 52–53
   maximizing value, 398
   public sector organizations, 373–74
   strategic assumption surfacing and testing, 70
   values and expectations, 67–71
Standardized customization, 170
Standard of living, 114
Star competitors, 218
Statutory consolidation, 420
Statutory mergers, 420
Steel industry, 122
Stock acquisition, 420
Stock market crash of 1987, 302, 305
Stoplight strategy, 220
Stora Kopparberg, 845
Strategic assumption surfacing and testing, 70
Strategic audits, 344–48
Strategic business units (SBUs)
   business profile matrix, 220–21
   business screen, 210–20
   cash cows, 218
   criteria, 213–15
   definition and characteristics, 211–15
   directional policy matrix, 222
   divestiture strategy, 236–37
   dogs, 218
   growth/share matrix, 217–19
   planning elements, 309
   question marks, 218
   reward systems, 327–28
   role in planning implementation, 318–20
   stars, 218
Strategic control, 47, 336–37
   basic elements, 336
   contingency plans, 341
   corrective action, 341
   definition, 8, 55
   focus, 314
   internal, 337–38